Praise for the first edition of *Wigmore on Alcohol*

"It will certainly be the new Alcohol Bible for decades to come, and be of great value to active practitioners and researchers."

—Dr. Kurt M. Dubowski, George Lynn Cross Distinguished Professor Emeritus of Medicine, University of Oklahoma

"In short, *Wigmore on Alcohol* is a wonderful research tool that will prove a valuable resource in both legal and scientific libraries."

—Justice Libman, Judge of the Ontario Court of Justice

"In summary, this work provides scientist and non-scientist, student and expert alike with a source of relevant articles to assist them in learning about, understanding or deepening their knowledge of alcohol toxicology."

—*Canadian Society of Forensic Science Journal*

"This book is a must for anyone who is working on medicolegal issues involving alcohol. It will be appreciated by lay persons interested in this topic as well as scientific and legal experts involved in alcohol-related medicolegal issues."

—Thomas L. Pazdernik, PhD, University of Kansas Medical Center

"I regret that *Wigmore on Alcohol* was not available to me during my years of active practice in forensic science."

—Doug Lucas, MSc, DSc (Hons), Retired Director of the Centre of Forensic Sciences, Toronto

"I worked in the insurance industry for many, many years and I have attended mediations, discoveries and trials. I have also published articles and presented at seminars. Your book would have been of such a help as a reference had it been available .... It is certainly one that should be used by the Insurance Industry, the Law Society and Police Departments across the country."

—Carolan Shannon, RN, Claims Consultant

Praise for *Wigmore on Cannabis*

"*Wigmore on Alcohol* and *Wigmore on Cannabis*, written by James Wigmore, are two fundamental and essential texts for any coroner and forensic toxicologist who wants to carry out his profession with seriousness and credibility."

—Giampiero Cortis, Tossicologo Forense, Sardinia, Italy

"Medical and legal practitioners will find this an indispensable tome with up-to-date scientific evidence related to cannabis and its use. Academic law libraries will also benefit from having this practical book in their collections, as it emphasizes the depth of analysis that has been undertaken and will continue to be required as new cannabis-related issues arise in our courts."

—Margo Jeske, *Canadian Law Library Review*

"The science of cannabis is a rapidly evolving area of research. This book is a valuable tool for finding published literature and keeping up to date on a variety of topics related to cannabis."

—Karen Woodall, PhD, Assistant Professor,
Forensic Toxicology, University of Toronto

"I found *Wigmore on Cannabis* to be an extremely useful, detailed, and accurate reference book that assisted me to gain comprehensive knowledge of this complex substance."

—Caro Smit, Founder and Director of South Africans Against
Drunk Driving (SADD), Alcohol and Drug Educator and
Counselor, Psychiatric Social Worker, Road Safety Expert

Praise for *Wigmore on Nicotine*

"Let us shout this important message from the hilltops."

—Ernest Snyman, Family Practitioner

"I look forward to adding it to my collection."

—Simon Keeling, Police Officer

WIGMORE ON ALCOHOL

SECOND EDITION

Also by James G. Wigmore

The Abridged Wigmore on Alcohol: Courtroom Alcohol Toxicology for the Medicolegal Professional

Wigmore on Cannabis: The Forensic Toxicology of Marijuana for Lawyers and Other Medicolegal Professionals

Wigmore on Nicotine: The Medicolegal Aspects of Our Most Addictive and Dangerous Legal Drug

SECOND EDITION

WIGMORE ON ALCOHOL

Courtroom Alcohol Toxicology for the Medicolegal Professional

JAMES G. WIGMORE

Forensic Toxicologist

Irwin Law
An imprint of University of Toronto Press
Toronto Buffalo London
utorontopress.com

ISBN 978-1-5522-1683-5 (paper) ISBN 978-1-5522-1684-2 (PDF)

Library and Archives Canada Cataloguing in Publication

Title: Wigmore on alcohol : courtroom alcohol toxicology for the medicolegal professional / James G. Wigmore, forensic toxicologist.
Names: Wigmore, James G., author.
Description: Second edition. | Includes bibliographical references and indexes.
Identifiers: Canadiana (print) 20240315855 | Canadiana (ebook) 20240315871 | ISBN 9781552216835 (softcover) | ISBN 9781552216842 (PDF)
Subjects: LCSH: Alcohol in the body — Measurement — Bibliography. | LCSH: Alcohol —Physiological effect — Bibliography. | LCSH: Medical jurisprudence — Bibliography. | LCGFT: Bibliographies.
Classification: LCC QP801.A3 W54 2024 | DDC 615.7/828—dc23

Cover images: Igor Normann | Adobe Stock

We wish to acknowledge the land on which the University of Toronto Press operates. This land is the traditional territory of the Wendat, the Anishnaabeg, the Haudenosaunee, the Métis, and the Mississaugas of the Credit First Nation.

University of Toronto Press acknowledges the financial support of the Government of Canada and the Ontario Arts Council, an agency of the Government of Ontario, for its publishing activities.

Canada Council for the Arts Conseil des Arts du Canada

Funded by the Government of Canada Financé par le gouvernement du Canada | Canada

This book is dedicated to my parents, Betty and Dick Wigmore, who were devoted to their seven sons, two daughters, and eighteen grandchildren. I would also like to dedicate this book to my mother's sister, Ruby, who was known affectionately to us as "auntie."

Summary Table of Contents

Detailed Table of Contents

List of Tables

(Reference number bold in brackets)

CHAPTER 1

CHAPTER 2

CHAPTER 3

- The Postmortem BAC and National Transportation Safety Board Findings of Various Pilots Killed in Fatal Civil Aviation Accidents **(60710)**
- Congener Concentration of Methyl, N-butyl, and Iso-butyl Alcohols in Mg/Standard Drink and Type of Alcoholic Beverage **(60811)**
- Symptoms of Hangover and Percent of Persons Affected **(60812)**
- Number of Wounds in Fatally Injured Stabbing Victims, the Male/Female Ratio, and Percent Positive BAC **(60903)**
- Circumstances of the Homicide and Percent of Victims with a BAC > 0.100 g/100 mL **(60907)**
- Percentages of Homicide Offenders, Victims, and Controls Positive for Alcohol According to Gender **(60916)**
- Mean BAC and Percent of Victims with BAC > 0.150 g/100 mL According to Type of Homicide **(60917)**
- Percentage of Female and Male Victims and Offenders Who Tested Negative and Positive for Alcohol, Alcohol and Drugs, and Drugs Only **(60918)**
- Percent of Postmortem Anatomical Findings in Hyperthermia Deaths **(61007)**
- Percent Occurrence of Autopsy Findings in 69 Hypothermia Victims **(61009)**
- Type of Maritime Accident While the Operator Was Under the Influence of Alcohol **(61109)**
- Percentages of the Type of Injuries in Under and Not Under the Influence of Alcohol in the Water Pool Floating Crew **(61110)**
- Mean Change in Rudder Alterations at BACs of 0.050 and 0.080 g/100 mL and Engine Commands Obeyed (0.080 g/100 mL BAC) for Cadets and Officers **(61112)**
- Some Blood Parameters (Mean Results) Before and Immediately After Tasering of Alcohol-Intoxicated Subjects **(61219)**
- Odds Ratio of Crash Characteristics of Motorcyclists Compared to Drivers **(61313)**
- Adjusted Odds Ratio (OR) of Moped and Motorcycle Drivers Responsible for Their MVC **(61314)**
- Mean (and Range) Percent Decrease in Driving Ability of Operating an E-Scooter at Various BACs **(61315)**
- Mean Mortality Rate, SAC, and Percent with SAC > 0.050 g/100 mL in Drivers of Automobiles, Motorcycles, and Mopeds **(61317)**
- Percent of Pedestrians with BAC > 0.150 g/100 mL According to Accident Type **(61401)**

CHAPTER 7

CHAPTER 8

CHAPTER 9

Foreword to the First Edition

BY DOUGLAS M. LUCAS

If one "Googles" *ethyl alcohol* (which will be referred to here simply as *alcohol*), it will be found described as, among other things, a "central nervous system depressant" drug. Although this will seem counterintuitive to many people (who drinks to get to sleep?), there is ample pharmacological literature to confirm this description. Indeed, there is undoubtedly no other single drug that has been the subject of so much research or has had so much written about it over such a long period of time.

The pleasures associated with the consumption of moderate doses of alcohol probably began to be enjoyed around 8000 BCE when it was discovered somewhere in central Asia that grapes, if allowed to stand and ferment, turn as if by magic into wine. As a result, it has been observed that "liquor drinking is a part of human behavior in which mankind has indulged forever" (Chaftez, 1965). The explanation for this may be found in the book of Proverbs: "Let him drink and forget his poverty, and remember his misery no more" (31:7).

Ancient literature, and stories about some ancients in more recent literature, contains references to the use of alcohol. For example, at some time in the seventh or eighth century BCE, Homer (or whoever wrote under that name) described behavior that may be observed in any tavern, even today: "The wine urges me on, the bewitching wine, which sets even a wise man to singing and to laughing gently and rouses him up to dance and brings forth words which were better unspoken" (*The Odyssey,* Book XIV, lines 527–30).

More recently, Chesterton rhymed in a couple of poems (1914a, 1914b): "And Noah he often said to his wife when he sat down to dine / I don't care where the water goes if it doesn't get into the wine"; and,

St. George he was for England
And before he killed the dragon
He drank a pint of English ale
Out of an English Flagon.

"Modern" (relatively) research on alcohol began with the alchemists who discovered the delights of distillation. The alcohol so derived seemed to represent a mystical union of fire and water and the ultimate secret of life itself. It is therefore not surprising that it was referred to by the Scottish as *uisge beatha*, "water of life," from which the term *whiskey* is derived. The demand for this product developed so extensively that distillation became the foundation for the first science-based industry.

As a result of all this history, this single drug has had enormous impact, both positive and negative, on society almost everywhere: "positive" through its stimulation of agriculture (grains for beer and whiskey, grapes and other fruits for wine, sugar for rum) in many geographic areas; the economy from its production, processing, distribution, and marketing throughout much of the world; and as a source of revenue for governments through widespread taxation of its sales; "negative" as a result of the effects of its misuse and abuse on health, transportation, crime, and law enforcement.

Alcohol and transportation have been in conflict since at least the days of Noah. Although not recorded on the manifest of "two of every sort—male and female" on board the Ark, yeast cells obviously stowed away and later industriously produced wine in the vineyards Noah planted: "Noah was the first tiller of the soil. He planted a vineyard; and he drank of the wine, and was drunken, and lay uncovered in his tent" (Genesis 9:20–21).

The volume of the scientific literature about alcohol presents a classic "good news/bad news" story. The good news is that, on almost any specific issue one chooses to review, there are multiple published studies to which one can refer. The bad news is that the sheer number of such studies can make finding the one or two most relevant articles an extremely challenging task. In particular, persons involved in litigation of cases in which alcohol use may have been a factor, such as lawyers, judges, coroners/medical examiners, and expert witnesses, frequently need to refer quickly to a particular study that they remember having seen but of which they cannot recall all the details. The author of this book, James Wigmore, is very familiar with such situations and has written this resource to serve as an *aide-mémoire*—to permit these persons to quickly find, review, and refresh their memory about the details of specific studies.

Wigmore has more than 30 years of experience as a forensic toxicologist specializing in the pharmacology of alcohol. During that period, he has almost obsessively collected, reviewed, summarized, and organized more than 9,000 articles related to his subject of interest published in over 190 scientific journals. From this database, he has selected some 700-plus studies covering a wide range of topics that regularly become issues in litigation. The criteria he has used for the selection of the articles to include in this book are the relevance of the studies to these issues and their reflection of the scientific consensus on the issues. For each included study, Wigmore has provided his own concise summary of its significance to the issues, written in a style that is appropriate for not only forensic toxicologists but others concerned with medicolegal issues. As much as possible, he has avoided unnecessary scientific jargon. He also has included with each summary some or all of the authors' conclusions as they appear in the original publication. For those who wish to use or cite a particular study, Wigmore firmly recommends consultation of the original publication through a variety of databases.

An indication of the range of issues covered is provided by the titles of the eight chapters. Topics range from the absorption, distribution, and elimination of alcohol, through the various materials used for analysis in forensic alcohol toxicology, to the effects of alcohol on a variety of human activities and behaviors. The latter discussion is not restricted to the effects on ability to drive—which is, of course, the commonest alcohol-related issue dealt with in the courts of most jurisdictions—but also covers such issues as aggression and violence, blackouts and memory, homicide, and sexual assault, among others.

Each chapter and subsection is introduced with a brief summary of the specific topic to orient the reader to the related issues. For example, the section (1.06) on Widmark calculations to estimate the amount of alcohol in a body based on a determined blood alcohol concentration (BAC), advises that such calculations tend to "underestimate the amount consumed and overestimate the BAC." Because this particular issue tends to take up an inordinate amount of court time in drinking-and-driving cases, it is helpful that the introduction to the section includes the sage comment that "another problem with calculating BAC from a drinking scenario is that alleged drinking patterns from drinking drivers are notoriously unreliable . . . and of little scientific value," with references to related studies.

Similarly, on another topic that has wasted enormous amounts of valuable court time, the blood-breath ratio (BBR), Wigmore introduces the relevant studies (3.04) with a pithy assertion: "Much unnecessary controversy has arisen in court regarding the BBR. BBRs < 2,100:1 are mainly due to the low BACs tested"; he then provides the relevant references.

Everyone who has studied any of the massive literature on the effects of alcohol on ability to drive will have a few favorite studies that have influenced their interest in the subject, and I am no exception. I was therefore delighted to see that Wigmore has included a long-time favorite of mine: reference number 50302 summarizes an article by Cohen et al from a 1958 issue of *British Medical Journal*, "The Risk Taken in Driving Under the Influence of Alcohol." This rather simple but elegant research showed that experienced bus drivers, when asked to drive their buses through a series of narrowing gaps until they reached a gap they deemed too narrow to pass, "were prepared to drive their vehicles through narrower gaps" with increasing BAC (although still low—0.05 g/100 mL). Willingness to accept increasing risk is a major factor in alcohol-related incidents (not only motor vehicle crashes), and for me this study has always represented a graphic demonstration of this aspect.

Proof that one can never be too old to learn is provided in reference number 60807—summarizing an article by Pittler et al published in 2003 in the *Canadian Medical Association Journal*—from which I learned, after more than 50 years in forensic science, "that artichoke extract does not prevent the signs and symptoms of alcohol induced hangover over and above placebo." Who knew?

The range of issues presented in this book is very broad. For example, discussion of the effects of alcohol range from the critical, such as homicides and sexual assaults, to the trivial, such as mosquito bites, sunburn, fear of snakes, and dart throwing. In other words, no matter what the reader's interest, there will be one or more references to it in this book. I regret that it was not available to me during my years of active practice in forensic science.

Douglas M. Lucas, MSc, DSc (Hon)

Retired Director, Centre of Forensic Sciences, Toronto, 1967–1994
Former Acting Assistant Deputy Minister of the Public Safety Division, 1992–1994
Recipient of the Gradwohl Award, the Derome Medal, and Robert F. Borkenstein Award
Retired Fellow and first Canadian President, American Academy of Forensic Sciences
Member/Chair, Canadian Society of Forensic Science, Alcohol Test Committee, 1967–2000

REFERENCES

CHAFTEZ, M.E. *Liquor, the Servant of Man*. Boston and Toronto: Little Brown & Co., 1965.

CHESTERTON, G.K. "The Englishman." *The Flying Inn*. London: John Lane Co., 1914b.

CHESTERTON, G.K. "Wine and Water." *The Flying Inn*. London: John Lane Co., 1914a.

Foreword to the Second Edition

BY A.W. JONES

The first edition of this book, *Wigmore on Alcohol*, was published in 2011, and much has happened in the business of scientific publishing over the past decade. Many journals no longer appear in the regular print format; they have become electronic, "online only," and one example of this change is the *Journal of Forensic Sciences*. Another trend in scientific publishing is "open access," which allows people to download PDF versions of individual articles gratis via the internet. One negative aspect of scientific publishing is the upsurge of predatory journals. These bombard scientists with unsolicited emails asking them to submit their next article for publication in some newly created journal. Most of these so-called opportunistic journals have gained a dubious reputation because they seem motivated more by monetary gains and profit rather than advancing scholarly publishing.

In this new edition of *Wigmore on Alcohol* the articles selected for review and evaluation are derived from well-established periodicals with experienced editors and mainstream publishers. The first edition of this book was compiled from information contained in ~700 journal articles, whereas this new edition is expanded to include more than 1,100 published articles.

In a nutshell, this book is concerned with research publications dealing with forensic aspects of alcohol. This book will prove particularly beneficial to all those who, in one way or another, are involved with investigation of alcohol-related crimes, especially driving under the influence of alcohol (DUI). Accordingly, the new edition of *Wigmore on Alcohol* is a valuable resource and a must-read for forensic practitioners, as well as those in the legal profession (attorneys, coroners, public prosecutors, and judges) and people called to testify in court as expert witnesses.

Although alcohol is a legal drug, it is often referred to as the Jekyll and Hyde of the drug world, because moderate drinking, such as one to two glasses of wine daily, is considered harmless, whereas heavy drinking and drunkenness wreck people's lives and lead to premature deaths. One of the biggest societal problems of irresponsible drinking is in connection with alcohol-impaired driving and associated road-traffic crashes. Statistics from different countries show that between 20% and 45% of the drivers killed in road-traffic crashes had an autopsy blood alcohol concentration (BAC) above the statutory limit for driving.

Road-traffic legislation in most nations defines a threshold concentration of alcohol in a sample of the driver's blood, breath, or urine above which it is an offense to drive a motor vehicle. This legal framework focuses attention on the evidence derived from analysis of alcohol (ethanol) in body fluids and whether this exceeds the legal limit for driving. In a criminal prosecution for DUI, a suspect's BAC trumps other evidence of impairment, such as the usual signs and symptoms of drunkenness. Accordingly, the laboratory methods of analysis used in DUI cases must be fit for their intended purpose.

Many questions arise during the prosecution of traffic offenders, such as how the biological specimens were collected, the way they were transported and stored at the forensic laboratory prior to analysis, and above all the accuracy, precision, and specificity of the analytical methods used. These and many other defense arguments are dealt with in this book. Another large section of the book is concerned with factors influencing the disposition and fate of ethanol in the body and the association between BAC and a person's ability to perform skilled tasks, such as driving.

Law firms that specialize in defending people accused of DUI need to have easy access to relevant scientific literature so that they can develop their case and perhaps raise a "reasonable doubt" about the veracity of prosecution evidence and win an acquittal for their client. Things like chain of custody of the specimens, the reliability of the analytical procedures used, whether the laboratory was accredited, and its performance in external proficiency tests are important things to consider. Reliability of the analytical methods used, such as uncertainty of the measurements, also deserves careful consideration when the results are interpreted in a legal context. The enforcement of concentration per se statutes creates a razor-sharp difference in penalty for those suspects with a measured BAC close to one of the statutory limits for driving.

Wigmore on Alcohol is not a textbook to read in the usual sense; instead it is a reference source and a tour de force of the scientific literature devoted to the forensic toxicology of alcohol. The book's subtitle, *Courtroom Alcohol Toxicology for the Medicolegal Professional*, gives a clue to the target readership for this book, namely people involved in litigation arising when alcohol-related crimes are prosecuted or defended, as exemplified by drunken driving, drug-related sexual assault, and deaths involving heavy drinking and drunkenness.

Wigmore on Alcohol takes an in-depth look at the pros and cons of the plethora of defense arguments that commonly arise when DUI suspects are prosecuted. Although most such challenges are bogus, they still need to be explained and rebutted by reference to experimental studies and the results from articles published in peer-reviewed journals. This book by James Wigmore simplifies this task.

The contents of the book are organized in a logical way, and it is easy to find relevant material on a vast array of topics. The author has compiled short summaries of more than 1,000 published articles, and in many instances, he has constructed tables of data summarizing the results reported. James Wigmore is well qualified to produce this book after close to 30 years of working as senior scientist at a major forensic science laboratory in Toronto and the experience he has gained from hundreds of court appearances as an expert witness in drunk-driving cases in the province of Ontario.

The 1,000-odd articles included in this second edition of *Wigmore on Alcohol* are derived from hundreds of peer-reviewed scientific journals. Both peer review and publication are important requirements for the admissibility of scientific evidence in civil and criminal litigation. After a manuscript survives peer review by at least two experts in the subject matter of the article, this gives it a stamp of approval, and the results and conclusions in the article are then considered more authoritative.

The author of this book (James Wigmore) has read widely and made a careful selection of the articles referenced in this second edition of his book. One might wonder what prompted him to select certain publications in preference to others; for example, was it the prestige of the journal where the article was published or the reputation of the lead author of the article concerned? Whatever the motivation, the author has done an excellent job in selecting the most important and relevant articles on the subject of forensic alcohol analysis and the pharmacology and toxicology of this dependence-producing drug.

For each reference, the names of the authors are listed followed by the title of the article and the full name of the journal where the work was published, including year, volume, and page numbers. Along with each citation, the number of figures, tables, and literature references in the article are also included. The second edition of *Wigmore on Alcohol* is divided into nine main sections or chapters, each containing hundreds of references and commentaries:

1. Absorption, Distribution, and Elimination of Alcohol
2. Blood Alcohol
3. Breath Alcohol
4. Urine, Saliva, Sweat, and Breast Milk Alcohol and Biomarkers of Alcohol Consumption
5. Effects of Alcohol on Driving Ability
6. Effects of Alcohol on Other Behaviors
7. Postmortem Alcohol
8. Other Alcohols and Related Compounds
9. Addiction/Alcohol Use Disorders, Withdrawal, Health Risks, FASD, and Public Safety Measures

The preparation of this book was an enormous undertaking and has meant collecting, collating, reading, summarizing, and sorting through thousands of journal articles. There is no doubt that the author possesses a broad knowledge of the entire discipline of forensic alcohol analysis and toxicology. The structure of the book is unique in a number of ways and in my opinion represents the best single reference source for medicolegal professionals. This tempts me to reiterate what is written in the foreword to the first edition of this book: namely, I wish this book had existed when I began my own career in forensic pharmacology and toxicology.

All in all, I can recommend this second edition of *Wigmore on Alcohol* to all those who deal with the host of scientific questions that arise when alcohol-related crimes are prosecuted. Accordingly, this book will appeal to many forensic practitioners, particularly analytical chemists, medical examiners, and toxicologists, as well as those in the legal professions, such as coroners, lawyers, solicitors, barristers, and judges. Judging the strengths and weaknesses of scientific test evidence, such as when traffic offenders are prosecuted and/or defended, has been made a lot easier by having this book available.

This book makes an essential reference source for people preparing to testify in court as expert witnesses in drunk-driving and other alcohol-related crimes. They would be wise to have a copy in their briefcases when they appear in court and/or on their desks at home when writing statements and/or affidavits prior to testimony.

Alan Wayne Jones, BSc, PhD, DSc,
Professor in Forensic Toxicology,
Department of Clinical Chemistry and Pharmacology,
University of Linköping, Sweden

Preface

It has been more than a decade since the first edition of my book *Wigmore on Alcohol* (*WOA*) was published by Irwin Law, and I have been overwhelmed by the positive reaction. So many people practicing in the area of forensic alcohol toxicology (professors, alcohol experts, coroners, pathologists, and lawyers) thanked me for researching and writing such a book as it has helped them immensely in their professional fields.

There were many requests for a second edition over the years, but the basic principles of the forensic aspects of alcohol have not changed substantially during that time. I also did not want to burden my readers with the costs and trouble of frequent new editions.

During the last decade I have not been idle. I continued to update my forensic alcohol database, in preparation for the second edition. I have also written and published additional books, *Wigmore on Cannabis* and *Wigmore on Nicotine*, which have provided me with more insight into our most popular recreational drug: alcohol. Areas such as addictions, withdrawal, fetal alcohol spectrum disorder, and public health issues have been added to the second edition.

I am particularly grateful and honored that the top forensic alcohol toxicologist and researcher in the world, Wayne Jones, wrote the foreword to the second edition. He has published more scientific studies in this area than any other researcher, which is reflected in this book.

Alcohol (ethanol, ethyl alcohol) is the most widespread drug found in medicolegal cases, including civil, criminal, and postmortem aspects. Alcohol is also a unique drug in that it is a simple molecule that is water soluble. It has been extensively studied for more than 100 years. Alcohol can be easily understandable to the nonscientist, although there are numerous popular misconceptions that this book aims to rectify.

I have been a forensic toxicologist specializing in alcohol for more than 35 years. During that time, I have developed a forensic alcohol toxicology database that is currently in ENDNOTES® and consists of more than 12,000 human studies. These published studies have been valuable and important in litigation and should form the basis of expert opinions.

Changes to *Wigmore on Alcohol*

The most obvious change from the first edition is that the number of scientific papers reviewed (i.e., references) in the book has increased by more than 50%, from 711 to more than 1,100. Many readers found the tables in the books to be informative and really liked them, and so the number of tables has been increased by more than 100%, from 85 to 186.

There is a totally new Chapter 9, which includes the topics of addiction, withdrawal, health risks, fetal alcohol syndrome, and public safety measures, topics that I have included in my books on cannabis and nicotine but were ignored in the first edition of *WOA* 10 years ago. I have also included a new section (5.08) on the effects of alcohol and cannabis on driving.

The additional references have been added to the end of the existing sections. The numbering and references of this edition are the same as in the first edition but with newer, updated references added typically to the end of the existing sections.

Some sections, such as those on

- Mouth Alcohol Effect (3.05),
- Transdermal Alcohol (4.03),
- Driving Simulator Studies (5.02),
- Blackouts/Memory (6.03),
- Falls (6.05),
- Sexual Assault (6.17),
- Postmortem Putrefaction (7.02), and
- Fatal BACs (7.04)

have been expanded greatly.

Another innovation for the second edition is the addition of quotations about alcohol at the beginning of every chapter and section. I find quotations add a lot to the knowledge of the forensic aspects of alcohol and alcohol's effect on human society. The quotations range from Abraham Lincoln and Albert Einstein to Homer Simpson and Rodney Dangerfield.

I have added five appendices to the second edition that the reader will find useful, especially Appendix 2, the table of the effects of alcohol with increasing BAC from the National Institute of Alcohol Abuse and Alcoholism, 2014.

The COVID-19 pandemic has affected everyone, and so it has affected various areas in the book. I have included nine studies on the effects of COVID-19, which range from the increase in poisonings due to the increased use and availability of alcohol-based hand sanitizers and decreases in breath alcohol testing of drivers, to increases in alcohol withdrawal syndrome, and suicides in countries that banned stores selling alcohol during lockdowns due to the pandemic.

How to Read *Wigmore on Alcohol*

I would recommend that readers peruse the entire book by reading and reflecting on the carefully selected quotes at the beginning of each chapter and section as they will provide a historical and cultural overview of alcohol and provide a general knowledge of its effects and how persuasive it is globally. And this is a lot of fun.

I would then read the chapter and section introductions as they are almost small scientific treatises on the various topics. Finally, I would get into the meat of the references in more detail and if interested read the original scientific study was well.

The Structure of *Wigmore on Alcohol*

The basic structure has not changed in the second edition, or in any of the other *Wigmore On* books. For the second edition of *WOA*, I have chosen more than 1,100 human studies that cover a wide range of forensic alcohol toxicology issues from more than 200 scientific journals, written mainly in English, but I have included some translated German and Swedish articles as well. The studies are divided into chapters and sections according to the various topics, such as the effects of alcohol on driving (Chapter 5), breath alcohol analysis (Chapter 3), and blood alcohol analysis (Chapter 2).

Each reference or study has a unique five-digit number assigned to it, of which the first digit is the chapter, where the reference is located, followed by two digits for the section in that chapter, and finally the last two digits denote the order that the reference appears in the section. For example, a reference number of **70211** means the reference is in Chapter 7, Section **02**, and is the 11th reference (**11**) in that section. If you look up that reference you will find:

Reference Number: 70211

WIGMORE, J.G. AND B.L.C. CHOW. "Case Report: Detection of Neo-Formation of Ethanol in a Postmortem Blood Sample Using N-Propanol and a Urine Sample." *Canadian Society Forensic Science Journal*, 33: 145–149, 2000 (1 table, 1 figure, 14 references)

Abstract: A thirty-one-year-old man was found dead several hours after a suicidal fall. An autopsy was conducted the next day, and peritoneal cavity blood and urine were collected. The blood was placed in a jar without preservative, and the urine in a tube with 1% NaF. The samples were received at the laboratory 19 days later. The blood alcohol, *n*-propanol, and acetaldehyde concentrations were 0.096, 0.004, and 0.003 g/100 mL, respectively. No volatile compounds were detected in the urine. The ratio of *n*-propanol detected to neo-formation of alcohol was approximately 25:1. *n*-Propanol should not be used as an internal standard for postmortem alcohol analysis.

> The blood ethanol concentration, therefore, is considered unreliable due to the *n*-propanol and acetaldehyde concentrations detected in the blood, the lack of preservation, the long transit time, the apparent lack of refrigeration, and the lack of ethanol or other volatile substances detected in the preserved urine sample. The victim therefore was not under the influence of ethanol or other common drugs at the time of the fall.

This is the format for all references in the book. The reference (or locator) number is the first line in bold, followed by the citation of the article (author, title, journal). Following in brackets are the number of tables, figures, and references (if any) that appeared in the published study. Next there is a short, condensed abstract of the study (written by me). Finally, there is a short quotation (mainly the author's conclusions) from the article.

For the citation, the authors' last names and initials appear in capital letters in the order that they were published. Typically, published scientific papers refer to the first author's last name and year of publication. If there are more than two authors, then the abbreviation "et al" is employed. So, reference 70211 would be referred to as "Wigmore and Chow, 2000."

The title of the reference follows the authors' names and is in quotation marks. Next follows the journal and information about the publication of the article in italics. For reference 70211, the article was published in volume 33 on pages 145 to 149 in the year 2000 in the *Canadian Society of Forensic Science Journal.*

The abstract that follows the journal citation of the reference is written by me and as far as possible avoids scientific jargon. Since the abstract is quite condensed and simplified, it may miss some of the subtleties of the original study, which in some instances may be of twenty pages or more in length. It is important, therefore, for any medicolegal proceedings that the *original published article* should be referred to and not just my short abstract.

The original paper can be obtained from a search online:

- Google Scholar (scholar.google.ca/)
- the US National Library of Medicine at PubMed (www.ncbi.nim.nih.gov/PubMed)
- National Research Council Canada Institute for Scientific and Technical Information (www.nrc-cnrc.gc.ca).

The articles may also be found at the publisher's website.

After the abstract, I have included a short quotation from the original article (except for the translated German and Swedish studies) that conveys in the authors' own words their results or conclusions. Thus, Wigmore and Chow, 2000 state that:

> The blood ethanol concentration, therefore, is considered unreliable due to the *n*-propanol and acetaldehyde concentrations detected in the blood, the lack of preservation, the long transit time, the apparent lack of refrigeration, and the lack of ethanol or other volatile substances detected in the preserved urine sample. The victim therefore was not under the influence of ethanol or other common drugs at the time of the fall.

I find that the quotations from the authors who wrote the actual scientific studies are useful in medicolegal proceedings. The lawyer doesn't have to go through pages and pages of scientific literature but can refer to the quotation and ask the witness where they agree with it or not, and why.

Breath/Blood Alcohol Measurement Units

The units for blood and breath alcohol concentrations have been converted in the abstracts into grams of alcohol in 100 millilitres of blood (g/100 mL). No distinction is made in using different units for breath and blood alcohol concentrations that exist in the legislation of many jurisdictions in the United States and other countries. This statutory sleight of hand refers to the breath alcohol concentration, for example, as grams of alcohol in 210 litres of breath (g/210 L). In the abstracts, the breath alcohol concentration has been reported in g/100 mL of blood using the 2,100:1 blood-breath alcohol ratio.

Some of the quotations from the original study may also mention other units of measuring blood alcohol concentration. In Canada, the statutory BAC units are in milligrams of alcohol in 100 millilitres of blood (mg/100 mL). Hospital alcohol results use the molecular weight of alcohol (46.07 grams) and report the alcohol concentration in millimoles of alcohol per liter of blood (mmol/L). Finally, many European countries use promille, which is the alcohol concentration in parts per thousand as wt/wt, and so the specific gravity of whole blood (1.055) has been employed to convert promille into g/100 mL. The conversions are as follows:

0.08 g/100 mL = 80 mg/100 mL = 17.4 mmol/L = 0.76 promille

I could not include all the papers published in a particular area of alcohol but have attempted to include the most relevant studies that reflect scientific consensus. This is not a historical review and so many of the major historical studies, such as the works by E.M.P. Widmark, have not been included. But in this edition I have included many historical quotes from these early studies as the beginnings of the chapters and sections.

Generally, I have not included review papers or papers that are based mainly on theoretical or academic models or discussions. I have kept mainly to the practical experimental studies.

Again, I would caution to always refer to the *original published paper*, and total reliance should not be placed on my abstract alone.

Acknowledgements

I was fortunate in the first 29 years of my professional career to work at one of the top forensic laboratories in North America, the Centre of Forensic Sciences (CFS) in Toronto, which was directed at that time by Doug Lucas. When I started there in the Toxicology Section in 1976, the court-going scientists who testified on alcohol were very experienced and dedicated and were extremely helpful to a new, inexperienced scientist like myself. The technologists and other staff, especially the library staff, were also of great assistance.

Jeff Teitelbaum, the forensic research librarian of the Global Forensic and Justice Center at Florida International University, has been of inestimable assistance in keeping me up to date with the current alcohol toxicology literature. His email address is forensiclibrary@fiu.edu.

Sherry Colbourne has provided much enthusiastic encouragement and support for more than 10 years on the writing and publishing of my books. She was responsible for getting my book published by Irwin Law. Karen Woodall and Rob Langille, my fellow "retired" colleagues from the Centre of Forensic Sciences, and my friends and walking companions, Andrew Bell and Justin Berrow, have also provided encouragement and support.

I am extremely grateful to my publisher, Jeff Miller of Irwin Law, who has supported me over the years in making my books a reality, and its wonderful editors and designers, including Lesley Steeve, Heather Raven, Rebecca Russell, and Dale Clarry.

Finally, I would also like to greatly acknowledge my amazing wife, Penelope, our wonderful children, Alexander (and spouse Ginny) and Kathleen (and spouse Kris), and our five grandchildren, Chloe, Simon, and Benji, and Calvin and Alice (respectively), who continue to inspire me, love me, and keep me properly grounded. It is in part for their future that I write, so that they will not forget the lessons of the past.

"It has long been recognized that the problems with alcohol relate not to the use of a bad thing, but to the abuse of a good thing."

— Abraham Lincoln

"Wine makes a man better pleased with himself. I do not say that it makes him more pleasing to others."

— Samuel Johnson

"There is a devil in every berry of the grape."

—the *Koran*

CHAPTER 1

Absorption, Distribution, and Elimination of Alcohol

> "But the truth is, that the elimination of alcohol by the skin and lungs in man (in any but the most trivial quantities) was brought indefinitely near in absolute disproof by the earlier researches of Dupré and myself. For the kidney elimination being proved to be practically nil."
>
> —Anstie, "Final Experiments on the Elimination of Alcohol from the Body" (1874)

The absorption, distribution, and elimination of alcohol are also known as the pharmacokinetics of alcohol. Pharmacokinetics is basically the study of what the body does to the drug: how the drug is absorbed, distributed, and metabolized by the various organs of the body. Although the pharmacokinetics of alcohol have been divided into the separate topics of absorption, distribution, and elimination, it should be emphasized that these processes occur nearly simultaneously in the body.

Alcohol is such a simple drug that its basic pharmacokinetics has been known for more than 150 years.

When the absorption of alcohol is greater than the elimination, the blood alcohol concentration (BAC) will increase. When absorption is slowed down such as with food, and absorption is equal to elimination, a plateau will occur, in which the BAC apparently does not change. When absorption is less than elimination, a decrease in BAC occurs, which is basically linear until all the alcohol has been eliminated from the body.

- Absorption > Elimination (BAC increases)
- Absorption = Elimination (BAC plateaus)
- Absorption < Elimination (BAC decreases)

If there is rapid absorption of alcohol from rapid oral drinking or intravenous infusion, then distribution may lag behind absorption and result in a significantly higher alcohol concentration in the arterial blood than the venous blood (arterio-venous lag).

The typical drinking patterns and pharmacokinetics of drinking drivers are also found in this chapter, as well as extrapolation or back calculations of the BAC of the drinking driver to an earlier time. Widmark (or forward) BAC calculations, which are generally much less reliable than back calculations, are in section 6. The effects of other drugs (e.g., cimetidine) and the effects of trauma are covered in sections 7 and 8, respectively.

1.01 ABSORPTION

> "Due to its low molecular weight and very high solubility in water, alcohol passes readily through all body membranes."
>
> — Cooke et al, "Absorption of Ethanol from the Stomach" (1969)

> "Alcohol is absorbed by the entire gastrointestinal tract. Its absorption is rapid in the stomach and even more rapid in the small intestines."
>
> — Mendoza et al, "Alcohol Absorption Following Jejunal Interposition in Patients with Previous Gastric Surgery" (1977)

Alcohol is generally absorbed after oral consumption via the stomach and small intestine. Alcohol is a unique drug in that it can be substantially absorbed via the stomach (10101–10103), although absorption from the small intestine is more rapid. The concentration of alcohol in the stomach decreases rapidly so that it is rarely beneficial to lavage or remove the contents of the stomach in alcohol-intoxicated patients, as usually only minimal amounts of alcohol remain in the stomach by the time the patient attends hospital (10105).

Food tends to slow the absorption of alcohol and decrease the maximum BAC but does not substantially prolong the time to the peak BAC (10106–10108). After fasting, however, a higher BAC is obtained after drinking a vodka tonic than beer or wine (10131).

Carbonation tends to cause a more rapid absorption of alcohol and increase the initial BACs (10109, 10110), but salty foods and warm temperatures of alcoholic beverages do not significantly change the rate of alcohol absorption (10111, 10112). Various gastric surgeries such as a gastric bypass may substantially increase the rate of alcohol absorption, and patients who undergo these operations should be warned of this possible effect (10114, 10129–10132).

Alcohol is not significantly absorbed by inhalation through the lungs (10120–10122) or via diffusion through the skin (10118, 10119, 10123, 10124). Hence, the frequent use of an alcohol-based hand sanitizer (ABHS) will not cause a significant BAC (10118, 10119, 10126–10128). In addition, the frequent use of ABHS in a daycare setting did not cause detectable breath alcohol content (BrAC) in either the children or staff (10126). This is of particular importance as ABHS is more frequently used as a result of COVID-19. However, the traces of alcohol inhaled or absorbed from ABHS may in some cases provoke a disulfiram ethanol reaction (10128).

Alcohol can be rapidly absorbed by intravenous infusion (10115, 10116) or a rectal enema (10117).

The eating of a large amount of chocolate-covered brandies will result only in nausea and a headache and not a significant BAC (10125).

Reference Number: 10101

BERGGREN, S.M. AND L. GOLDBERG. "The Absorption of Ethyl Alcohol from the Gastro-Intestinal Tract as a Diffusion Process." *Acta Physiologica Scandinavia,* 1/2: 246–270, 1940/1941 (4 tables, 4 figures, 47 references)

Abstract: The absorption of alcohol from the stomach was determined in cats and humans. Several human subjects were administered up to 300 mL of a 5% or 8% alcohol solution via a stomach tube. The stomach alcohol concentration was then determined over time. A mathematical model (based on Fick's law) of the diffusion process was presented. In human subjects with a closed pylorus, approximately 40% of the alcohol is absorbed after 30 minutes, 70% after 60 minutes and 100% after 120 minutes. If the stomach is emptied, 100% can be absorbed within 30 minutes. Tests were also conducted on patients with gastritis and achlorhydria (associated with severe anemias) and stomach cancer. No significant differences in alcohol absorption from the stomach were observed compared to normal subjects.

Table. Percent of Alcohol Absorbed from the Stomach and Stomach Emptying Time in Five Normal Subjects After Instillation of 300 mL of 5% Alcohol Solution

Subject Number	Percent Alcohol Absorbed from Stomach		Time of Stomach Emptying (minutes)
	30 minutes	60 minutes	
1	70%	96%	25
2	58%	85%	-
3	41%	72%	25
4	100%	–	5
5	45%	78%	9

Source: Adapted from Berggren and Goldberg (1940/1941).

The absorption of ethyl alcohol from the stomach follows the laws of diffusion. This means that the greater the concentration of alcohol ingested, the more rapidly will absorption take place with a higher and earlier blood alcohol maximum.

Reference Number: 10102

COOKE, A.R. "The Simultaneous Emptying and Absorption of Ethanol from the Human Stomach." *Digestive Diseases*, 15: 449–454, 1970 (2 tables, 3 figures, 12 references)

Abstract: A total of 237 test meals (117 of water and 120 of 7.5% volume of solute per volume of solvent [v/v] ethanol) were given to seven healthy, fasting subjects. The volume of the meals was 350 mL. Gastric contents were aspirated at various times and the alcohol concentration was measured by an ADH procedure. The emptying of ethanol meals and water meals proceeded at the same rate, up to about 30 minutes when about 90% of the meal had left the stomach. Absorption of ethanol was related directly to the time present in the stomach. The emptying was exponential in rate.

The findings of this study in conjunction with those of a previous study, suggests that similar amounts of ethanol can be absorbed by the stomach within 30 min whether emptying is delayed or allowed to proceed normally. Both studies indicate that the stomach is an important site of ethanol absorption.

Reference Number: 10103

CORTOT, A., G. JOBIN, F. DUCROT, C. AYMES, V. GIRAUDEAUX, AND R. MODIGLIANI. "Gastric Emptying and Gastrointestinal Absorption of Alcohol Ingested with a Meal." *Digestive Diseases and Sciences*, 31: 343–348, 1986 (6 figures, 14 references)

Abstract: The gastric evacuation and GI absorption of alcohol was measured by the intubation of seven male subjects. A homogenized meal containing [14C]PEG and 1.0 g/kg ethanol was given intragastrically. BACs were found to increase rapidly in the first hour and plateaued thereafter at a BAC of about 0.060 g/100 mL. The meal probably delayed gastric emptying of alcohol and prolonged its presence in the stomach which resulted in more absorption through the stomach wall.

> The main finding of the present study is that alcohol ingested with a meal is mainly (70%) absorbed by the stomach and to a lesser extent by the duodenum (25%); the amount of alcohol passing the angle of Treitz is thus negligible. Previous data on the site of alcohol absorption are surprisingly scarce and were obtained with inadequate methods. Some very old studies only rely on alcohol blood concentrations or on animal data.

Reference Number: 10104

HALSTEAD, C.H., E.A. ROBLES, AND E. MEZEY. "Distribution of Ethanol in the Human Gastrointestinal Tract." *American Journal of Clinical Nutrition*, 26: 831–834, 1973 (2 figures, 16 references)

Abstract: Chronic alcoholics often have abnormalities of intestinal absorption that revert to normal after abstinence of alcohol and a normal diet. In this study, five chronic alcoholics and two normal subjects were given 0.8 g/kg ethanol either PO or IV. A sampling tube was placed in the stomach and intestine and the fluids were analyzed by GC. For ethanol consumed PO, the gastric alcohol concentration peaked at 7–8 g/100 mL after 45 minutes. The duodenum and proximal jejunum peaked at 1–5 g/100 mL after 45 minutes. After 120 minutes, the concentration of ethanol in the serum and all GI sites were similar and declined in parallel to 0.02–0.05 g/100 mL by 300 minutes. For ethanol given IV, over 0.5 hours as a 20% v/v solution, the serum levels peaked at 0.128 g/100 mL after 45 minutes and fell to 0.055 g/100 mL. The concentration of ethanol in gastric, jejunal, and ileal contents peaked between 30 and 90 minutes, somewhat higher than the serum. After 120 minutes all sites were comparable to serum in ethanol concentration.

> In the present subjects, after an initial equilibrium period following its acute administration, ethanol was distributed equally in the vascular space, stomach, and small intestine. After oral ingestion, maximal ethanol levels were found in the stomach, duodenum, and proximal jejunum. High ethanol levels were sustained for up to 1 hr at these sites.

Reference Number: 10105

POLLACK JR, C.V., R.C. JORDEN, F.B. CARLTON, AND M.L. BAKER. "Gastric Emptying in the Acutely Inebriated Patient." *Journal of Emergency Medicine*, 10: 1–5, 1992 (3 tables, 37 references)

Abstract: Eleven female and thirty-nine male alcohol-inebriated patients (ages eighteen to sixty-five years) with a BrAC > 0.150 g/100 mL (as determined with an Alco-Sensor) underwent the evacuation of the stomach using a nasogastric tube in order to ascertain if significant amounts of alcohol can be removed prior to absorption. The time since the last drink was reported to range from 20 to 660 minutes (mean 290 minutes). Venous BACs were also measured and ranged from 0.108 to 0.637 g/100 mL. The volume of aspirate ranged from 50 to 700 mL (mean 190 mL) and the gastric alcohol concentration ranged from 0.1 to 2.9% v/v, mean 0.6% v/v. There was no significant correlation between the patient's stated drinking history or BAC and the aspirate volume or alcohol concentration. The authors estimated the increase in BAC that would result from the absorption of the measured alcohol in the gastric contents. However, the volume of distribution of alcohol used in this calculation was based only on the plasma volume (5% of body weight), rather than total body water (approximately 60% of body weight). The corrected increases in BAC ranged from 0.0003 to 0.014 g/100 mL.

Table. Self-Reported Types of Alcoholic Beverage Consumed by Fifty Intoxicated Patients as a Percentage

Beverage Type	Percent of Patients
Beer only	32%
Beer and liquor	20%
Beer, wine and liquor	6%
Liquor only	32%
Liquor and mouthwash	2%
Wine only	4%
Wine and liquor	2%
Mouthwash only	2%

Source: Adapted from Pollack Jr., et al (1992).

The occasional inebriated patient might benefit from gastric emptying in the ED. These data, however, do not support routine gastric evacuation solely for the management of ethanol ingestion, as the benefit would be small and would not justify the risk and inconvenience of the intervention.

Reference Number: 10106

WATKINS, R.L. AND E.V. ADLER. "The Effect of Food on Alcohol Absorption and Elimination Patterns." *Journal of Forensic Sciences*, 38: 285–291, 1993 (1 table, 2 figures, 14 references)

Abstract: Six male and three female subjects consumed 0.69 g/kg ethanol as a 15% v/v solution as quickly as possible (mean time 12 minutes). The subjects consumed the alcohol after either a 6-hour fast or after consuming a pepperoni pizza. The subjects provided a breath sample into an Intoxilyzer 4011A every 8 minutes. The time to maximum BAC was assumed to be the time in which the BrAC reached within 0.003 g/100 mL of the maximum. The mean time to maximum was 41 minutes for both fasting and food conditions. The mean maximum BAC was 0.079 g/100 mL on empty stomach and 0.062 g/100 mL on a full stomach. The mean rate of alcohol elimination was 0.020 g/100 mL/h (range 0.017–0.023 g/100 mL/h) on an empty stomach and 0.017 g/100 mL/h (range 0.014–0.020 g/100 mL/h) with food.

As expected, the presence of food in the stomach reduced the peak BrACs (averaging 21.5% lower). However, regardless of stomach condition the time to reach maximum BrAC was relatively short, on average being 41 min. The most important finding of this study was the short time required to reach the maximum BrAC and the failure of food to prolong the rising phase (upward sloped lag of the BrAC curve).

Reference Number: 10107

FINNIGAN, F., R. HAMMERSLEY, AND K. MILLAR. "Effects of Meal Composition on Blood Alcohol Level, Psychomotor Performance and Subjective State after Ingestion of Alcohol." *Appetite*, 31: 361–375, 1998 (2 tables, 3 figures, 46 references)

Abstract: Fifty-one male subjects (ages eighteen to forty years) were divided into six experimental groups; alcohol-carbohydrate, placebo-carbohydrate, alcohol-protein, placebo-protein, alcohol-fast and placebo-fast groups. Alcohol consumption was between 88.5–118.3 mL of vodka (37% v/v alcohol) calculated to obtain a BrAC of approximately 0.060 g/100 mL. BrACs were determined every 20 minutes with an Alcolmeter AE-D3. High protein or high carbohydrate meals (with minimal fat content) were consumed prior to alcohol consumption. Various psychomotor tests were conducted, and subjective state was measured before and after the alcohol administration. The mean peak BrACs were approximately 0.060 g/100 mL (fasting), 0.041 g/100 mL (protein) and 0.035 g/100 mL (carbohydrate). Two hours later the BrACs were 0.040 g/100 mL (fasting) and 0.028 g/100 mL (protein and carbohydrate).

These findings imply that the benefits of eating before drinking are modest at best, do not nearly eliminate performance impairment and that high carbohydrate foods are not noticeably superior to high protein foods. Indeed, the former may be more problematic in practice as high carbohydrate meals can make people feel less drunk while performing as badly as without food.

Reference Number: 10108

JONES, A.W. AND A. NERI. "Evaluation of Blood-Ethanol Profiles after Consumption of Alcohol Together with a Large Meal." *Canadian Society of Forensic Science Journal*, 24: 165–173, 1991 (2 tables, 3 figures, 34 references)

Abstract: Sixteen male subjects (ages thirty-one to fifty-four years) consumed 1.43 g/kg ethanol over 90 minutes together with a large meal consisting of raw herrings, meatballs, cheese, roast beef, ice cream, and coffee. Capillary blood samples were taken at 5, 45, 110, 170, 225, 405, 650, and 775 minutes after drinking ceased. The BACs were determined by the enzymatic method and the peak BACs ranged from 0.097 to 0.141 g/100 mL. The mean rate of elimination was 0.016 g/100 mL/h (range 0.013–0.021 g/100 mL/h). Approximately 80% of the final peak BAC was reached 0–10 minutes after drinking ceased. One subject vomited 60 minutes after the end of drinking and showed no effect on the BAC curve.

Table. Mean Percent of Maximum BAC Obtained in Drinking Subjects After Consumption of Alcohol Ceased

Time after consumption of alcohol ceased (min)	Mean percent of maximum BAC obtained
5	83%
45	91%
109	95%
175	98%

Source: Adapted from Jones and Neri (1991).

These results suggest that part of the dose of alcohol is rapidly absorbed into the blood despite the presence of undigested food in the stomach. However, the absorption of the remaining dose of alcohol might proceed for several hours.

Reference Number: 10109

RIDOUT, F., S. GOULD, C. NUNES, AND I. HINDMARCH. "The Effects of Carbon Dioxide in Champagne on Psychometric Performance and Blood-Alcohol Concentration." *Alcohol and Alcoholism*, 38: 381–385, 2003 (1 table, 2 figures, 23 references)

Abstract: Six male and six female subjects consumed 0.6 g/kg alcohol (approximate volume 325 mL) as champagne or degassed champagne, which was consumed within 20 minutes. The champagne was degassed by whisking in an electric blender. The alcohol content of the champagne was 11.6 g/dL, and the degassed champagne was 11.4 g/dL. Frequent blood samples were collected using an indwelling catheter and PACs were determined by GC. The subjects conducted various psychomotor tests such as CRT, CFF, and CTT. The mean PACs after consumption of degassed champagne were significantly lower than the mean PACs after consumption of champagne for the first 20 minutes after consumption ceased. There was a significant increase in CTT (reaction time) with champagne compared to degassed champagne.

Table. Mean Plasma Alcohol Concentration (PAC) After the Consumption of Champagne or Degassed Champagne

Time after alcohol consumption ceased (min)	Mean PAC after champagne consumption (g/100 mL)	Mean PAC after degassed champagne consumption (g/100 mL)
5	0.052	0.038
10	0.057	0.044
15	0.062	0.057
20	0.058	0.052
25	0.062	0.062

Source: Adapted from Ridout et al (2003).

Although this was very much a pilot study, employing a small number of subjects, the results support the popular belief that champagne may be more intoxicating than wine, although the mechanism remains unclear. Further research into the effects of CO_2 in alcoholic drinks could be of relevance to car drivers and others who wish to monitor their BACs.

Reference Number: 10110

ROBERTS, C. AND S.P. ROBINSON. "Alcohol Concentration and Carbonation of Drinks: The Effect on Blood Alcohol Levels." *Journal of Forensic and Legal Medicine,* 14: 398–405, 2007 (8 tables, 3 figures, 31 references)

Abstract: Nine female and twelve male subjects (ages eighteen to twenty-seven years) consumed 1.1 g/kg and 1.4 g/kg alcohol respectively as vodka neat (38% v/v alcohol), vodka diluted with water (19% v/v), and vodka with carbonated water (19% v/v) within 5 minutes. BrACs were determined every 15 minutes with an Alcolmeter S-D2. The mean peak BrACs were 0.066, 0.077, and 0.080 g/100 mL respectively. The mean absorption rates were 0.002, 0.003, and 0.005 g/100 mL/minute respectively. Subjects absorbed alcohol at a slower rate for undiluted vodka than diluted vodka.

Although this study has shown a significant link between alcohol concentration and alcohol absorption rates, it was performed in laboratory conditions that do little to mimic drinking situations.

Reference Number: 10111

EARLL, J.M., H.H. WESTMORELAND, C.A. WENDT, L.A. WENDT, AND M. PHILLIPS. "The Influence of Temperature on Alcohol Absorption Rates in Humans." *Military Medicine*, 150: 612–613, 1985 (1 figure, 3 references)

Abstract: Six subjects (ages eighteen to fifty-five years) consumed 0.4 g/kg alcohol diluted with water to 200 mL as a hot (60°C) or cold (–2°C) drink after a 4-hour fast. The alcohol was consumed within 3 minutes. BrACs were determined every 3 minutes by an Alco-Sensor III. The subjects rinsed their mouths with tap water at least twenty times before the first breath sample was collected. Although the subjects reported that the hot drink was more potent and had a more rapid onset than the cold drink, neither the peak BrACs nor the time to peak BrACs were statistically different.

If there is any enhancement of alcohol absorption by increasing the temperature of the imbibed fluid, it was not of a magnitude to be clinically important, nor was the difference statistically significant.

Reference Number: 10112

TALBOT, R. AND L. LA GRANGE. "The Effects of Salty and Nonsalty Food on Peak Breath Alcohol Concentration and Divided Attention Task Performance in Women." *Substance Abuse*, 20: 77–84, 1999 (1 table, 21 references)

Abstract: Twelve female subjects (ages twenty-one to fifty years) consumed either a placebo or 0.6 g/kg ethanol with 60 g of pretzels that contained either low (210 mg) or high (800 mg) amounts of sodium, after a 4-hour fast. BrACs were determined every 15 minutes using an Alco-Sensor II. Various psychomotor tests were conducted. The mean peak BrACs were 0.071 g/100 mL with low and 0.079 g/100 mL with high sodium pretzels. Sodium had no effect on the psychomotor tasks including RT.

It therefore seems appropriate to warn women (and men) that the consumption of salty foods while drinking alcohol does not contribute to a slower absorption of alcohol or prevent the BAC from exceeding the legal driving limit.

Reference Number: 10113

ROINE, R.P., T.G. GENTRY, R.T. LIM JR., E. HELKKONEN, M. SALASPURO, AND C.S. LIEBER. "Comparison of Blood Alcohol Concentrations after Beer and Whiskey." *Alcoholism: Clinical and Experimental Research*, 17: 709–711, 1993 (1 table, 1 figure, 18 references)

Abstract: Eleven male subjects (ages twenty-four to forty-eight years) consumed 0.3 g/kg alcohol as beer (4.3% v/v), white wine (11%), dry sherry (17%), and whiskey (40%), after an overnight fast, with a standard breakfast, or after a standard breakfast. The alcohol was consumed within 10 minutes. The volumes of alcoholic beverages for a 70 kg subject were 614, 240, 157, and 67 mL respectively for beer, wine, sherry, and whiskey. BrACs were determined with a Lion Alcometer SD-2 every 10 to 20 minutes.

Table. Mean Peak BrACs After Consumption of Whiskey or Beer Under Different Food Conditions

Food Conditions	Mean peak BrAC after whiskey consumption (g/100 mL)	Mean peak BrAC after beer consumption (g/100 mL)
One hour after a meal	0.023	0.031
With a meal	0.022	0.028
Fasting overnight	0.048	0.039

Source: Adapted from Roine et al (1993).

These findings are of practical importance, because most people normally consume alcoholic beverages with or following meals; therefore, they should be made aware that, under these circumstances, they may be more affected by a dilute beverage, such as beer, than by a concentrated one, such as whiskey for a given dose of alcohol.

Reference Number: 10114

KLOCKHOFF, H., I. NASLUND, AND A.W. JONES. "Faster Absorption of Ethanol and Higher Peak Concentration in Women after Gastric Bypass Surgery." *British Journal of Clinical Pharmacology*, 54: 587–591, 2002 (1 table, 1 figure, 30 references)

Abstract: Twelve women who had undergone gastric bypass surgery (at least 3 years earlier) and twelve matched controls (mean age forty years) consumed 0.3 g/kg alcohol within 5 minutes after an overnight fast. Venous blood samples were collected via an indwelling catheter every 10 minutes and BACs were determined by headspace GC. The mean peak BAC was 0.074 g/100 mL for the women who had the gastric surgery and 0.058 g/100 mL for controls. The time to maximum BAC was 10 minutes (range, 10 to 20 minutes) for the women with gastric surgery and 30 minutes (range, 20 to 50 minutes) for the controls.

> In conclusion, we suggest that after gastric bypass surgery, patients should be warned about drinking alcohol too quickly because even relatively small amounts of alcohol, such as two small glasses of wine (0.3 g/kg) might produce unexpectedly high BAC shortly after the end of drinking. Also, when other surgical procedures are performed on the gut such as gastric resection and gastrectomy, a more rapid absorption of ethanol can be expected.

Reference Number: 10115

DUNDEE, J.W., M. ISAAC, AND J. TAGGART. "Blood Ethanol Levels Following Rapid Intravenous Infusion." *Quarterly Journal of Studies on Alcohol*, 32: 741–747, 1971 (4 figures, 13 references)

Abstract: Subjects were administered 8% v/v ethanol IV within 2 to 8 minutes to help induce anesthesia at a dose of 0.8 g/kg. Venous and arterial blood samples were collected, and BACs were determined by GC. Arteriovenous equilibrium occurred in 3 to 4 minutes and total body equilibrium in 0.5–1 hour. This is a result of ethanol being of low molecular weight and infinitely soluble in water. The rate of elimination is linear; the mean rate was found to be 0.015 g/100 mL/h. There was little variation in the fall of BAC between individuals 0.5–4 hours after infusion. In the first 0.5 hour after infusion there are redistributional changes in BAC.

> During the period of infusion, the alcohol concentration was higher in arterial than in venous blood. The peak arterial concentration as well as the arteriovenous difference depended on the speed of injection.

Reference Number: 10116

MAHDI, A.S. AND A.J. MCBRIDE. "Intravenous Injection of Alcohol by Drug Injectors: Report of Three Cases." *Alcohol and Alcoholism*, 34: 918–919, 1999 (6 references)

Abstract: Three male polydrug uses (ages twenty-nine to thirty-five years) reported injecting alcohol IV. The alcohol was injected rather than consumed because of the rapid onset of effect and the perceived lack of odor of alcohol on the breath. The only described side-effects were a burning pain and local inflammation at the injection site.

> Two other unusual routes of alcohol ingestion have been reported in the media recently, snorting vodka among middle-class English club-goers and the use of vodka-soaked tampons by teenage girls in Eastern Finland. Intravenous injection has some common features with these other methods, e.g., rapid onset of effects, low doses required for intoxication and the reduced likelihood of recent alcohol consumption being identified.

Reference Number: 10117

WILSON, C.I., S.S. IGNACIO, AND G.A. WILSON. "An Unusual Form of Fatal Ethanol Intoxication." *Journal of Forensic Sciences*, 50: 676–678, 2005 (1 figure, 9 references)

Abstract: A fifty-five-year-old man was found dead, naked in 4 to 6 inches of fecal stained water in a bathtub with a rectal enema containing red wine. Three nearly empty 3 L bottles of wine were found near the body. The postmortem BAC was 0.400 g/100 mL and the VHAC was 0.410 g/100 mL, which tends to indicate that the victim died in the rising (absorptive) BAC phase.

> In summary, we report what we believe to be the first case in the English medical literature of an individual fatality from the use of a wine enema. Location of the victim as well as the presence of various articles indicative of enema use is helpful in determining the mechanism of death.

Reference Number: 10118

MILLER, M.A., A. ROSON, AND C.S. CRYSTAL. "Alcohol-Based Hand Sanitizer: Can Frequent Use Cause an Elevated Blood Alcohol Level?" *American Journal of Infection Control*, 34: 150–151, 2006 (6 references)

Abstract: A thirty-eight-year-old physician used an alcohol-based hand sanitizer (ABHS) which contained 62% alcohol, twenty-five times over 2 hours. Five milliliters of ABHS were applied each time to the hands and forearms and allowed to dry. The SAC immediately after the last application was less than the detectable limit (< 0.005 g/100 mL).

> We report a case of a 38-year-old physician with a negative blood ethanol level despite repetitive and high-volume use of a 62% ethanol based ABHS.

Reference Number: 10119

WIGMORE, J.G. "The Purell Defence: Can the Use of Alcohol-Containing Hand Sanitizers Cause an Elevated Breath or Blood Alcohol Concentration?" *Canadian Society of Forensic Science Journal*, 42: 147–151, 2009 (1 table, 15 references)

Abstract: A forty-three-year-old US congressman ran a red light and was stopped by the police. He did not pass the SFST, and his BrAC was 0.150 g/100 mL. The defence raised the issue that the BrAC was due to the use of an alcohol-containing hand rub (Purell) and RFI affecting the breath-testing instrument used by the police. A review of dermal absorption of alcohol was conducted in papers published since 1942.

> The dermal absorption of alcohol has been studied for over sixty years. The research has shown that only negligible amounts of alcohol are absorbed even after excessive use of an alcohol-containing hand sanitizer. No forensically significant blood or breath alcohol concentration in adults will occur via dermal absorption of alcohol.

Reference Number: 10120

LEWIS, M.J. "Inhalation of Ethanol Vapour: A Case Report and Experimental Test Involving the Spraying of Shellac Lacquer." *Journal of the Forensic Science Society,* 25: 5–9, 1985 (1 figure, 3 references)

Abstract: The subject was arrested for impaired driving, but prior to his arrest he had been spraying an ethanolic solution of shellac onto a car body. The BAC as measured by GC was 0.090 g/100 mL. A reconstruction test was conducted on this subject. The concentration of ethanol in the shellac was 86% weight of solute per volume of solvent (w/v). The subject was tested in a small garage with no ventilation. No face mask was worn. The spraying involved a mist of droplets saturating the air. The minimum ethanol concentration of the air was 450–2,500 ppm. The subject had three exposures of 15, 5, and 19 minutes and he endured the exposures for as long as possible. After the end of the exposures the BACs obtained were 0.002 g/100 mL (breath, Alcotector AED-1), 0.001 g/100 mL (blood, GC), and 0.0001 g/100 mL (urine, GC).

> It is difficult to draw general conclusions from an experiment such has been conducted. However, it was the consensus of opinion of the observers present that the subject had endured as much exposure as he could accept. This was particularly evident in the second and third spraying sessions. In this respect, it may be concluded that the BAC found immediately following the last session (the longest and most adverse) represented the maximum level obtainable. Clearly, in relating it to other circumstances, consideration must be given to the nature of any solute present in the ethanol, those with irritant properties (in spray form) being likely to limit acceptable exposure.

Reference Number: 10121

MASON, J.K. AND D.J. BLACKMORE. "Experimental Inhalation of Ethanol Vapour." *Medicine, Science, and the Law*, 12: 205–208, 1972 (2 tables, 2 figures, 9 references)

Abstract: One male subject sat in an enclosed room for 150 minutes in which two liters of alcohol was placed in a dish that measured 54 by 43 cm. Blood samples were collected from the ear and urine samples were collected every 30 minutes. BACs and UACs were determined using the GC method of Curry. All results except the last ear prick blood were zero and that BAC was only 0.005 g/100 mL. The experiment was repeated with three male volunteers with the room temperature elevated to between 30–34°C to allow for a greater saturation of alcohol. In addition, blood samples were collected via venipuncture, which is less prone to contamination. The subjects sat in the room for 165 minutes and during that time 590 mL of alcohol evaporated, resulting in a theoretical air alcohol concentration of 0.0017 g/100 mL atmosphere. All BACs and UACs were zero. In the last experiment one subject consumed 150 mL of 70 proof alcohol and blood and urine samples were collected before and after exposure to alcohol vapors. There was no effect of inhalation of alcohol on the BAC or UAC curves.

In these experiments, the authors were unable to demonstrate the presence of ethanol in blood or urine as a result of inhalation of ethanol vapour. Only once was a positive result obtained (5 mg per 100 mL blood) and this was clearly due to artefact.

Reference Number: 10122

CAMPBELL, L. AND H.K. WILSON. "Blood Alcohol Concentrations Following the Inhalation of Ethanol Vapour Under Controlled Conditions." *Journal of the Forensic Science Society,* 26: 129–135, 1986 (2 tables, 1 figure, 14 references)

Abstract: One male subject (weight 63 kg) was exposed to 1.9 g/m³ ethanol vapor for 3 hours in an exposure chamber. The alcohol vapor was generated by inducing an air stream saturated into the chamber passing over 90% ethanol. Frequent blood samples were collected from an arm with a cannula that was extended outside of the chamber through a porthole to prevent alcohol contamination. BACs were determined by headspace GC and the BACs were all less than 0.0002 g/100 mL.

From the experimental results and the estimated values, it appears that exposure to ethanol vapour at the UK occupational exposure limit of 1,900 mg/m³ will not produce significant blood alcohol concentrations.

Reference Number: 10123

SCHROT, M., K. PUSCHEL, AND C. EDLER. "Drunken by a Bath in Champagne?—Error: No Relevant Ethanol Absorption Through Intact Skin [German]." *Blutalkohol*, 47: 275–281, 2010 (1 table, 2 figures, 15 references)

Abstract: One male and two female subjects bathed for 45 minutes in alcohol baths of varying alcohol concentrations which were heated to 40°C. The baths contained 20 L of sparkling wine in 100 L of water (2% v/v alcohol), two baths of 135 L of sparkling wine (12.5% v/v alcohol) and 15 L of pure alcohol in 105 L of water (12.5% v/v alcohol). BrACs were measured with an Alcotest 6510 while the subjects were up to their necks in the bath. A positive BrAC was detected for all subjects in the bath and ranged from 0.014 to 0.240 g/100 mL, which decreased to < 0.030 g/100 mL after 1–3 minutes of exposure to fresh air. The ambient air around the bathtub was so saturated with alcohol than the assistants (who did not bathe) had a BrAC of 0.020–0.030 g/100 mL. A blood sample was collected at the end of bathing and a positive BAC (0.010 g/100 mL) was detected only in the subject who bathed in the pure alcohol/water mixture. The authors state that intact human skin is not significantly permeable to ethyl alcohol.

Table. BrACs of a Subject Who Bathed in 135 L of Sparkling Wine (12.5% v/v alcohol) Heated to 40°C. At the End of Bathing the BAC Was Zero

Time (minutes)	BrAC (g/100 mL)
0	0.000
5	0.240
10	0.083
20	0.162
30	0.094
45	0.096
5 minutes after end of bath	0.045
10 minutes after end of bath	0.000

Source: Adapted from Schrot et al (2010).

Reference Number: 10124

HANSEN, C.S., L.H. FAERCH, AND P.L. KRISTENSEN. "Testing the Validity of the Danish Urban Myth that Alcohol Can be Absorbed Through Feet: Open Labelled Self Experimental Study". *British Medical Journal*, 341: c6812, 3pp, 2010 (1 table, 1 figure, 3 references)

Abstract: One female and two male alcohol-free subjects (ages thirty-one to thirty-five years) immersed their bare feet into a washing-up bowl containing 2.1 liters of vodka (37.5% v/v alcohol). Blood samples were collected from an indwelling catheter every 30 minutes for 3 hours. PACs were determined using a photometric method with a detection limit of 0.010 g/100 mL. No positive PACs were detected throughout the 3 hours of foot soaking. No skin problems were observed during the experiment, and after the experiment, the skin on the subject's feet was clean and smooth.

> Our results suggest that the transcutaneous intake of alcohol (vodka, 37.5% by volume) through feet is not possible. We therefore conclude that the Danish urban myth about being able to get drunk by submerging feet in strong alcoholic beverages is just that, a myth.

Reference Number: 10125

GRUHN, K.M. AND O. PRIBILLA. "Blood Alcohol Concentrations after Consumption of Brandy Chocolates." [German]. *Blutalkohol*, 21: 363–365, 1984 (3 references)

Abstract: Five healthy, fasting subjects consumed as many chocolate-covered brandies as possible within 1 hour. The amount of alcohol contained in each candy was 10.4% by weight. The subjects consumed between twenty-five and forty chocolate brandies each and could consume up to 500 mL of tea, coffee, or lemonade. Blood samples were collected every 20 minutes for 2 hours, and the BACs were determined by GC. The highest BAC obtained was only 0.001 g/100 mL. All subjects complained of nausea and severe headaches as a result of hyperglycemia.

Reference Number: 10126

KINNULA, S., T. TAPIANINEN, M. RENKO, AND M. UHARI. "Safety of Alcohol Hand Gel Use among Children and Personnel at a Child Day Care Center." *American Journal of Infection Control*, 37: 318–321, 2009 (1 table, 1 figure, 18 references)

Abstract: The BrACs of forty-seven children using 1.5 mL of an alcohol-based hand sanitizer (70% ethyl alcohol) and 35 children using 3.0 mL of an alcohol hand gel (AHG) were determined using an Alcolmeter. No positive BrACs (> 0.001 g/100 mL) were detected even though the contact between the hand and mucous membrane (eyes, mouth, and nose) of the children varied between 0–30 in 15 minutes (mean 2.4 contacts). All children were between three and seven years of age.

> Alcohol was not absorbed when the children at the CDCCs [Child Day Care Center] used an AHG for hand disinfection in the experimental trial, even though there were as many as 30 contacts between the hands and the mucous membranes. There was no sign of any elevated alcohol concentrations in the children's alcometer measurements, although theoretically the amount of alcohol in the AHG could have caused a measurable rise in blood alcohol level.

Reference Number 10127

BESSONNEAU, V. AND O. THOMAS. "Assessment of Exposure to Alcohol Vapor from Alcohol-Based Hand Rubs," *International Journal of*

Environmental Research and Public Health, 9: 868–879, 2012 (1 table, 5 figures, 27 references)

Abstract: The alcohol vapor concentration arising from the use of two different alcohol-based hand sanitizers (ABHS) was determined from air samples collected every 10 seconds from the breathing zone and analyzed by bubbling the samples through a potassium dichromate/sulphuric acid solution. Both hygienic and surgical hand disinfection techniques were employed. The ambient alcohol vapor concentration peaked around 20 to 30 seconds after use of ABHS, and the highest mean concentration was 20 mg/L.

Based on the maximum of 30 hand sanitizers reported per working day, the corresponding absorbed dose would be around 950 mg, approximately one-tenth the dose of ethanol absorbed after one glass of wine (9.6 g).

Reference Number: 10128

BREWER, C. AND E. STREET. "Is Alcohol in Hand Sanitizers Absorbed Through the Skin or Lungs? Implications for Disulfiram Treatment." *Alcohol and Alcoholism*, 55: 354–356, 2020 (10 references)

Abstract: Various experiments were conducted on three subjects using a hand sanitizer (70% ethyl alcohol) and heated vodka (40% ethyl alcohol). The hand sanitizer was applied to the hand, and the hand was then sealed in a plastic bag for 20 minutes. The BrAC as measured with a Lion Alcolmeter 500 was zero. In tests where the hand sanitizer was used close to the nose, a BrAC of 7 mcg/100 mL occurred within 1 minute, which decreased to zero after 5–10 minutes. This was due to residual alcohol in the oral cavity being dissipated upon exposure to fresh air.

Despite the small number of subjects and measurements, this anecdotal study strongly indicates that contrary to repeated claims, significant cutaneous absorption of ethanol from even frequent use of hand sanitizers or other ethanol-containing liquid does not occur. However, especially in confined spaces, and at close quarters, the inadvertent (or *a fortiori*, deliberate) inhalation of ethanol vapor from sanitizers or other sources may transiently produce levels of ethanol absorption that are high enough to cause a mild DER. Even without further and more detailed studies, the traditional warnings in textbooks, papers, formularies, and product information sheets should probably be modified accordingly.

Reference Number: 10129

CHANGCHIEN, E.M., G.A. WOODARD, T. HERNANDEZ-BOUSSARD, AND J.M. MORTON. "Normal Alcohol Metabolism after Gastric Banding and Sleeve Gastrectomy: A Case-Cross-Over Trial." *American College of Surgeons*, 215: 475–479, 2012 (4 tables, 3 figures, 16 references)

Abstract: Two male and seven female morbidly obese patients (mean age forty-six years) who underwent laparoscopic adjustable gastric banding (LAGB) and one male and six female patients (mean age forty-eight years) who underwent laparoscopic sleeve gastrectomy (LSG) were tested pre-operatively and 3 and 6 months postoperatively after consuming one glass (5 oz) of wine. BrACs were determined every 15 minutes after wine consumption using an AlcoHAWK professional breath alcohol tester. The mean peak BrAC and time to a zero BrAC were statistically unaffected by the operations in spite of the fact that the patients during this time period achieved a mean loss of excess weight by approximately 45%. This may have been due to the weight loss being mainly fat, which alcohol does not distribute into.

Table. Mean Peak BrAC in Patients with Laparoscopic Adjustable Gastric Banding (LAGB) and Laparoscopic Sleeve Gastrectomy (LSG)

Operation	Pre-operation	3 months post-operation	6 months post-operation
LAGB	0.034 g/100 mL	0.037 g/100 mL	0.035 g/100 mL
LSG	0.031 g/100 mL	0.029 g/100 mL	0.033 g/100 mL

Source: Adapted from Changchien et al (2012).

> This is the first study to date that longitudinally examines alcohol metabolism among patients undergoing restrictive-type bariatric procedures. We found no significant change in either peak BAC or time to sober six months after LAGB or LSG. Despite achieving weight loss typical of these procedures, the participants did not experience any increased symptoms of intoxication. Furthermore, there was no significant increase in drinking frequency or drinks per sitting postoperatively.

Reference Number: 10130

STEFFEN, K.J., S.G. ENGEL, G.A. POLLERT, L. CAO, AND J.E. MITCHELL. "Blood Alcohol Concentrations Rise Rapidly and Dramatically Following Roux-en-Y

Gastric Bypass." *Surgery for Obesity and Related Disorders*, 9: 470–473, 2013 (1 table, 1 figure, 10 references)

Abstract: Five female subjects (mean age forty-one years) who had undergone Roux-en-Y gastric bypass (RYGB) 3 to 4 years prior consumed 0.3 g/kg alcohol within 5 minutes after a 4-hour fast. Blood samples were collected very frequently up to 60 minutes after consumption, and BACs were measured by an enzymatic method. The mean BACs were 0.043, 0.087, 0.114, 0.127, 0.126, 0.143, 0.109, 0.080, and 0.049 g/100 mL at 1, 2, 3, 4, 5, 7, 7.5, 10, 20, and 60 minutes after consumption of alcohol, respectively.

All five participants substantially exceeded the legal driving limit of 80 mg/dL (0.08%) within minutes following a dose of alcohol that should under normal circumstances produce a BAC significantly under 0.08% in individuals who have not undergone RYGB. Clinicians should educate patients to modify alcohol intake accordingly and to avoid engaging in potentially hazardous activities after drinking.

Reference Number: 10131

MITCHELL JR., M.C., E.L. TEIGEN, AND V.A. RAMCHANDANI. "Absorption and Peak Blood Alcohol Concentration After Drinking Beer, Wine, or Spirits." *Alcoholism: Clinical and Experimental Research*, 38: 1200–1204, 2014 (1 table, 1 figure, 15 references)

Abstract: Fifteen male subjects (ages twenty-five to sixty-five years) consumed 0.5 g/kg alcohol as beer (5.1% v/v alcohol), wine (12.5% v/v alcohol), or vodka tonic (20% v/v alcohol) within 20 minutes after an overnight fast. Venous blood was collected from an indwelling catheter at 0, 10, 20, 30, 40, 60, 90, 120, 150, 180, 210, 240, 360, and 480 minutes. The BACs were determined by headspace GC. The mean peak BACs (and mean time to peak) were 0.077 g/100 mL (36 minutes), 0.062 g/100 mL (54 minutes), and 0.050 g/100 mL (62 minutes) for vodka/tonic, wine, and beer, respectively. There was a 10% reduction in bioavailability of alcohol for beer compared to vodka/tonic.

Findings indicate that BAC is higher after drinking vodka/tonic than beer or wine after fasting. A binge pattern is significantly more likely to result in BAC above 80 mg/dL after drinking vodka/tonic than beer or wine. Men drinking on an empty stomach should know BAC will vary depending on beverage type and the rate and amount of EtOH.

Reference Number: 10132

ACEVEDO, M.B., J.C. EAGON, B.D. BARTHOLOW, S. KLEIN, K.K. BUCHOLZ, AND M.Y. PEPINO. "Sleeve Gastrectomy Surgery: When 2 Alcoholic Drinks Are Converted to 4." *Surgery for Obesity and Related Diseases*, 8: 7pp, 2017 (2 tables, 2 figures, 36 references)

Abstract: Breath and blood alcohol concentrations were measured on nine patients before and eight after RYGB surgery, and eleven patients after SG surgery, after consuming 0.5 g/kg alcohol within 10 minutes after an overnight fast. Blood samples were collected from an indwelling catheter and analyzed for alcohol by GC. BrACs were also determined using an Alco-Sensor IV. The mean peak BACs were 0.059 g/100 mL prior to gastric surgery and 0.101 g/100 mL (after SG surgery) and 0.112 g/100 mL (after RYGB surgery), with the mean time to peak of 35.6, 18.7, and 15.0 minutes respectively. The mean rates of elimination were 0.021, 0.020, and 0.017 g/100 mL/h for before and after SG and RYGB surgery, respectively. The BACs in the SG and RYGB groups were higher than presurgery for the first 35 minutes from the start of drinking. The BrAC was highly and linearly correlated with arterialized BAC ($r^2 = 0.93$), but the BAC was underestimated by 27% on average, probably due to serum alcohol being analyzed rather than blood (i.e., 10% lower BBR and 16% lower blood/serum ratio).

It is important to clarify that the underestimation of BAC by breath analyzers is not unique to the bariatric population; similar differences have been reported in lean nonsurgical candidates when a BAC:BrAC ratio < 2300:1 is used. Although the BAC:BrAC ratio varies widely among people (from 1800:1 to 3200:1), and changes as to a function of time after drinking alcohol, breath analyzers use a constant ratio. The Alco-Sensor IV, which like most breath analyzers is used to provide evidence of whether a driver has consumed alcohol over the legal limit to drive, uses a ratio of 2100:1. A ratio of 2300:1 would be more accurate, but the 2100:1 ratio has been selected because very few individuals have a BAC:BrAC ratio < 2100:1; consequently, the BrAC is almost always lower than the real BAC. Therefore, a person is not at a disadvantage by providing an evidential BrAC instead of venous blood. However, there is another more important issue for the validity of this technique in investigation of the effects of gastric surgeries on alcohol pharmacokinetics—the recommended lag period of approximately 15 minutes from the end of drinking to obtaining the first BrAC. This recommendation is to avoid contamination of the sample with alcohol in oral tissue. However, because peak BAC after RYGB and SG occurs within minutes of drinking, waiting 15 minutes for the first sample means the peak BAC levels will be missed using breathalyzers.

1.02 DISTRIBUTION

"Ethanol is not bound to plasma proteins extensively enough to modify drug distribution."

— Morasso et al, "Amoxicillin Kinetics and Ethanol Ingestion" (1988)

Alcohol distributes throughout the total body water (10201, 10202) and is in a higher concentration in tissues that have a high-water concentration like blood or the brain (10207). It is in a negligible concentration in tissues with a low water concentration like fat or bone. The distribution of alcohol throughout the body after it is consumed orally is as follows:

Stomach/small intestines → Liver → Right side of heart → Lungs → Left side of heart → Body tissues (including the brain) → Right side of heart

Two effects may occur during rapid absorption of alcohol such as when there is rapid drinking on an empty stomach or IV infusion. The first is that the arterial blood concentration can initially exceed the venous blood alcohol concentration. This AV lag is not significant for typical drinking patterns over a period of hours (10203, 10204, 10205). Brain alcohol concentration is more closely related to arterial blood alcohol concentration (as reflected by breath alcohol analysis) than venous blood during AV lag (10206, 10208). The second effect of rapid absorption can be an overshooting in the BAC, and the distribution of alcohol to the tissues is slower than the absorption of alcohol into the blood (10203). As the distribution becomes more uniform with time, there can be a sudden decrease in BAC, greater than could occur due to elimination of alcohol by the liver alone. This effect is known in German as *diffusionssturz* (diffusion drop). This distribution effect may explain some of the apparent high rates of elimination of alcohol reported in various cases.

Loss of body water due to dehydration after exercise had no significant effect on alcohol pharmacokinetics, although dehydrated individuals feel less intoxicated and have a greater willingness to drive (10209).

Reference Number: 10201

ENDRES, H.G.E. AND O. GRUNER. "Comparison of D_2O and Ethanol Dilutions in Total Body Water Measurements in Humans." *Clinical Investigator,* 72: 830–837, 1994 (3 tables, 3 figures, 44 references)

Abstract: The total body water was determined in fifteen male and five female subjects (ages twenty-three to thirty-one years), by the ethanol dilution and D_2O methods. Subjects consumed 0.8 g/kg ethanol within 20 minutes after a 12-hour fast. Blood samples were collected by an indwelling catheter every 20 minutes and the BACs and SACs were determined by the GC and ADH methods. The alcohol elimination rate for male and female subjects was approximately 0.014 and 0.012 g/100 mL/h respectively.

Particularly the comparison with D_2O dilution shows once again that ethanol is diluted only in body water. This confirms that the ethanol concentration in whole blood (water content about 80%) is smaller than that in plasma (water content about 92%) or body water (100% water content).

Reference Number: 10202

JONES, A.W., R.G. HAHN, AND H.P. STALBERG. "Pharmacokinetics of Ethanol in Plasma and Whole Blood: Estimation of Total Body Water by the Dilution Principle." *European Journal of Clinical Pharmacology*, 42: 445–448, 1992 (2 tables, 1 figure, 22 references)

Abstract: Fifteen male subjects (ages fifty-five to sixty-eight years) were administered 0.6 g/kg ethanol IV over 1 hour. Frequent blood samples were collected using an indwelling catheter and whole blood and serum alcohol concentrations were determined by GC. Hematocrit and water content of the blood were also determined. The plasma alcohol concentration was on average 9.8% higher than the whole blood alcohol concentration. The average rate of alcohol elimination was 0.019g/100 mL/h for plasma and 0.017g/100 mL/h for blood.

The TBW in male subjects decreases with age, being about 60% of body weight in 20 to 30 y men and 50% of body weight in men over 60 y. We found that TBW by ethanol dilution is 50.5% of body weight for men with mean age of 62 y. This result agrees well with literature reports of isotope dilution techniques with D_2O or tritiated water as tracers.

Reference Number: 10203

HAHN, R.G., A. NORBERG, AND A.W. JONES. "Overshoot of Ethanol in the Blood After Drinking on an Empty Stomach." *Alcohol and Alcoholism*, 32: 501–505, 1997 (2 tables, 2 figures, 12 references)

Abstract: Six female subjects (ages twenty to forty-one years) were administered 0.4 g/kg ethanol IV or orally within 15 minutes. Both tests were conducted weeks apart after an overnight fast. Frequent blood samples were collected from the cubital vein and the BACs were determined by headspace GC. Three of the six women had an overshoot in BAC after the oral consumption, which varied initially from 21%–50%.

In emergency medicine, it is not uncommon to treat teenagers who have become severely intoxicated because of rapid consumption of only a few alcoholic drinks. The present study suggests that one mechanism to explain the pronounced inebriation is that absorption of ethanol from an otherwise empty stomach occurs faster than the distribution into the total body water. This results in higher BACs than would otherwise be expected.

Reference Number: 10204

JONES, A.W., L. LINDBERG, AND S-G. OLSSON. "Magnitude and Time-Course of Arterio-Venous Differences in Blood-Alcohol Concentration in Healthy Men." *Clinical Pharmacokinetics*, 43: 1157–1166, 2004 (2 tables, 3 figures, 36 references)

Abstract: Nine healthy male subjects (ages twenty-six to sixty-seven years) consumed 0.6 g/kg alcohol within 2 to 15 minutes. Blood samples were collected every 15 to 20 minutes from indwelling catheters in a radial artery and cubital vein in the same arm. BACs were determined by headspace GC and blood water content was also determined. The mean maximum BAC was 0.098 g/100 mL in the arterial blood and 0.084 g/100 mL in the venous blood. The AV difference was greatest 10 minutes after the end of drinking (mean 0.020 g/100 mL, range 0.009 to 0.040 g/100 mL). This AV difference decreased with increasing time, and at a mean time of 90 minutes (range 45 to 105 minutes) the AV difference was zero. The mean rate of elimination was 0.012 g/100 mL/h in the arterial blood and 0.011 g/100 mL/h in the venous blood. The AUC was the same for both the arterial and venous BAC curves. There were no differences in blood water content.

> The magnitude and duration of AV differences reported in the present study after a rapid consumption of alcohol will not necessarily be the same as under real-world drinking conditions when the alcohol is consumed in smaller portions over a longer time period. Drinking alcohol over several hours allows more time for equilibration to occur between the arterial blood and tissue water. Under social drinking conditions, it seems more likely that the amount of alcohol contained in the last drink determines the magnitude of the AV differences in alcohol concentration.

Reference Number: 10205

JONES, A.W., A. NORBERG, AND R.G. HAHN. "Concentration-Time Profiles of Ethanol in Arterial and Venous Blood and End-Expired Breath During and After Intravenous Infusion." *Journal of Forensic Sciences*, 42: 1088–1094, 1997 (1 table, 6 figures, 28 references)

Abstract: The arterial BACs, venous BACs, and BrACs were determined in thirteen male subjects (mean age thirty-one years) who were administered 0.4 g/kg alcohol IV within 30 minutes. Frequent samples of arterial and venous blood were collected, and BACs were determined by head-space GC. BrACs were determined with a BAC DataMaster (based on a BBR of 2300:1). During the loading phase, the arterial BAC > venous BAC by approximately 0.01 g/100 mL. Within 5 minutes from the end of the infusion of alcohol, the AV differences were negligible. In the late postabsorptive phase the arterial BAC < venous BAC by 0.001 to 0.005 g/100 mL. The mean peak concentrations were 0.095 g/100 mL for arterial blood, 0.085 g/100 mL for venous blood, and 0.088 g/100 mL for breath. The mean rate of alcohol elimination was 0.015, 0.015, and 0.016 g/100 mL/h for those samples respectively. The BrAC > venous BAC until approximately 30 minutes after IV infusion ceased and the greatest overestimation was 0.007 g/100 mL. The BrAC < BAC in the postabsorptive phase.

> Accordingly, the use of a fixed ratio of 2100:1 would tend to underestimate BAC during the postabsorptive period. The analysis of venous blood samples gives a minimum estimate of the exposure of the brain to alcohol

which is important to remember when alcohol-induced impairment of body functions is being considered. This follows because the effects of alcohol on performance and behavior are more closely correlated with the concentration reaching the brain tissue as reflected in ABAC and BrAC.

Reference Number: 10206

FEIN, G. AND D.J. MEYERHOFF. "Ethanol in Human Brain by Magnetic Resonance Spectroscopy: Correlation with Blood and Breath Levels, Relaxation, and Magnetization Transfer." *Alcoholism: Clinical and Experimental Research*, 24: 1227–1235, 2000 (2 tables, 4 figures, 55 references)

Abstract: Eighteen male and two female subjects (mean age thirty-two years) consumed 0.85 g/kg alcohol within 15 minutes. Six to seven blood samples were collected via an indwelling catheter and SACs were determined with an enzymatic method. BrACs were determined using an Alco-Sensor IV. Brain alcohol concentrations were determined using proton magnetic resonance spectroscopy. The mean peak BAC was 0.112 g/100 mL which was obtained at a mean of 92 minutes after the start of drinking. The mean alcohol elimination rate was 0.019 g/100 mL/h. The correlation between BrAC and brain alcohol concentration was r = 0.79. The correlation between BAC and brain alcohol concentration was r = 0.58.

The correlation of brain EtOH measures are stronger with BrAC than with BAC, owing possibly to the fact that BrAC more closely reflects arterial rather than venous blood concentrations and thus more closely tracks brain EtOH levels. The correlation suggests that 1H MRS allows direct measurement of transient changes of EtOH levels in the brain formerly only possible indirectly through inference from BrAC levels.

Reference Number: 10207

HETHERINGTON, H.P., F. TELANG, J.W. PAN, M. SAMMI, D. SCHUHLEIN, P. MOLINA, AND N.D. VOLKOW. "Spectroscopic Imaging of the Uptake Kinetics of Human Brain Ethanol." *Magnetic Resonance Medicine*, 2: 1019–1026, 1999 (1 table, 7 figures, 29 references)

Abstract: Eight male subjects (ages twenty-eight to forty-two years) consumed 0.5 g/kg alcohol within 7 minutes. Blood samples were collected every 10 minutes from an indwelling antecubital vein catheter. The BACs were determined enzymatically in deproteinized blood. Brain alcohol concentrations were determined spectroscopically by NMR. The mean peak BACs ranged from 0.030–0.063 g/100 mL. The mean brain/blood alcohol ratio ranged from 9.31 at 15 minutes and decreased to 0.91 at 85 minutes after drinking started.

Table. Mean Brain/Venous Blood Alcohol Ratios at Various Times Since Drinking Started

Time since drinking started (min)	Mean brain/venous blood alcohol ratio
15	9.31
25	2.49
35	1.51
45	1.23
55	1.09
65	1.04
75	0.92
85	0.91

Source: Adapted from Hetherington et al (1999).

This relationship is due to the relatively rapid passage of alcohol into and out of the brain as opposed to skeletal muscle. Thus, the venous drainage of skeletal muscle displays longer time constants for uptake and release. The variations in early time points largely reflect intersubject variability of gastric absorption, resulting in differences in the kinetics of brain uptake and venous appearance. As the absorption phase is completed and the venous blood levels peak, the brain/blood alcohol ratio equalizes and the variability between subjects decreases.

Reference Number: 10208

THIERAUF-EMBERGER, A., J. ECHLE, M. DACKO, AND T. LANGE. "Comparison of Ethanol Concentrations in the Human Brain Determined by Magnetic Resonance Spectroscopy and Serum Ethanol Concentrations." *International Journal of Legal Medicine*, 134: 1713–1718, 2020 (2 tables, 1 figure, 23 references)

Abstract: Three male subjects (ages twenty-four to twenty-nine years) consumed vodka diluted with lemonade over 30 minutes, calculated to obtain a serum alcohol concentration of 0.100 g/100 mL, after a light breakfast. Five blood samples were collected from the end of drinking until 160 minutes later, and the SACs were determined by headspace GC. MRS measurements of ethanol concentrations in the brain were determined. Approximately 7 minutes were required to take two measurements.

Table. Brain and Serum Alcohol Concentrations (Mean of Three Subjects)

	End of Drinking	70 Minutes Later
Serum Alcohol Concentration (g/100 mL)	0.066	0.104
Occipital Cortex (g/100 mL)	0.059	0.049
Cerebellum (g/100 mL)	0.057	0.040

Source: Adapted from Thierauf-Emberger et al (2020).

Ethanol concentrations in brain regions normalized to the water content were lower than the measured serum ethanol concentrations and rather homogenous within the three participants and the various regions of the brain. The maximum ethanol concentration in the brain (normalized to water content) was 0.68 g/L. It was measured in the frontal cortex, in which the highest results were gained. The maximum serum concentration was 1.19 g/L. The course of the brain ethanol curve seems to be flatter than the one of the serum ethanol concentrations.

Reference Number: 10209

IRWIN C., A. GOODWIN, M. LEVERITT, A.K. DAVEY, AND B. DESBROW. "Alcohol Pharmacokinetics and Risk-Taking Behavior Following Exercise-Induced Dehydration." *Pharmacology, Biochemistry and Behavior*, 101: 609–616, 2012 (1 table, 6 figures, 61 references)

Abstract: Twelve male subjects (mean age twenty-three years) consumed 0.4 g/kg alcohol within 10 minutes after exercise (cycle ergometer), which caused a body water loss of approximately 2.5% (1.8 kg of sweat), and without exercise. Two series of tests were conducted in the non-dehydration (euhydrated) conditions. Blood samples were collected from an indwelling catheter. PACs were determined by an enzymatic method and were converted into a BAC using a factor of 1.14. BrACs were determined with an Alcolizer LE breathalyzer. Subjective measures of intoxication were also measured. Peak BrACs were obtained 15 to 30 minutes post-ingestion, and the means were 0.069 g/100 mL (dehydration) and

0.072 and 0.070 g/100 mL (non-dehydration conditions). There were no differences in alcohol pharmacokinetics in the dehydration or non-dehydration conditions. The subject's self-reported intoxication was lower and willingness to drive higher for the dehydration experiment.

> These results suggest that acute changes in total body water content as a result of exercise-induced sweat loss have no impact on alcohol pharmacokinetics when a moderate dose of alcohol is consumed. The lack of observed differences in pharmacokinetic response between the different trial conditions was evident regardless of whether fluid loss was considered as changes in body weight or estimated total body water loss. One possible explanation for this may be that the diuresis due to alcohol was much greater in euhydrated subjects particularly in the first 60 minutes following alcohol ingestion (720 mL for euhydrated trials and 120 mL for dehydrated trial).

1.03 ELIMINATION

> "Experimental results are presented which demonstrate that the oxidation of ethyl alcohol is a specific liver function and that oxidation of alcohol does not take place in the muscles."
>
> —Lundsgaard, "Alcohol Oxidation as a Function of the Liver" (1938)

The vast majority of alcohol is eliminated by the liver at constant rate. Alcohol is converted mainly by the ADH enzyme system in the liver into acetaldehyde, then into acetic acid, and eventually to carbon dioxide and water, as shown by the following chemical equation:

$$CH_3CH_2OH \rightarrow CH_3CHO \rightarrow CH_3COOH \rightarrow CO_2 + H_2O$$

The rate of alcohol elimination can be increased by chronic use of alcohol (10301, 10302). Prior or co-ingestion of food cannot only slow the absorption of alcohol but can increase the elimination rate as well (10304). A high protein diet also tends to increase the rate of elimination of alcohol (10307). Women generally have a higher rate of alcohol elimination than men (10305, 10306, 10318). The phase of menstrual cycle does not affect the elimination rate (10316). Other routes of elimination via the lungs or kidney or gastric mucosa are of minor significance (10314, 10315) and hence heavy exercise (10308, 10309) or renal failure (10310, 10311) do not significantly affect elimination of alcohol. Liver disease such as cirrhosis can lower the rate of alcohol elimination but typically not below the lower range of persons without liver disease (10302, 10312, 10313, 10317). Patients with chronic hepatitis C have an average rate of elimination of 0.015 g/100 mL/h (10318). Chinese subjects tended to have a lower rate of elimination (10319).

Due to the variability in the rates of alcohol elimination over time, a single drinking test conducted at a later time to determine an individual's precise rate of alcohol elimination is not forensically appropriate (10303).

Reference Number: 10301

OLSEN, H., J. SAKSHAUG, F. DUCKERT, J.H. STROMME, AND J. MORLAND. "Ethanol Elimination-Rates Determined by Breath Analysis as a Marker of Recent Excessive Ethanol Consumption." *Scandinavian Journal of Clinical and Laboratory Investigation*, 49: 359–365, 1989 (5 tables, 24 references)

Abstract: Fifteen skid row alcoholics admitted to a detoxification center and twelve age-matched social drinkers had the rate of elimination determined in breath by an Alcotest 7010 at least 2 hours after admission. The mean of triplicate breath samples was determined at least six times over a period of 2 to 4 hours. Blood samples were also taken and analyzed for biochemical markers of excessive alcohol consumption such as Gamma glutamyl transferase (GGT), MCV, hematocrit, etc. The BrACs of the alcoholics ranged from 0.078 to 0.261 g/100 mL and of social drinkers from 0.056 to 0.110 g/100 mL. The rates of elimination of alcoholics ranged from 0.013 to 0.031 g/100 mL/h. The median rate was 0.025 g/100 mL/h. For social drinkers the range of elimination rates was 0.012 to 0.017 g/100 mL/h with a median rate of 0.014 g/100 mL/h. The rate of elimination of seven alcoholics with a BAC range from 0.078 to 0.150 g/100 mL varied from 0.020 to 0.031 g/100 mL/h. Thirteen out of fifteen alcoholics had a rate of elimination greater than the highest rate of elimination in the social drinkers.

Table. Comparison of Rates of Alcohol Elimination in Alcoholics and Social Drinkers

Type of drinker and initial BAC range (g/100 mL)	Range of elimination rates (g/100 mL/h)	Median elimination rate (g/100 mL/h)
All alcoholics (0.078–0.261)	0.013–0.031	0.025
Alcoholics, high BACs (0.160–0.261)	0.013–0.031	0.025
Alcoholics, moderate BACs (0.078–0.150)	0.020–0.030	0.025
Social drinkers (0.056–0.110)	0.012–0.017	0.014

Source: Adapted from Olsen et al (1989).

Our study demonstrated that breath analysis could be useful in detecting increased EER. Factors such as breathing technique, temperature, etc. which might influence the conversion from breath- to blood-concentrations could be controlled and kept constant. The results were immediately available. The detoxification period may be used to gain objective information about previous drinking history of a patient; information that could be useful for the further planning of treatment.

Reference Number: 10302

JONES, A.W. AND B. STERNEBRING. "Kinetics of Ethanol and Methanol in Alcoholics during Detoxification." *Alcohol and Alcoholism*, 27: 641–647, 1992 (1 table, 3 figures, 28 references)

Abstract: Sixteen male and four female alcoholics (ages thirty-three to fifty-seven years) who were admitted to a hospital in Malmo for detoxification had venous blood samples collected every 3 to 6 hours for 24 hours. Blood alcohol and methanol concentrations were determined by headspace GC. The admission BACs ranged from 0.238 to 0.489 g/100 mL (mean 0.386 g/100 mL). The admission BMCs ranged from 0.0016–0.0028 g/100 mL (mean 0.0011 g/100 mL). BACs and BMCs were not correlated. The BMCs remained relatively constant until the BAC < 0.030 g/100 mL. The rate of alcohol elimination ranged from 0.013 to 0.036 g/100 mL/h (mean 0.023 g/100 mL/h).

Table. Initial BACs and Mean Alcohol Elimination Rate of Alcoholics (Female Alcoholics (F)), with Liver Disease

Subject number (liver disease)	Initial BAC (g/100 mL)	Mean elimination rate (g/100 mL/h)
1 (hepatitis)	0.443	0.018
2 (cirrhosis)	0.489	0.023
4 (hepatitis)	0.454	0.017
10 (F) (hepatopathy)	0.471	0.022
18 (hepatopathy)	0.377	0.013
19 (hepatopathy)	0.390	0.023
20 (hepatitis)	0.238	0.020

Source: Adapted from Jones et al (1992).

For healthy individuals who drink alcohol occasionally, it is generally agreed that the average rate of ethanol elimination from the blood is about 15 mg/dL/hr (Widmark, 1932). The mean rate of ethanol elimination in the dependent alcoholics in this study was 23 mg/dL/hr and the spread of values for individual subjects was 13–36 mg/dL/hr. The disappearance rate of ethanol therefore increased 53% on average (range –13% to +140%). as a consequence of chronic ingestion of alcohol.

Reference Number: 10303

YELLAND, L.N., J.P. BURNS, D.N. SIMS, A.B. SALTER, AND J.M. WHITE. "Inter- and Intra-Subject Variability in Ethanol Pharmacokinetic Parameters: Effects of Testing Interval and Dose." *Forensic Science International*, 175: 65–72, 2008 (6 tables, 2 figures, 35 references)

Abstract: Twelve male subjects (ages eighteen to thirty years) consumed a low dose of alcohol (LD) of 0.44 g/kg and 0.70 g/kg alcohol (high dose) at 1, 11, and 12 weeks later. The alcohol was consumed within 20 minutes, approximately 1 hour after the consumption of a standard breakfast. Venous blood samples were collected via an indwelling catheter and BACs were determined by direct injection GC. The mean alcohol elimination rate was 0.014, 0.016, 0.016, and 0.015 g/100 mL/h for the four occasions respectively (SD was 0.002–0.003 g/100 mL/h). Intra subject variances ranged from 0.002 to 0.006 g/100 mL/h depending on the dose and time interval between dosing. The maximum difference between rates of elimination also varied between 0.003 to 0.010 g/100 mL/h.

> Our results show forensically significant variability in ethanol pharmacokinetic parameters both between and within individuals. This indicates that neither population average ethanol pharmacokinetic parameters, nor individual specific parameters obtained from a single controlled drinking experiment are likely to produce a highly accurate BAC using forward or back-extrapolation, regardless of whether the dose is matched.

Reference Number: 10304

HAHN, R.G., A. NORBERG, J. GABRIELSSON, A. DANIELSSON, AND A.W. JONES. "Eating a Meal Increases the Clearance of Ethanol Given by Intravenous Infusion." *Alcohol and Alcoholism*, 29: 673–677, 1994 (1 table, 2 figures, 18 references)

Abstract: Six male and six female subjects (mean age thirty-eight years) were given 0.4 g/kg ethanol over 45 minutes either after fasting or after a light breakfast Approximately 4 hours after the first infusion, the fasting subjects consumed a standard lunch. When the BrACs of the subjects were zero, then an additional infusion of 0.4 g/kg ethanol was administered. Blood samples were taken frequently, and the BACs were determined by headspace GC. Subjects also reported their subjective feelings of intoxication. The fasting subjects had a mean rate of elimination of 0.013 g/100 mL/h before lunch and 0.018 g/100 mL/h after lunch. The other group that had breakfast but no lunch had a mean rate of elimination of 0.015 and 0.014 g/100 mL/h respectively.

> In conclusion, we found that the intake of food increased the clearance of ethanol and diminished the feelings of intoxication even when ethanol was administered by intravenous infusion.

Reference Number: 10305

DETTLING, A., F. FISCHER, S. BOHLER, F. ULRISCHS, G. SKOPP, M. GRAW, AND H-T. HAFFNER. "Ethanol Elimination Rates in Men and Women in

Consideration of the Calculated Liver Weight." *Alcohol,* 41: 415–420, 2007 (1 table, 1 figure, 52 references)

Abstract: Sixty-four female and sixty-eight male subjects (ages eighteen to fifty-three years) consumed between 0.79 and 0.95 g/kg alcohol after a breakfast. Numerous blood samples were collected from an indwelling catheter and SACs were determined by an enzymatic and GC method. Liver weight was calculated based on a normal body mass index. The mean peak BAC was 0.082 g/100 mL for female subjects and 0.084 g/100 mL for male subjects. The mean elimination rate was 0.018 g/100 mL/h for female subjects and 0.016 g/100 mL/h for male subjects. The mean liver weight was 1.5 kg for female subjects and 2.0 kg for male subjects. The mean elimination rate per kg liver was 5.00 g/hr/kg liver for female subjects and 4.85 g/hr/kg liver for male subjects, which is not a statistically significant difference.

This means, because women have significantly more liver tissue in comparison to a smaller distribution volume, they can break alcohol down more quickly, which results in high elimination rates in women.

Reference Number: 10306

DETTLING, A., S. WITTE, G. SKOPP, M. GRAW, AND H.T. HAFFNER. "A Regression Model Applied to Gender-Specific Ethanol Elimination Rates from Blood and Breath Measurements in Non- Alcoholics." *International Journal of Legal Medicine*, 123: 381–385, 2009 (4 tables, 1 figure, 32 references)

Abstract: The elimination rate of eighty-one female and ninety-six male subjects was determined by linear regression in breath by an Alcotest 7110 and by venous blood samples. The subjects were tested at least 2 hours after the end of drinking and the BACs ranged from 0.045 to 0.145 g/100 mL. There were at total of 1,065 BAC and 933 BrAC measurements. The mean rate of elimination for women in blood was 0.020 g/100 mL/h (range 0.013 to 0.028 g/100 mL/h) and 0.019 g/100 mL/h for men (range 0.010 to 0.025 g/100 mL/h).

The basis of the back calculation used in forensic cases in Germany today stems from Freudenberg from 1966. In his report the minimal rate of elimination of ethanol was determined to be 0.10 g/kg/h. The formula used included 99.4% of cases which correspond to a 0.3% probability of an overestimate. The maximum elimination rate was determined to be 0.20 g/kg/h using an equation of the same kind.

Reference Number: 10307

WISSEL, P.S. Dietary Influences on Ethanol Metabolism. *Drug-Nutrient Interactions*, 5: 161–168, 1987 (5 tables, 1 figure, 24 references)

Abstract: The alcohol elimination rate was determined in seven male subjects (ages twenty to forty-nine years) after a high protein, high carbohydrate diet; a high protein, low carbohydrate diet; and a low protein, hypocaloric diet for 10 to 12 days each. At the end of each diet the subjects consumed 0.7 g/kg alcohol within 10 minutes. Blood samples were collected every 0.5–1 hour and the SACs were determined by an enzymatic method. The rate of elimination was determined by the slope of the SAC curve. The elimination rate was between 0.016–0.022 g/100 mL/h (mean 0.019 g/100 mL/h), 0.014–0.016 g/100 mL/h (mean 0.014 g/100 mL/h), and 0.010–0.013 g/100 mL/h (mean 0.012 g/100 mL/h) for the three diets respectively.

> It is likely that protein deprivation and/or calorie deficiency mediates ethanol metabolism through diminished hepatic ADH concentration or altered mitochondrial NAD/NADH ratios, or a combination of both. Protein and calorie deficiency in humans may deplete hepatic ADH in a manner similar to the rodent. Calorie deprivation, with the adaptive Cori cycle and possible altered mitochondrial function, may alter the reaction of ethanol to acetaldehyde via diminished capacity to contribute NAD.

Reference Number: 10308

NYMAN, E. AND A. PALMLOV. “On the Effect of Muscular Exercise on the Metabolism of Ethyl Alcohol.” *Scandinavian Archives of Physiology*, 68: 271–294, 1934 (26 tables, 5 figures, 28 references)

Abstract: A detailed series of experiments were conducted on seven male subjects. The subjects consumed 0.4–0.7 g/kg ethanol and then either rested or exercised on a bicycle ergometer. Ventilation rates increased three to four times over the resting conditions. Capillary blood samples were taken, and the alcohol concentration was determined by the Widmark method.

From the above experiments it will appear that we have not been able to show any increased rate of disappearance of ethyl alcohol from the human body during muscular exercise as compared to rest within those limits of doses and amounts of work which we used. The only exception is the minute, theoretically calculated, increase in disappearance which in our case did not exceed 2 to 3 per cent, owing to the forced ventilation during muscular exercise. This increase, however, is of such small value that with the method we have used we were not as a rule able to demonstrate its effect.

Reference Number: 10309

BARNES, E.W., N.J. COOKE, A.J. KING, AND R. PASSMORE. "Observations on the Metabolism of Alcohol in Man." *British Journal of Nutrition*, 19: 485–489, 1965 (7 tables, 6 references)

Abstract: A study on the effects of exercise on the rate of elimination of alcohol was conducted on nine male subjects (ages twenty to twenty-one years) at rest and after eight miles of walking on a treadmill. Blood samples were collected every hour and the BACs were determined with an enzymatic method. The mean rate of alcohol elimination was 0.011 g/100 mL/h at rest and during exercise.

Alcohol (31.5 g/65 kg) was given to nine subjects and the metabolic changes followed for 6h on two occasions, once with complete rest and once with periods of exercise amounting to an 8-mile walk. No specific dynamic effect of the alcohol was observed, and the exercise did not increase the rate of elimination of alcohol.

Reference Number: 10310

WALLE, A.J., O. GRUNER, AND W. NIEDERMAYER. "Measurement of Total Body Water in Patients on Maintenance Hemodialysis Using an Ethanol Dilution Technique." *Nephron*, 26: 286–290, 1980 (2 tables, 2 figures, 27 references)

Abstract: Ten female and eighteen male patients (ages twenty-five to sixty-seven years) with terminal renal failure consumed on average 0.5 g/kg ethanol diluted to 30% v/v within 10 minutes, after a 6-hour fast. Venous blood samples were collected after 90, 105, 120, and 150 minutes. The average rate of elimination was 0.013 g/100 mL/h for blood and

0.014 g/100 mL/h for serum samples. The patients were on maintenance hemodialysis.

> In patients with terminal renal failure the elimination curves of ethanol from the serum or the blood appear to follow zero order kinetics, at least during the time interval between 90 and 180 minutes after the ingestion of ethanol, thus allowing for a simple extrapolation of the serum ethanol concentration to time zero.

Reference Number: 10311

JONES, A.W. AND R.G. HAHN. "Pharmacokinetics of Ethanol in Patients with Renal Failure before and after Hemodialysis." *Forensic Science International*, 90: 175–183, 1997 (1 table, 3 figures, 29 references)

Abstract: Four male and three female patients (mean age sixty-five years) with terminal renal failure were administered 0.4 g/kg ethanol IV over 45 minutes after an overnight fast. A second dose of ethanol was administered IV 4 to 5 hours later after the patients had undergone hemodialysis and after consuming a standard hospital lunch. Frequent blood samples were collected via an indwelling catheter and blood and plasma alcohol concentrations were determined by headspace GC. The water content of the blood was also determined. The mean rate of alcohol elimination was 0.016 g/100 mL/h before hemodialysis and 0.019 g/100 mL/h after. The plasma/blood alcohol was 1.07:1 (range 1.05–1.10). The apparent increase rate of elimination may be due in part to food consumption.

> We confirmed that the rate of elimination of alcohol from blood in patients with renal failure is of the same order of magnitude as in healthy controls, namely 0.15 g/L/h, which agrees with the results reported by Walle et al.

Reference Number: 10312

ASADA, M. AND J.T. GALAMBOS. "Liver Disease, Hepatic Alcohol Dehydrogenase Activity, and Alcohol Metabolism in the Human." *Gastroenterology*, 45: 67–72, 1963 (2 tables, 2 figures, 25 references)

Abstract: Four normal controls and fourteen patients with acute or chronic liver disease were given 0.5 or 1.0 mL/kg ethanol IV. BACs were determined by a potassium dichromate method, at 30 and 120 minutes after infusion. Liver biopsies were conducted to determine ADH activity.

The rate of elimination was 0.024 g/100 mL/h for the normal subjects and 0.025 g/100 mL/h for patients with liver disease.

There was no relationship between hepatic alcohol dehydrogenase activity and the rate of alcohol metabolism (milligrams per deciliter per hour) when it was administered intravenously. There was no apparent impairment of the rate of alcohol metabolism in patients with acute and chronic active liver disease as compared to normals. Although none of the patients tested was moribund, most of them with liver disease were jaundice and active cell necrosis was demonstrated in liver biopsy.

Reference Number: 10313

LIEBERMAN, F.L. "The Effect of Liver Disease on the Rate of Ethanol Metabolism in Man." *Gastroenterology*, 44: 261–266, 1963 (1 table, 1 figure, 21 references)

Abstract: The rate of metabolism of ethanol was measured in ten normal subjects and twenty-one patients with advanced alcoholic cirrhosis. Subjects were given 75–100 mL of absolute ethanol and 90–150 minutes were allowed for complete absorption. Five mL of blood was drawn every 30 minutes and BACs were determined by a potassium dichromate method. The ethanol space was found to be equivalent to the body water compartment.

Table. Range and Mean Rate of Alcohol Elimination in Healthy Persons and Those with Liver Diseases

Condition of liver	Range of elimination rates (g/100 mL/h)	Mean alcohol elimination rate (g/100 mL/h)
Controls (no liver disease)	0.012–0.020	0.015
Cirrhosis (no jaundice)	0.010–0.019	0.015
Cirrhosis (with jaundice)	0.006–0.016	0.010
Viral hepatitis (with jaundice)	0.012–0.016	0.014

Source: Adapted from Lieberman (1963).

The rate of metabolism of ethanol was measured in 10 persons without liver disease and in 21 patients with advanced alcoholic cirrhosis. Only those patients with the most advanced liver disease as indicated by the presence of jaundice, exhibited a significantly reduced rate. The cirrhotic patients without jaundice metabolized ethanol normally, although they had clinical and laboratory evidence of serious liver disease.

Reference Number: 10314

DERR, R.F. "First-Pass Metabolism of Ethanol in the Human Stomach: A Negligible Reaction." *Biochemical Archives*, 10: 197–201, 1994 (1 table, 20 references)

Abstract: A simulation pharmacokinetic model of first-pass oxidation of ethanol in the human stomach is presented. Ethanol must pass through the gastric unstirred layer (880 um thick) and the gastric mucosa (34 um thick) before reaching the systemic circulation.

Ethanol excretion by the lung and kidney accounted for only 0.94 and 0.40% of the ethanol dose respectively. These results are consistent with the well-known fact that ethanol elimination by the lung and kidney in the human are relatively minor and for most purposes can be neglected. Since ethanol oxidation in the gastric mucosa is even less, 0.12% of the dose, it may likewise be neglected in most cases, and is obviously neither the sole site of, nor a major contributor to the first-pass metabolism of ethanol.

Reference Number: 10315

LAI, C-L., Y-C. CHAO, Y-C. CHEN, C-S. LIAO, M-C. CHEN, Y-C. LIU, AND S-J. YIN. "No Sex and Age Influences on the Expression Pattern and Activities of Human Gastric Alcohol and Aldehyde Dehydrogenases." *Alcoholism: Clinical and Experimental Research*, 24: 1625–1632, 2000 (4 tables, 2 figures, 56 references)

Abstract: Endoscopic gastric biopsy samples were obtained from seventy male and forty-five female Han Chinese subjects, ages twenty to seventy-nine years. The expression patterns (from gel electrophoresis) of the alcohol dehydrogenase (ADH) and acetaldehyde dehydrogenase (ALDH) were determined as well as the enzymatic activities to ethanol and acetaldehyde. Both the expressions patterns and enzymatic activities of ADH and ALDH were unaffected by age or sex of the subject. The liver, not the stomach, is the main site for first pass metabolism (FPM) of alcohol.

In conclusion, the ADH or ALDH activities in human stomach do not appear to differ significantly in relation to sex and age. Recent studies have indicated that when the expression pattern and kinetic properties of the ADH family as well as the total organ ethanol-oxidizing activities at both high and low alcohol concentrations are taken into consideration, the stomach may account for a minor fraction of FPM in humans after alcohol ingestion. Thus, gastric ADH and ALDH are unlikely to play a causative role in producing the reported variations of the FPM of alcohol with respect to sex or age.

Reference Number: 10316

DETTLING, A., A. PREISS, G. SKOPP, AND H-T. HAFFNER. "The Influence of Luteal and Follicular Phases on Major Pharmacokinetic Parameters of Blood and Breath Alcohol Kinetics in Women." *Alcohol*, 44: 315–321, 2010 (3 tables, 6 figures, 28 references)

Abstract: Fourteen female subjects (ages twenty to thirty years) consumed alcohol over 2 hours to obtain a target BAC of 0.080 g/100 mL during their luteal and follicular phases of their menstrual cycle. BrACs were determined every 10 to 20 minutes using an Alcotest 7110 evidential breath alcohol testing instrument. Near simultaneous venous blood samples were collected using an indwelling catheter and BACs were determined by two enzymatic and two GC methods. In addition, blood estradiol, progesterone, and testosterone concentrations were determined. The mean rate of alcohol elimination was 0.0194 g/100 mL/h in the follicular phase and 0.0193 g/100 mL/h in the luteal phase. The Widmark r factor was 0.7101 in the follicular phase and 0.7173 in the luteal phase. There were no significant correlations between the rate of elimination of alcohol and the blood progesterone, estradiol, or testosterone concentrations.

As a conclusion, there seems to be no differences in the ethanol pharmacokinetic parameters during the menstrual cycle.

Reference Number: 10317

MCKAY, J., M.D. RAWLINGS, I. COBDEN, AND O.F.W. JAMES. "The Acute Effects of Alcohol on Acetanilide Disposition in Normal Subjects, and in Patients with Liver Disease." *British Journal of Clinical Pharmacology*, 14: 501–504, 1982 (1 table, 1 figure, 18 references)

Abstract: Ten healthy subjects (ages twenty to sixty-two years) and ten patients with chronic compensated non-alcoholic liver disease consumed 50 mg/kg acetanilide alone and with the consumption of 75 or

100 mL of vodka. Blood samples were collected at 30, 60, 90, and 120 minutes after alcohol consumption, and BACs were determined by GC. The alcohol elimination rate was 0.011–0.019 g/100 mL/h (median 0.015 g/100 mL/h) in normal subjects and 0.016–0.022 g/100 mL/h (median 0.020 g/100 mL/h) in subjects with liver disease.

> We conclude therefore that single doses of ethanol—in quantities that are consumed during social drinking—inhibit the microsomal oxidation of acetanilide both in normal subjects and in patients with chronic liver disease. This may have considerable therapeutic implications for patients taking a wide variety of drugs, who may also consume alcoholic beverages from time to time.

Reference Number: 10318

MANOLAKOPOULOS, S., M. ECONOMOU, S. BETHANIS, N. MATHOU, C. TRIANTOS, J. VLACHOGIANNAKOS, E. VOGIATZAKIS, A. AVGERINOS, AND D. TZOURMAKLIOTIS. "A Single Alcohol Ingestion Does Not Affect Serum Hepatitis C Virus RNA in Patients with Chronic Hepatitis C." *Liver International*, 26: 1196–1200, 2006 (2 tables, 2 figures, 18 references)

Abstract: Seven male and three female patients (ages thirty-two to fifty-two years) with chronic hepatitis C consumed 50 g of alcohol within 30 to 40 minutes. Serum HCV RNA, transaminase, GGT, and alcohol concentrations were measured at 1, 2, 8, and 24 hours and one week later. Peak SACs occurred at 1 hour after drinking ceased, and the mean rate of alcohol elimination was approximately 0.015 g/100 mL/h.

> In conclusion, our results clearly suggest that a single consumption of 50 g alcohol does not affect serum markers of hepatocellular necrosis or viral replication and possibly may not aggravate liver injury in patients with chronic hepatitis C.

Reference Number: 10319

LI, Y.C., N.N. SZE, S.C. WONG, K.L. TSUI, AND L. SO. "Experimental Study of the Temporal Profile of Breath Alcohol Concentration in a Chinese Population after a Light Meal," *PLoS ONE*, 14: 15pp, 2019 (7 tables, 5 figures, 31 references)

Abstract: Thirty-four male and eighteen female Chinese (ages twenty-one to sixty-one years) in Hong Kong consumed a standard meal after a 4-hour fast. Thirty minutes later the subjects consumed 500 mL of orange juice spiked with 0, 20, 40, or 60 grams of alcohol (1 standard drink = 10 grams), over 20 to 30 minutes. BrACs were measured with an Alcotest 9510 (EC/IR) evidential breath testing instrument every 15 to 30 minutes using the mean EC/IR result. A total of 119 drinking sessions were conducted. The mean peak BrAC after alcohol dosing ranged between 0.016 and 0.186 g/100 mL. The time from the start of alcohol consumption to the elimination phase ranged from 17 to 109 minutes. BACs less than 0.012 g/100 mL were not included in the data analysis. The mean rate of alcohol elimination was 0.011 g/100 mL/h for women and 0.009 g/100 mL/h for men.

> In this study, a baseline model of zero-order alcohol elimination was tested. Results of the parameter estimates of the baseline model were consistent to that of the conventional Widmark equation. A breath alcohol elimination rate after a light meal of 0.0042 mg/100 mL/hr (equivalent to a blood elimination rate of 9.7 mg/100 mL/h) was set out. In the second part of this study, a gamma model of non-linear breath alcohol elimination was examined. Results indicted that factors such as gender, body weight, and alcohol dose are correlated with the pattern and scale of alcohol elimination. Theoretically, the non-linear model performed better than the conventional linear model in certain conditions. For example, the proposed profile is applicable to the situation where a light meal is served (not empty stomach). Considering the ethical issue, the alcohol dose was limited to 60 g only.

1.04 PHARMACOKINETICS OF DRINKING DRIVERS

> "Courts are indeed plagued by the instant expert who whether out of a misguided eagerness to earn his fee or an overreaction to his own self-described credentials may expound far reaching opinions."
>
> — Lovell, "Breath Tests for Determining Alcohol in the Blood" (1972)

> "The lower court justices seem to have chosen to ignore a golden rule in DUI litigation, namely that what the suspect says he or she has drunk is not reliable evidence."
>
> — Jones, "Are a Blood Alcohol Concentration of 256 mg/dL and Minimal Signs of Impairment Reliable Signs of Alcohol Dependence?" (1994)

The pharmacokinetics of drinking drivers can be determined by:

- observations or surveys of actual drinking patterns

- realistic laboratory drinking tests of consumption of alcohol over a period of hours
- multiple blood samples from drinking drivers
- multiple breath samples from drinking drivers over a prolonged period of time
- blood and urine samples from drinking drivers
- postmortem blood and urine samples from drinking drivers killed in motor vehicle collisions (MVCs)

All of these studies show that the vast majority (> 95%) of drinking drivers are not in the rising phase of the BAC curve at the time of the driving or the arrest as is commonly alleged in criminal court. This allows for the forensic validity of presumptions, or time of testing laws and the back calculations of BAC (10401–10411).

The hip flask defence may be evaluated by use of blood and urine alcohol concentration changes and by an increasing urine EtG concentration from multiple samples, which would be difficult to obtain in most medicolegal cases (10412).

Reference Number: 10401

COOPER, P.J. AND J.P. ROTHE, "Drinking Establishment, Driving Risk, and Ethno-Pharmacology." *Proceedings of 35th International Congress on Alcohol and Drug Dependence, Oslo, Norway,* Vol 2, 6pp, 1988 (5 tables, 5 figures, 12 references)

Abstract: A study was conducted of the characteristics of 2,392 accident involved drivers, 854 telephone interviews of drinking drivers, and of 854 bartenders in the Lower Mainland of British Columbia. Some results are shown in the below table.

Table. Location of Drinking by Drivers, Time Over Which Drinking Occurred, Percent Drinking Beer, and Time Waited Before Driving

Location of Drinking	Drinking Time (h)	Percent Drinking Beer	Time Waited Before Driving (min)
Pub	2.0	73%	24
Hotel/bar	2.0	86%	29
Restaurant	2.2	36%	37
Home	1.8	39%	38

Source: Adapted from Cooper and Rothe (1988).

The subjective impressions people have of the extent of their drinking thus may not match the reality represented by actual blood-alcohol accumulation. The people we talked to tended to express alcohol consumption solely in terms of quantity, while seemingly ignoring the equally important factor of time.

Reference Number: 10402

YORK, J.L., J. WELTE, AND J. HIRSCH. "Gender Comparison of Alcohol Exposure on Drinking Occasions." *Journal of Studies on Alcohol*, 64: 790–801, 2003 (3 tables, 3 figures, 49 references)

Abstract: A detailed telephone survey regarding alcohol consumption was conducted on 1,028 male and 805 female current drinkers. Female drinkers reported a mean consumption of 2.2 standard drinks and male drinkers reported a mean consumption of 3.2 drinks for a typical drinking occasion. The duration of drinking episode was 122 minutes for women and 126 minutes for men. Estimated BACs were calculated for the reported drinking episode using TBW and an alcohol elimination rate of 0.012 g/100 mL/h for men and 0.016 g/100 mL/h for women. Of the 1,833 current drinkers, forty-one men (3.8%) and twenty-one women (1.4%) were determined to have alcohol abuse (pathological drinkers). Pathological drinkers consumed a mean of eight drinks per day for men and five drinks a day for women. The mean drinking time was 186 minutes for male pathological drinkers and 166 minutes for female pathological drinkers. The estimated peak BACs for pathological drinkers were 0.127 g/100 mL (men) and 0.117 g/100 mL (women) compared to 0.037 g/100 mL (men) and 0.032 g/100 mL (women) for non-pathological drinkers. The most frequent hourly drinking rate was two drinks per hour for men (33%) and one drink per hour for women (30%).

The findings of the current study are in general agreement with previous survey reports that women are less involved in alcohol than are men.

Reference Number: 10403

FORNEY, R.B. AND F.W. HUGHES. "Alcohol Accumulation in Humans after Prolonged Drinking." *Clinical Pharmacology and Therapeutics*, 5: 619–621, 1963 (2 figures, 6 references)

Abstract: A study was conducted of twenty-two female and thirty-five male subjects who consumed either 1 or 2 fl. oz. of 50% v/v alcohol/150 lb of body weight per hour. Drinking commenced after a breakfast of toast and fruit juice. Lunch consisted of meat sandwiches. BrACs were measured every 30 minutes with a Breathalyzer. When 1 fl. oz./h is consumed the BrAC did not exceed 0.050 g/100 mL after five hours. When 2 fl. oz./h were consumed the BAC exceeded 0.050 g/100 mL after 1.5 hours and exceeded 0.100 g/100 mL after 3 hours.

> While the consumption of approximately 1 drink per hour will not usually prove dangerous, a second drink per hour will more than double the concentration in the blood.

Reference Number: 10404

GANERT, P.M. AND W.D. BOWTHORPE. "Evaluation of Breath Alcohol Profiles Following a Period of Social Drinking." *Canadian Society of Forensic Science Journal*, 33: 137–143, 2000 (3 tables, 10 figures, 25 references)

Abstract: Six male and four female subjects consumed between 9–18 fl. oz. of liquor (40% alcohol v/v) over 3 hours at their own rate of drinking. BrACs were determined every 5 to 15 minutes with an Intoxilyzer 5000C. The time to peak BrAC after the end of drinking was between 4 to 22 minutes (mean 12 minutes). The increase in BrAC after the end of drinking was between 0 and 0.022 g/100 mL (mean 0.005 g/100 mL). The time from the end of drinking to the start of the linear decline (i.e., a plateau) was between 0 and 124 minutes (mean 69 minutes). The rate of alcohol elimination was between 0.015 to 0.022 g/100 mL/h (mean 0.019 g/100 mL/h).

> In a drinking experiment involving ten subjects under realistic social conditions the time to the maximum BAC was obtained on average 12 minutes (range 4 to 20 minutes) after the end of drinking. This is significantly shorter than for experiments not involving drinking under social conditions.

Reference Number: 10405

COWAN, J.M., M.E. DENNIS III, AND L.F. SMITH. "A Comparison of Equal Alcohol Doses of Beer and Whiskey on Eleven Human Test Subjects." *Canadian Society of Forensic Science Journal*, 37: 137–145, 2004 (6 tables, 6 figures, 10 references)

Abstract: Four female and seven male subjects (ages twenty-three to fifty-two years) consumed 1.23 g/kg (lean body weight) as whiskey (diluted with carbonated soda and ice) and beer (5% v/v alcohol) on two occasions after a fast of at least 10 hours. The alcohol was consumed socially over a period of 2 hours and 45 minutes. BrACs were determined every 15 to 20 minutes with an Intoxilyzer 5000. The maximum BrACs occurred within 15 minutes after the end of drinking. The mean rate of alcohol elimination for either alcoholic beverage was 0.019 g/100 mL/h. The mean peak BrACs were 0.113 and 0.112 g/100 mL for whiskey and beer respectively. The mean percent body fat was 24% for women and 17% for men.

While there were individual subject differences, on average, equal doses of ethanol per kg of lean body weight given in the same manner, over the same length of time, yielded statistically indistinguishable alcohol concentration results, regardless of subject gender or type of alcoholic beverage consumed.

Reference Number: 10406

JONES, A.W. "Ultra-Rapid Rate of Ethanol Elimination from Blood in Drunken Drivers with Extremely High Blood Alcohol Concentrations." *International Journal of Legal Medicine,* 122: 129–134, 2008 (2 tables, 1 figure, 62 references)

Abstract: The alcohol elimination rate was determined in 1,090 drunken drivers in Sweden from whom two to three blood samples were collected approximately 1 hour apart. The mean elimination rate was 0.019/100 mL/h and the 97.5 percentile was 0.011 and 0.031 g/100 mL/h. There were twenty-four cases (2.2%) with the apparent rate of elimination of less than 0.010 g/100 mL/h, probably due to the driver not in the post-absorptive state. Twenty-one drivers had a high rate of alcohol elimination. Their mean BAC was 0.405 g/100 mL (range 0.271 to 0.518 g/100 mL). Their mean rate of alcohol elimination was 0.033 g/100 mL/h and ranged from 0.020 to 0.062 g/100 mL/h.

With only a single blood sample available from each drunken driver, which is usually the case in forensic situations, the elimination rate of alcohol is unknown. In criminal trials when beyond a reasonable doubt is required, it is advisable to work with a range of values to give the suspect the benefits of the doubt. Experience from hundreds of controlled drinking experiments has shown that the vast majority of individuals as well as drunken drivers eliminate alcohol from the bloodstream at a rate between

0.10 g/L/h and 0.25 g/L/h. In alcoholics during detoxification, the elimination rate of alcohol might be considerably faster, as high as 0.35 g/L/h in some individuals.

Reference Number: 10407

NEUTEBOOM, W., AND A.W. JONES. "Disappearance Rate of Alcohol from the Blood of Drunk Drivers Calculated from Two Consecutive Samples; What Do the Results Really Mean?" *Forensic Science International*, 45: 107–115, 1990 (3 tables, 29 references)

Abstract: A study was conducted of 1,314 double blood samples taken from suspected impaired drivers in the Netherlands from February 1982 to September 1987. The blood was collected in Vacutainers containing NaF and analyzed by ADH. In forty-seven cases (2%) of the total database, the BAC was increasing. The rate of elimination varied from 0.010 to 0.064 g100 mL/h, with a mean of 0.022 g/100 mL/h and the mean rate of alcohol elimination tended to increase with increasing BAC (especially in drivers with a BAC > 0.250 g/100 mL). At BACs < 0.050 g/100 mL the rate of alcohol elimination in drivers ranged between 0.010 and 0.019 g/100 mL/h.

Table. Range of Elimination Rates of Arrested Drinking Drivers

Range of elimination rates (g/100 mL/h)	Number (and percentage) of drivers
0.010–0.0159	226 (17.2%)
0.016–0.0199	341 (26.0%)
0.020–0.0259	460 (35.0%)
0.026–0.0299	158 (12.0%)
0.030 +	129 (9.8%)

Source: Adapted from Neuteboom and Jones (1990).

The extremely high elimination, highest 0.64 mg/mL/h as well as 4 other drunk drivers with values above 0.50 mg/mL/h can hardly represent the rate of hepatic metabolism of alcohol in a human being. The results certainly reflect the change in BAC over the time period studied but this might be influenced by ongoing distribution and equilibration of alcohol between blood and tissue water. The high average BAC of drunk drivers suggests an over-representation of problem drinkers and alcoholics.

Reference Number: 10408

GULLBERG, R.G. AND A.J. MCELROY. "Comparing Roadside with Subsequent Breath Alcohol Analyses and Their Relevance to the Issue of Retrograde Extrapolation." *Forensic Science International*, 57: 193–201, 1992 (1 table, 4 figures, 20 references)

Abstract: Seven law enforcement officers in Seattle tested 161 suspected drivers with an Intoximeter Alco-Sensor III (PBT1) at the roadside. The arrested drivers were then tested on a BAC DataMaster (two tests, 2 to 3 minutes apart) between 18 and 114 minutes later (mean 53 minutes). An additional test was conducted with the Alco-Sensor III after the evidential test (PBT2). All BrACs were truncated to two decimal places. No PBT2 test results were more than 0.010 g/100 mL greater than PBT1. If 0.015 g/100 mL/h was added to the PBT2 results, there was a slight overestimation of PBT1 by 0.005 g/100 mL. This overestimation disappeared when there was a long time between test results.

> There was certainly no evidence that individuals were on the ascending portion of their concentration time curves at the time of driving. As a result, forensic breath alcohol analysis employing duplicates along with other appropriate quality control procedures appears to provide very good estimations of BrAC values when conducted within 2 h of driving.

Reference Number: 10409

JONES, A.W. "Ethanol Distribution Ratios between Urine and Capillary Blood in Controlled Experiments and in Apprehended Drinking Drivers." *Journal of Forensic Sciences*, 37: 21–34, 1992 (2 tables, 9 figures, 32 references)

Abstract: Eighty healthy male subjects consumed 0.51, 0.68, or 0.85 g/kg ethanol as neat whisky within 15, 20, or 25 minutes respectively after a 10-hour fast. Capillary blood samples were collected every 30 to 60 minutes for 6 to 8 hours and urine was collected every 60 minutes. BACs and UACs were determined by an ADH procedure. Additionally, 654 drinking drivers provided two urine samples and one capillary blood sample. The mean UAC/BAC ratio varied between 1.4 and 1.7 when the BACs > 0.050 g/100 mL. The mean UAC/BAC ratio was not dependent on the age of the individual (between twenty to sixty years). In only twelve drivers

(3.2%) was the UAC/BAC ≤ 1.0, indicating that these drivers were still in the absorption phase.

Despite these limitations, UAC/BAC ratios provide useful evidence to pinpoint the phase of ethanol metabolism at the time of sampling. If the UAC/BAC ratio is less than unity, or not more than 1.2, this suggests but does not prove the existence of a rising BAC. If the UAC/BAC ratio exceeds 1.3 this suggests that the subject was in the postabsorptive stage at the time of sampling. Moreover, if the concentration of alcohol in two successive voids 30 to 60 min apart shows a decreasing concentration by 0.10 mg/mL or more, then the bulk of the dose of alcohol was probably consumed at least 2 h earlier.

Reference Number: 10410

JONES, A.W. AND F.C. KUGELBERG. "Relationship Between Blood and Urine Alcohol Concentrations in Apprehended Drivers Who Claimed Consumption of Alcohol After Driving with and Without Supporting Evidence." *Forensic Science International*, 194: 97–102, 2010 (3 tables, 1 figure, 34 references)

Abstract: A study was conducted of the UACs and BACs of twenty drivers who claimed a drink after (hip flask) without any supporting evidence and twenty drivers who had supporting evidence of a drink after (e.g., eyewitnesses, empty bottle). Two urine samples and a blood sample were collected from each driver and analyzed by headspace GC. A drink after was determined if the first UAC was close or less than the BAC and the second UAC increased by 0.021 g/100 mL or more. The mean UAC/BAC ratio was 1.04 in drivers with supporting evidence and 1.46 in drivers without supporting evidence. In approximately ten of the twenty drivers (50%) with supporting evidence the UAC was less or similar to the BAC, and so a drink after could have occurred. In none of the drivers without supporting evidence was the UAC/BAC ratio less than 1.3, which indicates no post-offence drinking of alcohol.

Long experience from investigating claims of post-offence drinking leads us to conclude that in the vast majority of cases this lacks any substance and is simply a last resort by DUIA offenders to evade justice. Unless supporting evidence exists (eye witnesses, police report, etc.) of post-offence drinking, the courts are encouraged to ignore this defence argument.

Reference Number: 10411

LEVINE, B. AND J.E. SMIALEK. "Status of Alcohol Absorption in Drinking Drivers Killed in Traffic Accidents." *Journal of Forensic Sciences*, 45: 3–6, 2000 (1 table, 11 references)

Abstract: A study of the heart BACs and UACs of 129 drivers killed within 15 minutes of a MVC was conducted in the state of Maryland over a 3-year period. Peripheral blood samples were also collected and compared to heart BACs. The average peripheral BAC/heart BAC was 1.02. The alcohol concentrations were determined by headspace GC. The BACs ranged from 0.010–0.350 g/100 mL (mean 0.160 g/100 mL). The mean UAC/BAC ratio was 1.38. Eleven of the 129 cases (8.5%) had a UAC/BAC ratio of less than 1.0, which would indicate a rising BAC at the time of death. The remaining UAC/BAC ratios indicated a plateau or a postabsorptive phase at the time of the FMVC (fatal motor vehicle collision).

Table. Range of Postmortem BACs and Percent of Fatally Injured Drivers with BAC/UAC Ratio < 1

BAC Range (g/100 mL)	Percent BAC/UAC<1
0.02–0.08	5.6%
0.09–0.15	8.3%
0.16–0.20	12.5%
0.21–0.25	9.7%
0.26 +	0.0%

Source: Adapted from Levine and Smialek (2000).

Based on the above study the following conclusions can be offered: (1) less than 10% of ethanol drinking drivers were in the absorption phase at the time of their fatal accident; (2) over 90% of ethanol drinking drivers were in the plateau or post-absorptive phases at the time of their fatal accident; (3) these data are consistent with studies from living individuals which indicate that only a small number of drivers are in the absorptive phase at the time of a particular event; and (4) these data are consistent with alcohol concentrations found in living drivers in Maryland.

Reference Number: 10412

HOISETH, G., G.H. NILSSON, R. LUNDBERG, C. FORSMAN, I. NYSTROM, C. OSCARSSPM, E. ERICSSON, M.D. CHERMA, J. AHLNES, F.C. KUGELBERG,

AND R. KRONSTAND. "Evaluating the Hip-Flask Defence Using Analytical Data from Ethanol and Ethyl Glucuronide: A Comparison of Two Models." *Forensic Science International*, 316: 8pp, 2020 (4 tables, 3 figures, 24 references)

Abstract: Fourteen female and twenty-one male subjects (ages twenty-one to twenty-eight years) consumed 0.51 g/kg alcohol as 5% v/v beer over 1 hour and 1 hour later consumed either 0.25, 0.51, or 0.85 g/kg alcohol as beer, wine, or spirits over 15–30 minutes. Breakfast was provided during the first hour of drinking, and lunch 30 minutes after the second ingestion of alcohol. Frequent blood and urine samples were collected, and the alcohol concentrations were determined by headspace GC. Blood EtG and EtS concentrations were also determined by UHPLC/MS/MS. The samples collected 180–240 minutes after the first dose were evaluated. The mean peak BACs of approximately 0.041 g/100 mL increased to a mean maximum BAC of 0.058 g/100 mL (0.25 g/kg), 0.090 g/100 mL (0.51 g/kg), and 0.127 g/100 mL (0.85 g/kg). One subject in the 0.51 g/kg second dose condition and nine subjects in the 0.25 g/kg second dose failed to show either an increase in UAC or a BAC/UAC ratio of less than 1.3. Only one subject in the 0.25 g/kg second dose group failed to show an increasing blood EtG concentration.

> In conclusion, the present study showed that the two investigated methods to evaluate the hip-flask defence could also be used when alcohol was already on board from a previous intake, but only if the last dose was sufficiently high.

1.05 BACK CALCULATIONS OF DRINKING DRIVERS

> "[I]f the first of the samples of breath was taken, or the sample of blood was taken, more than two hours after the person ceased to operate the conveyance and the person's blood alcohol concentration was equal to or exceeded 20 mg of alcohol in 100 mL of blood, the person's blood alcohol concentration within those two hours is conclusively presumed to be the concentration established in accordance with subsection (1) or (2), as the case may be, plus an additional 5 mg of alcohol in 100 mL of blood for every interval of 30 minutes in excess of those two hours."
>
> —*Criminal Code of Canada*, s 320.31(4)

"In this article I have demonstrated that the rate of elimination of alcohol from blood varies as much between individuals as within the same individual from drinking occasion to occasion. This makes it rather pointless to try to determine a person's elimination rate after the fact although such post-offence drinking experiments are often commissioned by defence lawyers."

— Jones, "Evidence-Based Survey of Elimination Rates of Ethanol from Blood With Applications in Forensic Casework" (2010)

Much unnecessary argument has occurred in courts regarding the back calculation or extrapolation of BAC to an earlier time in arrested drinking drivers. The use of a plateau to allow for the variability of breath alcohol analysis (10501, 10506), to prevent the possibility of a falsely high estimated BAC (10502), as well as using a range of possible rates of elimination are warranted (10511).

Recently, in Canada, the law was changed such that the court could determine the BAC if the time between the operation of the motor vehicle and the collection of the breath or blood sample was more than 2 hours. An additional 0.005 g/100 mL could be added to the result for every additional 30 minutes. Thus, a low elimination rate of 0.010 g/100 mL/h is employed is this situation (*Criminal Code of Canada*, section 320.31(4)).

A proposed steepling effect or zigzag pattern of BAC has been found to be due to typical breath sampling variability and do not exist from a pharmacokinetic point of view (10507, 10508). The use of a truncated breath alcohol result decreased the time to maximum BrAC and increased the length of the plateau (10509). An example of a back calculation of the driver's BAC in Sweden is presented (10510).

It is rather pointless to determine a person's specific elimination rate sometime after the fact; as such, a range of elimination rates should be employed for BAC calculations (10511).

Reference Number: 10501

LOOMIS, T.A. "Blood Alcohol in Automobile Drivers: Measurement and Interpretation for Medicolegal Purposes I. Effect of Time Interval between Incident and Sample Acquisition." *Quarterly Journal of Studies on Alcohol*, 35: 458–472, 1974 (2 tables, 4 figures, 10 references)

Abstract: Eighteen drinking drivers had their BrACs determined at the roadside using a Breathalyzer Collection Unit (a $CaCl_2$ absorption tube) and then later at the police station using a Breathalyzer. The BrAC in the $CaCl_2$ tube was determined by GC. The time interval between the roadside test and the Breathalyzer result ranged from 12 to 61 minutes (mean 39 minutes). The roadside BrACs ranged from 0.070 to 0.270 g/100 mL (mean 0.168 g/100 mL). The Breathalyzer results ranged from 0.080 to 0.290 g/100 mL (mean 0.162 g/100 mL). The mean difference between the roadside BrAC and the Breathalyzer was 0.006 g/100 mL. In addition, twenty-seven subjects consumed alcohol over a period of time and had Breathalyzer tests conducted and BACs determined from blood samples. The mean rate of alcohol elimination in sixteen subjects as determined by BrAC was 0.011 g/100 mL/h and as determined by BAC was 0.013 g/100 mL/h. An interval of up to 2 hours was found in which the BrACs did not change by more than 0.010 g/100 mL. The Breathalyzer results should not be reported to three decimal places as the accuracy of the instrument is not sufficient for this purpose.

The conclusion from the above example is that if a BAC in an automobile driver is determined at any time within 2 hr following an incident, that BAC is not practically different from what it was at the time of the incident. Furthermore, in medicolegal cases a BAC determined in excess of 2 hr following an incident should not be considered equivalent to the BAC at the time of the incident.

Reference Number: 10502

LUND, A. "The Rate of Disappearance of Blood Alcohol in Drunken Drivers." *Blutalkohol,* 16: 395–398, 1979 (1 table, 1 figure, 3 references)

Abstract: Blood samples were collected 1 hour apart from 432 drinking drivers in Copenhagen between 1965 and 1970. The BACs were determined by the Widmark, ADH, and GC methods. The decrease in BAC ranged between 0 and 0.039 g/100 mL/h and the average was 0.018 g/100 mL/h. An increase in BAC was not observed in any driver.

After deduction of these two hours, a possible surplus time is used for backward calculation applying 0.10 promille as the BAC-fall per hour. The above-mentioned time deduction and the low BAC fall rate ensure that the possibility of obtaining a too high BAC value by the backward calculation is virtually eliminated.

Reference Number: 10503

AL-LANQAWI, Y., A. MORELAND, F. MCEWEN, F. HALLIDAY, C.J. DURNIN, AND I.H. STEVENSON. "Ethanol Kinetics: Extent of Error in Back Extrapolation Procedures." *British Journal of Clinical Pharmacology*, 34: 316–321, 1992 (2 tables, 3 figures, 20 references)

Abstract: Twenty-four male subjects consumed 0.7 g/kg alcohol within 5 minutes. Venous blood samples were collected from an indwelling venous catheter at 0, 0.25, 0.5, 0.75, 1, 1.3, 1.7, 2, 3, 4, 5, 6, 7, 8, and 9 hours after alcohol was consumed. Plasma alcohol concentrations were determined by GC. The mean peak PAC was 0.116 g/100 mL and the mean time to peak was 1 hour. The mean rate of alcohol elimination was 0.019 g/100 mL/h. Back extrapolation starting at 4 and 6 hours post consumption was conducted using 0.015, 0.019, and 0.024 g/100 mL/h as rates of elimination. When 0.015 g/100 mL/h was used, the back extrapolation resulted in underestimation of PAC in the majority of subjects. Using the PAC at 6 hours, the mean error was –0.0035 g/100 mL calculated to 5 hours and –0.021 g/100 mL for the calculation to 1 hour.

Table. Mean Difference (Estimated BAC–BAC) Using Different Elimination Rates With Increasing Back Calculation Time

	Mean Difference (g/100 mL) Using Back Calculation Duration of		
Elimination Rate (g/100 mL/h)	1 hour	2 hours	3 hours
0.0150	–0.004	–0.005	–0.012
0.0186	0.000	+0.002	–0.001
0.0238	+0.005	+0.013	+0.015

Source: Adapted from Al-Lanqawi et al (1992).

Thus, for the majority of the population the use of an elimination rate of 150 mg/L/h for back extrapolation would underestimate the true blood alcohol concentration and therefore would be unlikely to result in invalid prosecution. From this study, it may be concluded that the accuracy and precision of the back extrapolation procedure depends on the rate of elimination assumed.

Reference Number: 10504

JACKSON, P.R., G.T. TUCKER, AND H.F. WOODS. "Backtracking Booze with Bayes—The Retrospective Interpretation of Blood Alcohol Data." *British Journal of Clinical Pharmacology*, 31: 55–63, 1991 (2 tables, 11 figures, 31 references)

Abstract: An application of Bayes theorem to back calculate BAC using different rates of absorption, volume of distribution (Vd), and elimination rates is presented. The best mathematical model is zero order elimination and first order absorption rates. This mathematical model is applied to a famous British case involving a FMVA in which the accused had a BAC of 0.059 g/100 mL 4.5 hours after the collision.

> In the simple case without continuing absorption the variability in the predicted blood ethanol concentration at the time of the incident was low. The proportion of the area below 80 mg/% was small and therefore the likelihood of making a conviction in error is small. However, when the model was extended to include ethanol absorption which continues after the cessation of drinking, the possibility of the blood ethanol concentration at time t(a) being below the legal limit ceases to be negligible.

Reference Number: 10505

STOWELL, A.R. AND L.I. STOWELL. "Estimation of Blood Alcohol Concentrations After Social Drinking" *Journal of Forensic Sciences*, 43: 14–21, 1998 (4 tables, 2 figures, 29 references)

Abstract: Twenty-four male subjects (ages twenty-two to fifty-six years) consumed 0.6–2.07 g/kg ethanol over 2.33–3.92 hours, at least 1 hour after consuming lunch. A blood sample was collected immediately prior to drinking (BAC1); 0.78–1.38 hours after drinking stopped (BAC2); and 2.13–4.27 hours after drinking stopped (BAC3). BACs were determined by headspace GC. BAC2 ranged between 0.032 and 0.200 g/100 mL (mean 0.108 g/100 mL) and BAC3 between 0.016 and 0.130 g/100 mL (mean 0.066 g/100 mL). Back calculations were conducted in which the BAC2 was estimated from the BAC3. The mean time difference between these two blood samples was 2.22 hours. BAC2 was within the estimated range 67%, 92%, and 100% of the time using elimination rates of 0.010–0.020, 0.010–0.025, and 0.008–0.028 g/100 mL/h respectively. Forward calculations were conducted using Widmark, Watson et al, Lewis and Forrest methods. The forward calculations of Forrest and Watson et al use a 80% v/v water factor of blood rather than 85% v/v probably due to confusion over w/w and v/v units.

Table. Percent Correct Estimation of BAC2 Using Back Calculation from BAC3 or Forward Calculation to BAC2 Using Widmark or Watson Formulae and Different Rates of Elimination

Rates of elimination (g/100 mL/h)	Percent correct using back calculation from BAC3 to BAC2	Percent correct using Widmark forward calculation to BAC2	Percent correct using Watson et al forward calculation to BAC2
0.0010–0.020	67%	50%	63%
0.0100–0.025	92%	79%	88%
0.0080–0.028	100%	96%	92%

Source: Adapted from Stowell and Stowell (1998).

Considering that BAC2 was measured approximately one hour after drinking stopped, when absorption and equilibration of alcohol may not have been complete, these results are surprising. They suggest that back estimations up to a relatively short time after cessation of drinking may not be subject to gross errors after a period of social drinking. This conclusion is supported by other studies involving even shorter periods of social drinking.

Reference Number: 10506

GULLBERG, R.G. "Considering Measurement Variability When Performing Retrograde Extrapolation of Breath Alcohol Results [Letter]." *Journal of Analytical Toxicology*, 18: 126–127, 1994 (1 figure, 7 references)

Abstract: A statistical and theoretical discussion of BAC back calculation from two breath alcohol results is presented. For the calculation, the SD of the duplicate breath samples should be considered. If the BrACs were 0.120 and 0.140 g/100 mL, the mean BrAC would be 0.130 g/100 mL. The SD of duplicates using 15,493 duplicate results in a field study was 0.007 g/100 mL. Therefore, no increase in the back calculation would occur before 1.5 hours.

If the driving incident occurred only 1 hour prior to breath alcohol analysis, and all of the other relevant assumptions are valid, then one would expect the BrAC at the time of the incident to be measurably the same as the

BrAC at the time of the analysis. Their values would be considered random variables from the same distribution.

Reference Number: 10507

GULLBERG, R.G. "Employing Simulated Data to Illustrate an Important Cause of the Steepling Effect in Breath Alcohol Analysis." *Medicine, Science, and the Law,* 34: 321–323, 1994 (1 table, 1 figure, 7 references)

Abstract: A statistical evaluation of the alleged steepling effect of BrACs was conducted using multiple breath samples. If the mean of the BrACs is employed rather than single measurements, the steepling effect is much reduced. If blood rather than breath samples were used the effect would be reduced even further.

Interpreting this phenomenon as originating from some other biological cause (pyloric spasms, etc.) is cautioned against unless total analytical variability is accounted for. Certainly, other biological factors contribute to the total variability as well, but one must keep in mind the influence of data collection and treatment.

Reference Number: 10508

JONES, A.W., L. JORFELDT, H. HJERTBERG, AND K.A. JONSSON. "Physiological Variations in Blood Ethanol Measurements during the Post-Absorptive State." *Journal of the Forensic Science Society*, 30: 273–283, 1990 (1 table, 2 figures, 28 references)

Abstract: Nine subjects (ages twenty-four to sixty-two years) consumed 0.8g/kg ethanol over 30 minutes When the postabsorptive state was determined by BrAC, and at least 2 hours after the end of drinking, ten consecutive samples of venous blood were drawn at 3 minutes intervals into Vacutainers with a catheter. Six males (ages sixty-seven to seventy-three years) were given 0.4 g/kg ethanol IV and arterial BACs were determined with a catheter implanted in the radial arm. BACs were determined by headspace GC. The rate of elimination of alcohol from venous blood varied from 0.009 to 0.025 g/100 mL/h and from arterial blood from 0.011 to 0.015 g/100 mL/h. No zigzag pattern (i.e., steepling effect) was observed from the venous samples drawn at 3 minutes intervals, and most variations were less than 0.001 g/100 mL. Variations of 0.004–0.006 g/100 mL occurred in subjects who had technical problems with the catheter.

A zigzag concentration time profile of ethanol was demonstrated when end-expired air was used as the biological specimen for analysis of ethanol. There were inter- and intra-subject variations in the amplitude of the spiking, being most pronounced during the absorption phase. Making a long series of 50 to 60 successive end-exhalations at 3–5 min intervals must prove tiresome for the volunteer subjects. Some might have unintentionally changed their breathing technique between successive breaths, e.g., by hypo- or hyper-ventilation, to generate sufficient vital capacity for the forced exhalation maneuver. This could easily account for some of the breath-to-breath variation in concentration of ethanol reported.

Reference Number: 10509

MCELRAE, A., C. SU, AND L. SMITH. "Truncation of Breath Alcohol Measurements and Its Effect on Peak Concentrations." *Canadian Society of Forensic Science Journal*, 44: 13–21, 2011 (3 tables, 3 figures, 21 references)

Abstract: Nine male and five female subjects (ages twenty-two to fifty-six years) consumed 1.0, 1.1, and 1.6 g/kg alcohol over 30, 90, and 180 minutes. Duplicate BrACs were determined with an Intoximeter EC/IR starting at 10 minutes after the end of drinking (EOD). The mean BrAC reported to three decimal places was compared to the lowest truncated result. The mean increase in BrAC after the EOD for the mean three-digit BrAC was 0.015, 0.006, and 0.005 g/100 mL for the 30-, 90-, and 180-minute drinking periods. Using the lowest truncated BrAC, there was no increase more than 0.010 g/100 mL for the 90- and 180-minute drinking times. The mean time to the maximum BrAC was reduced from 41 minutes to 26 minutes, and the length of the plateau was increased from 22 to 39 minutes using the truncated BrAC results.

However, it is important to understand the forensic implications of reporting BAC results in this manner. Reduced peak times, decreased number of subjects that had rising BACs following EOD, and extended concentration plateau resulted when measurements were truncated to the second decimal. Consequently, consideration should be given to this effect when forming opinions regarding the possibility of "on the rise" BACs and when estimating the BAC at the time of driving.

Reference Number: 10510

JONES, A.W., "Biomarkers of Recent Drinking, Retrograde Extrapolation of Blood-Alcohol Concentration and Plasma-to-Blood Distribution Ratio in a Case of Driving under the Influence of Alcohol." *Journal of Forensic and Legal Medicine*, 18: 213–216, 2011 (1 table, 34 references)

Abstract: A female driver was involved in a FMVC with a truck at 1:00 a.m. that killed her male passenger. At 2:10 a.m. a blood sample was collected from a catheter in the driver, which had been previously swabbed with isopropyl alcohol. The PAC as determined by the hospital was 8 mmol/L, which was equivalent to a BAC of 0.031 g/100 mL (using a ratio of 1.2). A venous sample collected at 5:45 a.m. was reported as negative (< 0.010 g/100 mL) by the forensic laboratory. As the driver was reported to have last consumed alcohol at lunch a back calculation using 0.010 g/100 mL/h was conducted, and the estimated BAC of the driver at the time of the FMVC was estimated to be 0.043 g/100 mL. Elevated blood EtG and EtS concentrations of 11 mg/L and 4 mg/L, respectively, were detected in the alcohol-negative blood sample.

> At the time of the crash the driver of the car had a BAC of at least 43 mg/100 mL [0.043 g/100 mL], which is more than twice the legal limit for driving in Sweden (20 mg/100 mL [0.020 g/100 mL]). When leaving the airport, the driver's BAC was at least 68 mg/100 mL [0.068 g/100 mL]. Despite forensic evidence pointing toward a punishable BAC in the female car driver at the time of the crash, the crown prosecution service in Sweden decided not to prosecute because responsibility for the crash had already been attributed to the driver of the truck.

Reference Number: 10511

JONES, A.W. "Evidence-Based Survey of the Elimination Rates of Ethanol from Blood with Applications in Forensic Casework." *Forensic Science International*, 200: 1–20, 2010 (9 tables, 11 figures, 223 references)

Abstract: A detailed evidence-based review of the elimination rate of alcohol and its forensic applications is presented. The typical range of rates of alcohol elimination is between 0.010 and 0.035 g/100 mL/h. A mean rate of elimination of alcohol of 0.015 g/100 mL/h occurs in moderate drinkers, and 0.019 g/100 mL/h in apprehended drinking drivers.

Table. Mean and Range of Rates of Elimination of Alcohol in Three Healthy Male Subjects Who Consumed 40 g of Alcohol on Ten Different Occasions

Subject #	Mean Rate of Elimination (g/100 mL/h)	Range of Rates of Elimination (g/100 mL/h)
1	0.013	0.012–0.016
2	0.017	0.015–0.021
3	0.015	0.013–0.018

Source: Adapted from Jones (2010).

A person's ability to eliminate alcohol from blood is not known in any individual case, and this should be borne in mind when backcalculations are performed so that the suspect gets any benefit of the doubt. In this article I have demonstrated that the rate of elimination of alcohol from blood varies as much between individuals as within the same individual from drinking occasion to occasion. This makes it rather pointless to try to determine a person's elimination rate after the fact, although such post-offence drinking experiments are often commissioned by defence lawyers. This would only confuse the situation because for meaningful results the drinking pattern must be replicated exactly in terms of dose of ethanol, type of drinks, speed of drinking, frequency of intake, and prior exposure to alcohol, as well as the type and amount of food eaten on each occasion. A more pragmatic approach would be to work with a mean and a range of elimination rates such as 10–25 mg/100 mL/h.

1.06 "WIDMARK" OR FORWARD CALCULATIONS

"It should be noted that the use of the Widmark's expression again only provides a calculation of the least amount of alcohol circulating in the body at the particular time and not, as claimed by some, the amount of alcohol actually consumed."

—McCallum et al, "Some Aspects of Alcohol in Body Fluids. Part I: Correlation Between Blood Alcohol Concentration and Alcohol Consumption" (1959)

"Whatever the mechanism, the fact remains that after prolonged heavy drinking, a considerable quantity of alcohol fails to reach the systematic circulation and this needs to be considered when Widmark calculations are made."

—Jones et al, "The Course of the Blood-Alcohol Curve After Consumption of Large Amounts of Alcohol Under Realistic Conditions" (2006)

The calculations to estimate the amount of alcohol in the body from a BAC are commonly known as Widmark (or forward) calculations, named after the Swedish scientist E.M.P. Widmark. His research on alcohol was published mainly in the 1920s and 1930s in German. The equation is as follows:

A = p x C x r
where
A = amount of alcohol absorbed and distributed in the body (grams)
p = body weight in kilograms
C = BAC in mg/g or g/kg
r = reduction or Widmark factor (ratio of alcohol in the body to the alcohol in the blood), approximately 0.7 for men and 0.6 for women

By adding a range of elimination rates and the time since the **start** of drinking to the equation, the amount of alcohol **consumed** can be estimated. By rearranging the equation, one can calculate C or BAC from a drinking scenario. Widmark equations tend to underestimate the amount consumed and overestimate the BAC (10601–10603). The overestimation of BAC is substantial when there is prolonged drinking over a long period of time (10605).

Another problem with calculating BAC from a drinking scenario is that alleged drinking patterns from drinking drivers are notoriously unreliable (correlation coefficient (r) = 0.023–0.027) and of little scientific value (10606–10609). In addition, the uncertain volume of hand-poured drinks make accurate BAC calculations difficult (10610, 10611).

Reference Number: 10601

FORREST, A.R.W. "The Estimation of Widmark's Factor." *Journal of the Forensic Science Society*, 26: 249–252, 1986 (1 table, 13 references)

Abstract: Widmark r values tend to be lower in females than in males and lower in obese persons. To directly measure r the subject should be given a dose of 0.5 g/kg alcohol in a 20%–30% v/v solution on an empty stomach to be consumed within 10 minutes. Frequent blood or breath samples should be taken at 10-minute intervals for the next 6 hours. The technique will only give an estimate of r at the time of the testing; r = body ethanol concentration/blood ethanol concentration. In health the water content of the blood is relatively constant at 80%. Hence r = total body water/body weight × 0.8. The total body water may be estimated by TBW = 0.724 × (body weight – body fat). The body fat can be estimated from the sum of skin fold thickness measured at four sites using a standard caliper. Total body water and hence r may be estimated by the equations of Watson et al.

Whilst estimates of Widmark's factor from weight and height will be particularly unreliable in individuals of grossly unusual physique, no matter what equations are used, such estimates will still be useful aids in the preparation of reports for the courts concerning 'hip flask' defences.

Reference Number: 10602

FRIEL, P.N., B.K. LOGAN, AND J. BAER. "An Evaluation of the Reliability of Widmark Calculations Based on Breath Alcohol Measurements." *Journal Forensic Science*, 40: 91–94, 1995 (1 table, 2 figures, 10 references)

Abstract: Sixty-one male and fifty-four female subjects consumed 0.51 g/kg or 0.43 g/kg alcohol respectively within 10 minutes. BrACs were determined with a BAC Verifier DataMaster II at 15, 30, 45, 60, and 75 minutes. Widmark calculations to estimate the alcohol consumption were conducted based on a r of 0.68 for males and 0.55 for females and a B60 of 0.015 g/100 mL/h. In seven of the 115 subjects (6%) a diffusion-drop or plunge was observed.

This study shows that under the conditions described above, Widmark's formula usually underestimates the actual ethanol dose when BrACs were employed. When 105 min and 125 min BrACs are used, the 95% confidence limits for calculated vodka dose were from 1 to 30 mL below the actual dose. Thus, one can state with a high level of confidence that the calculated dose at these times does not overestimate the true dose, and may in fact underestimate it by as much as 30 mL of vodka.

Reference Number: 10603

GULLBERG, R.G. AND A.W. JONES. "Guidelines for Estimating the Amount of Alcohol Consumed from a Single Measurement of Blood Alcohol Concentration: Re-Evaluation of Widmark's Equation." *Forensic Science International*, 69: 119–130, 1994 (3 tables, 6 figures, 14 references)

Abstract: A study was conducted of 108 male subjects (ages twenty to sixty-three years) who consumed between 0.51–0.85 g/kg alcohol within 15 to 25 minutes after an overnight fast. Capillary or venous blood samples were collected every 15 to 30 minutes and the BACs were determined by an enzymatic method. The mean Vd was 0.689 L/kg, and the mean rate of elimination was 0.013 g/100 mL/h. Widmark's equation was used to estimate the amount consumed from the BACs obtained at 1, 2, and 5 hours post-drinking. The estimated amount consumed was within ± 25%, ±10%, and ± 15% for the 1-, 2-, and 5-hours post-drinking BAC (at 95% CI).

For most practical purposes Widmark's equation provides a fast and reliable way to estimate the quantity of alcohol consumed provided that the limits of uncertainty are considered. Much can be said for using the simplest pharmacokinetic model when this is supported by extensive empirical results, such as those presented here.

Reference Number: 10604

WATSON, P.E., I.D. WATSON, AND R.D. BATT. "Predictions of Blood Alcohol Concentrations in Human Subjects. Updating the Widmark Equation." *Journal of Studies on Alcohol*, 42: 547–556, 1981 (2 figures, 16 references)

Abstract: Equations are derived for expressing the relationship between alcohol intake and BAC in terms of total body water (TBW) and blood water fraction. These equations are more exact than Widmark's and, if used in conjunction with regression equations to calculate total body water, will give more accurate predictions of BAC. Data from various drinking experiments were employed to compare BACs estimated from the classic Widmark equation and from using TBW.

Table. Comparison of Accuracy Range of the Widmark and TBW (Watson et al) Equations with Measured BAC in Drinking Subjects

Accuracy range	Percent correct using Widmark	Percent correct using TBW (or Watson et al)
±5%	27%	44%
±10%	51%	62%
±15%	72%	87%

Source: Adapted from Watson et al (1981).

Hence not only does the Widmark equation overestimate the blood alcohol level in most cases, but it also predicts C_0 values much less precisely, particularly in women.

Reference Number: 10605

JONES, A.W., J.G. WIGMORE, AND C.J. HOUSE. "The Course of the Blood-Alcohol Curve After Consumption of Large Amounts of Alcohol Under Realistic Conditions." *Canadian Society Forensic Science Journal*, 39: 125–140, 2006 (3 tables, 1 figure, 52 references)

Abstract: A review and appreciation of the German article by Zink and Reinhardt (*Blutalkohol*, 21: 422–442, 1984) is presented. Twelve male subjects (mean age thirty-five years) consumed large doses of alcohol (3.0–5.7 g/kg) in a social setting over 5 to 10 hours. The total amount of alcohol consumed was equivalent to between 23 to 41 fl. oz. of 40% v/v liquor. Venous blood samples were collected every 15 to 30 minutes and SACs were determined by GC and enzymatic methods. The mean time to peak BAC was 2 minutes after the last drink. The rate of elimination of alcohol was 0.018 g/100 mL/h (range 0.012 to 0.027 g/100 mL/h). Widmark's r value ranged from 0.77 to 1.32 (mean 1.05). The percent overestimation in BAC using typical Widmark calculations ranged from 10% to 138%. No steepling effect was observed.

Table. Comparison of Measured BAC and Estimated BAC (Using the Widmark Equation and Rates of Elimination of 0.010 to 0.020 g/100 mL/h), Showing the Greatest BAC Overestimations

BAC Curve Number	Equivalent Fluid Ounces of 40% v/v Alcohol Consumed	Drinking Time (hr)	Maximum Observed BAC (g/100 mL)	Estimated BAC Range from Widmark Equation (g/100 mL)
3	40	10.3	0.401	0.630–0.730
4	40	9.7	0.244	0.490–0.580
5	39	6.0	0.305	0.640–0.700
7	41	7.3	0.289	0.550–0.630
11	34	6.3	0.226	0.430–0.490
13	35	6.3	0.207	0.390–0.450

Source: Adapted from Jones et al (2006).

Whatever the mechanism, the fact remains that after prolonged heavy drinking, a considerable quantity of alcohol fails to reach the systematic circulation and this needs to be considered when Widmark calculations are made. The rate of alcohol elimination when this is calculated from the slope of the BAC curve in the post-absorptive phase (0.16 g/kg/h in the Z&R study) underestimates a person's overall elimination capacity. Z&R suggested that a Widmark factor of 1.0 and a lower limit of 0.7 should be used when the dose of alcohol ingested exceeds 2.0 g/kg.

Reference Number: 10606

CAREY, K.B. AND J.T.P. HUSTAD. "Are Retrospectively Reconstructed Blood Alcohol Concentrations Accurate? Preliminary Results from a Field Study." *Journal of Studies on Alcohol*, 63: 762–766, 2002 (1 figure, 19 references)

Abstract: BrACs were determined with an Alco-Sensor IV and compared with estimated BACs (eBACs) from forty-four drinking subjects (64% male) near a university campus. The eBACs were determined from drinking scenarios obtained via telephone interviews the next day. The NHTSA equation was employed, which uses a rate of alcohol elimination of 0.017 g/100 mL/h. The difference between the eBAC and the BrAC ranged from −0.067 to +0.130 g/100 mL. The correlation between BrAC and eBAC decreased with increasing BrAC. At a BrAC < 0.080 g/100 mL, the r = 0.79, and when the BrAC > 0.080 g/100 mL, the correlation was r = 0.23.

The observation that eBACs become less accurate when higher BACs are estimated is consistent with the findings of Sommers and colleagues (2000, 2002) in two samples of hospitalized patients. At higher BACs a person must recall more drinks and estimate longer time periods. The encoding of more frequent events or temporal monitoring may be affected by increasing cognitive impairment due to intoxication.

Reference Number: 10607

SOMMERS, M.S., J.M. DYEHOUSE, S.R. HOWE, K. WEKSELMAN, AND M. FLEMING. "Nurse, I Only Had a Couple of Beers: Validity of Self-Reported Drinking Before Serious Vehicular Injury." *American Journal Critical Care*, 11: 106–114, 2002 (3 tables, 34 references)

Abstract: A 40-month study was conducted of forty-three female and 138 male non-alcohol-dependent patients injured in a motor vehicle accident with an admission BAC as determined by GC > 0.010 g/100 mL. There were 130 drivers, forty-five passengers, and six unknown passenger/drivers. Of the 181 patients, seven male patients (4%) with a BAC > 0.010 g/100 mL denied alcohol consumption. The BACs ranged between 0.012 and 0.315 g/100 mL (mean 0.165 g/100 mL). Sufficient information was obtained from the self-reported drinking pattern of eighty-six male and twenty-seven female patients to determine an estimated BAC based on a rate of alcohol elimination of 0.017 g/100 mL/h. For all patients the correlation between the measured BAC and the estimated BAC was r = 0.264. Drivers underreported drinking more often than non-drivers, and male patients underreported drinking more often than female patients. For all patients the estimated BAC was on average 0.076 g/100 mL lower than the actual BAC. For male drivers the estimated BAC was on average 0.105 g/100 mL lower than the actual BAC, and for female drivers it was 0.069 g/100 mL lower. Patients with an admission BAC > 0.100 g/100 mL were more likely to underreport drinking than drivers with lower BACs. All drinking histories were obtained when the patient was sober and not at admission.

Table. Mean Differences in Estimated BAC (from Self-Reported Drinking) Minus the Actual BAC in Patients Injured in a MVC

Patient Characteristic	Mean Difference (Estimated BAC–Actual BAC) (g/100 mL)
Male Driver	−0.105
Male Non-driver	−0.052
Female Driver	−0.069
Female Non-driver	+0.058
All Patients	−0.076

Source: Adapted from Sommers et al (2002).

We found that most subjects were not trying to conceal their drinking entirely but rather were either unable or unwilling to describe the exact quantity and frequency of alcohol consumption. Possibly, the subjects did not understand the concept of a standard drink. If they underestimated the number of standard drinks contained in their serving of alcohol, they would have underreported their drinking. In addition, some subjects may have underreported their drinking because they could not remember their drinking patterns because of confusion from the injury or because of alcohol intoxication itself. Because of these factors, we do not think that the data support the hypothesis that underreporting was a function of fear of prosecution alone.

Reference Number: 10608

MARTIN, T.L., J.G. WIGMORE, AND K.L. WOODALL. "A Comparison of Blood Alcohol Concentrations Estimated from Drinking Histories of Drivers Charged with Over 80 and Their Intoxilyzer 5000C Results." *Canadian Society of Forensic Science Journal,* 37: 187–195, 2004 (1 table, 3 figures, 36 references)

Abstract: Two hundred and thirty self-reported drinking scenarios from arrested drinking drivers in Ontario between 2000 and 2002 were obtained and compared to the first or the lowest Intoxilyzer 5000C result. There were 197 male (87%) and thirty-three female drivers. Beer was reported to have been consumed by 70% of the male drivers and 33% of the female drivers. Wine was reported to have been consumed by 7% of the female drivers and 0.1% of the male drivers. Estimated blood alcohol concentrations (eBACs) were calculated using the Widmark formula (rho = 0.7 for men and 0.6 for women). The Intoxilyzer results ranged from 0.080 to 0.310 g/100 mL. The eBACs ranged from 0 to 0.255 g/100 mL (mean 0.070 g/100 mL) and from 0 to 0.270 g/100 mL (mean 0.022 g/100 mL) using a rate of alcohol elimination of 0.010 and 0.020 g/100 mL/h respectively. The eBACs were more than 0.010 g/100 mL lower than the Intoxilyzer result in 84% and 96% of the reported drinking scenarios when a rate of elimination of 0.010 g/100 mL/h or 0.020 g/100 mL/h was employed respectively. The correlation coefficients (r) were 0.25 and 0.27 using rates of elimination of 0.010 and 0.020 g/100 mL/h respectively.

Estimated BACs based on submitted drinking scenarios from drivers charged with an over 80 offence were significantly lower than a measured BAC using an approved breath testing instrument, the Intoxilyzer 5000C. We suggest that this discrepancy lies not with the Intoxilyzer 5000C but is due to an unreliability of self-reported drinking scenarios in these cases. Whether this stems from memory loss, decreased attention, carry-over of a pre-existing BAC, misrepresentation or misunderstanding of the amount of alcohol consumed (due to non-standard size drinks being ingested) is unknown. It is also possible that a combination of these factors could result in a significantly underestimated eBAC calculated from a drinking scenario in a single case.

Reference Number: 10609

JONES, A.W. "Are a Blood Alcohol Concentration of 256 mg/dL and Minimal Signs of Impairment Reliable Indications of Alcohol Dependence?" *Medicine Science and the Law,* 34: 265–270, 1994 (20 references)

Abstract: A thirty-eight-year-old woman was involved in a minor traffic accident at approximately 1:00 p.m. and was arrested for impaired driving in Sweden. After she could not provide an acceptable breath sample into the Intoxilyzer 5000, two blood samples were collected. The reported BAC was 0.2565g/100 mL. Since the woman claimed she only had 1.5 glasses of wine at lunch, the BAC was determined in the second blood sample (which confirmed the first alcohol analysis). A DNA profile of the blood samples was conducted that matched the DNA profile of the driver. A lower court dismissed the charges against the woman as the defense expert stated that in tests conducted 7 months later the woman had no biochemical markers of excessive alcohol consumption. A higher court convicted the woman when in addition to the blood results the deficient BrAC result stored in the Intoxilyzer was equivalent to 0.226 g/100 mL.

The lower court justices seem to have chosen to ignore a golden rule in DUI litigation, namely that what the suspect says he or she has drunk is not reliable evidence.

Reference Number: 10610

STEPHENS, A. "A Survey of Hand-Poured Measures of Spirit." *Science and Justice*, 26: 191–194, 1996 (5 tables, 1 figure)

Abstract: Fifty-one male and forty-nine female members of the general public were asked to pour a single (25 mL) and double (50 mL) shot of spirits into three different types of glasses. The three types of glasses were a tall slender glass, a broad short tumbler, and a stemmed wine glass. The volume poured ranged from 6–75 mL for the single shot and 16–130 mL for the double shot. On average more volume was poured into the board short glass (30 mL and 55 mL) than the tall slender glass (27 mL and 51 mL) for the single and double shot pours respectively.

Given the often uncertain volume of hand-poured drinks in cases regarding Blood Alcohol Calculations it is hoped that this work will help those involved in carrying out such calculations to reach informed opinions as to the feasibility of some individuals' recollections.

Reference Number: 10611

WALKER, D., L. SMARANDESCU, AND B. WANSINK. "Half Full or Empty: Cues That Lead Wine Drinkers to Unintentionally Overpour." *Substance Use and Misuse*, Early Online: 1–8, 2013 (3 tables, 2 figures, 27 references)

Abstract: Forty-six female and twenty-seven male wine drinkers (mean age twenty-nine years) were required to pour as much wine as they normally would for one serving under seven different conditions. The average volume of wine poured under baseline conditions was 3.85 fl. oz., compared to 4.42 fl. oz. (wide glass), 4.43 fl. oz. (holding the glass), and 4.31 fl. oz. (white wine).

In conclusion, our research shows that contextual cues related to the shape or color of glass in which wine is poured, or pouring position, influence the amount of wine that is self-poured. In addition, this work shows that individuals, at least retrospectively, are generally accurate in their guesses about how much the environmental cues influenced their pours in a relative sense. This has important implications for the group of individuals who perceived a strong influence of contextual cures after they overpoured significantly. This is a very interesting finding to inform safe driving campaigns. Effective PSAs should be formulated to inform drivers of the different quantities of alcohol contained in different types of glasses (specifically wider glasses) but also about the fact that it they think they overfilled their glass, they probably did so by up to 12%.

1.07 EFFECTS OF OTHER DRUGS

"I would conclude that no agent known to us today plays an effective and practical role in any of the calculations that are used in forensic aspects of alcohol ingestion and especially in what is called back calculation."

—Lester, "Factors Influencing the Metabolism and Disappearance of Alcohol" (1965)

> "Because of the small quantity of alcohol excreted by any route, any therapeutic attempt aimed at increasing the elimination of alcohol is of little or no effect. The only procedure by which the blood alcohol level can be rapidly lowered is by extracorporeal or peritoneal dialysis."
>
> — Committee on Medical Legal Problems, "Alcohol and the Impaired Driver. A Manual on the Medicolegal Aspects of Chemical Tests for Intoxication with Supplement on Breath Alcohol Tests" American Medical Association, National Safety Council, Chicago, (1976)

Other drugs typically do not have a significant effect on the pharmacokinetics of alcohol, especially when the tests are conducted under realistic drinking conditions (10701–10704). Among the reasons for the lack of effect of other drugs on alcohol pharmacokinetics are:

- Alcohol is a simple drug that is distributed through the total body water and has a general effect (i.e., it is not bound to a specific carrier protein or receptor).
- Alcohol is at a concentration in the blood of 100 times to 10,000 times that of most other drug concentrations.

Some of the alleged effects of various drugs occurred only in vitro or with animal studies (10714). Various "sobering-up" preparations such as fructose or other sugars (10715, 10718, 10720), B vitamins (10713), the ADH and catalase liver enzymes (10722), energy drinks (10719), or oxygenated water (10716, 10721) have been shown to be ineffective at significantly increasing the rate of alcohol elimination. The ADH inhibitor (4-methylpyrazole) commonly used for the treatment of methanol poisoning can lower the rate of alcohol elimination (10705).

Reference Number: 10701

KENDALL, M.J., F. SPANNUTH, R.P. WALT, G.J. GIBSON, K.A. HALE, R. BRATIHWAITE, AND M.J.S. LANGMAN. "Lack of Effect of H_2-Receptor Antagonists on the Pharmacokinetics of Alcohol Consumed After Food at Lunchtime." *British Journal Clinical Pharmacology*, 37: 371–374, 1994 (1 table, 1 figure, 16 references)

Abstract: Twenty-four healthy male subjects (ages eighteen to forty years) were administered a placebo or ranitidine (150 mg, 4 times daily), cimetidine (400 mg, 4 times daily), or famotidine (20 mg, 4 times daily). After a seven-day administration of the drug or placebo, the subjects consumed

50 g of ethanol with a standard lunch. The ethanol dosage was between 0.5 and 0.8 g/kg. Frequent blood samples were collected by an indwelling cannula. The BACs were determined by GC. There were no significant differences in maximum BAC between any drug and placebo (range, 0.053 to 0.056 g/100 mL).

The absence of any pharmacokinetic interaction with any of the three drugs studied supports the view that these widely used agents do not have any significant interaction with alcohol.

Reference Number: 10702

OEHMICHEN, M., T. NORPOTH, G. STICHT, H. KAFERSTEIN, M. KNEIP, R. IFFLAND, AND M. STAAK. "Interaction of H_2-Receptor Antagonists (Cimetidine and Ranitidine) and High Blood Alcohol Concentrations. Experimental Investigations." *Blutalkohol*, 33: 305–320, 1996 (5 tables, 3 figures, 50 references)

Abstract: Twelve male subjects (ages twenty-four to thirty-one years) consumed either cimetidine, ranitidine, or placebo and consumed 1.4 g/kg ethanol within 90 minutes. The alcohol was consumed after a standard breakfast. Frequent blood samples were collected, and the BACs were determined in duplicate by GC. Various psychomotor tests were conducted. The mean peak BACs were 0.133, 0.130, and 0.135 g/100 mL for placebo, cimetidine, and ranitidine respectively. The mean rates of ethanol elimination were 0.017, 0.017, and 0.016 g/100 mL/h for placebo, cimetidine, and ranitidine respectively.

There is neither an effect of H_2RA on the kinetics of alcohol nor an effect of alcohol on the kinetics of H_2RA. Neither cimetidine nor ranitidine affect the psychomotor function of healthy sober male volunteers. With maximum blood alcohol concentrations of more than 1.1 promille, no additional deficiencies of psychomotor tests are demonstratable that cannot be explained from the alcohol.

Reference Number: 10703

BROWN, A.ST J.M., AND P.F.W. JAMES. "Omeprazole, Ranitidine and Cimetidine Have No Effect on Peak Blood Ethanol Concentrations, First Pass Metabolism, or Area Under the Time-Ethanol Curve Under Real-Life

Conditions." *Alimentary Pharmacology Therapeutics*, 12: 141–145, 1998 (4 tables, 2 figures, 19 references)

Abstract: Twelve female and eleven male subjects were administered 300 mg ranitidine, 800 mg cimetidine, or 20 mg omeprazole nightly for 2 weeks. The subjects then consumed 0.6 g/kg ethanol as beer (4.8% v/v alcohol) over 1 hour, 0.6 g/kg ethanol IV, and de-alcoholized beer immediately after the consumption of a standard meal with or without prior drug administration. Frequent blood samples were collected via an indwelling catheter and BACs were determined by GC. The mean peak BACs were 0.033 g/100 mL (control), 0.035 g/100 mL (cimetidine), 0.030 g/100 mL (ranitidine), and 0.036 g/100 mL (omeprazole).

> Under these real-life conditions, the concomitant administration of cimetidine, ranitidine, or omeprazole is unlikely to have any significant, physical, social or forensic implications since they do not significantly change ethanol elimination.

Reference Number: 10704

DITTMANN, V., O. PRIBILLA, AND T. WAGNER. "Ethanol Elimination in Man Under the Influence of Frequently Prescribed Beta Receptor Blockers [German]." *Blutalkohol*, 22: 364–370, 1985 (2 tables, 3 figures, 13 references)

Abstract: Four female and seven male subjects consumed 1.0 g/kg ethanol over 40 minutes, after consumption of a standard meal. Blood was collected from an indwelling cannula in the vein of an arm every 30 minutes and the BACs were determined by the ADH and GC methods. The same drinking procedure was repeated on four occasions with either pindolol (5 mg), propranolol (40 mg), atenolol (50 mg), or a placebo. There were no significant effects of the three B blockers on the BAC curve. The mean rate of elimination was 0.017 g/100 mL/h for placebo and 0.016 g/100 mL/h for B blockers. During the absorption phase, simultaneous ingestion of B blocker and ethanol sometimes produced a major drop in systolic and diastolic blood pressure; several subjects complained of a feeling of giddiness, and one subject collapsed.

Reference Number: 10705

SALASPURO, M.K., K.O. LINDROS, AND P.H. PIKKARAINEN. "Effect of 4-Methylpyrazole on Ethanol Elimination Rate and Hepatic Redox Changes in Alcoholics with Adequate or Inadequate Nutrition and in Nonalcoholic Controls." *Metabolism, Clinical and Experimental,* 27: 631–639, 1978 (1 table, 3 figures, 47 references)

Abstract: Nine non-alcoholics, six alcoholics with adequate nutrition, and seven alcoholics with inadequate nutrition were administered 0.8 g/kg alcohol IV within 30 minutes. Three hours later, 774 mg/kg 4-methylpyrazole (4-MP) was injected IV and an additional 0.2 g/kg alcohol was administered. Blood samples were collected every 30 minutes for the duration of the experiment. Blood alcohol, acetaldehyde, lactate, pyruvate, and galactose concentrations were measured. The mean rate of alcohol elimination was approximately 0.016, 0.024, and 0.020 g/100 mL/h in controls, alcoholics (adequate nutrition), and alcoholics (poor nutrition) respectively. After 4-MP administration the mean elimination rates decreased to 0.011, 0.014, and 0.017 g/100 mL/h respectively. In two alcoholics with poor nutrition, 4-MP only decreased the alcohol elimination rate by 2% and 3% respectively.

> In conclusion, the present results indicate that the contribution of a non-ADH pathway is pronounced in chronic alcoholics with inadequate nutrition, probably due to the secondary decrease in hepatic ADH activity caused by their deficient diet. The net effect is that redox-related metabolic changes in the liver are especially diminished in chronic alcoholics with inadequate nutrition.

Reference Number: 10706

JACOBSEN, D., C.S. SEBASTIAN, D.F. DIES, R.L. BREAU, E.G. SPANN, S.K. BARRON, AND K.E. MCMARTIN. "Kinetic Interactions Between 4-Methylpyrazole and Ethanol in Healthy Humans." *Alcoholism: Clinical and Experimental Research*, 20: 804–809, 1996 (2 tables, 3 figures, 31 references)

Abstract: Four fasted male subjects consumed either a placebo, 0.5 or 0.7 g/kg alcohol 1 hour after a placebo, or 10, 15, 20 mg/kg 4-methylpyrazole. Frequent venous blood samples were collected, and the BACs were determined by GC. The mean rate of alcohol elimination was 0.012, 0.016, and

0.012 g/100 mL/h with placebo and 0.007, 0.010, and 0.008 g/100 mL/h after 10, 15, and 20 mg/kg 4-MP.

Table. Mean Alcohol Elimination Rate After Various Doses of 4-Methylpyrazole

Group number (4-MP dose mg/kg)	Mean alcohol elimination rate after placebo (g/100 mL/h)	Mean alcohol elimination rate after 4-MP (g/100 mL/h)
1 (10 mg/kg)	0.012	0.007
2 (15 mg/kg)	0.016	0.010
3 (20 mg/kg)	0.012	0.008

Source: Adapted from Jacobsen et al (1996).

In conclusion, these studies have shown that doses of 4-MP shown to be safe in healthy humans will inhibit human ADH activity in vivo. Thus, the metabolism of methanol, and ethylene glycol to their toxic metabolites should be prevented by these levels of 4-MP, which should be therapeutic in these poisonings.

Reference Number: 10707

MELIA, A.T., J. ZHI, R. ZELASKO, D. HARTMANN, C. GUZELHAN, R. GUERCIOLINI, AND J. ODINK. "The Interaction of the Lipase Inhibitor Orlistat with Ethanol in Healthy Volunteers." *European Journal Clinical Pharmacology,* 54: 773–777, 1998 (4 tables, 1 figure, 15 references)

Abstract: Orlistat is an inhibitor of GI lipases and therefore inhibits the absorption of dietary fat. Thirty healthy male subjects (ages twenty to thirty years) were divided into three equal groups. One received 120 mg orlistat daily for six days and placebo alcohol, one received 120 mg orlistat daily for six days and alcohol, and the other placebo orlistat and alcohol. The subjects consumed 41.7 g of alcohol diluted with OJ to 300 mL and was consumed in three equal doses before, during, and after standard meals. Frequent blood samples were collected, and the SACs were determined by GC. The mean peak SACs for orlistat and orlistat placebo groups were virtually identical (0.041 to 0.043 g/100 mL).

In conclusion, inhibition of dietary fat absorption during short-term treatment (6 days) with orlistat was not altered by the concomitant ingestion of a social amount of ethanol. Short term treatment with orlistat had no significant influence on ethanol pharmacokinetics.

Reference Number: 10708

STROMBERG, C., T. SEPPALA, AND M.J. MATTILA. "Acute Effects of Maprotiline, Doxepin and Zimeldine with Alcohol in Healthy Volunteers." *Archives International Pharmacodynamics*, 291: 217–228, 1988 (3 tables, 5 figures, 27 references)

Abstract: Nine male and three female subjects (ages nineteen to twenty-five years) were administered 75 mg maprotiline, 25 mg doxepin, 200 mg zimeldine, and placebo with alcohol or alcohol placebo at 1-week intervals. The dose of alcohol was 1 g/kg, which was consumed within 40 minutes. Blood samples were collected at 2.5 and 5.5 hours after alcohol consumption and BACs and plasma drug concentrations were determined. BrACs were also determined with an Alcolmeter AE-D1. Various psychomotor tests were conducted. The mean BACs at 2.5 hours did not statistically differ among drug treatments and placebo (i.e., 0.082 to 0.091 g/100 mL).

> In conclusion, maprotiline in a single dose seems to be fairly safe in situations where special psychomotor skills are required (e.g., car driving). This holds true for doxepin as well, although it is subjectively clearly sedative. On the other hand, the addition of alcohol leads to a potentially dangerous interaction, and in this situation maprotiline takes a slight advantage over doxepin, probably because of its slower absorption, which yields a flatter plasma concentration vs time curve.

Reference Number: 10709

TILLONEN, J., N. HOMANN, M. RAUTIO, H. JOUSIMIES-SOMER, AND M. SALASPURO. "Ciprofloxacin Decreases the Rate of Ethanol Elimination in Humans." *Gut*, 43: 347–352, 1999 (4 tables, 2 figures, 43 references)

Abstract: Eight healthy male subjects (ages twenty-one to thirty-one years) were administered 0.63 g/kg ethanol IV before and after oral ingestion of 750 mg of ciprofloxacin twice daily for one week. Ciprofloxacin is an antibiotic that concentrates in the intestinal mucosa. Frequent blood samples were collected via an indwelling catheter and the BACs were determined by headspace GC. Fecal samples were also collected. The mean rate of alcohol elimination was 0.015 g/100 mL/h before treatment and 0.014 g/100 mL/h after treatment. The mean decrease in the alcohol elimination rate after antibiotic use was 9.4% (range 5.1%–17.6%).

In conclusion ciprofloxacin treatment decreases the ethanol elimination rate by 9.4% in man, with a concomitant decrease in faecal ADH activity and acetaldehyde production in vitro. Due to a lack of evidence that ciprofloxacin interferes with hepatic ethanol metabolism, our findings can be explained by the reduction in aerobic and facultative anaerobic bacteria in the lumen and mucosal surfaces of the human large intestines. The findings support evidence of the significant role of colonic bacteria in extrahepatic ethanol metabolism and acetaldehyde production in man.

Reference Number: 10710

KECHIAGIAS, S., K.A. JONSSON, AND A.W. JONES. "Impact of Gastric Emptying on the Pharmacokinetics of Ethanol as Influenced by Cisapride." *British Journal of Clinical Pharmacology*, 48: 728–732, 1999 (2 figures, 22 references)

Abstract: Ten male subjects (ages twenty-one to twenty-eight years) consumed 0.3 g/kg alcohol on an empty stomach (after a 10-hour fast), or 1 hour after a meal, or 1 hour after a meal after treatment with 10 mg of cisapride three times a day for 4 days. The alcohol was consumed within 5 minutes and multiple venous blood samples were collected via an indwelling catheter. BACs were determined by headspace GC. Paracetamol (1.5 g) was also administered to determine the rate of gastric emptying. Cisapride is used in the treatment of GERD and promotes gastric emptying. The mean maximum BACs were 0.044, 0.018, and 0.026 g/100 mL for fasting, food, and food with cisapride respectively.

In conclusion, our study demonstrates that taking the drug cisapride causes a small increase in both C_{max} and AUC when ethanol (0.3 g/kg) was ingested 1 h after eating a meal. The mechanism appears to be accelerated gastric emptying and more rapid saturation of metabolizing enzymes and thus a diminished first-pass metabolism. The increases in peak BAC and AUC after cisapride treatment were not remarkable and was less than that observed when ethanol was consumed on an empty stomach. This example of drug-alcohol interaction probably lacks clinical or forensic significance, and the ethanol-induced performance decrements will be more pronounced when alcohol is consumed on an empty stomach.

Reference Number: 10711

GLEITER, C.H., K-H. ANTONIN, W. SCHOENLABER, AND P. BIECK. "Interaction of Alcohol and Transdermally Administered Scopolamine." *Journal of Clinical Pharmacology*, 28: 1123–1127, 1988 (2 tables, 3 figures, 13 references)

Abstract: Six male and six female subjects (ages twenty to twenty-eight years) were administered a placebo or scopolamine transdermally via a patch and alcohol calculated to obtain a BAC of 0.080 or 0.130 g/100 mL. The alcohol was consumed within 30 minutes and frequent blood and urine samples were collected. The BACs were determined by an ADH method. Various psychomotor tests were conducted. The mean peak BACs were 0.080 g/100 mL with scopolamine and 0.081 g/100 mL with placebo and 0.133 g/100 mL with scopolamine and 0.129 g/100 mL with placebo respectively for the low and high alcohol dose. The mean rate of alcohol elimination was not affected by scopolamine and was 0.013 g/100 mL/h for the low dose of alcohol and 0.018 g/100 mL/h for the high dose.

> In conclusion, TTS-scopolamine did not significantly potentiate the effect of an acute dose on CRT and CFFF. There was no effect of TTS-scopolamine on alcohol elimination or of alcohol on scopolamine elimination.

Reference Number: 10712

ALLEN, D., M. LADER, AND H.V. CURRAN. "A Comparative Study of the Interactions of Alcohol with Amitriptyline, Fluoxetine and Placebo in Normal Subjects." *Progress. Neuro-Psychopharmacology and Biological Psychiatry*, 12: 53–80, 1988 (2 tables, 11 figures, 11 references)

Abstract: Six male and six female subjects were administered a placebo, amitriptyline (25–50 mg), or fluoxetine (20–40 mg) for seven days. On the eighth day subjects consumed vodka within 1 hour to produce a calculated BrAC of approximately 0.080 g/100 mL. BrACs were measured by an Alcometer AE-M2 1 hour after the end of drinking. Various psychomotor tests were conducted.

> The mean BrACs were 0.081, 0.078, and 0.077 g/100 mL after placebo, amitriptyline or fluoxetine treatments, which is not statistically significant. We conclude that amitriptyline and fluoxetine in the doses used in this study differ very little in their effects on physiological or psychomotor

activity before alcohol. Subjective ratings did show some differences and in general amitriptyline was less-well tolerated than either fluoxetine or placebo. After alcohol, significant effects were found with most measures, but these were mostly consistent with the effects of alcohol.

Reference Number: 10713

ALKANA, R.L., E.S. PARKER, H.B. COHEN, H. BIRCH, AND E.P. NOBLE. "Interaction of Sted-eze, Nikethamide, Pipradrol, or Ammonium Chloride with Ethanol in Human Males." *Alcoholism: Clinical and Experimental Research*, 4: 84–92, 1980 (6 tables, 6 figures, 31 references)

Abstract: Six male subjects (ages twenty-one to thirty-six years) consumed 0.8 g/kg alcohol within 15 minutes, 4 hours after a light breakfast and either four tablets of Sted-eze or a placebo. Each tablet of Sted-eze contains 160 mg of vitamin B1, 160 mg of vitamin B2, 45 mg of niacin, and 1 g of yeast. BrACs were determined by a Breathalyzer in duplicate on five occasions. Various psychomotor tasks were conducted. In addition, eight male subjects (ages twenty-one to thirty-five years) consumed 0.8 g/kg alcohol under identical conditions and then consumed either 2.5 mg of pipradol, 1 g of ammonium chloride, or 1.25 g of nikethamide. BrACs were again determined by a Breathalyzer and various psychomotor tests were conducted. Pipradol is an amphetamine-related stimulant. Nikethamide is a powerful CNS stimulant similar to strychnine. Ammonium chloride induces diuresis. The mean peak BrACs were approximately 0.095 g/100 mL under all conditions.

These results indicate that none of the tested drugs represent effective sobering agents at the doses employed.

Reference Number: 10714

VONLANTHEN, R., J.H. BEER, AND B.H. LAUTERBURG. "Effect of Methylene Blue on the Disposition of Ethanol." *Alcohol and Alcoholism*, 35: 424–426, 2000 (3 figures, 26 references)

Abstract: Eleven male subjects (ages nineteen to thirty-one years) consumed 0.5 g/kg alcohol with and without prior administration of 50 mg of methylene blue (24, 18, 12, and 1 hour prior to alcohol consumption). Frequent blood samples were collected via an indwelling catheter and PACs were determined by headspace GC. Blood lactate and pyruvate concentrations were also determined. Methylene blue has been shown to increase alcohol elimination in rats and hepatocytes cultures. The mean peak PACs were virtually identical with and without prior administration of methylene blue (approximately 0.064 g/100 mL). The mean rate of alcohol elimination was 0.019 g/100 mL/h and 0.018 g/100 mL/h without and with prior administration of methylene blue respectively.

In summary, whereas methylene blue stimulates the oxidation of ethanol to CO_2 in isolated hepatocytes and intact rats, no effect of methylene blue on the disposition of ethanol and its metabolic consequences could be demonstrated in humans, possibly because the dose of methylene blue that can be safely administered to humans is too low to be effective.

Reference Number: 10715

DUNDEE, J.W., J.G. BOVILL, AND M. ISAAC. "Failure to Demonstrate an Increased Removal of Alcohol from the Blood Stream by Fructose." *Medicine Science and the Law,* 11: 146–148, 1972 (1 figure, 11 references)

Abstract: A rapid infusion of 0.8 g/kg ethanol was administered to thirty controls and to twelve patients who were also given 100 g fructose IV. No significant increase in the rate of elimination of alcohol was detected with fructose. The mean rate of alcohol elimination was 0.015 g/100 mL/h without fructose and 0.017 g/100 mL/h with fructose. Fructose may alter absorption of alcohol consumed orally and thus may give some benefit. This amount of ethanol infused caused an appreciable incidence of sickness and headache. Fructose caused retrosternal pain and a constriction in the chest, which was frightening to patients.

Studies of blood ethanol levels after rapid infusion of 0.8 g/kg failed to demonstrate any significant increase in the rate of removal of alcohol from the blood by 100 g fructose given intravenously.

Reference Number: 10716

LAAKSO, M., T. HUOPANIEMI, J. HYVARINEN, K. LINDROS, R. ROINE, H. SIPPEL, AND R. YLIKAHRI. "Inefficacy of Oxygenated Drinking Water in Accelerating Ethanol Elimination in Humans." *Life Sciences*, 25: 1369–1372, 1979 (1 table, 9 references)

Abstract: In liver slices and perfused rat livers, the alcohol elimination rate had been shown to increase with increasing oxygen concentration.

Ten male and three female subjects (ages twenty to thirty-five years) after a 3-hour fast were administered 0.8 g/kg alcohol IV in saline with either drinking 200 mL of water or oxygenated water every 10–30 minutes. The third experimental condition was that the subjects were administered alcohol IV with 5% glucose and drank fruit juice or oxygenated fruit juice every 10 minutes. Blood samples were collected every 30 minutes and analyzed by GC. Elimination rates were calculated using linear regression. The mean elimination rates for the three conditions were 0.011, 0.013, and 0.017 g/100 mL/h for control (non-oxygenated) and 0.011, 0.012, and 0.019 g/100 mL/h for oxygenated conditions respectively.

Oxygenated drinks did not increase the elimination rate of ethanol in humans.

Reference Number: 10717

VARGA, M., L. BURIS, AND M. FODOR. "Ethanol Elimination in Man under the Influence of Hepatoprotective Silibinin." *Blutalkohol*, 28: 405–408, 1991 (1 figure, 26 references)

Abstract: Twenty-six healthy subjects of both sexes consumed either brandy or vodka to obtain BACs of between 0.100 to 0.150 g/100 mL. Three weeks later, the subjects consumed the same amount of alcohol but were given a single therapeutic does of 1.05 g of silibinin. Silibinin is a bioflavonoid used to treat chronic alcoholic liver damage. BACs were determined six times over 5 hours from fingertip blood and analyzed by GC. The rate of alcohol elimination was 0.0150 g/100 mL/h before and 0.0151 g/100 mL/h after silibinin treatment.

Although the bioflavonoid silibinin is known as a hepatoprotective agent in the prevention of chronic alcoholic liver damage, it can be stated that silibinin has no influence on acute alcohol elimination in spite of the biochemical hypothesis and considerations. Therefore, it is not suitable nor recommended to administer silibinin as a sobering-up drug.

Reference Number: 10718

MULLINS, M.E., R.A. GRIMSBO, AND E. O'LEARY. "A Natural Sobriety Enzyme: A Party Pill or Snake Oil?" *Veterinary and Human Toxicology*, 41: 102–103, 1999 (3 figures, 3 references)

Abstract: Five male and three female subjects consumed four to six 12 fl. oz. beers *ad libitum* over 90 minutes. The BACs and BrACs were determined 15 minutes after the last drink. The BrACs were determined by the Intoxilyzer 5000 and the BACs by GC. One-half of the subjects ingested twelve capsules of Alcozyme with a glass of water and the other half consumed only water. Forty minutes later the BACs and BrACs were determined again. The BACs and BrACs correlated well with $r^2 = 0.95$. There were no differences in BrACs or BACs with or without Alcozyme. In addition, an in vitro study showed no reduction in the aqueous alcohol concentration when Alcozyme was added to the solution.

Alcozyme fails to meet its expressed and implied claims to accelerate ethanol metabolism or to produce sobriety after consuming ethanol.

Reference Number: 10719

FERREIRA, S.E., M.T. DE MELLO, S. POMPEIA, AND M.L.O. DE SOUZA-FORMIGONI. "Effects of Energy Drink Ingestion on Alcohol Intoxication." *Alcoholism: Clinical and Experimental Research*, 30: 598–605, 2006 (1 table, 3 figures, 45 references)

Abstract: Twenty-six male subjects (mean age twenty-three years) consumed 0.6 or 1.0 g/kg alcohol after a standard meal with and without the consumption of the energy drink Red Bull (3.57 mL/kg). BrACs were determined with an Alco-Sensor IV. Subjective effects of alcohol and various psychomotor tests were determined. The mean peak BrACs were 0.044 g/100 mL (no energy drink) and 0.050 g/100 mL (energy drink) at the low alcohol dose and 0.097 g/100 mL and 0.099 g/100 mL respectively at the higher alcohol dose.

Table. A Comparison of the Mean Maximum BrAC with Alcohol Alone and Alcohol and Energy Drink at Alcohol Doses of 0.6 and 0.8 g/kg

Condition	Mean maximum BrAC at 0.6 g/kg alcohol dose (g/100 mL)	Mean maximum BrAC at 0.8 g/kg alcohol dose (g/100 mL)
Alcohol alone	0.044	0.097
Alcohol and energy drink	0.050	0.099

Source: Adapted from Ferreira et al (2006).

When compared with the ingestion of alcohol alone, the ingestion of alcohol plus energy drink significantly reduced subjects' perception of headache, weakness, dry mouth, and impairment of motor coordination. However, the ingestion of the energy drink did not significantly reduce the deficits caused by alcohol on objective motor coordination and visual reaction time. The ingestion of the energy drink did not alter the breath alcohol concentrations in either group.

Reference Number: 10720

PZAVLIC, M., K. LIBISELLER, P. GRUBWEISER, H. ULMER, T. SAUPER, AND W. RABL. "Another Soberade on the Market: Does Outox Keep Its Promise?" *Wiener Klinische Wochenschrift*, 119: 104–111, 2007 (4 tables, 2 figures, 33 references)

Abstract: Fourteen female and sixteen male subjects (ages twenty to forty years) consumed beer, wine, and vodka *ad libitum* over 2 hours (average dose, 1.06 g/kg) and either 250 mL of placebo or Outox. The second drinking session was conducted under identical conditions to the first. Outox contains fructose, citric acid, malic acid, ascorbic acid, and carminic acid. Blood and urine samples were collected, and the alcohol concentrations were determined by headspace GC. BrACs were also determined using an Alcotest 7110 MK III A. The mean BAC was 0.101 (placebo) and 0.098 g/100 mL (Outox). The mean rate of alcohol elimination was 0.017 g/100 mL/h (placebo) and 0.018 g/100 mL/h (Outox).

In addition, significant variances in the decrease of alcohol concentration were observed among the volunteers, therefore individuals cannot be sure if and to what extent Outox can possibly diminish their personal alcohol concentration. Consequently, the claim of Outox being a soberade cannot be proven from a scientific point of view.

Reference Number: 10721

RHEE, S.-J., J-W. CHAE, B-J SONG, F.S. LEE, AND K-I. KWON. "Effect of Dissolved Oxygen in Alcoholic Beverages and Drinking Water on Alcohol Elimination in Humans." *Alcohol*, 47: 27–30, 2013 (2 tables, 1 figure, 13 references)

Abstract: Fifteen male subjects (ages twenty to thirty years) consumed 540 mL of a Korean alcoholic beverage (19% v/v alcohol) with water, or oxygenated alcoholic beverage with alcohol, or oxygenated alcoholic beverage and oxygenated water over approximately 45 minutes. They also consumed food. BrACs were determined with an Alcometer SD-400. The times to peak BrAC were similar under all three conditions (0.113, 0.099, and 0.099 g/100 mL, respectively).

> No variable was significant when the normal and oxygenated alcoholic beverages were compared, implying that the dissolved oxygen in the alcoholic beverage had no effect on alcohol elimination. This seems to counter the results of the effect of dissolved oxygen in the alcoholic beverage on the alcohol pharmacokinetics. However, the total quantity of alcohol consumed was very high compared with the previous study, suggesting that there is a limit as to what the oxygen dissolved in only an alcoholic beverage can do.

Reference Number: 10722

WUNDER, C., S. HAIN, S.C. KOELZER, A. PAULKE, M.A. VERHOFF, AND S.W. TOENNES. "Lack of Effects of a Sobering Product Eezup on the Blood Ethanol and Congener Alcohol Concentration." *Forensic Science International*, 278: 101–105, 2017 (1 table, 2 figures, 25 references)

In 2013 a new alcohol-sobering product was promoted on the German market called Eezup. Each package contained two 4 g granulate sticks; users were instructed to dissolve one in the mouth before drinking and one after drinking as it would neutralize alcohol in the breath. The ingredients listed on the packages were vitamin B (4.6 mg), B2 (6.7 mg), and B6 (7.5 mg), zinc (20mg), vitamin E (22.5 mg), vitamin C (390 mg), rice protein (1.5 g), and fructose (5.2 g), as well as alcohol dehydrogenase (200 IU) and catalase (500 IU). Eleven male (median age thirty-one years) and six female (median age twenty-seven years) subjects consumed 1.1–2.0 L of beer after a standard breakfast and after using Eezup or a placebo. Twenty blood samples were collected on each occasion via an indwelling catheter, and plasma alcohol concentrations were determined by headspace GC/MS. The median maximum PAC was 0.09 g/100 mL after taking Eezup and 0.05 g/100 mL after placebo. The mean elimination rate was 0.017 g/100 mL/h for placebo and 0.018 g/100 mL/h for Eezup.

> In contrast to other so-called sobering products described in the literature, Eezup additionally contains the enzymes alcohol dehydrogenase (ADH) and catalase. Since both enzymes are involved in the alcohol metabolism,

Eezup has been assumed to work as an agent that could accelerate the rate of ethanol elimination. However, since Eezup is taken orally these enzymes are denatured by the stomach acid. To avoid this effect, users are instructed to keep the Eezup granulate in their mouths for 30 seconds before swallowing it, perhaps assuming that the enzymes are absorbed by the mucosal tissue. As these enzymes are large protein molecules, their passing of cell membranes is most unlikely. It is well known that the oral administration of proteins or peptides for therapeutic purposes is extremely difficult.

1.08 EFFECTS OF TRAUMA

"If ethanol is fully absorbed and distributed in all body fluids and tissues, neither massive blood loss nor administration of resuscitating fluids is expected to have any significant effect on a preexisting BAC or the rate of ethanol metabolism."

— Jones, "Impact of Trauma, Massive Blood Loss and Administration of Resuscitation Fluids on a Person's Blood-Alcohol Concentration and Rate of Ethanol Metabolism" (2016)

The effects of trauma and its clinical treatment on the pharmacokinetics of alcohol are described in this section. Since alcohol distributes throughout total body water (approximately 40 L) and not just the blood volume (approximately 5 L), the transfusion of blood (10801) or other fluids (10802, 10807) have no significant effect on the BAC. The use of activated or superactivated charcoal does not affect the BAC (10803, 10804).

Studies of the elimination rates of patients being treated in hospital has shown that trauma patients generally eliminate alcohol at higher rates. The elimination rate is decreased substantially if blood flow to the liver is restricted (10807). Burn patients with hypermetabolism may eliminate alcohol at a higher rate (10808). If blood samples are collected from the same arm as intravenous infusions, the blood sample may be diluted and cause a decrease in the apparent BAC (10809), but antemortem infusion of IV fluids have been found to decrease the postmortem BAC by about 10% (10810).

Reference Number: 10801

DITT, J. AND G. SCHULZE. "The Course of the Blood Alcohol Curve in Men After Blood Loss and Infusion of a Blood Substitute [German]." *Acta Medicinae Legalis et Socialis*, 16: 71–76, 1963 (4 figures)

Abstract: A series of thirty-two tests were conducted on twenty-eight male subjects (ages twenty-one to forty years). The subjects consumed an average of 340 mL of 38% v/v alcohol and 500 mL of beer within 2 hours, while eating bread rolls. BACs were determined in blood and ranged from 0.073 to 0.272 g/100 mL. In ten subjects 500 mL of blood was removed and from fourteen subjects it was increased to 750 mL. The amount of blood removed was 7% of the body weight, equivalent to 8%–18% of the total blood volume. In addition, the removed blood was infused back into the subjects several hours later. Also in some subjects, 500 mL of a blood volume substitute (Stereofundin) was infused after the blood removal. None of the above conditions affected the course of the BAC curve. The rate of elimination of alcohol was determined to be from 0.013 to 0.022 g/100 mL/h with a mean of 0.016 g/100 mL/h. Some subjects were unaccustomed drinkers and this large amount of alcohol frequently caused nausea and vomiting, which produced long BAC plateaus and absorption blockade.

Reference Number: 10802

LI, J., T. MILLS AND R. ERATO. "Intravenous Saline Has No Effect on Blood Ethanol Clearance." *Journal of Emergency Medicine*, 17: 1–5, 1999 (2 figures, 35 references)

Abstract: Five female and five male subjects (ages twenty-three to thirty-six years) consumed 0.81 g/kg ethanol after at least a 2-hour fast. Four days later the subjects consumed the same dose of ethanol but were administered 1 L of saline IV. The rate of elimination of alcohol was determined by breath samples collected every 20 minutes. The BrACs were determined by an Alco-Sensor III. Linear regression was used to determine the rate of elimination. The rate of alcohol elimination was 0.016 g/100 mL/h (without saline IV) and 0.015 g/100 mL/h (with saline IV).

> In summary, use of IV fluid therapy in alcohol-intoxicated patients is commonplace and has several potential justifications. Nevertheless, routine treatment of all intoxicated patients with IV fluids is potentially dangerous

since many of these patients may in reality be overhydrated, hypophosphatemic, or have underlying alcohol-induced cardiomyopathy. Intoxicated patients who require fluid or nutritive replenishments may be able to receive such replenishment by mouth. This study additionally demonstrates that IV fluids do not accelerate physiologic ethanol clearance rate.

Reference Number: 10803

HULTEN, B.A., A. HEATH, T. MELLSTRAND, AND T. HEDNER. "Does Alcohol Absorb to Activated Charcoal?" *Human Toxicology*, 5: 211–212, 1985 (1 table, 1 figure, 9 references)

Abstract: Alcohol poisoning is a common cause of morbidity and mortality in industrialized countries. Alcohol is rapidly absorbed from the gut and is absorbed poorly on activated charcoal; however, in 1981 dogs that were given ethanol at the same time as activated charcoal had significantly reduced BACs. In this study eight healthy men consumed 88 g of ethanol mixed with orange or pineapple juice in the early morning on a empty stomach. Thirty minutes after consumption subjects consumed either 20 g of activated charcoal as a slurry or an equivalent volume of water. Blood samples were taken 15, 30, 45, 60 minutes, and every hour for 8 hours. Plasma alcohol concentration was measured by GC. The mean elimination rate was 0.017 g100 mL/h with charcoal and 0.016 g/100 mL/h without charcoal. There were no significant differences in AUC with and without charcoal.

Table. Maximum Plasma Alcohol Concentration in Subjects with and Without Administration of Activated Charcoal

Subject number	Maximum PAC without activated charcoal (g/100 mL)	Maximum PAC with activated charcoal (g/100 mL)
1	0.115	0.111
2	0.106	0.115
3	0.142	0.129
4	0.122	0.162
5	0.123	0.128
6	0.123	0.098
7	0.102	0.123
8	0.092	0.123
Mean	**0.114**	**0.124**

Source: Adapted from Hulten et al (1985).

Activated charcoal has no place in the treatment of alcohol poisoning.

Reference Number: 10804

KATONA, B.G., E.G. SIEGEL, J.R. ROBERTS, W.K. FANT, AND M. HASSEN. "The Effect of Superactivated Charcoal and Magnesium Citrate Solution on Blood Ethanol Concentrations and Area under the Curve in Humans." *Clinical Toxicology,* 27: 129–137, 1989 (2 tables, 1 figure, 21 references)

Abstract: Nine male subjects (ages twenty-one to thirty-seven years) consumed 0.6 g/kg within 15 to 20 minutes after a standard breakfast. Blood samples were collected via a heparin lock at 0.5, 1, 1.5, 2, 3, and 4 hours after ingestion and the BACs were determined by GC. One week later under identical conditions, the subjects consumed 60 g of super activated charcoal (SAC) and 300 mL of 5.8% magnesium citrate solution 1 hour after consumption of alcohol. One subject consumed a second dose of the solution at 3 hours. The mean peak BACs were 0.046 g/100 mL for the control group and 0.049 g/100 mL for the superactivated charcoal group.

SAC or AC in situations where ethanol is the lone ingested substance. SAC showed a statistically significant effect in decreasing the blood ethanol concentration at the 2-hour determination. It did not significantly affect AUC or time to peak ethanol concentration. Our data supports not using it.

Reference Number: 10805

GERSHAM, H. AND J. STEEPER. "Rate of Clearance of Ethanol from the Blood of Intoxicated Patients in the Emergency Department." *Journal of Emergency Medicine,* 9: 307–311, 1991 (3 tables, 16 references)

Abstract: A study was conducted of 150 patients admitted to an inner-city hospital in the United States in which at least three blood samples were collected. Forty-five percent of those admitted had head and/or other trauma. The blood samples were collected on average 2 hours apart (range 1.0–7.13 hours). The SACs were determined by an enzymatic procedure. Two patients were excluded as a large bolus ingestion of alcohol within 30 minutes prior to admission caused the SACs to increase with time. The mean rate of alcohol elimination was 0.020 g/100 mL/h (range 0.010–0.037g/100 mL/h).

We have determined the rate of ethanol clearance in an intoxicated unselected population presenting to an inner-city ED to be 20.43 ± 6.86

mg/dL/h. While 20 mg/dL/h is a reproducible mean, the ED physician should also keep in mind that the variation in clearance rate is considerable (SD 6.86 mg/dL/h in our study) and that only 68.26% of the population will have clearances between 13.57 and 27.29 mg/dL/h. Therefore, it an accurate prediction of the rate of clearance is required, it will be necessary to draw a second ethanol level after several hours have elapsed. We find no justification for the measurement of liver, pancreatic or biliary function tests as a predictor of ethanol clearance in these patients.

Reference Number: 10806

BRENNAN, D.F., S. BETZELOS, R. REED, AND J. FALK. "Ethanol Elimination Rates in an ED Population." *American Journal of Emergency Medicine*, 13: 276–280, 1995 (2 tables, 1 figure, 31 references)

Abstract: A study of twenty-four intoxicated patients in which multiple breath samples were collected over a period of 0.5–12.1 hours was conducted. The BrACs were determined by an Intoxilyzer 1400. The initial BrACs were between 0.058 and 0.447 g/100 mL. The mean rate of elimination for chronic alcohol users was 0.020 g/100 mL/h. The mean rate of elimination for non-chronic alcohol users was 0.019 g/100 mL/h. There were problems with the Intoxilyzer 1400, and it required factory servicing. The Intoxilyzer 1400 was not suited for the rigors of daily ED use.

The rate of ethanol elimination in a ED population is 19.6 (95% CI, 16.9 to 22.3) mg/dL/h, corresponding closely to rates reported for other populations. Although some clinical factors have a statistical effect on elimination rate, their clinical significance appears small, and the prediction of ethanol elimination was not shown to be enhanced by consideration of other parameters.

Reference Number: 10807

KLEEMAN, W.J., M. SEIBERT, A. TEMPKA, M. WOLF, J-P. WELLER, AND H-D. TROGER. "Arterial and Venous Alcohol Elimination in Ten Patients with Polytrauma/Shock [German]." *Blutalkohol*, 32: 162–173, 1995 (1 table, 10 figures, 18 references)

Abstract: A study was conducted of the venous and arterial BACs of ten patients admitted to hospital with multiple injuries and suffering from hemorrhagic shock. Patients received up to 6 L of Ringer's lactate solution and 3 L of plasma IV. Blood samples were collected every hour and the BACs were determined by GC and ADH methods. The mean rate of alcohol elimination from venous and arterial blood was 0.019 g/100 mL/h. A BAC plateau occurred in one patient with total hepatic failure who died and in one patient whose hepatic blood supply was interrupted during an operation. There was a flattening of the BAC curve at BACs less than 0.021 g/100 mL. Back calculations of BAC can be conducted in patients who have multiple injuries, hemorrhagic shock, and are given fluids IV.

Table. Hourly Venous (and Arterial) BACs of Three Patients Who Suffered Polytrauma at 1 to 4 Hours After Admission to Hospital

Patient and IV fluids administered	Hourly venous (arterial) BAC (g/100 mL) at 1 to 4 hours after admission				Mean venous (arterial) rate of alcohol elimination (g/100 mL/h)
	1	2	3	4	
A (suicide attempt with a knife) 1,000 mL of Ringer's lactate at scene, additional 2,000 mL of Ringer's lactate, 3 units of fresh frozen plasma, 2 of erythrocyte concentrations +	0.085 (0.085)	0.071 (0.070)	0.043 (0.050)	0.032 (0.032)	0.018 (0.018)
F (MVC, trapped in car) 2,500 mL of Ringer's lactate, 500 mL of plasma	0.216 (0.223)	0.200 (0.198)	0.180 (0.180)	0.169 (0.167)	0.016 (0.019)
G (fall from first story of a building) 3 units of fresh frozen plasma, 3 erythrocyte concentrations, 3,000 mL of Ringer's lactate +	0.092 (0.090)	0.071 (0.068)	0.053 (0.051)	0.035 (0.033)	0.019 (0.019)

Source: Adapted from Kleemann et al (1995).

Reference Number: 10808

ZDOLSEK, H.J., F. SJOBERG, B. LISANDER, AND A.W. JONES. "The Effect of Hypermetabolism Induced by Burn Trauma on the Ethanol-Oxidizing Capacity of the Liver." *Critical Care Medicine*, 27: 2622–2625, 1999 (1 table, 2 figures, 24 references)

Abstract: Eight burn patients (ages twenty-four to fifty-eight years) suffering from burns to 18% to 72% of the total surface area of their bodies and nine healthy male subjects (ages twenty to thirty-one years) were administered 0.35 to 0.60 g/kg alcohol IV over 1 hour. Frequent blood samples were collected from the cubital vein and SACs were determined by headspace GC. None of the patients had a history of heavy alcohol consumption or liver disease. The alcohol was administered daily for the first week post-burn. The elimination rate was calculated from the ratio of g/kg alcohol administered and the time to a zero SAC (assuming a zero-order elimination rate). The mean rate of elimination in the burn victims was 0.020 g/100 mL/h (range, 0.016–0.026 g/100 mL/h) in the first day after the burn and increased to 0.026 g/100 mL/h (range, 0.021–0.031 g/100 mL/h) on day seven. The rate of elimination of control subjects ranged between 0.008 to 0.012 g/100 mL/h (mean, 0.011 g/100 mL/h). After severe burn injury oxygen consumption has been found to be increased in as soon as 7 to 10 hours reaching peak values 3 to 4 days post-burn. In addition, protein catabolism, urea genesis, lipolysis, and gluconeogenesis are increased and there is an extensive loss of water from the burned areas.

> We conclude that the increased elimination of ethanol in burn patients mainly reflects an increased activity in the mitochondrial electron transport chain. Clinically the elimination of ethanol may serve as a measure of the oxidative metabolic capacity of the liver.

Reference Number: 10809

RILEY, D., J.G. WIGMORE, AND B. YEN. "Dilution of Blood Collected for Medicolegal Alcohol Analysis by Intravenous Fluids." *Journal of Analytical Toxicology,* 20: 330–331, 1996 (1 table, 9 references)

Abstract: Two case reports are presented of blood samples diluted by IV in which there was administration of fluids in drinking trauma victims. In one case a forty-two-year-old female driver had a BAC of 0.134 g/100 mL in one blood sample and 0.066 g/100 mL in the other. The second blood sample was diluted and the Hb concentration had decreased from 15.2 to 9.3 g/100 mL. In the second case, a twenty-four-year-old injured snowmobile driver had a BAC of the first sample of 0.263 g/100 mL, which was reduced to 0.111 g/100 mL in the second. The Hb concentrations were 16.0 and 6.8 g/100 mL respectively.

The two reported cases show the possibility of the dilution of the blood sample by IV fluids, resulting in the lowering of the actual BAC. In order to minimize this phenomenon blood samples should be collected distally from the IV infusion or from the other arm.

Reference Number: 10810

KINTZ, P. "Influence of Antemortem Perfusion on Autopsy Blood Ethanol Concentration." *Forensic Toxicology*, 30: 76–79, 2012 (10 references)

Abstract: A twenty-three-year-old man was stabbed during a fight, which resulted in hemorrhagic shock and associated cardiac arrest. The victim was administered 3.25 L of IV fluids for 50 minutes and also received 50 mg of adrenaline. (Intravenous fluids are typically administered in the same amount as fluids lost by other routes to maintain blood pressure.) He was pronounced dead within minutes after the infusion was stopped. His postmortem BAC (right subclavian venous blood) was 0.010 g/100 mL. The BAC of the assailant was estimated to have been 0.165 to 0.190 g/100 mL, and the assailant stated that both he and the victim drank the same amount of alcohol.

Considering the relatively small amount of fluid added compared to the mean distribution volume of ethanol in our case, the effect of antemortem perfusion can be considered as minimal. The dilution factor was estimated to be less than 10%. The blood alcohol concentration of the victim was judged to have never had been as high as around 1.5–2.0 g/L, as was suggested by the assailant.

CHAPTER 2

Blood Alcohol

> "The quantitative procedure for the determination of alcohol in the human organism constitutes one of the best methods which Science has ever put into the hand of Justice."
>
> —Derome, "Quantitative Determination of Alcohol in the Human Organism" (1930)

> "The blood and urine test to determine intoxication has reached a stage of scientific development and reliability where it may serve a most useful purpose of assisting courts and juries to discover the truth in cases in which intoxication is an issue. Although the science never stands still and there will be constant improvements in respect to the test, it has passed its experimental period and affords a safe basis of determining intoxication where the alcoholic concentration is in the higher levels. The use of the test will liberate the innocent by the same means that it will convict the guilty."
>
> —Ladd and Gibson, "The Medico-Legal Aspect of the Blood Tests to Determine Intoxication" (1939)

The above two quotes emphasize the importance of reliable and accurate methods of determining BAC for medicolegal purposes. These tests have removed subjective opinions and replaced them with the actual amount of alcohol in a person's system. The quote from Derome in 1930 would probably be modified today to include DNA analysis as well.

This chapter is organized into five sections: the methods of BAC analysis, the distribution of alcohol into the various components of blood (serum, plasma, red blood cells), the effect of storage conditions (e.g., temperature) on BAC, the effects of the use of "alcoholic" swabs, and endogenous BACs. The average adult human has approximately five liters of whole blood. The major components of whole blood (and approximate percentage) are:

- plasma 54.3%
- red blood cells (erythrocytes) 45.0%
- white blood cells (leukocytes) 0.7%

2.01 METHODS OF ANALYSIS/ANALYTICAL FACTORS

> "There seems no doubt that gas chromatography is the technique of choice for the measurement of blood alcohol."
>
> —Briggs , "Problems in the Chemical Analysis of Blood Alcohol" (1973)

> "Few, if any drugs or toxic substances can be determined in blood and other body fluids with the same high degree of accuracy as alcohol."
>
> —Jones, "Alcohol, Its Analysis in Blood and Breath for Forensic Purposes, Impairment Effects and Acute Toxicity" (2019)

Currently, the most common method and gold standard of forensic analysis of alcohol is by headspace gas chromatographic (GC) (20101–20103). Various enzymatic methods of alcohol analysis are also employed, usually in a hospital setting using antemortem blood (20109–20113). As expressed by Jones in 2019, alcohol analysis is typically much more accurate than analysis of any other drugs and chemicals.

Approximately 8% of samples collected from drinking drivers were clotted due to the delay in mixing the blood with the anticoagulant or failure to mix the blood thoroughly (20115). The alcohol concentration of clotted blood for alcohol analysis tends to be lower as there is loss of alcohol during the homogenization of the blood (20104, 20116). Hemolyzed blood was found to have a lower blood alcohol concentration due to its conversion to acetaldehyde compared to fresh blood samples (20117). A low result is also obtained by the hospital enzymatic method in plasma samples that are hemolyzed (20118). Capillary blood alcohol concentrations tend to be on average 0.004 g/100 mL lower than venous BACs (20121).

Excess NaF in blood samples tends to lower the alcohol result by 2%–3% (20122). The specific gravity of water decreases by only 0.2% between 4°C and 22°C, and thus the equilibration time of samples removed from the refrigerator into room temperature has minimal effect on the blood alcohol analysis (20123).

The accuracy of BAC determination using headspace GC is typically ±5% (20119–20120).

Other methods of alcohol analysis include direct injection GC (20107, 20108) and HPLC (20114). Newer methods of alcohol analysis also include headspace GC coupled with MS (20124), and proton nuclear magnetic spectroscopy (20125–20126).

Reference Number: 20101

CHRISTMORE, D.S., R. KELLY, AND L.A. DOSHIER. "Improved Recovery and Stability of Ethanol in Automated Headspace Analysis." *Journal of Forensic Sciences,* 29: 1038–1044, 1984 (3 tables, 3 figures, 6 references)

Abstract: A study was conducted of analysis spiked aqueous, urine, serum, and whole blood samples by a Perkin-Elmer F-45 Automated Headspace Analyser. The column used was a 1.8 m stainless steel column (2 mm ID) packed with 5% Carbowax 20 M on Carbopak B. The operating temperatures were heating block, 60°C; injector, 100°C; oven, 65°C, and detector, 150°C. *n*-Propanol was used as an internal standard. The additions of sodium dithionate to prevent acetaldehyde formation and ammonium sulphate to prevent salting-out effects were found to improve recovery and precision of the ethanol analysis.

> In conclusion, we have developed a headspace GC method for determination of alcohol in blood in which the analyte is stable under analytical conditions for at least 3h; the method is accurate, linear and extremely precise and sensitive.

Reference Number: 20102

JONES, A.W. AND J. SCHUBERTH. "Computer-Aided Headspace Gas Chromatography Applied to Blood-Alcohol Analysis: Importance of Online Process Control." *Journal of Forensic Sciences,* 34: 1116–1127, 1989 (3 tables, 6 figures, 16 references)

Abstract: A headspace GC method used to determine the blood alcohol concentration of arrested drinking drivers in Sweden is described. A volume of 0.1 mL of blood is pipetted and diluted eleven-fold with a solution of *n*-propanol internal standard and sealed into a glass vial. The vial is heated to 40°C for 18 minutes and the headspace is injected onto three separate columns (Carbopak C, 80–100; Carbopak B, 60–80; and 15% Carbowax 20M).

HS-GC has emerged as the method of choice for analysis of ethanol as well as other low molecular weight volatiles in body fluids for research and medicolegal purposes. The present method is similar to many well-established HS-GC techniques described in the literature. Special precautions must be taken to eliminate the risk of mix-up of specimens and to ensure a high degree of quality control of the day-to-day analytical results. To this end, aliquots of blood are removed from two different Vacutainer tubes from each suspected driver. Furthermore, three laboratory assistants each make a single determination working independently with different sets of equipment.

Reference Number: 20103

CHIAROTTI, M. AND N. DE GIOVANNI. "Acetaldehyde Accumulation during Headspace Gas Chromatographic Determination of Ethanol." *Forensic Science International*, 20: 21–25, 1982 (2 tables, 1 figure, 13 references)

Abstract: Acetaldehyde is formed from ethanol if the whole blood sample is heated above 40°C for several hours. The use of headspace automatic samplers can be the cause of serious errors if the equilibration temperature is 50°C or higher, since the elapsed time between the first and the second analysis may be several hours.

Table. Decrease in BAC with Increasing Equilibration Time at 50°C and 60°C Temperatures During GC Analysis

Equilibration time (minutes)	10	50	90	120
BAC at 50°C (g/100 mL)	0.100	0.098	0.095	0.096
BAC at 60°C (g/100 mL)	0.100	0.099	0.098	0.091

Source: Adapted from Chiarotti and De Giovanni (1982).

In conclusion preheating at 45°C or lower, is advisable when an automatic headspace sampler is used, and when capillary blood samples are used.

Reference Number: 20104

SENKOWSKI, C.M. AND K.A. THOMPSON. "The Accuracy of Blood Alcohol Analysis Using Automated Headspace Gas Chromatography When Performed on Clotted Samples." *Journal of Forensic Sciences*, 35: 176–180, 1990 (1 table, 2 figures)

Abstract: The effect of blood clotting on the BAC was determined in twenty sets of blood that were collected from drinking subjects whose BACs ranged from 0.020–0.150 g/100 mL. Each set consisted of four tubes, including two that contained an anticoagulant and were thoroughly mixed, one that contained no anticoagulant, and one that contained anticoagulant and was not mixed. BACs were determined by headspace GC. The clotted BAC had a mean deviation from the unclotted BAC of –0.001 g/100 mL (range –0.006 g/100 mL to +0.001 g/100 mL). The tendency of the clotted BAC to be lower may be due to loss of alcohol (volatiles) during the homogenization process.

The data demonstrate that a valid determination can be performed on a clotted blood sample.

Reference Number: 20105

MILLER, B.A., S.M. DAY, T.E. VASQUEZ, AND F.M. EVANS. "Absence of Salting Out Effects in Forensic Blood Alcohol Determination at Various Concentrations of Sodium Fluoride Using Semi-Automated Headspace Gas Chromatography." *Science and Justice*, 44: 73–76, 2004 (3 tables, 9 references)

Abstract: Blood and aqueous samples containing various concentrations of alcohol and sodium fluoride were analyzed by headspace GC. The analytical method involves using 250 uL of sample and diluting six-fold with an aqueous *n*-propanol internal standard. This dilution would minimize salting-out effects. A HP 5890 Series II GC with FID was employed. The GC column was 6 ft × ⅛-inch ID stainless steel column (GP 60/80, Carbopak C, 0.2% Carbowax 1500). The results of the aqueous alcohol samples decreased slightly from 0.154 to 0.152 g/100 mL as the NaF concentration increased from 0 to 30 g/100 mL. When blood samples collected from drinking subjects were analyzed at a NaF concentration of 5 g/100 mL there was a decrease of approximately 9% in apparent BAC.

These data demonstrate that the salting-out challenge to blood alcohol measurements determined by headspace gas chromatography with *n*-propanol as an internal standard is a bogus challenge. Indeed, under these analytical conditions, the presence of NaF in the blood collection tubes depresses the measurement ethanol value resulting in the reporting of a value more beneficial to the defendant.

Reference Number: 20106

ZUBA, D. "Measurement Uncertainty in Determination of Blood Alcohol Concentration." *Problems Forensic Science*, 54: 113–136, 2003 (2 tables)

Abstract: The analytical variability of the headspace GC method and ADH methods routinely used at the forensic laboratory in Poland were determined. The headspace GC method employs *t*-butanol (1,1, dimethylethanol) as an internal standard. Detailed formulae and calculations are presented. The main sources of analytical variability for the headspace GC method are the volume of the blood sample (45%) and ethanol concentration of the standard solution (16%). Henry's constant accounts for 0.9% of the variability. The volume of the internal standard accounts for 0.5% of the variability. The conclusion of the study is that the analytical variability of the headspace GC method is 5% at BACs of 0.100 g/100 mL or greater.

The performed theoretical analysis and the experimental results show that the uncertainty of alcohol concentration determination should be assumed to be 0.05 promille for concentrations lower than 1.0 promille and 5% for higher concentrations. This assumption allows us to take into account all of the errors that can occur during the performing of the analyses, in the obtained results.

Reference Number: 20107

TANGERMAN, A. "Highly Sensitive Gas Chromatographic Analysis of Ethanol in Whole Blood, Serum, Urine, and Fecal Supernatants by the Direct Injection Method." *Clinical Chemistry*, 43: 1003–1009, 1997 (1 table, 6 figures, 23 references)

Abstract: A direct injection GC method is described to determine the ethanol concentration in blood, serum, urine, and fecal supernatants. The GC has a glass liner in the injection port to prevent contamination of non-volatile compounds and allows injection of a large sample volume (10 uL). Plugging of the syringe was a serious problem.

> In conclusion, the direct injection method as presented here is a highly sensitive, rapid, and reliable gas chromatographic procedure for measuring ethanol in various biological specimens.

Reference Number: 20108

VARGA, M., G. SOMOYGI, J. POSTA, AND L. BURIS. "Effect of Different Columns and Internal Standards on the Quality Assurance of the Gas Chromatographic Determination of Blood Ethanol." *European Journal of Clinical Chemistry and Clinical Biochemistry*, 31: 773–776, 1993 (4 tables, 1 figure, 14 references)

Abstract: A study was conducted of the effect of using two different columns and two different internal standards on the accuracy and precision of BAC determinations. Blood samples from drinking drivers were analyzed by direct injection. The GC was an HP5710 with FID. A glass or steel column was used both packed with Porapak S. Either isopropanol or *t*-butanol were used as an internal standard. No significant differences were observed between either columns or either internal standard.

> Thus, the use of different types of GC columns or different internal standards is acceptable.

Reference Number: 20109

CAPLAN, Y. AND B. LEVINE. "The Analysis of Ethanol in Serum, Blood and Urine. A Comparison of the TDx REA Ethanol Assay with Gas Chromatography." *Journal of Analytical Toxicology*, 10: 49–52, 1986 (4 tables, 13 references)

Abstract: Studies were performed to evaluate two Abbott TDx ethanol analyses. Both assays involved radiative energy attenuation (REA) and differed only in the dye used for the chromogen. The methods were compared to headspace gas chromatography. Good correlation was obtained ($r = 0.98$) for ethanol analysis in serum, urine, and fresh blood. However, in ninety-two postmortem blood samples, the TDx analysis had to be repeated in thirteen samples and there were three false positive and three false negative results obtained.

In conclusion, the authors feel that both TDx ethanol assays are acceptable methods for analyzing serum, urine, and fresh blood.

Reference Number: 20110

CARY, P.L., P.D. WHITTER, AND C.A. JOHNSON. "Abbot Radiative Energy Attenuation Method For Quantifying Ethanol Evaluated and Compared with Gas Liquid Chromatography and the Du Pont ACA." *Clinical Chemistry*, 30: 1867–1870, 1984 (3 tables, 1 figure, 8 references)

Abstract: REA involves the production of NADH from ethanol using ADH. The NADH reacts with iodonitrotetrazolium (INT) to produce formazen-INT. Formazen-INT yields a red color with an absorbance peak of 492 nm. This absorbance overlaps the excitation and emission spectrum of fluorescein, and the fluorescence intensity decreases logarithmically with increasing concentration of formazen-INT. Methanol, isopropanol, and acetone concentrations of up to 0.320 g/10mL of saline had no result greater than the zero-ethanol calibration.

REA correlations with GLC and ACA results are better for serum and urine than for blood. The error in postmortem blood was as high as 0.011 g/100 mL for the REA method.

We found the TDx REA assay for ethanol a useful method for quantifying ethanol in blood, serum, and urine in clinical and forensic specimens.

Reference Number: 20111

JORTANI, S.A., AND A. POKLIS. "Evaluation of the ADx REA Assay for Determination of Ethanol in Serum and Urine." *Journal of Analytical Toxicology*, 17: 307–309, 1993 (2 tables, 1 figure, 7 references)

Abstract: Serum, urine, and aqueous alcohol solutions were analyzed by the ADx REA method and GC. The ADx assay is similar to the TDx assay but the reagent packs are not interchangeable. The calibration curve was stable for 1 month. There was no evidence of carry-over of ethanol between samples. The ADx assay is linear to 0.300 g/100 mL. No significant interaction was observed with methanol, *n*-butanol, isopropanol, ethylene glycol, and acetone.

Overall, the ADx assay was found to be a useful method for rapid toxicology ethanol determination in clinical laboratories.

Reference Number: 20112

WINEK, C.L., W.W. WAHBA, R.M. WINDISCH AND C.L. WINEK JR. "Serum Alcohol Concentrations in Trauma Patients Determined by Immunoassays versus Gas Chromatography." *Forensic Science International*, 139: 1–3, 2004 (1 table, 16 references)

Abstract: Blood samples were collected from sixty-seven patients suffering from traumatic injury. Serum/plasma alcohol concentrations were determined by an enzymatic method (Dimension Clinical Chemistry) and a GC method. Forty-three of the sixty-seven injured patients had a zero S/PAC as determined by both methods. The S/PACs (enzymatic) ranged from 0.022 to 0.460 g/100 mL and were between 0.017 and 0.448 g/100 mL for the GC method for the other twenty-four samples. The enzymatic method ranged from 16% higher to 16% lower than the results of the GC method when the S/PAC > 0.100 g/100 mL.

> In conclusion, this study shows that in living patients with trauma, there were no false positives or significant increase in BAC as a result of using enzymatic method of analysis compared to the most reliable GLC. This study should put to rest the false, unsubstantiated notion that trauma is associated with an increase in LDH and lactate levels which leads to an elevated BAC when analysed by an enzymatic method.

Reference Number: 20113

KRISTOFFERSON, L. AND A. SMITH-KIELLAND. "An Automated Alcohol Dehydrogenase Method for Ethanol Quantification in Urine and Whole Blood." *Journal of Analytical Toxicology*, 29: 387–389, 2005 (2 tables, 1 figure, 11 references)

Abstract: Spiked urine samples were analyzed by an ADH method using the Hitachi 917 instrument. In addition, 305 forensic urine samples and 3,186 forensic blood samples were analyzed by this method and compared with headspace GC. The LOD and LOQ were 0.001 g/100 mL and 0.004 g/100 mL respectively. The ADH method gave lower results than headspace GC with increasing alcohol concentration. At spiked BAC of 0.150 g/100 mL, the Hitachi 917 would give a result of 0.146 g/100 mL at a concentration of between 0.020 to 0.300 g/100 mL.

> In conclusion, the automated enzymatic ADH method has proven to be suitable and highly efficient for a quantitative screening of ethanol.

The results of the external quality control specimens confirmed that the method was acceptable for ethanol determinations in urine and blood specimens. When used for forensic applications, the method should always be combined with a different method in order to confirm a positive ethanol result.

Reference Number: 20114

PELLEGRINO, S., F.S. BRUNO, AND M. PETRARULO. "Liquid Chromatographic Determination of Ethyl Alcohol in Body Fluids." *Journal of Chromatography B*, 729: 103–110, 1999 (2 tables, 4 figures, 12 references)

Abstract: An enzymatic HPLC method to determine aqueous, serum, and whole blood alcohol concentrations is described. The analysis is based on the conversion of ethyl alcohol to acetaldehyde to ADH-NAD in the presence of phenylhydrazine, which is then converted into acetaldehyde-phenylhydrazone. This derivative is suitable for reverse-phase LC at UV wavelengths of 276 nm. The results were compared with headspace GC. The LOD for whole blood was 0.0008 g/100 mL and the LOQ was 0.002 g/100 mL. The CV was 2.3% at a BAC of 0.100 g/100 mL. Methyl alcohol, *n*-propanol, isopropanol, and *n*-butanol did not interfere with the alcohol result.

The proposed method, however, does not allow the determination of other alcohols and this may be a limitation in situations that are clinically similar to ethanol intoxication.

Reference Number: 20115

RUDRAM, D.A. "The Incidence of Clotted Blood Samples in Road Safety Act Cases." *Journal of Forensic Science Society*, 14: 19–22, 1974 (5 references)

Abstract: In a two-month period in 1970, 2,202 duplicate specimens of blood were received and 7.8% were clotted. Comparison of alcohol content of clotted and unclotted blood samples showed no significant difference as analyzed by direct injection GC if the clotted blood sample was homogenized. The clotting of the blood specimen was due to the delay in mixing the blood with the anticoagulant or failure to mix the blood and anticoagulant thoroughly.

It is quite clear from these results that it is possible for the ethanol content of clotted blood specimens to be determined accurately and without systematic bias. Any failure to analyze such specimens is a reflection on the analyst's ability rather than any intrinsic failings of the sample.

Reference Number: 20116

KOSECKI, P.A., P. BROOKE, L. ABBOTT, AND E. CANONICO. "The Effect of Sample Hemolysis on Blood Ethanol Analysis Using Headspace Gas Chromatography." *Journal of Forensic Sciences*, 66: 1136–1142, 2021 (2 tables, 1 figure, 42 references).

Abstract: Hemolysis is the rupture of red blood cells and release of their contents into the blood plasma. It can occur during the freezing/thawing of the blood, during transportation or homogenization of a clotted blood sample, or when an aqueous internal standard is added to the blood sample for analysis. Postmortem blood is mainly hemolyzed. Blood was collected into three 10 mL gray-top Vacutainers (100 mg NaF, 20 mg potassium oxalate) from a volunteer who drank two 12 fl. oz. beers (9% v/v alcohol). After collection each tube was inverted ten times to mix the preservatives/anticoagulants in the tube with the blood. One tube was divided into two and either vigorously shaken for 5 minutes (hemolyzed) or not (nonhemolyzed). The hemolyzed blood sample was homogenized prior to analysis. Thirty analyses were conducted on each hemolyzed and nonhemolyzed blood sample using a 100 uL sample and 1 mL of *n*-propanol internal standard aqueous solution. The samples were analyzed by headspace GC using dual capillary columns and dual FIDs. The mean BAC determined was 0.1042 g/100 mL for both hemolyzed and nonhemolyzed samples.

Based on both theoretical arguments and the experimental data presented, hemolysis would not be expected to impact a blood ethanol measurement. It appears that hemolysis of whole blood samples does not result in a statistically significant difference in measured blood ethanol concentration when blood samples are diluted with an internal standard and analysed with headspace gas chromatography.

Reference Number: 20117

KRISTOFFERSEN L. L-E. STORMYHR, AND A. SMITH-KIELLAND. "Headspace Gas Chromatographic Determination of Ethanol: The Use of Factorial Design to Study Effects of Blood Storage and Headspace Conditions on Ethanol Stability and Acetaldehyde Formation in Whole Blood and

Plasma." *Forensic Science International,* 161: 151–157, 2006 (2 figures, 3 tables, 17 references)

Abstract: Blood samples from a single alcohol-free individual were spiked with alcohol to BACs of 0.021, 0.074, and 0.127 g/100 mL and stored in Vacutainers containing 0.4% w/v NaF. Plasma, hemolyzed blood (frozen), and fresh (nonhemolyzed) blood samples were analyzed for alcohol and acetaldehyde by headspace GC using *t*-butanol as an internal standard. The samples were analyzed at equilibration temperatures of 50°C and 70°C. Forensic blood samples were also analyzed. Hemolyzed blood had a higher acetaldehyde concentration and lower alcohol concentration than fresh blood during storage and at higher equilibration temperatures. This effect did not occur in plasma samples, indicating the presence of red blood cells caused the decrease in alcohol and increase in acetaldehyde concentrations.

Table. Hemolyzed (Frozen) Blood and Nonhemolyzed (Fresh) Blood Alcohol and Acetaldehyde Concentrations After Six Days' Storage and Equilibration Temperature of 70°C

Experiment Number	Initial (Spiked) BAC (g/100 mL)	Equilibration Time (min)	Hemolyzed Blood Alcohol (Acetaldehyde) Concentrations (g/100 mL)	Fresh Blood Alcohol (Acetaldehyde) Concentrations (g/100 mL)
10	0.021	15	0.017 (0.004)	0.019 (0.002)
12	0.021	25	0.016 (0.005)	0.018 (0.002)
14	0.127	15	0.115 (0.005)	0.118 (0.002)
16	0.127	25	0.117 (0.006)	0.117 (0.003)

Source: Adapted from Kristofferson et al (2006).

This work demonstrates by the use of factorial designs that the decrease in blood ethanol concentrations due to chemical oxidation resulted in a nearly equivalent increase in acetaldehyde concentration. Furthermore, this non-enzymatic oxidation of ethanol was dependent on both storage conditions before analysis and the headspace equilibration temperature during analysis. Although the differences may seem small, they are important in forensic science, where legal limits demand a high degree of accuracy in the determination of blood ethanol concentrations.

Reference Number: 20118

LIPPI, G., M. MERCADANTI, R. MUSA, AND R. ALOE. "The Concentration of Plasma Ethanol Measured with an Enzymatic Assay Is Decreased in Hemolyzed Specimens [Letter]." *Clinica Chimica Acta*, 413: 356–357, 2012 (1 figure, 10 references)

Abstract: Alcohol concentrations were determined in two blood samples with a heparin anticoagulant collected from patients. The plasma alcohol concentrations were determined with a Siemens RXL MAX instrument (based on an enzymatic ADH method). The blood samples were divided into three aliquots, one without mechanical hemolysis and the other two with increasing mechanical hemolysis. Mechanical hemolysis was done by aspirating the samples through a very thin needle (30-gauge, 0.3 × 8mm), which simulated a traumatic blood collection. The samples were then centrifuged at 2000 Xg for 15 minutes before analysis, and the plasma was analyzed. The hemolysis index of each sample was determined. A decrease in the measured plasma alcohol concentration (PAC) occurred with increasing hemolysis. The median decreases were 8% and 15% of the samples with increasing hemolysis, respectively. It is probable that the acetaldehyde dehydrogenase (ALDH) enzymes released from the lysed RBCs accelerate the catabolism of acetaldehyde and lower the apparent PAC.

> In spite of the significant bias observed in hemolyzed specimens (i.e., > 10% variance from the reference sample with no interferent), we conclude that results of ethanol testing, at least when assessed with enzymatic assays, should be suppressed in samples containing > 38.0 g/L of cell-free hemoglobin, since the interference would generate unreliable results for both the clinical reasoning and arbitral decision-making.

Reference Number: 20119

HWANG, R-J., J. BELTRAN, C. ROGERS, J. BARLOW, AND G. RAZATOS. "Measurement of Uncertainty for Blood Alcohol Concentration by Headspace Gas Chromatography." *Canadian Society of Forensic Science Journal*, 50: 114–124, 2017 (4 tables, 2 figures, 16 references)

A detailed measurement of uncertainty of ethanol, methanol, acetone, and isopropanol by headspace GC using a dual capillary column determined that the accuracy was ± 5%.

One expanded uncertainty value incorporates all four analytes, simplifies the calculation, and streamlines the reporting process of the estimation of error.

Reference Number: 20120

BOSWELL, H.A. AND F.L. DORMAN. "Uncertainty of Blood Alcohol Concentration (BAC) Results as Related to Instrumental Conditions: Optimization and Robustness of BAC Analysis Headspace Parameters." *Chromatography*, 2: 691–708, 2015 (5 tables, 10 figures, 21 references)

Abstract: Aqueous alcohol concentrations between 0.020 and 0.300 g/100 mL were analyzed by an Agilent Technologies 7890B Series GC with two capillary columns (DB-ALC1 and DB-ALC2) and FID using a headspace autosampler. Various parameters of the HSGS analysis were tested with two internal standards (*t*-butanol and *n*-propanol).

This study concludes that an improvement in accuracy and precision for blood alcohol concentration can be obtained using altered headspace parameters that produce lower percent relative standard deviations at the common threshold of 0.08 g/dL and lower detection limits. *t*-Butanol (RSD = 1.3%) produced a slightly lower percent relative standard deviation when compared to *n*-propanol (RSD = 1.5%); however, both performed optimally at an altered headspace parameter of 85°C headspace oven temperature and 15 psi headspace vial pressurization, relative to the recommended setting by the OEM. Despite these values, *n*-propanol was less affected by the alteration of the headspace parameters in producing accurate and precise blood alcohol concentrations.

Reference Number: 20121

TAYLOR, L., V. REMESKEVICIUS, L. SASKOY, T. BRODIE, J. MAHMUD, H. MOIR, J. BROUNER, C. HOWE, B. THATTI, S. O'CONNELL, G. TROTTER, AND B. ROONEY. "Determination of Ethanol in Micro-Volumes of Blood by Headspace Gas Chromatography: Statistical Comparison between Capillary and Venous Sampling Sites." *Medicine, Science, and the Law*, 11pp, 2020 (6 tables, 31 references)

Capillary blood (100 uL and 10 uL) and venous blood samples (5 mL) were collected from six female and thirty-four male drinking subjects (ages twenty to forty-five years) at least 1 hour after drinking ceased and analyzed for alcohol by headspace GC. The capillary BAC was on average 0.00375 g/100 mL lower than the venous BAC. The 100 uL capillary BAC was on average +0.0041 g/100 mL higher than the 10 uL volume capillary BAC.

On 10 April 2015, the statutory option for drink driving was removed (section 8, subsection 2 of the Road Traffic Act, 1988). Initially this Act stated that if a breath specimen contained no more than 50 ug/100 mL (115 mg/dL) ethanol, then the breath sample could be replaced with a sample of either blood or urine, and should an individual provide such a specimen, then the original breath specimen be discarded. This option was originally brought to compensate for issues with the reliability of the alcohol reading in breath samples. However, a review of the drink and drug driving laws by Sir Peter North in 2010 found that due to the increasing accuracy of evidential breath analyzers, the statutory option was no longer necessary and that an evidential breath reading alone was sufficient to ensure a conviction.

Reference Number 20122

JONES, A.W. AND M. FRANSSON. "Blood Analysis by Headspace Gas Chromatography: Does a Deficient Sample Volume Distort Ethanol Concentration?" *Medicine Science and the Law*, 43: 241–247, 2003 (2 tables, 2 figures, 25 references)

Abstract: The effect of sodium fluoride (NaF) concentration on headspace gas chromatography analysis (HS-GC) of alcohol using either *n*-propanol or *t*-butanol as an internal standard was determined on blood, water, and urine samples. The method of analysis involved using 0.1 mL of sample diluted with 1 mL of internal standard solution. This method would minimize the salting-out effect due to the 10:1 dilution of the sample. Using this method, there was a decrease in the apparent ethyl alcohol concentration in spiked water, urine, and blood samples, respectively, when the NaF concentration was increased from 0 to 20% w/v. The highest NaF concentration was obtained by placing only 0.5 mL of sample into a 12 mL glass tube containing 100 mg of NaF, which sometimes occurs when only a partial blood sample is collected.

Table. The Effect of a High NaF Concentration (i.e., A Deficient Sample) on the Apparent Alcohol Concentration

Spiked Sample	Alcohol Concentration w/o NaF (g/100 mL)	Alcohol Concentration with NaF (g/100 mL)	Percent Decrease in Alcohol Concentration with Excess NaF
Water	0.0999	0.0976	2.4%
Urine	0.0999	0.0955	3.5%
Blood	0.0943	0.0927	1.7%

Source: Adapted from Jones and Fransson (2003).

In conclusion, this study showed that an unusually small volume of blood in the tubes sent for analysis of ethanol and an excess of NaF caused a slight lowering (by 2–3%) of the apparent concentration of ethanol determined by a HS-GC compared with blood without NaF. The explanation appears to be a preferential salting-out of an internal standard (*n*-propanol or *t*-butanol) compared with the 2-carbon ethanol, making the peak area ratios (ethanol/internal standard) smaller, resulting in a lower apparent concentration of ethanol as determined from the calibration curve. When a deficient volume of blood or urine is sent for determination of ethanol by HS-GC, the drunk driver gains a slight advantage compared with a tube filled with blood and no excess NaF.

Reference Number: 20123

KOSECKI, P.A., P. BROOKE, AND E. CANONICO. "The Effect of Sample Temperature Variations during Sample Preparation on Measured Blood Ethanol Concentration." *Journal of Forensic Sciences*, 66: 2478–2483, 2021 (4 tables, 27 references)

Abstract: Spiked blood samples refrigerated at 4°C were placed at room temperature for 1, 2, 3, 4, and 24 hours prior to pipetting, diluting 10:1 with aqueous *n*-propanol internal standard and analyzed by headspace GC. The mean BAC for all five equilibration times was 0.153 g/100 mL. The effects of different equilibration times at room temperature were also studied for the calibrators and internal standard solution. All results were 0.197 g/100 mL. The density of water at 4°C is 0.9999750 g/cm^3 and at 22°C is 0.997773 g/cm^3, a 0.2% difference.

Differences in equilibration time for refrigerated samples do not affect blood ethanol measurement. Sample temperature variations are captured in a comprehensive uncertainty analysis. Temperature variations between calibrators and samples do not affect blood ethanol measurement.

Reference Number: 20124

WUNDER, C., W. POGODA, A. PAULKE, AND S.W. TOENNES. "Assay of Ethanol and Congener Alcohols in Serum and Beverages by Headspace Gas Chromatography/Mass Spectrometry." *MethodsX*, 8, 7 pp, 2021 (5 tables, 1 figure, 6 references)

Abstract: A headspace gas chromatography/mass spectrometry (HS-GC-MS) method to measure alcohol and congener content in 0.25 mL of serum was described. The internal standard mixture consisted of ethanol D6, methanol D4, *t*-butanol, and 2-pentanol. The equilibration time for the headspace vials was 70C for 20 minutes. The interday precision was less than 11% (%RSD).

The analysis of ethanol and of its congeners in blood plays an important role in forensic cases, especially when allegations are made that alcohol has been consumed after an accident. In alcoholic beverages, congeners are by-products and are generated during fermentation.

Reference Number: 20125

DIEHL, B.W. AND E. ZAILER, "Alternative Determination of BAC by Means of 1H- NMR." *Toxichem Krimtech* 80: 320–322, 2013 (2 figures, 1 table, 4 references)

Abstract: A new method of determining blood alcohol concentration by nuclear magnetic resonance (1H-NMR) spectroscopy is described. A capillary blood drop of only 20 uL is required for BAC analysis using this method. It is also non-destructive and requires only a 180-second analysis time. At BACs of less than 0.100 g/100 mL, the maximum deviation is 0.007 g/100 mL.

A drinking test demonstrates the identical BAC values and composition of capillary and intravenous blood. A forensic usability with the specified limits can be met.

Reference Number: 20126

ZAILER, E. AND B.W.K. DIEHL. "Alternative Determination of Blood Alcohol Concentration by 1H NMR Spectroscopy." *Journal of Pharmaceutical and Biomedical Analysis*, 119: 59–64, 2016 (5 figures, 22 references)

Abstract: Whole blood and serum alcohol concentrations were measured by proton nuclear magnetic resonance (1HNMR) spectroscopy. Only 20 μL of sample is required to which 120 μL of internal standard and 1 mL of D_2O were added. The CV% of the method was 1.5% and was linear to 0.300 g/100 mL. The limit of detected was 0.002 g/100 mL. The correlation coefficient compared to headspace GC and enzymatic methods was 0.9751.

> Our study presented an alternative method to determine the BAC in whole blood by the use of 1H NMR is an applicable tool for BAC determination in whole blood with very good results in precision, accuracy, linearity, and robustness. The clinical study with real DUI blood samples showed that the BAC values measured with 1H NMR were comparable with these measured with HS-GC and ADH. In order to reach more expressive results fresh DUI samples should be analyzed to prevent a changing amount of ethanol in the blood samples during storage.

2.02 SERUM, PLASMA, RED BLOOD CELLS

> "The plasma contains a higher alcohol content that the corpuscles in the ratio of about 2:1, but the urine is usually higher than the plasma."
>
> —Miles, "The Comparative Concentrations of Alcohol in Human Blood and Urine at Intervals After Ingestion" (1922)

> "Now as I have found out, the distribution of alcohol (physiological as well as the added alcohol) in blood is not impartial between serum and other cellular elements, ever in serum, its concentration is higher than in the cellular elements."
>
> —Aoki, "Modification of Widmark's Micromethod for the Determination of Blood Alcohol" (1925)

Alcohol distributes among the components of whole blood according to their water content. Serum is the watery component of whole blood that does not have the red blood cells or clotting factors. Plasma is the watery component of blood that does not have red blood cells but still retains the clotting factors. The components of plasma are:

- Water 92%
- Proteins (albumin, globulins) 8%

There is no significant difference between plasma and serum alcohol concentration (20202, 20206). Plasma and serum will have a higher alcohol concentration than whole blood. Hematocrit or the amount of red blood cells in whole blood does not significantly affect the serum/plasma:whole blood alcohol ratio (20202, 20203). Red blood cells have a lower alcohol concentration than whole blood (20205).

Reference Number: 20201

HODGSON, B.T. AND N.K. SHAJANI. "Distribution of Ethanol: Plasma to Whole Blood Ratios." *Canadian Society Forensic Science Journal*, 18: 73–77, 1985 (2 tables, 6 references)

Abstract: The analysis of blood in hospital by ADH requires separating the serum from the RBCs. In hemolyzed samples, blood is deproteinized before analysis. In this study four drinking subjects had two blood samples collected into Vacutainers containing fluoride and oxalate. The samples were then deproteinized with TCA or centrifuged at 1,200 rpm for 5 minutes. The samples were then analyzed by direct injection GC. The mean serum:blood ethanol ratio was 1.11:1 (range, 1.08–1.16). The mean deproteinized blood:blood ethanol ratio was 1.05:1 (range, 0.97–1.09).

The present study indicates that plasma concentrations are 11% higher than those in whole blood but the finding that supernatant alcohol concentrations are only 5% higher than those in whole blood means that forensic experts should investigate the methodology closely. This is particularly advisable for analyses performed by laboratories using the ADH method. In these cases, the sample preparation steps should be confirmed as either simple centrifugation of the blood or precipitation of the blood proteins followed by centrifugation. Either procedure leads to an overestimation of the whole blood concentration, an undesirable situation forensically. An expert should make the conversion to whole blood with the appropriate factor keeping in mind the variations in that factor.

Reference Number: 20202

WINEK, C.L. AND M. CARFAGNA. "Comparison of Plasma, Serum, and Whole Blood Ethanol Concentrations." *Journal of Analytical Toxicology*, 11: 267–268, 1987 (1 table, 3 references)

Abstract: A study was conducted of fifty blood samples analyzed for ethanol by direct injection GC. Samples were collected in the field by law enforcement agencies and consisted of at least one heparinized and one coagulated blood sample. Blood hematocrits were measured and ranged from 20% to 54%, mean 46%. Blood hematocrit had no significant effect on the serum/plasma:whole blood ratios. The ratio of the concentration of ethanol in serum to that in plasma was 1.00, with a range of 0.98:1 to 1.04:1. The mean serum/whole blood and plasma/whole blood alcohol ratios were both 1.12. The serum/whole blood alcohol ratio has a range of 1.09 to 1.18:1. The plasma/whole blood alcohol ratio has a range of 1.09 to 1.17:1. The BACs tested ranged from 0.040 to 0.442 g/100 mL.

Table. The BACs, SACs, and SAC/BAC Ratios in Arrested Drinking Drivers with the Lowest and Highest Hematocrits

Hematocrit	BAC (g/100 mL)	SAC (g/100 mL)	SAC/BAC Ratio
20	0.040	0.047	1.18
22	0.187	0215	1.15
41	0.061	0.070	1.13
41	0.132	0.146	1.11
53	0.303	0.349	1.15
53	0.222	0.256	1.15
54	0.064	0.072	1.16
54	0.145	0.170	1.17
54	0.204	0.234	1.15

Source: Adapted from Winek and Carfagna (1987).

The results of this study are in general agreement with other published studies using smaller subject samples.

Reference Number: 20203

JONES, A.W., R.G. HAHN, AND H.P STALBERG. "Distribution of Ethanol and Water Between Plasma and Whole Blood; Inter- and Intra-Individual Variations After Administration of Ethanol by Intravenous Infusion."

Scandinavian Journal Clinical Laboratory Investigation, 50: 775–780, 1990 (2 tables, 2 figures, 19 references)

Abstract: Seventeen hospital patients (mean age sixty-two years) were given ethanol IV over 60 minutes. Blood samples were collected at 5, 15, 30, 45, 60, 90, 120, 150, 180, 210, 240, 270, 300, 330, and 360 minutes after the start of infusion. The ethanol concentration of whole blood, plasma and erythrocytes were determined by headspace GC. Water concentration was also determined by the dry weight method. Hematocrit was also measured. The mean water content of whole blood was 80.1% w/w ±1.03, of plasma, 91.8% ±0.49, and of erythrocytes, 68.1% (range 65% to 73%). The mean concentration of alcohol in plasma was 0.062 g/100 mL (range, 0.008 to 0.149 g/100 mL) and in whole blood, 0.056 g/100 mL (range, 0.007 to 0.136 g/100 mL). The mean plasma:whole blood alcohol ethanol ratio was 1.12:1 (range 1.09 to 1.17:1). The serum:whole blood ratio was the same as plasma.

Neither of the ethanol ratios were correlated with the hematocrit values. This is not surprising because erythrocytes contain 68% w/w water and, therefore, also take up ethanol. This suggests that even extreme variation in hematocrit value will not appreciably influence the water content of whole blood or the equilibrium distribution of ethanol.

Reference Number: 20204

HAK, E.A., B.J. GERLITZ, P.M. DEMONT, AND W.D. BOWTHORPE. "Determination of Serum Alcohol: Blood Alcohol Ratios." *Canadian Society of Forensic Science Journal*, 28: 123–126, 1995 (1 figure, 8 references)

Abstract: Two blood samples were obtained from 134 subjects (ages twenty-two to fifty-four years) as simultaneously as possible. One sample was separated into serum and the other was retained as whole blood. The alcohol concentrations were determined by headspace GC. The BACs ranged between 0.022 and 0.155 g/100 mL. The mean SAC:BAC ratio was 1.15:1 (range 1.10 to 1.25). Three of the 134 SAC:BAC ratios (2%) were greater than 1.20:1.

For forensic purposes, when converting serum alcohol concentration to blood alcohol concentrations using a range of serum alcohol:blood alcohol ratios of 1.10 to 1.25 would encompass most individuals.

Reference Number: 20205

CHARLEBOIS, R.C., M.R. CORBETT, AND J.G. WIGMORE. "Comparison of Ethanol Concentrations in Blood, Serum, and Blood Cells for Forensic Application." *Journal of Analytical Toxicology*, 20: 171–178, 1996 (4 tables, 3 figures, 33 references)

Abstract: The serum, whole blood, and red blood cells alcohol concentrations from 235 drinking subjects were compared. Alcohol concentrations were determined by headspace GC. The BACs ranged between 0.014 and 0.202 g/100 mL (mean 0.081 g/100 mL). The mean SAC:BAC ratio was 1.14 (range 1.04–1.26). The mean CAC:BAC ratio was 0.871 (range 0.67–1.00). There is also a detailed literature review presented in this area including many German studies.

Because the SAC:BAC ratios were normally distributed, using a conversion factor higher than the mean will increase the proportion of underestimated BACs, increase with the magnitude of underestimates, and decrease the magnitude of overestimates. For example, when a conversion factor for SAC:BAC of 1.18 (mean + 1SD) was used, 83.8% of the BACs were underestimated by 17 mg/dL at most, whereas the largest overestimate was 6 mg/dL.

Reference Number: 20206

PENETAR, D.M., J.F. MCNEIL, E.T. RYAN, AND S.E. LUKAS. "Comparison Among Plasma, Serum, and Whole Blood Ethanol Concentrations: Impact of Storage Conditions and Collection Tubes." *Journal of Analytical Toxicology*, 32: 505–510, 2008 (2 tables, 2 figures, 21 references)

Abstract: Three female and two male subjects (ages thirty-eight to forty-five years) consumed 0.7 g/kg alcohol within 15 minutes. Blood samples were collected via an indwelling catheter at 20, 40, 60, 120, and 180 minutes after drinking ceased. At each time, blood was collected into a 10 mL red, 7 mL lavender (12 mg EDTA), 7 mL gray-1 (30 mg NaF), and 7 mL gray-2 (15 mg NaF, 12 mg potassium oxalate) Vacutainer tubes. Samples for plasma (gray-2 and lavender top containers) were immediately centrifuged. Samples for serum (red and gray-1 tops) were allowed to clot before centrifuging. Alcohol concentrations were determined by direct injection GC using a capillary column and *n*-propanol as an internal standard. There were no significant differences in PAC or SAC. The SAC and

PAC:BAC ratios were between 1.04 and 1.16 (mean 1.11) at all collection times. The samples were stored for up to ten days at 4°C or at room temperature. The mean BAC (120 minutes) was initially 0.071 g/100 mL, and 0.066 g/100 mL and 0.066 g/100 mL after storage for ten days at room temperature and 4°C respectively.

> Collecting blood samples in different types of tubes did not affect the ethanol levels as there were no systematic differences among plasma, serum or whole blood ethanol levels in tubes with or without either preservatives and/or anticoagulants. Theoretically the addition of sodium fluoride preservative in the gray-top collection tubes would prevent degradation of the ethanol levels over time, but any differences observed in our study were not statistically significant. This would indicate that such additives are not important in ethanol analyses that take place within 1–10 days of collection, even in samples that are stored at room temperature.

2.03 STORAGE/PRESERVATION

> "Alcohol is a good preservative for everything but brains."
>
> —Mary Pettibone Poole, "A Glass Eye at a Keyhole" (1938)

> "The lack of alcohol gain in all of the samples and particularly in those from alcohol-free subjects once again dispels a popular defense myth."
>
> —Glover, "The Effect of Heat on Blood Samples Containing Alcohol" (2002)

The effects of storage conditions and preservatives on the BAC of antemortem samples are discussed in this section. Typically, there is no increase in BAC with storage in blood samples as antemortem blood samples are usually sterile and do not have elevated blood glucose concentrations as found in postmortem blood samples. The red blood cells in the blood sample in the presence of oxygen will convert alcohol in the presence of oxygen to acetaldehyde in a temperature-dependent manner and decrease the BAC (20307, 20308) as follows:

$$CH_3CH_2OH \rightarrow CH_3CHO$$

Since serum and plasma samples have no red blood cells, this reaction does not occur and thus these samples are more stable for alcohol during storage than whole blood (20306). Blood samples with NaF stored in the passenger side and trunk of a police car for 30 days with temperatures ranging up to 47°C showed no increase in BAC, only decreases of approximately 0.02 g/100 mL (20305). The absence of preservative (NaF) will cause the whole blood glucose concentrations to decrease rapidly (20311), thus removing a major substrate of alcohol fermentation by microorganisms in the sample. The use of expired blood tubes will have no effect on BAC (20309).

Freezing and rethawing the blood sample during storage will not affect the BAC (20301). Frequent opening of the blood tube during storage will cause a greater decrease in BAC (20303, 20313, 20315). A blood tube that is at least one-half full and unopened has a greater stability in BAC (20314). The loss of alcohol during storage is first order and the decrease in BAC is greater at the start of storage (20316).

Forensic laboratories that also conduct alcohol analysis on postmortem blood samples are cautioned that if microorganisms from postmortem blood samples are introduced into the antemortem blood by diluters or pipettes, there can be a substantial decrease in BAC of the antemortem sample (20310).

Plasma alcohol samples should be stored at –20°C to maintain stability (20312).

Hospital blood tubes that contain gel and are serum separator tubes (SST) can leach *n*-propanol into the samples (20318). DUI blood samples that were damaged in a refrigerator fire had a lower BAC and higher acetaldehyde concentration (20319).

On 12 June 2019, a manufacturer of gray top Vacutainers reported that 0.03% of its tubes had no NaF or anticoagulant added, but this should have minimal effect on antemortem or DUI blood samples (20320).

Reference Number: 20301

MEYER, T., P.K. MONGE, AND J. SAKAHAUG. "Storage of Blood Samples Containing Alcohol." *Acta Pharmacologica et Toxicologica*, 45: 282–286, 1979 (4 tables, 8 references)

Abstract: Samples of blood were preserved with 1% potassium fluoride. The samples were stored at –20°C for six months and stored at 3°C for another five months and reanalyzed for alcohol by GC. Formation of ethanol did not occur with any sample preserved by fluoride. Freezing and rethawing the blood had no effect on BAC.

The present experiments show that freezing is a suitable method for the storage of blood containing alcohol in the range of 0.001–2.99 mg/g of sample over for forensic purposes reasonable period of time.

Reference Number: 20302

SHAJANI, N.K., B.A. IMAGE, AND E.B. CHU. "The Stability of Ethanol in Stored Forensic Blood Samples." *Canadian Society of Forensic Science Journal* 22: 335–339, 1989 (1 table, 4 figures, 18 references)

Abstract: Spiked blood samples were stored in gray top Vacutainers XF947 (now 367001) for 31 weeks at either room temperature or 4°C. BACs were determined by GC. Twenty-six forensic blood samples were also analyzed after at least 1 year storage at 4°C.

It is clear that alcohol is lost from blood samples in storage even when the samples are stored at 4°C. However, the magnitude of the loss is less than 10% over a period of at least one year.

Reference Number: 20303

JONES, A.W. "Are Changes in Blood Ethanol Concentration During Storage Analytically Significant? Importance of Method Imprecision." *Clinical Chemistry Laboratory Medicine*, 45: 1299–1304, 2007 (1 table, 1 figure, 31 references)

Abstract: The stability of alcohol in blood samples stored at 4°C with NaF was determined for up to 1 year. BACs were determined by headspace GC using *n*-propanol as an internal standard. The CV of the method was 1.1%. All blood samples showed a decrease in BAC with time. The average decrease was approximately 0.003 g/100 mL/month regardless of the initial BAC. In tubes that were opened frequently during storage the decrease in BAC was 0.022 g/100 mL compared to 0.010 g/100 mL in unopened tubes over 6.5 months.

In this study no evidence was found that BEC increased during storage of specimens at 4°C in properly sealed tubes containing 1% w/v sodium fluoride as a preservative. This finding is important to bear in mind if and when analytical results are challenged in the courts, such as when a person is charged with drunken driving.

Reference Number: 20304

PETKOVIC, S., S. SAVIC, D. ZGONJANIN, AND I. SAMOJLIK. "Ethanol Concentrations in Antemortem Blood Samples Under Controlled Conditions." *Alcohol and Alcoholism*, 43: 658–660, 2008 (2 tables, 8 references)

Abstract: Blood samples were collected from alcohol-free subjects from the cubital vein after using a 70% ethanol swab and then distilled water before venipuncture. The samples were stored at 4° and 20°C for 12 to 48 hours with and without 1% NaF. All BACs < 0.001 g/100 mL upon storage with or without preservative.

On the basis of this study, the authors are somewhat surprised that no ethanol production occurs in everyday practice in improperly processed antemortem blood samples. This implies that measured BACs reflect concordance with ethanol levels at the time of sampling.

Reference Number: 20305

GLOVER, P.L. "The Effect of Heat on Blood Samples Containing Alcohol." *Proceedings of the 16th International Conference on Alcohol, Drugs and Traffic Safety, T2002 CD-ROM, D. Mayhew, and C. Dussault (eds),* 5pp, 2002 (3 tables, 9 references)

Abstract: Ten tubes of blood were collected from four drinking and two non-drinking subjects using 7 mL Vacutainers containing EDTA and NaF. The samples were stored under various conditions and placed in the trunk and passenger side of a police patrol car. The ambient temperatures were measured every 5 minutes for 78 days and ranged between 17°C and 47°C. Control samples were stored at 4°C for 30 days. BACs were determined by headspace GC using *n*-propanol as an internal standard. The alcohol-free samples remained alcohol free under all storage conditions. The initial BACs of 0.123, 0.077, 0.079, and 0.062 g/100 mL decreased to 0.108, 0.064, 0.066, and 0.045 g/100 mL respectively after 78 days' storage. The greatest decrease in BAC occurred after 3 days of storage in the police car.

Table. Change in BAC After 7- and 78-Days' Storage in the Trunk of a Police Car at Temperatures up to 47°C

Subject	Initial BAC (g/100 mL)	BAC after 7 days' storage (g/100 mL)	BAC after 78 days' storage (g/100 mL)
A	0.000	0.000	0.000
B	0.000	0.000	0.000
C	0.123	0.113	0.108
D	0.077	0.065	0.062
E	0.079	0.066	0.064
F	0.062	0.047	0.042

Source: Adapted from Glover (2002).

The lack of alcohol gain in all of the samples and particularly in those from alcohol-free subjects once again dispels a popular defense myth. A comparison of the Day 0 Control and Day 30 Control values show the stability of the sample when stored under refrigeration. The more interesting observation was the decrease in concentration that occurred during the initial 72 hours.

Reference Number: 20306

WINEK, T., C.L. WINEK, AND W.W. WAHBA. "The Effect of Storage at Various Temperatures on Blood Alcohol Concentration." *Forensic Science International*, 78: 179–185, 1996 (4 tables, 6 references)

Abstract: Human serum samples spiked to SACs of 0.150, 0.205, and 0.320 g/100 mL were stored in Vacutainers containing potassium oxalate only or oxalate and a preservative (sodium fluoride). The samples were then stored at 27, 32, or 38°C for up to 35 days. In addition, whole blood samples collected by the police, of which thirty-seven out of forty (93%) had no preservative, were also stored under the same conditions. The alcohol concentrations were determined by headspace GC. There were no significant changes in SAC after 35 days' storage whether the serum was preserved or not. For the whole blood samples there was a mean loss of 10%–19% of the initial BAC. One blood sample had a 67% loss from the initial BAC after 35 days' storage.

Therefore, in samples collected aseptically, production of alcohol by microorganisms does not seem to play an important role. Certainly, this study confirms the importance of storage temperature on BAC and is of particular significance for geographical areas with high ambient temperatures. A whole blood sample analysed after exposure to elevated temperatures may produce lower BAC than it originally contained at the time of the collection.

Reference Number: 20307

CHEN, H-M., W.W. LIN, K.H. FERGUSON, B.K. SCOTT, AND C.M. PETERSON. "Studies of the Oxidation of Ethanol to Acetaldehyde by Oxyhemoglobin Using Fluorigenic High Performance Liquid Chromatography." *Alcoholism: Clinical and Experiment Research*, 18: 1202–1206, 1994 (6 figures, 29 references)

Abstract: The blood associated increase in acetaldehyde concentration was studied on spiked blood samples at BACs between 0.010 to 0.150 g/100 mL. In blood samples without alcohol there was no increase in acetaldehyde concentrations stored at room temperature for 7 days. Only the RBC component of the blood showed an increase in acetaldehyde concentration upon storage and not the plasma. Hemoglobin alone increased acetaldehyde concentrations and there was a linear relationship between the amount of Hb and the increase in acetaldehyde. Cyanide prevented the acetaldehyde increase but sodium citrate and iodoacetate did not.

These experiments confirm that a continued elevation in acetaldehyde levels occurs because of the presence of ethanol in blood if oxygen is present. Whole blood itself contains a certain level of acetaldehyde even in humans or animals not consuming ethanol. This baseline level of acetaldehyde remains stable at room temperature storage for up to 1 week. Once ethanol is added to blood, there is an immediate increase due to the acetaldehyde in the ethanol itself, followed by a further increase with time. The increase in WBAA with time can be accounted for by the oxidation of ethanol in the presence of oxyhemoglobin.

Reference Number: 20308

WIGMORE, J.G. "Blood Ethanol Concentrations are Less Stable than Serum or Plasma Upon Storage Because of Oxyhemoglobin-Mediated Oxidation of Ethanol to Acetaldehyde [Letter]." *Journal of Analytical Toxicology*, 33: 182–183, 2009 (7 references)

Abstract: A letter to the editor was published regarding the paper of Penetar et al (20206) on the RBC-mediated oxidation of ethanol to acetaldehyde, which does not occur in serum or plasma. Whole blood will therefore have a greater decrease in alcohol concentration than serum or plasma during storage.

This is of particular importance in cases in which a second blood ethanol analysis (as requested by defence lawyers or other officials) is conducted on a whole blood sample which may have been stored for several months or more.

Reference Number: 20309

ZITTEL, D.B., AND G.G. HARDIN. "Comparison of Blood Ethanol Concentrations in Samples Simultaneously Collected into Expired and Unexpired Venipuncture Tubes." *Journal of Analytical Toxicology*, 30: 317–318, 2006 (2 tables, 4 references)

Abstract: Blood samples were collected from forty male and eight female drinking subjects into two 10 mL venipuncture tubes containing 100 mg NaF and 20 mg potassium oxalate (Tri-Tech). One tube was used before the manufacturer's expiry date and the other tube was expired (between 8 to 74 months). BACs were determined by headspace GC. In the tubes that were 74 months past the expiry date the mean BAC was 0.161 g/100 mL compared to 0.161 g/100 mL in blood samples collected in the unexpired tubes. There was no correlation between expiry date and volume (or fill) of blood collected.

The study data indicate, as judged by the correlation coefficient of 0.997 and by paired two-tailed Students t-test that ethanol concentration in the unexpired and expired venipuncture tubes were statistically identical ($p \geq 0.05$). The correlation between time since expiration and sample volume was 0.086, indicating that the time since expiration had minimal influence on sample volume at least up to 74 months beyond the expiration date.

Reference Number: 20310

DICK, G.L. AND H.M. STONE. "Alcohol Loss Arising from Microbial Contamination of Drivers' Blood Specimens." *Forensic Science International*, 34: 17–27, 1987 (2 tables, 1 figure, 17 references)

Abstract: Some drivers' blood specimens containing 1% sodium fluoride deteriorated as a result of microorganism contamination, resulting in a decrease in BAC. Blood diluters were assumed to be the source of microbial cross contamination from one blood sample to another. Spiked blood samples were then inoculated with strains of *Pseudomonas sp.* and *S. marcescens* and stored under various conditions. Even in 1% sodium fluoride at 4°C a BAC of 0.150 g/100 mL could be reduced to zero after 84 days of storage. It is recommended that postmortem blood samples be analyzed in separate batches from drivers' blood.

> The presence of sodium fluoride in blood specimens at the customary concentration of 1% w/v did not prevent alcohol loss either at 4°C or ambient temperature in microbially-contaminated specimens, did not prevent alcohol loss in uninoculated specimens at ambient temperature, and presented no consistent advantage over zero concentration.

Reference Number: 20311

RUITER, J.E., F. WEINBERG, AND A. MORRISON. "The Stability of Glucose in Serum." *Clinical Chemistry*, 9: 356–359, 1963 (2 tables, 8 references)

Abstract: Blood samples were collected from twenty-five patients and allowed to clot for 0.5 to 2 hours. The blood was then centrifuged. Part of the serum was removed and stored separately, and part was allowed to remain in contact with the clot. The serum glucose concentration was determined at 0, 24, and 48 hours storage at room temperature. The glucose concentration of the serum removed from the clot did not change and ranged between 63 to 171 mg/dL. The serum glucose concentration in the sample in contact with the clot decreased to less than 10 mg/dL in most samples after a 48-hour storage.

Table. Change in Serum Glucose Concentration After 24 and 48 Hours of Storage at Room Temperature and in Contact with the Blood Clot

Serum Number	Initial Glucose Concentration (mg/dL)	Glucose Concentration After 24 hr (mg/dL)	Glucose Concentration After 48 hr (mg/dL)
1	100	49	<10
2	77	42	<10
3	104	24	<10
4	135	70	<10

Serum Number	Initial Glucose Concentration (mg/dL)	Glucose Concentration After 24 hr (mg/dL)	Glucose Concentration After 48 hr (mg/dL)
5	119	31	< 10
6	65	<10	< 10
7	85	24	< 10
8	60	18	< 10
9	164	92	15

Source: Adapted from Ruiter et al (1963).

Glycolysis is profound and prompt.

Reference Number 20312

KOCAK, F.E., O.O. ISIKLAR, H. KOCAK, AND A. MERAL. "Comparison of Blood Ethanol Stabilities in Different Storage Periods." *Biochemia Medica*, 25: 57–63, 2015 (2 tables, 2 figures, 24 references)

Abstract: Blood samples were collected from 84 drinking drivers into 4 mL Vacutainers containing sodium fluoride and EDTA. The blood was centrifuged at 3000× for 15 minutes, and the plasma was divided into two parts. One was analyzed for alcohol immediately, and the other was stored at –20°C for 2, 3, 4, or 5 months. The BACs were determined by an enzymatic method. The mean decrease in PAC was –7.8, –11.2, –20.5, and –25.2% for 2, 3, 4, and 5 months' storage, respectively.

According to our results, plasma ethanol samples can be kept at -20C for up to 3–4 months until re-analysis. However, each laboratory should also establish its own work-flow rules and criterion for reliable ethanol measurement in forensic cases.

Reference Number: 20313

SHAN, X., N.B. TISCIONE, I. ALFORD, AND D.T. YEATMAN. "A Study of Blood Alcohol Stability in Forensic Antemortem Blood Samples." *Forensic Science International*, 211: 47–50, 2011 (3 tables, 1 figure, 8 references)

Abstract: A study was conducted of the stability of BAC in 30 DUI cases, each with two tubes of blood preserved with NaF and potassium oxalate. BACs were determined by headspace GC. One tube was analyzed shortly after receiving the blood, and the other tubes were analyzed after storage at 4°C for 13 to 39 months. The tubes were then stored at room temperature for 6 months and then stored at 38°C for 7 or 28 days. Under all storage conditions, there was a loss in BAC and no increases were detected. In addition, all the BAC-negative cases remained negative under all storage conditions.

Our study with real DUI blood samples showed that (1) alcohol-negative preserved antemortem blood samples remained negative during storage regardless of storage temperature; (2) long-term storage either under refrigeration or at or above room temperature decreased BAC, especially if the tube had been previously opened, indicating that reanalysis of blood alcohol after long-term storage would result in lower BAC results than the true values at the time of blood collection.

Reference Number 20314

TISCIONE, N.B., R.E. VACHA, B. ALFORD, D.T. YEATMAN, AND X. SHAN. "Long-Term Blood Alcohol Stability in Forensic Antemortem Whole Blood Samples." *Journal of Analytical Toxicology*, 39: 419–425, 2015 (3 tables, 6 figures, 17 references)

Abstract: The long-term stability of 117 antemortem whole blood samples, preserved with NaF and stored at room temperature for 5.4 to 10.3 years, was determined. Tube A was analyzed by HS-GC and then reanalyzed by the same method. The sealed tube B was analyzed by HS-GC-FID-MS. Seven samples initially negative for alcohol remained negative for alcohol. All samples with an initial positive BAC showed a decrease in alcohol concentration over time. The decrease ranged from 0.005 to 0.243 g/100 mL. Tubes that were not previously opened and more than 1/2 full had a better BAC stability. The mean decrease in BAC was 0.080 g/100 mL (previously opened, < 6mL volume); 0.044 g/100 mL (previously opened, > 6 mL volume), 0.065 g/100 mL (unopened, < 6 mL volume), and 0.027 g/100 mL (unopened, > 6 mL volume).

When blood samples are reanalyzed after long-term room temperature storage, the results should be interpreted with these conclusions in mind. If the tube was unopened and more than half full, the sample should demonstrate a predictable loss in ethanol concentration. The expected ethanol loss would be in the range of 0.01 and 0.05 g/dL in most cases regardless of the original concentration.

Reference Number 20315

LAURENS, J.B., F.J.J. SEWELL, AND M.M. KOCK. "Pre-Analytical Factors Related to the Stability of Ethanol Concentration During Storage of Ante-Mortem Blood Alcohol Concentrations." *Journal of Forensic and Legal Medicine*, 58: 155–163, 2018 (9 figures, 35 references)

Abstract: Sixty-five percent of South African road accidents are alcohol-related. Blank pooled whole blood samples were spiked with alcohol concentrations of 0.010, 0.050, 0.200, 0.300, 0.400, 0.550, and 0.700 g/100 mL. The samples were stored at 4°C or 22°C with or without NaF and with or without the addition of *Candida albicans*. BACs were measured by GC/MS. There was a temperature-dependent decrease in alcohol concentration after storage. *C. albicans* spiked blood showed no change in BAC after storage for 9 weeks at 4°C with or without NaF. In blood samples stored at 22°C, there was a decrease in BAC even with *C. albicans* added.

> In general, there was no indication of a significant increase in blood alcohol concentration at either legal limit, whether the specimens were stored under refrigeration or at room temperature, or in the presence or absence of NaF. The ethanol concentrations of the specimens not stored under refrigeration in the presence of NaF typically showed a decreasing trend, except in the case of the 0.50 g/L room temperature specimens without sodium fluoride, which exhibited a drastic decrease followed by an increase to approximately 0.40 g/L. It was noted that the rate of decrease in ethanol concentration was more dependent on the temperature than on the presence or absence of fluoride, although the presence of NaF did have a stabilizing effect on the ethanol concentration. Hence, it is recommended that specimens for blood alcohol analysis be stored under refrigeration at or below 4°C in the presence of at least 1% NaF to ensure the stability of the ethanol concentration for up to 29 weeks.

Reference Number 20316

KOSECKI, P.A., L.A. ABBOTT, AND M.E. RAINES. "Large-Scale Reanalysis of Refrigerated Antemortem Blood Samples for Ethanol Content at Random Intervals." *Journal of Forensic Sciences*, 66: 1966–1972, 2021 (3 tables, 3 figures, 18 references)

Abstract: The alcohol concentration of 371 antemortem blood samples stored in gray-top Vacutainers for various times up to 1 year at 4°C were determined by headspace GC. In 349 cases, the second unopened tube was analyzed, and in twenty-two cases blood from the already opened tube was analyzed. In twenty-five cases, the first and second analyses were alcohol-negative. The average change in BAC was –0.004 g/100 mL. The average loss was slightly greater in the previously opened tube (0.0042 g/100 mL) compared with 0.0039 g/100 mL for the unopened tubes. Blood samples that were initially analyzed within 30 days of blood collection had a greater decrease in BAC than blood samples that were initially analyzed in greater than 30 days. The loss of alcohol due to oxidation in a sealed blood tube is first order, in which the loss of alcohol is greatest initially and tapers off.

> On average refrigerated antemortem blood samples analyzed in the normal flow of case work and then reanalyzed within approximately one year can be expected to show on average a small decrease in ethanol concentration, 0.004 g/dL. The expected decrease is affected by the time between the blood draw and the first analysis. The decrease in ethanol concentration for samples analyzed soon after the blood draw should be slightly greater than the decrease in samples with delayed analyses, if the sample is reanalyzed after storage. For most refrigerated antemortem blood samples reanalyzed for ethanol concentration within one year, the ethanol concentration should be within the measurement of uncertainty in the measurement of blood ethanol concentration compared with the average loss of ethanol with refrigerated storage; reanalysis of samples can result in measured concentrations that are greater than or less than the original analysis without representing an actual increase or decrease in ethanol concentration.

Reference Number: 20317

KOSECKI, P.A. AND M.E. RAINES. "Testing Antemortem Blood Samples for Ethanol After Four to Seven Years of Refrigerated Storage." *Journal of Forensic Sciences*, 1–8, 2022 (1 table, 4 figures, 25 references).

Abstract: BACs were determined in twenty-nine previously opened DUI gray-top Vacutainers (100 mg sodium fluoride, 20 mg potassium oxalate) and forty-one unopened blood DUI tubes by a dual column headspace GC after 4 to 7 years of refrigerated storage. The first analysis of the blood samples occurred within 35 days of the blood draw. The initial BACs ranged from 0.094 to 0.301 g/100 mL. All decreases in BAC were less than 0.020 g/100 mL. The mean decrease in BAC was –0.014 g/100 mL for the previously opened containers and –0.010 g/100 mL for the unopened blood tubes.

> Antemortem blood samples stored refrigerated for more than four years and up to seven years showed no further loss of ethanol beyond what is expected to occur after one to three years of refrigerated storage. Delayed analysis or reanalysis of refrigerated antemortem blood samples years after a blood draw should result in lowered measured ethanol concentration than would have otherwise been measured with a timely analysis. There is no indication that a delayed test of refrigerated antemortem blood up to seven years would result in a falsely high reported blood ethanol concentration. It may be reasonable to state that antemortem blood samples stored refrigerated after blood draw and tested between four and seven years later most likely represent an underestimation of the blood ethanol concentration at the time of the blood draw. Furthermore, if a delayed blood ethanol test indicates that the blood ethanol concentration was greater than a per se level such as 0.08 g/dL in most of the United States, it is extremely unlikely that the concentration was less than that level at the time of the blood draw.

Reference Number 20318

BOUMBA, V.A. AND T. VOUGIOUKIAKIS. "Impact of Blood Collection Tubes on Erroneous 1-Propanol Detection and on Forensic Ethanol Analysis." *Journal of Forensic Toxicology and Pharmacology*, 4: 5pp, 2015 (1 table, 2 figures, 29 references)

Abstract: Blood samples were stored in orange-cap, lavender-top, or SST II (with a separator gel) tubes and analyzed for alcohol and *n*-propanol by headspace GC using acetonitrile as an internal standard. A high apparent *n*-propanol concentration was detected in blood samples stored in the SST II tubes, which increased over 3 days of storage.

> The usage of blood collection tubes with separator gel is highly discouraged for forensic blood ethanol or other alcohol analysis. Interference artifacts such as erroneous 1-propanol can jeopardize analytical results and as a consequence conduct to misleading interpretations in forensic expert witness reports.

Reference Number 20319

KOSECKI, P.A., E. CANONICO, AND P. BROOKE. "Testing Antemortem Blood for Ethanol Concentration from a Blood Kit in a Refrigerator Fire." *Journal of Forensic Sciences*, 65: 2198–2200, 2020 (3 figures, 13 references)

Abstract: Two blood samples were collected from a DUI suspect after providing two Intoxilyzer 8000 test results of 0.103 and 0.092 g/100 mL. The blood kit was stored in a refrigerator that caught fire that lasted for 15 to 20 minutes. As received at the forensic laboratory, the outer cardboard box of the blood kit was partially burned and the plastic clam shell inner container was melted at one end. The blood tubes were intact and analyzed for alcohol by dual column headspace GC. The mean BAC was 0.093 g/100 mL, and a high blood acetaldehyde concentration was also detected.

Even under extreme conditions of the blood kit being in a refrigerator fire, the measured blood ethanol content agreed well with the paired breath ethanol test.

Reference Number 20320

RODDA, L.N., S. PEARRING, C.E. HARPER, N.B. TISCIONE, AND A.W. JONES. "Inferences and Legal Considerations Following a Blood Collection Tube Recall." *Journal of Analytical Toxicology*, 4pp, 2020 (30 references)

Abstract: On 12 June 2019, the manufacturers of evacuated gray-top blood tubes issued a notice that 300 of 247,000 tubes manufactured from that lot may not have had the sodium fluoride (100 mg) and 20 mg potassium oxalate added. Of the 300, 272 empty tubes were returned, leaving only twenty-eight tubes (0.01%) unaccounted for.

In summary, the possibility of reporting falsely high blood ethanol concentrations in gray-top tubes without coagulant and preservative is overwhelmingly low when samples are taken from living persons. Typical phlebotomy practices coupled with extensive observations, documentation, and standard operating protocols commonly used in forensic laboratories are among safeguards to ensure specimen integrity. Standard refrigeration of specimens (4°C) have been shown to mitigate any increases in ethanol concentrations, even in postmortem blood. Concentration of ethanol, and many other drugs actually decrease during storage without a fluoride preservative. While anticoagulant is required to maintain the integrity of a whole blood specimen, the optimal concentration of fluoride preservative or even its scientific necessity remains an open question when specimens are drawn from living persons. However, for convenience and the advantage of working with just one type of tube for both postmortem and antemortem specimens, the authors of this communication are not recommending laboratories change their current practices.

2.04 SWABS/BLOOD COLLECTION

"I would advise each person who performs blood tests for intoxication to repeat procedures that will permit him to vouch personally for the fact that alcohol applied to the skin does not materially affect the analysis for alcohol. I am not advocating the use of alcohol as an antiseptic, however, inasmuch as this might be responsible for needless arguments."

—Heise, "How Extraneous Alcohol Affects the Blood Test for Alcohol. Pitfalls to be Avoided When Withdrawing Blood for Medicolegal Purposes" (1959)

"With clock-like regularity and a tenacity worthy of greater goals, numerous attacks have been aimed at the suitability of body material specimens for alcohol determination. Among the most vigorously pursued objections, real or imaginary are those directed at the supposed contamination of blood specimens by improper skin disinfection."

—Dubowski, "Unsettled Issues and Practices in Chemical Testing for Alcohol" (1963)

The first reference (20401) is probably one of the most miscited of all studies on the use of alcohol swabs. It is often cited to show that alcohol swabs should not be used and to discuss the risks involved with their use before the collection of blood samples. The study, however, only warns against the storage of reusable glass syringes in absolute alcohol for sterilization. Reusable glass syringes are no longer used in hospitals, and so this cautionary note is no longer valid. Other studies have confirmed that the use of ethyl alcohol swabs will only contaminate the blood sample if a sloppy technique is used (20402–20407, 20411). Isopropyl alcohol swabs will cause no interference with GC or enzymatic analyses for alcohol (20408, 20409, 20410).

Reference Number: 20401

HEISE, H.A. "How Extraneous Alcohol Affects the Blood Test for Alcohol Pitfalls to Be Avoided When Withdrawing Blood for Medicolegal Purposes." *American Journal of Clinical Pathology*, 32: 169–170, 1959 (1 table, 1 reference)

Abstract: Of the hundreds of blood samples analyzed, only two were contaminated by ethanol and contained more than 1.0 g/100 mL. These two were the result of reusable syringes being kept in ethanol to ensure sterility. In this study blood samples were collected from alcohol-free subjects after swabbing the skin with (1) distilled water (apparent BAC = 0); (2) no antiseptic (apparent BAC = 0.002 g/100 mL); (3) blood taken when skin was still wet with ethanol with cotton swab (apparent BAC = 0.005 g/100 mL); and blood collected immediately after pouring ethyl alcohol on the skin (apparent BAC = 0.0012 g/100 mL). The BACs were determined using the non-specific potassium dichromate method.

> I would advise each person who performs blood tests for intoxication to repeat procedures that will permit him to vouch personally for the fact that alcohol applied to the skin does not materially affect the analysis for alcohol. I am not advocating the use of alcohol as an antiseptic, however, inasmuch as this might be responsible for needless arguments.

Reference Number: 20402

WINEK, C.L. AND T. EASTLY. "Factors Affecting Contamination of Blood Samples for Ethanol Determinations." *Legal Medicine Annual*, 147–162, 1976 (7 tables, 3 figures, 25 references)

Abstract: A study was conducted to evaluate the potential of altering the BAC due to blood transfusions and by the use of an alcoholic swab. The BACs of 1,450 blood donors were determined by GC. A positive BAC was found in twenty-eight donors (2%) and ranged between 0.007 and 0.148 g/100 mL (mean 0.030 g/100 mL). Eight technicians drew blood from drinking and non-drinking subjects using standard and sloppy techniques. The sloppy technique included injecting the needle through the skin that was still wet with ethanol and withdrawing the needle through an ethanol-soaked swab. In 100 samples using the standard collection technique, the greatest increase in BAC was 0.002 g/100 mL. Using the sloppy technique, the increase in BAC ranged between 0.012 and

2.225 g/100 mL. In vitro studies showed that a 1/10 drop of approximately 1 μL of 70% ethyl alcohol per milliliter of blood increased the BAC by approximately 0.068 g/100 mL.

In the past, legal decisions concerning contamination have not been in agreement with scientific findings. Almost all studies using the standard hypodermic syringe indicate that contamination is minimal (less than 10 mg/100 mL or 0.01 percent) but, to the lay juror, if a little contamination may occur, then a lot more may be possible. It has been solely from this legal viewpoint that cases have been dismissed.

Reference Number: 20403

MCIVOR, R.A. AND S.H. COSBEY. "Effect of Using Alcoholic and Non-Alcoholic Skin Cleansing Swabs When Sampling Blood for Alcohol Estimation Using Gas Chromatography." *British Journal of Clinical Practice*, 44: 235–236, 1990 (3 references)

Abstract: Four blood samples were collected from twenty alcohol-free subjects after using an alcohol-free, 70% isopropyl alcohol, 95% ethyl alcohol, and 95% ethyl alcohol (and soaked swab) swabs respectively prior to the collection of the sample. The venipuncture was conducted when the skin was still wet and the beveled tip of the needle was orientated upwards. In one case the needle was withdrawn through an ethyl alcohol soaked swab. The BACs were determined by a headspace GC using *n*-propanol as an internal standard. A positive BAC was found in only one sample, and it was only 0.0004 g/100 mL. A positive isopropyl alcohol was also detected, and it was 0.003 g/100 mL.

These results show that contamination is highly unlikely if alcohol-based swabs are used to cleanse the skin. Even if applied immediately before venipuncture, contamination is unlikely and if it does occur produces blood alcohol levels below 1 mg%.

Reference Number: 20404

OGDEN, EJ.D., J. GERSTNER-STEVENS, J. BURKE, AND S.J. YOUNG. "Venous Blood Alcohol Sampling and the Alcohol Swab." *Police Surgeon*, 42: 4–5, 1992 (1 table, 4 references)

Abstract: Twenty subjects with a zero BAC had venous blood samples collected after swabbing the arm with 99.9% ethanol. The skin area was deliberately left wet with alcohol dripping from the elbow when the sample was collected. The blood was analyzed by GC and no BACs > 0.001 g/100 mL were detected. To increase a 10 mL blood sample to a BAC of 0.010 g/100 mL requires 0.00126 mL of ethanol to be drawn into the syringe.

> As the internal diameter of a standard needle (21 gauge) used for phlebotomy is 0.8 mm and it would require the intake of a column of alcohol 2.5 mm long into the needle to achieve this volume. This study has demonstrated that even with liberal use of alcohol for skin preparation not even this alcohol volume is entrained into the syringe.

Reference Number: 20405

JONES, A.W. AND K.A. JONSSON. "Alcohol as a Disinfectant Resulted in Zero Per Thousand (Promille) in Blood [Swedish]." *Larkartidningen*, 95: 4052, 1998 (5 references)

Abstract: Three female and seven male alcohol-free subjects had blood samples taken from the cubital vein using a twenty-one-gauge needle. The blood was collected in vacutubes containing fluoride as a preservative. A 70% ethyl alcohol disinfectant was used. In five of the subjects the crook of the arm was swabbed before the collection of the blood sample. In the other five subjects the needle was drawn through a cotton swab soaked in the ethyl alcohol disinfectant. No positive BACs were detected by GC. The authors conclude that the risk of contamination of blood collected after the use of even a 70% ethyl alcohol disinfectant is very small.

Reference Number: 20406

MALINGRE, M., T. VERVERS, S. BOS, C. VAN KESTEREN, AND H. VAN RIJA. "Alcohol Swabs and Venipuncture in a Routine Hospital Setting: No Effect on Blood Ethanol Measurement [Letter]." *Therapeutic Drug Monitoring*, 27: 403–404, 2005 (6 references)

Abstract: BACs were measured in a hospital in the Netherlands of fifty patients (< 12 years of age) after using a swab dipped in absolute ethanol before venipuncture. No positive BACs were detected by headspace GC. BACs were also determined in twenty adult patients who had not consumed alcohol for at least 24 hours. Again, no positive BACs were detected.

In conclusion, we investigated the effect of alcohol swabs on blood ethanol concentration in a routine hospital setting. Our data shows that there is no effect, and thus alcohol swabs are not an obstruction in case of blood ethanol analysis in a clinical setting.

Reference Number: 20407

RYDER, K.W. AND M.R. GLICK. "The Effect of Skin Cleansing Agents on Ethanol Results Measured With the Du Pont Automatic Clinical Analyzer." *Journal of Forensic Sciences*, 31: 574–579, 1986 (1 table, 2 figures, 7 references)

Abstract: Neither benzalkonium chloride nor polyvinylpyrrolidone solutions affect the ACA result (enzymatic method). Skin cleansers containing either ethanol or isopropanol will not affect the accuracy of the ACA result if proper phlebotomy technique is used (i.e., letting the skin dry before venipuncture). The cross reactivity of isopropanol indicating ethanol result on ACA is 3.9%. Ethanol was only detected if an ethanol-soaked swab was pressed over the venipuncture site while the needle was withdrawn from the skin. In nine subjects this technique was used, and the detected ethanol concentration ranged from 0.010–0.638 g/100 mL.

We have shown, however, that inadvertently cleansing the skin with an ethanol- or isopropanol-containing agent (not in accord with manufacturer's recommendations) does not necessarily invalidate the ethanol result measured with the ACA. Such results must be interpreted both in light of the skin cleansing agent and the phlebotomy technique used.

Reference Number: 20408

TAYLOR, G.F., G.H. TURRILL, AND N.G. CARTER. "Blood Alcohol Analysis: A Comparison of the Gas-Chromatographic Assay with an Enzymatic Assay." *Pathology*, 16: 157–159, 1984 (1 figure, 6 references)

Abstract: The serum alcohol concentrations of 192 patients as analyzed by direct injection GC were compared to an enzymatic procedure. The correlation coefficient was 0.983. The mean SAC as determined by GC was 0.150 g/100 mL and the mean SAC as determined by the enzymatic method was 0.151 g/100 mL. The day-to-day CV was 7.6%. In another test, thirty blood samples were collected from subjects who had blood taken from one arm that was swabbed with either 70% ethanol or 70%

isopropanol, and from the other arm which was untreated. The mean SAC for the unswabbed arm as analyzed by the enzymatic method was 0.116 g/100 mL and for the swabbed arm, 0.117 g/100 mL.

> These findings are inside the previously reported within run variation and indicate that swabbing with either ethanol or isopropanol has no effect on the enzymatic determination of ethanol.

Reference Number: 20409

LEVESKY, M.E. AND M.A. MILLER. "Isopropyl Alcohol Skin Prep Pads: The Extreme Case [Letter]." *Journal of Emergency Medicine*, 33: 280, 2007 (1 table, 1 reference)

Abstract: Two 8 mL blood samples were collected and to one tube was added 1.5 mL of 70% isopropyl alcohol. This amount of isopropanol caused the blood to hemolyze and resulted in abnormal electrolyte findings, but the BAC as determined by an enzymatic method showed only traces of ethanol.

> If our hospital's method of assaying ethanol levels is typical in terms of its specificity for ethanol, we find it very unlikely that any amount of isopropanol contamination in a BAL sample would produce a significant false positive BAL.

Reference Number: 20410

TUCKER, A. AND C. TRETHEWY. "Lack of Effect on Blood Alcohol Level of Swabbing Venipuncture Sites With 70% Isopropyl Alcohol." *Emergency Medicine Australasia*, 22: 9–12, 2010 (2 tables, 15 references)

Abstract: Paired venous blood samples were collected from fifty-six uncontrolled (drinking status unknown) subjects. One arm was swabbed with 70% isopropyl alcohol and allowed to dry. The other arm was swabbed with saline. BACs were determined by an enzymatic method (Synchron LX system). There were no statistically significant differences in BAC measured from either arm. The mean BAC was 0.003 g/100 mL for the isopropyl alcohol swabbed arm and 0.003 g/100 mL for the saline swabbed arm.

> Current practice mandates a non-alcohol-containing swab before the collection of forensic blood alcohol tests. The present study demonstrated

that, using the enzymatic method for BAL analysis, the use of 70% isopropyl alcohol swabs did not significantly affect BAL when used before venipuncture.

Reference Number: 20411

LIPPI, G., A-M. SIMUNDIC, G. MUSILE, E. DANESE, G. SALVAGNO, AND F. TAGLIARO. "The Alcohol Used for Cleansing the Venipuncture Site Does Not Jeopardize Blood and Plasma Alcohol Measurements with Head-Space Gas Chromatography and an Enzymatic Assay." *Biochemia Medica*, 27: 398–403, 2017 (1 table, 30 references)

Eighteen female and five male alcohol-free subjects (mean age forty-nine years) had a blood sample collected from both arms using 2 mL of a 70% v/v ethyl alcohol swab. From one arm the blood was collected without drying the swabbed area of the arm, and the other arm was dried first before collecting the blood using a 19-gauge straight needle. Blood and plasma alcohol concentrations were determined by headspace GC and an enzymatic method, respectively. All the blood and plasma alcohol concentrations were below the limit of detection for both methods.

It seems reasonable to conclude that using ethanol-containing antiseptics before venipuncture may not be causes of spurious or false positive results of alcohol measurement at least when ideal venipunctures can be performed.

2.05 ENDOGENOUS BACS

"It seems not unreasonable to conclude that ethanol is present normally in man to the extent of not more than 1.5 mg per litre."

—Lester, "The Concentration of Apparent Endogenous Ethanol" (1962)

"If the liver did not eliminate alcohol, the continuous low production of alcohol would cause intoxicating alcohol concentration in the body within a short time. Nature protects against the danger of endogenous alcohol intoxication."

—Bode, "The Metabolism of Alcohol: Physiological and Pathophysiological Aspects" (1978)

Traces of alcohol that occur in the blood of living subjects are probably due in part to the microorganisms producing small amounts of alcohol in the gut. Typical endogenous BACs are less than 0.001 g/100 mL (20502–20505). The Widmark (i.e., potassium dichromate) analysis produces higher endogenous BACs than headspace GC (20507)

Autobrewing or endogenous production of high BACs has little forensic merit in adults (20504–20506), but young children with low body weight, small bowel malformations, and liver disorders may have significant endogenous BACs (20508).

Reference Number: 20501

WALKER, G.W. AND A.S. CURRY. "Endogenous' Alcohol in Body Fluids." *Nature*, 210: 1368, June 25, 1966 (3 references)

Abstract: A letter to *Nature* was published describing a GC method to measure low BACs.

> Preliminary results of a survey of the occurrence of ethanol in the blood and urine of normal persons who have not taken alcohol indicate that the amounts present are less than 0.1 mg per cent.

Reference Number: 20502

MEZEY, E., A.L. IMBEBO, J.J. POTTER, K.C. RENT, R. LOMBARDO, AND P.R. HOLT. "Endogenous Ethanol Production and Hepatic Disease Following Jejunoileal Bypass for Morbid Obesity." *American Journal of Clinical Nutrition*, 28: 1277–1283, 1975 (2 table, 29 references)

Abstract: One or more blood samples were collected from eight normal subjects, nine obese patients prior to surgery, and twenty obese patients 2 weeks to 40 months after jejunoileal bypass surgery. The blood was preserved with NaF and separated into serum and was stored frozen until analysis by GC. Both serum alcohol and acetone concentrations were determined. The LOD was 0.0001 g/100 mL. In addition, some dog studies were conducted. The SAC was negative in the eight normal individuals and nine obese patients prior to surgery. A SAC > 0.0001 g/100 mL was found in seven of twenty fasting patients after surgery and ranged between 0.00015 to 0.0041 g/100 mL (mean 0.0012 g/100 mL). The serum acetone concentration ranged between 0.18 and 0.43 mg/100 mL for the eight normal fasting subjects. In four patients with rapid weight loss the fasting serum acetone concentration varied between 0.003 and 0.015 g/100 mL.

> The presence of only mild elevations of ethanol in the serum of dogs and in only one-third of the patients together with the lack of persistence of the elevation after repeated blood samples, suggests that ethanol produced by bacteria in the intestine is an unlikely cause of the hepatic lesions complicating jejunoileal bypass in morbid obesity.

Reference Number: 20503

SPRUNG, R., W. BONTE, E. RUDELL, M. DOMKE, AND C. FRAUENRATH. "On the Problem of Endogenous Alcohols [German]." *Blutalkohol,* 18: 65–70, 1981 (2 tables, 35 references)

Abstract: A review was conducted of studies on endogenous blood ethanol concentrations in both animals and humans. The problem with earlier studies is that the method of determining BAC was usually nonspecific. In this study, the endogenous BAC was determined in 130 normal sober subjects, ten normal subjects on 4 successive days, and in thirty hospitalized patients with metabolic diseases including diabetes, liver cirrhosis, and hepatitis. The endogenous ethanol, acetaldehyde, and acetone blood concentrations were determined by a dual column headspace GC. In the normal subjects, the BACs were all below 0.000075 g/100 mL. In the patients, the endogenous BACs were between 0.00006 and 0.00052 g/100 mL. There was no statistical difference in the BACs between the healthy subjects or the patients.

Reference Number: 20504

LOGAN, B.K. AND A.W. JONES. "Endogenous Ethanol Auto-Brewery Syndrome as a Drunk-Driving Defence Challenge." *Medicine. Science and the Law*, 40: 206–215, 2000 (2 tables, 3 figures, 67 references)

Abstract: A general review of endogenous blood alcohol concentrations and the auto-brewery syndrome was conducted.

> Scores of defence strategies, some more far-fetched than others, have arisen during the prosecution of drunk drivers, and many of these were discussed in a recent review article. The idea of a person generating enormous amounts of ethanol in the gut such that the peripheral venous blood

ethanol concentration could reach 50 mg/dL or 80 mg/dL is one of the least convincing arguments, especially in non-Asian subjects.

Reference Number: 20505

AL-AWADHI, A., I.A. WASFI, AND Z. ALL-HATALI. "Autobrewing Revisited: Endogenous Concentrations of Blood Ethanol in Residents of the United Arab Emirates." *Science and Justice,* 44: 149–152, 2004 (2 tables, 1 figure, 15 references)

Abstract: The endogenous BACs of 1,563 residents of the United Arab Emirates who attended the Abu Dhabi Police clinic were determined by headspace GC-MS. The mean endogenous BAC was 0.000113 g/100 mL and the maximum BAC detected was 0.0035 g/100 mL. Ninety-eight percent of the endogenous BACs detected were less than 0.001 g/100 mL.

The values of blood ethanol reported in this study and those reported by others, indicate that they are far too low to have any forensic significance.

Reference Number: 20506

GATT, J.A. AND P. MATTHEWMAN. "Autobrewing: Fact or Fantasy?" *Science and Justice*, 40: 211–215, 2000 (16 references)

Abstract: In four cases in the UK the autobrewery syndrome was proposed as a defense to drinking and driving. In one case the defendant was tested and had a fasting BAC of zero. One hour after drinking 100 mL of 4% glucose solution and eating 1 g of glucose the BAC was apparently 0.019 g/100 mL. The defense expert stated the subject was predisposed to autobrewery because the defendant was prescribed cyclosporine. However, 5 g of glucose could only result theoretically in a BAC of 0.005 g/100 mL in a 70 kg male. It was strongly suspected that the defendant had altered the blood samples. The defense did not proceed in this area in court. In another case the subject was a carrier of *Candida albicans*. The defense expert did a poorly conducted test that showed a BAC of 0.010 g/100 mL. The defense expert had never heard of the Widmark factor and calculated a BAC based on plasma volume only and not total body water. The other two cases did not go to trial. It was calculated that a 45 kg woman would have to have 100% fermentation of 25 g of glucose per hour to match the elimination rate of alcohol. This would generate 11.25 L of carbon dioxide per hour.

The present authors' experience with these cases has not revealed any additional evidence that the phenomenon of autobrewery can exist in healthy individuals and agrees with the conclusion of Forrest and Walls and Brownlie.

Reference Number: 20507

SIMIC, M., N. AJDUKOVIC, I. VESELINOVIC, M. MITROVIC, AND N. DJURENDIC-BRENESEL. "Endogenous Ethanol Production in Patients with Diabetes Mellitus as a Medicolegal Problem." *Forensic Science International*, 216: 97–100, 2012 (1 figure, 27 references)

Abstract: Blood samples were collected from 100 patients (of both genders) diagnosed with diabetes mellitus in the early morning after an overnight fast and analyzed for alcohol by the specific headspace gas chromatography (HS-GC) method. In another thirty diabetic patients, blood and urine samples were analyzed for alcohol by the less specific Widmark method (wet chemical potassium dichromate oxidation) and by HS-GC. Blood samples were also collected from thirty healthy subjects (controls) and analyzed for alcohol by both the Widmark and HS-GC methods. Urine alcohol concentrations were also determined by both methods in thirty diabetic patients and fifteen controls. The mean endogenous BACs were approximately ten to twenty times greater for analysis by the nonspecific Widmark method compared to the specific HS-GC and may account for some high endogenous BACs reported in earlier studies. All endogenous BACs as determined by HS-GC were less than 0.001 g/100 mL. The highest endogenous UAC as detected by HS-GC was 0.003 g/100 mL. The blood glucose concentration (range 72 to 810 mg/100 mL) had no correlation with the endogenous BAC (i.e., auto-production of alcohol did not depend on the blood glucose concentration).

Table. Mean Endogenous BACs as Determined by the Widmark and HS-GC Methods

	Mean BAC (g/100 mL) as Determined by the Widmark Method	Mean BAC (g/100 mL) as Determined by the HS-GC Method
Control Subjects	0.0007	0.00004
Diabetic Patients	0.0027	0.00027

Source: Adapted from Simic et al (2012).

From the forensic point of view, such low values of ethanol cannot affect brain function and the ability of drivers of motor vehicles to safely participate in traffic.

Reference Number: 20508

JANNSSON-NETTELBLADT, E., S. MEURLING, B. PETRINI, AND J. SJOLIN. "Endogenous Ethanol Fermentation in a Child with a Short Bowel Syndrome." *Acta Paediartica*, 95: 502–504, 2006 (15 references)

Abstract: A three-year-old girl was operated on several times as a result of a malformation of the small bowel and as a result had more than half of her colon and a large portion of her jejunum removed, leaving only about 17 cm of small intestine. This is referred to as the Short Bowel Syndrome (SBS). She consumed a carbohydrate-rich fruit juice containing *Lactobacillus* two to four times a day. The parents detected the odor of an alcoholic beverage on her breath and she behaved intoxicated. A breath alcohol result was 15 mmol/L (70 mg/100 mL). Her gastric contents contained *S. cerevisiae*. She responded well to anti-fungal agents and a new diet with lower carbohydrate content.

Thus patients with SBS may be at risk of developing auto-brewery syndrome, a syndrome that should be added to the differential diagnosis list of D-lactic acidosis.

CHAPTER 3

Breath Alcohol

> "The exhalation of volatile substances from the lungs is exactly analogous to their evaporation from solutions in water, and the pulmonary cells seems to be purely passive in this process."
>
> — Cushny, "On the Exhalation of Drugs by the Lungs" (1910)

> "The levels of alcohol in breath and brain are controlled by the level in arterial blood. Therefore, during active absorption, breath should be more reliable than peripheral venous blood for predicting the level of alcohol in the brain."
>
> — Harger and Hulpieu, "The Pharmacology of Alcohol" (1956)

Breath alcohol analysis is commonly used in law enforcement as it has many advantages over blood alcohol testing as follows:

- Breath alcohol testing is noninvasive. No needles are required to collect blood, and hence there is no possibility of injury or transmission of disease.
- The breath alcohol results are known immediately, compared to the several days or even weeks for the blood results to be reported by the forensic laboratories. The police, therefore, are immediately aware of what charge to lay and whether medical treatment may be required for the drinking driver (e.g., alcohol poisoning).
- Two separate breath samples are analyzed independent of each other, rather than just one blood sample.

- Breath alcohol correlates better with brain alcohol concentration (arterial blood) and will give a better indication of impairment due to alcohol during the rising BAC phase.
- There are no continuity and/or storage and transportation issues. The breath sample is provided directly into the breath alcohol instrument. No special blood tubes, swabs, identity seals, biohazard refrigeration, or special transportation is required as for blood samples.
- No medical staff or phlebotomists are required for breath alcohol analysis. The breath tests may be conducted at the police station or mobile van, allowing the time between the arrest and testing to be reduced significantly.
- There is no problem with real or alleged blood or needle "phobia" of the arrested driver who is being breath tested.

This chapter deals with the many issues that arise in criminal court, such as the mouth alcohol effect, the blood/breath alcohol ratio, the ability to provide a suitable breath sample, and the specificity of breath alcohol tests.

3.01 METHODS OF ANALYSIS, DUPLICATION, AND TRUNCATION OF RESULTS

> "It seems to me that the mean concentration of alcohol in two separate breath tests is a better estimate of alcohol load in the body than the mean of duplicate determination on a single Vacutainer blood."
>
> — Jones et al, "Magnitude of Sampling and Analytical Variations in Blood and Breath" (1990)

> "Breath alcohol testing in law enforcement has made remarkable progress in the half century since its introduction. With few exceptions, the quantitative evidential test devices in current use are more than sufficiently accurate, precise, and specific for their intended use, even by evidentiary standards applicable to criminal and quasi-criminal litigation."
>
> —Dubowski, "The Technology of Breath-Alcohol Analysis" (1992)

Breath alcohol detection technology has changed dramatically over the more than 50 years since the Breathalyzer (using a wet chemical method) was first introduced (30101, 30102). The chemical reaction that was the basis of the Breathalyzer was based on potassium dichromate (yellow-orange color) and sulfuric acid, which reacts with alcohol to form chromic sulfate (blue-green color), potassium sulfate, acetic acid, and water as follows:

$$2K_2Cr_2O_7 + 8H_2SO_4 + 3CH_3CH_2OH \rightarrow$$
$$2Cr_2(SO_4)_3 + 2K_2SO_4 + 3CH_3COOH + 11\,H_2O$$

Electrochemical (fuel cell) sensors (30103–30106) also convert alcohol into acetic acid but measure the electric current generated rather than a color change as with the Breathalyzer. Other methods of breath alcohol detection include infrared (30107–30111) and a combination of the IR and fuel cell (30112). The *n*-type semiconductor (Taguchi) detector has been found not to be suitable for evidential or even screening applications (30113). Future methods of detection of alcohol may include portable MS (30114) or full IR spectrum scan (30115). The differences between two successive breath tests and the truncation of breath test results are included in this section (30116–30125).

In order of their reliability and validity of breath testing results, the devices are:

1. quantitative evidential breath alcohol instruments
2. screening or roadside breath testing devices based on fuel cell
3. passive breath alcohol detectors
4. automobile ignition interlock devices
5. IR light sent through the compartment of a moving car

Handheld fuel-cell-based (electrochemical) detectors have been found to be very accurate and reliable in field use (30126–30128). The most common error message of these devices is an insufficient breath volume (30128).

An Ambient Fail message by the Intoxilyzer 5000C has been found to occur more frequently in drivers with a high BAC, and hence more alcohol vapor is breathed into the room air (30129).

The increasing use of alcohol-based hand sanitizer (ABHS) due to COVID-19 can cause a high transient BrAC, especially if the hands are still wet with the hand sanitizer and are used to hold the instrument or mouthpiece, but a second breath test will be a good safeguard against this effect (30130–30132).

In one reported case, the driver was carrying refined spirits in their car and obtained a result of 0.059 g/100 mL while sitting in their car. When another test was conducted outside their car (away from the alcohol fumes in their car) 12 minutes later it was 0.018 g/100 mL (30133).

The Canadian Federal Advisory Board to the minister of justice regarding breath alcohol testing recommends that the required quality control information that must be reviewed to assess the proper working order of the approved instrument in Canada are the blank test results, the calibration check results, the instrument error messages that occurred during the breath testing sequence, and the duplicate subject breath test results and not maintenance records spanning many years (30135).

Reference Number: 30101

BORKENSTEIN, R.F. AND H.W. SMITH. "The Breathalyzer and Its Applications." *Medicine Science and the Law*, 2: 13–23, 1961 (2 figures, 9 references)

Abstract: The Breathalyzer, the most successful and widely used instrument for the medicolegal determination of alcohol in the breath, was designed and developed by RF. Borkenstein in 1954. It was based on the photometric measurement of the decrease in yellow color of potassium dichromate solution in reaction with alcohol.

The oxidation of alcohol using acid dichromate forms the basis of most of the available methods for the determination of alcohol. A degree of specificity for certain reactants is obtained through the choice of conditions. Using $K_2Cr_2O_7$ in 50% by volume H_2SO_4 at 50°C or at room temperature with a suitable catalyst, alcohol is quantitatively oxidized to acetic acid within 90 seconds. Variations in acid concentration (plus or minus 5%) or time (between 75 and 150 seconds) do not appreciably alter the results. The instrument automatically compensates for variations in the $K_2Cr_2O_7$ content of the solution.

Reference Number: 30102

LANDAUER, A.A. "The Accuracy Reliability and Validity of the Breathalyzer." *Australian New Zealand Journal of Criminology*. 5: 250–254, 1972 (3 tables, 7 references)

Abstract: In this study, thirty-three male subjects consumed 1 mL/kg in 25% v/v ethanol mixed with lime juice. Drinking was completed within 15 minutes. To prevent nausea subjects were allowed to eat a few dry biscuits. Thirty minutes after the subjects finished drinking, a breath sample was taken, and 20 minutes later a blood sample was taken. The BAC range was 0.041–0.109 g/100 mL. The correlation (*r*) between blood and breath was 0.925. A second breath sample was taken in twenty subjects as close as possible to the blood sample. The greatest time difference was 7 minutes. The correlation with blood was 0.943. The largest false high difference was a Breathalyzer result of 0.047 g/100 mL and a BAC of 0.041 g/100 mL, or 0.006 g/100 mL higher.

> The results of this experiment indicate that the Breathalyzer can be a reliable instrument in assessing a person's BAL. It is true that the apparatus was operated under ideal physical conditions by a highly skilled police officer and that the breath samples were collected from co-operative subjects who had drank relatively low quantities of alcohol.

Reference Number: 30103

BAY, H.W., K.F. BLURTON, H.C. LIEB, AND H.G. OSWIN. "Electrochemical Measurements of Blood Alcohol Levels." *Nature*, 240: 52–53, 1972 (1 figure, 8 references)

Abstract: In this device the detector cell contains an anode, a counter electrode, and a reference electrode containing concentrated sulfuric acid as an electrolyte. Ethanol is oxidized to acetic acid via acetaldehyde as an intermediate involving the transfer of four electrons. The device requires 1.2 L of breath to be exhaled to obtain a deep lung sample. The standard deviation (SD) is 0.0035 g/100 mL for a range of alcohol standards from 0.050–0.200 g/100 mL. The stability is 3% per month. Monthly calibration is adequate.

> Our studies with this instrument indicate that the electrochemical oxidation of alcohol is a more accurate technique for the measurement of alcohol in breath samples than the instruments based on colorimetric methods of detection. The electrochemical detector cell may be built into a rugged portable unit which may be used by a police officer at the scene of a traffic offence either as a screening instrument or as an evidential device.

Reference Number: 30104

HODGSON, B.T. AND M.D. TAYLOR. "Evaluation of the Breathalyzer 7410-CDN Evidential Breath Alcohol Analyzer." *Canadian Society of Forensic Science Journal*, 31: 263–267, 1998 (3 tables, 1 figure, 4 references)

Abstract: An evaluation of the Breathalyzer 7410 CDN evidential breath alcohol analyzer was conducted according to ATC standards. The

Breathalyzer 7410 (a fuel cell device) was compared to the Intoxilyzer 5000C (an IR device) in drinking subjects. BACs were also determined by headspace GC in some subjects. The time difference between the blood and breath sampling was 3 to 7 minutes. In vitro simulator tests of the Breathalyzer 7410 were conducted at target values between 0.050 and 0.350 g/100 mL. At 0.350 g/100 mL, the mean result was 0.348 g/100 mL (SD 0.006 g/100 mL, coefficient of variation [CV] 1.6%). In six drinking subjects the Breathalyzer 7410 results were between 0.010 and 0.030 g/100 mL lower than the BAC.

Table. Comparison of BACs and BrACs as Determined by the Breathalyzer 7410 in Six Drinking Subjects

Subject #	BAC (g/100 mL)	BrAC (g/100 mL)
1	0.145	0.130
2	0.071	0.061
8	0.130	0.109
9	0.120	0.100
10	0.115	0.085
11	0.096	0.078

Source: Adapted from Hodgson and Taylor (1998).

The Breathalyzer 7410-CDN underestimates the corresponding blood alcohol concentration by 10 to 30 milligrams in 100 millilitres of blood, values similar to those found with other evidential breath alcohol analyzers.

Reference Number: 30105

INNS, P., P.J. MORRISON, AND K. PAJOUMOND. "Evaluation of Fuel Cell Alcometer for Forensic and Pharmacokinetic Purposes." *British Journal of Clinical Pharmacology*, 7: 439P–440P, 1979 (1 reference)

Abstract: One hundred and eighty-eight paired blood-breath alcohol concentrations were determined over a BAC range of 0.001–0.100 g/100 mL. BACs were determined by GC and BrACs by the Lion Alcometer (a fuel cell device). The correlation was 0.986. The CV% for ten replicate samples in breath was 2.7% and in blood was 2.4%.

The alcometer provides a rapid and reproducible index of the blood ethanol concentration which, when breath samples are used is non-invasive. It is therefore suitable for both forensic and pharmacokinetic work.

Reference Number: 30106

VOAS, R.B., E. ROMANO, AND R. PECK. "Validity of the Passive Alcohol Sensor for Estimating BACs in DWI-Enforcement Operations." *Journal of Studies on Alcohol,* 67: 714–721, 2006 (3 tables, 1 figure, 24 references)

Abstract: A comparison was made between the BrACs determined by a Passive Alcohol Sensor (PAS III) and an Alco-Sensor IV in 12,587 crash-involved and control drivers in California and Florida. The overall PAC-Alco-Sensor IV Spearman correlation was 0.79. The correlation was higher for crash-involved than for control drivers.

Conversely the significance of this interaction in the crash model suggests that, in those cases, PAS readings underestimate the BAC level for drivers age 65 or older in crashes. Although reasons for this underestimation are not known it is reasonable to speculate that crash victims age 65 or older expel a reduced volume of air, perhaps coupled with a larger susceptibility to the physical consequences of the crash.

Reference Number: 30107

COWAN, J.M. "Does the Intoxilyzer 4011AS-A Conform to the Beer-Lambert Law?" *Journal of the Forensic Science Society,* 28: 179–184, 1988 (1 table, 1 figure, 4 references)

Abstract: A study was conducted of two Intoxilyzers model 4011AS-A (3.39 microns and 3.48 microns IR wavelength) using an alcohol simulator at concentrations of 0.100, 0.200, 0.300, and 0.400 g/100 mL. Both instruments showed excellent conformity with Beer-Lambert law. The absorbance versus alcohol concentration graph indicates an $r = 0.9998$ for one instrument and $r = 0.9999$ for the other. The slope of the two lines was different and was determined by the absorptivity and the path length of the particular Intoxilyzer tested. Absorptivity is affected by the source lamp intensity, the cleanliness of the filters and sample chamber, and the wavelength of light.

The two Intoxilyzer 4011AS-A instruments tested showed excellent compliance with the Beer-Lambert law.

Reference Number: 30108

GOLDBERGER, B.A. AND Y.H. CAPLAN. "Infrared Quantitative Evidential Breath Alcohol Analysers: in Vitro Accuracy and Precision Studies." *Journal of Forensic Sciences*, 31: 16–19, 1986 (4 tables, 5 references)

Abstract: In this study four different types of IR breath alcohol analyzers were tested using simulators. The instruments tested were Alcotest 7010, BAC Verifier, Intoxilyzer 5000, and Intoximeter 3000. A stock solution of 60.50 g/L ethanol was diluted to give simulator test values of 0.050, 0.100, 0.150, 0.250, and 0.400 g/100 mL. Twenty simulator tests were conducted at each concentration. All instruments had a CV of less than 2% and SD of 0.001–0.002 g/100 mL.

Statistical analyses indicate that the Alcotest 7010, BAC Verifier, Intoxilyzer 5000 and the Intoximeter 3000 met or exceeded the performance requirements adapted from the U.S. Department of Transportation Standard for quantitative breath-alcohol analyzers. Additionally, the infrared absorption technique utilized by these breath-alcohol analyzers yielded results similar to those reported in a previous validation study of Breathalyzer Models 900 and 900A.

Reference Number: 30109

RAZATOS, G., R. LUTHI, AND S. KERRIGAN. "Evaluation of a Portable Evidential Breath Alcohol Analyzer." *Forensic Science International*, 153: 17–21, 2005 (7 tables, 4 figures, 3 references)

Abstract: An evaluation was conducted of the Intoxilyzer model 8000 (portable) and compared to the Intoxilyzer 5000 in New Mexico. The differences between the IR 8000 and IR 5000 are a smaller sample chamber 29 mL versus 81 mL), faster processor (29 MHz versus 4 MHz), increased storage capacity, no moving parts (except for a fan), pulse IR source rather than a chopper wheel, and the use of 9.0 um and 3.0 um IR detection. The IR 8000 did not respond to in vitro solutions of acetone, isopropanol, methylene chloride, toluene, or benzene. The IR 8000 mean results were within 1% of the in vitro target values between 0.040 and 0.550 g/100 mL. Linear regression of 714 comparisons between the IR 8000 and IR 5000 showed an r^2 of 1.000. Using a wet bath simulator there was no effect of testing at 3,467 or 3,534 meters in altitude. The large majority of police officers (91%) who participated in the evaluation ranked the IR 8000 higher than the IR 5000, and 9% ranked it equally.

The Intoxilyzer 8000 (IR 8000) was approved as for evidential use based upon analytical performance, technical specifications, data management and data communication compatibility, and ease of transition of both law enforcement and scientific staff in terms of training, repairs and certification of instruments and officers.

Reference Number: 30110

FRANSSON, M., A.W. JONES, AND L. ANDERSSON. "Laboratory Evaluation of a New Evidential Breath-Alcohol Analyser Designed for Mobile Testing—The Evidenzer." *Medicine, Science and the Law*, 45: 61–70, 2005 (4 tables, 4 figures, 24 references)

Abstract: Ten female and ten male subjects (mean ages thirty-six and forty-four years respectively) consumed 0.4 g/kg alcohol within 15 minutes. BrACs were determined with the new mobile evidential IR instrument the Evidenzer (3.37-, 3.41-, 3.47-,3.52-, and 3.80-microns wavelength IR) and Intoxilyzer 5000S (3.39-, 3.48-, and 3.80-microns wavelength IR). Blood samples were collected every 15 to 30 minutes and BACs were determined by GC. It is important for roadside testing that the instrument used has a high specificity as organic solvents such as gasoline and windshield and brake fluids may be present. The CV% was 4.7 for the Evidenzer and 4.8 for the Intoxilyzer 5000S and 0.65 for blood. The mean blood-breath ratios (BBR) for the Intoxilyzer 5000S were 1,805, 2,319, 2,492, 2,654, and 3,443:1 at 15, 45, 75, 105, 165, and 225 minutes respectively. The mouth alcohol effect disappeared within 9 to 11 minutes in the drinking subjects. The authors conclude that the problem of mouth alcohol is greatly exaggerated.

The Evidenzer was easy to operate and gave accurate and precise results compared with the more well-established EBT (Intoxilyzer 5000S). Mouth alcohol had dissipated by 11 minutes after the end of drinking, which supports the current deprivation and observation period of 15 minutes. In tests made 45 minutes or more after the end of drinking, the breath alcohol instruments gave readings less than the venous blood alcohol concentration.

Reference Number: 30111

LINDBERG, L., S. BRAUER, P. WOLLMER, L. GOLDBERG, A.W. JONES, AND S.G. OLSSON. "Breath Alcohol Concentration Determined with a New Analyzer Using Free Exhalation Predicts Almost Precisely the Arterial Blood Alcohol Concentration." *Forensic Science International*, 168: 200–207, 2007 (2 tables, 7 figures, 31 references)

Abstract: Fifteen male and female subjects (ages twenty-six to sixty-seven years) consumed 0.6 g/kg alcohol within 15 minutes after a 2-hour fast. Breath, arterial, and venous blood samples were collected every 10 to 15 minutes for 5 to 7 hours. BACs were determined by headspace GC. BrACs were measured with a prototype IR device that uses 3.32, 3.40, and 3.48 microns and a reference wavelength and two additional wavelengths for detected water and carbon dioxide. The IR filters are on a rotating disk. BrACs are measured in a cuvette with a low flow resistance. The subject exhales freely into the cuvette from 2–12 cm. The measurement of the BrAC is triggered automatically by the increasing CO_2 concentration. The instrument uses the ratios between water and alcohol to determine the BrAC. Venous blood alcohol concentration (VBAC) underestimates arterial blood alcohol concentration (ABAC) and BrAC during absorption and overestimates it during post-absorption of alcohol. No gender or hemoglobin-related differences in BBRs were found.

> In conclusion, we have presented a new technique, which allows rapid evidential breath alcohol analysis by free exhalation.

Reference Number: 30112

HODGSON, B.T. AND M.D. TAYLOR. "Evaluation of the Drager Alcotest 7110 MKIII Dual C Evidential Breath Alcohol Analyser." *Canadian Society of Forensic Science Journal*, 34: 95–101, 2001 (3 tables, 1 figure, 5 references)

Abstract: An in vivo and in vitro evaluation of the Alcotest 7110 MKIII Dual C evidential breath alcohol analyzer was conducted according to the ATC standards. This instrument uses both an IR detector at 9.5 microns and a fuel cell detector. For police use in Canada the result used is the IR value and the fuel cell value is used for interferent detection. Eight male and three female subjects were tested on the MKIII, the Intoxilyzer 5000C, and a BAC DataMaster C. The BrACs ranged from 0.053–0.129 g/100 mL. The mean differences in the MKIII results compared with the BAC

DataMaster ranged from −0.0029 to +0.0013 g/100 mL and with the Intoxilyzer 5000C ranged from −0.0069 g/100 mL to −0.0015 g/100 mL. The MKIII Dual C gave either a zero result or interferent result from simulator solutions of acetaldehyde, methanol, isopropanol, toluene, and diethyl ether.

> The MKIII Dual C maintained its initial calibration throughout the evaluation, a period of approximately 5 months. No mechanical or electrical problems were encountered, and the instrument performed without breakdown.

Reference Number: 30113

BREAKSPERE, R.J. AND P.M.WILLIAMS. "Breath Alcohol Instrumentation: A Proposal in Commercial Taxonomy." *Proceedings 13th International Conference on Alcohol Drugs Traffic Safety*, Vol 1. C. N. Kloeden, and A. J. McLean (eds), Australia, 1995 (1 table)

Abstract: A short general review was conducted of fuel cell, semiconductor, IR, GC, and colorimetric-based instruments to determine the BrAC.

> Semiconductors are non-specific to alcohol, non-linear in response to alcohol vapor concentration and unstable in sensitivity with time; and their effective working life is rarely longer than one year, but actually depends to a large extent on how often they are used. Further since the surface effect by which they operate is dependent on the atmospheric partial pressure of oxygen, semiconductors have been found to vary in sensitivity to alcohol with changes in climate and even more so at changing altitudes of operation.

Reference Number: 30114

WILSON, P.F., C.G. FREEMAN, M.J. MCEWAN, D.B. MILLIGAN, R.A. ALLARDYCE, AND G.M. SHAW. "Alcohol in Breath and Blood: A Selected Ion Flow Tube Mass Spectrometric Study." *Rapid Communications Mass Spectrometry*, 15: 413–417, 2001 (3 figures, 21 references)

Abstract: Breath and/or blood headspace samples were analyzed for alcohol using the SIFT-MS method (Selective Ion Flow Tube-Mass Spectrometry). Five male subjects (ages thirty-three to fifty-seven years) consumed 50 mL of whiskey. Two blood samples were collected and analyzed by an REA enzymatic method and compared to SIFT-MS. The mean peak BACs were approximately 0.040 g/100 mL. The subjects provided a 5-second breath sample directly into the SIFT-MS sampling port. Additional breath samples were collected into 6 L, 1 L, and 250 mL Mylar bags and analyzed later. Poor results were obtained with the 250 mL Mylar bag because of the much smaller volume-to-surface ratio, which allowed adsorption of alcohol onto the bag walls. SIFT-MS was shown to correctly analyze spike blood/aqueous samples equilibrated at 34°C ($r^2 = 0.98$). The Henry's Law constant was found to be 209 ±7 mmol/kg*bar.

Perhaps the most telling feature of Figure 3 is the very good agreement found between the results from the alcohol content of the direct breath sample, the blood headspace sample determined by SIFT-MS and the hospital analysis of blood using radiative energy attenuation technology. For all of these methods all of the data points lie on the decay curve expected for oxidation. This confirms that ethanol exhaled from the lungs in the alveolar portion of the individual breaths is in full equilibrium with ethanol in the blood.

Reference Number: 30115

LAAKSO, O., M. HAAPALA, T. PENNANEN, T. KUITUNEN, AND J-J. HIMBERG. "Fourier-Transformed Infrared Breath Testing After Ingestion of Technical Alcohol." *Journal of Forensic Sciences*, 52: 982–987, 2007 (5 tables, 2 figures, 14 references)

Abstract: The BrACs and other volatile components of breath were analyzed in thirty-five men (ages thirty-five to sixty-five years) who had consumed technical alcohol in the city of Helsinki and were staying in a men's dormitory by a portable FT-IR Gas Analyser. The device measures IR wavelength from approximately 2.5–10 microns. The gas cell volume is 200 mL, and the absorption path length was two meters. The cell was heated to 50°C. A breath CO_2 concentration of 3% was used to determine a proper breath sample. The sample with the highest CO_2 concentration was used in the final analysis. Acetone, isopropanol, MEK, MIK, and ethanol were detected. The breath CO_2 concentration varied greatly due to the inebriation of the subjects.

The portable FT-IR analyzer was suitable for out-of-laboratory use. Because of the multicomponent analysis software, the analyzer could rapidly quantify all of the detectable components in breath. High ethanol and acetone concentrations were measured in the participants' breath as well as traces of other components of denatured alcohol.

Reference Number: 30116

DUBOWSKI, K.M. "Duplicate Breath-Alcohol Testing [Letter]." *American Journal of Forensic Medicine and Pathology*, 9: 272, 1988

Abstract: A letter to the editor was published regarding duplicate breath alcohol testing standards adopted by the National Safety Committee on Alcohol and other Drugs.

Reported breath alcohol analysis results should be truncated to two decimal places, and all results obtained shall be reported. Consecutive breath alcohol analysis results within 0.02g/210 L without regard to sign, shall be deemed to be in acceptable agreement.

Reference Number: 30117

GULLBERG, R.G., "A Concern Associated with Single Breath Alcohol Analysis for Forensic Purposes [Letter]." *Journal of Forensic Sciences*, 38: 1263–1265, 1993 (1 table, 5 references)

Abstract: A letter to the editor regarding duplicate breath alcohol analyses was published. A total of 39,496 duplicate breath analyses in the State of Washington during 1992 were studied. BrACs were determined by 205 BAC DataMasters (IR evidentiary instruments) and evaluated at hypothetical per se BrACs of 0.04, 0.08, 0.10, and 0.20 g/100 mL. If the per se BrAC was 0.100 g/100 mL, then only 1.4% of the individuals tested were at risk of being convicted if only a single BrAC was measured, in comparison to duplicate results.

One important observation is that the proportion of cases placed at risk due to a single analysis protocol appears to increase with concentration. The likely explanation for this is that measurement variability is proportional to concentration.

Reference Number: 30118

GULLBERG, R.G. "Predicting the Second Breath Alcohol Measurement from the First: An Application of Regression Analysis [Letter]." *Journal of Forensic Sciences* 36: 10–14, 1991 (2 figures, 10 references)

Abstract: A regression analysis of 2,668 pairs of BrACs from 150 IR instruments in Washington State during April 1990 was conducted. The equation of best fit is BrAC2 = 0.966 BrAC1 + 0.04. The 95% confidence interval is ±0.024 g/100 mL. For a first BrAC of 0.150 g/100 mL, the second BrAC would be predicted to be 0.149 g/100 mL with a range from 0.125–0.173 g/100 mL.

This information can be useful in situations in which a person provides one breath sample, and one wants to estimate what the second sample would have been based on the first result.

Reference Number: 30119

GULLBERG, R.G. "Repeatability of Replicate Breath Alcohol Measurements Collected in Short Time Intervals." *Science and Justice*, 35: 5–9, 1995 (3 tables, 1 figure, 14 references)

Abstract: A study on the effect of short time intervals between successive breath tests on the BrAC was conducted. Four male and four female subjects provided ten consecutive breath samples into a BAC DataMaster Verifier (an IR device) within 10 to 12 minutes after consuming alcohol. In addition, one subject provided ten breath samples within 4 minutes.

Finally, it is important to note that allowing at least two minutes between breath samples for evidential purposes will help to address the issue of mouth alcohol bias. Two minutes is generally adequate to allow the measurements to be significantly different if mouth alcohol is biasing one of the results. This is due to the first-order or exponential elimination of mouth alcohol. Therefore, it is not advised that jurisdictions perform duplicate analysis one minute apart. However, extremely short sampling techniques do not appear to influence replicate variability significantly and should not be the basis for rejection.

Reference Number: 30120

GULLBERG, R.G. AND B.K. LOGAN. "Reproducibility of Within Subject Breath Alcohol Analysis." *Medicine Science and the Law*, 38: 157–162, 1998 (1 table, 2 figures, 14 references)

Abstract: Six male and two female subjects (ages twenty-four to fifty-one years) consumed between 0.46–1.4 g/kg ethanol within 38 to 88 minutes. Twenty-two to sixty-nine BrACs were determined in each subject by a

BAC DataMaster. The BrACs ranged from 0.042–0.118 g/100 mL, the SD was between 0.0008 and 0.0045 g/100 mL, and the CV was between 1.9% and 4.7%. The mean SD increased with increasing BrAC.

Duplicate breath alcohol samples can be reasonably assumed random samples from a normal distribution and justify parametric statistical treatment. The steepling phenomenon is due largely to sampling variability and is capable of being reduced to acceptable levels with adequate attention given to sampling criteria and procedural technique.

Reference Number: 30121

GULLBERG, R.G. "Evaluation the Variability of Duplicate Breath Alcohol Analyses as a Function of Subject Age." *Medicine, Science and the Law*, 33: 110–114, 1993 (1 table, 1 figure, 13 references)

Abstract: A study was conducted of 30,324 duplicate breath results from arrested drivers in Washington State between January and October 1991. The drivers were divided into different age groups and the BrACs were determined by a BAC DataMaster. The percentage of duplicates not within ±0.02 g/100 mL is shown in the table below.

Table. Mean BrAC and Percent Duplicate Breath Tests Not Within 0.02 g/100 mL with Increasing Age of Arrested Drinking Driver

Age range (yrs)	Mean BrAC (g/100 mL)	Percent not within ±0.020 g/100 mL
10–19	0.131	3.2
20–29	0.156	5.4
30–39	0.172	5.8
40–49	0.176	5.0
50–59	0.174	4.2
60–69	0.170	3.0
70–79	0.148	1.9
80+	0.116	11.8

Source: Adapted from Gullberg (1993).

The subject's increasing age, along with greater risk of respiratory deficiencies, does not appear to influence duplicate test variability on the particular instrument employed when duplicate tests are capable of being provided.

Reference Number: 30122

WIGMORE, J.G., C.J. HOUSE, AND R.M. LANGILLE. "Duplicate Breath Alcohol Testing: Should the Statutory Wait in Canada of at Least 15 Minutes Between Tests Be Changed?" *Canadian Society of Forensic Science Journal*, 38: 1–8, 2005 (1 table, 4 figures, 26 references)

Abstract: A 1-year retrospective study was conducted of 2,759 duplicate Intoxilyzer 5000C tests in the City of Toronto during 1995 with a statutory wait of at least 15 minutes between tests. The time between tests ranged from 19–73 minutes (median 22 minutes). The absolute differences ranged between 0 and 0.042 g/100 mL (median 0.007 g/100 mL) and showed a skewed distribution. The second test was 0.010 g/100 mL or more less than the first test in 839 cases (30%), but only 75 (3%) of the second tests were 0.010 g/100 mL or greater than the first test. The number of duplicates that were not within the recommended 0.020 g/100 mL (truncated) occurred in 7.5% of the cases. When the data were corrected using a mean rate of alcohol elimination of 0.019 g/100 mL/h to account for the decrease in BAC between the two tests due to elimination, the skewness was greatly reduced and the number of duplicate tests outside the recommended range was reduced to 1.6%. At least 15 minutes between tests is not required to prevent the mouth alcohol effect. The average time in custody before the breath testing was 1.1 hours, and so there would be no exogenous source of alcohol to cause a mouth alcohol effect. Endogenous sources of mouth alcohol (such as blood in the mouth, regurgitation, etc.) are of small magnitude and short duration.

Table. Percent of Duplicate Breath Tests of Drinking Drivers in Which the Second Breath Test Is 0.010 g/100 mL or More Lower Than the First

	Uncorrected	Corrected (for time between tests and elimination (0.019 g/100 mL/h))
Untruncated BrAC	30%	7%
Truncated BrAC	46%	11%

Source: Adapted from Wigmore and House (2005).

The at least fifteen minutes wait between breath tests as specified in the *Criminal Code* since 1969, is an unnecessary and outdated requirement. A shorter wait of between two to five minutes, as used in other jurisdictions, would be just as effective in preventing the potential biasing effect of mouth alcohol and allow for a better agreement of duplicate breath samples, and a more efficient and rapid processing of arrested drinking drivers.

Reference Number: 30123

GULLBERG, R.G. "The Relationship Between Duplicate Reproducibility and Concentration in Breath Alcohol Testing Programs [Letter]." *Journal of Analytical Toxicology*, 16: 272–273, 1992 (1 table, 1 figure, 3 references)

Abstract: A study was conducted of 12,621 duplicate BrACs employing the BAC Verifier DataMaster in the State of Washington. The breath samples were collected within 3 minutes of each other, and the results truncated. The number of duplicates not within ±10% of the mean or within 0.020 g/100 mL were determined at increasing BrACs. At BrACs between 0.050 and 0.090 mg/ 100 mL, 5.4% of the duplicates did not meet the ±10% conditions and only 0.7% did not meet the 0.020 g/100 mL conditions. At BrACs between 0.300 and 0.340 g/100 mL, 0% did not meet the ±10% requirement but 16.5% did not meet the 0.020 g/100 mL criteria.

Measurement variability is clearly proportional to concentration in breath alcohol analysis. This condition of proportional variability may have some analytical component but is probably caused by biological and sampling factors such as the length and quality of exhalation that may vary with concentration.

Reference Number: 30124

GULLBERG, R.G. "Statistical Evaluation of Truncated Breath-Alcohol Test Measurements." *Journal of Forensic Sciences*, 33: 507–510, 1988 (1 table, 1 figure, 7 references)

Abstract: A study was conducted of 500 breath alcohol tests measured by a BAC Verifier, reported to three decimal places, in order to determine the error when the result is truncated to two decimal places. The magnitude of the error can range from 0–0.009 g/100 mL. The reporting error as a result of truncation follows a uniform distribution and would appear to be random in nature.

Therefore, when one is considering a two-digit breath alcohol test result, there is an equal probability that the third unobserved digit is a nine or a one. The defense could not logically suggest there is a greater probability that the third digit is a zero. Likewise, the prosecution could not logically suggest a greater probability that the third digit is a nine. There would be equal probabilities assigned to the outcome of the third unobserved digit. Regardless of the magnitude of the truncation error, it will always be in the individual's favor.

Reference Number: 30125

LANGILLE, R.M. AND J. PATRICK. "Precision of Breath Alcohol Testing in the Field Using the Intoxilyzer 5000C and the Paradox of Truncation," *Canadian Society of Forensic Science Journal*, 39: 55–64, 2005 (1 table, 6 figures, 11 references)

Abstract: A study of 8,585 duplicate breath tests analyzed by Intoxilyzer 5000C instruments in Toronto between 1995 and 1998 was conducted. Ninety-seven percent (8,309) of the duplicate breath tests were within 0.02 g/100 mL (untruncated). After truncation an additional 178 (2%) of the tests were within 0.02 g/100 mL. Eighty-three percent of the tests (7,146) had the second BrAC lower than the first. The mean calibration check of the Intoxilyzer 5000C did not vary with increasing difference between BrACs between 0.021 to 0.029 g/100 mL, indicating that the differences in BrACs are not due to analytical factors. The overall mean BrAC was 0.157 g/100 mL but was 0.185 g/100 mL for duplicate results > 0.02 g/100 mL.

Table. Mean First and Second Calibration Check (Cal Ck) Results and Difference Between the First and Second BrAC of Arrested Drinking Drivers

Difference between 1st and 2nd BrACs (g/100 mL)	Mean 1st Cal Ck (g/100 mL)	Mean 2nd Cal Ck (g/100 mL)
0.021	0.0997	0.0991
0.022	0.0992	0.0985
0.023	0.0998	0.0979
0.024	0.0991	0.0985
0.025	0.0968	0.0973
0.026	0.0984	0.0980
0.027	0.0992	0.0987
0.028	0.0988	0.0986
0.029	0.0993	0.0990

Source: Adapted from Langille and Patrick (2005).

Properly trained qualified breath technicians operate the Intoxilyzer 5000C with a high degree of precision and can obtain two untruncated alcohol breath tests that are no more than 20 mg/dL apart with little difficulty. Nevertheless, the practice of truncation treats differences due to quality of sample in a uniform matter and provides the most conservative determination of a breath alcohol result.

Reference Number: 30126

ZUBA, D. "Accuracy and Reliability of Breath Alcohol Testing by Handheld Electrochemical Analysers." *Forensic Science International*, 178: e29–e33, 2008 (4 figures, 21 references)

Abstract: BrACs were determined in 370 drinking drivers in Poland using IR evidential instruments (Alcomat, Alkometr A2.0 [3.39-micron IR]) and handheld electrochemical (EC) devices (Alcotest 7410, Alco-Sensor IV). BACs were also determined and corrected for time delays using a 0.016 g/100 mL/h elimination rate. The correlation coefficients were $r = 0.978$ (EC versus IR) and $r = 0.940$ (EC versus BAC).

The results indicate good correlation between the readings of the portable EC breath analyzers, the Alcotest 7410 and the AlcoSensor IV, and the results of confirmatory analyses using both stationary IR instruments, the Alcomat and the Alkometr A2.0, and blood analysis. It means that if a police officer follows proper procedure and the metrological properties of a breath analyzer are periodically verified, the readings of portable instruments are accurate and can be used for evidential purposes. On the other hand, the confirmatory analyses have to be performed as these are common in forensic toxicology.

Reference Number: 30127

POLLISSAR, N. L., W. SUWANVIJIT, AND R.G. GULLBERG. "The Accuracy of Handheld Pre-Arrest Breath Test Instruments as a Predictor of the Evidential Breath Alcohol Test Results." *Journal of Forensic Sciences*, 60: 482–487, 2015 (5 tables, 4 figures, 10 references)

Abstract: A comparison was conducted of 1,779 duplicate evidential breath alcohol results, found in Washington State between 2008 and 2011, using a BAC DataMaster and 929 Alco-Sensor FST and 850 Alco-Sensor III preliminary breath testers (PBTs). Both PBTs use ED detectors, but the Alco-Sensor III is an older version with no blank tests conducted and greater manipulation required by the operator. The duplicate DataMaster results compared to a single PBT result had a Pearson correlation (*r*) of 0.92. The overall correct classification of PBT in identifying drivers with a mean DataMaster result exceeding 0.080 g/100 mL was 93%. The mean difference between the AS FST and DM was 0.0044 g/100 mL, and for the AS II it was 0.010 g/100 mL. The mean time between PBT and the DM results was 53 minutes (range 19– 408 minutes). The accuracy at determining a BAC > 0.080 g/100 mL was nearly 100% at a PBT result of 0.110 g/100 mL. The difference between the PBT and DM was equivalent to an apparent elimination rate of 0.011 g/100 mL/h.

> The PBT instrument is an objective and important evidential tool for the investigation and prosecution for drunk driving cases. The accuracy of the PBT in predicting the subsequent evidential breath alcohol results from the Datamaster has been statistically demonstrated. The PBT is another important tool that should be more widely employed in an effort to provide a more objective evidence-based enforcement.

Reference Number: 30128

LEONARD, R.J. "Evaluation of the Analytical Performance of a Fuel Cell Breath Alcohol Testing Instrument: A Seven-Year Comprehensive Study." *Journal of Forensic Sciences*, 57: 1614–1620, 2012 (5 tables, 4 figures, 19 references)

Abstract: An evaluation was conducted on 54,255 breath alcohol test sequences conducted on 129 Alco-Sensor IV-XL portable evidential breath test instruments in Orange County, California, between 2003 and 2009. A dry gas alcohol standard was conducted on the instruments at least every 10 days. The mean percent bias of the instruments was 2.4% at an alcohol concentration of 0.110 g/100 mL. Of the 54,225 test sequences, 1,544 (3%) were negative for alcohol for both results (< 0.010 g/100 mL). The mean BrAC or all the tests was 0.141 g/100 mL. Of the 38,580 duplicate breath tests, 97.5% were within ± 0.020 g/100 mL. The mean difference between the two breath tests was 0.006 g/100 mL (range 0–0.332 g/100 mL). A third test was conducted in 949 test sequences, and the mean BrACs were 0.200, 0.195, and 0.193 g/100 mL for breath tests 1, 2, and 3, respectively. There were 14,333 error messages (26%).

Table. Percent Occurrence of Error Messages for Alco-Sensor IV-XL

Reason for Error Message	Percent Occurrence
Insufficient breath volume	33%
Blank test too high	30%
Test timeout	11%
Test sequence not completed	10%
Radio frequency interference (RFI)	7%

Source: Adapted from Leonard (2012).

This study demonstrates that the use of a portable fuel cell instrument in the field is capable of producing very precise results well within required limits. Uncertainty exists with these measurements as with any measurement, with the largest contributor in breath testing coming from biological or sampling variations such as breathing patterns, breath temperature and humidity, and breath volume. Despite the impact that each of these variables can potentially have on the alcohol concentration of a breath sample, duplicate tests still agreed within ± 0.020 g/210L of each other in 97.5% of all tests performed over a seven-year period and within ± 0.010 g/210 L of each other in 86.3% over the same period. These results demonstrate the exceptional precision of duplicate tests by a fuel cell instrument (and specifically the precision of the AlcoSensor IV-XL) in measuring breath samples for alcohol.

Reference Number: 30129

PALMENTIER, J.-P.F.P., R.M. LANGILLE, C.J. HOUSE, AND J. PATRICK. "Ambient Fail Exception Messages During Breath Testing of Suspected Impaired Drivers Using the Intoxilyzer 5000C: A 10-Year Retrospective Analysis." *Canadian Society of Forensic Science Journal*, 48: 46–57, 2015 (1 table, 4 figures, 8 references)

Abstract: An analysis was conducted of Ambient Fail Messages (AFM) that occurred during the breath teasing of 21,016 drivers conducted on fourteen Intoxilyzer 5000Cs by the Toronto Police Service between 1997 and 2006. An AFM occurred in 531 breath tests (2.5%): 510 tests had a single AFM and 21 had two AFM. The mean BAC of AFM drivers was 0.208 g/100 mL compared to 0.150 g/100 mL for drivers without an AFM. Calibration check results were not affected by the occurrence of an AFM.

The ambient conditions needed to generate an AFM are transient in nature and more likely to occur when testing subjects with elevated BACs. We concur with Person that ambient alcohol present when the instrument is being used is not a problem and claims to the contrary are unfounded.

Reference Number: 30130

EMESON, B. L., T. WHITFUL, C.R. BAUM, K. GARLIN-KANE, AND K. SANTUCCI. "Effects of Alcohol-Based Hand Hygiene Solutions on Breath Alcohol Detection in the Emergency Department." *American Journal of Infection Control*, 44: 1672–1674, 2016 (2 figures, 8 references)

Abstract: Ten alcohol-free subjects provided breath samples into an Alco-Sensor III immediately after and at 1-minute intervals under four conditions: (1) two pumps of foam ABHS (70% ethanol), (2) one pump of gel ABHS, (3) one pump of foam ABHS and the donning of gloves immediately afterwards, and (4) one pump of foam ABHS and allowing the hands to dry. Each subject conducted their own breath tests. At 1 minute after use the mean BrACs were 0.151 g/100 mL (foam), 0.161 g/100 mL (gel), 0.003 g/100 mL (gloves), and 0.005 g/100 mL (drying). Prolonged positive BrACs at 11 and 16 minutes were observed in two subjects.

These results confirm that ABHS use by the clinical provider using breath alcohol detection equipment may alter the results, even beyond the immediate period. Although these data do not confirm a mechanism for this effect, it is unlikely to be related to transdermal absorption.

Reference Number: 30131

ALI, S.S., M.P. WILSON, E.M. CASTILLO, P. WITUCKI, T.T. SIMMONS, AND G.M. VILKE. "Common Hand Sanitizers May Distort Readings of Breathalyzer Tests in the Absence of Acute Intoxication." *Academic Emergency Medicine*, 20: 212–215, 2013 (1 figure, 17 references)

Abstract: Seventy-five participants in a San Diego emergency department were tested and had a first BrAC as determined by an Alco-Sensor III of zero. They were divided into three groups of twenty-five subjects who provided a second breath test immediately after (1) using one pump (1.5 mL) of Purell hand sanitizer (62% v/v alcohol) and drying hands by rubbing briskly, (2) one pump of the hand sanitizer without drying, and (3) two pumps of the hand sanitizer without drying. The subjects blew into the Alco-Sensor III for only 2 seconds before the manual override collection button was pressed. The median BrACs (and range) for the second breath test were 0.004 g/100 mL (0–0.019), 0.051 g/100 mL (0.020–0.109), and 0.119 g/100 mL (0.020–0.166) for groups 1, 2, and 3 respectively. It is thought that the results are due to alcohol vapors from the hands, which are holding the Alco-Sensor III, being blown into the fuel cell instrument.

The use of an alcohol-based hand sanitizer can cause false-positive readings of a breathalyzer when the operator uses the hand sanitizer correctly. The breathalyzer readings are further elevated if more sanitizer is used or if it not allowed to dry appropriately. Health care workers and others who rely on these machines to make judgments about the alcohol level of others should be careful not to use hand sanitizers immediately before operating a breathalyzer machine and to use it according to manufacturer's recommendations when they do.

Reference Number: 30132

STRAWSINE, E. AND B. LUTMER. "The Effect of Alcohol-Based Hand Sanitizer Vapors on Evidential Breath Alcohol Test Results." *Journal of Forensic Sciences,* 63: 1284–1290, 2018 (4 tables, 2 figures, 27 references)

Abstract: In Missouri about 40% of the police agencies have alcohol-based hand sanitizers (ABHS) in the breath room, but only 3.8% have a general order specifying that the ABHS is not to be used prior to the breath alcohol test. Breath test operators rubbed their hands with two pumps of either a gel (70% ethanol) or foam (62% alcohol) until dry then opened a plastic package containing a mouthpiece. Ninety alcohol-free subjects provided breath samples into an Intox DMT, Intoxilyzer 800, or Intox EC/IR. A positive BrAC result (0.007 g/100 mL or greater) occurred in 6%, 2%, and 7.5% of the tests respectively. The highest false BrACs were 0.020, 0.021, and 0.041 g/100 mL for the first test.

Operator use of ABHS before conducting a breath test has the potential to lead to positive breath alcohol results if applied to the hands of the operator shortly before testing. These positive results are due to a transient mouth alcohol effect created by the inhalation of alcohol vapors by the subject. The evidential breath alcohol instruments do not always abort testing and print a status code when exhalation profiles indicated mouth alcohol contamination. Therefore, it is recommended that ABHS not be kept in the same room as an evidential breath instrument to minimize its use and the concomitant contamination of the room air. It is also suggested a minimum of 15 min pass between the exposure of hand sanitizer vapors and the testing of a subject to align with the National Safety Council's recommendation of a 15-min observation period of the subject.

Reference Number: 30133

STRAKA, L., F. NOVOMESKY, M. MARCINKOVA, AND J. KRAJCOVIC. "An Unusual Case of Highly False-Positive Breath-Alcohol Test in a Motor Vehicle Driver." *Romanian Journal of Legal Medicine,* 25: 293–296, 2017 (25 references)

Abstract: A random breath test using the AlcoQuant 6020 Plus, a fuel cell device, was conducted on a fifty-three-year-old male driver in the interior of his car as it was so cold outside. He registered a BrAC of 59 mg/L and 12 minutes later, outside his car, he registered an 18 mg/L result. He denied alcohol use for two days. A blood sample was collected 60 minutes later and the BAC was negative.

After police investigation, it was concluded that the driver was carrying refined spirit in the vehicle the day before the road-side control and some part of the spirit was spilled in the car while loading the spirit-containing barrels. The case reaffirms that in order to exclude possible false-positive breath alcohol analysis due to environmental alcohol inhalation, blank sample of air in the motor vehicle (or any confined space) should be obligatory prior to any breath alcohol analysis. In addition, current literature on the possibilities of false-positive results is reviewed.

Reference Number: 30134

MLYNCZAK, J., J. KUBICKI, AND K. KOPCZYNSKI. "Stand-Off Detection of Alcohol in Car Cabins." *Journal of Applied Remote Sensing*, 8: 7pp, 2014. (1 table, 4 figures, 20 references)

Abstract: The remote detection of alcohol vapor in a closed car cabin was conducted using a laser beam at a wavelength of 3.39 microns. The beam is sent through a chopper wheel, through the car cabin, and is reflected back to a cooled detector by a mirror on the other side of the road. The infrared (IR) beam passes through the car interior twice and so increases sensitivity. Simulated breath alcohol vapors at various concentrations were tested. Driving a car with open windows or having tinted windows may prevent detection. A false positive may occur if there is open liquor in the car or if passengers have consumed alcohol.

> The results of the investigations presented in this paper show that the developed device works properly. It is able to detect alcohol vapor in which a human being with a concentration of alcohol in blood of at least 0.1 promille is present.

Reference Number: 30135

CANADIAN SOCIETY OF FORENSIC SCIENCE ALCOHOL TEST COMMITTEE. "Alcohol Test Committee Position Paper, Documentation Required for Assessing the Accuracy and Reliability of Approved Instrument Breath Alcohol Results." *Canadian Society of Forensic Science Journal*, 45: 101–103, 2012 (11 references)

Abstract: The Alcohol Test Committee (ATC) position paper on the documentation required for assessing the accuracy and reliability of approved instrument breath alcohol test results was published. The required quality control information, which must be reviewed to assess the proper working order of the approved instrument in Canada, are the blank test results, the calibration check results, the instrument error messages that occurred during the breath testing sequence, and the duplicate subject breath test results.

> Review of these specified requirements is sufficient to assess the accuracy and reliability of a subject's breath test results. Deviations from the Operational Procedures recommended by the ATC would be recognizable by reviewing the materials outlined above; in such cases, further information may be required.

3.02 BREATH ALCOHOL SIMULATORS

> "In one ampoule one can (A) analyse a sample of room air as a blank to ensure freedom from contamination of all parts of the equipment, including the bubbler and ampoule of dichromate solution; (B) analyse a standard solution of alcohol and water at a known temperature; (C) analyse several samples of breath from a subject."
>
> —Borkenstein and Smith, "The Breathalyzer and Its Applications" (1961)

The main type of alcohol simulators used to calibrate and check the accuracy of breath test instruments currently are wet bath simulators, which are typically heated to 34°C ±0.2°C (30201, 30202). The volume of alcohol standard placed in the simulator (usually 500 mL) is not critical for the accurate testing (30203). Room temperatures between 17°C to 27°C also do not have a significant effect on the accuracy of the alcohol simulator (30204). The use of the breath alcohol simulator containing 500 mL of solution was found to only decrease in concentration by on average 5% after 218 calibration checks over a period of 12 days in the recirculation mode as employed by an Intoxilyzer 5000 (30205). Alcohol standard solution stored in glass or polyethylene bottles were found to be stable for up to 26 years (30206–30208, 30212). Another type of breath alcohol simulator is compressed or dry gas, which contains alcohol in an inert gas such as nitrogen and contains no water vapor (30209–30211).

Dry gas alcohol standard tanks when exposed to –20°C for two days had a decrease in pressurization and an increase in alcohol concentration by up to 51%. It is recommended that freeze indicators be applied to each tank (30213). Temperatures above 52°C can cause the tank to vent and shorten its storage life (30214).

Calibration testing of the portable, roadside fuel cell breath alcohol screeners can be increased from every week to once a month (30215–30217).

Reference Number: 30201

DUBOWSKI, K.M. AND N.A. ESSARY. "Evaluation of Commercial Breath-Alcohol Simulators: Further Studies." *Journal of Analytical Toxicology*, 15: 272–275, 1991 (2 tables, 4 figures, 10 references)

Abstract: Studies of two alcohol simulators were conducted on the Alcolmeter SL-2, Alco-Sensor III, ALERT J4, BAC Verifier DataMaster II, Intoxilyzer 5000D, and Intoxilyzer PAC-1200. The two simulators tested were the Toxitest II and 34C, and the respective temperatures were 33.98 ±0.040°C and 33.99 ±0.008°C respectively. The nominal sample chamber volumes were 1.3 mL for Alcolmeter, 1.3 mL for Alco-Sensor, 0.4 mL for ALERT, 50 mL for BAC Verifier, 400 mL for Intoxilyzer 4011 AS-A, 81 mL for 5000D, and 39.6 mL for PAC-1200.

Fifty simulator tests with the Intoxilyzer 5000D showed the alcohol concentration was reduced by 6.4% for non-recirculation mode and 2.0% for recirculation.

> The results of our evaluation demonstrate greatly improved performance of commercial simulators over those available a decade ago. Current generation simulators can be satisfactorily used without tandem coupling, for calibration of breath alcohol analyzers and for control tests.

Reference Number: 30202

DUBOWSKI, K.M. AND N.A. ESSARY. "Field Performance of Current Generation Breath-Alcohol Simulators." *Journal of Analytical Toxicology*, 16: 325–327, 1992 (2 tables, 2 figures, 10 references)

Abstract: A study was conducted of 779 alcohol simulator tests at six Intoxilyzer 5000D in Oklahoma at concentrations of 0.060, 0.080, 0.090, 0.100, 0.110, and 0.120 g/100 mL. The ToxiTest II was the simulator used in this study. The Intoxilyzers employ a recirculation mode. Every Intoxilyzer result was within 0.010 g/100 mL of the target alcohol simulator value. A regression of analysis showed the line of best fit was $y = 0.984x + 0.0015$ ($r = 0.99$).

> We conclude from these findings that the field performance of current generation breath-alcohol simulators as control-test devices parallels and approximates that found in our laboratory studies and that these devices can amply meet control-test requirements for quantitative evidential breath-alcohol testing.

Reference Number: 30203

SPECK, P.R., A.J. MCELROY, AND R.G. GULLBERG. "The Effect of Breath Alcohol Simulator Solution Volume on Measurement Results." *Journal of Analytical Toxicology*, 15: 332–335, 1991 (2 tables, 1 figure, 12 references)

Abstract: A series of experiments were conducted regarding the effect of varying simulator solution volume from 400 to 600 mL on an evidential breath alcohol tester. A Guth model 34C simulator and a BAC Verifier DataMaster were used, and ten tests were conducted at each volume.

Table. Effect of Varying Simulator Solution Volume on Breath Alcohol Calibration Checks

Volume of Simulator Solution (mL)	Mean of Cal Ck Results (g/100 mL)
400	0.105
450	0.103
500	0.105
550	0.103
600	0.104

Source: Adapted from Speck et al (1991).

The present study demonstrates that when keeping the simulator solution volume constant from aliquot to aliquot there is greater variability in the measurements than when varying the volumes from 400 to 600 mL. The result, however, is a statistical artifact and not a real difference.

Reference Number: 30204

ANDERSSON, L. AND A.W. JONES. "Room Temperature Influences on the Performance of Some Breath Alcohol Simulators." *Proceedings ICADTS T2000, Stockholm, May 22–26, 2000, Poster 1*, 6pp (1 table, 4 figures, 6 references)

Abstract: Four simulators (Alcotest model CU34, Guth model 210021 and Guth Model 34C, and a modified Guth 34C) were tested at different room temperatures (17°C, 22°C, and 27°C). The wet gas alcohol and water concentrations were determined by a specially constructed IR device. Tests were conducted to determine the problems of the unregulated temperature of the metal simulator head and the condensation of water in the connecting tubing and the upper part of the jar. The head temperature of the Guth 34C ranged from 30.3°C to 39°C at ambient room temperatures between 16.5°C to 27.6°C. The solution temperature of the Guth 34C varied from 34.00°C to 33.90°C for the same ambient room temperature range. At 17°C, 22°C, and 27°C ambient room temperature the average deviation from target (100%) for the Guth 34C was –2.6%, –0.7%, and 0.1% respectively.

However, the primary mode of calibrating breath alcohol analyzers should still entail the use of wet-bath simulators so that the gas standard has the same composition as the biological specimen (breath) intended to be measured, that is, alcohol in air saturated with water vapor.

Reference Number: 30205

WALKER, B., M. BUTLER, AND M. PLATE. "Assessment of the Calibration of the Intoxilyzer 5000C Following Extensive Use of an Alcohol Standard." *Canadian Society of Forensic Science Journal*, 37: 155–162, 2004 (3 tables, 6 references)

Abstract: An average of 218 calibration checks were conducted on each of seven Intoxilyzer 5000C using aqueous alcohol standards (500 mL) in Guth simulators in the recirculation mode over a period of 12 days. One milliliter of alcohol standard was collected at the beginning of testing and on the twelfth day of use, and the alcohol concentration was determined by headspace GC. The mean calibration check results ranged from 0.099 g/100 mL (0.089–0.105 g/100 mL) on the first day of testing to 0.096 g/100 mL (0.090–0.103 g/100 mL) on day eleven. The initial alcohol concentration was 1.20 mg/mL (1.19–1.22 mg/mL) and decreased to 1.14 mg/mL (1.11–1.17 mg/mL). The average depletion was 5% over the 12-day period. The maximum number of arrested drivers tested per week per Intoxilyzer instrument in Ontario was twenty-eight by Ottawa, twenty-two by Toronto, fifteen by Peel Regional, and six by York Regional police services. The alcohol standard solution was changed weekly in field use.

> This study demonstrates that while alcohol depletion does occur through use of the Intoxilyzer 5000C, the alcohol standard remains suitable for the assessment of the calibration of the instrument even after extensive use. Furthermore, typical usage of the Intoxilyzer 5000C in the field would not be expected to create a situation in which the alcohol standard cannot properly assess the calibration when a range of 90 to 110 mg/100 mL is used as an acceptable range for calibration checks.

Reference Number: 30206

PELLA, P.A. AND B.I. DIAMONDSTORE. "Stability of Aqueous Ethanol Solutions Stored in Glass Ampules." *Journal of Forensic Sciences* 20: 537–538, 1975 (1 table, 4 references)

Abstract: Five milliliters of aqueous ethanol solution were placed into a flamed sealed 10 mL glass ampoule. The initial ethanol concentration was 60.04 mg/mL; 5 months later the concentration was 60.29 mg/mL, and 2 years and 4 months later the measured concentration was 60.51 mg/mL.

The results indicate that aqueous ethanol solutions can be maintained in a flame-sealed ampule without any significant change in ethanol concentration. Reference ethanol solutions stored in this manner appear to be excellent for ensuring long-term stability.

Reference Number: 30207

CHOW, B.L.C. AND J.G. WIGMORE. "Technical Note: The Stability of Aqueous Alcohol Standard Used in Breath Alcohol Testing After Twenty-Six Years Storage." *Canadian Society of Forensic Science Journal*, 38: 21–24, 2005 (1 table, 1 figure, 9 references)

Abstract: Four 500 mL polyethylene bottles of alcohol standard solution at manufactured concentrations of 0.484, 2.420, 3.025, and 3.630 mg/mL each were analyzed by headspace GC after 26 years' storage at room temperature. The mean percent change (and range) in alcohol concentration were +4.4 (–6.5 to +8.3), +0.6 (–13.9 to +5.5), –2.0 (–15.6 to +3.5), and –26.3 (–39.1 to +3.9) for the four alcohol concentrations respectively. The percent decrease in alcohol concentration increased with increasing alcohol concentration and may be due to, in part, Fick's law of diffusion.

Dilute aqueous alcohol standards at concentrations of 3.025 mg/mL and less are remarkably stable when stored at room temperature for approximately 26 years. The greatest decrease in alcohol concentration was 15.6%, which if uniform, indicates an annual loss of approximately 0.6% per year. Much higher losses of alcohol concentration occurred at the highest alcohol standard tested (3.630 mg/mL) in which the greatest annual loss, if uniform, was 1.5% per year.

Reference Number: 30208

KUCMANIC, J. "Long-Term Stability of Ethanol Solutions for Breath-Alcohol Tests." *Journal of Analytical Toxicology*, 33: 328–331, 2009 (1 table, 8 references)

Abstract: The long-term stability of dilute aqueous standard alcohol solutions (1.21 mg/mL concentration) stored at room temperature for up to 5 years was determined. The 500 mL of solution was stored in high density polyethylene bottles sealed with a shrink wrap and foam seal. Currently in Ohio the alcohol standard has a 1-year expiry date. Two Intoxilyzer 8000 instruments were employed to determine the stability and the mean target results ranged from 0.098 to 0.100 g/100 mL over that time. GC analyses were also conducted initially on the solutions.

> It can be concluded that the stability of the wet bath solution packaged in high-density polyethylene bottles with a theoretical concentration of 0.100 g/210L is in excess of five years and surpasses the stability expiration of one year from the date of manufacture when stored at normal room temperature.

Reference Number: 30209

DUBOWSKI, K.M. AND N.A. ESSARY. "Vapor-Alcohol Control Tests with Compressed Ethanol-Gas Mixtures: Scientific Basis and Actual Performance." *Journal of Analytical Toxicology*, 20: 484–491, 1996 (7 tables, 4 figures, 20 references)

Abstract: A study was conducted of the accuracy and precision of compressed ethanol-gas standards on the Alcotest 7110 and Intoxilyzer 1400. Compressed ethanol-gas mixtures must be free of water vapor to retain microhomogenity and is therefore referred to as dry gas.

> Lastly, it is relevant to reaffirm a key point concerning atmospheric pressure in relation to breath- and vapor-alcohol analysis. As indicated by the theory and borne out by the experimental results of this study the expansion of compressed dry gas-alcohol mixtures to ambient conditions and, hence, the resultant VACs are partly controlled by atmospheric pressure. In contrast the measurement of alcohol in breath is independent of the ambient atmospheric pressure, as is the evolution of wet gas from simulators and VAC measurements in wet gas samples.

Reference Number: 30210

SILVERMAN, L.D., K. WONG, AND S. MILLER. "Confirmation of Ethanol Compressed Gas Standard Concentrations by an NIST-Traceable, Absolute Chemical Method and Comparison with Wet Breath Alcohol Simulators." *Journal of Analytical Toxicology*, 21: 369–372, 1997 (3 tables, 2 figures, 6 references)

Abstract: Compressed gas standards do not contain water vapor because water condenses at high pressures. A method is described to determine the ethanol concentration in compressed gas. It involves bubbling the compressed gas through a sulfuric acid and potassium dichromate solution followed by titration. For compressed gas the units of measurement are in ppm. The ppm can be multiplied by 2605 to determine the BrAC (g/dL) at 760 mm Hg air pressure.

An approximate correction can be made based on altitude using a chart on the label.

However, most breath alcohol testers are equipped with a pressure sensor and automatically correct dry gas values for ambient pressure.

Reference Number: 30211

MATTHIAS, D.J., D.C. HARVEY, AND D.E. DEFRAGE. "Concentration Verification of Ethanol/Nitrogen Compressed Gas Cylinders Prior to Use for Periodic Determinations of Accuracy in California." *Journal of Analytical Toxicology*, 25: 215–218, 2001 (4 references)

Abstract: The concentration of a compressed gas ethanol breath standard (EBS) cylinder was determined using a modified Alcotest 7110 MK II-C (AEV). The instrument has a one IR wavelength at 9.5 microns and was modified by removing the breath sampling tube and adding an absolute pressure transducer to compensate for changes in barometric pressure. The AEV was calibrated using a wet bath simulator and the results were compensated for water vapor as EBS contains only nitrogen and ethanol. The concentration of the EBS cylinder must be within 2% of the target concentration of 0.100 g/100 mL.

Previously gas chromatographic analysis has been used to verify cylinder gas concentrations, but several technical issues made the method difficult to use. To our knowledge this is the first method that uses a modified IR breath alcohol testing instrument for EBS cylinder verification. The method does not require a special set-up or instrumentation, eliminating the need to purchase a dedicated bench-top unit.

Reference Number: 30212

DE SOUZA, V., J.M. RODRIGUES, R.D. BANDEIRA, L.A. DAS NEVES VALENTE, M.V.B. SUSA, V.F. DA SILVA, AND R.A.L. DA SILVA. "Evaluation of the Stability of Ethanol in Water Certified Reference Material: Measurement Uncertainty Under Transport and Storage Conditions." *Accreditation Quality Assurance*, 13: 717–721, 2008 (5 tables, 2 figures, 6 references)

Abstract: The short-term stability (transport) and long-term stability (storage) of 0.5, 0.9, 1.1, and 4.6 mg/g water alcohol solution were determined. Analysis was conducted using direct injection GC with *n*-propanol as an internal standard. The solutions were stored in 500 mL glass bottles and were used to calibrate breath alcohol testing instruments. In the short-term stability study the solution was stored at 60°C and 4°C for 1 week. In the long-term stability study the solution was stored at 20°C for 1 year. There were no significant changes in ethanol concentration of any solution.

According to the statistical parameters used in both studies, the stability of ethanol in water CRM was confirmed for all of the mass factions studied.

Reference Number: 30213

ROSLAND, M., J. MONTPETIT, AND V. MENDES. "Practical Use of Commercially Available Compressed (Dry Gas) Alcohol Standards." *Canadian Society of Forensic Science Journal,* 50: 197–207, 2017 (5 tables, 6 figures, 7 references)

Abstract: Newer generation breath testing equipment allows for the use of dry gas (ethanol and nitrogen) in a compressed gas tank rather than wet bath alcohol simulators. Ten and nine compressed dry gas alcohol standard tanks from Airgas and Ilomo respectively were exposed to -20°C temperature for 48 hours. The tanks were then equilibrated at room temperature for 48 hours. During freezing the Airgas tanks lost pressure and increased the alcohol concentration from 5 to 51%. The Ilomo tanks had no change in alcohol concentration. It is thought that during freezing the valve released nitrogen but not alcohol, which remained in a liquid form at that temperature. It is recommended that a freeze indicator be applied for each tank. A change in atmospheric pressure resulted in a less than 1% change in the Intox EC/IR II and the BAC DataMaster DMT test results. There was no change in the alcohol concentration as the tanks emptied during use.

The results demonstrated that 1) the concentration of alcohol was found to remain stable as the tank emptied, 2) both instruments correctly compensated for the change in atmospheric pressure due to elevation change; and 3) when dry gas tanks from different manufacturers were subjected to –20°C for 48 hours, some tanks were found to have a decreased pressure and an increase in alcohol concentration. Some tanks exposed to freezing temperatures for an extended period may not produce the appropriate reading and as such, precautions should be taken when shipping or storing dry gas tanks in cold temperatures.

Reference Number: 30214

KNOTT, B. "The Facts About Workplace Evidential Breath Tester Calibration." *Data Focus*: 17–24, Spring 2013 (3 figures)

A good review was conducted of calibration checks and calibration of workplace EBTs using pressurized gas. Always let dry gas standards equilibrate at room temperature. It is recommended that dry gas not be stored at temperatures above 125°F (such as a hot car trunk) as each 10°F increase in temperature causes a 1 psi increase in pressure and may cause the tank to vent and having a shorter storage life.

The only way a user can be certain that an EBT is reading correctly is by performing a calibration check and if this unit is out of specification, performing a calibration followed by a successful calibration check.

Reference Number: 30215

ROSLAND, M. AND R. PON. "A Statistical Evaluation of Calibration Check Intervals." *Canadian Society of Forensic Science Journal*, 43: 41–46, 2010 (4 tables, 8 references)

Abstract: A statistical analysis was conducted on 612 calibration checks of thirty-six Alco-Sensor IV DWF used by two police agencies in 2002 and 2003. Calibration checks were conducted using dry gas. The Alco-Sensor IV DWF required calibration 1.3% of the time within 31 days of the previous calibration.

This study demonstrates that the AS IV DWF is no more likely to require calibration up to and including a 5-week interval when compared to a 2-week interval. The extension of the calibration interval by the ATC from biweekly to 31 days is supported by this data for the AS IV DWF. A similar further study can be conducted to determine the relationship between calibration interval and the frequency of the calibration check being within or outside the acceptable range at times beyond 5 weeks for other approved screening devices.

Reference Number: 30216

BOOKER, R., G.P. LEHMANN, AND S.L. KORKOSH. "Calibration Stability of the Alco-Sensor FST Over a Seven Week Period." *Canadian Society of Forensic Science Journal*, 45: 176–178, 2012 (1 table, 5 references)

Abstract: The calibration stability of five Alco-Sensor FST screening devices was checked at 1-week intervals for 7 weeks. Two wet bath simulator tests (using a 0.100 g/100 mL alcohol standard) were conducted on each occasion. Results outside 0.095 to 0.105 g/100 mL would require a re-calibration of the devices, which was not necessary during the 7 weeks of testing. The five Alco-Sensor FSTs were exposed to simulated operational conditions, including transportation in a motor vehicle, breath testing, changes in ambient temperatures, and in one case being accidentally dropped. The following table shows the alcohol standard test results of the five devices at 1-, 4-, and 7-week periods.

Table. Calibration Check Results for Five Screening Devices at 1, 4, and 7 Weeks

Screening Device Number	Calibration check results at 1 week (g/100 mL)	Calibration check results at 4 weeks (g/100 mL)	Calibration check results at 7 weeks (g/100 mL)
1	0.100/0.099	0.101/0.100	0.105/0.105
2	0.102/0.102	0.103/0.105	0.105/0.104
3	0.102/0.102	0.105/0.105	0.104/0.104
4	0.103/0.104	0.101/0.104	0.105/0.104
5	0.102/0.102	0.100/0.100	0.103/0.103

Source: Adapted from Booker, Lehmann, and Korkosh (2021).

The results of this study indicate that a monthly calibration check schedule is scientifically suitable for the Alco-Sensor FST.

Reference Number: 30217

TREMBLAY, J. "A Comparison of Paired Calibration Check Results of Alco-Sensor IV RBT IV and Intoxilyzer 5000C in Real Cases." *Canadian Society of Forensic Science Journal*, 46: 112–119, 2013 (4 tables, 2 figures, 23 references)

Abstract: A comparison was conducted of 481 paired calibration checks with the Alco-Sensor IV RBT IV and 1,125 paired calibration checks with the Intoxilyzer 5000C used by the police in Quebec between 2007 and 2012. The calibration checks were conducted using a wet bath simulator with an alcohol standard solution heated to 34 ±0.2°C. Two calibration checks and duplicate breath tests were conducted on the arrested drinking drivers. All calibration checks were between 0.095 and 0.105 g/100 mL. The SD was 0.0023 g/100 mL for the Alco-Sensor and 0.0018 g/100 mL for the Intoxilyzer 5000C.

> The comparison of paired calibration check results made in this study demonstrate that the uncertainty associated to Alco-Sensor IV-RBT IV and the Intoxilyzer 5000C results is well below the acceptable range around the target value. Therefore, alleging that the results of analysis are associated with a 10 mg/100 mL margin of error is an overestimation of the actual error associated with measurements obtained on these two approved instruments.

3.03 ABILITY TO PROVIDE BREATH SAMPLE

> "[T]he OMA [Ontario Medical Association] responded by warning motorists against trying to use medical problems as an excuse to dodge the breathalyser. There are almost no medical conditions that would prevent a driver from providing a sufficient sample of breath, said Dr. Ted Boadway, the OMA's director of health policy. If a driver is unable to breathe he or she has no business being behind the wheel of a car, whether drinking or not."
>
> —*Canadian Medical Association Journal*, "Don't Use Medical Excuses to Escape Breathalyzer, MDs Warned" (1997)

Older, short individuals and persons with various lung diseases may not be able to provide a suitable breath sample into screening or evidential breath alcohol instruments. Spirometric measures such as FVC or FEV_1 can indicate whether the person could physically provide a proper breath sample or not (30301–30307). One of the most common types of lung disease is chronic obstructive pulmonary disease (COPD) in which the airways are narrowed or constricted as occurs with asthma. COPD mainly causes a reduction of FEV_1. The use of an asthma inhaler will not affect the breath test if conducted a few minutes after use. Also, the use of the inhaler will not cause a "flood" of alcohol into the breath causing a false high result (30308, 30309). Local dental anesthetic may make it more difficult to obtain a proper seal and provide a suitable breath sample if it was injected within 2 hours prior to the breath sampling (30310). The use of manual sample to collect a breath sample before the minimum automatic parameters can cause the breath result to be up to 40% lower (30311). Nasal breath samples may be collected in cases of unconscious drivers in hospital (30312).

Another type of lung disease is called interstitial lung disease (ILD), which is an umbrella term for lung scarring or fibrosis resulting in lung stiffness and shortness of breath. The presence of a lung disease, however, does not explain why some individuals cannot provide a proper breath sample. It is thought to be due to poor instruction by the police as to how to provide a breath sample, which should include to inhale as deeply as possible and blow as *long* as possible (not as *hard* as possible) (30302, 30305, 30308, 30313–30314).

Reference Number: 30301

GOMM. P.J. AND C.G. BROSTER. "Study into the Ability of Healthy People of Small Stature to Satisfy the Sampling Requirements of Breath Alcohol Testing Instruments." *Medicine, Science, and the Law*, 33: 311–314, 1993 (1 table, 4 figures, 1 reference)

Abstract: A study was conducted of forty-eight healthy subjects (ages nineteen to sixty years) who were less than 5'5" in height (166 cm). The average height was 157 cm. The FEV_1, FVC, and PEFR were measured, and the subjects then provided breath samples into the Lion Intoximeter 3000 and the Alcolmeter S-L2A.

> When healthy people of small stature—less than 5'5" in height (166 cm)—with no respiratory problems are required to provide breath samples for alcohol analysis, they should be able to satisfy the requirements of the test instruments if their FEV_1 is greater than 2.3 L or their FVC is greater than 2.6 L. The results from the people who took part in this study show that for healthy people a PEFR of greater than 330 L/minute is also a likely indication of their ability to satisfy the sampling requirements. However, we have shown in the previous study that peak flow rates are not of use in patients with restrictive pulmonary diseases such a pulmonary fibrosis.

Reference Number: 30302

MILLS, R.J., W.D.S. MCLAY, AND J.D.H. BANKIER. "Breath Sampling by the Camic Breath Alcohol Analyser in the Presence of Respiratory Impairment." *Police Surgeon*, 39: 19–22, 1991 (3 tables, 3 figures, 6 references)

Abstract: Tests were conducted on seven patients with obstructive or restrictive lung diseases as to their ability to provide a proper sample into the Camic Breath Alcohol Analyser. The subject must blow continuously for at least 6 seconds. In Britain, the subject is given 3 minutes to provide a proper sample. The minimum pressure to provide a sample was determined to be 11 cm of H_2O, the flow was 10–15 L/minute, and the volume of sample was 1.1–1.5 L. Of seven patients, three were unable to provide samples: a thirty-four-year-old female with severe restriction, a fifty-seven-year-old female with severe obstruction, and a seventy-one-year-old male with gross obstruction.

Subjects with respiratory impairment of sufficient severity obstructive or restrictive, have difficulty in providing an adequate sample for the Camic device. Many subjects in these categories could comply if they were encouraged to take a maximal inspiration before blowing into the machine.

Reference Number: 30303

HURST, T.S. "Ability of Subjects with Impaired Respiratory Function to Provide a Satisfactory Breath Sample for the Alcotest 7410 Breath Alcohol Device." *Canadian Society of Forensic Science Journal*, 31: 269–274, 1998 (4 figures, 9 references)

Abstract: A study was conducted of fifty-three male and fifty female subjects (ages twenty-two to eighty-six years) who had varying degrees of respiratory impairment to determine if they could provide suitable breath samples into the Alcotest 7410. All subjects were alcohol-free. The Alcotest 7410 requires a flow of 6 L/minute (7 cm water pressure) to be maintained until 1.2 L of breath is vented. The subjects were given three attempts to provide a breath sample. All subjects with a FVC > 2 L or FEV_1 > 1.75 L could eventually provide a breath sample, except for one subject who had a medical problem that prevented them from forming an adequate seal at the mouth. No subject with a FVC < 1.25 L could provide a sample.

Several of the subjects who failed had a rapid, shallow breathing pattern which precluded them from exhaling for a long enough period to satisfy the device's requirement. It seems from our findings that persons who show evidence of an inability to form an adequate mouth seal or who have a vital capacity of less than 2 liters may have a valid reason why they cannot provide an adequate breath sample into the Alcotest 7410.

Reference Number: 30304

ODELL, M.S., C.F. MCDONALD, J. FARRAR, J.S. NATSIS, AND J.F. PRETTO. "Breath Testing in Patients with Respiratory Disability." *Journal of Clinical and Forensic Medicine*, 5: 45–48, 1998 (3 tables, 9 references)

Abstract: A study of the ability of sixty-seven subjects with known respiratory disability (i.e., $FEV_1 < 1.5$ L or FVC < 2.7 L) to provide a suitable breath sample into the Lion Alcolmeter and Drager Alcotest 7110 was conducted. The mean minimum volume of breath sample required for the Alcotest 7110 was 840 mL and five subjects could not provide the minimum volume of breath into the Alcotest 7110. These subjects had FVCs between 0.65 to 1.75 L. Forty-nine subjects (73%) were unable to provide a minimum breath sample into the Lion Alcolmeter as the mean minimum volume of sample required for this instrument was 1.55 L is nearly two times that of the Alcotest 7110.

Table. Age, Gender, FVC, and Clinical Diagnosis of Subjects Unable to Provide a Satisfactory Breath Sample into the Alcotest 7110

Age (yrs)	Gender	FVC (L)	Clinical Diagnosis
67	F	0.85	Kyphoscoliosis/Respiratory failure
59	F	1.40	Bronchiectasis
64	F	1.75	Asthma
64	F	0.65	Post-polio syndrome
82	M	1.15	Myasthenia gravis

Source: Adapted from Odell et al (1998).

These results indicate that the Drager Alcotest 7110 instrument used by the Victoria Police is able to be used at the limits of respiratory function likely to be encountered in drivers.

Reference Number: 30305

CROCKETT, A.J., M. ROZEE, R. LASLETT, AND J.H. ALPERS. "Minimum Lung Function for Breath Alcohol Testing Using the Lion Alcolmeter SD-400." *Science and Justice*, 39: 173–177, 1999 (2 tables, 1 figure, 7 references)

Abstract: One hundred and seventy-six female and 155 male subjects (median age sixty-five years) referred to a clinical respiratory function laboratory were tested to determine if proper breath samples could be provided into a Lion Alcolmeter SD- 400 after two attempts. The subjects had various respiratory diseases, including emphysema, pneumonia, and COPD. The FVC and FEV_1 were also determined. The minimum flow rate for this device was 19.6 L/minute, which was required to be maintained for at least 2 seconds until 0.7 L of breath was vented. Sixteen percent of the subjects could not provide a proper breath sample. Most of the subjects who failed were elderly women.

Table. Characteristics of Subjects Unable to Provide Proper Breath Samples into the Alcolmeter SD-400

Female:Male Ratio	6.4:1
Mean age (25%, 75% Quartiles)	72.5 yrs (64–79 yrs)
Mean FVC (25%, 75% Quartile)	1.83 L (1.55–2.27 L)
Mean FEV1 (25%, 75% Quartiles)	0.98 L (0.79–1.29 L)

Source: Adapted from Crockett et al (1999).

The ability of an individual to provide an adequate sample is influenced by both subject and operator's characteristics. The degree of co-operation, the cognitive abilities of the subject, the instructions relating to how to perform the test and type of encouragement offered during the test by the operator may all impact on the outcome.

Reference Number: 30306

HONEYBOURNE, D., A.J. MOORE, A.K. BUTTERFIELD, AND L. AZZAN. "A Study to Investigate the Ability of Subjects with Chronic Lung Diseases to Provide Evidential Breath Samples Using the Lion Intoxilyzer 6000 UK

Breath Alcohol Testing Device." *Respiratory Medicine*, 94: 684–688, 2000 (3 tables, 1 figure, 5 references)

Abstract: Ten controls, ten subjects with chronic obstructive pulmonary disease (COPD), and ten subjects with restrictive pulmonary disease (RPD) were tested on their ability to provide acceptable breath samples into the Intoxilyzer 6000 UK. The subject had to provide a minimum breath volume of 1.2 L at a flow rate of at least 12 L/minute and then meet the slope parameters. The subjects had exactly 3 minutes to provide a breath sample and then had to provide another breath sample only a few minutes later. This is the automatic UK procedure for evidential breath alcohol testing. The subject had to provide both breath samples. Subjects were tested before and after the consumption of alcohol. Alcohol was consumed within 15 minutes to obtain a BrAC of approximately 0.080 g/100 mL. Two asthmatics, four COPD subjects, and three with RPD failed to provide both breath samples. Of the nine failures, eight had a FVC > 1.5 L (range 1.64–3.03 L). Most subjects who provided proper breath samples had a FEV_1 > 1 L. The consumption of alcohol had no effect on the ability of the subjects to provide acceptable breath samples.

In conclusion, this study has shown that some subjects with lung diseases may have difficulty providing evidential breath samples using the Lion Intoxilyzer 6000 UK.

Reference Number: 30307

STEPHENS, A. AND S.D.A. FRANKLIN. "Level of Lung Function Required to use the Camic Datamaster Breath Alcohol Testing Device." *Science and Justice,* 41: 49–52, 2001 (3 figures, 8 references)

Abstract: Two hundred and fifty-nine subjects (ages six to eighty-five years) had their PEFR, FVC, and FEV_1 measured. Their ability to provide suitable breath samples into a Camic DataMaster was also determined. The DataMaster requires a minimum flow rate of 1.5 L/minute for at least 2 seconds and a minimum sample volume of 1.5 L. Nine subjects (4%) could not provide suitable breath samples.

This study has found that the best indications of an individual's ability to successfully provide a sample into a Camic Datamaster are the individual's values for FVC and FEV_1 coupled with the percentage of predicted values for such parameters. It is argued that any individual with values found within the region of the graph bounded by the FVC <1.09 L and actual FVC < 45% of predicted will be likely to have problems providing a sample.

Reference Number: 30308

HARDING, G.J. AND N.A. JARAD. "Alcohol Breath Testing: How Do Lung Diseases Interfere?" *Airways Journal*, 2: 204–207, 2004 (2 tables, 5 figures, 17 references)

Abstract: A general review was conducted on the ability of a person with lung disease to provide a proper breath sample into breath alcohol testing devices. There are seventeen references. Subjects may not be able to provide a suitable sample if their $FEV_1 < 1.0$ L, FVC < 1.2 L, they were unable to exhale for 6 seconds continuously, or they were unable to understand and follow instructions accurately.

Careful instruction at the time of testing may help prevent failures in subjects with borderline spirometry. MDIs should not affect breath alcohol testing if the inhaler is used correctly or with a spacer, and there is no evidence of any interfering effect 10 min after use. Unless exceptional circumstances exist, the main reasons for failing to provide a sample are procedural or physiological.

Reference Number: 30309

GOMM, P.J., M.D. OSSELTON, Z.C.G. BROSTER, N. MCI JOHNSON, AND K. UPTON. "The Effect of Salbutamol on Breath Alcohol Testing in Asthmatics." *Medicine Science and the Law*, 31: 226–228, 1991 (1 table, 1 figure, 2 references)

Abstract: Eight asthmatics (five male, three female) ages twenty-seven to seventy-one years and three control subjects consumed five 125 mL glasses of wine (9% v/v alcohol) over 1 hour. Thirty minutes later, BrACs were determined by an Intoximeter 3000. Simultaneous venous blood samples were collected, and BACs were determined by headspace GC. Measurements of FEV_1 and FVC were determined. The BBRs of these subjects were determined before and 5 minutes after inhaling 200 ug of salbutamol. The range of BBRs in asthmatics before salbutamol use was 2,082 to 2,773:1, and after salbutamol use, 2,174–2,900:1.

In asthmatics who were known to be capable of using the evidential breath alcohol testing devices, improvements in pulmonary function following the use of salbutamol had no effect on either breath or blood alcohol concentrations after the consumption of alcohol. It is likely that in some asthmatic subjects who are normally unable to use breath alcohol testing devices, the use of a bronchodilator inhaler will cause an improvement in respiratory capacity such that the requirements of evidential breath alcohol testing devices can be satisfied. Under such circumstances patients may have confidence that subsequent breath alcohol measurements will be reliable and not prejudiced by producing increased breath alcohol levels.

Reference Number: 30310

PEARSON, G.J. AND W.C. KEYS. "Local Dental Anaesthesia and Evidential Breath Testing: The Effect of Injection of Local Anaesthetic on Lip Seal." *Medicine Science and the Law*, 29: 298–302, 1989 (2 tables, 3 figures, 1 reference)

Abstract: Seven male and seven female subjects (ages twenty-one to sixty-four years) after providing proper samples into the Lion Intoximeter 3000, were given 1 mL of 2% lignocaine hydrochloride with 1/80,000 adrenaline (Xylocaine) injected into the apex of both the right and left side of the dental arch. This had the effect of totally anesthetizing the entire upper lip area. At 15 minute intervals for 120 minutes, the subjects attempted to provide breath samples. Ten out of fourteen (71%) were successful in providing two breath samples 15 minutes after injection. After 2 hours every subject could provide satisfactory samples.

Administration of local anaesthetic as an infiltration injection for the upper incisors results in loss of sensory and motor activity to the tissues and causes the upper lip to become flaccid. This does make the provision of a suitable sample of air more difficult than when no local anaesthetic has been given. However, over 75 percent of the subjects were able to provide two specimens of breath within one hour of local anaesthetic administration. In all cases, this was substantially before the time that the effect of the local anaesthetic had worn off.

Reference Number: 30311

BISHOP, S.C., G. JOHNSON, L. SMITH, D.D. FIORENTINO, T. GARCIA, R. GARCIA, C. BREYER, AND W.D. LOOMIS. "Manual versus Automatic Sampling Variations of a Preliminary Alcohol Screening Device." *Journal of Analytical Toxicology*, 33: 521–524, 2009 (4 tables, 1 figure, 14 references)

Abstract: Breath alcohol exhalation profiles consist of three phases—the first is airway deadspace, followed by a transitional phase, and then an alveolar phase. Six female and four male subjects (ages twenty-four to forty-one years) consumed vodka over 45 minutes. BrACs were determined with an Alco-Sensor IV Black Dot after the automatic 1.5 L of breath was exhaled (approximately 5 to 7 seconds duration) and by use of a manual collection (after 1.5 seconds exhalation). The manually collected BrACs were between 21 to 40% lower than the automatic 1.5 L collection (mean 28%).

At no instance did the manually sampled breath result produce a higher BrAC reading than the automatic breath result in any of the data sets for all 10 subjects. According to the manufacturer, because of this potential for sample variability, many agencies have chosen to disable the manual sampling function.

Reference Number: 30312

GERBERICH, S.G., B.K. GERBERICH, D. FIFE, J.J. CICERO, G.P. LILJA, AND L.C. VAN BERKOM. "Analyses of the Relationship Between Blood Alcohol and Nasal Breath Alcohol Concentrations: Implications for Assessment of Trauma Cases." *Journal of Trauma*, 29: 338–343, 1989 (3 figures, 34 references)

Abstract: The BrACs were determined both nasally and orally in thirty-five trauma patients using the Alco-Sensor III, before and after a venous blood sample was collected. Sixty-three percent of the patients were alcohol positive. The BACs ranged between 0 and 0.320 g/100 mL (mean 0.090 g/100 mL). The mean nasal and oral BrACs were 0.080 and 0.100 g/100 mL respectively. The correlation of BAC to nasal BrAC was $r = 0.99$. The correlation of BAC to oral BrAC was $r = 0.99$. Clinical assessment of alcohol compared to BAC was $r = 0.59$.

Using the study methodology, both the nasal and oral breath alcohol samples provided highly reliable estimates of venous BAC.

Reference Number: 30313

DOWLING, S., D. REYNOLDS, A. O'REILLY, G. NOLAN, C. GALLAGHER, AND D. CUSACK. "A Clinical Investigation into the Ability of Subjects with a Lung Disease to Provide Breath Specimens Using the Drager 6510." *Journal of Forensic and Legal Medicine*, 72: 6pp, 2020 (2 figures, 15 references)

The Alcotest 6510 requires the subject to provide a continuous breath specimen for at least 2 seconds at approximately 13 L/min to trigger the device and will sample the breath specimen when the flow drops to 10 L/min. A minimum volume of 1.2 L of breath is required. The mouthpiece is designed to provide minimum back pressure. The ability of nineteen controls, nineteen patients with asthma, twenty with COPD, and twenty-one with interstitial lung disease (ILD) was tested. The subjects were allowed three attempts and instructed to take a deep breath, make a seal with the lips around the mouthpiece, and blow at a steady rate until instructed to stop. Overall, 87.3% of the participants were successful at the first attempt, an additional 7.6% took two attempts, and 5.1% took three attempts. The overall failure rate was 1.3% and involved a female nonsmoker, 61.5 years of age who had a predicted FVC of 60% and with ILD.

> All patients with asthma and COPD and the vast majority with interstitial lung disease successfully provided a breath specimen using the roadside screening device. Age, gender, BMI, and PFT results of participants were not a factor in determining the success of a breath test. The presence of a lung disease did not indicate if a driver would be unable to provide a breath specimen at the roadside. The failure of the unsuccessful participant may have been due to incorrect technique and lack of understanding of what was required and not lung capacity. Further studies are needed to characterize the small minority of patients who may have difficulty providing a breath specimen. Also, all the participants were in good health and the lung disease groups were given a bronchodilator; it may be beneficial to perform the study without administering it to investigate their abilities if not taking their medication correctly.

Reference Number: 30314

SECCOMBE, L.M., P.G. ROGERS, L. BUBBLE, B. KARET, G. COSSA, M.J. PETERS, AND E.M. VEITCH. "The Impact of Severe Lung Disease on Evidential Breath Analysis Collection." *Science and Justice*, 56: 256–259, 2016 (3 tables, 1 figure, 18 references)

The Alcotest 7110 (requiring 775–925 mL of sample at 4 L/minute) had a 92% success rate for subjects providing suitable breath samples, whereas the Lion Intoximeter 6000 (requiring 1.2 L at 12 L/minute) had a success rate of only 60%. Twenty-four patients with ILD (mean age sixty-seven years) and twenty-six patients with COPD (mean age sixty-six years) were required to provide a suitable breath sample into the Lion Intoxilyzer 8000 evidential breath tester used in Australia. The subjects were given three attempts within 15 minutes to comply. The Intoxilyzer 8000 required 1 L of breath volume at 8 L/min. Altogether six subjects with ILD and two with COPD (16%) were unable to provide a suitable breath sample. The FVCs of these subjects ranged between 1.09–2.10 L (mean 1.40 L). A limitation of the police use of the instrument is that they do not request that the subject take a full inhalation.

> The higher failure rate in subjects with severe ILD as compared to COPD is likely to be a function of their pathophysiology in relation to respiratory mechanics. While patients with ILD experience external elastic loading, patients with COPD experience a loss of lung elasticity as evidenced by a reduce[d] FEV_1/FEV ratio. In ILD, decreased lung compliance results in a rapid and shallow breathing pattern to maintain adequate ventilation in the presence of increased physiological dead space. Although the ILD subject may achieve a FVC in excess of the 1 L minimum required in normal circumstances, the time required to exhale at 8 L/min against the resistance for breath analysis (about 7.5 seconds) can be a limiting factor in a severe ILD patient. In addition, deep inspiration in ILD patients results in a stretching of lung parenchyma, which often elicits a very rapid dry cough. Patients with COPD typically present with significant airway narrowing and los[s] of lung elasticity. Compared to ILD patients, this appears to allow for greater tolerance to increased expiratory resistance and particular time.

3.04 BLOOD:BREATH RATIO (BBR) AND COMPARISON OF BREATH AND BLOOD ALCOHOL CONCENTRATIONS

> "First, the data indicated that the 2.1 to 1 relationship between breath and blood as regards alcohol concentration is too low for breath testing instruments utilizing volumetric samples of deep lung breath samples obtained by forced exhalations. Instead, a 2.3 to 1 relationship is indicated."
>
> —Franklin, "A Comparison of Whole Blood:Breath Correlation With Blood Plasma:Breath Correlations for Alcohol Concentration" (1969)

> "Some of the extremely low or high values reported in the literature are unrealistic with reference to the physiochemical properties of ethanol and composition of whole blood and breath. The abnormally high or

low blood/breath ratios of alcohol often cited in court proceedings at DUI trials are probably caused by gross errors in the sampling and/or the analysis of specimens."

—Jones, "Enforcement of Drink-Driving Laws by Use of Per Se Legal Alcohol Limits: Blood and/or Breath Concentration as Evidence of Impairment" (1988)

Breath alcohol testing instruments in the United States and Canada and many other western countries are calibrated on a blood:breath ratio (BBR) of 2,100:1. If the subject's BBR is < 2,100:1 then the actual BAC would be overestimated. If the subject's BBR > 2,100:1 the BAC would be underestimated. The mean BBR in laboratory studies has been found to be approximately 2,300:1 and would underestimate the actual BAC by approximately 10%. Both laboratory (30401–30405) and field studies (30406–30411) have shown that breath instruments calibrated on 2,100:1 routinely underestimate the BAC.

Much unnecessary controversy has arisen in court regarding the BBR. BBRs < 2,100:1 are mainly due to the low BACs that were tested (30402, 30411). For example, a BAC of 0.005 g/100 mL and a BrAC of 0.009 g/100 mL would indicate an apparent BBR of 1,167:1, even though the breath alcohol is only 0.004 g/100 mL higher than the blood. Some of the low BBRs reported have been due to using a rebreathing technique, rather than using the end-expiratory technique of collecting breath samples that is commonly used in police breath alcohol testing of drinking drivers (30413).

Additionally, since low breath alcohol results occur when the subject provides shallow or inadequate breath samples (30412), the BBR distribution is skewed to the positive direction and typical Gaussian or normal distribution statistics cannot be applied and would tend to overestimate the number of low BBRs. In field use, the routine use of truncated breath results and the lowest of duplicate analysis also prevent significant overestimation (30410, 30411). In summary, the conditions in the field that cause BAC > BrAC are:

- Social drinking over several hours (no AV lag)
- Breath testing instruments in many countries (including Canada and the United States) are calibrated on the low BBR of 2,100:1 rather that the more realistic 2,300–2,400:1 found in drinking drivers.

- Uncooperative, inexperienced, or nervous subjects can provide poor breath samples, resulting in falsely low BrACs.
- Breath results are typically truncated (e.g., 0.108 g/100 mL is reported as 0.100 g/100 mL).
- The lower of duplicate breath results is generally used for court (rather than the average).
- Testing at high BACs (e.g., the average BAC of arrested drinking drivers is 0.150–0.180 g/100 mL rather than 0.009 g/100 mL).
- End-expiratory breath tests are conducted rather than rebreathing, which increased the BrAC.

Breathing technique can affect the BBR, but it is only of short duration (30413). The effect of breath temperature on the BBR is much less than usually cited (30415, 30419, 30420). Other factors such as gender (30408, 30418, 30419, 30421–30423), exercise (30417), or AV lag (30416, 30423) do not substantially affect the BBR for the testing of drinking drivers under typical field conditions. There was no difference in BBR between White, Hispanic, or African American subjects (30423).

The use of the BrAC for back calculation is as reliable as using the BAC (30426).

Reference Number: 30401

JONES, A.W. "Electrochemical Measurement of Breath-Alcohol Concentration: Precision and Accuracy in Relation to Blood Levels." *Clinica Chimica Acta*, 146: 175–183, 1985 (3 figures, 20 references)

Abstract: A study was conducted of thirty male subjects who consumed whiskey neat within 15 to 20 minutes in a fasting state. Doses of 0.54, 0.72, and 0.90 g/kg ethanol were given to 8, 6, and 16 subjects respectively. Triplicate samples of fingertip blood were taken at 30- to 60-minute intervals and analyzed by an enzymatic oxidation procedure. BrACs were measured by the electrochemical cell with an Alcolmeter. The blood/breath correlation was $r = 0.98$.

> This is supported by the present results; a blood/breath ratio of almost exactly 2,300:1 was found to give the closest estimate of blood ethanol. In practice however, the use of a lower ratio minimizes the risk of false positive estimates of blood ethanol concentration. This is particularly important when breath- alcohol determinations are used for medico-legal purposes.

Reference Number: 30402

JONES, A.W. "Enforcement of Drink-Driving Laws by Use of 'Per Se' Legal Alcohol Limits: Blood and/or Breath Concentration as Evidence of Impairment." *Alcohol, Drugs and Driving*, 4: 99–112, 1988 (4 figures, 49 references)

Abstract: A general review was conducted on blood and breath alcohol testing of drinking drivers, alcohol-related driving impairment, and legal aspects. At low BACs small variations in the measurement of alcohol will cause large variations in the BBR.

> Some of the extremely low or high values reported in the literature are unrealistic with reference to the physiochemical properties of ethanol and composition of whole blood and breath. The abnormally high or low blood/breath ratios of alcohol often cited in court proceedings at DUI trials are probably caused by gross errors in the sampling and/or the analysis of specimens.

Reference Number: 30403

WEATHERMON, A.R., J.R. MCCUTCHEON, AND J.M. COWAN. "Results of Analyses for Alcohol of Near Simultaneously Collected Venous Blood and Alveolar Breath Specimens." *Alcohol, Drugs and Driving,* 9: 19–25, 1993 (2 tables, 3 figures, 1 reference)

Abstract: Six male and four female subjects (ages twenty-five to forty-three years) consumed 0.9 g/kg ethanol over 60 minutes after a 10-hour fast. Blood and breath samples were collected simultaneously starting 30 minutes after the alcohol consumption ceased and were collected every 20 minutes on an additional three occasions. BACs were determined by headspace GC and BrACs by an Intoxilyzer 5000. A total of forty blood/breath alcohol comparisons were conducted. The BAC > BrAC in thirty-eight comparisons (95%) and the BrAC > BAC in only two occasions (once by 0.001 and the other by 0.009 g/100 mL). The time the subjects blew into the Intoxilyzer 5000 ranged from 12–30 seconds.

Table. Mean BAC, BrAC and BBR in Ten Drinking Subjects

Subject Number	Mean BAC (g/100 mL)	Mean BrAC (g/100 mL)	BBR
1	0.079	0.065	2,552
2	0.085	0.070	2,550
3	0.069	0.063	2,300
4	0.084	0.076	2,321
5	0.059	0.053	2,338
6	0.086	0.076	2,376
7	0.086	0.081	2,230
8	0.085	0.072	2,479
9	0.073	0.068	2,254
10	0.072	0.059	2,563

Source: Adapted from Weathermon et al (1993).

The results of this study indicates there is a good correlation ($r = 0.861$) between venous blood alcohol concentration and alveolar breath alcohol concentration. At a mean alveolar breath alcohol concentration (0.071 g/210 L) the breath underestimated the mean venous blood concentration (0.080 g/100 mL) by 0.010 g/210 L.

Reference Number: 30404

TAYLOR, M.D. AND B.T. HODGSON. "Blood/Breath Correlations: Intoxilyzer 5000C, Alcotest 7110 and the Breathalyzer 900A Breath Alcohol Analyzers." *Canadian Society Forensic Science Journal,* 28: 153–164, 1995 (4 tables, 6 figures, 21 references)

Abstract: A study was conducted of the correlation of the Intoxilyzer 5000C and the Alcotest 7110 compared to the Breathalyzer model 900A and compared to the BAC in twelve male and six female drinking subjects. The alcohol was consumed over 2 hours. Blood and breath samples were collected within 20 minutes of each other, and the BACs were determined by headspace GC. The BACs ranged between 0.047 and 0.167 g/100 mL. The Intoxilyzer 5000C was on average 0.004 g/100 mL lower than the Breathalyzer. The Alcotest was on average 0.003 g/100 mL higher. The correlation between BAC and BrAC was $r = 0.9497$ for the Breathalyzer, 0.9423 for the Intoxilyzer, and 0.9385 for the Alcotest. The Alcotest 7110 was the most difficult instrument to provide a proper breath sample.

Table. BACs and BrACs (Truncated BrAC) and BBR and the Effe„ct of Truncation of the BBR in Drinking Subjects with the Highest and Lowest BBR

Subject Number	BAC (g/100 mL)	BrAC (truncated) (g/100 mL)	BBR (truncated)
2	0.096	0.068 (0.060)	2,965 (3,360)
7	0.089	0.080 (0.080)	2,336 (2,336)
8	0.051	0.044 (0.040)	2,434 (2,678)
10	0.082	0.061 (0.060)	2,823 (2,870)
15	0.134	0.114 (0.110)	2,468 (2,558)
17	0.047	0.033 (0.030)	2,991 (3,290)

Source: Adapted from Taylor and Hodgson (1995).

Our results indicate the IR instruments will provide reliable estimates of the blood alcohol concentration but only if operators obtain suitable samples of breath. Notwithstanding the automation designed into these instruments, it is still essential that the operators instruct and closely monitor subjects when they are providing samples.

Reference Number: 30405

WATTERSON, J.H., AND K.N. ELLEFSEN. "Examination of Some Performance Characteristics of Breath Alcohol Measurements Obtained with the Intoxilyzer 8000C Following Social Drinking Conditions." *Journal of Analytical Toxicology*, 33: 514–520, 2009 (4 tables, 2 figures, 20 references)

Abstract: Five male and five female subjects (ages nineteen to twenty-seven years) consumed between 0.6 to 0.7 g/kg alcohol within 1 hour. The alcoholic beverages consumed included beer, rum, wine, or vodka coolers. BrACs were determined within 5 minutes of consuming alcohol with an Intoxilyzer 8000C. Blood samples were collected at least 30 minutes after drinking ceased and BACs were determined by the enzymatic method. The BrAC–BAC results ranged from −0.032 to +0.003 g/100 mL with untruncated results and from −0.032 to −0.004 g/100 mL with the truncated BrACs.

Overall, the Intoxilyzer 8000C was shown to be able to provide precision that is well within the standard limits currently adopted in Canadian jurisdictions. This precision appeared to be insensitive to breath sample volumes over the 2–3 L range in the subjects examined here based on these limits. Further, the truncated breath alcohol measurements using the Intoxilyzer 8000C reliably underestimated the venous in these samples by an average of 17.4% (12 mg/dL). Although the Invalid Sample message was valuable in some cases (5 out of 23) for indicating the presence of residual mouth alcohol, it is clear that a mandatory delay before breath testing commences should be enforced to minimize the likelihood of falsely elevated BrAC measurements.

Reference Number: 30406

HARDING, P.M., R.H. LAESSIG, AND P.H. FIELD. "Field Performance of the Intoxilyzer 5000: A Comparison of Blood- and Breath-Alcohol Results in Wisconsin Drivers." *Journal of Forensic Sciences*, 35: 1022–1028, 1990 (1 table, 3 figures, 17 references)

Abstract: A field study was conducted of 395 blood and breath samples taken within 1 hour of each other. The BrACs were determined by Intoxilyzer 5000, a three wavelength IR device. BACs were determined by direct injection GC using *n*-propanol as internal standard. The time between blood and breath sampling was 9 to 60 minutes (mean 36 minutes). The BrACs were reported to two decimal places (i.e., truncated) and BAC to three decimal places. The BrAC ranged from 0.021 g/100 mL higher to 0.074 g/100 mL lower than the corresponding BAC (mean = –0.018 g/100 mL). BrAC and BAC were considered in agreement if the results differed by less than 0.010 g/100 mL. Two-hundred and sixty-four (67%) of BrACs were lower than BAC, 123 (31%) of the results were in agreement, and eight (2%) were higher. When an allowance was made for the time interval for these eight cases, the highest overestimation of BAC by BrAC was 0.007 g/100 mL.

Table. BrAC and BAC Comparisons (Where the BrAC > BAC by More Than 0.01 g/100 mL), the Time Interval Between the Tests of Arrested Drinking Drivers, and the BAC Corrected for the Time Interval Using 0.019 g/100 mL/h Elimination Rate

BrAC (g/100 mL)	BAC (g/100 mL)	Time Difference (minutes)	Adjusted BAC (g/100 mL)
0.28	0.262	58	0.280
0.15	0.129	53	0.146
0.31	0.298	31	0.308

BrAC (g/100 mL)	BAC (g/100 mL)	Time Difference (minutes)	Adjusted BAC (g/100 mL)
0.21	0.198	41	0.211
0.19	0.169	50	0.186
0.16	0.149	58	0.167
0.15	0.133	48	0.148
0.10	0.082	34	0.093

Source: Adapted from Harding et al (1990).

No evidence was found of falsely elevated BrAC results that could be attributed to unusually low individual blood to breath alcohol ratios, endogenous or exogenous interfering compounds in the breath, residual mouth alcohol or electromagnetic interference. Overestimation of the BAC by the Intoxilyzer 5000 was infrequent and of small magnitude. Indeed, most of the differences shown in Table 1 could be eliminated if the amount of alcohol theoretically eliminated in the time lapse between breath and blood specimen collection were added to the BAC.

Reference Number: 30407

STERN, E.L., MOONEY, R., E. UKESTAD, AND S. JEJURIKAR. "Field Study Comparison of Intoxilyzer 5000 Breath Alcohol Tests with GLC and Urine Alcohol Tests." *Proceedings 11th International Conference on Alcohol Drugs Traffic Safety, National Safety Council, Chicago*, 250–259, 1990 (6 tables, 4 figures)

Abstract: A field study was conducted of 327 drivers in which both blood and breath samples were collected and 279 drivers in which urine and breath samples were collected between 1987 to 1988 in the state of Minnesota. Duplicate breath tests were conducted by an Intoxilyzer 5000. Physiologically the highest BrAC should give the most accurate result, but in Minnesota as well as many other jurisdictions, the lowest truncated BrAC is reported. BACs and UACs were analyzed by headspace GC. For the blood tests, 287 drivers had blood drawn after the breath tests with an average time interval of 34 minutes and a maximum of 2 hours, and twelve subjects had blood drawn prior to the breath test. Of the 327 blood-breath alcohol pairs, only one had a BAC of less than 0.100 g/100 mL when both BrACs > 0.100 g/100 mL. In this subject, the BAC was 0.072 g/100 mL 1 hour and 45 minutes after the two BrACs of

0.107 and 0.113 g/100 mL respectively. When the lowest truncated BrAC is used and adjusted for elimination (0.019 g/100 mL/h) the apparent BrAC would be 0.067 g/100 mL compared to a BAC of 0.72 g/100 mL.

> These data suggest that if a subject has a complete breath test yielding a 0.1 or greater, there is little likelihood that a subsequent blood test will yield a result less than 0.1.

Reference Number: 30408

JONES, A.W. AND L. ANDERSSON. "Variability of the Blood/Breath Alcohol Ratio in Drinking Drivers." *Journal of Forensic Sciences*, 41: 916–921, 1996 (5 tables, 4 figures, 20 references)

Abstract: A study was conducted of the BAC and Intoxilyzer 5000S results of 793 arrested drivers between 1992 and 1994 in Sweden. The BACs were determined in triplicate by headspace GC and the results were converted from wt/wt to wt/vol. Blood was collected within 1 hour of the breath test and the results were adjusted using an elimination rate of 0.019 g/100 mL/h. The BBRs for male and female drivers were not statistically different. Only thirty-four drivers (4.3%) had a BBR of less than 2,100:1. The mean BBR in forty-six samples in which the blood was collected within 15 minutes of breath was 2,337:1 (range 1,971–2,703:1).

> This creates a dilemma for those close to a critical legal limit because of the roughly 10% advantage obtained by those who were tested on a breath alcohol analyzer, compared with analysis of venous blood. The consequences for the individual might be guilty or not guilty depending on whether a breath- alcohol or blood- alcohol test was used for forensic purposes.

Reference Number: 30409

CURRIER, G.W., A.J. TRENTON, AND P.G. WALSH. "Relative Accuracy of Breath and Serum Alcohol Readings in the Psychiatric Emergency Service." *Psychiatric Services*, 57: 34–36, 2006 (1 figure, 10 references)

Abstract: The SACs and BrACs of thirty-two patients admitted to a psychiatric ER during 2003 were determined. BrACs were measured with an Alco-Sensor III and SACs by an enzymatic method. The difference in the time of the collection of the two samples ranged from

0.23 to 4.8 hours. An alcohol elimination rate of 0.018 g/100 mL/h was employed to correct for the time differences. The BrACs ranged from 0.020 to 0.210 g/100 mL (mean 0.150 g/100 mL). The SACs ranged from 0.060 to 0.320 g/100 mL (mean 0.230 g/100 mL). In only one case was the BrAC > SAC (by approximately 0.010 g/100 mL). The relative accuracy of BrAC decreased with increasing SAC.

Although a low false-positive rate makes the breath test acceptable for legal purposes, the blood alcohol level is more appropriate for clinical use in emergency settings because breath tests can underestimate the level of toxicity.

Reference Number: 30410

STOWELL, A.R., A.R. GAINSFORD, AND R.G. GULLBERG. "New Zealand's Breath and Blood Alcohol Testing Programs: Further Data Analysis and Forensic Implications." *Forensic Science International*, 178:83–92, 2008 (3 Tables, 10 Figures, 22 References)

Abstract: BACs and BrACs were determined in 11,837 drivers arrested by police in New Zealand between 2000 and 2007. The mean delay between breath and blood sampling was 0.73 hours (range 0.17 to 3.18 hours). The evidential breath instruments used in this study were the Intoxilyzer 5000, Seres 679T, or Seres 679EN2 Ethylometre. No alcohol standard tests were conducted in the field with these instruments, only the internal electronic tests. The BBR distribution was not normal or Gaussian and had a high skewness or kurtosis. The mean BrAC > BAC in 31% of the cases, but when adjusted for alcohol elimination it was reduced to 2.8%. Harmful false positives in which the BrAC > 0.100 g/100 mL and the BAC < 0.100 g/100 mL occurred in 0.14% of cases and was reduced to 0.04% when the lowest truncated BrAC was employed. The apparent BBR for the Intoxilyzer 5000 was 2,407:1.

Table. Harmful False Positive Cases (BAC < 0.100 g/100 mL, BrAC (Intoxilyzer 5000) > 0.100 g/100 mL) of Arrested Drinking Drivers Including the Time Interval Between Tests and the BAC Adjusted for the Elimination of Alcohol (0.019 g/100 mL/h)

BrAC1 (g/100 mL)	BrAC2 (g/100 mL)	BAC (g/100 mL)	Time Difference (minutes)	Adjusted BAC (g/100 mL)
0.103	0.099	0.086	43	0.100
0.104	0.100	0.090	31	0.100
0.104	0.100	0.088	26	0.096
0.101	0.101	0.078	59	0.097
0.102	0.102	0.084	45	0.098

Source: Adapted from Stowell et al (2008).

Many jurisdictions, including New Zealand, report the lower of the two BrAC results for legal purposes. For these jurisdictions, the more relevant false positive rate would be one based on the lower BrAC result. When using the lower BrAC result along with the time adjusted (0.019 g/dL/h) mean BAC results, the overall false positive percentage was 1.8% compared with 2.8% when using the mean BrAC result. In addition, the harmful false positive percentage (assuming the 0.100 g/dL critical level) dropped to 0.04% compared to 0.14% when using the mean BrAC result. This has important forensic implications for those jurisdictions reporting the lower BrAC result as a legal surrogate for the BAC measurement and demonstrates the additional benefit afforded the defendant.

Reference Number: 30411

WIGMORE, J.G., M.J. WARD, AND J. WELLS. "Assessing Breath Test Estimation of Blood Alcohol Concentration [Letter]." *Journal of Analytical Toxicology*, 13: 244–245, 1989 (1 figure, 7 references)

Abstract: The distribution of blood:breath alcohol ratios using the Cobb and Dabb (1985) London study of drinking drivers is described. The BBRs show a positively skewed normal curve, and so using typical standard deviations the number of BBRs < 2,100:1 would be overestimated. Truncation of breath test results increased the mean BBR from 2,340:1 to 2,450:1 and increased the number of underestimations of BAC.

Lastly, the study of Alobaidi, Hill and Payne cited by Simpson, illustrates the large variability than can occur in blood/breath alcohol ratios when low BACs are used. For example, in Table 3 of that study, a blood/breath alcohol ratio of 1123:1 is obtained at a BAC of 0.0093 g% and a converted breath alcohol result of 0.0174 g%. There is only one result where the BAC is in excess of 0.080 g% and that is for a BAC of 0.0817 g% and a breath alcohol concentration of 0.0868 g% resulting in a blood/breath alcohol ratio of 1980:1. If the breath result is reported to two significant figures, it becomes 0.08% and does not overestimate the BAC.

Reference Number: 30412

GULLBERG, R.G. "Statistical Evaluation and Reporting of Blood Alcohol/Breath Ratio Distribution Data." *Journal of Analytical Toxicology*, 15: 343–344, 1991 (1 figure, 11 references)

Abstract: A statistical analysis of 111 apparent BBRs was conducted. The ratios were determined by comparing truncated BrACs to truncated BACs and truncating the resultant BBR. A Gaussian distribution using ±2 SD should only be used if the skewness of the distribution is less than or equal to 1. In this data the skewness is 1.03; when the data are transformed into natural log, the skewness becomes 0.55. The original 95% confidence interval of the BBR is from 1,837 to 2,981; after transformation into natural log, the 95% confidence interval is from 2,287 to 2,395:1.

A close look at many of the BAC/BrAC distributions reveal a significant positive skewness, More meaningful assessment would be possible if investigators would report the skewness value along with the mean and SD for such data. With highly skewed data, the mean is no longer a good index of central tendency. The distributional properties are actually a combination of biological and analytical factors. However, the positive skewness is most likely due to the tendency to obtain low BrAC values from inadequate or shallow breath samples.

Reference Number: 30413

JONES, A.W. "How Breathing Technique Can Influence the Results of Breath Alcohol Analysis." *Medicine Science and the Law*, 22: 275–280, 1982 (1 table, 18 references)

Abstract: Eight male subjects (ages twenty to twenty-eight years) consumed either beer or whiskey to obtain a BAC of approximately 0.100 g/100 mL. Testing commenced 1 hour after drinking ceased and after three consecutive breath tests taken 15 minutes apart showed a decrease in BrAC. BrACs were determined by a GC Intoximeter Mk II. The temperature and volume of breath exhaled were also measured. The breathing techniques and the change in BrAC were as follows: deep inspiration (insp), slow expiration (exp) (2%); deep exp without insp (0.3%); nose insp, breath holding 30 seconds (12.6%); normal insp breath holding 30 seconds (15.7%); hyperventilation for 20 seconds (–10.6%); nose exp before deep insp (1.4%); and mouth closed for 5 minutes before nose insp (7.7%).

The other techniques of breathing gave results that were not significantly different from control breaths. And even with breathing techniques that did bring about a change, the recovery to control values occurred almost immediately subjects began breathing normally again.

Reference Number: 30414

JONES, A.W. "Role of Rebreathing in Determination of the Blood-Breath Ratio of Expired Ethanol." *Journal of Applied Physiology*, 55: 1237–1241, 1983. (3 tables, 2 figures, 23 references)

Abstract: Twenty-three male subjects drank beer or whiskey to obtain a BAC of about 0.150 g/100 mL. One hour from the end of drinking blood samples were taken. Breath alcohol was measured by a GC Intoximeter Mk. II. Breath temperature and breath volume were measured. Rebreathed air was collected in 4 L Saran bags heated to 40°C. The subjects inhaled and exhaled the same air five times with the nose clamped. The mean blood/breath ratio was 2,225 SD = 111 for end expiratory air and 1,947 SD = 110 for rebreathed air. The expiratory air temperature was always higher after rebreathing than for single exhalation (35.21°C, SD = 0.4 versus 34.45°C, SD = 0.44). Rebreathing five times increased the ethanol concentration in breath 10%, but after three normal breaths of room air the ethanol concentration decreased to end expiratory concentrations. Holding the breath for 30 seconds increased the breath ethanol concentration by 10%.

It becomes clear that blood-breath ratio of ethanol is a meaningless concept unless specified in terms of a particular breath sampling procedure.

Reference Number: 30415

JONES, A.W. "Effects of Temperature and Humidity of Inhaled Air on the Concentration of Ethanol in a Man's Exhaled Breath." *Clinical Science,* 63: 441–445, 1982 (1 table, 19 references)

Abstract: Ten male subjects (ages twenty to twenty-nine years) consumed whiskey to obtain a peak BAC of approximately 0.100 g/100 mL. One hour later and when three successive breath tests taken 15 minutes apart showed a decrease in BrAC after inhaling ordinary room air (23°C, 55% relative humidity (RH)); cold, dry air (5°C, 0%RH); cold moist air (5°C, 100% RH); hot, dry air (80°C, 0% RH); and hot moist air (80°C, 100% RH), subjects provided breath samples into a GC Intoximeter Mk II. The temperature of the expired air was also determined.

Table. Change in BrAC with Change in Breath Temperature in Drinking Subjects and Compared with Theoretical 6.5%/°C

Condition of inhaled air	Mean initial breath temp. (°C)	Mean breath temp. after inhalation (°C)	Change in breath temp. (°C)	Expected change in BrAC using 6.5%/°C (%)	Observed change in BrAC (%)
Cold, dry air	34.6	33.2	–1.4	-9.1	-9.6
Hot, dry air	34.6	34.6	0.0	0.0	-4.3
Cold, wet air	34.5	33.4	–1.1	-7.2	-6.4
Hot, wet air	34.3	36.1	+1.8	+11.7	-10.3

Source: Adapted from Jones (1982).

The end-expired temperature rose to 36.1°C average almost 2°C above control tests when subjects breathed hot wet air. Yet the concentration of ethanol in end-expired air dropped by about 10%. A possible explanation for this finding is that small water droplets present in an aqueous aerosol in hot, wet air are deposited on the first part of the airway and act as an absorption sink for expired alcohol. Based on the rise in expired temperature, expired ethanol should have increased by 11.7%.

Reference Number: 30416

JONES, A.W. "Relationship Between Blood and Breath Alcohol Concentration in a Subject Absorbing Alcohol at the Time of Testing [Letter]." *Journal of Analytical Toxicology*, 15: 44–45, 1991 (1 figure, 12 references)

Abstract: A case report of a subject who consumed beer and whiskey over a period of 3 hours and 20 minutes is presented. The total dose was 1.56 g/kg and the maximum BAC obtained was approximately 0.180 g/100 mL. Venous blood samples were collected on seven occasions throughout the drinking and the BAC was determined by headspace GC. BrACs were determined by an Intoximeter 3000, 10 minutes after each drink was finished and after the mouth was rinsed with warm water. The BAC increased at an average rate of 0.052 g/100 mL/h. The apparent blood/breath ratio was almost exactly 2,100:1 at the first and sixth sampling times and 2,300–2,400:1 at the other sampling times.

Obviously, the results from a single subject cannot be extrapolated to the population of drinking drivers. However, the experimental design described here is suitable to determine blood-breath ratios of ethanol during a drinking spree. This empirical approach will help resolve the issue of whether breath tests underestimate or overestimate the venous BAC during the absorptive state. Hopefully, this will put a stop to wild speculation on this subject.

Reference Number: 30417

HIGASHIKAWA, Y. AND S. SUZUKI. "Effect of Exercise After Drinking on Breath Alcohol Concentrations." *Japanese Journal of Forensic Toxicology*, 22: 205–208, 2004 (2 tables, 3 figures, 10 references)

Abstract: Ten male and two female subjects (ages twenty-three to fifty years) consumed, on two occasions, 700 mL beer (with a snack) within 15 minutes after an overnight fast. BrACs were measured with a BRAC DPA-5 analyzer. The subjects either rested or did a 1-minute stair exercise. BrACs were measured after exercise. Five Widmark parameters including Co, B, t (c = 0) were measured. The rates of alcohol elimination ranged from 0.009 to 0.015 g/100 mL/h (resting) and 0.010 to 0.014 g/100 mL/h (exercise).

As results, for all parameters tested statistically significant differences could not be found between the two groups with and without exercise. Therefore, we can conclude that the physical exercise does not increase breath alcohol levels; the claim made by a driver that a high breath alcohol level over 0.15 mg/ml is due to its temporary increase caused by physical exercise should be denied.

Reference Number: 30418

COWAN, J.M., W.E. VAN TASSEL, AND M.E. DENNIS III. "Is There a Gender Factor? A Comparison of Blood:Breath Differences and Ratios Between Men and Women." *Proceedings of the 17th International Conference on Alcohol, Drugs and Traffic Safety*, August 8–13, 2004, Glasgow, Scotland, Oliver, J., Williams, P., and Clayton, P. (eds), CD, 5pp (1 table, 5 figures, 14 references)

Abstract: The BrACs and BACs of twenty-eight female and 105 male subjects were determined nearly simultaneously approximately 45 to 75 minutes after the end of drinking. The study was conducted over a period of 13 years. BrACs were determined by four different models of Intoxilyzer 5000 and model 8000. BACs were determined by GC. The BBR for female subjects ranged between 2,198 and 2,520:1. The BBR for male subjects ranged from 2,235 to 2,596:1. All BrACs < BACs. There was no effect of differences in hematocrit between male and female subjects on the BBR, even though it has been alleged that the differences in hematocrit between men and women would affect the BBR.

The differences between BAC and BrAC and the blood:breath ratio for blood and breath samples taken nearly simultaneously are the same for men and women. Women do not produce disproportional higher breath alcohol concentration test results compared to men. There is no gender factor related to breath alcohol testing.

Reference Number: 30419

COWAN, J.M., J.M. BURIS, J.R. HUGHES, AND M.P. CUNNINGHAM. "The Relationship of Normal Body Temperature, End-Expired Breath Temperature, and the BAC/BrAC Ratio in 98 Physically Fit Human Test Subjects." *Journal of Analytical Toxicology*, 34: 238–242, 2010 (3 tables, 5 figures, 13 references)

Abstract: Fourteen female and eighty-four male subjects (ages twenty-one to fifty-one years) consumed alcohol (whiskey mixed with a carbonated beverage) over 45 minutes and between 45 and 75 minutes later had their BrACs and end-expired breath temperature measured with an Intoxilyzer 8000. Blood samples were collected as well, and BACs were determined in duplicate by headspace GC. In addition, oral, tympanic, and temporal temperature were also measured. The mean BBRs were 2,379 for male subjects (range 2,125–2,765) and 2,385 for female subjects (range 2,258–2,535) and were not significantly different. The BAC/BrAC correlation was $r = 0.938$. The mean end-expired breath temperature was 34.5°C (range 33.3–35.5°C) for male subjects and 34.6°C (range 33.8–35.3°C) for female subjects. The mean oral temperature was 36.6°C (range 35.8–37.2°C) for male subjects and 36.9°C (range 35.9–37.3°C) for female subjects. The correlation between body versus expired breath temperature was $r = 0.431$ for male subjects and $r = 0.582$ for female subjects. The subject with the lowest body temperature (36.0°C) did not have the lowest breath temperature but did have the highest BBR (2,765).

> For the physically fit subjects studied, their BrAC results were consistently lower than their BAC results, and these results were very well-correlated. However, neither normal body temperature nor end-expired breath temperature was strongly associated with BAC/BrAC ratios.

Reference Number: 30420

WIGMORE, J.G. "Up to Their Necks in Hot Water: Body Temperature and the BAC/BrAC Ratio [Letter]." *Journal of Analytical Toxicology*, 34: 605–606, 2010 (14 references)

Abstract: A letter to the editor regarding the effects of elevated body temperature on the BAC/BrAC ratio was published. The Fox and Hayward study (*Journal of Forensic Sciences*, 34: 836–841, 1989) showing a 8.62% increase in BrAC for every 1°C increase in body temperature is problematic due to the artificial method of increasing body temperature by immersing nine male subjects up to their necks in stirred water heated up to 42°C. Hydrostatic pressure by immersion in water causes a shifting of the blood from the extremities to the central regions (including the lungs), an increase in intrapulmonary pressure, a decrease in vital capacity and residual volume, and an increase in the closing volume of the lung.

> Extensive field studies of drinking drivers in police custody have shown that overestimation of the BAC by BrAC is infrequent and of small magnitude. This indicates that, in actual drinking drivers, the effect of elevated body temperature is not a significant issue. Either few drinking drivers have an elevated body temperature when tested by the police, or its effect on BrAC is not as great in vivo as shown in vitro, or a combination of both.

Reference Number: 30421

KORKOSH, S.L., J.A. HACKETT, AND J.C. MONTPETIT. "Blood Alcohol and Breath Alcohol Comparisons Using the Intox EC/IR II." *Canadian Society of Forensic Science Journal,* 45: 195–200, 2012 (2 tables, 13 references)

Sixteen male and eleven female subjects consumed alcohol at RCMP-sponsored qualified technician training courses in Halifax, Vancouver (HV), and Winnipeg (W) and obtained BACs of between 0.031 to 0.153 g/100 mL. Blood samples were collected within 4 minutes after the breath tests and analyzed by headspace GC. BrACs were determined using an Intoximeter EC/IR II. The blood and breath samples were collected at least 30 minutes after drinking ceased. The instrumental criteria for the acceptance of a breath sample as determined by the RCMP National Forensic Service is that a minimum flow rate of 12 L/minute and a minimum volume of 1.5 L must be provided, followed by a drop in flow rate of 5% from the maximum flow rate. The mean BBR using all the data with a truncated BrAC result was 2,675:1 and ranged between 2,170:1 and 3,360:1. The mean BBR for female subjects was 2,658:1 compared to 2,688:1 for male subjects. The percentage underestimation of BAC by the Intox EC/IR II ranged from 15 to 28% in subjects with a BAC of 0.080 g/100 mL or more. There were no overestimations of BAC. The mean BBR increased in twelve subjects from 2,411:1 for untruncated BrACs to 2,566:1 for truncated results.

Table. Truncated BrAC, BAC, and BBR for Subjects with a BAC of 0.08 g/100 mL or Greater

Subject no. and Location	Gender	Truncated BrAC (g/100 mL)	BAC (g/100 mL)	Blood:breath alcohol ratio (BBR)
3HV	M	0.090	0.107	2,497:1
6HV	M	0.120	0.134	2,345:1
7HV	F	0.110	0.134	2,558:1
8HV	F	0.130	0.153	2,472:1
9HV	M	0.110	0.142	2,711:1
10HV	F	0.080	0.096	2,520:1
11HV	F	0.070	0.084	2,520:1
12HV	M	0.060	0.083	2,905:1
1W	M	0.080	0.101	2,651:1
3W	M	0.050	0.080	3,360:1
4W	M	0.070	0.094	2,820:1

Subject no. and Location	Gender	Truncated BrAC (g/100 mL)	BAC (g/100 mL)	Blood:breath alcohol ratio (BBR)
5W	M	0.100	0.133	2,793:1
6W	M	0.090	0.123	2,870:1
7W	M	0.080	0.100	2,625:1
8W	F	0.070	0.091	2,730:1
9W	F	0.060	0.087	3,045:1
10W	F	0.090	0.107	2,497:1
12W	F	0.120	0.146	2,555:1
13W	F	0.100	0.135	2,835:1
14W	M	0.100	0.119	2,499:1
15W	M	0.080	0.107	2,809:1

Source: Adapted from Korkosh, Hackett, and Monpetit (2012).

In conclusion, breath analysis using the Intox EC/IR II underestimates the BAC like other approved instruments used in Canada.

Reference Number: 30422

JAFFE, D.H., M. SIMAN-TOV, A. GOPHER, AND K. PERLEG. "Variability in the Blood/Breath Alcohol Ratio and Implications for Evidentiary Purposes." *Journal of Forensic Sciences,* 58: 1233–1237, 2013 (2 figures, 1 table, 22 references)

Abstract: Two hundred and fifty-two blood/breath alcohol comparisons were determined in thirty-three male and twenty-eight female subjects (ages twenty-one to thirty-seven years) who consumed 0.89 to 1.02 g/kg alcohol within 15 minutes. This type of rapid drinking does not usually occur in drinking drivers and would be expected to increase the arterio-venous differences in BAC and BrAC and lower the apparent BBR. Blood and breath samples were collected at baseline and 29, 40, and 58 minutes after drinking ceased. BACs were measured by headspace GC and BrACs were measured with an Alcotest 7110 MK III IL. Two breath tests were conducted 6 to 9 minutes apart and had to be within 10% of each other. Blood and breath samples were collected within 1 minute of each other. Overall, the correlation coefficient between BAC and BrAC was $r = 0.984$. No gender differences in BBR were observed. Environmental conditions such as temperature or humidity did not affect the BBR.

Table. Mean Blood Breath Ratio (BBR) and Percent of BBRs< 2,100 at 29, 40, and 58 Minutes After Drinking Ceased

Time Since End of Drinking (minutes)	Mean BBR	Percent BBRs < 2,100
29	2,164	33%
40	2,291	15%
58	2,345	12%

Source: Adapted from Jaffe et al (2018).

This study confirmed a high degree of correlation between BAC and BrAC as measured using the Draeger 7110 MKIII IL breath analyzer. We show that even after adjustment for various stages of alcohol absorption, variability between subjects of the BAC/BrAC ratio is relatively small and decreases with time from alcohol consumption. These results reinforce the utility of the Draeger 7110 MKIII IL breath analyzer for evidentiary purposes.

Reference Number: 30423

JONES, A.W. AND J.M. COWAN. "Reflections on Variability in the Blood-Breath Ratio of Ethanol and Its Importance When Evidential Breath-Alcohol Instruments Are Used in Law Enforcement." *Forensic Science Research*, 9pp, 2020 (3 tables, 4 figures, 44 references)

Abstract: Eighty-five men and fifteen women (mean age twenty-nine years) consumed a mixed alcoholic beverage (50.5% v/v liquor mixed with a carbonated drink) and obtained a mean maximum BAC of 0.097 g/100 mL. Between 45–75 minutes after the end of drinking, two consecutive breath samples were analyzed by an Intoxilyzer 8000 and the mean BrAC was compared with venous blood BAC. The BAC was measured by headspace GC. Body and end expiratory breath temperatures were measured as well. The mean breath temperature was 34.5°C (range 33.3–35.6°C) and the mean body temperature was 36.7°C (range 35.8–37.3°C). The mean BBR was 2,382 (range 2,125–2,765) and the Pearson regression coefficient of BAC and BrAC was $r = 0.948$. The mean BBR for females was 2,396 compared to 2,380 for males (not statistically significant). The mean BBR was 2,398 for Caucasians, 2,364 for Hispanics, and 2,344 for African Americans (not statistically significant). BBR was positively associated with BAC ($r = 0.298$) and negatively associated with breath temperature ($r = -0.423$) and body temperature ($r = -0.324$). The longer the subject blew into the Intoxilyzer 8000, the lower the BBR.

> BBRs determined in controlled laboratory studies are not necessarily the same as in apprehended drivers for several reasons. Many evidential breath alcohol testing protocols mandate that the subject makes a continuous exhalation into the instrument for a minimum time of 6 s. Volunteers participating in laboratory studies are more willing to provide a representative specimen of end-exhaled breath, whereas the apprehended drivers tend to provide the minimum possible volume of breath to complete the analysis. Furthermore, the BAC reached in laboratory studies ranges from 0.05 to 0.15 g/100 mL whereas the apprehended drivers in most countries have a mean BAC of 0.15–0.18 g/100 mL.

Reference Number: 30424

JONES, A.W. "Evidential Breath Alcohol Analysis and the Venous Blood-to-Breath Ratio [Letter]." *Forensic Science International* 2016 (15 references)

Abstract: A detailed letter to the editor was published in regard to the low BBRs obtained by the Hartung et al 2015 study (*Forensic Science International*, 258: 64–67, 2015)

> In conclusion, there are many aspects of the Hartung et al article that are deficient and require clarification. Their suggestion to abandon the use of evidential breath alcohol testing in Germany above a BAC of 0.50 g/kg is not supported by the facts. Both the BAC and BrAC are objective tests to verify overconsumption of alcohol by drivers. These scientific tests are far superior to making a clinical examination of offenders, in my opinion, forensic practitioners in Germany should re-think the official procedure used for blood-alcohol analysis and instead of analyzing serum and estimating BAC they should analyse ethanol in whole blood directly and stop using a variable conversion factor of 1.263:1.

Reference Number: 30425

DRUMMOND-LAGE, A.P., R.G. DE FREITA, G. CRUZ, L. PERILLO, M.A. PAIVA, AND A.J.A. WAINSTEIN. "Correlation Between Blood Alcohol Concentration (BAC) Breath Alcohol Concentration (BrAC) and Psychomotor Evaluation in a Clinical Monitored Study of Alcohol Intake in Brazil." *Alcohol*, 66: 15–20, 2018 (6 tables, 1 figure, 26 references)

Abstract: Ten female and five male subjects (mean age 23.9 years) consumed vodka (40% v/v alcohol) at a dose of 0.5 g/kg within 10 minutes.

Breath and blood samples were collected at 30, 60, 90, 120, 150, 180, 210, 240, and 270 minutes and were analyzed for alcohol by an Alco-Sensor III and headspace GC respectively. Psychomotor tests were conducted throughout by non-medical transit authority trained personnel and a legal medical doctor. The mean peak BrAC occurred at 30 minutes (0.26 mg/L) compared to 60 minutes for blood (48 mg/100 mL).

> The results of this monitored study of alcohol intake indicate a correlation between the BAC and BrAC during the post-absorption phase of ethanol pharmacokinetics and we observed a conversion factor comparable to that in the literature. The evaluations of psychomotor changes performed by the medical authority (M) were superior to those performed by the transit authority (NM). However, at the concentrations of alcohol reached in this study, i.e., below the limit considered to be a criminal infraction, the evaluations of psychomotor alterations were ineffective in terms of detection of drunkenness compared with the BAC and BrAC results, regardless of the identity of the examiner.

Reference Number: 30426

JURIC, A., A. FIJACKO, L. BAKULIC, T. ORESIC, AND I. GMAJNICKI. "Evaluation of Breath Alcohol Analysers by Comparison of Breath and Blood Alcohol Concentrations." *Arhj Hig Rada Toksikol*, 69: 69–76, 2018 (4 tables, 4 figures, 32 references)

Abstract: A comparison was conducted of 714 drinking drivers in 2011 between the BrACs as determined by an Alcotest 7410 and BACs measured by headspace GC. Blood was obtained 0–303 minutes after breath and BACs were corrected using an elimination rate of 0.015 g/100 mL/h. The UAC from the drivers was compared to the BAC to confirm the drivers were in the post-absorptive phase. In addition, a drinking experiment was conducted with twenty-one men and forty-one women (ages twenty-six to sixty-one years) comparing the BrACs (Alcotest 6810) and BACs (headspace GC). The BACs ranged from 0.007 to 0.206 g/100 mL. Blood and breath samples were collected within 3 to 4 minutes of each other.

> We have shown a high correlation between BrAC and BAC in both parts of the study. These results allow us to conclude that breathalysers are as reliable for back-calculation as are the BAC obtained by the FID-HS method when there is available only one sample of blood and data about the time,

type and volume of consumed alcoholic beverage available. The advantage of measurement with the Drager Alcotest 7410 plus and 6810 is that this is a quick, accurate, and non-invasive method. Its disadvantage is that unlike with blood samples, the measurement cannot be repeated. As long as the police follow manufacturer's instructions (take measurements at least 15 minutes after alcohol consumption), the measurement error is minimal.

3.05 MOUTH ALCOHOL

"Much caution is necessary however in applying this test. It must not be tried during at least the first quarter hour after a dose has been taken."

—Anstie, "Prognosis and Treatment of Certain Acute Diseases with Special References to the Indications Afforded by the Graphic Study of the Pulse" (1867)

"A so-called deprivation period of at least 15 minutes after the end of alcohol ingestion, or from the time of first observation of a tested subject, prior to breath alcohol analysis has been universally employed in all forensic and well-controlled experimental applications of breath alcohol analysis. Nevertheless, articles in the scientific literature periodically rediscover mouth alcohol interference with breath analysis and claim that such effects are of long duration and substantial magnitude. Thus, Spector reported breath alcohol experiments (apparently with only 2 subjects) and concluded that determinations of the concentration of ethanol in so-called alveolar gas are highly inaccurate for at least the first 20 minutes after exposure to ethanol and that further, rinsing the mouth with water does not eliminate these false readings."

—Dubowski, "Studies in Breath Alcohol Analysis: Biological Factors" (1975)

Safeguards against the mouth alcohol effect include deprivation periods, duplicate breath testing, and mouth alcohol detectors (slope and CO_2). The duration and magnitude of the mouth alcohol effect is reduced when the alcohol content of the last drink is low (e.g., beer, which is 5% v/v alcohol) (30501, 30503), when the drink is swallowed (30502), when the person has a pre-existing BAC (30504), and when the person is chewing gum (30505). A realistic laboratory experiment in which alcohol-free subjects swallowed beer showed a mean BrAC increase of only 0.005 g/100 mL after 5 minutes and 0 after 10 minutes (30503). In summary:

- Swallowing rather than rinsing (or gargling) the mouth with an alcohol-containing solution or beverage will reduce the mouth alcohol effect.
- Alcoholic beverages of a lower alcohol concentration (e.g., beer (5% v/v alcohol) or stomach contents (usually < 2% v/v) have a greatly reduced mouth alcohol effect than higher concentration of spirits or mouthwash (20%–40% v/v alcohol).
- Talking and having the mouth open will cause greater evaporation and decrease the mouth alcohol effect.
- Multiple (duplicate or more) breath samples will reduce the mouth alcohol effect.
- Gum, chewing tobacco, or food in the mouth will cause a lesser mouth alcohol effect (due to the increase in salivary flow rate).
- A pre-existing BAC will shorten the bias time of the mouth alcohol effect.
- Aerosol sprays have a lesser mouth alcohol effect than liquids.
- Acidic gastric contents from GERD in the oral cavity cause hypersalivation ("waterbrash"), which reduces the mouth alcohol effect.

A field study of testing arrested drivers at the roadside without a deprivation period using a screener without a mouth alcohol detector showed that under these extreme conditions, a potential mouth alcohol effect occurred in only 0.2% of the drivers (30506). An invalid sample was found in 2% of the drivers tested by the police with an Intoxilyzer 5000, but it was determined that this was due to varying breath sampling (e.g., "suck and blow") and not a prolonged mouth alcohol effect (30507).

Duplicate or multiple breath samples also decrease the mouth alcohol effect, and proper duplicate breath results protects against the mouth alcohol effect in the field (30519, 30520).

Nasal decongestant sprays, asthma inhalers, food and soda, energy drinks, and breath freshener strips may contain small amounts of alcohol and produce a slight mouth alcohol effect but only for a few minutes' duration (30508–30512). Blood in the mouth (30513), GERD or hiatus hernias (30514, 30515, 30518, 30528), dentures (30516), Invisalign (30527) or tongue piercings (30517), chewing gum (30522), snuff or chewing tobacco (30521), homeopathic mother tinctures (30523), and chocolate-covered liquors (30529) do not cause a significant increase in the duration or magnitude of the mouth alcohol effect.

E-liquids used in e-cigarettes may contain up to 16% v/v alcohol (30524), but the mouth alcohol effect after vaping these liquids disappears within 3 minutes (30525).

The detection of water vapor before alcohol in breath samples may be another type of mouth alcohol detection system (30526).

Reference Number: 30501

CADDY, G.R., M.B. SOBELL, AND L.C. SOBELL. "Alcohol Breath Tests: Criterion Times for Avoiding Contamination by 'Mouth Alcohol.'" *Behavour Research Methods and Instrumentation*, 10: 814–818, 1978 (2 figures, 14 references)

Abstract: A study was conducted of twelve subjects who swished 0.5 fl. oz. of either beer (4% v/v), wine (12% v/v), bourbon (43% v/v), vodka (45% v/v), or ethyl alcohol (95% v/v) for 15 seconds. The beverage was then expectorated from the mouth. Breath samples were taken by the IR Intoxilyzer or the GC AlcoAnalyzer. The mean times by which alcohol will have no effect on breath analysis are beer 555 seconds; wine 735 seconds; vodka or bourbon 915 seconds; and ethyl alcohol 1,095 seconds. When the subjects rinsed the mouth continuously with warm water, the mouth alcohol effect was reduced to 5 to 7 minutes (300 to 420 seconds). The greater expiration required for the Intoxilyzer caused an earlier reduction of the mouth alcohol effect than the AlcoAnalyzer.

> The finding that differences in the rate of mouth alcohol dissipation may be plotted as an inverse function of ethanol concentration and that continuous mouth rinsing with warm water is efficacious in accelerating the rate of mouth alcohol dissipation have definite methodological implications for the conduct of scientific research involving the determination of BAC using breath-analysis procedures.

Reference Number: 30502

WIGMORE, J.G. AND G.M. LESLIE. "The Effect of Swallowing or Rinsing Alcohol Solution on the Mouth Alcohol Effect and Slope Detection of the Intoxilyzer 5000." *Journal of Analytical Toxicology*, 25: 112–114, 2001 (2 tables, 1 figure, 17 references)

Abstract: Nine female and twenty-one male alcohol-free subjects had their BrACs determined by an Intoxilyzer 5000C 5 and 10 minutes after rinsing or swallowing 10 mL of diluted gin (20% v/v alcohol). The subjects kept their mouths closed and did not talk throughout the experiment. The mean BrACs after rinsing were 0.091 g/100 mL (0.023–0.225 g/100 mL) and 0.014 g/100 mL (0–0.035 g/100 mL) after 5 and 10 minutes respectively. The mean BrACs after swallowing were 0.036 g/100 mL (0–0.18 g/100 mL) and 0.004 g/100 mL (0–0.024 g/100 mL) after 5 and 10 minutes respectively. At 5 minutes all BrACs were higher after rinsing than swallowing except for one subject. At 10 minutes 63% of the BrACs >0.010 g/100 mL after rinsing compared to 7% after swallowing. The Intoxilyzer correctly detected mouth alcohol in 90%, 66%, 63%, and 30% of the samples at 5 minutes after rinsing and swallowing and 10 minutes after rinsing and swallowing respectively.

Table. Mean BrAC in Alcohol-Free Subjects After Rinsing or Swallowing a 20% v/v Alcohol Solution

Time after alcohol use (min)	Mean BrAC after rinsing (g/100 mL)	Mean BrAC after swallowing (g/100 mL)
5	0.091	0.036
10	0.014	0.004

Source: Adapted from Wigmore and Leslie (2001).

The extent and duration of the mouth alcohol effect has been shown to be less after swallowing an alcoholic beverage than after rinsing. In practical use, the deprivation time required before conducting a breath alcohol test may be of shorter duration than indicated in previous studies on the mouth alcohol effect based on rinsing.

Reference Number: 30503

LANGILLE, R.M. AND J.G. WIGMORE. "The Mouth Alcohol Effect After a Mouthful of Beer Under Social Conditions." *Canadian Society of Forensic Science Journal*, 33: 193–198, 2000 (2 tables, 13 references)

Abstract: Fifteen male and fifteen female alcohol-free subjects consumed a mouthful of beer (5% v/v alcohol) from a 341 mL bottle. The subjects then provided breath samples into an Intoxilyzer 5000C at 5 and 10 minutes after the consumption of beer. The volume of the mouthful was on average 85 mL (26–146 mL) for men and 37 mL (16–141 mL) for women. The subjects were allowed to talk and the mean BrAC was 0.005 g/100 mL (0–0.013 g/100 mL) for male subjects and 0.005 g/100 mL (0–0.016 g/

100 mL) for female subjects at 5 minutes. At 10 minutes after the mouthful of beer was swallowed the BrAC was zero for all subjects. There was no effect of the volume of beer consumed and the BrAC.

Table. Volume of a Mouthful of Beer and Percent Positive BrACs (> 0.006 g/100 mL) in Male and Female Subjects Under Realistic Conditions

	Male Subjects	Female Subjects
Mean volume of mouthful of beer (range) in mL	85 (26–146)	37 (16–41)
Percent positive BrAC after 5 min	47%	40%
Percent positive BrAC after 10 min	0%	0%

Source: Adapted from Langille and Wigmore (2000).

Under more realistic conditions (i.e., swallowing a mouthful of beer and talking freely) any significant mouth alcohol effect disappeared within ten minutes. Even after five minutes a BrAC > 0.010 g/210L occurred in only eight subjects (27%) and the highest false positive BrAC was 0.016 g/210L. Thus, in the field during roadside breath alcohol screening, a full 15–20 minutes deprivation time may not be required if the subject has consumed beer.

Reference Number: 30504

GULLBERG, R.G. "The Elimination Rate of Mouth Alcohol: Mathematical Modeling and Implications in Breath Alcohol Analysis." *Journal of Forensic Sciences*, 37: 1363–1372, 1992 (2 tables, 3 figures, 21 references)

Abstract: Three male volunteers provided short (2–3 seconds) breath samples into a BAC Verifier DataMaster every 30 seconds after rinsing the mouth with 5 mL of 40% v/v alcoholic beverage for 10 seconds. The subjects then consumed alcohol and 50 minutes later repeated the mouth alcohol procedure. The elimination of mouth alcohol over time follows a first order exponential model. The time that mouth alcohol is required to be non-biasing were 14.5, 8.0, and 8.0 minutes for alcohol-free subjects, and 8.5, 6.5, and 4.0 minutes when the subjects had consumed alcohol.

A 15 min observation period appears to be more than adequate to prevent a biased measurement from mouth alcohol at forensically important levels. However, the forensic science context of breath alcohol measurements demands that both an observation period and duplicate analyses be present to provide confidence in unbiased results.

Reference Number: 30505

WIGMORE, J.G. AND I.M. BUGYRA. "Decreasing the Mouth Alcohol Effect by Increasing the Salivary Flow Rate." *Canadian Society of Forensic Science Journal*, 36: 211–216, 2003 (2 tables, 1 figure, 12 references)

Abstract: Nineteen female and eleven male alcohol-free subjects rinsed their mouths with 20 mL of 20% v/v alcohol for 20 seconds and then expectorated. The subjects kept their mouths closed and provided breath samples 5 and 10 minutes later into an Intoxilyzer 5000C, with and without chewing one piece of a sugar-free gum. The gum was chewed for 5 minutes and then discarded before providing the first breath sample. Chewing this type of gum has been found to increase the baseline salivary flow rate from 0.5 mL/min to 5.5 mL/min, which then decreases to 2.0 mL/min after 5 minutes and to 1.4 mL/min after 10 minutes. The mean BrACs (range) at 5 minutes were 0.155 g/100 mL (0.031 to 0.277 g/100 mL) without gum and 0.022 g/100 mL (0 to 0.091 g/100 mL) with chewing gum. Chewing gum caused a mean 85% reduction in apparent BrAC due to the mouth alcohol effect. At 10 minutes all subjects who had chewed gum had a BrAC < 0.011 g/100 mL, whereas without chewing gum only three subjects (10%) had a BrAC < 0.011 g/100 mL.

Increasing salivary flow rate has been shown to cause a substantial reduction in the duration and magnitude of the mouth alcohol effect. Although more research is required into the use of salivary promoters (especially under forensic conditions), it has the potential to reduce the time required before conducting a breath alcohol test. This may allow more rapid testing of subjects under field conditions and may allow research into determining BrACs shortly after drinking ceased rather than a 15–20-minute delay.

Reference Number: 30506

WILKIE, M.P., J.G. WIGMORE, AND J.W. PATRICK. "The Performance of the Approved Screening Device, the Alcotest 7410 GLC in the Field: Low Incidence of False Positive Results in the Identification of Drinking Drivers." *Canadian Society of Forensic Science Journal*, 36: 165–171, 2003 (2 tables, 2 figures, 20 references)

Abstract: A retrospective field study was conducted of 811 drinking drivers in Toronto between 1998–1999 who obtained a FAIL (BrAC ≥ 0.100 g/100 mL) on the approved screening device, the Alcotest 7410 GLC. These results were compared to the BrACs as determined by the evidential instrument, the Intoxilyzer 5000C, in tests conducted between 0.1 to 2.6 hours later. There were 103 Alcotest 7410 GLCs and thirteen Intoxilyzer 5000Cs used in the study. The BrACs as determined by the Intoxilyzer 5000C ranged between 0 to 0.310 g/100 mL (mean 0.134 g/100 mL). Seventeen drivers (2.1%) had a BrAC < 0.080 g/100 mL and 117 drivers had a BrAC < 0.100 g/100 mL. When the BrACs were adjusted for the time lag using a rate of alcohol elimination of 0.019 g/100 mL/h, then only two drivers (0.2%) had an estimated BrAC < 0.080 g/100 mL and twelve drivers (1.5%) had a BrAC < 0.100 g/100 mL.

The Alcotest 7410 GLC has a low false positive screening rate when operated under field conditions by the police. Of the 811 drivers who obtained a FAIL on the ASD, only two drivers (0.2%) had an estimated BrAC < 0.080 g/210 L at the time of the ASD test. Thus, the Alcotest 7410 GLC is a robust and reliable instrument for screening drivers who are suspected of having elevated blood alcohol concentrations while operating a motor vehicle.

Reference Number: 30507

PALMENTIER, J-P F.P., J.G. WIGMORE, R.M. LANGILLE, AND J. PATRICK. "Incidence of Invalid Sample Screen Messages on the Intoxilyzer 5000C Obtained from Arrested Drinking Drivers in Toronto. Is a 15 to 20 Minute Wait Period Warranted?" *Canadian Society of Forensic Science Journal*, 39: 101–114, 2006 (5 tables, 4 figures, 31 references)

Abstract: One hundred and ninety-six Invalid Sample (IS) messages (2%) were obtained from 184 drivers on the Intoxilyzer 5000C in Toronto between 1999 and 2003. The time between single IS messages ranged from 2 to 61 minutes (mean 5 minutes). Most drivers who obtained an IS were male (86%) and between twenty to forty-nine years of age (81%). The BrACs ranged from 0.039 to 0.316 g/100 mL. Seventy percent of the IS occurred at BrACs > 0.150 g/100 mL. The time interval between arrest and IS ranged from 27–145 minutes (mean 78 minutes). The table shows the effect of an Invalid Sample within 2 to 4 minutes (rather than 15 minutes) before the second breath test. The second BrAC < first BrAC indicates that there was no significant mouth alcohol effect (i.e., high $BrAC_2$) even when a wait of 15–20 minutes did not occur.

Table. The Effect of an Invalid Sample Message on the Second BrAC Conducted 3 to 5 Minutes Later in Arrested Drinking Drivers

$BrAC_1$ (g/100 mL)	Time After IS $BrAC_2$ Tested (minutes)	$BrAC_2$ (g/100 mL)
0.225	3	0.204
0.196	3	0.172
0.263	4	0.241
0.099	4	0.076
0.168	3	0.144

Source: Adapted from Palmentier et al (2006).

This five-year retrospective study has shown that IS screen messages obtained in the field could be due to variations in the breath exhalation pattern of the sample provided into the instrument and not exogenous mouth alcohol. However, highly transient endogenous mouth alcohol could potentially still cause an IS message, but this effect would be of limited magnitude and short duration. A 15 to 20 minutes wait period does not appear to be routinely required after an IS message occurs. Similarly, MIS messages do not appear to be more likely the result of mouth alcohol. If a breath technician observes an arrested drinking driver varying their breath exhalation pattern e.g., huffing and puffing, or sucking back a breath sample into the Intoxilyzer 5000C resulting in an IS screen message and there is no suspicion of mouth alcohol, then a 15-to-20-minute wait until a subsequent breath test can be conducted is not required.

Reference Number: 30508

LOGAN, B.K., S. DISTEFANO, AND G.A. CASE. "Evaluation of the Effect of Asthma Inhalers and Nasal Decongestant Sprays on a Breath Alcohol Test." *Journal of Forensic Sciences*, 43: 197–199, 1998 (1 table, 1 figure, 8 references)

Abstract: A study was conducted on the effect of eight asthma inhalers (Azmacourt, Vanceril, Vancenase, Ventolin, Becloent, Beconase, Rhinocort, and Primatene Mist) and four non-prescription decongestant sprays (4-way Nasal Spray, Duration 12-Hour Nasal Spray, Afrin Nasal Spray, and Vicks Inhaler) on the breath alcohol result. BrACs were determined by the DataMaster, an IR evidential breath tester. The sprays were used according to the manufacturer's instructions. Breath samples were provided immediately after use of the spray and 2 and 15 minutes later. The only spray that affected the BrAC was Primatene Mist (33% v/v ethanol), and this effect disappeared after 4.5 minutes. Azmacourt, which contains 1% v/v ethanol, had no effect on the BrAC. None of the other sprays contained ethanol and had no effect on the BrACs.

Firstly, the only constituent of inhaler medication which might exert an effect on the DataMaster is ethanol, which is present in only a few such products. Secondly even when alcohol is present a relatively high concentration is required (33% v/v) to have any effect, which in any event may be detected by the instrument as mouth alcohol. Thirdly we confirm that the observation of a 15 min deprivation period prior to the test will eliminate any possibility of interference from alcohol present in an inhaler medication.

Reference Number: 30509

IGNACIO-GARCIA, J.M., J.M. IGNACIO-GARCIA, J. ALMENARA-BARRIOS, M.J. CHOCRON-GIRALDEZ, AND C. HITA-IGLESIAS. "A Comparison of Standard Inhalers for Asthma with and Without Alcohol as a Propellant on the Measurement of Alcohol in Breath." *Journal of Aerosol Medicine*, 18: 193–197, 2005 (4 tables, 8 references)

Abstract: The effect of asthma inhalers on the BrACs of thirty male and thirty-nine female alcohol-free asthmatics were determined with an Alcotest 7110. Only one inhaler (Buto-asma) contained ethanol (19.72 mg/dose) as a propellant. No false positive BrACs were obtained after use of the dry or powder asthma inhalers, which contain lactate monohydrate as a vehicle. Asthma inhalers containing trichlorofluoromethane, dichlorodifluoromethane, and norflurane gave similar false positive BrACs as the ethanol-containing spray. All BrACs were 0 after 5 minutes. The use of a spacer decreased the false positive BrAC.

This study confirms that the observation of a 5–10 min deprivation period prior to the test eliminates any possibility of interference from alcohol or propellants present in an inhaler medication for asthma. These data are relevant for breath tests made with drivers apprehended during routine controls, traffic violations, and those involved in traffic accidents.

Reference Number: 30510

LOGAN, B.K. AND S. DISTEFANO. "Ethanol Content of Various Foods and Soft Drinks and their Potential for Interference with a Breath-Alcohol Test." *Journal of Analytical Toxicology*, 22: 181–181, 1998 (2 tables, 10 references)

Abstract: A study of the alcohol concentration of various soft drinks, bread, and various bakery goods and their effect on the BAC DataMaster was conducted. Subjects rinsed their mouths for 20 seconds with various beverages, expectorated, then provided breath samples. Subjects also chewed bite-size samples of bread for 20 seconds then provided breath samples without swallowing the bread. Alcohol solutions of 0.149 g/100 mL or less were not detected as invalid. The alcohol concentrations of soft drinks varied from 0 (Mandarin Orange Slice) to 0.084 g/100 mL for (Calestoga Lime Flavor); and for bread from 0 (mini-pretzel) to 1.070 g/100 mL (apple-walnut bread). The mouth alcohol disappeared after 3.5 minutes. The highest BrAC produced by the bread was 0.027 g/100 mL and 0.046 g/100 mL in one case.

When all three protections, slope detector, duplicate testing and 15-min deprivation period are present, the potential for mouth-alcohol interference from bread or soft drinks is reduced to zero.

Reference Number: 30511

LUTMER, B., C. ZURFLUH, AND C. LONG. "Potential Effect of Alcohol Content in Energy Drinks on Breath Alcohol Testing." *Journal of Analytical Toxicology*, 33: 167–169, 2009 (1 table, 12 references)

Abstract: The alcohol concentration of twenty-seven energy drinks including Red Bull and Rock Star were determined by headspace GC. Twenty-four (89%) had low concentrations of alcohol detected (0.005–0.230 g/100 mL). The concentrations were high enough in eleven (41%) to give a positive BrAC to the Alco-Sensor FST when consumed less than a minute before testing (0.006–0.015 g/100 mL). No beverage with an alcohol concentration of less than 0.064 g/100 mL gave a positive BrAC. It was calculated that a 175-lb male would have to consume 200 fl. oz. of 180 Energy (0.23% w/v) quickly to obtain a BAC of 0.020 g/100 mL.

The recent consumption of certain energy drinks can give a slight but positive response on a breath alcohol test taken shortly after consumption. This is due to the mouth alcohol effect the beverage cause on the individuals consuming them. Although the levels of alcohol found in the energy drinks tested were significantly higher than previously found on non-alcoholic beverages, any positive response on a breath-testing instrument still disappeared after a minimum 15-min observation period was observed.

Reference Number: 30512

MOORE, R.L. AND J. GULLIEN. "The Effect of Breath Freshener Strips on Two Types of Breath Alcohol Testing Instruments." *Journal of Forensic Sciences*, 49: 829–831, 2004 (1 table, 18 references)

Abstract: Breath strips are edible films that contain breath freshening ingredients such as peppermint oil, which dissolve rapidly when placed on the tongue. Two alcohol-free subjects placed twelve different types of breath strips on the tongue for 30 seconds and then provided breath samples into the BAC DataMaster and Alco-Sensor IV-XL. None of the breath strips gave positive results for the Alco-Sensor (fuel cell detector). A result of 0.006–0.010 g/100 mL was obtained with the DataMaster at 30 seconds, which became zero at 150 seconds.

The results of these tests indicate that while there may be a small amount of potential interference with the results of an infrared breath test, the interference from a single strip is quite small and short-lived Therefore, use of a single breath strip more than a few minutes prior to giving a breath sample would not be expected to alter the results.

Reference Number: 30513

WIGMORE, J.G. AND M.P. WILKIE. "A Simulation of the Effect of Blood in the Mouth on Breath Alcohol Concentrations of Drinking Subjects." *Canadian Society of Forensic Science Journal,* 35: 9–16, 2002 (2 tables, 2 figures, 21 references)

Abstract: Twenty-six male subjects consumed alcoholic beverages *ad libitum* over approximately 1 hour after lunch. At least 1.5 hours later a breath sample was collected and then a venous blood sample. The subject then placed approximately 3 to 5 mL of blood into the mouth and held it there for 30 seconds. The subjects then either expectorated or swallowed the blood. A second breath sample was collected within 1 minute after the blood was removed from the mouth and within 10 minutes of the first breath sample. BACs were determined by headspace GC and BrACs by the Breathalyzer Model 900 or 900A. The BACs ranged between 0.044 and 0.168 g/100 mL (mean 0.095 g/100 mL). The mean BrAC was 0.087 g/100 mL before blood in the mouth and 0.084 g/100 mL after blood in the mouth, which is a statistically significant decrease ($p < 0.05$). However, when the BrAC results were truncated to two decimal places, there was no significant differences in the BrACs. The apparent BBR based on comparing the first BrAC with the BAC ranged between 1,947 to 2,654:1 (mean 2,319:1). If the lower of the two truncated Breathalyzer results were used then there was no overestimation of the BAC by the BrAC.

Table. Weight of Alcohol in 30 mL (1 oz) of Various Alcohol Solutions Indicating the Potential Magnitude of the Mouth Alcohol Effect

Alcohol solution	Alcohol concentration of the solution	Weight of alcohol in 30 mL (1 oz of solution) in grams
Blood	0.08 g/100 mL	0.02
Beer	5% v/v	1.19
Wine	12% v/v	2.84
Mouthwash	20% v/v	4.74
Spirits	40% v/v	9.48

Source: Adapted from Wigmore and Wilkie (2002).

The presence of blood in the mouth of a drinking subject tends to slightly decrease the BrAC. However, this slight decrease has no practical significance in evidential breath alcohol testing of drinking drivers when the results are reported to two decimal places. We conclude that blood in the mouth has no forensically relevant effect upon the measured breath alcohol concentration.

Reference Number: 30514

KECHAGIAS, S., K-A. JONSSON, T. FRANZEIN, L. ANDERSSON, AND A.W. JONES. "Reliability of Breath-Alcohol Analysis in Individuals with Gastroesophageal Reflux Disease." *Journal of Forensic Sciences*, 44: 814–818, 1999 (2 tables, 2 figures, 30 references)

Abstract: Five male and five female subjects (ages twenty-eight to fifty-six years) who had gastroesophageal reflux disease (GERD) including a hiatus hernia consumed between 0.31–0.44 g/kg ethanol within 15 minutes on two occasions. Frequent blood and breath samples were collected from the subjects in a supine position. BrACs were determined by an Alcometer SD-400 and BAC DataMaster. For one series GERD was induced by use of an abdominal compression belt. The mean maximum BrACs were 0.042 g/100 mL with and 0.044 g/100 mL without inducing GERD. The subjects who experienced reflux complained of adverse sensations in the throat, including coughing and hoarseness. This was incapacitating for subjects for a short time after the reflux was induced. The authors suggest that if a gastric reflux occurs 90 minutes or more after the end of drinking, the BrAC result would not be affected as the gastric fluid alcohol concentration at the time is relatively low and is similar in concentration to the mucous secretion in the mouth and upper airway.

> We conclude that the risk of a person experiencing gastric reflux during the time he or she participates in a breath alcohol test procedure is very low. Even if reflux does occur, our study shows that it is not very likely that an abnormally high BrAC reading will be obtained.

Reference Number: 30515

GULLBERG, R.G. "Breath Alcohol Analysis in One Subject with Gastroesophageal Reflux Disease." *Journal of Forensic Sciences*, 46: 1498–1503, 2001 (1 table, 5 figures, 6 references)

Abstract: A twenty-three-year-old male was arrested for DWI and was tested on a BAC DataMaster with the resulting BrACs of 0.114 and 0.123 g/100 mL. As he provided medical evidence of gastroesophageal reflux disease (GERD), a drinking experiment was conducted. The subject consumed 1 g/kg alcohol within approximately 1 hour. BrACs were determined frequently over the next 1.5 hours and two venous blood samples were collected. Breath exhalations expirograms were also determined. The BrACs before and after the blood samples were 0.096 and 0.089 g/100 mL (compared to a BAC of 0.086 g/100 mL), and 0.075 and 0.076 g/100 mL (compared to a BAC of 0.081 g/100 mL).

> No bias is expected where the operator observes a 15 min. period, does not observe any regurgitation of material into the mouth, and duplicate analyses agree acceptably well. Moreover, any belching immediately prior to exhalation will not significantly bias a test result since any gas from the stomach will be exhaled into and out of the instrument sample chamber

being replaced by the final end-expiratory sample arriving from the deep lungs. Belching during a continuous exhalation is highly improbable.

Reference Number: 30516

HARDING, P.M., M.C. MCMURRAY, R.H. LAESSIG, D.O. SIMLEY II, P.J. CORRELL, AND J.K. TSUNEHIRO. "The Effect of Dentures and Denture Adhesives on Mouth Alcohol Retention." *Journal of Forensic Sciences*, 37: 999–1007, 1992 (1 table, 4 figures, 15 references)

Abstract: A study was conducted of twenty-four alcohol-free denture wearing subjects who were given 30 mL of 40% v/v brandy to retain in the mouth for 2 minutes prior to expectoration. Subjects were tested with dentures removed, with dentures held loosely in place, and with dentures plus an adhesive. The subjects provided breath samples into an Intoxilyzer 5000 at 4-minute intervals after expectoration. The mouth alcohol slope detector of the Intoxilyzer 5000 is not infallible, and an apparent BrAC of 0.180 g/100 mL was not detected as mouth alcohol. The mean time to zero BAC was 13 minutes for no dentures, 14 minutes for dentures and no adhesives, and 15 minutes for dentures and adhesives.

The use of dentures, either with or without the concurrent use of denture adhesives does not significantly affect mouth alcohol retention time and contribute to BrAC readings beyond twenty minutes. Dentures need not be treated as foreign objects in the mouth and removed prior to conducting a BrAC test, which includes a 20 min pretest alcohol deprivation period as part of the test protocol.

Reference Number: 30517

LOGAN, B.K. AND R.G. GULLBERG. "Lack of Effect of Tongue Piercing on an Evidential Breath Alcohol Test." *Journal of Forensic Sciences*, 43: 239–240, 1998 (1 figure, 7 references)

Abstract: Two female subjects (ages nineteen and twenty-four years) had their tongues pierced for 5 weeks and 8 months respectively and had oral jewelry inserted. The two female subjects and two female controls (without tongue piercing) rinsed their mouths with Listerine mouthwash (28% v/v alcohol) for 30 seconds. The subjects then provided breath samples into a DataMaster IR instrument. The BrACs were all less than 0.100 g/100 mL after 2 minutes and less than 0.010 g/100 mL after 9 minutes.

> Based on previous research of factors that can lead to mouth alcohol interference, and the experimental results on these two subjects, we found no basis to believe that tongue piercing, or the wearing of oral jewelry would interfere with the results of the breath test, or that such jewelry need be removed prior to administering a breath alcohol test for evidential purposes.

Reference Number: 30518

HELM, J.F. "Esophageal Acid Clearance." *Journal of Clinical Gastroenterology,* 8 (Suppl 1): 5–11, 1986 (5 figures, 33 references)

Abstract: A general review was conducted on esophageal acid clearance. There are thirty-three references. Esophageal acid clearance is a two-step process: first one to two peristaltic sequences empty virtually all acid volume from the esophagus (usually within 10–15 seconds) and then the minimal residual acid is neutralized by swallowed saliva.

> The ability of saliva to neutralize acid is primarily due to bicarbonate. Saliva flow normally increases concurrent with the onset of heartburn. Hypersalivation with heartburn commonly referred to as waterbrash, may be a protective response to gastroesophageal reflux.

Reference Number: 30519

BUCZEK, Y. AND J.G. WIGMORE. "The Significance of Breath Sampling Frequency on the Mouth Alcohol Effect." *Canadian Society of Forensic Science Journal,* 35: 185–193, 2002 (3 tables, 4 figures, 21 references)

Abstract: On three occasions nineteen female and eleven male alcohol-free subjects rinsed their mouths with 20 mL of 20% v/v alcohol for 20 seconds and then expectorated. The subjects then provided breath samples every 2, 4, and 8 minutes respectively into an Intoxilyzer 5000C instrument. The rate of detection of mouth alcohol by the Intoxilyzer 5000C increased from 53% at BrACs < 0.050 g/100 mL to 100% at BrACs > 0.199 g/100 mL.

Table. Mean and Range of BrACs Obtained from Alcohol-Free Subjects at 16 Minutes After Expectoration for Breath Sampling Frequencies of Every 2, 4, and 8 Minutes and Percent of Subjects with a Positive BrAC

Breath Sampling Frequency	Mean BrAC (g/100 mL)	Range of BrACs (g/100 mL)	Percent of Subjects with a Positive BrAC
Every 2 minutes	0.001	0.000–0.012	13%
Every 4 minutes	0.004	0.000–0.019	33%
Every 8 minutes	0.007	0.000–0.045	47%

Source: Adapted from Buczek and Wigmore (2002).

Abstract: The results of the present study show that as the breath sampling frequency increases, the duration and magnitude of the mouth alcohol effect decreases.

Reference Number: 30520

STERLING, K. "The Rate of Dissipation of Mouth Alcohol in Alcohol Positive Subjects." *Journal of Forensic Sciences*, 57: 802–805, 2012 (1 table, 2 figures, 13 references)

Abstract: Five male and two female subjects at BrACs of between 0.030 to 0.060 g/100 mL rinsed their mouths with 20% vodka on five separate occasions and provided one breath sample into an Alco-Sensor IV XL (a fuel cell device) at 1, 2, 3, 4, and 5 minutes apart respectively. In another testing sequence the effect of multiple breath sampling on the mouth alcohol effect was determined by having the subjects again rinse their mouths and provide a breath sample every minute. Both testing sequences were repeated after the subjects were given additional alcohol to obtain BrACs of between 0.060 to 0.130 g/100 mL. No correlation was found between the actual existing BrAC and the rate of dissipation of mouth alcohol. The average time for the subjects to reach steady state values was 9.35 minutes (range 4–13 minutes). This study confirms that findings of Buczek and Wigmore (30519) that providing a breath sample itself causes additional decreases in the mouth alcohol effect.

Table. Mean and Percent Decrease in BrAC with Increasing Time Between Duplicate Breath Tests

Breath Sampling Times (minutes)	Mean Decrease in BrAC (g/100 mL)	Mean Percent Decrease in BrAC (g/100 mL)
1 and 2 minutes	0.000	20.5%
1 and 3 minutes	0.096	30.9%
1 and 4 minutes	0.120	43.0%
1 and 5 minutes	0.165	52.4%

Source: Adapted from Sterling (2012).

As a 15-min observation period and duplicate breath testing with at least a 2-min wait are each sufficient to protect against mouth alcohol individually, it can be concluded that the combination of the two is sufficient to protect against mouth alcohol in instruments that do not contain mouth alcohol detectors (fuel cell devices).

Reference Number: 30521

DECHANO, W.D. "The Effects of Dosed Tobacco in Evidentiary Breath-Testing Using Non-Drinking Subjects." *Science and Justice*, 52: 142–144, 2012 (3 tables, 11 references)

Abstract: Snuff and pouches of chewing tobacco were dosed with 2 and 4 mL of brandy (40% v/v alcohol) respectively. Seven female and ten male subjects were tested with an Intoxilyzer 8000 with and without having the chewing tobacco in their mouths. Of the seventeen subjects, nine had a zero BrAC and two had a maximum BrAC of 0.050 g/100 mL. Mouth alcohol was detected in six subjects. Only one breath test was conducted with the dosed chewing tobacco, and so the duration of the effect was not determined.

However, if the officer does not observe that there is dosed tobacco in the subject's mouth, it is unlikely that there would be a valid test produced provided that the previously mentioned safeguards are in place.

Reference Number: 30522

TREMBLAY, J. AND G. NOLIN. "Lack of Response of Breath Alcohol Screening Devices to Sugar Alcohols Contained in Chewing Gum." *Canadian Society of Forensic Science Journal*, 47: 46–54, 2014 (2 tables, 32 references)

Abstract: Seventy-five different brands of sugarless gum containing up to 74% sugar alcohols (polyols) were tested on the Alco-Sensor IV DWF, Alco-Sensor FST, Alcotest 7410 GLC, and Intoxilyzer 400D. All of the devices use an electrochemical detector. The subjects provided breath samples before and after five pieces of gum were chewed in the mouth until the maximum flavor was obtained. The breath samples were provided while the gum was still in the mouth. The gums contained sugar alcohols such as mannitol, maltitol, sorbitol, and xylitol. Of the 300 breath results obtained, 298 gave a zero response after chewing gum. The only positive result occurred with Trident Splash Strawberry and Kiwi, which contained 0.05% w/w ethanol. The results were all less than 0.01 g/100 mL and were zero less than 1 minute later.

Chewing gum prior to providing a breath sample gives a null result on breath alcohol screening devices in the vast majority of cases. A positive result is not due to sugar alcohols found in sugar-free gums but rather to the small amount of ethanol present. The effect was only seen for one flavour and only lasted for less than one minute. Chewing gum in realistic conditions prior to providing a breath sample in a breath alcohol screening device will not produce a false positive result, especially when administered by a peace officer in the field (gum removed, explanations given, and breath provided more than one minute later). Although the study focused on breath alcohol screening devices, there is no reason to believe that different results would have been obtained if they had been carried out on approved instruments.

Reference Number: 30523

BOATTO, G., C. TRIGNANO, L. BURRAI, A. SPANU, AND M. NIEDDU. "Effects of Homeopathic Mother Tinctures on Breath Alcohol Testing." *Journal of Forensic Sciences,* 60: S1, S231–S233, 2015 (1 table, 13 references)

Abstract: The effect of three homeopathic mother tinctures containing various amounts of alcohol (35%, 60%, and 90% v/v respectively) on the Alcotest 7110 MKIII was tested. Thirty alcohol-free subjects consumed fifty drops of the alcohol-containing tincture added to 10 mL of water in accordance with directions on the label. The subjects were divided into three groups of ten, each group consuming one type of tincture before providing a breath test into a Drager Alcotest 7110 MKIII. The subjects provided breath tests at 1, 3, 5, 15, 30, and 60 minutes after the alcohol was consumed. The incidence and duration of false positive BrACs increased with increasing alcohol concentration of the tincture. No false positive BrACs were detected in the 35% v/v alcohol tincture even at 1 minute, nor after 3 minutes for the 60% v/v alcohol tincture, nor after 5 minutes for the 90% v/v alcohol tincture. At 1 minute 30% of the BrACs were not identified as mouth alcohol for the 60% tincture, and 60% of the BrACs were not identified as mouth alcohol for the 90% tincture. The highest false positive BrAC was 0.082 g/100 mL. The instruments were calibrated on a 2,300:1 blood:breath alcohol ratio and the legal limit in Italy is 0.05 g/100 mL.

> These percentages are not high enough to determine a measurable alcohol result after 15 min. from administration of recommended dosages. In these conditions, the possibility to have a measurable response after an observation period is definitely nonexistent. Therefore, this study underscores the importance of applying an observation period (15–20 min) period to breath alcohol testing.

Reference Number: 30524

POKLIS, J.L., C.E. WOLF II, AND M.R. PEACE. "Ethanol Concentration in 56 Refillable Electronic Cigarettes Liquid Formulations Determined by Headspace Gas Chromatography with Flame Ionization Detector (HS-GC-FID)." *Drug Testing and Analysis*, 9: 1637–1640, 2017 (2 tables, 11 references)

Abstract: The alcohol concentration of fifty-six commercially available e-liquids was determined by headspace GC. E-liquids typically contain propylene glycol and/or glycerin, nicotine, and flavoring agents. Only one e-liquid listed alcohol as a component. A positive alcohol concentration was found in fifty-three of the fifty-six (95%) e-liquids tested and ranged between 0.07 to 206 mg/mL (16% alcohol v/v).

> Ethanol is a common component found in e-liquid regardless of the labeled active ingredient(s). The ethanol detected in these products may be used in flavorant or a solvent, however, the reason for inclusion cannot be fully ascertained. The implications of vaporizing ethanol as an e-liquid component are largely uninvestigated.

Reference Number: 30525

MINH, A.E. "Effects of Vaping E-Juices with and Without Alcohol on the Accuracy of the Alco-Sensor FST Approved Screening Device." *Canadian Society of Forensic Science Journal*, 54: 77–85, 2021 (5 tables, 13 references)

Abstract: Two female and three male alcohol-free smokers took ten puffs from an EC and then blew into an Alco-Sensor FST, a fuel cell breath alcohol screener used by the police in the detection of drinking drivers. Two e-liquids were employed, Lightning Loops (0% alcohol v/v) and Honeydew (21.9% alcohol v/v). No false positive breath alcohol results occurred with the inhalation of alcohol-free Lightning Loops. Immediately after inhalation of the alcohol-containing e-liquid, the BrACs were 0.017, 0.022, and 0.038 g/100 mL, and 2 Warns occurred in the other subjects (i.e., BrAC 0.050 g/100 mL or greater). Two-and-one-half minutes after vaping, the BrACs were zero. For drinking subjects, the BrAC results were not substantially elevated after 1 minute.

> Alcohol is a common component found in commercial E-juices but is often not marked on the product label owing to a lack of regulation. The Mad Vapore Honeydew E-juice was found to contain the highest alcohol concentration of E-juices available and was used in this study to elicit the maximum potential mouth alcohol effect. Our study demonstrated that vaping alcohol-containing E-juices can falsely increase an individual's existing BAC or provide a false positive reading in an alcohol-free individual. It was determined that the effects were short lived and dissipated in less than 3 min after vaping ceased. The dissipation time for mouth alcohol with vaping was substantially shorter than that associated with alcohol consumption.

Reference Number: 30526

LINDBERG, L., D. GRUBB, D. DENCKER, M. FINNHULT, AND S-G. OLSSON. "Detection of Mouth Alcohol During Breath Alcohol Analysis." *Forensic Science International*, 240: 66–72, 2015 (7 figures, 15 references)

Abstract: Six men and two women (ages thirty-five to seventy-one years) consumed 0.4 g/kg alcohol as diluted gin (20% v/v alcohol) and provided breath samples into an IR breath analyzer (3.32, 3.40, 3.49 um filters). Additional filters were added: 3.70 um as a reference, 2.58 um to detect water vapor, and 4.40 um to detect carbon monoxide. The subjects rinsed their mouths with undiluted gin (40% v/v alcohol) for 30 seconds and then expelled the gin at 90 minutes after the state of drinking. The subjects then provided breath samples for up to 40 minutes. In the absence of mouth alcohol, the water vapor in the breath is always exhaled ahead of the alcohol vapor. After the mouth alcohol rinse, the exhaled alcohol from the oral cavity precedes the water vapor. This effect disappears gradually between 5 to 8 minutes in the presence of a positive BAC in the subject.

> We have used a modified prototype breath analyzer, which simultaneously measures water vapor, alcohol, and air flow in the exhaled air. This gave us the unique ability to differentiate the occurrence of the gases in exhaled fractional volumes during an alcohol breath test. In this study we showed that by using water vapor as a reference gas to position alcohol in different fractions of the exhaled volume, it is without doubts, possible to reliably detect MA contamination, which falsely increases the obtained BrAC.

Reference Number: 30527

KRAMER-SARRETT, M. "The Effect of Invisalign Use on Mouth Alcohol Retention." *Canadian Society of Forensic Science Journal*, 49: 52–57, 2016 (3 tables, 15 references)

Abstract: Invisalign is a removable, clear, custom dental aligner, also known as a tray, which is worn in the mouth and has been alleged to cause a prolonged mouth alcohol effect. Two female and one male subject (ages twenty-nine to thirty-four years) were tested after rinsing beer (4.9–8.5% v/v alcohol), wine (13.5% v/v alcohol), or liquor (40–43% v/v alcohol) in their mouths for 1 minute, with or without the Invisalign in their mouths, and expectorated. The subjects provided breath samples into an Alco-Sensor IV, 30 seconds later and then every minute until the BrAC was zero. At 15 minutes only the wine and liquor rinsing with the Invisalign were positive (< 0.020 g/100 mL) as well as one liquor rinsing without the Invisalign (0.009 g/100 mL).

> Based on these finding Invisalign use does not significantly affect breath alcohol concentration when a pretest alcohol deprivation period of 15 minutes is performed.

Reference Number: 30528

BOOKER, J.L. AND K. RENFROE. "The Effects of Gastroesophageal Reflux Disease on Forensic Breath Alcohol Testing." *Journal of Forensic Sciences*, 60: 1516–1522, 2015 (2 tables, 5 figures, 14 references)

Abstract: GERD, in which gastric contents reflux into the esophagus, is estimated to occur in 14 to 20% of the adult population. Five control subjects and ten GERD subjects (seven males, eight females) consumed 1.7 g/kg and 1.5 g/kg alcohol within 30 minutes on two occasions. Breath and blood samples (indwelling catheter) were collected every 20 minutes for 8 hours. BrACs were measured with an Intoxilyzer 5000 and BACs were determined by headspace GC. The elimination rate ranged from 0.010 to 0.020 g/100 mL/h (mean 0.015 g/100 mL/h). Only three of the ten GERD subjects showed elevated BrACs that may be due to GERD, and in only one was it replicated in the second drinking session.

GERD is not a factor to be considered whether the subject is postabsorptive. GERD elevated BrAC elevation occurs when alcohol is present in the stomach at a very high concentration. GERD related leakage elevated above the concurrent BAC by more than 0.030 g/dL more than one hour after dosing was completed. No elevation above 0.030 was noted more than 2 h after dosing was completed. GERD-related alcohol leakage from the stomach into a breath sample is therefore an essentially irrelevant source of potential error in forensic breath testing.

Reference Number: 30529

POTOCKA-BANAS, B.K., T. JANUS, AND S. MAJDANIK. "Expert Opinions Concerning Breath Testing After Consumption of Chocolates Filled with Alcohol and Selected Preparations Containing Alcohol." *Problems of Forensic Science*, 75: 256–267, 2008 (7 tables, 4 references)

Abstract: The response of the Alco-Sensor IV LEC and the Alkometer A2.0 (IR) was determined after the consumption of two types of chocolates filled with alcohol, breath fresheners, gastric drops, and non-alcoholic and alcoholic (6.7% ABV) beer. One and five liquor-filled chocolates were consumed. The IR instrument only detected mouth alcohol occasionally after the consumption of beer. There are numerous tables showing the rapid disappearance of the mouth alcohol effect, most within 5 minutes.

The results of the performed experiment confirm the need to maintain the obligatory waiting time (15 min) before or between measurements of breath alcohol concentration, which was recommended many years ago. It allows most of the presented problems to be evaded.

Reference Number: 30530

ERNSTGARD, L., A. PEXARAS, AND G. JOHANSON. "Washout Kinetics for Ethanol from the Airways Following Inhalation of Ethanol Vapors and Use of Mouthwash." *Clinical Toxicology*, 58: 171–177, 2020 (3 tables, 2 figures, and 31 references)

Abstract: Six female and five male subjects (ages twenty-one to thirty-six years) were exposed to 856 mg/m^3 alcohol vapor for 15 minutes (the Swedish Occupational Exposure Limit is 100 mg/m^3). Breath samples were collected in Tedlar bags at 15 seconds after exposure and every 10 seconds for 90 seconds thereafter and analyzed for alcohol by GC. The average BrAC of the first breath sample after exposure was 0.091 mg/L compared to 0.10 mg/L, which is the Swedish legal limit driving (equivalent to a BAC of 21 mg/100 mL). The $t_{1/2}$ was 0.42 minutes. Capillary blood samples were collected and the mean BAC was 0.00073 mg/g, indicating no significant inhalation of alcohol into the blood. One hour later the subjects rinsed their mouths with 20 mL of Listerine mouthwash (21.6% wt/v alcohol) for 30 seconds and then expectorated. Breath samples were collected into the Tedlar bags (with the mouths closed between samples) and BrACs were determined by GC. The BrAC of the first breath sample collected a few seconds after expectoration was 4.4 mg/L. The $t_{1/2}$ was 1.9 minutes. It took 11 minutes for the BrAC to drop to 0.1 mg/L. The mean capillary BAC at 19 minutes after expectoration was 0.00043 mg/g, again indicating no significant alcohol absorption into the systemic blood circulation.

This study shows that, in practice, inhalation of ethanol, even if carried out immediately before the breath alcohol test does not result in an overestimate of the true BrAC value. In contrast, use of mouthwash might overestimate BrAC. People suspected of drunken driving, sometimes use mouthwash as an excuse when found positive in a breath alcohol test. However, in our study the BrAC fell below the Swedish statutory limit (0.1 mg/L) in less than 16 min in all 11 subjects. This suggests that the use of mouthwash does not explain positive alcohol breath test as, in practice, it takes longer to get the car started, be stopped by the police and carry out the breath test. In any case, a positive alcohol breath test can easily be verified by repeating the test after 15 min or using a 14 min period of observation before testing, as already applied in many countries (e.g., California, Canada).

3.06 SPECIFICITY

"Four patients undergoing halothane anaesthesia were tested before and two hours after surgery, all results were 0 BAC. This study demonstrates the importance of testing a driver's defence by experimentation, speculative defences by medical and scientific experts may mislead the court."

—Dunbar et al, "Evidential Breath Testing of Drivers—Day Surgery and Halothane Anaesthesia" (1985)

"There is no empirical evidence that occupational exposure to solvents contained in paint products are retained in the lungs such that a false alcohol reading will be registered on the Intoxilyzer 5000. When one considers the quick dissipation of solvents from the lungs coupled with the 15-min observation requirement for a valid breath test, paint solvent's effect on the Intoxilyzer 5000 seem remote at best."

—Imobersteg et al, "The Effects of Occupational Exposure to Paint Solvents on the Intoxilyzer 5000" (1993)

According to the Report of the Subcommittee on Alcohol Technology, Pharmacology, and Toxicology (P. Harding and K. Dubowski, co-chairs), of the National Safety Council Committee on Alcohol and Other Drugs, issued in Seattle, Washington, on 22 February 2010, in order for a non-alcohol compound to produce a significant response on a breath alcohol testing instrument it must:

- Be a volatile organic compound capable to be measured in the breath of a living conscious human being
- Be present in sufficiently high concentration to be measured by the instrument after a 15- to 20-minute pretest observation period
- Be able to produce a response on the instrument that is indistinguishable from alcohol (e.g., interferent detection system, proper duplicate results)

In addition,

- Have no distinctive odor or physical appearance on the driver, such as the smell of solvents, or glue or paint traces on the driver or clothing

Potential endogenous volatile organic compounds (other than alcohol) include acetone, methanol, and isopropanol. Concentrations of methanol and isopropanol in the blood of drinking drivers are typically less than 0.001 g/100 mL (30601, 30602, 30605) and therefore will not cause a significantly elevated breath result (30607). High blood acetone concentrations may occur in diabetics and people with other medical conditions but do not affect current breath testing instruments (30602–30605).

Exogenous volatile compounds such as paint solvents, toluene, or gasoline disappear rapidly from the breath upon exposure to fresh air (i.e., short half-life) and so do not cause elevated breath alcohol test results in the field (30608–30614). These compounds also have characteristic odors and significant toxicity. Halothane anesthesia during day surgery does not affect breath test results after 2 hours of exposure to fresh air (30615). Various other substances such as chewing tobacco, breath mints, and nicotine gum also do not affect breath test results (30616) and neither does the use of pepper spray (30617).

The Intoxilyzer 8000 met the specificity requirements (in regard to acetone) of the Alcohol Test Committee (30618). Methyl tert-Butyl Ether (MTBE) and ethanol gasoline do not affect breath alcohol testing or disappears rapidly from the breath upon exposure to fresh air (30619, 30620).

Two case reports involving acetone, isopropanol, methanol, and toluene were correctly identified by the Intoxilyzer 8000 (30621–30622).

Endogenous breath methane and hydrogen in patients with small intestinal bacterial overgrowth (SIBO) does not affect fuel cell breath testing devices (30623).

Reference Number: 30601

BARZ, J., W. BONTE, C. KEULTJES, AND J. SIELAND. "Concentrations of Ethanol, Methanol, Propanol-2 and Acetone in Blood Samples of Impaired Drivers." *Acta Medicinae Legalis et Socialis*, 40: 49–60, 1990 (5 figures, 2 references)

Abstract: The blood ethanol, methanol, isopropanol, and acetone concentrations were determined in 1,628 samples from impaired drivers after being stored for 3 years at 3°C and whose BAC > 0.105 g/100 mL. The blood methanol concentrations ranged between 0.0001–0.0054 g/100 mL, isopropyl alcohol from 0.000006–0.0003 g/100 mL, and acetone from 0.00003–0.0016 g/100 mL. The storage time did not seem to affect the blood methanol and isopropyl alcohol concentrations, but the acetone concentrations decreased by 50%.

> Nevertheless, the importance of high methanol and propanol-2 concentrations as biochemical markers for chronic alcohol abuse even in blood samples after a longer storage period could be confirmed. This result is very significant, because it gives more information about drivers who are suspected to have alcohol problems than the blood ethanol level alone.

Reference Number: 30602

JONES, A.W., A. SAGARDUY, E. ERICSSON, AND H.J. ARNQVIST. "Concentrations of Acetone in Venous Blood Samples from Drunk Drivers, Type-1 Diabetic Outpatients, and Healthy Blood Donors." *Journal of Analytical Toxicology*, 17: 182–185, 1993 (2 tables, 3 figures, 23 references)

Abstract: A study was conducted of the blood acetone concentration of 500 drunk drivers, 250 type 1 diabetics, and 288 healthy blood donors. The blood acetone concentration was determined by headspace GC using *n*-propanol internal standard. The blood was also salted out using 1.5 g of sodium chloride. The blood acetone concentration was stable for up to 8 days when stored at 4°C. When water was stored in gray top Vacutainers for several days, an acetone concentration of 0.00096 g/100 mL was detected. In addition, trace amounts of *t*-butanol were found. The mean plasma/whole blood acetone ratio was 1.23:1. The mean blood acetone concentration was 0.00032 g/100 mL (0.00005–0.0062 g/100 mL) for drunken drivers; 0.00026 g/100 mL (0.00001–0.0828 g/100 mL) for type 1 diabetics, and 0.00016 g/100 mL (0.000015–0.0015 g/100 mL) for blood donors.

> In conclusion, the results of this study demonstrate a very low probability that a driver on the highway would have an abnormally high concentration of acetone in his or hers blood or breath. Defence challenges that focus on the lack of specificity of infrared breath-alcohol analyzers towards acetone are therefore unwarranted even when single wavelength IR analyzers are used for medicolegal purposes.

Reference Number: 30603

SLAMA, G., F. BRUZZO, J.P. DUPEYRON, M. LASSECHERE, M., AND F. DAUCHY. "Ketone Bodies Do Not Give a Falsely Positive Alcohol Tests." *Diabetic. Medicine*, 6: 142–143, 1989 (6 references)

Abstract: Nine hospitalized ketotic diabetic patients had blood and breath samples collected to determine if acetone and other ketone bodies could affect the blood or breath alcohol tests. The plasma acetone concentrations ranged between 0.005 and 0.057 g/100 mL. The plasma glucose, 3-hydroxybutyrate, and acetoacetate concentrations were also elevated. No positive BrACs were detected in any patient using the Drager tubes (sulfuric acid-dichromate) or a fuel cell device. No positive BACs were detected using the GC, TDx-REA, or a chemical nitrochromic oxidation method.

> We conclude that in diabetic patients as well as in non-diabetic people, it is most unlikely that ketone bodies in the expired air or in the circulating blood can lead to a false diagnosis of excess alcohol intake.

Reference Number: 30604

BRICK, J. "Diabetes, Breath Acetone and Breathalyzer Accuracy: A Case Study." *Alcohol, Drugs and Driving*, 9: 27–28, 1993 (2 references)

Abstract: A case report is presented of a forty-two-year-old male diabetic whose blood sugar concentration had unintentionally decreased substantially. The subject had impaired gross motor control; slurring speech; slow, deliberate gait; and was unable to stand without staggering. The blood glucose was 49 and 53 mg/dL. Four breath samples were collected into two Breathalyzers and all results were below 0.010 g/100 mL. Within 45 minutes after the administration of insulin and chocolate, the subject returned to normal.

> Thus, even under conditions of relatively severe physiological and behavioral distress, it is unlikely that the endogenous formation of ketones (ketoacidosis) in a diabetic would contribute more than 0.01 g% error to the Breathalyzer or similar instruments.

Reference Number: 30605

KRISHAN, S. AND S.M.W. LUI. "A Study of Acetone Interference in Intoxilyzer 5000C." *Canadian Society of Forensic Science Journal*, 35: 159–164, 2002 (1 table, 4 figures, 6 references)

Abstract: Sixty different aqueous solutions containing various concentrations of acetone (1–0.500 g/100 mL) and ethyl alcohol (0–0.200 g/100 mL) were tested on an Intoxilyzer 5000C using a Guth simulator. An interferent message was displayed by the Intoxilyzer when the aqueous acetone concentration was 0.035 g/100 mL or greater. Even though an interferent message occurred at these concentrations, the Intoxilyzer correctly adjusted the alcohol results for acetone concentrations up to 0.100 g/100 mL. At an aqueous acetone concentration of 0.500 g/100 mL, an Invalid Sample message was displayed.

> The results of this study reveal that the Intoxilyzer 5000C is effective in measuring breath alcohol in the presence of acetone interference up to 100 mg/100 mL. The alcohol measurements were not falsely elevated (i.e., within experimental error of ± 10 mg/100 mL) when acetone concentrations in the simulator solutions ranged from 0 to 100 mg/100 mL. This implies that within this acetone range the Intoxilyzer 5000C is capable of adjusting to the acetone effect and of producing accurate alcohol results even when the Interferent message appears.

Reference Number: 30606

JONES, A.W. AND H. LOWINGER. "Relationship Between the Concentration of Ethanol and Methanol in Blood Samples from Swedish Drinking Drivers." *Forensic Science International*, 37: 277–285, 1988 (3 figures, 29 references)

Abstract: A study was conducted of 519 samples of blood from impaired drivers. The blood was analyzed for ethanol by headspace GC using 10 uL of blood and 100 uL of *n*-propanol internal standard. Blood was analyzed for methanol by headspace GC using 1.0 mL of blood and 1.0 mL of saturated potassium carbonate solution in order to achieve greater sensitivity. The BACs ranged from 0.011 to 0.379 g/100 mL and the blood methanol concentrations ranged from 0.0001 to 0.0023 g/100 mL. The blood concentrations of ethanol and methanol were positively correlated, $r = 0.47$; however the large scatter of results precludes making reliable estimates of blood methanol concentrations from BAC. But higher blood methanol concentrations are definitely associated with higher BACs. It is suggested that the methanol detected is not from congeners in the alcoholic beverage but from endogenous sources.

> Frequent exposure to methanol and its toxic products of metabolism formaldehyde and formic acid might constitute an additional health risk associated with heavy drinkers in predisposed individuals. The determination of methanol in blood of drinking drivers in addition to ethanol could indicate long-standing ethanol intoxication and therefore potential problem drinkers or alcoholics.

Reference Number: 30607

WIGMORE, J.G. "The Effect of an Elevated Serum Methanol Concentration on the Intoxilyzer 5000C Results of a Drinking Driver." *Canadian Society of Forensic Science Journal*, 41: 171–174, 2008 (1 table, 19 references)

Abstract: A forty-year-old man was involved in a motor vehicle collision and was taken to hospital. A blood sample was collected at 10:41 p.m. and the SAC was 0.346 g/100 mL (equivalent to a BAC of 0.298 g/100 mL). An elevated serum methyl alcohol concentration of 0.004 g/100 mL was also detected, probably due to chronic heavy drinking or alcoholism. At 1:17 a.m. and 1:38 a.m. the BrACs were 0.240 and 0.250 g/100 mL respectively. No Interferent was detected and the BrACs were not falsely elevated by the high serum methanol concentration.

> These results are in agreement with one of the most detailed reports on the specificity of breath alcohol testing, which concludes that endogenous compounds found in the human breath do not significantly affect current breath alcohol testing instruments.

Reference Number: 30608

DENNEY, R.C. "Solvent Inhalation and Apparent Alcohol. Studies on the Lion Intoximeter 3000." *Journal of the Forensic Science Society*, 30: 357–361, 1990 (2 tables, 7 references)

Abstract: Reconstruction experiments were conducted on two male subjects who claimed that Intoximeter 3000 results were inflated due to inhaled solvents arising from the spray painting of cars. Five to seven liters of solvents were sprayed over a period of 135 minutes. The solvents contained methanol, toluene, and xylene. In one subject only trace results were detected; in the other, a maximum apparent BrAC of 0.020 g/100 mLL was detected which fell to traces 30 minutes later.

Table. Apparent BrAC in an Alcohol-Free Subject Exposed to 135 Minutes of Paint Spraying

Conditions	Alcolmeter S-D2 Results (g/100 mL)	Intoximeter 3000 Results (g/100 mL
At the end of 135 min of paint spraying	0.005	0.009
After 15 min exposure to fresh air	0.000	0.005
After 30 min exposure to fresh air	0.000	0.001

Source: Adapted from Denney (1990).

They confirm that recovery from the inhalation of solvents is normally rapid and could only be expected to lead to very slightly inflated breath alcohol levels on evidential breath tests carried out less than 30 minutes after exposure to the solvents has ceased. Under normal circumstances the arresting and processing of drinking drivers by the police prior to the evidential breath testing takes more than this length of time. As a consequence, "inhaled solvents" is not a viable defence.

Reference Number: 30609

GILL, R., S.E. HATCHETT, C.G. BROSTER, M.D. OSSELTON, R.D. RAMSEY, H.K. WILSON, AND A.H. WILCOX. "The Response of Evidential Breath Alcohol Testing Instruments with Subjects Exposed to Organic Solvents and Gases. I. Toluene, 1,1,1-Trichloroethane and Butane." *Medicine, Science, and the Law*, 31: 187–200, 1991 (5 tables, 7 figures, 27 references)

Abstract: Four male and two female subjects (ages twenty to twenty-one years) were exposed in a controlled atmosphere chamber to 100 ppm toluene, 100 ppm 1,1,1-trichloroethane, or 600 ppm butane for approximately 4 hours. Blood samples were collected throughout the experiment and were analyzed by headspace GC. After exposure subjects provided breath samples into the Lion Intoximeter or Camic breath alcohol instruments.

Breath tests using the Lion and Camic evidential breath alcohol testing instruments showed no interference when the subjects had been exposed to toluene or 1,1,1-trichloroethane. After butane exposure, apparent alcohol responses were observed shortly after the subject left the exposure chamber (1 to 5 min) but these responses rapidly fell in subsequent tests. The analytical results confirmed that butane concentrations in breath and blood fell rapidly post- exposure as the subjects breathed clean air.

Reference Number: 30610

GILL, R., H.E. WARNER, C.G. BROSTER, M.D. OSSELTON, H.K. WILSON, AND A.H. WILCOX. "The Response of Evidential Breath Alcohol Testing Instruments with Subjects Exposed to Organic Solvents and Gases. II. White Spirit and Nonane." *Medicine, Science, and the Law,* 31: 201–213, 1991 (7 tables, 8 figures, 18 references)

Abstract: White spirit is also called mineral turpentine, mineral spirits, turps substitute, or Stoddard solvent and is produced by the distillation of the petroleum fraction of crude oil. Four male and one female subjects (ages twenty to thirty-seven years) inhaled 100 ppm white spirits in an atmospheric chamber for 4 hours. An additional two subjects (forty-two and thirty-five years old) painted in the closed atmospheric chamber and were exposed to a maximum 185 ppm. The subjects provided samples into the Lion Intoximeter or Camic breath alcohol instruments, post exposure. Blood samples were also collected. The maximum response of the instruments was 4 ug/100 mL (0.009 g/100 mL) 0–3 minutes post exposure. After 10 minutes the responses of the instruments were all 1 ug/100 mL (0.002 g/100 mL) or less.

The results of the present work show that false positive results are unlikely to occur in breath alcohol testing arising from exposures to white spirit in workplaces where conditions are properly controlled in line with recommended OELs. In domestic situations such careful controls may not apply, and the painting experiment undertaken in a non-ventilated small room was designed to represent a situation of high exposure. Even here, the apparent alcohol were very small.

Reference Number: 30611

IMOBERSTEG, A.D., A. KING, M. CARDEMA, AND E. MULRINE. "The Effects of Occupational Exposure to Paint Solvents on the Intoxilyzer 5000: A

Field Study [Letter]." *Journal of Analytical Toxicology*, 17: 254–255, 1993 (5 references)

Abstract: A field study was conducted of two subjects who worked in an automobile body shop, painting cars. The spraying was conducted in a 30 × 25 foot room, ventilated by two fans and a single sliding door. The subjects wore mist/vapor masks. Subjects were tested on two separate days and approximately 5 gallons of solvent-based paint was sprayed. The paints contained butyl acetate, xylene, toluene, propylene glycol, *n*-butyl alcohol, ethyl alcohol, isobutyl alcohol, and diacetone. Within 10 minutes after exposure, all Intoxilyzer 5000 results were 0. Subjects stated that they occasionally had dizziness, euphoria, and slurred speech after heavy exposure, which quickly dissipated in clean air.

There is no empirical evidence that occupational exposure to solvents contained in paint products are retained in the lungs such that a false alcohol reading will be registered on the Intoxilyzer 5000. When one considers the quick dissipation of solvents from the lungs coupled with the 15-min observation requirement for a valid breath test, paint solvent's effect on the Intoxilyzer 5000 seem remote at best.

Reference Number: 30612

COOPER, S. "Infrared Breath Alcohol Analysis Following Inhalation of Gasoline Fumes." *Journal of Analytical Toxicology*, 5: 198–199, 1981 (1 table, 8 references)

Abstract: A subject inhaled gasoline fumes for 15 minutes and then provided a breath sample after 10 minutes of exposure to fresh air. There was no result of the subject's inhalation of gasoline on an Intoxilyzer 4011 (IR device). However, when gasoline fumes were introduced directly into the sample chamber, the result went off scale. The subject's behavior after 15 minutes inhalation included difficulty in breathing, light headedness, decreased concentration, and a few random incoherent remarks.

After regular inhalation of the fumes had ceased, gasoline rapidly dissipated from the subject's breath.

Reference Number: 30613

DALLEY, R. "DUI and Petrol Consumption [Letter]." *Journal of the Forensic Science Society*, 25: 53–54, 1985

Abstract: A subject rinsed their mouth with 8 mL of ESSO gasoline and provided breath samples into a Lion Intoximeter 3000. The apparent BrAC was 7 ug/100 mL (0.016 g/100 mL BAC) 1 minute after rinsing and 2 ug/100 mL (0.005 g/100 mL BAC) 2 minutes after rinsing. After 15 minutes the apparent alcohol concentration was 0.

> It may be of interest that although care was taken not to swallow any petrol, the taste of petrol remained in the mouth for 6 to 8 hours.

Reference Number: 30614

STEPHENS, A. AND S. PHEASEY. "Petrol Effects on the New Camic Machine [Letter]." *Journal of the Forensic Science Society*, 34: 106, 1994

Abstract: A letter to the editor was published regarding the effect of gasoline in the mouth on the IR Camic breath alcohol testing device. The subject rinsed his mouth with unleaded gasoline and the initial test result after 2 minutes was 0.076 g/100 mL, which decreased to 0 at 28 minutes. The presence of an interfering substance at readings above 0.023 g/100 mL was detected by the Camic device.

> The ability of the new machines to respond to the presence of interfering substances, at very low levels, on the breath of individuals giving samples will surely be advantageous both to the individual whose breath samples are truly contaminated with detectable substances other than ethanol, and to the courts, by reducing the number of cases where such an argument is used as a defence.

Reference Number: 30615

DUNBAR, J.A., W.A. MACRAE, J.H. MURPHIE, D. WHITTET, AND A.M. MATHER. "Evidential Breath Testing of Drivers—Day Surgery and Halothane Anaesthesia." *Medicine Science and the Law,* 25: 162–164, 1985 (1 table, 4 references)

Abstract: A thirty-eight-year-old man was given halothane during day surgery and was released at 4:00 p.m. At 8:48 p.m. breath tests were conducted on an IR Camic Breath Analyzer with the result of 71 ug/100 mL (approximately 0.160 g/100 mL BAC). The accused stated he had only one beer. An in vitro 2% concentration of halothane in oxygen gave a reading of 41 ug/100 mL (0.094 g/100 mL), and a 1% concentration gave a reading of 29 ug/100 mL (0.067 g/100 mL) on the IR instrument. Approximately

60 to 80% of absorbed halothane in humans is eliminated unchanged in exhaled gas in the first 24 hours after exposure. Four alcohol-free patients undergoing halothane anesthesia were tested before and 2 hours after surgery; all results were 0 BrAC.

A number of substances may on theoretical grounds of absorption at 3.4 microns be proposed as explanations for breath samples above the prescribed limit of 35 mcg/100 mLs. This study demonstrates the importance of testing a driver's defence by experiment. Speculative defence by medical and scientific experts may mislead the courts.

Reference Number: 30616

PENNINGTON, J.C. "The Effect of Non-Ethanolic Substances on the Alcolmeter S-L2." *Canadian Society of Forensic Science Journal*, 28: 131–135, 1995 (1 table, 5 references)

Abstract: An in vitro and in vivo study was conducted on the specificity of a screening device, the Alcolmeter S-L2 (fuel cell). Alcohol-free subjects inhaled, insufflated, chewed, or held in the mouth the following substances before providing a breath sample into the Alcolmeter: Ventolin, Beclovent, Dristan nasal mist, Excel gum, Nicorette gum, Skoal chewing tobacco, Halls menthol lozenge, Certs breath mints, and Cinnamon Pearl Drops. All results on the Alcolmeter were 0–0.002 g/100 mL. Simulators employing various concentrations of acetaldehyde, ether, isopropanol, methyl chloride, trichloroethylene, acetone, ethylene glycol, methanol, and toluene were then tested on the device, and only acetaldehyde, ether, isopropanol, and methanol gave positive results.

The study results demonstrate the Alcolmeter S-L2 has sufficient specificity for police officers to rely upon the FAIL, WARN, PASS or READY readings for assistance in their investigations for possible impaired drivers.

Reference Number: 30617

LUTMER, B.M. "The Effect of Water Soluble OC Pepper Spray on Select Infrared and Electrochemical Breath Alcohol Instruments." *Canadian Society of Forensic Science Journal*, 42: 266–275, 2009 (5 figures, 23 references)

Abstract: Pepper spray consists of the natural extract of chili peppers (oleoresin capsicum), which is emulsified with propylene glycol and suspended in water. The spray is pressurized with nitrogen or carbon dioxide. After use, there is difficulty in breathing or talking for 3 to 15 minutes and a burning sensation on the skin for 45 to 60 minutes. There is significant absorption of water-soluble OC at the 3.4 microns IR wavelength used by evidential breath alcohol testers. The effect of OC spray was determined in three nondrinking and nine drinking subjects. The subjects were tested before and after OC spray use with a BAC DataMaster and Alco-Sensor FST. There was no significant effect on the results. A solution of 9% OC spray was placed in a simulator at 34°C and tested on the BAC DataMaster, DataMaster DMT, Alco-Sensor FST, and Intox EC/IR. All in vitro results were zero.

Given the results obtained, it can be reasonably concluded that evidential breath alcohol instruments are not affected by the use of oleoresin capsicum aerosol on a subject. Therefore, the use of OC pepper spray on subjects should not affect subsequent breath alcohol test results.

Reference Number: 30618

MARTIN, T.L. "An Evaluation of the Intoxilyzer 8000C Evidential Breath Alcohol Analyzer." *Canadian Society of Forensic Science Journal*, 44(1): 22–30, 2011 (3 tables, 2 figures, 10 references)

Abstract: An evaluation of the Intoxilyzer 8000C was conducted according to Alcohol Test Committee (ATC) standards. This evidential instrument employs IR at 3.4 and 9.4 microns to determine BrAC. In vitro concentrations of 0.005 and 0.010 g/100 mL acetone had no effect on the results. An acetone concentration of 0.050 g/100 mL produced an Interferent Detect message. A simulator target BAC of 0.102 g/100 mL resulted in a mean Intoxilyzer 8000C result of 0.100 g/100 mL (range 0.099 to 0.102 g/100 mL). A comparison of near simultaneous BrACs of ten drinking subjects (range 0.060 to 0.124 g/100 mL) comparing the Intoxilyzer 5000C and 8000C resulted in an r^2 of 0.968. The Intoxilyzer 8000C was designated an approved instrument in Canada on 29 August 2007.

The successful assessment of the Intoxilyzer 8000C according to the ATC Equipment Evaluation Procedures demonstrates that the instrument conforms to rigid standards. When operated properly by a qualified individual the Intoxilyzer 8000C is an accurate and reliable means of performing breath alcohol testing.

Reference Number: 30619

BUCKLEY, T.J., J.D. PLEIL, J.R. BOWYER, AND J.M. DAVIS. "Evaluation of Methyl tert-Butyl Ether (MTBE) as an Interference on Commercial Breath-Alcohol Analyzers." *Forensic Science International*, 123: 111–118, 2001 (1 table, 3 figures, 29 references)

Abstract: In vitro simulator studies were conducted with and without alcohol and at vapor concentrations of MTBE from 0–991 ug/L on the Breathalyzer Model 900A and Alcotest 7110 (electrochemical and IR (9.5 microns) detectors). MTBE is a gasoline oxygenate additive. A literature review was also conducted on reported MTBE concentrations in subjects exposed to gasoline. The highest reported breath MTBE concentration in a subject exposed to gasoline was 245 ug/L. A continuous reaction was observed after 90 seconds with the Breathalyzer Model 900A when samples of MTBE were analyzed. At 144 ug/L MTBE, the Breathalyzer result was increased by 5%, and at 245 ug/L the increase was 10%. The Alcotest 7110 was not affected by MTBE and gave either a mouth alcohol or interferent message.

Using a simulated breath matrix (100% humidification) prepared in summa polished canisters, it has been established that MTBE presents a positive bias in the measurement of percent blood alcohol on an older technology Breathalyzer relying on in situ chemical oxidation of ethanol and spectrophotometric detection. It may be possible to identify the MTBE interference by noting an increase in the instrument percent blood alcohol reading after the initial reading. The same increase does not occur when ethanol alone is present. These results suggest that the colorimetric reaction of MTBE and ethanol occur on a different time scale. The new technology instruments employing infrared and electrochemical sensors showed no bias and/or successfully identified the interference.

Reference Number: 30620

RAN, R. AND M.E. MULLINS. "Can Handling E85 Motor Fuel Cause Positive Breath Alcohol Test Results?" *Journal of Analytical Toxicology*, 37: 430–432, 2013 (1 figure, 9 references)

Abstract: E85 fuel contains 85% alcohol and 15% gasoline and is available in approximately 2,500 gas stations in the United States. Three male and two female alcohol-free subjects (ages twenty-four to twenty-six years) dispensed or handled approximately 8 US gallons of E85 fuel under four conditions. BrACs were measured every 2 minutes for 10 minutes, using a BAC Track 550, which uses a non-specific semiconductor detector. The highest BrAC detected was 0.04 g/100 mL in one subject immediately after pouring the fuel from one container into another and decreased to zero after 2 minutes.

> Handling E85 motor fuel produced low, transient elevations in breath alcohol measurements up to 6 min in a minority of subjects. Because standard police procedure includes waiting 15–20 min after a traffic stop before administering a breath alcohol test, it is unlikely that handling E85 motor fuel prior to arrest would result in erroneous prosecution for DWI.

Reference Number: 30621

WALLAGE, H.R. AND I.M. BUGYRA. "Interferent Detect on the Intoxilyzer 8000C in an Individual with an Elevated Blood Acetone Concentration due to Ketoacidosis." *Canadian Society of Forensic Science Journal*, 50: 157–163, 2017 (2 tables, 14 references)

Abstract: A seventy-two-year-old male chronic alcoholic abuser who had not eaten for 1 day was arrested and provided a Fail into an Alcotest 6810, a fuel cell device. He provided two breath samples into the Intoxilyzer 8000C, which resulted in an Interferent Detect and an Invalid Sample. Paramedics were called and the serum alcohol analysis using the enzymatic method was 0.172 g/100 mL. The hospital GC-FID analysis was 0.161 g/100 mL alcohol and 18 mg/dL acetone. The blood alcohol analysis conducted at the Centre of Forensic Sciences was 0.131 g/100 mL alcohol and 21 mg/dL acetone. A positive isopropanol concentration was also detected (< 5 mg/dL). The blood beta-hydroxybutyrate concentration was 46.8 mg/dL.

> In conclusion, all of the instrumentation performed as expected.

Reference Number: 30622

WOODALL, K.L. AND J-P.F.P. PALMENTIER. "Intoxilyzer 8000C Breath Results Obtained from a Suspected Impaired Driver Following Reported Occupational Solvent Exposure." *Canadian Society of Forensic Science Journal*, 50: 84–89, 2017 (21 references)

Abstract: A sixty-eight-year-old man was observed to be driving erratically and when stopped by the police had a strong odor of alcohol, slurring speech, and difficulty keeping his balance. He was arrested at 12:49 a.m. At approximately 2:02 a.m. he provided a breath sample into an Intoxilyzer 8000C (two wavelength IR device), which registered a BAC of 0.158 g/100 mL and an Interferent Detected. Another breath test at 2:04 a.m. registered a BAC of 0.159 g/100 mL and another Interferent Detected. No BACs were recorded on the test record. Blood samples were collected at hospital at 4:25 a.m. and analyzed by HS/GC and found to contain 0.101 g/100 mL alcohol, 17 mg/dL acetone, 10 mg/dL isopropanol, 26 mg/dL methanol, and < 2.5 mg/dL toluene. He worked for a company and was exposed to acetone and toluene.

This case provides an example of two Interferent Detect messages obtained from a driver and demonstrates the ability of the Intoxilyzer 8000C to detect the presence of volatile substances other than ethanol on the breath of a drinking driver.

Reference Number: 30623

KRAMER-SARRETT, M., E. LIN, K.S. CHUA, N. PICHETSHOTE, A. REZAIE, AND M. PIMENTAL. "Examination of the Effects of Breath Hydrogen and Methane Levels on the EC/IR II." *Canadian Society of Forensic Science Journal*, 50: 125–130, 2017 (1 table, 2 figures, 6 references)

Abstract: Twenty-nine female and twenty-one male patients (ages eighteen to eighty-three years) with a pre-existing or suspected diagnosis of having a small intestinal bacterial overgrowth (SIBO) were tested on an Intox EC/IR (fuel and IR device) before and after the consumption of lactulose. The patients had breath hydrogen concentrations ranging from 1 to 176 ppm and breath methane concentrations from 0 to 107 ppm. All patients tested zero, except for one patient who admitted drinking heavily the night before. When this positive patient was retested, his Intox EC/IR result decreased even though his breath hydrogen and methane concentrations did not, which indicated that the positive result was probably due to alcohol. One expert had testified that a false result would be produced on fuel cell testing devices due to SIBO. In vitro testing has shown previously that hydrogen and methane gases have no effect on the fuel cell.

Based on these findings, breath hydrogen and methane do not have any impact on breath alcohol results with the EC/IR II.

3.07 BREATH CONTAINERS

"The technology of breath alcohol analysis has evolved from collection of breath in balloons and analysis by cumbersome wet chemical methods to automated portable microprocessor-controlled instruments providing immediate results. These instruments are capable of providing reliable results when operated in a non-laboratory environment by individuals with little or no scientific background or training."

— Harding, "Methods for Breath Analysis" (1996)

The accuracy and precision of alcohol analysis of the breath collected into breath containers, typically containing silica gel, is less than that of the evidential breath alcohol instruments (30701). Silica gel is also affected by moisture and storage conditions (30703) and there is difficulty in extracting the alcohol uniformly and consistently from the silica gel for analysis (30702).

As the technology of evidential breath tests improves, such as automatic operation and printed test results, the use of a secondary and less accurate measurement using obsolete breath containers is no longer warranted and has finally been removed from the *Criminal Code of Canada*.

Reference Number: 30701

BERGH, A.K. "Observations on ToxTrap Silica Gel Breath Capture Tubes for Alcohol Analysis." *Journal of Forensic Science*, 30: 186–193, 1985 (5 tables, 4 references)

Abstract: A study of using simulator solutions and Intoxilyzer 4011 to determine the accuracy of using silica gel ToxTraps to preserve breath alcohol was conducted. The Intoxilyzer has a volume of 721 mL at 55°C, which is equivalent to 675 mL at 33.8°C (the mean simulator temperature). Analysis of ToxTrap was by GC after addition of *n*-propanol internal standard solution and equilibration overnight. The ToxTraps weighed from 190–212 mg, mean 202 mg. The tubes after desiccation for 2–3 hours at 135°C were found to weigh 162–179 mg, mean 171 mg. Tubes that were not heat desiccated gave results of 0.069–0.084 g/100 mL at a simulator concentration of 0.100 g/100 mL. ToxTrap did display instrumental variation from 4% higher to 5 and 6% lower, respectively, using other Intoxilyzers. Under optimum conditions at a simulator concentration of 0.200 g/100 mL, the SD of the Intoxilyzer is 0.002 g/100 mL and of the

ToxTrap is 0.005 g/100 mL. The presence of moisture in the silica gel decreased accuracy and precision markedly.

Table. Range of Silica Gel Breath Tube Results Compared to the Target Value, with and Without Prior Desiccation

Target value (g/100 mL)	Desiccation pre-treatment	Range of silica gel breath tube results (g/100 mL)
0.100	No	0.069–0.084
0.100	Yes	0.095–0.106
0.200	No	0.141–0.188
0.200	Yes	0.184–0.208

Source: Adapted from Bergh (1985).

Much manipulation is involved in the analysis of silica gel samples. Each manipulative step contains potential sources of error.

Reference Number: 30702

CHIAROTTI, M., N, DE GIOVANNI, AND A. CARNEVALE. "The Use of Silica Gel in Evidential Tests in Drunken Driver Problems Related to Alcohols Adsorption and Elution." *Blutalkohol*, 22: 264–271, 1985 (2 tables, 4 figures, 11 references)

Abstract: Two types of silica gel tubes were tested; the Lion tube (160 mg of silica crystal, 18 mesh) and the Drager tube (370 mg of silica crystal, 14 mesh). Simulator tests were conducted. Silica gel analysis was by headspace GC with the addition of 1 mL of 0.05% *n*-propanol to the silica gel crystals. The ethanol/*n*-propanol area ratio increased with elution time and reached a constant value after 20 hours for the Drager tubes and after 3 hours for the Lion tubes. There is a different ethanol and *n*-propanol adsorption on to the silica gel. There is little increase in ethanol concentration with time, but a much greater decrease in *n*-propanol concentration.

Our experimental data (obtained on different kinds of silica gel) show that increase in time elution is necessary. 3hrs. are not enough for reproducible results and longer elution time is required. For practical problems, we tested 20 hrs. with good results, because silica gel: water: ethanol: *n*-propanol system had certainly reached a state of equilibrium.

Reference Number: 30703

GOLDBERGER, B.A., Y.H. CAPLAN, AND J.R. ZETTL. "A Long Term Field Experience with Breath Ethanol Collection Employing Silica Gel." *Journal of Analytical Toxicology*, 10: 194–197, 1986 (2 tables, 3 figures, 7 references)

Abstract: A study of 143 breath samples retained for 1.25–2.75 years was conducted. Breath samples were collected into silica gel containers (Tox-Trap lot nos. 11, 12, 15, 21, and 27) using a single Intoxilyzer 4011AS instrument. Vapor ethanol samples collected on lot 27 served as calibrators. The silica gel was analyzed by headspace GC. When the silica gel samples were compared to the direct result the silica gel was on average 7.5% low. The CV% was 16.3%. For all samples $r = 0.900$. The Student T test indicated significant differences for the paired samples. Analysis of silica gel for ethanol should be performed as soon as possible. Calibrators should be used from the same lot as the unknowns to avoid lot-to-lot variability.

Several explanations for the underestimation of the ethanol content are possible: loss of ethanol during storage, loss of ethanol during collection from sample chamber or tubing, inability to desorb ethanol following long-term storage, lot-to-lot variability, analytical error during re-analysis, operator error, and/or condensation in instrument tubing. Reasons for overestimation of the ethanol content may include lot-to-lot variability, analytical error during re-analysis, operator error, and/or condensation in instrument tubing.

Reference Number: 30704

ANDREWS, S.A. AND H.J. COLVIN. "Verification of Intoximeter 3000 Breath Alcohol Concentration by Magnesium Perchlorate Tube Method in Long-Term Field Program." *Journal of Analytical Toxicology*, 13: 113–116, 1989 (2 tables, 2 figures, 9 references)

Abstract: A two-year study was conducted in Alaska of 1,024 comparisons of Intoximeter 3000 results with magnesium perchlorate tubes (MPT). Eighteen Intoximeters were used in this study. Analysis of MPT involved 3 mL of *n*-propanol internal standard added to the tube; the contents were shaken, and the tube was recapped. The capped MPT stood for 1 hour to allow the mixture to reach room temperature. The contents were then transferred to a 22 mL vial containing 1 g NaCl. The samples were equilibrated at 60°C for 30 minutes. The MPT tubes were stored from 5 to 745 days and the differences in 90-day groups were negligible.

In most cases the MPT-GC values confirmed the Intoximeter readings within ±0.03 g/210L. Of those cases not within the limits, the problem lies in the Intoximeter, the magnesium perchlorate tube, the collection procedure, or the MPT-GC breath alcohol analysis.

Reference Number: 30705

PARKER, K.M. AND J.L. GREEN. "Delayed Ethanol Analysis of Breath Specimens: Long-Term Field Experience with Commercial Silica Gel Tubes and Breathalyzer Collection." *Journal of Forensic Science*, 35: 1353–1359, 1990 (4 figures, 10 references)

Abstract: A five-year study was conducted of 1,109 Breathalyzer results compared to the delayed silica gel result of suspected impaired drivers. Collection errors occurred in 2.5% of the silica gel samples. A total of 642 results were compared, and 81% were within ±0.030 g/100 mL. At 0.100 g/100 mL, sixty-six out of seventy-five (88%) were within this range. At BACs > 0.210 g/100 mL, the confirmation rate was 65%. The average recovery of ethanol from the silica gel was 82% with a CV of 4%.

When fixed tolerance limits of ± 0.03 were used, 81% of the direct results were confirmed. The confirmation percentage was best in the critical range of direct results, 0.05 to 0.15 g/210L. The collection tubes showed no substantial variability in retaining ethanol during storage and releasing ethanol for analysis.

CHAPTER 4

Urine, Saliva, Sweat, and Breast Milk Alcohol and Biomarkers of Alcohol Consumption

> "When alcohol is taken into the body, it is rapidly absorbed and passes to all fluids and tissues of the body in approximately equal amount, so that within an hour and a half, practically all absorbed and an analysis of blood, urine or tissue will give a fairly accurate measure of alcohol present."
>
> —McNally and Embree, "Alcohol in the Human Body" (1928)

In addition to the more commonly used breath and blood alcohol testing of drinking drivers, other samples such as urine and saliva have been employed. Transdermal (sweat) alcohol monitoring of persons on parole or probation with the condition of no alcohol consumption is becoming more frequent. Biomarkers of alcohol consumption found in the hair or urine are also used for this purpose. Since alcohol distributes throughout the total body water, it is not surprising that alcohol, if consumed by a lactating woman, will appear in her breast milk.

4.01 URINE

> "Macduff: What are three things does drink especially provoke?
> Porter: Marry, sir, nose-painting, sleep, and urine."
>
> —William Shakespeare, *Macbeth*

> "I drink too much. The last time I gave a urine sample it had an olive in it."
>
> —Attributed to Rodney Dangerfield

"The ratio of the concentration of alcohol in blood to that of urine varies only slightly with specific gravity; the ratio that was determined here is 1:1.3. Absorption of alcohol from the bladder into the blood does not occur to a significant extent at the concentration found in the urine after drinking alcohol."

— Haggard et al, "The Use of Urine in the Chemical Test for Intoxication" (1940)

Urine is the only sample that can be collected from living subjects that can indicate the blood alcohol concentration (BAC) at a time prior to the collection of the sample, as it is stored isolated in the bladder before voiding (40101). The phase of the BAC curve can be determined as follows:

- UAC < BAC (absorption phase, BAC increasing)
- UAC > BAC (postabsorption phase, BAC plateau or decreasing)

Alcohol causes an increase in urine flow (diuresis) only during the first several hours after drinking (40102, 40103). Urine samples collected from drinking drivers can be used to determine BAC (40101, 40104). Falsely high urine alcohol concentrations (UAC) may occur if the urine sample is collected from a diabetic with a yeast infection (40105, 40106). The use of refrigeration and NaF will prevent this alcohol formation (40105, 40106, 40107). Freezing and rethawing urine samples and improperly sealed containers will cause a decrease in UAC (40107, 40108). Alcohol intoxication can increase the risk of bladder rupture after minor trauma (40109) or even result in idiopathic bladder rupture (40110).

The possibility of alcohol formation from glucose in a urine sample that was stored refrigerated for 41 days of a DUI suspect resulted in a lesser charge (40111).

Whole body CT scans of trauma patients showed alcohol-positive patients had a larger mean urinary bladder volume than patients with no alcohol (40112).

Reference Number: 40101

BIASOTTI, A.A. AND T.E. VALENTINE. "Blood Alcohol Concentration Determined from Urine Samples as a Practical Equivalent or Alternative to Blood and Breath Tests." *Journal of Forensic Sciences*, 30: 194–207, 1985 (6 tables, 1 figure, 34 references)

Abstract: The average production of urine is 0.55–1.25 mL/minute. With alcohol consumption the average production is approximately 7–12 mL/minute. The impulse to void occurs at 150 mL of urine in the bladder and pronounced discomfort occurs at 450 mL. Under normal circumstances the impulse to void occurs in 2–4.5 hours. In law enforcement practice the average time for the second urine sample was 25 minutes due to the diuretic effect. Assuming that urine is 100% water and blood is 82%, the urine/blood ethanol ratio should be 1.22. In impaired driving cases the two urine samples showed that most people reached the BAC plateau or the elimination phase (199/204 or 98%). In only two cases was the difference between the first and second sample greater than 0.020 g/100 mL. This contradicts the frequent claims of rapid consumption of alcohol just before driving.

Urine is a reliable and accurate alternative to sampling blood for alcohol determination when second samples collected within 1 h from voiding are provided by cooperative subjects and converted using a ratio of 1.3:1.

Reference Number: 40102

JONES, A.W. "Excretion of Alcohol in Urine and Diuresis in Healthy Men in Relation to Their Age, the Dose Administered and the Time After Drinking." *Forensic Science International,* 45: 217–224, 1990 (4 tables, 1 figure, 22 references)

Abstract: Eight male subjects consumed either 0.51, 0.68, or 0.85 g/kg ethanol as neat whiskey within 15 to 25 minutes. Urine was collected immediately before drinking and every 60 minutes for 7 to 8 hours and analyzed for ethanol by an ADH method. Only 0.7 to 1.5% of the alcohol consumed was excreted unchanged in the urine. Ethanol caused an up to tenfold increase in urine flow only in the first 2 hours after drinking and returned to normal after the peak UAC was reached, even when the BAC was still elevated.

The volume of urine collected 30 to 60 min after an initial void might give a clue to the time lapse after drinking when the samples were collected and therefore the phase of alcohol metabolism. An objective test of whether the BAC profile was rising or falling during the collection period is useful forensic information. A moderate diuresis is expected for the first 2 h after drinking and suggest a rising BAC, whereas a normal urine flow 30–60 mL/h suggests that the post absorptive phase was well established. This kind of information might be useful in evaluating alleged drinking after the offence.

Reference Number: 40103

BENDTSEN, P. AND A.W. JONES. "Impact of Water-Induced Diuresis on Excretion Profiles of Ethanol, Urinary Creatinine and Urinary Osmolality." *Journal of Analytical Toxicology*, 23: 565–569, 1999 (4 figures, 29 references)

Abstract: Five male and two female subjects (mean age thirty-six years) consumed 1 L of beer (0.55 g/kg alcohol) within 30 minutes. Urine samples were collected frequently between 30 and 360 minutes after drinking ceased. At 120 minutes after the end of drinking the subjects consumed either 0.5 or 1 L of water. UACs, urinary osmolality, and urinary creatinine concentrations were determined. The mean peak UAC was 0.070 g/100 mL (0.051–0.098 g/100 mL) obtained at 60 minutes after the end of drinking. The maximum alcohol-induced diuresis occurred in the absorption phase and was 11.4 mL/minute (range, 4.7–16.6 mL/minute). The maximum water-induced diuresis was 4.7 mL/minute (range, 0.7–6.8 mL/minute). The total amount of alcohol recovered in the urine was 1.5% of the total dose. Urinary creatinine and osmolality decreased after alcohol consumption and again after consumption of water.

Because neither UAC nor BAC are seemingly lowered after drinking 500–1000 mL water, the urine/blood ratios of ethanol should also remain unchanged despite a marked water-induced diuresis. This is important to consider when the UAC/BAC ratio of ethanol is used to derive information about the likely time of consumption of alcohol in relation to sampling and also whether a person's BAC might have been rising or falling sometime prior to sampling.

Reference Number: 40104

JONES, A.W. "Reference Limits for Urine/Blood Ratios of Ethanol in Two Successive Voids from Drinking Drivers." *Journal of Analytical Toxicology*, 26: 333–339, 2002 (2 tables, 4 figures, 39 references)

Abstract: Two urine samples were collected from 450 drinking drivers in Sweden approximately 66 minutes apart (range 30–130 minutes). A venous blood sample was collected at a time generally between the collection of the two urine samples. UACs and BACs were determined by headspace GC. The mean BAC was 0.197 g/100 mL. The mean initial UAC was 0.260 g/100 mL and the mean second UAC was 0.240 g/100 mL. The UAC/BAC ratios were calculated from 429 drinking drivers with a BAC > 0.050 g/100 mL. The median UAC/BAC ratio for the first void was 1.325 The median UAC/BAC ratio for the second void was 1.226. The first UAC > second UAC in 393 cases (87%).

Dividing the UAC of the first void by 1.33 gives an idea of the average BAC during the time that the urine was being produced and stored in the bladder. Accordingly, the concentration determined in the first urine sample collected after driving is a good representation of the BAC at the time of driving. This unique advantage of urine over other body fluids for forensic analysis: namely to give an indication of the BAC at an earlier point in time (i.e., the time of driving or crash) has surprisingly not been fully appreciated.

Reference Number: 40105

SULKOWSKI, H.A., A.H.B. WU, AND Y.S. MCCARTER. "In-Vitro Production of Ethanol in Urine by Fermentation." *Journal of Forensic Sciences*, 40: 990–993, 1995 (1 table, 3 figures, 11 references)

Abstract: Three yeasts and six bacteria species were added to a blank urine sample containing no alcohol or sugar. The samples were incubated at 0°, 25°, and 35°C for 24, 48, and 144 hours, without or without 1.0 mg/mL of glucose, fructose, galactose, or sucrose. In addition, some samples were preserved with 0.89% sodium fluoride. UACs were determined by an enzymatic method (centrifugal analyzer). The maximum UAC was obtained with samples spiked with glucose and *Candida albicans* and stored at 35°C for 24 hours (UAC was 0.052 g/100 mL). At 0°C or with NaF, no alcohol was formed.

The time vs. ethanol plot for any yeast showed that the production of ethanol was higher at 24 than at 48 h. After 48 h, the ethanol levels began to drop off dramatically. An explanation for this is that once the yeast consumes all of the available sugar, the organisms begin to digest the ethanol, thereby lowering ethanol concentrations.

Reference Number: 40106

JONES, A.W., A. EKLUND, AND A. HELANDER. "Misleading Results of Ethanol Analysis in Urine Specimens from Rape Victims Suffering from Diabetes." *Journal Clinical and Forensic Medicine*, 7: 144–146, 2000 (1 table, 14 references)

Abstract: Two female sexual assault victims (ages fifteen and eighteen years) had blood and urine samples collected approximately 15 and 19 hours respectively after the assault. Both victims had type 1 diabetes. The BAC of the first victim was zero and the urine contained 0.082 g/100 mL alcohol and 0.011 g/100 mL acetone. The BAC of the second victim was also zero and the urine contained 0.102 g/100 mL alcohol. This urine sample also contained a metabolite of flunitrazepam (Rohypnol) and cannabinoids. After several months storage at 4°C the UACs had increased to 0.550 and 0.800 g/100 mL respectively.

First, care is needed when urinary ethanol is measured in diabetic patients with genital candidiasis. Second, the tubes used to collect specimens of urine for alcohol analysis should always contain at least 1% sodium or potassium fluoride to prevent fermentation of any glucose that might be present.

Reference Number: 40107

NEUTEBOOM, W. AND P.G.M. ZWEIPFENNING. "The Stability of the Alcohol Concentration in Urine Specimens." *Journal of Analytical Toxicology*, 13: 141–143, 1989 (2 tables, 7 references)

Abstract: A study was conducted of the stability of alcohol in urine specimens from twenty impaired drivers and alcohol-negative urine samples from eighteen volunteers. The samples were placed in 100 mL polyethylene bottles preserved with 1% NaF and stored at 5°C or frozen (–10°C). Samples were analyzed in quadruplicate by ADH. After 12 months at 5°C, a mean decrease of 4.5% was observed. For samples frozen and thawed and refrozen three times over 12 months, there was a 4.4% decrease. No formation of ethanol was observed in the urine samples.

The chosen conditions for storage (i.e., 100-mL polyethylene bottles with screw caps, addition of sodium fluoride (1% w/v) and a temperature of -10°C) are suitable for storing urine specimens for at least 12 months before alcohol determination for forensic purposes.

Reference Number: 40108

SREERAMA, L. AND G.G. HARDIN. "Improper Sealing Caused by the Styrofoam Integrity Seals in Leakproof Plastic Bottles Lead to Significant Loss of Ethanol in Frozen Evidentiary Urine Samples." *Journal of Forensic Sciences*, 48: 672–676, 2003 (5 tables, 2 figures, 19 references)

Abstract: Spiked urine samples (n = 100), actual case urine samples (n = 345) and urine samples collected from drinking subjects were stored under various conditions. The UACs are reported in this paper as g/67 mL of urine, which is equivalent to a UAC/BAC ratio of 1.5. UACs were determined by headspace GC using *n*-propanol as an internal standard. In the case of urine samples that were stored for approximately 2 years at –20°C and thawed either at room temperature or at 4°C, the mean decrease in UAC was 32%. In spiked urine samples stored at –20°C for 1 month the average decrease in UAC was approximately 20% and was independent of initial UAC. The decrease in UAC was found to be due to the styrofoam seals placed around the top of the jars. Urine samples stored for up to 1 year at –20°C in Vacutainer blood tubes or in plastic bottles without the Styrofoam seal had a decrease in UAC of 2 to 3%.

> Clearly, the use of leak proof 100 mL plastic bottles without Styrofoam integrity seals results in prevention of loss of ethanol from these bottles during storage and/or thawing processes, and the poor sealing of the containers was responsible for the observed loss of ethanol concentration when the contents were frozen. Thus, paying close attention to, and experimental evaluation of loss in ethanol, in any particular system used by a laboratory can prevent the loss of ethanol.

Reference Number: 40109

HARD, A.M., N.G. CROFTS, L.M. LEE, J.V.J. GIRARD, AND R.J. SWEETLAND. "Isolated Bladder Rupture After Minor Trauma in a Patient With Alcohol Intoxication." *Journal of Emergency Medicine*, 12: 409–411, 1994 (1 figure, 10 references)

Abstract: A fifty-three-year-old male alcoholic attended hospital on two occasions as a result of abdominal pain and being unable to void for 19 hours. It was determined that there was a rupture in the dome of his bladder.

Alcohol intoxication increases the risk of bladder rupture by several means. Intoxication decreases the sensation of, and the behavioural response to, bladder filling. Both the sheer volume of alcohol and its diuretic effect increases bladder filling, often to the point of massive overdistensions. This overdistension may lead to an atonic decompensated bladder so stretched and thinned that even minor trauma may cause it to rupture.

Reference Number: 40110

DOOLDENIYA, M.D., R. KHAFAGY, H. MASHALY, A.J. BROWNING, S.K. SUNDARAM, AND C.S. BIYANI. "Lower Abdominal Pain in Women After Binge Drinking." *British Medical Journal*, 335: 992–993, 2007 (1 table, 1 figure, 11 references)

Abstract: Three women (ages twenty-four, thirty-two, and thirty-seven years respectively) were treated for lower abdominal pain after binge drinking. They were eventually diagnosed with idiopathic rupture of the bladder.

Alcohol consumption increases the volume of urine held within the bladder and dulls the senses such that the patient has reduced urge to void despite the increased bladder volume. Minor trauma such as from a fall will further increase the pressure and can cause rupture. It has been thought that women, because of the short length of the urethra and less pronounced sphincter mechanism would have a tendency to leak rather than rupture. We suggest that with the increase in alcohol consumption in women today the complications previously seen only in men should now also be considered.

Reference Number: 40111

BURNS, D.T. AND M.K. WALKER. "The Stability of Urine for the Forensic Analysis of Samples in Alleged Driving Under the Influence of Alcohol Cases—A Review and Case Report." *Journal of the Association of Public Analysts*, 48: 10 pp, 2020 (30 references)

Abstract: A urine sample was collected in Northern Ireland by the police from a driver suspected of DUI, which was the second of two successive voids. The urine sample was placed improperly into a plastic jar that did not contain NaF. The sample was placed in a police refrigerator for 41 days and sent to the forensic laboratory, which reported a UAC of not less than 125 mg/100 mL. The statutory limit is 107 mg/100 mL. It was postulated that a random urine sample from a healthy subject could contain 60 mg/dL glucose, which if fully converted could contain 30 mg/100 mL to the UAC.

The instant case was listed before a District Judge in the Magistrate's court. Expert reports and witness statements were exchanged. The defendant is not diabetic, however, based on the above literature it was argued that normal urine generally contains some glucose, and that a random sample of urine might contain sufficient glucose, if fully fermented, to jeopardize the safety of a conviction. The judge adjourned the case indicating that he required oral evidence from the police property officer on the storage conditions of the sample. In the meantime, the COVID-19 pandemic supervened, and it appears the defendant accepted responsibility for a lesser charge which did not result in the loss of his driving license and the matter did not come to trial.

Reference Number: 40112

GUMBEL, D., F. SCHNEIDLER, M. FRANK, B. BOCKHOLDT, P. HINZ, M. NAPP, R. SPITZMULLER, A. EKKERNKAMP, AND S. LANGER. "Urinary Bladder Volume Measured in Whole-Body CT Scans Is a Useful Marker for Alcohol Intoxication." *Alcohol*, 65: 45–50, 2017 (2 tables, 5 figures, 24 references)

Abstract: Whole body CT scans were conducted in the ER on 831 individuals with suspected multiple injuries in Germany. Manual #D-CT volumetry of the urinary bladder, BAC, serum creatinine, and hematocrit were determined. Fifty-three patients with a positive BAC were compared to 778 with a negative BAC or signs of intoxication. Patients with a positive BAC had a higher rate of falls than negative BAC patients. The mean urinary bladder volume (UBV) was 307.4 mL for patients with a negative BAC and 474.5 mL in patients with a positive BAC.

Table. Clinical Results of Negative and Positive BAC ER Patients

	Negative BAC Patients	Positive BAC Patients
UBV (mL)	307.4	474.5
Creatinine ratio (mL/μmol)	4.0	6.8
Hematocrit ratio (mL/%)	7.7	11.7
Hematocrit (%)	40.5	40.8
Serum creatinine (μmol/L)	86.6	79.7

Source: Adapted from Gumbel et al (2017).

Identification of clinically relevant alcohol intoxication in patients transferred to the ED is often challenging, due to an initial evaluation protocol focusing primarily on the treatment of life-threatening injuries. In this scenario, increased UBV may serve as an adjunct to clinical evaluation and should raise suspicion of alcohol intoxication, especially in cases where the UBV exceeds 416.3 mL. Accuracy can be improved by using the creatinine quotient, as it has been shown to be an even more sensitive marker for alcohol intoxication.

4.02 SALIVA (ORAL FLUID)

"Alcohol is excreted in the saliva in a concentration that closely approximates that of the blood. Alcohol by exciting sensory nerve endings in the mouth reflexly stimulates a flow of saliva which is followed by a poststimulatory depression of secretion."

—Beazell and Ivy, "The Influence of Alcohol on the Digestive Tract. A Review" (1940)

Saliva contains more alcohol than blood due to its higher water content (40201). Rapid saliva testing may be conducted in the clinical or forensic setting (40210), but it may be difficult to collect from some subjects (40202, 40206, 40208, 40209). The use of saliva test strips by drinking subjects to self-monitor their own BAC is not recommended due to the high error rate (40207, 40211).

Reference Number: 40201

JONES, A.W. "Inter- and Intra-Individual Variations in the Saliva/Blood Alcohol Ratio During Ethanol Metabolism in Man." *Clinical Chemistry*, 25: 1394–1398, 1979 (2 tables, 3 figures, 23 references)

Abstract: A study was conducted of forty-eight healthy male subjects who consumed 0.72 g/kg ethanol as neat whiskey over 20 minutes. Capillary blood and unstimulated mixed saliva secretions were taken concurrently at 30–60 minutes intervals for 7 hours. The mean saliva/blood alcohol ratio was 1.077 (n = 336), with a 95% confidence interval of 1.065–1.088. If whole blood contains 850 g and saliva 994 g of water/L, then the theoretical blood/saliva ratio should be 1.17. The saliva/blood alcohol ratio is not affected by the phase of ethanol absorption, distribution, and elimination.

In contrast to both the urine/blood and breath/blood alcohol ratios, which vary according to the phase of ethanol metabolism, the mean saliva/blood alcohol ratios shows no such variation. The applicability of saliva as a biological specimen for ethanol determination in clinical and medicolegal work should perhaps be reconsidered in view of this finding.

Reference Number: 40202

MCCOLL, K.E.L., B. WHITING, M.R. MOORE, AND A. GOLDBERG. "Correlation of Ethanol Concentration in Blood and Saliva." *Clinical Science*, 26: 283–286, 1979 (1 table, 2 figures, 6 references)

Abstract: Twelve male subjects (ages twenty to thirty-five years) consumed 100 to 200 mL of vodka over 15 minutes. Mixed saliva, parotid saliva, mixed saliva samples obtained after rinsing the mouth with tap water, and blood samples were collected and the alcohol concentrations were determined by GC. In addition, blood and mixed saliva samples were collected from thirty-three patients attending a hospital ER and showed clinical evidence of alcohol intoxication. For the drinking subjects the correlation between mixed saliva alcohol concentrations and the PACs at 20–240 minutes after drinking were r between 0.95 and 0.97. For hospital patients the correlation was $r = 0.96$. Saliva samples were difficult to obtain from severely intoxicated patients.

The examination of mixed saliva obtained at 20 min after completion of drinking onwards allows the accurate non-invasive determination of the blood ethanol concentration. Suitable samples may be difficult to collect in severely intoxicated patients.

Reference Number: 40203

HAECKEL, R. AND U. PEIFFER. "Comparison of Ethanol Concentration in Saliva and Blood from Police Controlled Persons." *Blutalkohol*, 29: 342–349, 1992 (4 figures, 24 references)

Abstract: Blood and saliva samples were collected from 105 arrested subjects. SACs and saliva alcohol concentrations were determined enzymatically. The SAC was converted into a whole blood alcohol concentration by using a factor of 1.2. The mean BAC was 0.168 g/100 mL. The mean saliva/blood concentration ratio for alcohol was 1.096. The water content of blood varied from 80.6 to 90.3% (CV = 5%).

Saliva should be taken together with breath samples from traffic participants who are controlled for ethanol consumption. These samples should be preserved in a refrigerator. Thus, if required, the analytical results can be confirmed, and interferences or drug interactions can be excluded. The advantage of saliva in favour of blood is that it can be determined nearly simultaneously with the breath sample without the intervention of a physician and does not hurt the person under suspicion.

Reference Number: 40204

SMOPLLE, K.H., G. HOFMANN, P. KAUFMANN, A. LUEGER, AND G. BRUNNER. "Q.E.D. Alcohol Tests: A Simple and Quick Method to Detect Ethanol in Saliva of Patients in Emergency Departments." *Intensive Care Medicine,* 25: 492–495, 1999 (1 table, 2 figures, 32 references)

Abstract: The saliva and blood alcohol concentrations of thirty female and seventy male patients (ages sixteen to sixty-one years) with suspected alcohol abuse were determined. A control group of fifteen patients who abstained from alcohol consumption for 24 hours was also tested. Saliva alcohol concentrations were determined by the QED Alcohol Test A350 and the BACs by an enzymatic method. The mean saliva alcohol concentration was significantly higher than the BAC by approximately 2.4%. Sufficient saliva for analysis was unable to be collected from seventeen subjects.

In conclusion, the two main findings of this study are 1) the results of the Q.E.D. Alcohol Test A350 correlate well with blood alcohol levels and 2) the saliva test gives an immediate quantitative indication of the level of alcohol in the blood. Since it is non-invasive and cheap, as well as easy to handle for emergency room personnel, it should prove useful in emergency rooms and ambulances, as well as for emergency physicians to determine whether alcohol is a cause of disturbed consciousness.

Reference Number: 40205

DEGUTIS, L.C., R. RABINOVICI, A. SABBAJ, R. MASCIA, AND G. D'ONOFRIO. "The Saliva Strip Test Is an Accurate Method to Determine Blood Alcohol Concentration in Trauma Patients." *Academy of Emergency Medicine,* 11: 885–887, 2004 (1 table, 10 references)

Abstract: The saliva alcohol concentration as determined by the AST QED A350 test strip was compared to the serum alcohol concentration as determined by GC in 100 trauma patients. The mean time between the collection of the two samples was 10 minutes. A positive SAC was found in forty-one patients. The mean SAC was 0.198 g/100 mL (range 0.022 to 0.446 g/100 mL). The mean saliva alcohol concentration was 0.168 g/100 mL (range 0.020 to 0.350 g/100 mL). The QED A350 does not measure the saliva alcohol concentration above 350 g/100 mL. The correlation between the two tests was $r = 0.879$. Eighteen patients had blood in the oropharynx and the correlation between the serum and saliva tests was $r = 0.976$.

Several factors support the wide use of AST in trauma patients. AST correlates well with serum BAC. AST results are not influenced by the presence of blood in the oral cavity. The noninvasive nature of AST minimizes the risk of needlestick injuries for staff and multiple needle punctures for patients. AST provides a determination of the BAC within 5 minutes. It should be noted that, although a breath analyzer also provides a rapid result, it requires calibration on a regular basis and patient cooperation.

Reference Number: 40206

BENDTSEN, P., J. HULTBERG, M. CARLSSON, AND A.W. JONES. "Monitoring of Ethanol Exposure in a Clinical Setting by Analysis of Blood, Breath, Saliva and Urine." *Alcoholism: Clinical and Experimental Research*, 23: 1446–1451, 1999 (1 table, 1 figure, 25 references)

Abstract: Admission and discharge blood, breath, urine, and saliva samples were collected from twenty-eight patients attending a detoxification center at the University Hospital in Linkoping, Sweden. Venous BACs and UACs were determined by headspace GC. BrACs were determined by an Alcolmeter S-D2. Saliva alcohol concentrations were determined by a QED saliva alcohol test. The mean UAC/BAC ratio was 1.44 (0.82–2.09). The rate of alcohol elimination was between 0.017–0.037 g/100 mL/h (mean 0.023 g/100 mL/h). The BAC/BrAC, BAC/UAC, and BAC/SAC correlations were 0.97, 0.75, and 0.92 respectively. When a BBR of 2,100:1 was used all BrACs were lower than the BAC.

In conclusion, the analysis of alcohol in breath offers a simple and reliable method of estimating the coexisting blood ethanol concentration in patients who attended a detoxification unit. Saliva alcohol analysis with the Q.E.D. failed to perform well, especially at high BAC levels, mainly because of difficulties in obtaining a significant amount of specimen in some patients.

Reference Number: 40207

JOHNSON, M.B. AND R.B. VOAS. "Potential Risks of Providing Drinking Drivers with BAC Information." *Traffic Injury and Prevention*, 5: 42–49, 2004 (1 table, 2 figures, 38 references)

Abstract: One hundred and twenty-nine drinking male and female college students were interviewed and self-administered a Guardian Angel (GA) saliva alcohol tester. The participants had to read and follow the instructions, i.e., place the test strip on the tongue for 10 to 15 seconds and wait 2 minutes and interpret the color change. The color change corresponded to BACs of low (0 to 0.040 g/100 mL), high (0.040 to 0.070 g/100 mL), and highest (0.080 g/100 mL+). BrACs were also determined with a handheld Breathalyser.

With respect to the three research issues that this pilot study was designed to study, it was found that: 1) with respect to test administration, 10% to 20% of drinkers in a naturalistic night-time setting will make errors in administering the test and that errors are associated with the user's BAC; 2) with respect to GA test accuracy when interpreted by drinkers in a naturalistic setting, it understates rather than overstates the user's BAC when compared to a breath test device; and 3) with respect to test interpretation, users of the GA unit reported feeling less drunk and possibly less impaired after using the device but did not change their view of the ability to drive legally.

Reference Number: 40208

DUTTA, S.K., M. ORESTES, S. VENGULEKUR, AND P. KWO. "Ethanol and Human Saliva: Effect of Chronic Alcoholism on Flow Rate, Composition and Epidermal Growth Factor." *American Journal of Gastroenterology*, 87: 350–354, 1992 (5 figures, 30 references)

Abstract: The stimulated parotid saliva flow rate and protein/electrolyte composition of the saliva were determined in twenty-four alcoholics (ages twenty-five to fifty-eight years) admitted for detoxification and then 1 week later. These were compared with sixteen matched control subjects.

The parotid saliva flow rate was stimulated with a 2% citric acid solution in the oral cavity and was collected with a Carlson-Crittenden cap. The mean stimulated parotid salivary flow rate was lower in eleven alcoholics (0.16 mL/min/gland) compared to the control subjects (0.46 mL/min/gland). After 1 week of detoxification the mean salivary flow rate increased to 0.32 mL/min/gland and was not statistically significant from controls. There was a significant reduction in total protein output (mg/min) in alcoholics.

Table. Mean Stimulated Parotid Saliva Flow Rate in Alcoholics and Healthy Subjects

Type of Subject	Mean stimulated parotid saliva flow rate (mL/min/gland)
Alcoholic Patients	0.16
Alcoholic Patients (1 week abstinence)	0.32
Healthy Controls	0.46

Source: Adapted from Dutta et al (1992).

We have previously reported more than 40% reduction in mean stimulated parotid saliva flow rate after ingestion of a single large dose (0.8 g/kg) of ethanol in healthy adult subjects. This observation suggests that ethanol, if ingested in large amounts can induce inhibition of stimulated parotid saliva secretion.

Reference Number: 40209

GJERDE, H., P.T. NORMANN, AND A.S. CHRISTOPHERSEN. "The Prevalence of Alcohol and Drugs in Sampled Oral Fluid Is Related to Sample Volume." *Journal of Analytical Toxicology*, 34: 416–418, 2010 (4 tables, 10 references)

Abstract: Saliva samples were collected from 10,816 Norwegian drivers during a roadside survey between 2005 and 2006 using the Intercept Oral Specimen Sampling Device and from 10,928 drivers between 2008 and 2010 using the Statsure Saliva Sampler. The prevalence of alcohol and drugs were found to be greater in saliva samples with a smaller volume of saliva collected. A positive oral fluid alcohol concentration was found in 4.5% of the samples < 0.6 mL in volume and decreased to 0.4% in samples > 1.25 mL in volume for the Statsure Saliva Sampler.

> Our recommendation is that samples of oral fluid with smaller volume than required by the analytical methods should not be discarded, but instead be analyzed using a smaller sample volume, if necessary, after dilution. If not analyzed positive drug cases will be missed, and the total prevalence of alcohol and drugs in the population being studied will be underestimated.

Reference Number: 40210

THOKALA, M.R., S.P.R. DORANKULA, K. MUDDANA, AND S.R. VELDANDLA. "Alcohol Saliva Strip Test." *Journal of Clinical and Diagnostic Research*, 8: 307–308, 2014 (10 references)

Abstract: A general description of the alcohol saliva test (AST) was presented. ASTs contain 12 mg of tetramethylbenzidine (TMB), 0.51 IU of alcohol oxidase, 0.35 IU of peroxidase, and 0.15 mg of protein. The color change in response to alcohol occurs within 20 seconds. The AST tests are not affected by the presence of blood in the mouth.

> Combining rapidity and reliability, alcohol saliva strip test (AST) has been put forward for the detection of alcohol in saliva for blood alcohol concentration (BAC).

Reference Number: 40211

GJERDE, H., A.L. BRETTEVILLE-JENSEN, AND H. FURUHAUGEN. "Poor Correlation Between Alcohol Concentration in Oral Fluid and Breath in Subjects Consuming Beverages Immediately Before Testing." *Biochemia Medica (Zagreb)*, 32: 5pp, 2022 (1 figure, 13 references)

Abstract: Oral fluid (OF) and breath samples were collected from eighty-nine nightclub patrons in Norway after drinking a glass of water to remove residual alcohol from the mouth. Oral fluid was collected using a Quantisal oral fluid collection device in which a small pad collects approximately 1 mL of OF. This is transferred to a collection tube containing 3 mL of a preservative/buffering solution. The alcohol concentrations were determined by an ADH method. BrACs were determined with an Alcolmeter 5000 (fuel cell sensor) calibrated on a BBR of 2,000:1. The manufacturers recommend that OF samples should be collected at least 10 minutes after consumption of food and beverage and that the breath tests should be taken at least 20 minutes after talking or taking anything by mouth. Of the eighty-nine participants, eighty-eight tested positive for both OF and breath alcohol. There were no false negative or false positive alcohol results when OF was compared to breath. The correlation between OF and breath alcohol concentrations was poor with an ICC of 0.40.

> The procedure for collecting oral fluid was suitable for the qualitative determination of alcohol intake but not for quantitative assessment. We recommend that oral fluid samples should not be used for estimating blood or breath alcohol concentrations in people who have recently consumed alcohol or non-alcoholic beverages, as recommended in the instructions for use.

4.03 SWEAT (TRANSDERMAL)/TEARS

> "The analyses showed a concentration amounting to about 80 p.c. of that of the blood. Since evaporation must have taken place and the value of this error can to some extent be calculated, the experiments give fairly reliable evidence that alcohol passes over into the sweat in a way corresponding to its occurrence in other body fluids."
>
> —Nyman and Palmlov, "The Elimination of Alcohol in Sweat" (1936)

> "Sweating does not get rid of alcohol from your body any quicker than normal. Alcohol is broken down by your liver into smaller byproducts, which are then expelled from your kidneys into your urine. Sweating is a result of the effects of alcohol on your body, but sweating does not 'get rid' of the alcohol from your body any quicker."
>
> —Babylon Health Team US, 1 October 2021

Since alcohol distributes throughout the total body water, it will appear in sweat. Sweat alcohol concentrations tend to lag behind breath or blood alcohol concentrations and obtain a lower peak alcohol concentration (40301, 40302, 40304). Various patches and devices have been developed over the years to monitor alcohol abstinence by alcohol analysis of the sweat (40303, 40305).

The most established, reliable, and studied transdermal alcohol monitoring device is SCRAM (Secure Continuous Remote Alcohol Monitor) (40307–40313).

Alcohol also appears in the tears (40306).

Reference Number: 40301

NYMAN, E. AND A. PALMLOV. "The Elimination of Ethyl Alcohol in Sweat." *Skandinavischae Archiv fur Physiologie*, 74: 155–159, 1936 (1 table, 7 references)

Abstract: Sweat samples were collected by various techniques from subjects in a highly heated room after the subjects consumed 0.5–0.7 g/kg ethanol. Sweat and blood alcohol concentrations were determined by the Widmark method. The sweat alcohol concentration was found to be approximately 80% that of BAC, but it is suggested that some alcohol may have evaporated from the sweat prior to the collection of the sample.

Since the amount of sweat even under extreme conditions will never exceed 10 L in a day it is easy to calculate that there can be no question of using sweating as a method of getting rid of alcohol from the body. Normally the daily amount of sweat is about 600–700 c.c.; hence less than 1 p.c. of the ingested quantity of ethyl alcohol can be eliminated under normal conditions.

Reference Number: 40302

PHILLIPS, M., J. GREENBERG, AND J. ANDRZEJEWSKI. "Evaluation of the Alcopatch, A Transdermal Dosimeter for Monitoring Alcohol Consumption." *Alcoholism: Clinical and Experimental Research*, 19: 1547–1549, 1995 (1 figure, 7 references)

Abstract: A study was conducted of thirteen male and one female subjects (mean age 32.5 years) who consumed alcohol over the next 7 to 8 days and had an Alcopatch attached to their ankles. The Alcopatch concentration was determined by headspace GC. The daily alcohol consumption ranged between 0.1 to 0.9 g/kg. Two of the subjects had outlier results and the correlation between the reported consumption of alcohol and the Alcopatch concentration was $r = 0.61$.

The Alcopatch may be most useful in the future as a measure of monitoring alcohol consumption in subjects whose self-reports are potentially unreliable. This includes alcoholics and persons under surveillance by the criminal justice system (e.g., for parole, probation, and offenses such as driving while intoxicated.).

Reference Number: 40303

DAVIDSON, D., P. CAMARA, AND R. SWIFT. "Behavioral Effects and Pharmacokinetics of Low-Dose Intravenous Alcohol in Humans." *Alcoholism, Clinical and Experimental Research*, 21: 1294–1299, 1997 (1 table, 2 figures, 29 references)

Abstract: Seven male and eight female subjects (ages twenty-one to fifty-eight years) were administered ethanol IV to obtain BACs of 0, 0.010, 0.020, and 0.040 g/100 mL. BACs were determined in blood (ADH method), breath (Intoximeter), and with a transdermal alcohol sensor (TAS). Subjective intoxication and various psychomotor tests were conducted.

The TAS curve typically shows a delay in time with respect to the breath alcohol and blood alcohol curves. This delay may be specific to the diffusion properties of alcohol from the skin and a reservoir effect of the tissue, compared with the more rapid expiration of alcohol from lungs or the equilibrium of alcohol within circulating blood.

Reference Number: 40304

BUONO, M.J. "Sweat Ethanol Concentrations Are Highly Correlated with Co-Existing Blood Values in Humans." *Experimental Physiology*, 84: 401–404, 1999 (2 figures, 14 references)

Abstract: Ten male subjects (mean age twenty-six years) consumed approximately 0.8–0.9 g/kg alcohol within 30 minutes. Blood and sweat alcohol samples were collected 1, 2, and 3 hours after the start of alcohol consumption. Sweat was collected from a 7 cm^2 area on the flexor surface of the forearm for 15 minutes immediately following pilocarpine iontophoresis using a Macroduct sweat collector. Capillary blood samples were collected from the fingertip midway through the sweat collection. Alcohol concentrations were measured by an enzymatic method. Water concentrations were also determined. The water content of the blood was approximately 80% and the sweat was 98%. The blood and sweat alcohol concentrations were highly correlated, $r = 0.98$, and when corrected for the water concentration the slope was 1.01.

These results suggest rapid equilibrium of ethanol across the sweat gland epithelium.

Reference Number: 40305

SAKAI, J.T., S.K. MIKULICH-GILBERTSON, R.J. LONG, AND T.J. CROWLEY. "Validity of Transdermal Alcohol Monitoring: Fixed and Self-Regulated Dosing." *Alcoholism: Clinical and Experimental Research*, 30: 26–33, 2006 (3 tables, 4 figures, 23 references)

Abstract: A comparison between BrACs and transdermal alcohol concentration (TAC) was conducted in twenty-four subjects who consumed 0, 0.28, and 0.56 g/kg alcohol within 10 minutes. BrACs were determined with an Alco-Sensor III and TACs with a SCRAM anklet. In the group that did not consume alcohol, all BrACs and TACs were zero. The mean peak BrACs for the two alcohol doses were 0.056 and 0.088 g/100 mL compared to 0.028 and 0.064 g/100 mL respectively for the TAC. On average the peak TAC occurred 2 and 3 hours respectively after the peak BrAC. The SCRAM anklet was also tested on ten alcohol-dependent and ten non-alcohol-dependent volunteers in the community who wore the anklet for 8 days. The SCRAM anklet weighs 227 g and is larger than the WrisTAS.

> Although in general, alcohol is known to rapidly diffuse across compartments, the elimination of transdermal alcohol is slowed; during absorption, TAC results were sometimes zero when breath results were not and during elimination, transdermal results remained positive after breath results had already returned to zero. This suggests the presence of a third compartment (such as fatty tissues), which takes up alcohol more slowly and holds alcohol after it is eliminated from the water compartment. Alternatively, this effect may relate in part to the anklet design. In an attempt to make the anklet water resistant, only a small external outlet on the anklet covering was provided and this may not easily allow fresh air into the sampling chamber between readings. This may also partially explain the protracted transdermal readings.

Reference Number: 40306

LUND, A. "The Secretion of Alcohol in the Tear Fluid." *Blutalkohol*, 21: 51–54, 1984 (1 table, 6 references)

Abstract: Twelve subjects consumed approximately 75 g of alcohol. Thirty to sixty minutes after drinking ceased, blood and tear samples were collected and analyzed for ethanol by ADH. Tear formation was stimulated by either cigarette smoke, ammonia vapor, or by tickling the nostril with a horse hair. Blood is 86% v/v water and tears are 99.5% v/v water, therefore the theoretical TAC/BAC ratio should be 1.16. The TAC/BAC ratio was determined in this experiment to be 1.14, SD = 0.037.

> A TAC/BAC ratio of 1.14 found in the present investigations means that TAC multiplied by 0.88 yields the most likely value for BAC. For the legal procedure it may be more relevant to state that an actual BAC with more than 99% security is equal to or higher than the analytically found TAC multiplied by 0.80, corresponding to the mean ratio value, added 3 SD.

Reference Number: 40307

KARNS-WRIGHT, T.E., J.D. ROACHE, N. HILL-KAPTURCZAK, Y. LIANG, J. MULLEN, AND D.M. DOUGHTERY. "Time Delays in Transdermal Alcohol Concentrations Relative to Breath Alcohol Concentrations." *Alcohol and Alcoholism,* 52: 35–41, 2017 (1 table, 1 figure, 25 references)

Abstract: BrACs and TACs were determined in thirty-two men and twenty-nine women (ages twenty-one to forty-seven years) after drinking one, two, three, four, or five beers. The five beers were consumed over 47 to 166 minutes. TACs were automatically recorded by the SCRAM device every 30 minutes. BrACs were measured every 15 to 30 minutes by an Alcotest 6810. The TAC showed lower peaks, long time to peaks, and longer duration than BrACs. The time lag to peak for TAC compared to BrAC was 82.5, 119.8, 131.2, 153.6, and 162.0 minutes for one, two, three, four, and five beers respectively. Both peak TACs and BrACs were higher in women than men.

> The times to peak were an increasing function of the number of beers consumed. At each level of beer consumption, the peak TAC average lower than peak BrAC and times to peak TAC were longer than for BrAC. The time to peak BrAC increased as a function of the beers consumed. No sex differences in the time lag between peak BrAC and TAC was detected. The congruence between TAC and BrAC and time lags between TAC and BrAC are related to the number of beers consumed. Peak values of TAC and BrAC became more congruent with higher doses but the time lag increased as a function of the amount of alcohol consumed. The time delay (or lag) and congruence between transdermal vs. BrACs increase as the number of beers increases. Though sex differences are evident in peak transdermal and BrACs, no sex differences were evident in the time lag and the congruence between transdermal and breath alcohol concentrations.

Reference Number: 40308

DOUGHTERY, D.M., N. HILL-KAPTURCZAK, Y. LIANG, T.E. KARNS, S.K. LAKE, S.E. CATES, AND J.D. ROACHE. "The Potential Clinical Utility of Transdermal Alcohol Monitoring Data to Estimate the Number of Alcoholic Drinks Consumed." *Addict Disorders and Their Treatment*, 14: 124–130, 2015 (1 table, 2 figures, 15 references)

Abstract: Twenty-one male and twenty-one female subjects (ages twenty-one to forty-seven years) consumed one to five beers within 2 hours over successive days. TACs were measured with a SCRAM device and BrACs with an Alcotest 6810.

> This study complements and extends our previous work using TAC data to estimate peak BrAC levels by developing a new mathematical model to accurately estimate the number of standard drinks consumed. The model that best estimated units of alcohol consumed included three parameters; time to peak TAC, AUC, and sex variables. We validated the model developed from data in one study to accurately predict the number of standard units of alcohol consumed in another independent study.

Reference Number: 40309

BARNETT, N.P., E.B. MEADE, AND T.R. GLYNN. "Predictors of Detection of Alcohol Use Episodes Using a Transdermal Alcohol Sensor." *Experimental and Clinical Psychopharmacology*, 22: 86–96, 2014 (2 tables, 3 figures, 26 references)

Abstract: Thirty-two female and thirty-four male heavy drinkers wore the SCRAMII (earlier model) or SCRAMx anklet to detect the TAC over a period of 1 to 28 days and the results were compared to self-reported alcohol consumption. Overall, 690 drinking sessions were reported and 502 (72.8%) were detected. If the drinking episode consisted of five or more drinks, then 93% of the episodes were detected. For drinking sessions of less than five drinks, women's drinking episodes were more likely to be detected than men's due to the higher TACs obtained by women. In this study a drinking episode was identified if one TAC > 0.020 g/100 mL and the absorption rate was < 0.050 g/100 mL/h or the elimination rate was < 0.025 g/100 mL/h if the peak TAC < 0.150 g/100 mL and < 0.035 g/100 mL/h if the peak TAC > 0.150 g/100 mL/h. The AMS criteria include three TAC readings > 0.020 g/100 mL and meet both the absorption and elimination criteria.

Although the research participants in this study were not mandated to wear the SCRAM, it is important to consider how these research findings are relevant for court-mandated alcohol monitoring. First, false negatives (i.e., failure to detect a real drinking episode) are more likely to happen when the drinking episode is smaller, whereas missing a drinking episode using SCRAM when the number of drinks is five or greater is unlikely. That is, heavy drinking episodes which are more likely to be associated with significant impairment, have a very high likelihood of being detected. Second, it is important to emphasize that false positive (i.e., identifying a drinking episode that did not occur) are likely to be lower in the real world using AMS' system for detecting alcohol use. AMS has more conservative criteria for detecting alcohol use and takes additional steps including visual inspection of suspected drinking events to determine the likelihood that drinking occurred; this more conservative approach has a very low likelihood of false positive.

Reference Number: 40310

DOUGHTERY, D.M., N. CHARLES, A. ACHESON, S. JONG, R.M. FURR, AND N. HILL-KAPTURCZAK. "Comparing the Detection of Transdermal and Breath Alcohol Concentrations during Periods of Alcohol Consumption Ranging from Moderate Drinking to Binge Drinking." *Experimental and Clinical Psychopharmacology*, 20: 373–381, 2012 (3 tables, 3 figures, 48 references)

Abstract: Binge drinking is defined as five+ drinks for men and four+ drinks for women over a 2-hour period that results in a BAC of 0.080 g/100 mL or greater. Approximately 1% of alcohol consumed is excreted through sweat. Eleven male and eleven female drinkers (ages twenty-one to forty-five years) consumed one, two, three, and four beers for women and one to five beers for men on successive days. BrACs were measured with an Alcotest 6810. The beers consumed were 12 oz. Corona beers (4.6% v/v alcohol). The TAC did not change from zero after one beer consumption for two women and one man. TACs increased linearly as a function of the number of drinks consumed. A formula to calculate the BrAC from TAC was developed ($r = 0.93$).

Table. Mean Peak TAC and BrAC Concentrations in 11 Male Drinking Subjects After Consuming 1–5 Beers

Number of Beers Consumed	Mean Peak TAC (g/100 mL)	Mean Peak BrAC (g/100 mL)
1	0.010	0.028
2	0.025	0.040
3	0.045	0.055
4	0.072	0.069
5	0.085	0.090

Source: Adapted from Doughtery et al (2012).

The present findings suggest TAC data is reliably related to alcohol consumption and has convergent validity with BrAC, a more commonly used measure of alcohol intake. Additionally, TAC monitoring has unique advantages over other methods of monitoring drinking behavior that can improve the quality of data obtained and decrease the interference of monitoring procedures with wearer's normal behavior. Therefore, TAC monitors could be used in both clinical and research contexts where determining a range of blood alcohol levels may be necessary.

Reference Number: 40311

LEFFINGWELL, T.R., N.J. COONEY, J.G. MURPHY, J.G. LUCZAK, G. ROSEN, D.M. DOUGHTERY, AND N.P. BARNMETT. "Continuous Objective Monitoring of Alcohol Use: Twenty-First Century Measurement Using Transdermal Sensors." *Alcoholism: Clinical and Experimental Research*, 37: 16–22, 2013 (22 references)

Abstract: Two devices have been developed for detecting transdermal alcohol, the Secure Continuous Remote Alcohol Monitor (SCRAM) and the Wrist Transdermal Alcohol Sensor (WrisTAS). The SCRAM device has a fuel cell detector that collects samples every 30 minutes, a skin temperature detector, and an IR device ensuring continuous contact with the skin. SCRAM can be worn while showering but not immersed in water. It can be worn for up to 6 months. WrisTAS had high malfunction rates and low true positive detection rates.

Transdermal alcohol sensors continuously collect reliable and valid data on alcohol consumption in vivo over the course of hours to weeks. Transdermal alcohol readings are highly correlated with breath alcohol measurements but transdermal alcohol levels lag behind breath alcohol levels by one or more hours owing to the longer time required for alcohol to be expelled through perspiration. By providing objective information about alcohol consumption, transdermal alcohol sensors can validate self-report and provide important information not previously available.

Reference Number: 40312

FAIRBAIRN, C.E., W.J. VENERABLE, I.G. ROSEN, AND S.E. LUCZAK. "Estimating the Quantity and Time Course of Alcohol Consumption from Transdermal Alcohol Sensor Data: A Combined Laboratory-Ambulatory Study." *Alcohol*, 81: 111–116, 2019 (2 tables, 31 references)

Abstract: Twenty-four male and twenty-four female heavy social drinkers (ages twenty-one to thirty years) were fitted with a SCRAM device after ensuring their BrAC was zero (Alco-Sensor IV) for 7 days. Self-reported drinking reports were obtained daily, and six times a day the subjects were prompted to take a picture of their surroundings. The subjects were also administered approximately 0.8 g/kg alcohol consumed over 36 minutes, and BrACs and TACs were determined. The average peak BrAC was 0.074 g/100 mL obtained within 60 minutes after the end of consumption.

More research is needed to understand the relationship between BrAC and TAC across a range of BrAC levels including very high alcohol doses. Further the vast majority of research to date has measured transdermal alcohol using the SCRAM bracelet. Although well suited to the binary characterization of drinking episodes within a forensic context, this bracelet may be suboptimal for assessing continuous real-time BrAC in voluntary populations. Not only may the SCRAM be uncomfortable and embarrassing for some participants, but its precise position with respect to the surface of the skin may be variable and thus potentially impact the precision of TAC readings.

Reference Number: 40313

RASH, C.J., N.M. PETRY, S.M. ALESSI, AND N.P. BARNETT. "Monitoring Alcohol Use in Heavy Drinking Soup Kitchen Attendees." *Alcohol*, 81: 139–147, 2019 (3 tables, 2 figures, 43 references)

Fifteen male and seven female heavy drinkers who attended a soup kitchen had their BrACs determined daily for 15 days using an Alco-Sensor

IV. Transdermal alcohol concentrations were also determined for 3 weeks using a SCRAMx. The percentage of non-drinking days was 93% using BrAC, 58% using SCRAM, and 57% using self-reports. The longest duration of consecutive non-drinking days averaged 10.3 days (BrAC), 7.2 days (SCRAM), and 5.7 days (self-report).

> These data suggest that transdermal monitors are well tolerated and documented substantial heavy drinking in this population. Soup kitchens users are in need of alcohol interventions, and soup kitchens may represent a novel opportunistic setting for intervention delivery for an important and growing health disparities population.

4.04 BREAST MILK

> "The above result show that the alcohol passes quickly into breast milk at a level which at equilibrium is equal to or greater than in blood."
>
> —Lawton, "Alcohol in Breast Milk" (1985)

If alcohol is consumed by a lactating woman, the alcohol will be distributed in the breast milk according to its water concentration but will not be stored or concentrated there (40401–40404). There may be less systemic availability of alcohol in lactating women and their peak BACs may be lower than for women who are not lactating (40405). Breast pumping after the consumption of alcohol may increase its rate of elimination (40406).

A three-week-old infant developed an abdominal distension due to alcohol being transferred from the breast milk of a mother who consumed Chinese yellow wine (40407).

Reference Number: 40401

KESANIEMI, Y.A. "Ethanol and Acetaldehyde in the Milk and Peripheral Blood of Lactating Women After Ethanol Administration." *Journal of Obstetrics and Gynaecology*, 81: 84–86, 1974 (1 table, 9 references)

Abstract: Twelve lactating women consumed 0.6g/kg ethanol as 15% v/v solution within 5 minutes. Blood and milk samples were taken 30, 60, 90, and 120 minutes after ethanol administration. Samples were analyzed for ethanol by headspace GC using *t*-butanol as an internal standard. The ethanol concentration in human milk is approximately the same as blood. No acetaldehyde was detected in the breast milk, although high acetaldehyde concentrations were detected in the mother's blood. (Note: there are no red blood cells in milk, therefore no significant amounts of acetaldehyde will be formed in comparison to whole blood).

> Clearly, continuous exposure of breast-fed baby to ethanol may be harmful, and while daily usage of alcohol cannot be recommended, occasional drinking of alcohol during lactation cannot be regarded as dangerous.

Reference Number: 40402

LAWTON, M.E. "Alcohol in Breast Milk." *Australian and New Zealand Obstetrics and Gynaecology*, 25: 71–73, 1985 (3 tables, 1 figure, 6 references)

Abstract: The average water content of breast milk is 87.5% and blood is 85%. Eight nursing mothers consumed 0.56–1.50 g/kg ethanol as quickly as possible. Blood and breast milk samples were analyzed by headspace GC. If a six-month-old child weighing 6.5 kg drank 180 mL of milk while the mother was at a BAC of 0.119 g/100 mL, the baby would have a BAC of 0.006 g/100 mL. Alcohol is not stored isolated in breast milk as it is in urine in the bladder.

Table. BAC and Breast Milk Alcohol Concentration in Lactating Women at 2 Hours After Alcohol Consumption

Subject Number	BAC at 2 hr (g/100 mL)	Breast Milk Alcohol Concentration at 2hr (g/100 mL)
3	0.065	0.068
4	0.119	0.129
5	0.035	0.039
6	0.044	0.046
7	0.035	0.036

Source: Adapted from Lawton (1985).

> The above result show that the alcohol passes quickly into breast milk at a level which at equilibrium is equal to or greater than in blood.

Reference Number: 40403

HO, E., A. COLLANTES, B.M. KAPUR, M. MORETTI, AND G. KOREN. "Alcohol and Breast Feeding: Calculation of Time to Zero Level in Milk." *Biology of Neonate*, 80: 219–222, 2001 (2 tables, 28 references)

Abstract: A table of times to reach a zero BAC is presented for women between 41 to 95 kg based on standard drinks (12 fl. oz beer (5%), 1.5 fl. oz spirits (40%), 5 fl. oz wine (11%)) and an average rate of alcohol elimination of 0.015 g/100 mL/h.

Since elimination of alcohol follows zero- order kinetics, drinking water, resting, or pumping and dumping of breast milk will not accelerate the elimination of alcohol. Unlike urine, which stores substances in the bladder, alcohol is not trapped in breast milk but is constantly removed as it diffuse back into the blood during elimination.

Reference Number: 40404

SCHUETZE, P., R.D. EIDEN, AND A.W.K., CHAN. "The Effects of Alcohol in Breast Milk on Infant Behavioral State and Mother-Infant Feeding Interactions." *Infancy*, 3: 349–363, 2002 (1 table, 44 references)

Abstract: The short-term effect of alcohol consumed by a lactating mother on the breast-fed infant was determined. Fourteen mothers breast-fed their infants without and with consumption of 0.3 g/kg alcohol within 15 minutes. BrACs were determined in the mothers with an Intoxilyzer 5000. The mean BrAC at 30 minutes was approximately 0.030 g/100 mL. The breast milk alcohol concentrations ranged from 0.012 to 0.048 g/100 mL.

The results of this study indicated that exposure to even small amounts of alcohol through breast milk can affect infant arousal. More specifically, after consuming breast milk containing small amounts of alcohol, infants spent proportionately less time in quiet sleep and more time in quiet alert state.

Reference Number: 40405

PEPINO, M.Y., A.L. STEINMEYER, AND J.A. MENNELLA. "Lactation State Modified Alcohol Pharmacokinetics in Women." *Alcoholism: Clinical and Experimental Research*, 31: 909–918, 2007 (3 tables, 3 figures, 62 references)

Abstract: Twenty lactating women, nine formula-feeding women, and fifteen women who had never given birth (nulliparous) consumed 0.4 g/

kg alcohol after a 12-hour fast and after a standard breakfast. BrACs were determined with an Alco-Sensor III. The mean peak BrACs after fasting were 0.069, 0.076, and 0.084 g/100 mL for the lactating, formula-feeding, and nulliparous women respectively. The mean peak BrACs after food were 0.039, 0.050, and 0.046 g/100 mL respectively. The mean rates of alcohol elimination were 0.015, 0.017, and 0.016 g/100 mL/h respectively for the fasted state and 0.018, 0.022, and 0.017 g/100 mL/h in the fed state.

> The systemic availability of alcohol is diminished during lactation, a finding that extends the previous work of da Silva et al (1993). Regardless of whether alcohol was consumed following a meal or on an empty stomach, the resultant BAC levels were significantly lower, and the UAC were significantly smaller in lactating women when compared with the 2 groups of nonlactating women. As expected the differences were most apparent when alcohol was consumed with food.

Reference Number: 40406

PEPINO, M.Y., AND J.A. MENNELLA. "Effects of Breast Pumping on the Pharmacokinetics and Pharmacodynamics of Ethanol During Lactation." *Clinical Pharmacology and Therapeutics*, 84: 710–714, 2008 (2 tables, 2 figures, 33 references)

Abstract: Eight lactating women breast pumped 1 hour before and eight lactating women breast-pumped approximately 0.6 hours after the consumption of 0.4 g/kg alcohol within 10 minutes under fasted and fed conditions. The mean rate of alcohol elimination was 0.015 g/100 mL/h (fed) and 0.013 g/100 mL/h (fasted) for the breast pump before group and 0.021 g/100 mL/h (fed) and 0.017 g/100 mL/h (fasted) for the breast pump after group.

Table. Mean Rate of Elimination of Alcohol (g/100 mL/h) for Eight Lactating Women Under Fed and Fasted Conditions and Using a Breast Pump Before or After Alcohol Consumption

	Mean rate of elimination (g/100 mL/h)	
Food conditions	Breast pump (before)	Breast pump (after)
Fed	0.015	0.021
Fasted	0.013	0.017

Source: Adapted from Pepino and Mennella (2008).

Breast feeding and breast pumping elicit neural, hormonal, and gut responses similar to those elicited by eating but the exact mechanisms underlying their effect on ethanol metabolism remain to be elucidated.

Reference Number: 40407

HON, K.L., A.K.C. LEUNG, E. CHEUNG, B. LEE, M.M.C. TSANG, AND A.R. TORRES. "An Overview of Exposure to Ethanol-Containing Substances and Ethanol Intoxication in Children Based on Three Illustrated Cases." *Drugs in Context*, 7: 5pp, 2018 (1 figure, 23 references)

Abstract: Three cases of unintentional alcohol ingestion in children are reported. A three-week-old male infant had an abdominal distension, which reduced the frequency of the passage of stools. This was due to alcohol being transferred from the breast milk of a mother who consumed Chinese yellow wine. A four-year-old girl obtained a BAC of 0.225 g/100 mL after licking and eating hand sanitizer jelly (75% ethyl alcohol) while unsupervised. The third case involved a ten-year-old boy who had a BAC of 0.201 g/100 mL after drinking spirits (40% v/v alcohol) from his parent's liquor cabinet.

Diagnosis of ethanol intoxication in children is based on detailed history of exposure, including the lactating mother. Physicians should be aware of the danger of ethanol intoxication is typically not necessary. Supportive measures include intravenous fluids, dextrose, and mechanical ventilation, which should be used when necessary.

4.05 BIOMARKERS (EtG TEST)

"The main purpose of an EtG test is to document alcohol abstinence.... It's important to note that the EtG test is not recommended for use in workplace testing programs as it does not measure current impairment from alcohol."

—Buddy T, "EtG Test for Confirming Alcohol Abstinence: What You Should Know About the EtG Test" (2022)

The metabolism of alcohol produces numerous biomarkers in blood, urine, or hair of either chronic heavy alcohol consumption (40501–40505) or of abstinence from alcohol (40506–40513). The formation of ethyl glucuronide occurs mainly in the liver as ethyl alcohol undergoes an enzymatic reaction with glucuronic acid to form ethyl glucuronide as follows:

$$CH_3CH_2OH + C_6H_{10}O_7 \rightarrow C_8H_{14}O_7$$

Another biomarker formed from alcohol is ethyl sulfate ($C_2H_6O_4S$). Only approximately 0.1% of the alcohol is metabolized to EtG and EtS. These biomarkers are so sensitive that the use of mouthwash (40509), alcohol-containing cosmetics (40510), the consumption of alcohol-free beer (40516), or baker's yeast and sugar (40517) can result in a detectable concentration of these biomarkers, although the levels obtained are well below the US standard of 500 ng/mL as evidence for deliberate alcohol ingestion (40518).

The consumption of traditional low alcohol beverages such as salgam and kefir did not result in any positive BACs, nor did it increase urinary EtS or EtG concentrations (40519).

In urine samples containing glucose and infected with *C. albicans*, the urine EtG concentration increased and then decreased upon storage, but the urine EtS concentration was unaffected (40520, 40521).

The percentage of alcohol converted into EtG in the blood did not increase when the alcohol dose was increased (40522). Recent alcohol consumption can be detected by blood EtG and EtS in traffic injury cases where the BAC was negative as a result of long delays in the collection of the blood sample (40523).

EtG is diffused from the blood through the surrounding tissues and outer and inner root sheaths into the completed hair in these regions, which seems to contribute essentially to the final concentration in the hair; in addition, EtG is added to the hair by sweat (40524). In many countries drivers convicted of DUI must undergo a hair EtG analysis to ensure they are not chronic heavy drinkers before license renewal (40525).

The use of a hair shampoo does not affect the hair EtG concentration (40526) but bleaching the hair with hydrogen peroxide causes a significant decrease (40527). Straightening the hair can cause either a decrease or increase in hair EtG concentrations by either thermal degradation of the EtG or a better extraction of EtG from the damaged hair matrix (40528).

The use of an ABHS for three to seventy times a day for 5 to 6 months does not significantly increase the hair EtG concentration (40529).

As has been done for COVID-19 infections in the population, the overall temporal alcohol use may be determined in wastewater-based epidemiology (WBE) by monitoring sewage EtS concentrations. EtG is too unstable in wastewater for reliable results (40530–40531).

Reference Number: 40501

PAPOZ, L., J. WEILL, Y. CHICH, C. GOT, AND Y. GOEHRS. "Biological Markers of Alcohol Intake Among 4,796 Subjects Injured in Accidents." *British Medical Journal*, 292: 1234–1237, 1986 (4 tables, 1 figure, 17 references)

Abstract: A study was conducted of 4,796 patients who attended the ER of twenty-one hospitals in France as a result of accidents during 1982–1983. The BAC, GGT, and corpuscular volume were determined in blood. There were 3,427 male and 1,369 female patients. BACs > 0.010 g/100 mL were found in 41% of the men and BACs > 0.080 g/100 mL were found in 25% of the men. Twenty-seven percent of the male accident victims were classified as chronic heavy drinkers according to GGT and corpuscular volume. Subjects injured in fights and domestic accidents were more likely chronic heavy drinkers.

> In France, therefore, the policy for preventing accidents should focus on chronic as much as on occasional drinking.

Reference Number: 40502

SAVOLA, O., O. NIEMELA, AND M. HILLBOM. "Blood Alcohol Is the Best Indicator of Hazardous Alcohol Drinking in Young Adults and Working-Age Patients with Trauma." *Alcohol and Alcoholism*, 39: 340–345, 2004 (5 tables, 49 references)

Abstract: The BACs or BrACs, self-reported drinking, and four biochemical markers of alcoholism in the blood (GGT, AST, CDT, and MCV) were determined in 349 trauma patients (ages sixteen to forty-nine years). The mean age was thirty-one years. According to the history of alcohol consumption, 8% of patients were dependent drinkers, 61% were frequent binge drinkers, and 17% were infrequent binge drinkers. Male patients had a higher mean BAC (0.200 g/100 mL) than female patients (0.170 g/100 mL). The correlation coefficient between reported alcohol consumption in the previous 24 hours was 0.866 for BAC, 0.336 for GGT, 0.233 for MCV, 0.328 for CDT, and 0.234 for AST.

BAC was the most accurate marker of hazardous alcohol drinking in trauma patients. Ninety-six percent of the alcohol-positive trauma patients reported hazardous alcohol drinking.

Reference Number: 40503

ROINE, R.P., U.M. KORRI, R. YLIKAHRI, A. PENTTILA, J. PIKKARAINEN, AND M. SALASPURO. "Increased Serum Acetate as Marker of Problem Drinking Among Drunken Drivers." *Alcohol and Alcoholism*, 23: 123–126, 1988 (2 tables, 21 references)

Abstract: Seven hundred and twenty-seven drunken drivers whose BAC > 0.050 g/100 mL had various biochemical markers of alcoholism determined in their blood. High blood acetate concentrations were found to correlate best with alcoholism. Increased serum acetate concentrations were detected in 18.8% of 527 first offenders compared to 32% of 200 repeat offenders.

Acetate derived from ethanol rise quickly and reaches a plateau which is maintained as long as ethanol is present. Blood acetate concentration is determined by the rate of hepatic oxidation of ethanol as by the rate of acetate's utilisation of peripheral tissues. It is independent of blood ethanol concentration and can easily be analysed in a routine laboratory. Acetate has earlier been shown to be a rather sensitive and specific marker of heavy drinking and alcoholism in patients admitted intoxicated to the emergency unit of our hospital.

Reference Number: 40504

ROINE, R.P., C.J.P. ERIKSSON, R. YLIKAHRI, A. PENTILLA, AND M. SALASPURO. "Methanol as a Marker of Alcohol Abuse." *Alcoholism: Clinical and Experimental Research*, 13: 172–175, 1989 (2 figures, 15 references)

Abstract: Serum methyl and ethyl alcohol concentrations were determined by headspace GC in sixteen skid-row alcoholics, sixteen alcoholics entering a detoxification center, 193 drinking drivers, and fifty social drinkers, all of whom had a SAC > 0.023 g/100 mL. The mean SMCs were 0.0018, 0.0020, 0.0007, and 0.0004 g/100 mL for the above groups respectively. The upper SMC limit for nonalcoholic social drinkers was determined to be 0.0008 g/100 mL. This upper limit was exceeded by 100% of the alcoholics entering detoxification, 75% of the skid-row alcoholics, 26% of the drinking drivers, and 4% of the social drinkers. The mean urine methanol concentration of seventy drinking drivers was 0.0006 g/100 mL and the correlation coefficient with SMC was 0.56. In addition, ten nonalcoholic subjects consumed 5.5 g/kg alcohol over 48 hours. The mean SMC increased from 0.0006 g/100 mL at 1 hour, to 0.0008 g/100 mL at 16 hours to 0.001 g/100 mL at 41 hours from the start of drinking. The SMC rapidly decreases once ethanol is completely oxidized from the blood.

> In conclusion methanol tends to accumulate during prolonged heavy drinking independently of blood-ethanol concentrations, and thus methanol determined either from urine or blood can be used as a laboratory marker in the screening of alcoholism.

Reference Number: 40505

ARNDT, T., B. GUESSREGEN, D. HALLERMANN, M. NAUCK, D. TERJUNG, AND H. WECKESSER. "Forensic Analysis of Carbohydrate Deficient Transferrin (CDT) by HPLC—Statistics and Extreme CDT Values." *Forensic Science International,* 175, 27–30, 2008 (2 figures, 9 references)

Abstract: The serum CDT/transferrin ratios from 19,236 serum samples were determined by HPLC. Most samples (75%) were submitted for traffic or employment medicine investigation.

> CDT/transferrin ratios are usually < 20%. Higher values can appear in rare cases. Chronic heavy alcohol abuse can cause CDT results of > 20%. CDT values > 30% should be considered as remarkable single observations after long-lasting extreme and chronic alcohol abuse.

Reference Number: 40506

DAHL, H., N. STEPHANSON, O. BECK, AND A. HELANDER. "Comparison of Urinary Excretion Characteristics of Ethanol and Ethyl Glucuronide." *Journal of Analytical Toxicology,* 26: 201–204, 2002 (2 figures, 15 references)

Abstract: Three female and three male subjects (ages twenty-five to fifty-four years) consumed 0.5 g/kg alcohol as beer (5.3% v/v alcohol) within 30 minutes, 90 minutes after consuming a standard breakfast. The subjects then drank the same volume of water within 10 minutes, 3 hours later. Frequent urine samples were collected, and the urine alcohol, creatinine, and ethyl glucuronide concentrations were determined. The UAC increased rapidly after alcohol consumption and the mean peak UAC was 0.078 g/100 mL at 1.5 hours. Both the alcohol and water-induced diuresis caused a decrease in the urine creatinine and ethyl glucuronide concentrations. Positive UACs were detected for 6.5 hours, whereas ethyl glucuronide was detected at low concentrations (< 0.1 mg/dL) for 22.5 to 31.5 hours. The amount of ethyl glucuronide in the urine corresponded to about 0.02% of the alcohol dose.

In conclusion, the results of the present study confirmed that EtG remains detectable in the urine for many hours after ethanol itself has been eliminated. Thus, testing urine for the presence of EtG provides a means to determine if a person has recently consumed alcohol. However, the results also showed that it is possible to lower the urinary concentration of EtG simply by drinking large amounts of water prior to voiding, whereas this strategy did not influence the concentration of ethanol or the EtG/creatinine ratio.

Reference Number: 40507

SCHMITT, G., P. DROENNER, G. SKOPP, AND R. ADERJAN. "Ethyl Glucuronide Concentration in Serum of Human Volunteers Teetotalers, and Suspected Drinking Drivers." *Journal of Forensic Sciences*, 42: 1099–1102, 1997 (2 tables, 3 figures, 9 references)

Abstract: A study was conducted of the serum ethyl glucuronide concentrations in ten abstinent patients, twelve healthy volunteers consuming 44–90 g of ethanol within 60 to 90 minutes, and fifty blood samples collected from suspected drinking drivers. The serum ethyl glucuronide (EtG) concentration was determined by GC/MS and the serum ethanol concentrations by headspace GC. In the drinking group the maximal serum ethanol concentration was 0.148 g/100 mL and EtG was 0.37 mg/dL. In all drinking-driving samples that contained ethanol, EtG was also detected. The highest EtG concentration was 1.2 mg/dL. There was no correlation with serum ethanol concentration.

EtG is detectable in serum exclusively after alcohol consumption. EtG peaks later and decreases slower as compared to ethanol. The formation of EtGC depends on the serum ethanol concentration. After ethanol elimination, the SEtGC declines exponentially with a half-life of 2 to 3 h. The kinetic profile explains why the SEC and SEtGC do not seem to correlate in 50 samples of drivers suspected of being under alcohol influence.

Reference Number: 40508

APPENZELLER, B.M.R., R. AGIRMAN, P. NEUBERG, M. YEGLES, AND R. WENNING. "Segmental Determination of Ethyl Glucuronide in Hair: A Pilot Study." *Forensic Science International,* 173: 87–92, 2007 (2 tables, 2 figures, 14 references)

Abstract: Eleven male and four female alcoholic patients provided hair and blood samples and had their drinking histories determined. Blood biomarkers such as MCV, GGT, and ASAT were determined. Segmental EtG hair concentrations were also determined by GC/MS.

These results clearly display the relevance of EtG determination in segmental hair analysis and demonstrate that variation in the concentration of EtG among hair segments may provide an overview of the drinking history of patients. An important advantage with respect to traditional blood biomarkers is that consumption trends for several months (depending on hair length) may be observed following a single non-invasive sampling.

Reference Number: 40509

CONSTANTINO, A., E.J. DIGREGORIO, W. KORN, S. SPAYD, AND F. RIEDERS. "The Effect of the Use of Mouthwash on Ethylglucuronide Concentrations in Urine." *Journal of Analytical Toxicology*, 30: 659–662, 2006 (3 tables, 1 figure, 6 references)

Abstract: Nine subjects gargled a total of 4 fl. oz. of mouthwash (12% v/v alcohol) over a period of 15 minutes and urine EtG concentrations were determined by LC-MS. Of the thirty-nine urine samples collected after gargling, twenty-two had a urine EtG concentration > 50 ng/mL and one was > 300 ng/mL. In another experiment, urine was collected every morning from eleven subjects who gargled with mouthwash three times a day for 5 days. Sixteen of the fifty-five submitted urine samples had an EtG concentration > 50 ng/mL.

Alcohol may be absorbed into the body from the use of alcohol containing mouthwash. EtG formed from the alcohol may be present in the urine samples of individuals whose only source of alcohol exposure was the use of such mouthwash. Findings of EtG in urine specimens must be investigated in order to determine the origin of alcohol exposure.

Reference Number: 40510

DE GIONVANNI, G. DONADIO, AND M. CHIAROTTI. "The Reliability of Fatty Acid Ethyl Esters (FAEE) as Biological Markers for the Diagnosis of Alcohol Abuse." *Journal of Analytical Toxicology*, 31: 93–97, 2007 (3 tables, 4 figures, 21 references)

Abstract: The fatty acid ethyl esters (FAEE) concentration was determined by MS in hair samples from twelve alcoholics, ten social drinkers, and ten teetotalers. FAEEs are non-oxidative metabolites of alcohol and are direct markers for they contain the intact ethyl group.

However, our experience suggests the results obtained induce some consideration about the reliability of these biological markers. It was observed that FAEE concentrations could not only be modified by frequent washes that allowed a decrease of these compounds, but their amount could increase for the environmental contamination mainly because of the frequent use of ethanol containing cosmetics.

Reference Number: 40511

HOISETH, G., J.P. BERNARD, N. STEPHANSON, P.T. NORMANN, A.S. CHRISTOPHERSEN, J. MORLAND, AND A. HELANDER. "Comparison between the Urinary Alcohol Markers EtG, EtS, and GTOL/5-HIAA in a Controlled Drinking Experiment." *Alcohol and Alcoholism*, 43: 187–191, 2008 (2 tables, 2 figures, 30 references)

Abstract: Ten male subjects (ages twenty-one to forty-six years) consumed 0.5 g/kg alcohol within 15 minutes and urine samples were collected over 15 hours. Urinary EtG and EtS and GTOL/5-HIAA concentrations were determined by LC-MS. The frequency of positive tests was 100% at 4 hours, 0% for UAC at 10 hours, 40% for GTOL/5-HIAA at 10 hours, and 100% for EtG and EtS at 20 hours.

In conclusion, measurement of EtG, EtS and GTOL/5-HIAA in urine were confirmed as useful tests to detect recent ingestion of ethanol. Positive results were obtained some time after ethanol had been eliminated and EtG and EtS registering the longest detection times. The GTOL/5-HIAA ratio was equally sensitive in the short run but showed a much shorter detection window. In cases where surveillance of an alcohol slip or relapse drinking is needed, EtG and EtS urine offer very sensitive alternatives or complements to ethanol testing.

Reference Number: 40512

HOISETH, G., L. MORINI, A. POLETTINI, A.S. CHRISTOPHERSEN, L. JOHNSEN, R. KARINEN, AND J. MORLAND. "Serum/Whole Blood Concentration Ratio for Ethylglucuronide and Ethyl Sulfate." *Journal of Analytical Toxicology*, 33: 208–211, 2009 (1 table, 29 references)

Abstract: The whole blood and serum EtG and ES concentration ratios were determined in nine male and four female patients admitted for alcohol detoxification. The BACs ranged from 0 to 0.370 g/100 mL (median 0.070 g/100 mL). The mean serum/blood ratios were 1.69:1 for EtG and 1.30:1 for EtS.

> In conclusion, the present study showed that the concentration of the ethanol metabolites, EtG and EtS was higher in serum than whole blood. This has to be considered when blood results obtained from forensic toxicology are compared to serum or plasma results from clinical laboratories.

Reference Number: 40513

THIERAUF, A., A. SERR, C.C. HALTER, A. AL-AHMAD, S. RANA, AND W. WEINMANN. "Influence of Preservatives on the Stability of Ethyl Glucuronide and Ethyl Sulphate in Urine." *Forensic Science International*, 182: 41–45, 2008 (2 tables, 2 figures, 21 references)

Abstract: Urine samples were inoculated with glucuronidase-positive *E. coli* after sterile filtration and preserved with thymol, chlorhexidine, boric acid, and chlorhexidine/methylparaben/sodium propionate and stored at 4°, 18°, or 36°C for 9 days. Urinary EtG concentrations decreased in unpreserved urine samples stored at 18° and 36°C with *E. coli* added.

> An increasing percentage of the diagnostic samples are not analyzed locally but shipped for testing worldwide. This study shows that cold storage as well as the addition of some of the preservatives investigated inhibits the degradation of EtG. The perpetuation of cool shipping conditions can be difficult and hence the use of preservatives is an available option of avail. Apart from thymol, all the preservatives studied here proved useful for the stabilization of EtG and EtS in urine specimens.

Reference Number: 40514

WURST, F.M., R. VOGEL, K. JACHAU, A. VARGA, C. ALLING, A. ALT, AND G.E. SKIPPER. "Ethyl Glucuronide Discloses Recent Covert Alcohol Use Not Detected by Standard Testing in Forensic Psychiatric Inpatients." *Alcoholism Clinical Experimental Research,* 27: 471–476, 2003 (3 tables, 1 figure, 38 references)

Abstract: Three female and thirty-two male psychiatric patients (ages twenty-six to fifty-six years) committed for substance abuse had BrACs, UACs, urinary EtG, CDT, and GGT/MCV measured over 12 months. Fourteen of the 146 urine samples had a positive EtG in which the patients admitted to consuming 40 to 200 g of alcohol 12–60 hours prior to testing. BrACs were positive in only one case.

A test like that for EtG is needed in numerous settings including alcohol and drug treatment (to detect lapse/relapse), in safety sensitive work settings where use is dangerous or in other settings where use may be inappropriate (e.g., such as driving, workplace, pregnancy), or for the testing of other groups (such as children or those with medical problems) where alcohol use would be unhealthy or unsafe).

Reference Number: 40515

HOISETH, G., L. MORINI, A. POLETTINI, A. CHRISTOPHERSEN, AND J. MORLAND. "Ethyl Glucuronide in Hair Compared with Traditional Alcohol Biomarkers—A Pilot Study of Heavy Drinkers Referred to an Alcohol Detoxification Unit." *Alcoholism Clinical and Experimental Research*, 33: 812–816, 2009 (3 tables, 40 references)

Abstract: Hair and serum samples were collected from twelve male and four female patients who had recently consumed alcohol and were undergoing detoxification treatment in hospital. Hair EtG concentrations and serum AST, ALT, GGT, and CDT were determined. The percent positive results were 94, 67, 67, 93, and 64% respectively. The estimated ethanol daily intake (EDI) and hair EtG concentration showed a positive correlation of $r = 0.56$.

Table. Sensitivity of Different Biomarkers in Detecting Heavy Alcohol Use in Sixteen Alcoholic Patients

Biomarker	Percent Positive Results
AST	67%
ALT	67%
GGT	93%
CDT	64%
Hair EtG	94%

Source: Adapted from Hoiseth et al (2009).

In conclusion, this study was the first to compare the sensitivity of EtG in hair to all the traditional biomarkers of alcohol consumption AST, ALT, GGT, and %CDT in a group of high consumers with detailed information on their alcohol consumption. In the present study, EtG showed the highest sensitivity together with GGT. In addition, hair EtG was the only marker than tended to give some information on the magnitude of alcohol consumption.

Reference Number: 40516

THIERAUF, A., H. GNANN, A. WOHLFARTH, V. AUWATER, M.G. PERDEKAMP, K-J. BUTTER, F.M. WURST, AND W. WEINMANN. "Urine Tested Positive for Ethyl Glucuronide and Ethyl Sulphate After the Consumption of Non-Alcoholic Beer." *Forensic Science International*, 202: 82–85, 2010 (1 figure, 19 references)

Abstract: Two female and two male subjects (ages twenty-three to thirty years) consumed 2.5 L of nonalcoholic beer (0.4% v/v alcohol) within 1 hour. Blood and urine samples were collected and analyzed for alcohol, EtG and EtS. No positive BACs or UACs were detected. No positive serum EtG or EtS concentrations were determined. The maximum urine EtG and EtS concentrations were 14.1 mg/L and 16.1 mg/L respectively.

The ethanol metabolites EtG and EtS can be found in urine after drinking non-alcoholic beer and therefore negative consequences may arise for monitored persons.

Reference Number: 40517

THIERAUF, A., A. WOHLFARTH, V. AUWATER, M.G. PERDEKAMP, F.M. WURST, AND W. WEINMANN. "Urine Tested Positive for Ethyl Glucuronide and Ethyl Sulfate After the Consumption of Yeast and Sugar." *Forensic Science International,* 202: e45–e47, 2010 (1 figure, 13 references)

Abstract: One male and one female subject (ages forty-three and thirty-one years) consumed 42 and 21 grams of baker's yeast respectively with approximately 50 grams of sugar on a slice of bread and drank approximately 300 mL of water. In addition, two female and two male subjects (ages thirty-one to sixty-four years) consumed twenty brewer's yeast tablets (Biolabor Bierhefe Tabletten) with sugar and water. In both experiments urine samples were collected over 20 hours and analyzed for alcohol, EtG, EtS and creatinine. The maximum urine EtG and EtS concentrations were 0.50 mg/L and 1.05 mg/L for the male subject and 0.12 mg/L and 0.17 mg/L for the female subject respectively after the consumption of baker's yeast. No positive UACs were detected. No positive urine EtG, EtS, or alcohol concentrations were detected in the subjects who consumed brewer's yeast.

> The consumption of baker's yeast with sugar and water can lead to the formation of EtG and EtS reaching relevant concentrations in urine and possibly in people that are monitored for the proof of alcohol abstinence, whereas the uptake of brewer's yeast tablets used in this experiment did not result in detectable amounts of EtG and EtS.

Reference Number: 40518

REISFIELD, G.M., B.A. GOLDBERGER, B.O. CREWS, A.J. PESCE, B.O. CREWS, G.R. WILSON, S.A. TEITELBAUM, AND R.L. BERTHOLF. "Ethyl Glucuronide, Ethyl Sulfate, and Ethanol in Urine After Intensive Exposure to High Ethanol Content Mouthwash." *Journal of Analytical Toxicology,* 35: 264–268, 2011 (2 tables, 12 references)

Abstract: Urinary ethyl glucuronide (EtG), ethyl sulfate (EtS), creatinine, and alcohol concentrations were determined in ten subjects who gargled with mouthwash (27% v/v alcohol) for 30 seconds four times a day for four consecutive days. All urine alcohol concentrations were below the limit of quantitation (0.020 g/100 mL). The maximum urine EtG detected was 173 ng/mL and the maximum EtS was 104 ng/mL.

> The urinary concentrations of EtG and EtS measured in this study were well below the commonly accepted (United States) threshold of 500 ng/mL, for evidence of deliberate ethanol ingestion.

Reference Number: 40519

TUMER, A.R., A. LALE, M. GURLER, M.S. YILDIRIM, A.D. KAYNAK, AND R. AKCAN. "The Effects of Traditional Fermented Beverages on Ethanol, Ethyl Glucuronide and Ethyl Sulphate Levels." *Egyptian Journal of Forensic Sciences*, 8: 33, 5pp, 2018 (8 tables, 18 references)

Abstract: Five women and seven men consumed 300 mL of traditional fermented beverages. Blood samples were collected before and 45 minutes after consumption, and urine samples were collected before and 4 hours after the consumption of alcohol. The samples were analyzed for alcohol by headspace GC in blood, and urinary EtG and EtS were measured by LC. The traditional alcoholic beverages (and alcohol concentration) were salgam (0.080 g/100 mL), boza (0.030 g/100 mL), kimiz (0.058 g/100 mL), and kefir (0.006 g/100 mL). There were no detectable BACs either before or after consumption and there was no change in urinary EtG or EtS concentrations.

> At the present study, it is demonstrated that consumption of 300 mL of traditional fermented beverages, Salgam, Boza, Kimiz and Kefir did not affect blood alcohol levels. Furthermore, this consumption does not cause any effect on concentrations of ethanol metabolites in urine.

Reference Number: 40520

HELANDER, A., I. OLSSON, AND H. DAHL. "Postcollection Synthesis of Ethyl Glucuronide by Bacteria in Urine May Cause False Identification of Alcohol Consumption." *Clinical Chemistry*, 53: 1855–1857, 2007 (1 table, 1 figure, 14 references)

Abstract: Fresh human urine samples with confirmed growth of three different types of bacteria (*E. coli*, *K. pneumoniae*, or *E. cloacae*) were stored at 4°C or 22°C. Alcohol was added to the urine, or glucose and *C. albicans*. EtG and EtS concentrations were measured by LC-MS. Urine EtG concentrations increased and decreased with storage in samples infected with *E. coli*, but EtS was not affected.

The presence of EtG in urine is not a unique indicator of recent drinking, but might originate from postcollection synthesis if specimens are infected with E.Coli and contain ethanol. Given the associated risks for false identification of alcohol consumption and false-negative EtG results due to bacterial degradation,we recommend that measurement of EtG be combined with EtS or in the future possibly replaced by EtS.

Reference Number: 40521

ARMER, J.M., L. GUNAWARDANA, AND R.L. ALLCOCK. "The Performance of Alcohol Markers Including Ethyl Glucuronide and Ethyl Sulphate to Detect Alcohol Use in Clients in a Community Alcohol Treatment Programme." *Alcohol and Alcoholism*, 52: 29–34, 2017 (1 table, 22 figures, 22 references)

Abstract: The performance of breath, urine alcohol, urine EtG, and EtS to detect alcohol consumption were evaluated in forty-two clients enrolled at a 12-week community alcohol treatment program in the UK, who provided these samples and recorded a daily drink diary. BrACs were determined with a Lion Alcometer 500, UACs by an ADH method, and urine EtG and EtS by an LC-MS/MS method. Urine creatinine concentrations were also measured by an enzymatic method. False positive and false negative urine EtG results may occur in the urine due to bacterial contamination, but the EtS results do not appear to be affected. The sensitivity to detect alcohol consumption within the previous 24 hours was 57% for BrAC, 71% for UAC, 100% for urine EtG (0.5 mg/L cutoff), and 100% for EtS (0.22 mg/L cutoff).

Clients in community alcohol treatment were recruited. In comparison to a diary of alcohol intake, urine EtG and EtS were able to detect all participants continuing to consume alcohol in the previous 24 h. All four markers have excellent diagnostic specificity for alcohol intake. A combination of tests including immediate availability of breath ethanol and collection of urine for EtG and EtS will increase relapse detection in clients in community alcohol treatment. Detection of continued alcohol intake could lead to initiation of early intervention and altered treatment strategies which could improve the numbers of clients successfully completing treatment.

Reference Number: 40522

FOSEN, J.T., J. MORLAND, AND G. HOISETH. "The Relationship Between Ingested Dose of Ethanol and Amount of Ethyl Glucuronide Formed in Blood." *Journal of Analytical Toxicology*, 44: 861–863, 2020 (1 table, 13 references).

Abstract: Ten subjects consumed 0.5 g/kg over 15 minutes and 1.0 g/kg over 60 minutes after an overnight fast. Blood samples were collected before and 1.5, 3.5, 5.5, 8.5, 11.5, and 24 hours after intake and were analyzed for alcohol by an enzymatic method and ethyl glucuronide by UPLC-MS-MS. The mean Cmax for EtG in the blood was 0.35 mg/L for the low dose and 1.06 mg/L for the high dose. The ratio between the AUC for EtG in the blood and the dose of alcohol administered is higher after the 1.0 g/kg dose than the 0.5 g/kg dose. But this is not seen when the AUC for EtG is compared to the AUC for alcohol.

> In conclusion, this study supported that the percentage of ethanol converted to EtG is not increasing when the doses increase. An explanation for the non-linear relation previously observed between the dose of ethanol ingested and the amount of EtG formed may be a relatively higher first-pass metabolism of ethanol at lower doses, but other explanations are also possible.

Reference Number: 40523

DENGIZ, H., N. DAGLIOGLU, AND I.E. GOREN. "Assessment of Recent Alcohol Consumption by Detecting Ethyl Glucuronide and Ethyl Sulfate Level Among Traffic Accident Patients." *Traffic Injury Prevention*, 21: 371–374, 2020 (3 tables, 23 references)

Abstract: Blood alcohol, EtS, and EtG concentrations were determined by headspace GC and LC/MS/MS respectively in 200 patients attending a hospital in Turkey due to injuries suffered in a motor vehicle collision. All patients were male with an average age of 34.4 years. Positive BAC, EtG, and EtS concentrations were found in 16.5%, 35.5%, and 23% of the patients respectively. EtG/EtS were found in all patients with a positive BAC. The mean BAC in the BAC positive injured patients was 0.118 g/100 mL.

Table. Mean Time to the Collection of the Blood Sample and EtG and EtS Concentrations in BAC Positive and BAC Negative Injured Patients

	BAC Positive	BAC Negative
Time from injury to collection of the blood sample	1.50 hours	4.50 hours
Mean EtG (mg/L)	2.72	0.658
Mean EtS (mg/L)	0.0990	0.0053

Source: Adapted from Dengiz et al (2020).

In our study it was found that positive EtG and EtS values of the patients with negative BAC results bring along the need for analyzing EtG and EtS minor metabolites along with ethanol in the blood in traffic accidents. On the other hand, detection of EtG and EtS concentrations can be used for the detection of negative ethanol detection and verification of abstinence from alcohol to elucidate the unexplained accidents if more studies with experimenter controlled exposure to alcohol performs in evaluating the sensitivity and specificity of these biomarkers.

Reference Number: 40524

SCRADER, J., M. ROTHE, AND F. PRAGST. "Ethyl Glucuronide Concentrations in Beard Hair After a Single Alcohol Dose: Evidence for Incorporation in Hair Root." *International Journal of Legal Medicine*, 126: 791–799, 2012 (3 tables, 3 figures, 45 references)

Abstract: After a 2-week abstinence, three male subjects (ages thirty-nine, forty-four, and fifty-three years) consumed 153–200 g of alcohol over 5.5 hours and obtained BACs of between 0.130 to 0.160 g/100 mL. Beard hair was collected every morning using an electric razor and analyzed for EtG using LC-ESI-MS/MS. The total weight of daily beard shavings ranged from 9 to 44 mg. The maximum EtG beard hair concentrations occurred between days two and four and ranged from 74 to 242 pg/mg. The anatomy of hair root growth and physiology of hair growth are discussed.

The results and the discussion lead to the conclusion that at least for daily shaved beard hair, incorporation of EtG from sweat is not the dominating route. Instead EtG is mainly incorporated within the hair root with highest concentrations in the isthmus and in the upper part of the suprabulbar region. Diffusion from the blood through the surrounding tissues and outer and inner root sheaths into the completed hair in these regions seems to contribute essentially to the final concentration in the hair. Nevertheless, deposition of EtG from sweat can play a more important role in longer hair where the hair shaft provides a larger area for deposition than the shaved hair stubble.

Reference Number: 40525

FRENI, F., M. MORETTI, S. SCARDO, C. CARELLI, C. VIGNALI, M.C. MONTI, AND L. MORINI. "Ethyl Glucuronide in Hair: A 5-Years Retrospective Cohort Study in Subjects Sanctioned for Driving Under the Influence of Alcohol and Psychoactive Substances." *Drug Testing Analysis*, 1–12, 2022 (4 tables, 5 figures, 42 references)

Abstract: The hair EtG concentration was determined by LC/MS/MS in 4,328 drivers charged with DUI and undergoing a license renewal process in Italy between 2015 and 2019. A hair EtG greater than 7.0 pg/mg (indicating moderate drinking was found in 22% of the drivers, and of those, 7% had a hair EtG concentration > 30 pg/mg (indicating chronic excessive alcohol drinking). A total of 460 drivers underwent at least four repeated hair EtG measurements over 18 months. The rate of positive hair EtG tests was 2.3 times greater for male than female drivers.

Our study allowed to highlight some risk factors related to alcohol drinking habits among drivers such as being male sex, age > 55 years, and coming from rural areas. A similar protocol could be applied to a larger territory maybe at a national level, in order to evaluate other potentially at risk populations. Moreover, data obtained from this study suggested that the introduction of hEtG test in the DLR protocol led to benefits in terms of limiting the alcohol misuse habits among subjects being evaluated. Indeed, a significant decrease was observed among young people living in urban and suburban areas.

Reference Number: 40526

BINZ, T.M., M.R. BAUMGARTNER, AND T. KRAEMER. "The Influence of Cleansing Shampoos on Ethyl Glucuronide Concentration in Hair Analyzed with an Optimized and Validated LC-MS/MS Method." *Forensic Science International*, 244: 20–24, 2014 (4 tables, 3 figures, 18 references).

Abstract: Special shampoos have been developed and advertised to "purify" and "detoxify" the hair before alcohol and drug testing to cause false low results. Twenty-five hair samples, all 5 cm in length, containing different EtG concentrations were divided into two groups. One was treated with shampoo (Ultra Clean, Ultra Klean, Folli-Klean, and Detox) and the other without any pretreatment. EtG concentrations were determined by an LC-MS/MS method.

The study showed that for the four different cleansing shampoos no influence on the concentration of EtG in hair was observed. EtG was still detectable in all samples after all of the selected shampoo treatments at equal levels. This clearly demonstrates that these shampoos cannot significantly remove EtG from hair after a single use.

Reference Number: 40527

AMMANN, D., R. BECKER, A. KOHL, J. HANISCH, AND I. NEHLS. "Degradation of the Ethyl Glucuronide Content in Hair by Hydrogen Peroxide and a Non-Destructive Assay for Oxidative Hair Treatment Using Infra-Red Spectroscopy." *Forensic Science International*, 244: 30–35, 2014 (5 figures, 31 references).

Abstract: Hair EtG content decreases significantly when treated by hydrogen peroxide during cosmetic hair bleaching, especially if ammonia is used. Attenuated Total Reflectance Fourier Transformed Infrared Spectroscopy (ATR-FTIR) could detect hair exposure to hydrogen peroxide non-destructively.

The EtG content in hair degrades when treated with alkaline hydrogen peroxide under conditions similar to cosmetic bleaching. The effect becomes more distinct in the presence of ammonia. Even before significant degradation of the EtG content, cysteic acid is formed in amounts detectable by routine ATR-FTIR spectroscopy. Thus, in doubtful cases the oxidative treatment of a hair sample can be tested and non-destructively and without loss of sample using widely available equipment. This test is applicable to archived samples and even to samples already having been extracted and dried.

Reference Number: 40528

KIRCHEN, L. AND M. YEGLES. "Influence of Hair Straightening on Ethyl Glucuronide Content in Hair." *Toxichem Krimtech*, 80 (Special Issue): 357–358, 2013 (1 table, 7 references)

Abstract: Sixteen positive EtG hair samples were treated with hair straighteners for 1 minute at 200°C. Tested and non-treated hair samples were analyzed for EtG by GC/MS-MICI. In eleven samples, there was an average decrease of 24% (range 1%–70%). In five cases, an average increase of 14% (range 8%–30%) occurred. A decrease in EtG is due to the thermal destruction of EtG during treatment. An increase in EtG may be due to a better extraction of EtG from the damaged hair matrix.

This preliminary study indicates that a heat source may influence EtG content in hair. This has to be considered for a correct interpretation of EtG results in hair.

Reference Number: 40529

SCHOLZ, C., M.R. BAUMGARTNER, AND M.M. MADRY. "Use of Ethanol-Based Hand Disinfectants: Source of Increased Ethyl Glucuronide Levels in Hair?" *Alcohol and Alcoholism*, 1–4, 2020 (1 table, 1 figure, 20 references)

Abstract: Ethyl glucuronide (EtG) is a phase II metabolite of alcohol and is one of the most important diagnostic markers of alcohol consumption. According to the Society of Hair Testing, if the concentration of EtG in the proximal hair sample is less than or equal to 5 pg/mg, then alcohol abstinence cannot be contradicted. If the hair EtG concentration exceeds 5 pg/mg, this strongly suggests alcohol consumption and > 30 pg/mg indicates chronic excessive alcohol consumption. Due to the increased use of ethanol-based hand disinfectants (EBHD) because of COVID-19, the effect of its use on hair EtG was determined. The proximal hair EtG concentration was determined by LC/MS/MS in nine female and one male health care professionals who used EBHD between 3 and 70 times per day for 5 to 6 months. Eight subjects were non-drinkers and two consumed two to four units of alcohol per month. A positive hair EtG concentration (2 pg/mg) was determined in only one subject, a non-drinking surgeon who used EBHD 60–70 times daily for 5 to 6 days a week.

Our study outcome extends the current knowledge as the tested hair samples derive from health professionals under real working conditions. The results indicate that the frequent EBHD use by nondrinkers is highly unlikely to produce a hair EtG concentration above the SoHT cutoff for repeated alcohol consumption. Therefore, alcohol abstinence testing by hair analysis is a valid tool despite exposure to disinfectants.

Reference Number: 40530

GAO, J., J. LI, G. JIAN, Z. YUAN, G. EAGLESHAN, A. COVACI, J.F. MUELLER, AND P.K. THAI. "Stability of Alcohol and Tobacco Consumption in a Real Rising Main Sewer." *Water Research*, 138: 19–26, 2018 (2 tables, 3 figures, 50 references)

Abstract: Wastewater-based epidemiology (WBE) is one method to monitor the consumption of psychoactive drugs such as nicotine and alcohol in the general population. Real sewers as a dynamic system regarding wastewater flow leads to turbulent mixing and variable hydraulic retention times. The stability of the biomarkers of alcohol consumption (EtG and EtS) and tobacco use (nicotine, cotinine, and 3-hydroxycotinine) in a real UC 9 sewer was measured. EtS degrades at approximately 8% per hour, whereas EtG has a half-life of 1.9 hours. De-conjugation of nicotine, cotinine, and 3HC leads to their formation in wastewater, but cotinine is relatively stable.

> Our study found that EtS can degrade approximately 8% per hour in a real rising main sewer. Therefore, degradation should be considered when EtS is used to estimate consumption of alcohol by WBE. EtG is unstable in the sewer and hence not a suitable biomarker for WBE. Rapid de-conjugation of glucuronide Nic, Cot, and OH-Cot interfered with the stability assessment for those chemicals. Further study may be required to assess the stability of these chemicals in the real sewer. A good understanding of the sewer catchment would improve the interpretation of WBE results.

Reference Number: 40531

RYAU, Y., D. BARCELO, L.P. BARRON, L. BIILSMA, S. CASTIGLIONI, P. DE VOOGT, E. EMKE, F. HERNANDEZ, F.Y. LAI, A. LOPES, M.L. DE ALDA, N. MASTONIANNI, K. MUNRO, J. O'BRIEN, C. ORT, B.G. PLOSZ, M.J. REID, V. YARGEAU, AND K.V. THOMAS. "Comparative Measurement and Quantitative Assessment of Alcohol Consumption Through Wastewater-Based Epidemiology: An International Study in 20 Cities." *Science of the Total Environment*, 565: 977–983, 2016 (3 tables, 3 figures, 47 references)

Abstract: The community alcohol consumption pattern was determined by wastewater-based epidemiology (WBE) by the analysis of EtS by LC/MS/MS in the wastewater of twenty cities in eleven countries, daily to a 1-week period. The average per capita alcohol consumption in the twenty cities ranged between 6.4 and 44.3 L/1000 inhabitants/day. EtS is a metabolite of ethanol that indicates recent consumption of alcohol up to 48 hours and is stable in wastewater. The margin of exposure for alcohol as determined by WBE was lowest for cities such as Granby and Montreal in Canada, Dresden (Germany), and Copenhagen (Denmark), and highest for Lugano (China) and Milan (Italy). But all sampled cities were in the high risk category (MOE > 10).

> An international study on the alcohol consumption through WBE in 20 cities with a combined population of 17 million people has been performed. WBE showed alcohol consumption levels and patterns in the studied cities providing the most recent snapshot of actual alcohol use in these communities. Comparisons of data with international reports, such as global status on alcohol and health and illicit drug estimates by wastewater analysis were also carried out, which showed WBE would be an important complement for the assessment of actual alcohol use at the community level.

CHAPTER 5

Effects of Alcohol on Driving Ability

"The author of this communication shows very clearly that the management of automobile wagons is far more dangerous for men who drink than the driving of locomotives on steel rails. Inebriates and moderate drinkers are the most incapable of all persons to drive motor wagons. The general palsy and diminished power of control of both reason and senses are certain to invite disaster in every attempt of guide such wagons. The precaution of railroad companies to have only total abstainers guide their engines will soon extend to owners and drivers of these new motor wagons."

—Editorial, *Quarterly Journal of Inebriety*, 1904

"Whether impairment is apparent depends upon the complexity of the driving task: however, because driving is an inherently complex behavior, it can be asserted scientifically that the faculties required in the operation of a motor vehicle will be impaired at a BAC of 0.050% or greater."

—Martin et al, "A Review of Alcohol-Impaired Driving: The Role of Blood Alcohol Concentration and Complexity of the Driving Task" (2013)

The adverse effects of alcohol on abilities related to driving have been known for more than 118 years. The main types of research in this area are:

- Laboratory studies of various components of the driving task
- Laboratory studies using increasingly more sophisticated computerized driving simulators
- Closed course driving of motor vehicles
- Actual highway driving or observations

- Field (epidemiological) studies of the incidence of alcohol-related driving and various types of motor vehicle collisions (MVCs)

There are various countermeasures that have substantially reduced alcohol-related MVC injury and death. This chapter also includes studies on physical tests of alcohol intoxication and standardized field sobriety tests (SFSTs).

Also included is a new section (5.08) on the effects of cannabis and alcohol combined on impaired driving. After all, tetrahydrocannabinol is just a 21-carbon alcohol.

5.01 LABORATORY STUDIES

"The problem with drinking and driving is the mourning after."

—Unknown, Alcoholsayings.com

"From a functional standpoint, this study might point to some of the harmful effects of ethanol on overlearned tasks, such as driving a car. Because ethanol impairs the response to unexpected events, it might increase the risk of alcohol-related traffic accidents. Intoxicated drivers might not be aware of this potential danger and might feel fit to drive because moderate doses of alcohol may not affect the overlearned aspects of driving a car."

—Grillon et al, "Effects of Ethanol on the Processing of Low-Probability Stimuli: An ERP Study" (1995)

There are numerous laboratory studies on the effect of alcohol on abilities related to driving. These studies are the least realistic in relation to driving but provide the best scientific control and can separate the various important parameters for driving such as dynamic visual acuity (50101), glare recovery time (50102), and vigilance tasks (50106). Heavy drinkers did not show significant behavioral tolerance when compared with social drinkers in saccadic velocity and digit symbol substitution tests (DSSTs) (50105). The studies in this section are generally arranged with increasing BAC tested.

A longer reaction time to auditory stimuli than to visual stimuli, perceptual judgment, and divided attention were also affected and found at BACs of 0.05 g/100 mL (50115, 50117, 50118).

My colleagues at the Centre of Forensic Sciences in Toronto conducted an extensive review of the effects of alcohol on driving ability and concluded that scientifically the facilities required for driving (a complex task) will be impaired at BACs of 0.050 g/100 mL or greater (50117).

Reference Number: 50101

SCHMAL, F., R. KUNZ, C. ORTMANN, W. STOLL, N. NIESCHALK, AND G. FECHNER. "Effect of Ethanol on Dynamic and Visual Acuity During Vertical Body Oscillation in Healthy Volunteers." *European Archives Otorhinolaryngology*, 257: 485–489, 2000 (2 tables, 2 figures, 47 references)

Abstract: Dynamic visual acuity (DVA) was measured in two female and ten male subjects (ages twenty-five to thirty-two years) during vertical body oscillations before and after consuming 0.65 g/kg alcohol within 30 minutes. Venous blood was collected immediately after consumption ceased and 40 minutes later, and BACs were determined by headspace GC. The mean BACs were 0.043 g/100 mL (0.009–0.094 g/100 mL) and 0.055 g/100 mL (0.033–0.079 g/100 mL) respectively. There were no significant differences in the performance of the tasks at either BAC, so the results were pooled; therefore the mean BAC was 0.049 g/100 mL. Visual orientation is the most important sensory input during locomotion (e.g., driving a car).

> In summary low doses of ethanol disturbed the visual guided oculomotor response during fixation of an earth-fixed target while the observer was subject to linear vertical acceleration. This effect led to an increasing delay between the beginning of body and eye movements. The consequence is an increasing phase shift and thus a decrease in DVA during whole body oscillation.

Reference Number: 50102

ADAMS, A.J., AND B. BROWN. "Alcohol Prolongs Time Course of Glare Recovery." *Nature*, 257, 481–483, 1975 (6 figures, 9 references)

Abstract: In this study, nine male subjects were given either 0.5 or 1.0 mL/kg of 95% v/v alcohol consumed within 20 minutes. A placebo was also given. BrACs were determined by an Intoxilyzer. Subjects were exposed to a high intensity light source and the time required to regain vision in a low intensity light field was measured. Impairment was detected as much as 3 hours after alcohol ingestion when the mean BrACs were 0.01 and 0.05 g/100 mL respectively. Glare recovery time was increased 30 to 50% with alcohol ingestion.

> We have demonstrated alcohol induced delays in glare recovery which we believe to be occurring at the retinal level. These delays have been demonstrated at surprisingly low BALs (approximately one cocktail on an empty stomach) and are dose related.

Reference Number: 50103

BREITMEIER, D., I. SEELAND-SCHULZE, H. HECKER, AND U. SCHNEIDER. "The Influence of Blood Alcohol Concentrations of Around 0.03% on Neuropsychological Functions—A Double-Blind, Placebo-Controlled Investigation." *Addiction Biology*, 12: 183–189, 2007 (4 tables, 50 references)

Abstract: Sixteen male subjects (ages twenty-two to twenty-nine) were administered either a placebo or 0.3 g/kg alcohol IV. BrACs were determined with an Alcotest 7410 and SACs were also determined. The SAC was converted into a BAC using the factor 1.236. Various neuropsychological tests were conducted including vigilance, divided attention, and vocabulary tests. The mean BrAC was approximately 0.035 g/100 mL and the mean BAC was 0.034 g/100 mL.

> The findings reported herein make it clear that already at BAC of around 0.03% cognitive functions are impaired with growing complexity of tasks, especially those which rely on perception and processing of visual information. This becomes even more evident the more complex and urgent a task becomes. This is of particular importance when steering a motor vehicle. Cognitive performances such as verbal intelligence, functional capacity, memory, and vigilance in relation to optical stimuli remain—as long as they are analyzed separately—uninfluenced.

Reference Number: 50104

HORNE, J.A., L.A. REYNER, AND P.R. BARRETT. "Driving Impairment Due to Sleepiness Is Exacerbated by Low Alcohol Intake." *Occupational Environmental Medicine,* 60: 689–692, 2003 (1 table, 3 figures, 16 references)

Abstract: Twelve male subjects (ages twenty to twenty-six years) were tested on a driving simulator for 2 hours in the afternoon under four conditions—normal sleep and alcohol; normal sleep and no alcohol (baseline condition); reduced night sleep (5 hours) and alcohol; and reduced night sleep and no alcohol. The subjects consumed 75 mL of 38% v/v alcohol within 15 minutes after consuming two cheese rolls. BrACs were measured with a Lion Alcometer SD400 at the start and completion of the driving task. EEGs and EOGs were also measured. The mean BrACs were 0.038 g/100 mL (sleep restricted) and 0.032 g/100 mL (no sleep restriction) at the start of the task and zero by the completion of the task.

> In conclusion, because of the natural afternoon dip in alertness, even after a normal night's sleep, a modest alcohol intake at lunchtime (giving BACs well within the pass range for police roadside breathalyser) presents a potential danger to driving at this time, especially under dull and monotonous conditions. This hazard with alcohol is markedly worsened if the afternoon sleepiness was further enhanced by sleep disturbance the previous night.

Reference Number: 50105

KING, A.C. AND J.A. BYARS. "Alcohol-Induced Performance Impairment in Heavy Episodic and Light Social Drinkers." *Journal of Studies on Alcohol*, 65: 27–36, 2004 (1 table, 4 figures, 83 references)

Abstract: Ten male and four female light social drinkers (LD) and sixteen male and four female heavy drinkers (HD), ages twenty-four to thirty-eight years, consumed either placebo, low (0.4 g/kg), or high (0.8 g/kg) alcohol within 15 minutes. BrACs were determined with an Alco-Sensor III and Alco-Sensor IV. Various psychomotor tests were conducted including DSST and eye movements. The mean peak BrACs were similar for both groups, 0.030–0.040 g/100 mL for the low and 0.070–0.080 g/100 mL for the high dose. The saccadic latency was slower for the HD group at both low and high doses but only at the high dose for the LD group. Both HD and LD had impairment of saccadic velocity and DSST at both doses.

> It may be speculated that HDs have greater alcohol-related behavioral tolerance to tasks of a stereotyped repetitive nature than those requiring the processing and execution of new strategies, higher cortical input or shifting of set. The later task processes are ostensibly more reflective of the DSST and saccadic eye task than the smooth pursuit task because of their sudden onset stimuli and multiple forms. It is interesting to note that the HD group did not show tolerance to alcohol's impairing effects on these tasks.

Reference Number: 50106

ROHRBAUGH, J.W., W. STAPLETON, R. PARASURAMAN, H.W. FROWEIN, B. ADINOFF, J.L. VARNER, E.A. ZUBOVIC, E.A. LANE, M.J. ECKARDT, AND H. LINNOILA.

"Alcohol Intoxication Reduces Visual Sustained Attention." *Psychopharmacology*, 96: 442–446, 1988 (2 tables, 2 figures, 37 references)

Abstract: Twelve male social drinkers (ages twenty-one to thirty-two years) consumed on four occasions, in random order, a placebo, 0.45, 0.80 and 1.05 g/kg ethanol within 30 minutes. In addition, three maintenance doses of 0.12 g/kg were administered every 30 minutes to maintain the BrAC. BrACs were determined by an Alco-Sensor III. The mean BrACs were 0.040, 0.080, and 0.090 g/100 mL respectively. The subjects were tested on a vigilance task of 486 trials. The eye movements and blinks were recorded. Ethanol effects were found to be centrally rather than peripherally mediated.

Table. Hit Rate (%) with Increasing Time on Task and BAC

Alcohol Dose (Mean BAC)	1–162 Trials	163–324 Trials	325–486 Trials
Placebo (0)	85%	78%	77%
Low (0.040 g/100 mL)	81%	77%	72%
Medium (0.080 g/100 mL)	79%	72%	68%
High (0.090 g/100 mL)	75%	65%	55%

Source: Adapted from Rohrbaugh et al (1988).

On a practical level, these data have relevance to the interpretation of accident statistics for driving and other tasks requiring continuous performance, to the extent to which tasks place continuous demands on central processing capacity. Our finding that ethanol's effects are exacerbated with time on task has implications for the translation of discrete laboratory tasks to field studies in which performance demands are more likely to be continuous. Even though the skills involved might appear unaffected when probed for brief periods, the interactive effects of ethanol and time on task may well render significant impairment during typical field conditions.

Reference Number: 50107

ANTEBI, D. "The Effects of Alcohol on Four Choice Serial Reaction Time." *Medicine Science and the Law*, 22: 181–188, 1982 (6 tables, 4 figures, 17 references)

Abstract: Sixteen male subjects (ages nineteen to twenty-five years) were divided into alcohol and nonalcohol groups. The alcohol group consumed 140 mL of 33% v/v alcohol within 10 minutes. The nonalcohol group consumed the same quantity of orange juice. BACs were determined in capillary blood samples just prior to testing. The mean peak BACs ranged from 0.050 to 0.060 g/100 mL. The task consisted of responding to numbers generated on a screen, corresponding to numbers on four buttons. The task was conducted on five occasions, once before drinking and subsequently at half-hour intervals. The task was of 4 minutes duration. The mean number of errors, total number of responses, and the total number of correct responses were not significantly affected. The mean number of gaps (RT > 1 second) and mean reaction time were significantly affected by this dose of alcohol. Only one of the eight subjects felt incapable of driving.

> In conclusion, I submit that as a significant proportion of the population is impaired with respect to reaction times and other parameters at a blood alcohol level of 50 mg percent, on should perhaps consider reducing the level at which a driver is committing an offence from the present 80 mg percent.

Reference Number: 50108

GENGO, F.M., C. GABOS, C. STRALEY, AND C. MANNING. "The Pharmacodynamics of Ethanol: Effects on Performance and Judgment." *Journal of Clinical Pharmacology*, 30: 748–754, 1990 (1 table, 5 figures, 22 references)

Abstract: Twenty healthy male subjects (ages twenty-one to thirty-five years) were given four different treatments, either a placebo or doses of ethanol calculated to achieve a BAC of 0.070, 0.100 or 0.140 g/100 mL. BrACs were determined by a Breathalyzer Model 900A. Subjects consumed the ethanol in two equal doses over 5 minutes. Digit symbol substitution test (DSST), simulated driving reaction time (SDRT), choice reaction time (CRT), and self-assessment of impairment (SRI) were measured. Testing was conducted on the increasing and decreasing BrACs.

In summary, the data presented do not support the existence of an acute tolerance to the effects of ethanol measured by objective psychometric tests. The data do support the existence of a hysteresis between subjective assessment of impairment and ethanol concentration. This may help to explain conflicting reports in the literature regarding the time course of ethanol concentration and the time course of its effects. Our data support the present assumption by the medico-legal community that equal impairment of psychomotor function occurs regardless of increasing or decreasing ethanol concentration. The threshold BAC associated with scores different from placebo scores obtained (0.03–0.06 gm/dL) is consistent with the policy of most states that restrict driving of individuals with blood alcohol concentration of 0.05 gm/dL or greater.

Reference Number: 50109

ANDRE, J.T. "Visual Functioning in Challenging Conditions: Effects of Alcohol Consumption, Luminance, Stimulus Motion and Glare on Contrast Sensitivity." *Journal of Experimental Psychology and Applications*, 2: 250–269, 1996 (6 tables, 8 figures, 61 references)

Abstract: Six female and six male subjects (ages twenty-three to twenty-eight years) consumed either a placebo or 1.3 mL/kg alcohol within 20 minutes. The subjects were tested on the effect of low luminance, alcohol consumption, stimulus motion, and glare on contrast sensitivity. Subjective feelings of intoxication were also determined. BrACs were determined with an Alco-Sensor IV. The mean BrAC during the testing session was 0.073 g/100 mL. An increase in BrAC was associated with a decrease in contrast sensitivity. Subjective feelings of intoxication were a poor measure of alcohol-related impairment of contrast sensitivity.

The interaction between luminance and alcohol consumption was probably the most interesting, because it illustrated the combined effects of the two factors that had the largest individual effects on contrast sensitivity. The effect of alcohol consumption was exacerbated in the low-luminance condition and the effect was even larger when the glare source was added. Interestingly, most drinkers tend to consume alcohol at night, the time when its effects will be most detrimental.

Reference Number: 50110

DALRYMPLE-ALFORD, J.C., P.A. KERR, AND R.D. JONES. "The Effects of Alcohol on Driving-Related Sensorimotor Performance Across Four Times of Day." *Journal of Studies on Alcohol,* 64: 93–97, 2003 (1 table, 30 references)

Abstract: Sixteen male subjects (mean age twenty-nine years) consumed 0.836 g/kg alcohol with a small meal within 20 minutes at 9:00 a.m., 1:00 p.m., 6:00 p.m. and 1:00 a.m. BrACs were determined with an Alcolmeter and were approximately 0.070 g/100 mL. The subjects were tested on seven tracking tasks (total duration 12 to 15 minutes) with and without alcohol at these four times of the day respectively. There was no interaction of alcohol effect and time of day.

> Alcohol levels just below the legal threshold for driving in New Zealand adults (80 mg/dL blood) produced marked impairments on several tracking tasks with the exception of a modest effect when predictable ballistic movements were required (step tracking preview). The sensitivity to alcohol to tasks that require lateral movements is consistent with the observation that alcohol-related accidents are more likely when the driver has to negotiate a bend, although other factors such as speed and perception will also be relevant in real-life situations.

Reference Number: 50111

NAWROT, M., B. NORDENSTROM, AND A. OLSON. "Disruption of Eye Movements by Ethanol Intoxication Affects Perception of Depth from Motion Parallax." *Psychological Science,* 15: 858–865, 2004 (4 figures, 41 references)

Abstract: Nine male and six female subjects (mean age twenty-four years) were tested for depth perception, pursuit eye movements, compensatory eye movements, and motion perception without and with consuming 0.8 g/kg alcohol within 40 minutes. BrACs were determined with an Intoxilyzer 5000 and Lifeloc FC10. The BrACs during testing ranged between 0.070 and 0.140 g/100 mL (mean 0.085 g/100 mL). Alcohol did not affect depth perception, tVOR eye movements, or motion perception but affected slow OKR eye movements and perception of depth from motion parallax.

> Indeed, the effects of ethanol intoxication on eye movement may have an underappreciated impact on the visual mechanisms necessary for

successful locomotion through a cluttered and hazard-filled environment. Although the current study suggests that intoxicated drivers may have difficulty determining the relative position of obstacles using motion parallax, this may be only one part of a broader but poorly understood set of visual perceptual problems caused by ethanol's effects on the eye movement system.

Reference Number: 50112

GRILLON C., R. SINHA, AND S.S. O'MALLEY. "Effects of Ethanol on the Processing of Low Probability Stimuli: An ERP Study." *Psychopharmacology,* 119: 455–465, 1995 (2 tables, 7 figures, 57 references)

Abstract: Seven male and nine female subjects (ages twenty-one to twenty-six years) consumed either a placebo or 0.85 g/kg ethanol within 20 minutes. Additional doses of ethanol (0.062 g/kg) were administered to maintain the BrAC. Testing was conducted when the BrACs were declining. The mean peak BAC was 0.084 g/100 mL. Subjects were tested on event-related potentials (ERPs) from fifteen electrodes in the scalp. Subjects pressed a button in response to the detection of a rare auditory stimuli embedded among frequent standard and rare novel auditory stimuli. Ethanol impaired the processing of task-irrelevant stimuli to a greater extent than task-relevant stimuli.

From a functional standpoint, this study might point to some of the harmful effects of ethanol on overlearned tasks, such as driving a car. Because ethanol impairs the response to unexpected events, it might increase the risk of alcohol-related traffic accidents. Intoxicated drivers might not be aware of this potential danger and might feel fit to drive because moderate doses of alcohol may not affect the overlearned aspects of driving a car.

Reference Number: 50113

WEGNER, A.J. AND M. FAHLE. "Alcohol and Visually Guided Saccades: Gap Effect and Predictability of Target Location." *Psychopharmacology,* 146: 24–32, 1999 (7 figures, 74 references)

Abstract: Eight male and five female subjects (ages nineteen to fifty-four years) had their eye movements (saccades) recorded sober and after consuming 0.8 g/kg alcohol after a 4-hour fast. BrACs were determined every 5 minutes by an Alcotest 7410 and testing was conducted after the peak BrAC had been obtained. The peak BrACs ranged between 0.080–0.130 g/100 mL. The saccades were measured under classical and gap conditions with predictable or unpredictable movements. Alcohol increased saccade reaction time (RT) for both conditions. Sober subjects took more advantage of the predictability of the target under gap conditions and had a 19% decrease in RT compared to an 8% decrease in intoxicated subjects.

In summary acute alcohol consumption significantly interferes with the oculomotor system. Visually guided saccades are slowed down both due to an increase in saccadic reaction time and a decrease in peak velocity.

Reference Number: 50114

CROMER, J.R., J.A. CROMER, P. MARUFF, AND P.J. SNYDER. "Perception of Alcohol Intoxication Shows Acute Tolerance While Executive Functions Remain Impaired." *Experimental and Clinical Psychopharmacology*, 18: 329–339, 2010 (3 tables, 4 figures, 47 references)

Abstract: Eleven female and nine male subjects (ages twenty-one to twenty-five years) consumed a placebo or one drink of alcohol over 15 minutes every 30 minutes until the BrAC as measured by an AlcoMate Pro was 0.100 g/100 mL. The subjects were tested on subjective perception of intoxication (Visual Analog Scale) and the computerized Groton Maze Learning Test (GMLT) on the rising and declining phases of the BAC curve. Subjective perception of intoxication, visuomotor speed, and visuospatial learning efficiency showed acute tolerance to alcohol. Executive functions and spatial short-term memory did not show acute tolerance.

Taken together, the results demonstrate that whereas subjective perception of intoxication recovers with declining BAC, accuracy of executive functions does not. These results have direct practical relevance as people often decide to operate motorized vehicles despite being intoxicated. Our study strongly suggests that one likely reason for this common decision is the mismatch between their perceived recovery from intoxication and continued impairments in higher order cognitive abilities.

Reference Number: 50115

CHENG, S-Y., H-Y. LEE, J-C. LEE, AND S-Y. TSAI. "Comparing the Effects of Light Alcohol Consumption on Human Response to Auditory and

Visual Stimuli." *Perceptual and Motor Skills*, 111: 589–607, 2010 (4 tables, 5 figures, 44 references)

Abstract: Twenty male subjects (ages twenty to twenty-five years) consumed a placebo, 0.2, 0.3, and 0.5 g/kg alcohol and 30 minutes later were tested on auditory and visual RT. BrACs were determined with a Lifeloc PBA3000 breath alcohol device and the mean BrACs were 0.000, 0.013, 0.019, and 0.038 g/100 mL respectively.

> Increasing the alcohol dose from zero to moderate resulted in an increase of the mean total response time for auditory stimuli of about 0.2 sec. in comparison to about 0.1 sec. for visual stimuli. Under moderate alcohol doses, workers such as visual display terminal operators, motor vehicle drivers, or operators of dangerous machinery who must respond quickly to visual and particularly to auditory alarms, may experience increased probability of accident owing to alcohol-induced slowed response and increased probability of erroneous judgments.

Reference Number: 50116

FRIEDMAN, T.W., S.R. ROBINSON, AND G.W. YELLAND. "Impaired Perceptual Judgment at Low Blood Alcohol Concentrations." *Alcohol*, 45: 711–718, 2011 (1 table, 5 figures, 28 references)

Abstract: Eleven female and ten male subjects (ages eighteen to twenty-seven years) were tested on a computerized Subtle Cognitive Impairment Test (SCIT) before and 35, 80, 125, and 170 minutes after consuming a placebo or a mean alcohol volume of 50 mL for male and 39 mL for female subjects. BrACs were measured with an Alco-Sensor 6510. The mean peak BrACs were 0.055 g/100 mL for male and 0.052 g/100 mL for female subjects. Impairment of perceptual judgment was equivalent on both the ascending and descending BAC limbs.

> In conclusion, this preliminary study has revealed that perceptual judgment is impaired at BACs that are below the legal limit for driving in most countries. Increased number of errors were not compensated for by a slowed volitional response time. These findings suggest that mild alcohol intoxication can impair performance on activities that involve making decisions quickly and accurately on the basis of fleeting sensory stimuli.

Reference Number: 50117

MARTIN, T.L., P.A.M. SOLBECK, D. J. MAYERS, R.M. LANGILLE, Y. BUCZEK, AND M.R. PELLETIER. "A Review of Alcohol-Impaired Driving: The Role of Blood Alcohol Concentration and Complexity of the Driving Task." *Journal of Forensic Sciences*, 58: 1238–1250, 2013 (124 references)

Abstract: A detailed and extensive review on the effects of alcohol on driving ability was conducted. There are 124 references. Major topics covered include laboratory studies, closed course studies, on-road studies, and functional and acute tolerance.

> It is uncontroversial that alcohol-related impairment is concentration dependent: the magnitude of impairment increases with increasing BAC. As demonstrated by the present review, there is convergent evidence, therefore a high degree of scientific confidence in support of the conclusion that a BAC of 0.050% impairs faculties required in the operation of a motor vehicle. This conclusion notwithstanding, the present review also demonstrates that impaired may occur at BACs < 0.050%. Whether impairment is apparent depends upon the complexity of the driving task: however, because driving is an inherently complex behavior, it can be asserted scientifically that the faculties required in the operation of a motor vehicle will be impaired at a BAC of 0.050% or greater.

Reference Number: 50118

TREMBLAY, M., F. GALLANT, M. LAVALLIERE, M. CHIASSON, D. SILVEY, D. BEHM, W.J. ALBERT, AND M.J. JOHNSON. "Driving Performance on the Descending Limb of Blood Alcohol Concentration (BAC) in Undergraduate Students: A Pilot Study." *Public Library of Science ONE*, 10(2): 15pp, 27 February 2015 (2 tables, 3 figures, 28 references)

Abstract: Two groups of ten subjects (twelve women and eight men in total) with a mean age of 21.6 years were divided into an alcohol group and a control group and tested on a driving simulator on the Useful Field of View (UFOV) test. The alcohol group consumed on average 5.3 drinks (30 mL 40% v/v alcohol) over 1 hour or one drink per 11 kg body weight. BrACs were measured with an Alcotest 7410 GLC. The alcohol group was tested before, and 4 and 24 hours after alcohol consumption. The BACs obtained were moderate (0.050 to 0.070 g/100 mL) and low (0.010 to 0.040 g/100 mL).

In order to better reflect the practices of undergraduate students after acute alcohol consumption, our methodology explored descending limb of blood alcohol concentration. Our findings add understanding of the behaviors linked to the overrepresentation of young drivers under the influence of alcohol in fatality statistics as moderate blood alcohol concentrations increased driving speeds and the number of errors committed by the drivers. Also, the useful field of view test was not sensitive enough to measure performance differences due to alcohol consumption. This tool is not a good predictor of crash risk in young adults and in young adults under the influence of alcohol.

Reference Number: 50119

GARRISON, H., A. SCHOLEY, F. OGDEN, AND S. BENSON. "The Effects of Alcohol Intoxication on Cognitive Functions Critical for Driving: A Systematic Review." *Accident Analysis and Prevention*, 154: 11pp, 2021 (2 tables, 3 figures, 43 references)

Abstract: As up to 35% of road collisions are alcohol related, a systematic review of the effects of alcohol on driving-related skills was conducted. A total of fourteen placebo controlled studies were assessed involving a total of 666 healthy participants. The main areas for alcohol impairment of driving include dividing attention, executive function, perception, psychomotor skills, reaction time, and vigilance. Deficits in visual perception occur at BAC of 0.030 g/100 mL. Vigilance was sensitive to BACs of 0.030 g/100 mL at longer time duration tasks. Deficits in divided attention occurred at BAC of 0.050 to 0.080 g/1000mL.

The findings of this review are consistent with epidemiological data indicating that, when compared to a sober driver, a drink-driver's relative crash risk is significantly elevated beginning at a BAC as low as 0.04%. More specifically, we found evidence of impairment in measures of aspects of attention, perception, and vigilance at BACs within the legal limit in many countries supporting the recommended limit of 0.05% for the general population and 0.02% for young and novice drivers. It is important for drivers to be aware that the BAC limits set in many countries are arbitrary, politically chosen and they do not necessarily align with levels compatible with safe driving, as the capacity to safely operate a motor vehicle begins to deteriorate at any level of alcohol consumption.

5.02 DRIVING SIMULATOR STUDIES

"Until the advent of the motor car over-indulgence in alcohol was regarded by the law as being merely a very minor crime. Persuasion and precept rather than a severe legal punishment were used to minimize the moral and social levels which it often caused. It soon became evident that the overuse of alcohol by drivers of motor cars and other vehicles was a source of many dangerous accidents."

—McGrath, "The Method and Significance of Blood Alcohol Estimations" (1939)

"The results of this study indicate that in individuals who habitually binge drink, those individuals may not feel like they are too intoxicated to drive. These subjective feelings are at odds with their actual driving performance under alcohol, which remains poor."

—Marczinski et al, "Effects of Alcohol on Stimulated Driving and Perceived Driving Impairment in Binge Drinkers" (2008)

Driving simulator studies tend to be more realistic than the laboratory studies described in the previous section. Similar results were obtained, however, in that there is increasing impairment of driving abilities with increasing BAC. Stopping distance was increased (50204), lane position was affected (50525, 50206, 50210, 50211), as was ability to negotiate curves (50208). Although habitual binge drinkers felt less impaired than social drinkers, they still performed as poorly in driving simulators (50211).

Recently more and more sophisticated and technical driving simulators have been driven by drinking drivers, as there are no safety risks (or insurance costs) for the subjects that can occur with closed course studies involving real automobiles (50213–50220). As found in real situations, the willingness to drive increases on the declining BAC phase when drinking drivers feel less impaired (50213).

Reference Number: 50201

LANDAUER, A.A. AND P. HOWATT. "Low and Moderate Alcohol Doses, Psychomotor Performance and Perceived Drowsiness." *Ergonomics,* 26: 647–657, 1983 (2 tables, 2 figures, 26 references)

Abstract: Eighteen male and eight female subjects (ages eighteen to thirty-five years) consumed four doses of ethanol within 10 minutes.

The doses were adjusted for gender. BrACs were measured by an Alcometer. The mean BACs were 0, 0.021, 0.050, and 0.073 g/100 mL. Subjects were tested under all four alcohol conditions on a TIM (tracking input manipulator); a driving simulator combined with a divided attention task. Testing commenced 25–35 minutes after the ethanol was consumed to allow for alcohol absorption. Subjects reported an increase in drowsiness for up to 3 hours after alcohol consumption.

Table. Mean Error Score and BAC in Simulated Driving.

Mean BAC (g/100 mL)	Mean Total Error Score
0	89
0.021	99
0.050	108
0.073	113

Source: Adapted from Landauer and Howatt (1983).

This study presents further evidence to the direct relationship between increased driving errors and mounting BACs. In particular, subjects were shown to make more errors in terms of anticipating signals, incorrect steering, and under or over steering whilst under the effect of low to moderate amounts of alcohol (BAC 0.020–0.073%). It is highly probable that these incorrect responses are significant causal factors in many traffic accidents.

Reference Number: 50202

BANKS, S., P. CATCHSIDE, L. LACK, R.R. GRUNSTEIN, AND R.D. MCEVOY. "Low Levels of Alcohol Impair Driving Simulator Performance and Reduce Perception of Crash Risk in Partially Sleep Deprived Subjects." *Sleep,* 27: 1063–1067, 2004 (2 tables, 2 figures, 27 references)

Abstract: Eleven female and nine male subjects (mean age twenty-three years) were tested on a driving simulator at 1:00 a.m. after being partially sleep-deprived (5 hours sleep) with and without consuming two to three standard drinks over 2 hours. BrACs were determined with an Alcotest 7410 Plus. The mean BrAC was 0.037 g/100 mL. The driving simulation lasted for 70 minutes and EEG microsleep analysis was also conducted. The mean number of crashes increased from 1.0 to 4.3 and the mean seconds of microsleep increased from 4.8 to 8.9 seconds.

In conclusion, in this study, alcohol consumption to a BAC considered in most jurisdictions to be safe, when combined with sleep loss, increased EEG-defined sleepiness, impaired driving simulator performance, and reduced subjects' ability to detect impairment in driving performance and assess crash risk. Women appeared to be more perceptive of increased crash risk or more willing to admit to their driving limitations under partial sleep deprived conditions. These results have may have implications for policy, including reduction in permissible BAC for drivers under 25 years of age and restricting young drivers to daytime driving (which has been successfully implemented in some areas).

Reference Number: 50203

BARKLEY, R.A., K.R. MURPHY, T. O'CONNELL, D. ANDERSON, AND D.F. CONNOR. "Effects of Two Doses of Alcohol on Simulator Driving Performance in Adults with Attention-Deficit/Hyperactivity Disorder." *Neuropsychology*, 26: 77–87, 2006 (3 tables, 42 references)

Abstract: Fifty adults with attention-deficit/hyperactivity disorder (ADHD) and forty control adults (mean age twenty-nine years) consumed either a low (0.040 g/100 mL BAC) or high (0.080 g/100 mL BAC) dose of alcohol and a placebo within 15 minutes. BrACs were determined 15 minutes later with an Intoximeter and the mean BrACs were within ±0.009 g/100 mL of the target BACs. The subjects were tested on a virtual reality driving simulator and other measures such as a continuous performance test (CPT).

With these limitations in mind, the present study extends earlier research in driving and ADHD by demonstrating a possibly greater adverse impact of alcohol consumption on the attention and driving performance of adults with ADHD than may be seen in community control adults. Such findings were evident on CPT performance and in the self and examiner ratings of driving performance in the simulator but not on the simulator scores themselves. Even so, we found that alcohol had a detrimental effect on these driving scores in both groups, increasing speed and variability, increasing collisions, and slowing brake RTs to critical events.

Reference Number: 50204

LIGUORI, A., R.B. D'AGOSTINO JR., S.I. DWORKIN, D. EDWARDS, AND J.H. ROBINSON. "Alcohol Effects on Mood, Equilibrium and Simulated Driving."

Alcoholism Clinical and Experimental Research, 23: 815–821, 1999 (1 table, 4 figures, 35 references)

Abstract: Ten female and eight male subjects (mean age thirty-two years) who had consumed on average seven drinks per week were tested on four occasions after consumption of a placebo, 0.5, or 0.8 g/kg alcohol after a 12-hour fast. The initial session was a practice session. Each session was separated by a least 7 days. The alcohol was consumed within 20 minutes and the BrACs were measured. The mean BrACs were 0.057 g/100 mL, which declined to 0.047 g/100 mL after testing (0.5 g/kg) and 0.097 g/100mL, which declined to 0.092 g/100 mL (0.8 g/kg). Various psychomotor tests were conducted (CFF, CRT) and the subjects were also tested on a computerized driving simulator. The average stopping distances upon appearance of a yellow barrier were 50 ft, 53 ft, and 60 ft for the placebo, 0.5, and 0.8 g/kg doses respectively.

> The present study found that a dose of alcohol that produces BrACs below the legal limit significantly impaired reaction time in a driving simulator but not on relatively simple task (CRT). The results demonstrate that psychomotor tasks such as CRT and CFF which are thought to measure individual components of driving (e.g., reaction time and visual discrimination) may be insensitive to alcohol doses that significantly impair more realistic simulations of driving that integrates these tasks.

Reference Number: 50205

RAKAUSKAS, M.E., N.J. WARD, E.R. BOER, E.M. BERNAT, M. CADWALLADER, AND C.J. PATRICK. "Combined Effects of Alcohol and Distraction on Driving Performance." *Accident Analysis and Prevention*, 40: 1742–1749, 2008 (2 tables, 3 figures, 44 references)

Abstract: Forty-five male drivers were administered a placebo (n = 21) or alcohol (n = 24) consumed rapidly and calculated to obtain a target BAC of 0.080 g/100 mL. BrACs were determined with an Alcotest 7410 Plus and the mean BrAC was 0.074 g/100 mL (range 0.053 to 0.108 g/100 mL). The subjects were tested on a driving simulator with the primary task of maintaining a safe stopping distance and the secondary goal of maintaining lane position. The task was of 2 minutes duration with a low demand distraction task (every 25 to 50 seconds) and a high demand distraction task (every 8 to 16 seconds).

Moderate alcohol doses affected how drivers allocated resources and adjusted performance thresholds. These results suggest that intoxicated drivers may adopt a strategy of deemphasizing lane position in order to invest released resources to protect the primary task of maintaining a constant headway. This may be construed as a combination of goal reduction and resource management. In effect this shedding of attention from one goal to favour another is kin to self-imposed removal of attentional resources from an aspect of driving performance safety. This method of coping with alcohol impairment is unsafe for two reasons; one, the reduction in lateral control could lead to a lane departure crash; or two, the withdrawal of attention by shifting to reactive weakens the ability to contend with sudden and unexpected hazards.

Reference Number: 50206

ALLEN, R.W., H.R. JEX, D.T. MCRUER, AND R.J. DIMARCO. "Alcohol Effects on Driving Behavior and Performance in a Car Simulator." *IEEE Transactions on Systems, Man and Cybernetics, SMC-5*: 498–505, 1975 (2 tables, 8 figures, 27 references)

Abstract: Seventeen male and one female subjects (ages twenty-one to sixty-five years) consumed either whiskey or vodka within 20 minutes to obtain a BrAC of 0.06 g/100 mL on the ascending phase of the BAC curve. An additional drink was consumed to obtain a peak BrAC of 0.110 g/100 mL. The subjects were also tested at a BAC of 0.06 g/100 mL on the descending phase. BrACs were determined with a GC Intoximeter Mk II. The subjects were divided equally into moderate and heavy drinkers. Testing was conducted in a driving simulator and involved a steering control task in which the car was "buffeted" by the wind and a visual detection task. The simulated scenario was driving an automobile on a rural road on a stormy night. There were no significant differences in impairment of performance on either the ascending or descending phase.

Line deviations increase with BAC level, which is explained by measures of lower driver control gain and increased remnant. Distraction of the sign response task further increased the impairment of path control by alcohol.

Reference Number: 50207

BUIKHUISEN, W. AND R.W. JONGMAN. "Traffic Perception Under the Influence of Alcohol." *Quarterly Journal of Studies on Alcohol*, 33: 800–806, 1972 (11 references)

Abstract: Male drivers were divided into a control group (n = 55) and an alcohol group (n = 50). The alcohol group consumed five drinks of 40% v/v spirits within 45 minutes. The BACs were determined by blood analysis with the following results: thirteen subjects had a BAC < 0.070 g/100 mL, twenty-four had a BAC from 0.070–0.090 g/100 mL, and thirteen had a BAC > 0.090 g/100 mL. Subjects then watched a 5-minute film taken from a moving car that contained twenty-five potentially dangerous situations especially staged for the experiment. Eye movement was recorded by a TV eye monitor.

> While watching a film taken from a moving car, intoxicated subjects observed fewer important traffic incidents, missed more incidents to the sides rather than the centre of the screen, more nonmoving objects and more incidents that were part of a complex situation than sober subjects.

Reference Number: 50208

GAWRON, V.J. AND T.A. RANNEY. "The Effects of Spot Treatments on Performance in a Driving Simulator Under Sober and Alcohol-Dosed Conditions." *Accident Analysis and Prevention* 22: 263–279, 1990 (6 tables, 6 figures, 34 references)

Abstract: Twelve subjects consumed alcohol to obtain BrACs of 0, 0.070, or 0.120 g/100 mL, as determined by an Intoximeter Mk II. The subjects were then tested in a driving simulator as to their ability to negotiate curves. The curves had various spot treatments or warning systems, such as a flashing light, chevron, post delineator, or herringbone road markings. There was no general overall effect of spot treatments on performance in a driving simulator.

> The pattern of results suggests that drivers' responses to the spot treatments as implemented in the driving simulator were not the same as those obtained on the road by Johnston (1983) but do support Thomson's (1985) contention that improved delineation systems are uneffectual because alcohol impaired drivers simply stop processing task-relevant information and miss the curve.

Reference Number: 50209

QUILLAN, W.C., D.J. COX, B.P. KOVATCHEV, AND C. PHILLIPS. "The Effects of Age and Alcohol Intoxication on Simulated Driving Performance, Awareness and Self-Restraint." *Age and Aging*, 28: 59–66, 1999 (4 tables, 3 figures, 33 references)

Abstract: Fourteen middle age (thirty-five to fifty years) and fourteen older (sixty to seventy-seven years) healthy males were tested on a driving simulator for 20 minutes with and without consumption of alcohol. The mean peak BrAC as determined by an Alco-Sensor IV was 0.080 g/100 mL. The older men were unwilling to drive while intoxicated because of fear of physical injury, whereas the middle-aged men were unlikely to drive while intoxicated due to fear of legal ramifications. Men over sixty years of age had a poorer performance on the driving simulator than middle-aged men when sober. Alcohol caused a poorer performance on the driving simulator for both age groups.

Ethanol consumption does not affect healthy, older male drivers more than middle-aged healthy male drivers in terms of blood alcohol concentrations, driving performance or awareness of either intoxication or impaired driving.

Reference Number: 50210

FILLMORE, M.T., J.S. BLACKBURN, AND E.L.R. HARRISON. "Acute Disinhibiting Effects of Alcohol as a Factor in Risky Driving Behavior." *Drug and Alcohol Dependence*, 95: 97–106, 2008 (2 tables, 4 figures, 52 references)

Abstract: Seven female and seven male subjects (ages twenty-one to thirty years) were tested on a computerized simulated driving task and a cued go/no go task with placebo or 0.6 g/kg alcohol consumed within 2 minutes. BrACs were determined with an Intoxilyzer and the mean peak BrAC was 0.089 g/100 mL.

Compared with placebo, the profile of driving under alcohol was characterized by greater deviation of lane position, increased line crossings, more failures to stop at red lights, faster more abrupt steering maneuvers, greater acceleration, and faster overall speed. Moreover, response conflict exacerbated impaired and risky driving behavior under alcohol by further increasing deviation of lane position and failures to stop at red lights. The study also showed that alcohol and response conflict produced a similar interactive impairing effect on the drivers; inhibitory control as measured by the cued go/no go task.

Reference Number: 50211

MARCZINSKI, C.A., E.L.R. HARRISON, AND M.T. FILLMORE. "Effects of Alcohol on Simulated Driving and Perceived Driving Impairment in Binge Drinkers." *Alcoholism: Clinical and Experimental Research*, 32: 1329–1337, 2008 (2 tables, 2 figures, 57 references)

Abstract: Twenty female and twenty male subjects (ages twenty-one to twenty-nine years) consumed a placebo or 0.65 g/kg alcohol within 7 minutes and were tested on a computerized driving simulator. The simulation was of 19 miles duration over winding roads and hills and a constant speed of 55 mph was to have been maintained. BrACs were measured with an Intoxilyzer 400. Twenty-four subjects were classified as binge drinkers and sixteen as nonbinge drinkers. The mean peak BrACs were approximately 0.090 g/100 mL. With alcohol, all subjects had difficulty maintaining their lane position and the appropriate speed and made multiple driving errors.

Table. Mean Simulated Driving Measures for Binge and Nonbinge Drinkers Under Placebo and Alcohol (0.65 g/kg) Conditions

Subjects/ Conditions	No. of Center Lane Crossings	No. of Road Edge Excursions	No. of Collisions
Binge Drinkers (placebo)	5.9	3.6	0.1
Binge Drinkers (alcohol)	14.9	11.3	0.9
Nonbinge Drinkers (placebo)	4.6	1.8	0.0
Nonbinge Drinkers (alcohol)	20.5	13.6	1.8

Source: Adapted from Marczinski et al (2008).

The results of this study indicate that in individuals who habitually binge drink, those individuals may not feel like they are too intoxicated to drive. These subjective feelings are at odds with their actual driving performance under alcohol, which remains poor.

Reference Number: 50212

MEDA, S.A., V.D. CALHOUN, R.S. ASTUR, B.M. TURNER, K. RUOPP, AND G.D. PEARLSON. "Alcohol Dose Effects on Brain Circuits During Simulated Driving: An fMRI Study." *Human Brain Mapping*, 30: 1257–1270, 2009 (3 tables, 6 figures, 50 references)

Abstract: Twenty male and twenty female subjects (mean age twenty-five years) on three occasions consumed a placebo, low dose of alcohol (target BAC = 0.050 g/100 mL), and a high dose of alcohol (target BAC = 0.100 g/100 mL). The subjects then drove a virtual reality driving simulator while undergoing functional magnetic resonance imaging (fMRI) of the brain. The alcohol was consumed within 10 minutes and testing was conducted 15 minutes later. BrACs were determined with a hand-held Intoximeter unit and the mean peak BrACs were 0.039 and 0.087 g/100 mL. There was an increase in passenger side white lane crossings, crashes, and increased mean speed with increasing alcohol dose.

> Further we found consistent behavioral changes while driving intoxicated supporting our imaging results. Our results demonstrated that speed and white line crossing errors mediated the fronto-basal-ganglia-temporal (green) component involvement across alcohol dosages. Overall, our findings might imply a significant impairment in attention, cognitive, goal direction, motor planning and emotional/working memory related functional capabilities while driving under the influence of alcohol.

Reference Number 50213

WEAFER, J. AND M.T. FILLMORE. "Acute Tolerance to Alcohol Impairment of Behavioral and Cognitive Mechanisms Related to Driving: Drinking and Driving on the Descending Limb." *Psychopharmacology*, 220: 697–706, 2012 (3 figures, 2 tables, 31 references)

Abstract: Ten female and ten male social drinkers (ages twenty-one to thirty-one years) consumed a placebo or 0.65 g/kg alcohol within 6 minutes and performed a test battery including computerized simulated driving and go/no go tests. BrACs were determined with an Intoxilyzer Model 400 and testing occurred at 35 minutes (ascending BAC) and 95 minutes (descending BAC) and the mean BrACs were 0.072 and 0.074 g/100 mL respectively. Impaired motor coordination and subjective tolerance showed acute tolerance whereas driving performance and inhibitory control did not.

Table. Mean Simulated Driving Performance Parameters and Reaction Time for Placebo (No Alcohol) and on the Ascending and Descending BAC Curve

	Mean Placebo	Ascending BAC	Descending BAC
Lane Position Standard Deviation (ft)	1.0	1.3	1.2
Lane Crossings	2.0	4.0	3.6
Steering Rate	7.5	8.9	8.0
Willingness to Drive	73.5	17.1	38.9
Reaction Time (ms)	331.5	343.3	346.8

Source: Adapted from Weafer and Fillmore (2012).

In conclusion, the study highlights the importance of examining alcohol impairment of individual skills related to driving performance and decisions to drive at later time points during a drinking episode. Acute tolerance can result in diminished impairment of some skills, but not others. Moreover, acute tolerance to the subjective effects of alcohol could reduce the ability to accurately appraise one's fitness to drive. As such, these findings have important implications, particularly in terms of education and prevention of intoxicated driving. Future policy changes could consider education regarding misperception of self-intoxication as well as information about the likelihood of sustained impairment of driving ability and inhibitory control in response to a dose of alcohol.

Reference Number: 50214

HARRISON, E.L.R. AND M.T. FILLMORE. "Alcohol and Distraction Interact to Impair Driving Performance." *Drug Alcohol Dependence*, 117: 31–37, 2011 (1 figure, 1 table, 35 references)

Abstract: Twenty female and twenty male subjects (ages twenty-one to thirty-five years) were divided into four groups and tested on a computerized driving simulator. The groups were alcohol, alcohol and divided attention, placebo, and placebo and divided attention. The subjects were tested on the driving simulator before treatment to establish baseline performance. The divided attention task was a two-choice reaction time (RT) task that was conducted while driving. The alcohol dose was 0.65 g/kg alcohol, which was consumed within 8 minutes. BrACs were determined with an Intoxilyzer 400 and the mean BrAC was 0.081 g/100 mL.

Drivers with alcohol and distraction had the greatest increase in standard deviation of lateral position (SDLP), which is a measure of swerving and poorer vehicle control.

Table. Mean SDLP in Centimeters and (Mean Speed in Kilometers per Hour) in Subjects Without and with Distraction

	Placebo	Alcohol
No Divided Attention	29 cm (92 km/h)	34 cm (95 km/h)
Divided Attention	27cm (78 km/h)	40 cm (94 km/h)

Source: Adapted from Harrison and Fillmore (2011).

In the present study it was demonstrated that the combination of alcohol and distraction interacted to decrease driving precision, and that drivers failed to reduce their speed to compensate for the additional impairment.

Reference Number: 50215

VAN DYKE, N.A. AND M.T. FILLMORE. "Distraction Produces Over-Additive Increases in the Degree to Which Alcohol Impairs Driving Performance." *Psychopharmacology,* 232: 4277–4284, 2015 (1 figure, 30 references)

Abstract: Fourteen female and thirty-six male licensed drivers (ages twenty-one to thirty-four years) consumed a placebo or 0.65 g/kg alcohol within 6 minutes and then were tested on a computerized driving test (5.9 miles duration) with distracted and undistracted conditions. The distracted driving included a two-choice detected task (responding to two red lights at the corners of the windshield. BrACs were measured with an Intoxilyzer 4000 and the mean BAC during the driving test was 0.067 g/100 mL. Driving speed was slightly faster with the distraction than non-distraction. The factor by which distraction increased the magnitude of alcohol impairment was 2.1 times for SDLP, 3.5 times for steering rate, and 2.6 times for exceeding the speed limit.

In conclusion, the findings from the present study provide some of the first pieces of evidence on the degree to which distractions can severely disrupt intoxicated drivers' ability to maintain proper control of their vehicle on the road by impacting even the most basic aspects of driving behavior. With continuing advancements in technology and the omnipresence of distractions while driving, it is becoming increasingly important to study the interaction between alcohol and distractions on driving. A clearer understanding of how common distractions impact intoxicated drivers, especially at BrACs that are currently legal for driving in the USA, is an important step to reducing traffic accidents and fatalities and improving overall traffic safety.

Reference Number: 50216

VAN DIJKEN, J.H., J.L. VELDSTRA, A.J.A.E.VAN DE LOO, J.C. VERSTER, N.N.J.J.M. VAN DER SLUISZEN, A. VERMEEREN, J.G. REMAEKERS, K.A. BROOKHUIS, AND D. DE WAARD. "The Influence of Alcohol (0.5%) on the Control and Maneuvering Level of Driving Behaviour, Finding Measures to Assess Driving Impairment: A Simulator Study." *Transportation Research Part F*, 73: 119–127, 2020 (1 table, 2 figures, 25 references)

Abstract: Twenty male and ten female drivers (mean age 45.4 years) consumed a placebo or alcohol and conducted a simulated driving test of 30–60 minutes duration including swerving, average speed, speed variation, reaction time to a traffic light turning yellow, and response to a suddenly merging car. The mean BAC as determined by a breathalyzer was 0.049 g/100 mL before and 0.035 g/100 mL after the driving tests. All participants in the sober condition braked for the light, whereas one in the alcohol condition did not. The RT to the traffic light was also longer in the alcohol condition.

The deteriorating effect of alcohol at the control level of driving behaviour was replicated, confirming the suitability of the standard deviation of lateral position and the variation in speed as measures of impairment. At the maneuvering level, the kept distance to the leading car during an overtaking maneuver appeared to be a suitable measure to assess impairment as well as reaction time to a traffic light. The current study also confirms the difficulties in evaluating complex driving behaviour and the need for more research on this subject.

Reference Number: 50217

WIEDERMANN, K., F. NAUJOKS, J. WORLE, R. KENNETER-MABIALA, Y. KAUSSNER, AND A. NEUKUM. "Effect of Different Alcohol Levels on Take-Over Performance in Conditionally Automated Driving." *Accident, Analysis and Prevention*, 115: 89–97, 2018 (6 tables, 7 figures, 57 references)

Abstract: Automated driving systems are more frequently being employed in new motor vehicles. These systems still require the driver as a fallback to intervene (conditionally automated driving) in case system limits are exceeded or malfunction. This study was conducted to determine the effect of different BACs on the drivers' ability to take back manual control. Seventeen female and nineteen male drivers (mean age thirty-three years) were tested on a takeover task (conditionally automated driving) on a high fidelity driving simulator at a BAC of 0.050 g/100 mL, 0.080 g/100 mL, or a placebo. The BACs were determined using a breathalyzer ACE AF33.

> The current study assessed alcohol-induced impairments of take-over performance during conditionally automated driving, demonstrating a significant worsening of both take-over time and quality at a BAC-level of 0.08%. For 0.05% BAC, there was only a descriptive tend of worsening compared with the alcohol placebo condition. These results demonstrate that the risks associated with alcohol consumption will not disappear as a result of vehicle automation and that efforts have to be undertaken that this risk is not underestimated.

Reference Number: 50218

YADAV, A.K. AND N.R. VELAGA. "Effect of Alcohol Use on Accelerating and Braking Behaviors of Drivers." *Traffic Injury Prevention*, 20: 353–358, 2019 (3 tables, 3 figures, 20 references).

Abstract: Sixty-two male and twenty female drivers (mean age twenty-five years) were tested on a driving simulator at BACs of 0.0, 0.030, 0.050, and 0.080 g/100 mL. The drivers were tested on the declining phase at BACs of 0.030 and 0.050 g/100 mL. BACs were determined in breath using a Lion Alcolmeter SD-500. Drivers tended to be more aggressive and impulsive under the influence of alcohol, and alcohol caused impairment of accelerating and braking behaviors.

Table. Results of Linear Mixed Models for Mean Acceleration and Brake Pedal Force

BAC (g/100 mL)	Acceleration Estimate (m/s^2)	Braking Estimate (Newtons)
0.03	0.013	1.09
0.05	0.026	1.32
0.08	0.027	1.44

Source: Adapted from Yadav and Velaga (2019).

The findings of the study suggest that alcohol significantly impaired drivers' control of the vehicle which led to greater pressure on the accelerator and brake pedals. The braking model indicates that alcohol-impaired drivers are more prone to aggressive braking while driving. Aggressive braking increases the likelihood of rear-end collisions and aggressive acceleration increases the likelihood of front-end collisions because alcohol impairment makes it difficult to judge safe spacing between the lead vehicle and the following vehicle. In conclusion, it can be said that alcohol impaired the motor coordination of the drivers. They tended to be more impulsive under the influence of alcohol and perceived driving to be a significantly less dangerous task.

Reference Number: 50219

YADAV, A.K. AND N.R. VELAGA. "Laboratory Analysis of Driving Behavior and Self-Perceived Physiological Impairment at 0.03%, 0.05% and 0.08% Blood Alcohol Concentrations." *Drug and Alcohol Dependence*, 205: 7pp, 2019 (4 tables, 2 figures, 44 references)

Abstract: Fifty-six male and nineteen female licensed Indian drivers (mean age 24.8 and 23.7 years respectively) were tested on a computerized driving simulator at BACs of 0.0, 0.080, 0.050, and 0.030 g/100 mL in the declining phase. The declining phase was chosen because the decision to drink and drive is increased as the perceived danger to drive after drinking is reduced. The average speed increased with increasing BAC from 63.9 km/h at a 0 BAC to 72.4 km/h at a BAC of 0.080 g/100 mL. Impairment in the drivers' mental alertness, visual ability, ability to judge, attention on the road while driving, and sense of surroundings increased with increasing BAC.

Mean speed was the only performance measure significantly affected at 0.03% BAC. At 0.05% BAC, mean speed and mean steering wheel angle were the two significantly impaired measures. At 0.08% BAC, all the driving performance measures showed significant impairment except steering wheel angle variability. Physiological characteristics of drivers deteriorated with rising BAC levels. Alcohol significantly impaired the physiology of Indian drivers resulting in impairment in their driving performance. Mean speed was the only performance measure insignificantly affected by all the BAC levels making it a suitable parameter to detect the alcohol-impaired state of the drivers.

Reference Number: 50220

LI, Z., X. LI, X. ZHAO, AND Q. ZHANG. "Effects of Different Alcohol Dosages on Steering Behavior in Curve Driving." *Human Factors*, 61: 139–151, 2019 (6 tables, 2 figures, 56 references)

Abstract: Twenty-five young healthy male drivers (ages twenty to thirty-five years) were tested on a simulator car that had three degrees of freedom (tilting, forward, and backward) while driving around a curve at BACs of 0.0, 0.030, 0.060, and 0.090 g/100 mL. The vehicle speed (VS), steering angle (SA), steering speed (SS), steering reversal rate (SRR), and peak to peak value of the steering angle (PP) were measured. The radii of the simulated curves were 200, 500, and 800 meters.

Table. Mean Measurement Results of 200-Meter Radius Curve at 0, 0.03, 0.06, and 0.09% BAC

Mean Measure	0.00%	0.03%	0.06%	0.09%
Vehicle Speed (km/h)	78	81	80	74
Steering Angle (rad)	0.38	0.46	0.58	0.67
Steering Speed (rad/s)	0.22	0.32	0.42	0.48
Steering Reversal Rate (r/s)	0.31	0.42	0.44	0.52
Peak to Peak Value of the Steering Angle (rad)	1.35	1.64	2.41	3.21

Source: Adapted from Li et al (2019).

For all of the curves, the SS, SRR, and PP had a tendency to increase as the BrAC increased. The large PP at a high BrAC accompanied by the high speed, SS, and SRR resulted in a high probability of lane exceedance. The use of measures of SS, SRR, and PP aided in the improvement of the accuracy of intoxication detection for the different types of curves.

5.03 CLOSED COURSE DRIVING STUDIES

"It is at once evident that the degree of intoxication important in this respect is not that it deprives a person of the power of speech, locomotion, etc., but rather his ability to operate a motor vehicle."

—Behrer and Wilzbach, "The Urine Alcohol Test and the Drunken-Driver in Cincinnati" (1943)

"The effects of alcohol on driving were found to be quite unrelated to previous drinking history and heavy drinkers showed as much impairment as light drinkers. In general, our results are consistent with the conclusions derived from laboratory studies that any measurable quantity of alcohol in the blood impairs, in some measure, the skills important in driving. It should be emphasized that the impairment is subtle and not at all obvious to the untrained observer."

—Lovibond et al, "Danger Level—The Warwick Farm Project" (1971)

Closed course studies involve having the drinking driver operate an actual car around a closed course. Usually, the course is flat with good visibility and no other cars or distractions are allowed in order to decrease the risk of damage or injury during testing. Even so, in one study damage was done to the front spoiler of the Mercedes test car by a drinking driver (50305).

Some of the differences in closed course driving compared to actual driving situations are:

- Speeds of the test vehicle are usually low, seldom exceeding 30 mph
- No distractions from passengers or other traffic
- No sudden emergencies
- The driver has been over the course many times (a confounding learning effect)
- Hawthorne effect—the drivers knew they were being tested and so did their best

Some closed course studies, however, have been designed to overcome these limitations, including a surprise or emergency component (50301, 50305). Heavy drinkers have been found to be as impaired as light drinkers (50304). No additional published closed course studies have been found for this second edition.

Reference Number: 50301

LAURELL, H. "Effects of Small Doses of Alcohol on Driver Performance in Emergency Traffic Situations." *Accident, Analysis and Prevention,* 9: 191–201, 1977 (7 figures, 28 references)

Abstract: According to Goldberg, in emergency situations the critical BAC for impairment is 0.020–0.040 g/100 mL, whereas in tasks requiring less complicated performance the critical BAC is 0.040–0.050 g/100 mL.

In this test the driving task involved emergency braking and evasive maneuver in response to lights. In order to perform the task correctly, the driver had to brake hard, release brake, swerve, realign car, and brake to a full stop. All drivers practiced this task for 2 hours. The drivers were twenty-six male subjects (ages nineteen to thirty-one years) who consumed 1.5 mL of whiskey/kg over 15 minutes. The tests were conducted 60 minutes after the start of drinking. Performance deteriorated at a BAC of 0.024–0.040 g/100 mL for pylons hit and stopping distance.

> Thus, if one is willing to accept the semi-laboratory driving performance as representative of full scale driving performance, then this study has shown the detrimental effects of very low BACs in situations demanding fast reaction times, attention, rapid decision, and precise and accurate action on the part of the driver.

Reference Number: 50302

COHEN, J., E.J. DEARNALEY, AND C.E.M. HANSEL. "The Risk Taken in Driving Under the Influence of Alcohol." *British Medical Journal*, 1438–1442, 1958 (3 tables, 15 references)

Abstract: A study was conducted of bus drivers with at least 12 years' experience on the job. They were divided into three groups: control, moderate alcohol (2 fl. oz. of 40% v/v alcohol) and large alcohol (6 fl. oz.). The alcohol was consumed within 30 minutes. The BACs were determined in blood using ADH. The mean BACs were 0.0, 0.004, and 0.058 g/100 mL respectively. Subjects were requested to drive their buses through increasingly narrow gaps.

> Our main results may be summarized as follows: Drivers who took alcohol became involved in greater hazards than alcohol-free drivers. As the amount of alcohol taken increased, the drivers were prepared to drive their vehicles through narrower gaps. This revealed that the alcohol had adversely affected their judgment. The performance of the drivers, as well as their judgment progressively deteriorated as they consumed more alcohol.

Reference Number: 50303

FLANAGAN, N.G., P.W. STRIKE, C.J. RIGBY, AND G. LOCHRIDGE. "The Effect of Low Doses of Alcohol on Driving Performance." *Medicine, Science, and the Law*, 22: 203–208, 1983 (1 table, 3 figures, 7 references)

Abstract: There is no safe level of alcohol consumption for driving. It is very difficult to predict BAC from alcohol intake and even a safe BAC may be associated with significant impairment of driving ability. In this study thirty-five male and eleven female subjects consumed 2–2.5 pints of beer with free choice of food over 1.25–1.5 hours. The BACs obtained were 0.030–0.060 g/100 mL. The driving test involved a closed course 1.5 miles long with eighty-two different types of tasks. The subject's own car was used for this course and subjects had practiced the course at a zero BAC. There was no penalty for slow driving.

> Most were surprised to find that their performance had deteriorated. The willingness to take a risk so well described by Cohen et al. (1958) was again demonstrated in our drivers by their attempts to negotiated hazards when their angle of approach was clearly unsuitable.

Reference Number: 50304

LOVIBOND, S.H. AND K. BIRD. "Danger Level—The Warwick Farm Project." *Proceedings of the 29th International Conference on Alcoholism and Drug Dependence*. L.G. Kiloh (ed), Butterworths (pub), Australia, 299–305, 1971 (4 figures)

Abstract: A brief description of the Warwick Farm Project is presented. Sixteen racing and rally drivers and twenty-six ordinary drivers consumed alcohol to obtain BrACs as determined by a Breathalyzer of 0.050, 0.080, or 0.100 g/100 mL. Subjects drove an instrumented car, and braking distance, speed, smoothness of control, lane control, and pylons knocked over were determined. At a BrAC of 0.100 g/100 mL, the braking distance was increased by 6 feet.

> The finding of an almost straight line deterioration of driving performance across blood alcohol levels is quite inconsistent with the notion of a threshold below which alcohol produces no effects. The effects of alcohol on driving were found to be quite unrelated to previous drinking history and heavy drinkers showed as much impairment as light drinkers. In general, our results are consistent with the conclusions derived from laboratory studies that any measurable quantity of alcohol in the blood impairs, in some measure, the skills important in driving. It should be emphasized that the impairment is subtle and not at all obvious to the untrained observer.

Reference Number: 50305

BARTL, G., C. BRANDSTATTER, A. HOSEMANN, AND C. REITER. "Saccadic Eye Movements and Reactions of Drivers with Low Alcohol Concentration" [German]. *Blutalkohol*, 35: 124–138, 1998 (1 table, 5 figures, 9 references)

Abstract: A closed course driving study was conducted on twenty-three sober and twenty-five drinking subjects. The course was 2.5 km long and the driving was conducted at night during the winter. The BrACs of the drinking drivers as determined by the Alcomat ranged between 0.054 and 0.092 g/100 mL (mean 0.070 g/100 mL). The subjects drove a Mercedes that was specially equipped to record the eye movements while driving. For the first 14 minutes the driver drove around the course at their own speed to familiarize themselves with the car. The last 30 seconds of the test drive consisted of a realistic traffic situation with traffic signs, pedestrians, a bicyclist, and a surprise gray foam barrier in the middle of the road. Five of the drinking drivers had an accident with the barrier compared to none of the sober drivers. One drinking driver caused damage to the front spoiler of the Mercedes when it got stuck on an icy patch on the side of the track. Drinking drivers recalled less of the traffic situation than sober drivers (3.7 items versus 5.9 items). The authors conclude that there is significant impairment in driving at low BACs.

Table. Mean RT and Collisions and Near Misses for Sober and Drinking Drivers in Response to a Surprise Obstacle

Subjects	Mean RT to Obstacle (seconds)	No. of Collisions with obstacle	No. of Near Misses with Obstacle
Sober Drivers	0.97	0	1
Drinking Drivers	1.29	5	2

Source: Adapted from Bartl et al (1998).

Reference Number: 50306

GAWRON, V.J. AND T.A. RANNEY. "The Effects of Alcohol Dosing on Driving Performance on a Closed Course and in a Driving Simulator." *Ergonomics*, 31: 1219–1244, 1988 (9 tables, 5 figures, 40 references)

Abstract: Subjects consumed alcohol in small doses over a 1-hour period to obtain BrACs as determined by a Breathalyzer 30 minutes later of 0, 0.070, or 0.120 g/100 mL. Six subjects drove for 2 hours over a closed-loop, two lane courses at a speed of 64 km/h. Twelve subjects drove for 2 hours in a simulator.

> BAC effects on the closed-course study were strong and generally consistent with previous research. BAC increased the frequency of lane position errors (deviations from the travel lane) and accidents. It also increased the variability of speed and lateral position. BAC effects on speed indicated a failure of drivers in the 0.12% BAC trial to reduce speed in curve negotiation.

Reference Number: 50307

SCHUSTER, R., G. SCHEWE, O. LUDWIG, L. FRIEDEL, AND J. HELLWEGE, "Driving Tests on Alcohol-Caused Unsafe Driving at Night" [German]. *Blutalkohol,* 28: 287–301, 1991 (5 tables, 4 figures, 19 references)

Abstract: Sixty-three male and one female subjects (average age twenty-six years) drove an unmodified car through six tasks around a closed course track. The subjects drove the car during the day sober, with a BAC of 0.116 g/100 mL, and a BAC of 0.146 g/100 mL and at night sober and at a BAC of 0.116 g/100 mL. The subjects consumed alcohol over 3 hours and drove 1 hour after the end of drinking. All subjects had declining BACs at the time of driving. The total driving ability at night for a BAC of 0.116 g/100 mL was only 25% that of driving during the day sober. The driving ability was additionally impaired by alcohol for unfavorable lighting conditions at night.

Table. Mean Number of Errors of Sixty-Four Drivers in a Closed Course at Day and Night with and Without the Consumption of Alcohol

Light conditions (and BACs g/100 mL)	Mean number of errors
Day (sober)	2.1
Day (0.116)	4.3
Day (0.146)	6.8
Night (sober)	3.2
Night (0.116)	8.0

Source: Adapted from Schuster et al (1991).

5.04 HIGHWAY DRIVING STUDIES

> "If the law [prohibition] were changed, we'd have to shut down our plants. Everything in the United States is keyed to a new pace. The speed at which we run our motor cars, operate our intricate machinery, and generally live would be impossible with liquor."
>
> —Henry Ford, "National Affairs: Mr. Ford" (1928)

> "At the most general level, it was suggested that high BACs both increase the time necessary to begin applying the brakes, as well as reduce the degree of control in the actual use of the brakes during the course of stopping. These two factors in combination probably account for a large part of the alcohol contribution to highway crashes."
>
> —Perrine, "Alcohol and Highway Crashes: Closing the Gap Between Epidemiology and Experimentation" (1976)

There are few studies, for obvious safety reasons, that allow a drinking subject to drive on the highways in real traffic. Some studies in Europe have been conducted in actual highway traffic but typically the BACs of the drivers were less than 0.06 g/100 mL (50401, 50402). One study showed that drinking drivers tend to steer their car to the left in response to an unexpected "bump" in the road (50403). Another study using Doppler radar showed that drinking drivers braked more abruptly and with less control than nondrinking drivers (50404).

Novice drivers were found to be impaired at BACs of 0.02 g/100 mL and above, which provides further evidence for a lower statutory BAC limit for these drivers (50405).

The top seven journals on alcohol impairment of driving ability over the last 50 years is presented (50406).

Reference Number: 50401

DEWAARD, D. AND K.A. BROOKHUIS. "Assessing Driver Status: A Demonstration Experiment on the Road." *Accident Analysis and Prevention*, 23: 297–307, 1991 (7 figures, 44 references)

Abstract: Twenty male subjects (ages twenty-five to forty years) consumed alcohol after lunch to obtain a BAC of not more than 0.050 g/100 mL. The BrACs were determined with a Breathalyzer and were a mean of 0.046 g/100 mL at the start of the test and 0.035g/100 mL at the end. The subjects drove an instrumented car for 15 minutes following a car around a heavy traffic ring road, then drove 70 km at 100 km/h, then another 100 minutes in traffic. The SD of lateral position increased by more than 5 cm (30% impairment) at these BACs.

> The effects of alcohol were additionally present when subjects had to respond to speed changes of a leading car; alcohol resulted in an impairment of 19% compared to baseline-delay.

Reference Number: 50402

DE GIER, J.J. "A Subjective Measurement of the Influence of Ethyl Alcohol in Moderate Levels on Real Driving Performance." *Blutalkohol*, 16: 363–370, 1979 (2 tables, 18 references)

Abstract: Ten male subjects (mean age twenty-nine years) consumed 0.45 g/kg ethanol over 5 minutes under double blind conditions. BACs were measured by saliva and analyzed by GC. The mean BAC obtained was approximately 0.050 g/100 mL. The subjects drove through the city streets of Utrecht during daylight hours for 60 km and an average duration of 86 minutes. During the test, two trained observers using a standard scoring method rated the driving. One hundred and twelve items reflecting behavior components of driving were rated as satisfactory, moderate, or insufficient.

> Thus, transformational of scoring results in order to assess a real comparison is possible. The method used in this study is able to show differences in driving behavior when subjects are under influence of moderate levels of a CNS depressant.

Reference Number: 50403

BRAGG, B.W.E., N. DAWSON, D. KIRBY, AND G. GOODFELLOW. "Detection of Impaired Drivers Through Measurement of Speed and Alignment." *Proceedings 8th International Conference on Alcohol Drugs and Traffic Safety*, T-80 Stockholm, L. Goldberg (ed), 1341–1353, 1981 (3 tables, 2 figures, 8 references)

Abstract: Speed and lateral placement were determined during a roadside survey in Ontario. Four hundred and sixty drivers were stopped and the BrACs were determined with an ALERT J-130 digital device. Thirty-two drivers (7%) had a BrAC > 0.080 g/100 mL and 400 (87%) had a BrAC

< 0.049 g/100 mL. Speed and alignment were determined by placing a 1 cm diameter pneumatic tube across the road. As drivers passed over the tubes and made a bump, the drinking drivers tended to move to the left and sober drivers to the right.

Table. BACs and Mean Lane Alignment of Drivers Exposed to an Unexpected Bump in the Road

BAC of Drivers (g/100 mL)	Percent of Drivers at that BAC	Mean Lane Alignment Shift Response
0–0.049	87%	5.9 cm (to right)
0.050–0.079	6%	2.1 cm (to left)
0.080+	7%	5.6 cm (to left)

Source: Adapted from Bragg et al (1981).

In summary, the results of this study indicate that the introduction of an unexpected stimulus, in this case 1 centimeter diameter pneumatic tubes, evoked driving reactions that differed significantly for impaired and sober drivers. In addition to providing further evidence of the utility for police of the speed/alignment device in the detection of impaired drivers, these results suggest a whole avenue of research to determine the unexpected event which will maximally differentiate, safely, between impaired and sober drivers.

Reference Number: 50404

PERRINE, W. "Alcohol and Highway Crashes. Closing the Gap Between Epidemiology and Experimentation." *Modern Problems Pharmacopsychology*, 11: 22–41, 1976 (1 table, 3 figures, 40 references)

Abstract: A general summary was conducted of the effects of alcohol on laboratory, simulator, and instrumented car studies. There are forty references. One reported experiment measured the speed and braking of drivers on a public highway by Doppler radar as they were stopped by police. The BACs of the drivers were then determined. The braking performance of drivers at high BAC was found to be abrupt, unsmooth, and less controlled than that of sober drivers.

At the most general level, it was suggested that high BACs both increase the time necessary to begin applying the brakes, as well as reduce the degree of control in the actual use of the brakes during the course of stopping. These two factors in combination probably account for a large part of the alcohol contribution to highway crashes.

Reference Number: 50405

JORGEN, S., N.N.J.J.M. VAN DER SLUISZEN, D. BROWN, AND E.F.P.M. VUUMAN. "Single- and Dual-Track Performance During On-the-Road Driving at a Low and Moderate Dose of Alcohol: A Comparison Between Young Novice and More Experienced Drivers." *Human Psychopharmacology Clinical and Experimental*, 33: e2661, 6pp, 2018 (1 figure, 33 references)

Abstract: Nine novice drivers with a driver's license of less than 1-month duration and nine experienced drivers with a driver's license of at least 1-year duration, ages eighteen to twenty-five years, were tested on an instrumented car (with dual control) over a 100 km public primary highway at BACs of 0.0, 0.020, and 0.050 g/100 mL. The BACs were determined in breath by a Lion Alcoholmeter SD-400. A driving instructor had the other control.

Table. Estimated Mean SDLP (in cm) of Experienced and Novice Drivers in Highway Road Tracking

BAC (g/100 mL)	Experienced Drivers	Novice Drivers
0.0	17.2	19.5
0.020	18.5	21.5
0.050	21.0	23.4

Source: Adapted from Jorgen et al (2018).

In conclusion, this study showed that road-tracking performance is already impaired at a BAC of 0.2 g/L in both novice and experienced drivers. In addition, secondary task performance is impaired in both groups at a BAC of 0.5 g/L. Furthermore, it was found that driving in novice drivers was already impaired at a BAC of 0.2 g/L under dual task conditions, whereas driving impairment in experienced drivers occurred at a BAC of 0.5 g/L. This provides further evidence for the lower legal limit of 0.2 g/L for novice drivers.

Reference Number: 50406

VALDERRAMA-ZURIAN, J.C., D. MELERO-FUENTES, F.J. ALVAREZ, AND F. HERRERA-GOMEZ. "Worldwide Research Output Trends on Drinking and Driving from 1956 to 2015." *Accident Analysis and Prevention*, 135: 5pp, 2020 (2 tables, 1 figure, 37 references).

Abstract: A detailed literature search was conducted for an article related to drinking and driving between 1956 to 2015. A total of 5,999 articles on drinking and driving were published between 1956 and 2015. The number of articles published have increased dramatically from 152 (1956–1965) to 2,302 (2006–2015). Authors from the United States published 2,257 articles, followed by Canada (6.1%), Germany (6.0%), and Australia (5.3%). The top three journals were *Accident Analysis and Prevention*, *Journal of Studies on Alcohol and Drugs*, and *Blutalkohol*.

Table. The Top Journals for Drinking and Driving Research

Journal	Years of Publication	Percent of All Articles Published
Accident Analysis and Prevention	50	7.70%
Journal of Studies on Alcohol and Drugs	60	4.48%
Blutalkohol	40	4.18%
Traffic Injury Prevention	20	2.75%
Addiction	60	2.33%
Forensic Science International	40	2.32%
Alcoholism: Clinical and Experimental Research	40	1.73%

Source: Adapted from Valderrama-Zurian et al (2020).

Road alcohol related injuries and deaths are a worldwide priority, as the figures are still unacceptable 60 years after. Probably this is the price to pay for progress. For many, this is a scourge for the population being hard to eradicate.

5.05 FIELD (EPIDEMIOLOGICAL) STUDIES

"The driver is innocent in the eyes of the law and presumably self-satisfied as long as he can conceal his impairment of intoxication. Concealment of intoxication is an ancient and highly developed game of skill. Do we want it played on our highways?"

—Ferguson, "Keynote Address" (1955)

"Blood alcohol concentrations (BACs) over 0.04% are definitely associated with an increased accident rate. The probability of accident involvement

> increases rapidly at BACs over 0.08% and becomes extremely high at BACs above 0.15%. When drivers with BACs over 0.08% have accidents, they tend to have more single vehicle accidents, more severe (in terms of injury and damage) accidents, and more expensive accidents than sober drivers."
>
> —Borkenstein et al, "The Role of the Drinking Driver in Traffic Accidents. The Grand Rapids Study" (1974)

The most famous field study of the effect of alcohol on drivers was the Grand Rapids study by Borkenstein et al, 1974 (50501), which showed an increasing risk of causing a motor vehicle collision with increasing BAC. Similar studies have confirmed and expanded on the results of the Grand Rapids study (50502–50506). The most common alcoholic beverages consumed by male drinking drivers (in decreasing frequency) are:

Beer > spirits > wine

Whereas the most common alcoholic beverages consumed by female drinking drivers (in decreasing frequency) are the reverse:

Wine > Spirits > Beer

Young drivers are at a greater risk of MVC at lower BACs than older drivers and this is the basis of zero tolerance laws for these drivers (50504, 50505). Red light running and wrong-way FMVCs were 6 times to 10 times more likely to involve a drinking driver (50507, 50508). Crash responsibility increased with increasing BAC of drivers killed in FMVCs (50509).

Even though alcohol is a depressant drug, drinking drivers tend to speed more, leading to more severe injuries than sober drivers (50510)

Drivers with the highest BACs (i.e., greater than 0.300 g/100 mL), who are typically alcohol-dependent, drink and drive any day of the week, unlike drivers at lower BACs who cluster on weekend evenings (50511–505112).

Lowering the statutory BAC from 0.08 to 0.05 g/100 mL would also increase the apprehension of drugged drivers as well (50513).

Alcohol causes impaired judgment, decreased attention, reduces alertness, and promotes a false sense of security, which limits the abilities of drinking drivers to compensate for hazardous weather driving conditions, which results in a 30 times greater risk of motor vehicle fatalities (50514).

There has been a narrowing gender gap in DUI arrests recently, such that the percent of female drivers court-mandated to attend alcohol safety programs has increased from 13% in 1992 to 19% in 2008 (50515).

In arrested drinking drivers who are seventy years of age or older, 88% of the drivers were male and 11% had a BAC of 0.200 g/100 mL or higher. The mean BAC decreased with the driver's age (50516).

During lockdown for COVID-19 the number of drinking and driving cases decreased. But the lockdown did not affect the rate of elimination of alcohol in drivers, which was 0.014 g/100 mL/h for female and 0.018 g/100 mL/h for male drivers (50517).

Reference Number: 50501

BORKENSTEIN, R.F., R.F. CROWTHER, R.P. SHUMATE, W.B. ZIEL, AND R. ZYLMAN. "The Role of the Drinking Driver in Traffic Accidents. The Grand Rapids Study." *Blutalkohol* 11(Suppl. 1): 1–131, 1974 (73 tables, 20 figures, 25 references)

Abstract: A study of the BACs of over 12,000 drivers who were either controls or involved in motor vehicle collisions was conducted. BACs were determined by breath samples of the drivers that were collected at the scene into plastic bags and analyzed later by the Breathalyzer.

Table. Relative Risk of Causing a Motor Vehicle Collision with Increasing BAC

Driver BAC (g/100 mL)	Relative Risk of Causing a MVC
0.060	2×
0.080	4×
0.100	7×
0.150	25×

Source: Adapted from Borkenstein et al (1974).

> Blood alcohol concentrations (BACs) over 0.04% are definitely associated with an increased accident rate. The probability of accident involvement increases rapidly at BACs over 0.08% and becomes extremely high at BACs above 0.15%. When drivers with BACs over 0.08% have accidents, they tend to have more single vehicle accidents, more severe (in terms of injury and damage) accidents, and more expensive accidents than sober drivers. BACs of 0.04% and below are apparently not inconsistent with traffic safety.

Reference Number: 50502

KRUGER, H-P. AND M. VOLLRATH. "The Alcohol-Related Accident Risk in Germany: Procedure, Methods and Results." *Accident Analysis and Prevention* 36: 125–133, 2004 (4 tables, 2 figures, 23 references)

Abstract: The BrACs were determined in 9,087 drivers stopped at roadside surveys in Germany between 1992 and 1994, and 1,968 drivers involved in traffic accidents in 1993. Approximately 10% of the roadside survey drivers had a positive BrAC. For all motor vehicle collisions, there was no apparent increase in risk at BACs < 0.050 g/100 mL. At BrACs between 0.050 and 0.080 g/100 mL, the risk was 2.8 times; between 0.080 and 0.110 g/100 mL, the accident risk was 15.6 times; between 0.110 and 0.159 g/100 mL, the risk was 15.1 times; and at BrACs > 0.160 g/100 mL, it was 37 times. The risk factor for accidents with increasing BrAC was similar to those found in the Grand Rapids study but are somewhat higher. This higher risk was attributed to higher traffic density in Germany.

> On the other hand, the structure of the risk function is comparable; an effect of alcohol cannot be shown for BACs below 0.05%. At larger BACs, accident risks rise exponentially with a relatively small increase for BACs below 0.08%, a larger increase below 0.16% and a dramatic increase above 0.16%. This structure is also quite comparable to that of risk studies conducted in other countries at other time-points, e.g. The Grand Rapids Study of Borkenstein et al. (1974).

Reference Number: 50503

BLOMBERG, R.D., R.C. PECK, H. MOSKOWITZ, M. BURNS, AND D. FIORENTINO. "The Long Beach/Fort Lauderdale Relative Risk Study." *Journal of Safety Research*, 40: 285–292, 2009 (3 tables, 1 figure, 22 references)

Abstract: A short review of studies determining the BACs of drivers involved in MVCs including the Evanston, Toronto, and New York City studies was conducted. In addition, a case-control study was conducted of 2,871 crash-involved drivers in Long Beach, California, and Fort Lauderdale, Florida, during 1997–1999. BACs were determined using an Alco-Sensor IV, the hospital results, or a Sniffer passive alcohol sensor in 81% of the crash-involved drivers and 98% of the control drivers. The relative risk of MVC is similar to that found by Borkenstein et al, 1974 (50501).

Table. Relative Risk of Motor Vehicle Collision Involvement with BAC of the Driver

Driver BAC (g/100 mL)	Adjusted Relative Risk of MVC Involvement
0.060	2×
0.080	3×
0.100	5×
0.150	22×

Source: Adapted from Blomberg et al (2009).

The study results regarding general relative risk due to alcohol confirm a notable dose-response relationship beginning at .04 to .05 BAC and increasing exponentially at BACs of .10 or greater.

Reference Number: 50504

PECK, R.C., M.A. GEBERS, R.B. VOAS, AND E. ROMANO. "The Relationship Between Blood Alcohol Concentration (BAC), Age, and Crash Risk." *Journal of Safety Research*, 39: 311–319, 2008 (6 tables, 1 figure, 33 references)

Abstract: An analysis was conducted on the MVC data from the Long Beach and Fort Lauderdale study on the effects of age and BAC on crash risk (22% involved injuries and 0.5% involved fatalities). The relative risk (RR) of a motor vehicle collision was greater for drivers less than twenty-one years of age than for older drivers.

Table. Relative Risk of a Motor Vehicle Collision in Drivers Ages < 21 Years and Older Drivers with Increasing BAC

BAC (g/100 mL)	Drivers Under 21 years (RR)	Drivers 21–55+ years (RR)
0.000	1.00	1.00
0.010	1.13	0.94
0.020	1.34	0.92
0.030	1.64	0.93
0.040	2.09	0.98
0.050	2.75	1.07
0.060	3.72	1.20
0.100	16.0	2.41
0.150	135	8.04

Source: Adapted from Peck et al (2008).

There are a number of reasons for believing that young and inexperienced drivers would be more vulnerable to the effects of alcohol. As noted in the introduction, the literature indicated that young novice drivers have less driving skill and less ability and maturity to assess risk and vulnerability. They would also have less experience drinking and perhaps more importantly less experience driving after consuming alcohol. All of these attributes would lead one to expect that young, inexperienced drivers would be more susceptible to the impairing effects of alcohol.

Reference Number: 50505

ZADOR, P.L., S.A. KRAWCHUK, AND R.B. VOAS. "Alcohol-Related Relative Risk of Driver Fatalities and Driver Involvement in Fatal Crashes in Relation to Driver Age and Gender: An Update Using 1996 Data." *Journal of Studies on Alcohol,* 61: 387–395, 2000 (4 tables, 1 figure, 24 references)

Abstract: The alcohol-related relative risk of driver involvement in fatal crashes by age and gender as a function of BAC was studied using the FARS data and the National Roadside Survey of drivers in the United States during 1996. For all age groups and genders, the relative risk of a driver being fatally injured in a single motor vehicle collision increased significantly at a BAC of 0.035 g/100 mL or more. Except for drivers ages sixteen to twenty years there was no significant differences in the risk of being killed in a single motor vehicle crash between male or female drivers.

Table. Relative Risk of Male and Female Drivers, Ages 16 to 20 Years, Being Killed in a Single Motor Vehicle Collision

BAC Range (g/100 mL)	Male drivers age 16–20 yrs (RR)	Female drivers age 16–20 yrs (RR)
0.010–0.019	1.55	1.35
0.020–0.049	4.64	2.86
0.050–0.079	17.32	7.04
0.080–0.099	51.87	42.63
0.100–0.149	240.89	42.63

Source: Adapted from Zador et al (2000).

With the new findings of this study, and the parallel results currently being observed in laboratory studies at the Southern California Research

Institute, one can state with confidence that driving at BAC levels below 0.10% is very dangerous.

Reference Number: 50506

CONNOR, J., R. NORTON, S. AMERATUNGA, AND R. JACKSON. "The Contribution of Alcohol to Serious Car Crash Injuries." *Epidemiology*, 15: 337–344, 2004 (5 tables, 20 references)

Abstract: The BrACs or BACs of 571 car drivers involved in crashes in which at least one occupant was admitted to hospital or killed were compared to 588 control drivers in Auckland, New Zealand, between 1998 and 1999. Structured interviews were also conducted. Approximately 24% of the crash drivers and 5% of the control drivers reported consuming some alcohol in the previous 6 hours. Thirty-seven percent of crash drivers had a positive BrAC (> 0.003 g/100 mL) compared to 2% of the control drivers. Two-thirds of the drinking drivers had a BAC > 0.150 g/100 mL. The odds ratio of being involved in a serious crash was 8.1 for BrACs < 0.050 g/100 mL and 81 at BrACs > 0.050 g/100 mL.

> Our study draws attention to the distribution of alcohol levels in crash drivers. Specifically, drivers who are under the legal limit (even at 50 mg/100 mL) make an important contribution to injury crashes, whereas drivers with blood alcohol concentrations of twice the limit or more are responsible for most of the burden of injury.

Reference Number: 50507

RETTING, R.A., R.G. ULMER, AND A.F. WILLIAMS. "Prevalence and Characteristics of Red-Light Running Crashes in the United States." *Accident Analysis and Prevention,* 31: 687–694, 1999 (7 tables, 1 figure, 24 references)

Abstract: A study was conducted of 3,753 red light running FMVCs in the United States between 1992 and 1996 using the FARS data. It is estimated that 260,000 red light running crashes occur in the United States annually resulting in 750 FMVCs. Red light running crashes were more likely to occur on urban roads and during the day compared to other FMVCs. All FMVCs occur primarily in good weather conditions. Fatally injured red light running drivers had a BAC > 0.100 g/100 mL in 35% of cases compared to 6% of other FMVC drivers.

This study has shed light on the prevalence and characteristics of red light running crashes in the United States. It is clear from analyses of FARS and GES data that red light running crashes occur in very substantial numbers. Results confirm earlier findings that red light runners are a deviant population, more likely than non-runners to be alcohol impaired and to have invalid licenses and prior violations. Results also show that red light running crashes differ markedly by time of time. Nighttime crashes are most likely to involve young males with poor driving records and alcohol impairment, with more than half the nighttime red light runners in fatal crashes having high BACs.

Reference Number: 50508

LATHROP, S.L., T.B. DICK, AND K.B. NOLTE. "Fatal Wrong-Way Collisions on New Mexico's Interstate Highways, 1990–2004." *Journal of Forensic Science*, 55: 432–437, 2010 (4 tables, 27 references)

Abstract: A study was conducted of the characteristics and BACs of 1,092 FMVCs and 79 wrong-way FMVCs in New Mexico between 1990 and 2004. The mean postmortem BAC (range) was 0.160 g/100 mL (0–0.362 g/100 mL) for drivers killed going the wrong way compared to 0.020 g/100 mL (0–0.198 g/100 mL) of drivers killed in FMVCs going the right way. The percentage of drivers killed over 0.080 g/100 mL was 57% and 6% for drivers going the wrong way and right way respectively.

Wrong-way collisions are only one type of catastrophe resulting from drinking and driving, but by better understanding these collisions, the argument for additional funding of drunk-driving prevention programs is further strengthened. New Mexico can only benefit from additional impaired driving prevention programs.

Reference Number: 50509

MOUNCE, N.H. AND O.J. PENDLETON. "The Relationship Between Blood Alcohol Concentration and Crash Responsibility for Fatally Injured Drivers." *Accident Analysis and Prevention*, 24: 201–210, 1992 (7 tables, 6 figures, 12 references)

Abstract: The probability of crash responsibility as a function of BAC in 595 fatally injured drivers in Texas was determined by a panel of three researchers. The percentage of drivers killed with a BAC > 0 was 38% in the 301 SMVCs and 22% in multi-vehicle MVCs. Over 90% of the drivers with a positive BAC were assigned full responsibility for their crashes. At a BAC of 0.250 g/100 mL or more, all fatally injured drivers were deemed fully responsible for their MVC.

Table. BAC Range of Drivers Killed in FMVCs and Percent Responsible for the Collision

BAC Range of Fatally Injured Driver (g/100 mL)	Percent Deemed Responsible for FMVC
0.00	80.6%
0.01–0.04	80.0%
0.05–0.09	100.0%
0.10–0.14	84.6%
0.15–0.19	88.6%
0.20–0.24	92.0%
0.250+	100.0%

Source: Adapted from Mounce and Pendleton (1992).

Specifically, as BAC increased, the probability of responsibility for the crash increased, and the average BAC was considerably greater among drivers determined to be at fault in weekday crashes than among those who were not at fault. However, this relationship was not as apparent for weekend accidents. Alcohol use was quite evident in crashes that occurred throughout the designated weekend period, even among the not responsible group of drivers.

Reference Number: 50510

STUBIG, T., M. PETRI, C. ZECKEY, S. BRAND, C. MULLER, D. OTTE, C. KRETTEK, AND C. HAASPER. "Alcohol Intoxication in Road Traffic Accidents Leads to Higher Impact Speed Difference, Higher ISS and MAIS and Higher Preclinical Mortality." *Alcohol*, 46: 681–686, 2012 (1 table, 4 figures, 52 references)

Abstract: An Accident Research Unit evaluated 37,635 MVCs that occurred in the Hanover area of Germany between 1999 and 2010. A total of 20,741 patients were injured and treated at the Hanover hospital in these MVCs, and 2.3% of the patients died. Blood or breath alcohol concentrations were determined in 1,769 (8.5%) of the patients and of those tested, 947 (54%) had a negative alcohol results (< 0.01 g/100 mL) and 823 (46%) had a positive alcohol result (mean BAC, 0.220 g/100 mL). The traumatized patients included pedestrians, motorcyclists, bicyclists, and car drivers. Of the patients with a negative alcohol result, 2.3% died compared to 4.6% of the patients with a positive alcohol result. The relative collision speed at impact was higher for the BAC positive patients (30 km/h) than for the BAC negative patients (25 km/h).

> Alcohol intoxication in trauma patients leads to a higher preclinical mortality. Furthermore, BAC positive vehicle users and pedestrians are more often injured and experience a higher relative speed (i.e., delta v) on impact. The subgroup analysis showed no alcohol dose related effect on injury severity and relative speed, but a correlation of increasing age of patient's age with higher alcohol concentrations.

Reference Number: 50511

WIGMORE, J.G., C.J. HOUSE, AND J.W. PATRICK. "Characteristics of Arrested Drinking Drivers with the Highest Intoxilyzer 5000C Results in Toronto: Drinking and Driving Not Only at Night or on Weekends." *Canadian Society of Forensic Science Journal,* 37: 1–8, 2004 (1 table, 3 figures, 24 references)

Abstract: The characteristics of 100 drinking drivers in the City of Toronto between 1995 and 1999 with the highest BrACs were determined. The BrACs were measured with the Intoxilyzer 5000C and ranged between 0.301 and 0.410 g/100 mL (median 0.335 g/100 mL). There were ninety male and ten female drivers between twenty-two and sixty-four years of age. Forty-seven drivers were involved in motor vehicle collisions (MVCs). There were no significant differences in the BrACs between the drivers involved in MVCs and those not involved in MVCs. Most of the drivers (51%) were involved with alcohol-related driving incidents between 12:00 p.m. (noon) and 8:00 p.m. and the incidents were spaced evenly throughout the week (and not as typically expected on weekends). This is shown in the following table.

Table. Day of Week and Percent of Total Drivers with BrACs > 0.300 g/100 mL

Day of the Week	Percent of Drivers
Monday	14%
Tuesday	13%
Wednesday	12%
Thursday	19%
Friday	13%
Saturday	16%
Sunday	13%

Source: Adapted from Wigmore, House and Patrick (2004).

This temporal pattern is similar to that found in alcohol-dependent individuals. Police countermeasures against drinking and driving should not only concentrate on weekends and nights as they would be mainly ineffective for a large proportion of drivers with the highest BrACs, hence the greatest risk of alcohol related motor vehicle collisions.

Reference Number: 50512

JONES, A.W. AND P. HARDING. "Driving Under the Influence with Blood Alcohol Concentrations over 0.4g%." *Forensic Science International*, 231: 349–353, 2013 (3 tables, 3 figures, 38 references)

Abstract: The characteristics of 156 drivers arrested in Sweden over a 25-year period and 233 drivers arrested in Wisconsin over a 3-year period with a BAC > 0.40 g/100 mL were determined. This represents 0.5% of all drivers arrested. Nine percent of the drivers in Sweden were female compared to 35% in Wisconsin. The mean ages of the drivers were between forty-three and forty-five years. In Wisconsin, 37% of the drivers were arrested between 12:00 p.m. (noon) and 6:00 p.m. The highest BAC was 0.546 g/100 mL in Sweden and 0.526 g/100 mL in Wisconsin. Forty percent of the drinking drivers were involved in motor vehicle crashes.

Table. Percent of Wisconsin Drinking Drivers and the Mean BAC According to the Day of the Week

Day of the Week	Percent of Arrested Drinking Drivers	Mean BAC (g/100 mL)
Monday	14%	0.428
Tuesday	13%	0.431
Wednesday	15%	0.422
Thursday	15%	0.433
Friday	16%	0.419
Saturday	9%	0.431
Sunday	18%	0.431

Source: Adapted from Jones and Harding (2013).

In this retrospective study we identified 389 traffic offenders with BACs > 0.4 g% in two jurisdictions. Forty-eight percent of the drivers in Sweden and 37% in Wisconsin were arrested between 12 noon and 6 p.m. and not as might have been expected, late at night or weekends. This confirms a Canadian study in which the characteristics of drivers with the highest breath alcohol concentrations were investigated. People with alcohol problems drink at all times of day or night depending on availability of alcoholic beverages, which might account for this observation. Some traffic offenders were sufficiently alert and coherent to be interviewed by the arresting police officers.

Reference Number: 50513

VOAS, R.B., J.H. LACEY, K. JONES, M. SCHERER, AND R. COMPTON. "Drinking Drivers and Drug Use on Weekend Nights in the United States." *Drug and Alcohol Dependence*, 130: 215–221, 2013 (2 tables, 35 references)

Abstract: A roadside survey was conducted in the United States on weekend nights from July to November 2007. Of the 8,384 drivers surveyed, 85% provided a breath sample, 70% an oral fluid sample, and 39% a blood sample. A regression analysis was conducted on 5,912 drivers who provided a breath sample and an oral fluid or blood test. Approximately 11% of non-drinking drivers were using illegal drugs and 26 to 33% of the drivers with a BAC > 0.080 g/100 mL also used illegal drugs. Medicinal drug use occurred in 4% of the non-drinking drivers and in 2% of the drivers with a BAC > 0.080 g/100 mL. The following table shows the odds ratio of detecting illegal drugs is much greater in drinking than non-drinking drivers and increases at higher BACs.

Table. Odds Ratio of Detecting Drugs in Drivers with a BAC < 0.08 g/100 mL or 0.08 g/100 mL+ Compared to Non-drinking Drivers

	Odds Ratio			
BAC (g/100 mL)	Any illegal drug	Marijuana detected	Cocaine detected	Prescription or over-the-counter drugs
< 0.08	4.1	4.2	4.2	0.7
0.08+	4.0	3.5	3.5	0.9

Source: Adapted from Voas et al (2013).

The relationship between a high BrAC and drug use also suggests that programs or laws that increase the arrests of drinking drivers, such as conducting sobriety checkpoints or lowering the BAC limit from 0.08 to 0.05 will increase the apprehension of drugged drivers. In sum, it appears that under the current alcohol-orientated DWI enforcement system, a substantial number of drug-using drivers is arrested. This offers opportunities for increasing the apprehension of drug-using drivers by strengthening alcohol enforcement.

Reference Number: 50514

REDELMEIER, D.A. AND F. MANZOOR. "Life-Threatening Alcohol-Related Traffic Crashes in Adverse Weather: A Double-Matched Case-Control Analysis from Canada." *British Medical Journal,* 9: e024415, 7pp, 2019 (2 tables, 3 figures, 83 references)

Abstract: A study was conducted of 2,088 alcohol positive patients admitted to the largest trauma hospital in Canada (Sunnybrook in Toronto) and compared to 8,111 alcohol negative patients between 1995–2015 due to life-threatening road traffic injuries. Adverse weather conditions (rain, fog, snow, freezing rain) occurred in 312 alcohol-related crashes (15%) compared to 13% of non-alcohol-related crashes. The majority of alcohol-related crashes involved patients as drivers, most occurred at night, and less than half used a seatbelt. The relative risk of a life-threatening alcohol-related traffic crash was 19% higher in adverse weather conditions (odds ratio [OR] 1.19 times). The crude OR of 25 times is associated with drunk driving in general, and when multiplied by the OR of

1.19 times for driving in adverse weather conditions when drunk it may increase the risk to 30 times (i.e., 25 × 1.19) for life-threatening injuries.

> Alcohol causes traffic crashes because of impaired judgment, decreased attention, reduced alertness, and many other factors that limit the ability to compensate for hazards. A further subtle mechanism is how alcohol lowers visual acuity when moving. Laboratory experiments indicate, for example, that three drinks of alcohol cause a one-line loss on a Snellen eye chart test due to faulty visual tracking and reduced dynamic visual acuity. Acute alcohol ingestion also causes decreased contract sensitivity, sluggish glare adaptation and impaired risk perception that is unnoticed when stationary. The net effect is that eyesight deficits may be irrelevant when seated indoors (static vision) critical when driving in adverse weather (high-speed optical flow) and part of the false sense of security associated with drinking and driving.

Reference Number: 50515

ROBERTSON, A.A., H. LIEW, AND S. GARDNER. "An Evaluation of the Narrowing Gender Gap in DUI Arrests." *Accident Analysis and Prevention*, 43: 1414–1420, 2011 (2 tables, 42 references)

Abstract: An evaluation of the ratio of male to female convicted drinking drivers who attended a court mandated alcohol safety program in Mississippi between 1992 and 2008 was conducted. Approximately 10,000 to 12,000 convicted DUI offenders are ordered to attend the alcohol safety program every year in that state. The percentage of female drivers attending the program increased from 13% in 1992 to 19% in 2008. Female drivers tended to have lower BACs than male drivers and so the lowering of the statutory BAC limits in the United States from 0.100 g/100 mL to 0.080 g/100 mL affected female drivers to a greater extent.

Table. Some Characteristics of Female Drivers Between 1992 and 2008

	1992	2008
Percentage of female licensed drivers	51%	52%
Percentage of women reporting current alcohol use	24%	29%
Percentage of female drivers court mandated to attend an alcohol safety program	13%	19%
Percentage of female drivers who reported a prior arrest	19%	36%

Source: Adapted from Robertson et al (2011).

In conclusion, there is no single explanation for the upward trend in female DUI arrests. Changes in women's substance use and driving behavior, as well as changes in law enforcement practices, contribute to the narrowing of the gender gap.

Reference Number: 50516

KIRSCH, B., C.G. BIRNGRUBER, AND R. DETTMEYER. "Senior Driving Under the Influence. A Five-Year Retrospective Study of Alcoholized Road-Users Aged 70 and Over." *Forensic Science International*, 277: 10–15, 2017 (6 figures, 24 references).

Abstract: The BACs were determined of forty-seven female and 357 male drivers, seventy years of age and older, which is 1.5% of 26,395 blood samples submitted of drivers by the German police between 2009 and 2013. More than 88% of the drivers were male and 63% had a BAC of more than 0.110 g/100 mL, and 11% had a BAC of greater than 0.200 g/100 mL. The mean BAC decreased with age.

Table. Distribution of Diseases in Drivers Aged 70 Years and Older

Type of Disease	Percent
Cardiovascular disease	83.2
Metabolic disorders	32.2
Neurological disorders	11.4
Pulmonary disease	8.6
Psychiatric disorders	7.3

Source: Adapted from Kirsch et al (2017).

Moreover, the collected data includes aspects such as the kind of traffic participation as well as neurological and physiological deficits of the road-users. If accidents were caused by drunk driving, the external circumstances and consequences of these accidents were analyzed too. The evaluation revealed that the standard medical examination protocol proved to be improbable to cover polypharmacy and multimorbidity of older alcoholized drivers. So an evaluation and adaptation of the common medical examination protocol must be considered.

Reference Number: 50517

HOSTIUC, S., D. RADU, L. SERETEAN, C. TIRDEA, R. SIMINIUC, AND G.C. CURCA. "Driving Under the Influence of Alcohol During the COVID-19 Pandemic." *Forensic Science International*, 329: 6pp, 2021 (2 tables, 3 figures, 22 references)

Abstract: BrACs and BACs were determined in 3,258 drivers in 2019 and 2,026 in 2020 in Bucharest, Romania. On 17 March 2020, a state of emergency due to COVID-19 was declared. Before COVID-19, the number of daily cases was 8.52, which decreased to 5.29 after COVID-19. Two breath/blood samples can be collected 1-hour apart. The average rate of elimination in the blood was 0.0184 g/100 mL/h (0.0143 g/100 mL/h in female and 0.0184 g/100 mL/h in male drivers).

During the lockdown, the number of alcohol tests in traffic decreased significantly. This reduction was not associated with statistically significant changes in BrAC or BAC. We have seen a substantial increase in the number of minimally elevated BrAC and negative BAC cases, changes that could be caused by an increased use of alcohol-based hand sanitizers.

5.06 PHYSICAL SIGNS/TESTS

"A person may, however, be under the influence of alcohol to an extent that seriously affects his powers and behavior, especially in such a responsible position as driving an automobile without presenting the entire common picture of drunkenness."

—Bogen, "Drunkenness: A Quantitative Study of Acute Alcohol Intoxication" (1927)

"It often happens that the police officer who arrests an intoxicated driver declares the latter to be obviously influenced, whereas another police official at a later point of time, for instance at the police station, may judge him to be slightly influenced. Finally, the physician who, at a still later time performs the blood test may give the diagnosis of not influenced. However, as a result of the intervals between these three phases of observation, it may happen that all three observers are right."

—Froentjes, "An Analysis of 10,000 Blood Tests in the Netherlands" (1963)

Physical signs of alcohol consumption include the odor of an alcoholic beverage, which decreases after a meal (50601) and increases with increasing BAC (50601, 50602). Postural ataxia or body sway increases with alcohol consumption, especially when the eyes are closed (50604). It is suggested that a staggering gait is a sign of extreme alcohol intoxication and generally indicates a BAC > 0.150 g/100 mL (50605). The most reliable physical test of alcohol intoxication is horizontal gaze nystagmus (50606–50608, 50610). The three main tests of the standardized field sobriety tests (50609) used by the police are:

- Horizontal gaze nystagmus (HGN)
- Walk and turn (WAT)
- One leg stand (OLS)

HGN and WAT were found not to be affected by sleep deprivation (50615).

The physical effects of alcohol intoxication are more obvious shortly after drinking alcohol ceases rather than several hours later (acute tolerance or Mellanby Effect) and may explain some of the discrepancies in the observations of the police at the scene and later observations (50613, 50614). In one extreme case a women arrested after a FMVC became rapidly unconscious at a BAC of 0.730 g/100 mL and was in a deep coma at hospital. Several hours later at a BAC of 0.520 g/100 mL she was conscious and able to respond to questioning. Finally, 11 hours later at a BAC of 0.190 g/100 mL she was fully coherent and showed no physical signs of alcohol intoxication (50617).

Persons with high chronic tolerance (usually heavy alcohol abusers or alcoholics) as well may not show obvious physical signs of alcohol intoxication even at high BACs (50612).

Police recognized alcohol involvement in 80% of the hospitalized drivers with a BAC of 0.160 g/100 mL or higher but only 14% were convicted of a DUI (50616).

Reference Number: 50601

MOSKOWITZ, H., M. BURNS, AND S. FERGUSON. "Police Officers' Detection of Breath Odors from Alcohol Ingestion." *Accident Analysis and Prevention*, 31: 175–180, 1999 (4 tables, 3 references)

Abstract: Eight male and six female subjects (ages twenty-one to thirty-five years) consumed vodka, bourbon, red wine, or beer on four separate occasions. BrACs were determined by an Intoximeter. Twenty police officers were asked to determine by breath odor whether the subjects had been drinking and what alcoholic beverage was consumed. The drinking subjects were hidden behind a curtain and blew through a plastic tube. When no food odors were present the detection rate was 60% at BrACs < 0.080 g/100 mL and 80% at BrACs > 0.080 g/100 mL. After the subjects consumed a meal the detection rate dropped to 55% and 67% respectively. There was no relationship between the type of alcoholic beverage and detection rate.

Table. Percent of Odor Detected in Drinking Subjects at Increasing BAC and Different Types of Alcoholic Beverages

Type of Beverage	Percent odor detected at BACs < 0.04 g/100 mL	Percent odor detected at BACs > 0.08 g/100 mL
Beer	50%	85%
Wine	28%	83%
Vodka	60%	59%
Bourbon	N/A	72%

Source: Adapted from Moskowitz et al (1999).

The finding that there were only small differences in the intensity of odor as a function of the type of beverage is of scientific interest. It suggests that fusel oils and other chemical constituents of many alcoholic beverages are not the prime determinant of odor after the beverage is fully absorbed. Note that although vodka has only a few parts per million of these chemicals and bourbon contains several thousand parts per million, there was little difference in the detection of these odors from these two substances. This suggests that what is detected in the breath may be a constituent of the metabolization of alcohol.

Reference Number: 50602

LI, Y-M. "Feasibility of Identification of Alcohol Intoxication by Nurses in Emergency Departments." *Kaohsiung Journal of Medical Science*, 19: 391–396, 2003 (4 tables, 1 figure, 21 references)

Abstract: The BACs, odor of alcohol, and accuracy of the nursing staff's identification of alcohol intoxication were determined in 945 injured drivers in Taiwan between 1997 and 1998. The BACs were determined in whole blood by the TDx method. Injured drivers with a BAC > 0.050 g/100 mL were considered alcohol positive and those with a BAC > 0.150 g/100 mL were considered intoxicated. Five hundred and five patients (53%) had a BAC > 0.050 g/100 mL and 152 (16%) had a BAC > 0.150 g/100 mL. The mean BAC was 0.178 g/100 mL for male (n = 365) and 0.105 g/100 mL for female (n = 140) injured drivers. Of the patients with a low BAC (0.013–0.050 g/100 mL) 88% were incorrectly identified, and in patients with a BAC > 0.150 g/100 mL, 15% were incorrectly identified. The overall accuracy of the nurse's assessment was 73%. An odor of an alcoholic beverage was found in 8, 12, 43, 59 and 85% of the patients with a 0 BAC and BACs of 0.013–0.050, 0.050–0.100, 0.100–0.150, and > 0.150 g/100 mL respectively.

> Nearly one-third of patients with vehicle-related injury presenting to our emergency departments had BACs of more than 50 mg/dL. This confirms that alcohol is a significant contributing factor to emergency department attendance. Blood alcohol testing is not routine in the emergency room in Taiwan. Therefore, the importance of alcohol as a risk factor for injuries is underestimated.

Reference Number: 50603

ADACHI, J., Y. MIZOI, T. FUKUNAGA, Y. OGAWA, Y. UENO, AND H. IMAMICHI. "Degrees of Alcohol Intoxication in 117 Hospitalized Cases." *Journal of Studies on Alcohol*, 52: 448–453, 1991 (3 tables, 3 figures, 13 references)

Abstract: A study of the correlation between the apparent degree of intoxication as determined by various physical tests, facial flushing, BAC, and blood acetaldehyde concentrations (n = 27) was conducted on 117 hospitalized male alcoholics in Japan. Ten healthy male volunteers were used as controls. BACs and acetaldehyde concentrations were determined by headspace GC. The BACs of the alcoholics ranged from 0.029 to 0.577 g/100 mL (mean 0.214 g/100 mL). Facial flushing was apparent in 75% of the subjects and correlated with relatively high concentrations of acetaldehyde in the blood. Forty-eight patients (41%) showed apparently normal reactions to walking and turning tests (mean BAC = 0.192 g/100 mL). More than half of alcoholics showed bloodshot eyes, only 10% showed watery eyes, and only 4% showed dilated pupils. The speech was normal in 79% of the alcoholics. The type of alcoholic beverage consumed by the alcoholics (usually either sake or distilled spirits) did not affect the odor of an alcoholic beverage on the breath. When the BAC was 0.350 g/100 mL or higher, alcohol intoxication was apparent in most alcoholics. The ten male control subjects consumed between 1.6 and 2.0 g/kg ethanol within 60 minutes. The peak BACs ranged from 0.202 to 0.269 g/100 mL. Two of the control subjects vomited, three were nauseous, and three seemed not affected by alcohol. Seven of the ten controls fell into a deep sleep commencing at 2 hours after alcohol consumption.

> Thus, our present findings indicate that a great difference exists in the physiological and behavioural effects of alcohol between healthy men and alcoholics. In addition, at BACs of 300 mg/dL or higher, healthy men might generally lose consciousness, whereas some of the alcoholics could still stand erect, walk or be in an enhanced mood.

Reference Number: 50604

NIESCHALK, M., C. ORTMANN, A. WEST, F. SCHMAL, W. STOLL AND G. FECHNER. "Effects of Alcohol on Body-Sway Patterns in Human Subjects." *International Journal of Legal Medicine*, 112: 253–260, 1999 (2 tables, 3 figures, 43 references)

Abstract: The sway pattern of seventeen male and thirteen female subjects (ages twenty-two to thirty-five years) on a computerized static platform before and after alcohol consumption was evaluated. The subjects had their feet 4 cm apart with their hands folded in front of their chest in a relaxed stance and with the eyes open or closed. Alcohol was consumed ad libitum over 2 hours. Thirty minutes later a blood sample was collected, and the BACs were determined by headspace GC. The BACs ranged from 0.023 to 0.167 g/100 mL. The sway area after alcohol consumption only increased slightly with the eyes open (i.e., visual control guaranteed for postural stabilization) compared with eyes closed. With alcohol and eyes closed, body sway was more pronounced anterio-posterior but did not reach statistical significance when compared with lateral sway. Subjects with BACs > 0.105 g/100 mL could be clearly distinguished from subjects with BACs < 0.084 g/100 mL by the increase in sway area.

> The achievement of the present study consists in the new finding that within the range of intoxication tested here, the alcohol induced ataxia could not entirely be compensated by visual stabilization.

Reference Number: 50605

PERHAM, N., S.C. MOORE, J. SHEPHERD, AND B. CUSENS. "Identifying Drunkenness in the Night-Time Economy." *Addiction*, 102: 377–380, 2007 (1 table, 5 references)

Abstract: The BrACs and physical attributes of drunkenness (PD) were conducted on 314 female and 579 male drinkers in a downtown area between 11:00 p.m. to 3:00 a.m. between 2004–2005. BrACs were determined with an Alcolmeter. The physical attributes of drunkenness included gait (normal, staggering, severely impaired), eye appearance (clear or glazed), and speech (clear, slurred, or incoherent) and a subjective rating of overall drunkenness (scale of 1 to 10). The lowest transition BAC was for glazed eyes (mean 0.106 g/100 mL) and was greatest for all three PDs (mean 0.222 g/100 mL). The transition BAC for glazed eyes and slurred speech together (mean 0.177 g/100 mL) was less than for staggering gait alone (mean 0.186 g/100 mL).

> However, assessment of drinkers' physical attributes depends on environmental as well as individual factors. For example, slurred speech and glazed eyes might not be easily detected in premises due to high levels of ambient noise and subdued lighting. Furthermore, both glazed eyes and slurred speech require that the rater is in close proximity to the drinker for them to be observed. The estimated transition BAC between walking normally and staggering was the highest individual PD and exceeded the criteria for severe intoxication for both men and women. As drinkers usually walk into licensed premises and up to the bar, evidence of a staggering gait provides door staff, licensees, and servers with a visible determinant of excessive intoxication.

Reference Number: 50606

CITEK, K., B. BALL, AND D.A. RUTLEDGE. "Nystagmus Testing in Intoxicated Individuals." *Optometry*, 74: 695–710, 2003 (7 tables, 5 figures, 33 references)

Abstract: Thirty-seven female and forty-nine male subjects (ages twenty-one to sixty-two years) consumed various amounts of alcohol and were tested by police officers as to horizontal gaze nystagmus (HGN) and vertical gaze nystagmus (VGN) while the subjects were standing, seated, and supine. BrACs were determined with an Intoxilyzer 5000 and BAC

Datamaster. The BrACs ranged from 0 to 0.189 g/100 mL. The accuracy of HGN testing at a BrAC of 0.080 g/100 mL was 77, 76, and 73% for standing, seating, and supine positions respectively. The accuracy of VGN was 56, 59, and 69% for standing, seated, and supine positions respectively.

> Consistent with previously published results, we confirm the validity of the HGN test in the standing posture to discriminate blood alcohol levels of 0.08% and 0.10%. We also established, with similar accuracy and reliabilities the use of the HGN test in the seated and supine postures. The average inter-evaluator reliability and accuracy demonstrate that HGN is a highly reliable test.

Reference Number: 50607

PENTILLA, A., M. KATAJA, AND M. TENHU. "Examination Model for Suspected Drunken Drivers." *Blutalkohol,* 12: 24–38, 1975 (2 tables, 7 figures, 31 references)

Abstract: A study was conducted of 494 impaired drivers; various physical tests were conducted, and the results compared to BAC. Nystagmus was the most valuable test for determining alcohol impairment. Walking a straight line and the Romberg test were the next best physical tests. The regression coefficient for six clinical tests was $r = 0.72$. The regression coefficient for ten clinical tests was $r = 0.73$.

> Walking along a line was superior to other walking tests in most models studied, which is obviously due to the more objective assessment of the test result. The results of numerous regression analyses indicated that the tests based on quite subjective criteria e.g., tests describing the quality of speech and behavior, relaxation of inhibitions and pulling oneself together, were practically worthless as stated earlier.

Reference Number: 50608

GODING, G.S. AND R.A. DOBIE. "Gaze Nystagmus and Blood Alcohol." *Laryngoscopic* 96: 713–717, 1986 (3 tables, 3 figures, 14 references)

Abstract: Thirty-seven male and nine female patients (ages sixteen to sixty-seven years) at an ER between 1985 and 1986 were tested for angle of onset of horizontal gaze nystagmus (AON) using a protractor and had their BACs determined. Twenty-five of the twenty-six patients with a BAC > 0.100 g/100 mL had an AON < 40 degrees. Four of the eleven patients with a BAC < 0.100 g/100 mL had an AON < 40 degrees but three of these patients were on other drugs as well. The estimated BAC (as determined by AON) and BrACs (as determined by a Breathalyzer 900A) were compared in 149 DWI suspects. The correlation between the eBAC from AON and BrAC was $r = 0.878$. The difference between eBAC and BrAC was greater than 0.020 g/100 mL in fifteen of the 149 DWI suspects.

Horizontal gaze nystagmus is an effective tool in estimating BAC when alcohol is the only drug taken. When using horizontal gaze nystagmus as a screening exam the tester must be aware of the effects of other drugs, the presence of complicating diseases and the artifact of nystagmus at extreme lateral gaze. In addition, the inability to fixate on a stationary object does not necessarily imply alcohol intoxication.

Reference Number: 50609

STUSTER, J. "Validation of the Standardized Field Sobriety Test Battery at 0.08% Blood Alcohol Concentration." *Human Factors*, 48: 608–614, 2006 (3 tables, 1 figure, 9 references)

Abstract: The SFST (HGN, WAT, and OLS) was administered to 297 motorists by seven police officers in San Diego. The estimated BAC > 0.080 g/100 mL using SFST was compared with blood, breath, or urine samples. Of the 297 tests, there were twenty-two false positive tests (7%) and four false negatives (1%). The most effective test was the HGN.

The results of this study provide statistically significant evidence of the validity of the Standardized Field Sobriety Test Battery to discriminate above or below 0.08% BAC. However, only moderate agreement was found when discriminating above or below 0.04% BAC.

Reference Number: 50610

MCKNIGHT, A.J., E.A. LANGSTON, A.S. MCKNIGHT, AND J.E. LANGE. "Sobriety Tests for Low Blood Alcohol Concentrations." *Accident Analysis and Prevention*, 34: 305–311, 2002 (2 tables, 19 references)

Abstract: Eighteen male and seventeen female subjects with BACs between 0 and 0.100 g/100 mL were tested as to what physical measures could detected impairment at BACs of 0.040 g/100 mL. BrACs were determined using a preliminary breath tester (PBT). In another experiment sixteen male and fourteen female subjects consumed alcohol to obtain BrACs of 0, 0.020, 0.040, 0.060, 0.080, and 0.100 g/100 mL. The subjects were evaluated by sixteen police officers. BrACs were determined with a PBT. Pupil size and peripheral vision tests were not affected at BrACs tested. The subjects were observed to have a red face, sweating face, and red eyes but the *r* values were 0.31, 0.34, and 0.42 respectively. Horizontal gaze nystagmus (HGN) had the highest *r* value (0.67).

> Finding measures of performance or appearance that are capable of detecting the effects of low blood alcohol level against large individual differences in the characteristics being measured proved extremely difficult. HGN emerged as the only valid indicator of blood alcohol level assessed, proving as effective in identifying subjects over a 0.04% BAC limit as those over a 0.08 or 0.10% limit. The basic HGN was also as valid when administered to seated subject as to a standing subject, an important advantage at low BACs, where the observed behavior of drivers is not likely to give probable cause to require the suspects to step out of a vehicle.

Reference Number: 50611

PENNER, D.W. AND B.B. COLDWELL. "Car Driving and Alcohol Consumption: Medical Observations on an Experiment." *Canadian Medical Association Journal*, 79: 793–800, 1958 (7 tables)

Abstract: A study was conducted of fifty adult males, of whom twenty-five were light drinkers, fifteen were intermediate drinkers, and ten were heavy drinkers. Separate and independent medical examinations were conducted by two physicians (MD1 and MD2). BACs were determined in blood. The physicians conducted a number of tests including Romberg, coordination, gait, speech, etc. Subjects also drove an instrumented car over a closed course. At BACs of 0.080–0.99 g/100 mL, MD1 considered that 50% of the subjects were impaired and MD2 considered 80% of the subjects were impaired. At BACs of 0.140–0.150 g/100 mL, MD1 and MD2 considered 50% of the subjects were impaired.

> Car driving is so complex that any evaluation of one or even more component parts does not necessarily represent the entire picture.

Reference Number: 50612

PERPER, J.A., A. TWERSKI, AND J.W. WIENAND. "Tolerance at High Blood Alcohol Concentrations: A Study of 110 Cases and Review of Literature." *Journal of Forensic Sciences*, 31: 212–221, 1986 (2 tables, 2 figures, 46 references)

Abstract: One hundred and ten alcoholics (87% male and mainly thirty to forty-nine years of age) who voluntarily entered a detoxification center were given psychomotor tests and blood samples were collected within 1 hour of admission. BACs were determined by an enzymatic method after the blood was centrifuged. The BACs ranged from 0–0.444 g/100 mL. Thirteen of the forty-four patients (24%) with a BAC of ≥ 0.200 g/100 mL showed no clinical signs of alcohol intoxication.

> One should not, however, conclude that apparent clinical sobriety in a chemically intoxicated alcoholics reflects safe or acceptable driving capabilities. Driving combines a complex array of physical and mental activities that require anticipatory judgments, estimates of distance, peripheral vision, and short reaction time to unexpected hazards, all of which are known to be adversely affected by alcohol.

Reference Number: 50613

GERCHOW, J. "Statistical and Experimental Studies on the Differing Assessment in Subjects During Rising and Falling BAC [German]." *Heifte Unfallheik*, 66: 90–95, 1961 (4 tables, 2 figures, 16 references)

Abstract: A study was conducted of 2,815 arrested impaired drivers in Germany who were assessed as to their degree of drunkenness by doctors at the time the blood sample was collected. The time from the end of drinking to the collection of the blood sample ranged from 15 minutes to over 5 hours. The percentage of the drivers who were obviously drunk decreased with increasing time since the end of drinking. The authors conclude that the degree of drunkenness cannot be determined by the BAC alone and that there is a significant difference in obvious physical symptoms of drunkenness at a specific BAC in the absorption or in the elimination phases.

Table. Percent of Drivers Showing Obvious Marked Drunkenness According to BAC and Time Since the Drinking Ended

	Percent of drivers showing obvious marked drunkenness in minutes after the end of drinking		
BAC Range (g/100 mL)	15 to 20	121 to 180	> 300
0.05–0.110	20%	5%	2%
0.110–0.160	41%	11%	10%
0.160–0.210	65%	22%	17%
0.210–0.260	81%	31%	22%
0.260–0.320	100%	45%	21%

Source: Adapted from Gerchow (1961).

Reference Number: 50614

FROENTJES, W. "An Analysis of 10,000 Blood Tests in the Netherlands." *Proceedings 3rd International Conference on Alcohol and Road Traffic*, BMA House, London, 179–188, 1963 (4 tables, 6 figures, 8 references)

Abstract: A study was conducted of 10,000 blood and urine samples submitted by the police from suspected drunken drivers. Samples were analyzed by an ADH and the Widmark method. In 8,889 cases, physicians performed a clinical examination and determined the driver to be not perceptibly influenced, slightly influenced, or obviously influenced. The greater the time since the drinking to the clinical examination, the greater the number of drivers were found not or slightly influenced by the examining doctors.

Table. Percent of Drivers Not Perceptibly Influenced by Alcohol According to BAC and Time Since Drinking Ended

	Percent of drivers not perceptibly influenced by alcohol at hours after drinking ended			
BAC Range (g/100 mL)	0–1 hrs	1–2 hrs	2–3 hrs	3–4 hrs
0.120–0.150	18%	31%	35%	38%
0.150–0.180	14%	20%	25%	31%
0.180–0.210	10%	13%	18%	16%
0.210–0.240	5%	7%	11%	14%

Source: Adapted from Froentjes (1963).

It is therefore essential that the judge should be aware of this phenomenon since, in special cases, misunderstanding and contradictions in the statements of witnesses may be explained in this way. It often happens that the police officer who arrests an intoxicated driver declares the latter to be obviously influenced, whereas another police official at a later point of time, for instance at the police station, may judge him to be slightly influenced. Finally, the physician who, at a still later time performs the blood test may give the diagnosis of not influenced. However, as a result of the intervals between these three phases of observation, it may happen that all three observers are right.

Reference Number: 50615

CITEK, K., A.D. ELMONT, C.L. JONS, C.J. KREZELOK, J.D. NERON, T.A. PLUMMER, AND T. TANNENBAUM. "Sleep Deprivation Does Not Mimic Alcohol Intoxication in Field Sobriety Testing." *Journal of Forensic Sciences*, 56: 1170–1179, 2011 (2 tables, 13 figures, 73 references)

Abstract: Field sobriety tests (including HGN, WAT, and OLS) and clinical tests were conducted on fourteen female and fifteen male subjects (ages twenty-one to fifty-two years) after a normal sleep or 24 to 32 hours of sleep deprivation (SD) and at BrACs (as measured by an Intoxilyzer 5000) of 0, 0.040, 0.070, and 0.060 g/100 mL. The highest BrAC obtained was 0.115 g/100 mL. Three subjects in the normal sleep or SD groups were administered an alcohol placebo. Mean pupil size increased from 4.47 mm to 5.41 mm with sleep deprivation and did not vary with BrAC. Mean diastolic blood pressure increased from 75.2 to 77.8 mm Hg with sleep deprivation but did not vary with BrAC. HGN and WAT did not change with sleep deprivation and was affected by BrAC. OLS count changed with SD but was not affected by BrAC.

While SD can affect cognitive ability and certain physiological responses, the results of this study suggest that there is no evidence that it affects the movements of motor skills assessed with FSTs in a manner that would lead a law enforcement officer to conclude that a suspect is intoxicated, unless intoxication also is present.

Reference Number: 50616

BRUBACHER, J.R., H. CHAN, M. FANG, D. BROWN, AND R. PURSSELL. "Police Documentation of Alcohol Involvement in Hospitalized Injured Drivers." *Traffic Injury and Prevention*, 14: 453–460, 2013. (4 tables, 55 references)

Abstract: The police documentation of alcohol involvement of 2,410 injured drivers attending a British Columbia trauma center or Vancouver General Hospital ED between 1999 and 2003 was determined. Overall, 857 (36%) of the injured drivers had a positive BAC. Of the 736 drivers with a BAC > 0.050 g/100 mL, the police reported alcohol involvement in 72%. The DUI conviction rate was 5% for drivers with a BAC between 0.080 to 0.160 g/100 mL and 14% for drivers with a BAC > 0.160 g/100 mL.

Table. BAC of Injured Drivers, Percentage Police Recognition of Alcohol Involvement, and DUI Conviction Rate

BAC (g/100 mL)	Police Recognition of Alcohol Involvement (%)	DUI Conviction Rate (%)
0	5.1%	0.6%
0.010–0.049	24.0%	1.7%
0.050–0.079	40.4%	1.9%
0.080–0.159	63.1%	4.7%
0.0160+	79.6%	13.6%

Source: Adapted from Brubacher et al (2013).

Police recognized and documented alcohol involvement in 72 percent of injured drivers with BAC > 0.05 percent. Police documentation of alcohol involvement was more common at higher BAC levels, in night time or single-vehicle crashes, for drivers who committed traffic violations or drove unsafely, and for drivers with a prior record of impaired driving. The low conviction rate of injured impaired drivers does not appear to be due to police inability to recognize alcohol involvement.

Reference Number: 50617

HAMMOND, K.B., B.H. RUMACK, AND D.O. RODGERSON. "Blood Ethanol: A Report of Unusually High Levels in a Living Patient." *Journal of the American Medical Association*, 226: 63–64, 1973 (1 figure, 12 references)

Abstract: A twenty-three-year-old female alcoholic weighing 125 pounds consumed approximately 26 fluid ounces of bourbon (50% v/v alcohol)

within 2 hours on an empty stomach at a local tavern. She had been discharged the previous week from an alcoholic rehabilitation center following a 2-month period of treatment. She drove from the tavern and was involved in a motor vehicle collision several minutes later. She was arrested and taken to jail where she rapidly loss consciousness. As a result, she was taken to hospital where it was determined that her admission BAC was 0.730 g/100 mL. She was in a class 1 coma (responds to deep pain only). Three hours after her admission, her BAC was 0.520 g/100 mL and she was conscious and able to respond to questions. Eleven hours later, she was fully coherent and showed no physical signs of alcohol intoxication, even though her BAC was 0.190 g/100 mL. This case report illustrates acute tolerance (i.e., the Mellanby Effect) in an impaired driving case.

> It is the lack of correlation between the blood levels and the patient's clinical condition that remains a puzzling feature and indicates the development of an unusually high degree of central nervous system tolerance in this patient.

5.07 COUNTERMEASURES

> "If terrorists killed as many people as drunk drivers, there would be a public outcry followed by political action. No one need to drink and drive. All the death, injury, and misery it causes is unnecessary."
>
> —Dunbar, "Random Breath Testing—Cutting the Gordian Knot" (1988)

> "Then I explored the myriad historical reasons for these phenomena. They include America's love of driving, the country's lack of public transportation and the enduring backlash against the Prohibition experiment of the 1920s. Meanwhile, industry interested in selling alcohol and cars have publicly opposed drunk driving but never in a manner that would seriously threaten the sales of its products. Finally, a strong American streak of individualism and libertarianism has hampered more aggressive attempts to curb drinking and driving."
>
> —Lerner, "One for the Road: Drunk Driving since 1900" (2011)

There has been a dramatic decrease in alcohol-related motor vehicle collisions in many countries over the past 30 years (50701, 50702, 50709, 50710). Some of the effective countermeasures against drinking and driving have been found to be statutory BAC limits of 0.080 g/100 mL and lower (50701–50705), zero tolerance for young/novice drivers (50706–50708), mandatory license suspensions (50704, 50711), MADD (50702,

50712), and checkpoints (50713). Mandatory jail sentences for first-time offenders do not appear to be effective (50714). In summary, some of the effective countermeasures against drinking drivers are:

- Statutory BAC limits at 0.08 g/100 mL or lower
- Mandatory license suspensions, especially at roadside (immediate roadside suspensions)
- Graduated license (zero tolerance) for novice/young drivers
- Grassroots organizations such as MADD
- Random spot-checks and increased enforcement
- Automobile ignition interlocks
- Mandatory alcohol screening
- Rideshares such as Uber
- Policies to reduce per capita alcohol consumption

Nearly 20% of designated drivers had a BAC ≥ 0.050 g/100 mL and 42% of servers reported that they would be willing to overserve a group of drinkers if there was a designated driver in the group (50715, 50716).

Immediate roadside suspensions, increased enforcement, and zero tolerance laws for young and inexperienced drivers have been found to decrease drinking and driving (50717–50718, 50720, 50721).

Motor vehicle trauma was decreased by nearly 24% on Friday and Saturday nights after Uber rideshare started in Houston in 2014 (50719).

The mass media campaigns by the alcohol industry to limit personal alcohol consumption have been found to lead to more positive views about alcohol, whereas a decrease in the alcohol excise tax in Finland caused a 12.4% rise in alcohol consumption and a 38% increase in alcohol-related FMVCs (50722, 50723).

Reference Number: 50701

NAGATA, T., S. SETOGUCHI, D. HEMENWAY, AND M.J. PERRY. "Effectiveness of a Law to Reduce Alcohol-Impaired Driving in Japan." *Injury Prevention*, 14: 19–23, 2008 (2 tables, 4 figures, 21 references)

Abstract: A new traffic law was passed in Japan in 2002 that reduced the per se BAC from 0.050 to 0.030 g/100 mL and increased the fines from $425.00 to $4,250.00. Moreover, the law made bartenders and passengers culpable in addition to arrested drivers. A time series analysis of alcohol-related traffic injuries and fatalities was conducted between 1998 and

2004. Alcohol impaired driving (AID) traffic fatalities decreased 38% and AID traffic injuries by 33%.

Despite some limitations, this study by applying time series analysis, shows that the new Japanese road traffic law implemented in June 2002 had an effect on declining traffic injuries and fatalities. This success was obtained in several ways, decreasing the permissible blood alcohol level, increasing penalties, and an active media campaign. By describing the success of the AID intervention in Japan, the findings of this study may be helpful for other countries in coping with the problem of AID.

Reference Number: 50702

ASBRIDGE, M., R.E. MANN, R. FLAM-ZALCMAN, AND G. STUDOTO. "The Criminalization of Impaired Driving in Canada: Assessing the Deterrent Impact of Canada's First Per Se Law." *Journal of Studies on Alcohol*, 65: 450–459, 2004 (3 tables, 1 figure)

Abstract: An auto-regressive integrated moving average model was applied to the number of driver FMVCs with and without alcohol in Ontario between 1962 and 1996. On 1 December 1969, Canada introduced it's first per se law (0.08 g/100 mL) and mandatory breath alcohol testing. Between 1962 and 1996, it was estimated there were 15,376 fatally injured drivers with alcohol and 32,197 fatally injured drivers without alcohol killed in Ontario. In 1976 the mandatory seatbelt law in Ontario was introduced. The emergence of MADD occurred in 1982. It is estimated that the Breathalyzer Law caused a reduction of 18% in FMVC drinking drivers, but not non-drinking FMVC drivers. The formation of MADD was associated with a reduction in all FMVC fatalities. The mandatory seatbelt law did not reduce alcohol-related FMVCs but did reduce nonalcohol-related FMVCs.

The current study, while demonstrating that Canada's 1969 Breathalyser Law led to a decline in drinking-driver fatalities in Ontario, also identifies additional influences such as per capita alcohol consumption, grassroots organizations (MADD) and other legislative activity (e.g., OMSL) that shape driver fatality rates. More important this research adds to the broader policy literature on drinking and driving by suggesting that impaired-driving legislation can produce an enduring long-term effect on fatalities and is not solely limited to short-term pulse effects.

Reference Number: 50703

TIPPETTS, A.S., R.B. VOAS, J.C. FELL, AND J.L. NICHOLS. "A Meta-Analysis of.08 BAC Laws in 19 Jurisdictions in the United States." *Accident Analysis Prevention*, 37: 149–161, 2005 (8 tables, 1 figure, 31 references)

Abstract: A meta-analysis was conducted on the effectiveness of 0.08 laws in nineteen US states in reducing FMVCs between 1982 and 2000. It is estimated that if all US states had a 0.08 law that approximately 947 lives would have been saved in 2000. The average reduction of alcohol-related FMVCs was 15%.

> The effectiveness of the .08 law, however, most probably does not come from a clear understanding by the public of the difference between .08 and .10 BAC levels. Most surveys indicate that the public has only a very rudimentary understanding of the BAC concept. Further, large segments of the public cannot identify their state's BAC limit. Thus, most of the deterrent effect of the .08 law may not be based on .08 as a specific level but on the general understanding that drinking and driving laws have become stricter. This is suggested by the fact that the .08 law appears to be as effective in reducing high BAC (greater than .10) driver involvement in fatal crashes as it does with drivers who have BAC levels in the .01 to .099 range.

Reference Number: 50704

BERNAT, D.H., W.T.M. DUNSMUIR AND A.C. WAGENAAR. "Effects of Lowering the Legal BAC to 0.08 on Single Vehicle Nighttime Fatal Traffic Crashes in 19 Jurisdictions." *Accident Analysis Prevention*, 36: 1089–1097, 2004 (3 tables, 33 references)

Abstract: The effects of lowering the BAC limit to 0.080 g/100 mL in nineteen US states on nighttime SMVC fatalities were determined.

> In summary, the best estimate of the effect of a state's change from 0.10 to 0.08 allowable blood alcohol concentration limit for drivers is a 5.2% reduction in alcohol-involved fatal crashes. Moreover, implementation of an administrative driver's license revocation policy is associated with a further 10.8% reduction. Both policies are recommended for states that which to reduce the public health burden of alcohol-related traffic crashes.

Reference Number: 50705

FELL, J.C. AND R.B. VOAS. "The Effectiveness of Reducing Illegal Blood Alcohol Concentration (BAC) Limits for Driving: Evidence for Lowering the Limit to .05 BAC." *Journal of Safety Research*, 37: 233–243, 2006 (3 tables, 1 figure, 64 references)

Abstract: A review of the scientific literature regarding the benefits of reducing the statutory BAC limit from 0.100 to 0.080 to 0.050 g/100 mL is presented.

> When all of the international evidence on lowering BAC limits is assembled, reviewed, and summarized, we have concluded that lowering the illegal BAC limit to .05 is an effective strategy in reducing impaired driving.

Reference Number: 50706

HINGSON, R., T. HEEREN, AND M. WINTER. "Lower Legal Blood Alcohol Limits for Young Drivers." *Public Health Reports*, 109: 738–744, 1994 (6 tables, 13 references)

Abstract: A study was conducted of the alcohol-related crashes in twelve US states that have established a lower BAC limit for drivers younger than twenty-one years, compared to twelve nearby states without such a change.

> Lowering BALs for adolescents to .00 or .02 percent reduced the proportion of fatal crashes that involved single vehicles at night among adolescents by at least 20 percent more than in comparison States. If all States were to lower BAL limits to .00 or .02 percent for adolescents, at least 375 fatal single-vehicle night crashes could be prevented each year among drivers ages 15–20. This law warrants consideration in all States.

Reference Number: 50707

VOAS, R.B., A.S. TIPPETTS, AND J.C. FELL. "Assessing the Effectiveness of Minimum Legal Drinking Age and Zero Tolerance Laws in the United States." *Accident Analysis Prevention*, 35: 579–587, 2003 (3 tables, 2 figures, 24 references)

Abstract: The effectiveness of zero tolerance (BAC < 0.020 g/100 mL) and a minimum drinking age of twenty-one years were studied in the United States between 1982 and 1997. A 19% reduction of fatally injured underage drinking drivers occurred as a result of the minimum age laws and a 24% reduction as a result of zero tolerance laws.

> Particularly striking are the substantial effects sizes for the MLDA and zero tolerance laws targeted at this age group. The zero-tolerance factor appears larger in this analysis. This may be because two-thirds of the states had already adopted MLDA laws by 1982 when this study began. Two of the three general drinking-and-driving laws that affect drivers of all ages also showed significant effect sizes for underage drivers.

Reference Number: 50708

CARPENTER, C. "How Do Zero Tolerance Drunk Driving Laws Work?" *Journal of Health Economics,* 23: 61–83, 2004 (7 tables, 1 figure, 36 references)

Abstract: A detailed study was conducted on the effectiveness of zero BAC laws on the drinking behavior of eighteen- to twenty-year-olds using FARS and other data between 1984 and 2001.

> I find strong evidence that the main effect of these laws among 18–20-year-olds was to curb heavy episodic drinking by males by about 13%. Further examination reveals that the reduction in heavy episodic drinking were accompanied by similarly sized increases in the likelihood of being a light drinker as well as a decrease in overall number of drinks consumed by young males.

Reference Number: 50709

MACDONALD, S. "The Influence of the Age and Sex Distributions of Drivers on the Reduction of Impaired Crashes: Ontario, 1974–1999." *Traffic Injury Prevention*, 4: 33–37, 2003 (3 figures, 20 references)

Abstract: In Ontario the rate of alcohol-impaired MVCs declined linearly from 24.5 per 10,000 licensed drivers in 1974 to 5.4 per 10,000 licensed drivers in 1999, a reduction of 78%. During the same period of time the average age of Ontario drivers increased from 39.4 years to 43.2 years. The rate of impaired MVCs generally decreases with increasing driver age. Approximately 11% of the decline in impaired crashes was due to the aging of drivers. In 1977, 40.2% of all licensed drivers were women, which increased to 46.8% in 1999. It is extrapolated that in 1974 the percentage of women was 39.3%. Women drivers are much less likely to be involved in alcohol-impaired MVCs. Approximately 9% of the decline in impaired crashes was due to the greater percentage of women drivers.

> The reduction of impaired crashes in Ontario from 1974 to 1999 was 78%, which substantially exceeds the decline by 45% for non-alcohol related crashes. This comparison suggests that roughly about one-half of the reduction in impaired crashes is due to targeted legislative initiatives, educational campaigns, and other factors directly related to drinking and driving.

Reference Number: 50710

WILLIAMS, A.F. "Alcohol-Impaired Driving and Its Consequences in the United States: The Past 25 Years." *Journal of Safety Research*, 37: 123–138, 2006 (2 tables, 5 figures, 118 references)

Abstract: The alcohol-impaired driving problem in the United States since the 1980s is discussed. Deaths in alcohol-related MVCs decreased 35% from 26,173 in 1982 to 17,105 in 2003. During the same time period, nonalcohol-related MVC deaths increased from 17,772 to 25,630. Fatally injured drivers with BAC > 0.080 g/100 mL decreased from 49 to 31%. The percentage of drivers killed in MVCs with a BAC > 0.080 g/100 mL ranged from 32% in Montana and North Dakota to 25% in Texas to 20% in Oklahoma to 15% in Indiana and 8% in Utah. The percentage of weekend nighttime drivers with a positive BAC from roadside surveys was 36% in 1973, 26% in 1986, and 17% in 1996. In 1973, 14% of drivers had a BAC > 0.050 g/100 mL, which decreased to 8% in 1986.

Table. Percent of Fatally Injured Drivers with BACs ≥ 0.08g/100 mL by Vehicle Type and Percent Change Between 1982 and 2003

Vehicle Type	Percent BAC ≥ 0.08 g/100 mL 1982	Percent BAC ≥ 0.08 g/100 mL 2003	Percent Change (1982–2003)
Passenger Vehicle Drivers (all)	51%	32%	–17%
Passenger Vehicle Drivers (ages 16–20 years)	53%	27%	–49%
Tractor Trailer Drivers	16%	4%	–75%
Motorcyclists	49%	30%	–39%

Source: Adapted from Williams (2006).

> Two primary reasons for the decline appear to be the emergence of citizen activities groups and the proliferation of effective laws. Citizen groups mobilize public support and attention to the problem and energize the activities of government and other agencies that typically have addressed the problem.

Reference Number: 50711

WAGENAAR, A.C. AND M.M. MALDONADO-MOLINA. "Effects of Drivers' License Suspension Policies on Alcohol-Related Crash Involvement: Long-Term Follow-Up in Forty-Six States." *Alcoholism: Clinical and Experimental Research*, 31: 1399–1406, 2007 (3 tables, 1 figure, 39 references)

Abstract: The effect of mandatory license suspension for DUI on alcohol involvement in fatal SMVCs was determined in forty-six US states between 1976–2002.

> We found that preconviction license suspensions had the same effect on drinking drivers below and above the legal limit (stratifying drivers into 2 groups, BAC = 0.01–0.07 g/dL and those over 0.08 g/dL, shows that both declined by 5%). Thus, this law appears to effectively deter both lower risk more moderate drinking drivers as well as high-risk heavy or problem drinkers. Laws mandating license suspension penalties after conviction for DUI do not appear to be an effective deterrent.

Reference Number: 50712

FELL, J.C. AND R.B. VOAS. "Mothers Against Drunk Driving (MADD): The First 25 Years." *Traffic Injury Prevention*, 7: 195–212, 2006 (1 table, 4 figures, 103 references)

Abstract: A historical overview of MADD is presented. MADD is described as one of the most successful public health grassroots citizen advocacy organizations in the United States. MADD was founded in 1980 and since then the number of alcohol-related fatalities in the United States has decreased from 30,000 to 16,694 in 2004. The percentage of drivers with a positive BAC in nighttime surveys has decreased from 36% in 1973 to 26% in 1986 to 17% in 1996.

Table. Number of Drunk-Driving Laws Passed by US States 1981 to 1986

Year	Number of Laws Passed
1981	44
1982	47
1983	129
1984	106
1985	223
1986	178

Source: Adapted from Fell and Voas (2006).

There is considerable evidence that MADD has made a difference in the United States regarding alcohol impaired driving. MADD has contributed to the public's view that drunk driving is socially unacceptable. MADD has played an important role in encouraging state legislatures to enact more effective impaired driving laws and has been a prominent player in landmark federal legislation (MDLA 21, zero tolerance .08 BAC per se). Because of these accomplishments, there are now official MADD affiliations in Guam, Puerto Rico, Canada, Sweden, and Japan.

Reference Number: 50713

LACEY, J.H., S.A. FERGUSON, T. KELLY-BAKER, AND R.P. RIDER. "Low-Manpower Checkpoints: Can They Provide Effective DUI Enforcement in Small Communities?" *Traffic Injury Prevention*, 7: 213–218, 2006 (4 tables, 13 references)

Abstract: Low manpower sobriety checkpoints were conducted weekly in two West Virginia counties during 2003 and 2004 and its effectiveness was compared to two adjacent counties that did not conduct checkpoints. The number of police officers involved at each checkpoint ranged from three to five. Passive alcohol sensors were used. Roadside surveys found that the percent of drivers with a BAC > 0.050 g/100 mL declined from 1.6 to 1.0% in counties with the checkpoints, while it increased from 1.4 to 2.8% in comparison counties.

This study demonstrated that a sobriety checkpoint enforcement program using only three to five police officers can be a very effective deterrent against drinking and driving in rural jurisdictions.

Reference Number: 50714

WAGENAAR, A.C., M.M. MALDONADO-MOLINA, M.M., D.J. ERICKSON, L. MA, A.L. TOBLER, AND K.A. KOMRO. "General Deterrence Effects of U.S. Statutory DUI Fine and Jail Penalties: Longer-Term Follow-Up in 32 States." *Accident Analysis and Prevention*, 39: 982–994, 2007 (7 tables, 47 references)

Abstract: The effect of US state statutory changes in DUI fines or jail penalties for first-time offenders on fatal SMVCs in thirty-two states between 1976 and 2002 was studied. Various statistical models were employed. Mandatory fines were associated with a decrease of 8% of drivers killed with BACs > 0.080 g/100 mL. Mandatory jail sentences for first-time offenders appeared to have little effect.

> To maximize population wide reductions in alcohol-related crashes, future state DUI policy making should focus on ensuring effective procedures for enforcement and implementation of administrative license suspensions and norms shaping standards like lower legal BAC limits with mandatory fines viewed as an adjunct. Jail penalties should be considered more as an incapacitant for multiple offending recidivists than a general deterrent, perhaps supplemented with other means of incapacitating one from driving such as impoundment of license plates of the vehicle, ignition interlocks, electronic monitoring, and other such measures.

Reference Number: 50715

REILING, D.M. AND M.R. NUSBAUMER. "An Exploration of the Potential Impact of the Designated Driver Campaign on Bartenders' Willingness to Over-serve." *International Journal of Drug Policies*, 18: 458–463, 2007 (2 tables, 30 references)

Abstract: A survey was conducted on 938 licensed servers in Indiana. Approximately 42% of the servers reported they may or would be willing to overserve if there was a designated driver in a group of drinkers.

> Servers had always been a key factor in drunk driving, and yet our findings suggest that some servers may be using the Designated Driver Campaign to shift responsibility from the server onto the patron. Clearly, what servers believe to be the consequences of a non-driving patron's intoxication must be examined, as well as the server's perceived responsibility in managing intoxication if the patron is with a designated driver. Specifically,

whether some servers use the Designated Driver Campaign as a license to over-serve must be determined. In other words, we need to know whether some servers are excusing their over-serving by claiming no-harm done if the drinker is not driving.

Reference Number: 50716

BARRY, A.E., B.H. CHANEY, AND M.L. STELLEFSON. "Breath Alcohol Concentrations of Designated Drivers." *Journal of Studies in Alcohol and Drugs*, 74: 509–513, 2013 (1 table, 40 references)

Abstract: The BrACs of 1,071 bar patrons in a southeastern US college community were determined with an Alco-Sensor IV over a 3-month period. A survey (including AUDIT-C, a measure of alcohol use disorder) was also conducted. Approximately 15% (165) patrons leaving the bar stated that they were the designated driver (DD). The mean BrAC of the DDs was 0.020 g/100 mL compared to 0.040 g/100 mL of the non-DDs. Sixty-five percent of the DDs had a zero BrAC, 17% had a BrAC between 0.020 and 0.049 g/100 mL, and 18% had a BrAC of 0.050 g/100 mL+. The mean AUDIT-C scores are shown in the following table. An AUDIT-C score of greater than five is indicative of an alcohol use disorder.

Table. Mean AUDIT-C Scores for the Three Groups of Designated Drivers (DDs)

Abstaining DDs	DDs with BAC < 0.050 g/100 mL	DDs with BAC > 0.050 g/100 mL
3.73	4.64	6.72

Source: Adapted from Barry, Chaney, and Stellefson (2013).

Considering the low BAC levels at which driving-related abilities are negatively affected, these findings identify the need for consensus across researcher, layperson, and communication campaigns that a DD must be someone who abstains from drinking entirely. This is especially important considering the alcohol-related driver impairment such as divided attention, is further exacerbated by the unsafe actions of drunken passengers (e.g., roughhousing with the driver). DDs who consumed alcohol (regardless of level) or are selected because they are deemed least intoxicated place both themselves and their passengers at greater risk for injury.

Reference Number: 50717

BEIRNESS, D.J. "Assessment of the Initial Impact of Mandatory Alcohol Screening on Alcohol-Involved Driver Fatalities in Canada." Final Report, Department of Justice Canada, 11pp, 5 May 2021 (2 tables, 3 figures, 9 references)

Abstract: Mandatory alcohol screening (common in many European countries) became law in Canada on 18 December 2018, in which the police no longer needed a reasonable suspicion to demand a roadside breath alcohol screening test to any driver. The number of alcohol-impaired (BAC of 0.080 g/100 mL or greater) and non-impaired drivers was determined in British Columbia, Alberta, Saskatchewan, Ontario, and Quebec between 2016–2019. The number of alcohol-impaired driving incidences reported by the police was also determined and declined between 2011–2018, followed by a 21.7% increase in 2019. This is probably due to more effective police enforcement as a result of MAS.

Table. Average Number of Alcohol-Impaired and Non-Impaired Fatally Injured Drivers Between 2016 and 2019

	Non-Impaired	Impaired	Percent Impaired
Pre: 2016–2018	750	171	18.6%
Post: 2019	704	104	12.9%
Percent Change (Pre-Post)	–6.1%	–39.3%	

Source: Adapted from Beirness (2021).

Mandatory Alcohol Screening was introduced in Canada to reduce the number of deaths and injuries caused by impaired driving. By providing police officers with the means and authority to screen large numbers of drivers for the presence of alcohol, MAS enhances both the perceived and actual probability that drivers who have been drinking will be detected and subject to sanctions, key factors in creating and maintaining a high level of general deterrence.

Reference Number: 50718

YAO, J., M.B. JOHNSON, AND K.H. BECK. "Predicting DUI Decisions in Different Legal Environments: Investigating Deterrence with a Conjoint Experiment." *Traffic Injury Prevention*, 15: 213–221, 2014. (4 tables, 4 figures, 43 references)

Abstract: One hundred and twenty-one seniors and graduate students at the University of Maryland were questioned on a Web-based survey as to the effects of nine different hypothetical levels of DUI enforcement and penalties on their decision to drink and drive.

Table. Countermeasures and Percent of Drivers Who Stated That This Countermeasure Was Important as to Their Decision to Drink and Drive

Countermeasure	% Importance to Decision to Drink and Drive
Increased enforcement	22%
Jail penalty	21%
License penalty	19%
Alternative way to get home	16%
Immediate penalty	9%
Increased Fines	7%
Lower BAC limit	6%

Source: Adapted from Yoa et al (2014).

Intensified enforcement, harsh jail penalty and immediate long license suspension were found to be the strongest deterrents to drinking and driving. Alternative ways to get home were also important in reducing people's willingness to drive. These factors accounted for most of the attribute effect on the DUI decision, whereas delayed punishment due to judicial processing, fine penalty, and legal blood alcohol concentration (BAC) limit had negligible effects. For the personal characteristics, college seniors and those who had previously driven after drinking were more likely to choose to drink and drive, whereas those who expect a jail penalty for a DUI offense were less likely to drive.

Reference Number: 50719

CONNER, C.R., H.M. RAY, R.M. MCCORMACK, J.S. DICKEY, S.L. PARKER, X. ZHANG, R.M. VERA, J.A. HARVIN, AND R.S. KITAGAWA. "Association of Rideshare Use with Alcohol-Associated Motor Vehicle Crash Trauma." *JAMA Surgery*, E1–E8, 2021 (1 table, 4 figures, 30 references)

Abstract: A study was conducted of 23,491 MVC trauma patients (2007–2019) and 93,742 impaired driving convictions (2007–2018) in Houston, Texas. Ride sharing Uber started in Houston in February 2014. Twenty-four million rides were analyzed. MVC trauma decreased by 23.8% during peak trauma periods (Friday and Saturday nights) after Uber started in Houston in 2014. There also was a decrease in impaired driving convictions between 2014 and 2019.

> In this study, introducing rideshare services in the Houston metropolitan area was associated with significant reductions in MVC traumas and impaired driving convictions. Increased use of rideshares may be an effective means of reducing impaired driving and decreasing rate of MVC traumas.

Reference Number: 50720

BLAIS, E., F. BELLAVANCE, A. MARCIL, AND L. CARNIS. "Effects of Introducing an Administrative .05% Blood Alcohol Concentration Limit on Alcohol-Related Collisions in Canada." *CIRRELT-2015-01*, 27pp, 2015 (4 tables, 2 figures, 48 references)

Abstract: An evaluation was conducted on the provincial administrative licensing laws of a BAC of 0.050 g/100 mL on alcohol-related fatal motor vehicle collisions. In 2010, 2,541 persons died in MVCs in Canada and 11,338 were seriously injured. Alcohol was involved in 38.7% and 18.9% of these MVCs respectively. Administrative BAC laws have reduced the percentage of fatally injured drivers with a BAC > 0.050 g/100 mL, > 0.080 g/100 mL, and > 0.150 g/100 mL by 4.1%, 3.5%, and 4.9% respectively. The introduction of administrative 0.050 g/100 mL laws did not change the law enforcement pattern.

> The results of the present study indicate that Canadian administrative .05% BAC laws were effective at reducing the percentage of fatally injured drivers with prohibited BAC limits at all levels. This improvement occurred without affecting the rate of DWI incidents reported by police officers and the likelihood to be charged for DWI once intercepted for such an offense.

Reference Number: 50721

STRASSGUTL, L. AND C. EVERS. "Long-Term Effects of the German Zero Tolerance Law for Novice Drivers." *Journal of Safety Research*, 80: 46–53, 2022 (7 tables, 2 figures, 24 references).

Abstract: A zero tolerance law (ZTL) for novice drivers was introduced in Germany in 2007. Its effect on alcohol-related crashes and traffic offenses was determined using police records between 2003 and 2018. Current novice drivers have a lower rate of alcohol-related crashes and offenses than novice drivers before the introduction of the law.

> The ZTL is associated with a long-term increase of traffic safety in Germany. Former novice drivers appear to have retained learned behavior toward drinking and driving. Thus, the ZTL might have an impact on perceived norms resulting in less acceptance of drinking and driving. Changes in society, like lower alcohol consumption and decreased importance of passenger cars among young people, further accelerated these effects. ZTL for novice drivers are an effective way to improve traffic safety. It is associated with a positive effect on traffic safety even when drivers were no longer directly affected by the measure. These findings suggest that policies are an effective tool to improve traffic safety and help towards achieving Vision Zero.

Reference Number: 50722

STEIN, I., A.M. BACHANI, AND C. HOE. "The Alcohol Industry's Involvement with Road Safety NGOs." *Globalization and Health*, 18: 9pp, 2022 (4 figures, 22 references).

Abstract: A review was conducted of the alcohol industry's involvement with 256 road safety non-government organizations (NGOs) in ninety-two countries. Eleven (4%) of the NGOs had direct ties to industry and three (1%) showed indirect ties. The majority of the alcohol involvement was with international alcohol manufacturers such as Diageo, Heineken, and AB InBev. The mass media campaigns promoted by the alcohol industry to limit personal alcohol consumption have been found to lead to more positive views about alcohol in both drinkers and non-drinkers. Of the 266 global initiatives to decrease drinking and driving, sponsored by the alcohol industry, only two (0.8%) were backed by evidence and recommended by public health experts.

> Road crashes are a major cause of death among all age groups and the leading cause of death among persons 5–29 years, according to the World Health Organization. One key risk factor is drink-driving. While the world's leading beer, wine and spirit producers have pledged to combat drink-driving, there is increasing evidence showing the alcohol industry's promotion of solutions which minimally impact sales. One strategy is forming partnerships with road safety non-governmental organizations (NGOs). Given this, the primary objective of this study is to understand the extent to which the alcohol industry is involved with road safety NGOs around the world.

Reference Number: 50723

KALSI, J., T. SELANDER, AND T. TERVO. "Alcohol Policy and Fatal Alcohol-Related Crashes in Finland 2000–2016." *Traffic Injury and Prevention,* 19: 476–479, 2018 (4 figures, 18 references)

Abstract: There were 3,477 fatally injured drivers who died in Finland between 2000 and 2016 of which 869 (25%) were intoxicated (i.e., BAC of 0.050 g/100 mL or greater). After an alcohol excise tax decrease of 33%, alcohol consumption rose by 12.4% from 2003–2005 and alcohol-related FMVCs increased 38%. There was a strong correlation ($r = 0.7$) between recorded alcohol consumption and the number of alcohol-related FMVCs. It was also found that the lower the price of alcohol, the more it was consumed.

When making political decisions regarding alcohol price and availability, the effect of these policies on road safety should be assessed. Increasing the price of alcohol is an effective way to reduce alcohol-related harm and alcohol-related traffic accidents. There are also other types of measures that are effective in relation to alcohol-related accidents; these include organizational interventions, policy interventions, and health education (including media and school/community education). These measures may have had an impact on alcohol consumption and drunk driving in Finland from 2000 to 2016. This study confirms results from Estonia that the alcohol excise tax rate is linked to alcohol-related traffic accidents. Alcohol-related traffic fatalities are only a small fraction of the public health problems caused by heavy drinking but have an impact on all road users. Price and availability restrictions are still effective even if introduced in the absence of any other policies.

5.08 CANNABIS AND ALCOHOL

"Alcohol use and marijuana use are each associated with significantly increased risks of fatal crash involvement. When alcohol and marijuana are used together, there exists a positive synergistic effect on fatal crash risk on the addictive scale."

—Chihuri et al, "Direct and Indirect Effects of Marijuana Use on the Risk of Fatal 2-Vehicle Crash Initiation" (2017)

"Tetrahydrocannabinol (THC) is just a 21-carbon alcohol."

—Wigmore, *Wigmore on Cannabis* (2018)

The statutory BAC limit varies among different countries from 0.02 to 0.08 g/100 mL. The statutory blood THC limit also varies; in Norway there are two statutory limits at 1.3 ng/mL and 3.0 ng/mL (50801). Likewise in Canada the blood THC statutory limits are between 2 to 5 ng/mL for a lesser offense and greater than 5 ng/mL is considered a greater *Criminal Code* offense (50808).

Alcohol was found as often in combination with THC (12%) in FMVCs as by itself (12.2%). Male drivers in FMVCs were two times as likely to test positive for THC than female drivers. The presence of THC was greater in the age group of 19–25 years and declined with increasing age. Alcohol-involved FMVCs were more likely to involve a single vehicle, but cannabis-involved FMVCs involved another vehicle (50802, 50803, 50804).

In a simulated driving task, both low levels of alcohol or THC were associated with an increase in mean speed and lateral variability, but at higher doses of THC the mean speed decreased (50805).

SFST was sensitive to THC and low levels of alcohol (50806).

Drivers who were positive for THC alone had a 16% increase in an unsafe driving action (UDA). When alcohol and THC were combined the OR of a UDA increased an additional 9% for each 0.010 g/100 mL increase in BAC greater than either alcohol or THC alone (50807).

Alcohol use and marijuana use are each associated with significantly increased risks of fatal crash involvement. When alcohol and marijuana are used together, there exists a positive synergistic effect on fatal crash risk on the additive scale (50808).

Due to the increase in risk of collision when alcohol and THC are used in combination, it has been recommended to lower the BAC limit when THC is detected as well (50809). In Canada the BAC statutory limit is 0.08 g/100 mL but is lowered to 0.05 g/100 mL when a blood THC concentration of greater than 2.5 ng/mL is detected.

Reference Number: 50801

PASIN, L.T. AND H. GJERDE. "Alcohol and Drug Use Among Road Users Involved in Fatal Crashes in Norway." *Traffic Injury Prevention*, 22: 267–271, 2021 (3 tables, 21 references)

Abstract: There were 330 fatal MVCs in Norway between 2016–2018 causing 349 deaths and 384 non-fatal injuries. When passengers are excluded, 308 drivers were fatally injured and 246 survived. Twenty-nine percent of the fatally injured road users had a BAC of 0.050 g/100 mL or greater, compared to 4.8% of the survivors. The most common other drugs detected were sedatives and hypnotics, THC, stimulants, and opioids. Norway has a statutory limit for alcohol at 0.020 g/100 mL and an impaired limit of 0.050 g/100 mL and 1.3 ng/mL and 3.0 ng/mL for blood THC concentrations respectively.

Table. Percentage of Road Users Impaired by Alcohol and/or THC

	BAC (0.05 g/100 mL+)	THC (3 ng/mL+)
Drivers of cars/vans	15.2%	7.5%
Drivers of trucks/buses/trains, etc.	0	0
Drivers of other vehicles (ATVs, etc.)	41.7%	0
Drivers of motorcycles/mopeds	8.0%	8.0%
Bicyclists	38.1%	0
Pedestrians	15.8%	10.5%

Source: Adapted from Pasin and Gjerde (2021).

The key finding in this study was that impairment by alcohol or drugs was more common among killed road users than among survivors involved in fatal crashes. In total, about one quarter of the killed road users were impaired by with alcohol or drugs. Impairment was more common among certain road users groups such as killed bicyclists and killed drivers of agriculture tractors, all-terrain vehicles and tracked vehicles, where about 40% were impaired. None of the killed drivers of trucks, buses, minibuses, trams and trains were impaired, while 20–30% of killed motorcycle riders and car drivers were impaired.

Reference Number: 50802

WOODALL, K.L., B.L.C. CHOW, A. LAUWERS, AND D. CASS. "Toxicological Findings in Fatal Motor Vehicle Collisions in Ontario, Canada." *Journal of Forensic Sciences*, 60(3): 669–674, 2015 (4 tables, 2 figures, 28 references)

Abstract: Detailed forensic toxicological analyses were conducted on 229 fatally injured drivers in Ontario between 2011 and 2012. The ages of the drivers ranged from fifteen to ninety-two years. Seventy-six percent were male and 24% were female drivers. No drugs or alcohol were detected in 44.1% of the drivers, alcohol only in 12.2%, drugs only in 28.4%, and in 15.3% both alcohol and drugs were detected. The most common drugs detected were cannabis (22% of the drug positive cases) followed by benzodiazepines (17%) and antidepressants (17%). Single MVCs accounted for 43% of FMVCs. The incidence and BAC of drivers was greater in single FMVCs compared to multiple, but the incidence of drugs did not vary between single and multiple FMVCs.

> This study indicates the importance of comprehensive toxicological testing in FMVC drivers. The findings reveal that although alcohol and cannabis are the most common findings, a wide variety of drugs are observed in this type of death investigation.

Reference Number: 50803

BEIRNESS, D.J., K.W. GU, N.J. LOWE, K.L. WOODALL, N.A. DESROSIER, B. CAHILL, A. PORATH, AND A. PEAIRE. "Cannabis, Alcohol and Other Drug Findings in Fatally Injured Drivers in Ontario." *Traffic Injury Prevention*, 22: 6pp, 2021 (1 table, 5 figures, 17 references)

Abstract: Toxicological analyses for alcohol, THC, and other drugs were conducted on 921 fatally injured drivers in Ontario between 2016 and 2018. Male drivers outnumbered female drivers 4:1 and the ages ranged from fifteen to ninety-seven years (mean 44.7 years). The largest number of driver fatalities occurred in the summer months (31.8%) and the least number in winter (18.8%). Overall alcohol was detected in 241 drivers (26.2%) and 79% of them had a BAC > 0.080 g/100 mL. THC was found in 251 drivers (27.2%) and the blood THC concentration ranged from < 1 ng/mL to > 100 ng/mL (mean 8.5 ng/mL). Male drivers were two times as likely to test positive for THC than female drivers. The presence of THC declined with increasing age, with drivers ages nineteen to twenty-five years having the greatest proportion of THC positive cases. Alcohol and THC positive cases were found in 107 drivers (12%).

Table. Percent of Fatally Injured Drivers in Ontario in Which Alcohol or THC Was Detected According to the Day of the Week

Day of Week	Percent Alcohol Detected	Percent THC Detected
Monday	17.6	24.3
Tuesday	16.1	24.2
Wednesday	25.0	29.8
Thursday	22.5	30.8
Friday	21.6	24.7
Saturday	40.7	35.2
Sunday	38.5	26.9

Source: Adapted from Beirness et al (2021).

Alcohol-involved driver fatalities were most prevalent on weekends and most likely to have involved a single vehicle, whereas fatalities involving cannabis and other drugs were more likely to involve more than one vehicle. This may be related to the patterns of use of different types of substances, the effects of different substances as well as the traffic volumes on different days and at different times of the day. For example, alcohol consumption is common on weekends and alcohol-involved fatalities frequently occur during late night hours on these days. Traffic volumes are lower at these times and impaired performance is less likely to involve a collision with another vehicle. The use of cannabis and other types of drugs, however, appear to be common throughout the day, including daytime hours when traffic volumes are higher. Even minor driving impairment at these times would be more likely to result in a collision with another vehicle.

Reference Number: 50804

POULSEN, H., R. MOAR, AND C. TRONCOSO. "The Incidence of Alcohol and Other Drugs in Drivers Killed in New Zealand Road Crashes 2004–2009." *Forensic Science International*, 223: 364–370, 2012 (6 tables, 2 figures, 45 references)

Abstract: Blood alcohol and other drug concentrations were determined in 1,046 drivers killed in MVCs in New Zealand between 2004 and 2009. The BAC limit for drivers less than twenty years of age in New Zealand is 0.030 g/100 mL and alcohol may be purchased at the age of eighteen years. Twenty-four percent of the victims were women and 76% were men.

Five hundred deceased drivers (48%) had alcohol or another impairing drug detected. One hundred and thirty-five drivers (27%) had consumed alcohol alone, ninety-six (19%) used cannabis alone, and 142 (28%) used alcohol and cannabis. The BACs of the 351 alcohol positive drivers ranged from 0.005 g/100 mL to 0.354 g/100 mL (mean 0.152 g/100 mL). The blood THC concentrations ranged from 0.1 ng/mL to 44 ng/mL (mean 5.6 ng/mL). The prevalence of alcohol used by deceased drivers in New Zealand has decreased from 41 to 34% over a ten-year period.

Table. Age of Drivers and Percent Alcohol and Cannabis Detected and with Blood Alcohol Concentration Greater than 0.200 g/100 mL

Age of Driver (yrs.)	Percent Alcohol Detected	Percent, BAC > 0.200 g/100 mL	Percent Cannabis Detected
< 20	29	3	35
20–29	47	13	44
30–39	46	20	41
40-49	31	10	31
50–59	22	8	12
≥ 60	14	3	1

Source: Adapted from Polsen, Moar, and Troncoso (2012).

Almost half of the drivers killed in New Zealand roads over a 5-year period had used a potentially impairing drug. Use of cannabis by these drivers was almost as prevalent as the use of alcohol. When compared with studies of a similar nature from other countries, the use of cannabis in New Zealand, either alone or in combination with other drugs, is very high. The proportion of drivers who had used impairing drugs such as sedatives, stimulants or opioids was similar to that seen in other studies.

Reference Number: 50805

LENNE, M.G., P.M. DIETZE, T.J. TRIGGS, S. WALMSLEY, B. MURPHY, AND J.R. REDMAN. "The Effects of Cannabis and Alcohol on Simulated Arterial Driving: Influences of Driving Experience and Task Demand." *Accident Analysis and Prevention*, 42: 850-866. 2010 (5 tables, 2 figures, 35 references)

Abstract: Twenty-five experienced (7 years +) and twenty-two young novice drivers (< 2 years) consumed a placebo, 0.4, and 0.6 g/kg alcohol and placebo, one joint (19 mg THC), or two joints (38 mg THC). The subjects alternated consuming alcohol after each puff of marijuana or inactive marijuana cigarette. The mean BACs were 0.000, 0.020, and 0.050 g/100 mL and the mean blood THC concentrations were 0, 7.4, and 12.0 ng/mL. The drivers were tested on a simulated computerized driving task.

Table. Mean SD of Lateral Position (Weaving) of Placebo, Low and High Doses of Cannabis and Alcohol

	Alcohol	Cannabis
Placebo	0.36	0.35
Low Dose	0.41	0.39
High Dose	0.41	0.43

Source: Adapted from Lenne et al (2010).

High levels of cannabis generally induced greater impairment than lower levels, while alcohol at the doses used had few effects and did not produce synergistic effects when combined with cannabis. Both cannabis and alcohol were associated with increases in speed and lateral position variability, high doses of cannabis was associated with decreased mean speed, increased mean and variability in headway and lower reaction time, while in contrast alcohol was associated with a slight increase in mean speed.

Reference Number: 50806

BOSKER, W.M., E.L. THEUNISSEN, S. COENE, K.P.C. KUYPERS, W.K. JEFFREY, H.C. WALLS, G.F. KAUERT, S.W. TOENNES, M.R. MOELLER, AND J.G. RAMAEKERS. "A Placebo-Controlled Study to Assess Standardized Field Sobriety Tests Performance During Alcohol and Cannabis Intoxication in Heavy Cannabis Users and Accuracy of Point of Collection Testing Devices for Detecting THC in Oral Fluid." *Psychopharmacology*, 223: 439–446, 2012 (2 tables, 1 figure, 21 references)

Abstract: Fifteen male and five female heavy cannabis users (mean age twenty-four years) consumed placebo alcohol, 0.5 or 0.7 g/kg alcohol, and additional placebo alcohol or 0.1 g/kg every 30 minutes to maintain the BAC for 4.5 hours. The subjects then smoked 400 ug/kg of THC in a marijuana cigarette containing 11% THC at 3 hours from the start of alcohol administration. Baseline serum THC before the experiment was 7.1 ng/mL. Blood and oral fluids were collected frequently for 4.5 hours.

SFSTs were conducted 2 hours after cannabis use. Oral fluid THC was detected with the Draeger Drug Test 5000 (cutoff 5 ng/mL) and Securetec Drugwipe 5 (cutoff 30 ng/mL). Cannabis intoxication was related to OLS impairment. Alcohol and cannabis was associated with HGN. The mean BACs were 0.000, 0.037, and 0.051 g/100 mL during SFST performance and the mean serum THC were 13.4, 14.4, and 11.6 ng/mL respectively.

Taken together, the results indicated that the SFST were mildly sensitive to THC use in heavy users, probably because many of the participants have developed behavioral tolerance to THC-induced impairment. SFST were sensitive to low levels of alcohol in combination with THC as indicated by increments in the number of participants rated as impaired on HGN, OLS and total SFST scored. The Draeger Drug Test 5000 achieved a high sensitivity for THC after acute THC administration in the present study but the sensitivity in the case of Securetec Drugwipe 5 was low.

Reference Number: 50807

DUBOIS, S., N. MULLEN, B. WEAVER, AND M. BEDARD. "The Combined Effects of Alcohol and Cannabis on Driving: Impact on Crash Risk." *Forensic Science International*, 248: 94–100, 2015 (3 tables, 2 figures, 58 references)

Abstract: The prevalence of driving under the influence of cannabis, alcohol, or both was determined in drivers ages twenty years or older who had a least one unsafe driving action (UDA) before the FMVC, compared to control drivers who did not have any UDA, using FARS data between 1999 and 2008. The prevalence of alcohol and THC increased from 2% in 1991 to 10% in 2008. Each 0.010 g/100 mL increase in BAC increased the OR of a UDA by approximately 10%. Drivers who were positive for THC alone had a 16% increase in UDA. When alcohol and THC were combined the OR of a UDA increased an additional 9% for each 0.010 g/100 mL increase in BAC greater than either alcohol or THC alone. Of the 7,734 drivers positive for THC, approximately 56% were positive for alcohol and 31% for another drug.

Driver positive for both agents had greater odds of making an error than drivers positive for either alcohol or cannabis only. Further research is needed to better examine the interaction between cannabis concentration levels, alcohol, and driving. This research would support enforcement agencies and public health educators by highlighting the combined effect of cannabis at low BAC levels.

Reference Number: 50808

CHIHURI, S., G. LI, AND Q. CHEN. "Interaction of Marijuana and Alcohol on Fatal Motor Vehicle Crash Risk: A Case Control Study." *Injury Epistemology*, 4:8 2017 (7 tables, 69 references)

Abstract: A case control study was conducted of the incidence of alcohol alone, THC alone, and THC + alcohol in 1,944 fatally injured drivers in the United States between 2006 and 2008 and 7,719 control drivers who participated in the 2007 US National Roadside Survey of Alcohol and Drug Use by Driver. Overall, 12.2% of the fatally injured drivers had a positive cannabis test compared to 5.9% of the control. A positive BAC was detected in 57.8% of the fatally injured drivers compared to 7.7% of the controls. The adjusted ORs were 16.33 for alcohol alone, 1.54 for THC alone, and 25.09 for alcohol and THC.

Table. Adjusted Odds Ratio of Fatal Crash Involvement According to Cannabis Testing Result and BAC

Cannabis Testing Result	BAC (g/100 mL)	Adjusted Odds Ratio of Fatal Crash Involvement
Negative	0	1.00×
Positive	0	1.56×
Negative	0.01–0.07	2.81×
Positive	0.01–0.07	4.38×
Negative	0.08+	61.11×
Positive	0.08+	95.26×

Source: Adapted from Chihuri et al (2017).

Alcohol use and marijuana use are each associated with significantly increased risks of fatal crash involvement. When alcohol and marijuana are used together, there exists a positive synergistic effect on fatal crash risk on the additive scale.

Reference Number: 50809

LIRA, M. C., T.C. HEEREN, M. BUCZEK, J.G. BLANCHETTE, R. SMART, R.L. PACULA, AND T.S. MAIMI. "Trends in Cannabis Involvement and Risk of Alcohol Involvement in Motor Vehicle Crash Fatalities in the United States, 2000–2018." *American Journal of Public Health,* 111: 1976–1985, 2021 (2 tables, 2 figures, 48 references)

Abstract: A study was conducted of the cannabis and alcohol involvement of 254,002 drivers, 52,053 passengers, and 16,718 other victims (i.e., pedestrians and cyclists) killed in FMVCs in the United States between 2000 and 2018. Alcohol was involved in approximately 40% of MVC fatalities between 2000 and 2018, but the percentage of crashes involving any cannabis increased from 9.0% in 2000 to 21.5% in 2018. The percentage of fatalities involving alcohol and cannabis increased from 4.8 to 10.3%. Crash cannabis involvement was more prevalent in the deceased who were younger than thirty-five years of age, Black, at night, and on weekends with a positive BAC.

Table. The Odds Ratio of Cannabis Being Involved with a FMVC According to BAC

BAC	OR of Cannabis-Involved FMVC
0	1.0×
0.01–0.049	1.56×
0.050–0.079	1.62×
0.080+	1.46×

Source: Adapted from Lira et al (2021).

Adopting a lower permissible BAC threshold for those with cannabis in their system may be a policy strategy to reduce MVC harms from concurrent and simultaneous use of alcohol and cannabis. Indeed, even without consideration for cannabis, the National Highway Traffic Safety Administration and National Academies of Sciences, Engineering, and Medicine have recommended decreasing the legal alcohol limit to 0.05% to reduce alcohol-involved MVC fatalities.

CHAPTER 6

Effects of Alcohol on Other Behavior

"The chief reason for drinking is the desire to behave in a certain way and blame it on alcohol."

—Attributed to Mignon McLaughlin

"Beer. Now there's a temporary solution."

—Homer Simpson, *The Simpsons*, "Homer's Odyssey"

Since alcohol is ubiquitous in most western societies, it is not surprising that many other human behaviors in addition to driving a motor vehicle are affected by alcohol. Some of the signs of the decreased inhibitions caused by alcohol intoxication that can lead to trauma/violence are:

- Boisterous
- Argumentative
- Confrontational
- Animated or exaggerated actions
- Obnoxious
- Saying/doing things that would not normally occur when sober
- Bravado
- Loud comments about other people in the vicinity

The high incidence of alcohol in many crimes such as sexual assault and homicide gives credence to the old saying that alcohol is but "distilled crime."

6.01 AGGRESSION/VIOLENCE

"Drunkenness being nothing but a voluntary madness."

—Seneca, *Epistulae ad Lucilium*

There appears to be an association between alcohol consumption and aggression from laboratory studies (60101–60104) and field studies (60105–60111). Alcohol may increase aggression and violent crimes as it can induce alcohol "myopia" (60112) and is usually involved in incidents of air rage (60113) and road rage (60114, 60115).

In a laboratory experiment, subjects administered a greater and longer "shock" to a subject as their BAC increased (60116). Women with heightened anger and hostility tended to drink more than women in a non-provocation situation (60117).

Twelve of thirteen victims assaulted by nightclub security agents had a BAC > 0.100 g/100 mL (60118), and a positive BAC was most frequently detected (57%) in hospitalized victims of physical aggression (60119).

Empty glass beer bottles are sturdier than full beer bottles and can fracture the human skull when thrown. Banning beer bottles in certain situations is justified (60120).

Alcohol was found to facilitate feelings of aggression whereas cannabis tended to diminish aggressive feelings in heavy users (60121).

Reference Number: 60101

SAYETTE, M.A., G.T. WILSON, AND M.J. ELIAS. "Alcohol and Aggression: A Social Information Processing Analysis." *Journal of Studies on Alcohol*, 54: 399–407, 1993 (4 tables, 34 references)

Abstract: Forty male subjects (ages twenty-one to thirty years) were assigned to either a control, placebo, low alcohol (0.45 g/kg), or a high alcohol (0.85 g/kg) group. The dose was consumed within 20 minutes and BrACs were determined by an Intoximeter 3000. The mean BrAC was 0.030 g/100 mL for the low and 0.080 g/100 mL for the high alcohol groups. Subjects viewed a series of eight videotapes depicting a dormitory TV room scenario in which a person changed the TV channel.

> The major finding of the present study is that a 0.85 g/kg dose of alcohol was associated with aggressive responses to a provocation. Moreover, latter skills in a social information processing model were implicated in aggressive responding.

Reference Number: 60102

DOUGHTERY, D.M., J.M. BJORK, R.H. BENNETT, AND F.G. MOELLER. "The Effects of a Cumulative Alcohol Dosing Procedure on Laboratory Aggression in Women and Men." *Journal of Studies on Alcohol*, 60: 322–329, 1999 (3 figures, 26 references)

Abstract: Thirteen female and thirteen male subjects (mean age thirty years) on two separate days consumed three placebo drinks or three alcohol drinks (0.35 g/kg each) at 1-hour intervals. The alcohol dose was reduced 8% for female subjects. The subjects were tested on aggression. BrACs were determined with an Intoximeter 3000-III. The mean peak BrAC for both male and female subjects was 0.108 g/100 mL.

> Our most important findings were that: 1) alcohol increased aggressive responding that was not specific to either gender; 2) aggressive responding increased during the ascending limb of the BAC curve and remained elevated for several hours after alcohol consumption; and 3) the aggression increasing effects of alcohol were particular to individuals who were aggressive under placebo conditions.

Reference Number: 60103

GUSTAFSON, R. "Male Alcohol-Related Aggression as a Function of Type of Drink." *Aggressive Behavior*, 25: 401–408, 1999 (1 table, 22 references)

Abstract: Ninety male subjects (ages nineteen to thirty-five years) consumed 1.0 mL of 100% alcohol as vodka (40%), red wine (12%), or beer (5.6%) or a placebo or control within 20 minutes. Aggression was measured with a computerized version of the Taylor Aggression Machine. BrACs were determined with a Lion Breathalyzer SD2. The mean BrACs were 0.105 g/100 mL (spirits), 0.092 g/100 mL (wine), and 0.094 g/100 mL (beer).

> The hypothesis of the present study was to a large extent confirmed. Under both nonprovocative and provocative conditions, alcohol intoxication induced by spirits elicited more aggression in terms of shock intensity and shock duration than did intoxication induced by either beer or wine.

Reference Number: 60104

PARROTT, D.J. AND P.R. GIANCOLA. "The Effect of Past-Year Heavy Drinking on Alcohol-Related Aggression." *Journal of Studies on Alcohol*, 67: 122–130, 2006 (2 tables, 1 figure, 50 references)

Abstract: One hundred and fifty-two male and 158 female subjects (ages twenty-one to thirty-five years) were surveyed as to their drinking history. The subjects were divided into a placebo or an alcohol group. The alcohol was consumed within 20 minutes (1.0 g/kg for male and 0.9 g/kg for female subjects). BrACs were determined with an Alco-Sensor IV. The subjects were tested for aggression using a modified Taylor Aggression Paradigm. The mean BrAC was 0.110 g/100 mL.

In conclusion, this is the first investigation to examine the moderating effects of a history of heavy episodic drinking on the alcohol-aggression relation in men and women. The results support the hypothesis that alcohol is more likely to increase aggression in persons (i.e., men) who tend to consume alcohol in large quantities.

Reference Number: 60105

LEONARD, K.E., R.L. COLLINS, AND B.M. QUIGLEY. "Alcohol Consumption and the Occurrence and Severity of Aggression: An Event-Based Analysis of Male-to-Male Barroom Violence." *Aggressive Behavior*, 29: 346–365, 2003 (4 tables, 43 references)

Abstract: One hundred and ninety men (ages eighteen to thirty years) who experienced an episode of aggression or threatening experience around a barroom were interviewed. Men who consumed five drinks or more were 1.5 times as likely to engage in high severity aggression and 2.0 times as likely to hurt or injure the other person compared to the men who consumed no alcohol.

These results suggest that alcohol expectancies may facilitate the occurrence of aggression. However, the results also support the contention that alcohol use may contribute to the severity of aggression occurring in bar contexts.

Reference Number: 60106

SHEPHERD, J., M. IRISH, C. SCULLY, AND I. LESLIE. "Alcohol Intoxication and Severity of Injury in Victims of Assault." *British Medical Journal*, 296: 1299, 1988 (1 table, 4 references)

Abstract: A study was conducted of the reported alcohol consumption of 470 consecutive patients attending the ER of an inner-city hospital as a result of injuries suffered due to an assault. The BACs were determined in 362 patients. There was increasing alcohol consumption of the victim with increasing severity of the injury. Eighteen percent of the victims with the least injury consumed more than 10 units of alcohol compared to 29% of those with the most severe injury.

This link between consumption of alcohol by a victim of assault and more serious injuries and multiple wounds may arise because aggression and loss of judgment induced by alcohol in the victim prolongs violence or simply because intoxicated victims are less able to avoid blows during an assault.

Reference Number: 60107

QUIGLEY, B.M., K.E. LEONARD, AND R.L. COLLINS. "Characteristics of Violent Bars and Bar Patrons." *Journal of Studies on Alcohol*, 64: 765–772, 2003 (3 tables, 31 references)

Abstract: A survey was conducted in Erie County, New York, between 1998 and 2000 of 327 frequent bar patrons (185 men) in which the bars they attended were divided into fifty-eight reported nonviolent bars and ninety-four reported violent bars. Bars in which violence occurred were reported to be smokier, more crowded, dirtier, darker, noisier, warmer, and to have poor ventilation. Violent bars were more likely to employ bouncers and to be staffed by more men than women. Violent bars were more likely to have pool tables, dancing, and illegal activities. The cost of drinks was reported to be lower in violent bars than nonviolent bars and the average age of the patrons was lower in violent bars.

Those who frequent violent bars were more likely to be younger, to have alcohol dependence problems (ADS) and to express anger more openly.

Reference Number: 60108

LUKE, L.C., C. DEWAR, M. BAILEY, D. MCGREEVY, H. MORRIS, AND P. BURDETT-SMITH. "A Little Nightclub Medicine: The Healthcare Implications of Clubbing." *Emergency Medicine*, 19: 542–545, 2002 (1 table, 1 figure, 24 references)

Abstract: A study was conducted of 777 patients attending the emergency department of the Royal Liverpool University hospital between 1997–1998 (0.8% of all attendees) after injuries suffered while attending a nightclub. The modes of transport to the hospital were by ambulance (38%), taxi (30%), private vehicle (18%), on foot (8%), and by police (3%). Most presentations were on weekends (64%) between the hours of 12:00 (midnight) and 8:00 a.m. (79%). The average length of stay was 2.25 hours. Most patients presented with laceration (39%) and soft tissue injuries (26%) in the face (46%), scalp (20%), and hands (17%). Two hundred and forty-nine patients (32%) were reported by hospital staff as being clinically intoxicated with alcohol.

There had been great popular anxiety about use of Ecstasy in club culture especially in the early 1990s, but we have found that alcohol—not substance misuse—and alcohol related assaults account for the majority (57%) of clubbers' use of medical emergency services. Assaults were associated with overt intoxication and a quarter of the assault victims in this study, although this figure needed recognition and documentation of overt patient intoxication by medical or nursing staff.

Reference Number: 60109

ZHANG, L., W.F. WIECZOEK., AND J.W. WELTE. "The Nexus Between Alcohol and Violent Crime." *Alcoholism: Clinical and Experimental Research*, 21: 1264–1271, 1997 (4 tables, 3 figures, 41 references)

Abstract: A study was conducted on the relationship of alcohol and violent crime in a 5-year study of delinquency of 625 males (ages sixteen to nineteen years) in Buffalo, New York.

The present research identifies two critical empirical observations. The first one is that the study reinforces the fact that alcohol and violence are correlated and joint behaviors. The second observation is that persons who used alcohol before committing a violent act are likely to have motives in addition to those associated with drinking.

Reference Number: 60110

NORSTROM, T. "Effects on Criminal Violence of Different Types and Private and Public Drinking." *Addiction*, 93: 689–699, 1998 (8 tables, 7 figures, 34 references)

Abstract: The assault and homicide rate and public and private consumption of various alcoholic beverages were determined in Sweden between 1956 and 1994. There was no association between wine consumption and violence, which may be due in part to it being the preferred drink of women.

> The outcome was fairly clear-cut: the variation in the assault rate seems to be related to changes in public consumption, whereas the variation in the homicide rate appears to be linked to changes in private consumption. The further decomposition suggests that beer and spirits (consumed on premises) were the more important beverages with respect to assaults. The corresponding finding with respect to homicide was that it is (private) spirits that matters primarily.

Reference Number: 60111

BYE, E.K. "Alcohol and Violence: Use of Possible Confounders in a Time-Series Analysis." *Addiction*, 102: 369–376, 2007 (3 tables, 1 figure, 50 references)

Abstract: An aggregate time series analysis was conducted on criminal violence rates and per capita alcohol consumption in Norway between 1880 and 2003 and 1911 and 2003. Possible confounders are the unemployment rate, divorce and marriage rates, total fertility rate, GNP, public assistance, and proportion of the population aged between fifteen and twenty-five years. Per capita alcohol consumption was significantly associated with the rate of violence. An increase in alcohol consumption of 1 L per person per year was associated with an increase in the rate of criminal violence of approximately 8%. Of the possible confounders only the divorce rate was associated with the violence rate.

> The results thus suggest that alcohol consumption has an independent effect on violence rates when other factors are controlled for. This support the assumption of a causal effect of alcohol consumption on violence and it appears that alcohol consumption is an important factor when we wish to explain changes in violence rates over time.

Reference Number: 60112

STEELE, C.M. AND R.A. JOSEPHS. "Alcohol Myopia. Its Prized and Dangerous Effects." *American Psychologist*, 45: 921–933, 1990 (1 table, 4 figures, 61 references)

Abstract: A general review was conducted of the social and psychological effects of alcohol consumption. Alcohol is implicated in numerous violent and antisocial behaviors such as homicides, FMVCs, spousal abuse, and burglaries.

> Alcohol makes us the captive of an impoverished version of reality in which the breadth, depth, and time line of our understanding is constrained. It causes what we have called an alcohol myopia, a state of shortsightedness, in which superficially understood, immediate aspects of experience have a disproportionate influence on behaviour and emotion, a state in which we can see the tree albeit more dimly but miss the forest altogether.

Reference Number: 60113

SMART, R.G. AND R.E. MANN. "Causes and Consequences of Air Rage in Canada." *Canadian Journal of Public Health*, 94: 251–253, 2003 (1 table, 5 references)

Abstract: Twenty-nine cases of air rage reported in the Canadian Press archives were examined. There were two reported incidents in 1998, fourteen in 1999, and thirteen in 2000. In all but two cases the perpetrators were male.

> Many air rage cases involved passengers drinking too much alcohol. In 15 cases, the perpetrator was said to be drunk and abusive. In most of those cases the perpetrator had come on board drunk or was using his own alcohol and had been cut off from drinking on the plane. In one case, a passenger boarded a small plane in Northern Ontario with several bottles of alcohol taped to his chest. He bashed his head on the roof, attempted to break windows, and had to be restrained. The number of drunk perpetrators may be underestimated as no alcohol or breath tests are used and the information about drinking comes from observations only.

Reference Number: 60114

MANN, R.E., R.G. SMART, G. STODUTO, E.M. ADALF, AND A. IALOMITEANU. "Alcohol Consumption and Problems Among Road Rage Victims and Perpetrators." *Journal of Studies on Alcohol*, 65: 161–168, 2004 (3 tables, 29 references)

Abstract: A telephone survey was conducted of 2,610 adults (18+ years) in Ontario between 2001 and 2002. In the last year 44% of respondents reported someone shouted, cursed, or made rude gestures during driving, and 6% reported being threatened with physical or personal injury. Various other demographics were also determined as well as alcohol consumption patterns (AUDIT). The AUDIT alcohol problem measure was the most consistent factor associated with road rage incidents.

There are many reasons for expecting an association between alcohol and road rage. Alcohol is associated with many other forms of violence and the link is believed to be a causal one.

Reference Number: 60115

BATTEN, P.J., D.W. PENN, AND J.D. BLOOM. "A 36-Year History of Fatal Road Rage in Marion County, Oregon: 1963–1998." *Journal of Forensic Sciences*, 45: 397–399, 2004 (6 references)

Abstract: Five cases of fatal road rage that occurred in Marion County, Oregon, between 1963 and 1998 are presented. All victims were male, and the causes of death were as a result of gunshot wounds in two cases, as a result of motor vehicle collisions in two cases, and natural causes in one case. Four of the five victims had a positive BAC (range 0.040 to 0.080 g/100 mL).

These cases have familiar themes: deadly weapons, automobiles, guns, alcohol and—in the only background information that we have—a hair trigger.

Reference Number: 60116

DUKE, A., P.R. GIANCOLA, D.H. MORRIS, J.C.D. HOLT, AND R.L. GUNN. "Alcohol Dose and Aggression: Another Reason Why Drinking More Is a Bad Idea." *Journal of Studies on Alcohol and Drugs*, 72: 34–43, 2011 (5 tables, 2 figures, 30 references)

Abstract: Ninety-five male and ninety-two female subjects (ages twenty-one to thirty-four years) were tested on a modified Taylor Aggression Paradigm (in which electric shocks were received from and administered to a fictitious opponent) after consuming between 0 to 1.0 g/kg alcohol within 20 minutes. The alcoholic beverage was 95% alcohol mixed 1:5 in orange juice. BrACs were measured with an Alco-Sensor IV and the mean peak BrACs were between 0 to 0.112 g/100 mL respectively. There was a highly significant positive trend between increasing BrAC and aggression in both genders. The mean "shock" intensity and duration increased with increasing BrACs as shown in the following table.

Table. Mean BrAC of the Subjects and Mean Delivered "Shock" Intensity and Duration

Mean BrAC (g/100 mL)	Mean "Shock" Intensity	Mean "Shock" Duration(s)
0.000	4.65	0.64
0.014	4.80	0.87
0.028	4.77	1.18
0.056	5.28	1.24
0.085	5.73	1.85
0.112	6.12	2.10

Source: Adapted from Duke et al (2011).

Numerous experimental studies have investigated the impact of alcohol on aggression. Only a few of these, however, have examined the effects of different doses of alcohol on aggression, and a clear picture of this dose-response relation has not yet been forthcoming. We believe that our findings help to clarify this literature by demonstrating a positive linear relation between alcohol and aggression in both men and women up to a dose of 1.0 g/kg. Our findings also have clear public health implications: Violence and excessive drinking go hand in hand.

Reference Number: 60117

MORRISON, P.M., N.E. NOEL, AND R.L. OGLE. "Do Angry Women Choose Alcohol?" *Addictive Behaviors*, 37: 908–913, 2012 (33 references)

Abstract: Twenty-eight female subjects (ages twenty-one to thirty years) were divided equally into provocation and non-provocation groups. In the provocation group a female confederate was both annoying and condescending to the subject for 8 minutes. In addition, the anagrams the subjects were supposed to solve within the 8 minutes were unsolvable. Afterwards a simulated test taste was conducted on all subjects in which they consumed beer (which was actually non-alcoholic) and ginger ale. The mean amount of beer consumed was 172 mL for the provocation (heightened anger and hostility) subjects and 119 mL for the non-provocation subjects.

> Results support a causal relationship between young women's anger and their specific choice to drink alcohol.

Reference Number: 60118

ROMAIN-GLASSEY, N., M. GUTT, A-S. FEINER, F. CATHIENI, M-C. HOFNER, AND P. MANGIN. "When Nightclub Security Agents Assault Clients." *Journal of Forensic and Legal Medicine,* 19: 341–344, 2012 (3 tables, 3 figures, 15 references)

Abstract: A study was conducted of seventy victims assaulted by nightclub security agents in Lausanne, Switzerland, between 2007 and 2009. More than 75% of the assaults occurred on the weekends. Ninety-three percent of the victims were male with a median age of twenty-six years. Bruises and abrasions were the most common injuries. BACs were determined in thirteen patients and was > 0.100 g/100 mL in twelve patients. The security agents involved were all men, and in 50% of the situations they were alone at the time of the assault.

> These findings raise questions about the ability of security agents of nightclubs to deal adequately with obviously risky situations and ensure client security. Considering our study, it appears that they can interact in a rather violent way. The observatory for safety in the City of Lausanne considers that this may be partly due to the fact that the security agents are frequently hired directly by the nightclubs rather than via security companies and hence are moonlighters who are neither professionals nor professionally trained for their tasks, as well as to high staff turnover.

Reference Number: 60119

DE FREITAS, E.A.M., I.D. MENDES, AND L.C.M. DE OLIVEIRA. "Alcohol Consumption Among Victims of External Causes in a University General Hospital." *Rev Saude Publica*, 42: 1–8, 2008 (3 tables, 22 references)

Abstract: BACs were determined in eighty-five trauma patients in an ER in southeastern Brazil in 2004, as well as self-reported alcohol consumption. CAGE and self-reported alcohol consumption were also determined in another 301 trauma outpatients. BACs were determined in serum by the TDx method. The BAC was positive in twenty-seven patients (32%), of which twenty-four (28%) had a BAC > 0.060 g/100 mL. A positive BAC was most frequent among victims of physical aggression (57.1%), traffic accidents (29.3%), and falls (18.2%). The CAGE was positive among 120 outpatients (39.9%).

In conclusion, among patients victims of external causes, about one-third consumed alcoholic beverages prior to trauma, the majority were chronic drinkers, male, young, and had low level of education and family income. The most frequent external cause was traffic accidents. Proportionately, previous consumption of alcoholic beverages was more usual among patient victims of violence. Victims with positive BAC showed injuries with greater severity and more frequently. The occurrence of accidents associated with previous alcohol consumption was more usual on weekends and at night.

Reference Number: 60120

BOLLIGER, S.A., S. ROSS, L. OESTERHELWEG, M.J. THALI, AND B.P. KNEUBUEHL. "Are Full or Empty Beer Bottles Sturdier and Does Their Fracture-Threshold Suffice to Break the Human Skull?" *Journal of Forensic and Legal Medicine*, 16: 138–142, 2009 (5 figures, 3 references)

Abstract: Six empty and four full 500 mL glass beer bottles were tested as to their breaking energy by dropping a 1 kg steel ball on them. The full bottle weighed 896 g and the empty one weighed 391 g. The full beer bottles burst at 30 Joules (J) of energy whereas the empty beer bottles shattered at 40 J of energy. The energy required to fracture the skull was between 14.1 J and 68.5 J. Typical one pint beer glasses shatter at 1.7 J and should not be able to fracture the skull.

Empty beer bottles are sturdier than full ones. However, both full and empty bottles are theoretically capable of fracturing the human neurocranium. We therefore conclude that half-litre beer bottles may indeed present formidable weapons in a physical dispute. Prohibition of these bottles is therefore justified in situations which involves risk of human conflicts.

Reference Number: 60121

PERNA, E.B.D.F., E.L. THEUNISSEN, K.P.C. KUYPERS, S.W. TOENNES, AND J.G. RAMAEKERS. "Subjective Aggression During Alcohol and Cannabis Intoxication Before and After Aggression Exposure." *Psychopharmacology*, 233: 331–3340, 2016 (1 table, 3 figures, 54 references)

Abstract: Twenty heavy alcohol users, twenty-one regular cannabis users, and twenty controls (mean age twenty-three years) were administered two aggression tests (PSAP, SC-IAJ) and subjective aggression was assessed before and after drug/placebo administration. The alcohol consumed was enough to obtain a BAC of 0.080 g/100 mL, and 300 ug/kg THC using a Volcano vaporizer (12% THC marijuana) was administered to the cannabis users. Blood testosterone and cortisol concentrations were determined as well. The mean serum THC, 11-OH-THC, and THC-COOH before aggression tests were 46.5, 3.9, and 27.7 ng/mL respectively. The mean BrAC was 0.079 g/100 mL.

> It is concluded that alcohol facilitated feelings of aggression, whereas cannabis diminished aggressive feelings in heavy alcohol and regular cannabis users respectively.

6.02 BICYCLING

> "The findings reported in this study suggest that alcohol plays an important role in fatal and serious bicycling injuries, and intoxication increases the risk of fatality. To a certain extent, the increased fatality among the intoxicated bicyclists is probably mediated by the association of intoxication with not wearing a helmet."
>
> —Li et al, "A Comparative Analysis of Alcohol in Fatal and Nonfatal Bicycling Injuries" (1996)

> "Tour de France contestants commonly drank alcohol well into the 1960s, particularly wine and beer. This was thought to help dull the pain of the intensive and long ride. However, this is now prevented due to doping regulations."
>
> —Sandwood, "Drinking and Cycling—Why They Shouldn't Be Mixed" (2020)

Alcohol increases the risk of being injured and killed in a collision for bicyclists in a similar manner to drinking drivers (60201–60206).

Nineteen percent of the late-night bicycle crashes involved alcohol compared to only 4% of late-night motorized vehicle crashes (60207). Bicycle riders who used alcohol showed unsafe riding patterns, no helmet use, and were 2.27 times as likely to have a severe injury than sober bicyclists (60208–60210).

The number of fatal bicycle collisions in the EU has increased in recent years and the statutory BAC limit for riding a bicycle range from 0.020 to 0.160 g/100 mL with a fine up to 1 month's salary (60211).

Reference Number: 60201

LI, G., S.P. BAKER, J.E. SMIALEK, AND C.A. SODERSTROM. "Use of Alcohol as a Risk Factor for Bicycling Injury." *Journal of the American Medical* Association, 285: 893–897, 2001 (3 tables, 17 references)

Abstract: The BACs of 124 bicyclists fifteen years or older who were fatally or seriously injured during the day in Maryland between 1985 and 1995 were determined. The roadside BrACs of 342 bicyclists at the same time of day, day of week, and month of year of the original accident were also determined with an Alco-Sensor III. A positive BAC (≥ 0.020 g/100 mL) was found in nineteen (13%) of the injured/killed bicyclists compared to ten (3%) of the controls. A positive BAC was found in 24% of the thirty-four fatally injured bicyclists. The rates of helmet use were 5% for bicyclists with a positive BAC compared to 35% of bicyclists without a positive BAC.

Table. Odds Ratio of Being Non-fatally or Fatally Injured with Increasing BAC in Bicyclists

BAC (g/100 mL)	Odds Ratio		
	Non-fatal Injuries	Fatal Injuries	Combined Injuries
≥ 0.002	2.9	21.9	5.6
≥ 0.080	10.1	no control had BAC ≥ 0.08g/100 mL)	20.2

Source: Adapted from Li et al (2001).

Our study expands the knowledge base of alcohol as an etiologic factor in causing trauma. The risk of bicycling injury increases significantly with BACs. In particular alcohol at levels of 0.08 g/dL and higher may subject bicyclists to a 20-fold heightened risk of fatal or serious injury.

Reference Number: 60202

OLKKONEN, S. AND R. HONKANEN. "The Role of Alcohol in Nonfatal Bicycle Injuries." *Accident Analysis and Prevention*, 22: 89–96, 1990 (4 tables, 1 figure, 28 references)

Abstract: A study was conducted of the BrACs of 140 adults injured in bicycle accidents during 1986 in Helsinki, Finland, compared to 700 control cyclists. The BrACs were determined by a Lion Alcometer SM-3 or S-D2. The mean BrAC in the accident victims was 0.200 g/100 mL and in controls it was 0.075 g/100 mL. Approximately 24% of the accident victims and 4% of controls had a positive BrAC.

Table. Risk (Odds Ratio) of Bicycle Injury Related to Alcohol (BAC > 0.010 g/100 mL) and Age

Age (years)	OR of bicycle injury
16–25	10.4
26–35	6.5
36–45	8.5
46+	5.7

Source: Adapted from Olkkonen and Honkanen (1990).

> In conclusion, the injury risk of an inebriated bicyclist seems to be at least ten-fold at BACs above 100 mg/dL. Also impaired health seems to be a risk factor. As an unprotected road user, an inebriated bicyclist greatly increases his own risk of injury but seldom causes danger to other road users.

Reference Number: 60203

ANDERSSON, A.L. AND O. BUNKETORP. "Cycling and Alcohol." *Injury, International Journal of Care Injured*, 33: 467–471, 2002 (3 tables, 21 references)

Abstract: Telephone interviews were conducted on 207 adults who attended a hospital in Goteborg, Sweden, between 1995 and 1996 as a result of injuries suffered in a bicycling accident. Ninety-five victims were found to be intoxicated by alcohol and 112 were determined to be sober.

> Cycling under the influence of alcohol is associated with a significant risk of head or face injuries. Few people seem to be aware of this risk. The weak legislation regarding alcohol and cycling does not seem to have any preventative effect. Measures to prevent injury should be directed

at altering the attitudes toward cycling intoxicated and promoting the wearing of a helmet. The alternative solution is a change in the law in both cases.

Reference Number: 60204

LI, G., C.SHAHPAR, C.A. SODERSTROM, AND S.P. BAKER. "Alcohol Use in Relation to Driving Records Among Injured Bicyclists." *Accident Analysis and Prevention,* 32: 583–587, 2000 (3 tables, 24 references)

Abstract: A study was conducted of the driving records of 120 injured bicyclists (mean age thirty-six years) attending a Maryland hospital between 1995 and 1998. At the time of admission 23% had a positive BAC that ranged between 0.010 and 0.350 g/100 mL (mean 0.160 g/100 mL). Of the bicyclists with a positive BAC, 30% had a record of DWI compared with 3% of the bicyclists with a zero BAC.

Despite the various limitations, this study provides compelling evidence that individuals who practiced risky driving behavior while riding a bicycle are more likely than others to do so while driving a motor vehicle.

Reference Number: 60205

LI, G., S.P. BAKER, S. STERLING, J.E. SMIALEK, P.C. DISCHINGER, AND C.A. SODERSTROM. "A Comparative Analysis of Alcohol in Fatal and Nonfatal Bicycling Injuries." *Alcoholism: Clinical and Experimental Research*, 20: 1553–1559, 1996 (3 tables, 3 figures, 47 references)

Abstract: A study was conducted of the BACs of sixty-three fatally injured bicyclists and 253 injured bicyclists treated at a trauma center between 1987 and 1994 in Maryland. Thirty percent of the fatal cases were positive for alcohol and 22% had BACs > 0.100 g/100 mL. Sixteen percent of the non-fatal cases had a positive BAC and 13% had a BAC > 0.100 g/100 mL. The risk of a fatal bicycle accident was 2.81 times as great if the BAC > 0.100 g/100 mL.

The findings reported in this study suggest that alcohol plays an important role in fatal and serious bicycling injuries, and intoxication increases the risk of fatality. To a certain extent, the increased fatality among the intoxicated bicyclists is probably mediated by the association of intoxication with not wearing a helmet.

Reference Number: 60206

LI, G. AND S.P. BAKER. "Alcohol in Fatally Injured Bicyclists." *Accident Analysis and Prevention*, 26: 543–548, 1994 (6 tables, 1 figure, 28 references)

Abstract: A study was conducted of the BACs of 1,711 bicyclists fifteen years of age or older who were fatally injured in the United States between 1987 and 1991. A BAC > 0.010 g/100 mL was found in 32% of the victims, and 23% had BACs > 0.100 g/100 mL. The alcohol involvement was greatest in the age group between twenty-five and thirty-four years, where 48% of the male and 26% of the female victims had a positive BAC.

> Consideration should be given to regulating the use of alcohol by the bicyclist on public roads. As in the case of bicycle helmet requirements now being considered in many jurisdictions, the primary effect of such regulations could be to safeguard the bicyclists themselves.

Reference Number: 60207

TWISK, D.A.M. AND M. REURINGS. "An Epidemiological Study of the Risk of Cycling in the Dark: The Role of Visual Perception, Conspicuity and Alcohol Use." *Accident Analysis and Prevention*, 60: 134–140, 2013 (3 tables, 3 figures, 28 references)

Abstract: A study was conducted of 128,000 cyclists in the Netherlands who were seriously injured and admitted to a Dutch hospital between 1993 and 2008. Various parameters were determined including age, time of crash, type of crash (involving motorized traffic (M) and not involving motorized traffic (NM)), and alcohol use. Cycling in the dark is more hazardous than daylight and the risk is greater for NM crashes in the dark. The proportion of cyclists ages eighteen to fifty-nine years has been increasing, and approximately 50% of injured cyclists in this age group who were injured on weekends and early mornings had been drinking.

Table. Percentage of Cyclists Under the Influence of Alcohol in Motorized and Non-motorized Crashes According to Light Condition

Light Condition	Motorized Crashes	Non-Motorized Crashes
Early morning darkness	7.5%	15.9%
Dawn	0.4%	2.3%
Daylight	0.4%	2.1%

Reference Number: 60206

Light Condition	Motorized Crashes	Non-Motorized Crashes
Dusk	1.9%	11.4%
Late night darkness	4.0%	19.0%

Source: Adapted from Twisk and Reurings (2013).

This analysis of epidemiological data shows that injury risks for cyclists are higher in the dark than in daylight, with alcohol use probably being an additional and increasingly important risk component. The difference between crash types with motorized traffic and single crashes indicates that low conspicuity and low visibility both play a role. However, experimental studies are needed to understand the relative contribution of these factors and the influence of alcohol and fatigue on task performance. These insights will provide further underpinnings for the selection and development of effective countermeasures such as improved lighting (both street lighting and bicycle lights), campaigns concerning hazards of alcohol use, low visibility, and conspicuity, and technical requirements for adequate bicycle lights.

Reference Number: 60208

CROCKER, P., O. ZAD, T. MILLING, AND K.A. LAWSON. "Alcohol, Bicycling, and Head and Brain Injury: A Study of Impaired Cyclists' Riding Patterns R1." *American Journal of Emergency Medicine*, 28: 68–72, 2010 (3 tables, 14 references)

Abstract: A 1-year study (2006–2007) was conducted of 126 no-head injury and seventy-two head injury adult bicyclists who presented at an ER in Austin, Texas, as the result of an accident. The median age of the bicyclists was thirty-two years (range eighteen to sixty-seven years) and 81% were male. Alcohol was consumed by 14% of the bicyclists without head injury and 34% of those with head injury. Serum alcohol concentrations ranged from 0.045 g/100 mL to 0.373 g/100 mL. Alcohol use caused a 3.2 times increase in the risk of head injury. Alcohol-consuming bicyclists were more likely to ride at night.

Riders who use alcohol appear to exhibit predictable and unsafe riding patterns in this mid-sized American city, and, confirming prior reports, are much more likely to have head or brain injury, lack medical insurance, and generate increased hospital charges.

Reference Number: 60209

SETHI, M., J. HEYER, S. WALL, C. DIMAGGIO, M. SHINSEKI, D. SLAUGHTER, AND S.G. FRANGOS. "Alcohol Use by Urban Bicyclists Is Associated with more Severe Injury, Greater Hospital Resource Use, and Higher Mortality." *Alcohol,* 53: 1–7, 2016 (4 tables, 1 figure, 29 references)

Abstract: Alcohol use (by history or BAC > 0.010 g/100 mL) was determined in 689 bicyclists presenting at Bellevue Hospital Center (BHC), a level 1 regional trauma center in New York City between 2012 and 2014. The injured bicyclists were 85% male with a mean age of 35.2 years. Blood was analyzed for alcohol in 277 injured bicyclists (40.5%) and a positive BAC was found in seventy-one. An additional thirty-three patients had a history of recent prior alcohol consumption. Alcohol use was 2.27 times as likely to be associated with more severe injury. Alcohol-use bicyclists were less likely to use helmets and more likely to fall from the bicycle. Bicyclists who used alcohol were less likely to be injured by an automobile.

> Bicycling under the influence of alcohol is associated with significant risk of collision, injury, critical injury, and mortality. Yet few people seem to be aware of this risk, as there is a dearth of research on alcohol intoxication in the context of bicycling injuries, limiting the ability of legislators and those involved in health policy to direct public health initiatives. Although arguments against legislation have been made so as not to limit bicycling or worse, promote intoxicated driving, a negative impact may be less likely in NYC in light of its vast public transportation system.

Reference Number: 60210

TONELLATO, D.J., J.R. RANSOHOFF, C. NASH, S.E.F. MELANSON, A.K. PETRIDES, N.V. TOLAN, S.A. GOLDBERG, E.W. BOYER, P.R. CHAI, AND T.B. ERICKSON. "Traumatic Pedestrian and Bicyclist Injuries Associated with Intoxication." *American Journal of Emergency Medicine*, 4pp, 2020 (2 tables, 24 references)

Abstract: A study was conducted of the alcohol (blood) and other drug (urine) involvement in ninety-four pedestrians and bicyclists admitted to hospital as a result of injuries between 2017 and 2019. Nearly three-quarters (73.3%) tested positive for alcohol and/or other drugs. Fentanyl was the most common drug detected (40.4%), followed by opiates (28.7%), THC (24.5%), and ethanol (22.3%). The mean positive SAC was 0.159 g/100 mL. Extremity bone fractures were more common in intoxicated patients (70%) compared to 32% in non-intoxicated patients.

> In our study of vulnerable road users, the presence of drugs and alcohol on toxicology screening correlated with higher risk of traumatic injury, bony fractures, operative procedures, and ICU admissions. Intoxicated pedestrians and bicyclists were particularly at higher risk for body extremity fractures than the control groups. Public health prevention focusing on traffic safety interventions and substance abuse educational programs are recommended for these higher-risk patients ideally initiated during hospitalization. Public health campaigns should also educate bicyclists and pedestrians of the risk of cycling or walking in areas with road traffic while under the influence of alcohol or illicit drugs. Emergency departments should anticipate differences in management for intoxicated pedestrians and bicyclists, especially in terms of severity of trauma and intensity of treatment required.

Reference Number: 60211

AIRAKSINEN, N.K., I.S. NURMI-LUTHJE, J.M. KATAJA, H.P.J. KROGER, AND P.M.J. LUTHJE. "Cycling Injuries and Alcohol." *Injury, International Journal of Care for the Injured,* 49: 945–952, 2018 (5 tables, 4 figures, 49 references).

Abstract: The proportion of cycling fatalities of all road fatalities in the EU has increased from 6 to 8%. A strong correlation has been found between cycling under the influence of alcohol and head injuries and is associated with higher medical costs. The BrACs of 217 injured cyclists treated at the North Kymi hospital in Finland between 2004 and 2006 were determined. One-third of the injured cyclists had a positive BrAC and 87% of those had a result greater than 0.120 g/100 mL. Forty-five percent of the male and 12% of the female injured cyclists had a positive alcohol result. Single cycling accidents accounted for 81% of the accidents. Head injuries occurred more often in cyclists with alcohol involvement (60%), compared to 29% in sober cyclists. A BAC of 0.150 g/100 mL or greater and between fifteen and twenty-four years of age were risk factors for head injuries. Alcohol-involved cyclists were between fifteen and seventy-five years of age.

Table. BAC Limits and Fines for Bicycling in Various EU Countries

Country	BAC Limit (g/100 mL)	Fine (Euros)
Belgium	0.050	140+
Britain	No limit	35+
France	0.050	135+
Poland	0.020	145+
Germany	0.160	One month's salary

Source: Adapted from Airaksinen et al (2018).

Cyclists involved with alcohol were, in most cases, heavily intoxicated and were not wearing a bicycle helmet. Head injuries were more common among these cyclists than among sober cyclists. As cycling continues to increase, it is important to monitor cycling accidents, improve the accident statistics and heighten awareness of the risks of head injuries when cycling under the influence of alcohol.

Reference Number: 60212

ASBRIDGE, M., R. MANN, M.D. CUSIMANO, J.M. TALLON, C. PAULEY, AND J. REHM. "Cycling-Related Crash Risk and the Role of Cannabis and Alcohol: A Case-Crossover Study." *Preventive Medicine*, 96: 80–86, 2014 (1 table, 2 figures, 30 references)

Abstract: A study was conducted of 393 non-fatally injured bicyclists who presented at ERs in Halifax and Toronto between 2009 and 2011. One hundred and fifty-three agreed to provide blood samples; of these 28.8% were positive for THC (> 0.2 ng/mL) and 21.6% were positive for alcohol (> 0.005 g/100 mL). Cannabis and alcohol-related cycling crashes were more likely to occur in the evening and at night. Cyclists who used cannabis were more likely to be male (98%) and younger (none older than sixty-five years of age). Fifteen percent of the cyclists reported cannabis use prior to the crash and 14.5% reported alcohol use. Alcohol use was associated with an odds ratio (OR) of crash of 4.00 times and 2.38 times for cannabis.

Table. Age or Gender of the Bicyclists Involved in a Cannabis or Alcohol-Related Crash

Age or Gender	Percent Involved in Cannabis-Related Bicycle Crash	Percent Involved in Alcohol-Related Bicycle Crash
16–20 yrs	10.3	3.5
21–35 yrs	44.7	36.8
36–50 yrs	34.5	40.3
51–65 yrs	10.4	15.8
65 yrs +	0	3.6
Male	98.3	92.9
Female	1.7	7.1

Source: Adapted from Asbridge et al (2014).

Cannabis and alcohol use each appear to increase the risk of a non-fatal injury-related crash among bicyclists and point to the need for improved efforts to deter substance use prior to cycling, with the help of regulation, increased education, and greater public awareness. However, cannabis results should be interpreted with caution as the observed association with a crash was contingent on how consumption was measured.

6.03 BLACKOUTS/MEMORY

"Drinking can cause memory loss . . . or even worse, memory loss."

—T-shirt slogan

"What we found was that remote memory was intact, but that people had trouble with short term memory, which meant that, during a blackout, a person would be able to recite the Ten Commandments and know the consequences of robbing a bank. It was simply that he would not remember these things for 30 minutes later or the next day. He knew right from wrong at the time of the act and this appears to be the crucial fact where the law is concerned."

—Goodwin, "Alcohol Amnesia" (1995)

The term alcoholic "blackout" is often misunderstood to mean loss of consciousness. Blackouts, however, are just the total loss of memory (amnesia), which can occur during heavy and rapid ingestion of alcohol

(60301–60305). The term "blankout" would be a better descriptor. Factors involving blackouts are:

- The consumption of liquor or liquor and beer are much more frequently associated with blackouts than the consumption of beer alone.
- On average, ten to fourteen drinks were consumed (mostly on an empty stomach) before a blackout occurred.
- The mean BAC that a blackout occurred at was approximately 0.230 g/100 mL.
- Most persons with blackouts are alcohol dependent.
- Most persons with blackouts relied on others to provide details at what transpired during that time.
- Blackouts involve anterograde amnesia, in which there is memory loss after a high BAC is obtained onward. In contrast, a blow or trauma to the head can cause retrograde amnesia, where the person cannot remember the past or their name, etc.

Grayouts and red-outs involving partial memory loss have also been associated with excessive alcohol consumption (60305, 60307, 60308). Alcohol can affect eyewitness memory (60309, 60310, 60316, 60317, 60320), but mild to moderate alcohol intoxication does not make an individual more susceptible to misleading information from a co-witness (60320).

Alcohol by itself is not a drug associated with automatism (60306). Alcoholic blackouts do not fulfill the typical legal requirements of automatism (60513).

Alcoholic blackouts are a strong future predictor of alcohol-related injuries (60514). Cannabis use is associated with more frequent alcoholic blackouts (60318).

Reference Number: 60301

GOODWIN, D.W., J.B. CRANE, AND S.B. GUZE. "Alcoholic Blackouts: A Review and Clinical Study of 100 Alcoholics." *American Journal of Psychiatry*, 126: 191–198, 1969 (2 tables, 1 figure, 12 references)

Abstract: Blackout is amnesia for events of any part of a drinking episode without loss of consciousness. Blackouts are associated positively with the severity and duration of alcoholism, the duration of alcohol consumption per drinking episode, gulping drinks, a history of head trauma, or neglect of meals. Of the sixty-four alcoholics who experienced blackouts, only one had experienced it with a moderate BAC.

> The quantities of alcohol that alcoholics can consume is remarkable; even more remarkable is how little they seem to be physically affected by such heavy drinking, at least during the early years.

Reference Number: 60302

GOODWIN, D.W. "Alcohol Amnesia [Editorial]." *Addiction*, 90: 315–317, 1995 (7 references)

Abstract: The experiences of D.W. Goodwin while studying alcohol amnesia are recounted.

> Our findings had legal implications. Blackouts have rarely been held in extenuation for crimes, but lawyers continually try. I receive calls; when I tell lawyers what we found, they usually do not call back. What we found was that remote memory was intact, but that people had trouble with short term memory, which meant that, during a blackout, a person would be able to recite the Ten Commandments and know the consequences of robbing a bank. It was simply that he would not remember these things for 30 minutes later or the next day. He knew right from wrong at the time of the act and this appears to be the crucial fact where the law is concerned.

Reference Number: 60303

WHITE, A.M., M.L. SIGNER, C.L. KRAUS, AND H.S. SWARTZWELDER. "Experiential Aspects of Alcohol-Induced Blackouts Among College Students." *American Journal of Drug Alcohol Abuse*, 30: 205–224, 2004 (2 tables, 19 references)

Abstract: Thirty-four female and sixteen male undergraduate students with a history of at least one alcohol-related blackout were interviewed. The types of alcohol consumed for the most recent blackout were liquor (40%), liquor and beer (42%), and beer only (2%). Female undergraduates consumed on average ten drinks and males consumed on average fourteen drinks before experiencing blackout. The mean estimated BACs were 0.350 g/100 mL for the female undergraduates and 0.300 g/100 mL for the male undergraduates. Two students reported being taken to hospital for alcohol poisoning. Most students (78%) remembered parts of the events that occurred during blackouts and virtually all subjects (94%) relied on other people to provide details about what transpired. None of the students had sexual intercourse with someone they did not know during their blackout. Thirty-two students (64%) had AUDIT scores suggesting alcohol dependence.

> Becoming aware that a blackout had occurred was often accompanied by a sense of dread or apprehension. Many subjects later learned that they had gotten into fights, had sexual experiences, or had been arrested during a blackout. Factors that would increase the slope and peak of a subject's BAC curve like gulping drinks or drinking on an empty stomach, seemed to precipitate blackouts.

Reference Number: 60304

LUCZAK, S.E., S.H. SHEA, A.C. HSUEH, J. CHANG, L.G. CARR.,AND T.L. WALL. "ALDH2*2 Is Associated with a Decreased Likelihood of Alcohol-Induced Blackouts in Asian American College Students." *Journal of Studies on Alcohol,* 67: 349–353, 2006 (1 table, 35 references)

Abstract: Four hundred and three Asian American college students of Chinese and Korean descent were genotyped at ALDH2 and ADH1B loci and assessed for self-reported incidence of blackouts and maximum number of drinks consumed in one day. Nineteen percent of lifetime alcohol drinkers experienced a blackout. The incidence of blackouts did not vary between men and women. Korean Americans were more likely to experience blackouts than Chinese Americans (26% versus 19%). A blackout was experienced by none of the individuals whose maximum daily alcohol consumption was 0–3 drinks and increased to 6% (4–6 drinks), 29% (7–10 drinks), and 36% (11+ drinks) as the daily alcohol consumption increased. Possessing an ALDH2*2 allele provide greater protection from lifetime blackouts as there is a more intense reaction to alcohol in these individuals.

> This stronger response to alcohol is hypothesized to be due to heightened levels of acetaldehyde. This may lead individuals with an ALDH2*2 allele to drink lower quantities of alcohol and thus their BACs may not reach a high enough level to induce blackouts.

Reference Number: 60305

PERRY, P.J., T.R. ARGO, M.J. BARNETT, J.L. LIESVELD, B. LISKOW, J.M. HERNAN, M.G. TRNKA, AND M.A. BRABSON. "The Association of Alcohol-Induced

Blackouts and Grayouts to Blood Alcohol Concentrations." *Journal of Forensic Sciences*, 51: 896–899, 2006 (1 table, 2 figures, 11 references)

Abstract: Fifty-one male and fourteen female arrested offenders (mean age thirty-one years) with a BAC > 0.080 g/100 mL were interviewed as to their drinking pattern, experience, and the occurrence of blackout or grayouts. Twenty (31%) offenders reported blackouts and thirteen (20%) described grayouts during the arrest procedure. Five subjects recalled vomiting during their drinking episode. Thirty-two offenders (49%) consumed alcohol on an empty stomach. The mean BACs were 0.180 g/100 mL (no memory loss), 0.220 g/100 mL (grayouts), and 0.230 g/100 mL (blackouts). The r^2 between BAC and memory loss was 0.27 for grayouts and 0.54 for blackouts.

The primary finding of the study was that there was a significant association in measured BAC with the level of amnesia reported by the subjects during a recent drinking episode. Thus, as the BAC increased the likelihood of a grayout or blackout increased.

Reference Number: 60306

KALANT, H. "Intoxicated Automatism: Legal Concept vs. Scientific Evidence." *Contemporary Drug Problems*, 23: 631–648, 1996 (32 references)

Abstract: A general review was conducted of legal concepts and scientific research on alcohol-induced blackouts and automatism. There are thirty-two references. Blackouts involve alcohol intoxication with high BACs (generally 0.250 g/100 mL or more).

Blackout, as noted at the outset of this paper, is frequently equated with automatism. This is a serious error of concept. Blackout means nothing more than the failure of subsequent recall of events that occurred during a limited time in which the person was intoxicated.

Reference Number: 60307

SWIHART, G., J. YUILLE, AND S. PORTER. "The Role of State-Dependent Memory in Red-Outs." *International Journal of Law and Psychiatry*, 22: 199–212, 1999 (32 references)

Abstract: A detailed review was conducted of "red-outs." There are thirty-two references. A red-out is amnesia for a violent crime carried out in a state of rage. Two case reports are presented.

> The presence of alcohol or other substances may provide an explanation for some of the instances of amnesia for a crime. However, the pattern of the amnesia is likely to be different from that of the red-out. Alcohol or substance inducted amnesia is more likely to involve a blackout: an inability to recall anything that occurred once a certain level of intoxication has occurred. The red-out is more likely to involve the following: amnesia for the most violent part of the crime with some memory for events both before and after the violent event.

Reference Number: 60308

NORDBY, K., R.G. WATTEN, R.T. RAANAAS, AND S. MAGNUSSEN. "Effects of Moderate Doses of Alcohol on Immediate Recall of Numbers: Some Implications for Information Technology." *Journal of Studies on Alcohol*, 60: 873–878, 1999 (3 figures, 46 references)

Abstract: Eleven male subjects (mean age twenty-five years) consumed a placebo, 0.65 mL, or 1.3 mL/kg alcohol within 1 hour. BrACs were determined by a Lion Alcolmeter SD-2 and the mean BrACs were 0, 0.050, and 0.100 g/100 mL respectively. Subjects were tested on the ability to recall an eight digit number presented either visually or auditorily. As the BrAC increased the memory recall decreased by up to 9% in the visual mode and 15% in the auditory mode.

> In conclusion, the results from the present study, tailored to the practical everyday task of dialing unfamiliar eight-digit domestic telephone numbers, show that even moderate doses of alcohol will affect the performance of an already fragile short-term memory system engaged whenever reproduction of digit strings is required.

Reference Number: 60309

YUILLE, J.G. AND P.A.TOLLESTRUP. "Some Effects of Alcohol on Eyewitness Memory." *Journal of Applied Physiology*, 75: 268–273, 1990 (2 tables, 25 references)

Abstract: A control group of twenty-seven subjects, a placebo group of forty-six subjects, and an alcohol group of forty-seven subjects witnessed a robbery staged by two actors. The alcohol dose was 1.32 mL/kg consumed within 30 minutes. The BrACs were determined in twelve of the alcohol subjects and ranged between 0.060 and 0.120 g/100 mL. An immediate interview regarding the details of the robbery was conducted immediately after the event in fifty-eight subjects. All subjects were interviewed 1 week later. A photospread was shown to the subjects at that time for identification of the suspect

> The results of this study provides a clear indication that alcohol has an effect on eyewitness memory. Although the levels of intoxication used here was mild, it produced consistent effects. Immediately after the event the control witnesses recalled 20.56% more information than those under the influence of alcohol. The accuracy of the information recalled was high in both alcohol and control groups, although slightly lower when alcohol was consumed.

Reference Number: 60310

SANTTILA, P., M. EKHOLM, AND P. NIEMI. "The Effects of Alcohol on Interrogative Suggestibility: The Role of State-Anxiety and Mood States as Mediating Factors." *Legal Criminological Psychology*, 4: 1–13, 1999 (3 tables, 25 references)

Abstract: Twelve female and thirty-nine male university students (ages nineteen to twenty-eight years) were divided into no-alcohol (control), low alcohol (0.13 mL/kg alcohol), medium alcohol (0.6 mL/kg), and high alcohol (1.32 mL/kg) groups. The subjects listened to a description of a traffic accident on an audiotape and then were tested for immediate recall and 50 minutes later for delayed recall. After listening to the tape, the subjects consumed one of the four alcohol doses. The mood of the subject was also determined. Alcohol decreased yielding to leading questions and had no effect in changing answers in response to negative social pressure.

> Does this mean that suspects who are intoxicated are fit to be interviewed by the police? The results of this study suggest that they are not necessarily more vulnerable to the effects of leading questions and negative social feedback than sober subjects if they are intoxicated at the time of the interrogation. It must be remembered, however, that the situation is completely different if the suspect was also intoxicated at the time of the offence. Alcohol disturbs encoding of an event and may therefore lead to increased suggestibility due to memory impairment.

Reference Number: 60311

GARFINKEL, S.N., Z. DIENES, AND T. DUKA. "The Effect of Alcohol and Repetition at Encoding on Implicit and Explicit False Memories." *Psychopharmacology*, 188: 498–508, 2006 (2 tables, 5 figures, 50 references)

Abstract: Sixteen female and sixteen male subjects (ages eighteen to thirty-four years) consumed either a placebo or 0.6 g/kg alcohol over 30 minutes before undergoing an encoding task consisting of ten lists of nine associated words (veridical items). Half of the lists were presented once, and half were repeated three times. BrACs were measured with an Alcometer S-D3M. The next day the subjects underwent an implicit and explicit (free recall) task.

> Thus, in summary the present study has shown a differential effect of alcohol and repetition on the generation of false memories and on accuracy judgments in recognition of false memories in comparison to placebo. Alcohol relative to placebo decreased the generation of false memories for items presented once; repeated presentations of items counteracted this effect of alcohol. On the other hand, alcohol decreased accuracy judgments for repeated items whilst an increase in accuracy judgment was seen with repeated presentation of items in the placebo participants. The activation and monitoring framework is used to explain these effects of repetition and alcohol.

Reference Number: 60312

GOLDING, J.M. AND G.S. BRADSHAW. "Alcohol in the Courtroom: The Intoxication Defense." *American Journal of Forensic Psychiatry*, 26: 37–56, 2005 (1 figure, 19 references)

Abstract: A mock criminal trial (either robbery or arson) was presented to sixty-two male and sixty-four female "jurors." In the written summary of the mock trial the defendant admitted to the crime, but it was argued that the defendant was too drunk to be held accountable. According to the summary, the defendant's BAC was determined at hospital to be 0.300 g/100 mL. Of the 126 participants, 98 (78%) found the defendant guilty. Most participants felt alcohol was no excuse for the crime.

> Not only did the intoxication defense prove ineffective with regard to the verdict in the case, but it undermined the credibility of the defendant. The defendant's claim that he had been drinking beyond legal limits led mock

jurors in the present study to disbelieve his additional statement that he had no intent to either rob the store or burn the building. That is, mock jurors held firm to the perception that alcohol can have deleterious effects on one's memory.

Reference Number: 60313

PRESSMAN, M.R. AND D.S. CAUDILL. "Alcohol-Induced Blackout as a Criminal Defense or Mitigating Factor: An Evidence-Based Review and Admissibility as Scientific Evidence." *Journal of Forensic Sciences*, 58: 932–940, 2013 (7 tables, 49 references)

Abstract: A detailed review was conducted of twenty-six studies on alcoholic blackout or amnesia. A case report of a homicide in which the defense was alcoholic blackout was described. Some of the findings for experimental studies in blackouts were that short-term memories are not stored or retained, the capacity for planning is intact, there were no external signs of a blackout, and physical symptoms of severe intoxication were not present. Alcoholic blackouts do not fulfill the requirements of automatism.

In summary, there is no objective or scientific method to verify the presence of an alcoholic blackout, while it is occurring or to confirm its presence retrospectively. Even if such a method were available, valid and reliable, an alcoholic blackout would not negate men rea as the experimental studies reviewed here report only short-term memory is impaired and other cognitive functions—planning, attention, long-term memory required to form criminal intent—are not impaired. This should disqualify a claim of alcohol blackout under Daubert and FRE 702. Its qualification under Frye is more difficult and depends on how general acceptance is defined, but there is not consensus in the field supporting a claim of automatism or unconsciousness. In light of these findings, expert scientific testimony on alcoholic blackouts would not appear to meet the standards for scientific evidence set by Frye or Daubert.

Reference Number: 60314

MUNDT, M.P., L.I. ZAKLETSKAIA, D.D. BROWN, AND M.F. FLEMING. "Alcohol-Induced Memory Blackouts as an Indicator of Injury Risk Among College Drinkers." *Injury Prevention*, 18: 44–49, 2012 (1 table, 1 figure, 36 references)

Abstract: Memory blackouts are common among college drinkers. The association of blackouts to alcohol-related injury was determined over 24 months using the College Health Intervention Study (CHIPS) of 796 undergraduate and 158 graduate college students between 2004 and 2009. The odds ratio (OR) of an alcohol-related injury increased with increasing number of blackouts (memory losses).

Table. Number of Blackouts and Odds Ratio of an Alcohol-Related Injury

Number of Blackouts	Odds Ratio of Alcohol-Related Injury
1–2	1.8×
3–5	2.6×
6+	3.9×

Source: Adapted from Mundt et al (2012).

Memory blackouts are a strong predictor of future alcohol-related injury among college drinkers. The link between memory blackouts and injury is mediated by younger age, prior alcohol-related injury, heavy drinking, and sensation seeking disposition. Our findings may have implications for prevention and intervention effects by healthcare professionals working with college students and other populations at high risk.

Reference Number: 60315

SCOTT, C.L. "Evaluating Amnesia for Criminal Behavior: A Guide to Remember." *Psychiatric Clinics of North America,* 35: 797–819, 2012 (2 tables, 95 references)

Abstract: A detailed review of memory (acquisition, storage, and retrieval of information) and evaluating claims of amnesia for criminal acts was conducted. A list of twenty-seven questions was presented to interview the offender in order to evaluate alcohol-related blackouts claims by offenders. Approximately 20 to 30% of defendants who have committed a violent crime claim amnesia for the event.

An alcohol blackout is not the same as passing out or falling asleep. Blackouts occur when a person is unable to recall critical elements of events, or even entire events that occurred while he or she was intoxicated and awake. People experiencing a blackout can participate in salient, emotionally charged events and even more routine actions that they cannot later remember. Persons who experience a blackout have anterograde memory impairments while intoxicated but retain memories that occurred before they became intoxicated. Two types of blackouts have been described: en bloc blackouts and fragmentary blackouts.

Reference Number: 60316

ALTMAN, C.M., D.E. MCQUISTON, AND N.S. COMPO. "How Elevated Blood Alcohol Concentration Level and Identification Format Affect Eyewitness Memory: A Field Study." *Applied Cognitive Psychology*, 33: 426–438, 2019 (1 table, 3 figures, 57 references)

Abstract: One hundred and thirty bar patrons were tested on a 20–25 minute test in a study on the effects of alcohol on cognition and motor control. About halfway through the test, they were interrupted by an accomplice who yelled at the tester and banged a chair. The bar patron was then tested whether they could identify the interrupter from a showup or lineup. BrACs were determined using a BACtrack 580 Pro Breathalyzer. A BrAC of 0.080 g/100 mL or more was found in fifty-nine patrons (44.7%). The highest BrAC was 0.240 g/100 mL. As the BAC increased the number of relevant informational units decreased and the number of inaccurate informational units increased.

The aim of this study was to examine witnesses' memory of a live staged interaction at elevated BAC levels and how identification format impacts witnesses' identification decisions. Two central findings emerged: a) Alcohol intoxication significantly affected witnesses' event memory by reducing both the quantity and quality of relevant information reported, and b) alcohol had no effect on identification accuracy regardless of identification format.

Reference Number: 60317

GAWRYLOWICZ, J., A.M. RIDLEY, I.P. ALBERY, E. BARNOTH, AND J. YOUNG. "Alcohol-Induced Retrograde Facilitation Renders Witnesses of Crime Less Suggestible to Misinformation." *Psychopharmacology*, 9pp 2017 (3 tables, 42 references)

Abstract: This study explored the effects of alcohol consumed after a witness event but prior to exposure from misinformation or false memories. Sixty male and twenty-three female subjects (ages eighteen to fifty-eight years) watched a video of a staged crime. Twenty subjects were control, twenty-eight subjects received alcohol (beer) and expected alcohol, and twenty-eight subjects received alcohol but expected no alcohol. The alcohol was consumed within 20–30 minutes and BrACs were determined with an Alcolmeter 500. The mean BrAC was 0.065 g/100 mL and ranged from 0.030 to 0.110 g/100 mL. Subjects were presented with misleading information and were tested to their accuracy of recall the next day. Control subjects were more likely to report misinformation compared to alcohol subjects.

> In summary, our findings indicate that the timing of alcohol consumption plays an important role in determining how accurate and reliable subsequent memory reports are. The assumption that alcohol inevitably impairs eyewitness memory performance is oversimplified. We suggest that in certain circumstances alcohol intoxication can protect eyewitnesses' memory by making individuals less suggestible to misinformation. Scientists who are conducting research in the field need to take this into account when designing their experiments and interpreting their findings, for example, by asking participants about subsequent drinking behavior between testing sessions.

Reference Number: 60318

VOLOSHYNA, D.M., E.E. BONAR, R.M. CUNNINGHAM, M.A. ILGEN, F.C. BLOW, AND M.A. WALTON. "Blackouts Among Male and Female Youth Seeking Emergency Department Care." *American Journal of Drug and Alcohol Abuse,* 44: 129–139, 2018 (2 tables, 100 references)

Abstract: The past 3-month blackout experiences were determined in 2,300 past-year drinking youth (ages fourteen to twenty years) who attended an ED. No blackouts were experienced by 72.8%, and 27.2% reported less than monthly blackouts. The OR of experiencing a blackout was 1.55 times with cannabis use, 3.82 times for incapacitated sexual assault, and 1.85 times for involvement with Greek life in college.

Table. Percent of Experiencing a Blackout Monthly or More in Various Groups of Youth Attending an ER

Group characteristic	Percent experiencing a blackout at least monthly
Female gender	49.7%
Caucasian race	82.5%
Hazardous drinking	94.5%

Group characteristic	Percent experiencing a blackout at least monthly
Tobacco use	73.2%
Cannabis use	86.3%
In college, involved in Greek life	33.9%
Ever had sexual intercourse	92.4%

Source: Adapted from Voloshyna et al (2018).

In summary, one-quarter of underage drinkers in this clinical setting reported blackouts in the past three months, with one-third of these youth reporting that blackouts occurred monthly or more frequently. The association between blackouts and other negative health risk behaviors and outcomes, such as other drug use and sexual assault, underscore the public health significance of this issue. Findings suggest that alcohol-focused prevention and interventions programs should incorporate poly-substance use and drinking motives, with content on sexual assault prevention also included. Although findings highlight how high-risk college students such as those in the Greek system may be at risk for blackouts, the fact that one-third of youth with a recent blackout were not in college suggests that interventions are needed to reduce blackouts among youth in other settings as well.

Reference Number: 60319

BARTLETT, G., J. GAWRYLOWICZ, D. FRINGS, AND I.P. ALBERY. "The Intoxicated Co-Witness: Effects of Alcohol and Dyadic Discussion on Memory Conformity and Event Recall." *Psychopharmacology,* 238: 1485–1493, 2021 (1 table, 2 figures, 39 references)

Abstract: One hundred and six female and sixteen male students (mean age twenty-four years) were administered vodka and orange juice or orange juice alone within 30 minutes. The drinking subjects rinsed their mouths with water and 10 minutes later provided a breath sample into a Lion Alcometer 5000. The mean BrAC was 0.060 g/100 mL. The subjects either watched a video alone or with one non-drinking and one drinking subject. The two subjects (or dyad) each watched a slightly different video. The video showed a student in an empty bookstore stealing money from a wallet. Memory recall, accuracy, and confidence were determined.

Contrary to the perceptions of laypeople and professionals working within the criminal justice system, our findings suggest that mild to moderate alcohol intoxication does not make individuals more susceptible to incorporate misleading information obtained from a co-witness. Our work also shows that alcohol does impact recall completeness but not accuracy, so mild to moderately intoxicated may be regarded as reliable source of information even if questioned in an intoxicated state. There is the potential for all witnesses, sober and intoxicated alike who discuss a crime with co-witness, to report information that they did not see but have just heard about from alcohol witness. Alcohol does not seem to exacerbate the memory conformity effect.

Reference Number: 60320

ALTMAN, C.M., N.S. COMPO, D. MCQUISTON, A.V. HAGSAND, AND J. CERVERA. "Witnesses' Memory for Events and Faces Under Elevated Levels of Intoxication." *Memory*, 14pp, 2018 (2 tables, 3 figures, 73 references)

Abstract: In a 2009 survey, 90% of police officers reported having interviewed an intoxicated witness within the past month. Sexual assault victims/witnesses often fail to report to the police as they fear their memory/credibility will be questioned due to their intoxication. In this study, seventy-five male and sixty-three female bar patrons (ages nineteen to sixty years of age) watched a 2-minute video on a laptop depicting a staged convenience store robbery. Their memory of the event was audio recorded. Their BrACs were measured with a BACtrack 580 Pro Breathalyzer: Professional Edition and ranged from 0.0 to 0.290 g/100 mL (mean 0.080 g/100 mL). As the participants' BAC increased the number of units remembered decreased. BAC had no effect on facial recognition. Open-ended questions provided more accurate and plentiful information from intoxicated witnesses.

Three central findings emerged: 1) alcohol clearly impaired memory for the criminal event by impacting both the quantity and quality of witnesses' reports, 2) alcohol (even at elevated levels) continues to differentially affect witnesses' memory for faces and events, that is, alcohol reduced witnesses ability to recall accurate and plentiful information but had no effect on identification regardless of lineup conditions, and 3) recall format may play an important role when interviewing intoxicated witnesses across a broad BAC spectrum, That is, both open-ended and cued questions elicited less accurate information from intoxicated witnesses; however participants reported more information in response to cued questions especially at higher BAC levels.

6.04 DROWNING/RECREATIONAL BOATING

"For a drunkard the sea only reaches his knees."

—Russian proverb

"Bacchus hath drowned more men than Neptune."

—Attributed to Thomas Fuller

"The important points that emerge from the observations are firstly, that people who drink alcohol, even in moderate amounts before entering water are at risk, secondly that this risk applies to swimmers and sailors alike, summer or winter, and thirdly, the public is apparently unaware of these dangers. Perhaps water safety organizations should emphasize the dangers of drinking rather than giving the time-honored advice about eating before swimming—which has not yet been shown to place the victim at risk."

—Editorial, *British Medical Journal*, 1979

The Russian proverb shows why alcohol causes swimmers to ignore the risks of drowning. The old English proverb (attributed to Thomas Fuller) has merit as alcohol consumption is a major risk factor for drowning due to the following factors:

- Increase in risk taking, or a decrease in the ability to assess risky situations
- Impairment of coordination and balance resulting in a greater risk of falling overboard or from docks or land
- Vasodilation effect of alcohol causes greater risk of drowning in cold water
- Alcohol intoxication may increase the risk of caloric labyrinthitis (inner ear disturbance) in which the person suddenly in cold water becomes disoriented and swims down rather than up
- Incoordination caused by alcohol intoxication makes swimming movements inefficient and energy demanding and there is a decrease in endurance

Typically, the alcohol-intoxicated victim either immediately sinks or only swims a short distance (60401–60403). In addition, alcohol increases the risk of injury from diving into the water (60404). Alcohol appears not to affect the formation of bubbles in the blood during decompression in scuba divers (60405) but does appear to increase body sway in a hyperbaric chamber (60406). The relative risk of a fatality in recreational boating increases markedly with increasing BAC (60408). A standardized field sobriety test (SFST) for boaters has been developed, as the walk and turn and one leg stand tests cannot be conducted onboard a boat (60410, 60411).

Forty-nine percent of spinal cord injuries in a swimming pool involved alcohol (60412). A positive BAC was detected in 35% of the victims of bath-related deaths and ranged from 0.017 to 0.508 g/100 mL (60413). Routine alcohol and drug screening should be conducted for all drowning victims (60414).

Alcohol was more involved in elderly (≥ 65 years of age) drownings in the bathtub or river than in the lake or ocean (60415).

A study of MVCs that led to drownings showed 46% of the victims had a positive BAC, which was less than the rate for unintentional drownings but greater than the rate for other FMVCs (60416).

Reference Number: 60401

STEENSBERG, J. "Epidemiology of Accidental Drowning in Denmark 1989–1993." *Accident Analysis and Prevention*, 30: 755–762, 1998 (3 tables, 33 references)

Abstract: A study of 349 cases of accidental drowning or immersion hypothermia (*immersio frigida*) was conducted in Denmark between 1989 and 1993. Forty-six percent of the victims were children (up to fourteen years of age). Forty-six percent of the adult male and 27% of the adult female victims had a positive postmortem BAC. The predominate risk factor for drowning for men was alcohol consumption.

> The influence of alcohol not only increases the risk of an accident but also is of importance for the prospects for survival as the victim is less likely to be able to rescue himself. The core temperature seems to fall more rapidly in an intoxicated person, thereby increasing the cooling effect. Already at arterial blood concentrations close to 0.150 g/100 mL, subjects experience a curiously different feeling towards the cooling of the skin that may explain the often-tragic results of the combination of alcohol and cold.

Reference Number: 60402

WENTWORTH, P., A.E. CROAL, L.A. JENTZ, M. ESHGHABADI, AND G. PLUCK. "Water-Related Deaths in Brant County 1969–1992: A Review of

Fifty-Seven Cases." *Canadian Society of Forensic Science Journal,* 26: 1–17, 1993 (6 tables, 3 figures, 19 references)

Abstract: A study was conducted of fifty-seven fresh water deaths in Brant County, Ontario, between 1969 and 1992. BACs were determined in thirty-eight (67%) of the cases and a positive BAC was detected in twenty-four victims. Four victims had BACs of approximately 0.400 g/100 mL.

Drowning under the influence of alcohol is common. Alcohol was present in approximately sixty percent of our cases who drowned. Giersten estimated twenty percent of drownings in Norway were alcohol related. Characteristically, these persons either sink immediately or swim only a short distance. Whether victims were good or indifferent swimmers does not seem to be a factor. Alcohol causes vasodilatation of the skin with a rise in skin temperature and this disparity between water temperature and the warm skin of intoxicated persons. Keatinge has shown that sudden cooling of the skin stimulates cold receptors in the skin which trigger uncontrollable hyperventilation, increased blood pressure, pulse rate, and produce extrasystoles. This reaction in a swimmer may lead to inhalation of water or fatal cardiac dysrhythmia. In intoxicated persons, cold receptors may be stimulated to produce such a reaction to sudden cooling.

Reference Number: 60403

CAIRNS, F.J., T.D. KOELMEYER, AND W.M.I. SMEETON. "Deaths From Drowning." *New Zealand Medical Journal*, 97: 65–67, 1984 (3 tables, 9 references)

Abstract: A study was conducted of 150 cases of accidental drowning. Eleven victims fell out of boats (nine of the boats were moored at the time), In twenty-two cases the boat was swamped or overturned, and in two cases there were collisions of boats. Of the 150 victims, the BAC was determined in ninety-seven, as advanced putrefaction was evident in the remaining cases. Of the ninety-seven cases, thirty-six (37%) had BACs > 0.100 g/100 mL, and forty-eight (50%) had a detectable BAC. In 75% of boating fatalities and 50% of the falls, the BAC > 0.100 g/100 mL.

Alcohol and boating do not mix. The drunken person on board a small craft, particularly a dinghy, is a liability to himself and other unfortunate occupants in that craft. These are avoidable deaths.

Reference Number: 60404

PERRINE, M.W., J.C. MUNDT, AND R.I. WEINER. "When Alcohol and Water Don't Mix: Diving Under the Influence." *Journal of Studies on Alcohol*, 55: 517–524, 1994. (1 table, 2 figures, 25 references)

Abstract: Thirteen male subjects (ages twenty-one to thirty-four years) consumed 1.45 g/kg ethanol divided into five equal drinks; each drink was consumed 20 minutes before each of five diving sessions. The BrACs were measured by an Intoxilyzer 1400 and the mean peak BrAC was 0.123 g/100 mL. Subjects were tested in the ability to perform a shallow dive, and each of 271 dives were videotaped and rated.

> The data obtained from this study clearly emphasize the increased risk of injury resulting from alcohol consumption prior to or during recreational diving. A significant increase in the number of dives in which the subject would have come into contact with the 3.5-foot (107 cm) bottom of a swimming pool was evident at an average BAC of 40 mg/dL, a comparatively low amount considering that most current laws prohibit operating a motor vehicle under the influence of alcohol with a BAC of 100 mg/dL or higher.

Reference Number: 60405

ECKENHOFF, R.G. AND C.S. OLSTAD. "Ethanol and Venous Bubbles After Decompression in Humans." *Undersea Biomedical Research*, 18: 47–51, 1991 (3 tables, 7 references)

Abstract: A study was conducted of thirty-four male sport divers who lived for 48 hours in an underwater habitat at 1.62 atmospheres of pressure. During decompression, eleven divers consumed 0.5 to 1.0 mL/kg ethanol; the other twenty-four divers were controls. The divers were then Doppler monitored for formation of bubbles in the blood for the next 12 hours.

> No differences due to ethanol in the timing or the magnitude of bubbles generated after prolonged shallow hyperbaric exposures could be detected. We were unable to test for an effect of ethanol on decompression sickness symptoms because of the lack of any such symptoms produced by these exposures.

Reference Number: 60406

JONES, A.W., R.D. JENNINGS, J. ADOLFSON, AND C.M. HESSER. "Combined Effects of Ethanol and Hyperbaric Air on Body Sway and Heart Rate in Man." *Undersea Biomedical Research*, 6: 15–25, 1979 (2 tables, 3 figures, 24 references)

Abstract: There are some similarities between the signs of ethanol intoxication and inert gas narcosis. Eight male subjects (all amateur divers) were tested in two experimental sessions (alcohol and alcohol free) using a randomized cross-over design. The alcohol dose was 0.72 g/kg ethanol consumed over 20 minutes. BACs were determined by capillary blood samples analyzed by the ADH technique. The mean BAC was 0.077 g/100 mL. All experiments were carried out in a dry compression chamber at normal or raised air pressure. Testing involved subjective estimation of intoxication, measurement of body sway, and heart rate. Increasing the air pressure to 4 and 6 ATA had no significant effect on the BAC curve or the elimination rate.

> In conclusion, it may be stated that a moderate dose of alcohol potentiates the increase in body sway and hence in the performance decrement caused by acute exposure to high pressure of air. These findings could be of practical significance in relation to alcohol use by sport divers before and between dives and may be one explanation of underwater accidents.

Reference Number: 60407

GLOVER, E.D., S. LANE, AND M.Q. WANG. "Relationship of Alcohol Consumption and Recreational Boating in Beaufort County, North Carolina." *Journal of Drug Education*, 25: 149–157, 1995 (8 references, 3 tables)

Abstract: Two hundred and eleven boaters were surveyed as to alcohol use and boating activities at three boating access locations in Beaufort County.

> The prevalence of alcohol use on boats was highest among persons water-skiing (62%), followed by sailing (59%) and cruising (56%). The amount of alcohol use while boating was significantly higher during water skiing activities than sailing with 83 percent of boaters consuming two or more drinks per outing. These findings suggest that boating activities such as water skiing, sailing and cruising should be more carefully monitored by boating authorities.

Reference Number: 60408

SMITH, G.S., P.M. KEYL, J.A. HADLEY, C.L. BARTLEY, R.D. FOSS, W.G. TOLBERT, AND J. MCKNIGHT. "Drinking and Recreational Boating Fatalities. A Population-Based Case-Control Study." *Journal of the American Medical Association*, 286: 2974–2980, 2001 (4 tables, 1 figure, 38 references)

Abstract: A study was conducted of 403 boating deaths that occurred from 1990 to 1998 in Maryland and North Carolina and were compared with control subjects from a random sampling of boaters. Of the 221 boating death victims, 55% had a positive BAC and 36% had a BAC > 0.050 g/100 mL. In the control boaters, 17% had a positive BAC and 7% had a BAC > 0.050 g/100 mL.

Table. Adjusted Odds Ratio (OR) of Dying While Boating by BAC Range

BAC Range (g/100 mL)	Adjusted OR of Dying While Boating
0.0	1.0
0.001–0.049	2.8
0.050–0.099	5.7
0.100–0.149	12.0
≥ 0.150	37.4

Source: Adapted from Smith et al (2001).

Alcohol can affect boater safety in multiple ways, influencing both the risk of ending up in the water (or crashing) and chances for survival in the water. Alcohol impairs balance and coordination, which can increase the risk of falling overboard whether a boat is underway or not. Impaired judgment resulting from an elevated BAC can also increase the likelihood of being in high-risk situations and unlike on the roadway, having a sober operator will not necessarily protect impaired occupants.

Reference Number: 60409

KHIABANI, H.Z., M.S. OPDAL, AND J. MORLAND. "Blood Alcohol Concentrations in Apprehended Drivers of Cars and Boats Suspected to Be Impaired by the Police." *Traffic Injury and Prevention*, 9: 31–36, 2008 (1 table, 2 figures, 24 references)

Abstract: Currently in Norway, both car and boat drivers have an illegal per se BAC of 0.021 g/100 mL. The BACs of 321 boat drivers and 3,061

car drivers suspected by the police to be under the influence of alcohol were determined in Norway between 2002 and 2004 (May-September). The median BAC in boat drivers was 0.188 g/100 mL (range 0.021 to 0.374 g/100 mL) compared to 0.165 g/100 mL (range 0 to 0.450 g/100 mL in car drivers. Three percent of arrested boat drivers were women compared to 11% of the arrested car drivers. The median BAC in female boat drivers was 0.135 g/100 mL compared to 0.185 g/100 mL for male boat drivers. There was no difference in the median BAC between male and female car drivers.

> Our results show that the median BAC in drivers of cars and boats in Norway, who were suspected by the police to be impaired, are very high and most probably will cause impairment of the drivers and give increased risks of boat and car accidents. The majority of apprehended car drivers are under the age of 30, while ages 30–50 stands for the majority of boat drivers. The age group 41–50 stands for the highest BAC in both groups.

Reference Number: 60410

MCKNIGHT, A.J., J.E. LANGE, AND A.S. MCKNIGHT. "Development of a Standardized Boating Sobriety Test." *Accident Analysis and Prevention*, 31: 147–152, 1999 (4 tables, 5 references)

Abstract: The standardized field sobriety test (SFST) used in traffic enforcement was adapted for the marine environment. The three measures used after laboratory and field testing were horizontal gaze nystagmus and the hand pat and alphabet tests. The hand pat test involved clapping the hands alternatively with the palm and back of the hand while counting. The alphabet test consisted of reciting the alphabet from A to Z. This type of testing allowed it to be conducted by a person seated in a boat.

> A standardized boating sobriety test (SBST) consisting of gaze nystagmus, hand-pat and the alphabet tests proved effective in distinguishing boaters above and below a 0.10% BAC legal limit.

Reference Number: 60411

FIORENTINO, D.D. "Validation of Sobriety Tests for the Marine Environment." *Accident Analysis and Prevention*, 40: 870–877, 2011 (3 tables, 16 references)

Abstract: Four seated physical sobriety tests (horizontal gaze nystagmus, finger to nose, palm pat, and hand coordination) were conducted on 330 boaters suspected of BUI between June and September 2009. BrACs were determined with an Intoximeter Alco-Sensor FST. The BrACs ranged from 0 to 0.320 g/100 mL (mean 0.072 g/100 mL). The correlation between BAC status (greater or less than 0.080 g/100 mL) and HGN, FTN, PP, and HC were 0.715, 0.298, 0.403, and 0.182 respectively. HGN and any one of the other tests correctly predicted BAC status in 85% of the cases.

The tests were administered at almost all hours of the day; with probable cause or at sobriety checkpoints; under clear or cloudy weather; with and without wind; at various water and air temperatures; on calm, choppy or rough water surface; and under various lighting conditions.

Reference Number: 60412

DEVIVO, M.J. AND P. SEKAR. "Prevention of Spinal Cord Injuries That Occur in Swimming Pools." *Spinal Cord*, 35: 509–515, 1997 (3 tables, 3 figures, 29 references)

Abstract: A detailed study was conducted of the circumstances surrounding spinal cord injuries that occur in swimming pools. There were 169 male and twenty-seven female victims (ages eleven to fifty-six years). Eighty-seven percent of the injuries occurred in private/residential pools. Most injuries (57%) occurred at water depths of less than four feet. Almost half of all injuries occurred during pool parties. There was self-reported alcohol involvement in 49% of the cases. Other drugs were only involved in 2% of the cases.

These results provide important clues to the development of a successful primary prevention program for spinal cord injuries that occur in swimming pools. The most appropriate target population for such a program would appear to be younger aged white males with high school education or less who quite often are still students.

Reference Number: 60413

YANG, K., B.H. CHOI, B. LEE, AND S.H. YOO. "Bath-Related Deaths in Korea Between 2008–2015." *Journal of Korean Medicine and Science*, 33: e108, 9pp, 2018 (4 tables, 2 figures, 20 references)

Abstract: The blood (right ventricle) and/or femoral vein alcohol concentration was determined by headspace GC in eighty-four bath-related deaths in Korea between 2008 and 2015. There were fifty-six male and twenty-eight female victims (ages eighteen to ninety-one years, mean age 61.3 years). The primary cause of death in fifty-seven (68%) victims was drowning in the bath, followed by natural causes in twenty-four (29%) victims and acute alcohol intoxication in three (3%) victims. A positive BAC was found in twenty-nine victims (35%) and ranged between 0.017 g/100 mL to 0.508 g/100 mL (mean 0.169 g/100 mL).

> In conclusion, our study revealed that the primary cause of mortality in two-thirds of bath-related deaths was drowning, while the remainder died of natural causes and acute alcohol intoxication. Although the diagnosis of bathtub drowning is still performed by a process of elimination, our results showed that multiple water inhalation signs as found on complete autopsy can confirm bathtub drowning. Two leading contributory causes of bath-related deaths were cardiovascular disease and alcohol intoxication (binge drinking before bathing). Preventative strategies for reducing bath-related deaths should target alcohol drinking before bathing. Moreover, long soaking times in bathtubs should be avoided, especially among elderly individuals with pre-existing cardiovascular disease.

Reference Number: 60414

STEPHENSON, L., P. STOCKHAM, C. VAN DEN HEUVEL, AND R.W. BYARD. "Characteristics of Drowning Deaths in an Inner City River." *Legal Medicine*, 47: 3pp, 2020 (1 table, 19 references).

Abstract: A study was conducted of twenty-eight male and six female drowning victims that occurred between 1988 and 2017 in the urban section of the River Torrens in Adelaide, South Australia. On average there was one drowning death per year with most of the victims being younger males. Of the twenty-two cases that had complete toxicology reports and occurred after 1994, 45% of the victims had a BAC greater than 0.050 g/100 mL (range 0.110–0.300 g/100 mL). There were fifteen accidental drownings, eleven suicides, one homicide, and one undetermined. The presence of an illicit drug was found in four cases. It is recommended that routine alcohol and drug testing should be conducted in all drowning victims.

> Although the numbers of cases were not high, the urban portion of the River Torrens had a much higher number of drowning events per kilometre

compared to other inland waterways in South Australia such as the Murray River. This is most likely due to the vulnerability that exists for intoxicated individuals in the city from falls into the water and the availability of the river as a means of suicide to members of the adjacent urban population.

Reference Number: 60415

PEARN, J.H., A.E. PEDEN, AND R.C. FRANKLIN. "The Influence of Alcohol and Drugs on Drowning Among Victims of Senior Years." *Safety*, 5: 8, 10pp, 2019 (3 tables, 1 figure, 47 references)

Abstract: A reduction in childhood drowning rates has occurred in Australia, but not in the elderly (sixty-five years or older). An evaluation was conducted of 651 closed coronal cases of unintended drownings in people in their senior years between 2002 and 2016. Nearly three-quarters of the victims were male. The greatest number of drowning deaths occurred in rivers (26.8%), swimming pools (17.2%), and leaches (15.3%). Toxicology, including alcohol, was conducted on 471 victims and a positive BAC was found in 24.6%.

Table. Percent of Elderly Drowning Victims Positive for Alcohol According to Location of Death

Location	Percent Alcohol Positive
Bathtub	47.4%
Beach	19.2%
Lake	18.6%
Ocean	16.3%
River	35.0%

Source: Adapted from Pearn et al (2019).

Alcohol consumption is present in approximately a quarter of all deaths, although this proportion is higher among those who drown in rivers and bathtubs. To the issue of alcohol consumption alone, we add the increased risk of drowning created by the synergy of alcohol and prescribed medications. We posit that this increased risk is causal, and not simply associative, similar to the proven causal risks of alcohol-impaired driving. Medical practitioners and drowning prevention advocates should encourage reduction of elimination of alcohol consumption when undertaking aquatic activity or when older people are near the water.

Reference Number: 60416

LUNETTA, P. AND K. HAIKONEN. "Land Motor Vehicle-Related Drowning in Finland: A Nation-Wide Population Based Survey." *Traffic Injury Prevention*, 21: 533–538, 2020 (1 table, 3 figures, 25 references).

Abstract: The WHO estimated that more than 1.3 million people die worldwide as a result of motor vehicle collisions, and 300,000 drown. This study examined 538 land motor vehicle collisions that led to drownings in Finland between 1971–2013. This was 4.9% of all unintentional drownings and 3.7% of FMVCs. The mean age of the victims was 37.1 years and the male to female ratio was 7.8:1. Nearly 46% of the victims had a positive BAC, which was less than the rate of unintentional drownings but greater than for FMVCs.

> Noticeably, in addition to the driver, a significant proportion of passengers also tested positive for alcohol. Alcohol (and psychoactive drug) use by the driver represents a risk factor for the crash itself by causing loss of control of the vehicle; however, once the vehicle has ended in the water, alcohol (and psychoactive drugs) becomes a risk factor for both the driver and passenger(s) by hampering safety action, escape procedures and swimming ability.

6.05 FALLS

"I do not know whether to accuse the wine of Bacchus or the rain of Jupiter. For both jeopardize the feet. This grave contains Polyxenos who, returning from a country feast, fell from a slippery slope. Let every toper dread rainy paths after dark."

—Ancient Greek orator at funeral of a drunkard, cited by M. Keller, "A Historical Overview of Alcohol and Alcoholism" (1979)

"One tequila, two tequila, three tequila, floor."

—George Carlin

"A drunk doesn't try to stand up, a drunk tries not to fall down."

—Matthew McConaughey

Although the skills required for walking are much less than for driving, there is still an increasing risk of falls at increasing BAC (60502). Alcohol also tends to increase the severity of head injuries occurring in falls in part due to the slower and less appropriate reactions of the intoxicated person (60503–60505, 60510). Alcohol increases body sway (60506) and impairs visual tracking for guiding stepping (60507). As a vasodilator, alcohol potentiates orthostatic hypotension (60508) and micturition syncope (60509). Alcohol intoxication increases the risk of falls and having more severe injury in the following ways:

- Reactions are slower and less appropriate (e.g., not protecting the head when falling)
- Walking becomes more impaired as there is an increase in body sway and poorer visual tracking
- Alcohol potentiates orthostatic hypotension and is a risk factor for micturition syncope
- Increase in risk taking or decrease in ability to assess risky situations

Alcohol intoxication also increases the risk of positional alcoholic asphyxia, which can occur in arrested persons who are handcuffed in a position that restricts their breathing (60511–60513).

Even low BACs (three drinks) can affect obstacle avoidance (and hence falls) in seniors (60514, 60518) and impairs segmental body movement coordination, which is important for walking (60515–60517).

Younger intoxicated persons have an increase in head and neck injuries, including traumatic brain injury (TBI) (60519). Patients who fell on stairs were three times more likely to have moderate/severe TBI compared to patients who fell while walking (60520).

The main risk groups for escalator injuries were elderly women and intoxicated younger men (< 60 years of age) (60521). Falls from balconies by intoxicated younger men appear to be a new source of injuries (60522).

Reference Number: 60501

DIENER, H.C., J. DICHGANS, M. BACHER, J. HULSER, AND H. LIEBICH. "Mechanism of Postural Ataxia after Intake of Alcohol." *Zeitschrift fur Rechtsmedizin,* 90: 159–165, 1983 (1 table, 2 figures, 15 references)

Abstract: In this study twelve subjects consumed 1 L of wine within 1 hour. The BACs obtained were 0.090–0.167 g/100 mL. The action of alcohol on postural stability is most easily seen if the subject does not have visual cues. With eyes open, alcohol-induced ataxia can be somewhat compensated for. The critical BAC was found to be between 0.060 and 0.090 g/100 mL.

Table. Mean Sway Parameters at 0 and 1 Hour (in Parentheses) After Alcohol Consumption

Sway Parameter	Eyes Open	Eyes Closed
Sway Area (cm^2)	1.9 (5.2)	3.6 (6.9)
Anterio-postural Sway (cm)	2.6 (3.9)	4.8 (6.6)
Lateral Sway (cm)	1.9 (2.4)	2.4 (2.9)

Source: Adapted from Diener et al (1983).

Summarizing the above results for use of everyday practice we conclude that the action of alcohol on postural stability is most easily seen without visual stabilization when the eyes are closed. The resulting increase in sway is predominately antero-posterior. The delay of reflex responses of the stabilizing leg muscles after sudden disturbances of upright stance shows the risk of alcohol consumption in highly demanding situations.

Reference Number: 60502

HONKANEN, R., L. ERTAMA, P. KUOSMANEN, M. LINNOILA, A. ALHA, AND T. VISURI. "The Role of Alcohol in Accidental Falls." *Journal of Studies on Alcohol*, 44: 231–245, 1983 (5 tables, 26 references)

Abstract: The BACs of 301 adults who were admitted to hospital due to injuries from a fall were determined by blood using a GC. The BrACs of 598 matched controls not injured in falls were determined using an ASD breath analyzer. A positive BAC occurred in 50% of the victims of falls and 15% of the controls. The relative risks were calculated. There was a steep risk increase with increasing BAC, which indicates that alcohol is a common cause of accidental falls.

Table. Relative Risk of an Accidental Fall with Increasing BAC

BAC Range (g/100 mL)	RR of Fall
0.00	1
0.05–0.100	3
0.100–0.150	10
0.160+	60

Source: Adapted from Honkanen et al (1983).

The risk of BACs above 100 mg/100 mL is so high that practically all cases with such BACs can be considered to have been caused by alcohol.

Reference Number: 60503

HARTSHORNE, N.J., R.C. HARRUFF, AND E.C. ALVORD. "Fatal Head Injuries in Ground-Level Falls." *American Journal of Forensic Medicine and Pathology*, 18: 258–264, 1997 (4 tables, 1 figure, 25 references)

Abstract: A study was conducted of fifty-two male and twenty-three female victims of fatal ground level falls between 1992 and 1996 in Washington State. BACs were determined in forty-eight victims and a positive BAC was found in twenty-three victims (48%). Sixty-one percent of the victims were greater than seventy years of age.

> Furthermore, acute alcohol intoxication seemed to play a role in causing a sizable proportion of falls particularly in men. Thus, it can be said that alcohol abuse is important, not only in increasing the incidences of ground-level falls but also in contributing to the severity of head injuries sustained.

Reference Number: 60504

JOHNSTON, J.J.E. AND S.J. MCGOVERN. "Alcohol Related Falls: An Interesting Pattern of Injuries." *Emergency Medicine Journal*, 21: 185–188, 2004 (2 tables, 2 figures, 16 references)

Abstract: A study was conducted of 351 victims (ages sixteen to sixty years) of a standing fall who attended hospital between 2001 and 2002. There were 113 patients who consumed alcohol and 238 who did not consume alcohol. SACs were determined in forty-seven patients. SACs were adjusted to the time of injury using 0.018 g/100 mL/h. The alcohol group had a higher incidence of head injuries (48%) compared to 9% for the non-alcohol group. The alcohol group had a lower incidence of limb injuries (39%) compared to 76% in the non-alcohol group. There was more severe injury (ISS) in the alcohol group than the non-alcohol group. In alcohol positive patients with a SAC < 0.200 g/100 mL the injury pattern was mainly soft tissue, at SACs between 0.200 and 0.250 g/100 mL, there were usually more severe limb fractures with an increasing number of head injuries. Mostly severe head injuries occurred in patients with a SAC > 0.250 g/100 mL.

> This study shows different patterns and severity of injury in alcohol related falls. In alcohol related falls there was a greater incidence of craniofacial injury and a greater severity of injury. These differences can be accounted for by the inhibition of protective reflexes. In the intoxicated patient the inability to put out the outstretched hand to break the fall resulted in a

lower incidence of limb injury and a greater force being transmitted to the head when it strikes the ground.

Reference Number: 60505

WYATT, J.P., D. BEARD, AND A. BUSUTTIL. "Fatal Falls Down Stairs." *Injury, International Journal of Care Injured,* 30: 31–34, 1999 (1 table, 3 figures, 31 references)

Abstract: A study was conducted of fatal falls down stairs in the south-east of Scotland between 1992 and 1997. There were twenty-four female and twenty-seven male victims (mean age sixty-nine years). BACs were determined in twenty-eight victims and twenty had a BAC > 0.080 g/100 mL. Two victims had BACs between 0.350 and 0.400 g/100 mL. Injury to the brain or spinal cord was responsible for the vast majority of the most severe injuries.

Alcohol was implicated in contributing in some way in many forms of trauma and death both in the U.K. and elsewhere. Alcohol was heavily implicated in causing many of the falls. In this situation the combination of increasing age (with attendant motility problems) and acute alcohol intoxication renders stairs very dangerous. Having contributed to causing falls, acute alcohol intoxication may have rendered individuals prone to more serious injuries by adversely affecting any natural tendency to protect themselves as they landed. In addition, chronic alcohol abuse (with associated liver disease) may also have been predisposed to increased bleeding after injury. In this fashion a relatively minor traumatic insult may have been transformed into a life-threatening problem.

Reference Number: 60506

THYSSEN, H.H., J. BRYNSKOV, AND E.C. JANSEN. "Alcohol and Postural Imbalance. A Forced Plate Study." *Zeitschrift fur Rechtsmedizin*, 87: 257–260, 1981 (1 table, 2 figures, 7 references)

Abstract: Nine female and seven male subjects (ages twenty to twenty-nine years) consumed one beer or 30 mL of spirits (20 g ethanol) every hour for 4 to 5 hours, after consuming a light meal. BACs were determined in blood collected twice each hour by a spectrographic method. Postural sway (Romberg test) was determined by strain meters placed on a metal plate. The BACs ranged from 0.010 to 0.170 g/100 mL.

Body sway increased with increasing BAC and was significant at BACs > 0.060 g/100 mL.

> The finding that postural imbalance is increased at a BAC over 0.6 mg/mL (0.6 promille) might be of vital interest to people highly dependent on a safe standing position in exposed situations.

Reference Number: 60507

CROWDY, K.A. AND D.E. MARPLE-HORVAT. "Alcohol Affects Eye Movements Essential for Visually Guided Stepping." *Alcoholism: Clinical and Experimental Research*, 28: 402–407, 2004 (3 figures, 22 references)

Abstract: The eye movements and performance of six adults (ages twenty-two to thirty-five years) were monitored as they progressed along a pathway of eighteen irregularly placed stepping stones before and after the consumption of 100 mL of alcohol (45% v/v). The alcohol was consumed within 5 minutes and BrACs were determined with an Alco-Sensor III. Testing was conducted at the time of the peak BrAC. No BrACs are listed. The mean walk time was 11 seconds before and 15 seconds after alcohol consumption. With alcohol the subjects stepped less accurately and occasionally missed a footfall target. Oculomotor abnormalities were also observed. There was an increase in the number of saccades required to fixate a target.

> We conclude that the effects of alcohol on the ability to use vision to guide stepping can be understood as arising at least in part from a direct effect of alcohol in the cerebellum, thus removing the cerebellar contribution to visuomotor control and so compromising the separate and coordinated (linked) performance of both the oculomotor and the locomotor controller.

Reference Number: 60508

NARKIEWICZ, K., R.L. COOLEY, AND V.K. SOMERS. "Alcohol Potentiates Orthostatic Hypotension: Implications for Alcohol-Related Syncope." *Circulation*, 101: 398–402, 2000 (2 tables, 1 figure, 23 references)

Abstract: Thirteen male and one female subject consumed either a placebo or 1.0 g/kg alcohol within 30 minutes on two occasions. The mean peak PAC was 0.105 g/100 mL 60 minutes after alcohol intake. The subjects were supine and exposed to increasing levels of lower body negative pressure (LBNP). Blood pressure, heart rate, and forearm vascular resistance (FVR) were measured.

> In summary, these data demonstrate that in healthy young subjects, short-term alcohol consumption elicits hypotension during orthostatic stress because of impairment of vasoconstriction. These findings have implications for understanding of the hemodynamic effects of alcohol, particularly for understanding the syncopal events that occur in association with alcohol intake.

Reference Number: 60509

LYLE, C.B., J.T. MONROE JR., D.E. FLINN, AND L.E. LAMB. "Micturition Syncope: Report of 24 Cases." *New England Journal of Medicine*, 265: 982–986, 1961 (2 tables, 20 references)

Abstract: A study of twenty-four cases of micturition syncope involving males between eighteen to forty-four years of age was conducted in the US Air Force between 1955 and 1960. Typically, a loss of consciousness occurs abruptly when a person voids immediately after arising from a period of recumbency. The syncope is brief, and recovery is rapid and complete. The most common pre-disposing factor was alcohol consumption, which occurred in fourteen cases.

> In persons assuming the upright position with a distended bladder, reflex vasoconstriction may obviate the usual drop in blood pressure of 5 to 20 mm that stimulates the carotid sinus and aortic adaptive mechanism. On voiding, this reflex vasoconstriction may be released with concomitant fall in pressure. However, in this situation the postural-adaptive mechanism is not allowed the usual period of adjustment afforded while the person gradually arises by first sitting. Instead, the compensatory reaction must take place while he is already erect and standing motionless. In the presence of pre-disposing factors lowering the peripheral arterial resistance—for example recumbency and alcohol intake—the adaptive mechanisms may occasionally fail with resulting circulatory collapse.

Reference Number: 60510

LAWRENCE, D.W., L.I. GIBBS, AND M.A. KOHN. "Spinal Cord Injuries in Louisiana Due to Falls from Deer Stands, 1985–1994." *Journal of Louisiana State Medical Society*, 148: 77–79, 1995 (1 figure, 10 references)

Abstract: During the deer hunting seasons of 1985 to 1991 there were twenty-eight deer stand falls resulting in permanent paralysis and thirteen cases of temporary neurological deficits. Of the forty-one victims (ages seventeen to sixty-one years) thirty-seven were male and four were female. Of the eighteen case reports that contained data on alcohol use, twelve (66%) were positive.

> Alcohol is a well-known risk factor for injuries of all types. Its consumption plays a role in these falls. Alcohol adversely affects motor co-ordination, decreases reaction time, and causes drowsiness—a hazardous situation for an unrestrained hunter high above the ground. Although alcohol use is discouraged by sporting and hunting clubs, its use is still common.

Reference Number: 60511

DEDONNO, A., A. DEFAZIO, M.G. GRECO, F. INTONA, AND R.A.G. MAGLIETTA. "Death in Head-Down Position in a Heavily Intoxicated Obese Man." *Legal Medicine*, 10: 204–209, 2008 (1 figure, 24 references)

Abstract: A seventy-eight-year-old obese man was found dead hanging upside down in a blackberry bush. The postmortem BAC was 0.210 g/100 mL.

> Interestingly, alcoholism has been identified as a risk factor (22/30 subjects, 73.4%, range 0.1–4.8 g/L, mean level 2.4 g/L) in cases of positional asphyxia in adults. Studies on the effects of alcohol have also described a decrease in arterial blood pressure and myocardial contractility, supraventricular and ventricular tachyarrhythmia, and inhibition of the medulla. In this case, therefore, acute alcohol intoxication undoubtedly aggravated the hemodynamic and pulmonary alterations induced by the head-down position. The alcohol level was extremely high indicating a heavy consumption of alcohol just before death. Moreover, there were signs of chronic liver disease compatible with alcohol abuse.

Reference Number: 60512

BELL, M.D., V.J. RAO, C.V. WETLI, AND R.N. RODRIGUEZ. "Positional Asphyxiation in Adults. A Series of 30 Cases from the Dade and Broward County Florida Medical Examiner Offices From 1982 to 1990." *American Journal of Forensic Medicine and Pathology,* 13: 101–107, 1992 (4 tables, 9 figures, 15 references)

Abstract: A study was conducted of 270 deaths resulting from asphyxia in Dade and Broward counties, Florida, between 1982 and 1990. Of these, thirty were classified as positional (or postural) asphyxia, in which the deceased was discovered in a position that restricts breathing and there is no evidence of internal airway obstruction (e.g., food aspiration). Positive BACs were determined in twenty-three cases, in which the mean BAC was 0.240 g/100 mL (range 0.010–0.480 g/100 mL); seventeen victims had a BAC > 0.100 g/100 mL.

> Acute alcohol intoxication is the major risk factor for positional asphyxiation. Its central nervous system depression causes relaxation of the muscles that keep the airway open during sleep, in particular, the genioglossal muscle which draws the tongue forward during inspiration and prevents its lapse into the pharynx.

Reference Number: 60513

TUMRAM, N. K., V.N. AMBRADE, AND P.G. DIXIT. "Compression Asphyxia in Upright Suspended Position." *American Journal of Forensic Medicine and Pathology*, 35: 80–82, 2014 (2 figures, 12 references)

Abstract: A thirty-eight-year-old man was found wedged and suspended in a gap between two bridges under construction. The victim had a postmortem BAC of 0.110 g/100 mL.

> The body was wedged in the gap between 2 static hard surfaces. The victim was unable to extricate himself from the position owing to impairment of cognitive responses and coordination due to influence of alcohol. The victim died as a result of static asphyxia due to compression of the chest and the abdomen. Compression asphyxia in upright suspended position under this circumstance is very rare and not reported preciously to the best of our knowledge.

Reference Number: 60514

HEGEMAN, J., V. WEERDESTEYN, B.J.F. VAN DEN BERNT, B. NIENNHUIS, J. VAN LIMBEEK, AND J. DUYSENS. "Even Low Alcohol Concentrations Affect Obstacle Avoidance Reactions in Healthy Senior Individuals." *BMC Research Notes*, 3: 243, 2010 (2 tables, 6 figures, 33 references)

Abstract: Nine male and four female older subjects (mean age sixty-two years) were tested on an obstacle avoidance task on a treadmill during the consumption of three drinks of alcohol or a placebo. BrACs were measured with an Alcotest 7410 Plus and the mean peak BrACs ranged from 0.030 to 0.060 g/100 mL. The treadmill was at a speed of 3 km/h and the obstacle was always presented to the left foot. The risk of hitting an obstacle was doubled after three drinks compared to placebo.

> In conclusion, the present results clearly show that alcohol levels, considered to be safe for driving, seriously hamper the ability to successfully avoid sudden obstacles in the travel path. It is suggested that many of the alcohol related falls are the result of the disruptive effects of alcohol on the online corrections of the ongoing gait pattern when walking under challenging conditions.

Reference Number: 60515

PATEL, M., F. MODIG, M. MASNUSSON, AND P.A. FRANSSON. "Alcohol Intoxication at 0.06 and 0.10% Blood Alcohol Concentration Changes Segmental Body Movement Coordination." *Experimental Brain Research*, 202: 431–443, 2010 (4 tables, 3 figures, 56 references)

Abstract: Thirteen female and twelve male subjects (ages nineteen to forty-one years) consumed a placebo, 0.6 (0.7) g/kg, and 1.0 (1.1) g/kg alcohol over 30 minutes. BrACs were measured with an Evidenzer breath alcohol instrument. The target BrACs were 0, 0.060, and 0.100 g/100 mL respectively. Posturography tests were conducted, and body movements were recorded at five locations (ankle, knee, hip, shoulder, and head) with eyes open and closed.

> To summarize, when balance was repeatedly perturbed by a proprioceptive disturbance, the normal movement pattern could not be maintained for a longer period of time, while under 0.10% BAC intoxication, but caused the CNS to use a body movement coordination pattern involving more independent knee movement. An inability to relate drunkenness with knee movement may be a contributing factor to falls in addition to the direct effect of alcohol intoxication.

Reference Number: 60516

HAFSTROM, A., M. PATEL, F. MODIG, M. MAGNUSSON, AND P.A. FRANSSON. "Acute Alcohol Intoxication Impairs Segmental Body Alignment in Upright Standing." *Journal of Vestibular Research*, 24: 297–304, 2014 (2 tables, 1 figure, 33 references)

Abstract: Acute alcohol intoxication is a major contributor to accidental falls requiring medical care. The least energy consuming and most common movement pattern to maintain postural stability is the simple-link or ankle strategy where there is a similar movement of all body segments with corrective movements around the ankle. Thirteen women and twelve men (mean age twenty-five years) consumed alcohol/placebo in elderflower juice to obtain BACs as measured by an Evidenzer IR device of 0.000, 0.060, and 0.100 g/100 mL. Body alignment was determined in perturbed and unperturbed positions, with and without visual information.

This study uncovered that alcohol intoxication from ethanol has significant effects on segmental body alignment and adaptation to balance perturbations. The effects of alcohol intoxication at 0.06 and 0.10% BAC were more evident during balance perturbations than in quiet standing. The more posterior and rigid knee positioning and the tendency for a more posterior and left deviated head position with increasing alcohol intoxication may be contributing factors to fall trauma in addition to the direct effect of alcohol intoxication. Furthermore, the changes in body alignment in the anteroposterior direction was more pronounced when visual information was available compared to when it was not, indicating an increased visual dependency with increasing levels of alcohol intoxication. Thus, acute alcohol intoxication resulted in inadequate balance control strategies with increased postural rigidity and impaired adaptation to perturbations. These factors probably contribute to the increased risk of falling when intoxicated with alcohol.

Reference Number: 60517

MODIG, F., P-A FRANSSON, M. MAGNUSSON, AND M. PATEL. "Blood Alcohol Concentration at 0.06 and 0.10% Causes a Complex Multifaceted Deterioration of Body Movement Control." *Alcohol*, 46: 75–88, 2012 (3 tables, 4 figures, 46 references)

Abstract: Body movements were recorded at the ankle, knee, hip, shoulder, and head in thirteen female and twelve male subjects (ages nineteen to forty-one years) during quiet standing and during balance perturbations (pseudo-random pulses of calf muscle vibration) at BrACs of 0, 0.060, and 0.100 g/100 mL. The alcohol was consumed over 30 minutes and BrACs were determined every 15 minutes using the Evidenzer (IR instrument). There was a relationship between increasing BAC and amplitude of body movements. Alcohol intoxication caused a greater stability to decrease in the lateral rather than the anterio-posterior direction. Alcohol also decreased the visual information to postural control.

> Alcohol intoxication at 0.06% BAC and 0.10% BAC causes a complex multifaceted deterioration of human postural control. The stability deterioration was expressed by a direct relationship between increased BAC and increased recorded body movements and a large stability decrease in lateral direction. Alcohol intoxication also influenced the movement pattern and reduced the ability for sensorimotor adaptation to such an extent in lateral direction that human postural control became progressively poorer to be able to handle repeated perturbations. Furthermore, vision provided a weaker contribution of postural control during alcohol intoxication.

Reference Number: 60518

BYE, E.K., S.T. BOGSTRAND, AND I. ROSSOW. "The Importance of Alcohol in Elderly's Hospital Admissions for Fall Injuries: A Population Case-Control Study." *Nordic Studies on Alcohol and Drugs,* 12pp, 2021 (3 tables, 51 references)

Abstract: A study was conducted of 424 patients, sixty years of age and older, attending an ER in Norway as a result of a fall and 1,859 controls in the general population. Self-reported drinking patterns and intoxication frequency were determined. Fall injuries were determined to be alcohol-related when the BAC was greater than 0.010 g/100 mL and/or the patient reported alcohol consumption within 6 hours prior to injury. The risk of a fall was 10.2 times more likely to occur among persons who reported drinking to intoxication monthly or more often. Sixty-four of the sixty-eight alcohol-related falls attending the ER reported drinking to intoxication.

> In general, the acute effects of alcohol on psycho-motor functions are diverse, and include impaired balance and reaction, and there is some evidence suggesting that there is an age-related worsening of performance in people who have consumed alcohol; in other words that older adults are more susceptible to alcohol related impairment, compared to younger adults. The strong association observed between drinking to intoxication and alcohol-related injuries among the patients observed in this study is in line with the assumption of a causal association between heavy episodic drinking and risk of fall injury.

Reference Number: 60519

CHATHA, H., I. SAMMY, M. HICKNEY, A. SATTOUT, AND J. HOLLINGSWORTH. "Falling Down a Flight of Stairs: The Impact of Age and Intoxication on Injury Pattern and Severity." *Trauma,* 20: 169–174, 2018 (2 tables, 2 figures, 19 references)

Abstract: An analysis was conducted of 481 patients who attended a major trauma center in the UK as a result of a fall down a flight of stairs between 2012–2015. Alcohol intoxication was determined by clinical history and assessment. Patients ages sixty-five years or greater were compared to younger patients. Intoxicated patients were more likely to be male and younger and sustain more neck and head injuries.

The association between alcohol intoxication and head injuries in patients who have fallen down a flight of stairs has been documented elsewhere and this study also found an increase in head and neck injuries including traumatic brain injury (TBI) in younger intoxicated patients. In this group of patients, it may therefore be prudent to have a high index of suspicion for TBI and a low threshold for CT of the brain.

Reference Number: 60520

HORAUF, J.-A., C. NAU, N. MUHLENFELD, R.D. VERBOKET, I. MARZI, AND P. STORMANN. "Injury Patterns After Falling Down Stairs—High Ratio of Traumatic Brain Injury Under Alcohol Influence." *Journal of Clinical Medicine,* 11: 697, 10 pp, 2022 (5 tables, 35 references)

Abstract: An evaluation was conducted of 118 patients admitted to a level 1 trauma center in Germany as a result of a fall down stairs between 2016 and 2019. The patients were divided into groups according to the number of steps fallen, low falls (1–5 steps, n = 20), intermediate falls (6–10 steps, n = 40), and high falls (> 10 steps, n = 58). A positive BAC was detected in 44.9% of the patients. The mean BAC was 0.245 g/100 mL. The fall height of the intoxicated and sober patients were comparable. Patients who fell on stairs had a three times higher risk of moderate/severe TBI compared to patients who fell while walking.

The present study shows that stair falls occur amongst all ages and result in a heterogeneous pattern of injury, TBIs being the most common. The high coincidence of stair falls and alcohol intoxication observed in this study poses an additional challenge for the treating physician. Due to the interdisciplinary approach with a high probability for neurosurgical and facial surgery, patients should preferably be treated in hospitals that have such departments.

Reference Number: 60521

SCHMINKE, L.H., V. JEGER, D.S. EVANELOPOULOS, H. ZIMMERMAN, AND A.K. EXADAKTYLOS. "Riding the Escalator: How Dangerous Really?" *Western Journal of Medicine*, 14: 141–145, 2013 (4 figures, 31 references)

Abstract: The first escalator was patented in 1892 and was installed initially as an amusement ride in Coney Island. The first escalators were built of wood. The largest escalators are in the St. Petersburg subway system; one is 142 m in length. About 10,000 escalator-related injuries occur in the United States annually. A Swiss study was conducted of 173 victims of escalator accidents presenting to the Bern University Hospital in 2000 to 2011. The victims were 50% men and the majority were sixty years of age or older. Fifty percent of the men showed alcohol intoxication compared to 7% of women. Escalator injuries occurred mainly on Tuesdays between noon and 7:00 p.m. for women and on Saturdays between 6:00 p.m. and midnight for men. The main risk groups were elderly women and intoxicated men (< 60 years of age). About 1% of the patients at the trauma center were victims of escalator injuries. Escalator use should be restricted for those under the influence of alcohol.

Escalator-related accidents can cause significant medical consequences. Even though most patients suffered multiple soft tissue injuries, many suffered severe injuries, injuries to multiple body parts, or had to be admitted to the hospital or undergo surgery. There were even 2 fatalities.

Reference Number: 60522

SCHAFFER, K.B., G. SCHWENDIG, F. NASRALLAH, J. WANG, AND J.F. KRAUS. "Falls From a Balcony While Intoxicated: A New Injury Among Young Adults?" *Injury Epidemiology*, 6: 4, 6pp, 2019 (2 tables, 24 references)

Abstract: Approximately 11,000 patients were admitted to a San Diego trauma center between 2010 and 2017 for the treatment of traumatic injuries. About one-third (36.2%) of the patients were treated for falls of any type and 532 were unintentional falls from a height. Balcony-related falls occurred in fifty-five cases (10.3%). Two-thirds of the patients were male and 58% were between eighteen and twenty-nine years of age. The average time from the fall to arrival at hospital was 1.75 hours (range 18 minutes to 17.5 hours). The majority of falls (63%) occurred between 9:00 p.m. and 4:00 p.m. BACs were determined and a positive BAC was detected in thirty-four (62%) of the patients (mean 0.200 g/100 mL). Seven of the eight patients under the legal drinking age had a positive BAC. Head injuries occurred in 64% of the patients and the mean length of hospital stay was eight days. "Balconing" is the practice of tourists in some European tourist spots jumping from the balcony or roof into a pool.

> Unintentional falls from balconies are a distinctive type of fall but not uncommon as previously thought. A closer look at the behaviors and demographics of the injured population shows the commonalities. In addition to falling off of balconies while under the influence of alcohol, victims are seldom alone prior to falling and often attended social events with peers. Because the fall event is sudden during these social events where others are also drinking and distracted with the party atmosphere, these occurrences are seldom witnessed and, in many cases result in a delay to medical treatment.

6.06 FIRE/BURNS

> "That a body composed four-fifths of water should take fire from a spark or a flame and continue to burn till only ashes are left, is surely incredible enough without the added wonder of spontaneity, or, as in the case of Mr. Krook, of the volatilization and condensation of some part of the victim into a thick yellow liquid . . . which is offensive to the touch and sight and more offensive to the smell. A stagnant, sickening oil etc.
>
> This oil drips from the wall of the room above that in which the accident occurred. If an intelligence so active and acute as that of Dickens was imposed upon by the pseudoscientific evidence in favour of this marvel, it is small wonder that a belief in it dies hard among the wonder-loving and superstitious people who form the majority of the public. I am, etc."
>
> —A letter to the *British Medical Journal* on 26 August 1905 by E. Muirhead Little regarding Charles Dickens's portrayal of the death of alcoholic Mr. Krook by spontaneous combustion in his novel *Bleak House*.

Alcohol intoxication increases the risk of fire injuries and deaths due to increasing the possibility of a fire through inattention or smoking and a decreased ability to escape the fire (60601–60603, 60605, 60606). In summary some of the factors of the involvement of alcohol in fire injuries/deaths are as follows:

- Heavy drinkers are more likely to be smokers
- Increased risk of fires through inattention due to alcohol intoxication
- Impairment in ability to react appropriately when the fire is discovered
- Alcohol intoxication decreases the ability to escape a fire
- The incidence of smoke inhalation is greater and there tends to be a longer stay in hospital and more complications in drinking fire victims
- Alcohol itself is flammable and high concentrations can be explosive unless the container has a metal flame arrester

The BAC of the victim does not appear to affect the lethal COHb concentration in fire victims (60606). High proof or high alcohol concentration alcoholic beverages can also be a fire hazard (60607, 60608). Spontaneous combustion is not a factor in fire deaths (60609, 60610).

Male fire victims were three times more likely to have a positive BAC than female victims, and alcohol was found to significantly reduce the likelihood of waking to a smoke alarm (60611).

In a large outdoor party celebrating a college basketball team win, numerous intoxicated persons (mean age 23.8 years) were treated for burns due to fire jumping (60612).

Reference Number: 60601

BARILLO, D.J., B.F. RUSH JR., R. GOODE, R-L. LIN, A. FREDA, AND E.J. ANDERSON JR. "Is Ethanol the Unknown Toxin in Smoke Inhalation Injury?" *American Surgeon*, 52: 641–645, 1986 (2 tables, 3 figures, 27 references)

Abstract: A study of thirty-nine fire deaths (twenty-seven adult and twelve children) was conducted in Newark, New Jersey, from 1983–1985. Blood cyanide, alcohol, and COHb concentrations were determined. A positive BAC was found in 80% of the adult victims. The average positive BAC was 0.204 g/100 mL. The average BAC for victims found near the bed was 0.268 g/100 mL and for victims found near the exit it was 0.088 g/100 mL.

> In conclusion we have observed that ethanol intoxication significantly impairs the ability of a victim to escape from smoke and fire. Mean blood

ethanol levels of victims found in bed (no escape attempt) are significantly higher than in victims found close to a point of escape. Carboxyhemoglobin and cyanide levels do not show a similar pattern. While carbon monoxide poisoning may be considered to be the primary cause of death in this series, ethanol intoxication proved to be the major contributing factor in mortality caused by smoke inhalation.

Reference Number: 60602

SQUIRES, T. AND A. BUSUTTIL. "Alcohol and House Fire Fatalities in Scotland, 1980–1990." *Medicine Science and the Law*, 37: 321–325, 1997 (3 tables, 1 figure, 16 references)

Abstract: A study was conducted of the BACs of 392 male and 302 female victims of house fires in Scotland between 1980 and 1990. A positive BAC was found in 268 (68%) of the male and 164 (54%) of the female victims. The mean BACs were 0.159 g/100 mL for males and 0.117 g/100 mL for female victims.

Alcohol affects the fire risk in several ways: an increase in the risk of fire outbreak, a reduction in the ability to react when fire is discovered and an adverse effect on both the potential for self-escape and the ability to assist other occupants.

Reference Number: 60603

HAUM, A., W. PERBIX, H.J. HACK, G.B. STARK, G. SPILKER, AND M. DOEHN. "Alcohol and Drug Abuse in Burn Injuries." *Burns*, 21: 194–199, 1995 (4 tables, 6 figures, 12 references)

Abstract: A study was conducted of forty-seven female and 178 male patients admitted to a trauma center for treatment of burn injuries between 1989 and 1992 in Cologne, Germany. BACs were determined with an enzymatic method and other drug concentrations were determined by HPLC. Seventy patients (31%) had a positive BAC. The fatality rate of patients with a positive BAC was 31% compared to 18% in patients with a zero BAC. Fifty-nine patients (26%) had a history of chronic alcoholism. The mean BAC in alcoholic fatalities was 0.129 g/100 mL and was 0.087 g/100 mL in non-alcoholic fatalities. A BAC > 0.060 g/100 mL was associated with a greater risk for fatalities.

Table. Characteristics of Non-intoxicated and Intoxicated Burn Patients

Patient Characteristics	Non-Intoxicated	Intoxicated (BAC ≥0.01 g/100 mL)
Mean Days of ICU Stay	23.9	28.3
Smoke Inhalation (%)	29.0	50.0
Alcoholics (%)	15.5	50.0
Fatality Rate (%)	18.1	31.5

Source: Adapted from Haum et al (1995).

We conclude that alcohol levels above 60 mg/100 mL mean a greater risk for fatal outcome.

Reference Number: 60604

KELLEY, D., AND J.B. LYNCH. "Burns in Alcohol and Drug Users Result in Longer Treatment Times with More Complications." *Journal of Burn Care and Rehabilitation*, 13: 218–220, 1992 (2 tables, 1 reference)

Abstract: A study of 131 burn patients was conducted at Vanderbilt University Medical Centre between 1988 and 1989. Nineteen patients (15%) were determined to be under the influence of drugs/alcohol at the time of the injury.

Patients who were using alcohol and/or drugs at the time of injury were found to have increased lengths of stay and more complications. They also required more surgical procedures than patients who were not using alcohol or drugs at the time of injury.

Reference Number: 60605

MCGWIN JR. G., V. CHAPMAN, M. ROUSCULP, J. ROBISON, AND P. FINE. "The Epidemiology of Fire-Related Deaths in Alabama." *Journal of Burn Care Rehabilitation*, 21: 75–83, 2000 (3 tables, 4 figures, 31 references)

Abstract: A study of 674 fire-related deaths in the state of Alabama was conducted between 1992 and 1997. Fire-related deaths were high among children under nine years of age and adults over sixty years of age. Of the 531 victims greater than eighteen years of age, BACs were determined in 247. More than half (55%) of the victims had a positive BAC (mean 0.120 g/100 mL). The COHb concentration of 334 victims was greater than 75% in the majority of the victims (61%). Fatal fires occurred more often during the weekend probably due to alcohol consumption.

We found that intoxicated persons were more likely to be found in the room where the fire originated. This finding supports the hypothesis that inebriated individuals may be unable to respond properly to a fire once it has started. Clearly, alcohol plays a role in fire-related deaths; fire prevention initiatives should provide ample information about this role.

Reference Number: 60606

ROGDE, S. AND J.H. OLVING. "Characteristics of Fire Victims in Different Sorts of Fires." *Forensic Science International*, 77: 93–99, 1996 (1 table, 3 figures, 7 references)

Abstract: A study was conducted of 286 fire fatalities in Norway between 1984 and 1993. In 131 victims (46%) the BAC > 0.010 g/100 mL, and in sixty cases, the BAC > 0.190 g/100 mL. The COHb concentration and the presence or absence of soot in the trachea were also determined.

Our data furthermore support their finding that the lethal COHb saturation is independent of the blood alcohol concentration. There is reason to believe that excessive alcohol consumption may be associated with both the cause of fire as well as the impaired ability to escape.

Reference Number: 60607

LINDEN, C.H. AND J.R. TUCKER. "Alcoholic Beverages: Proof and Flammability [Letter]." *American Journal of Emergency Medicine*, 16: 544–555, 1998 (7 references)

Abstract: A letter regarding the proof and flammability of alcoholic beverages was published. Original proof was the beverage with the lowest alcohol concentration that could be ignited when mixed with gunpowder. This concentration was 57%. At room temperature after a brief 1 second application of flame there was a continuous flame produced at alcohol concentrations > 55% and a momentary flash produced at 46 to 56%. With prolonged application of flame, ignition occurred as low as 20% alcohol concentration. When heated, an alcohol concentration of 20% produced a continuous flame.

Even with prolonged flame exposure or prior heating, beverages such as beer and wine which had an alcohol concentration of less than 20% cannot be ignited by the flame of a butane lighter. Although it is theoretically possible for then to ignite at temperatures between the boiling point of alcohol and that of water, under most conditions of use they are not likely to be flammable or to pose a risk of fire.

Reference Number: 60608

GEAR, A.J.L., W.D. NGUYEN, H.N. HIMEL, AND R.F. EDLICH. "Flaming Dr. Pepper—Another Cause of Recreational Burn Injury [Letter]." *American Journal of Emergency Medicine*, 15: 108–111, 1997 (1 table, 6 figures, 8 references)

Abstract: A fourteen-year-old boy accidentally spilled a flaming Dr. Pepper drink on his face. He was admitted to hospital although his burns were superficial. His admission BAC was 0.045 g/100 mL. A flaming Dr. Pepper is an alcoholic drink consisting of 0.5 fl. oz. of rum (75.5% alcohol v/v) and 0.5 fl. oz. of amaretto, which are placed in a shot glass and ignited with a match. In a well-lit room the flame is nearly invisible. The flaming shot glass is then submerged into a glass containing about 6 fl. oz. of beer, which extinguishes the flame. The drink tastes similar to Dr. Pepper. One-half of one ounce of 75.5% alcohol v/v rum burns for an average of 21 minutes. Bacardi has put a warning label on the bottle of 75.5% alcohol v/v rum and also has a metal flame arrester on the bottle.

> With the high frequency of recreational use of alcohol, it would appear prudent for manufacturers of 151 proof rum to provide warning labels on their products, in addition to flame arresters. Although we realize that these precautions will not ultimately solve the problem, they will serve to heighten public awareness of the flammability of 151 proof rum and reduce the frequency of this potentially disfiguring and fatal burn injury.

Reference Number: 60609

DE MOULIN, D. "Spontaneous Combustion: An Odd Chapter in the History of Burns." *Archives Chirurgicum Neeland*, 27: 223–227, 1975 (2 figures, 17 references)

Abstract: A brief history of the theory of spontaneous combustion of humans is presented. In the early nineteenth century few people doubted the possibility of igniting spontaneously as a result of chronic alcohol abuse.

> The alcohol, enjoyed in quantity for years had apparently made the body extremely combustible. Exceptionally, the combustion was incomplete, and the victim survived the accident for a few days. The frightening

prospect of flaming death was eagerly evoked by zealous members of the temperance movement in first half of the last century.

Reference Number: 60610

LEVI-FAICT, T.W. AND G. QUATREHOMME. "So-Called Spontaneous Human Combustion." *Journal of Forensic Sciences*, 56: 1334–1339, 2011 (1 table, 4 figures, 38 references)

Abstract: A forty-seven-year-old male alcoholic was found dead in the middle of a room in his house in the prone position. His body was partially carbonized. The middle section of the body was reduced to ashes, but the extremities were virtually intact. The postmortem BAC was 0.320 g/100 mL and the VHAC was 0.300 g/100 mL. No significant postmortem blood COHb concentrations were detected. The objects surrounding the body, including newspaper, wood, straw, and alcohol bottles, were virtually intact. It is suggested that spontaneous human combustion (SHC) should be referred to as isolated body combustion or isolated central body combustion. A short history of SHC is presented.

So-called Spontaneous Human Combustion is not spontaneous but needs a source of heat near the body. Typically, it affects elderly, overweight alcoholic Caucasian (Western Europe and North American) women. Only parts of the body are reduced to ashes, including bones, whereas other parts are stunningly well or totally preserved. The immediate vicinity of the victim is nearly intact. The cause of death is nearly always natural and burning of the body usually occurs after death. Frequently (but not always) there is a high blood alcohol concentration. There is no evidence of assault or foul play. The main forensic issue is to rule out a criminal behavior.

Reference Number: 60611

BRUCK, D., M. BALL, AND I.R. THOMAS. "Fire Fatality and Alcohol Intake: Analysis of Key Risk Factors." *Journal of Studies on Alcohol and Drugs*, 72: 731–736, 2011 (2 tables, 28 references)

Abstract: The BACs and other characteristics were determined in sixty-four male and thirty-one female adult fatal fire victims who died in Victoria, Australia, between 1998 and 2006. Fifty-five (58%) victims had a positive BAC (mean 0.220 g/100 mL, range 0.060 to 0.410 g/100 mL). Male fire victims were three times more likely to have a positive BAC than female fire victims. There was a higher likelihood of the smoke alarm being activated for alcohol positive than alcohol negative fire victims. Alcohol significantly reduces the likelihood of waking to a smoke alarm. It is recommended that a 520 Hz square wave alarm should replace the 3000+ Hz pure sound fire alarm as it would awaken more alcohol-intoxicated persons.

> A new finding is that the alcohol-affected fire fatalities were significantly less likely to have a condition preventing escape than a sober fatality. This is important information because it suggests that the risk of dying in a fire for the alcohol-affected people who are capable of being alerted and physically capable of escape, may be reduced if they can be alerted more quickly.

Reference Number: 60612

HAWKINS, E.R. AND J.H. BRICE. "Fire Jumpers: Description of Burns and Traumatic Injuries From a Spontaneous Mass Gathering and Celebratory Riot." *Journal of Emergency Medicine*, 38: 182–187, 2010 (1 table, 1 figure, 20 references)

Abstract: On 3 and 5 April, 2005, approximately 52,000 people gathered in Chapel Hill, North Carolina, to celebrate their collegiate basketball team victories. The partying intensified into a celebratory riot with large amounts of alcohol consumed and dozens of bonfires lit. A total of thirty-two male and seventeen female celebrants required medical treatment. The average age of those treated was 23.8 years (range eighteen to seventy-two years) and 65% consumed alcohol. Nearly 30% of those presenting at hospital had burns associated with fire jumping.

Table. Diagnosis of Celebrants Requiring Medical Treatment

Diagnosis	Percent
Burn	28%
Laceration	27%
Alcohol intoxication	14%
General musculoskeletal injury	18%
Fracture	8%
Subdural hematoma	12%

Source: Adapted from Hawkins et al (2010).

This report serves to increase awareness among emergency physicians and EMS personnel, especially those in college towns of injuries from similar spontaneous mass gatherings and celebratory riots in response to outcomes of their local sports teams. In addition to common musculoskeletal and medical complaints, we found a higher than expected number of celebratory fire jumping and bonfire associated injuries. Educational efforts aimed at college students before scheduled sports events should disclose the potential for such injuries and discourage this behavior. Finally, officials responsible for planning for mass-gathering events should have location-specific response plans and should practice those plans on a regular basis to ensure familiarity and efficiency of response when needed.

6.07 FLYING

"In any case, the results of the present studies do not support the idea that BAC values under 0.04% are safe in flight. Apparently even a quite low BAC can result in pilot errors under circumstances that, while may differ from pilot to pilot are likely to occur under difficult flight conditions."

—Ross et al, "Pilot Performance with Blood Alcohol Concentrations Below 0.04%" (1992)

"A JetBlue pilot was removed from the cockpit of a Fort Lauderdale-bound flight by police at Buffalo Niagara International Airport in New York on Wednesday after registering a blood-alcohol level of 0.17%, more than four times the Federal Aviation Administration's limit of 0.04%."

—Jeff Dean, NPR, 2 March 2022

Impairment of ability to fly an airplane generally occurs at lower BACs than for driving a car, as shown in flight simulator studies (60701–60705) and actual flying (60706). Simulated altitude did not affect BACs or cause significant synergistic effects with alcohol (60708).

The prevalence of alcohol violations by safety sensitive employees of major American airlines was 0.03% for the flight crew and 0.19% for air traffic controllers (60709).

Case reports are presented of twenty-three pilots with positive BACs who died in civil aviation accidents between 2000 and 2007, and of a pilot who was involved in a motor vehicle collision with a BAC of 0.105 g/10mL regarding FAA medical certificates (60711).

Reference Number: 60701

SMITH, F.J. AND D. HARRIS. "Effects of Low Blood Alcohol Levels on Pilots' Prioritization of Tasks During a Radio Navigation Task." *International Journal Aviation Psychology*, 4: 349–358, 1994 (1 table, 24 references)

Abstract: Eight male pilots (mean age thirty-seven years) flew a 40-minute cross-country, radio navigation task on an Aerosoft 2000 flight simulator. Four pilots consumed alcohol within 10 minutes. BrACs were determined with a Lion Alcometer S-D2. The overall mean BrAC was 0.021 g/100 mL.

> Pilots' radio communication performance was found to be significantly impaired at a mean BAL of 20.63 mg%. Flying and navigation performance were not significantly impaired. These findings are consistent with the hypothesis that as the task demands exceed pilot available processing capacity, decrements were most likely in lower priority tasks. Radio communication is the task of lowest priority in the task hierarchy of aviate, navigate, communicate.

Reference Number: 60702

ROSS, L.E. AND J.C. MUNDT. "Multiattribute Modeling Analysis of the Effects of a Low Blood Alcohol Level on Pilot Performance." *Human Factors*, 30: 293–304, 1988 (2 tables, 1 figure, 10 references)

Abstract: Twelve male pilots consumed a placebo or 0.5 g/kg ethanol over 25 minutes. A maintenance dose of 0.062 g/kg ethanol was given 25 minutes later, just prior to testing in an ATC 610 flight simulator. BrACs were determined by an Intoxilyzer Model 5000 and the mean BrAC was 0.043 g/100 mL (range 0.036–0.048 g/100 mL). Four different task segments were identified: VOR tracking, vectoring, descent, and collision avoidance.

> Decrements in pilot performance such as were found in this study may not routinely place an aircraft in imminent risk of an accident, but the margin of safety would be reduced and under circumstances of increased demands on the pilot, it is highly likely that the probability of an accident would be increased significantly.

Reference Number: 60703

ROSS, L.E., L.M. YEAZEL, AND A.W. CHAU. "Pilot Performance with Blood Alcohol Concentrations Below 0.04%." *Aviation, Space Environmental Medicine*, 63: 951–956, 1992 (1 table, 4 figures, 3 references)

Abstract: Thirty-six male pilots were tested on a flight simulator under four different flight scenarios, with and without alcohol. The pilots consumed 150 mL of alcohol or placebo within 25 minutes and were given a maintenance dose of 0.062 g/kg ethanol to maintain the BrAC. The mean BrACs as determined by an Alco-Sensor III were 0.024–0.039 g/100 mL.

> In any case, the results of the present studies do not support the idea that BAC values under 0.04% are safe in flight. Apparently even a quite low BAC can result in pilot errors under circumstances that, while may differ from pilot to pilot are likely to occur under difficult flight conditions.

Reference Number: 60704

BILLINGS, C.E., T. DEMOSTHENES, T.R. WHITE, AND D. O'HARA. "Effects of Alcohol on Pilot Performance in Simulated Flight." *Aviation, Space Environmental Medicine*, 62: 233–235, 1991 (8 tables, 29 references)

Abstract: Four air carrier pilots consumed a placebo or alcohol to obtain BACs of 0, 0.025, 0.050, or 0.075 g/100 mL. BrACs were determined by an Intoxilyzer. Subjects were then tested on a 727-flight simulator.

> Piloting performance in simulated flight in a Boeing 727 simulator evaluated by observation of discrete errors, was linearly and inversely correlated with blood alcohol concentration. Serious errors increased under the influence of as little as 0.025% blood alcohol. The results of this study do not differ materially from those of a previous study of alcohol effects in actual flight in much simpler aircraft.

Reference Number: 60705

MORROW, D., J. YESAVAGE, V. LEIRER, N. DOLHERT, J. TAYLOR, AND J. TINKLENBERG, J. "The Time-Course of Alcohol Impairment of General Aviation Pilot Performance in a Frasca 141 Simulator." *Aviation Space Environmental Medicine*, 64: 697–705, 1993 (8 tables, 29 references)

Abstract: Fourteen younger pilots (mean age twenty-six years) and fourteen older pilots (mean age thirty-eight years) consumed a placebo or alcohol (to obtain a BrAC of 0.100 g/100 mL) and were tested at 0, 2, 4, 8, 24, and 48 hours later on a flight simulator. BrACs were determined with an Alco-Sensor III. The mean BrACs were 0.071 g/100 mL (2 hours), 0.042 g/100 mL (4 hours), and 0 at 8 hours, showing a mean rate of alcohol elimination of approximately 0.015 g/100 mL/h. Flying performance was impaired for up to 8 hours (even when the BrAC was zero).

> Second, we found that alcohol (and pilot age) increased variability in performance. While increased variability reduces the sensitivity of statistical tests of mean differences in performance between conditions, it may also be an important finding in itself. Increased variability in performance during alcohol sessions suggests that some pilots are more susceptible to carry over effects of alcohol on flying performance.

Reference Number: 60706

WICK, R.L. "Alcohol and Pilot Performance Decrements." *Alcohol, Drugs and Driving,* 8: 207–215, 1992 (4 figures, 20 references)

Abstract: A study was conducted of the effect of alcohol on the flying ability of experienced and inexperienced pilots. Tests were conducted in a Cessna 172 for an instrumented night landing at an airport in Columbus, Ohio. Pilots flew at BACs of 0, 0.040, 0.080 and 0.120 g/100 mL. The author, also a pilot, was in the seat of the Cessna next to the subject and could correct major errors in the airplane. The inexperienced pilots had a greater decrement in flying ability than the experienced pilots.

Table. Major Procedural Error Frequency in Experienced and Inexperienced Pilots at BACs of 0, 0.04, 0.08, and 0.12 g/100 mL

	BAC			
	0.0	0.04 g/100 mL	0.08 g/100 mL	0.12 g/100 mL
Experienced Pilots	4	18	30	52
Inexperienced Pilots	30	45	65	78

Source: Adapted from Wick (1992).

> The data show degraded performance at all alcohol levels investigated. Because alcohol is a depressant i.e., a sedative drug, performance degradation may be viewed as a continuum. In other words, there is no reason to think that blood alcohol levels less than 0.04% are safe or satisfactory for flying.

Reference Number: 60707

LI, G., S.P. BAKER, M.W. LAMB, Y. QIANG, AND M.L. MCCARTHY. "Characteristics of Alcohol-Related Fatal General Aviation Crashes." *Accident Analysis and Prevention*, 37: 143–148, 2005 (4 tables, 33 references)

Abstract: A study was conducted of 233 fatally injured pilots in general aviation accidents in Maryland, New Mexico, and North Carolina who died between 1985 and 2000. Twenty-five pilots (11%) had a positive BAC and fifteen (6%) had a BAC > 0.040 g/100 mL. The mean BAC was 0.075 g/100 mL and the highest BAC was 0.136 g/100 mL. A positive BAC (> 0.020 g/100 mL) was associated with more nighttime crashes (18% versus 6%). Alcohol-related aviation crashes were more likely to involve flying under visual flight rules (VFR) into cloudy weather (i.e., instrument meteorological conditions) (64% versus 41%). Pilot error was a contributing factor for all alcohol-related crashes and 96% of all crashes.

The heightened involvement of alcohol in nighttime crashes which has been reported in previous studies may reflect the fact that alcohol is often consumed in the evening with supper and implies that preventative efforts should target night flights.

Reference Number: 60708

COLLINS, W.E., H.W. MERTENS, AND E.A. HIGGINS. "Some Effects of Alcohol and Simulated Altitude on Complex Performance Scores and Breathalyzer Readings." *Aviation, Space Environmental Medicine*, 58: 328–332, 1987 (2 tables, 2 figures, 11 references)

Abstract: Seventeen male subjects consumed a placebo or 2.2 mL/kg of vodka (50% v/v alcohol) over 20 minutes on four separate occasions. BrACs were determined with an Omicron Intoxilyzer. Subjects performed seven tasks in the Multiple Task Performance Battery and wore an oxygen mask providing either gas at ground level or simulated altitude of 12,500 ft (13.5% O_2, 86.5% N_2). The mean BrACs were virtually identical for either ground level or simulated altitude (i.e., 0.077 and 0.078 g/100 mL respectively).

In this study, the ingestion of alcohol resulted in significant impairment in complex performance tasks for the first 3–4h after the drinking period. As a separate effect, the simulated altitude of 12,500 ft (3,810m) produced a smaller but statistically significant decrement in performance skills under both placebo and alcohol conditions. Thus, performance was adversely affected both by altitude and by alcohol but there was no synergistic interaction between the two. Moreover, the breathalyzer readings showed no difference between ground and simulated altitude conditions.

Reference Number: 60709

LI, G., S.P. BAKER, Y. QIANG, G.W. REBOK, AND M.L. MCCARTHY. "Alcohol Violations and Aviation Accidents: Findings from the U.S. Mandatory Alcohol Testing Program." *Aviation, Space, Environmental Medicine*, 78(5): 510–513, 2007 (1 table, 1 figure, 14 references)

Abstract: Between 1995 and 2002 the major airlines reported a total of 511,745 random alcohol tests to the FAA of which 329 had a BAC > 0.040 g/100 mL and 111 refused, resulting in an overall prevalence rate of 0.09%. The prevalence rate varied from 0.03% for flight crews to 0.19% for non-federally employed air traffic controllers. Alcohol violations were associated with a 2.56 times risk of accident involvement (although not statistically significant) and were attributable to 0.13% of aviation accidents.

Table. Prevalence of Alcohol Violations by Occupation Among US Major Airline Employees with Safety-Sensitive Functions, 1995–2002

Occupation	Percent Violations
Flight Crew	0.03%
Flight Attendants	0.06%
Maintenance Personnel	0.09%
Aviation Screeners	0.07%
Air Traffic Controllers	0.19%

Source: Adapted from Li et al (2007).

The heightened relative risk of accident involvement accorded to alcohol violations suggests alcohol misuse appears to be a valid risk factor for aviation accidents. The tiny population attributable risk of alcohol violations indicates that, in reality, alcohol misuse as a contributing factor has been virtually eradicated from US major airline accidents. The FAA's alcohol misuse prevention program is likely to have played a role in effectively maintaining the prevalence of alcohol violations in aviation employees at very low levels and minimizing alcohol involvement in aviation accidents.

Reference Number: 60710

BOTCH, S.R. AND R.D. JOHNSON. "Alcohol-Related Aviation Accidents Involving Pilots with Previous Alcohol Offenses." *DOT/FAA/AM-08/22,* Office of Aerospace Medicine, 8pp, Final Report, October 2008 (1 table, 7 references)

Abstract: A study was conducted of twenty-three pilots who died between 2000 and 2007 in civil aviation accidents in the United States and had a positive BAC and previous alcohol/drug offenses.

Table. The Postmortem BAC and National Transportation Safety Board Findings of Various Pilots Killed in Fatal Civil Aviation Accidents

Pilot Number	Postmortem BAC (g/100 mL)	NTSB Findings
2	0.124	The pilot's misjudgment of his altitude and distance from the airport was due to impairment by alcohol
6	0.171	Physical impairment due to alcohol was a factor.
8	0.054	Contributing factors were the pilot's impairment due to alcohol.
10	0.365	The pilot's misjudged distance and speed that led to a long landing and his inadequate recovery, from a bounced landing, all due to the effects of impairment from alcohol consumption, which resulted in an in-flight collision with terrain during an aborted landing attempt. A contributing factor was the Federal Aviation Administration's failure to identify existing evidence of substance (alcohol) dependence in the pilot due to an inadequate and incomplete process of screening medical applications.
11	0.061	Factors in the accident were the pilot's ostentatious display and impairment due to alcohol.
16	0.373	The pilot's failure to maintain aircraft control due to the effects of impairment from alcohol consumption. A contributing factor was the Federal Aviation Administration's failure to identify existing evidence of substance (alcohol) dependence in this commercial pilot due to an inadequate and incomplete process of screening medical applications.

Source: Adapted from Botch and Johnson (2008).

The number of pilots involved in aviation accidents from 2000 to 2007 who have a history of alcohol offences accounted for 9% (215 of 2391) of the aviation accidents during that time period that were received at CAMI for toxicological analysis. Of the pilots with previous alcohol offenses 11% (23 of 215) had consumed ethanol prior to the fatal incident. Providing more detailed documentation to Aviation Medical Examiners to aid in the determination of eligibility for medical certification is important and could potentially save the lives of pilots, their passengers, and people on the ground. Additionally, identifying pilots with substance abuse problems is not only paramount for providing a safe environment to fly but also benefits pilots who may not have previously addressed these issues.

Reference Number: 60711

JACOBSON, M.D. "Alcohol-Related Motor Vehicle Encounter with a Cow." *The Federal Air Surgeon's Medical Bulletin*, 53: 8–9, 2015 (9 references)

Abstract: A forty-year-old male first class pilot with 900 total flying hours was driving a motor vehicle alone at night when he hit a cow, which triggered his airbag. He lost consciousness briefly and was hospitalized for 3 days. His BAC at the ER was 0.105 g/100 mL. Each time a pilot applies to the FAA for a medical certificate, they must acknowledge (Block 18V) arrests, convictions, or administrative actions in regard to a DUI. Since no legal BAC was conducted in this case, he was not required to report the accident. More than 32,000 aviators with a history of drug/alcohol abuse or dependence currently hold FAA medical certificates.

Due to the blood alcohol level, his airline employer requested a formal evaluation for alcohol/substance disorder. A substance abuse professional reported that the airman had a history of controlled alcohol use without consequent legal issues or offences. Since the airman did not meet DSM-IV criteria for alcohol dependence, the substance abuse profession's findings were inconclusive, and a recommendation of total abstinence from alcohol was rendered.

6.08 HANGOVER (VEISALGIA)

"It's not a hangover. It's wine flu.

—Owls Quotes

"A hangover is just your body telling you that you are an idiot."

—Unknown

The scientific name for a hangover is "veisalgia," which comes from the Norwegian "kveis" which means "uneasiness following debauchery" and the Greek "algia" which means "pain" (60812).

Hangover symptoms typically occur 8 to 16 hours after drinking ceased (60801, 60810) and may be related to methanol (60804, 60805, 60811), which forms while the alcohol blocks the liver enzymes that metabolize methanol. Once the alcohol is eliminated, the liver enzymes then metabolize methanol forming toxic formaldehyde and formic acid. As such, the hangover effects may be mitigated by additional alcohol consumption in the morning of the hangover, known as an "eyeopener" or "hair of the dog" (60805, 60806), which will prevent further formaldehyde from being produced. However, the consumption of alcohol in the morning to relieve a hangover is a CAGE symptom of alcohol dependence (i.e., the "E" of the acronym).

Other hangover cures appear to be of little value (60807, 60808). Hangover may cause impairment of some aspects related to driving even when the BACs are zero (60802, 60809, 60810). Some of the symptoms of hangover are:

- Thirst
- Tiredness
- Headache
- Dizziness or faintness
- Nausea
- Stomach ache
- Racing heart
- Loss of appetite

Hangovers may serve as a protective factor against chronic excessive alcohol consumption (60803).

Subjective intoxication and sleep quality were stronger predictors of hangover than BAC (60813) or UAC (60814).

Subjects with hangover and a zero BrAC have increased reaction time and impaired selective attention compared to the control groups, but not all subjects with hangover had impaired driving abilities (60815, 60816).

Reference Number: 60801

HOWLAND, J., D.J. ROHSENOW, D, ALLENSWORTH-DAVIES, J. GREECE, A. ALMEIDA, S.J. MINSKY, J.T. ARNEDT, AND J. HERMOS. "The Incidence and Severity of Hangover the Morning After Moderate Alcohol Intoxication." *Addiction*, 103: 758–765, 2008 (3 tables, 49 references)

Abstract: One hundred and seventy-two subjects consumed in the evening either a placebo, beer (7.2% v/v alcohol), bourbon (40% v/v alcohol), or vodka (40% v/v alcohol) over approximately 1.5 hours. The mean BrAC obtained was 0.110 g/100 mL. The subjects then slept for approximately 8 hours and the presence and intensity of the hangover were determined the next morning at 7:00 a.m. In the placebo conditions, 97% reported no hangover and 3% reported a mild hangover. In the alcohol condition, 24% reported no hangover, 44% reported a mild hangover, and 32% reported a moderate hangover. The OR of hangover was 1.41× for bourbon and 0.85× for beer compared to vodka.

> Our findings on the propensity for hangover, the findings from the previous experimental study and those from surveys of drinkers suggest that 25%–30% of drinkers may be resistant to hangover.

Reference Number: 60802

FINNIGAN, F., D. SCHULZE, J. SMALLWOOD, AND A. HELANDER. "The Effects of Self-Administered Alcohol-Induced Hangover in a Naturalistic Setting on Psychomotor and Cognitive Performance and Subjective State." *Addiction*, 100: 1680–1689, 2005 (3 tables, 2 figures, 38 references)

Abstract: Thirty-five female and thirty-six male subjects (mean age twenty-five years) were divided into hangover and control groups. Both groups were tested on various psychomotor and cognitive tests such as simple vigilance and probe-memory recall. The hangover group would telephone the experimenter when they had a night of heavy drinking and would be tested in the morning. BrACs were determined with a Lion SD 400P alcometer. Fourteen (40%) of the hangover subjects had a positive BrAC (range 0.002–0.124 g/100 mL) the next morning and were analyzed separately. All hangover subjects reported hangover symptoms such as headache, nausea, and fatigue.

In summary, the findings presented here show clear acute and hangover effects on psychomotor tasks but not on more demanding cognitive tasks.

Reference Number: 60803

WALL, T.L., S.M. HORN, M.L. JOHNSON, T.L. SMITH, AND L.G. CARR. "Hangover Symptoms in Asian Americans with Variations in the Aldehyde Dehydrogenase (ALDH2) Gene." *Journal of Studies on Alcohol,* 61: 13–17, 2000 (2 tables, 27 references)

Abstract: Eighty-two female and fifty-eight male students (ages twenty-one to twenty-six years) of Chinese, Japanese, and Korean descent were surveyed as to drinking history and severity of hangovers. Blood samples were also collected and the ALDH2 genotypes were determined. ALDH2*2 homozygotes have been found to experience extreme reactions, including nausea and vomiting, after moderate alcohol ingestion. ALDH2*2 heterozygotes have reported less severe reactions but still have unpleasant responses (such as facial flushing) to moderate alcohol consumption. Seventeen of the students were removed from the analysis as they had not consumed any alcohol within the past 6 months.

In summary, results demonstrated that Asian Americans with ALDH2*2 alleles estimated more severe hangovers, with a similar but non-significant trend toward more frequent hangover symptoms. These findings suggest that hangovers may serve as a potential protective factor in the development of excessive or problematic drinking in this population; however, additional research regarding hangover is needed.

Reference Number: 60804

BENDTSEN, P., A.W. JONES, AND A. HELANDER. "Urinary Excretion of Methanol and 5-Hydroxytryptophol as Biochemical Markers of Recent Drinking in the Hangover State." *Alcohol and Alcoholism*, 33: 431–438, 1998 (2 tables, 1 figure, 35 references)

Abstract: Nine female and eleven male social drinkers (mean age thirty-nine years) consumed either 50 or 80 g of ethanol as white wine (11% v/v alcohol) or beer (5.2% v/v alcohol) over 2 hours with a meal. BrACs were determined 15 minutes after the end of drinking and several times in the next morning by an Alcolmeter S-D2. Urine samples were collected after drinking, before bedtime, and several times in the morning. Urine methanol, 5-HTOL, and 5HIAA were determined. The UMC was on average 0.077 mg/100 mL (pre-drinking) and 0.306 mg/dL and 0.506 mg/dL the next morning for the 50 and 80 g dose respectively. The 5HTOL and 5HIAA ratio was 6.36 pre-drinking, and 134 and 296 in the morning for the 50 and 80 g dose respectively. Mild hangover symptoms occurred after consuming 50 g and increased after consuming 80 g.

Since the peak of methanol excretion in the urine coincides with the time when hangover symptoms are worse, it has been suggested that methanol or metabolites thereof, play a role in the development of hangover. This is further supported by observations that alcoholic beverages rich in methanol, such as brandy, whisky, and red wine, cause more severe hangover symptoms than equivalent doses of pure ethanol.

Reference Number: 60805

JONES, A.W. "Elimination Half-Life of Methanol During Hangover." *Pharmacology and Toxicology*, 60: 217–220, 1987 (1 figure, 29 references)

Abstract: Four subjects consumed 1–1.5 L of red wine (9.5 g/100 mL ethanol and 100 mg/L methanol). Breath ethanol and methanol concentrations were measured by GC. The BBR for methanol was 3,231:1. After the BAC dropped below the KM of ADH (0.010 g /100 mL), the $t_{1/2}$ of methanol was 213, 110, 133 and 142 minutes in the four subjects respectively.

It is generally known that the consumption of alcoholic beverages rich is congeners (including methanol) causes more severe hangover than equivalent doses of pure ethanol or vodka. The most effective treatment for hangover, at least for short periods is to drink more ethanol. The resulting increase in blood ethanol may serve to block the conversion of methanol into formaldehyde and formic acid.

Reference Number: 60806

HOON, J.R. "Hair of the Dog." *Journal of the American Medical Association*, 229: 184–185, 1974 (4 figures, 2 references)

Abstract: Two male subjects suffering from severe hangovers in the morning were administered 1.5 oz. of an alcoholic beverage (40% v/v). A gastrocamera took pictures of the stomach before and after the administration of alcohol. There was a remarkable calming of the stomach after the alcohol consumption.

I do not advocate morning drinking; I merely point out that in the two subjects presented it worked to relieve suffering (and I have some gastrocamera photographic evidence of this point).

Reference Number: 60807

PITTLER, M.H., A.R. WHITE, C. STEVINSON, AND E. ERNST. "Effectiveness of Artichoke Extract in Preventing Alcohol-Induced Hangovers: A Randomized Controlled Trial." *Canadian Medical Association Journal*, 169: 1269–1273, 2003 (2 tables, 1 figure, 26 references)

Abstract: Five men and ten women were randomly allocated to receive the artichoke extract or placebo and then a crossover after a 1-week washout period. The subjects drank between 3.3 to 15.9 units of alcohol after consuming the extract/placebo and subjectively rated their hangover scores the next morning (10 hours later). The mean scores for the overall hangover rating and the individual hangover symptoms did not differ significantly between artichoke or placebo treatments.

These data suggest that artichoke extract does not prevent the signs and symptoms of alcohol-induced hangover over and above placebo. There are also some indications that artichoke extract does not speed up recovery time. The discrepancy between the data from our randomized controlled trial and other information may be seen as a reminder of the power of expectations and make-believe.

Reference Number: 60808

WIESE, J., S. MCPHERSON, M.C. ODDEN, AND M.G. SHLIPAK. "Effect of Opuntia ficus indica on Symptoms of the Alcohol Hangover." *Archives Internal Medicine*, 164: 1334–1340, 2004 (4 tables, 3 figures, 47 references)

Abstract: Thirty-two female and twenty-two male subjects (mean age twenty-seven years) consumed a placebo or 1600 IU of *Opuntia ficus indicia* (OFI) and then consumed up to 1.75 g/kg alcohol within 4 hours. The alcohol consumed included vodka, gin, and rum (low congener containing), and bourbon, scotch, and tequila (high congener containing). The same type of alcoholic beverage was consumed for both placebo and drug conditions. BrACs were determined with an Alco-Sensor IV 1 hour after drinking ceased. The mean BrACs were 0.131 g/100 mL (placebo) and 0.124 g/100 mL (OFI). Hangover (veisalgia) symptoms were measured at 10:00 a.m. the next morning. Various measurements of hangover were determined as well as C-reactive protein and serum electrolytes in the blood sample collected in the morning. BrACs were all < 0.001 g/100 mL in the morning. The subjects who consumed the high congener alcoholic beverage had more severe hangover symptoms. The congeners may contribute to hangover by contributing to the inflammatory response. CRP levels were elevated during hangover, which indicate inflammation may play a role in hangover. OFI is an extract from the skin of the prickly pear fruit and has been shown to decrease oxidative injury.

> In this randomized, placebo-controlled, crossover trial, we found hangover symptoms severity to be moderately reduced by an extract of the prickly pear plant Opuntia ficus indica. This effect was observed chiefly through the reduction in the symptoms of nausea, dry mouth, and anorexia.

Reference Number: 60809

ANDERSON, S. AND J. DAWSON. "Neurophysiological Correlates of Alcoholic Hangover." *South African Journal of Science*, 95: 145–147, 1999 (2 tables, 2 figures, 13 references)

Abstract: Eight female and eight male subjects (ages nineteen to twenty-four years) had various psychomotor tests conducted before and 12 to 16 hours after consumption of 1 g/kg alcohol. The control group consisted of five male and five female subjects (ages nineteen to twenty-four years). Hangover-induced impairment was found even when the BAC was zero.

> What are the implications of our preliminary findings? Of concern is the possibility that an individual with hangover could remain compromised for 16 or more hours following cessation of alcohol intake. Certainly, the presence of even mild, neurophysiological impairment in individuals with hangover could have serious ramifications for those who make heavy demands on attentional resources in pursuit of recreational or occupational interests.

Reference Number: 60810

KIM, D-J., S-J. YOON, H-P. LEE, B-M. CHOI, AND H.J. GO. "The Effects of Alcohol Hangover on Cognitive Functions in Healthy Subjects." *International Journal of Neuroscience*, 113: 581–594, 2003 (4 tables, 30 references)

Abstract: Thirteen male social drinkers (ages twenty to twenty-nine years) consumed 1.5 g/kg alcohol within 30 minutes at 7:00 p.m. and slept from 11:00 p.m. to 7:00 a.m. the following morning. Various neuropsychological tests were conducted before the consumption of alcohol and at 8:00 a.m. the morning after the consumption of alcohol. BACs were determined using an enzymatic method. The mean BACs were 0.004 g/100 mL before the consumption of alcohol, 0.075 g/100 mL 1 hour after the consumption of alcohol, and 0.007 g/100 mL the following morning (13 hours after alcohol consumption). The mean subjective hangover score was 2 before alcohol consumption and 8 during the hangover state. A hangover is characterized by the constellation of unpleasant physical and mental symptoms that occur between 8 and 16 hours after drinking.

> According to the results of the present study there was no change in simple motor function including motor, rhythm, and tactile functions. Also, there was no change in simple speech functions including receptive speech, expressive speech, writing, reading and arithmetic functions during hangover state. However, those functions measured by visual acuity, memory, and intellectual process subscale were decreased significantly during experimentally induced hangover state.

Reference Number: 60811

RODDA, L.N., J. BEYER, D. GEROSTAMOULOS, AND O.H. DRUMMER. "Alcohol Congener Analysis and the Source of Alcohol: A Review." *Forensic Science, Medicine, and Pathology,* 9: 194–207, 2013 (2 tables, 154 references)

Abstract: An extensive review was conducted on the medicolegal and forensic value of alcohol congener analysis (ACA). Beer and spirits contain about 800 congeners, whereas wine has approximately 600 congeners. It is recommended that blood for the congener analysis of drinking drivers to determine the validity of a hipflask defense should be collected within 1 to 3 hours of cessation of drinking and a BAC of > 0.08 g/100 mL must be present. The following table lists the concentration of some congeners found in common alcoholic beverages.

Table. Congener Concentration of Methyl, N-butyl, and Iso-butyl Alcohols in Mg/Standard Drink and Type of Alcoholic Beverage

	Concentration (mg/std drink)		
Alcoholic Beverage	Methyl alcohol	n-Butyl alcohol	Iso-butyl alcohol
Beer	3–7	0–2	2–28
Wine	1–14	0–<1	2–10
Fortified Wine	8–21	<1–1	4–6
Brandy	60–153	0–12	2–14
Whiskey	<1–11	0–<1	<1–16
Rum	<1–4	0	<1–15
Vodka	0–5	<1	<1–5

Source: Adapted from Rodda et al (2013).

Fermentation by-product ACA is a technique used in Germany to investigate after-drinking defense claims by examining the feasibility of the claimed alcoholic beverage consumption. This review expresses concerns surrounding the current ACA approach due to limitations, uncertainties, the difficult nature of carrying out the evaluation, varying methodologies used by experts and the limited knowledge of the variations in pharmacokinetics of these congeners in humans. For example, many of the fermentative by-product congeners can either be produced endogenously, by bacterial putrefaction during storage, or obtained from sources other than the consumption of the claimed alcoholic beverage.

Reference Number: 60812

WIESE, J.G., M.G. SHILPAK, AND W.S. BROWNER. "The Alcohol Hangover." *Annals of Internal Medicine,* 132: 897–902, 2000 (3 tables, 63 references)

Abstract: In this review, a literature search was conducted on MEDLINE between 1965 and 1999 and found more than 4,700 studies had been published on the effects of alcohol, but only 108 on hangover. The scientific name for hangover is veisalgia (from *kveis*: Norwegian meaning "uneasiness following debauchery" and the Greek *algia*, meaning "pain"). Common symptoms are listed in the table. Hangover may be due to acetaldehyde, congeners, dehydration, or other hormonal changes.

Table. Symptoms of Hangover and Percent of Persons Affected

Symptom	Percent Persons Affected
Headache	66%
Feeling poor	60%
Diarrhea	36%
Loss of appetite	21%
Tremulousness	20%
Fatigue	20%
Nausea	9%

Source: Adapted from Wiese et al (2000).

For the patient with occasional hangovers, recommended interventions include the discussion of potential therapies for alcohol hangover (adequate hydration) and a reminder that 1.5 g/kg of alcohol (approximately 5 to 6 drinks for an 80-kg man and 3 to 5 drinks for a 60-kg woman) will almost always lead to hangover. Patients should also be educated about the physiologic effects of hangover. Most patients understand the impairment inherent in acute alcohol intoxication, but few appreciate the cognitive and visual-spatial impairment that may accompany alcohol hangover. Patients who work with heavy equipment or are involved in transportation should be warned of the potential hazards.

Reference Number: 60813

VERSTER, J.C., L.D. KRUISSELBRINK, K.A. SLOT, ET AL. "Sensitivity to Experiencing Alcohol Hangovers: Reconsideration of the 0.11% Blood Alcohol Concentration (BAC) Threshold for Having a Hangover." *Journal of Clinical Medicine,* 9: 179, 7pp, 2020 (1 table, 2 figures, 25 references)

Abstract: A hangover is a combination of mental and physical symptoms such as nausea and headache, which occurs the day after a single episode of heavy drinking, which occurs when the BAC approaches zero. The Alcohol Hangover Research Group states that a 0.11% BAC is the threshold for having a hangover. In this study, the strongest predictors of hangover were subjective intoxication (48.5%), sleep quality (7.2%), and estimated BAC (1.2%).

Taken together, the research reviewed here suggests that the level of subjective intoxication and the increase in alcohol consumption relative to a regular drinking occasion are stronger predictors of next-day hangover severity than (estimated) BAC. Furthermore, a substantial number of alcohol drinkers experience hangover symptoms at BAC levels well below 0.11%. Therefore, we argue that the current consensus regarding the BAC 0.11% threshold value as a criterion for having a hangover should be abandoned.

Reference Number: 60814

VAN DE LOO, M.M., G. KORTE-BOUWS, K. BROOKHUIS, J. GARSSEN, AND J. VERSTER. "Urine Ethanol Concentration and Alcohol Hangover Severity." *Psychopharmacology*, 234: 73–77, 2017 (2 tables, 11 references)

Abstract: Thirty-six social drinkers (ages eighteen to thirty years) were divided into a group of eighteen who claimed they regularly had hangovers and a group of eighteen who claimed they never had hangovers. Urine samples were collected the morning after the subjects consumed no alcohol or enough alcohol to produce a calculated BAC of over 0.080 g/100 mL. Both groups consumed the same amount of alcohol, on average approximately eleven to twelve drinks. UACs were determined by direct injection GC. The mean UACs were 0.0003 g/100 mL after no alcohol and 0.0185 g/100 mL after alcohol consumption for the hangover group and 0.0001 g/100 mL and 0.0034 g/100 mL for the no hangover group respectively. There was a significant correlation between UAC and hangover symptom in the hangover group but no correlation in the hangover immune group.

Next day urine ethanol concentration was significantly higher on hangover day compared to control day. Also, urine ethanol concentration was significantly higher in the hangover group when compared to the hangover immune group. In the hangover-immune group none of the correlations of urine ethanol concentration with individual hangover symptoms was significant. In contrast, in the hangover group, significant correlations were found with a variety of hangover symptoms, including nausea, headache, concentration problems, regret, sleepiness, shaking, weakness, dizziness, sweating, confusion, thirst, heart racing and sleep problems.

Reference Number: 60815

DEVENNEY, L.E., K.B. COYLE, AND J.C. VERSTER. "Memory and Attention During an Alcohol Hangover." *Human Psychopharmacology Clinical and Experimental*, 34: e2701, 7pp, 2019 (3 tables, 44 references)

Abstract: An alcohol hangover can be defined as the combination of mental and physical symptoms that are experienced the day after an episode of heavy alcohol consumption as the BAC approaches zero. Thirty-nine male and thirty-five female drinkers (mean age 22.4 and 25.1 years respectively) were divided into a hangover group and a control group. The hangover group had consumed a mean of 13.8 units of alcohol the night before, whereas the control group had consumed no alcoholic beverages. The subjects were tested on various cognitive tests including selective attention, divided attention, and mood, between 9:00 a.m. and 11:30 a.m. the next morning. All subjects had a zero BrAC when tested.

The hangover group had increased reaction times compared with the control group. Selective attention (Stroop and Eriksen's Flanker test performance) was significantly impaired during alcohol hangover. However, the number of did not differ significantly between the groups in any task. Mood assessment revealed that the hangover group reported significantly higher levels of drowsiness and clumsiness compared with the control group. Selective attention was significantly impaired during alcohol hangover. The differences between the hangover and control group did not reach significance for other forms of attention or memory.

Reference Number: 60816

ALFORD, C., C. BROOM, H. CARVER, S.J. JOHNSON, S. LANDS, R. REECE, AND J.C. VERSTER. "The Impact of Alcohol Hangover on Simulated Driving Performance During a Commute to Work—Zero and Residual Alcohol Effects Compared." *Journal of Clinical Medicine*, 9: 1435, 14 pp, 2020 (2 tables, 1 figure, 46 references)

Abstract: Twenty-one male and thirty-one female students (mean age 20.9 years) drove for 20 minutes in a driving simulator (STISDrive TM) twice in the morning, once after a night of no alcohol consumption and once after a night of alcohol consumption. BrACs were measured with a Lion Alcometer 400/500. Twenty-six subjects had a zero BrAC after a night of drinking and twenty-six had a positive BrAC (mean 0.047 g/1000mL). For the combined hangover group there was significant impairment in eight out of fifteen driving variables, including divided attention task, driving control, and driving violations. The residual alcohol group drove significantly faster than the zero BrAC group, but having a zero BrAC did not improve driving abilities compared to the residual BrAC group.

Overall, this evaluation of driving hangover performance has been successful in demonstrating the marked impact of alcohol hangover in impairing driving performance, even though participants overall were below the legal limit for driving in several countries. The key findings are that significant impairments were seen in a range of driving measures, including complex attention and driving control for those with residual alcohol as well as those with zero alcohol, with only limited differences between groups. The level of impairment seen here, which was comparable to driving while intoxicated at or above a BAC of 0.05%, indicates the dangers of driving whilst hangover, even when breath alcohol is at zero.

6.09 HOMICIDES/VIOLENT DEATHS

"Aristotle advocated this approach for drunken murders. Such a man deserves double punishments because he has doubly offended, viz being drunk to the evil example of others, and in committing the crime of homicide."

—Critchlow, "Blaming the Booze: The Attribution of Responsibility for Drunken Behavior" (1983)

"As a consequence, both judicial pronouncements and learned commentaries are populated by imaginary creatures—blind drunks who can see, dead drunks who move openly among the living, intoxicated automatons who perform complex, purposeful tasks and mad drunks who knowingly focus their aggression on specific targets."

—Mitchell, "The Intoxicated Offender—Refuting the Legal and Medical Myths" (1988)

Alcohol is a risk factor for homicides and other violent deaths, especially in those involving sharp instruments, blunt force, or fights (60907). Alcohol intoxication of the victims may:

- Increase risk taking or decrease awareness of potentially violent situations
- Make them less capable of defending themselves or escaping
- Make them less aware of severity of injury
- Make them less capable of obtaining help or applying pressure to the wound
- Promote greater bleeding (especially in chronic alcoholics) due to the vasodilation effect of alcohol

Reference Number: 60816

There tends to be a greater involvement of alcohol with gunshot homicide victims than suicide victims (60909). The rate of binge drinking on the weekends has been found to be associated with the homicide rate (60914). Alcohol intoxication is associated with fatal traumatic basal subarachnoid hemorrhage (60910, 60911). Chronic alcohol abusers with high BACs can bleed to death with relatively minor cuts (60913).

Binge drinking and homicide mortality were 10 to 20% higher on Fridays and Saturdays than on any other day of the week (60914). Homicide victims and offenders were more likely to have negative toxicology findings during the weekends than on weekdays (60918).

Drinking increased the odds of carrying a gun to protect themselves in their weakened intoxicated state. The mean level of intoxication was nearly two times for violent conflicts than nonviolent conflicts (60915). In South Africa, the largest number of alcohol positive cases were stabbing-related homicides at shebeens (60917).

In one highly intoxicated tourist (BAC = 0.275 g/100 mL), the murderer was the hotel folding bunk bed (60919).

Reference Number: 60901

WEBB, E., J.P. WYATT, J. HENRY, AND A.A. BUSUTTIL. "A Comparison of Fatal with Non-Fatal Knife Injuries in Edinburgh." *Forensic Science International,* 99: 179–187, 1999 (1 table, 3 figures, 32 references)

Abstract: A study of twenty stabbing deaths (seventeen male and three female victims) and 100 non-fatal stabbings (ninety-six male and four female victims) was conducted in Edinburgh, Scotland, between 1992 and 1996. Most of the fatal stabbings involved wounds to the chest or neck. A positive BAC was found in thirteen of the eighteen deaths analyzed and the BACs ranged from 0.066 to 0.357 g/100 mL.

> Firstly, alcohol may render a person less capable of defending himself or escaping quickly from a potentially violent situation. Secondly having been stabbed, alcohol may blur an individual's perception of the severity of their injuries and adversely affect their initial response in terms of seeking urgent medical attention. Thirdly the influence of alcohol may reduce a stabbed person's ability to apply pressure and limit bleeding from an external wound. Fourthly the presence of alcohol may limit the ability of someone to call for emergency medical help this is particularly pertinent in those cases where there were no witnesses to the stabbing incident.

Reference Number: 60902

KATKICI, U., M.S. OZKOK, AND M. ORSAL. "An Autopsy Evaluation of Defence Wounds in 195 Homicidal Deaths due to Stabbing." *Journal of the Forensic Science Society,* 34: 237–240, 1994 (5 tables, 20 references)

Abstract: A study was conducted of 195 deaths due to stabbing in which seventy-five (39%) of the victims had defense wounds. Defense wounds were seen frequently in cases in which there were many stab wounds but in only 3% of the cases with a single stab wound. BACs > 0.050 g/100 mL were found in fifty-five cases. Defense wounds were present in 44% of these cases. At BACs > 0.150 g/100 mL defense wounds were present in 24% of these cases.

Absence of defence wounds does not therefore rule out the possibility of homicide, but their existence definitely shows homicidal intent.

Reference Number: 60903

KARLSSON, T. "Sharp Force Homicides in the Stockholm Area, 1983–1992." *Forensic Science International*, 94: 129–139, 1998 (4 tables, 3 figures, 13 references)

Abstract: A study was conducted of 133 male and forty-one female homicide victims of sharp force injuries in Sweden between 1983–1992. Of eighty-eight cases in which BACs > 0.030 g/100 mL the perpetrator was sober in only eight cases (9%). No female perpetrator killed a female victim.

Table. Number of Wounds in Fatally Injured Stabbing Victims, the Male/Female Ratio, and Percent Positive BAC

Number of stab wounds	Male/female victim ratio	Percent of victims with BAC > 0.03 g/100 mL
1	6.8	80%
2–9	26.0	53%
10+	8.7	54%

Source: Adapted from Karlsson (1998).

Alcohol seemed to be an especially important variable in cases where only one wound was inflicted; in these cases, the inebriation among victims often was in the post-absorption phase. The low number of wounds could possibly be related both to a lower degree of intent or emotional charge, and the victim's severe intoxication making him unable to defend himself.

Reference Number: 60904

BILGREN, S., N. TURKMEN, B. EREN, AND R. FEDAKER. "Peripheral Vascular Injury-Related Deaths." *Turkish Journal of Trauma and Emergency Surgery*, 15: 357–361, 2009 (4 tables, 3 figures, 22 references)

Abstract: A study was conducted of sixty-three cases of deaths due to vascular injuries (0.9% of all autopsies) in Turkey between 1996 and 2006. Fifty-seven victims (91%) were men and the victims ranged in age between sixteen to sixty-six years (mean thirty-six years). The most frequent types of injury were stab wounds (59%) and shotgun wounds (22%). The most frequent type of case was homicide (69%). A positive BAC was detected in eighteen male and one female victim (range 0.044 to 0.256 g/100 mL).

In accordance with previous studies, 30.2% of the cases had detectable levels of alcohol in the blood. We think alcohol contributes to the mortality of extremity vascular injury. Alcohol consumption may compromise the capacity for self-protection as well as escape from the scene of injury. Furthermore, the vasodilator effect of alcohol may cause increased bleeding and accelerate death.

Reference Number: 60905

ROGDE, S., H.P. HOUGEN, AND K. POULSEN. "Homicide by Blunt Force in 2 Scandinavian Capitals." *American Journal of Forensic Medicine and Pathology*, 24: 288–291, 2003 (3 tables, 5 figures, 8 references)

Abstract: A study was conducted of seventy-seven blunt-force homicides in Oslo and Copenhagen between 1985 and 1994. Fifty-four of the victims were male and twenty-three were female. Approximately one-half of the male victims were killed by an acquaintance. A positive BAC was found in 56% of the male and 39% of the female victims. Approximately five male but no female victims had a BAC > 0.300 g/100 mL.

In conclusion, the victims of blunt force homicide are often men killed by an acquaintance during a fight under the influence of alcohol. The female victim, however, is often killed by her spouse or previous spouse, thus not differing significantly from victims of other homicide methods.

Reference Number: 60906

STRAUCH, H., I. WIRTH, U. TAYMOORIAN, AND G. GESERICK. "Kicking to Death—Forensic and Criminological Aspects." *Forensic Science International*, 123: 165–171, 2001 (7 tables, 3 figures, 29 references)

Abstract: A study was conducted of 103 male and forty-nine female victims who were kicked to death in Berlin between 1980 and 1997. BACs were determined in ninety-three adult victims, and all had a positive BAC, most ranging between 0.160 and 0.350 g/100 mL. Bleeding to death and head injuries were the most common causes of death. Both the victims and offenders generally came from the lower socio-economic strata.

Physical confrontation between offender and victim had been preceeded by consumption of alcohol in 84 of 110 cases. Occasional drug taking was admitted by six offenders. Seven of 155 offenders had a record of psychiatric disease. Among 95 offenders with criminal records, eight had been convicted for bodily harm, two for bodily harm by kicking, one for manslaughter and another one for attempted murder of his ex-wife. Details of criminal records remained unknown for 49 offenders.

Reference Number: 60907

GOODMAN, R.A., J.A. MERCY, F. LOYA, M.L. ROSENBERG, J.C. SMITH, N.H. ALLEN, L. VARGAS, AND R. KOLTS. "Alcohol Use and Interpersonal Violence: Alcohol Detected in Homicide Victims." *American Journal of Public Health*, 76: 144–149, 1986 (3 tables, 1 figure, 35 references)

Abstract: BACs were determined by GC in 4,092 homicide victims in Los Angeles from 1970–1979. Alcohol was detected in 1,883 (46%) of the victims. The BACs ranged from 0.001 to 0.870 g/100 mL and in 30% of the victims the BAC > 0.100 g/100 mL. Alcohol was detected in 75% of those killed in bars or restaurants and in 68% of those involved in a physical fight. Alcohol involvement was greatest in those killed with cutting instruments (59%) compared to 29% of those who were strangled and 45% of those killed by firearms.

Table. Circumstances of the Homicide and Percent of Victims with a BAC ≥ 0.100 g/100 mL

Homicide Circumstances	Percent of Victims with BAC ≥ 0.100g/100 mL
Physical Fight	52.5%
Verbal Argument	38.1%
Gang-Related	21.5%
Crime-Related	19.9%
Sex-Related	21.3%
Child Abuse/Neglect	3.9%

Source: Adapted from Goodman et al (1986).

Alcohol use could relate to an increased risk of homicide victimization in several ways. Alcohol could increase the likelihood of risk-taking and provocative behaviour by some potential victims; this might in turn lead to violent interactions and homicide.

Reference Number: 60908

SLADE, M., L.J. DANIEL, AND C.J. HEISLER. "Application of Forensic Toxicology to the Problem of Domestic Violence." *Journal of Forensic Sciences,* 36: 708–713, 1991 (3 tables, 25 references)

Abstract: Toxicological analyses were conducted on samples from twenty cases of domestic violence that ended in homicide in San Francisco between 1985 and 1988. The average BAC was 0.130 g/100 mL for suspects and 0.210 g/100 mL for victims (range 0.060–0.400 g/100 mL). A positive BAC was found in 70% of the suspects and 45% of the victims.

The data in the current study clearly shows that in the case of lethal domestic violence, it is highly probable that alcohol or other drug use will not be confined exclusively to either the suspect or the victim.

Reference Number: 60909

MOUG, S.J., J.A. LYLE, AND M. BLACK. "A Review of Gunshot Deaths in Strathclyde—1989 to 1998." *Medicine, Science, and the Law,* 41: 260–265, 2001 (3 tables, 3 figures, 16 references)

Abstract: A study was conducted of seventy-one gunshot fatalities (sixty-six male, five female victims) between 1989 and 1998 in Strathclyde,

Scotland. The median age of the victims was thirty-one years (ages seventeen to eighty years). Twenty-five percent of the fatalities were due to suicides and 75% were due to homicides. A positive postmortem BAC was found in sixteen of the twenty-five homicide victims tested (64%) and five of the twelve suicide victims tested (42%). The BACs were higher in the homicide victims than suicides. The homicide victim is usually a younger male shot in the early hours of the morning after consuming a large amount of alcohol.

Toxicological analysis revealed alcohol was present in the majority of homicide cases. Homicide victims were more likely to have consumed alcohol than suicide victims as well as having consumed greater volumes. In some cases, the blood alcohol level could be consistent with coma (more than 300 mg/100 mL of blood).

Reference Number: 60910

DOWLING, G., AND B. CURRY. "Traumatic Basal Subarachnoid Hemorrhage." *American Journal of Forensic Medicine and Pathology*, 9: 23–31, 1988 (2 tables, 6 figures, 47 references)

Abstract: Six fatal cases of traumatic basal subarachnoid hemorrhage are reported, and a literature review is presented. There are forty-seven references. Six male victims (ages twenty-eight to sixty-one years) died of blows to the face and head causing basal subarachnoid hemorrhage. BACs were determined in four cases and ranged between 0.090 and 0.280 g/100 mL, and in one of the other cases drinking was involved. Alcohol intoxication may be associated with traumatic basal subarachnoid hemorrhage due to its dilatation effect on cerebral arteries, slowing of the reflexes and coordination, and greater likelihood of fighting.

The importance of recognizing a traumatic basal subarachnoid hemorrhage lies in the fact that the manner of death in these cases is homicidal or accidental rather than natural. In four of the six cases in this series criminal charges have been laid against the assailants.

Reference Number: 60911

CAMERON, J.M. AND A.K. MANT. "Fatal Subarachnoid Hemorrhage Associated with Cervical Trauma." *Medicine Science and the Law*, 12: 66–70, 1972 (5 figures, 6 references)

Abstract: Four case reports of death due to traumatic vertebral artery hemorrhage are described. The victims were all male (ages thirty-one to fifty-five years) and all received blows to the head that ruptured the vertebral artery. The blood is released into the subarachnoid space and the injury causing the rupture may leave no external marks. Two victims had high levels of alcohol intoxication (one victim UAC 0.249 g/100 mL; the other victim BAC 0.390 g/100 mL and UAC 0.390 g/100 mL).

> There would appear little to dispute that alcoholic intoxication is an important contributory factor not merely because of the dilatation of the cerebral vessels but also because of the delayed reaction by the cervical muscles (in common with other muscular reactions) to stimuli.

Reference Number: 60912

BYARD, R.W. "Lethal Injuries Occurring During Illegal Break-Ins." *American Journal of Forensic Medicine and Pathology*, 26: 121–124, 2005 (3 figures, 6 references)

Abstract: Two cases of illegal break-ins that resulted in the death of the intruder are presented. The first victim (a thirty-year-old male) cut himself on broken window glass in the groin while exiting and bled to death. His postmortem BAC was 0.040 g/100 mL and a high blood methamphetamine concentration of 1.5 mg/L was also detected. The second victim (a twenty-two-year-old man) cut his arm on a broken window while trying to break into a house and also bled to death. His postmortem BAC was 0.170 g/100 mL.

> In summary, the reported cases demonstrate similar features in individuals who died of accidentally inflicted stab wounds after attempting to gain access to, or illegally entering premises. Impairment from drugs or alcohol most likely predisposed to injury and interfered with instituting first aid and/or seeking appropriate help. The vasodilatory and adrenergic effects of alcohol and amphetamines may also have predisposed to enhanced bleeding with more rapid exsanguination. Neither of the victims had any other significant injuries or underlying organic illnesses that could have caused death.

Reference Number: 60913

BRATZKE, H. AND T. GILG. "Fatal Hemorrhage from a Single Scalp Wound" [German]. *Archives fur Kriminologie*, 180: 101–106, 1987 (2 figures)

Abstract: Three case reports are presented of fatal deaths due to massive bleeding from a single accidental scalp wound (e.g., from hitting the head with the edge of a bed or bathtub). All three victims were alcoholics. At the scene large amounts of blood were found even though the scalp wounds were only 4 to 6 cm long. The first victim was a forty-two-year-old male with a BAC of 0.325 g /100 mL and a UAC of 0.410 g/100 mL. The second victim was a sixty-three-year-old female with a BAC of 0.225 g/100 mL and UAC of 0.265 g/100 mL. The blood and urine methanol concentrations were 0.005 and 0.005 g/100 mL respectively, which were in the typical range for alcoholics. The third victim was a fifty-seven-year-old female with a BAC of 0.260 g/100 mL and UAC of 0.340 g/100 mL. The blood methanol concentration was 0.001 g/100 mL and the blood acetone and isopropanol concentrations were 0.016 g/100 mL and 0.009 g/100 mL respectively. The authors suggest that the acute and chronic effects of alcohol impair the clotting ability of the blood and the intoxication prevents the victim from seeking medical assistance.

Reference Number: 60914

PRIDEMORE, W.A. "Weekend Effects on Binge Drinking and Homicide: The Social Connection Between Alcohol and Violence in Russia." *Addiction* 99: 1034–1041, 2004 (1 table, 1 figure, 36 references)

Abstract: Vodka represents about 75% of the estimated 15 L of alcohol consumed per person in Russia during 1997. All death certificates of those ages twenty to sixty-four years who died in the Udmurt Republic in Russia between 1994 and 1998 were examined. Deaths due to alcohol poisoning were used as a proxy for binge drinking. There was a correlation ($r = 0.75$) between alcohol poisonings and homicides. Alcohol and homicide mortality were 10 to 20% higher on Fridays and Saturdays than at other times of the week. The number of homicide and alcohol poisonings were relatively evenly distributed between the warm and cold seasons.

The paper examines the important link between alcohol consumption and violent crime. We see that both binge drinking and homicide mortality in Russia are higher on weekends, when the intermediate context of socializing is more likely, thus revealing indirect evidence for a social connection between the two and illustrating the consequences of reduced societal controls on consumption and the negative behaviors that may follow.

Reference Number: 60915

PHILLIPS, S., J. MATUSKO, AND E. TOMASOVIC. "Reconsidering the Relationship Between Alcohol and Lethal Violence." *Journal of Interpersonal Violence*, 22(1): 66–84, 2007 (4 tables, 38 references)

Abstract: Detailed interviews were conducted on 100 male inmates (mean age twenty-seven years) convicted of aggravated assault or homicide with another man after a violent conflict. The inmates also described nonviolent conflicts they had within 2 years of the offense. Drinking increased the odds of carrying a gun, which promotes violent escalation of the conflict. The mean level of alcohol intoxication in violent conflicts was almost twice that of nonviolent conflicts (2.71 versus 1.44).

Research suggests that protection is the most common motivation for carrying a gun. Men who have been drinking are less able to protect themselves in a fight, as inebriation slows reactions and dulls motor functions; a drunk is an easy mark. Thus, alcohol-induced vulnerability might lead men to pack heat to deter adversaries and ensure protection.

Reference Number: 60916

HEDLUND, J., J. FORSMAN, J. STURUP, AND T. MASTERMAN. "Pre-Offense Alcohol Intake in Homicide Offenders and Victims: A Forensic Toxicological Case Control Study." *Journal of Forensic and Legal Medicine*, 56: 55–58, 2018 (2 figures, 26 references)

Abstract: The BACs of 105 homicide offenders and 200 victims in Sweden between 2007–2009 were determined and compared to 1,629 controls who died in MVCs between 2006–2014. Homicide offenders were more likely to be male (91.4% versus 64.0%), and younger (mean age 38.4 years versus 44.6 years) than homicide victims. The mean age of the MVC victims (controls) was 48.7 years. The presence of alcohol increased the risk of offending (OR = 3.6 times) and victimization (OR = 2.1 times). The risk of offending and victimization in women with alcohol was three times greater than for men with alcohol.

Table. Percentages of Homicide Offenders, Victims, and Controls Positive for Alcohol According to Gender

	Women	Men
Offender	33.3%	30.2%
Victim	19.4%	18.4%
Control	4.0%	11.3%

Source: Adapted from Zhedlund et al (2018).

The results of the present study are consistent with prior findings suggesting alcohol to be an important risk factor for homicide offending and victimization. Surprisingly, however, associations were more pronounced in females, although additional studies that control for potential confounders are warranted to facilitate speculation about causality.

Reference Number: 60917

AUCKLOO, M.B K.M. AND B.B. DAVIES. "Post-mortem Toxicology in Violent Fatalities in Cape Town, South Africa: A Preliminary Investigation." *Journal of Forensic and Legal Medicine*, 63: 18–25, 2019 (6 tables, 47 references).

Abstract: The femoral blood alcohol concentrations were determined by headspace GC in 102 homicide victims who died in Cape Town, South Africa, in 2015. Drug screens were also conducted in femoral blood as well as urine, bile, and vitreous humor. The victims were 98% male and a mean age of thirty-one years. The female victims (2%) were White and died due to gunshots. The methods of homicide were gunshot (47%), stabbing (30%), assault (19%), and combination (2%). The BAC was positive in 41% of the cases with a mean BAC of 0.175 g/100 mL (range 0.020 to 0.400 g/100 mL). The most common other drugs detected were methamphetamine, diphenhydramine, and methaqualone.

Table. Mean BAC and Percent of Victims with BAC > 0.150 g/100 mL According to Type of Homicide

Type of Homicide	Mean BAC (g/100 mL)	Percent > 0.150 g/100 mL
Gunshot	0.140	11%
Stabbing	0.190	41%
Assault	0.170	9%

Source: Adapted from Auckloo and Davies (2019).

An increased risk to being a victim of violence and thus fatal injury has been reported with alcohol use, drug use, or both. Alcohol-related injury is a major public health concern in South Africa. Literature reveals that ethanol is the most frequently detected substance among victims of violent fatalities, however, the assessment of the role of alcohol was not evaluated. In our study, 95% of the alcohol-positive cases had BACs > 0.05 g/100 mL (the legal limit for driving in South Africa) spreading over the higher stages of alcohol intoxication. Interestingly, the largest number of alcohol-positive cases were stabbing related homicides. A large number of these cases were reported to take place at local shebeens—illicit bars or clubs where alcohol is often sold without a license—which highlights the need for addressing violence and illegal activities in these locations.

Reference Number: 60918

HEDLUND, J., J. AHLNER, M. KRISTIANSSON, AND J. STURUP. "Population-Based Study on Toxicological Findings in Swedish Homicide Victims and Offenders from 2007 to 2009." *Forensic Science International*, 244: 25–29, 2014 (4 tables, 39 references)

Abstract: Blood alcohol and other drug concentrations were determined in 273 homicide victims and 257 offenders in Sweden between 2007 and 2009. The homicide rate is relatively low in Sweden, only one per 100,000 population. A positive BAC was detected in 36% of the victims and 42% of the offenders. The only significant difference in the toxicological results between the victims and the offenders was in the detection of benzodiazepines in offenders, which was over two times that detected in victims. The homicide-suicide perpetrator group had the highest incidence of negative toxicological results (62%).

Table. Percentage of Female and Male Victims and Offenders Who Tested Negative and Positive for Alcohol, Alcohol and Drugs, and Drugs Only

	Negative	Alcohol	Alcohol and Drugs	Drugs
Female Victims	47.7%	36.4%	3.4%	12.5%
Male Victims	40.7%	33.3%	14.1%	11.9%
Female Offenders	40.0%	30.0%	0%	30.0%
Male Offenders	37.3%	23.6%	19.1%	20.8%

Source: Adapted from Hedlund et al (2014).

> Victims and offenders were more likely to display negative toxicology during week days compared to weekends, and also if the offense took place during the daytime. Only a small difference was detected when indoor and outdoor crime scenes were compared. A substantial difference was detected when daytime incidents during weekdays were compared to evenings or nighttime incidents on weekends.

Reference Number: 60919

DOMENECH, M.S., H.M. ALCAZAR, A.A. PALLARES, I.G. VICENTE, J.C. GARCIA, C.V.GUTIERREZ, AND J.M. MUNIZ. "The Murderer Is the Bed: An Unusual Case of Death by Traumatic Asphyxia in a Hotel Folding Bunk Bed." *Forensic Science International*, 220: e1–e4, 2012 (6 figures, 10 references)

Abstract: A fifty-one-year-old male tourist was found dead, trapped in a lower folding bunk bed in a hotel in Spain. His postmortem peripheral BAC was 0.275 g/100 mL.

> In conclusion, in this very unusual case, all the collected data strongly supported the hypothesis of an accidental death by traumatic asphyxia.

6.10 HYPOTHERMIA

> "And though your clothes be ne'er so bad,
> all raged, rent and torne,
> Against the cold you may be clad
> with a little Barley-Corne"
>
> —English folk song

A high proportion of adult hypothermia victims have been intoxicated by alcohol (61002–61005). The vasodilatation effect of alcohol may cause an increase in heat loss and less awareness of that loss in hypothermia victims (61001, 61005). Alcohol intoxication impairs judgment and prevents many hypothermia victims from seeking shelter (61011). Some of the postmortem signs of hypothermia are:

- Red or purple skin
- Swelling of ears, hands, or other frostbites
- Violet patches on knees or elbows
- Dilated veins on extremities
- Stomach erosions or hemorrhages ("Wisniewski flecks")

- Myocardial degenerative foci
- Elevated blood/urine acetone concentrations

Paradoxical undressing of hypothermia victims is an unusual feature of this type of death (61003, 61006, 61007, 61108). In one case, the crime scene appeared to be due to paradoxical undressing in hypothermia, but it was determined that the victim had been beaten to death (61009). Another unusual behavior related to hypothermia is terminal burrowing behavior (61010).

High doses of alcohol and amitriptyline can induce severe hypothermia (61012).

Reference Number: 61001

GRAHAM, T. "Alcohol Ingestion and Man's Ability to Adapt to Exercise in a Cold Environment." *Canadian Journal of Applied Sport Science*, 6: 27–31, 1981 (3 tables, 2 figures, 26 references)

Abstract: Six male subjects (mean age twenty years) consumed 2.5 mL/kg of 40% v/v alcohol, the same dose of alcohol and 50g/150 mL of d-glucose powder, or an equivalent volume of water within 30 minutes. The subjects then performed intermittent bicycle ergometer work in a –5°C cold chamber for 3 hours. Frequent blood samples were collected, and the BAC and blood glucose concentration were measured. The mean peak BACs were 0.060 g /100 mL (without) and 0.043 g/100 mL (with glucose). There were no significant differences in the blood glucose concentration between the groups and no one became hypoglycemic.

This study confirmed that alcohol ingestion (although the subjects did not exceed blood concentrations that are classified as legal intoxication) resulted in exaggerated heat loss when performing mild exercise in a cold environment. Despite the colder body temperatures, the subjects did not perceive the environment as more stressful. Thus, a situation is created where a person might not take adequate precautions to guard against hypothermia Fortunately it appears that once the blood alcohol level declines (one to two hours post-ingestion), the ability to thermoregulate approaches the control state.

Reference Number: 61002

HIRVONEN, J. "Necropsy Findings in Fatal Hypothermia Cases." *Forensic Science*, 8: 155–164, 1976 (3 tables, 4 figures, 21 references)

Abstract: A study of twenty-two hypothermia deaths was conducted between 1971 and 1975 in Finland. There were eighteen male and four female victims (ages fifteen to eighty-nine years). Alcohol was detected in twelve cases (55%). The mean postmortem BAC was 0.150 g/100 mL (range 0.125–0.249 g/100 mL).

> The survey of external signs in our series of hypothermia cases on the whole confirmed earlier reports. The most frequent signs were reddish livores, purple colour and swelling of ears, face, hands, and feet (frostbites) and violet patches on knees and elbows.

Reference Number: 61003

WEDIN, B., L. VANGGAARD, AND J. HIRVONEN. "Paradoxical Undressing in Fatal Hypothermia." *Journal of Forensic Sciences*, 24: 543–553, 1979 (5 tables, 5 figures, 15 references)

Abstract: A study was conducted of thirty-three cases of hypothermia deaths involving paradoxical undressing in Sweden between 1964 and 1973. A positive BAC was found in 54% of male victims. The mean BAC was 0.160 g/100 mL and the UAC was 0.270 g/100 mL. A high blood acetone concentration was detected in two cases.

> It is concluded that paradoxical undressing might be explained by changes in peripheral vasoconstriction in the deeply hypothermic person. It represents the last effort of the victim and is followed almost immediately by unconsciousness and death.

Reference Number: 61004

GALLAHER, M.M., D.W. FLEMING, L.R. BERGER, AND C.M. SEWELL. "Pedestrian and Hypothermia Deaths Among Native Americans in New Mexico. Between Bar and Home." *Journal of the American Medical Association*, 267: 1345–1348, 1992 (1 table, 2 figures, 28 references)

Abstract: A study was conducted of 347 pedestrian and 166 hypothermia deaths of Native Americans in New Mexico from 1980 to 1989. BACs were determined in 252 (80%) of pedestrian and 134 (82%) of the hypothermia deaths. Of those tested in pedestrian deaths, 91% had a positive BAC, and the median BAC was 0.240 g/100 mL (range 0.100–0.710 g/100 mL). BACs were positive in 90% of those tested in hypothermia deaths, where the median BAC was 0.180 g/100 mL (range 0.030–0.560 g/100 mL).

Native Americans are at an especially high risk for both hypothermia and pedestrian deaths in New Mexico. These two seemingly disparate categories of death are linked by a common high-risk profile—a highly intoxicated male who dies off reservation while traveling on foot.

Reference Number: 61005

HANZLICK, R., K. POWELL, AND K. TOOMEY. "Hypothermia Related Deaths—Georgia, January 1996–December 1997 and United States, 1979–1995." *Journal of the American Medical Association,* 281: 124–125, 1999 (1 table, 1 figure, 9 references)

Abstract: Three case reports of hypothermia deaths in Fulton County, Georgia, are presented. In one case the postmortem BAC was 0.370 g/100 mL. Between 1979 and 1995, there were on average 723 hypothermia deaths in the United States each year. Approximately half of all hypothermia deaths occur in persons over sixty-five years of age.

Alcohol abuse results in vasodilatation and interferes with peripheral vasoconstriction, an important physiologic mechanism of defence against the cold.

Reference Number: 61006

KINZINGER, R., M. RISSE, AND K. PUSCHEL. "Cold-'Craziness': Paradoxical Undressing in Hypothermia" [German]. *Archives fur Kriminologie,* 187: 47–56, 1991 (2 tables, 4 figures, 29 references)

Abstract: Two male alcoholic fatal hypothermia victims (ages thirty-four and fifty-two years) were found totally undressed in a park in Essen, Germany. The postmortem BACs were 0.315 and 0.295 g/100 mL respectively. The UACs were 0.460 and 0.360 g/100 mL respectively. At autopsy typical signs of hypothermia-related deaths were found, including Wisniewski gastric mucosal hemorrhages. In addition, thirty fatal hypothermia cases between 1979 and 1989 were reviewed. The victims were six women and twenty-four men (ages fourteen to eighty-five years). Paradoxical undressing occurred in five (17%) of the cases. All of these victims were male (ages thirty-four to sixty-six years) and all had high BACs (0.125–0.310 g/100 mL). The authors conclude that alcohol intoxication is an important factor in fatal hypothermia cases and of paradoxical undressing.

Reference Number: 61007

BRANDSTROM, H., A. ERIKSSON, G. GIESBRECHT, K-A. ANGQUIST, AND M. HANEY. "Fatal Hypothermia: An Analysis from a Sub-Arctic Region." *International Journal of Circumpolar Health,* 71: 18502, 7pp, 2012 (2 tables, 3 figures, 25 references)

Abstract: An analysis was conducted of 149 male and fifty-eight female victims of hypothermia in northern Sweden between 1992 and 2008. A positive femoral vein BAC was detected in ninety (43%) of the victims. The mean BAC was 0.156 g/100 mL and the mean UAC was 0.253 g/1,000 mL. Fifty-seven victims were identified as alcoholics. Some degree of paradoxical undressing was found in sixty-three (30%) of the victims; most had just removed their shoes.

Table. Percent of Postmortem Anatomical Findings in Hypothermia Deaths

Postmortem Finding	Cases Positive
Excoriations (hand and feet)	33%
Gastric erosion	34%
Fatty infiltration of the liver	46%
Pancreatitis	1%
Coronary artery disease	64%
Cardiomyopathy	9%

Source: Adapted from Brandstrom et al (2012).

> We noted a high annual incidence (1.35 per 100,000 inhabitants) of fatal hypothermia in Northern Sweden. Factors associated with fatal hypothermia were alcohol intoxication, paradoxical undressing, and proximity to inhabited areas, whereas pancreatitis was uncommon. We concluded that, with the identification of groups at high risk for fatal hypothermia, it should be possible to reduce risk through thoughtful interventions, particularly related to the highest risk subjects: rural, alcohol-imbibing, and psychiatric diagnosis-carrying citizens.

Reference Number: 61008

KETTNER, M., A. SCHNABEL, AND F. RAMSTHALER. "Suspected Paradoxical Undressing in a Homicide Case." *Forensic Science, Medicine, and Pathology*, 8: 426–429, 2012 (1 figure, 19 references)

Abstract: A fifty-one-year-old man was found dead and naked on a road with his clothing scattered all about. The death was initially suspected to be due to hypothermia as a result of the low ambient temperatures at the time, causing paradoxical undressing. His BAC was 0.040 g/100 mL and UAC was 0.170 g/100 mL. The man, however, had been severely beaten and died of his injuries. The assailant was convicted of manslaughter.

Clothing scattered in the surrounding of a discovered body is always suspicious of paradoxical undressing and thus a hypothermia-related death.

Reference Number: 61009

ROTHSCHILD, M.A. AND V. SCHNEIDER. "Terminal Burrowing Behaviour—A Phenomenon of Lethal Hypothermia." *International Journal of Legal Medicine*, 107: 250–256, 1995 (4 tables, 4 figures, 50 references)

Abstract: A study was conducted of sixty-nine cases (fifty-five male and eleven female victims) of deaths due to hypothermia that occurred between 1978 and 1994 in Berlin. Thirty-three hypothermia victims were found in buildings and thirty-one in the open. Seventeen victims were inadequately clothed and five were completely naked with the clothes strewn about the ground beside the body (paradoxical undressing). Paradoxical undressing is thought to occur due to a cold-induced paralysis of the nerves in the walls of the blood vessels, which leads to vasodilation and flow of the central blood to the extremities, which causes a feeling of warmth and removal of clothing by the victim just before death. In fourteen of these seventeen cases there was evidence of terminal burrowing behavior, which gave rise to the suspicion of an attempt to hide the body. A postmortem BAC > 0.100 g/100 mL was found in forty-nine victims (59%). Terminal burrowing behavior is thought to be a primitive reaction pattern controlled by the brain stem and appears to be an attempt by the victim of getting out of danger and into safety. An elevated postmortem blood acetone concentration was found in forty victims (58%) and ranged between 0.001 and 0.019 g/100 mL.

Table. Percent Occurrence of Autopsy Findings in 69 Hypothermia Victims

Autopsy Finding	Occurrence
Wisniewski ulcers (gastric)	86%
Red-purple blotches on skin	68%
Abrasions	49%
Pancreas changes	23%
Stripped hemorrhages in iliopsoas muscle	12%

Source: Adapted from Rothschild et al (1995).

This terminal burrowing behaviour only occurred in 20% of our cases of death due to hypothermia. As in other findings of hypothermia this phenomenon also seems to be dependent on how fast the body temperature decreases. Moderately cold ambient temperatures and a slower decrease of body temperature induced a terminal burrowing behaviour more often than environmental temperatures far below 0°C with a rapid state of severe hypothermia. There was no significant effect from alcohol or other substances on the occurrence of the paradoxical undressing or the terminal burrowing behaviour.

Reference Number: 61010

TAYLOR, A.J., G. MCGWIN JR, G.G. DAVIS, R.M. BRISSIE, T.D.HOLLEY, AND L.W. RUE III. "Hypothermia Deaths in Jefferson County, Alabama." *Injury Prevention*, 7: 141–145, 2007 (1 table, 3 figures, 25 references)

Abstract: Sixty-three hypothermia deaths that occurred in Jefferson County, Alabama, between 1983 to 1999 were evaluated. Sixty-four percent of the victims were male and 70% were Black. A positive postmortem BAC was detected in 30% of the victims and twelve (19%) had BACs of between 0.150 and 0.400 g/100 mL. Alcohol intoxication may have impaired judgment and caused them to fail to seek shelter and prevent the hypothermia.

We observed that hypothermia deaths fell roughly into two categories: elderly persons found indoors and middle-aged males found outdoors and having detectable BACs.

Reference Number: 61011

CHAPPELL, A.G. "Severe Hypothermia due to Combination of Psychotropic Drugs and Alcohol." *British Medical Journal*, 356, 5 February 1966 (2 references)

Abstract: A forty-three-year-old woman was admitted to hospital suffering from severe hypothermia (body temperature 28°C) after consuming a large quantity of red wine and amitriptyline. She recovered after treatment.

The following case is reported since it records complete recovery from severe hypothermia coma and emphasizes once more the dangers of combinations of various psychotropic drugs especially when taken with alcohol.

6.11 MARITIME SHIPPING

"What will we do with a drunken sailor?
What will we do with a drunken sailor?
What will we do with a drunken sailor?
Early in the morning"

—Sea shanty

"The Safety Board concluded that the master of the EXXON VALDEZ was impaired by alcohol at the time the vessel grounded on Bligh reef and that impairment of his judgement due to alcohol consumption caused him to leave the bridge at a critical time."

—Brenner et al, "The EXXON VALDEZ Accident" (1991)

Alcohol can cause impairment of ability to safely operate and navigate a ship (61101–61104, 60112). No impairment was detected in cadets 8 hours after a night of heavy drinking (61105). Two groundings of ships that occurred when the master was intoxicated with alcohol are reported (61106, 61107).

Alcohol increases temperature loss, which can lead to fatal hypothermia and drowning in commercial fishing deaths (61108). Commercial fishing vessels represented nearly two-thirds of the charges of navigating under the influence of alcohol in South Korea (61109). Most of the maritime accidents associated with alcohol were due to collisions (80%) followed by strandings (12%) (61109). The rate of alcoholism was 2.5 times greater in the Russian maritime crews compared to the land population (61110).

The main cause of injuries in cruise ship passengers were falls and 25% of the victims had a positive alcohol tox screen (61111).

Reference Number: 61101

MARSDEN, G. AND J. LEACH. "Effects of Alcohol and Caffeine on Maritime Navigational Skills." *Ergonomics*, 43: 17–26, 2000 (1 table, 36 references)

Abstract: Twelve experienced seamen (ages thirty-five to fifty-two years) consumed either 75 mL of whiskey (40% alcohol) and 250 mg of caffeine; alcohol alone; caffeine alone; or control and were tested on maritime navigational skills. Alcohol caused impairment in visual search and navigational problem solving. Caffeine enhanced performance on visual search but did not improve accuracy of navigational problem solving.

Furthermore, errors made under the alcohol condition were more serious in nature than those found under any of the other conditions. For example, one subject when laying off a course to steer placed the angular correction for leeway which was 5° to the leeward side of the vessel's track rather than the windward, effectively producing a course error of 10° overall. Another subject omitted to allow for the draught of the vessel above the echo-sounder transducer when calculating the depth of water for anchoring purposes, which in a real situation would have put the vessel aground.

Reference Number: 61102

HOWLAND, J., D.J. ROHSENOW, B. GOMEZ, T.W. MANGIONE, AND A.K. LARAMIE. "Effects of Low-Dose Alcohol Exposure on Simulated Merchant Ship Piloting by Maritime Cadets." *Accident Analysis and Prevention,* 33: 257–265, 2001 (1 table, 5 figures, 38 references)

Abstract: Thirty-eight cadets enrolled in the Marine Maritime Academy were tested on a simulator of a large merchant vessel before and after consumption of a placebo or 0.5–0.6 g/kg alcohol. The alcohol was consumed within 15 minutes and testing was commenced 20 minutes later. BrACs were determined with an Alco-Sensor III.

The mean BrACs were 0.047 g/100 mL (0.038–0.059 g/100 mL) at the start of the simulation and 0.051g/100 mL (0.040–0.063 g/100 mL) at the completion of the simulation.

This study found significant decrements in simulated merchant ship operation at BACs between 0.04 and 0.05 g%. The scores of cadets who received this relatively low dose of alcohol was 21% lower on average than the scores of peers who received placebo.

Reference Number: 61103

RITZ-TIMME, S., M. THORNE, G. GRUTTERS, M. GRUTTERS, J.A. REICHELT, N. BILZER, AND H-J. KAATSCH. "What Shall We Do with the Drunken Sailor? Effects of Alcohol on the Performance of Ship Operators." *Forensic Science International*, 156: 16–22, 2006 (1 table, 2 figures, 16 references)

Abstract: Twenty male and one female ship captains (ages twenty-seven to sixty-two years) were tested on a ship-piloting simulator before and after the consumption of alcohol over 45 minutes to obtain BACs of approximately 0.100 g/100 mL. BrACs and BACs were determined, and the mean BAC was 0.100 g/100 mL (range 0.075 to 0.141 g/100 mL).

None of the participants were capable to operate the simulated ship with an adequate safety after ingestion of alcohol. The observed impairment in the analysis of situations, in foresight, concentration, navigation, risk disposition and accurateness is not compatible with an adequate safety for men, property, and environment in water traffic.

Reference Number: 61104

KIM, H., C-S. YANG, B-W. LEE, Y-H. YANG, AND S. HONG. "Alcohol Effects on Navigational Ability Using Ship Handling Simulator." *International Journal of Industrial Ergonomics,* 37: 733–743, 2007 (1 table, 18 figures, 22 references)

Abstract: Eight deck officer cadets in their senior year consumed a placebo and two doses of alcohol (to obtain calculated BACs of 0.050 and 0.080 g/100 mL) within 5 minutes. Thirty minutes later, the subjects spent 50 minutes on a bridge simulator and tested their navigational skills. BrACs were measured with a Win-Bio Breathalyzer CA-2000. Additional experiments were conducted with an experienced pilot. At a BAC of 0.080 g/100 mL the average radius of the navigation track was increased by 11 m. Rudder use declined with alcohol consumption. Breath alcohol testing surveys of ship operators in Korea between 2000 and 2003 showed approximately 0.3 to 0.5% had a BAC $\geq$ 0.08 g/100 mL.

The study found that alcohol intake significantly impairs the physical and mental ability of the ship operators. In particular, alcohol intake was found to have a direct correlation with changes in bio-signals such as heart rate, not to mention the decline of ship operation performance. Alcohol intake also increased mental workload according to the subjective mental workload evaluation.

Reference Number: 61105

ROHSENOW, D.J., J. HOWLAND, S. MINSKY, AND J.T. ARNEDT. "Effects of Heavy Drinking by Maritime Academy Cadets on Hangover, Perceived Sleep, and Next-Day Ship Power Plant Operation." *Journal of Studies on Alcohol*, 67: 406–415, 2006 (2 tables, 4 figures, 43 references)

Abstract: Fifty male and eleven female cadets (ages twenty-one to twenty-six years) were tested on a maritime diesel power plant simulator after consuming placebo beer or beer (mean BrAC = 0.115 g/100 mL) and getting 8 hours of sleep (i.e., hangover effect). The beer was consumed between 8:30 p.m. and 10:00 p.m. the evening before the morning simulation.

Despite the beliefs of the maritime cadets that their performance in the power plant simulator was impaired the morning after a night of heavy drinking, objective measures of performance showed no impairment as a function of residual effects of a BrAC ≥ .11g% alcohol. Cadets were equivalent in the amount of time it took them to solve an engine failure scenario.

Reference Number: 61106

BRENNER, M. AND J.R. CASH. "Speech Analysis as an Index of Alcohol Intoxication—The EXXON Valdez Accident." *Aviation Space, Environmental Medicine,* 62: 893–898, 1991 (1 table, 2 figures, 14 references)

Abstract: On March 24, 1989, the *EXXON Valdez* was grounded on Bligh reef spilling 258,000 barrels of oil. The master of the vessel had a BAC of 0.060 g/100 mL and a UAC of 0.090 g/100 mL 10.5 hours after the collision. The master had been previously treated for alcohol problems and was arrested for impaired driving in 1985 and 1988. The breath alcohol test result of the last impaired driving arrest was 0.190 g/100 mL. Recordings of the master's radio transmission were used to determine if his speech could be used as an indication of alcohol intoxication. Alcohol can cause slow speech, speech errors, misarticulations of difficult sounds, and changes in vocal quality. The rate of speaking of the master decreased from 5.1 syllables/second (33 hours before the grounding) to 3.9 syllables/

second immediately before and after the accident. The master had trouble pronouncing the sounds and made *s* to *sh*, *iz* to *is*, and *r* and *l* mistakes.

> The Safety Board concluded that the master of the EXXON VALDEZ was impaired by alcohol at the time the vessel grounded on Bligh Reef and that impairment of his judgment due to alcohol consumption caused him to leave the bridge at a critical time.

Reference Number: 61107

CURCULIC, D., A. BOSNAR, V. STEMBERGA, M. COKLO, N. NIKOLIC, AND E. GRGUREVIC. "Interpretation of Blood Alcohol Concentration in Maritime Accidents—A Case Report." *Forensic Science International*, Suppl. Series 1: 35–37, 2009 (1 figure, 9 references)

Abstract: On 1 February 2008 at 5:00 a.m. a merchant ship (the *Cappadocia*) stranded on the breakwater of the Rijeka harbour in Croatia. The master of the ship admitted to drinking two to three beers at 2:30 p.m. the day before. The BrAC of the master at 9:10 a.m. as determined with an Alcotest 7410 was 0.165 g/100 mL. The master failed the SFST conducted by the examining doctor. Blood and urine samples were collected sometime after 10:45 a.m. The BAC was 0.115 g/100 mL and the UAC was 0.020 g/100 mL. The UAC was not consistent with the BAC or BrAC, and it was found upon analyses of creatinine and SG that it had been diluted.

> Alcohol impairment of car drivers is known to be the most important cause of car crashes. Driving a boat may demand at least the same degree of performance skill as driving a car. Our observations indicate a need for stricter and more precise legislation as well as more frequent police control that will hopefully results in prevention of serious maritime accidents caused by alcohol consumption.

Reference Number: 61108

BYARD, R.W. "Commercial Fishing Industry Deaths—Forensic Issues." *Journal of Forensic and Legal Medicine*, 20: 129–132, 2013 (40 references)

Abstract: An overview of the forensic issues in commercial fishing deaths was conducted. Some of the causes of death include fires, explosions, cable/net entanglement, marine predators/large fish thrashing in the boat, and falls into the water or in the boat.

As noted, alcohol use has been documented in a significant percentage of victims in fishing industry deaths and may have led to multiple adverse effects including navigation errors, misinterpretation or ignoring of weather conditions, misuse of machinery or loss of balance. Once in the water, alcohol will increase temperature loss hastening the onset of lethal hypothermia. While drowning is a quite likely terminal event, hypothermia may play a significant role. Sudden and unexpected cold-water immersion may cause death within minutes due to cold shock or within 3–15 minutes due to so-called swimming failure.

Reference Number: 61109

LEE, S. "Navigating Under the Influence and the Threat to Maritime Safety in Korea." *Asia-Pacific Journal of Ocean Law and Policy*, 5: 228–236, 2020 (3 tables)

Abstract: On 28 March 2019, after having left Yongho wharf at Busan Post, the Russian flagged cargo ship *Sea Guard* (59,998 tons, 15 Russian sailors) collided with three docked yachts and eventually the Gwangan Bridge. The captain's BAC was 0.086 g/100 mL, nearly three times the 0.030 g/100 mL limit in the *Maritime Safety Act* of Korea. A study was conducted of 530 cases of navigating under the influence of alcohol between 2014 and 2018 at sea in Korea. Fishing vessels represented 314 cases (64.3%), fifty-five (10.4%) involved leisure vessels, and nine (1.7%) involved cargo ships. There were sixty-six maritime accidents due to vessel operation under the influence of alcohol. The BACs of the operators were 0.030–0.100 g/100 mL (53.2%), 0.100–0.200 g/100 mL (33.6%), and 0.200 g/100 mL or greater (7%).

Table. Type of Maritime Accident While the Operator Was Under the Influence of Alcohol

Type of Accident	Number	Percent
Collision	53	80.3%
Stranding	8	12.1%
Sinking	2	3.0%
Fire	0	0.0%
Capsized	1	1.5%
Other	2	3.0%
Total	66	100.0%

Source: Adapted from Lee (2020).

Such accidents caused by the operation of a vessel under the influence of alcohol at sea can bring about marine environmental pollution as well as casualties and physical damage. It is necessary to prevent accidents by raising consciousness about the operation of vessels under the influence of alcohol at a time when critics point out that under the current legislation, despite the growing social damage due to alcohol abuse, penalties are lighter than the gravity of the offense. The Gwangan Bridge collision has led to growing calls for stronger punishment.

Reference Number: 61110

SHAPOVALOV, K.A. "Injuries of the Floating Crew of the Northern Water Pool in a State of Alcohol Intoxication." *International Maritime Health*, 64: 41–50, 2013 (3 tables, 83 references).

Abstract: An analysis was conducted of 180 accidents and 1,686 injuries requiring hospitalization on board the ships of the northern water pool of Russia. The diagnosis of alcoholism is 2.5 times greater among the floating crew compared to the land population.

Table. Percentages of the Type of Injuries in Under and Not Under the Influence of Alcohol in the Water Pool Floating Crew

Type of Injury	Under the Influence of Alcohol	Not Under the Influence of Alcohol
Bruises	10.4%	16.3%
Wounds	19.2%	15.5%
Head Injuries	14.6%	3.6%
Burns	4.5%	5.7%
Fractures	14.6%	41.0%

Source: Adapted from Shapovalow (2013).

Alcoholic injuries have been recorded at the time of walking on the cat-walk and the decks (54.2%), mooring operations (15.1%), maintenance and repairing the deck machinery, water preparation (6.6%) as well as boat and loading-unloading works (4.3%). Falls from height constituted 36.6% of the injuries. Alcohol in 3.2 times increased the weight of the combined injuries. The deaths from the alcohol related injuries in marine conditions (43.4%) significantly exceed the indicators in the group of non-alcoholic injuries (7.0%). Alcoholic intoxication has been noted in 35.0% of the cases of the floating crew injuries, hospitalized in the surgical department.

Reference Number: 61111

BANSAL, V., D. FORTLAGE, J.G. LEE, L.L. HILL, B. POTENZA, AND R. COIMBRA. "Significant Injury in Cruise Ship Passengers. A Case Series." *American Journal of Preventive Medicine* 33: 219–221, 2007 (2 tables, 11 references)

Abstract: The number of cruise ship passengers in San Diego, California, has increased from 92,000 in 2003 to 235,000 in 2005. In 2006, eight injured passengers (ages twenty-six to eighty years) received medical care at a university level 1 trauma center. All but one passenger were female. All eight patients suffered injuries from falls and two (25%) had a positive alcohol tox screen. One patient died.

In this case series, falls were the sole cause of major injury among cruise ship passengers. Improved surveillance and characterization of injuries among cruise ship passengers is needed to inform safety policies and develop programs to prevent passenger injury.

Reference Number: 61112

GUG, S.-G., J-H. YUN, D. HARSHAPRIYA, AND J-J. HAN. "A Prefatory Study on the Effects of Alcohol on Ship Maneuvering, Navigational and Decision-Making Abilities of Navigators." *The Journal of Navigation*, 1–13, 2022 (1 table, 10 figures, 24 references)

Abstract: Five senior cadet students (mean age twenty-three years) and five experienced navigational officers (mean age thirty-nine years) were tested on the operation of a simulator LNG carrier of 283 m in length at a 0.0, 0.050, and 0.080 g/100 mL BAC. BrACs were measured with an Alcoscan AL8800. The participants were required to change the rudder angle and speed of the vessel for several course alterations.

Table. Mean Change in Rudder Alterations at BACs of 0.050 and 0.080 g/100 mL and Engine Commands Obeyed (0.080 g/100 mL BAC) for Cadets and Officers

Conditions	Cadets	Officers
Rudder Alterations at a BAC of 0.050 g/100 mL	+25%	+29%
Rudder Alterations at a BAC of 0.080 g/100 mL	+45%	+35%
Engine Telegraph Commands Obeyed at a BAC of 0.080 g/100 mL	–30%	–50%

Source: Adapted from Gug et al (2022).

The results obtained from the ship simulations clearly showed the effects of alcohol on motor functions, logical thinking, and decision-making capabilities of navigators regardless of how experienced they are. When the BAC levels were zero (0.00% BAC), both cadets and officers had no trouble following the desired course with the proper speed and rudder alterations. However, the ability to make the correct decisions at the right time was drastically deteriorated when the blood alcohol concentration was increased. The vessel was at risk and participants were not able to keep the vessel within the safe limits of the fairway when they were intoxicated.

6.12 MISCELLANEOUS

"A bartender is just a pharmacist with a limited inventory."

—Albert Einstein

"I wonder what the blood alcohol level is of all those mosquitoes that keep biting me."

—Unknown

Alcohol affects a plethora of human activities, from the whimsical such as mosquito attraction (61201), sunburn (61202), laughter (61203), and restaurant tipping (61204) to the more serious, such as surgical performance (61209). Other miscellaneous behaviors that are affected by alcohol include gambling (61205), fear of snakes (61206), managerial performance (61208), reading (61210), and writing (61214). Alcohol has been found to hinder rather than assist in the artistic/creative process (61218).

Prolonged conducted electrical discharge using a TASERX26 did not change blood parameters in alcohol-intoxicated adults and did not contribute to metabolic acidosis (61219).

Champagne corks can travel at a speed of 50 km/h, and they cause 1.4% of the eye injuries in Hungary (61220).

Drinking homemade prison liquor made from potato peels, known as Pruno, can cause botulism (61221).

The rates of alcoholism in physicians is lower than the general population, but most patients do not recognize alcohol intoxication in their physicians (61222).

Holding a Beer Fest near a zoo is not a good idea as one participant was found mauled to death by a Himalayan black bear. The victim's VHAC was 0.200 g/100 mL and UAC was 0.420 g/100 mL (61223).

Reference Number: 61201

SHITAI, Y., T. TSUDA, S. KITAGAWA, K. NAITOH, T. SEKI, K. KAMIMURA, AND M. MOROHASHI. "Alcohol Ingestion Stimulated Mosquito Attraction." *Journal of American Mosquito Control Association*, 18: 91–96, 2002 (2 tables, 8 figures, 19 references)

Abstract: The percentage of mosquitoes landing on the forearms of twelve male and one female subject (ages twenty to fifty-eight years) were determined before and after the ingestion of one 350 mL serving of beer (5.5% v/v alcohol). Skin temperature, sweat production, and sweat alcohol concentrations were also determined. The mean percentage of mosquitoes landing on the forearm was 41% before and 51% after the ingestion of beer. The increase in percentage of mosquitoes landing did not correlate with sweat alcohol concentration or with the temperature of the skin. There was no increase in sweat production after alcohol consumption.

> In conclusion our research indicated that humans attract more mosquitoes after ingesting ethanol. We can conclude that sweat production or skin temperature after ethanol ingestion does not attract mosquitoes, but the attraction might be due to the presence of unknown chemical substances on the skin after ethanol ingestion.

Reference Number: 61202

WATHAN, M.M., D.S. SEWELL, R.A. MARLOW, M.L. WARTHAN, AND R.F. WAGNER JR. "The Economic Impact of Acute Sunburn." *Archives Dermatology*, 139: 1003–1006, 2003 (2 tables, 8 references)

Abstract: Eighteen male and thirty-eight female sunburned beachgoers (ages eighteen to fifty-six years) were interviewed on a Galveston, Texas, beach between July and August 1999. Thirteen (23%) drank alcohol. Five men and four women missed a total of nine and eight days of work respectively due to sunburn. Drinkers reported greater initial sunburn pain than nondrinkers as well as more pain the next day. Drinkers also had a significantly greater body surface area sunburned than nondrinkers and were more likely to develop blisters.

Anecdotal reports about alcohol use at the beach have long been associated with severe sunburn. The study adds further evidence that alcohol use at the beach may lead to more severe sunburn. Although the mechanism is currently unknown, alcohol users in this survey did not report spending significantly more time in the sun than nondrinkers. Alcohol may blunt the immediate sensation of sunburn preventing subtle behavioral changes that could decrease further exposure to UV light and additional skin damage.

Reference Number: 61203

LOWE, G. AND S.B. TAYLOR. "Effects of Alcohol on Responsive Laughter and Amusement." *Psychological Reports*, 80:1149–1150, 1997 (5 references)

Abstract: Twenty-four male and twenty-four female social drinkers consumed either two 360 mL bottles of 8.2% v/v alcohol beverage or an alcohol-free beverage within 30 minutes. The subjects then watched a 20-minute humorous film. The frequency of the audience laughter and post-film subjective feelings of amusement were determined. The mean frequency of laughter score was forty-seven for the alcohol group and twenty-eight for the non-alcohol group.

These results, together with previous findings, provide empirical support for the commonly held notion that drinking increases the frequency of laughter and humour. In conjunction with evidence that laughter and humour can serve as a moderator of stress and enhance immune function such observations suggest that the positive influence of moderate consumption of alcohol on health and longevity may operate, at least partly, via psychological variables such as mood enhancement and stress buffering.

Reference Number: 61204

LYNN, M. "The Effects of Alcohol Consumption on Restaurant Tipping." *Personality and Social Psychological Bulletin*, 14: 87–91, 1988 (1 table, 14 references)

Abstract: A study was conducted of the tipping behavior of 207 dining patrons at a moderately priced Italian restaurant in a large Midwestern US city. The percent tip was negatively correlated with bill size. From a regression analysis, drinkers tipped more than nondrinkers, however, as a percent tip, there was no effect of alcohol consumption.

There are at least two potential explanations for alcohol's effect on helping. First, alcohol improves people's moods, and this positive affect may increase helping. Second, alcohol decreases people's ability to process information and in situations in which the most salient cues call for helping, this may reduce people's ability to process additional cues that would inhibit the behavior.

Reference Number: 61205

SJOBERG, L. "Alcohol and Gambling." *Psychopharmacology*, 14: 284–298, 1969 (5 tables, 3 figures, 18 references)

Abstract: One hundred and ten subjects (ages twenty to twenty-eight years) were assigned to a placebo group or 0.4, 0.5, or 0.7 g/kg alcohol. The alcohol was consumed within 20 minutes and the BACs were determined by capillary blood samples. The subjects were tested on their willingness to gamble or take a risk on simulated lottery tickets. The mean peak BACs were 0.034, 0.060, 0.067, and 0.074 g/100 mL respectively.

The two experiments showed that decision making studied by means of ratings in a gambling situation was affected by the administration of alcohol. A small dose enhanced willingness to gamble and a large dose lowered willingness.

Reference Number: 61206

RIMM, D., D. BRIDDELL, M. ZIMMERMAN, AND G. CADDY. "The Effects of Alcohol and the Expectancy of Alcohol on Snake Fear." *Addictive Behaviours*, 6: 47–51, 1981 (1 table, 9 references)

Abstract: Six male and fifty female subjects consumed either a placebo or 0.5 g/kg ethanol within 20 minutes. The subjects were told randomly whether they had consumed alcohol or not. Breathalyzer tests were conducted. Subjects were exposed to a four-foot-long caged boa and their fear/anxiety response was determined.

In the present investigation, significant decrease in subjective anxiety vis a vis a harmless snake was associated with mild alcohol intoxication.

Reference Number: 61207

KOPPEL, C. AND F. MARTENS. "Clinical Experience in the Therapy of Bites from Exotic Snakes in Berlin." *Human and Experimental Toxicology*, 11: 549–552, 1992 (1 table, 40 references)

Abstract: Between 1980 and 1991, fifty-one snake bites were reported in Berlin. Eleven patients who had been bitten by exotic poisonous snakes were treated in intensive care. Eight of the patients had BACs between 0.120 and 0.420 g/100 mL at the time of admission. All patients survived with treatment.

> In Germany there is no legal restriction on keeping poisonous exotic snakes in private households. The personality structure of people keeping exotic snakes and suffering snake bites seemed to be rather similar; they were mainly people who were not very successful in their lives or their professions. One reason for keeping an exotic poisonous snake seemed to be to attract attention. In some patients the poisonous snakes were to some extent regarded as a substitute for a weapon. Many of these individuals had a history of ethanol abuse. The combination of ethanol intake and feeding the snake seemed to be the major cause of snake bites.

Reference Number: 61208

STREUFERT, S., R. POGASH, J. ROACHE, W. SEVERS, D. GINGRICH, R. LANDIS, L. LONARDI, AND A. KANTNER. "Alcohol and Managerial Performance." *Journal of Studies on Alcohol*, 55: 230–238, 1994 (2 tables, 42 references)

Abstract: Forty-eight managers were administered alcohol or a placebo to determine the effect of alcohol on managerial performance. Subjects consumed alcohol throughout the day to maintain a BrAC of either 0.050 or 0.100 g/100 mL. BrACs were determined frequently with an Intoxilyzer 5000. The experiment was conducted between 7:00 a.m. and 4:30 p.m. The subjects participated in a simulated test of managerial functioning.

> To summarize: Alcohol consumption even at the .05 BAC appears to result in a deterioration of competency to handle complex tasks such as planning and strategy, both under normal and emergency conditions. In contrast, simpler components of managerial activity are not necessarily affected until the BAC reaches higher levels (here .10) or may not be affected at all.

Reference Number: 61209

DORAFSHAR, A.H., D.J. O'BOYLE, AND R.F. MCCLOY. "Effects of a Moderate Dose of Alcohol on Simulated Laparoscopic Surgical Performance." *Surgical Endoscopy,* 16: 1753–1758, 2002 (3 figures, 21 references)

Abstract: Twenty-eight male medical students (mean age twenty-two years) were administered either a placebo or 1.05 g/kg alcohol within 15 minutes. The subjects were tested on the MIST Virtual Reality surgical simulator 1 hour before, 1 hour after, and 10 hours (after a night's sleep) after the alcohol/placebo ingestion. BrACs were determined with an Alcolmeter S-D2 and the mean peak BrAC was approximately 0.085 g/100 mL.

> The observation of an impairment of simulated surgical performance 1–2 h following ingestion of a moderate dose of alcohol is consistent with the literature on the effects of alcohol on a wide variety of information processing tasks. The observed absence of both a hangover effect on performance when the BAC had returned to near zero following a night's sleep and of an effect on estimated sleep duration during the night following alcohol ingestion is also consistent with previous reports.

Reference Number: 61210

WATTEN, R.G., AND I. LIE. "The Effects of Alcohol on Eye Movements During Reading." *Alcohol and Alcoholism*, 32: 275–290, 1997 (3 figures, 28 references)

Abstract: Eighteen male subjects (mean age twenty-six years) consumed a placebo, 0.65, or 1.35 mL/kg vodka over 1 hour. BrACs were determined with an Alcometer SD-2 and the mean BrACs were 0.050 and 0.100 g/100 mL. The movement of the eyes while reading was determined by an IR corneal reflection monitoring system. The duration of eye fixations (saccadic pauses) and number of fixations increased with increasing BrAC.

> The increased duration of fixation as a function of elevated BAC levels is probably the result of the depressant effects of alcohol on the brain stem.

Reference Number: 61211

WOODROW, K.M. AND L.G. ELTHERINGTON. "Feeling No Pain: Alcohol as an Analgesic." *Pain*, 32: 159–163, 1988 (3 tables, 9 references)

Abstract: Eighteen female subjects (ages twenty-one to thirty years) were injected with 0.4 mg atropine, 0.5 mL saline, or 0.17 mg/kg morphine subcutaneously and consumed 1.0 mL/kg alcohol at 1-week intervals. The threshold and tolerance to pain were measured using an Achilles tendon device. The BrACs were determined with a Breathalyzer and the mean was approximately 0.070 g/100 mL. The mean threshold effects were similar for all four conditions. The mean tolerance effect was 3.61 for alcohol, 2.96 for morphine, 0.61 for saline, and 0.04 for atropine.

The most significant finding of this study was the demonstration that the alcohol equivalent of 2 cocktails induced analgesia comparable to that of 11.6 mg of subcutaneous morphine. Significantly, excellent analgesia occurred at blood concentrations of approximately 70 mg/100 mL, which is less than the legal limit of intoxication in California.

Reference Number: 61212

PERRINO JR., A.C., E. RALEVSKI, G. ACAMPORA, J. EDGECOMBE, D. LIMONCELLI, AND I.L. PETRAKIS. "Ethanol and Pain Sensitivity: Effects in Healthy Subjects Using an Acute Pain Paradigm." *Alcoholism: Clinical and Experimental Research,* 32: 952–958, 2008 (1 table, 2 figures, 33 references)

Abstract: Forty-one FHN (family history of alcoholism: negative) subjects and nineteen FHP (family history of alcoholism: positive) subjects were administered a placebo or two doses of alcohol IV to obtain BrACs of 0.040 or 0.100 g/100 mL. BrACs were measured with an Alcotest 7410 Plus. The analgesic effects of alcohol to a noxious electrical stimulus were assessed.

The findings from this study provide support for the primary hypothesis and demonstrate that in young healthy adults, with and without a family history of alcoholism, IV ethanol administration at the 0.100 g/dL level elevate pain tolerance though not pain threshold, in a noxious electrical stimulation paradigm. Ethanol administration at the lower concentration of 0.04 g/dL did not produce a significant effect on pain sensitivity.

Reference Number: 61213

GREEN, R.S. AND R. MAIER. "The Urban Cowboy Syndrome Revisited: Case Report." *Southern Medical Journal* 96: 1262–1264, 2003 (1 figure, 7 references)

Abstract: A thirty-two-year-old man who consumed an undetermined amount of alcohol was injured while sitting on a mechanical bull. The man suffered symphysis, diastasis, urethral injury, and significant retroperitoneal hematoma resulting in cardiovascular instability. This was the most severe mechanical bull injury reported to date.

The urban cowboy syndrome refers to injuries that combine mechanical bull riding, alcohol use and subsequent orthopedic injury.

Reference Number: 61214

PHILLIPS, J.C., R.P. OGEIL, AND F. MULLER. "Alcohol Consumption and Handwriting: A Kinematic Analysis." *Human Movement Science*, 29: 619–632, 2009 (3 tables, 2 figures, 77 references)

Abstract: Twenty male subjects (mean age twenty-four years) wrote four cursive "l"s twenty times on a Wacom SD420 graphic tablet before and 20 minutes after consuming alcohol over 30 minutes. The mean BrACs as determined with an Alcotest 6510 were 0.048 g/100 mL 20 minutes after drinking ceased. Ten subjects were determined to be non-alcohol dependent and ten were alcohol dependent as assessed by AUDIT scores. The mean stroke length was 21.9 mm before and 23.3 mm after the consumption of alcohol. The mean stroke duration was 332.9 ms before and 315.8 ms after the consumption of alcohol. Alcohol dependent subjects tended to have slower writing.

The present article demonstrated alcohol related changes in handwriting that were in keeping with cerebellar dysfunction. There appeared to be a dysmetric of control of writing stroke length and alterations in the relative proportions of acceleration and deceleration. However, some effects were marginal, and could also reflect the involvement of other brain structures. For instance, alcohol intoxication initially reduces glucose metabolism in the cortex and then at higher doses reduces glucose metabolism in cerebellar and subcortical structures.

Reference Number: 61215

SAYETTE, M.A., E.D. REICHLE, AND J.W. SCHOOLER. "Lost in the Sauce. The Effects of Alcohol on Mind Wandering." *Psychological Science*, 20: 747–752, 2009 (36 references)

Abstract: Fifty-four male subjects consumed either a placebo or 0.82 g/kg alcohol within 30 minutes and were tested on a mind wandering reading task (Tolstoy's *War and Peace*). The mean BrAC before testing was 0.067 g/100 mL.

This study suggests that a moderate dose of alcohol simultaneously increases mind wandering while reducing the likelihood of noticing that one's mind has wandered. Participants who drank alcohol were mind-wandering without awareness of doing so about 25% of the time that they were engaged in the reading task. This frequency was more than double than for participants in the placebo condition.

Reference Number: 61216

NORLANDER, T., A. NORDMAKER, A., AND T. ARCHER. "Effects of Alcohol and Frustration on Experimental Graffiti." *Scandinavian Journal of Psychology*. 39: 201–207, 1998 (1 table, 29 references)

Abstract: Twenty-one male and twenty-one female subjects (ages nineteen to thirty-two years) were divided into three groups: control, alcohol, and alcohol and frustration. The alcohol dose was 1 mL/kg consumed within 20 minutes. BrACs were determined with a Lion SD2. The mean BrACs ranged from 0.056 to 0.081 g/100 mL. The subjects were tested on scrawling or aggressive graffiti.

Both the male and female subjects showed more scrawling graffiti under conditions of Alcohol and Frustration. However, female subjects displayed significantly higher levels in all conditions.

Reference Number: 61217

RIEMANN, R., R. VOLK, A. MULLER, AND M. HERZOG. "The Influence of Nocturnal Alcohol Ingestion on Snoring." *European Archives Otorhinolaryngology*, 267:1147–1156, 2010 (9 figures, 30 references)

Abstract: Ten male non-snorers (mean age twenty-seven years) and ten male snorers (mean age thirty-seven years) consumed a placebo or two doses of alcohol calculated to obtain BACs of approximately 0.050 and 0.080 g/100 mL at night before bedtime. BrACs were measured with an Alcotest 7410. Snoring noises and duration were recorded. The mean incidence of total snoring (TSI) in snorers increased from approximately 2%

(placebo) to 4% (low alcohol dose) to 10% (high alcohol dose). In non-snorers there was no significant increases with alcohol.

> The presented study demonstrates that healthy men, who already snore without alcohol intake, revealed a dose dependent increase in loudness and incidence of snoring after nocturnal alcohol ingestion whereas non-snoring healthy male did not present an induction of snoring.

Reference Number: 61218

BEVERIDGE, A. AND G. YORSTON. "I Drink, Therefore I Am: Alcohol and Creativity." *Journal of Royal Society of Medicine*, 92: 646–648, 1999 (19 references)

Abstract: A short overview of alcohol use/misuse and artists is presented. Alcohol has featured in the life of many writers such as Dylan Thomas, F. Scott Fitzgerald, Ernest Hemingway, and Jack Kerouac.

> If one is struck by the large number of artists who drank to excess, one is also struck by the appalling personal and physical price they paid. Biographies reveal a grim catalogue of mental illness, physical disease, family breakdown, suicide, and premature death. Artists have certainly been aware of the downside of drinking. Indeed, most artists seem to have produced their work while sober.

Reference Number: 61219

MOSCATI, R., J.D. HO, D.M. DAWES, AND J.R. MINER. "Physiological Effects of Prolonged Conducted Electrical Weapon Discharge in Ethanol-Intoxicated Adults." *American Journal of Emergency Medicine*, 28: 582–587, 2010 (2 tables, 4 figures, 18 references)

Abstract: Various blood laboratory parameters were measured in eight male and four female subjects (ages thirty-four to fifty-two years) who consumed alcohol at their own pace until the BrAC > 0.080 g/100 mL or they showed obvious intoxication. BrACs were measured with an Alco-Sensor IV. Blood samples were collected before and up to 24 hours after being exposed to a 15-second conducted electrical weapon (CEW) discharge using a TASER X26 and various blood parameters were measured.

Table. Some Blood Parameters (Mean Results) Before and Immediately After Tasering of Alcohol-Intoxicated Subjects

Parameter	Before Tasering	After Tasering
pH	7.37	7.31
Lactate (mmol/L)	1.98	4.19
Bicarbonate (mmol/L)	25.2	24.4
PCO_2	43.4	48.5

Source: Adapted from Moscati et al (2010)

> Our study results indicate that prolonged CEW exposure on alcohol-intoxicated adult subjects result in no clinically significant changes in physiologic markers of acidosis. Suggestions that CEW use on intoxicated subjects may contribute synergistically to the development of a potentially serious metabolic acidosis were not borne out.

Reference Number: 61220

SHARP, D. "Safe Bubbly [Comment]." *Lancet*, 364: 2165, 2004 (1 figure, 5 references)

Abstract: The American Academy of Ophthalmology issued a seasonal reminder of the risk of opening a bottle of champagne and that champagne corks are the most common holiday-related hazard to the eyes. Champagne corks caused 1.4% of eye injuries in Hungary and 0.07% of eye injuries in the United States. It has been calculated that champagne corks can hit the eye at a speed of 50 km/h.

> The safe opening method certainly means pointing the bottle away from people, including yourself, and serving it cool, keeps the inside pressure down a bit.

Reference Number: 61221

THORNTON, D., M.B. HILL, D. VITEK, ET AL. "Botulism from Drinking Prison-Made Illicit Alcohol—Utah 2011." *Morbidity and Mortality Weekly Report*, 61, 782–784, 2012 (7 references)

Abstract: Eight prisoners (ages twenty-four to thirty-five years) were hospitalized from botulism poisoning after drinking homemade liquor ("Pruno") made from a potato that was stored in a plastic bag for several days. The toxin was probably produced under the anaerobic conditions in the bag. Botulism causes signs of double vision, blurred vision, impaired gag reflex, and weakness.

The report documents an outbreak of severe illness with prolonged outbreak of severe illness with prolonged morbidity and great public expense that occurred in prison from pruno alcohol made illicitly by inmate. When a potato or other root vegetable is added to pruno, the risk for foodborne botulism increases.

Reference Number: 61222

SENDLER, D.J. "Physicians Working Under the Influence of Alcohol: An Analysis of Past Disciplinary Proceedings and Their Outcomes." *Forensic Science International* 285: 29–37, 2018 (1 table, 30 references).

Abstract: The prevalence rate of alcoholism for Austrian physicians was 9.5% for men and 4% for women, which is lower than the general population. Between 2010 and 2016, three female and fourteen male physicians were subject to disciplinary action due to providing medical treatment while under the influence of alcohol. One hundred and fifty-seven patients were potentially affected, but only four patients were harmed. But it is estimated that 10% of the 157 patient's health care was compromised by the physician's intoxication due to a mistake in medical procedure, diagnosis, or miscommunication. Only eleven patients noticed symptoms of intoxication and confronted the treating physician.

Surprisingly, this study showed that very few of the affected patients noticed that the physician treating them was intoxicated and incapable of performing his or her duties. Another important finding is the relative lack of involvement of the supporting nursing staff, which failed to report their clinical co-worker's problem with providing care under the influence of alcohol. As a result, physicians who were subjected to disciplinary action faced modest professional and legal consequences—most returned to work without any complications within six months from the incident. These results demonstrate that the problem of physicians working under the influence of alcohol might be more widespread than it appears. Furthermore, our study furthers widespread understanding that many supporting staff fear retaliation from their clinical supervisors who might regularly overuse alcohol and provide medical care. Therefore, the actions of these irresponsible clinicians remain underreported packing hundreds of patients at risk of misdiagnosis and poor treatment outcome.

Reference Number: 61223

MIHAILOVIC, Z., S. SAVIC, I. DAMJIANJUK, A. STANOJEVIC, AND M. MILOSEVIC. "A Case of a Fatal Himalayan Black Bear Attack in the Zoo." *Journal of Forensic Sciences*, 56: 806–809, 2011 (5 figures, 19 references)

Abstract: A twenty-two-year-old man was found naked and dead after being mauled by a Himalayan black bear in a cage at the Belgrade Zoo. The traditional Belgrade Beer Fest had been held near the zoo. The victim was seen to have been drinking a lot of beer and acting aggressively. He disappeared at approximately 2:00 a.m. and his body was found at 7:00 a.m. His postmortem vitreous humor alcohol concentration was 0.200 g/100 mL and urine alcohol concentration was 0.420 g100 mL. Cannabinoids were also detected in the urine.

Regarding safety precautions, the Beer Fest was dislocated from the area near the Belgrade Zoo to a safer location, but no further action was performed concerning protection of the available parts of wild animals' cages.

6.13 MOTORCYCLING

"Under normal environmental conditions, the operation of a motorcycle is more difficult than that of a four-wheeled passenger vehicle. In general, the motorcyclist will be involved in an accident at a lower BAC than the same individual in a four-wheeled passenger vehicle."

—Sun et al, "Lowering the Legal Blood Alcohol Limit for Motorcyclists" (1998)

"MOPEDS: Motorized Objects Propelling Ethanol Drinking Subjects."

—Christmas et al, "MOPEDS: Motorized Objects Propelling Ethanol Drinking Subjects" (2011)

The operation of a motorized two-wheel vehicle requires more skill (including balance) than the operation of a four-wheel vehicle and so there are laboratory and field studies that show greater impairment for drivers of motorcycles at lower BACs than for drivers of automobiles (61301–61304, 61309). In multi-vehicle collisions alcohol increased the risk of a fatality of the motorcyclist by 126% (61311). More severe motorcycle crashes occurred on roads with loops and curves (61312). Motorcycle DUIs were found to be given less harsh penalties than motor vehicle DUIs (61313).

Alcohol also causes impairment and increases the risk of risky behavior leading to collision in e-bike and moped drivers as well (61314–61317).

Reference Number: 61301

COLBURN, N., R.D. MEYER, M. WRIGLEY, AND E.L. BRADLEY. "Should Motorcycles Be Operated Within the Legal Alcohol Limits for Automobiles?" *Journal of Trauma*, 35: 183–186, 1993 (1 table, 3 figures, 18 references)

Abstract: Two female and twelve male licensed motorcyclists (ages twenty-one to forty-six years) consumed two standard drinks (either 12 oz beer or 1.25 oz of 40% spirits) over repeated 20-minute intervals until there was a 50% decrease in performance on a motorcycle simulator. BrACs were determined by an Intoxilyzer 5000 and in serum by GC. The mean peak BrACs were between 0.054 and 0.132 g/100 mL.

> We conclude that basic motorcycle handling skills are impaired at currently legal blood alcohol levels. Reaction times and total errors increased at a BAC of 0.062–0.088 mg/ dL, well below that defined as the legal limit of intoxication (0.1 mg/dL). Road errors also increased while motorcyclists were operating within the legal alcohol levels. Riders more frequently left the roadway at a BAC of 0.038–0.059 mg/dL.

Reference Number: 61302

CHIANG, H-H. AND Y-H. YOUNG. "Impact of Alcohol on Vestibular Function in Relation to the Legal Limit of 0.25 mg/L Breath Alcohol Concentration." *Audiology and Neurotology*, 12: 183–188, 2007 (2 tables, 27 references)

Abstract: Twenty male subjects (ages twenty-two to thirty years) consumed 0.5 g/kg alcohol within 10 minutes and were tested on a VEMP (vestibular evoked myogenic potential) test and caloric and visual suppression tests. BrACs were measured with an Intoximeter RBT IV and the BrACs ranged from 0.041 to 0.069 g/100 mL (mean 0.058 g/100 mL). The vestibular system gathers information for body position in space and helps maintain balance, which is important particularly for motorcyclists.

> From our perspective of vestibular function, the 0.25 mg/L BrAC limit gains clinical significance because the VOR performance deteriorates further when the BrAC exceeds 0.25 mg/L. However, impaired performance

of SCR and vestibulocerebular interaction has occurred when BrAC < 0.25 mg/L suggesting that a lower legal threshold is appropriate.

Reference Number: 61303

WATSON, W.A. AND J.C. GARRIOTT. "Alcohol and Motorcycle Riders: A Comparison of Motorcycle and Car/Truck DWIs." *Veterinary and Human Toxicology*, 34: 213–215, 1992 (1 table, 1 figure, 9 references)

Abstract: A study was conducted of the BrACs of eighty motorcycle drivers and ninety-two car/truck drivers who were arrested for impaired driving during 1984–1985 in San Antonio, Texas. These BrACs were determined with an Intoxilyzer 1000. The mean BrAC was 0.140 g/100 mL for motorcycle drivers and 0.160 g/100 mL for car/truck drivers. In addition, the mean BAC was 0.110 g/100 mL for fifteen alcohol positive motorcycle drivers involved in accidents, compared to 0.170 g/100 mL for thirty-six alcohol positive car/truck drivers involved in accidents.

The results of this study suggest that the pharmacologic effects of alcohol is more significant for the motorcyclists than the driver of a 4-wheeled vehicle.

Reference Number: 61304

SUN, S.W., D.M. KAHN, AND K.G. SWAN. "Lowering the Legal Blood Alcohol Limit for Motorcyclists." *Accident Analysis and Prevention,* 30: 133–136, 1998 (2 tables, 1 figure, 12 references)

Abstract: A study was conducted of forty motorcycle accidents (MCA) victims and 411 motor vehicle accident (MVA) victims admitted to a trauma center in New Jersey during 1992. All victims were operators, not passengers, and the blood samples were collected within 30 minutes of the accident. Thirty-three percent (12) of the MCA victims and 35% (117) of the MVA victims had a positive BAC. The mean BAC was 0.124 g/100 mL (0.014–0.313 g/100 mL) for the MCA victims and 0.180 g/100 mL (0.005–0.395 g/100 mL) for the MVA victims. The difference in BACs between the two groups was statistically significant.

Under normal environmental conditions, the operation of a motorcycle is more difficult than that of a four-wheeled passenger vehicle. In general, the motorcyclist will be involved in an accident at a lower BAC than the same individual in a four-wheeled passenger vehicle.

Reference Number: 61305

LUNA, G.K., R.V. MAIER, L. SOWDER, M.K. COPASS, AND M.R. ORESKOVICH. "The Influence of Ethanol Intoxication on Outcome of Injured Motorcyclists." *Journal of Trauma*, 24: 695–700, 1984 (2 tables, 1 figure, 21 references)

Abstract: An 18-month study was conducted of 139 injured motorcyclists admitted to hospital. Type and severity of injury was determined by the physician and standardized using the AIS and Injury Severity Score. BACs were determined in ninety-two patients and thirty-five (38%) had BACs > 0.100 g/100 mL and were classified as intoxicated. The mean BAC was 0.189 g/100 mL. The mortality rate was 10% for all motorcyclists, 23% for motorcyclists with BAC > 0.100 g/100 mL, and 6% for motorcyclists not intoxicated. Intoxicated motorcyclists were found to be 50% more at fault for their accidents than non-intoxicated motorcyclists.

> In conclusion, the presence of acute ethanol intoxication in motorcyclists can be demonstrated to have several effects—all deleterious. The intoxicated cyclist tends not to wear a helmet, be at fault for an accident and have an increased risk for severe head injury. Patients with severe head injury are at risk for death with the presence of alcohol intoxication providing an apparent synergistic deleterious effect.

Reference Number: 61306

OUELLET, J.V., H.H. HURT JR., AND D.R. THOM. "Alcohol Involvement in Motorcycle Accidents." *SAE Technical Paper Series 870602*, 121–129, International Congress and Exposition, Detroit Michigan, Feb 23–27, 1987 (9 tables, 8 figures, 11 references)

Abstract: A study was conducted of 900 fatal and non-fatal motorcycle accidents in which fifty-four drivers and five passengers were killed. BACs were determined by admission blood samples, police, or coroner's samples, or by the calculation of BAC by using the victim's alleged consumption. BACs were corrected by the addition of 0.015 g/100 mL/h from the time of the accident to the time of the blood sample. An additional study of 300 motorcycle fatalities was included, which showed fatty metamorphosis of the liver indicating alcohol abuse was present in forty-four of the 235 cases in which autopsies were conducted.

> The typical accident involving a nondrinking motorcyclist is a low speed, daytime, multiple vehicle collision, usually the result of another vehicle

violating the motorcycle right of way. By contrast, the typical alcohol involved accident occurs during late afternoon until an hour or so after the bars close; it is likely to be a single motor vehicle accident with the motorcycle running off the road at high speeds and is far more likely to be fatal.

Reference Number: 61307

KASANTIKUL, V., J.V. OUELLET, T. SMITH, J. SIRATHRANONT, AND V. PANICHABHONGSE. "The Role of Alcohol in Thailand Motorcycle Crashes." *Accident Analysis and Prevention*, 37: 357–366, 2005 (7 tables, 1 figure, 21 references)

Abstract: A prospective study of 1,082 accident-involved motorcycle riders was conducted in Thailand between 1999 and 2000. BACs, UACs, or BrACs (Alcometer SD400) were determined. Three hundred and ninety-three drivers (36%) had been drinking. The mean BAC (SD) of the 229 drivers who tested positive for alcohol was 0.135 g/100 mL (0.088 g/100 mL), and 164 (72%) had a BAC > 0.080 g/100 mL. Drinking drivers were more seriously injured in accidents than non-drinking drivers. Drinking drivers were more likely to be in non-intersection collisions than non-drinking drivers. Running red lights before the crash was twice as likely for drinking than non-drinking drivers. There was little difference in speed between the two groups.

Alcohol-involved riders were their own worst enemy. They were the primary cause factor in three-fourths of their accidents, and the only cause factor in one-third. Alcohol contributed to causing the accident in nearly 90% of the cases in which the rider had been drinking. Attention failures appear to be a major reason behind this culpability. Over half (54%) of the drinking riders appeared to be inattentive to the driving task before the crash. Evidence of inattention was often evident in single vehicle crashes in curves, or when the rider ran off the road or struck the rear of another vehicle or violated red traffic signals.

Reference Number: 61308

PEEK-ASA, C. AND J.F. KRAUS. "Alcohol Use, Driver and Crash Characteristics Among Injured Motorcycle Drivers." *Journal of Trauma Injury and Infection, Critical Care*, 41: 989–993, 1996 (4 tables, 1 figure, 21 references)

Abstract: The characteristics and BACs of 3,236 injured motorcyclists attending hospital in California between 1991 and 1992 were determined. Fifty-six percent (1,827) had their BACs determined within 4 hours of the collision. A positive BAC was found in 42% of those tested. The mean BAC was 0.173 g/100 mL (range 0.010 to 0.470 g/100 mL). The mean age of the drinking motorcyclist was thirty years compared to twenty-nine years for the non-drinking motorcyclist. Among drinking motorcyclists, 56% had a single MVC compared to 34% of non-drinking motorcyclists.

Driver characteristics indicate that drinking drivers were less likely to have a valid motorcycle license, were less likely to be wearing a helmet, were more likely to crash at night, and were more likely to be speeding. This profile indicates that drinking drivers have a profile that includes many high-risk behaviours.

Reference Number: 61309

GRAHAM, J.W. "Fatal Motorcycle Accidents." *Journal of Forensic Sciences*, 14: 79–86, 1969 (5 tables, 1 figure, 10 references)

Abstract: BACs were measured in 193 motorcycle drivers who survived less than 6 hours after the MVC between 1962 and 1966. Forty-six percent of the motorcyclists had a measurable BAC. Seventy-five percent of the motorcyclists with positive BAC were responsible for the MVC. Ninety-four percent of the motorcyclists with a BAC > 0.150 g/100 mL were responsible for the accidents.

In view of the special skill and awareness required to operate a motorcycle, blood alcohol concentrations associated with impairment of general driving ability are likely to have a greater influence on motorcycle operators.

Reference Number: 61310

PREUSSER, D.F., A.F. WILLIAMS, AND R.G. ULMER. "Analysis of Fatal Motorcycle Crashes: Crash Typing." *Accident Analysis and Prevention*, 27:845–851, 1995 (2 tables, 2 figures, 18 references)

Abstract: An analysis of 2,074 fatal motorcycle crashes that occurred in the United States during 1992 was conducted. A positive BAC was detected in 72% of the ran off road, 34% of the ran traffic control, 49% of the oncoming, and 37% of the bike-down accidents.

In general, however, the crash type analysis confirms that the most important and feasible means of reducing motorcyclist injuries are through laws requiring helmet use, and through enforcement of speed limit and alcohol-impaired driving laws.

Reference Number: 61311

SAVOLAINEN, P., AND F. MANNERING. "Probabilistic Models of Motorcyclists' Injury Severities in Single-and Multi-Vehicle Crashes." *Accident Analysis and Prevention,* 39: 955–963, 2007 (6 tables, 1 figure, 32 references)

Abstract: A probabilistic model was employed on the severity of a motorcyclists' injuries in single and multi-vehicle MVCs in Indiana between 2003–2005. Alcohol involvement results in a 10% reduction in minor or no injury and a 12% increase in non-incapacitating injuries in SMVCs. In the multi-vehicle crashes in which the motorcyclist was at fault, the likelihood of a fatality is 126% higher with alcohol. Crashes were found to be less severe on wet pavement conditions, near intersections, and when passengers were on the motorcycle, perhaps due to the motorcyclist driving more cautiously.

There were also some disturbing findings. Perhaps key among these is the finding that older motorcyclists were more likely to be involved severe injury crashes—even when controlling for all other elements of the crash in a multivariate analysis. This supports some recent aggregate data trends and would seem to contradict the long—held belief that young and inexperienced motorcyclists are more likely to be involved in severe crashes.

Reference Number: 61312

RIFAAT, S.M., R. TAY, AND A. DE BARROS. "Severity of Motorcycle Crashes in Calgary." *Accident Analysis and Prevention*, 49: 44–49, 2012 (2 tables, 2 figures, 34 references)

Abstract: An evaluation was conducted of 466 motorcycle crashes that occurred in Calgary between 2003 and 2005. Approximately 1% of the crashes were fatal and 49% involved injury. More severe crashes occurred on roads with loops and curves rather than on roads with traditional grid patterns. Alcohol use increased the possibility of severe injuries.

Our study finds that alcohol impairment and speeding are significant factors determining the severity outcomes of motorcycle involved crashes on local streets. Therefore, the common issues of speeding and alcohol impairment while driving or riding needs to be considered in a broader perspective, including on local streets. In most jurisdictions, traffic law enforcement tends to be focused on main roads where the traffic volumes are higher and enforcement is more visible. Some efforts need to be invested in ensuring that these risky behaviors are also targeted on local streets. In addition, anti-speeding and drink-driving education campaigns should also include motorcycle riders as a target audience.

Reference Number: 61313

YANG, J., X. GUO, M. XU, L. WANG, AND D. LORD. "Alcohol-Impaired Motorcyclists Versus Car Drivers: A Comparison of Crash Involvement and Legal Consequences from Adjudication Data." *Journal of Safety Research*, 79: 292–303, 2021 (8 tables, 1 figure, 54 references)

Abstract: An analysis was conducted of 10,451 motorcycle and 6,402 car DUIs with a BAC of 0.080 g/100 mL or greater between 2012 and 2016 at Jiangsu High People's Court of China. The percentage of DUI offenders with a BAC between 0.080 and 0.130 g/100 mL was 36.6% for motorcyclists and 31.7% for car drivers.

Table. Odds Ratio (OR) of Crash Characteristics of Motorcyclists Compared to Drivers

Crash Characteristic	OR
Crash involvement	1.83 ×
Single vehicle crashes	1.22 ×
SMVCs that cause injuries or death	6.92 ×

Source: Adapted from Yang et al (2021).

Theorists and researchers have previously noted that motorcyclists' risk of crash and injury against BAC climbs more steeply than the risk for car drivers. This is further demonstrated by our findings that alcohol-impaired riding results in more crashes than alcohol-impaired driving. Moreover, motorcycles are found to have a significantly higher likelihood of being responsible for single-vehicle crashes. Among the single-vehicle crashes caused by motorcyclists, 40.2% result in injuries or death, which confirms that alcohol-impaired riding makes motorcyclists extremely vulnerable in a collision. The perniciousness of DUI offences to other traffic participants are considered as an adjudicative factor in sentencing. By comparing judicial outcomes, judges are found more lenient with motorcycle offenders in practice. Specifically, with controls for BAC and other risk factors, there is an approximately 50% decrease in the likelihood of motorcyclists being sentenced to a harsh penalty.

Reference Number: 61314

MOSKAL, A., J-L MARTIN, AND B. LAUMON. "Risk Factors for Injury Accidents Among Moped and Motorcycle Riders." *Accident Analysis and Prevention*, 489: 5–11, 2012 (4 tables, 32 references)

Abstract: A comparison was conducted of the risk factors for 181,319 moped and 181,228 motorcycle collisions that occurred in France between 1996 and 2005. The adjusted odds ratios were determined comparing those motorcycle/moped drivers responsible for their motor vehicle collisions to those not responsible.

Table. Adjusted Odds Ratio (OR) of Moped and Motorcycle Drivers Responsible for Their MVC

BAC (g/100 mL)	Moped OR	Motorcycle OR
0.050–0.080	2.7 ×	3.7 ×
0.080–0.120	5.5 ×	7.4 ×
0.120–0.200	8.0 ×	9.8 ×
0.200+	10.3 ×	11.4 ×

Source: Adapted from Moskal et al (2012).

For both moped and motorcycle riders, being male, not wearing a helmet, exceeding the legal limit for alcohol and traveling for leisure purposes increased the risk of accident involvement. The younger and the oldest users had a greater risk of accident involvement. The largest risk factor was alcohol, and we identified a dose-effect relationship between alcohol consumption and accident risk with an estimated odds ratio of over 10 for motorcycle and moped riders with a BAC of 2 g/L or over.

Reference Number: 61315

ZUBE, K., T. DALRUP, M. LAU, R. MAATZ, A. TANK, I. STEINER, H. SCHWENDER, AND B. HARTUNG. "E-Scooter Driving Under the Acute Influence of

Alcohol—A Real Fitness Study." *International Journal of Legal Medicine*, 10pp, 26 February 2022 (1 table, 5 figures, 26 references)

Abstract: A closed course study was conducted on twenty-eight female and twenty-nine male e-scooter riders (ages eighteen to forty-nine years) before and after the consumption of three different amounts of alcohol over a period of 4 days of testing. The BACs were measured according to the current German forensic guidelines (GC and enzymatic methods) at the end of each e-scooter ride and the maximum BAC obtained ranged from 0.54 to 1.70 g/kg (median 1.6 g/kg). The course consisted of a narrowing track, a gate passage, driving in circles, a narrowing track, a slalom ride, and nine obstacles. The maximum speed allowed for the e-scooter was 20 km/h. The gate passage and slalom obstacles might mimic avoiding pedestrians (or their dogs) or parked cars.

Table. Mean (and Range) Percent Decrease in Driving Ability of Operating an E-Scooter at Various BACs

BAC Range	Mean Percent Decrease in E-Scooter Driving Ability Compared to Sober Driving	Range of Percent Decrease in E-Scooter Driving Ability Compared to Sober Driving
0.021–0.040	41%	9–62%
0.041–0.060	44%	27–47%
0.061–0.080	44%	29–47%
0.081–0.100	62%	51–73%
0.101–0.120	72%	64–78%
0.121–0.140	80%	73–85%

Source: Adapted from Zube et al (2022).

Even low BACs were demonstrated to pose risks when driving an e-scooter in road traffic. At BACs ranging from 0.21 to 0.60 g/kg, a higher risk of driving dangerously was seen. Referring to the mentioned results from the slalom and gate passage, an increased danger for pedestrians can be assumed at a BAC of at least 0.81 g/kg.

Reference Number: 61316

CENTOLA, C., M. TAGLIABUE, A. SPOTO, M. PALPACELLI, A. GIORGETTI, R. GIORGETTI, AND G. VIDOTTO. "Enhancement of Unsafe Behaviors in Simulated Moped-Riding Performance Under the Influence of Low Dose of Alcohol." *Accident Analysis and Prevention*, 136: 105409, 8pp, 2020 (2 figures, 84 references)

Abstract: Thirteen female and eleven male drivers (ages twenty-four to forty-two years) consumed a placebo or alcohol over 20 minutes and were tested on three driving scenarios in a motorcycle driving simulator. BrACs were measured with an Alcotest 6510 and the mean BrAC was 0.028 g/100 mL. The consumption of this low dose of alcohol by light drinkers resulted in measurable performance impairment, especially in the increase of dangerous behaviors and a reduction in safe maneuvers.

Currently, the scientific evidence deriving from epidemiological data and experimental studies, the former being more abundant than the latter, suggests that more caution and attention should be addressed to the category of motorcyclists. The recognized differences between cars and motorcycles cannot be ignored; this factor, together with all the other issues discussed, suggests that the legal equivalence of two- and four-wheeled vehicles is not recommended in countries in which the BAC limit is greater than or equal to 0.05 g/dL.

Reference Number: 61317

CHRISTMAS, A.B., R.A. BRINTZENHOFF, T.M. SCHMELZER, K.E. HEAD, AND R. SING. "MOPEDS: Motorized Objects Propelling Ethanol Drinking Subjects." *The American Surgeon*, 77: 304–306, 2011 (2 tables, 1 figure, 12 references)

Abstract: Between 1995 and 2006 there were 8,772 admissions to Carolinas Medical Center for injuries caused by motor vehicle collisions, of which 7,186 (87%) involved an automobile, 973 (12%) involved a motorcycle, and 113 (1%) involved a moped. SACs, injury severity, and mortality were determined.

Table. Mean Mortality Rate, SAC, and Percent with SAC > 0.050 g/100 mL in Drivers of Automobiles, Motorcycles, and Mopeds

	Automobile	Motorcycle	Moped
Mortality Rate	6.7%	8.5%	9.7%
Percent SAC > 0.05 g/100 mL	23.4%	24.8%	39%
Mean SAC	N/A	0.122	0.185

Source: Adapted from Christmas et al (2011).

In this study, we discovered a greater association between moped collisions and positive serum ethanol levels compared with automobile and motorcycle collisions. Although we strongly suspect that many of these riders are drunk driving recidivists, we do not have license suspension data.

6.14 PEDESTRIANS

"[T]he alcoholic concentration of the urine, breath or tissues as the most important single factor at the correct conclusion as to the degree of alcoholic intoxication of a patient.... Not infrequently, according to newspaper reports, chauffeurs administer to the unfortunate victim of their carelessness, some liquor in order to create the impression that the pedestrian was run over because he had imbibed too freely. The telltale breath of the injured person has no doubt time and again been considered sufficiently convincing evidence to convict the one and absolve the other."

—Bogen, "The Measurement of Drunkenness" (1927)

"Highly intoxicated participants showed some lack of awareness of impairment, a tendency to engage in risky road-crossings, and difficulty integrating speed and distance information in a timely manner, necessary to select safe gaps in the traffic."

—Oxley et al, "The Effect of Alcohol Impairment on Road-Crossing Behavior" (2006)

The quote by Bogen in 1927 again emphasizes the importance of determining the postmortem BAC of pedestrian victims, as a large proportion of injured and killed pedestrians, especially at night, had been consuming alcohol (61401, 61403, 61405). The risk of being hit by an automobile increases with the increasing BAC of the pedestrian (61402). At high BACs, the pedestrian is more likely to not to have been in the erect position when hit (61406).

Hit and run drivers of pedestrians were three times more likely to have a positive BAC and were more likely to flee the scene if the pedestrian was less than eleven years of age (61407–61409).

Pedestrians with high BACs may not feel the severity of their injuries after being hit by a motor vehicle (61408).

In a laboratory study, pedestrians with a BAC of between 0.070 to 0.100 g/100 mL had difficulty in selecting safe gaps in traffic flow and engaged in risky road crossings (61410). Alcohol impairs judgment and coordination leading to risky street crossing behavior and more severe injuries (61411). Being distracted and alcohol impaired were associated with unsafe road crossing behavior at intersections with traffic lights (61412).

Walking under the influence (WUI) pedestrians were involved in 6.6% of all collisions, 9.4% of incapacitating injuries, and 22.1% of pedestrian fatalities (61413). In addition, a BAC ≥ 0.080 g/100 mL was found in 26.4% of residents, 35.3% of visitors, and 64.3% of homeless persons (61414).

Areas with more off-premise alcohol outlets were associated with an increase in pedestrian collisions (61415). Most of the pedestrian fatalities on US freeways occurred in urban areas at night and 34% of the victims had a BAC ≥ 0.08 g/100 mL (61416). Older age causes a high probability of pedestrian collision due to cognitive decline and lower walking speed (61417).

Reference Number: 61401

JORDAN, P.W. AND W. YOUNG. "The Incidence of Alcohol Amongst Injured Pedestrians." *Australian Road Research Proceedings*, 1: 87–99, 1982 (11 tables, 7 figures, 19 references)

Abstract: A review was conducted of ten studies of the BACs of fatally injured pedestrians showed that 28 to 61% had BACs > 0.100 g/100 mL. This paper also studied the BACs of injured pedestrians from 1977 to 1979 in Victoria, Australia. Of the 812 after-dark pedestrian accidents, 36% had BAC = 0 and 40% had BAC > 0.150 g/100 mL.

Table. Percent of Pedestrians with BAC > 0.150 g/100 mL According to Accident Type

Pedestrian type	Percent with BAC> 0.150 g/100 mL
All Pedestrians	5–6%
Accident Involved Pedestrians	22%
Fatally Injured Pedestrians	31%
Fatally Injured Pedestrians (at night)	43%

Source: Adapted from Jordan and Young (1982).

It is hypothesized that alcohol influences the type of accident in two ways. Firstly, the pedestrian with a high BAC may be more likely to cross the road at the most convenient and closest point and avoid walking to the nearest intersection or traffic control device. Secondly, it can be assumed that the pedestrian with a high BAC is less able to judge the gap in two directions of traffic and hence tends to be involved in more farside accidents.

Reference Number: 61402

IRWIN, S.T., C.C. PATTERSON, AND W.H. RUTHERFORD. "Association Between Alcohol Consumption and Adult Pedestrians Who Sustain Injuries in Road Traffic Accidents." *British Medical Journal*, 286: 522, 1983 (1 table, 5 references)

Abstract: The BrACs of patients who were pedestrians injured in MVCs were determined by a Lion Alcolmeter or by a blood sample. One week after the accident, and within 30 minutes of the time of the accident, controls were obtained by asking passersby of approximately the same age and sex to provide a breath sample. The patient's BACs ranged from 0.060–0.340 g/100 mL. In twenty-seven patient-control pairs there was no alcohol detected. In eleven patient-control pairs, the patient had a positive BAC and the control was negative. In twelve patient-control pairs, the patient was negative for alcohol and the controls were positive. The relative risk of a pedestrian with a BAC > 0.080 g/100 mL being involved in an accident is 3.6 times. A correlation was found between increasing BAC and more severe injury.

Our study confirms the central finding of three case-control studies reported above, that there is a strong positive association between blood alcohol concentration and road accidents to pedestrians.

Reference Number: 61403

FONTAINE, H. AND Y. GOURLET. "Fatal Pedestrian Accidents in France: A Typological Analysis." *Accident Analysis and Prevention* 29: 303–312, 1997 (4 tables, 4 figures, 20 references)

Abstract: An analysis was conducted of 1,289 pedestrians killed in France between 1990 and 1991. Sixty-two percent of the victims were male. BACs were determined in 585 fatally injured adult pedestrians and 203 (51%) had a BAC > 0.080 g/100 mL. Nine out of ten accidents associated with adult intoxicated pedestrians occurred at night. Intoxicated pedestrians were more frequent in the countryside (48%) than in the city (23%).

The classification of pedestrians involved in fatal accidents identifies four groups; elderly pedestrians who were crossing a road in an urban area; children involved in daytime accidents in urban areas whilst playing or running; intoxicated pedestrians involved in night-time accidents in the country whilst walking on the carriageway; pedestrians involved in secondary accidents and changes of transport mode.

Reference Number: 61404

OSTROM, M. AND A. ERIKSSON. "Pedestrian Fatalities and Alcohol." *Accident Analysis and Prevention*, 33: 173–180, 2001 (1 table, 7 figures, 28 references)

Abstract: A study was conducted of 236 pedestrian fatalities in Umea Sweden between 1977–1995. The majority of the victims were male (58%) and the mean age was fifty-seven years (range of one to ninety-five years). There was an average of fifteen fatalities per year, although the lowest number of fatalities occurred in the last two years. BACs were determined in 201 pedestrians and were detected in forty-four (22%). The mean BAC was 0.150 g/100 mL (range 0.010–0.350 g/100 mL). In the victims aged fifteen to twenty-four years, 65% had a positive BAC.

Notably among the 11 alcohol-positive vehicle drivers the majority had run over an alcohol positive pedestrian and a relation between alcohol positive drivers and pedestrian victims has been reported.

Reference Number: 61405

PREUSSER, D.F. AND R.D. BLOMBERG. "Pedestrians and Alcohol." *Abstracts and Reviews in Alcohol and Driving*, 2: 6–10, 1981 (1 table, 1 figure, 8 references)

Abstract: The BACs of eighty fatally injured pedestrians and 143 non-fatally injured pedestrians were determined. These data were compared to the BACs of non-accident-involved pedestrians. The study was conducted in New Orleans from March 1975 to April 1976. Approximately 50% of fatally and non-fatally injured pedestrians had been drinking prior to the accident; 45% of the fatal and 36% of the non-fatal had BAC > 0.100 g/100 mL. The relative risk of pedestrian crash injury in the general population with increasing BAC is shown in the below table.

Table. Relative Risk of Pedestrian Crash Injury with Increasing BAC in the Population at Large

BAC (g/100 mL)	Relative Risk
0.000–0.049	1×
0.050–0.099	2×
0.100–0.149	4×
0.150–0.199	11×
0.200–0.249	40×

Source: Adapted from Preusser and Blomberg (1981).

It was concluded that pedestrian drinking is a major factor in adult pedestrian-vehicle crashes. The problem parallels the driver-alcohol problem in that it typically involves middle-age males and occurs at night and on weekends. However, this evidence suggests that the BACs of accident-involved drinking pedestrians are higher on average, than the BACs of drinking drivers, and the pedestrian risk curve, while similar in shape to the one for drivers, does not begin its dramatic rise until higher BACs are reached. Concerning the accidents themselves, it was concluded that many alcohol-involved crashes result from pedestrian risk taking and are probably related to alcohol's effect on judgment. Others appear to result from direct psychomotor impairment and were characterized by staggering, falling, and a general loss of psychomotor control.

Reference Number: 61406

KARGER, B., K. TEIGE, M. FUCHS, AND B. BRINKMANN. "Was the Pedestrian Hit in an Erect Position Before Being Run Over?" *Forensic Science International*, 119: 217–220, 2001 (2 tables, 3 figures, 18 references)

Abstract: Thirty-two fatally injured pedestrians, who were run over in the supine position, were compared to twenty-one pedestrians who were hit in the erect position and then run over (combined) between 1977 and 1997. The mean age in the run-over group was thirty-six years compared to fifty-one years for the combined group. The mean BAC in the run-over victims was 0.214 g/100 mL compared to 0.153 g/100 mL in the combined group. Twenty-four percent of the run over victims had a BAC > 0.300 g/100 mL compared to none of the combined group.

This excessive degree of intoxication possibly combined with tiredness was obviously the motivation for some persons in the run over group to just lie down on or near the road to sleep.

Reference Number: 61407

SOLNICK, S.J., AND D. HEMENWAY. "The Hit and Run in Fatal Pedestrian Accidents: Victims, Circumstances and Drivers. Accident." *Analysis and Prevention,* 27: 643–649, 1995 (4 tables, 33 references)

Abstract: An analysis was conducted of approximately 18,000 fatal pedestrian accidents in the United States between 1989–1991. Approximately 20% of the drivers involved left the scene of the accident. About 50% of the hit-and-run motorists were eventually identified. Drivers are much less likely to leave the scene when the victims is either quite young (< 11 years of age) or elderly (> 65 years of age).

Alcohol also appears as an important influence on leaving the accident scene when the analysis is restricted to drivers from whom information is available. Identified hit and run drivers are more likely to be young and male, to live outside the South, and to have invalid licenses or previous DWI convictions. For drivers tested, those who left the scene were three times more likely to have positive BACs.

Reference Number: 61408

WERFEL, P. "Beware of Patients Under the Influence." *Journal of Emergency Medical Services*, 22: May 2000

Abstract: A case report is presented by a paramedic who arrived at the accident scene of a pedestrian hit by a car. The victim was a thirty-seven-year-old male who was still walking at the scene but complained of pain in his legs. The victim smelled of alcohol and had slurred speech. He was walked into the ambulance and taken to hospital. The victim decompensated in the hospital and died. The autopsy showed four pelvic fractures and numerous lacerations to the internal organs.

Early in my EMS career I learned that intoxicated patients are walking, breathing lawsuits. There range from two-beer attorneys to unconscious drunks. We must remain more suspicious than usual in these cases because intoxicated patients generally give us unreliable information.

Reference Number: 61409

MACLEOD, K.E., J.B. GRISWOLD, L.S. ARNOLD, AND D.R. RAGLAND. "Factors Associated with Hit-and-Run Pedestrian Fatalities and Driver Identification." *Accident Analysis and Prevention*, 45: 366–372, 2012 (4 tables, 16 references)

Abstract: An analysis was conducted of nearly 40,000 hit-and-run pedestrian fatalities that occurred in the United States between 1998 and 2007 using the FARS data. Drivers were more likely to flee from the scene if the pedestrian was younger (< 11 years of age) and less likely to hit-and-run for older (> 65 years of age) pedestrians. Drivers were less likely to hit-and-run if the pedestrian was hit at a crosswalk. Hit-and-run drivers were more likely to be male, young, have prior violations, and have a suspended license.

Table. Odds Ratio (OR) of Hit-and-Run for Driver Characteristics

Driver Characteristics	OR of Hit-and-Run
BAC of 0.100 g/100 mL or higher	3.9 ×
Invalid license	4.3 ×
Prior DWI	1.8 ×
Prior suspensions	1.5 ×

Source: Adapted from MacLeod et al (2012).

Alcohol use and early morning, the time frame when persons may be leaving bars and parties, were among the leading factors that increased the risk of hit-and-run. Pedestrian alcohol use, which was not evaluated, may also contribute to this risk. Reducing alcohol-related crashes could substantially reduce pedestrian fatality as a result of hit-and-run.

Reference Number: 61410

OXLEY, J., M. LENNE, AND B. CORBEN. "The Effect of Alcohol Impairment on Road-Crossing Behavior." *Transportation Research Part F*, 9: 258–268, 2006 (1 table, 2 figures, 32 references)

Abstract: This study measured the road-crossing behavior of seventeen adults with a zero BAC, five with a low BAC (< 0.060 g/100 mL), and nineteen with a high BAC (0.070–0.100 g/100 mL) on a computerized test simulator with fifteen traffic scenes. Walking time was also measured at normal and fast paces. The subjects consumed 0.75 mL/kg alcohol over 16 minutes and BACs were determined in breath.

> Highly intoxicated participants showed some lack of awareness of impairment, a tendency to engage in risky road-crossings, and difficulty integrating speed and distance information in a timely manner, necessary to select safe gaps in the traffic. These results are discussed in terms of the effect of alcohol impairment on perceptual and cognitive capacities and the ability to compensate for impairment.

Reference Number: 61411

DULTZ, L.A. AND S.G. FRANGOS. "The Impact of Alcohol in Pedestrian Trauma." *Trauma* 15: 64–75, 2012 (5 tables, 72 references)

Abstract: A review was conducted of the effect of alcohol on traffic-related injuries. Alcohol use by pedestrians impairs judgment and coordination leading to risky street-crossing behaviors. Injured pedestrians who consumed alcohol tend to be young, single, male heavy drinkers. The US Uniform Accident and Sickness Drinking Provision Law (UPPL) allows insurers to deny reimbursement for medical service if the patient is intoxicated. As a result, US trauma centers do not routinely measure BAC.

> Pedestrians struck by motor vehicles are more severely injured than motor vehicle occupants and account for a large proportion of fatalities. Pedestrians who are drunk sustain more severe injuries, require more imaging, encounter more complications, and require longer hospital LOS. The prevention focus may need to evolve in the ensuing years from strategies focusing primarily on motor vehicle occupants to one that targets the vulnerabilities and distractions of pedestrians and which emphasize a safe co-existence within their shared environment.

Reference Number: 61412

REISH, L., L.M. CARSON, AND A.F. RAY. "Associations Between Social Drinking Events and Pedestrian Behavior—An Observational Study." *Journal of Transport and Health*, 20: 8pp, 2021 (3 tables, 1 figure, 24 references)

Abstract: The road-crossing behavior of 1,101 pedestrians was observed at three crosswalks near social drinking venues in Washington, DC. The most prevalent risky crossing behaviors were walking against the pedestrian walk signal (32%), distraction (17%), and walking outside of the crosswalk (15%). Overall, 52% of the pedestrians exhibited at least one unsafe road-crossing behavior. Atypical gait due to probable alcohol intoxication was observed in three pedestrians.

> This study reinforces the prevalence of unsafe road crossing behaviors and identifies several opportunities for future research by examining environmental influences of intersection characteristics and investigating types of distraction and alcohol impairment.

Reference Number: 61413

HEZAVEH, A. M. AND C.R. CHERRY. "Walking Under the Influence of the Alcohol: A Case Study of Pedestrian Crashes in Tennessee." *Accident Analysis and Prevention*, 121: 64–70, 2018 (4 tables, 2 figures, 42 references)

Abstract: An analysis was conducted of 11,309 pedestrian/car crashes in Tennessee between 2011 and 2016 of which 746 involved a pedestrian walking under the influence (WUI) of alcohol. WUI pedestrians were involved in 6.6% of all collisions, 9.4% of incapacitating injuries, and 22.1% of pedestrian fatalities. A BAC was determined in 131 WUI crashes and ranged between 0.010 and 0.660 g/100 mL (mean 0.171 g/100 mL). Men were 1.90 times more likely to be involved in WUI crashes than women. The odds of a weekend WUI was 1.52 times higher than on weekdays and 2.73 times more likely to occur at night without lighting.

> Comparisons indicate that the WUI crashes had their characteristics, which distinguished them from non-WUI crashes. Analysis indicates that 83% of the WUI crashes occurred in the night, moreover, 54%, 69%, and 85% of WUI crashes respectively occurred on weekends, midblock section of the road and areas with no traffic control device. Results of a binary logit regression indicates that pedestrian's age, males, posted speed limit, and nighttime crashes had a positive association with the WUI crashes. On the other hand, urban content, intersection crashes, driver maneuvers (i.e., parking-related, turning and straight) and daylight had a negative association with WUI crashes.

Reference Number: 61414

HICKOX, K.L., N. WILLIAMS, L.F. BECK, T. COLEMAN, J. FUDENBERG, B. ROBINSON, AND J. MIDDAUGH. "Pedestrian Traffic Death Among Residents, Visitors, and Homeless Persons—Clark County, Nevada, 2008–2011."

Morbidity and Mortality Weekly Report, 63(28): 597–602, 2014. (2 tables, 1 figure, 10 references)

A study was conducted of 140 pedestrian traffic deaths that occurred in Clark County, Nevada, between 2008 and 2011. The victims were divided into 107 residents, nineteen visitors, and fourteen homeless persons. A BAC of 0.080 g/100 mL+ was found in 26.4% of the residents, 35.3% of the visitors, and 64.3% of the homeless persons. Pedestrian deaths occurred between 6:00 p.m. and 11:59 p.m. in 41.1% of the residents and 78.6% of the homeless persons.

Higher pedestrian death rates among homeless persons in Clark County might be related to high rates of alcohol and drug abuse, mental illness and increased time spent walking along roadways; further research of this population is needed to more fully understand behaviors and environments that increase their risk. Interventions to decrease pedestrian deaths among homeless persons can be enhanced by a deeper understanding of the association between homeless pedestrian deaths and excessive alcohol use, nighttime collisions, and not residing in shelters. Homeless service providers, especially those providing services to unsheltered homeless persons in Clark County should understand that pedestrian death is a health risk for their clients and consider collaborating with organizations that have expertise in pedestrian safety to identify and implement effective interventions.

Reference Number: 61415

NESOFF, E.D., A.J. MILAM, C.C. BRANZAS, S.S. MARTINS, A.R. KNOWLTON, AND D.M. FURR-HOLDEM. "Alcohol Outlets, Neighborhood Retail Environments, and Pedestrian Injury Risk." *Alcohol: Clinical and Experimental Research* 42: 1979–1987, 2018 (2 tables, 1 figure, 53 references)

Abstract: A spatial analysis was conducted of the location of 848 alcohol off-premise and 726 on-premise alcohol outlets and 398 corner and 192 convenience stores that do not sell alcohol in Baltimore City and 841 pedestrian injury accidents between 2014–2015. When controlled for confounding factors, each additional off-premise alcohol outlet was associated with a 12.3% increase in the rate of neighborhood pedestrian injury. On-premise alcohol outlets were not associated with pedestrian injury.

Off-premise alcohol outlets are associated with pedestrian injury rate, even when controlling for other retail locations. This study provides new information in disentangling the mechanisms by which the neighborhood environment around alcohol outlets and other retail establishments influence pedestrian injury risk. Findings reinforce the unique importance of alcohol outlets in understanding neighborhood pedestrian injury risk and may provide evidence for informing policy on liquor store licensing, zoning, and enforcement.

Reference Number: 61416

WANG, J. AND J.B. CICCHINO. "Fatal Pedestrian Crashes on Interstates and Other Freeways in the United States." *Journal of Safety Research*, 74: 1–7, 2020 (6 tables, 30 references)

Abstract: Between 2015 and 2018 more than 800 pedestrians on average died annually on the interstates and other freeways in the United States. An analysis was conducted of 2,518 pedestrian deaths, about 14% of the total pedestrian deaths in the United States between 2015 and 2017. Most of the fatalities on the freeways or interstates occurred in urban areas at night. More than three-quarters of the pedestrians killed were male and 34% had a BAC of 0.080 g/100 mL or greater.

Crossing was the most common activity that pedestrians were doing when fatally injured on interstates and other freeways. Most of these pedestrians were crossing at nonjunctions, in urban areas and between areas that had residential and commercial or other land uses on opposite sides of the roadway. Alcohol impairment was a prominent issue among pedestrians fatally injured while crossing interstates and other freeways, with 40% of these pedestrians having a BAC of 0.08 g/dL or higher. Mixed residential and commercial land use is associated with greater pedestrian activity and more pedestrian crashes on a variety of roadway types and the density of alcohol outlets has been associated with alcohol-related pedestrian crashes. Localities with mixed land use adjacent to interstates and other freeways and particularly those with alcohol outlets near these roadways should consider physically obstructing access in open areas or promoting other means of travel such as transit, taxis, or ridesharing. Isolating pedestrians from traffic by constructing overpasses or underpasses would allow pedestrians to cross safely, but these facilities are expensive and need to be carefully designed to encourage their use.

Reference Number: 61417

KEMNITZER, C., C.N. POPE, S. NWOSU, L. WEI, AND M. ZHU. "An Investigation of Driver, Pedestrian, and Environmental Characteristics and Resulting Pedestrian Injury." *Traffic Injury Prevention*, 20: 510–514, 2019 (2 tables, 20 references)

Abstract: An analysis was conducted of 11,241 pedestrian crashes that occurred in Ohio between 2013 and 2017. No pedestrian injures occurred in 34% of the crashes, 43% had non-incapacitating injuries, 19% had incapacitating injuries, and 4% were fatal. The OR of pedestrian injury were 1.44 times if the pedestrian was sixty-five years of age or older, and 1.64 times if alcohol/drug use was suspected. Older age causes a high probability of pedestrian collision due to cognitive decline and lower walking speed.

The odds of pedestrian injury increased when the driver was male, the driver was under the influence of alcohol, the cause of the crash was pedestrian darting, the pedestrian was struck while in the travel lane, the pedestrian was 65 or older, the pedestrian was under the influence of alcohol, or under dark conditions on an unlit roadway. Factors that lowered the odds of injury was pedestrian age 0–4, and vehicle maneuvers other than driving straight ahead.

6.15 RAILWAYS

> "Soon after he invented the locomotive, George Stephenson complained that the personnel operating his monsters were tanked up on something besides steam in their boilers. He cited the accident hazard caused by train operators who drank."
>
> —Borkenstein, "The Evolution of Modern Instruments for Breath Alcohol Analysis" (1960)

A large proportion of pedestrians killed by trains were intoxicated by alcohol (61501–61504). Intoxicated passengers have engaged in risky behavior on trains and subways (61505, 61506).

Railway suicides occurred in 61% of train pedestrian fatalities and 50% of the railway suicide victims had consumed alcohol (61507, 61508).

Reference Number: 61501

CINA, S.J., J.L. KOELPIN, C.A. NICHOLS, AND S.E. CONRADI. "A Decade of Train-Pedestrian Fatalities: The Charleston Experience." *Journal of Forensic Sciences*, 39: 668–673, 1994 (1 table, 9 references)

Abstract: A study was conducted of twenty-five consecutive pedestrian fatalities in Charleston County, South Carolina, between 1982 and 1992. Eighty percent of the victims had a blood or tissue alcohol concentration of greater than 0.100 g/100 mL. Eighty percent of the victims were killed between 11:00 p.m. and 6:00 a.m.

> Given the strong association with alcohol consumption noted above, this temporal relationship can be predicted. A significant number of our victims may have falling into an alcohol induced stupor while lying on the tracks; this would explain their failure to respond to the train's warning signal. This scenario reinforced the point that the majority of people witnessed to be laying across the train tracks are probably not suicidal.

Reference Number: 61502

LERER, L.B., AND R.G. MATZOPOULOS. "Fatal Railway Injuries in Cape Town, South Africa." *American Journal of Forensic Medicine and Pathology*, 18: 144–147, 1997 (6 tables, 16 references)

Abstract: A study was conducted of the BACs of 285 fatally injured victims of railway-related accidents in Cape Town, South Africa, between 1992 and 1994. There were thirty-two suicides (8%), forty-three criminal violence (11%), thirty-eight falling from the train (10%), and 227 pedestrian (60%) fatal accidents.

Table. BACs of Railway-Related Fatalities

BAC Range (g/100 mL)	Violence, Robbery, Sexual Assault	Suicide	Fell out of Train	Crossing Tracks
0	57%	90%	54%	55%
> 0.01–0.10	14%	7%	12%	10%
0.11–0.20	3%	3%	12%	13%
0.21–0.30	17%	0%	15%	15%
> 0.30	9%	0%	8%	7%

Source: Adapted from Lerer and Matzopoulos (1997).

The low numbers of suicide with elevated blood alcohol levels confirms the belief that intoxication is a good indicator of accidental death rather than suicide with respect to railway mortality.

Reference Number: 61503

PELLETIER, A. "Deaths Among Railroad Trespassers. The Role of Alcohol in Fatal Injuries." *Journal of the American Medical Association*, 277: 1064–1066, 1997 (2 tables, 1 figure, 11 references)

Abstract: A study was conducted of 128 railroad-related deaths involving trespassers in North Carolina between 1990–1994. A positive BAC was found in 82% of the victims. The average BAC was 0.260 g/100 mL (range 0.030–0.490 g/100 mL).

During 1990 through 1994 most train related deaths that occurred among persons who were trespassing on railroad property in North Carolina occurred among unmarried male pedestrians aged 20 to 49 years who had less than a high school education and who were intoxicated at the time of the injury. Relatively few incidents involved children or the elderly.

Reference Number: 61504

NIXON, J., A. CORCORAN, L. FIELDING, AND J. EASTGATE. "Fatal and Nonfatal Accidents on the Railways—A Study of Injuries to Individuals, with Particular Reference to Children and to Nonfatal Trauma." *Accident Analysis and Prevention,* 17: 217–222, 1985 (5 Tables, 13 References)

Abstract: A 5-year study was conducted of eighty-four fatal and 211 non-fatal cases involving railways in Queensland, Australia. The ages of the fatally injured victims ranged from twelve months to seventy-three years. BACs ranged from 0.011 to 0.408 g/100 mL and were detected in twenty-three (30%) of victims age seventeen years and over. The median BAC was 0.197 g/100 mL, and in five cases the BAC > 0.300 g/100 mL. Suicide was thought to occur in ten (13%) of the cases. In non-fatal injuries, the largest category was falls from a moving or stationary train.

The railway track is obviously a dangerous place for the inebriated and in a number of fatal cases, the victim was crossing the track by foot or in a motor vehicle and was struck by a train. Alcohol was also implicated as a causal factor in a number of falls on and from trains.

Reference Number: 61505

STRAUCH, H., I. WIRTH, AND G. GESERICK. "Fatal Accidents Due to Train Surfing in Berlin." *Forensic Science International*, 94: 119–127, 1998 (3 tables, 3 figures, 10 references)

Abstract: A study was conducted of forty-one train surfing accidents in Berlin between 1989 and 1995, of which eighteen were fatal. Autopsies were conducted in fourteen of the cases. There were thirteen male and one female victims (ages thirteen to twenty-five years). A positive BAC was found in eight of the victims and six had a BAC > 0.115 g/100 mL. The highest BAC was 0.275 g/100 mL.

A speed-controlled permanent door locking system has been installed in two of the old series 476 and 477, so that train surfing is possible only on trains of the 475 series. These trains account for about 10% of all rolling stock and are to be decommissioned in 1998. S-Bahn surfing in Berlin, consequently, is expected to be no more than a temporary phenomenon.

Reference Number: 61506

LIN, P.T. AND J.R. GILL. "Subway Train-Related Fatalities in New York City: Accident Versus Suicide." *Journal of Forensic Sciences*, 54: 1414–1418, 2009 (4 tables, 4 figures, 16 references)

Abstract: A study was conducted on 211 (53% female) victims fatally injured in New York City subway accidents between 2003 and 2007. It was determined that 111 (52%) were suicides and 76 (36%) were accidental. A positive BAC was detected in 42% of the accidental victims (mean 0.200 g/100 mL) and 14% of the suicide victims (mean 0.160 g/100 mL). There were six persons who died falling off the train while attempting to urinate and five of them were intoxicated (possible micturition syncope).

Toxicology may help distinguish between accident and suicide. The greatest discrepancies occurred with the detection of cocaine, ethanol and antidepressants. Cocaine and ethanol were more commonly associated with accidents while antidepressants were more commonly associated with suicides. The blood-alcohol concentration was slightly higher among accidental deaths.

Reference Number: 61507

SOUSA, S., L. SANTOS, R.J. DINIS-OLIVEIRA, T. MAGALHAES, AND A. SANTOS. "Pedestrian Fatalities Resulting from Train-Persons Collisions." *Traffic Injury Prevention*, 16: 208–212, 2015 (2 tables, 1 figure, 25 references).

Abstract: A study was conducted of ninety-seven pedestrian fatalities due to trains in the northern region of Portugal between 2008 and 2012. Approximately 61% of the cases were classified as suicide, 31% as accidents, and 8% as undetermined. Suicides most often occurred on weekday afternoons and accidents in the evening or at night. Alcohol was the most common drug detected (50%), and 60% of the cases in which alcohol was detected were suicides. Cannabinoids were detected in only one accident case.

> In conclusion, like other European countries, suicide was the main etiology of the train-person fatalities, but this suicide method only represented a small percentage of total suicides registered in the region. Being under influence of alcohol or drugs was found to have a considerable impact in these cases, especially in suicides.

Reference Number: 61508

LASOTA, D., A. AL-WATHINANI, P. KRAJEWSKI, D. MIROWSKA-GUZEL, K. GONIEWICZ, A.J. HERTELENDY, K.A. ALHAZMI, W. PAWLOWSKI, A. KHORRAM-MANESH, AND M. GONIEWICZ. "Alcohol and the Risk of Railway Suicide." *International Journal of Environmental Research and Public Health*, 17: 70003, 10pp, 2020 (2 tables, 50 references)

Abstract: Suicide is one of the top ten causes of deaths globally and 22% of the suicides can be attributed to alcohol use. Alcohol use is the strongest predisposing factor for impulsive and aggressive behavior compared to all other drug use. An evaluation was conducted of sixty victims of railroad suicide in Warsaw, which included an alcohol analysis of postmortem blood, VH, and muscle tissues. Almost 77% of railway suicides were men. The ages of the victims ranged from seventeen to eighty-nine years (mean age 45.38 years). Alcohol was detected in thirty victims (50%) and the BACs ranged from 0.080 to 0.420 g/100 mL (mean 0.097 g/100 mL). Sober suicide victims were in general older than drinking victims. The older the victim the higher the detected BAC. Alcohol-related railway suicides are significantly lower in autumn.

The observed relationship between age and the presence of alcohol in suicide victims may be the cause of railway suicides. Knowledge of the mechanisms of seasonal variability of suicidal behavior can help to develop effective strategies to prevent railway suicides.

6.16 SAUNA (HYPERTHERMIA)

"Drinking alcohol while sauna bathing can create serious health risks and should be avoided. Alcohol consumption increases the risk of hypotension and fainting in the sauna as well as the risk of arrhythmia and sudden and hyperthermia death, especially in people with coronary heart disease."

—Hannusela et al, "Benefits and Risks of Sauna Bathing" (2001)

Alcohol is a risk factor in sauna or hyperthermia deaths. The effects of alcohol potentiate the decrease in blood pressure and increase in heart rate caused by heat (61601, 61602) and hence can cause hypotension, dizziness, and cardiac arrhythmias (61603, 60106). Up to 91% of the men who died of hyperthermia in saunas were intoxicated by alcohol (61606, 61608). The recommended characteristics of a sauna (Finnish bath) are as follows:

- Temperature of between 80° to 100°C at face level and 30°C at floor level
- The relative humidity should be between 10% to 20%
- Good ventilation of three to eight air exchanges per hour.
- Short stays in the sauna of 5 to 20 minutes interspersed with a cooling-off period, followed by oral intake of fluids
- Never sauna alone and don't consume alcohol.

Reference Number: 61601

MEKJAVOC, I.B., C.A. GAUL, M.D. WHITE, AND K.D. MITTLEMAN. "Cardiovascular Responses During 70 Degree Head-Up Tilt. The Effect of Elevated Body Temperature and High Alcohol Blood Levels." *Physiologist*, 30: S-56–S-57, 1987 (2 figures, 6 references)

Abstract: Six male subjects consumed either a control (OJ) or 2.5 mL of 40% v/v alcohol/kg. The subjects were then immersed in a euthermic or hyperthermic water bath for 60 minutes or until their rectal temperature reached 38.5°C. BACs were measured in blood and urine and were

0.099 g/100 mL for the euthermic and 0.078 g/100 mL for the hyperthermic conditions. ECG and blood pressure were measured before and after the subjects were tilted head-up at 70 degrees.

> The present study demonstrates that alcohol acts synergistically with elevated body temperature increasing peripheral perfusion by decreasing peripheral resistance as indicated by the reduction in mean arterial blood pressure, with a concomitant rise in heart rate.

Reference Number: 61602

ROINE, R., O.J. LUURILAS, A. SUOKAS, E. HEIKKONEN, P. KOSKINEN, R. YLIKAHRI, L. TOIVONEN, M. HARKONEN, AND M. SALASPURO. "Alcohol and Sauna Bathing: Effects on Cardiac Rhythm, Blood Pressure, and Serum Electrolyte and Cortisol Concentrations." *Journal of Internal Medicine*, 231: 333–338, 1992 (2 tables, 2 figures, 22 references)

Abstract: Ten healthy male subjects (ages twenty-four to forty years) consumed either fruit juice or 1.5 g/kg ethanol within 2 hours. The subjects were then placed in a dry sauna at 85°C for three 10-minute periods. After an overnight sleep, subjects were again placed in the sauna. Blood pressure, body temperature, ECGs, and various blood electrolyte concentrations were determined. BACs were between 0.070 and 0.100 g/100 mL. Two subjects suffered from nausea and dizziness after alcohol consumption during sauna bathing. Body temperature increased by 1.5–1.8°C, which led to a 62%–93% increase in mean heart rate. Alcohol caused a significant fall in systolic blood pressure.

> In conclusion, sauna bathing even in combination with heavy alcohol consumption does not appear to be arrhythmogenic in healthy male subjects. Whether this is true for patients suffering from atherosclerotic or other heart disease or subjects with known rhythm disturbances needs further evaluation.

Reference Number: 61603

HANNUSELA, M.L. AND S. ELAHHAM. "Benefits and Risks of Sauna Bathing." *American Journal of Medicine*, 110: 118–126, 2001 (2 tables, 2 figures, 130 references)

Abstract: A general review was conducted of the benefits and risks of taking a sauna (Finnish bath). The recommended temperature of a sauna is 80 to 100°C at the level of the face and 30°C at the floor. The relative humidity of the air should be between 10 and 20%.

Drinking alcohol while sauna bathing can create serious health risks and should be avoided. Alcohol consumption increases the risk of hypotension and fainting in the sauna as well as the risk of arrhythmia and sudden and hyperthermia death, especially in people with coronary heart disease. Almost all (221 of 228) hyperthermia deaths in Finland from 1970 to 1986 took place in saunas and were considered accidents. Most of the victims were middle-aged men, 84% were under the influence of alcohol and 27% had cardiovascular disease.

Reference Number: 61604

KORTELAINEN, M-L. "Hyperthermia Deaths in Finland in 1970–1986." *American Journal of Forensic Medicine and Pathology* 12: 115–118, 1991 (3 tables, 1 figure, 18 references)

Abstract: A study was conducted of 184 male and forty-four female hyperthermia victims (mean age fifty-two years) who died in Finland between 1970–1986. Most of the victims were found in a sauna. A positive BAC was found in 91% of the male and 59% of the female victims.

Middle-aged men were overrepresented among the hyperthermia victims dying in the sauna and usually had large postmortem concentrations of alcohol in the blood.

Reference Number: 61605

RODHE, A. AND A. ERIKSSON. "Sauna Deaths in Sweden, 1992–2003." *American Journal of Forensic Medicine and Pathology*, 29: 27–31, 2008 (1 table, 3 figures, 13 references)

Abstract: The characteristics of fourteen female and sixty-three male victims (mainly middle-aged) whose deaths were related to sauna baths in Sweden between 1992 and 2003 were determined. The postmortem BAC was determined in sixty-nine victims and a positive BAC was found in forty-nine victims (71%). The mean BAC was 0.160 g/100 mL. Most of the victims who died on weekends had a positive BAC.

According to the present and other studies, it seems as if middle-aged men especially those with heavy alcohol consumption are overrepresented among sauna-related deaths but whether this is due to different or more frequent sauna bathing of this group is unknown. In addition to heavy alcohol intake, the results in this study indicate that bathing alone in a sauna is also a risk factor since all victims but 2 found dead in the sauna had been bathing alone. Bathing alone is a risk factor that can be avoided which should perhaps be emphasized more.

Reference Number: 61606

KENTTAMES, A. AND K. KARKOLA. "Death in Sauna." *Journal of Forensic Sciences*, 53: 724–729, 2008 (3 tables, 4 figures, 22 references)

Abstract: A study was conducted of 393 deaths that occurred in a sauna around Helsinki between 1990 and 2002. Exposure to heat was the underlying cause of death in 25% of the victims. Alcohol intoxication was the underlying cause of death in 34%, and the mean BAC was 0.306 g/100 mL (range 0.169–0.401 g/100 mL). Men who died of hyperthermia were almost always intoxicated (91%).

The proportion of women in sauna deaths has increased and the role of alcohol as a risk factor has grown. The prevention and control of deaths in the sauna should focus on less alcohol drinking or drinking afterwards. Furthermore, a drunken sauna bather should not be left alone in the sauna.

Reference Number: 61607

WHITE, M.D., C.E. JOHNSTON, M.P. WU, G.K. BRISTOW, AND G.G. GIESBRECHT. "Ethanol Ingestion Prolongs Orthostatic Intolerance in Hyperthermic Humans." *Aviation, Space Environmental Medicine*, 69: 577–582, 1998 (2 tables, 1 figure, 16 references)

Abstract: Three female and four male subjects (mean age twenty-five years) consumed either OJ or OJ and 1 mL/kg ethanol within 15 minutes after a 4-hour fast. Subjects were then immersed in 40°C water and then tested for orthostatic intolerance (OI) by a 63 degree head-up tilt. Esophageal temperature, heart rate, blood pressure, and BrACs were determined. BrACs were determined with an Alco-Sensor IV and corrected by –8.62% per degree Celsius increase in body temperature. The mean BrAC was approximately 0.075 g/100 mL. Esophageal temperature was 37.07°C (control) and 37.05°C (ethanol) both prior to immersion, and 39.01°C (control) and 38.97°C (ethanol) post-immersion. No OI was seen pre-immersion with or without ethanol, but ethanol increased OI after immersion.

> In conclusion our data indicate that prolonged immersion in warm water presents a significant health hazard through orthostatic intolerance to sudden postural changes from supine to standing position for at least 25 minutes post-immersion. These effects seem to be exacerbated by ethanol ingestion and may be more prevalent in males than females.

Reference Number: 61608

YANG, K.-M., B-W. LEE, J. OH, AND S.H. YOO. "Characteristics of Sauna Deaths in Korea in Relation to Different Blood Alcohol Concentrations." *Forensic Science, Medicine and Pathology*, 14: 307–313, 2018 (3 tables, 1 figure, 20 references)

Abstract: Sauna baths are known as *Jjimjilbangs* (or heating room) and are popular in Korea to relieve fatigue and cure hangovers. Traditionally in Korea the sauna is taken while resting on a stone or wooden floor rather than sitting up on a bench. Between 2008 and 2015 there were 103 sauna deaths. Eighty-five percent of the victims were men, with an age range of twenty-six to eighty-six years (mean fifty-five years). Eighty-one percent had a positive BAC (> 0.010 g/100 mL) and 74% had a BAC > 0.080 g/100 mL and were deemed to be intoxicated. Intoxicated victims were 11.3 times as likely to have been found in the prone position and 2.4 times more likely to be in the side position than non-intoxicated victims. Acute alcohol intoxication was diagnosed as the cause of death in four victims (BACs were 0.320, 0.330, 0.340, and 0.380 g/100 mL respectively).

> Saunas are usually used for relaxation and refreshment. The benefits of sauna bathing have been shown in epidemiological studies. However, the hazardous role of alcohol consumption in saunas has not been fully emphasized, especially at lower BACs; thus, the significance of the relationship between alcohol consumption and sauna death has been unknown. Our study suggests that sauna deaths have different characteristics in the I and NI groups, according to BAC at autopsy. The results presented herein support evidence that sauna death is still undoubtedly a diagnosis of exclusion. The cause of death of individuals with no alcohol detected in their blood may be attributed to heart disease such as ischemic heart disease. However, individuals (especially men) with alcohol intoxication were associated with the prone position at the scene of death. This suggests that respiratory

dysfunction caused by acute alcohol intoxication and body position could lead to sauna death despite lower BACs. Furthermore, considering the high prevalence of alcohol intoxication in sauna death. Monitoring sauna bathing after alcohol consumption is a key step in preventing sauna deaths.

6.17 SEXUAL ASSAULT

"It provokes the desire, but it takes away the performance."

—William Shakespeare, *Macbeth*

"We conclude that the stereotype of DFSA has arisen largely from media hysteria, misleading scientific reports and drug detector kits with poor specificity, all of which are adding to public concerns that sexual assault associated with covert drugging is widespread. Although public health campaigns focusing only on covert drug administration are laudable, they are detracting from the much greater risk of being sexually assaulted following voluntary drug and/or alcohol consumption."

—Benyon et al, "The Involvement of Drugs and Alcohol in Drug-Facilitated Sexual Assault" (2008)

Laboratory studies have shown that alcohol tends to decrease inhibitions and affects the perception of sexual availability (61701–61703). Alcohol is by far the most common drug found in sexual assault victims (61704, 61706, 61707). The drugs detected in the blood and urine in the victims of suspected drug-facilitated sexual assault (in decreasing frequency detected) are as follows:

Alcohol > Cannabis > Cocaine > Ecstasy > Amphetamine > Heroin > Ketamine

Alcohol consumption by the offender was associated with more aggressive assaults, night assaults, stranger assaults, and outdoor assaults (61705, 61708) and assailants were less likely to wear a condom (61723). Approximately 40% of the women victims of fatal sexual assaults had a positive postmortem BAC (61712).

About 25% of sexual assault victims had a positive BAC, perhaps due in part to long delays in collecting the samples. Victims with visible trauma were 3.4 times more likely to have acetone detected compared to non-visible trauma victims (61713).

Of the urine/blood samples collected within 12 hours of the sexual assault, about 85% were positive for alcohol. The higher the BAC of the victim, the more likely the victim felt they were drugged, although no cases of drug facilitated sexual assault (DFSA) were detected (61714).

Of the drug/alcohol toxicology screens conducted on alleged DFSA cases, GHB was detected in only one case (1.3%) and suggests that spiked drinks are not as common as portrayed in the media (61715).

In a mock DFSA case, jurors only convicted 9% of the time if they were only presented with a negative toxicology report (61716).

Biomarkers of alcohol consumption (EtG, EtS), which can be detected for 2 to 3 days, were found in 94% of the victims, but a positive UAC was detected in only 42%. The detection of EtG or EtS may lend credence to the claims of the victim of assault occurring while the victim was intoxicated by alcohol (61717).

Extrapolation of BAC occurs frequently in sexual assault court cases due to the long delays in collecting the sample and may be used if the victim was incapable of consenting (61718), as drinking alcohol prior to sexual activity influences consent, especially in regard to casual or new sexual partners (61719).

A review of legal issues in sexual assault cases in the United Kingdom suggests that blackout, unconsciousness, vomiting, and back calculation of BAC may show extreme intoxication and inability to consent (61720). The best and most reliable method of determining BACs is by the collection of a blood sample close to the time of assault (61721) and neither forensic toxicologists nor psychologists/psychiatrists should be asked if the alleged victims were too impaired to consent as this should be the matter for the factfinders to determine (61721).

In Denmark, of the 277 cases of sexual violence, 59% were dropped before prosecution and a conviction occurred in only 19% of the cases (61722).

Reference Number: 61701

ABBEY, A., T. ZAWACKI, AND P. MCAUSLAN. "Alcohol's Effect on Sexual Perception." *Journal of Studies on Alcohol*, 61: 688–697, 2000 (2 tables, 3 figures, 35 references)

Abstract: Eighty-eight male and eighty-eight female undergraduate students (mean age twenty-six years) were administered either a placebo or 1.25 mL/kg of 40% v/v vodka consumed within 15 minutes. The BrACs were determined before and 10 minutes after consumption ended. The mean BrAC was 0.033 g/100 mL. At random, one male and one female student conversed with each other for 15 minutes and then filled in a questionnaire. In addition, the conversations were videotaped and rated by observers. Men perceived that their female companions behaved in a more sexual manner than the women perceived.

This study demonstrates that two drinks are enough to affect perception of disinhibition and sexuality. Students who feel sexy and uninhibited when drinking are at risk for having sex with someone they do not know well, having unprotected sex, being the victim of forced sex or feeling comfortable forcing sex on someone.

Reference Number: 61702

ABBEY, A., P.O. BUCK, T. ZAWACKI, AND C. SAENZ. "Alcohol's Effects on Perceptions of a Potential Date Rape." *Journal of Studies on Alcohol*, 64: 669–677, 2003 (1 table, 1 figure, 39 references)

Abstract: Ninety male and ninety female university students (mean age twenty-six years) were administered alcohol, a placebo, or a non-alcoholic beverage and then read a 1,000 word story that described a potential date rape situation in which both the man and the woman had been drinking. The mean BrACs as determined with the Alco-Sensor IV was 0.073 g/100 mL. The subjects then filled in a questionnaire.

Participants who consumed alcohol during the study felt that the male character acted more appropriately than did those who did not consume alcohol. Also, the more positive participants' attitudes about casual sex, and the more sexually aroused they thought the female character was, the more appropriately they thought the male behaved.

Reference Number: 61703

DAVIS, K.C., C.S. HENDERSHOT, W.H. GEORGE, J. NORRIS, AND J.R. HEIMAN. "Alcohol Effects on Sexual Decision Making: An Integration of Alcohol Myopia and Individual Differences." *Journal of Studies on Alcohol*, 68: 843–851, 2007 (3 figures, 28 references)

Abstract: Thirty female and thirty-one male subjects (mean age twenty-four years) consumed no alcohol or 0.99 g/kg (male) or 0.790 g/kg (female) within 10 minutes. BrACs were determined with an Alco-Sensor IV. A hypothetical sexual risk scenario was read and measures of sexual decision making were determined. The mean BrAC was 0.092 g/100 mL.

> Not only do these findings further establish the importance of alcohol myopia theory for understanding intoxicated sexual risk taking by providing support for theoretically relevant mediating mechanisms, they also expand our current understanding of alcohol facilitated sexual risk by integrating individual difference characteristics into the alcohol myopia theory of sexual risk and by using experimental protocols that induce high levels of sexual arousal and intoxication. Findings indicated that intoxicated participants were more attentive to impelling cues like sexual arousal than sexual risk.

Reference Number: 61704

SCHWARTZ, R.H., R. MILTEER, M.J. SHERIDAN, AND C.P. HORNER. "Beach Week: A High School Graduation Rite of Passage for Sun Sand, Suds and Sex." *Archives Pediatric and Adolescent Medicine*, 153: 180–183, 1999 (3 tables, 5 references)

Abstract: Twenty-five White female high school graduates who attended beach week at a North Carolina beach were interviewed. BrACs were also determined by an Alco-Sensor before and after a beach party. Thirty-four graduates completed the survey 2 to 3 months later. Of the twenty-five girls who attended the party, fifteen (60%) had a BrAC > 0.080 g/100 mL upon leaving. Daily cigarette smoking (54%), daily drunkenness (75%), and sex (46%) were the norm among the respondents of the survey. Eighty-six percent of the girls who had sex were drunk. Months after beach week, 32% of the respondents had negative feelings, 12% were depressed, and 18% were concerned about getting a bad reputation among classmates.

> Second, girls tended to drink more alcohol during beach week parties than they did during parties held in their home community. There was a clear relationship between frequency and extent of alcohol intake and sexual intercourse among our survey respondents.

Reference Number: 61705

ABBEY, A., A.M. CLINTON-SHERROD, P. MCAULSAN, T. ZAWACKI, AND P.O. BUCK. "The Relationship Between the Quantity of Alcohol Consumed and the Severity of Sexual Assaults Committed by College Men."

Journal of Interpersonal Violence, 18: 813–833, 2003 (3 tables, 1 figure, 42 references)

Abstract: A study was conducted of 113 male undergraduates (ages eighteen to fifty-three years) who reported that they had committed a sexual assault at age > fourteen years. Most sexual assaults occurred when the participants and their victims were eighteen years of age. Most of the assaults occurred in the woman's home (36%). Only one assault occurred with a woman who was just met at a party or bar; most of the men knew the women. The man's alcohol consumption was linearly related to increased aggressiveness and the victim's alcohol consumption was linearly related to more severe forms of assault.

Alcohol's role may also vary based on the type of relationship. In casual relationships, perpetrators may seek out intoxicated women because they view them as easy targets and fair game. In close relationships, alcohol may be perceived as a signal for sexual intimacy. Researchers have found that when college students read stories about couples on dates, alcohol consumption is associated with the perception that consensual sex will occur.

Reference Number: 61706

SCOTT-HAM, M. AND F.C. BURTON. "A Study of Blood and Urine Alcohol Concentration in Cases of Alleged Drug-Facilitated Sexual Assault in the United Kingdom Over a 3-Year Period." *Journal of Clinical Forensic Medicine*, 13: 107–111, 2006 (2 tables, 1 figure, 17 references)

Abstract: The blood and/or urine alcohol concentrations were determined in 391 victims of alleged DFSA in the United Kingdom between 2000 and 2002 from samples collected within 12 hours of the assault. A backcalculated BAC was determined using 0.018 g/100 mL/h. A positive alcohol concentration was found in 316 victims (81%). A backcalculated BAC of > 0.150 g/100 mL was determined in 158 victims (60%).

Of the 391 cases analysed in which the samples were taken within 12 h of the incident, the majority (81%) contained alcohol and 60% had a high back-calculated figure (where high was defined as greater than 150 mg%). Assuming that none of the alcohol consumed had been added clandestinely, these results show the high alcohol concentrations being obtained during social drinking. These results therefore emphasize the need for education of the dangers of excessive alcohol consumption. As highlighted elsewhere, the advice would be to drink slowly, steadily and moderate drinking to a degree that judgment and control are not unduly impaired.

Reference Number: 61707

WELLS, D. "Drug Administration and Sexual Assault: Sex in a Glass." *Science and Justice*, 41: 197–199, 2001 (7 references)

Abstract: Two case reports are presented involving the use of alcohol and flunitrazepam in suspected sexual assault cases in Victoria, Australia. In one case a twenty-seven-year-old female inexperienced drinker met her girlfriend in a bar and a male at the adjoining table joined them. When she returned from the washroom, she finished the drink she had left at the table and began to feel dizzy, confused, and nauseated. She awoke 9 hours later in her bed, partially undressed with no recollection of how she got there. A forensic examination was conducted 3 hours later and her BrAC was 0.120 g/100 mL. The police contacted her girlfriend who stated that the woman got progressively more drunk and the girlfriend drove her home, partially undressed her and placed her in bed. The woman had vomited a number of times throughout the night. In the second case an unknown male over a 3.5-year period attempted to sexually assault twenty-one women after giving them a beverage. Flunitrazepam was detected in the blood of two of the women in which there was no large delay in the forensic examination.

Ethanol is a common factor in a large number of (particularly first) sexual encounters; this applies to both consenting and nonconsenting acts. Not infrequently there is a history of significant amounts of ethanol being consumed by both parties. Ethanol may affect memory, conscious state and will also produce a range of after-effects very similar to that of other central nervous system (CNS) depressants.

Reference Number: 61708

BRECKLIN, L.R. AND S.E. ULLMAN. "The Role of Offender Alcohol Use in Rape Attacks. An Analysis of National Crime Victimization Survey Data." *Journal of Interpersonal Violence*, 16: 3–21, 2001 (4 tables, 25 references)

Abstract: The role of the offender pre-assault alcohol use (as perceived by the victim) was determined in 362 sexual assaults between 1992 and 1996 in the United States. The average age of the female victim was twenty-eight years. Alcohol and/or drugs were used by 61% of the offenders. Alcohol use was associated with less likelihood of rape completion.

Results revealed that offender preassault alcohol use was associated with stranger assaults, night assaults, outdoor assaults and more victim resistance as hypothesized, based on past research.

Reference Number: 61709

EGAN, V. AND G. CORDAN. "Barely Legal: Is Attraction and Estimated Age of Young Female Faces Disrupted by Alcohol Use, Make Up and the Sex of the Observer?" *British Journal of Psychology*, 415–427, 2009 (1 table, 2 figures, 25 references)

Abstract: The attractiveness of composite pictures of immature and mature females with and without makeup were determined in 120 persons without alcohol and 120 persons who had consumed alcohol in bars and cafes. The BrACs were determined with a Lion Alcometer SD-400 and ranged between 0 to 0.400 g/100 mL. The mean BrACs were 0.141 g/100 mL and 0.135 g/100 mL for female and male participants respectively. Twenty-one persons had BrACs of between 0.210 and 0.400 g/100 mL and were classified as unambiguously drunk.

Placed in its forensic context, this study tentatively concludes that alcohol consumption and make-up use do not inherently interfere with age-perception task nor inflate subsequent age estimations. Alcohol disrupted the processing of maturity-immaturity cues for females but not male participants.

Reference Number: 61710

HALSEY, L.G., J.W. HUBER, R.D.J. BUFTON, AND A.C. LITTLE. "An Explanation for Enhanced Perceptions of Attractiveness After Alcohol Consumption." *Alcohol*, 44: 307–313, 2010 (2 figures, 29 references)

Abstract: Acute consumption of alcohol tends to increase the ratings of attractiveness to faces and may explain in part the increase in sexual encounters after alcohol consumption. Thirty-three male and thirty-six female subjects (mean age twenty-two years) were tested on the attractiveness of twenty paired faces and to whether twenty single faces were symmetrical or not. The faces were shown on a computer screen and the testing was conducted at local bars. BrACs were determined with an

Alcosign CA-1000 and the subjects were deemed to be sober if the BrAC < 0.050 g/100 mL and intoxicated if BrAC> 0.080 g/100 mL. Thirty-six subjects were classified as sober and twenty-eight as intoxicated. Male subjects made fewer mistakes than female subjects in determining whether the individual faces were symmetrical or not.

> Confirming previous results, sober participants had a preference for symmetrical versus asymmetrical faces. Intoxicated participants also had a preference for symmetrical faces. However, the preference of intoxicated participants for symmetrical faces was less than of sober participants. Intoxicated participants were also less able to detect when faces were asymmetrical than were sober participants.

Reference Number: 61711

DAVIS, K.C., W.H. GEORGE, J. NORRIS, R.L. SCHACHT, S.A. STONER, C.S. HENDERSHOT, AND K.F. KAJUMULO. "Effects of Alcohol and Blood Alcohol Concentration Limb on Sexual Risk-Taking Intentions." *Journal of Studies on Alcohol and Drugs*, 70: 499–507, 2009 (1 table, 2 figures, 43 references)

Abstract: Seventy-seven male and seventy-three female subjects (mean age twenty-five years) were tested as to perceived intoxication and sexual arousal and with a written sexual risk assessment after consuming a control drink or alcohol (0.82 g/kg for men and 0.68 g/kg for women). The alcohol was consumed within 9 minutes and BrACs were determined with an Intoxilyzer 5000. The subjects were tested on the ascending BAC (mean 17 minutes after drinking ended) or the descending BAC limb (mean 103 minutes after drinking ended). The mean BrACs at the time of testing at each BAC limb was approximately 0.072 g/100 mL.

> The current work also provides evidence regarding the importance of alcohol's biphasic effects on unprotected sexual intentions. An interaction of beverage condition and limb condition indicated that alcohol's effects on perceived intoxication varied significantly by limb and those on the ascending limb reporting greater perceived intoxication than those on the descending limb. Thus, individuals whose BACs were still rising reported greater perceived intoxication followed by greater perceived sexual arousal and greater unprotected sex intentions than did those individuals whose BACs were falling. Individuals on the descending limb may thus be less likely to engage in sexual risk taking than their ascending counterparts because of their relatively lower levels of perceived intoxication and arousal.

Reference Number: 61712

DEMING, J.E., R.E. MITTLEMAN, AND C.V. WETLI. "Forensic Science Aspects of Fatal Sexual Assaults on Women." *Journal of Forensic Sciences*, 28: 572–576, 1983 (2 tables, 1 figure, 4 references)

Abstract: A study was conducted of forty-one female victims of fatal sexual assaults in Dade County, Florida, between 1959 and 1981. The victims were between ten and eighty-eight years of age (mean age forty-two years). Only two victims were known prostitutes. A positive BAC was found in 40% of the victims (range 0.010–0.290 g/100 mL, mean, 0.140 g/100 mL).

A blood alcohol concentration averaging 0.14 g/100g (in those that were positive for alcohol) is quite striking in view of the possibility that some of the victims may in fact have contributed to their own demise in terms of emotional labiality and the lack of judgment that may accompany alcohol intoxication. The relative inability to escape may also render the victim as an easy target.

Reference Number: 61713

WIGMORE, J.G. AND M.J. WARD. "The Incidence of Ethanol and Acetone in the Blood and Urine of Victims of Sexual Assault." *Canadian Society of Forensic Science Journal,* 19: 49–58, 1986 (5 figures, 2 tables, 35 references)

Abstract: The blood and urine alcohol and acetone concentrations in 255 victims of sexual assault were determined by headspace GC. Approximately 25% of the blood and 28% of the urine samples had an alcohol concentration greater than 0.010 g/100 mL. Acetone (0.001 g/100 mL or greater) was detected in 4% of the blood and 21% of the urine samples. A control group of blood donors had acetone detected in 0.5% of the blood samples. The sexual assault victims were divided into 153 cases with no visible trauma and 102 cases with visible trauma. As shown in the following table the incidence of acetone was approximately 3.4 times greater in victims with visible trauma. Alcohol decreased the incidence of acetone to a great extent.

Table. Percent Blood and Urine Acetone Detected in Sexual Assault Victims with Visible and No Visible Trauma

Condition	% Blood Acetone Detected	% Urine Acetone Detected
No Visible Trauma	2.6	15.7
Visible Trauma	9.2	43.4

Source: Adapted from Wigmore and Ward (1985).

Victims of sexual assault react to the physical and physiological stress of assault by fatty acid mobilization and subsequent ketone body production. These individuals were ten times more likely to have an increased concentration of acetone in the urine than a normal comparison population. Within this group, acetone was detected three times more frequently in victims that experienced some degree of physical injury than in the less traumatized individuals.

Reference Number: 61714

HAGEMANN, C.T., A. HELLAND, O. SPIGSET, K.A. ESPNES, K. ORMSTAD, AND B. SCHEI. "Ethanol and Drug Findings in Women Consulting a Sexual Assault Center—Associations with Clinical Characteristics and Suspicions of Drug-Facilitated Sexual Assault." *Journal of Forensic and Legal Medicine*, 20: 777–784, 2013 (4 tables, 38 references)

Abstract: The toxicological findings (using urine and/or blood) were determined in 264 female sexual assault victims attending at a sexual assault center in Trondheim, Norway, between 2003 and 2010. Serum alcohol concentrations were determined and converted into a BAC using a factor of 1.14. Urine alcohol concentrations were converted into a BAC using a factor of 1.345. Alcohol and/or drugs were detected in 155 (59%) of the victims. Of the 120 victims who had samples collected within 12 hours of the assault, 102 (85%) were positive for alcohol. The estimated BAC at the time of the assault (using 0.015 g/100 mL/h elimination rate) ranged between 0.044 and 0.395 g/100 mL (mean 0.192 g/100 mL). No positive cases of proactive DFSA were found. Victims testing positive for alcohol more often report a public place of assault and stranger assault. The higher the estimated BAC at the time of the assault, the greater the frequency of suspicion of DFSA by the victim.

We believe that victims of sexual assault should have easy and fast access to emergency health care with a trained staff and should be encouraged to seek immediate help. Toxicological screening should be routinely offered to achieve a comprehensive assessment in each individual case. Based on the current study, it should be communicated that the perceived danger of surreptitious drugging with so-called date rape drugs such as GHB and flunitrazepam is most likely overrated, whereas the dangers of voluntary excessive intake of alcohol (and drugs) should be emphasized more.

Reference Number: 61715

GREENE, S.L., C.M. SHIEW, P. STREETE, S.J. MUSTCHIN, D. HUGGET, B. EARL, AND P.I. DARGAN. "What's Being Used to Spike Your Drink? Alleged Spiked Drink Cases in Inner City London." *Postgraduate Medical Journal*, 83: 754–758, 2007 (3 tables, 18 references)

Abstract: Drug and alcohol analyses were conducted on sixty-seven blood and seventy-five urine samples collected from sixty-four female and fourteen male sexual assault victims who attended an inner city hospital in London within 12 hours after allegedly consuming a spiked drink. Victims reported symptoms of nausea, vomiting, ataxia, dizziness, slurred or slow speech, blurred vision, and headache. Alcohol was detected in 90% of the victims. The mean serum alcohol concentration was 0.165 g/100 mL (range 0.040–0.310 g/100 mL). Illicit or medical drugs of unexplained origin were detected in 10% of the victims. GHB was detected in one male victim at a club where he drank what he considered to be an alcoholic beverage but then started behaving bizarrely and then became drowsy.

The use of sedative drugs to spike drinks may not be as common as portrayed in the mainstream media. Sedative drugs commonly associated with drink spiking were detected in only a small minority of study participants. A similar number of cases detected involving the stimulant MDMA serves as a reminder that the disinhibiting effects of MDMA and similar drugs may also impair personal judgment and lead to unlawful assault. Routine toxicological screening of ED patients with alleged exposure to a spiked drink is not supported by the results from this study but should be undertaken in selected cases for medico-legal purposes.

Reference Number: 61716

JENKINS G. AND R.A. SCHULLER. "The Impact of Negative Forensic Evidence on Mock Jurors' Perceptions of a Trial of Drug-Facilitated Sexual Assault." *Law and Human Behavior*, 31: 369–380, 2007 (3 tables, 40 references)

Abstract: One hundred female and seventy-one male undergraduate university students (ages eighteen to fifty-one years) were presented with a written mock trial transcript of a sexual assault case in which the victim had consumed alcohol and allegedly was administered a drug by the accused and sexually assaulted. The participants received one of three versions of the forensic evidence: a negative toxicology report, a negative toxicology report with expert testimony explaining the results, and no report (control). Overall, 80% of the participants found the defendant not guilty and 20% found him guilty. Participants who had the negative forensic toxicology report alone were significantly less likely to find the defendant guilty (9%) than those who had no toxicology report (22%) or with a negative toxicology report and expert testimony (30%).

Table. Conviction Rate in a Mock DFSA Case According to Evidence Presented to the Jury

What the Jury Saw	Percent Found Accused Guilty
Negative toxicology report alone	9%
No toxicology report	22%
Negative toxicology report and expert testimony	30%

Source: Adapted from Jenkins and Schuller (2007).

Overall, the results of this study revealed that the introduction of a negative forensic report into evidence at trial without the contextualizing evidence of an expert witness produced greater verdict leniency and a more favorable evaluation of the defendant's case. In contrast, no difference between the control condition that omitted the report and the condition in which expert testimony was introduced to contextualize the negative forensic report were found on any of the dependent measures. Thus, it appears that the information provided by the expert witness completely negated the impact of the negative forensic on participants' decisions.

Reference Number: 61717

HEGSTAD, S., A. HELLAND, C. HAGEMANN, L. MICHELSEN, AND O. SPIGSET. "EtG/EtS in Urine from Sexual Assault Victims Determined by UPLC-MS-MS." *Journal of Analytical Toxicology*, 37: 227–232, 2013 (3 tables, 3 figures, 25 references)

Abstract: Urine alcohol, creatinine, ethyl glucuronide (EtG), and ethyl sulphate (EtS) concentrations were determined in fifty-nine female victims of sexual assault (ages fourteen to sixty-one years) who attended a hospital in Trondheim, Norway, between 2010 and 2011. Urinary EtG and EtS concentrations were determined by ultra-high-performance liquid chromatography tandem mass spectrometry. Forty-eight of the victims (81%) reported alcohol consumption prior to the sexual assault. The mean time from alcohol consumption to the time of the collection of the urine sample was 20.9 hours (range 1.5 to 108 hours). A positive UAC was found in twenty urine samples (42%) and ranged from 0.037 to 0.280 g/100 mL. Positive EtG/EtS concentrations were found in forty-five samples (94%). In no cases were positive urine EtG/EtS concentrations detected in urine samples from victims who reported no alcohol consumption. Self-reported alcohol consumption by sexual assault victims appears to be reliable. Using urine EtG/EtS, alcohol consumption can be detected for approximately 2 to 3 days after alcohol consumption.

The improved detection times and sensitivity for EtG and EtS remain positive considerably longer that urinary ethanol. The improved detection times and sensitivity for EtG and EtS may provide a more complete assessment of toxicological involvement in the investigation of cases of sexual assault because the delay in reporting is particularly common in cases of drug facilitated sexual assault. The detection of EtG and EtS may lend credence to possible claims by victims of being assaulted while intoxicated.

Reference Number: 61718

BELSKY, T.P. "Does It Add Up? Analyzing the Use of Extrapolation Calculations to Determine the Ability to Consent in Alcohol-Related Sexual Assault Cases." *Naval Law Review Military Justice Edition*, LXII, 54–75, 2013 (134 references)

Abstract: Current US military standards prohibit sexual activity with someone who is incapable of consenting due to impairment by any drug, intoxicant, or similar substance. Increasingly, alcohol calculations conducted by a toxicologist are employed in those matters to prove or dispute that the victim was incapable of consenting. The general scientific principle of extrapolation are presented in this article. Extrapolation evidence has been accepted under Daubert.

> Additionally, there is a strong argument that the primary information concerning a victim's ability to consent is not the BAC but the physical signs of intoxication he or she exhibits. In this sense, a BAC is even less probative of the victims' mental state, which makes the risk of it being outweighed by unfair prejudice all the greater. Given both the arguments discussed, there are very serious and as of yet not litigated questions as to whether extrapolation evidence is admissible in sexual assault cases in an effort to establish the victim's mental state at the time of the alleged assault.

Reference Number: 61719

JOZKOWSKI, K.N. AND J.D. WIERSMA. "Does Drinking Alcohol Prior to Sexual Activity Influence College Students' Consent?" *International Journal of Sexual Health*, 27: 156–174, 2015 (3 tables, 58 references)

Abstract: The effect of alcohol consumption on external and internal consent prior to sexual activity was determined in a survey of 175 male and 654 female college students (mean age 20.4 years).

> Some argue that consent promotion approaches may be particularly problematic because consent promotion programming often does not adequately address alcohol consumption in conjunction with consent negotiation. Simple messages of just get consent, yes means yes or no means no, fail to address how to just get consent in general and how to assess someone's ability to even give consent when they have consumed alcohol. Our findings suggest that drinking alcohol prior to sexual activity influences consent both in terms of the cues utilized to assess consent as well as the feelings individuals have as part of the decision process to consent to sex, particularly with casual or new sexual partners.

Reference Number: 61720

COWAN, S. "The Trouble with Drink Intoxication, (In)capacity, and the Evaporation of Consent to Sex." *Akron Law Review*, 41: Article 4, 899–922, 2015 (94 references)

Abstract: A legal review was conducted of the legal issues relating to intoxicated consent in cases of sexual assault in the United Kingdom. The level of alcohol use in sexual assault cases is high, and in the student population up to 81% of the cases can involve alcohol.

> This is not to say that either memory loss or vomiting always in themselves imply incapacity to consent. But there are strong reasons to think that if someone is suffering from these kinds of problems, this would indicate extreme intoxication so that lack of capacity to consent would be indicated. In other words, if following alcohol consumption, the complainant has experienced one or more of a cluster of possible symptoms—vomiting, inability to speak or move, memory loss, or periods of unconsciousness for example—it may be assumed that she did not have capacity to consent, unless the defendant can show and the jury believes that she in fact was not extremely intoxicated and had in fact given consent. Again, if a back calculation of intoxication level could be used to a high degree of certainty, this could be one piece of relevant probative evidence to take into account.

Reference Number: 61721

CONNELL, M. "Expert Testimony in Sexual Assault Case: Alcohol Intoxication and Memory." *International Journal of Law and Psychiatry*, 8pp, 2015 (3 tables, 69 references)

Abstract: An overview of toxicological evidence in US court martial trials involving alcohol and facilitated sexual assault is presented. Under the Uniform Code of Military Justice regarding rape, consent cannot be given where the accused knew or should have known the victim was incapable of consenting due to impairment. Three tables are shown presenting impairment as the BAC increases but varies as to when impairment of memory occurs. According to the three tables, the BACs when impairment of memory occurs ranges from 0.060–0.150 g/100 mL, 0.090–0.250 g/100 mL, and 0.060–0.099 g/100 mL respectively. Generally, fragmentary memory loss occurs around 0.150 g/100 mL and blackouts at 0.220–0.240 g/100 mL. Binge drinking is common in the military; about 43% of active US military personnel reported binge drinking. Pre-game drinking occurred in about one-third of college students and typically involves about two drinks. The most reliable method of determining BAC is by blood samples collected close to the time of the sexual assault. Retrograde

BAC extrapolation and estimates of BAC according to amount consumed, time, weight, and gender are also discussed.

Neither forensic toxicologists nor psychologists/psychiatrists should be asked if the alleged victim was too impaired to consent. This is a matter for the factfinders to determine. Although courts may allow such testimony, there are arguably questions about the expert's foundation for such opinion, its reliability, and ultimately whether it goes beyond the expertise of forensic toxicologists or psychologist/psychiatrists. Finally, the testimony may be confusing to the factfinders if the expert is using a different definition of too impaired to consent that the definition the court members will be asked to apply. To whatever extent the expert appears to be offering an opinion on the ultimate issue, the foundation of that opinion should be vigorously scrutinized.

Reference Number: 61722

INGEMANN-HANSEN, O., O. BRINK, S. SABROE, V. SORENSEN, AND A.V. CHARLES. "Legal Aspects of Sexual Violence—Does Forensic Evidence Make a Difference?" *Forensic Science International*, 180: 98–104, 2008 (1 figure, 4 tables, 47 references)

Abstract: A study was conducted of the legal outcomes in 277 cases of sexual violence that occurred in Denmark between 1999 and 2004. Charges were filed in 151 cases (55%). Eighty-nine cases (59%) were dropped before prosecution, mainly because of insufficient evidence. A conviction occurred in 19% of the cases. A forensic medical examination was conducted in 216 victims, including collection of samples to test for sperm, DNA, and to conduct toxicological analyses. A positive BAC was found in sixty-two cases.

Determinant for conviction was use of severe coercion by the perpetrator. No forensic findings were associated with conviction. The police authorities filed charges in 55% of the cases, and 19% of all cases ended with conviction. In 19% of cases, the forensic clinician did not find sperm detected by the genetics laboratory.

Reference Number: 61723

O'NEAL, E.N., S.H. DECKER, C. SPOHN, AND K. TELLIS. "Condom Use During Sexual Assault." *Journal of Forensic and Legal Medicine*, 20: 605–609, 2013 (3 tables, 35 references)

Abstract: The characteristics of 841 sexual assault complaints that occurred in Los Angeles and St Louis in 2008 and 2004 respectively were determined. A condom was used in approximately 12 to 16% of the assaults. This is a higher prevalence of condom use than in previous studies and may be due to the "CSI Effect," due to fear of DNA analysis in the semen being used to identify the assailant. Approximately 21 to 33% of the suspects had consumed alcohol prior to the assault. Suspects who consumed alcohol during the assault were less likely to use condoms due to lower self-control.

> Condom use during sexual assault appears to be motivated by three contextual factors. Younger suspects and suspects who use a weapon during assaults are more likely to use a condom. The suspect's use of alcohol is negatively related to condom use. The low rates of condom use found in this study, coupled with the dangers of unprotected sexual contact, suggest that public health efforts must address the needs of victims of sexual assault more carefully.

6.18 SNOWMOBILING

> "The high incidence of alcohol involvement in snowmobile operator fatalities combined with the known impairing effects of alcohol, suggest that the operation of motorized snow vehicle after drinking is an extremely dangerous activity."
>
> —Beirness, "Alcohol Involvement in Snowmobile Operator Fatalities in Canada" (2001)

> "Alcohol is a major factor in snowmobile fatalities. Consuming any amount of alcohol before you ride affects your ability to make good decisions. Alcohol also increases fatigue, slows reaction time and increases your risk of hypothermia."
>
> —Ontario.ca, "Off-Road Vehicles and Snowmobiles" (2022)

Alcohol impairs the ability to operate motor vehicles, including snowmobiles. Up to 75% of fatal snowmobile collisions have been found to involve alcohol, which is much greater than alcohol involvement in FMVCs (61804–61806). The main mechanisms of recreational snowmobile injury (in decreasing frequency) are:

> Collision with another snowmobile or loss of control > Collision with a tree or a car > Collision with a fence post > Fall from a moving snowmobile

Increased community-based police enforcement on the snowmobile trails have been shown to reduce alcohol-related injuries and death (61807). Unshielded vehicle crashes, particularly involving snowmobiles, have the highest risk of blunt traumatic brachial plexus injuries (61808).

Twenty-seven percent of non-geriatric injured snowmobilers had a positive BAC compared to 9% of the injured geriatric (≥ 65 years of age), but geriatric patients had a 4.1% mortality rate compared to 0.6% for non-geriatric patients (61809).

Reference Number: 61801

WALLER, J.A. AND K.R. LAMBORN. "Snowmobiling: Characteristics of Owners, Patterns of Use and Injuries." *Accident Analysis and Prevention*, 7: 213–223, 1975 (12 tables, 14 references)

Abstract: A study was conducted of 133 snowmobilers who were injured in northern Vermont between 1971–1973, who were compared to 126 snowmobilers not injured in accidents. No BACs were determined.

> As seen in Table 2, injured drivers age 18 or older were twice as likely to report that they had been drinking and drinking heavily just before their injury event as were uninjured drivers to report that they had consumed alcohol in their last excursion ($p < 0.005$).

Reference Number: 61802

ROWE, B. AND G. BOTA. "Serious Snowmobile Trauma in a Northern Ontario Community: A Case Series." *Annals Royal College of Physicians and Surgeons of Canada,* 24: 501–505, 1991 (6 tables, 18 references)

Abstract: A study was conducted of 144 victims injured in snowmobile accidents admitted to hospital and of twelve deaths that occurred between 1985 and 1990 in the Sudbury Region of Ontario. The presence of alcohol was determined by patient records or postmortem BACs. Thirty-four percent of victims had a positive alcohol history. Sixty-three percent of victims injured between 1:00 a.m. and 8:00 a.m. had a positive alcohol history.

Table. Percent of Alcohol History Positive in Seriously Injured Snowmobilers and Time of Day

Time	Percent Alcohol History Positive
0801–1600	11%
1601–2400	37%
0001–0800	63%

Source: Adapted from Rowe and Bota (1991).

The most distressing information that we found was the high proportion of alcohol-impaired drivers operating snowmobiles. Alcohol use was related with higher ISS scores and occurred more often from 1600 to 0800 hours.

Reference Number: 61803

STEWART, R.L. AND G.B. BLACK. "Snowmobile Trauma: 10 Years' Experience at Manitoba's Tertiary Trauma Centre." *Canadian Journal of Surgery*, 47: 90–94, 2004 (3 tables, 30 references)

Abstract: A study was conducted of 260 male and thirty-four female patients admitted to the Health Sciences Centre in Winnipeg between 1988 and 1997 due to injuries suffered from a snowmobile collision. The mean age of the patients was twenty-nine years and 62% were between nineteen and twenty-five years of age. Alcohol use was associated with 88% of the injuries sustained by patients. A BAC > 0.080 g/100 mL was found in 207 (70%) patients. Sixteen percent of the collisions occurred on groomed trails and 31% on roads. The manufacturer's recommended maximum nighttime speed of 50 km/h was exceeded by 82% of the injured patients.

The recreational use of snowmobiles remains a significant cause of serious injury. Such trauma is caused by human factors and is therefore potentially preventable. Our research has confirmed that the previously described risk factors of alcohol consumption, excessive speed and poor lighting are still important risk factors. We have identified for the first time a major risk factor: riding on roadways. Trail site monitoring is likely to be ineffective, as the majority of accidents do not occur on designated snowmobile trails.

Reference Number: 61804

ROWE, B., R. MILMNER, C. JOHNSON, AND G. BOTA. "The Association of Alcohol and Night Driving with Fatal Snowmobile Trauma: A Case-Control

Study." *Annals of Emergency Medicine*, 24: 842–848, 1994 (5 tables, 24 references)

Abstract: A study was conducted of 108 snowmobile drivers who died as a result of an accident in Ontario between 1985 and 1990 and compared to a sample of fatally injured drivers in automobile and motorcycle accidents. The adjusted odds ratio of alcohol use and snowmobile fatalities was 4.3 times.

Table. Alcohol Involvement in Fatally Injured Snowmobile, Motorcycle, and Motor Vehicle Drivers

Type of Fatality	Alcohol Detected	BAC > 0.08 g/100 mL	Mean BAC (g/100 mL)
Snowmobile	73%	65%	0.158
Motorcycle	39%	35%	0.140
Motor Vehicle	38%	31%	0.177

Source: Adapted from Rowe et al (1994).

Regardless of the method of measurement, alcohol was detected in significantly more snowmobile fatalities than motorcycle or motor vehicle fatalities and exceeded the legal limit in nearly two-thirds of all snowmobile cases. This may result because drivers of snowmobiles do not consider that the risks of alcohol use and driving apply to the use of these off-road vehicles. Alternatively, the chance of being detected by law enforcement officials is small in many remote and rural settings, therefore removing a known deterrent.

Reference Number: 61805

ERIKSSON, A. AND U. BJORNSTIG. "Fatal Snowmobile Accidents in Northern Sweden." *Journal of Trauma*, 22: 977–982, 1982 (9 figures, 16 references)

Abstract: The BACs of thirty-six victims of fatal snowmobile accidents between 1973 and 1981 were determined. Twenty-eight operators were men and two were women; the other six fatalities were passengers. The most common cause of fatalities was driving through thin ice (fifteen cases) and collision with a fixed object, which occurred in seven cases. In twenty-three cases, a positive BAC was detected. The mean BAC was 0.160 g/100 mL.

For the fatal accidents, it has been established that drunken driving is an important factor. The figures for blood alcohol levels are disturbing, particularly in view of the relative youth of the drivers involved.

Reference Number: 61806

WENZEL, F.J. AND R.A. PETERS. "A Ten Year Survey of Snowmobile Accidents, Injuries and Fatalities in Wisconsin." *Physician and Sports Medicine.* 14: 140–149, 1986 (1 table, 4 figures, 24 references)

Abstract: A study was conducted of 5,185 snowmobile accidents in Wisconsin between 1972 and 1982. Alcohol consumption was involved in 7% of non-fatal accidents and 61% of fatal accidents.

Both the percentage of accidents and the number of deaths related to drugs and alcohol increased significantly over the period of the present study. To combat this problem the kinds of penalties imposed on drunken drivers of autos should be extended to snowmobiling.

Reference Number: 61807

ROWE, B.H., S.A. THERRIEN, J.A. BRETZLAFF, V.S. SAHAI, K.V. NAGARAJAN, AND G.W. BOTA. "The Effect of a Community-Based Police Surveillance Program on Snowmobile Injuries and Deaths." *Canadian Journal of Public Health,* 89: 57–61, 1998 (4 tables, 27 references)

Abstract: The impact of the increase in police enforcement of snowmobilers (STOP) in Sudbury on snowmobile injuries and deaths is presented. During the winters of 1990–1992 (pre STOP) there were fifteen deaths, compared to four for the winters of 1993–1995 (STOP). It is estimated that hospital admission costs related to snowmobile fatalities decreased from $401,700.00 to $194,528.00.

The results of this study confirm that a volunteer police-assisted enforcement program on snowmobile trails reduces deaths and admissions from snowmobile injuries in a community where these events burden health care delivery. Changing behaviors, attitudes and beliefs surrounding alcohol and snowmobiling has been the main thrust of the campaign.

Reference Number: 61808

LEONARD, S., T. WOEHRLE, H. NIKIZAD, J. VEARRIER, M. ODEAN, C. RENIER, J. BOLLINS, AND S. EYER. "Blunt Traumatic Brachial Plexus Injuries in a Northern Rural US Setting: Increased Likelihood in Unshielded Motor-Power Crashes." *Trauma Surgery & Acute Care Open*, 5: e000558, 3pp, 2020 (1 table, 2 figures, 12 references)

Abstract: Blunt traumatic brachial plexus injuries (BTBPI) are severe peripheral nerve injuries that occur in the neck and upper chest, occur in about 1% of trauma patients, and cause weakness, chronic pain, and loss of feeling/movement in the shoulder and hand. The major cause of BTBPI is high-velocity crashes and occurs most frequently in young men (ages nineteen to thirty-five years). A total of sixty-three patients were found to have BTBPI between 1995 and 2016 in northern Minnesota, Wisconsin, and Michigan. Alcohol was found to be involved in 41% of the BTBPIs and the average ISS was 20.2.

Table. Odds Ratio of BTBPIs in Motor Vehicle Collisions and Characteristics of BTBPI Crashes

Vehicle	All Injuries	BTBPI (%)	OR	Male	Alcohol Related
Motor Vehicle	5,734	22% (0.4)	Ref	82%	50%
All-Terrain Vehicle	1,590	10% (0.6)	1.64	90%	30%
Snowmobile	1,367	24% (1.8)	4.64	92%	38%
Motorcycle	1,260	7% (0.6)	1.45	86%	43%

Source: Adapted from Leonard et al (2020).

Unshielded vehicle crashes, particularly snowmobiles, have the highest risk of BTBPI in our rural region. The overall incidence of these injuries appears to be declining.

Reference Number: 61809

GOLDWAG, J.L., E.D. PORTER, A.R. WILCOX, Z. LI, T.D. TOSTESON, A.O. CROCKETT, A.B. WOLFFING, D.J. MANCINI, E.D. MARTIN, J.W. SCOTT, AND A. BRIGGS. "Geriatric Snowmobile Trauma: Longer Courses After Similar Injuries." *Journal of Surgical Research*, 262: 85-92, 2021 (1 figure, 6 tables, 26 references).

Abstract: A comparison was conducted between 2,347 non-geriatric (ages eighteen to sixty-four years) and 124 geriatric (sixty-five+ years) snowmobilers who presented at a trauma center between 2011 and 2015 due to snowmobile-related trauma. Twenty-seven percent of the non-geriatric injury victims had a positive BAC compared to 9.1% of the geriatric victims. AUD was detected in 6.6% of the non-geriatric injured snowmobilers and 0.9% of the geriatric snowmobilers. The vast majority (93%) of the patients had a GCS > 9. There were no significant differences between the two groups in injury severity. Geriatric patients had a longer hospital length of stay (median 5 days versus 3 days), and the number of ventilation days (median 7.5 versus 3 days) than non-geriatric patients. Geriatric patients had a 4.1% mortality rate compared to 0.6% for non-geriatric patients.

> After snowmobile-associated trauma, geriatric patients had similar rates of severe injury as their nongeriatric counterparts, but have unique injury patterns, longer hospitalizations and suffer higher mortality. Colder climate areas need to be aware of this emergency trauma population that may benefit from specialized geriatric specific trauma center care to improve outcomes.

6.19 SPORTS

> "It is recommended that alcohol should be avoided by the serious athlete."
>
> —O'Brien and Lyon, "Alcohol and the Athlete" (2000)

> "From an industry perspective, this is a sound investment. Alcohol promotion through commercials in sports programming or sponsorship of sports teams and events provides companies with tremendous exposure—before, during and after an event. It creates positive associations between drinking and the traits associated with athletes and teams: strength, loyalty, endurance, success, health, vitality, fun, fitness and speed. Promotion of youth-oriented events such as snowboarding, extreme sports and biking create an aura of coolness around a product—and grab attention of a new generation of future drinkers."
>
> —Mediasmarts, "Who's on First? Alcohol Advertising and Sports" (2012)

Alcohol does not appear to be an ergogenic aid and does not significantly improve physical performance (61901–61905). As such, alcohol was excluded in the World Anti-Doping Agency prohibited list effective 1 January 2018.

Reference Number: 61809

Collegiate athletes were more likely to have been heavy consumers of alcohol and engage in binge drinking (61807, 61908). Heavy alcohol consumption also occurs in fans of many different sporting events (61909–61913) and has been implicated in an increase in injuries (61911) and drinking and driving (61912, 61913). A 41% increase in alcohol-related FMVCs has been found in the United States after the Super Bowl telecast, which exceeds the relative increase found on New Year's Eve (61913).

A positive BrAC was found in 40% of the fans leaving a major league baseball or football game and the OR of having a BrAC ≥ 0.08 g/100 mL was 17.0 times if the fan attended a tailgate party (61915). Thirty-three empty vodka bottles were found after a male collegiate volleyball game compared to four empty vodka bottles after a female collegiate volleyball game (61916).

The percentage of athletes injured in sports was greater in drinking athletes compared to non-drinkers. In cricket, 63% of the drinkers had injuries compared to 0% of the non-drinkers (61917).

The presence of alcohol in the blood is an important cause of accidents in recreational downhill skiing (61918–61919).

Reference Number: 61901

MCNAUGHTON, L. AND D. PREECE. "Alcohol and Its Effect on Sprint and Middle Distance Running." *British Journal of Sports Medicine*, 20: 56–59, 1986 (2 figures, 25 references)

Abstract: Five sprinters and five middle distance runners consumed a placebo or alcohol to obtain BrACs as determined by the Alcotest 7310 and Breathalyzer of 0, 0.010, 0.050, and 0.100 g/100 mL. The time required to run 100, 200, and 400 meters for the sprinters and 800 and 1,500 meters for the middle distance runners were determined.

> Alcohol is not an ergogenic aid in so much that it does not improve performance. Clearly in all but the 100 m sprint, differing levels of alcohol had differing, but consistently detrimental, effects on timed performance but neither was there any positive effect on running. We would therefore not recommend the use of alcohol in sprinting performance.

Reference Number: 61902

HOURNARD, J.A., M.E. LAGENFELD, R. WILEY, AND J. SIEFERT. "Effects of Acute Ingestion of Small Amounts of Alcohol Upon 5-Mile Run Times." *Journal of Sports Medicine*, 27: 253–257, 1987 (4 tables, 23 references)

Abstract: Eighteen well-trained male runners consumed a placebo, 0.22, and 0.44 mL/kg alcohol on three occasions separated by 1 week and were tested on a treadmill. BACs were determined from fingertip blood and the mean BACs were 0, 0.014, and 0.029 g/100 mL respectively. The time for a five mile run, heart rate, and perceived exertion were measured. The mean time to run five miles was 30:42, 30:56, and 31:11 (minutes: seconds) for the three conditions respectively.

Thus alcohol does not appear to be an ergogenic aid for endurance exercise.

Reference Number: 61903

KENDRICK, Z.V., M.B. AFFRIME, AND D.T. LOWENTHAL. "Effects of Caffeine or Ethanol on Treadmill Performance and Metabolic Responses of Well-Trained Men." *International Journal of Clinical Pharmacology and Therapeutics*, 32: 536–541, 1994 (3 tables, 30 references)

Abstract: Four male subjects (ages twenty-four to twenty-nine years) consumed either a placebo, 2.5 mg/kg caffeine, or 25 mL of ethanol 10 minutes prior and at 30 minutes of a 60-minute treadmill run. The treadmill was adjusted to elicit an oxygen consumption of 80 to 85% of the subject's maximal oxygen consumption. All subjects completed the treadmill run for caffeine and placebo conditions but three out of four subjects could not complete the task after the second alcohol dose.

In summary, the administration of caffeine had no effect on treadmill performing for 60 minutes and the metabolic responses of well-trained subjects to exercise. In contrast, ethanol adversely influenced the treadmill performance which was proposed to result from an ethanol-induced hypoglycemia.

Reference Number: 61904

REILLY, T. AND F. HALLIDAY. "Influence of Alcohol Ingestion on Tasks Related to Archery." *Journal of Human Ergology*, 14: 99–104, 1985 (1 table, 2 references)

Abstract: Small doses of alcohol have been used by participants in archery and pistol shooting sports to improve aiming and shooting skills. Small doses of alcohol have also been consumed by professional soccer players before games. Alcohol is banned by the IOC. For archery, deflection of the arrow tip by 0.02 millimeters at 90 meters would cause the arrow to miss the target. Nine male subjects (ages twenty to twenty-four years) on three occasions in a randomized order consumed a placebo or two different doses of vodka within 15 minutes. Fifty minutes later, fingertip blood was collected and the BACs were determined by a spectrophotometer. The mean BACs were 0.019 and 0.048 g/100 mL respectively. The subjects were tested for extended arm steadiness, reaction time (RT), muscular strength, and endurance. Significant slowing of RT was produced by both doses of alcohol, and there was no appreciable effects on muscle strength or endurance. Arm steadiness decreased with increasing BAC.

> Several trends were noticeable in the EMG analysis. The most relevant general trends were firstly, that holding time prior to loose was extended significantly under both alcohol treatments. This would be of no benefit to the archer and it may denote poorer concentration on the task of aiming.

Reference Number: 61905

REILLY, T. AND J. SCOTT. "Effects of Elevating Blood Alcohol Levels on Tasks Relating to Dart Throwing." *Perceptual and Motor Skills*, 77: 25–26, 1993 (1 table, 2 references)

Abstract: Ten males (ages twenty to twenty-six years) who had some basic dart-throwing experience were tested under four conditions: sober, placebo, low BAC (0.020 g/100 mL), and high BAC (0.050 g/100 mL). BACs were determined by finger-prick blood with an Analox device. Subjects were tested for balance, hand steadiness, rotary pursuit, and dart throwing. Seventy-five darts were thrown and the score was the number of bulls-eyes recorded.

Table. Effect of Alcohol on Dart Throwing

Measure	Placebo	BAC 0.02 g/100 mL	BAC 0.05 g/100 mL
Time off-balance (s)	7.3	7.4	9.4
Hand, unsteady (s)	3.6	4.8	5.5
Dart score	13.7	14.4	12.5

Source: Adapted from Reilly and Scott (1993).

While there were negative effects from the light alcohol dose on hand-eye coordination, effects were positive on balance and throwing. The higher BAC level produced poorer performance on all tasks. These results indicate some improvement with a light dose of alcohol for dart throwers but decrements in performance when BAC levels reached 0.05%.

Reference Number: 61906

OAKLAND, C.D.H. "Ice Skating Injuries: Can They Be Reduced or Prevented?" *Archives of Academic Emergency Medicine*, 7: 95-99, 1990 (2 figures, 7 references)

Abstract: Over a 1-year period, 241 male and 233 female skaters (ages three to sixty-two years) attended a hospital as a result of skating injuries. There were seventy-seven fractures and eight dislocations. Thirty skaters had been drinking at the bar in the skating arena before the injury.

This study attempted to identify any predisposing factors which contributed to a skater's injuries. Thirty of our patients had consumed alcohol on the premises and of these, 10 had a fracture and 5 required admission as a result of head injury. The next most common factor was poor ice conditions which has been identified before in a large Swiss study. It is the usual practice at ice rinks to divide up the skating into sessions with time in between to clear and smooth the ice. It would appear that these sessions might be reduced in length, particularly at busy weekend periods.

Reference Number: 61907

LEICHLITER, J.S., P.W. MEILMAN, C. PRESLEY, AND J.R. CASHIN. "Alcohol Use and Related Consequences Among Students with Varying Levels of Involvement in College Athletics." *Journal of American College Health*, 46: 257–262, 1998 (2 tables, 27 references)

Abstract: Alcohol is the most widely used drug on US college campuses with annual prevalence rates of over 80%. Alcohol consumption patterns and athletic involvement were determined by surveys of 51,483 students at 125 colleges during 1994 and 1996. The percentage of men who did not participate in intercollegiate sport was 76% and the percentage of women was 97%.

Our findings offered considerable support for the hypothesis that athletes consumed more alcohol and face more consequences from use than non-athletes do. The number of alcoholic drinks the respondents consumed per week and the percentage of students reporting episodes of binge drinking increased as the level of involvement in intercollegiate athletics increased from nonparticipant to participant to team leader. When we analyzed the results by gender, we found significant differences between male team members and leaders on binge drinking.

Reference Number: 61908

NELSON, T.F. AND H. WECHSLER. "School Spirits: Alcohol and Collegiate Sports Fans." *Addictive Behaviors*, 28: 1–11, 2003 (3 tables, 32 references)

Abstract: A survey was conducted in 1999 of students attending 128 four-year colleges and universities in the United States regarding extracurricular activities and substance use. According to the survey, 3,445 were classified as sports fans and 8,405 as non-sports fans. Forty-three percent of the sports fans were male compared to 33% of the non-sports fans. Sports fans were 1.55 times more likely to engage in binge drinking and were 0.85 times less likely to be abstainers from alcohol than non-sports fans.

Sports fans were less likely to abstain from alcohol than their nonfan peers and were more likely to engage in binge drinking. They also exhibited a more extreme drinking style. As a result of this heavier drinking behavior, sports fans were more likely to experience a variety of problems. Schools where many students had a strong sports interest were more likely to have high rates of binge drinking than schools where fewer students were interested in sports. In addition, students at sports schools were more likely to experience negative consequences from the alcohol use of others. Nearly half of students who attended sports schools reported three or more problem due to others' use of alcohol.

Reference Number: 61909

CLARKE, S.W., K.E. GLINDEMANN, AND D.M. WIEGAND. "The Epidemiology of Alcohol Consumption at College Football Tailgate Parties: Implications for Traffic Safety." *Proceedings of 17th International Conference on Alcohol, Drugs and Traffic Safety, August 8–13, 2004,* Glasgow, Scotland, Oliver, J., Williams, P., and Clayton, P. (eds), CD, 6pp (18 references)

Abstract: The characteristics of 719 men and 366 women attending more than 165 tailgate parties at US college football games were determined. BrACs were measured in 282 tailgaters with a LifeLoc FC20. BrACs ranged from 0 to 0.253 g/100 mL (mean 0.075 g/100 mL). The mean BrACs were greater for men (0.096 g/100 mL) than for women (0.045 g/100 mL). Despite university policies, 24% indicated they would consume alcohol during the game. Thirty percent intended to drive after the game.

> Overall, results indicated that a number of variables were related to intoxication levels at pre-game tailgate parties, including gender, age, and driving intentions. Men were more intoxicated than women, older adults (≥ 35 years of age) were less intoxicated than younger adults (18–34 years of age), and there was no difference between intoxication levels of drivers and non-drivers at pre-game tailgate parties.

Reference Number: 61910

WRIGHT, N.R. "A Day at the Cricket: The Breath Alcohol Consequences of a Type of Very English Binge Drinking." *Addiction Research and Theory*, 14: 133–137, 2006 (1 figure, 8 references)

Abstract: The drinking behavior and BrACs of twelve male cricket spectators (ages thirty-four to fifty-nine years) were determined during a cricket match between 11:00 a.m. to 6:00 p.m. BrACs were determined with an Intoximeter SD400P. The drinkers consumed between nine and twenty-two units of alcohol. All spectators had an initial BrAC of zero. The BrACs at the end of the match ranged between 0 to 0.140 g/100 mL.

> The pharmacokinetics of alcohol during social drinking is an under-researched area. New medical texts e.g. Paten and Touget (2005) continues to base best estimates of the time course of breath or blood alcohol concentrations on data from laboratory-style experiments in which alcohol is taken at a high concentration, bolus, after fasting. The BACs recorded in this study are much lower than predicted by studies that have employed these artificial conditions.

Reference Number: 61911

MATTICK, A.P., R. MEHTA, H. HANRAHAN, AND J.J. O'DONNELL. "The Football World Cup 2002—Analysis of Related Attendance to an Irish Emergency Department." *Irish Medical Journal*, 96: 90–91, 2003 (2 tables, 7 references)

Abstract: A total of forty-seven patients attended the University College Hospital, Galway, Ireland, with World Cup-related injuries during the televised finals. The majority of the attendances were due to minor trauma such as an assault or fall. Alcohol was involved in twenty-five (53%) of the patients. The incidence of trauma and alcohol involvement was lowest when the game was televised at 7:30 a.m.

> World Cup 2002 was a major televised sporting event with some of the matches watched live by up to half the population of Ireland. During the competition the Emergency Department at University College Hospital Galway saw 47 directly related attendances, most of which were around the times of the Ireland matches. The majority of these were minor trauma cases and the overall impact on the Emergency Department was limited.

Reference Number: 61912

WOLFE, J., R. MARTINEZ, AND W.A. SCOTT. "Baseball and Beer: An Analysis of Alcohol Consumption Patterns Among Male Spectators at Major-League Sporting Events." *Annals Emergency Medicine*, 31: 629–632, 1998 (1 table, 1 figure, 15 references)

Abstract: A study was conducted of the BrACs of 729 male spectators of drinking age who attended a major league baseball game during 1993. The subjects also filled in a questionnaire. The BrACs were determined with an Alcomonitor after having the subjects rinse their mouths with water. A positive BrAC was found in 41% of the subjects and a BAC > 0.080 g/100 mL was found in 8.4%. A total of 4.6% of the subjects who had a BAC > 0.080 g/100 mL during the fifth inning of the game claimed to be driving home. The greatest alcohol use occurred in the twenty- to thirty-five-year-old age group.

Table. Percent of Spectators Consuming Alcohol and with BrAC > 0.08 g/100 mL at the Entrance and at the Fifth Inningof a Baseball Game

Age range (yrs)	Percent consuming alcohol (and percent BrAC > 0.08 g/100 mL) at entrance	Percent consuming alcohol (and percent BrAC > 0.08 g/100 mL) at fifth inning
20–35	39 (8)	60 (13)
36–50	30 (4)	34 (8)
51–65	24 (0)	44 (25)
66+	20 (0)	0 (0)

Source: Adapted from Wolfe et al (1998).

These studies suggest that consumption of alcoholic beverages at sporting events can be a problem even at venues that do not sell alcohol and that the risk of alcohol-related injury extend to the roads and highways surrounding stadiums. This evidence supports the need for effective alcohol management policies at all venues in which there is a possibility of alcohol consumption.

Reference Number: 61913

REDELMEIER, D.A. AND C.L.STEWART. "Driving Fatalities on Super Bowl Sunday." *New England Journal of Medicine*, 348: 368–369, 2003 (1 figure, 4 references)

Abstract: The number of fatally and non-fatally injured drivers for twenty-seven consecutive Super Bowl Sundays were determined before and after the televised game and on control Sundays. The Super Bowl is the most popular regular TV show in the United States with an audience of 130 million Americans. There was a 41% relative increase in the average number of fatalities after the telecast. There was an average of seven additional deaths on the average Super Bowl Sunday compared to control Sundays. There was also an increase in non-fatal injuries. There was an increase in alcohol-positive fatally injured drivers as well.

The 41 percent relative increase in fatalities after the Super Bowl telecast exceeds the relative increase in fatalities on New Year's Eve that has prevailed for the past two decades in the United States. Hence, one option could be for sponsors to support subsidized public transit after the telecast.

Reference Number: 61914

DEAKIN, C.D., F. THOMPSON, C. GIBSON, AND M. GREEN. "Effects of International Football Matches on Ambulance Call Profiles and Volumes During the 2006 World Cup." *Emergency Medicine Journal*, 24: 405-407, 2007 (1 table, 3 figures, 6 references)

Abstract: The type and volume of calls to the Hampshire Ambulance Service in Winchester, England, were determined during a 2006 World Cup soccer match in which England played. There was a 50% increase in calls on the Saturday when England played Paraguay. An increase was seen in falls (19%), collapse (44%), and MVCs (118%).

Call profile analysis showed increases in alcohol-related emergencies including collapse, unconsciousness, assault and road traffic accidents. The increase in assaults was particularly marked at the end of each match and increased in the late evening.

Reference Number: 61915

ERICKSON, D.J., T.L. TOOMEY, K.M. LENK, G.R. KILIAN, AND L.E.A. FABIAN. "Can We Assess Blood Alcohol Levels of Attendees Leaving Professional Sporting Events?" *Alcoholism: Clinical and Experimental Research*, 35: 689–694, 2011 (3 tables, 1 figure, 15 references)

Abstract: The BrACs of 362 adults attending a major league baseball or football game were determined using an Intoxilyzer SD 400. A zero BrAC was found in 216 (60%) and a BrAC > 0.080 g/100 mL was found in 8% of the attendees. The mean BrAC was 0.039 g/100 mL (range 0.005 to 0.217 g/100 mL). The odds ratio (OR) of having a BrAC > 0.080 g/100 mL compared to a zero BrAC were 17.0 times for attending a tailgate party, 9.3 times for ages twenty-one to thirty-five years, and 3.0 times for testing on Mondays. The percentage of attendees who had their last drink between 1 to 4 minutes before the interview was 9%, between 5 and 15 minutes was 40%, and more than 15 minutes were 51%.

We found it was feasible to implement a protocol for collecting BAC information from attendees outside sports stadiums that was adapted from procedures for collecting BAC levels in other settings. Our findings suggest that tailgating and serving practices within professional sporting events may be contributing to a significant number of attendees having elevated BAC levels including BAC levels over the legal driving limit of 0.08. These elevated BAC levels could contribute to greater levels of alcohol-related problems during and following sporting events.

Reference Number: 61916

PODSTAWSKI, R., E. WESOLOWSKA, AND D. CHOSZCZ. "Empty Alcohol Containers and Breath Alcohol Analysis Measures of Alcohol Consumption at a College Volleyball Championship." *Journal of Studies on Alcohol and Drugs*, 76: 152–157, 2015 (5 tables, 21 references)

Abstract: A study was conducted of the alcohol consumption of 1,768 male and 915 female students (ages ninteen to twenty-four years) who attended interdepartmental volleyball games at a university in Poland between 2012–2013. Alcohol consumption was measured by the empty alcoholic beverage containers after the game and by determining the BrAC in 325 students using an Alkohit X600 used by the Polish police. The highest BrAC detected was 0.051 g/100 mL for male spectators and 0.059 g/100 mL for female spectators. After the male volleyball matches, thirty-three empty bottles of vodka were retrieved compared to four empty bottles after the female matches.

Table. Number of Empty Alcoholic Beverage Containers After Different Levels of Volleyball Games

Game Level	Number of Beer Cans	Number of Vodka Bottles
Male quarterfinals	189	12
Female quarterfinals	100	1
Male semifinals	181	8
Female semifinals	101	0
Male final	234	7
Female final	64	2

Source: Adapted from Podstawski et al (2015).

Male league games were accompanied by more alcohol consumption than were female league games, and male spectators drank more than female spectators. The most drinking occurred among men watching the male league, and the least amount of drinking occurred among women watching the female league. Alcohol intoxication increased with the rank of the match, mostly among men watching the male league. The sex of players and spectators seems to be a mediating factor in the relationship between the rank of a match and the amount of alcohol consumed.

Reference Number: 61917

O'BRIEN, C.P. AND F. LYONS. "Alcohol and the Athlete." *Sports Medicine*, 29: 295-300, 2000 (1 table, 1 figure, 34 references)

Abstract: Alcohol is the most widely used drug among the athletic population, but typically the weekly consumption was below the upper safe limit of consumption of twenty-two units per week for men. Alcohol is an ergolytic (performance impairing) drug, but small doses can temporarily cause cardiac arrhythmias, which are potentially fatal.

Table. Percent of the Drinkers and Non-drinkers Injured According to Sport

Sport	Drinkers Injured	Non-drinkers Injured
Tennis	83%	33%
Rugby	76%	66%
Gaelic Football	71%	18%
Hurling	71%	14%
Basketball	69%	16%
Cricket	63%	0%

Source: O'Brien and Lyons (2000).

Alcohol consumption also appears to have a causative effect in sports related injury with an injury incidence of 54.8% in drinkers compared with 23.5% in nondrinkers ($p < 0.005$). This may be due in part to the hangover effect of alcohol consumption, which has been shown to reduce athletic performance by 11.4%. Alcohol is a potentially lethal drug and is a banned substance for certain Olympic sports. Education is the cornerstone for appropriate social use of this drug. Athletes and coaches need to be aware of sports related adverse effects of alcohol consumption and its role in sports injury and poor physiological performance. It is recommended that alcohol should be avoided by the serious athlete.

Reference Number: 61918

MENZ, V., M. PHILIPPE, E. POCECCO, G. RUEDL, T. WOLDRICH, R. SOMMERSACHER, AND M. BURTSCHER. "The Use of Medication and Alcohol in Recreational Downhill Skiers: Results of a Survey Including 816 Subjects in Tyrol." *Journal of Science and Medicine in Sport*, 22: 522–526, 2019 (3 tables, 3 figures, 32 references)

Abstract: A survey of 816 recreational downhill skiers (ages six to eighty-seven years) was conducted at various ski resorts in Tyrol, Austria, during the 2014 winter season. Compared to female skiers, male skiers were nearly twice as likely to have consumed alcohol on the day of skiing (30% versus 16%). Fifty percent of female skiers and 64% of male skiers consumed alcohol the evening before skiing. Medication was used by 20% of the female and 22% of the male skiers. There was a high percent of concomitant alcohol and medication use (21%–35%).

Gaudio et al. regard the presence of alcohol in the blood as an important cause of accidents during skiing as the technical ability and ski control are unpredictably influenced. This is not surprising considering the fact that alcohol is markedly influencing the central nervous system with cognitive and motor impairment contributing to reduced concentration and reaction time and also affecting the risk and sensation seeking behavior. Additionally, when combining exercise as alpine skiing and alcohol overall performance is reduced whereas onset of fatigue is increased which may be associated with an increased risk of falls.

Reference Number: 61919

GAUDIO, R.M., S. BARBIERI, P. FELTRACCO, ET AL. "Impact of Alcohol Consumption on Winter Sports-Related Injuries." *Medicine, Science and the Law*, 50: 122–125, 2010 (1 table, 8 figures, 10 references).

Abstract: A study was conducted of 4,450 patients with skiing and snowboarding injuries between 2004 and 2009 in the Dolomite Mountains. BACs were determined in 200 patients suffering from serious injuries and consisted of eighty-four skiers (mean age 33.5 years) and 116 snowboarders (mean age twenty-two years). A high BAC was detected in 43% of the 200 patients.

Table. Mechanisms of Injuries in Skiing and Snowboarding

Mechanism	Percent
Falling and jumping	39
Falling	32
Collision object/person	17
Avoiding collision with others	10
Unknown	2

Source: Gaudio et al (2010).

The presence of alcohol in the blood is among the important causes of accidents, with unpredictable and indefinite influence on technical ability or ski control. Moderate to high BAC could be a serious danger especially for beginner skiers who lose their balance quickly and are unable to compensate in time the heavy impact of a fall onto the snow surface.

6.20 SUICIDES

"Drunkenness is temporary suicide: the happiness that it brings is merely negative, a momentary cessation of unhappiness."

—Bertrand Russell

"In fact, 27% of the decedents had a BAC greater than 0.20 g/dL, a concentration generally associated with significant to severe impairment. Despite the impairment, these individuals were able to form intent to commit suicide as evidenced by the presence of a suicide note."

—Levine et al, "Alcohol Concentration and the Ability to Form Intent" (2005)

Alcohol consumption is a risk factor in suicide attempts (62001, 62002). A positive postmortem BAC has been found in a large percentage of suicide victims (62003–62012). In the United States, the main suicide methods (in decreasing frequency) have been found to be:

Gunshot wound > Hanging > Drug overdose > CO poisoning

The presence of a high BAC does not necessarily indicate that the victim was incapable of committing suicide (62006, 62007) or of forming intent (62004). Victims who left a suicide note were more likely to have consumed alcohol than victims who did not leave a note (43% versus 24%) (60210).

Fifty percent of Russian roulette deaths had a BAC ≥ 0.100 g/100 mL (60213).

Alcohol is involved in numerous different methods of suicide, such as hanging (62015–62017), CO poisonings (62008, 62015), firearms (62010, 62013, 62018), and jumping from a height (62010, 62018).

The odds ratio of a suicide attempt after consuming alcohol was 6.34 times, which increased to 16.2 times after drinking a larger amount of alcohol (62019).

It is estimated that suicide occurs in 1.5% to 15% of all FMVCs. A positive BAC was found in 79% of the negligent drivers compared to 11% of suicide drivers (62020).

A total lockdown including liquor stores in India due to COVID-19 resulted in an increase in suicides in persons with alcohol withdrawal syndrome (62021).

Reference Number: 62001

BORGES, G. AND H. ROSOVSKY. "Suicide Attempts and Alcohol Consumption in an Emergency Room Sample." *Journal of Studies on Alcohol*, 57: 543–548, 1996 (3 tables, 33 references)

Abstract: The BrACs of nineteen female and twenty-one male attempted suicide patients and 372 control patients (involved in usually non-alcohol-related accidents) were determined with an Alco-Sensor III within hours of admission to an ER in Mexico during 1986. A positive BrAC was found in twenty-two (6%) of the controls and ten (28%) of the attempted suicide patients.

According to our results, alcohol consumption prior to the suicide attempt is a more important risk factor than habitual consumption.

Reference Number: 62002

BORGES, G., C.J. CHERPITEL, S. MACDONALD, N. GIESBRECHT, T. STOCKWELL, AND H.C. WILCOX. "A Case-Crossover Study of Acute Alcohol Use and Suicide Attempt." *Journal of Studies on Alcohol*, 65: 708–714, 2004 (1 table, 1 figure, 33 references)

Abstract: A detailed interview was conducted on 102 attempted suicide victims attending hospital in the United States, Canada, Australia, and Mexico. Fifty-two percent of the victims were male, and 59% were under the age of thirty years. Thirty-six victims (35%) reported alcohol consumption within 6 hours of the suicide attempt (49% of the men and 20% of the women).

We found a positive association between alcohol use 6 hours prior and suicide attempts in 102 ER cases in four countries. The RR estimate for the effect of acute alcohol was found to be 9.6 (95% CI 5.7–16.3). Exploratory analyses of hourly risk periods suggested that this effect is mainly concentrated within the first hour after alcohol consumption.

Reference Number: 62003

CROMBIE, I.K., D.J. POUNDER, AND P.H. DICK. "Who Takes Alcohol Prior to Suicide?" *Journal of Clinical and Forensic Medicine*, 5: 65-68, 1998 (4 tables, 13 references)

Abstract: The BACs of 248 male and 101 female suicide victims at Dundee, Scotland, between 1988–1995 were determined. A positive BAC was found in 48% of the male and 37% of the female victims (range 0.005–0.410 g/100 mL). A BAC > 0.150 g/100 mL was found in 17% of the hanging victims, 20% of the car exhaust victims, 20% of the drug overdose victims, and 19% of the drowning victims.

> In conclusion, this study confirms that alcohol consumption is a common precursor to suicide. Consumption was not associated with a particular method of suicide nor social factors such as employment status, marital status, or social class. The effect of age on the incidence of alcohol use was weak. However, alcohol use was more common among those with no previous psychiatric history. This suggests that alcohol intoxication may play a more important role in the events leading to suicide among those with no previous psychiatric history.

Reference Number: 62004

LEVINE, B., J.M. TITUS, K.A. MOORE, AND D. FOWLER. "Alcohol Concentration and the Ability to Form Intent." *Science and Justice*, 45: 195–197, 2005 (1 table, 5 references)

Abstract: A study was conducted in Maryland over a 2-year period of thirty-seven cases in which the victim had a positive BAC and committed suicide after leaving a suicide note. The mean BAC of the victims was 0.140 g/100 mL and ranged from 0.010 to 0.370 g/100 mL.

> In fact, 27% of the decedents had a BAC greater than 0.20 g/dL, a concentration generally associated with significant to severe impairment. Despite the impairment, these individuals were able to form intent to commit suicide as evidence by the presence of a suicide note.

Reference Number: 62005

MICHALODIMITRAKIS, M.N, R. LA GRANGE, AND A.M. TSATSAKIS. "Suicide by Alcohol Overdose." *Journal of Clinical and Forensic Medicine,* 4: 91–94, 1997 (25 References)

Abstract: An elderly Swedish male cancer patient committed suicide by consuming alcohol. Two empty 1.5 L bottles of whiskey were found in the room. The postmortem BAC was 0.900 g/100 mL and the VHAC was 0.620 g/100 mL.

Taking into account the above facts, the conclusion of the medical examination was that the cause of his death was acute alcohol intoxication, occasioned intentionally to commit suicide.

Reference Number: 62006

DAVIS, A.R. AND A.H. LIPSON. "Central Nervous System Tolerance to High Blood Alcohol Levels." *Medical Journal of Australia*, 144: 9–12, 1986 (2 tables, 34 references)

Abstract: A 5-week study was conducted of the BACs of thirty-two male patients (ages twenty-nine to sixty-one years) who attended an alcohol detoxification center. BrACs were determined with an Alco-Sensor III and by a blood sample taken within 10 minutes of the breath test. Seventeen patients (53%) had BACs > 0.300 g/100 mL; the highest BAC was 0.450 g/100 mL. All thirty-two patients were ambulatory and provided a breath sample as instructed. They also engaged in conversation and all provided a history of chronic alcohol abuse.

Medical opinions based on the Miles scale, have been expressed in good faith for legal purposes. In 1981, for example, an inquest was held into the death of a 21-year-old man with a blood alcohol level of 3 g/L who was found hanged in a police cell. He had been detained for being intoxicated. Foul play was suspected when the court was advised that it was highly improbable that the deceased would have been capable of performing any of the proposed actions that were necessary to hang himself. Suicide would have been a reasonable alternative if the deceased suffered from alcoholism. In the three years before his death, the dead man had been charged with drunkenness on seven occasions and detained as being intoxicated on three occasions.

Reference Number: 62007

COOKE, C.T., G.A. CADDEN, AND K.A. MARGOLIUS. "Death by Hanging in Western Australia." *Pathology*, 27: 268–272, 1995 (2 tables, 1 figure, 28 references)

Abstract: A study was conducted of 280 hanging deaths in Western Australia between 1988 and 1992. Toxicological analyses were conducted in 267 of the cases. Alcohol was detected in ninety-three cases (35%). The highest BAC determined was 0.525 g/100 mL.

Finding a very high alcohol level may raise the question of the ability of the deceased to undertake the possibly intricate manipulation needed to successfully complete suicide by hanging. Naturally, each case needs to be assessed on its merit with particular attention being paid to the alcohol consumption history of the deceased, and the likelihood of possible assistance by someone else. It is well known that significant tolerance to the effects of alcohol may develop following regular use, so that even complex tasks may be undertaken with apparently little impairment.

Reference Number: 62008

BUSUITTIL, A., J.O. OBAFUNWA, AND A. AHMED. "Suicidal Inhalation of Vehicular Exhaust in the Lothian and Borders Region of Scotland." *Human, Experimental Toxicology*, 13: 545–550, 1994 (2 tables, 5 figures, 20 references)

Abstract: A study was conducted of seventy-one male and eight female suicide victims (ages nineteen to seventy-four years) who died of CO poisoning using a vehicle between 1987–1992 in Scotland. The mean COHb saturation was 74% (35%–90%). A positive BAC was found in thirty-seven victims (0.014–0.397 g/100 mL). There was no significant correlation between COHb saturation, age, and BAC.

Suicidal exhaust fume inhalation is more of a rural phenomenon an observation similar to the report from England and Wales in 1989. This probably reflects the greater availability of space and privacy in the rural areas.

Reference Number: 62009

BLUMENTHAL, R. "Suicidal Gunshot Wounds to the Head. A Retrospective Review of 406 Cases." *American Journal of Forensic Medicine and Pathology*, 28: 288–291, 2007 (2 figures, 14 references)

Abstract: A retrospective review of 406 victims of suicidal gunshot wounds to the head that occurred in Pretoria between 1997 and 2000 was conducted. Eighty-two percent of the victims were male and most were between twenty-one to forty years of age. Handguns were used by 95% of the victims and 92% of the deaths occurred indoors. The majority of gunshot entry wounds were to the right temple (41%) followed by the mouth (18%), the back of the head (17%), the left temple (11%), and the submental region (10%). Postmortem BACs were determined in 87% of the victims and 40% had a positive BAC. Most positive BACs were between 0.060

and 0.150 g/100 mL, although four victims had BACs between 0.360 and 0.750 g/100 mL.

These findings are consistent with most of the previously published literature. The right temple was the most common site of gunshot entrance would. A handgun was used in 96% of the cases. The findings show a predominance of adult white males as victims. A slight increase in the incidence of fatal self-harm seemed to have occurred around spring and autumn. Of all the cases, 92% of the fatal gunshot wounds to the head occurred indoors and 81% were contact gunshot wounds. The blood alcohol concentration was positive in 40% of those analysed.

Reference Number: 62010

COOPER, P.N. AND C.M. MILROY. "Violent Suicide in South Yorkshire, England." *Journal of Forensic Sciences*, 39: 657–667, 1994 (4 tables, 44 references)

Abstract: A study was conducted of sixty-four female and 182 male victims (ages fifteen to ninety-four years) of violent suicides. The most common method of suicide was hanging (129 cases), jumping from a height (forty-three cases), and drowning (twenty-five cases). A positive BAC was detected in thirty-eight of the 130 cases tested (29%). Of the thirty-eight positive cases, twenty-four (63%) had BACs > 0.100 g/100 mL. Victims leaving suicide notes were more likely to have consumed alcohol than victims not leaving a suicide note (43% versus 23%).

The importance of alcohol in accidental, homicidal and suicidal deaths particularly in young males is well recognized. Indeed the suicide rate in a community has been shown to correlated with the level of alcohol consumption. In this study, the individuals most likely to be intoxicated by alcohol at the time of death were young males and the methods favored by this group (self-immolation and railway deaths) showed among the highest prevalence of alcohol positivity.

Reference Number: 62011

BENNETT, A.T. AND K.A. COLLINS. "Suicide: A Ten-Year Retrospective Study." *Journal of Forensic Sciences,* 45: 1256–1258, 2000 (3 tables, 9 references)

Abstract: A study was conducted of 678 suicides in South Carolina between 1988 and 1997. There were 539 male (80%) and 139 female (20%) victims. Their ages ranged from twelve to ninety-four years of age (mean thirty-nine years). A suicide note was found in 22% of the cases. The number of suicides declined from late November to early January. They did not tend to occur around the holidays. The methods of suicide include gunshot wounds (65%), hanging (12%), overdose (11%), and CO poisoning (4%). A positive BAC was found in 258 (38%) of the victims and was greater than 0.100 g/100 mL in 155 victims (23%).

Many potentially suicidal people seek comfort, escape and relief in alcohol prior to committing suicide.

Reference Number: 62012

SHIELDS, L.B.E., D.M. HUNSAKER, J.C. HUNSAKER III, AND M.K. WARD. "Toxicologic Findings in Suicide. A 10-Year Retrospective Review of Kentucky Medical Examiner Cases". *American Journal of Forensic Medicine and Pathology*, 27: 106–112, 2006 (6 Tables, 50 References)

Abstract: A study was conducted of 2,864 suicides that occurred in Kentucky between 1993 and 2002. Blood and urine samples were collected in 95% and 72% of the victims respectively. The victims ranged in age between eleven and ninety-six years (mean forty-two years) and were mainly male (82%). A positive BAC was found in 41% of the male victims and 27% of the female victims. The causes of death were mainly gunshot (77%), hanging (14%), and drug overdose (10%).

Ethanol may influence suicidal behavior through a variety of actions. Its pathophysiological and dysfunctional effects may increase aggressiveness, disinhibit suicidal impulses and interfere with cognition by impairing the development of coping strategies.

Reference Number: 62013

SHIELDS, L.B.E., J.C. HUNSAKER III, AND D.M. STEWART. "Russian Roulette and Risk-Taking Behavior. A Medical Examiner Study." *American Journal of Forensic Medicine and Pathology*, 29: 32–39, 2008 (4 tables, 40 references)

Abstract: A study was conducted of twenty-four incidents of fatal gunshot wounds to the head while playing Russian roulette in Kentucky between 1993–2002. All victims were male with a mean age of twenty-five years (range fourteen to forty-seven years). A positive BAC was detected in 75%

of the victims of Russian roulette compared with 39% of suicidal victims of gunshot wounds.

Table. BACs of Russian Roulette Victims and Victims of Suicidal Gunshot Wound Deaths

BAC (g/100 mL)	Russian Roulette Deaths	Suicidal GSW Deaths
Negative	25%	61%
< 0.100	25%	12%
≥ 0.100	50%	27%

Source: Adapted from Shields et al (2008).

The group mentality prompting Russian roulette may convince reluctant individuals to participate as a means of gaining peer acceptance and approval. Players' judgments are often clouded by the effects of ethanol and drugs, inciting those so influenced to engage in a risky and potentially fatal behavior. The pathophysiologic effects of ethanol exacerbate psychologic distress, increase aggressiveness and constrict cognition by interfering with the development of coping strategies.

Reference Number: 62014

JORDAN, F.B., K. SCHMECKPEPER, AND M. STROPE. "Jail Suicides by Hanging. An Epidemiological Review and Recommendations for Prevention." *American Journal of Forensic Medicine and Pathology*, 8: 27–31, 1987 (1 table, 4 figures, 9 references)

Abstract: A study was conducted of seventeen suicides by hanging while in custody in Oklahoma between 1981 and 1983. All victims were male, and a positive BAC was found in 65% of the cases. Most victims were jailed for nonviolent crimes.

The intoxicated person therefore may be in double jeopardy: first due to poor impulse control at high blood alcohol levels; second, due to the heightened potential for dysthymic feelings as the brain serotonin level plunges.

Reference Number: 62015

HAYWARD, L., S.R. ZUBRICK, AND S. SILBURN. "Blood Alcohol Levels in Suicide Cases." *Journal of Epidemiology and Community Health*, 46: 256–260, 1992 (2 tables, 9 references)

Abstract: The postmortem BACs were determined in 414 male and 101 female suicide victims (mean age forty-one years) in Western Australia between 1986 and 1988. A positive BAC was found in 36% of the victims and 25% had a BAC > 0.050 g/100 mL. The average BAC was 0.120 g/100 mL for male victims and 0.080 g/100 mL for female victims. The UACs were also determined in 45% of the victims and only forty-nine victims had a higher BAC than UAC. A positive BAC was found in 49% of the CO poisonings, 38% of the firearm fatalities, 31% of the drownings, and 8% of the jumping suicides. Victims with a BAC > 0.050 g/100 mL were younger (thirty-seven versus forty-three years of age), more likely male (28% versus 11%), more likely to have experienced a breakup of a relationship (62% versus 40%), and more likely to experience a job loss (21% versus 6%) than victims with a BAC < 0.050 g/100 mL.

> Many of these people had been drinking for some time prior to their death and it is possible that in such cases the depressant and disinhibitory effects of alcohol, combined with depression arising from a recent loss of a relationship, and lack of attempt to seek professional help, created an emotional state when they sought to take their lives.

Reference Number 62016

ZERBINI, T., J. DE CARVALHO PONCE, D.M. SINGAWA, R.B. CINTRA, D.R. MUNOZ, AND V. LEYTON. "Blood Alcohol Levels in Suicide by Hanging Cases in the State of Sao Paulo, Brazil." *Journal of Forensic and Legal Medicine*, 19: 294–296, 2012 (3 figures, 20 references)

Abstract: A study was conducted of 184 victims of suicide by hanging that occurred in Sao Paulo, Brazil, during 2007. The victims were mainly male (84%), and 67% were between fifteen to forty-four years of age. A positive BAC was found in 41% of the male hanging victims and 17% of the female hanging victims. The mean BAC was 0.180 g/100 mL.

> Alcohol causes attention deficit, diminished cognition, autobiographical memory and disinhibition, in addition to dysphoria, depression and aggressiveness, impulsiveness and self-destructive behavior. The mean BAC

found in the present study (1.80 g/L) is consistent with self-destructive behavior associated with impulsiveness, which can lead to suicide especially among males.

Reference Number: 62017

ZUPANC, A.M. A.V. PASKA, AND P. PREGELJI. "Blood Alcohol Concentration of Suicide Victims by Partial Hanging." *Journal of Forensic and Legal Medicine*, 20: 976–979, 2013 (2 tables, 1 figure, 40 references)

Abstract: A study was conducted of the postmortem BAC of 184 victims of partial hanging and 112 victims of complete hanging that occurred in Slovenia between 2000 to 2007. Partial hanging occurs where the suicide victim is not found fully suspended but part of the body is in touch with the floor or other object such as a chair. The mean BAC was 0.057 g/100 mL for the partial hanging and 0.040 g/100 mL for the complete hanging victims.

Partial hanging is almost twice as common as complete hanging. Higher BAC in the group of suicide victims who used partial hanging and more BAC positive suicide victims in the group who used non-violent suicide methods could indicate the role of alcohol is the selection of suicide method. Other explanations are also possible such as motor functions being diminished by alcohol, decreased intention to die associated with higher BAC, increased possibility to be rescued, or increased age of suicide victims associated with partial hanging. It is also necessary to question whether the victim actually always make a choice as to which form of hanging to use. If this is not the case, then alcohol and increasing age may cause a less efficient attempt, which then presents as partial hanging.

Reference Number 62018

PARK, C.H.K., S.H. YOO, J. LEE, S.J. CHO, M.-S. SHIN, E.Y. KIM, S.H. KIM, K. HAM, AND Y.M. AHN. "Impact of Acute Alcohol Consumption on Lethality of Suicide Methods." *Comprehensive Psychiatry*, 75: 27–34, 2017 (4 tables, 1 figure, 48 references)

Abstract: The postmortem BACs of 315 suicide victims who died in South Korea during 2015 were determined. The victims were divided into a suicide method of low lethality (SMLL) (e.g., drug overdose, sharp objects) and a suicide method of high lethality (SMHL) (e.g., hanging, jumping from a height, firearms). There were seventy victims in the SMLL and 245 in the SMHL. SMHL occurred more often in victims with a BAC between 0.150 to 0.199 g/100 mL. The number of suicide victims decreased as the BAC > 0.200 g/100 mL.

Table. BAC Range of Victims and the Lethality Ratio

BAC Range (g/100 mL)	Lethality Ratio (High:Low)
0.011–0.049	2.86
0.050–0.099	2.31
0.100–0.149	3.20
0.150–0.199	7.71
0.200–0.249	7.33
0.250–0.299	3.60
0.300+	4.25

Source: Adapted from Park et al (2015).

> In this retrospective study, we demonstrated the non-linear, bell shaped distribution of SMHL to SMLL ratios across the BAC range; SMHL were more likely to be used by suicide completers with the mid range BAC levels (0.150–0.199%). This finding indicates that less severely intoxicated people may need to be more closely monitored in terms of suicidality. For example, if drunk emergency patients with suicidal risk are seen in the emergency room, if not fully drunk, it may be desirable that they stay there until they sober up. In addition, advancing age and a history of psychiatric illness were independent predictors for SMLL. Acute alcohol use may influence the selection of suicide methods of different lethality by affecting impulsivity and executive dysfunctions.

Reference Number 62019

BAGGE, C.L., H-J. LEE, J.A. SCHUMACHER, K.L. GRATZ., J.L. KRULL, AND G. HOLLOMAN JR. "Alcohol as an Acute Risk Factor for Recent Suicide Attempts: A Case-Crossover Analysis." *Journal of Studies on Alcohol and Drugs*, 74: 552–558, 2013 (1 table, 25 references)

Abstract: The alcohol consumption pattern of 192 suicide attempters admitted to a level 1 trauma hospital in Mississippi, prior to their attempt, was determined. Twenty-five percent of the patients reported alcohol use within 6 hours prior to the suicide attempt. The odds ratio of attempting suicide soon after drinking was 6.34 times and with a larger amount of drinking increased to 16.2 times.

> The results of our study suggest that drinking (especially relatively higher levels of drinking) is a unique acute risk factor for suicide attempts, controlling for other important acute exposures (i.e., other drug use and negative life events). These results suggest that clinicians should consider current levels of drinking during risk assessment among populations at high risk for suicide attempts.

Reference Number: 62020

HERNETKOSKI, K. AND E. KESKINEN. "Self-Destruction in Finnish Motor Traffic Accidents in 1974–1992." *Accident Analysis and Prevention*, 30: 697–704, 1998 (1 table, 3 figures, 25 references).

Abstract: It is estimated that suicides occur in 1.5 to 15% of all traffic fatalities. The annual rate of suicides in Finnish men is forty per 100,000, compared to ten per 100,000 for Finnish women. Fatal motor vehicle collisions between 1974 and 1992 were studied, in particular from 1974–1975, 1984–1985, 1987–1988, and 1991–1992. During these two 4-year periods, a total of 2,240 cases occurred, which were classified into suicides (6.2%), unclear (4.1%), negligent (15.7%), and true accidents (74.0%). During that time period the percent of suicides in FMVCs increased from 1.1 to 7.4%. Forty-three percent of the negligent drivers had a previous drinking-driving offense, compared to 11% of the drivers in both the unclear and suicide groups. Seventy-nine percent of the negligent drivers used alcohol at the time of the FMVC compared to 22% of the suicide and 36% of the unclear groups. In the suicide group, 49% of the drivers were classified as depressed compared to 19% of the unclear group and 6% of the negligent drivers.

> The majority of the motor vehicle suicides covered by this study was committed by young males. Bearing in mind that suicide is the most common cause of death among young men in Finland, this finding is not at all surprising. Finnish men generally also use more violent means of committing suicide than women and a motor vehicle certainly fills that criterion.

Reference Number: 62021

AHMED, S., M.O. KHAIUM, AND F. TAZMEEM. "COVID-19 Lockdown in India Triggers a Rapid Rise in Suicides Due to the Alcohol Withdrawal Symptoms: Evidence from Media Reports." *International Journal of Social Psychiatry*, 66: 827–829, 2020 (22 references)

Abstract: A total lockdown including liquor stores was enforced in India between 25 March 2020 to 3 May 2020 to prevent the spread of COVID-19. As of 5 May 2020, at least twenty-three people committed suicide and several more attempted suicide due to suffering from alcohol withdrawal syndrome because of the unavailability of alcohol.

The lockdown due to the coronavirus pandemic in India has spotted one of the most critical yet lesser recognized public health issues of the Southern part of India (e.g., Karnataka, Kerala, Telandana), that is high alcohol consumption and high alcohol dependency of people. Although mass media campaigns have already been used in India to minimize the intake of alcohol, research suggests the quality of these campaigns was not up to the mark.

CHAPTER 7

Postmortem Alcohol

> "Even still more serious consequences may be the result of false positive alcohol reactions. In the case of a 3-month-old dead infant, an alcohol concentration of about 0.2% was verified but the blood contained alcohol-producing micro-organism. It is probable that two years ago, the mother would have been accused of infanticide by means of alcohol."
>
> —Gormsen, "Alcohol Production in the Dead Body. Further Investigations" (1954)

> "It is important to be understood that the mere finding of alcohol in a specimen of putrefied blood does not indicate that antemortem ingestion of alcohol has taken place."
>
> —Bucklin, "Medical Examiner's File" (1976)

The analysis and interpretation of postmortem alcohol testing is more complicated than for blood samples collected from living subjects. Other factors such as postmortem diffusion and putrefaction (partially as a result of high postmortem blood sugar concentrations) can affect the alcohol results. Blood can be collected from a variety of areas such as the heart, iliac (leg) vein, or hematoma (blood clot), rather than just venous blood, which is routinely collected from living persons in drinking-driving cases. As well the alcohol concentration can be determined in vitreous humor, liver, bile, or muscle. Postmortem biomarkers of alcohol ingestion can assist in determining whether the postmortem BAC was caused by putrefaction.

In general the postmortem BAC is not as stable as blood collected from living subjects for the following reasons:

- Postmortem blood is no longer sterile.
- Numerous bacteria/yeasts migrate from the gut postmortem.
- Postmortem blood can have very high glucose concentration.
- In cases of blunt force trauma these three processes are accelerated and BACs of up to 0.190 g/100 mL have been detected in alcohol-free victims.

7.01 METHODS OF ANALYSIS

"Widmark's method has been found inadequate if more than 48 hours have elapsed between death and autopsy."

—Bonnichsen et al, "Alcohol in Post Mortem Specimens. II Comparative Determination by Widmark's and Zeisel-Fanto's Methods and by ADH method" (1954)

Headspace gas chromatography is the current preferred method of alcohol analysis in postmortem blood samples as it is for antemortem samples. It is recommended, however, that *t*-butanol be employed as the internal standard rather than *n*-propanol, which is commonly used for antemortem samples, as *n*-propanol is a putrefactive product (70102, 70103, 70105). Headspace GC has also been employed to detect the alcohol concentration in brain tissues (70106).

A solid-phase extraction method with headspace GC has been described (70104).

A false positive alcohol concentration was detected by an enzymatic method in perimortem blood samples, but were zero in the postmortem blood samples analyzed by headspace GC (70107).

Reference Number: 70101

CHRISTOPOULOS, G., E.R. KIRCH, AND J.E. GEARIEN. "Determination of Ethanol in Fresh and Purified Postmortem Tissues." *Journal of Chromatography*, 87: 455–472, 1973 (14 tables, 4 figures, 18 references)

Abstract: Postmortem blood and tissues were analyzed for ethanol by GC and Widmark methods. The Widmark method should not be used in postmortem blood. One Widmark analysis showed a reading as high as 0.105 g/100 mL of oxidizable material, calculated as ethanol, and the GC analysis showed no ethanol. In postmortem blood samples, the glucose concentration ranged from 0 to 1,200 mg/dL. Of five ethanol negative postmortem blood samples that were preserved in 1% NaF and stored at room temperature, three samples produced ethanol with time and one showed an increase to 0.048 g/100 mL. Samples with 1% NaF that were refrigerated showed no increase after 45 days. Urine samples stored at room temperature with no preservatives showed only slight increases in ethanol, up to 0.015 g/100 mL, and the fluctuations in UAC with time were small compared to the changes in BAC. It is recommended that blood samples be preserved with 1% NaF and refrigerated.

Widmark's method is reliable for the determination of ethanol only in the absence of distillable volatiles such as methanol, acetaldehyde, isopropyl alcohol, 1-propanol and 1-butanol.

Reference Number: 70102

O'NEAL, C.L., C.E. WOLF II., B. LEVINE, G. KUNSMAN, AND A. POKLIS. "Gas Chromatographic Procedures for Determination of Ethanol in Postmortem Blood Using T-Butanol and Methyl Ethyl Ketone as Internal Standards." *Forensic Science International*, 83: 31–38, 1996 (3 tables, 2 figures, 8 references)

Abstract: Three GC procedures for the determination of alcohol in postmortem blood are described using either methyl ethyl ketone (MEK) or *t*-butyl alcohol as internal standards and headspace GC, or using *t*-butyl alcohol and headspace GC. For *t*-butyl alcohol headspace method, a RTX-BAC2 column was used measuring 30 m × 0.53 mm ID × 2.0 um. A sample of 0.2 mL and 1.8 mL of internal standard were pipetted into the headspace vials.

Our study demonstrates that using t-butanol or methyl ethyl ketone as internal standards resulted in precise ethanol determinations in postmortem blood, whether applied to procedures with packed or capillary columns, with direct injection or headspace gas chromatography. Additionally, the use of these internal standards with capillary headspace gas chromatography allows for the identification of other volatiles in postmortem specimens, specifically *n*-propanol that may aid in distinguishing antemortem ingestion from postmortem synthesis of ethanol.

Reference Number: 70103

BONVENTRE, J., S. VALANJU, AND M.L. BASTOS. "Evaluation of Ethanol Analysis on Brain and Liver by Head-Space Gas Chromatography." *Forensic Science International*, 19: 75–83, 1982 (1 table, 38 references)

Abstract: A headspace GC method is described for the determination of ethanol concentration in brain and liver tissues. A Multifract F-40 was used and the internal standard was *t*-butanol. The effect of the fat content of the sample on the alcohol analysis was determined using spike samples of water (0%), skimmed milk (0.05%), homogenized milk (3.5%), and heavy cream (35% fat content respectively). As the fat content increased, the internal standard peak height decreased compared with the peak height of ethyl alcohol. At a spiked ethyl alcohol concentration of 0.156 g/100 mL the measured results were 0.155, 0.163, 0.196, and 0.305 g/100 mL for water, skim milk, homogenized milk, and heavy cream respectively. *t*-Butanol is more fat soluble than ethyl alcohol. The ratio of the ethanol concentration of the brain and blood is between 0.97–1.32. There was a poor correlation between blood and liver ethanol concentration. This is thought to be due to the natural oxidative losses of ethanol in the liver and the variable fat content of the sample.

The direct headspace chromatographic method as applied to the determination of ethanol in the brain is a reliable indication of antemortem concentration of ethanol in the central nervous system. This is true despite the postmortem changes that may occur in the body or in vitro. The methodology does not yield as reliable results for the analysis of ethanol in the liver, which presents the additional problem of remarkable postmortem oxidation of ethanol.

Reference Number: 70104

DE MARTINIS B.S. AND C.C.S. MARTIN. "Automated Headspace Solid-Phase Microextraction and Capillary Gas Chromatography Analysis of Ethanol in Postmortem Specimens." *Forensic Science International*, 128: 115–119, 2002 (2 tables, 2 figures, 26 references)

Abstract: A headspace GC method using solid-phase microextraction to determine the alcohol concentration in postmortem blood, urine, and vitreous humor is described. Isobutanol was used as an internal standard.

In the present work, we have demonstrated that HS-SPME using a polar 85 um polyacrylate coated fibre and capillary gas chromatography is an effective and suitable methodology for the determination of ethanol and other volatile compounds in blood, urine and vitreous humor. The procedure presented was simple, sensitive, reproducible and allowed excellent quantitation performance.

Reference Number: 70105

RAWAT, B.R. "Head Space Gas Chromatography (GC-HS) Analysis of Postmortem Unpreserved Blood Samples and Identification of Volatiles Produced." *The Indian Police Journal*, 55: 36–45, 2008 (2 tables, 2 figures, 17 references)

Abstract: Seven postmortem, unpreserved blood samples were analyzed by headspace GC in cases without an alcohol consumption history. The most common volatiles detected were isopropanol, acetaldehyde, and methanol. *n*-Propanol was detected in the blood sample with the highest BAC (0.106 g/100 mL).

The two most important factors are microbial alcohol production and alcohol diffusion from gastric residue or airways contaminated by vomits. Distinguishing between alcohol ingestion in life and microbial production after death is a common problem. Within a few hours of death gut bacteria penetrates the portal venous system and after about six hours contaminates the systemic vessels in the blood, glucose and lactate provides the substrates for microbial ethanol production by the pathway opposite to that of its catabolism in the living body. Higher environmental temperate after death, terminal hyperglycemia, terminal septicemia, abdominal trauma and severe trauma with wound contamination provide particularly fertile conditions for ethanol synthesis. At room temperature blood ethanol values of around 150 mg/100 mL can be reached in a few days, although more typically values are below 70 mg/dL.

Reference Number: 70106

CHUN, H-J., J.L. POKLIS, A. POKLIS, AND C.E. WOLF. "Development and Validation of a Method for Alcohol Analysis in Brain Tissue by Headspace Gas Chromatography with Flame Ionization Detector." *Journal of Analytical Toxicology*, 40: 653–658, 2016 (3 tables, 3 figures, 21 references)

Abstract: A headspace GC method for the determination of methanol, ethanol, acetone, isopropanol, and *n*-propanol was developed using *t*-butanol as the internal standard. The brain sample was weighed and diluted four-fold with distilled water and then homogenized. One GC capillary column was used (Restek BAC 1). Ethyl formate was found to co-elute with ethanol, methylene chloride with acetone, and *n*-heptane and iso-octane with *t*-butanol. Matrix effects were minimized by using the four-fold dilution of the brain tissue. The CV for all volatiles was < 10%.

Another alternative specimen for alcohol analysis is brain tissue. Where blood is easily lost due to ante-mortem trauma, the brain may be preserved due to its encasement in the protective skull. The isolated location and lack of glucose storage also make the brain an attractive specimen for analysis as it is less susceptible to postmortem alcohol diffusion, such as from the stomach to heart blood and post-mortem alcohol formation. Whereas there is concern over differences in alcohol concentration in post-mortem blood collected from various sites, the regional distribution of alcohol in the brain does not differ significantly. As a highly vascularized tissue with a rich blood supply, the brain displays rapid alcohol equilibrium with blood and thus may be a good indicator of ante-mortem BAC.

Reference Number: 70107

BISHOP-FREEMAN, S.C., R.L. BERTHOLF, R.H. POWERS, L.C. MAYHEW, AND R.E. WINECKER. "False-Positive Enzymatic Alcohol Results in Perimortem Specimens." *Laboratory Medicine*, 51: 394–401, 2020 (2 tables, 25 references).

Abstract: The most common method of analysis used in hospitals to determine the serum alcohol concentration is based on the enzymatic (ADH) oxidation of alcohol to acetaldehyde and the production of NADH, which is measured to quantitate the alcohol concentration. Serum samples with an elevated lactate and lactate dehydrogenase concentrations can also produce NADH, which results in a false positive alcohol result. A six-year-old boy who drowned and a two-year-old girl who died of respiratory failure and a heart attack had SACs of 0.076 g/100 mL and 0.053 g/100 mL respectively. The postmortem BAC in both cases as determined by headspace GC, however, were zero.

The 2 cases reported, in which enzymatic testing indicated the presence of significant concentrations of ethanol in pediatric patients and yet those results were clearly demonstrated by GC-FID to be false-positive results, show that laboratory and medical professionals need to better understand enzymatic assays. Clinical laboratory workers using enzymatic ethanol assays should be aware of potential causes of false-positive or falsely elevated ethanol results, including elevated lactate and LD levels. Also, they should question results that do not fit the clinical picture. Laboratory policies or result flags may be instituted to alert clinicians to order a second ethanol analysis by a different technique, using the same or future serum specimens if possible to allow for ethanol metabolism. Ultimately, it may be necessary to contact the laboratory directly and speak to a toxicologist regarding the reliability of a specific ethanol measurement. Definitive analytical methods, such as dual-column headspace gas chromatography should be considered for confirmation of ethanol results that may have legal consequences. These perimortem pediatric cases showed that the potential exists for interferences to complicate an ED diagnosis and to negatively impact families already trying to cope with a tragedy.

7.02 PUTREFACTION/PRESERVATION

"High blood alcohol levels may develop during putrefaction and levels up to 0.200 per cent will not necessarily indicate that alcohol was imbibed prior to death."

—Plueckhahn, "The Evaluation of Autopsy Blood Alcohol Levels" (1967)

"Postmortem specimen contamination with ethanol-producing microorganisms increase with an increasing extent of trauma to the body. Therefore, postmortem ethanol formation is far more likely to occur in cases involving severe trauma to the body."

—Canfield et al, "Postmortem Ethanol Testing Procedures Available to Accident Investigators" (2007)

Postmortem blood is more prone to putrefaction and endogenous formation of alcohol than antemortem blood in part due to its potentially high glucose content and exposure to microorganisms (70201, 70202). The glucose can be fermented by yeast, bacteria, and fungi through various steps into acetaldehyde and carbon dioxide and eventually to alcohol as follows:

$$C_6H_{12}O_6 \rightarrow 2\ CH_2CHO + 2\ CO_2 \rightarrow 2\ CH_3CH_2OH$$

Yeasts, the most efficient fermenters, can convert approximately 0.100 g/100 mL of glucose into approximately 0.040 to 0.050 g/100 mL of alcohol, whereas bacteria and fungi can only produce approximately 0.010 to 0.020 g/100 mL of alcohol from the same amount of glucose. Typically, postmortem neoformation of alcohol results in low BACs (70203–70205). Postmortem alcohol concentrations can increase or decrease with storage (70206, 70207, 70210). Postmortem production of alcohol can be indicated by analysis and comparison of alcohol concentrations of other specimens, detection of other volatiles (mainly *n*-propanol) (70206, 70208, 70210–70211, 70215–70219, 70223, 70226), or biomarkers (70212, 70220).

Urine and vitreous samples are invaluable to assist in the determination of potential postmortem production of alcohol as these samples typically contain little or no glucose and are isolated from the body cavity and GI tract (70203, 70206, 70210, 70221, 70223, 70226, 70227).

Fifty percent of the trauma victims of the USS *Iowa* explosion had a positive postmortem BAC due to putrefaction, which was detected by analysis of urine, vitreous humor, or other body tissues (70214).

The main higher alcohols and other volatiles that could indicate postmortem production of alcohol are:

- *n*-propanol
- *n*-butanol
- iso-butanol
- amyl alcohol
- isoamyl alcohol
- acetaldehyde

Postmortem clotted blood in the major vessels occurred approximately seven times more frequently in alcohol-positive than alcohol-negative victims of asphyxial deaths (70213).

If the postmortem blood has a high glucose concentration such as from a diabetic patient, 2% NaF may be required rather than the usual 1% NaF (70222).

Postmortem BACs are generally lower than the antemortem blood usually taken at hospital as there can be a delay of up to 45 hours before death so that the elimination of alcohol in that time delay would cause the postmortem BAC to be lower (70224).

Large increases in the alcohol concentration of up to 1,470% can occur in postmortem muscle and kidney tissues unless they are preserved with NaF (70225).

In a case of a diabetic death the BAC increased from 0.002 to 0.234 g/100 mL over 14 days, even though the blood sample had 1% NaF and was stored at 4°C, whereas the UAC, without NaF, increased from 0.600 to 1.062 g/100 mL (70228).

It should always be kept in mind that the evaluation of a postmortem BAC is a complex and multifactorial process that deserves a thorough analysis and a careful interpretation (70229).

Reference Number: 70201

PLUECKHAHN, V.D. "The Significance of Alcohol and Sugar Determinations in Autopsy Blood." *Medical Journal of Australia*, 46–51, January 10, 1970 (8 tables, 3 figures, 17 references)

Abstract: The glucose and alcohol concentrations were determined in heart and femoral blood from 500 non-diabetic sudden or accidental death victims in Geelong, Australia, between 1965 and 1969. BACs were determined with a GC method. The blood samples were stored under various temperatures and with various concentrations of sodium fluoride. The high glucose concentration from the right side of the heart is primarily due to agonal glycogenolysis in the liver. Bacteria and fungi were found in 54% of the autopsy blood samples. In fifty postmortem blood samples that were stored for 7 days at room temperature (20–25°C) with no preservative, a BAC > 0.050 g/100 mL was found in seven cases. The BAC caused by neoformation in these cases ranged from 0 to 0.131 g/100 mL. The highest BACs were found from the heart blood.

Table. Postmortem Glucose Concentrations in Fifty Blood Samples Collected from the Right Heart, Left Heart, and Femoral Vessel

Blood Sample	Range and Mean of Glucose Concentration (mg/100 mL)
Right Heart	21–728 (201)
Left Heart	0–195 (62)
Femoral	0–112 (48)

Source: Adapted from Plueckhahn (1970)

Sodium fluoride in a concentration of 1.0% is an adequate preservative for autopsy blood samples and will prevent the generation of ethyl alcohol in a blood sample stored at room temperature for seven days.

Reference Number: 70202

PLUECKHAHN, V.D. "The Significance of Blood Alcohol Levels at Autopsy." *Medical Journal of Australia*, 118–124, July 15, 1967 (11 tables, 8 references)

Abstract: In five cases where death was caused by incineration, no alcohol was generated by trauma or burning in absence of putrefaction. In three of the cases there was almost complete charring of the lower body and the extremities and blood had to be collected from the heart rather than the femoral vein. High BACs may develop during putrefaction to as high as 0.200 g/100 mL. Alcohol levels in samples of blood taken from the intact heart are as significant as those from the femoral vein.

Ethyl alcohol or other alcohols may be generated and broken down in the human body after death and during storage of blood taken at autopsy. This may occur through any one or a combination of three principal mechanisms—namely by the action of enzymes, bacteria or fungi.

Reference Number: 70203

LEVINE, B., M.L. SMITH. J.E. SMIALEK, AND Y.H. CAPLAN. "Interpretation of Low Postmortem Concentrations of Ethanol." *Journal of Forensic Sciences*, 38: 663–667, 1993 (2 tables, 9 references)

Abstract: A study was conducted of the alcohol concentration of blood, urine, and vitreous humor in 381 postmortem cases as analyzed by headspace GC. A postmortem BAC of > 0.04 g/100 mL would reasonably be expected to indicate that antemortem alcohol consumption occurred.

One assumption in the interpretation of this data is that a positive VHAC and UAC indicate antemortem consumption and not postmortem ethanol formation. Although glucose is present in the vitreous humor, microorganism contamination of the fluid is limited during the early stages of the decomposition process. In healthy individuals no glucose should appear in the urine. One report of in vitro formation of ethanol in urine was from a diabetic patient infected with Candida albicans.

Reference Number: 70204

HADLEY, J.A. AND G.C. SMITH. "Evidence for an Early Onset of Endogenous Alcohol Production in Bodies Recovered from the Water. Implications for Studying Alcohol and Drowning." *Accident Analysis and Prevention,* 35: 763–769, 2003 (1 table, 3 figures, 40 references)

Abstract: The height, body weight, combined lung volume, BAC, and length of time immersed in the water were determined in 562 drowning victims in Maryland between 1982 to 1999. Decreasing lung weight is associated with an increasing putrefactive process. There was an increase in positive postmortem BACs with decreasing lung weight and an increase in submersion time. It is suggested that submersion times as short as 12 hours can cause postmortem endogenous BACs. A formula was developed to subtract presumed endogenous BAC formation based on the length of time of submersion. The maximum endogenous BAC subtracted is 0.040 g/100 mL after 168 hours (1 week) of submersion.

The subtraction procedure discussed above, in which an assumed amount of endogenous (that increases over submersion time) is subtracted from each observed BAC, seems to be the best alternative. Finally, the present results demonstrate that endogenous alcohol is not a concern for bodies that are submersed for as long as 1 week in the colder waters of winter.

Reference Number: 70205

FRANCISCO, J.T. AND T.E. BALDWIN. "Are Post Mortem Alcohols Valid?" *Medical Times*, 100 145–155, 1972 (2 Tables, 4 References)

Abstract: A study was conducted of sixty-six postmortem cases where serial blood samples were collected up to 93 hours after death to determine if BACs change after death. BACs were determined by GC. Of the sixty-six cases, fifty-five (83%) had differences between samples of within ±0.010 g/100 mL, and sixty-one (92%) were within ±0.020 g/100 mL.

Another interesting and very important observation is that in no case did alcohol appear in a previously negative sample. This was true even in a sample drawn 93 hours after death and 49 hours after the first sample. There were 22 cases having negative alcohol on the initial sample and all cases gave the same result in subsequent samples. The average postmortem interval for these samples was 32 hours.

Reference Number: 70206

OLSEN, T. AND W.L. HEARN. "Stability of Ethanol in Postmortem Blood and Vitreous Humor in Long-Term Refrigerated Storage." *Journal of Analytical Toxicology,* 27: 517–519, 2003 (2 tables, 5 references)

Abstract: Thirty-two paired, alcohol-positive postmortem blood and vitreous humor samples collected from autopsies performed in 1996 and 1997 and stored under refrigerated conditions were re-analyzed by headspace GC using *n*-propanol as an internal standard in 2002. The blood was stored in 50 mL polypropylene containers that contained NaF and potassium oxalate. The vitreous humor samples were stored in 10 mL gray top Vacutainers. The decrease in BACs ranged from 0.010 to 0.290 g/100 mL after storage and the percentage decrease ranged from 4 to 100%. The VHAC decreased from 0.100 to 0.040 g/100 mL and the percentage loss ranged from 0 to 19%. In five blood samples that were stored in gray top Vacutainers the decrease in BAC ranged from 0 to 0.010 g/100 mL and the percentage decrease from 0 to 11%.

Vitreous humor samples stored in 10 mL gray top Vacutainer tubes for prolonged storage were more stable than postmortem blood samples stored in 50 mL polypropylene tubes. Vitreous humor is an acceptable alternative to blood when performing ethanol analysis on samples stored under refrigeration. This is extremely important if ethanol analysis needs to be repeated at a later date. If blood is to be reanalyzed after prolonged storage, a filled gray top Vacutainer tube will give more reliable results than blood samples stored in a large tube with a large headspace.

Reference Number: 70207

FERRARI, L.A., J.M.TRISZCZ, AND L. GIANNUZZI. "Kinetics of Ethanol Degradation in Forensic Blood Samples." *Forensic Science International*, 161: 144–150, 2006 (4 tables, 5 figures, 20 references)

Abstract: The effect of temperature, percentage of airspace in the container (%CA), initial BAC, and postmortem time interval on the degradation of alcohol in postmortem blood samples was determined. The tests were conducted on postmortem blood samples with no preservatives at various BACs between 0.050 to 0.430 g/100 mL in 3 mL glass containers. The testing was conducted at 0, 5, 20, 35, and 65%CA and at temperatures of 25°C, 4°C, and –10°C. BACs were determined by headspace GC using *t*-butanol as an internal standard. At 35%CA, the initial BAC decreased by 50% after 21 days' storage at 4°C and after 9 days of storage at 25°C. At 65%CA, the initial BAC decreased 50% after 1.6 days at 10°C and 1.2 days at 25°C. A formula was developed to predict the initial BAC based on these parameters.

This study only analyses cases of alcohol loss in postmortem samples of blood (without decomposition) with no preserving agents. Blood samples were analysed in relation to time, %CA and storing temperature; formation of alcohol in blood due to microbial activity was not considered. The addition of preserving agents decreases the probability of alcohol production.

Reference Number: 70208

MORIYA, F. AND Y. HASHIMOTO. "Endogenous Ethanol Production in Trauma Victims Associated with Medical Treatment." *Japanese Journal Legal Medicine*, 50: 263–267, 1996 (4 tables, 23 references)

Abstract: Four cases of trauma are described in which it is suspected that alcohol was produced in association with the medical treatment of the victim. In one case a forty-year-old male was stabbed in the abdomen with a knife and underwent a peritonectomy but died 12 hours later. The corpse was refrigerated for 12 hours before autopsy. The BACs were 0.046 g/100 mL (heart blood), 0.054 g/100 mL (pericardial sac), 0.115 mg/100 mL (intra-abdominal blood), and 0.014 g/100 mL (VH). The *n*-propanol concentrations ranged from not detected (VH) to 0.003 g/100 mL (intra-abdominal blood). The heart BACs in the other cases were 0.016, 0.032, and 0.023 g/100 mL. Of the thirty-four autopsies of trauma victims between 1991 and 1995, elevated BACs were detected in four cases.

In conclusion we have demonstrated the possibility of endogenous ethanol production in individuals who had suffered traumatic and hemorrhagic shock and undergone medical treatment. We suggest that for proper interpretation of the presence of exogenous ethanol, various body fluids and tissues be analysed for both ethanol and *n*-propanol irrespective of postmortem interval, especially in cases of traumatic or unnatural deaths.

Reference Number: 70209

JONES, A.W., R. ANDERSSON., J. SAKSHAUG, AND J. MORLAND. "Possible Formation of Ethanol in Postmortem Blood Specimens After Antemortem Treatment with Mannitol [Letter]." *Journal of Analytical Toxicology*, 15: 157–158, 1991 (1 figure, 8 references)

Abstract: Two case reports are presented of accident victims ages seventy-three and eighty-three years who were treated with mannitol and died later. Mannitol is a water-soluble carbohydrate with a molecular weight of 182, which is used to lower intracranial pressure prior to surgery in patients with head trauma. The postmortem BAC of the first victim was 0.053 g/100 mL and the BAC of the second victim (autopsy performed 6 days after death) was 0.064 g/100 mL and the UAC was 0.

The elevated concentrations of mannitol in blood after emergency treatment furnishes a rich substrate for bacterial action and subsequent production of ethanol.

Reference Number: 70210

YAJIMA, D., H. MOTANI, K. KAMEI, Y. SATO, M. HAYAKAWA, AND H. IWASEH. "Ethanol Production by *Candida Albicans* in Postmortem Human Blood Samples: Effects of Blood Glucose Levels and Dilution." *Forensic Science International,* 164: 116–121, 2006 (1 table, 6 figures, 20 references)

Abstract: Peripheral blood from four subjects was collected aseptically and incubated at 56°C for 30 minutes to deactivate complement and white blood cells and to inhibit coagulation during the experiments. The blood samples were inoculated with *C. albicans* and stored under various conditions for up to 12 days at 24°C. Blood ethanol and *n*-propanol concentrations were determined by headspace GC using *t*-butanol as an internal standard. Two postmortem cases are reported in which the blood of traumatized victims increased in storage at 4°C from 0.059 to 0.490 g/100 mL and from 0.210 g/100 mL to 0.960 g/100 mL respectively, while the *n*-propanol concentration increased to only 0.003 g/100 mL. There was no ethanol or *n*-propanol detected in the samples stored without the addition of glucose. The blood glucose concentration decreased to 0 after 4 to 8 days' storage. No ethanol or *n*-propanol was detected in the blood samples that were preserved with 1 to 2% NaF and the blood glucose concentration did not decrease.

When we discuss postmortem ethanol production we should consider together such factors as the situation surrounding death, the subject's history, information on sample collection and the ethanol concentration in the vitreous humor; *n*-propanol is just one factor that we need to consider.

Reference Number: 70211

WIGMORE, J.G. AND B.L.C. CHOW. "Case Report: Detection of Neo-Formation of Ethanol in a Postmortem Blood Sample Using N-Propanol and a Urine Sample." *Canadian Society Forensic Science Journal*, 33: 145–149, 2000 (1 table, 1 figure, 14 references)

Abstract: A thirty-one-year-old man was found dead several hours after a suicidal fall. An autopsy was conducted the next day and peritoneal cavity blood and urine were collected. The blood was placed in a jar without preservative and the urine in a tube with 1% NaF. The samples were received at the laboratory 19 days later. The blood alcohol, *n*-propanol, and acetaldehyde concentrations were 0.096, 0.004, and 0.003 g/100 mL respectively. No volatile compounds were detected in the urine. The ratio of *n*-propanol detected to neoformation of alcohol was approximately 25:1. *n*-Propanol should not be used as an internal standard for postmortem alcohol analysis.

The blood ethanol concentration, therefore, is considered unreliable due to the *n*-propanol and acetaldehyde concentrations detected in the blood, the lack of preservation, the long transit time, the apparent lack of refrigeration, and the lack of ethanol or other volatile substances detected in the preserved urine sample. The victim therefore was not under the influence of ethanol or other common drugs at the time of the fall.

Reference Number: 70212

CANFIELD, D., J. BRINK, R. JOHNSON, R. LEWIS, AND K. DUBOWSKI. "Clarification of Ethanol-Positive Case Using Urine Serotonin Metabolite Ratio." *Journal of Analytical Toxicology*, 31: 592–595, 2007 (1 table, 19 references)

Abstract: A two-car MVC resulted in both cars being engulfed in flames and three deaths. Shortly after death, blood and urine samples were collected and the alcohol concentrations were zero. Additional blood and urine samples were collected at autopsy 60 hours later from the driver and the BAC was 0.080 g/100 mL and the UAC was 0.070 g/100 mL. The body had not been refrigerated and was in an advance state of putrefaction. The urine 5HTOL/5HIAA ratio was zero, indicating that the alcohol was formed postmortem.

> Postmortem ethanol production can and does occur in fatal accidents. Therefore, care is necessary in investigating fatal accidents involving severe trauma to the body or in cases where long delays occurred prior to the collection of specimens for toxicological analysis.

Reference Number: 70213

FRACASSO, T., B. BRINKMANN, J. BEIKE, AND H. PFEIFFER. "Clotted Blood as a Sign of Alcohol Intoxication: A Retrospective Study." *International Journal of Legal Medicine*, 122: 157–161, 2008 (3 tables, 1 figure, 41 references)

Abstract: A comparison study was conducted at autopsy between sixty-nine victims of asphyxial death with a BAC > 0.106 g/100 mL and sixty-nine victims of asphyxial death with a 0 BAC between 1994 and 2006. The blood from central vessels was found to be clotted in 49% of alcohol-positive victims compared to 6% of the alcohol-negative victims.

> Therefore, to explain our findings, there only remains the published influences in the fibrinolytic process. In other words, the inhibition of fibrinolysis by intermediate and high alcohol concentration is responsible for advanced degrees of postmortem coagulation even in groups where this is normally rate or extremely rare. Our results show that a BAL > 1 promille is apparently nine times more often associated with postmortem clotted blood in the heart and central vessels in cases of asphyxial deaths.

Reference Number: 70214

MAYES, R., B. LEVINE, M.L. SMITH, G.N. WAGNER, AND R. FROEDE. "Toxicologic Findings in the USS *Iowa* Disaster." *Journal of Forensic Sciences*, 37: 1352–1357, 1992 (2 tables, 8 references)

Abstract: The toxicologic results of tests conducted on the forty-seven victims of the explosion on the USS *Iowa* in 1989 during gunnery exercises are presented. Autopsies were conducted 48 to 96 hours after death. A good correlation was found between cause of death and the COHb saturations in the victims. BACs were determined by headspace GC. Alcohol was detected in twenty-three of the victims (50%) due to postmortem changes. Thirteen victims had BACs < 0.030 g/100 mL. The highest BAC detected was 0.190 g/100 mL, although the bile and urine alcohol concentrations were less than 0.010 g/100 mL.

> Although there was no suspicion that the use or abuse of drugs played a role in the tragedy, comprehensive drug testing was requested on each case. Except for the presence of nicotine in 11 individuals, no drugs were detected in the 47 victims.

Reference Number: 70215

NANIKAWA, R. AND S. KOTOKU. "Medico-Legal Evaluation of the Ethanol Levels in Cadaveric Blood and Urine." *Yonago Acta Medica*, 15: 61–69, 1971 (4 tables, 7 figures, 13 references)

Abstract: A series of experiments were conducted on rabbits and mice regarding postmortem BAC changes under various adverse conditions, including burning and drowning. Included are five human postmortem cases. The femoral BAC of rabbits that were sacrificed by fire until the skin was lightly carbonized showed a decrease of 11%. In one postmortem case of a human killed in a fire, the heart BAC was 0.348 g/100 mL, the femoral BAC was 0.320 g/100 mL, and the UAC was 0.348 g/100 mL. The femoral BAC was thought to be lower due to the fire causing evaporation of alcohol in the peripheral blood. *n*-Propanol is considered to be a marker of putrefaction and should not be used as an internal standard in postmortem alcohol analysis.

> The ethanol is produced in all organs and body fluids of dead bodies and the production is observed least in urine. In autopsy cases of the bodies, which have been dead more than 24 hours at the temperature of 20°C, consideration should be given to the postmortem production of ethanol. The higher the temperature and the longer the time after death is, the higher the ethanol concentration becomes. Ethanol and *n*-propanol are produced in parallel with each other, postmortem and the ethanol is less than twenty times the amount of *n*-propanol. As *n*-propanol is unable to be found in vivo, it becomes a standard to know the amount of the ethanol produced after death.

Reference Number: 70216

BOUMBA, V.A., N. KOURKOUMELIS, P. GOUSIA., V. ECONOMOU, C. PAPDOPOULOU, AND T. VOUGIOUKLAKIS. "Modeling Microbial Ethanol Production by

E. coli Under Aerobic/Anaerobic Conditions: Applicability to Real Postmortem Cases and to Postmortem Blood Derived Microbial Cultures." *Forensic Science International*, 232: 191–198, 2013 (4 tables, 3 figures, 26 references)

Abstract: Human blood samples with and without the addition of 200 mg/100 mL glucose were inoculated with pure *E. coli* strains or postmortem derived microbial cultures. Alcohol and other volatiles were determined by GC. After 5 days of storage at 25°C, the conditions for *E. coli* were changed from aerobic to anaerobic. No alcohol was produced at 4°C storage. The highest mean BAC was 0.065 g/100 mL and 0.003 g/100 mL of *n*-propanol was also detected. A model was developed describing alcohol production and applied to sixty postmortem cases. The two most common volatiles detected were *n*-propanol and *n*-butanol.

> The statistical evaluation of the results revealed that the formulated models were presumably correlated to 1-propanol and 1-butanol which were recognized as the most significant descriptors of the modeling process. The significance of 1-propanol and 1-butanol as descriptors was so powerful that they could be used as the only independent variables to create a simple and satisfactory model. The current models showed a potential for application to estimate microbial ethanol—within an acceptable standard error—in various tested cases where ethanol and other alcohols have been produced from different microbes.

Reference Number: 70217

CECILLIASON, A.-S., M.G. ANDERSSON, E, LUNDIN, AND H. SANDLER. "Microbial Neoformation of Volatiles: Implications for the Estimation of Post-Mortem Interval in Decomposed Human Remains in an Indoor Setting." *International Journal of Legal Medicine*, 11pp, 6 October 2020 (4 figures, 40 references).

Abstract: The postmortem femoral vein blood of 412 deceased found in an indoor setting in Sweden between 2011 and 2017 were analyzed by head-space GC for ethanol, *n*-propanol, 1-butanol, and acetaldehyde. Acetaldehyde was found in 83%, ethanol in 37%, *n*-propanol in 21%, and 1-butanol in 4% of the cases. Neoformation of ethanol was indicated in eighty-five of 203 cases (42%) with external signs of decomposition and in six of the 209 cases (3%) without visible signs of decomposition. Forty-two percent of the decomposed bodies had *n*-propanol and/or 1-butanol detected in the femoral blood.

The decomposition process is divided into two major chemical processes: autolysis (mediated by internal enzymes and chemicals) and putrefaction (mediated by bacteria). Putrefaction is fermentation in which microorganisms use organic compounds available in the dead body as electron acceptors to generate adenosine triphosphate for energy. Ethanol is a well-known product of fermentation, although other volatiles are also produced post-mortem such as acetaldehyde, acetone, 1-butanol, *n*-propanol and isopropanol. The alcohol produced during decomposition depends on the microorganisms present and the substrates available. Ethanol can also be used as a carbon or energy source by a variety of microorganisms. The origin of ethanol in a post-mortem blood sample may be difficult to interpret, especially in decomposed human remains and without knowledge of whether or not ante-mortem intake of ethanol occurred. *N*-propanol has be presented as a marker of putrefaction, as it reflects bacterial activity after death. Another alcohol that is a possible marker of putrefaction is 1-butanol, often produced in parallel with *n*-propanol and ethanol. In cases where ethanol is produced by the common yeast (*Candida albicans*), *n*-propanol may not always be detected in post-mortem blood.

Reference Number: 70218

BOUMBA, V.A., N. KOURKOUMELIS, K.S. ZIAVROU, K. FRAGKOULI, AND T. VOUGIOUKLAKIS. "Patterns of the Most Abundant Volatiles Detected in Post-Mortem Blood." *Romanian Journal of Legal Medicine* 20: 147–154, 2012 (3 tables, 2 figures, 40 references)

Abstract: The most abundant volatiles detected during postmortem forensic blood alcohol analyses were alcohol, acetaldehyde, *n*-propanol, isopropanol, and acetone. Signs of putrefaction occurred in fifty-seven cases (i.e., with), and no signs in 426 cases (i.e., without) at autopsy. The highest postmortem BAC detected was 0.208 g/100 mL in the cases that showed signs of putrefaction.

The detection of certain volatiles in autopsy blood samples has been used in the field of forensic toxicology in order to aid: the specification of the origin of post-mortem ethanol; the evaluation of the probable cause of natural death; the determination of the cause of intoxications; the support of a pathological diagnosis; even the determination of the location of clandestine burials and human remains.

Reference Number: 70219

BOUMBA, V.A. "Modeling Postmortem Ethanol Production/Insights into the Origin of Higher Alcohols." *Molecules*, 27: 700, 14pp, 2022 (4 tables, 50 references)

Abstract: The decomposition of the human body is a complicated process in which microbes of the gut and respiratory tract invade the body and produce alcohol, higher alcohols (*n*-propanol, *n*-butanol, isobutanol, amyl- and iso-amyl alcohol), as well as other fermentation products. The main groups of microbes involved are bacterial, clostridia, and yeasts. It is suggested that a postmortem blood *n*-propanol concentration of greater than 0.104 mg/dL indicates that postmortem alcohol production has occurred. Numerous mathematical formulae are listed to determine how much alcohol could be produced from the detected postmortem blood concentrations of the higher alcohols and the type of microorganism involved.

Main conclusions of this contribution are, firstly, that the higher alcohols are qualitative and quantitative indictors of microbial ethanol production, and, secondly that the respective models of microbial ethanol production are tools offering additional data to interpret properly the origin of the ethanol concentrations measured in postmortem cases.

Reference Number: 70220

APPENZELLER, B.M.R., M. SCHUMAN, AND R. WENNIG. "Was a Child Poisoned by Ethanol? Discrimination Between Ante-Mortem Consumption and Post-Mortem Formation." *International Journal of Legal Medicine*, 122: 429–434, 2008 (1 table, 2 figures, 10 references)

Abstract: A baby girl (age fourteen months) died 12 hours after admission to hospital after a coma following dehydration. Her antemortem blood glucose concentration was 0.420 g/100 mL due to the administration of IV glucose solutions. The body was refrigerated 3 days at 4°C before autopsy. Her postmortem heart BAC was 0.200 g/100 mL. The liver and kidney alcohol concentrations were 3.23 g/kg and 2.54 g/kg respectively. No ethyl glucuronide (a direct metabolite of antemortem alcohol ingestion) was detected in the girl's liver. In fermentation tests, the alcohol concentration was 0.121 g/100 mL over 7 days after a vial of glucose solution was inoculated with the deceased's blood, which decreased to 0.048 g/100 mL after 14 days.

> As a conclusion, the present work demonstrates that postmortem formation of ethanol can reach high concentrations in blood and tissues as far as sufficient glucose is present in the body for fermentation. Microorganisms cannot only produce ethanol but also consume the ethanol present, resulting in the fact that no maximum level exists to discriminate between antemortem ethanol consumption and postmortem formation.

Reference Number: 70221

MURTY, O.P. "Postmortem Production of Alcohol in Viscera." *International Journal of Medical Toxicology and Legal Medicine*, 4: 34–35, 2002 (1 table, 2 figures, 14 references)

Abstract: A thirty-eight-year-old male trauma victim who was in a coma for 1 month and eventually succumbed to his injuries had various postmortem samples collected and analyzed for alcohol/drugs after several months of storage. The viscera BAC was 0.064 g/100 mL and the vitreous humor alcohol concentration was zero. A 1% NaF concentration did not prevent alcohol formation.

> Ethanol is also generated in a dead body spontaneously as a result of putrefactive processes. The degree of culpability often hangs round this point. Under conditions of normal refrigeration, formation of oxidisable substances is not significant. For 24 to 48 hours, such production is not detectable easily but after one week to two weeks such production is significant. Thus, in cases that have undergone putrefaction, other than submersion, positive alcohol findings with values in the intoxicated range are indicative of consumption.

Reference Number: 70222

SUTLOVIC, D., M. VERSIC-BRATINCEVIC, AND M. DEFINIS-GOJANOVIC. "Blood Alcohol Stability in Postmortem Blood Samples." *American Journal of Forensic Medicine and Pathology*, 35: 55–58, 2014 (11 references)

Abstract: The BACs of seventy-nine postmortem blood samples preserved with NaF were measured by headspace GC before and after 191–468 days of storage at –20°C. Most samples showed a decrease in BAC by up to 61%. Only a few blood samples showed an increase in BAC by up to 11%.

There were good agreements in the BAC in 2 performed measurements, but the observed deviation in few cases was up to 10% (confirmed in 39% samples) and was not acceptable when dealing with forensic samples. It is necessary to store the blood sample in a tube of suitable volume with minimal or no headspace to defer alcohol oxidation. Also, if a sample comes from a diabetic patient, the analyst is advised to add more than 2% of sodium fluoride to inhibit microorganisms from producing ethanol out of glucose and ethanol oxidation in general.

Reference Number: 70223

LIN, Z., H. WANG, A.W. JONES, F. WANG, Y. ZHANG, AND Y. RAO. "Evaluation and Review of Ways to Differentiate Sources of Ethanol in Postmortem Blood." *International Journal of Legal Medicine*, 134: 2081–2093, 2020 (3 figures, 119 references)

Abstract: The complete fermentation of 180 grams of glucose results in the formation of 92 g of alcohol. Thus, the average blood glucose concentration of 100 mg/dL could result in a BAC of 0.050 g/100 mL. The endogenous synthesis of alcohol depends on many factors such as the postmortem interval (PMI), the ambient temperature, humidity, and the extent of trauma. Autolysis begins in the lower abdomen and cecum and allows bacteria and other microorganisms to spread to blood vessels and tissues in close proximity. Some methods of assisting in determining the source of postmortem alcohol include analysis of femoral blood and other fluids such as urine and vitreous humor, detection of other volatiles such as *n*-propanol, and analyses for EtG, EtS, and serotonin.

The possibility exists that a positive autopsy BAC might reflect both scenarios—AM ingestion and PM synthesis. When an evidence-based opinion on the source of ethanol in PM blood is necessary, the golden rule in PM toxicology is to consider all relevant information in the case, including the cause and manner of death, age and gender of the deceased, results from the autopsy, such as the condition of the body and any factors that might promote the synthesis of ethanol after death. The main scenarios that may cause PM synthesis of ethanol are summarized as follows: 1) Bodies which are without appropriate storage and autopsied beyond 24 h after death are likely to generate ethanol by spread of gut bacteria and fermentation processes. 2) Badly decomposed and foul smelling bodies with evidence of bloating and purge fluids are instances when production of ethanol is expected. 3) In bodies subjected to massive trauma with open blood vessels and a long delay before recovery, refrigeration and autopsy, along with exposure to elevated environmental temperatures, are other factors that promote PM synthesis of ethanol.

Reference Number: 70224

GREENE, N., M.B. ESSER, R. VESSELINOV, K.M. AUMAN, T.J. KERNS, AND M.H. LAUERMAN. "Variability in Antemortem and Postmortem Blood Alcohol Concentration Levels Among Fatally Injured Adults." *American Journal of Drug and Alcohol Abuse*, 8pp, 2020 (1 table, 3 figures, 31 references)

Abstract: Antemortem plasma alcohol concentrations and postmortem BACs were determined in forty-five male and seven female injury-related deaths between 2006 and 2016. The PAC obtained antemortem in hospital was converted into a whole blood alcohol concentration (as determined postmortem) by a conversion factor of 14%. Twenty-two victims died from transportation-related injuries and twenty by homicide. The median antemortem BAC was 0.100 g/100 mL compared to the median postmortem BAC of 0.060 g/100 mL. The mean length of hospital stay before death was 2.2 hours but ranged up to 45 hours. The two cases with the greatest decreases in postmortem BACs compared to antemortem BACs were cases with a length of hospital stay before death of 38 and 45 hours respectively.

The findings from this study suggest that postmortem BACs generally underestimate the magnitude of alcohol involvement in fatal injuries. Therefore, postmortem BACs may not accurately represent a person's BAC at the time of injury. Nevertheless, for many decadents, death investigations are the only source of information about factors contributing to injury-related deaths, and the death investigations can provide important information to help prevent alcohol-related fatal injuries. However, these efforts may be thwarted when death records do not have BAC data. When possible, more routine alcohol testing in acute care facilities, and recording of this information in medical records would improve the surveillance of alcohol-related nonfatal and fatal injuries.

Reference Number: 70225

JOHNSON, R.D., R.J. LEWIS, M.K. ANGIER, AND N.T. VU. "The Formation of Ethanol in Postmortem Tissues." *FAA Civil Aerospace Medical Institute Report*, Oklahoma City, 14pp, 2004 (3 tables, 10 figures, 32 references)

Abstract: The alcohol and other volatile concentrations were determined by headspace GC in four postmortem muscle and five postmortem kidney samples after homogenization in water. The tissues were mainly from trauma victims. The samples were stored with or without 1% NaF and for up to 96 hours at 4°C or 25°C. Without preservatives, tissues stored at 4°C for 96 hours showed an average increase in alcohol concentration by an average of 1,470%. At 25°C, a 1,432% increase in alcohol concentration occurred after 48 hours. No increases were observed after the addition of 1% NaF.

> It is clear from these experiments that all 9 unadulterated specimens from actual aviation accident victims contained microbes capable of ethanol production. We have demonstrated that even at 4°C, significant amounts of postmortem ethanol can form in the absence of a preservative. Additionally, we have demonstrated that the addition of sodium fluoride to the postmortem tissue specimens during the homogenization process prevents the formation of ethanol at storage temperatures of 4°C and 25°C. Therefore, we believe that sodium fluoride should be added as a precaution to all postmortem specimens. However, caution must always be used when interpreting ethanol results from postmortem samples since, even with these precautions, we cannot rule out the phenomenon of ethanol production in a small percentage of cases where larger numbers of microbes are present when the sample is received.

Reference Number: 70226

PAJUNEN, T., E. VUORI, AND P. LUNETTA. "Epidemiology of Alcohol-Related Unintentional Drowning: Is Post-mortem Ethanol Production a Real Challenge?" *Injury Epidemiology*, 5: 39, 5pp, 2018 (3 tables, 28 references)

Abstract: A full medicolegal autopsy and toxicological analyses were conducted in 967 unintentional drowning victims in Finland to determine the extent of postmortem alcohol production. Comparing the BAC, UAC, and VHAC, only four victims (0.4%) had evidence of postmortem production of alcohol, and their postmortem BACs ranged from 0.025 to

0.048 g/100 mL. The postmortem time interval from the submersion of the body to autopsy ranged from 1 to 50 days.

In medico-legal cases involving potential criminal or civil litigation, a detailed case by case assessment of PM ethanol remains crucial. It should include evaluation of the victim's medical history and the circumstances leading to drowning, and also comparison of BAC, UAC, VAC and analysis of putrefactive alcoholic indicators (e.g., *n*-propanol) and of ethanol metabolites (e.g., glucuronide), as well as including bacterial culture, molecular analysis, and fermentation test to identify micro-organisms capable of producing PM ethanol. The present survey, however, suggests that, at least in Finland, PM endogenous alcohol production has a limited impact on epidemiological research on drowning and alcohol.

Reference Number: 70227

OSHAUG, K., R. KRONSTRAND, F.C. KUGELBERG, L. KRISTOFFERSEN, J. MORLAND, AND G. HOISETH. "Frequency of Postmortem Ethanol Formation in Blood, Urine and Vitreous Humor—Improving Diagnostic Accuracy with the Use of Ethyl Sulphate and Putrefactive Alcohols." *Forensic Science International*, 331: 6pp, 2022 (4 tables, 35 references)

Abstract: Putrefactive alcohols (i.e., *n*-propanol and *n*-butanol) were determined in 8,001 postmortem blood samples in Sweden and ethyl sulfate in 2,504 blood samples in Norway. Vitreous humor and urine samples were also analyzed. From the Norwegian data, 15.3% of all ethanol positive blood, 9.4% of urine, and 7.4% of VH were positive for alcohol but negative for EtS. Putrefactive alcohols were found in 24.4% of the Swedish blood samples. Postmortem ethanol formation occurred more frequently in central than peripheral blood. The highest postmortem BACs in which the EtS (and EtG) concentrations were negative were 0.180 g/100 mL and 0.160 g/100 mL respectively.

Ethanol is formed postmortem by microbial activity. The frequency of postmortem ethanol formation was found to be highest in blood, followed by urine and then vitreous humor. A possible explanation is the protective environment of the vitreous humor and to a certain degree, also urine, which makes postmortem ethanol formation unlikely in urine and even less likely in vitreous humor. Ethanol concentrations originating from postmortem formation were generally lower in urine than blood and lowest in vitreous humor. Various factors such as trauma to the eye or pelvis and its surrounding structures, urinary tract infections and glycosuria may facilitate postmortem formation. Nevertheless, the frequencies observed within this study raise the question on whether postmortem formation in vitreous humor and, to some extent also in urine, is perhaps more common than previously assumed.

Reference Number: 70228

SUTLOVIC, D., M. MESTIC, Z. KOVACIC, S. GUSIC, T. MLINAREK, I. SALAMUNIC, AND S. SARDELIC. "Microbial Ethanol Production in Postmortem Urine Sample." *Medicine, Science, and the Law*, 53: 243–246, 2013 (2 tables, 18 references).

Abstract: A seventy-five-year-old female diabetic suffering from heart disease died of natural causes in her home. Blood and urine samples were collected at autopsy 3 days after death and only the blood sample had NaF added to it. The samples were stored in a refrigerator at 4°C and analyzed for alcohol by headspace GC. The initial blood and urine alcohol concentrations were 0.002 g/100 mL and 0.600 g/100 mL respectively, and the acetone concentrations were 51 mg/dL and 63 mg/dL respectively. The alcohol in the blood and urine samples continued to increase with storage time, whereas the acetone concentrations decreased. Various microorganisms, including *Candida glabrata*, were identified in the blood and urine.

Table. Postmortem Blood and Urine Alcohol and Acetone Concentrations and Days After Autopsy

Days After Autopsy	Blood Alcohol Concentration	Blood Acetone Concentration	Urine Alcohol Concentration	Urine Acetone Concentration
0	0.002	0.051	0.600	0.063
7	0.089	0.040	0.976	0.053
14	0.234	0.037	1.063	0.048

Source: Adapted from Sutlovic et al (2013).

According to the Guidelines for Obtaining Specimens for Postmortem Toxicological Analysis, blood and urine samples should be collected in a separate tube containing 2% sodium fluoride. To inhibit microorganisms producing ethanol from glucose, and oxidation of ethanol with a consequent incorrect diagnosis of cause of death, it is necessary to add more than 2% sodium fluoride in blood and urine samples from diabetic patients.

Reference Number: 70229

QUINTAS, M.J., P. COSTA, P. MELO, A. CASTRO, J.M. FRANCO, AND H.M. TEIXEIRA. "Postmortem In Vitro Ethanol Production—It Could Be More Common Than We Think!" *Forensic Science International*, 247: 113–116, 2017 (2 figures, 10 references)

Abstract: A fifty-five-year-old man died of a myocardial infarction and an autopsy was conducted 14 hours later. Peripheral blood was collected from the common iliac veins (not the femoral veins) and was stored in standard plastic tubes containing 100 mg of NaF and 20 mg of potassium oxalate. The samples were stored at 4°C and arrived at the forensic laboratory 5 days later, where they were kept at –20°C for 2 months. The samples were analyzed by two column headspace GC using *n*-propanol as an internal standard. The initial BAC was 0.018 g/100 mL and increased to 0.026 g/100 mL 8 hours later. Two days later the BAC was 0.062 g/100 mL and increased further to a maximum of 0.085 g/100 mL 3 days later. The yeast *Candida parapsilosis* was detected in the blood.

> In conclusion, taking into account the relevant medico-legal consequences of BAC determinations and reflecting on cases as the one hereby reported, it is tempting to wonder about if and how we should be reporting these results. In any case, we should always keep in mind that evaluating a postmortem BAC is a complex and multifactorial process that deserves a thorough analysis and a careful interpretation.

7.03 POSTMORTEM DIFFUSION

"Blood taken from a peripheral source is the most reliable for blood alcohol estimations after death."

—Bowden and McCallum, "Blood Alcohol Content: Some Aspects of Its Post Mortem Uses" (1949)

"In case work the diffusion of ethanol from gastric fluid in the airways into the blood will rarely be a practical problem because it is uncommon for people to die with a bellyful of alcohol."

—Pounder and Yonemitsu, "Postmortem Absorption of Drugs and Ethanol from Aspirated Vomitus—An Experimental Model" (1991)

Postmortem diffusion of alcohol from the stomach to surrounding areas of the body can occur, although not to a large extent to blood collected from the intact chambers of the heart (70301–70305). Blind-stick collection of blood samples at postmortem is not recommended (70306). Postmortem diffusion should be suspected when:

Stomach alcohol concentration >> BAC > UAC

Postmortem diffusion of solvents can occur through the skin (70307, 70308, 70311). Since alcohol is distributed in the total body water (approximately 40 L in men), postmortem BACs can still be useful in cases of large volumes of blood or fluids administered IV before death (70309)

In one case with a high gastric alcohol concentration (17% v/v alcohol) the alcohol diffused into the surrounding blood and tissues and caused the femoral BAC to be 0.210 g/100 mL and the cardiac blood to be 0.180 g/100 mL, but the VHAC and UAC were zero (70310).

Subclavian blood (from the root of the neck) can be easily collected at the scene. Although the study indicates that subclavian blood is as valid as femoral blood to determine the BAC, in one postmortem case the femoral BAC and the VHAC were zero and the femoral blood was 0.081 g/100 mL (70312).

Reference Number: 70301

PLUECKHAHN, V.D. AND B. BALLARD. "Diffusion of Stomach Alcohol and Heart Blood Alcohol Concentration at Autopsy." *Journal of Forensic Sciences*, 12: 463–470, 1967 (1 table, 13 references)

Abstract: Various quantities of alcohol (up to 20% v/v) were instilled into the stomach of 20 cadavers and BACs were determined in femoral, right and left heart blood, and samples from the pericardial sac and pleural cavity approximately 20 hours later. The maximum increase in BAC was 0, 0.015, 0.027, 0.554, and 0.178 g/100 mL respectively. Of 230 autopsies, the highest stomach alcohol concentration was 2.95%, showing that people do not die with a bellyful of strong liquor. The diffusion of alcohol from the stomach to the intact chambers of the heart is minimal.

At death the concentrations of alcohol in the stomach are usually surprisingly low even when large amounts of alcohol have been consumed immediately prior to death.

Reference Number: 70302

IWASAKI, Y., M. YASHIKI, A. NAMERA, T. MIYAZAKI, AND T. KOJIMA. "On the Influence of Postmortem Alcohol Diffusion from the Stomach Contents to the Heart Blood." *Forensic Science International*, 94: 111–118, 1998 (3 tables, 1 figure, 9 references)

Abstract: The alcohol concentration of the mixed left and right heart blood, urine, and stomach contents were determined in 147 cases by GC between 1987 and 1996. In thirty-nine cases the BAC was less than 0.011 g/100 mL and the StAC > 0.105 g/100 mL. Postmortem diffusion from the stomach into the heart was less than 10%.

In cases where the BAC is higher than the UAC and the StAC is much higher that the BAC, the influence of alcohol diffusion from the stomach contents and postmortem alcohol production to BAC should be taken into consideration.

Reference Number: 70303

BUDD, R.D. "Validity of Post Mortem Chest Cavity Blood Ethanol Determinations." *Journal of Chromatography*, 449: 337–340, 1988 (2 tables, 12 references)

Abstract: A comparison of the alcohol concentration of scooped thorax, chest, or pleural blood compared to heart blood was studied in fifteen postmortem cases. Chest cavity blood can be a valid sample when precautions such as prompt autopsy and refrigeration arc taken to minimize postmortem diffusion and putrefaction and when there is no perforation of the stomach wall or the diaphragm. In eleven cases the mean chest cavity/heart BAC was 1.02 (range 0.75–1.40). In the other four cases there were large differences in the alcohol concentration. The greatest difference occurred in a case in which the stomach wall and diaphragm were perforated. In this case the heart BAC was 0.090 g/100 mL and the chest BAC was 0.210 g/100 mL.

In ethanol determinations if there is any question about compromise of a chest cavity, thorax, or pleural cavity blood specimen, this blood should not be used or at least should be corroborated by the determination of ethanol concentration in other body fluids and tissues.

Reference Number: 70304

PELISSIER-ALICOT, A-L., N. COSTE, C. BARTOLI, M-D. PIERCECCHI-MARTI, A. SANVOISIN, J. GOUVERNET, AND G. LEONETTI. "Comparison of Ethanol Concentrations in Right Cardiac Blood, Left Cardiac Blood and Peripheral Blood in a Series of 30 Cases." *Forensic Science International*, 156: 35–39, 2006 (2 tables, 15 references)

Abstract: The postmortem right cardiac, left cardiac, and peripheral blood alcohol concentrations and gastric, urine, and vitreous humor alcohol concentrations were determined by headspace GC using *t*-butanol as an internal standard in thirty medicolegal cases. The degree of putrefaction, chest or abdominal injury, and regurgitation of gastric contents into the airways were noted. *n*-Propanol was found in eight cases and ranged from 0.005 to 0.007 g/100 mL. The right cardiac BAC in those cases ranged from 0.007 to 0.139 g/100 mL. The left cardiac BAC can be significantly higher than the right cardiac BAC or peripheral BAC, which may be due to the close proximity of the left cardiac chambers to the stomach. In three cases the peripheral BAC was greater than the right or left cardiac BAC due to unsuccessful resuscitation attempts.

Table. Left Heart Blood, Right Heart Blood, and Peripheral Blood Alcohol Concentrations in Cases with an Autopsy Finding of Regurgitation of Gastric Contents

Case No.	Right Heart BAC (g/100 mL)	Left Heart BAC (g/100 mL)	Peripheral BAC (g/100 mL)
7	0.123	0.346	0.118
8	0.081	0.168	0.063
10	0.010	0.017	0.019
11	0.061	0.208	0.073
12	0.182	0.231	0.172
26	0.016	0.037	0.019
27	0.005	0.012	0.005

Source: Adapted from Pelissier-Alicot et al (2006).

Independently of these mechanical aspects, these results are of considerable practical value because they suggest it is preferable to sample cardiac blood from the right chamber rather than from the left, in order to limit as much as possible an erroneously high interpretation of ethanol levels due to redistribution, in particular if peripheral blood is not available.

Reference Number: 70305

WINEK JR., C.L., C.L. WINEK, AND W.W. WAHBA. "The Role of Trauma in Postmortem Blood Alcohol Determination." *Forensic Science International*, 71: 1–8, 1995 (3 tables, 11 references)

Abstract: A study was conducted of nineteen postmortem cases in which the BACs > 0.500 g/100 mL in Allegheny County between 1980 and 1986. Eight of the nineteen cases were traumatic deaths due to laceration and transection of the stomach and/or esophagus. In two cases the elevated BACs of 0.827 and 0.739 g/100 mL suggest contamination. In seven out of twenty-eight trauma cases in which blood samples were collected by transthoracic cardiac puncture, the TT blood was significantly higher than the heart blood.

It is recommended that in cases of traumatic injury HB samples should be collected from the intact heart chamber. It is also good practice to collect additional biological samples from other sites in cases of traumatic injury to rule out the possibility of contamination and to ensure the BAC used for forensic interpretation is accurate.

Reference Number: 70306

LOGAN, B.K. AND G. LINDHOLM. "Gastric Contamination of Postmortem Blood Samples During Blind-Stick Sample Collection." *American Journal of Forensic Medicine and Pathology*, 17: 109–111, 1996 (1 table, 6 references)

Abstract: A forty-five-year-old woman with a history of cardiovascular disease and diabetes was found dead in her residence. A blood sample was drawn through the chest wall with a hypodermic needle (blind-stick). The sample was brown in color and was found to contain 0.220 g/100 mL ethyl alcohol, 0.620 g/100 mL amitriptyline, and 0.04 mg/dL nortriptyline. These concentrations are associated with fatalities. Another autopsy was conducted and subclavian blood was collected. This blood contained 0.010 g/100 mL ethyl alcohol, 0.03 mg/dL amitriptyline, and 0.001 mg/dL nortriptyline. The cause of death was pancreatitis.

The potential as illustrated in this case for the contamination of blood with stomach contents or gastric aspirate during blind-stick sample collection is a further argument against this practice. We strongly recommend that blind-stick sample collection be eliminated in favour of a simple cut-down procedure for the collection of subclavian or femoral blood for toxicologic testing.

Reference Number: 70307

CAUGHLIN, J.D. "An Unusual Source for Postmortem Findings of Methyl Ethyl Ketone and Methanol in Two Homicide Victims." *Forensic Science International*, 67: 27–31, 1994 (1 table, 3 references)

Abstract: Two case reports are presented of homicide victims whose bodies were fingerprinted using a 20% methyl ethyl ketone and 80% methanol solutions.

In the first case the vitreous humor contained 0.004 g/100 mL MEK and 0.013 g/100 mL methanol. The blood from the heart contained 0.4 mg/dL MEK and 0.036 g/100 mL methanol. In the second case the vitreous humor contained 0.001 g/100 mL MEK and 0.201 g/100 mL methanol. The blood from the subclavian vein contained 0.2 mg/dL MEK and 0.027 g/100 mL methanol.

Fingerprint specialists need to exercise caution when fingerprinting bodies postmortem so as not to contaminate any specimen with volatile substances such as MEK or methanol. As well, the toxicologist should be aware of any treatment of the body which may affect interpretation of analytical results.

Reference Number: 70308

JONES, A.W. AND J. RAJS. "Appreciable Blood-Ethanol Concentration after Washing Abrased and Lacerated Skin with Surgical Spirit [Letter]." *Journal of Analytical Toxicology*, 21: 587–588, 1997 (11 references)

Abstract: A case report is presented of a fifty-six-year-old woman who was knocked off her bicycle and run over by a bus. The victim was surgically scrubbed with 70% v/v ethanol to clean the damaged skin, which covered 33% of her body. The victim died before the operation commenced. The blood alcohol concentration as determined by headspace GC was 0.046 g/100 mL and the vitreous humor alcohol concentration was zero.

We are reporting this case to warn others about the risk of ethanol being absorbed into the bloodstream if damaged skin is washed with surgical spirits. A BEC of 0.046 g/100 mL might have ramifications in civil litigation when responsibility for the accident is investigated and insurance claims are made.

Reference Number: 70309

WEILER, G. "Are Postmortem Alcohol Determinations Useful in Cases of Severe Hemorrhagic Shock Treated with Numerous Blood Transfusions? [German]." *Blutalkohol*, 16: 306–309, 1979 (9 references)

Abstract: A case report is presented of a thirty-nine-year-old female alcoholic in a highly intoxicated state who fell on her buttocks onto broken glass on the floor. Massive bleeding took place and the woman lost consciousness after 15 minutes. The patient was admitted to hospital 30 minutes after the trauma, surgery was conducted, and the woman received 1 L of blood substitute and 8.5 L of blood. The woman died 12 hours later. An autopsy was performed 29 hours after death and the femoral BAC was determined to be 0.141 g/100 mL and the bile was 0.163 g/100 mL. Urine was unavailable.

It is suggested that even in this extreme case of hemorrhagic shock with large volumes of blood and fluid administered IV that the BAC may not be substantially affected and can still provide useful information.

Reference Number: 70310

MARTI, V., M. AUGSBURGER, C. WIDMER, AND C. LARDI. "Significant Postmortem Diffusion of Ethanol: A Case Report." *Forensic Science International*, 328: 5pp, 2021 (3 tables, 2 figures, 16 references)

Abstract: A depressed forty-nine-year-old man (173 cm tall, weight 58.4 kg) was found dead after suicidal hanging with a rope, 15 hours after death. The stomach content contained 400 g of a transparent liquid with a strong aromatic smell. The bladder contained 45 mL of liquid. The femoral BAC was 0.210 g/100 mL, but the urine and VHAC were zero. The cardiac BAC was 0.180 g/100 mL and the cardiac muscle alcohol concentration was 1.12 g/kg. The gastric alcohol concentration was 168 g/kg (17% v/v alcohol).

Based on the results of all investigations, the cause of death was attributed to mechanical asphyxia by hanging. Considering the unusual discrepancy between the ethanol concentrations in our samples, which was very high in stomach content, high in femoral blood and negative in urine and vitreous humor, we assumed that femoral blood ethanol concentrations measured in our samples was the result of postmortem (PM) diffusion and did not reflect the femoral blood ethanol concentration at the time of death, which should have been negative as shown by urine and vitreous humor concentrations. Therefore, the man had the ability to act when he hung himself.

Reference Number: 70311

GHADIPASHA, M. AND M. AKHGARI. "Case Report: An Unusually High Blood Alcohol Level in a Burnt Child Homicide Victim." *International Journal of Medical Toxicology and Forensic Medicine*, 9: 45–49, 2019 (1 figure, 15 references)

Abstract: The body of a six-year-old girl was found in a bathtub in a neighbor's house. Two bottles of denatured alcohol had been poured over the body and ignited. The cause of death was stab wounds and the body was burned to mask the homicide. No vitreous humor or femoral blood were available. Her heart blood had an alcohol concentration of 1.055 g/100 mL and methyl alcohol concentration of 0.071 g/100 mL. No postmortem blood COHb or HCN were detected. The offender had a BAC of 0.258 g/100 mL.

The leading cause of death was stab wounds. Burning seemed to be a tool for covering up the homicide. Use of alcoholic fire accelerant and contamination of the corpse with alcohol was the main reason to detect high blood alcohol levels.

Reference Number: 70312

SASTRE, C., V. BAILLIF-COUNION, F. MUSCARELLA, C. BARTOLI, J. MANCINI, M-D. PIERCECCHI-MARTI, G. LEONETTI, AND A-L. PELISSIER. "Can Subclavian Blood Be Equated with a Peripheral Blood Sample? A Series of 50 Cases." *International Journal of Legal Medicine*, 127: 379–384, 2013 (1 table, 17 figures)

Abstract: Subclavian blood is easy to sample at the scene of death when an autopsy is not required. But it is very difficult at the scene to determine whether subclavian blood is arterial or venous. Samples were collected at fifty medicolegal autopsies including right cardiac blood, left cardiac blood, subclavian blood, femoral blood, gastric content, bile, urine, and vitreous humor for alcohol by headspace GC. The degree of putrefaction was determined, as well as any known resuscitation attempts and aspiration of gastric contents. Regurgitation can occur during agonal process or a postmortem relaxation of the esophageal sphincter. No chest or abdominal trauma were noted. The greatest difference was a femoral BAC and VHAC of zero and a subclavian BAC of 0.081 g/100 mL in a case with little putrefaction detected.

> Our present results confirm those of our previous study of 30 cases, which demonstrated for the first time that ethanol concentrations in right cardiac blood were not significantly different to those of peripheral blood. The results of this second study also demonstrates that subclavian blood concentrations are comparable to those measured in femoral blood. This is a strong argument in support of using subclavian blood as an alternative sample when femoral blood is not available.

7.04 FATAL BACs

> "All things are poison, and nothing is without poison, the dosage alone makes it so a thing is not a poison."
>
> —Attributed to Paracelsus

> "Ethanol is a weak drug. One must use tens of grams of the substance to produce a pharmacological effect, as opposite to most other drugs that act in the body at milligrams or submilligrams per kilogram doses."
>
> —Fadda and Rossett, "Chronic Ethanol Consumption from Neuroadaptation to Neurodegeneration" (1998)

Alcohol is a CNS depressant and at high BACs can cause respiratory or cardiac failure. The rate of alcohol poisoning deaths in the United States was on average 8.8 deaths per 1 million population over the age of fifteen years and ranged from 5.3 per million in Alabama to 46.5 per million in Alaska. Contrary to the great publicity and media attention surrounding alcohol poisoning deaths in college students, this age group had the lowest rate of alcohol poisoning (2.6 per million) (70417).

The range of postmortem BACs in acute fatal alcohol poisoning vary widely but usually occur at BACs of approximately 0.300 g/100 mL or greater (70401–70405, 70411–70412). A BAC ≥ 0.400 g/100 mL occurred in 1.1% of trauma patients treated in hospital with a positive BAC (70413). With clinical treatment, persons can survive extremely high BACs (70410). Obese people died at a mean BAC of 0.320 g/100 mL in alcohol poisoning cases compared to a mean BAC of 0.350 g/100 mL in normal weight victims (70414).

The UAC/BAC ratio is generally lower for acute alcohol poisoning than for non-poisoning cases (70408). The postmortem femoral BAC may also be low in cases of fatal alcohol poisonings in the absorption phase (70407). The incidence of alcohol poisoning appears to be related to the per capita sales of spirits and not total alcohol consumption (70409).

Two fatal alcohol poisoning cases occurred as a result of ingestion of alcohol-based hand sanitizer, which could pose an increased risk during the COVID-19 pandemic (70415–70416).

Reference Number: 70401

KAYE, S. AND H.B. HAAG. "Terminal Blood Alcohol Concentrations in Ninety-Four Fatal Cases of Acute Alcoholism." *Journal of the American Medical Association*, 165: 451–452, 1957 (1 table, 7 references)

Abstract: The postmortem BAC and survival time were determined in ninety-four victims of fatal acute alcohol intoxication between 1948 and 1955. The majority of the victims were male alcoholics between twenty-five and fifty years of age. The postmortem BACs ranged from 0.180 to 0.600 g/100 mL. The longer the survival time, the lower the postmortem BAC.

Table. Postmortem BAC and Survival Time in Ninety-Four Victims of Acute Alcohol Poisoning

Postmortem BAC Range (g/100 mL)	Time Interval to Death (hrs)
0.180–0.250	10–15
0.250–0.300	8–12
0.300–0.350	6–10
0.350–0.400	6–10
0.400–0.450	3–8
0.450–0.500	3–8
0.500–0.550	1–4
0.550–0.600	1–2

Source: Adapted from Kaye and Haag (1957).

Calculated antemortem concentrations at some previous time varied between 500 and 600 mg of alcohol per 100 mL of blood. From this, and in keeping with findings of others, it appears that patients with levels of alcohol of about 500 mg per 100 ml of blood and above are foredoomed; in the absence of effective therapy, although at death the blood alcohol level may be only a fraction of this figure.

Reference Number: 70402

PACH, J., Z. MAREK, M. BOGUSZ, AND W. STASKO. "The Clinical Appearance and Blood Alcohol Level in Acute Poisoning and Blood Alcohol Level in Fatal Non-Treated Poisoning." *Acta Pharmacologica Toxicologica*, 41: 362–368, 1977 (1 table, 4 figures)

Abstract: A study was conducted of sixty-six male and six female fatal alcohol poisoning victims and ninety-eight male and fourteen female patients who were admitted to hospital and survived between 1974 and 1975 in Krakow, Poland. The mean BAC in the fatal cases was 0.368 g/100 mL and was 0.320 g/100 mL in the non-fatal cases. In general, the age of the deceased was older than of living patients. There was no fatal alcohol poisonings in persons less than twenty years of age.

The mortality in acute ethanol poisoning depends mainly on the age of the subjects, general health state and environmental factors. The ingested dose and subsequent blood ethanol level seems to have a minor role in predicting of death.

Reference Number: 70403

TAYLOR, H.L. AND R.P. HUDSON. "Acute Ethanol Poisoning: A Two Year Study of Deaths in North Carolina." *Journal of Forensic Sciences,* 22: 639–653, 1977 (12 tables, 1 figure, 27 references)

Abstract: A 2-year study was conducted of 502 fatalities in North Carolina where the BAC exceeded 0.300 g/100 mL. Alcohol poisoning occurred most frequently during fall and winter, which correlates well with increased liquor sales those months. Most deaths occur at home but there is a significant number that occur in parked motor vehicles. Deaths occur mostly during weekends and holidays.

A little more than 50% of the fatalities involving blood ethanol levels of from 300 to 399 mg/100 mL have either a well-documented history or pathologic findings of chronic alcoholism. In those deaths with greater than 400 mg/100 mL blood ethanol levels, there is a frequency of chronic alcoholism of greater than 70%. In very few of all these deaths is there sufficient evidence of the decedent not being a chronic alcoholic.

Reference Number: 70404

HEATLEY, M.K. AND J. CRANE. "The Blood Alcohol Concentration at Post-mortem in 175 Fatal Cases of Alcohol Intoxication." *Medicine Science and the Law,* 30: 101–105, 1990 (2 tables, 3 figures, 10 references)

Abstract: A 10-year study was conducted of 175 cases in which death was determined by pathologists as being the result of acute alcohol poisoning. The postmortem BACs as determined by GC ranged from 0.048 to 0.767 g/100 mL (mean 0.355 g/100 mL). The age of the deceased ranged from nineteen to eighty-one years (mean forty-nine years). Eighty-two (47%) of cases showed histological evidence of inhalation of vomit or stomach contents. The UAC was determined in 140 cases. The UAC > BAC in all but two cases where the BAC < 0.300 g/100 mL. The mean BAC of victims who died from aspiration was significantly lower (0.326 g/100 mL) than those who did not die from aspiration (0.382 g/100 mL).

Death from the effects of acute alcohol intoxication can occur at levels lower than those frequently quoted in forensic textbooks. Where there is an element of aspiration lower BACs may cause death, underpinning the importance of histology in these cases. Individuals with a history of alcohol abuse or evidence of alcoholic liver disease tended to have higher BACs at death than the remainder of the study group.

Reference Number: 70405

JONES, A.W. AND P. HOLMGREN. "Comparison of Blood-Ethanol Concentration in Deaths Attributed to Acute Alcohol Poisoning and Chronic Alcoholism." *Journal of Forensic Sciences*, 48: 874–879, 2003 (2 tables, 3 figures, 50 references)

Abstract: The postmortem femoral BACs were determined by headspace GC in 693 victims of acute alcohol poisonings and 825 victims of chronic alcoholism in Sweden. The range of BACs in the acute alcohol poisoning victims was between 0.074 to 0.680 g/100 mL (mean 0.360 g/100 mL). The range of BACs in the chronic alcoholism victims were between 0.010

to 0.560 g/100 mL (mean 0.170 g/100 mL). Elevated blood acetone concentrations (0.010–0.068 g/100 mL) were found in twenty-eight (4%) of the acute alcohol poisoning victims. Elevated blood acetone concentrations (0.010–0.140 g/100 mL) were found in ninety-eight (12%) of the chronic alcoholic victims. Elevated blood isopropanol concentrations (0.010–0.085 g/100 mL) were found in twenty-two victims (3%) of acute alcohol poisoning. Elevated blood isopropyl alcohol concentrations (0.010–0.069 g/100 mL) were found in fifty (6%) of the chronic alcoholic victims. There was no correlation between the BAC and blood acetone concentrations.

In conclusion, we report that the median blood-ethanol concentration in deaths attributed to acute alcohol poisoning was 0.36 g/100 mL and the 5th and 95th percentiles were 0.22 and 0.55 g/100 mL. These values can be compared with a median blood-ethanol of 0.15 g/100 mL in deaths attributed to chronic alcoholics with 5th and 95th percentiles of 0.014 and 0.41 g/100 mL. These concentrations are probably underestimates of the highest blood ethanol concentration reached before death and likewise the total amount of alcohol consumed owing to metabolism of alcohol taking place until the time of death.

Reference Number: 70406

HIEDA, Y., H. TAKESHITA, J. FUJIHARA, AND K. TAKAYAMA. "A Fatal Case of Pure Ethanol Ingestion." *Forensic Science International*, 149: 243–247, 2005 (1 table, 2 figures, 18 references)

Abstract: A forty-five-year-old man (weighing 58 kg) was found dead in a car with two empty 500 mL bottles of dehydrate ethanol (> 99.5% v/v). The man had tried to commit suicide on prior occasions. The alcohol concentration was measured by headspace GC using dioxane as an internal standard. The right heart BAC was 0.805 g/100 mL and the left heart BAC was 0.755 g/100 mL. The UAC was 0.799 g/100 mL.

In conclusion, the primary cause of death was determined to be an acute alcohol intoxication caused by ingestion of about 1 L of pure alcohol. Direct actions of ethanol i.e., depression of the central nervous system and/or systemic acidosis were considered to be the main cause of death. Severe hemorrhagic necrotizing pancreatitis was considered to have developed concomitantly following the effects of pure alcohol.

Reference Number: 70407

DRESSLER, J., G. HAUCK, AND K. LEHMAN. "On the Diagnosis of Fatal Ethanol Intoxication During the Absorption Period [German]." *Blutalkohol*, 28: 302–303, 1991 (3 references)

Abstract: An eighty-seven-year-old male consumed 1 L of rye whiskey over 2 hours. Fifteen minutes after the end of drinking he was seen snoring loudly in bed. Two hours later he was found dead in bed. His femoral BAC was 0.152 g/100 mL and the UAC was 0.077 g/100 mL. The pulmonary vein BAC was 0.316 g/100 mL. If blood from a central vessel was not analyzed then the diagnosis for the cause of death would be a heart attack rather than fatal ethanol poisoning. In cases of death due to alcohol poisoning in which the victim is in the absorption phase, the normally used femoral BAC will be too low.

Reference Number: 70408

JONES, A.W. AND P. HOLMGREN. "Urine/Blood Ratios of Ethanol in Deaths Attributed to Acute Alcohol Poisoning and Chronic Alcoholism." *Forensic Science International*, 135: 206–212, 2003 (2 tables, 4 figures, 31 references)

Abstract: The postmortem UAC/BAC ratios were determined in 628 victims of acute alcohol poisonings and 647 chronic alcoholics. The mean UAC/BAC ratio was higher in deaths due to chronic alcoholism (1.30) compared to acute alcohol poisoning (1.18). The UAC/BAC ratios were not correlated with the age of the deceased in chronic alcoholism deaths.

The UAC/BAC ratio also gives an indication about the status of alcohol absorption and elimination in the body at the time of death. Finding a low UAC/BAC ratio along with other information e.g., appreciable amounts of alcohol in the gastric contents (> 5 g/L) or empty liquor bottles at the death scene gives hints of recent consumption of alcohol. By contrast, if the UAC/BAC ratio exceeds 1.3 this indicates that alcohol was already absorbed and distributed in all body fluids at the time of death.

Reference Number: 70409

POIKOLAINEN, K., K. LEPPANEN, AND E. VUORI. "Alcohol Sales and Fatal Alcohol Poisonings: A Time-Series Analysis." *Addiction,* 97: 1037–1040, 2002 (1 table, 2 figures, 8 references)

Abstract: The rate of alcohol poisonings and retail alcohol sales were determined in Finland between 1983 and 1999. During that time period there were 5,107 male and 1,072 female victims of alcohol poisonings.

Fatal alcohol poisonings were found to peak during weekends and in the May Day, Midsummer and Christmas celebrations. Regression analysis of quarterly series lead to a model showing that 1% increase in the sales of spirits increases the number of fatal alcohol poisonings by 0.4%. At the population level, increases in the sales of spirits and periods of hard drinking seem to increase deaths from alcohol poisoning. The findings could be of use in efforts to decrease hard drinking.

Reference Number: 70410

BERILD, D. AND H. HASSELBALCH. "Survival After a Blood Alcohol of 1127 mg/dL" [Letter]. *Lancet,* August 15th, 1981, 363 (3 references)

Abstract: A fifty-nine-year-old man with no history of alcoholism consumed 2.5 bottles of whiskey over several hours in a suicide attempt. Upon admission to hospital, the patient was deeply comatose with a temperature of 32°C. The patient required artificial ventilation, fluid therapy, and vasopressin for shock and acidosis. The serum alcohol concentration was 1.127 g/100 mL upon admission, and 0.566 g/100 mL 12 hours later. The apparent elimination rate was 0.040 g/100 mL/h. The patient survived and 1 month later showed no physical or intellectual damage.

In acute ethanol intoxication a blood ethanol of 500 mg/dL carries only a 50% probability of survival and death is usually caused by respiratory depression. To our knowledge, the highest blood-ethanol hitherto measured in a patient is 780 mg/dL.

Reference Number: 70411

TORMEY, W.P. AND T.M. MOORE. "Ethanol as a Single Toxin in Non-Traumatic Deaths—A Toxicology Perspective." *Legal Medicine,* 15: 122–125, 2013 (4 tables, 35 references)

Abstract: Alcohol was the only toxin detected in 285 autopsy cases conducted in Ireland in 2010. Of these, fifty-five male and seventeen female victims were analyzed in more detail as to the effect of alcohol upon these deaths. Traumatic cases such as hanging, drowning, and fires were excluded. The ages of the victims ranged between twenty-three and seventy-six years. The highest postmortem BAC detected was 0.556 g/100 mL. The median BAC range in male victims was 0.200 to 0.249 g/100 mL. UACs were determined in fifty-five cases and the UAC/BAC ratios ranged between 0.13 to 2.02:1. VHACs were determined in ten cases and the BAC/VHAC ratio ranged from 0.76 to 1.09:1 (median, 0.84).

> Whether there is a level of ethanol in blood that is universally safe is unknown but the level of ethanol that is lethal in those with no other demonstrable abnormality at autopsy is also uncertain. The wide variations in blood ethanol levels found in these non-traumatic deaths suggest that lethal ethanol toxicity may have a lower threshold than is conventionally acknowledged.

Reference Number: 70412

LI, R., L. HU, L. HU, X. ZHANG, R. PHIPPS, D.R. FOWLER, F. CHEN, AND L. LI. "Evaluation of Acute Alcohol Intoxication as the Primary Cause of Death: A Diagnostic Challenge for Forensic Pathologists." *Journal of Forensic Sciences*, 62: 1213–1219, 2017 (4 tables, 3 figures, 44 references).

Abstract: A detailed analysis was conducted of 149 acute alcohol intoxication deaths (AAI) that occurred in the state of Maryland between 2004 and 2012. The victims were 122 (88%) males and twenty-seven (18%) females and ranged in age between sixteen and sixty-five years (mean thirty-seven years). Liver examination showed cirrhosis (5.4%), steatosis (64.4%), fibrosis (20.1%), and alcoholic hepatitis (30.2%). The mean peripheral BAC was 0.400 g/100 mL (range 0.180 to 0.690 g/100 mL). Obese victims had a lower peripheral BAC (0.370 g/100 mL) than average weight victims (0.420 g/100 mL). Only 19% of the deaths were assessed to have occurred in the absorption phase.

Table. Comparison of Mean Fatal Peripheral BAC, Heart BAC, UAC, and VHAC

Sample	Mean Alcohol Concentration (g/100 mL)	Mean Ratio in Comparison to Peripheral Blood (g/100 mL)
Peripheral Blood	0.400	–
Heart Blood	0.410	1.03
Urine	0.460	1.15
Vitreous Humor	0.480	1.20

Source: Adapted from Li et al (2017).

The mechanisms in death due to alcohol intoxication are generally considered to be suppression of the respiratory center in the brain stem, with a concomitant lowered arterial oxygen consumption, carbon dioxide production and the respiratory workload. Our data also demonstrated that intoxicated overweight people were more frequently found in the prone position compared to normal or underweight people. People with postmortem BAC < 0.30% were mostly overweight, or obese with a mean BMI of 31.3 and were more frequently found in the prone position at the time of death. Fatal positional asphyxia has been reported to be associated with drunkenness or other intoxicants or disabilities. In most of the reported cases, the victim was intoxicated or incapacitated to a degree that it was impossible to move out of that abnormal position. To our best knowledge of our authors, the significance and the role of prone position or intoxicated individuals has not been studied. Our data suggest that prone position or intoxicated people, especially when they were overweight or obese may further compromise respiratory function and lead to die from lower lethal blood alcohol concentration.

Reference Number: 70413

AFSHAR, M., G. NETZER, E. SALISBURY-AFSHAR, S. MURTHI, AND G.S. SMITH. "Injured Patients with Very High Blood Alcohol Concentrations." *Injury*, 47: 83–88, 2016 (1 table, 5 figures, 36 references)

Abstract: The BAC was determined in 44,502 patients admitted to a major trauma center in Illinois between 2002 and 2011. A BAC of 0.400 g/100 mL or greater was found in 147 (1.1%) of the BAC positive cases. Nearly one-quarter of the high BAC patients returned to the trauma center with another injury. The ISS, TBI, and GCS were measured as well to determine the severity of trauma. The patients with a high BAC had more blunt trauma injuries (53% were due to falls) than patients with lower BACs. The high BAC patients also had lower rates of severe injury and in-hospital deaths than the lower BAC patients.

> Most published reports of BAC > 400 mg/dL were in forensic medicine and comprised of postmortem cases of alcohol poisoning deaths and suggested a high likelihood for death in BAC > 400 mg/dL. In one report with 213 cases of acute alcohol deaths, 62% of fatalities had BAC above 400 mg/dL and the remainder had levels between 300 and 400 mg/dL. While alcohol levels in excess of 300 mg/dL indicated severe alcohol intoxication with concomitant respiratory depression, our study suggests that higher BACs in trauma were tolerated, with many of these patients navigating steps or operating motor vehicles immediately prior to injury. Risky alcohol users were previously shown to tolerate BACs above 200 mg/dL, with minimal psychomotor vigilance impediment. In the case of the highest BAC in ten years at the trauma centre, the patient was 30 years old, and presented with a BAC of 613 mg/dL and arrived breathing spontaneously and unassisted with stable physiologic parameters after a fall. Patients admitted to the trauma centre with a BAC > 400 mg/dL were engaged in risky activities further supporting the need for focused care in this group.

Reference Number: 70414

WINGREN, C.J. AND A. OTTOSSON. "The Association Between Obesity and Lethal Blood Alcohol Concentrations: A Nationwide Register-Based Study of Medicolegal Autopsy Cases in Sweden." *Forensic Science International*, 244: 285–288, 2014 (2 tables, 17 references)

The prevalence of obesity globally in 2013 has been estimated to be about 37% in men and 38% in women. Obesity may increase oxygen consumption and carbon monoxide production and respiratory workload. It has been proposed that when determining the cause of death in an obese individual without any obvious sign of death that respiratory depression be considered. The association between body mass index (BMI) and lethal BAC was determined in 1,545 cases where alcohol intoxication was the primary cause of death, which occurred in Sweden between 1999 and 2013. The mean postmortem femoral fatal BAC was 0.350, 0.340, and 0.320 g/100 mL for normal weight (18.5 to < 25), overweight (25 to < 30), and obese (> 30) individuals respectively. The percentage of victims with a BAC > 0.300 g/100 mL was 72%, 69%, and 58% for normal weight, overweight, and obese persons respectively. The association between obesity and lower fatal BAC occurred regardless of age, gender, other drugs, or decomposition.

Table. Fatal BACs of 1,545 Persons of Different BMI Who Died from Alcohol Intoxication in Sweden (1999–2013)

Body Type (BMI)	Percent with BAC > 0.300 g/100 mL	Mean BAC at Death (g/100 mL)	Range of Fatal BACs (g/100 mL)
Underweight (< 18.5)	65%	0.350	0.220–0.570
Normal weight (18.5 to < 25)	72%	0.350	0.070–0.800
Overweight (25 to < 30)	69%	0.340	0.100–0.590
Obese (> 30)	58%	0.320	0.090–0.520

Source: Adapted from Wingren and Ottosson (2014).

We showed an association between obesity and lower lethal BACs confirming our initial hypothesis. The results indicate that obese and overweight individuals have an increased risk to die from lower BACs than subjects of normal weight.

Reference Number: 70415

SCHNEIR, A.B. AND R.F. CLARK. "Death Caused by Ingestion of an Ethanol-Based Hand Sanitizer." *Journal of Emergency Medicine*, 1–3, 2013 (1 figure, 21 references)

Abstract: A thirty-six-year-old male alcohol abuser was admitted to an ER due to alcohol intoxication. He was alert but uncooperative and had slurred speech and nystagmus. His BrAC was 0.278 g/100 mL. Approximately 4.5 hours later he was stabilized and his BrAC was 0.188 g/100 mL. He was found unresponsive 30 minutes later in the bathroom of the ER waiting room with an empty 354 mL container of Purell hand sanitizer (62% v/v ethyl alcohol). His serum alcohol concentration was 0.526 g/100 mL. He was treated for alcohol poisoning but died 7 days later.

Subsequent to this case presented, our institution decided to eliminate removable hand sanitizer containers. Balancing the benefit of hand sanitizers with their potential for abuse remains challenging. Despite limiting hand sanitizers to wall dispensers in the patient care areas in our institution, multiple patients have been observed in our ED ingesting the contents from these wall dispensers.

Reference Number: 70416

PERESKA, Z., N. SIMONOVSKA, A. BABULOVSKA, A. BERAT-HUSEINI, K. NAUMOSKI, AND K. KOSTADINOSKI. "Acute Severe Poisoning with Disinfectant in Senior Patient-Case Report and Overview of Literature Considering Age Influence on Treatment Decision in Alcohol-Based Intoxication." *SAGE Open Medical Case Reports*, 9: 1–6, 2021 (1 table, 35 references)

Abstract: An unconscious sixty-six-year-old woman with immunocompromising comorbidities and five previous suicide attempts was admitted to a North Macedonia hospital. Her SAC was 0.526 g/100 mL due to the ingestion of a 70% ethanol hand sanitizer. She was administered hemodialysis, which reduced her SAC to 0.200 g/100 mL. She recovered after 48 hours and was transferred to a psychiatric hospital.

> Considering the decreased biotransformation in the elderly, immunocompromising comorbidities, reports of fatal outcome in poisoned elderly patients with disinfectants under standard fluids supportive protocol, hemodialysis was initiated with registered associated hypercoagulability which resulted in complete stabilization after 48 h of admission. Treatment protocols of poisoning with ethanol-based disinfectant in the elderly should consider timely performing hemodialysis at lower alcholemia levels than recommended.

Reference Number: 70417

KANNY, D., R.D. BREWER, J.B. MESNICK, L.J. PAULOZZI, T.S. NAIMI, AND H. LU. "Vital Signs: Alcohol Poisoning Deaths—United States, 2010–2012." *Morbidity and Mortality Weekly Report*, 63: 5pp, 2015 (1 figure, 2 tables, 24 references)

Abstract: Between 2010 and 2012 there was an average of 2,221 alcohol poisoning deaths per year in the United States, which is a rate of 8.8 deaths per million population aged fifteen years or older. Approximately 75% of deaths involved adults thirty-five to sixty-four years of age and 75% were males. Contrary to the great publicity and media attention surrounding alcohol poisoning deaths in college students, this age group had the lowest rate of alcohol poisoning (2.6 deaths per million). The rate of alcohol poisoning per 1 million population ranged from 5.3 in Alabama to 6.9 in Ohio to 46.5 in Alaska.

Table. Race/Ethnicity and Percentage of Total Alcohol Poisoning Deaths and Rate Per 1 Million US Population

Race/Ethnicity	% of Total Alcohol Poisoning Deaths	Rate per 1 Million Population
White, non-Hispanic	67.5%	8.8
Black, non-Hispanic	8.6%	6.2
Hispanic	15.2%	9.0
American Indian/Alaskan Native	6.9%	49.1
Asian/Pacific Islander	1.5%	2.2

Source: Adapted from Kanney et al (2015).

Deaths from alcohol poisoning is a serious and preventable public health problem in the United States. A comprehensive approach to the prevention of excessive drinking that includes evidence-based community and clinical prevention strategies is needed to decrease alcohol poisoning deaths and other harms attributable to excessive alcohol use.

7.05 HEMATOMAS

"Make not thyself helpless drinking in the beer shop ... falling down thy limbs will be broken, and no one will give thee a hand to help thee up."

— Ancient Egyptian papyrus, cited in Zuska, "Wounds Without Cause" (1981)

Subdural hematomas (clots) can be a useful specimen for alcohol determination, especially in cases in which the victim had a long survival time (70501–70505), as the hematoma can be isolated from the general blood circulation (and the alcohol elimination by the liver) and can retain its alcohol concentration for a prolonged period of time.

The presence of a positive BAC increases the risk of subdural hematoma death (70506).

Reference Number: 70501

BUCHSBAUM, R.M., ADELSON, L., AND I. SUNSHINE. "A Comparison of Post-Mortem Ethanol Levels Obtained from Blood and Subdural Specimens." *Forensic Science International*, 41: 237–243, 1989 (3 tables, 7 references)

Abstract: A study was conducted of seventy-five postmortem cases where blood and subdural hematomas were analyzed for ethanol by headspace GC. The time intervals between trauma and death ranged from 1 to 50 hours. In thirty-eight cases the time interval was not known. In cases where the time interval to death was less than 9 hours, the subdural clot analysis did not provide any additional information as to the BAC and the subdural clot alcohol concentrations were similar. In twelve of sixteen (75%) cases where the time interval to death was greater than 9 hours, the subdural blood was positive for alcohol when the BAC was negative.

Table. Subdural Blood Alcohol Concentrations in Cases Where the Postmortem BAC Was Zero and When the Survival Time of the Victims was ≥ 9 Hours

Case Number	Survival Time (hrs)	Subdural BAC (g/100 mL)
23	9	0.05
24	10	0.02
26	13	0.12
28	16	0.01
29	16	0.04
30	19	0.03
32	26	0.06
33	26	0.26
34	32	0.07
35	38	0.07
36	41	0.06
37	50	0.04

Source: Buchsbaum et al (1989).

This study of 75 autopsied persons from whom both blood and subdural ethanol levels were obtained shows the usefulness of the subdural ethanol level especially where there is a prolonged or unknown post-traumatic time interval. Use of such a test is recommended in these situations.

Reference Number: 70502

EISELE, J.W., D.T. REAY, AND H.J. BONNELL. "Ethanol in Sequestered Hematomas: Quantitative Evaluation." *American Journal of Clinical Pathology*, 81: 352–355, 1984 (1 table, 4 references)

Abstract: The antemortem, postmortem, and sequestered hematoma alcohol concentrations were determined in fifteen victims of trauma. The postmortem blood and sequestered hematoma concentrations were also determined in four cases of immediate death due to trauma. The postmortem blood was obtained from the proximal aorta. Postmortem alcohol concentrations were determined by GC. The antemortem alcohol concentrations were determined in serum by GC. The time between the ante- and postmortem samples ranged between 5 and 172 hours. The SACs ranged from 0.022 to 0.674 g/100 mL and the blood hematoma alcohol concentrations ranged between 0 and 0.190 g/100 mL.

The results presented above demonstrate that blood in sequestered intracranial hematomas may reflect the presence or absence of ethanol in the circulating blood at the time of injury but does not yield an accurate estimate of the concentration of that ethanol. The control group validates the proposal that at the time of bleeding, the level in the hematoma blood approximate those in the circulating blood. With the passage of time, however, the level in the hematomas decrease in an unpredictable manner.

Reference Number: 70503

SMIALEK, J.E., W.U. SPITZ, AND J.A. WOLFE. "Ethanol in Intracerebral Clot: Report of Two Homicidal Cases Involving Prolonged Survival After Injury." *American Journal of Forensic Medicine and Pathology*, 1: 149–150, 1980 (3 references)

Abstract: Head injuries are a common result of physical violence and may lead to subdural, epidural, subarachnoid, or intracerebral hematomas. The hematoma is sequestered from the circulating blood and is no longer metabolized. In one case, a forty-four-year-old male was involved in a bar room fight. He survived for 9 hours. The BAC at death was 0.040 g/100 mL. The BAC of the clot was 0.110 g/100 mL. In another case, a twenty-three-year-old male survived 33 hours after being beaten with a baseball bat. The blood and urine alcohol concentrations at death were zero. The BAC of the clot was 0.040 g/100 mL.

The blood clot is another potential resource for information in an unnatural death investigation where intoxication is suspected or indicated by the behaviour of the victim.

Reference Number: 70504

RIGGS, J.E., J.L. FROST, AND S.S. SCHOCHET JR. "Ethanol Level Differential Between Postmortem Blood and Subdural Hematoma." *Military Medicine*, 163: 722–724, 1998 (3 figures, 10 references)

Abstract: A sixty-nine-year-old male fell down an inside stairway at home at about 10:00 p.m. He suffered a 2.5 cm laceration on the left side of his nose but no other visible injury. He was examined at the hospital at 11:00 p.m. and released at 12:00 midnight. He was found dead in bed at 11:30 a.m. the next day. The autopsy revealed a large acute subdural hematoma. The postmortem iliac vein BAC was 0.070 g/100 mL and the subdural hematoma alcohol concentration was 0.040 g/100 mL.

The most reasonable explanation is that he sustained a subsequent injury after returning home from the hospital. The ethanol level differential between the blood in the sequestered hematoma in this case indicate that this individual consumed alcohol after being discharged from the emergency department. If he had not consumed ethanol after being discharged from the emergency department the ethanol level in the subdural hematoma would have been higher that in the peripheral blood. Because he consumed alcohol after leaving the hospital the risk of a subsequent fall and injury is markedly increased.

Reference Number: 70505

CASSIN, B.J. AND W.U. SPITZ. "Concentration of Alcohol in Delayed Subdural Hematoma." *Journal of Forensic Sciences*, 28: 1013–1015, 1983 (4 references)

Abstract: A young woman who was drinking beer at a bar was hit by a car 30 minutes after finishing drinking. One hour after the accident the hospital did an analysis and detected a BAC of 0.120 g/100 mL. The woman remained unconscious and died 21 hours after admission. At autopsy, the tests for alcohol were negative in the peripheral and the hematoma blood samples. There may be delayed intracranial hematoma following head injury. Therefore, the subdural hematoma in this case may not have formed until sometime after the accident.

The occurrence of delayed intracranial hemorrhage is not a new discovery, but there has been no published discussion of its medicolegal implications. Tests for alcohol and drugs on subdural hematomas discovered at autopsy may be useful in its recognition or confirmation. In cases of prolonged survival following injury, initially positive concentrations of alcohol and drugs may become negative, which is frequently the case in our experience.

Reference Number: 70506

HENINGER, M. "Subdural Hematoma Occurrence. Comparison Between Ethanol and Cocaine Use at Death." *American Journal of Forensic Medicine and Pathology,* 34: 237–241, 2013 (7 tables, 24 references)

Abstract: A study was conducted of 967 subdural hematoma (SDH) deaths that occurred in Fulton County, Georgia, between 2003 and 2010. One hundred and sixty-two victims (17%) had a postmortem BAC of 0.100 g/100 mL or greater, sixty-nine victims (7%) had a BAC < 0.100 g/100 mL, and 561 had no alcohol detected. Cocaine/metabolites were detected in 113 cases. SDH occurred in 7 to 9% of the victims with BAC between 0 and 0.100 g/100 mL, and 18% in victims with a BAC of 0.100 g/100 mL+. SDH was found in 11% of the cases negative for cocaine and 9% of the cases with cocaine present.

Ethanol-related atrophic changes altering the anatomy of the dura and arachnoid membranes make an SDH more likely. The alcoholic is more likely to fall and more likely to acquire an SDH. Ethanol is also associated with drivers more frequently acquiring head injuries and SDH. Cocaine causes hypertensive-related intracerebral hemorrhage (stroke) that occasionally breaks through, resulting in an SDH and often with underlying vascular defects. Victims of homicide involving head trauma and SDH are somewhat more likely to be using cocaine than ethanol. But in not a single case in this entire 8-year study of SDH in 967 cases is there any reason to attribute the SDH to the spontaneous direct effects of cocaine.

7.06 VITREOUS HUMOR

"The eyes are the window to your soul."

—William Shakespeare, Quotes 55

"Given the seriousness of the problem and the potential importance of the analytical result, it is important that ethanol measurements in postmortem blood are corroborated by the analysis of other body fluid. Vitreous humor from the eye and bladder urine are helpful here. Vitreous, which is easily obtained is valuable because it is well protected from bacterial infiltration after death."

—Pounder, "Dead Drunk or Dead Sober?" (1998)

Vitreous humor (eye fluid) is another useful postmortem sample for alcohol analysis as it is isolated from potential contamination from the chest cavity and has a low glucose concentration. It is a gelatinous substance that consists of 98% water and 2% collagen fibers, electrolytes, carbohydrates, and other proteins (70611).

The VHAC lags behind the BAC and requires 1–2 hours to equilibrate with the BAC, and so if the BAC > VHAC, it can indicate that the person died in the rising BAC phase (70602, 70603, 70608). Various ratios have been proposed to convert the VHAC into a BAC (70602, 70604, 70605, 70608–70611). There is no difference in VHAC from either the left or right eye (70601). VHAC can be diluted in drowning victims (70606) and can be contaminated by embalming fluids (70607).

Onsite testing at autopsy using the enzymatic QED saliva test strips showed poor results when used with postmortem saliva as it is frequently contaminated with blood but showed a good correlation with the BAC ($r = 0.9931$) when used with vitreous humor (70612).

A low blood or vitreous humor EtG concentration can indicate postmortem production of alcohol (70613).

Reference Number: 70601

SOUSA, A.P., D.N. VIEIRA, M.M.F. OLIVEIRA, E.P. MARQUES, AND P.V. MONSANTO. "Comparison Between Ethanol Levels of Vitreous Humor of Both Eyes in the Same Individual." *Proceedings of the 35th The International Association of Forensic Toxicology, Padova, Italy*, 574–578, 1997 (4 tables, 2 figures, 6 references)

Abstract: Vitreous humor was collected from the right and left eyes of forty alcohol-positive cadavers within 48 hours of death. The vitreous humor was frozen at –18°C and the VHACs were determined by headspace GC within 3 days of autopsy. The mean VHAC was 0.174 g/100 mL for both right and left eye.

In cadavers with a postmortem interval less than 48 hours the ethanol levels obtained in vitreous humor of both eyes showed no statistically significant differences, when samples are performed within the first three days after autopsy. Therefore, in these cases, samples of vitreous humor of the right or left eyes can be indistinctly used for forensic purposes.

Reference Number: 70602

YIP, D.C.P. AND S.F. SHUM. "A Study on the Correlation of Blood and Vitreous Humor Alcohol Levels in the Late Absorption and Elimination Phases." *Medicine Science and the Law,* 30: 29–33, 1990 (1 table, 1 figure, 6 references)

Abstract: The blood, urine, and vitreous humor alcohol concentration were determined in eighty-six postmortem cases. The alcohol concentrations were determined by GC. Only BACs > 0.030 g/100 mL were selected to determine BAC/VHAC ratios since at low BACs, slight analytic errors may lead to gross errors in the calculation of the distribution ratio.

> We conclude that if an adequate error margin is allowed for the equation B = 0.76V + 4.7 can be safely used to estimate the minimum blood alcohol concentration in cases where cadaveric blood is unsuitable or unavailable for alcohol estimation. This would underestimate the level in cases of death occurring in the absorption phase, but in a medico-legal setting it would be more desirable for a Forensic Pathologist to base his opinion on minimum levels in which he can be confident. In cases where urine is not available, the B/V ratio can be used to infer the phase in which the deceased died: a B/V ratio greater than 0.95 indicates death in the absorption phase. It should be noted that the reverse of the proposition is not valid.

Reference Number: 70603

NORHEIM, G. "Postmortem Alcohol in Vitreous Humor." *Blutalkohol,* 9: 187–191, 1972 (1 table, 1 figure, 9 references)

Abstract: A study was conducted of seventy-three postmortem cases in which no putrefaction was evident where both blood and vitreous humor samples were collected. BACs and VHACs were determined by ADH. The BACs ranged from 0.021 to 0.466 g/100 mL. The mean BAC/VHAC ratio was 0.84, with a range from 0.53 to 1.11. The BAC/VHAC variation was greatest at low BACs. It is suggested that a BAC/VHAC ratio > 1 indicates recent alcohol consumption before death.

The relation between the alcohol content in the two fluids may in some instances be of value for estimation of the time from alcohol consumption to death.

Reference Number: 70604

CAPLAN, Y.H. AND B. LEVINE. "Vitreous Humor in the Evaluation of Postmortem Blood Ethanol Concentrations." *Journal of Analytical Toxicology*, 14: 305–307, 1990 (3 tables, 1 figure, 9 references)

Abstract: A 6-month study was conducted of 347 paired postmortem blood and vitreous humor samples that were analyzed for ethanol by headspace GC. In 205 cases in which the BAC > 0.100 g/100 mL, the mean VHAC/BAC ratio was 1.17. In forty-one cases, a positive BAC was associated with a negative VHAC, and in thirty-four (83%) the BAC < 0.030 g/100 mL and the VHAC = 0 g/100 mL. A BAC as high as 0.120 g/100 mL was associated with a VHAC = 0.

Table. Percent of Cases in Which the Postmortem BAC Was Positive and the VHAC Was Negative

BAC (g/100 mL)	Cases where VHAC < 0.01 g/100 mL
0.01	57.0%
0.02	50.0%
0.03	20.0%
0.04	11.0%
0.05	13.0%
>0.05	1.3%

Source: Adapted from Caplan and Levine (1990).

Vitreous humor should be collected in all postmortem cases when possible. The mean ratio of vitreous humor to blood ethanol concentration is 1.17, which is consistent with theoretical considerations and previously reported data. Blood ethanol concentrations less than 0.03 g/dL are frequently associated with negative vitreous humor ethanol concentrations implying that postmortem fermentation may have occurred.

Reference Number: 70605

JONES, A.W. AND P. HOLMGREN. "Uncertainty in Estimating Blood Ethanol Concentrations by Analysis of Vitreous Humor." *Journal of Clinical Pathology*, 54: 699–702, 2001 (1 table, 1 figure, 24 references)

Abstract: The VHAC and femoral venous BACs were determined in 672 postmortem cases. The alcohol concentrations were determined by headspace GC using *t*-butanol as an internal standard. The mean VHAC was 0.158 g/100 mL and the mean FVBAC was 0.134 g/100 mL. The mean VH/FVBAC ratio was 1.19 (95% confidence interval, 0.63–1.75).

If the VH ethanol content is halved this could be considered beyond a reasonable doubt, to provide an FVB result not exceeding the true concentration.

Reference Number: 70606

SINGER, P.P., G.R. JONES, R. LEWIS, AND R. JOHNSON. "Loss of Ethanol from Vitreous Humor in Drowning Deaths." *Journal of Analytical Toxicology*, 31: 522–525, 2007 (1 table, 23 references)

Abstract: Two case histories are reported of drowning deaths in which the body remained underwater for 2 to 4 weeks. The postmortem central BAC and UAC were 0.260 and 0.330 g/100 mL respectively and the VHAC was 0.050 g/100 mL. In the other victim the BAC and UAC were 0.280 and 0.320 g/100 mL respectively and the VHAC was 0.080 g/100 mL. Urine 5HTOL/5HIAA concentration ratios indicated antemortem alcohol consumption occurred rather than putrefaction.

These cases demonstrate that in cases of prolonged immersion in water, ethanol can diffuse out of the eye and, therefore, low vitreous/blood ethanol ratios should not automatically be interpreted as evidence of postmortem ethanol formation in the blood. Determination of the urine 5-HTOL/5-HIAA ratio can assist in determining whether ethanol has been consumed prior to death.

Reference Number: 70607

SCOTT, W., I. ROOT, AND B. SANBORN. "The Use of Vitreous Humor for Determination of Ethyl Alcohol in Previously Embalmed Bodies." *Journal of Forensic Sciences*, 9: 913–916, 1974 (1 table, 4 references)

Abstract: A study was conducted of thirty-eight cases in which a blood sample was collected postmortem and the body was then embalmed. After embalming, the vitreous and blood ethanol and methanol concentrations were determined by GC. The embalming fluid contained only methanol, not ethanol. Post-embalming VH methyl alcohol concentrations ranged from 0.040 to 0.420 g/100 mL.

The methyl alcohol levels in the post embalming specimen have been given in order to indicate that there is considerable diffusion of embalming fluid into the vitreous, but that the degree of this diffusion does not correlate with either a higher or lower level of alcohol in the vitreous humor than in the blood.

Reference Number: 70608

IOAN, B.G., V. JITARU, R. DAMIAN, AND S.I. DAMIAN. "Study on the Relationship Between the Concentration of Ethanol in the Blood, Urine and Vitreous Humor." *Romanian Journal of Legal Medicine*, 23: 211–216, 2015 (4 tables, 3 figures, 19 references)

Abstract: Blood, urine, and vitreous humor alcohol concentrations were determined in 202 forensic cases between 2010 and 2012 in Romania using a potassium dichromate method. The correlation between UAC/BAC was $r = 0.905$ and the VHAC/BAC was $r = 0.887$. The average VHAC/BAC ratio was 1.07:1. The equilibrium of VHAC/BAC is 1–2 hours so it provides an opportunity to assess the BAC 1–2 hours prior to death.

Vitreous humor is one of the biological products most widely used in forensic toxicology. The vitreous is particularly useful in cases where the body is severely damaged, affected by putrefaction or where the toxicological exam is done after embalming the body and BAC determination becomes irrelevant. The isolated location of the eyeball makes the vitreous humor not to be exposed to bacterial contamination and alcohol diffusion from gastric and pulmonary levels. The intact eyeball is relatively avascular and isolated from other tissues and fluids, so that vitreous humor is a sterile product, useful for quantitative determinations. The level of alcohol in the vitreous humor (VAC) is not influenced by the formation of alcohol during putrefaction and the electrolyte and metabolites concentrations of drugs in this environment remains stable post-mortem for a longer period of time than in blood. Due to these features, the quantitative determination of VAC is an excellent way to interpret the value of alcohol as a measure of quality control.

Reference Number: 70609

PAPIERZ, P., J. BERENT, L. MARKUSZEWSKI, AND S. SZRAM. "A Comparative Study of the Ethyl Alcohol Concentration in Vitreous Humor in Relation to Ethyl Alcohol Concentration in Blood and Urine." *Problems of Forensic Science,* LVIII, 34–44, 2004 (6 figures, 14 references)

Abstract: Femoral blood, urine from the bladder, and vitreous humor were collected from fifty-five deceased who died in the alcohol absorption phase and 435 deceased in the alcohol elimination phase at the Department of Forensic Medicine of the Medical University in Lodz, Poland, between 2000 and 2003. The alcohol concentration was determined by GC. In addition, the BACs and UACs were confirmed by an ADH method. The correlation between VHAC and BAC was $r = 0.91$ in cases in the absorption phase compared to $r = 0.94$ in cases in the alcohol elimination phase.

1. A high coefficient of correlation was ascertained between alcohol concentration in vitreous humor and blood and also between alcohol concentration in vitreous humor and urine. 2. The conducted study demonstrates that there is a direct correlation between the alcohol concentrations in blood and urine. 3. The introduction of a division of the analyzed material into two sub groups of alcohol absorption phase and alcohol elimination phase minimises the scatter of single cases around the regression line, improves the correlation coefficient, and decreases the error of estimating blood alcohol concentration in the absorption phase. 4. Vitreous humor is of major importance in postmortem alcohol determination.

Reference Number: 70610

SZEREMETA, M., E. MIRONIUK, M. JANICA, P. DROBULIAKOVA, K. LOMPERTA, M. SZCZYPEK, AND A. NIEMCUNOWICZ-JANICA. "Vitreous Humor as an Alternative Material for the Determination of Alcohol Concentration in Human Corpses." *Archiwum Medycyny Sadowej i Kryminologii,* 68: 108–118, 2018 (1 table, 4 figures, 39 references)

Abstract: Vitreous humor and femoral blood alcohol concentrations were determined in sixty-two postmortem cases of sudden and violent deaths autopsied between 2012 and 2016 in Poland. There were no visible signs of putrefaction and none of the deceased were diabetic. The VHAC ranged from 0.010 to 0.460 g/100 mL and the femoral BAC between 0.010 and 0.450 g/100 mL. The mean BAC/VHAC ratio was 0.96 and $r = 0.96$.

> Vitreous humor is a very good material for assessing the degree of alcoholaemia in the deceased and should be routinely used in forensic toxicology, especially when collecting blood samples is not possible.

Reference Number: 70611

SAVINI, F., A. TARTAGLIA, L. COCCIA, D. PALESTINI, C. D'OVIDIO, U. DE GRAZZIA, G.M. MERONE, E. BASSOTTI, AND M. LOCATELLI. "Ethanol Determination in Post-Mortem Samples: Correlation Between Blood and Vitreous Humor Concentration." *Molecules*, 25: 2724, 9pp, 2020 (2 tables, 3 figures, 28 references)

Abstract: The postmortem femoral blood and vitreous humor alcohol concentrations were determined by headspace GC using *n*-propanol as an internal standard in thirty-one cases of suspected alcohol poisoning. The VHAC/BAC ratio varied from 0.81 to 1.91:1. The VHAC > BAC in 74% of the cases, and VHAC < BAC in 26% of the cases. The correlation (r^2) between VHAC and BAC was 0.92. Postmortem blood water content increased from 60 to 90% as loss of cell membrane integrity causes tissue liquefaction and increases the glucose and consequence invasion by bacteria and other microorganisms causing ethanol production.

Table. Postmortem Vitreous Humor and Blood Alcohol Concentrations and the VAC/BAC Ratio in Cases in Which the BAC > 0.100 g/100 mL

VHAC (g/100 mL)	BAC (g/100 mL)	VHAC/BAC Ratio
0.168	0.131	1.28
0.223	0.211	1.06
0.150	0.164	0.91
0.161	0.142	1.13
0.131	0.123	1.07
0.150	0.148	1.01
0.201	0.210	0.96
0.187	0.197	0.95
0.136	0.124	1.10
0.198	0.223	0.89

VHAC (g/100 mL)	BAC (g/100 mL)	VHAC/BAC Ratio
0.149	0.130	1.15
0.278	0.260	1.07
0.105	0.120	0.88
0.168	0.160	1.05
0.110	0.109	1.01
0.206	0.199	1.04
0.106	0.097	1.09
0.210	0.172	1.22
0.180	0.150	1.20

Source: Adapted from Savini et al (2020).

Vitreous humor is a gelatinous substance that consists of 98% H_2O and of 2% collagen fibers, glycosaminoglycans as hyaluronic acid, cells, electrolytes, carbohydrates and other proteins. Vitreous humor is considered advantageous because due to [the fact the] eyeball is less exposed to bacterial contamination, it is easy to sample (VH is sampled by syringe from the center of the eyeball with slow aspiration) and shows sample stability over time after death. Additionally, vitreous humor is less subject to post-mortem ethanol formation: being encapsulated in the eyeball the eye water is less subject to post-mortem alcohol generation and the ethanol levels in vitreous humor remain constant. However, some limitations are present also for VH such as a limited volume of samples and the presence of the retinal blood barrier, which limits the passage inside and outside.

Reference Number: 70612

ENGELHART, D.A. AND A.J. JENKINS. "Evaluation of an Onsite Alcohol Testing Device for Use in Postmortem Forensic Toxicology." *Journal of Analytical Toxicology*, 25: 612–615, 2001 (1 table, 2 figures, 16 references)

Abstract: The onsite enzymatic QED saliva alcohol test was attempted in fifty postmortem cases. For twenty-three cases (46%) oral fluid was not attainable and for ten cases (20%) the OD was contaminated with blood. The correlation between the OF and blood alcohol was poor ($r = 0.8345$). Vitreous humor samples were collected from 165 out of 171 cases and were analyzed in the QED saliva alcohol test and headspace GC and compared to the postmortem BAC. The correlation was good ($r = 0.9931$). The average VHAC/BAC ratio by GC was 1.16:1 compared to 1.22 using QED results.

Although the ability of the QED saliva alcohol test to accurately measure clinical saliva ethanol levels and its correlation to blood ethanol levels has been well documented, this is the first reported study evaluating the QED device in the postmortem setting. The results demonstrate that postmortem saliva/oral fluid ethanol levels are very difficult to obtain because of insufficient or contaminated samples. There, in most cases, postmortem oral fluid will not provide a reliable estimation of blood ethanol levels. However, the ability to determine accurate postmortem vitreous ethanol levels with the QED device was demonstrated by comparison to GC results. Over the concentration range of 0.01–0.35 g/dL, the QED device proved to be as sensitive and accurate as headspace GC analysis. Use of vitreous humor specimens for the analysis was also found to be reliable since only 6 of the 171 tests performed were aborted because of the high viscosity of the specimens.

Reference Number: 70613

VEZZOLI, S., M. BERNINI, AND F. DE FERRARI. "Ethyl Glucuronide in Vitreous Humor and Blood Postmortem Specimens: Analysis by Liquid Chromatography-Electrospray Tandem Mass Spectrometry and Interpreting Results of Neo-Formation of Ethanol." *Annali dell'Istituto Superiore di Sanità*, 51: 19–27, 2015 (5 tables, 2 figures, 30 references)

Abstract: Postmortem femoral blood and vitreous humor from sixty-three autopsy cases were analyzed for alcohol, *n*-propanol, acetaldehyde, and EtG. In seventeen cases alcohol and EtG were absent in both the blood and VH. Nineteen cases had a positive BAC ranging from 0.005 to 0.030 g/100 mL, but the EtG concentration in blood and VH was lower than 0.01 mg/L indicating postmortem production, and in eight cases *n*-propanol and/or acetaldehyde were detected.

The determination of EtG in biological material is important in those cases where the intake of ethanol appears doubtful, as it allows us to exclude the possibility of any post-mortem formation of ethanol.

7.07 URINE

"Ethyl alcohol is not likely to be produced by bacterial contamination of urine."

—Blackmore, "The Bacterial Production of Ethyl Alcohol" (1968)

Postmortem urine samples tend to be more stable than blood since it is isolated in the bladder from the gut and contains virtually no glucose. However, putrefaction of the urine sample can occur, especially in diabetics with yeast infections (70702–70704). The UAC, since it is a pooled sample, represents the BAC of the deceased sometime prior to death. A UAC < BAC indicates that the deceased died in the absorption phase. A positive UAC (with no putrefaction) and a zero BAC may indicate that the deceased survived for a period of time prior to death (70701).

- UAC < BAC deceased died on absorption phase and drinking probably occurred shortly prior to death.
- UAC > BAC deceased died during postabsorptive phase and drinking probably occurred hours or more prior to death.

The use of a Foley catheter in emergency treatment can dilute the UAC (70705).

In a case of a diabetic death in which the BAC was preserved with 1% NaF, the postmortem BAC was negative, but the urine, which was not preserved with NaF, increased to a maximum of 0.280 g/100 mL after 41 days when stored at 2°C–8°C and the urine acetone concentration increased to 0.092 g/100 mL (70706).

The mean UAC/BAC ratio was 1.3:1 (70707).

There is new evidence for the old lore regarding bladder urine volume and alcohol/drug intoxication. The mean urine volume was 92 mL for the not intoxicated and 215 mL for the intoxicated. The highest mean urine volume was 321 mL for positive cocaine case (70708).

Reference Number: 70701

ALHA, A.R. AND V. TAMMINEN. "Fatal Cases with an Elevated Urine Alcohol but Without Alcohol in the Blood." *Journal of Forensic Medicine,* 11: 3–5, 1964 (1 reference)

Abstract: Fifteen cases of fatalities were found with UAC as high as 0.220 g/100 mL but the BACs were only from 0.003 to 0.027 g/100 mL.

> The present paper demonstrates that considerably high levels of alcohol, even up to over 2% (200 mg/100 mL) may be found in the urine although no alcohol is present in the blood. This is the case, in particular, in patients with brain injuries who have survived for some time after the accident. In these cases, the determination of the urine alcohol content may be of

great supplementary significance in the establishment or exclusion of the role of alcohol.

Reference Number: 70702

GRUSZECKI, A.C., A. ROBINSON, S. KLODA, AND R.M. BRISSIE. "High Urine Ethanol and Negative Blood and Vitreous Ethanol in a Diabetic Woman. A Case Report, Retrospective Case Survey, and Review of the Literature." *American Journal of Forensic Medicine and Pathology*, 26: 96–98, 2005 (10 references)

Abstract: A nineteen-year-old woman with a history of poorly controlled juvenile diabetes was admitted to hospital with a severe diabetic ketoacidosis. She died soon after admission. Antemortem blood glucose concentration was 553 mg/dL and the urine was positive for ketones (> 80 mg/dL) and glucose (> 1,000 mg/dL). The postmortem blood and vitreous humor acetone concentrations were 0.004 g/100 mL and 0.006 g/100 mL respectively. No alcohol was detected in the postmortem blood or vitreous humor, but the UAC was 0.320 g/100 mL.

This case demonstrates a potential difficulty in toxicologic analysis and interpretation using urine only. The presence of a high level of ethanol detected in urine could potentially be misleading. Our case was accurately interpreted because blood and vitreous fluids were also screened for ethanol. This case of a noncompliant juvenile-diabetic woman illustrates a rare finding of glucose fermentation to form ethanol in urine by *C. glabrata* in vivo.

Reference Number: 70703

CULLEN, S.A. AND R.W. MAYES. "Alcohol Discovered in the Urine After Death: Ante-mortem Ingestion or Post-Mortem Artefact?" *Medicine, Science and the Law,* 45: 196–200, 2005 (1 table, 1 figure, 10 references)

Abstract: The postmortem BACs and UACs were determined in forty-four bodies recovered from the sea in which there was no evidence of antemortem alcohol consumption. The time immersed in the sea varied from 1 to 72 days. A positive UAC (range 0.005 to 0.059 g/100 mL) occurred after at least 19 days of immersion. The postmortem BACs ranged up to 0.103 g/100 mL after at least 19 days of immersion. The correlation coefficient for the time the body was immersed and the alcohol concentrations were 0.83 for BAC and 0.65 for UAC. Blood and urine samples are more frequently available after a length of time in the water than for a similar time on dry land. It is not indicated how the alcohol analyses were conducted and if *n*-propanol was detected in these cases.

> If alcohol is discovered in the urine of a fatality, where the body has been recovered more than three days after death, and if the urine alcohol level is less than the blood alcohol, post mortem artefacts should be suspected.

Reference Number: 70704

HELANDER, A., O. BECK, AND A.W. JONES. "Distinguishing Ingested Ethanol from Microbial Formation by Analysis of Urinary 5-Hydroxytryptophol and 5-Hydroxyindoleacetic Acid." *Journal of Forensic Sciences*, 40: 95–98, 1995 (4 figures, 19 references)

Abstract: Ethanol metabolism alters the 5HTOL/5HIAA ratio. This ratio increases and does not return to normal in the urine until several hours after ethanol is no longer detectable. This study used urine samples spiked with glucose and *Candida albicans* and postmortem samples. The spiked urine samples were stored at 20°C for 7 days and the highest UAC produced was 0.788 g/100 mL, however the 5HTOL/ 5HIAA ratio was unaltered.

> In conclusion, the present results show that determination of the 5HTOL/5HIAA ratio in urine provides a useful method to distinguish between ethanol that might have been produced postmortem or generated in vitro from the ethanol excreted as a result of drinking.

Reference Number: 70705

WIGMORE, J.G. "An Unusual Postmortem Urine—Blood Alcohol Ratio: Beware of Urine Dilution from Catheter Use." *Canadian Society of Forensic Science Journal*, 39: 25–27, 2006 (16 references)

Abstract: A man in his twenties was stabbed multiple times outside a tavern after a day of heavy drinking. He received emergency medical treatment at hospital but died soon after. The femoral BAC was 0.280 g/100 mL and the UAC was 0.060 g/100 mL. It was determined that the urine was diluted by fluid from a Foley catheter used at the hospital.

> The abnormally low UAC/BAC ratio in this stabbing victim, which was inconsistent with the reported drinking history, was probably due to the

dilution of the urine sample by the irrigation fluid used to flush the Foley catheter. Urinary catheter use in trauma victims may cause abnormal urine/blood alcohol concentration ratios.

Reference Number: 70706

ANTONIDES, H. AND L. MARINETTI. "Ethanol Production in a Postmortem Urine Sample." *Journal of Analytical Toxicology*, 35: 516–518, 2011 (3 tables, 1 figure, 7 references)

Abstract: A sixty-six-year-old woman with a history of obesity, diabetes, chronic renal failure, and prescription drug abuse died in hospital. The hospital and postmortem blood had an acetone concentration of 0.005 g/100 mL. No isopropanol or ethanol were detected in the blood. The postmortem urine acetone and ethanol concentrations were 0.080 g/100 mL and 0.100 g/100 mL respectively. The blood was preserved with NaF but not the urine. The postmortem UAC increased to a maximum of 0.280 g/100 mL after storage for 41 days at 2°C–8°C. The urine acetone concentration increased to a maximum concentration of 0.092 g/100 mL. The vitreous humor glucose concentration was 217 mg/100 mL. The cause of death was ruled to be due to complications of diabetes, atherosclerotic cardiovascular disease, hepatic stenosis, and bacteremia (*S. aureus*).

Because of the decedent's history of diabetes and cause of death, the ethanol and acetone results are attributed to the presence of microorganisms and substrates in the urine specimen. The inconsistent results demonstrate the importance of proper storage of the specimen and second matrix confirmation of an analyte.

Reference Number: 70707

HILMI, M., P.S. LAI, L.S. KHOO, N. SHAZUAWANI, S.F. SIEW, AND S. KUNASILAN. "Relationship of Blood and Urine Alcohol Levels in Postmortem Blood Samples and Prevalence of Alcohol Level Above Legal Limit in Hospital Kuala Lumpur." *SM Journal of Forensic Research and Criminology*, 1: 1012, 4pp, 2017 (8 tables, 11 references)

Abstract: The postmortem heart (subclavian) blood and urine alcohol concentrations were determined in 229 cases in 2016. Putrefied cases were excluded. A positive BAC and UAC were detected in forty-eight cases. The correlation between BAC and UAC was $r = 0.609$. The mean

BAC was 179.5 mg/100 mL compared to 247.4 mg/100 mL for the mean UAC. The average BAC:UAC ratio was 1.29:1.

> Ethanol may be formed as a putrefactive product by a wide range of microorganisms. Ethanol production can be prevented by refrigeration of the body within 4 h after death. Endogenous production does not generally exceed 0.3 g/L if samples are correctly stored. Right cardiac blood has higher ethanol content than in left cardiac blood because of postmortem hepatic glycogenolysis which produces glucose in the right heart via the hepatic veins and the inferior vena cava. The case history, degree of putrefaction and ethanol levels in different body fluids could be useful to determine whether detected ethanol has originated from the postmortem or antemortem.

Reference Number: 70708

ROHNER C., S. FRANCKENBERG, N. SCHWENDENER, A. OESTREICH, T. KRAEMER, M.J. THALI, G.M. HATCH, AND T.D. RUDER. "New Evidence for Old Lore—Urinary Bladder Distension on Post-Mortem Computed Tomography is Related to Intoxication." *Forensic Science International*, 225: 48–52, 2013 (1 table, 5 figures, 17 references)

Abstract: The bladder urine volume, determined physically at autopsy by the pathologist, was compared with the urine volume calculated by computed tomography (CT) in 259 autopsy cases. Autopsy and toxicology reports in these cases were evaluated to determine if there was any correlation between urine volume at autopsy and alcohol/drug intoxication of the deceased. The mean difference between measured urine volume and CT computed urine volume was only 0.8 mL and the correlation was good ($r = 0.92$). The mean volume of urine increased with alcohol/drug intoxication, and the mean urine volume was greater in cases in which a fatal alcohol/drug intoxication occurred (as seen in the following table). The study found that if there was a urinary bladder volume cutoff of 182 mL, there was a 40% sensitivity and 87% specificity of detecting alcohol/drug intoxication. If a higher cutoff urine volume of 330 mL was used, the sensitivity of detecting drug/alcohol intoxication decreased to 25% but specificity increased to 97%.

Table. Case Type and Mean Bladder Urine Volume

Case Type	Mean Urine Volume (mL)
Not intoxicated	92
Intoxicated	215
Non-fatal intoxication	161
Fatal intoxication	255
Opiate/methadone positive	222
Cocaine positive	321

Source: Adapted from Rohner et al (2013).

> We have found that CT provides a reliable method to quantify urinary bladder volume. In our population, there was a statistically significant correlation between urinary bladder distension on the post-mortem CT and cases of intoxication. This means that the occurrence of urinary bladder distension as single finding on post-mortem imaging should raise suspicion of intoxication and result in subsequent toxicological analysis.

7.08 OTHER TISSUES/FLUIDS

> "Arterial or venous femoral and cardiac blood, urine, vitreous humor, gastric content and organs (namely the liver and lungs and always after evisceration) are the most important samples to be collected. Several other alternative specimens (e.g., blood clots, blood from thoracic or abdominal cavities, cerebrospinal fluid, brain, spleen, bile, bone, synovial fluid, bone marrow, maggots, skeletal muscle) can occasionally be collected in particular circumstances."
>
> —Dinis-Oliveria et al, "Guidelines for Collection of Biological Samples for Clinical and Forensic Toxicological Analysis" (2016)

Numerous types of postmortem specimens can be collected to assist in the determination of the BAC of the victim at the time of death, including brain (70801, 70802), skeletal muscle (70804, 70805), putrefactive blisters (70806), bone marrow (70807, 70808, 70816), liver (70809), synovial (knee) fluid (70810, 70812, 70815), bile (70813), and testicle (70814). The possibility of an increase in the postmortem tissue alcohol concentration should be assessed (70814).

If the stomach alcohol concentration is > 0.8% and the brain:blood ratio is < 0.8, the deceased died in the absorption alcohol phase (70818).

The mean femoral blood alcohol ratios of pleural effusions, lung fluid, CSF, bile, urine, and VH are listed in a table (70818).

Reference Number: 70801

BUDD, R.D. "Post Mortem Brain Alcohol Levels." *Journal of Chromatography*, 259: 353–355, 1983 (2 tables, 3 references)

Abstract: A study was conducted of fifty-one coroner's case where brain and blood alcohol concentrations were measured. Five grams of brain tissue were homogenized into 5 mL of 10% sodium tungstate, and 5 mL of *t*-butanol internal standard was added. The sample was centrifuged and 3 μL of aliquot was injected directly into a GC fitted with a porapak Q column.

The mean brain:blood ratio was 1.24 SD 1.01. Eighty-two percent of the values ranged from 0.08–1.50. The correlation between brain and blood alcohol concentrations was $r = 0.9$. Brain tissue may be used to determine BAC since ethanol rapidly equilibrates between blood and brain.

> In conclusion, brain ethanol concentrations can be rapidly and accurately determined by gas chromatography and can be used to determine a blood ethanol concentration range.

Reference Number: 70802

MOORE, K.A., G.W. KUNSMAN, B.S. LEVINE, M.M. HERMAN, J. CERVENAK J., AND T.M. HYDE. "A Comparison of Ethanol Concentrations in the Occipital Lobe and Cerebellum." *Forensic Science International*, 86: 127–134, 1997 (2 tables, 21 references)

Abstract: A study of the alcohol concentration of blood, occipital lobe, and cerebellum was conducted in eighteen postmortem cases. The alcohol concentrations were determined by headspace GC and the BACs ranged between 0.011 and 0.260 g/100 mL. The average occipital alcohol concentration/BAC ratio was 0.7 when the BAC > 0.040 g/100 mL.

> We concluded, that as long as samples which consist primarily of gray matter are used for analysis, brain ethanol concentration can be used judiciously to give a rough approximation of blood ethanol levels.

Reference Number: 70803

DE MARTINIS, B.S., C.M.C. DE PAULA, A. BRAGA, H.T. MOREIRA, AND C.G.S. MARTIN. "Alcohol Distribution in Different Postmortem Body Fluids." *Human Experimental Toxicology,* 25: 83–97, 2006 (3 tables, 2 figures, 14 references)

Abstract: The heart, subclavian and femoral blood, urine, and vitreous humor alcohol concentrations were determined in twenty-one victims of natural and violent death in Brazil during 2003. The alcohol concentrations were determined by headspace GC. The average time from death to sampling was 6 hours (range 3 to 8 hours). The heart BACs ranged from 0.013 to 0.363 g/100 mL. There were no statistically significant differences between the alcohol concentrations among the various sampling sites. In general, there was a slight alcohol concentration increase from heart blood < subclavian blood < vitreous humor < femoral blood < urine. The femoral BAC/ VHAC ratio ranged from 0.71 to 2.40.

> Our results are consistent with most of the studies performed in relatively cold climate locations that evaluated the postmortem alcohol distribution in different sampling sites and that suggest vitreous humor as an alternative sample for postmortem alcohol investigation. However, further studies considering a larger number of cases and longer time of death are necessary to ensure that such specimens can be used as an alternative to blood.

Reference Number: 70804

GARRIOTT, J.C. "Skeletal Muscle as an Alternative Specimen for Alcohol and Drug Analysis." *Journal of Forensic Sciences,* 36: 60–69, 1991 (7 tables, 13 references)

Abstract: Postmortem blood, vitreous humor, and skeletal muscle alcohol and drug concentrations were determined in a random group of medical examiner cases. Alcohol concentration was determined by direct GC injection.

> When the blood concentration was greater than 0.10 g/dL, the muscle to blood ratio was 1.0 or less (average 0.94), and when the blood concentration was less than 0.10 g/dL, the ratio was greater than 1.00 (average 1.48). The author proposes that this ratio is dependent upon the time course of absorption and distribution, as has been observed for vitreous humor but with a more rapid equilibrium.

Reference Number: 70805

TRELA, F. AND M. BOGUSZ. "Usefulness of Ethanol Determination in Perilymph and Skeletal Muscle in the Case of Advanced Putrefaction of the Body." *Blutalkohol*, 17: 198–206, 1980 (3 tables, 3 figures, 24 references)

Abstract: The main substrates of endogenous ethanol formation are glucose, lactate, and pyruvate. Inner ear fluid is valuable as a material for ethanol determination as it is protected from decomposition and the glucose levels are low (34–79 mg/dL). Between 300 and 350 uL of perilymph may be obtained by splitting off the pyramid of the temporal bone. Thirty-seven deceased, all in an advanced stage of putrefaction (e.g., greenish skin, swelling of face) were examined. Muscle tissue was steam distilled and analyzed by ADH. Perilymph was analyzed by ADH. The mean blood/perilymph alcohol ratio was 1:1.32, and the mean blood/muscle ratio was 1:1.78.

The analysis of perilymph and muscle appeared useful for interpretation of data obtained from blood analysis and was particularly valuable in cases when blood sampling was impossible due to putrefactive decomposition.

Reference Number: 70806

GRELLNER, W. AND R. IFFLAND. "Assessment of Postmortem Blood Alcohol Concentrations by Ethanol Levels Measured in Fluids from Putrefactive Blisters." *Forensic Science International*, 90: 57–63, 1997 (3 tables, 2 figures, 19 references)

Abstract: A study was conducted of forty-five putrefied bodies (twenty-nine male, sixteen female victims) with postmortem intervals between 3 to 23 days. The degree of putrefaction was assessed as slight (n = 4), moderate (n = 14), and marked (n = 20). Fluids from putrefactive blisters (PBF) as well as femoral vein blood or femoral muscle tissue were collected. Alcohol concentrations were determined by headspace GC, and the water content of the blood, PBF, or tissue was determined. Relevant concentrations of putrefactive alcohols (1,2-propanol, 1-butanol) occurred only in cases of advanced decomposition. The correlation between PBF and blood/muscle alcohol concentrations was $r = 0.725$. The tendency for higher PBF alcohol concentrations occurred only in cases of advance putrefaction. In one case the PBF alcohol concentration was 0.216 g/100 mL and the BAC was 0.026 g/100 mL.

> Due to the variability observed in this study, ethanol values measured in fluids from putrefactive blusters cannot be used for an exact calculation of the postmortem BAC with certainty required in criminal law. Nevertheless, with a high degree of probability, ethanol values in PBF > 0.15% point to corresponding blood values, at least where advance putrefaction is excluded.

Reference Number: 70807

ISOKOSKI, M., A. ALHA, AND K. LAIHO. "Bone Marrow Alcohol Content in Cadavers." *Journal of Forensic Medicine*, 15: 9–11, 1968 (1 table, 5 references)

Abstract: Blood and bone marrow alcohol concentration were determined in six cases by the Widmark and ADH methods. In fresh cadavers the bone marrow content was 12 to 44% of the BAC. When the BAC = 0, the bone marrow alcohol concentration was also zero. In the bone marrow of a femur stored for 1 year with an initial BAC = 0, the alcohol concentration was 0.015 to 0.047 g/100 mL.

> It is possible to conclude from the alcohol content of bone marrow specimen taken soon after death whether alcohol played a role. The extent of this role cannot, however, be estimated If the bone marrow sample is from a body dead for a long time, it is impossible to determine the role of alcohol.

Reference Number: 70808

MAEDA, H., B-L. ZHU, T. ISHIKAWA, S. ORITANI, T. MICHIUE, D-R. LI, D. ZHAO, AND M. OGAWA. "Evaluation of Post-Mortem Ethanol Concentrations in Pericardial Fluid and Bone Marrow Aspirate." *Forensic Science International*, 161: 141–143, 2006 (2 figures, 13 references)

Abstract: Blood samples from the left and right heart and iliac vein as well as pericardial fluid and bone marrow aspirate were collected in 140 postmortem cases. The alcohol concentrations were determined by GC/MS. The right heart BAC was > 0.010 g/100 mL in forty-four cases. In all cases, the pericardial alcohol concentrations were approximately equal to the peripheral and heart BACs (r > 0.9) and on average were 0.010 to 0.030 g/100 mL higher. A high stomach alcohol concentration and aspiration of alcohol vomit mildly affected the pericardial levels. Bone marrow aspirates were obtained in only twenty cases. The right heart BAC/bone marrow aspirate alcohol ratios were 0.74 to 1.39 (mean 1.03).

In conclusion, the study showed that pericardial fluid and bone marrow aspirate can be used as alternative materials when adequate blood specimens are not available and may be particularly useful for analysis of volatile substances.

Reference Number: 70809

JENKINS, A.J., B.S. LEVINE, AND F. SMIALEK. "Distribution of Ethanol in Postmortem Liver." *Journal of Forensic Sciences*, 40: 611–613, 1995 (1 table, 2 figures, 11 references)

Abstract: A study was conducted of the relationship between heart blood and liver alcohol concentrations in 103 postmortem cases. Alcohol concentrations were determined by headspace GC. The BACs ranged between 0.010 and 0.540 g/100 mL and the liver alcohol concentrations between 0 and 0.410 g/100 mL. In seventy-one cases in which the BAC > 0.040 g/100 mL, the average liver/heart blood alcohol ratio was 0.56 (range 0–1.40). In six cases of acute ethanol poisoning the average liver/heart blood alcohol ratio was 0.65 (range 0.47–0.85). Assuming blood has a water content of 78.6% and the liver 73.2%, the theoretical ratio should be 0.797.

Liver is a specimen usually readily available at autopsy. In cases of trauma or when blood samples are contaminated, it may be the only specimen available for toxicological analysis. This underscores the importance of conducting postmortem studies of drug (including ethanol) disposition in this organ.

Reference Number: 70810

OHSHIMA, T., T. KONDO, Y. SATO, AND T. TAKAYASU. "Postmortem Alcohol Analysis of the Synovial Fluid and Its Availability in Medico-Legal Practices." *Forensic Science International*, 90: 131–138, 1997 (4 tables, 2 figures, 10 references)

Abstract: A study was conducted of the synovial fluid (from the knee joint), blood, and urine alcohol concentrations in twelve postmortem cases. The alcohol concentrations were determined by Py-GC. The BAC/synovial alcohol concentration (SAC) ratio was 0.76:1 (range 0.60–0.94), and the UAC/SAC ratio was 1.03:1 (range 0.90–1.21). The correlation coefficients were 0.97 and 0.99 respectively. The amount of synovial fluid in each knee joint ranges from 0.5 to 3.0 mL.

In comparison with vitreous humor, the collection of SF does not generate cosmetic problems. Thus, the author proposes that alcohol analysis using SF provides useful information in autopsy cases in which suitable blood and/or urine specimens for alcohol analysis cannot be obtained.

Reference Number: 70811

WINEK, C.L., J. BAUER, W.W. WAHBA, AND W.D. COLLOM. "Blood Versus Synovial Fluid Ethanol Concentrations in Humans." *Journal of Analytical Toxicology*, 17: 233–235, 1993 (2 tables, 1 figure, 10 references)

Abstract: A comparison of the BAC and the synovial fluid ethanol concentration was conducted in twenty-eight postmortem cases. The alcohol analysis was by direct injection GC. Synovial fluid was collected by a 10 mL syringe inserted into the medial side of the knee just under the patella. The average postmortem blood/synovial fluid ethanol concentration ratio was 0.99 (range 0.4–1.72). The average percentage of water in the synovial fluid was 95% (range 89%–98%).

Factors that may affect blood-synovial fluid ratio and cause such a wide range variation may include the time elapsed between dosing and death, time elapsed between death, and collection of sample and time to achieve equilibrium between BEC blood and synovial fluid ethanol levels. Other factors include age and water content of synovial fluid.

Reference Number: 70812

WINEK, C.L., D. HENRY, AND L. KIRKPATRICK. "The Influence of Physical Properties and Lipid Content of Bile on the Human Blood/Bile Ethanol Ratio." *Forensic Science International*, 22: 171–178, 1983 (2 tables, 1 figure, 4 references)

Abstract: A study was conducted of 189 postmortem cases where blood and bile were collected. The blood/bile ethanol ratio was 1.03, SD 0.29, and the range of ratios was between 0.32 and 2.91. When the bile alcohol concentration is > 0.175 g/100 mL, the BAC is generally > 0.150 g/100 mL.

The wide range observed makes it undesirable to use observed bile ethanol concentrations to predict a specific blood concentrations. However, under certain conditions, bile ethanol levels may be used to estimate blood concentrations within a range of values.

Reference Number: 70813

PIETTE, M., L. DECOMINCK, J. TIMPERMAN, F. THOMAS, AND W. MAJELYNE "Correlation between Postmortem Ethanol Levels in the Blood and Testicle." *Zeitschrift fur Rechtsmedizin*, 88: 39–48, 1982 (5 tables, 1 figure, 42 references)

Abstract: A study was conducted of 633 postmortem cases in which blood and testicle alcohol concentrations were determined since 1957 in Belgium. Alcohol concentrations were determined in 0.5 mL of blood or 0.5 g of tissue by direct injection GC. The correlation between BAC and TAC was $r = 0.92$ and had a mean ratio of 1.05:1 and a median ratio of 0.96:1. The water content of the testicle remains more stable than the blood, and the testicle is completely isolated from the outside world by a protective covering, the albuginea.

> If it has been impossible to collect blood because of its absence consecutively to decomposition, the testicle value will still make it possible to assess approximately the alcholemia.

Reference Number: 70814

LEWIS, R.J., R.D. JOHNSON, M.K. ANGIER, AND N.T. VU. "Ethanol Formation in Unadulterated Postmortem Tissues." *Forensic Science International*, 146: 17–24, 2004 (3 tables, 3 figures, 31 references)

Abstract: Postmortem tissues (muscle or kidney) from nine trauma victims of fatal airplane crashes were homogenized in water with or without the addition of 1% NaF. The samples were then stored at 4°C or 25°C for 24 to 96 hours. Alcohol concentrations were determined by headspace GC using *t*-butanol as an internal standard. For samples preserved with 1% NaF there were no significant increases in alcohol concentration whether the samples were stored at 4°C or 25°C. In samples without NaF, the initial tissue alcohol concentrations increased from 0.001–0.028 g/100g to between 0.025 to 0.090 g/100g when stored at 25°C for 48 hours to between 0.028 to 0.080 g/100g when stored at 4°C for 96 hours.

It is clear from these experiments that all nine unadulterated specimens from actual aviation accident victims contained microbes capable of ethanol production. We have demonstrated that even at 4°C, significant amounts of postmortem ethanol can form in the absence of a preservative. Additionally, we have demonstrated that the addition of sodium fluoride to postmortem tissue specimens during the homogenization process prevents the formation of ethanol at storage temperature of 4° and 25°C. Therefore, we believe that sodium fluoride should be added as a precaution to all postmortem specimens.

Reference Number: 70815

BUYUK, Y., M. EKE, A.S. CAGDIR, AND H.K. KARAASLAN. "Post-Mortem Alcohol Analysis in Synovial Fluid: An Alternative Method for Estimation of Blood Alcohol Level in Medico-Legal Autopsies." *Toxicology Mechanisms and Methods*, 19: 375–378, 2009 (4 tables, 1 figure, 8 references)

Abstract: Heart blood and synovial (knee) fluid samples were collected at fifty autopsies and the alcohol concentrations were determined by headspace GC. A positive BAC was found in fourteen cases and ranged from 0.057 to 0.455 g/100 mL. The mean BAC/SAC ratio was 0.90 and the correlation coefficient was 0.984. One case involved a blood methanol concentration of 0.417 g/100 mL and a corresponding SMC of 0.448 g/100 mL (BMC/SMC ratio of 0.93).

As a conclusion, this current study shows the applicability of synovial fluid alcohol concentration for estimation of blood alcohol concentration within a range. When compared to the other specimens such as vitreous humor, bone marrow, bile and muscle, it is easier to obtain the synovial fluid and this procedure does not lead to cosmetic problems in autopsy cases. For these reasons we propose that synovial fluid can be used in alcohol analysis of autopsy cases in which the appropriate sampling of blood is not possible.

Reference Number: 70816

ISKIERKA, M., M. ZAWADZKI, P. SZPOR, AND T. JUREK. "Comparison of Post-Mortem Ethanol Level in Blood and Bone Marrow." *Journal of Forensic and Legal Medicine*, 61: 65–68, 2019 (1 table, 1 figure, 22 references)

Abstract: Postmortem femoral and bone marrow (ilium) alcohol concentrations were determined by headspace GC in 100 autopsies in Poland between 2015 and 2017. A positive blood and bone marrow alcohol concentration was found in fifty-six cases. The mean BAC was 0.68 mg/g and the mean bone marrow alcohol concentration was 0.59 mg/g. In victims who were greater than sixty years of age, the bone marrow alcohol concentration was slightly greater than the femoral BAC. The correlation between blood and bone marrow alcohol concentrations was $r = 0.98$.

To sum up, despite many unresolved issues related to bone marrow pharmacokinetics, this material can be used to evaluate the presence of ethyl alcohol in the body when routine biological materials are not available. The correlation coefficients of blood versus bone marrow indicate strong relationships between the biological materials under discussion, which demonstrates the usefulness of bone marrow examination in forensic and medical toxicology.

Reference Number: 70817

BRICK, J. "Time of Death Relative to Alcohol Use: Application of Brain:Blood Ratios and Gastric Ethanol." *Journal of Addiction Medicine and Therapeutic Science*, 2: 19–22, 2016 (2 tables, 13 references)

Abstract: The blood, brain, and stomach alcohol correlations were determined in twenty-three fatal accident cases in New Jersey. The brain:blood ratio ranged from 0.563 to 1.234 (average 0.87). A stomach concentration > 0.8% alcohol and brain:blood ratio < 0.8 indicates that alcohol was still being absorbed in ten of the cases.

In forensic examination, peripheral blood such as from the femoral artery is the preferred matrix for post-mortem alcohol analysis. Central sites, including heart and chest blood also seem acceptable under normal conditions, when postmortem redistribution is unlikely and samples are not obtained from a blind-stick. There are many conditions in which postmortem alcohol samples may be limited to fluids or tissues other than blood. There are also conditions wherein the blood sample may be compromised resulting in an unusually high alcohol concentration relative to other tissue. For example, if death was the result of major thoracic impact subsequent to an automobile collision, extensive hemorrhaging or lacerations (e.g., of the stomach or intestinal wall) may result. High gastrointestinal alcohol concentrations may then contaminate blood obtained from the chest cavity or unknown location near the heart, such as a sample obtained by a blind puncture. However, the brain or vitreous humor alcohol concentration would be relatively less affected in such a case.

Reference Number: 70818

THELANDER, G., F.C. KUGELBERG, AND A.W. JONES. "High Correlation Between Ethanol Concentrations in Postmortem Femoral Blood and in Alternative Biological Specimens but Large Uncertainty When the Linear Regression Model Was Used for Prediction in Individual Cases." *Journal of Analytical Toxicology*, 44: 415–421, 2020 (3 tables, 1 figure, 39 references)

Abstract: The postmortem alcohol concentration was determined of femoral blood, VH, urine, bile CSF, lung fluid, and pleural effusions in duplicate by headspace GC using two different fused silica capillary columns and *n*-propanol and *t*-butanol as internal standards.

Table. Median Femoral BAC Ratio and *r* for Various Postmortem Tissues

Specimen	Median Ratio (compared to Femoral BAC)	Regression Coefficient (*r*)
Pleural Effusions	1.04	0.849
Lung Fluid	0.85	1.029
CSF	1.19	0.858
Bile	1.00	0.902
Urine	1.32	0.783
VH	1.19	0.796

Source: Adapted from Thelander et al (2020).

In conclusion, this study showed that femoral BAC and the concentrations of ethanol in alternative biological specimens were highly correlated. The mean femoral BAC could be predicted from the linear regression model with a good precision, but there was considerable uncertainty of the estimated value in any individual new case. The principal reason for analyzing ethanol in alternative biological specimens in PM toxicology is to give supporting evidence and strengthen the conclusion that the deceased had consumed an alcoholic beverage before death.

7.09 BIOMARKERS

"The results indicate that EtG analysis can be performed on mummy hair samples even several hundred years after deaths to identify evidence for significant alcohol consumption during life."

—Musshof et al, "Ethyl Glucuronide Findings in Hair Samples from Mummies of the Capuchin Catacombs of Palmero" (2013)

The use of biomarkers of alcohol consumption in various postmortem samples to assess antemortem alcohol consumption has been determined. EtG has been tested in postmortem blood, urine, vitreous humor, and other tissues (70901–70905, 70911) and has been found to decrease in concentration with putrefaction (70903, 70904). Other biomarkers such as EtS (70905), CDT (70906, 70907, 70912), FAEE (70908), and PEth (70910) have been studied as well.

In cases where the central blood/peripheral blood EtG ratio was < 3, drinking occurred 3 to 8 hours prior to death (70913).

Dental EtG concentrations can also determine alcohol use (70914). Hair EtG concentrations have been detected in thirty-eight mummies dating from 1599 in the Capuchin Catacombs in Palermo to determine alcohol use (70915).

Reference Number: 70901

HOISETH, G., R. KARINEN, A.S. CHRISTOPHERSON, L. OLSEN, P.T. NORMANN, AND J. MORLAND. "A Study of Ethyl Glucuronide in Post Mortem Blood as a Marker of Ante Mortem Ingestion of Alcohol." *Forensic Science International*, 165: 41–45, 2007 (1 table, 1 figure, 32 references)

Abstract: Postmortem ethyl glucuronide and alcohol concentrations were determined in 146 victims in Norway between 2000 and 2004. In the ninety-three cases in which antemortem ingestion of alcohol was assured, EtG was detected even when the postmortem BAC was low. In fifty-three cases (mainly children ages two to seven years) no postmortem alcohol or EtG were detected. Eleven cases had suspected postmortem putrefaction and *n*-propanol was detected in eight of the cases. In the putrefied cases, no EtG was detected.

Table. Median Blood EtG Concentration Detected in Various Postmortem Cases

Postmortem Cases	Median Blood EtG Concentration (mg/L)
Antemortem alcohol ingestion—high BAC	4.80
Antemortem alcohol ingestion—intermediate BAC	3.60
Antemortem alcohol ingestion—low BAC	0.77
No antemortem alcohol consumption—no putrefaction	< LOQ
No antemortem alcohol consumption—putrefaction	< LOQ

Source: Adapted from Hoiseth et al (2007)

In conclusion, this study indicates that EtG in blood may be used as a marker of ante-mortem alcohol ingestion in cases where post-mortem production of ethanol is questioned. Some factors, especially the stability of EtG during putrefaction remain to be further studied.

Reference Number: 70902

KETEN, A., A.R. TURNER, AND A. BALSEVEN-ODABAST. "Measuring of Ethyl Glucuronide in Vitreous Humor with Liquid Chromatography-Mass Spectrometry." *Forensic Science International*, 193: 101–105, 2009 (2 tables, 2 figures, 27 references)

Abstract: Blood, urine, and vitreous humor were collected from 110 post-mortem cases. Alcohol concentrations were determined by HS-GC and EtG by LC-MS. BACs ranged from 0.033 to 0.358 g/100 mL. The two deceased persons with the highest vitreous humor EtG concentrations (1.23 mg/L and 1.26 mg/L) were alcohol addicts.

It can be concluded that VH can be used in postmortem EtG analyses to reveal alcohol intake. It is easier to collect VH than blood and urine in postmortem investigations. There was a significant relation between VH EtG levels and urine EtG levels. Therefore, it can be suggested that blood and VH specimens can be used together for EtG analyses in cases in which urine specimens cannot be obtained.

Reference Number: 70903

HOISETH, G., R. KARINEN, L. JOHNSEN P.T. NORMANN, A.S. CHRISTOPHERSON, AND J. MORLAND. "Disappearance of Ethyl Glucuronide During Heavy

Putrefaction." *Forensic Science International*, 176: 147–151, 2008 (2 tables, 2 figures, 22 references)

Abstract: Blood samples with and without preservatives and stored at room temperature or 30°C to 40°C were spiked with ethanol, EtG, or already had an endogenous EtG concentration detected. In the samples stored at 30° to 40°C, the EtG concentration decreased to zero within 21 days. The samples are stable at room temperature with fluoride preservative.

In conclusion, analysis of EtG in blood is a helpful tool to determine in vivo ingestion of ethanol in post-mortem cases. This study showed that it has a high specificity but a lower sensitivity in post-mortem cases. Therefore, a positive result probably verifies the ingestion of ethanol, while a negative result, especially in heavy putrefied cases, must be interpreted with caution. Analysis of an additional medium or also of EtS would be valuable in these cases.

Reference Number: 70904

SCHLOEGL, H., S. DRESEN, K. SPACZYNSKI, M. STOERTZEL, F.M. WURST, AND W. WEINMANN. "Stability of Ethyl Glucuronide in Urine, Post-Mortem Tissue and Blood Samples." *International Journal of Legal Medicine*, 120: 83–88, 2006 (4 tables, 4 figures, 21 references)

Abstract: The stability of ethyl glucuronide (EtG) was determined in urine samples from nine volunteers and in postmortem blood, liver, and skeletal muscle from nine deceased. EtG analysis was conducted by LC-MS/MS. Eight of the volunteers had consumed alcohol. The EtG concentration of urine stored for 5 weeks at 4°C changed from –12% to +43% (mean, +9.2%) and changed from –30% to +83% (mean 23%) after storage at 22°C. No EtG was detected in the urine of the non-drinker even after the same storage conditions. In postmortem samples there was a decrease in EtG with time.

A post-mortem formation of EtG was not found in these in vitro experiments, which would support the hypothesis that EtG concentrations in body liquids or tissue like liver and skeletal muscle prove an alcohol consumption of the victim prior to death.

Reference Number: 70905

POLITI, L., L. MORINI, F. MARI, A. GROPPI, AND E. BERTOL. "Ethyl Glucuronide and Ethyl Sulfate in Autopsy Samples 27 Years After Death." *International Journal of Legal Medicine*, 122: 507–509, 2008 (1 table, 9 references)

Abstract: The EtG and EtS concentrations were determined by LC-MS in liver, kidney, a blood clot, and a hair strand of a fifty-year-old alcoholic whose corpse was exhumed 27 years later. The EtG concentrations were 141, 249, and 219 ng/g in liver, kidney, and blood clot respectively. EtG and EtS concentrations were not able to be determined in the hair strand.

> For the first time, at least to our knowledge, EtS was identified in postmortem samples. Moreover, EtG was identified in the liver, kidney, blood clot and hair 27 years after death of a known alcoholic.

Reference Number: 70906

MALCOLM, R., R.F. ANTON, S.E. CONRADI, AND S. SUTHERLAND. "Carbohydrate-Deficient Transferrin and Alcohol Use in Medical Examiner Cases." *Alcohol*, 17: 7–11, 1999 (1 table, 1 figure, 25 references)

Abstract: Postmortem hemolyzed blood samples were collected from nineteen male and six female victims of mainly trauma, 2 to 37 hours after death. Alcohol abuse by the victims was determined by microscopic examination of the liver and coroner's reports/records. Serum carbohydrate-deficient transferrin (CDT) concentrations and alcohol concentrations were determined. The CDT concentration for hemolyzed samples were on average 40% lower than the non-hemolyzed samples. Sixteen of the victims were determined to have alcohol abuse by pathology reports. Fifteen of these seventeen victims had positive CDT levels. There were three cases in which the alcohol was negative and no liver pathology, but the CDT concentrations were above threshold.

> At present our data suggest that if CDT levels are used to detect antemortem alcohol abuse in postmortem samples that a positive test should raise the index of suspicion, but that confirmatory history should be obtained from knowledgeable reporters.

Reference Number: 70907

OSUNA, E., M.D. PEREZ-CARCELES, M. MORENO, A. BEDATE, J. CONEJERO, J.M. ABENZA, P. MARTINEZ, AND A. LUNA. "Vitreous Humor Carbohydrate-Deficient Transferrin Concentrations in the Postmortem Diagnosis of Alcoholism." *Forensic Science International*, 108: 205–213, 2000 (2 tables, 2 figures, 32 references)

Abstract: The postmortem vitreous humor CDT, ALT, GCT, and AST concentrations were determined in thirty-eight alcoholic and twenty-eight non-alcoholic males (ages twenty-two to eighty-seven years). The range of vitreous humor CDT among alcoholics ranged from 4.7 to 24.5 U/L (mean 9.8) and was 3.4 to 13.9 U/L (mean 7.0) among non-alcoholics.

> In conclusion, the present results suggest that levels of CDT in vitreous humor are useful in cases where the postmortem diagnosis of alcoholism is made difficult by the non-specificity of the data available. The study must be considered as preliminary since, in conjunction with future studies it will help on the selection of markers which might be of use in the postmortem diagnosis of alcoholism.

Reference Number: 70908

REFAAI, M.A., P.N. NGUYEN, T.S. STEFFENSEN, R.J. EVANS, J.E. CLUETTE-BROWN, AND M. LAPOSTA. "Liver and Adipose Tissue Fatty Acid Ethyl Esters Obtained at Autopsy Are Postmortem Markers for Premortem Ethanol Intake." *Clinical Chemistry*, 48: 77–83, 2002 (1 table, 7 figures, 22 references)

Abstract: Postmortem BACs, liver, and adipose tissue fatty acid ethyl esters (FAEE) concentrations were determined in fifteen deceased with a positive BAC, seven chronic alcoholics with a zero BAC, and nine social drinkers with a zero BAC. Alcohol and fatty acids esterify to form FAEEs. Liver and adipose FAEEs were determined as in some victims no postmortem blood was available. Liver samples were selected as it tends to remain intact for a longer period of time postmortem whereas the pancreas degrades rapidly. The postmortem BACs ranged from 0.016 to 0.232 g/100 mL. The correlation between BAC and liver FAEE was 0.751 and with adipose tissue was 0.721. The mean total FAEE concentration in liver samples were 14,521, 5,315, and 5,485 pmol/g for the alcoholics with a positive BAC, alcoholics with a 0 BAC, and social drinkers with a 0 BAC respectively. The mean total FAEE in adipose tissue was 2,723, 2,993, and 649 pmol/g for these groups respectively.

> In conclusion, we describe two new indices that can be used as postmortem markers for premortem ethanol intake, either in cases in which there is no blood available to determine the ethanol concentration or when there is a desire to confirm the blood ethanol concentration.

Reference Number: 70909

APPENZELLER, B.M.R., M. SCHMAN, M. YEGLES, AND R. WENNIG. "Ethyl Glucuronide Concentration in Hair is not Influenced by Pigmentation." *Alcohol and Alcoholism,* 42: 326–327, 2007 (1 figure, 16 references)

Abstract: The effect of hair pigmentation on EtG concentration was determined in twenty-one postmortem cases of varying BACs in which the relative part of the white hair shaft ranged from 28 to 84%. The percentage of grizzled persons (white, grey, or dark streaked with grey hair) diagnosed as alcoholics ranged from 18 to 50%.

> We demonstrated here that unlike many other substances, the EtG determination in hair has not to take into account the hair colour for the correct interpretation of hair testing results.

Reference Number: 70910

BECK, O., M. MELLRING, C. LOWBEER, S. SEFERAJ, AND A. HELANDER. "Measurement of the Alcohol Biomarker Phosphatidylethanol (PEth) in Dried Blood Spots and Venous Blood—Importance of Inhibition of Post-Sampling Formation from Ethanol." *Analytical and Bioanalytical Chemistry,* 413: 5601–5606, 2021 (3 figures, 42 references)

Abstract: Phosphatidylethanol (PEth) is a specific alcohol biomarker used as a measure of alcohol consumption in medicolegal and clinical studies and in cases where the driver is banned from consuming alcohol or the person is on parole. PEth was measured in spiked dried blood samples, finger-prick microsamples, and venous blood samples stored in EDTA collection tubes at 4°C. The venous blood sample was spiked with 0.200 g/100 mL alcohol before analysis. There is a large interindividual scatter in PEth response and half-life after alcohol withdrawal.

The results of the present study confirmed previous observations that PEth can be formed in whole blood samples after collection, if they contain ethanol. This represents a major drawback when PEth is used as an alcohol biomarker, because it has clinical and forensic applications and a positive test result can have serious consequences. The results further confirmed that sampling and storing blood on standard filter paper (DBS) seemingly eliminated this risk, whereas post-sampling formation of PEth from ethanol occurred with all three commercial devices for volumetric dried blood microsampling. It is therefore recommended to use an inhibitor of PLD, for example $NaVO_3$, whether venous blood is collected in a vacutainer tube or finger-pricked capillary blood using devices for microsampling; otherwise, a PEth value can be questioned and disputed.

Reference Number: 70911

NEUMANN, J., T. KELLER, F. MONTICELLI, O. BECK, AND M. BOTTCHER. "Ethyl Glucuronide and Ethanol Concentrations in Femoral Blood, Urine, and Vitreous Humor from 117 Autopsy Cases." *Forensic Science International*, 318: 7pp, 2021 (4 tables, 3 figures, 25 references)

Abstract: Vitreous humor, femoral blood, and urine samples were collected from 117 autopsy cases and analyzed for alcohol by headspace GC and EtG by LC/MS/MS. The main purpose of determining EtG concentrations is to determine if the postmortem production of alcohol occurred. This can also be detected by the alcohol analysis of VH, urine, or other specimens. Alcohol was detected in all three matrices in thirty-nine cases and EtG was present in sixty-two cases. In twenty-three cases of discrepant results between specimens, the highest femoral blood alcohol concentration was 0.011 g/100 mL. The mean VH/FB alcohol ratio was 1.30. The mean VH/urine alcohol concentration was 0.89. The urine/FB alcohol ratio was greater than 1.25 in thirty-three of the forty cases indicating the subject was in the elimination phase.

In conclusion, this study confirms the value of using VH as a specimen in forensic investigations regarding recent exposure to ethanol. EtG can be used not only for investigating post-mortal ethanol formation but potentially also for estimating the level of recent alcohol drinking.

Reference Number: 70912

RAINO, J., S. AHOLA, P. KANGASTUPA, J. KULTTI, H. TUOMI, P.J. KARHUNEN, A. HELANDER, AND O. NIEMELA. "Comparison of Ethyl Glucuronide and Carbohydrate-Deficient Transferring in Different Body Fluids for Post-Mortem Identification of Alcohol Use." *Alcohol and Alcoholism*, 49: 55–59, 2014 (2 tables, 38 references)

Abstract: Postmortem EtG and CDT concentrations were measured in vitreous humor, urine, serum, and cerebrospinal fluid from forty-eight male and twelve female deceased individuals. Medical and police records showed that thirty-eight cases had a positive history of excessive alcohol consumption. A positive BAC (mean 0.122 g/100 mL) was detected in twenty-one of the thirty-eight cases (68%). The highest sensitivity for detecting excessive alcohol consumption was obtained with urine and VH EtG analysis (92%). A positive BAC had a 68% sensitivity.

> Taken together, the present findings support the use of EtG measurements for detecting ante-mortem alcohol consumption in cause-of-death investigations. Vitreous humor and urine appear to be the most suitable specimens for such analyses. However, since urine samples are more likely to show analytical problems, vitreous humor could be recommended as the primary specimen for forensic purposes.

Reference Number: 70913

SANTUNIONE, A.L., P. VERRI, F. MARCHESI, C. RUSTICHELLI, F. PALAZZOLI, D. VANDELLI, M. LICATA, AND E. SILINGARDI. "The Role of Ethyl Glucuronide in Supporting Medico-Legal Investigations: Analysis of This Biomarker in Different Postmortem Specimens from 21 Selected Autopsy Cases." *Journal of Forensic and Legal Medicine*, 53: 25–30, 2018 (3 tables, 24 references)

Abstract: Since EtG takes longer to leave the body than alcohol, it is a more sensitive indicator of recent drinking than BAC. Postmortem urine, central blood, and liver EtG concentrations were determined in twenty-one cases by LC/MS/MS between 2012 and 2015. Urine, central, and femoral BACs were determined by headspace GC. The postmortem interval until autopsy ranged between 1 and 6.5 days. The femoral BAC ranged between 0.023 and 0.350 g/100 mL. The CB/PB EtG ratio was always < 3 and the L/PB EtG ratio was always > 5 in cases where drinking occurred

2 to 3 hours prior to death. In cases when drinking occurred 3 to 8 hours prior to death, the CB/PB EtG ratio was < 3 and the L/PB EtG ratio was < 5.

These findings underline the possibility for a non-lipophilic and non-basic molecule such as EtG, to be subjected to factors altering postmortem concentrations. EtG could have a high affinity for some tissues from which it can be redistributed during the postmortem period. From this point of view, the liver is an obvious candidate: EtG could be progressively redistributed from the liver parenchyma via gradient diffusion into the central blood vessels without affecting the peripheral vessel. Moreover, the possibility of residual metabolic activity in the early hours after death must also be considered.

Reference Number: 70914

ZEREN, C., A. KETEN, S. CELIK, I. DAMLAR, N. DAGHOGLU, A. CELIKER, AND B. KARAASLAN. "Demonstration of Ethyl Glucuronide in Dental Tissue Samples by Liquid Chromatography/Electro-Spray Tandem Mass Spectrometry." *Journal of Forensic and Legal Medicine*, 20: 706–710, 2013 (2 tables, 4 figures, 28 references)

Abstract: Twenty-nine male patients of the Dental Clinic of Mustafa Kemal University (ages thirty-five to sixty years) were grouped into alcohol abstainers, non-hazardous alcohol users, and hazardous alcohol users. EtG concentrations were determined by LC-MS/MS in powderized extracted teeth. The EtG concentrations ranged from below the limit of detection to 23.39 pg/mg dental tissue. EtG was less than the LOD in all six abstainers and EtG concentration was related to self-reported alcohol use.

The findings of the present study demonstrate that dental tissue could be used for revealing of alcohol intake. There was a correlation between EtG levels detected in the dental tissue and alcohol intake behavior suggesting that dental tissue could be used for alcohol intake behavior in the longer periods. Especially in postmortem forensic medical investigations, obtaining dental tissue is always possible compared to blood, urine and intraocular (i.e., vitreous) fluid. Dental tissue can be used in the cases of deterioration of body integrity as in decomposed or severely injured cases.

Reference Number: 70915

MUSSHOF, F., C. BROCKMANN, B. MADEA, W. ROSENDAHL, AND D. PIOMBINO-MASCALI. "Ethyl Glucuronide Findings in Hair Samples from the Mummies of the Capuchin Catacombs of Palermo." *Forensic Science International*, 232: 213–217, 2013 (1 table, 3 figures, 30 references)

Abstract: EtG concentrations were determined by LC-MS in hair samples from thirty-eight mummies in the Capuchin Catacombs in Palermo. The first mummified bodies date from 1599 and the last in the early 1900s. All hair samples were analyzed in two separate segments. A (0–3 cm long) and B (the remainder of the hair). No positive EtG results were detected in the six child mummies but were detected in fourteen adults (44%) in both segments.

The results indicate that EtG analysis can be performed on mummy hair samples even several hundred years after deaths to identify evidence for significant alcohol consumption during life.

CHAPTER 8

Other Alcohols and Related Compounds

"In chemistry, the term alcohol refers to a whole class of organic compounds that include a hydroxyl group—consisting of an oxygen atom and hydrogen atom—bonded to a carbon atom. In common parlance, however, the word alcohol usually refers to a specific chemical with the formula C_2H_5OH, which chemists call ethanol."

— Sam Wong, "Alcohol," *New Scientist*

The other common alcohols, such as isopropyl (rubbing) or methyl (wood) alcohol, are covered briefly in this chapter. In addition, the major metabolite of ethyl alcohol (acetaldehyde), as well as acetone and ethylene glycol are included.

8.01 ACETALDEHYDE

"Acetaldehyde, whose metabolism is inhibited by disulfiram also possesses potentially neurotoxic effects that could have explained the delirium and laboratory abnormalities exhibited by our patient. Acetaldehyde is known to form bound adducts with many tissue constituents within the body."

— Park and Riggio, "Disulfarim-Ethanol Induced Delerium" (2001)

Acetaldehyde is readily formed in vitro from alcohol in whole blood samples (80101). Elevated blood acetaldehyde concentrations can also result from consumption of alcohol and the use of Antabuse or calcium carbimide as the conversion of acetaldehyde to acetic acid is inhibited (80102–80105). This is seen in the following chemical equation:

$$CH_3CH_2OH \rightarrow CH_3CHO \rightarrow CH_3COOH \rightarrow CO_2 + H_2O$$

(Thus, the toxic acetaldehyde substantially increases in the blood, causing the adverse effects.)

A fatal case of Antabuse-alcohol interaction has been reported (80106). The consumption of inky cap mushrooms also causes an Antabuse effect (80105). The different enzymatic metabolism of alcohol, in which higher blood acetaldehyde concentrations occur in many Asians, has been found to cause a reduction in alcohol consumption similar to the Antabuse effect (80107). Some of the symptoms caused by elevated blood acetaldehyde concentrations are:

- Pronounced flushing of face and body
- Increase in heart rate
- Palpitations
- Decrease in blood pressure
- Nausea
- Dizziness

The disulfiram-alcohol reaction may cause severe hypertension and bronchoconstriction (80109) and cause acute liver injury (80110).

The use of an ABHS in 339 AUD patients treated with Antabuse caused a disulfiram-alcohol reaction in 19 percent (80111).

Reference Number: 80101

ERIKSSON, C.J.P. "Problems and Pitfalls in Acetaldehyde Determination." *Alcoholism: Clinical and Experimental Research*, 4: 22–29, 1980 (4 tables, 65 references)

Abstract: Artefactual formation of acetaldehyde occurs in blood. It is recommended that blood be deproteinized rapidly (< 5 seconds) after collection to avoid false high results.

The determination of acetaldehyde in biologic samples is complicated by a variety of formation and disappearance reactions occurring in the present methods of acetaldehyde analyses. The acetaldehyde formation (ethanol oxidation) in deproteinized supernatant of tissue preparations is prevented by the use of thiourea. During deproteinization, however, it is not inhibited by thiourea, and this remains the main problem in blood acetaldehyde determinations.

Reference Number: 80102

JONES, A.W., S. SKAGERBERG, S. BORG, AND E. ANGGARD. "Time Course of Breath Acetaldehyde Concentrations During Intravenous Infusions of Ethanol in Healthy Men." *Drugs and Alcohol Dependence* 14: 113–119, 1984 (3 figures, 15 references)

Abstract: Acetaldehyde determination in biological samples is a simple procedure but artifacts can occur in whole blood. In this study four healthy men were given 10% ethanol IV. Giving ethanol IV eliminates any possible mouth alcohol effects. The breath/blood acetaldehyde ratio was 185:1. Breath contained approximately 2,000 times more ethanol than acetaldehyde.

The breath acetaldehyde time course followed the changes in blood and breath ethanol for widely varying infusion regimens. Breath analysis is a useful analytical technique because serial determinations can be made every 2–3 min and the results reflect, at least in part, the concentration of free acetaldehyde in the pulmonary arterial blood and therefore the central nervous system. This assumes that acetaldehyde freely passes the blood-brain barrier, although this may not be so.

Reference Number: 80103

JONES, A.W., J. NEIMAN, AND M. HILLBOM. "Elimination Kinetics of Ethanol and Acetaldehyde in Healthy Men During the Calcium Carbimide-Alcohol Flush Reaction." *Alcohol and Alcoholism*, Suppl 1: 213–217, 1987 (2 tables, 1 figure, 25 references)

Abstract: Ten healthy male subjects took either a placebo or a calcium carbimide tablet (50 mg) and 2 hours later consumed 0.25 g/kg ethanol. The ethanol was consumed within 5 minutes. Breath acetaldehyde and ethanol concentrations were measured by GC and converted into blood concentrations. The maximum BAC was 0.036 g/100 mL with placebo and 0.044 g/100 mL with calcium carbimide. The maximum acetaldehyde concentration was 3.4 µM with placebo and 190 µM with calcium carbimide. The mean rate of elimination was 0.014 g/100 mL/h with placebo and 0.014 g/100 mL/h with calcium carbimide.

The present results do not support a significant role of acetaldehyde in regulating the overall metabolism of ethanol. In spite of the 50-fold rise in blood acetaldehyde during the CC-alcohol flush reaction, the rate of ethanol metabolism was only diminished by about 5%. However, it should be emphasized that the most pronounced elevation of acetaldehyde levels persisted only for the first 60 min of ethanol oxidation, decreasing thereafter with a half-life of 23.5 min on average. The reason for this wearing-off phenomenon is not clear.

Reference Number: 80104

PEACHEY, J.E., D.H. ZILM, AND H. CAPPELL. "Burning Off the Antabuse: Fact or Fiction." *Lancet*, 943–944, 25 April 1981 (1 table, 8 references)

Abstract: Six subjects were assigned to each of the following drug treatments over 48 hours; 0.7 mg/kg calcium carbimide twice daily, placebo every morning and 3.5 mg/kg disulfiram, or placebo twice daily. Twelve hours after the last dose the subjects consumed 0.15 g/kg ethanol followed by 0.05 g/kg ethanol every hour for 3 hours. BACs and blood acetaldehyde concentrations were determined in blood, which was collected every 8 minutes. The mean BACs ranged between 0.002 and 0.008 g/100 mL. The blood acetaldehyde concentrations decreased from 0.75–1.02 µg/mL to 0.03–0.25 µg/mL after repeated ethanol dosing.

The diminished intensity of the reaction, as measured by heart rate and flushing reactions, with repeated alcohol exposure supports the claim that alcoholics make of being able to burn-off the effects of Antabuse.

Reference Number: 80105

MAYER, J.H., J.E. HERLOCHER, AND J. PARISAN. "Esophageal Rupture After Mushroom Alcohol Ingestion [Letter]." *Journal of American Medical Association*, 285: 1323, 1971 (10 references)

Abstract: A fifty-three-year-old man who consumed inky-cap mushrooms (*Coprinus atramentoridis*) combined with 355 mL of beer attended hospital as a result of several hours of flushing, nausea, and hematemesis. Sharp pain radiated into his back, and he appeared acutely ill. A 3 cm linear tear was found in his esophagus distal into the left pleural cavity. The tear was closed with a single layer of 3-0 chromic catgut.

Indeed, poisoning has rarely followed ingestion of the black-spotted inky cap. Combination with alcohol, however, often produces a severe clinical response not unlike disulfiram (Antabuse)-ethanol reaction.

Reference Number: 80106

AMADOR, E. AND A. GAZDAR. "Sudden Death During Disulfiram-Alcohol Reaction." *Journal of Studies on Alcohol*, 28: 649–654, 1967 (1 figure, 19 references)

Abstract: A forty-four-year-old man with AUD who had been taking 0.5 g of disulfiram daily for 8 weeks collapsed after having consumed a quart and a pint of whiskey over 2 days. He was admitted to hospital and 30 minutes later complained of crushing retrosternal pain that radiated down his left arm. Cardiac arrest occurred suddenly 2 hours later and he died. There was no significant gross or microscopic evidence of coronary disease. The postmortem BAC was 0.050 g/100 mL and the blood acetaldehyde was 0.004 g/100 mL.

> A disulfiram-alcohol reaction was the event immediately preceding death in the present case. It appears reasonable to attribute the patient's death to this reaction because of the close temporal association between the two events and high concentration of blood acetaldehyde, and the anatomical absence of other known causes of sudden death.

Reference Number: 80107

TU, G.C. AND Y. ISRAEL. "Alcohol Consumption by Orientals in North America Is Predicted Largely by a Single Gene." *Behavioral Genetics*, 25: 59–65, 1995 (2 tables, 4 figures, 45 references)

Abstract: One hundred and forty-nine North American born Oriental subjects were genotyped for $ALDH_2(+)$ (normal) or the $ALDH_2(-)$ gene (atypical). Self-rated alcohol consumption was also determined in Oriental and Caucasian subjects. The Caucasian subjects were not genotyped but were assumed to be virtually all $ALDH_2(+)$. The $ALDH_2(-)$ Oriental males consumed two-thirds less alcohol than $ALDH_2(+)$ Oriental males. Acculturation in North America affected the alcohol consumption only to a small degree.

> In conclusion data presented indicate that aldehyde dehydrogenase-2-allele exerts a profound influence on alcohol consumption behaviors in Oriental males in North America.

Reference Number: 80108

HOMANN, N., H. JOUSIMIES-SOMER, H., K. JOKELAINEN, R. HEINE, AND M. SALASPURO. "High Acetaldehyde Levels in Saliva After Ethanol Consumption Methodological Aspects and Pathogenetic Implications." *Carcinogenesis*, 18: 1739–1743, 1997 (4 figures, 45 references)

Abstract: Six male and four female subjects (ages eighteen to thirty years) consumed 0.5 g/kg ethanol within 20 minutes after a standard breakfast and before and after rinsing the mouth with chlorhexidine twice daily for 3 days. Frequent breath and saliva samples were collected. Saliva alcohol, acetaldehyde, and bacteria were determined. The mean peak saliva acetaldehyde concentration was 0.16 mg/dL, which decreased to 0.10 mg/dL after 3 days of chlorhexidine use. The mean peak saliva alcohol concentration was not affected by the treatment (0.083 g/100 mL).

> In the present study, we have demonstrated the production of considerable amounts of acetaldehyde in saliva during normal social drinking. As acetaldehyde is mutagenic and carcinogenic the long term effects of locally produced acetaldehyde may be one explanation for the enhanced cancer risk of the upper gastrointestinal tract among heavy drinkers.

Reference Number: 80109

ZAPATA, E. AND A. ORWIN. "Severe Hypertension and Bronchospasm During Disulfiram-Ethanol Test Reaction [Letter]." *British Medical Journal*, 305: 870, 1992 (3 references)

A forty-five-year-old male heavy drinker was administered 200 mg of disulfiram each day. On the sixth day he was challenged with three doses of 100 mL of beer each (4.1% v/v alcohol). His blood pressure rose to 270/150 mm Hg and he developed bronchoconstriction, which required two doses of salbutamol. The BP then dropped to the normal range.

> Severe hypertension and bronchoconstriction during a disulfiram-ethanol reaction are possible; the first is those with risk factors for hypertension other than alcohol, the second in patients with a history of bronchospasm.

Reference Number: 80110

RAMER, L., M. TIHY, N. GOOSSENS, J-L. FROSSARD, L. RUBBIA-BRANDT, AND L. SPAHR. "Disulfiram-Induced Acute Liver Injury." *Case Reports in Hepatology*, Article ID 8835647, 4pp, 2020 (2 figures, 18 references).

Abstract: A forty-seven-year-old woman with AUD was administered 200 mg of disulfiram after psychosocial support and benzodiazepines failed to control the alcohol abuse. She was then administered 200 mg of disulfiram every other day, but due to nausea, fatigue, and abdominal discomfort, the disulfarim was discontinued. Drug-induced liver injury had occurred due to disulfiram.

> Although disulfiram is not recognized nowadays as a major tool to treat alcohol dependence, it is described as a relatively safe treatment with no liver-related deaths reported in recent years. Nevertheless, the risk of hepatoxicity needs to be kept in mind and transaminases need to be regularly monitored when stating a treatment with disulfiram. The typical pattern of injury is hepatocellular and the fatality rate may reach 10 to 15% if jaundice complicates the course of such DILI. In case of any doubt about the diagnosis of disulfiram-induced liver injury, a liver biopsy may help to confirm the diagnosis by excluding alternative causes of acute injury including alcoholic liver disease.

Reference Number: 80111

GHOSH, A., T. MAHINTAMANI, Y.P.S. BLAHARA, F.E. ROUB, D. BASU, B.N. SUBODH, S.K. MATTOO, E. MISHRA, AND B. SHARMA. "Disulfiram Ethanol Reaction with Alcohol-Based Hand Sanitizer: An Exploratory Study." *Alcohol and Alcoholism*, 1–8, 2020 (1 table, 1 figure, 11 references)

Abstract: An assessment was conducted of 339 AUD patients treated with disulfiram during the COVID-19 pandemic between March and June 2020. Of this group, eighty-two (24%) were adherent to disulfiram during this time period and forty-two (12.3%) had used an ABHS and disulfiram concurrently. Eight of the forty-two patients (19%) showed signs of a disulfiram-ethanol reaction and four also showed signs of isopropanol toxicity (IT). One patient was sprayed with ABHS and developed a severe systemic reaction.

> Our study revealed that nearly one in five patients developed DER or IT with alcohol-based hand sanitizers. Forty percent of those developing

reaction required medical attention. Two out of three patients who had local reactions with the usual amount of sanitizer developed more severe and systematic reactions with a higher dose, suggested a possible dose-response relationship of alcohol hand rub and disulfiram-ethanol reaction. The application of a higher dose may lead to more extensive local absorption or systemic absorption through pulmonary vasculature during the evaporation of the sanitizer. Local absorption of clinical significant amounts of alcohol from intact skin is still a debatable entity, but it may occur from moist skin.

8.02 ACETONE

"The discovery of acetone is shrouded in the past of alchemical history. Probably it was produced for the first time in the Middle Ages. In any event, it was well known at the beginning of the seventeenth century and was used for various medical purposes. Although it could be produced by the dry distillation of several metallic acetates, the most frequently used source was lead acetate, and consequently acetone was known as spirit of Saturn."

— Gorman, "The History of Acetone, 1600–1850" (1962)

Acetone occurs in the body naturally from the enzymatic and nonenzymatic conversion of acetoacetic acid to acetone and carbon dioxide:

$$CH_3COCH_2COOH \rightarrow CH_3COCH_3 + CO_2$$

High endogenous acetone concentrations can occur as a result of diabetes and starvation (80201, 80202, 80204), as these conditions cause an excess of acetoacetic acid and hence acetone.

Acetone is also the major metabolite formed after ingestion of isopropyl alcohol. The reverse reaction can occur, and low concentrations of isopropanol can also be formed from acetone (80202–80204). Acetone can be used as an indicator of hypothermia deaths (80206, 80207) and is found in sexual assault victims (61713).

Acetone is readily available in common household products such as nail polish remover, glues, and paints, but acetone poisoning rarely occurs (80808–80809). The symptoms of acetone poisoning include:

- Headache
- Slurred speech
- Lethargy

- Lack of coordination
- Fruity, sweet odor on breath
- Low blood pressure
- Deep stupor
- Coma

The postmortem blood concentrations of beta-hydroxybutyrate and acetone are significantly higher in diabetes-related deaths than alcohol-related and other causes of deaths (80210).

Reference Number: 80201

SULWAY, M.J. AND J.M. MALINS. "Acetone in Diabetic Ketoacidosis." *Lancet*, ii: 736–740, 1970 (3 tables, 5 figures, 47 references)

Abstract: A study was conducted of twenty-seven hospitalized diabetic patients. Plasma acetone concentrations were determined by GC. The plasma acetone concentrations varied between 0.015 to 0.075 g/100 mL. Six patients were fully conscious and alert with plasma acetone concentrations up to 0.037 g/100 mL. Acetone is eliminated slowly.

> Failure to recognize the very high levels of plasma-acetone in diabetic ketoacidosis has been due to the inadequacy of older methods for the determination of the blood ketone bodies.

Reference Number: 80202

BAILEY, D.N. "Detection of Isopropanol in Acetonemic Patients Not Exposed to Isopropanol." *Clinical Toxicology*, 28: 459–466, 1990 (2 tables, 9 references)

Abstract: A study was conducted of five patients with Type 1 diabetes in which all patients were hypoglycemic and four were acidotic. Serum isopropanol and acetone concentrations were determined by GC. The serum isopropanol concentration ranged between 0.003 and 0.030 g/100 mL and the acetone concentration between 0.006–0.032 g/100 mL. An additional 131 serum samples from thirty-two ketotic patients were also analyzed. All had acetone but no isopropanol detected.

> Nevertheless, it is tempting to speculate that some cases of suspected IPA ingestion by chronic alcoholics may in fact be due to in vivo conversion of acetone to this compound.

Reference Number: 80203

JONES, A.E. AND R.L. SUMMERS. "Detection of Isopropyl Alcohol in a Patient with Diabetic Ketoacidosis." *Journal of Emergency Medicine*, 19: 165–168, 2000 (2 tables, 1 figure, 12 references)

Abstract: A twenty-nine-year-old male alcohol abuser with previously undiagnosed diabetes was admitted to hospital after 3 days of illness. The physical examination revealed a well-nourished person who was extremely agitated and made incomprehensible noises. Blood and urine samples were collected. The blood acetone concentration was 0.097 g/100 mL and the blood isopropyl alcohol concentration was 0.005 g/100 mL. The patient recovered upon treatment and is currently managed with an appropriate amount of insulin.

It is proposed that metabolism is shifted toward the production of IP from ACT from massive hypoglycemia coupled with a state of induced alcohol dehydrogenase as is with chronic alcohol ingestion.

Reference Number: 80204

JONES, A.W. AND L. ANDERSSON. "Biotransformation of Acetone to Isopropanol Observed in a Motorist Involved in a Sobriety Check." *Journal of Forensic Sciences,* 40: 686–687, 1995 (1 figure, 11 references)

Abstract: A fifty-four-year-old man was stopped at a police check and given a roadside screening breath test using an Alcolmeter S-L2. The result was greater than the BAC limit in Sweden (0.021 g/100 mL). Twenty minutes later, another breath test was conducted this time on an Intoxilyzer 5000, and an interfering substance was detected on the breath. A blood sample taken 10 minutes later and analyzed by headspace GC showed no ethanol, but 0.045 g/100 mL acetone and 0.017 g/100 mL isopropanol. The man had hyperglycemia and latent diabetes and had not eaten all day.

This case scenario gives a well-documented example of the metabolic conversion of acetone to isopropanol in an ostensibly healthy individual driving on the highway.

Reference Number: 80205

IRWIN, J. AND S.D. COHLE. "Sudden Death Due to Diabetic Ketoacidosis." *American Journal Forensic Medicine and Pathology*, 9: 119–121, 1988 (1 table, 7 references)

Abstract: Two case reports are presented of sudden deaths due to diabetic ketoacidosis in two obese women (thirty-five and thirty-eight years old) with no known history of diabetes. In the first case, the postmortem vitreous humor acetone concentration was 0.035 g/100 mL and the glucose was 744 mg/dL. In the second case the postmortem blood and vitreous humor acetone concentrations were both 0.022 g/100 mL and the glucose was 552 mg/dL.

Emotional or physical stress, fasting and dehydration (all characterized by high catecholamine levels) may be the factors that combined with insulin deficiency, initiate DKA.

Reference Number: 80206

TERESINSKI, G., G. BUSZEWICZ, AND R. MADRO. "Acetonaemia as an Initial Criterion of Evaluation of a Probable Cause of Sudden Death." *Legal Medicine*, 11: 18–24, 2009 (1 table, 5 figures, 43 references)

Abstract: Between 1996 and 2003 there were 17,138 routine headspace GC analyses for ethanol conducted at the Medical University in Lublin. Other volatiles such as acetone, methyl alcohol, *n*-propanol, and isopropanol concentrations were also evaluated. One hundred and two cases (0.6%) had a postmortem blood acetone concentration of greater than 0.045 g/100 mL. Elevated *n*-propanol concentrations were detected in putrefaction cases, but putrefaction did not cause acetonemia. High isopropanol concentrations were found only in putrefaction cases and in individuals intoxicated with alcohol.

Concentrations of ketone bodies (or even of acetone) in the autopsy material serve as a marker of biochemical disturbances which are not usually accompanied by detectable macro- and microscopic anatomical changes. They may be particularly relevant for the diagnostics of unexplained deaths of alcoholics and individuals consuming alcohol substitutes as well as in cases of death due to excessive hypothermia.

Reference Number: 80207

TERESINSKI, G., G. BUZEWICZ, AND R. MADRO. "Biochemical Background of Ethanol-Induced Cold Susceptibility." *Legal Medicine*, 7: 15–23, 2005 (1 table, 3 figures, 45 references)

Abstract: Blood acetone and alcohol concentrations were determined in sixty-six hypothermia victims and thirty victims who died of other causes in Poland between 1996 and 2002. The hypothermia victims were divided into those with a postmortem BAC < 0.105 g/100 mL and those with a BAC > 0.105 g/100 mL. The mean blood acetone concentration was 0.010 g/100 mL (range 0.0001 to 0.049 g/100 mL) in hypothermia victims with a BAC < 0.105 g/100 mL and was 0.0004 g/100 mL (range 0.00005 to 0.002 g/100 mL) in hypothermia victims with a BAC > 0.105 g/100 mL. The severity of ketosis was inversely proportional to BAC. Signs of prolonged cold exposure (i.e., frostbite, gastric hemorrhages) were less frequently observed in hypothermia victims with BACs > 0.105 g/100 mL.

> The analysis showed that in the cases in which death caused by overcooling was suspected, the inverse relation between ketonaemia and the severity of insobriety was observed. Moreover, signs of prolonged cold exposures were less frequent in unsober victims. These findings supported the hypothesis that the antiketonaemic effects of alcohol might be treated as one of the reasons of increased sensitivity of intoxicated individuals to cold (beside the direct effects of ethanol on increased heat loss—the dilation of the peripheral blood vessels, inhibition of shivering thermogenesis due to muscle relaxation, central nervous system depression and behavioral factors). The possibilities to detect acetone during ethanol determination by gas chromatography make hyperacetonaemia a very convenient initial criterion of past hyperthermia.

Reference Number: 80208

UMEH, C., R.C. GUPTA, R. GUPTA, H. PAUR, S. KAZOURRA, S. MAGUWUDZE, A. TORBELA, AND S. SAIGAL. "Acetone Ingestion Resulting in Cardiac Arrest and Death." *Cureus, Open Access Case Report*, 5pp, 2021 (1 table, 23 references)

Abstract: Acetone is a colorless volatile chemical with a distinct aromatic odor and taste. It is found naturally at low levels in the healthy body. It is also found in common household products such as nail polish remover, glues, detergents, and cleaners. A forty-one-year-old woman with COPD was found asystole by EMS after consuming two-thirds of a bottle of acetone. She was administered chest compressions and epinephrine, which restored her heartbeat. She was admitted to an ER, unconscious, with a blood pH of 7.24 and high serum osmolality, anion, and osmolar gaps. The next day the patient developed hyperglycemia (614 mg/dL) due to the acetone metabolism. Her GCS remained at 3 and her EEG showed no cortical activity. She was extubated on day 15 as per her family's wishes and died on day 19 after admission.

We presented a case that proved to be a fatal following ingestion of a large dose of acetone. Mortality secondary to acetone is very rare. Our patient presented with cardiopulmonary arrest, hypotension, tachycardia, hyperglycemia, AKI, thrombocytopenia, and elevated liver enzymes; she also had extensive esophageal and gastric erosion with associated upper gastrointestinal bleeding. Management of acetone poisoning involves mainly supportive case.

Reference Number: 80209

MOHAMMADZADEH, H., H. MOHAMMADI, M. ALI TAVAKOLI, AND S. SADEGHI. "Sudden Death Due to Acetone Toxicity." *Pharmaceutical and Biomedical Research*, 7: 217–220, 2021 (1 figure, 10 references)

Abstract: A twenty-five-year-old male nurse was found dead at the ER where he worked. He had no medical history such as diabetes and had smoked for 4 years previous. He had nausea and diarrhea on the day before his death. At autopsy, he had severe pulmonary congestion, diffuse necrosis of hepatocytes, infiltration of inflammatory cells in the liver, and brain vascular hyperemia. His postmortem acetone concentrations were 35 mg/dL in the VH, 28 mg/dL in the blood, and 77 mg/dL in the urine. No other drugs were detected.

This report highlighted rare sudden death due to solvents poisoning. Contrary to public opinion, acetone is a toxic and dangerous substance; thus, it is necessary to improve and implement public safeguards concerning acetone usage, as well as its handling and disposal.

Reference Number: 80210

MIDTLYNG, L., G. HOISETH, H. LUYTKIS, L. KRISTOFFERSON, I.L. NYGAARD, M.C. STRAND, M. ARNETAD, AND M. VEVELSTAD. "Relationship Between Betahydroxybutyrate (BHB) and Acetone Concentrations in Post-mortem Blood and Cause of Death." *Forensic Science International*, 32: 6pp, 2021 (1 table, 3 figures, 26 references)

Abstract: The postmortem BHB (by UHPLC-MS/Ms) ethanol, acetone, and isopropanol (by headspace GC) concentrations were determined in thirty-eight diabetic-related, thirty-five alcohol-related, and 303 other causes of death cases in Norway between 2012 and 2015. The median ages of the victims were forty-six, fifty-six, and sixty years respectively. Men comprised about 70% of each group. The median BHB concentration was significantly higher in diabetes deaths (671 mg/L) compared to 304 mg/L for alcohol-related deaths and 113 mg/L for all other deaths. The median blood acetone concentration was 26.7 mg/dL for the diabetic-related deaths compared to 0 mg/dL for the other two groups. Of the eighty-four deaths where acetone was detected, a pathological BHB blood concentration of greater than 250 mg/L was found in 80% of the cases. Isopropanol was detected in thirteen cases and always occurred with acetone. The BACs in the alcohol-related deaths were mostly low if not detected, indicating that alcoholic ketoacidosis is a frequent cause of death in this group.

This study shows that the postmortem blood concentrations of BHB and acetone were significantly higher in diabetes-related deaths, compared to alcohol-related and other causes of death. There was, however, a considerable overlap between the groups. Although the BHB and acetone concentrations were highly correlated, BHB was the most sensitive indicator of pathologically significant ketoacidosis.

8.03 METHYL ALCOHOL

"Methanol, which has long been used in mummification in ancient Egypt was obtained from the distillation of wood, which in Greek roots was called methylene or wood wine."

— Nekoukar et al, "Methanol Poisoning as a New World Challenge: A Review" (2021)

Methyl alcohol was originally made by the destructive distillation of wood, hence the common name: wood alcohol. Endogenous blood methyl alcohol concentrations are typically less than 0.001 g/100 mL (80301), but after chronic heavy drinking may increase to approximately 0.005 g/100 mL (80302, 80303). Methyl alcohol is converted by the enzymes that metabolize alcohol into more toxic metabolites, formaldehyde, and formic acid (formate):

$$CH_3OH \rightarrow HCHO \rightarrow HCOOH$$

Methyl alcohol poisoning can be treated by alcohol or fomepizole administration (80304–80306, 80311, 80312, 80315), which inhibit the enzymatic conversion of methanol to the toxic metabolites (formaldehyde and formic acid). Methyl alcohol generally is not well absorbed in adults either by the skin or inhalation (80307, 80308), unless large quantities are employed (80314, 80318), but can be absorbed by these routes in infants (80310).

ABHS that contain methanol rather than ethanol pose an additional health problem and have been banned by the CDC (80316–80317).

Some of the symptoms of acute methanol poisoning are:

- Headache
- Dizziness
- Blurring/loss of vision
- Acidosis
- Dilation of pupils
- Decrease in blood pressure
- Coma

Vitreous humor methanol, ethanol, and formate concentrations can be measured in vitreous humor, and blood or vitreous humor formate concentrations > 0.5 g/L are highly correlated with fatal methanol outcomes (80311–80312).

Chronic dermal and inhalational exposure to methanol in an electronics plant can lead to optic damage and long-term visual impairment (80319).

Co-ingestion of ethanol can prevent fatal methanol poisoning compared to methyl alcohol ingestion alone (80320–80321).

One teenager who announced that the ingestion of ethanol and methanol were similar and consumed 500 mL of 95% methanol on social media died approximately 18 hours later (80322).

A stepmother was convicted of first-degree murder of a twenty-one-month-old child by administering the child methanol in a sippy cup. His postmortem heart blood methanol and formate concentrations were 0.214 g/100 mL and 0.100 g/100 mL respectively (80323).

Reference Number: 80301

STRANGER, J., M. GRAW, K. BESSERER, AND H.T. HAFFNER. "Nutritive Influences on Endogenous Methanol Concentrations and Endogenous Methanol Formation." *Blutalkohol*, 36: 269–275, 1999 (2 tables, 1 figure, 15 references)

Abstract: Four male subjects (ages twenty to twenty-four years) were administered a 7% isotonic alcohol solution IV at a rate of 0.35 g/kg/h after fasting and after eating a low or high pectin diet. For the fasting conditions, the subjects were given 20–30 g of Glauber's salt and ample fluid to clear the intestines. BrACs were monitored by an Alcotest 7110 to maintain a BrAC of approximately 0.053 g/100 mL. Frequent blood samples were collected, and the serum methanol concentration was determined by headspace GC. The mean endogenous serum methanol concentrations were 0.00004 g/100 mL (fasting), 0.00007 g/100 mL (low pectin), and 0.00011 g/100 mL (high pectin). After administration of ethanol the serum methanol concentrations increased to 0.00022, 0.00024, and 0.00041 g/100 mL respectively. The highest serum methanol concentration detected in any subject was 0.00055 g/100 mL.

> On the whole, the results detected here seem to ascertain the tendency that endogenous methanol concentrations depend on the kind of food consumed. The difference, however, is not seen in the intraindividual methanol concentrations that rises from investigation to investigation but rather in the elevation of the mean values of the groups combined with a strongly increasing standard deviation.

Reference Number: 80302

TINTINALLI, J.E. "Serum Methanol in the Absence of Methanol Ingestion [Letter]." *Annals Emergency Medicine*, 26: 393, 1995 (5 references)

Abstract: A fifty-year-old male was admitted to hospital after a 3-day drinking binge. He consumed at least seven bottles of wine, rum, or whiskey a day. The initial serum ethanol and methanol concentrations were

0.275 g/100 mL and 0.005 g/100 mL respectively. The patient denied consuming methanol. Six hours later the serum methanol concentration was not detected.

> The cause of the detectable serum methanol in our patient is unknown but in the absence of confirmation of ingestion of methanol products and in association with a drinking binge of extreme magnitude it could well have been due to the metabolic process described above.

Reference Number: 80303

WARGOTZ, E.S. AND M. WERNER. "Asymptomatic Blood Methanol in Emergency Room Patients." *American Journal of Clinical Pathology*, 87: 773–775, 1987 (1 table, 16 references)

Abstract: Blood samples were collected from 687 patients attending a hospital in Washington, DC, between September and December 1985. The SACs and SMCs were determined by direct injection GC. The LOD for SMC was 0.0015 g/100 mL. The anion gap was determined as well. A positive SAC was found in 373 patients (54%) and ranged from 0.003 to 0.613 g/100 mL (mean 0.254 g/100 mL). A positive SMC was found in eighteen (4.8%) of the alcohol-positive patients and ranged from 0.0023 to 0.0040 g/100 mL. All eighteen patients had a history of chronic alcohol abuse.

> We found that about 1 in 20 ethanol positive emergency room patients also has blood methanol in the range of 2.3–4.0 mg/dL (0.72–1.25 mmol/L). At these concentrations methanol is believed to be nontoxic to humans. Therefore, it is not unexpected that no signs or symptoms of toxicity are observed.

Reference Number: 80304

LIU, J.J., M.R. DAYA, O. CARRASQUILLO, AND S.N. KALES. "Prognostic Factors in Patients with Methanol Poisoning." *Clinical Toxicology*, 36: 175–181, 1998 (2 tables, 1 figure, 21 references)

Abstract: A study was conducted of thirty-seven male and thirteen female patients (ages eighteen to seventy-four years) who were treated for methanol poisoning at two Toronto hospitals between 1982–1992. All fifty patients were treated with ethanol and sodium bicarbonate IV and hemodialysis. Eighteen patients died (36%) and thirty-two survived.

Of the thirty-two survivors, seven (22%) suffered visual sequelae. Ten patients had a positive BAC upon admission (0.046–0.276 g/100 mL) and all survived. The deceased patients had a higher mean blood methanol concentration (0.266 g/100 mL) than the survivors (0.131 g/100 mL). The most specific symptom associated with methanol poisoning was a visual complaint.

> In conclusion, severe acidosis with initial arterial pH < 7 and coma or seizure on presentation are associated with higher mortality in methanol poisoning. Our study appears to suggest that residual visual sequelae were seen in patients with prolonged metabolic acidosis.

Reference Number: 80305

KERNS II, W., C. TOMASZEWSKI, K. MCMARTIN, M. FORD, J. BRENT, AND THE META STUDY GROUP. "Formate Kinetics in Methanol Poisoning." *Clinical Toxicology*, 40: 137–143, 2002 (2 tables, 1 figure, 19 references)

Abstract: Serial blood samples were collected in six male and five female methanol-poisoned patients (ages eighteen to sixty-one years) and plasma methyl alcohol and formate concentrations were measured as well as pH. Formate kinetics was determined in six patients. All patients received hemodialysis, fomepizole, folate, and sodium bicarbonate. The mean initial plasma methanol concentration was 0.183 g/100 mL (range 0.023–0.612 g/100 mL). The mean initial formate concentration was 5 mg/dL (range 0.15–11 mg/dL). The endogenous $t_{1/2}$ for formate was 3.4 hours without dialysis and 2.5 hours with dialysis. The difference was not statistically significant. Hemodialysis is beneficial primarily for those drugs eliminated from the kidneys, especially when there is renal dysfunction. In lieu of formate analysis (not routinely available), low pH, low sodium bicarbonate, and elevated anion gap can be indications of formate accumulation in methanol-poisoned patients.

> Our data question the utility of hemodialysis for the case of a late-presenting, acidemic methanol-poisoned patient. In such a patient there is formate accumulation but insignificant amounts of circulating methanol remaining to be removed by hemodialysis. Treatment with folic acid and or bicarbonate may be more important than hemodialysis for formate elimination in such a case.

Reference Number: 80306

PALATNICK, W., L.W. REDMAN, D.S. SITAR, AND M. TENEBEIN. "Methanol Half-Life During Ethanol Administration: Implications for Management of Ethanol Poisoning." *Annals Emergency Medicine*, 26: 202–207, 1995 (1 table, 3 figures, 28 references)

Abstract: Three methyl alcohol poisoned patients (ages forty-eight, four, and twenty-three years) were treated with 0.6 g/kg alcohol IV and a maintenance infusion of 0.07 g/kg/h. Additional bolus doses of alcohol were also administered to maintain the BAC above 0.100 g/100 mL. No hemodialysis was conducted. The initial serum methanol concentrations were 0.135, 0.024, and 0.110 g/100 mL respectively. The serum methyl alcohol half-life was 31.0, 30.3, and 46.5 hours respectively. There was difficulty in maintaining a uniform SAC during therapy.

> The implication of ethanol monotherapy are considerable. By prolonging methanol excretion, it results in a longer ICU stay and longer duration of ethanol therapy. As an example, consider a hypothetical patient with a serum methanol concentration of 40 mg/dL (12.5 mmol/L) who has neither acidosis nor visual symptoms. With a median methanol half-life of 43.1 hours, the patient would require at least 2 days of vigilant care if treated with ethanol monotherapy; if hemodialysis were added only several hours of care would be needed. As we observed in our patients and others have noted in the literature, maintaining a therapeutic ethanol concentration can be difficult. As a result, serum ethanol concentration fluctuates placing the patient at risk for periods of subtherapeutic or toxic serum ethanol concentrations.

Reference Number: 80307

BATTERMAN, S.A. AND A. FRANTZBLAU. "Time-Resolved Cutaneous Absorption and Permeation Rates of Methanol in Human Volunteers." *International Archives Occupational Environmental Health*, 70: 341–351, 1997 (4 tables, 5 figures, 33 references)

Abstract: Five female (ages forty-one to sixty-three years) and seven male (ages twenty-two to fifty-four years) subjects immersed their left hand in 99.8% pure methanol up to the wrist for 2 to 16 minutes. Blood samples were collected frequently from the unexposed arm and the blood methanol concentration was determined by headspace GC.

After prolonged exposure, the hand became white and very dry. The baseline blood methanol concentration was between 0.00004 and 0.00047 g/100 mL. The maximum blood methanol concentrations were obtained approximately 1.9 hours after exposure. The maximum blood methanol concentration detected in one individual with the most severe prior skin damage to the hand was approximately 0.0016 g/100 mL.

Our data shows that absorption rates are 6 times higher for exposure to hands.

Reference Number: 80308

CHUWERS, P., J. OSTERLOH, T. KELLY, A. D'ALESSANDRO, P. QUINLAN, P., AND C. BECKER. "Neurobehavioral Effects of Low-Level Methanol Vapor Exposure in Healthy Human Volunteers." *Environmental Research*, 71: 141–150, 1995 (4 tables, 53 references)

Abstract: Eleven female and fifteen male subjects were exposed to 200 ppm methanol or water vapor (control) for 4 hours. Various psychomotor tests were conducted, and serum and urine methanol concentrations were determined by headspace GC. The mean peak serum methanol concentration was 0.00065 g/100 mL after 4 hours exposure. The control mean peak serum methanol concentration was 0.00015 g/100 mL.

The finding of this study demonstrates that the toxic metabolite of methanol, formate, does not increase as a result of 4 hours of 200 ppm exposure to methanol, and such exposure probably does not cause subtle neurotoxic effects.

Reference Number: 80309

AUFDERHEIDE, T.P., S.M. WHITE, W.J. BRADY, AND H. STUEVEN. "Inhalation and Percutaneous Methanol Toxicity in Two Firefighters." *Annals of Emergency Medicine*, 22: 1916–1918, 1993 (17 references)

Abstract: Two male volunteer firefighters were exposed to methanol vapor and liquid from two tanker cars in a train derailment. Both were treated at hospital for heat exhaustion and possible chemical exposure. The initial blood methanol concentrations 2 hours after exposure were 0.019 and 0.013 g/100 mL respectively. The patients were treated with ethanol and folic acid and were discharged 48 hours later with no adverse consequences.

This report further emphasizes guidelines recommending that HAZMAT first-responders access accident sites upwind at a safe distance from the scene.

Reference Number: 80310

KAHN, A. AND D. BLUM. "Methyl Alcohol Poisoning in an 8-Month Boy: An Unusual Route of Intoxication." *Journal of Pediatrics*, 94: 841–843, 1979 (8 references)

Abstract: An eight-month-old boy had warm compresses of methyl alcohol applied to his chest, which was also rubbed with olive oil. This was conducted as a home remedy for the child, except that methyl alcohol was used rather than the usual ethyl alcohol. The boy was admitted to hospital in a coma. The blood glucose concentration was 293 mg/100 mL and pH was 6.50. The blood methanol concentration was 0.040 g/100 mL. Although the boy received clinical treatment including administration of ethanol IV, he died.

In our patient, poisoning was presumably due to percutaneous absorption of toxin, although additional inhalation cannot be excluded.

Reference Number: 80311

ROY, M., B. BAILEY, D. CHALUT, P-E. SENECAL, AND P. GAUDREAULT. "What Are the Adverse Effects of Ethanol Used as an Antidote in the Treatment of Suspected Methanol Poisoning in Children?" *Journal of Toxicology and Clinical Toxicology* 41: 155–161, 2003 (3 tables, 2 figures, 24 references)

Abstract: Thirty-nine boys and twenty-one girls (ages six months to eighteen years) were administered ethanol either orally (thirty-nine cases) or IV (twenty-one cases) for the treatment of suspected methyl alcohol poisoning between 1980 and 2000. The patients received from 0.2 to 19.1 g/kg alcohol (mean 2.4 g/kg) over a period of 1.5 to 64 hours (median 16 hours). Twelve patients had no detectable SMCs. The SMCs ranged from 0.0 to 0.280 g/100 mL (mean 0.013 g/100 mL). The SACs varied widely and ranged from 0.0 to 0.230 g/100 mL. Most patients consumed methanol from windshield washer fluid (30%) or fondue fluid (22%). None of the sixty patients developed symptomatic hypoglycemia, however the majority of the patients (50 of 60) had dextrose administered IV. The only adverse effects of ethanol administration were 10% of the patients became more drowsy and 3% had hypotension. There was no morbidity or mortality in these patients.

> Thus, our results suggest that the incidence of adverse effects is at most low when ethanol is used as an antidote in children in a tertiary care hospital setting. Furthermore, our study also illustrated that children treated with ethanol for methanol poisoning usually have a good prognosis despite the wide variation in ethanol levels.

Reference Number: 80312

WU CHEN, N.B., E.R. DONOGHUE, AND M.I. SCHAFFER. "Methanol Intoxication: Distribution in Postmortem Tissues and Fluids Including Vitreous Humor." *Journal of Forensic Sciences*, 30: 213–216, 1985 (1 table, 1 figure, 11 references)

Abstract: A forty-four-year-old man was found unconscious and admitted to hospital. Upon admission the serum methanol concentration was 0.540 g/100 mL. Treatment included ethanol infusion and hemodialysis, but the patient died. At autopsy the blood methanol concentration was 0.142 g/100 mL. The average rate of methanol elimination was 0.011 g/100 mL/h. The concentration of methanol in the vitreous humor was 0.173 g/100 mL.

> The methanol blood to vitreous humor ratio was 0.82; this compares favorably with the ethanol blood to vitreous humor ratio of 0.89 that Coe reported.

Reference Number: 80313

JONES, G.R., P.P. SINGER, AND K. RITTENBACH. "The Relationship of Methanol and Formate Concentrations in Fatalities Where Methanol Is Detected." *Journal of Forensic Sciences*, 52: 1376–1382, 2007 (3 tables, 5 figures, 24 references)

Abstract: A study was conducted of 153 cases in which postmortem blood and VH methanol concentrations were detected in Alberta between 1986 and 2005. Methyl alcohol, ethanol, and formate concentrations were determined by headspace GC. Formate concentrations were determined by adding concentrated sulfuric acid. Diisopropyl ether was used as the internal standard. One hundred and seven deaths were attributed to methanol toxicity and the cases are listed. The correlation between blood and VH methanol concentrations was $r = 0.9859$, but the correlation for formate was $r = 0.2646$. Postmortem blood methyl alcohol concentrations in fatal cases ranged from 0.070 to 0.790 g/100 mL (mean 0.330 g/100 mL). Postmortem blood formate concentrations ranged from 0.053 to 0.140 g/100 mL (mean 0.086 g/100 mL). Eighty-eight percent of the methanol victims were male and most had a history of chronic alcohol abuse.

Formate concentrations in blood or vitreous humor > 0.5 g/L are highly correlated with fatal outcomes in methanol poisoning cases unlike methanol concentrations alone.

Reference Number: 80314

AVELLA, J., E. BRIGLIA, G. HARLEMAN, AND M. LEHRER. "Percutaneous Absorption and Distribution of Methanol in a Homicide." *Journal of Analytical Toxicology*, 29: 734–737, 2005 (2 tables, 18 references)

Abstract: A naked forty-six-year-old woman was found dead in the foyer of a house 11 feet below a balcony, laying in a pool of 95% methanol (SNAP Octane Booster). When the body was moved, a clear liquid (methanol) emanated from her mouth. It was determined that the husband had killed the women with blunt trauma and staged the body so that it would appear to be suicide. He stated before she jumped, she consumed methyl alcohol in a suicide attempt. The femoral blood contained 0.031 g/100 mL or methanol, pulmonary artery blood contained 0.111 g/100 mL, vitreous humor contained 0.196 g/100 mL, and brain contained 0.002 g/100 mL methanol. No methyl alcohol was detected in the stomach, small intestines, bile, or urine. It was estimated that approximately 22 mL of 95% methyl alcohol would be required to obtain the detected femoral blood methanol concentration. The body surface area was calculated, and it was estimated that 7 to 12 minutes would be required for dermal absorption of this amount of methyl alcohol.

These conditions were unusual and extremely favorable for the percutaneous absorption of methanol. The analysis of multiple tissues, especially femoral blood, brain, stomach contents and urine were instrumental in refuting the husband's claim that his wife consumed the methanol containing gasoline additive. The pathologist concluded that the cause of death was blunt impact trauma and methanol poisoning. The toxicological results and the findings of other investigators were subsequently used as part of a successful prosecution of homicide.

Reference Number: 80315

DALLY, A.M. "Fatal Methanol Intoxication—Two Exceptional Cases." *Toxichem Krimtech*, 82(1): 27, 2015 (5 figures, 10 references)

Abstract: Two cases of fatal methanol poisonings are discussed. A fifty-three-year-old woman was admitted to hospital as a result of dizziness, nausea, and impaired vision. Her admission plasma methanol concentration was 0.150 g/100 mL. No alcohol was detected. She was treated for methanol poisoning using ethyl alcohol therapy but lapsed into a coma and died of irreversible CNS lesions 1 month later. Hair EtG indicated ethanol abstinence. In the second case, a middle-aged man was found dead in a public toilet. A bottle found beside the body contained pure methanol. His postmortem methyl alcohol concentration was 0.370 g/100 mL. No positive BAC was detected. A postmortem blood diphenhydramine concentration of 0.45 mg/dL was determined. Hair EtG analysis did not show alcohol abuse.

In methanol poisonings, neither kind of hemodialysis (continuous vs. intermittent) nor choice of antidote (ethanol vs. fomepizole) seem to have an influence on the mortality. Severity of metabolic acidosis, state of consciousness, and serum ethanol on admission were the only significant parameters associated with mortality in the Czech mass poisoning event.

Reference Number: 80316

TSE, T.J., S.K. PURDY, J. SHEN, F.B. NELSO, R. MUSTAFA, D.J. WIENS, AND M.J.T. REANEY. "Toxicology of Alcohol-Based Hand Rubs Formulated with Technical-Grade Ethanol." *Toxicology Reports*, 8: 785–792, 2021 (2 tables, 1 figure, 8 references)

Abstract: The use of technical grade ethanol in alcohol-based hand rubs (ABHRs) was temporarily permitted in Canada and the United States in April 2020 due to the COVID-19 pandemic. Technical grade ethanol can contain contaminants not detected in pharmaceutical grade (USP) ethanol and can contain methanol, isopropanol, ethyl acetate, and benzene. There were nineteen recall incidences of ABHR in Canada and 165 in the United States between 2020 and 2021 due to the detection of methanol.

It is important for both doctors and the public to be aware that the interim ABHRs are higher in contaminants, even if they come from food sources (e.g., local distilleries). Although the elevated concentrations for most of the contaminants found may not elicit detrimental health effects, the combined effects for these contaminants have not been studied. Defatting of the skin can further human health risks for elevated dermal absorption of these contaminants. There is the potential for addictive adverse effects, or effects because of underlying health conditions. The main contaminants for health concern that may be present in ABHRs appear to be methanol due to risk of dermatitis and added exposure routes related to this, acetaldehyde due to teratogenicity, and benzene due to mutagenicity and carcinogenicity. Although most products are deemed safe-to-use in the interim, there have been cases where dangerous levels of contaminants have been reported.

Reference Number: 80317

YIP, L., D. BIXLER, D.E. BROOKS, ET AL. "Serious Adverse Health Events, Including Death, Associated with Ingesting Alcohol-Based Hand Sanitizers Containing Methanol—Arizona and New Mexico, May–June 2020." *Morbidity and Mortality Weekly Report*, 69: 1070–1073, 2020 (1 table, 10 references)

Abstract: The Centers for Disease Control recommends that alcohol-based hand sanitizers (ABHS) contain either 60% to 95% ethanol or > 70% isopropanol. Between 1 May to 30 June 2020, fifteen cases of methanol-containing ABHS poisonings occurred and were admitted to hospital. The mean age of the patients was forty-five years (range twenty-one to sixty-five years) and thirteen were male. The first blood methyl alcohol concentrations detected ranged from 0.021 to > 0.500 g/100 mL. All patients had metabolic acidosis and blood pH ranged from 6.70 to 7.25. All patients were treated with fomepizole and nine received hemodialysis. Four patients died (three had seizures at the time of admissions) and three were discharged with visual impairment.

Severe methanol poisoning resulting in permanent disability or death can occur after swallowing alcohol-based hand sanitizer containing methanol. The public should check their products against FDA Updates on Hand Sanitizers Consumers Should not Use website. If the product is on this list, its use should be discontinued immediately, and the product should be disposed of in hazardous waste containers; these products should not be flushed down a toilet or poured down a drain. All alcohol-based hand sanitizers should only be used to disinfect hands and should never be swallowed. Children using hand sanitizers should be supervised, and these products should be kept out of reach of children when not in use. Swallowing alcohol-based hand sanitizer products, including those that do not contain methanol, might also lead to serious illness and outcomes, including death. Consumers who have been exposed to alcohol-based hand sanitizers containing methanol should stop using them immediately and seek immediate medical attention if they experience any concerning symptoms.

Reference Number: 80318

MOJICA, C.V., E.A. PASOL, M.L. DIZON, W.A. KIAT JR., T.R.U. LIM, J.C. DOMINGUEZ, V.V. VLAENCIA, AND B.J.P TUANO. "Chronic Methanol Toxicity Through Topical and Inhalational Routes Presenting as Vision Loss and Restricted Diffusion of the Optic Nerves on MRI: A Case Report and Literature Review." *eNeurologicalSci*, 20: 4pp, 2020 (1 figure, 18 references)

Abstract: A fifty-seven-year-old woman was admitted to ICU with tachycardia, severe metabolic acidosis (pH 6.898), and a high anion gap of 20. She underwent emergency hemodialysis for the acidosis and developed vision loss. She reported using a clear odorless liquid on her entire body and scalp every day for 3 months. Although labeled as being ethanol, the liquid was 95.5% methyl alcohol.

We present an uncommon case of vision loss in the background of chronic exposure to methanol through dermal and inhalational routes. Methanol was isolated late in the course of this patient. As such, this case highlights the need for high index of suspicion for methanol in presence of vision loss and severe metabolic acidosis with high anion gap despite lacking history of toxic ingestion. This case adds to the increasing number of reports of methanol intoxication from vapor and skin contact. The symptoms and course of the patient were similar to those seen in toxic ingestion of methanol.

Reference Number: 80319

RYU, J., K.H. LIM, D-R. RYU, H.W. LEE, J.Y. YUN, S-W. KIM, J-H. KIM, K. JUNG-CHOI, AND H. KIM. "Two Cases of Methyl Alcohol Intoxication by Sub-Chronic Inhalation and Dermal Exposure During Aluminum, CNC Cutting in a Small-Sized Subcontracted Factory." *Annals of Occupational and Environmental Medicine*, 28: 65–72, 2016 (2 figures, 24 references)

Abstract: Two cases of methyl alcohol poisoning occurred in a small cell-phone parts manufacturing plant in Korea. Methanol was used as a solvent and was evaporated in the ill-ventilated plant. The patients (a twenty-eight-year-old woman and a twenty-seven-year-old man) were exposed to the methanol dermally as well and by their hands to the eyes and other parts of the body. The patients had visual disturbances and were treated in hospital by hemodialysis and sodium bicarbonate and ethanol IV. Their urine methyl alcohol concentration was 0.0008 g/100 mL. The ambient air methanol concentration at their workplace was 1,030.1–2,220.5 ppm, which exceeded the 200 ppm safety limit. They were diagnosed with optic neuropathy due to methyl alcohol poisoning and still have visual impairment.

Workers who were hired as dispatched employees in a small-sized subcontracted factory were exposed to high concentrations of methyl alcohol. The workplace had a poor ventilation system. In addition, workers did not wear proper personal protection equipment. Working environment measurements and annual checkups for workers were not performed. They were in a blind spot to occupational safety and health. More attention is needed to protect vulnerable workers' health.

Reference Number: 80320

YOSHIZAWA, T., Y. KAMIJO, Y. FUJITA, Y. SUZUKI, T. HANAZAWA, K. USUI, AND T. KISHINO. "Mild Manifestations of Methanol Poisoning Half a Day After Massive Ingestion of a Fuel Alcohol Product Contain 30% Ethanol and 70% Methanol: A Case Report." *Acute Medicine and Surgery*, 5: 28–291, 2018 (10 references)

Abstract: A thirty-seven-year-old man consumed a fuel alcohol product containing 70% methanol and 30% ethanol in a suicide attempt. He was admitted to hospital 12 hours later and presented with mild somnolence and acidosis. Upon admission, his serum methanol concentration was 0.224 g/100 mL and serum ethanol was 0.0005 g/100 mL. He was administered repeated doses of fomepizole and hemodialysis (twice). After the first hemodialysis, the serum methanol concentration dropped to 0.094 g/100 mL and then 0.037 g/100 mL after the second round of hemodialysis.

The presented case involved delayed treatment with fomepizole and HD by at least half a day after ingestion of a product containing 70% MeOH and 30% EtOH. The EtOH in the product may have effectively delayed MeOH metabolism. If the patient had arrived earlier after ingestion of the product, he might have been possibly treated only with HD but not fomepizole.

Reference Number: 80321

TIAN, M., H. HE, Y. LIU, R. LI, B. ZHU, AND Z. CAO. "Fatal Methanol Poisoning with Different Clinical and Autopsy Findings: Case Report and Literature Review." *Legal Medicine*, 54: 6pp, 2022 (3 tables, 3 figures, 40 references)

Abstract: Two men, forty-seven years old and thirty-three years old, shared a meal at a private restaurant and both drank about 250 mL of a liquid during the meal. The liquid was high purity methyl alcohol. The men eventually died on the third and fifth days after ingestion respectively. The first victim had typical signs of methanol poisoning but the second victim only had slight signs. The postmortem blood, urine, and stomach content methanol and ethanol concentrations were determined by head-space GC using *t*-butanol as an internal standard. Methanol metabolites were not determined.

Table. Concentration of Methanol and Ethanol in Postmortem Blood, Urine, and Stomach Contents and Immediate Cause of Death.

	Victim 1	Victim 2
Blood methanol (g/100 mL)	0.089	0.0008
Blood ethanol (g/100 mL)	0.009	0.0040
Urine methanol (g/100 mL)	0.137	0.0009
Urine ethanol (g/100 mL)	0.002	0.0170
Stomach contents methanol (g/100 mL)	0.117	0.0006
Stomach contents ethanol (g/100 mL)	0.508	0.0250
Immediate cause of death	Cerebral hernia secondary to cerebral edema	Cerebral hemorrhage

Source: Adapted from Tian et al (2022).

The present case report highlights the importance of individual differences in the manifestations of methanol poisoning. Individual genotypes may be among the many factors that influence methanol metabolism and the various clinical and postmortem manifestations of methanol toxicity. Methanol intoxication is a complex and multifactorial process that warrants thorough investigation and careful analysis. Therefore, a combination of multiple diagnosis methods, including autopsy, quantitative detection of methanol and formic acid may more accurately diagnose methanol poisoning and should be tailored by forensic pathologists on an individual basis.

Reference Number: 80322

WATERS, B., K. HARA, N. IKEMATSU, M. TAKAYAMA, A. MATSUSUE, M. KASHIWAGI, AND S-I. KUBO. "An Unusual Case of Suicide by Methanol Ingestion." *Forensic Science International*, 289: e9–e14, 2018 (2 tables, 5 figures, 18 references).

Abstract: A female student in her late teens purchased a 500 mL container of fuel alcohol (95% methanol, 5% ethanol) at a drugstore 2 days before her death. At 8:30 a.m. she documented on social media her ingestion of the fuel alcohol and stated that the drinking of methanol was similar to ethanol. At 11:30 p.m. she began groaning, then convulsing and foaming at the mouth. At 12:10 a.m. her parents called for an ambulance. She presented at hospital at 12:39 a.m. in a deep coma (GCS 3), vomiting with cyanosis. Despite medical treatment she died at 2:15 a.m. Her postmortem methyl alcohol concentration of peripheral blood, cardiac blood, and cerebrospinal fluid were 0.214, 0.224, and 0.253 g/100 mL respectively. The peripheral blood ethanol concentration was 0.002 g/100 mL. The postmortem peripheral and cardiac blood formate concentrations were 49 and 51 mg/dL respectively. All measurements were conducted by headspace GC.

Methanol ingestion is characterized by a prolonged latent period from ingestion to the onset of symptoms, up to 30 h in some cases. Hallmark symptoms of methanol exposure include nausea, vomiting, neurological deterioration, visual disturbance, coma and seizures. One unique aspect of this case was the use of social media and witness statements to map a timeline of the decedent's experience from ingestion of the fuel methanol until death. Evidence of the nauseating effects of methanol can be found in the deceased's posts on a popular social media site, where she commented on how the fuel methanol was not very different from drinking ethanol and mentioned that she was feeling nauseous and vomiting.

These symptoms occurred shortly after ingestion, supporting previous reports that the initial effects of methanol mimic those of ethanol, including nausea.

Reference Number: 80323

BENO, J.M., R. HARTMAN, C. WALLACE, D. NEMETH, AND S. LAPOINT. "Homicidal Methanol Poisoning in a Child." *Journal of Analytical Toxicology*, 35: 524–528, 2011 (2 tables, 15 references)

Abstract: A case of homicidal methyl alcohol poisoning of a twenty-one-month-old male child is presented. The baby was found dead in his crib. The postmortem heart blood, venous blood, urine, and vitreous humor methanol concentrations were 0.214, 0.231, 0.306, and 0.276 g/100 mL respectively. The postmortem heart blood and urine formic acid concentrations were 0.100 g/100 mL and 0.635 g/100 mL respectively. Methanol was detected in the baby's sippy cup. The stepmother, who had previously stated to witnesses that the child had "ruined her life," was convicted of first-degree manslaughter.

Based on the child's venous blood methanol concentration of 0.23% at the time of death and the clearance rate for methanol, which is reported to be 8 mg/dL/h, his blood methanol concentration around the time he was put to bed on the night he was poisoned is estimated to have been in excess of 0.45% (w/v). If methanol had significant CNS depressant activity, it is unlikely that the child would have awoken the next morning.

8.04 ISOPROPYL ALCOHOL

"Isopropyl alcohol (C_3H_8O) was the first commercial synthetic alcohol. First produced in 1920, a group of chemists at the Standard Oil Company in New Jersey discovered it whilst studying by-products of petroleum. IPA is now one of the most widely used solvents in the world."

— Bell-Young, "What Is Isopropyl Alcohol?" (2018)

The main metabolic route in the body after ingestion of isopropyl alcohol is the conversion of it into acetone (80402–80404, 80406):

$$CH_3CHOHCH_3 \rightarrow CH_3COCH_3$$

Under more extreme conditions, such as diabetic or alcoholic ketoacidosis, the reverse reaction may occur, and acetone may be converted into low concentrations of isopropyl alcohol (80401). As with the other alcohols, there is no significant absorption of isopropyl alcohol through the skin or by inhalation in adults (80407, 80408). High blood isopropyl alcohol concentrations can be obtained from hand sanitizers containing isopropyl alcohol but only if it is consumed orally (80405). One person became addicted to sucking on isopropanol swabs to relieve stress (80409).

The symptoms of isopropyl alcohol are more marked than alcohol intoxication and include:

- Persistent nausea
- Vomiting (of blood)
- Abdominal pain
- Depressed respiration
- Coma

The cardiac blood isopropanol and acetone concentrations in a case of pure isopropyl alcohol poisoning were 46.4 mg/100 mL and 159.0 mg/100 mL respectively (80410). As the postmortem blood alcohol concentration increased, the isopropanol concentration increased (80411).

Reference Number: 80401

DAVIS, P.L., L.A. DAL CORTIVO, AND J. MATURO. "Endogenous Isopropanol: Forensic and Biochemical Implications." *Journal of Analytical Toxicology*, 8: 209–212, 1984 (2 tables, 2 figures, 15 references)

Abstract: An in vitro study was conducted of acetone added to ADH and NADH incubated at 37°C at pH 7.3 and 8.8. Approximately 10 times more isopropanol was produced at pH 7.3 than 8.8. Eight postmortem (mainly diabetics or chronic alcoholics) cases are also presented showing production of isopropanol from acetone. The postmortem blood acetone concentrations ranged from 0.007 to 0.062 g/100 mL and the isopropanol concentrations ranged from 0.001 to 0.029 g/100 mL.

It is clear from both sets of data that the forensic investigator must cautiously evaluate isopropanol and acetone findings, lest an erroneous conclusion be made regarding cause and manner of death. Since misinterpretation may have far-reaching legal and social implications.

Reference Number: 80402

PAPPAS, A.A., B.H. ACKERMAN, K.M. OLSEN, AND E.H. TAYLOR. "Isopropanol Ingestion: A Report of Six Episodes with Isopropanol and Acetone Serum Concentration Time Data." *Clinical Toxicology*, 29: 11–21, 1991 (4 tables, 1 figure, 25 references)

Abstract: Case reports of five patients admitted to hospital for isopropanol poisoning are presented. Standard patient treatment included gastric lavage with 2 L of saline followed by administration of activated charcoal and magnesium citrate, and maintenance fluids were also given IV. Frequent serum samples were collected and analyzed for acetone and isopropanol. Peak isopropanol serum concentrations were from 0.016 to 0.220 g/100 mL and peak serum acetone concentrations were from 0.141 to 0.585 g/100 mL. Mean $t_{1/2}$ for isopropanol was 4.2 hours, and mean $t_{1/2}$ for acetone was 11.3 hours. The presence of ethanol appeared to increase the isopropanol $t_{1/2}$ by 2 times.

Profound prostration and narcosis was noted in three of the six ingestions, but none developed renal failure or died. Hypotension and respiratory arrest though were observed in three of the six cases indicating that careful attention must be paid to sudden and rapid changes in blood pressure and respiratory status.

Reference Number: 80403

DANIEL, D.R., B.H. MCANALLEY, AND J.C. GARRIOTT. "Isopropyl Alcohol Metabolism After Acute Intoxication in Humans." *Journal of Analytical Toxicology*, 5: 110–112, 1981 (1 figure, 19 references)

Abstract: A study was conducted of two patients admitted to hospital for isopropanol poisoning where multiple blood samples were taken over a period of time. The blood was analyzed for acetone and isopropanol by direct injection FID GC. The initial blood isopropanol concentrations were 0.170 and 0.100 g/100 mL. Isopropanol was eliminated from the blood according to first order kinetics. The half lives in these two cases were 155 and 187 minutes respectively. Acetone was eliminated at a much slower rate and was still at a high concentration after the blood isopropanol concentration reached zero.

This observation may provide an explanation for the generally assumed long-term toxic effects of isopropyl alcohol. Acetone causes central nervous system depression, drowsiness, weakness, nausea and headache, symptoms nearly identical to those reported for isopropyl alcohol. Thus, the long-term effects in some cases may be due to acetone, although assumed to be from persistent isopropyl alcohol.

Reference Number: 80404

GAUDET, M.P. AND G.L. FRASER. "Isopropanol Ingestion: Case Report with Pharmacokinetic Analysis." *American Journal of Emergency Medicine*, 7: 297–299, 1989 (1 figure, 11 references)

Abstract: A thirty-four-year-old female alcoholic was found unconscious after consuming rubbing alcohol (70% v/v isopropyl alcohol) left unattended in hospital. Frequent blood samples were collected over the next 43 hours and the ethanol, acetone, and isopropanol concentrations were determined by GC. The initial blood alcohol and isopropanol concentrations were 0.120 and 0.300 g/100 mL respectively. The $t_{½}$ of isopropanol was 7.3 hours. There was a 4-hour delay before any measurable blood acetone concentrations were detected.

We also emphasize the need to limit access to seemingly benign but potentially toxic substances within the confines of the hospital especially where alcoholic, suicidal or delirious patients are treated.

Reference Number: 80405

EMADI, A., AND L. COBERLY. "Intoxication of a Hospitalized Patient with an Isopropanol-Based Hand Sanitizer [Letter]." *New England Journal of Medicine*, 356: 530–531, 2007 (4 references)

Abstract: A forty-three-year-old male alcoholic was admitted to hospital with chest pains; he was hypotensive and delirious. His serum isopropanol concentration was 0.014 g/100 mL and serum acetone concentration was 0.269 g/100 mL.

When asked why he ingested the hand cleaner, he pointed to the label which read; Active ingredient, 63% v/v isopropyl alcohol. He explained that this percentage is higher than that in vodka.

Reference Number: 80406

JONES, A.W. "Driving Under the Influence of Isopropanol" [Letter]. *Clinical Toxicology,* 30: 153–155, 1992 (16 references)

Abstract: A man was arrested for impaired driving. The examining doctor noted that he displayed moderate intoxication. A blood sample was taken and analyzed by headspace GC. The blood was found to contain no ethanol, but 0.220 g/100 mL acetone and 0.096 g/100 mL isopropanol. The man admitted to consuming almost pure isopropanol 24 hours prior to his arrest.

The toxic and fatal concentration of acetone currently cited in clinical and forensic toxicology literature may need revision.

Reference Number: 80407

KAWAI, T., T. YASUNGI, S. HORIGUCHI, Y. UCHIDA, O. IWAMI, H. IGUCHI, O. INOUE, T. WANTANBE, H. NAKATSUKA, AND M. IKEDA. "Biological Monitoring of Occupation Exposure to Isopropyl Alcohol Vapor by Urinalysis for Acetone." *International Archives of Occupational and Environmental Health*, 62: 409–413, 1990 (3 tables, 25 references)

Abstract: A study was conducted of ninety-nine printers exposed to isopropanol vapors at the workplace compared to thirty-four workers not exposed to isopropanol. Urine samples were collected at the end of the shift and urine acetone and isopropanol concentrations were determined by GC. The workers were also equipped with a diffusive sampler to monitor exposure. The urine acetone concentration ranged between 0.0 to 0.00016 g/100 mL in non-exposed workers compared to up to 0.002 g/100 mL for exposed workers. Urine isopropanol concentrations were not detected in non-exposed workers and were only detected in thirty out of ninety-nine workers (30%). The highest urine isopropanol concentration was 0.0002 g/100 mL.

It is of practical interest that the occupational exposure to IPA can be biomonitored by means of urinalysis for acetone even when the IPA exposure is as low (up to 66 ppm) as one sixth to one seventh of the current occupational exposure limit of 400 ppm.

Reference Number: 80408

TURNER, P., B. SAEED, AND M.C. KELSEY. "Dermal Absorption of Isopropyl Alcohol from a Commercial Hand Rub: Implications for Its Use in Hand Decontamination." *Journal of Hospital Infection*, 56: 287–290, 2004 (1 table, 1 figure, 15 references)

Abstract: Four male and six female subjects used a hand sanitizer (53% v/v isopropyl alcohol) every 10 minutes for 4 hours. A blood sample was collected within 5 minutes of the final application of the hand rub and blood isopropyl alcohol concentrations were determined by GC. A low, measurable blood isopropanol concentration was found in nine of the subjects and ranged from 0.00005 to 0.00018 g/100 mL.

The hand rub was generally well tolerated although most reported that their hands felt sticky. One participant noted mild erythema and itching of her hands at the end of the study period.

Reference Number: 80409

SHARMA, A. AND J.D. MORROW. "Isopropyl Alcohol Swabs as a Preferred Substance of Abuse." *Journal of Psychoactive Drugs*, 49: 258–261, 2017 (13 references).

Abstract: A thirty-six-year-old mother of three with AUD, a major depressive disorder, and substance abuse attended an outpatient client because she felt compelled to suck isopropyl alcohol swabs daily. At the time, she was sucking 150 to 200 BD brand isopropanol swabs a night. She initially enjoyed the smell of the swabs, which were used to clean her infants, and then started putting the swabs in her mouth to use both hands, and it escalated from there. She reported not feeling intoxicated but at times felt dizzy, nauseated, had a headache, and a burning sensation in her stomach. Each swab contained 0.8 mL of 70% isopropyl alcohol.

One important differential diagnosis we considered in this case was obsessive-compulsive disorder. This patient's use of alcohol swabs was somewhat stereotyped and ritualized and her strong preference for a specific brand was particularly striking. After all, if intoxication with alcohol was her goal, ethanol-based beverages were readily available to her and isopropyl alcohol can be easily obtained in liquid form in any supermarket. However, stereotyped behavior is an important component of all addictive disorders and marked brand preference is both well-documented and correlated with severity of both nicotine and alcohol use disorders.

Reference Number: 80410

DUMOLLARD, C., J-F. WIART, F. HAKIM, C. DERMARLY, P. MORBIDELLI, D. ALLORGE, AND J-M. GAULIER. "Putatively Lethal Ingestion of Isopropyl Alcohol-Related Case: Interpretation of Post Mortem Isopropyl Alcohol and Acetone Concentrations Remains Challenging." *International Journal of Legal Medicine*, 135: 175–182, 2021 (2 tables, 38 references)

Abstract: A thirty-three-year-old man with a past history of drug addiction, psychosis, and a previous suicide attempt was found dead with a 1.5 L plastic bottle containing 1.1 L of 99% isopropyl alcohol. Autopsy took place 5 days after death and early putrefaction of the body prevented peripheral blood samples from being collected. Biological samples were collected (see table), and the cardiac blood isopropanol and acetone concentrations as determined by headspace GC were 46.4 and 159.0 mg/dL respectively. No ethyl alcohol was detected. Blood isopropyl alcohol half-life ranges from 2.5 to 8 hours. Blood acetone elimination half-life is about 22 hours. The lethal dose of isopropanol is estimated to be from 200 to 400 mL.

Table. Isopropanol and Acetone Concentrations in Various Postmortem Samples

Sample	Isopropanol Concentration (mg/dL)	Acetone Concentration (mg/dL)
Heart blood	46.4	159.0
Vitreous humor	26.0	234.0
Urine	46.5	304.0
Bile	99.1	136.0
Stomach contents (volume 100 mL)	23.0	213.0

Source: Adapted from Dumollard et al (2021).

The interpretation of post mortem isopropyl alcohol and acetone concentrations as well as IPA-to-acetone ratios, remains challenging mainly due to overlapping values between documented IPA poisoning cases and other cases not related to IPA poisoning. When isopropanol is detected in post mortem samples, by taking into account analytical findings in multiple biological specimens (and their confrontation with literature data), complete case history and search of possible IPS presence at the scene of death may provide reasonable explanations of a possible cause of death. Finally, in the current situation of the COVID-19 [pandemic] where ABHRs are more easily accessible, it is noteworthy that in cases of death suspected to be in relation with ABHR ingestion, post mortem detection of other constituents of the liquid (i.e., ethanol and *n*-propanol) simultaneously with IPA and acetone can be helpful for diagnostic.

Reference Number: 80411

BOROWSKA-SOLONYNKO, A. SIWINSKA-ZIOLKOWSKA, M. PIOTRKOWICZ, M. WYSMOLEK, AND M. DEMKOW. "Analysis of the Origin and Importance of Acetone and Isopropanol Levels in the Blood of the Deceased for Medicolegal Testimony." *Archiwum medycyny sadowej i kryminologii,* 64: 230–245, 2014 (8 figures, 13 references)

Abstract: Postmortem blood concentrations of alcohol, acetone, and isopropanol were determined in 2,475 cases in Warsaw between 2008 and 2009 by headspace GC. Blood acetone concentrations were detected in 202 cases. No alcohol was detected in eighty-seven (43%) of these cases. Isopropanol was detected with acetone in 68% of the cases. The median postmortem blood acetone and isopropyl alcohol concentrations were 20.5 mg/dL and 16.5 mg/dL respectively.

1. Acetone is detected in ca 1/10 of all routine blood tests performed to determine the presence of ethyl alcohol. 2. The concomitant presence of isopropanol and acetone in the blood is found with equal frequency in sober individuals, people with low blood concentrations of ethyl alcohol and intoxicated people. 3. There was no correlation between the blood concentrations of ethyl alcohol and acetone, however there was a clear rise in the blood concentration of isopropanol along with an increase in the concentration of ethanol in the blood.

8.05 ETHYLENE GLYCOL

"Not to be confused with Polyethylene glycol, Diethylene glycol, Propylene glycol, or Glycol."

—Ethylene glycol, *Wikipedia*

Ethylene glycol is a sweet smelling and sweet tasting liquid (hence the name "glycol") used mainly as an antifreeze. A typical indication of ethylene glycol poisoning is the formation of oxalate crystals in the urine and other tissues (80502–80509). Ethylene glycol is converted by various enzymes (including ADH) into glycolaldehyde, glycolic acid, and eventually oxalic acid:

$$CH_2OHCH_2OH \rightarrow CH_2OHCHO \rightarrow CH_2OHCOOH \rightarrow COOHCOOH$$

Alcohol or fomepizole is recommended as a treatment for ethylene glycol poisonings to block the formation of the toxic metabolites (80502–80508, 80511) in a similar manner as methanol poisoning is treated. Crystals in the urine or metabolites may not form when there is a massive ingestion of ethylene glycol and death occurring shortly after (80510). Some of the clinical symptoms of ethylene glycol poisoning include:

- Vomiting
- Cyanosis
- Headache
- Increase in heart rate
- Decrease in blood pressure
- Pulmonary edema
- Hypoglycemia
- Coma

Ethylene glycol is also used as an antifreeze coolant and chemical solvent. Ethylene glycol poisoning is typically divided into three phases: CNS involvement (0.5–12 hours), cardiopulmonary toxicity (12–36 hours), and renal toxicity (24–72 hours).

A twenty-six-year-old woman consumed brake fluid (ethylene glycol) in a suicide attempt. She was treated with dialysis and was discharged from hospital 10 days later with residual facial nerve palsy (80512).

The half-life of ethylene glycol is 3 hours, compared to 10 hours for glycolic acid. The serum glycolic acid concentration was a better indicator of fatalities than the serum ethylene glycol concentration (80513).

Reference Number: 80501

ROBINSON, D.W. AND D.S. REIVE. "A Gas Chromatographic Procedure of Quantitation of Ethylene Glycol in Postmortem Blood." *Journal of Analytical Toxicology*, 5: 69–72, 1981 (4 figures, 6 references)

Abstract: A gas chromatographic method for the determination of ethylene glycol in postmortem blood using FID is described. The ethylene glycol in 2 mL of postmortem blood is esterified with *n*-butyl boronic acid in acetone and 1 µL is injected into a salinized 180 cm long, 2 mm i.d. glass column containing 3% OV-25 on 100/200 mesh. Care must be taken to eliminate the presence of water to ensure a complete reaction. In a positive postmortem blood sample, which was analyzed four times over a period of 4 months, a consistent ethylene glycol concentration of 45 mg/dL was measured using this method.

Quantitation of ethylene glycol in postmortem blood using esterification by means of a *n*-butyl boronic acid, provides reproducible, sensitive and reliable results. The simplicity of this method should make it acceptable for forensic or clinical analysis of ethylene glycol.

Reference Number: 80502

HANTSON, P., R. VANBINST, AND P. MAHIEU. "Determination of Ethylene Glycol Tissue Content After Fatal Oral Poisoning and Pathologic Findings." *American Journal of Forensic Medicine and Pathology*, 23: 159–161, 2002 (1 table, 1 figure, 15 references)

Abstract: A twenty-three-year-old man was admitted to hospital 5 hours after the ingestion of ethylene glycol (radiator antifreeze). On admission, the plasma and urine ethylene glycol concentrations were 0.116 and 0.092 g/100 mL respectively. Despite aggressive therapy including ethyl alcohol administration, the patient was declared brain dead 27 hours after ingestion. The plasma ethylene glycol concentration was 0.036 g/100 mL immediately prior to death. The postmortem pleural fluid ethylene glycol concentration was 0.070 g/100 mL. At autopsy, ethylene-glycol induced acute tubular necrosis and deposits of calcium oxalate crystals were observed.

Ethylene glycol is metabolized initially by conversion via ADH to glycolaldehyde which is in tissue rapidly metabolized to glycolic acid. Accumulation of glycolic acid seems to be the major determinant of metabolic acidosis observed in human cases of ethylene glycol poisoning.

Reference Number: 80503

ROSANO, T.G., T.A. SWIFT, C.J. KRANICK., AND M. SIKIRICA. "Ethylene Glycol and Glycolic Acid In Postmortem Blood from Fatal Poisonings." *Journal of Analytical Toxicology*, 33: 508–513, 2009 (1 table, 8 figures, 38 references)

Abstract: A GC and GC-MS method are described to measure the ethylene glycol (EG) and glycolic acid (GA) concentrations in postmortem blood. The method is linear from 0.005 to 4.0 g/100 mL with a LOD of 0.0025 g/100 mL. In twelve cases of suspected EG poisoning, the postmortem blood EG concentration ranged from 0.0058 to 0.779 g/100 mL (mean 0.183 g/100 mL) and the GA concentration ranged from 0.081 to 0.177 g/100 mL (mean 0.136 g/100 mL).

Measurement of GA is recommended in the postmortem investigation of EG poisoning as EG determination alone may not provide a sensitive index for detection in determination of severity of EG poisoning. Birefringent oxalate crystals in kidney sections provided a consistent histological clue for EG poisonings in unsuspected cases.

Reference Number: 80504

CASAVANT, M.J., M.N. SHAH, AND R. BATTELS. "Does Fluorescent Urine Indicate Antifreeze Ingestion by Children?" *Pediatrics*, 107: 113–114, 2001 (8 references)

Abstract: Fluorescein is a fluorescent dye added to most antifreeze so automobile mechanics can locate a leak using a black light. Forty-six urine samples collected from children were evaluated for fluorescence by three physicians using a Woods light (black light). Approximately 80%–90% of the samples were considered fluorescent although none of the children had ethylene glycol poisoning.

Most urine samples obtained from children are fluorescent. Interrater variability exists. Some plastic and some glass tubes are fluorescent. Fluorescent urine is not an indication of ethylene glycol ingestion by children.

Reference Number: 80505

WALDER, A.D. AND C.K.G.TYLER. "Ethylene Glycol Antifreeze Poisoning." *Anaesthesia*, 49: 964–967, 1994 (2 tables, 2 figures, 28 references)

Abstract: Three case reports of ethylene glycol poisoning and a general review of its toxicology are presented. Ethylene glycol is not toxic, but the toxicity is due to its metabolite glycolic acid, which is formed by ADH in the liver. Further metabolism of glycolic acid is slow. The lethal dose of ethylene glycol is 1.4–1.6 mL/kg. There are three stages of ethylene glycol poisoning. The first is 0.5–12 hours after ingestion and is due to the ethanol-like effect of ethylene glycol. The second, 12 to 48 hours after ingestion, is cardiopulmonary failure caused by the acid metabolite. The final phase is renal failure caused by calcium oxalate crystal deposition. In addition to other clinical treatments, ethanol is employed to inhibit the production of the glycolic acid.

Haemodialysis when available remains the treatment of choice for removal of the ethylene glycol molecule and its toxic metabolites in severe poisoning. However, successful treatment depends on rapid diagnosis and institution of cardiovascular and respiratory support, ethanol therapy and gastric lavage.

Reference Number: 80506

KARLSON-STIBER, C., AND H. PERSSON. "Ethylene Glycol Poisoning: Experiences from an Epidemic in Sweden." *Journal of Toxicology and Clinical Toxicology*, 30: 565–574, 1992 (5 tables, 1 figure, 22 references)

Abstract: Thirty-six cases of ethylene glycol poisoning occurred in Sweden between January and May 1987. Serum ethylene glycol concentrations were determined in twenty-four cases and the presence of oxalate crystals in urine or kidney was found in another six cases. There were thirty male and six female victims (ages twenty to sixty-nine years) of whom thirty poisonings were due to suicide attempts. Metabolic acidosis was found in 86% of the patients. There was no correlation between serum ethylene glycol concentration and the degree of renal failure. The time elapsed between ingestion and treatment is a major factor in the severity of symptoms and fatal outcomes. Renal damage was seen in 67% of the victims. Six patients died (17%). Four patients with serum ethylene concentrations between 0.062 and 0.124 g/100 mL with minimal acidosis were treated with ethanol alone.

In this series the severity of the metabolic acidosis correlated with the severity of poisoning, defined as renal failure and mortality. The absence of a positive correlation between the measured serum ethylene glycol concentrations and the clinical course is consistent with the experimental observations that the toxicity of ethylene glycol derives from its metabolites. Central nervous system symptoms were more common and more important than circulatory disturbances. All six patients who died had severe neurological impairment and in four, brain damage was considered the direct cause of death.

Reference Number: 80507

DAVIS, D.P., K.J. BRAMWELL, R.S. HAMILTON, AND S.R. WILLIAMS. "Ethylene Glycol Poisoning: A Case Report of a Record-High Level and a Review." *Journal of Emergency Medicine*, 15: 653–667, 1997 (3 tables, 2 figures, 194 references)

Abstract: A twenty-eight-year-old man was brought unresponsive to the ER. He was seen earlier drinking at a bar and appeared drunk. Monohydrate and dihydrate calcium oxalate crystals were observed in the urine as well, the urine fluorescent under the Wood's lamp. The patient was administered ethanol IV, and hemodialysis was conducted. The initial serum ethylene glycol concentration was 0.888 g/100 mL. A review of ethylene glycol toxicity was presented.

Ethylene glycol is a commonly available and fortunately uncommonly ingested substance with wide ranging and severe toxic effects on the body. There effects are primarily a result of the metabolic acidosis, tissue deposition of calcium oxalate crystals, or direct effects of the multitude of metabolites. The presentation of ethylene glycol intoxication is non-specific but may include altered level of consciousness, metabolic acidosis, respiratory and gastrointestinal symptoms, and renal failure.

Reference Number: 80508

SIVILOTTI, M.L.A., M.J. BURNS, K.E. MCMARTIN, AND J. BRENT. "Toxicokinetics of Ethylene Glycol During Fomepizole Therapy: Implications for Management." *Annals of Emergency Medicine*, 36: 114–125, 2000 (4 tables, 4 figures, 45 references)

Abstract: Nineteen patients presenting to ED with initial serum ethylene glycol concentrations between 0.024 and 0.446 g/100 mL were studied. Twelve patients also had a positive SAC, but only four had a SAC > 0.100 g/100 mL. The median time from the ingestion of ethylene glycol to the administration of fomepizole was 11.4 hours (range 6.6–20.8 hours).

Seventeen patients were hemodialyzed for various periods of time. One patient died. During fomepizole administration the serum ethylene glycol half-life was 19.7 hours, and this was not affected by the presence of alcohol. The half-life of ethylene glycol was 8.6 hours in the absence of alcohol or fomepizole. The serum fomepizole concentration had to be greater than 10 μmol/L to inhibit ethylene glycol elimination. Fomepizole has been described as an expensive antidote.

In summary pharmacokinetic evidence is presented to demonstrate that fomepizole effectively inhibits ADH in human subjects with EG poisoning.

Reference Number: 80509

ARMSTRONG, E.J., D.A. ENGELHART, A.J. JENKINS, AND E.K. BALRAJ. "Homicidal Ethylene Glycol Intoxication. A Report of a Case." *American Journal of Forensic Medicine and Pathology*, 27: 151–155, 2006 (1 table, 4 figures, 7 references)

Abstract: A seventy-five-year-old hypertensive diabetic man was admitted to an ER with signs of nausea and intoxication. He was administered hemodialysis at 9 hours after admission but died 28 hours later. Six serial antemortem blood samples showed blood ethylene glycol concentrations decreasing from 0.711 to 0.019 g/100 mL (shortly before death). At autopsy calcium oxalate crystals were observed in the kidneys and brain. The postmortem ethylene glycol concentration in the heart blood, femoral blood, CSF, and vitreous humor were 0.01, 0.015, 0.957, and 0.029 g/100 mL respectively. The postmortem propylene glycol concentrations were 0.028, 0.018, 0.083, and 0.017 g/100 mL respectively. The victim also had multiple blunt traumas. The female companion-caretaker was charged with homicide.

The cause of death was determined to be acute intoxication by EG, with another condition of multiple blunt trauma impacts to the head, trunk and extremities. The manner of death was ruled as homicide. The history and clinical findings are supportive of an unintentional ingestion of an EG/PG containing substance.

Reference Number: 80510

GARG, U., C. FRAZEE, L. JOHNSON, AND J.W. TURNER. "A Fatal Case Involving Extremely High Levels of Ethylene Glycol Without Elevation of Its

Metabolites or Crystalluria." *American Journal of Forensic Medicine and Pathology,* 30: 273–275, 2009 (2 tables, 14 references)

Abstract: A fifty-eight-year-old man with a history of chronic alcohol abuse who had previously tried to commit suicide was found dead in a garage with a can of ethylene glycol antifreeze and a suicide note beside him. His postmortem ethylene glycol concentrations were 2.340 g/100 mL in blood, 2.261 g/100 mL in urine, and 1.028 g/100 mL in vitreous humor. No ethylene glycol metabolites such as oxalic acid were found in the urine. No crystals were found in the urine.

In conclusion, we report a fatal case of ethylene glycol intoxication with an extremely high concentration of ethylene glycol in the absence of toxic metabolites and crystalluria. To our knowledge, this is the first case with these findings and may have forensic and clinical applications. For example, ethylene glycol poisoning cannot and should not be ruled out based upon urine studies or microscopic examination of kidney as crystals may be absent if the death occurs before crystals could form.

Reference Number: 80511

ACHAPPA, B., D. MADI, T. KANCHAN, AND N.K. KISHANLAL. "Treatment of Ethylene Glycol Poisoning with Oral Ethyl Alcohol." *Case Reports in Medicine,* Article ID, 7985917, 3pp, 2019 (18 references).

Abstract: A seventy-year-old woman who accidentally consumed car coolant attended hospital as a result of unsteady gait and drowsiness. Gastric lavage was conducted. Crystalluria was observed, which is a major indicator of ethylene glycol poisoning. The patient had metabolic acidosis as well. She was administered 100 mL of alcohol before hemodialysis and showed no more crystal in the urine after 48 hours.

The reported case highlights on the importance of oral ethyl alcohol therapy where intravenous ethyl alcohol and fomepizole are not available. Oral ethanol when supplemented with timely hemodialysis (HD) leads to clinical improvement with no residual complications. The elimination half life of ethylene glycol is approximately 3 hours; hence patients presenting to the hospital much later are not likely to be benefited from ethanol therapy irrespective of the route of administration. In such cases, hemodialysis must be chosen as the main modality of treatment to remove the metabolites of ethylene glycol from the system.

Reference Number: 80511

Reference Number: 80512

BASNAYAKE, B.M.D.B., A.W.M. WAZIL, N. NANAYAKKARA, R.M.B.S.S. MAHANAMA, P.N.S. PERMATHILAKE, AND K.K.M.C.D.K. GALADUWA. "Ethylene Glycol Intoxication Following Brake Fluid Ingestion Complicated with Unilateral Facial Nerve Palsy: A Case Report." *Journal of Medical Case Reports*, 13: 203, 4pp, 2019 (23 references).

Abstract: Brake fluid is a type of transmission fluid that is composed of ethylene glycols and glycol ethers. Ethylene glycol is also used as an antifreeze coolant and chemical solvent. Ethylene glycol poisoning is typically divided into three phases: CNS involvement (0.5–12 hours), cardiopulmonary toxicity (12–36 hours), and renal toxicity (24–72 hours). A twenty-six-year-old woman was transferred from a local hospital with a history of reduced urine output, shortness of breath, abdominal pain, and vomiting over a period of 2 days. It was eventually determined that she consumed brake fluid in a suicide attempt after a conflict with her husband. No ethylene glycol or metabolite concentrations were measured. She was treated with dialysis and discharged after 10 days with residual facial nerve palsy.

> Ethylene glycol intoxication is a potential life-threatening conditions, and it the patient reveals history of ingestion, an immediate and aggressive protocol-based management needs to be instituted. However, in the usual scenario when the patient denies self-poisoning by ingestion, it is crucial to interpret the available investigations of severe metabolic acidosis, high anion gap, high osmolar gap and oxaluria in order to arrive at the accurate etiology. Unusual presentations like cranial neuropathies need to be checked out and considered.

Reference Number: 80513

TUERO, G., J. GONZALEZ, L. SAHUQUILLO, A. FREIXA, I. GOMILA, M.A. ELORZA, AND B. BARCELO. "Value of Glycolic Acid Analysis in Ethylene Glycol Poisoning: A Clinical Case Report and Systematic Review of the Literature." *Forensic Science International*, 290: e9–e14, 2018 (2 tables, 1 figure, 20 references)

Abstract: Ethylene glycol is an alcohol used in antifreeze and industrial products. EG is metabolized by the alcohol dehydrogenase and other liver enzyme to form glycolaldehyde, glycolic acid, glyoxylic acid, and oxalic acid. Metabolic acidosis is caused by the glycolic acid, and calcium oxalate crystals can cause acute renal failure. A literature review of the outcome of 137 ethylene glycol poisoned patients was conducted as to the serum and urine ethylene glycol and glycolic acid concentrations. The half-life of EG is approximately 3 hours, compared to 10 hours of glycolic acid. The serum glycolic acid concentration but not the EG differed significantly between fatal and non-fatal poisonings.

Table. Mean Serum and Urine Ethylene Glycol and Glycolic Acid Concentrations in Fatal and Non-fatal Cases

	Non-Fatal (mg/L)	Fatal (mg/L)
Serum Ethylene Glycol	1,945.2	1,904.2
Urine Ethylene Glycol	1,383.5	5,551.0
Serum Glycolic Acid	903.9	1,473.7
Urine Glycolic Acid	3,899.8	4,566.2

Source: Adapted from Tuero et al (2018).

EG poisoning is a medical emergency and a diagnostic challenge for both the clinician and the toxicologist. Communication between the two has an impact on the diagnosis and prognosis of these patients. In all suspected cases of EG poisoning, it would be advisable to carry out the simultaneous analysis of EG and GA.

CHAPTER 9

Addiction/Alcohol Use Disorders, Withdrawal, Health Risks, Fetal Alcohol Spectrum Disorder, and Public Safety Measures

"Lyke tan leather hyded:
She had her so guyded
Betweene the cup and the wall.
That she was there wythall
Into a palsy fall;
With that her hed shaked.
And her hands quaked:
Ones hed wold haue asked
To se her naked:
She dranke so of the dregges,
The dropsy was in her legges;
Her face glystrying like glass;
All foggy fat she was;
She had also the gout
In all her ioyntes about;
Her breath was sour and stale.
And smelled all of ale."

—Description of a Woman with Alcohol Use Disorder,
"The Tunnyng of Elynour Rummyng" by John Skelton (1463–1529)

"O God, that men should put an enemy in their mouths to steal away their brains! That we should with joy, pleasance, revel and applause, transform ourselves into beasts!"

—William Shakespeare, Othello

From a forensic toxicology viewpoint, the detection of a zero BAC is as significant in a person with alcohol use disorder (AUD) as a high BAC, as the person's unusual behavior or injury/death may have been caused by alcohol withdrawal syndrome and not a high BAC.

9.01 ADDICTION/ALCOHOL USE DISORDER

> "Then on the next day there is the breath reeking of the wine-cask, and a nearly total obliviousness of everything, from the annihilation of the powers of the memory. And this, too is what they call seizing the moment of life, whereas, in reality, while other men lose the day that has gone before, the drinker has already lost the one that is to come."
>
> —Pliny the Elder, Natural History 14.28. (22)-Drunkenness

> "We now diagnose with confidence the existence of concealed drinking habits in thousands of cases which would have passed undetected not many years since. One of the most remarkable features of these secret drinkers is their inordinate propensity to tell lies, and their favorite falsehood, when they are detected, is to lay the blame of their evil habit on some apocryphal medical prescription of stimulants. Those observers, however, who have carefully studied the genesis of alcoholic excesses are aware that the habit in the immense majority of cases, from the temptation supplied by states of bodily or mental dejection and misery, and very often from a peculiar weakness of the nervous system, which is inherited."
>
> —Anstie, "On the Physiological and Therapeutical Action of Alcohol" (1865)

> "First you take a drink, then a drink takes a drink, then the drink takes you."
>
> —F. Scott Fitzgerald, *The Great Gatsby*

Some definitions may be of assistance in this section. Binge drinking is usually defined as five or more drinks for men and four or more drinkers for women on a single occasion, whereas heavy drinking is binge drinking on five or more days in the past month. Alcohol use disorder (AUD) is a problematic pattern of drinking that requires to two to three (mild AUD), to four to six (moderate AUD), or seven to eleven (severe AUD) diagnostic criteria as listed in the DSM-5 (see Appendix 4) to be diagnosed. A typical North American drink is defined as 14 g of alcohol, or 1.5 fl. oz. of liquor (40% ABV), 12 fl. oz. of beer (5% ABV), or 5 fl. oz. of wine (12% ABV).

An alcohol dose can also be defined as one unit, which is defined as 8 g of alcohol or equivalent to approximately 0.9 fl. oz. of liquor, 7 fl. oz. of beer, or 3 fl. oz. of wine. This is the amount of alcohol that can be eliminated in 1 hour by an average adult man.

Chronic alcohol use changes the structure of the brain, including altered reward circuitry. This causes an increase in craving and compromised frontal white matter, which affects decision making, impulse control, and executive functioning (90112).

An uncontrollable and irresistible desire to consume alcohol was first described by Benjamin Rush in 1784. Delirium tremens was first reported in 1813 (90101). Alcohol use disorders are among the most prevalent disorders globally and are characterized by compulsive heavy drinking and affects 1.7 percent of women and 8.6% of men globally (90102, 90104).

Persons with a ALDH2*2 gene (rare in Europeans but found in 40% of the East Asian population) have impaired alcohol metabolism, which results in a high concentration of acetaldehyde forming and thereby decreasing the risk of AUD. Countries in which there is a permissive attitude to heavy drinking and inexpensive, readily available alcohol have a greater incidence of AUD (90102).

Alcohol consumption during adolescence (ten to nineteen years of age) increases the risk of AUD later in life (90103).

In high income countries only 10% of the persons diagnosed with AUD receive treatment (90105).

Persons with AUD have more legal, social, and workplace problems (90106), have four times the rate of serious arguments with family, are more likely to be depressed, and have more suicide attempts than persons without AUD (90107–90110).

Some successful therapies for the long-term treatment for alcoholism include self-help groups such as Alcoholics Anonymous, medications (e.g., disulfiram and naltrexone), cognitive behavioral therapy, and classical addiction therapy (90111–90112).

During the 1918 influenza pandemic heavy alcohol use was found to be a risk factor for a worse outcome. This is also occurring with the COVID-19 pandemic in which chronic alcohol use can impair the immune system, suppress cough, increase risk taking, and increase exposure to the virus at parties (90113).

Reference Number: 90101

MANN, K., D. HERMANN, AND A. HEINZ. "One Hundred Years of Alcoholism: The Twentieth Century." *Alcohol and Alcoholism*, 35: 10–15, 2000 (67 references).

Abstract: An uncontrollable and irresistible desire to consume alcohol was first described by Benjamin Rush in 1784. Delirium tremens (DT) was reported in 1813. The early temperance movements were based on the degeneration theory, that anyone who consumed excessive amounts of alcohol would suffer from alcohol-related problems and that this social vice would trigger a cascade of social, moral, and medical problems that would increase with each generation causing an eventual extinction of that family. In the first thirty years of the twentieth century, political activity such as the Anti-Saloon League resulted in Prohibition (1919–1933), which in the United States ultimately failed. The disease concept of alcoholism was promoted and revised. In the last decade of the twentieth century, substantial progress has been made in the treatment of alcohol use disorder.

> Finally, the history of the last 100 years warns us that ethics are not an option, as Edwards stated in a 1999 conference at the Central Institute of Mental Health, Mannheim. That alcoholism had been considered a disease in Germany since 1915, did not prevent the dehumanizing treatment of patients with alcohol dependence during the Nazi era. It is an integral part of the professional mission to assist patients in their efforts to be treated equally inside and outside of medical therapy. Our increasing knowledge about the disposition towards alcohol dependence and a high relapse risk can help identify patients with demands for special therapeutic efforts; it should never be used to stigmatize these subjects.

Reference Number: 90102

CARVALHO, A.F., M. HELLIG, A. PEREZ, C. PROBST, AND J. REHM. "Alcohol Use Disorders." *Lancet*, 394: 781–792, 2019 (2 tables, 2 figures, 140 references)

Abstract: AUDs are among the most prevalent mental disorders globally and are characterized by compulsive, heavy drinking and loss of control over alcohol intake. In 2016, AUDs affected 8.6% of men and 1.7% of women globally. Yet AUDs remain some of the most undertreated of mental disorders, in part because of the stigma attached to it. The development of AUD can be affected by genetic risk factors. Alcohol dehydrogenase (ADH) and the mitochondrial form of aldehyde dehydrogenase (ALDH2) are the two major liver enzymes that metabolize alcohol. Carriers of the ALDH2*2 gene have impaired alcohol metabolism, which results in a buildup to acetaldehyde after the consumption of alcohol and causes flushing, headache, tachycardia, and vomiting (similar to Antabuse) and protects against developing AUD. This gene is carried by 40 percent of the East Asian population but is rare in Europeans. Some environmental factors also contribute to the development of AUD. AUD tends to be more prevalent in countries with a permissive attitude to heavy drinking and with wide availability of cheaper alcohol.

Thus, alcohol use disorders and their associated heavy drinking are clearly major public health problems, which could be reduced by treatment. However, as indicated in the section on risk factors, the wider environment has an important role in the cause and course of alcohol use disorders. For instance, on the basis of experience in the treatment of other mental disorders such as depression, a reduction in the stigma associated with alcohol use disorders would probably result in an increased number of individuals seeking treatment. A supportive environment in the community might also be important and is currently being explored in a large-scale implementation trial in three countries in the Americas: Colombia, Peru, and Mexico. Moreover, the overall permissiveness of cultures is important, either via informal control, such as in the classic Mediterranean cultures, where alcohol is restricted to meals and showing signs of intoxication is met with disapproval or by formal control such as restrictions on availability and a ban on marketing. Another effective way to reduce alcohol consumption and alcohol-attributable harm is to increase prices by taxation.

Reference Number: 90103

NIXON, K. AND J.A. MCCLAIN. "Adolescence as a Critical Window for Developing an Alcohol Use Disorder: Current Findings in Neuroscience." *Current Opinions Psychiatry*, 23: 227–232, 2010 (61 references)

Abstract: The World Health Organization (WHO) defines adolescence as the phase of childhood from ten to ninteen years of age. By grade 12, 73% of adolescents will have experimented with alcohol and 30% will have been drunk within the past month. Alcohol consumption during adolescence greatly increases the risk of AUD in later life.

The adolescent's decreased response to the negative aspects of alcohol consumption (motor impairment, sedation, anxiety, and social depression) coupled with increased or altered response to the positive and rewarding effects of alcohol may promote excessive intake. Repeated exposure to excessive intake and the adolescent's enhanced susceptibility to alcohol induced damage, whether through toxicity, teratogenicity, or other effects on plasticity further dysregulates behavioral control of consumption. Thus, the adolescent's unique response to alcohol combined with increased susceptibility to alcohol-induced neurodegeneration interact to facilitate excessive alcohol consumption, the hallmark of AUD.

Reference Number: 90104

AGABIO, R., C. PISANU, G.L. GESSA, AND F. FRANCONI. "Sex Differences in Alcohol Use Disorder." *Current Medicinal Chemistry*, 24: 1–10, 2017 (1 table, 72 references)

Abstract: In the 1980s, the prevalence of AUD was five times greater in men than women. Currently the difference between men and women with AUD has narrowed to 2:1. There are no sex differences in the diagnostic criteria of AUD. Due to their lower body weight and higher fat composition compared to men, women obtain a higher BAC than men for the same alcohol dose. Women can have a telescoping effect where there is an accelerated progression from the first use of alcohol to the onset of AUD into treatment compared to men. The risks of developing health problems due to AUD is higher for women than men.

Women and men largely differ in several aspects of AUD. For instance, women and men perceive rewarding effects of different intensity after the consumption of similar amounts of alcohol, and the effects perceived by AUD women may change across different phases of their life. AUD is more frequent among men, than women, but the substantial number of AUD women requires specific studies dedicated to the specific needs of female patients. The effects of environmental and genetic risk factors as well as comorbidity also vary between men and women. Women are at higher risk for negative consequences induced by alcohol consumption than men and may also differ in their response to psychotherapy and to AUD medications. Finally, AUD women are less likely to seek treatment than AUD men. However, despite this large body of evidence, in the majority of studies, men are overrepresented in comparison with women and the results obtained in men are considered to be completely translatable to women. Accordingly, women receive a therapy that is less based on the principles of evidence-based medicine than men.

Reference Number: 90105

PROBST, C., J. MANTHEY, A. MARTINEZ, AND J. REHM. "Alcohol Use Disorder Severity and Reported Reasons Not to Seek Treatment: A Cross-Sectional Study in European Primary Care Practices." *Substance Abuse Treatment, Prevention and Policy*, 10: 32, 10pp, 2015 (4 tables, 3 figures, 53 references)

Abstract: Of 1,008 patients diagnosed with AUD by a general practitioner in six European countries within the past 12 months, 810 (80%) did not receive treatment and 251 of these gave a reason for not seeking treatment. The most frequent reasons cited for not seeking treatment were lack of problem awareness (55.3%), stigma or shame (28.6%), encounter barriers (22.8%), and coping alone (20.9%). Alcohol is the most important risk factor for morbidity and mortality, but in high income countries less than 10% of persons classified with AUD received treatment. It is estimated that if alcohol treatment was increased by 40 percent there would be a 10% reduction in alcohol-related mortality in the EU in the first year alone.

Table. Barriers That Were Cited by People with AUD: Why Treatment Was Not Sought

Barriers Encountered	Percentage
Wished not to stop drinking	72.9
No trust in treatment system	9.9
The help was not offered	5.6
Treatment was not affordable	4.7
Treatment was not seen as an option	4.0
Lack of possibility or knowledge	3.0

Source: Adapted from Probst et al (2015).

General health care patients from six European countries were asked for reasons why they did not seek help for AUDs. The study showed that lacking problem awareness was the major reason for not seeking treatment, especially in less severe cases that are however prone to physical harm from heavy drinking. A more regular monitoring of patients' alcohol consumption and offering brief interventions for individuals with mild AUDs could potentially improve their heath and reduce societal harm. For more severe cases, treatment barriers were reported more frequently. For these cases GPs could serve as a junction point to specialized care.

Reference Number: 90106

MALATHESH, B.C., C.N. KUMAR, A. KANDASAMY, S. MOIRANGTHEM, S.B. MATH, AND P. MURTHY. "Legal, Social, and Occupational Problems in Persons with Alcohol Use Disorder: An Exploratory Study." *Indian Journal of Psychological Medicine*, 43: 234–240, 2021 (6 tables, 48 references).

Abstract: A cross-sectional study was conducted of eighty-seven male and four female adults with AUD admitted to an addiction unit for treatment in India. The patients were 86 percent Hindu, 3 percent Muslim, and 11 percent Christian. The most common legal, occupational, and social problems experienced by AUD patients were drunk driving, being detained by the police, work absenteeism, a serious altercation with their spouse, and using public transit while drunk.

Table. Percent of Patients with AUD Who Reported Various Legal Problems

Legal Problem	Percent
Detained by police	39.6
Formal complaint lodged at police station	23.1
Detained in judicial custody	8.8
Past suicide attempt	47.3
Using firearm while intoxicated	3.3
Drink and drive	59.3
MVC while intoxicated	22.2
Involvement with gangs	12.1
Any legal problems	81.3

Source: Adapted from Malathesh et al (2021).

To conclude, patients with AUDs face a plethora of legal, social and occupational problems. A higher quantity of alcohol consumed per day is associated with higher chances of having the aforementioned problems, and they in turn, further worsen the AUD. There is need to routinely screen patients with AUD for adverse legal, social, and occupational problems. Along with treatments aimed at reducing alcohol use, we should also have targeted interventions to address the aforementioned problems, with the help of a multidisciplinary team, which otherwise [would] be incomplete management of patients with AUD and there will be higher chances of relapse and failed rehabilitation of patients. If the assessment and management strategies for the aforementioned problems become a mandatory part of the management of AUD, it will go a long way in reducing the harm to patients and the community at large.

Reference Number: 90107

KOLVES, K., B.M. DRAPE, J. SNOWDON, AND D. DE LEO. "Alcohol Use Disorders and Suicides: Results from a Psychological Autopsy Study in Australia." *Alcohol*, 64: 29–35, 2017 (4 tables, 29 references)

Abstract: A structured clinical interview for DSM-IV was obtained from close relatives of 259 suicide victims (ages thirty-five years or greater) in Queensland, New South Wales, to determine if the victim had AUD. Fifty-six victims (22%) had AUD and 203 did not. Suicide victims with AUD were significantly younger (49.3 years) than non-AUD cases (54.3 years).

Table. Odds Ratio Comparing AUD and Non-AUD Suicides

	OR (AUD vs Non-AUD)
Substance use disorder (not alcohol)	2.82 ×
Aggression (OAS)—general score	1.18 ×
Serious arguments with family members in previous 12 months	3.90 ×

Source: Adapted from Kolves et al (2017).

Every fifth person who died by suicide had an AUD. When compared to non-AUD suicides, AUD suicides had a higher prevalence of other substance-use disorders, history of suicide attempt, higher scores of aggression, serious arguments with spouse/partner and other family members, infidelity, being a victim of a crime in the last 12 months, being younger, and not coming from a non-English speaking background. Furthermore, comparison of AUD suicides and sudden deaths showed that AUD suicides were more likely to have mood disorders, previous suicide attempts, expressions of hopelessness, higher scores in physical aggression toward self, romantic relationship breakup, and serious arguments with other family members. Our findings support that aggressive behavior, comorbidity of other psychiatric disorders as predisposing factors, and recent interpersonal conflict can trigger suicide in people with AUD. There is a need for proper diagnosis, risk assessment and treatment for suicidal people with AUD.

Reference Number: 90108

PFEIFER, P., C. BARTSCH, A. HEMMER, AND T. REISCH. "Acute and Chronic Alcohol Use Correlated with Methods of Suicide in a Swiss National Sample." *Drug and Alcohol Dependence*, 178: 75–79, 2017 (3 tables, 42 references)

Abstract: The postmortem BACs of 2,946 suicide victims who died in Switzerland between 2011 and 2013 were determined and 39.5% of the victims had a positive alcohol result. Alcohol use disorder was diagnosed in 366 victims (12.4%). The prevalent rate of AUD in Switzerland is about 3.7%. The mean BAC in AUD victims was 0.186 g/100 mL compared to 0.056 g/100 mL in non-AUD victims. Victims with AUD were more often in medical treatment before suicide and more likely to have drug intoxication as the method of suicide.

Table. Mean BAC and Percent Positive According to the Method of Suicide

Method of Suicide	BAC Positive	Mean BAC (g/100 mL)
Drug intoxication	46%	0.114
Hanging	32%	0.128
Firearms	41%	0.134
Jumping from a height	28%	0.125
Jumping in front of moving object	42%	0.131

Source: Adapted from Pfeifer et al (2017).

Considering the age of the decedents, the highest percentage of suicide victims in AUD were found in the age group from 46 to 65 years. The predominance of this middle-aged group with AUD has also been found in preceding suicide autopsy studies. In midlife, the consequences of alcohol misuse becomes evident, and in this age group, many patients suffer more often from various negative psychological or somatic distress. In consequence suicide may progressively appear as a possible solution to avoid those negative consequences. Sedative use disorder was significantly more prevalent in subjects with AUD compared to the rest of the study population. Further, subjects with AUD have been hospitalized more often for psychiatric inpatient treatment within the last month before their death compared to NAUD. This is an interesting finding as it confirms a recent study that found a high percentage of subjects with alcohol misuse to seek medical help before committing suicide.

Reference Number: 90109

CONNER, K.R. AND C.L. BAGGE. "Suicidal Behavior. Links Between Alcohol Use Disorder and Acute Use of Alcohol." *Alcohol Research: Current Reviews*, 40: el–e4, 2019 (28 references)

Abstract: The risk of suicide attempt is 3.13 times greater for those with AUD compared to those without. Women receiving AUD treatment were at sixteen times greater risk of suicide, and men receiving AUD treatment were nine times at risk of suicide compared to the general population. In the United States, approximately 36% of male and 29% of female suicide victims have a postmortem BAC of 0.010 g/100 mL or greater. The risk of suicide increases with the degree of acute use of alcohol (AUA), from 2.71 times at low BACs to 37.18 times at BACs of 0.100 g/100 mL or greater.

A seminal review posited several mechanisms by which AUA may increase risk for suicidal behavior, including alcohol-related increases in psychological distress, depressed mood, aggressiveness, and impulsivity. The role of alcohol in cognitive constriction, a narrowing of attention to one's present emotional state and circumstances is another likely mechanism. Recent research has shown that during the 24-hour period preceding a suicide attempt, AUA in a given hour is associated with increased intensity of suicidal ideation in the next hour. Research has also shown that AUA is associated with a rapid transition from acute suicidal impulse to action, suggesting that the role of AUA in promoting suicidal ideation and disinhibition is a mechanism of risk for suicidal behavior.

Reference Number: 90110

MCHUGH, R.K. AND R.D. WEISS. "Alcohol Use Disorder and Depressive Disorders." *Alcohol Research, Current Reviews*, 40: el–e8, 2019 (57 references)

Abstract: Depressive disorders are the most common psychiatric disorders among people with AUD. The co-occurrence of these disorders are more severe and problematic to treat than either alone. People with AUD are 2.3 times more likely to have a major depressive disorder in the previous year than people without AUD. Women are also nearly two times as likely to experience a major depressive disorder than men. Unfortunately, the effects of antidepressant drugs alone on drinking outcome was modest.

People with AUD have a heightened risk for depressive disorders, which are the most common co-occurring psychiatric disorders for this population. AUD and depressive disorders appear to share some behavioral, genetic, and environmental risk factors, yet these shared risks remain poorly understood. Diagnosis and treatment of the commonly co-occurring AUD and depressive disorders have many challenges. Diagnosis is particularly challenging because of overlapping symptoms such as the depressant effects and alcohol and because of the features that are common to both alcohol withdrawal and depressive disorders such as insomnia psychomotor agitation.

Reference Number: 90111

SMREKAR, M., S. CUKLIEK, A.M. HOSNIAK, B. LLIC, AND S.L. FICKO. "Alcoholism: Success of Long-Term Treatment—A Systematic Review." *Croatian Nursing Journal*, 2: 63–71, 2018 (1 table, 1 figure, 23 references)

Abstract: A systematic review of scientific studies published between 2000 and 2017 showed six studies that evaluated the success of long-term treatment for alcoholism. Treatment of AUD is one of the biggest challenges since only about 50% of all patients achieved long-term abstinence by currently available therapies. People who abstain from alcohol for 3 to 6 months are more likely to establish and maintain long-term abstinence. The four medications approved for the treatment of alcoholism in Europe are acamprosate, disulfiram, naltrexone, and malmefene. The following interventions have a positive impact on the abstinence rate: aftercare telephone monitoring, regular medical check-ups, participation in self-help groups, pharmacotherapy, and outpatient long-term intensive therapy for alcoholics (psychiatric care, cognitive behavioral therapy, patient-centered psychiatry, and classical addiction therapy).

Alcoholics Anonymous is a widely used intervention for alcohol use disorders. Many patients find the social support provided by 12-step self-help groups useful in maintenance of abstinence, especially if they have no other social support. Most Western experts for helping alcohol addicts agree that the best chance for recovery and healing are alcoholics who have attended Alcoholics Anonymous meetings long enough and frequently enough as well. From just under 60% of alcoholics who after the completion of treatment continued to attend Alcoholics Anonymous meetings, 41% of them continued stable abstaining.

Reference Number: 90112

STILLMAN, M.A. AND J. SUTCLIFF. "Predictors of Relapse in Alcohol Use Disorder: Identifying Individuals Most Vulnerable to Relapse." *Addiction and Substance Abuse*, 1: 3–8, 2020 (33 references).

Abstract: Chronic alcohol abuse affects the brain structure, such as altered reward circuitry (which increases craving for alcohol), modified stress pathways, and compromised frontal white matter (which affects decision making, impulse control, and executive functioning). Craving and relapse are two core features of AUD. Comorbid depression, deficits in social cognition, interpersonal relationships, and facial emotion recognition ability may be predictive of relapse. Negative mood is associated with increased craving.

Clinicians should encourage AA attendance, treat depressive symptoms, address coping mechanisms, and enhance social support in the first year of abstinence. Monitoring individuals whose alcohol problems and impulsivity improve unusually quickly may be vital in determining at-risk patients.

Reference Number: 90113

BAILEY, K.L., D.R. SAMUELSON, AND T.A. WYATT. "Alcohol Use Disorder: A Pre-Existing Condition for COVID-19?" *Alcohol*, 90: 11–17, 2021 (99 references).

Abstract: In the 1918 influenza pandemic, heavy alcohol intake was recognized as a risk factor for poor outcome. Alcohol use can also cause behavioral changes that increase the risk of COVID-19. In Thailand, fifteen people in their twenties gathered for a farewell party. Eleven drank alcohol out of the same glass and developed COVID-19, whereas the four who did not drink did not contract COVID-19. The disease was spread in large gatherings with heavy drinking such as Mardi Gras in New Orleans. Alcohol is associated with dyspnea (shortness of breath), as is COVID-19, and alcohol also suppresses coughing and clearing of the virus. Alcohol may also interfere with the cilia mucous clearance cells, especially when combined with smoking, and impairs the immune function of the lungs. Heavy alcohol use predisposes those with acute respiratory distress syndrome to develop multi-system organ failure.

> Alcohol affects nearly every cell in the lung. Most of these changes potentially put those that drink heavily at higher risk of COVID-19 infection, and more severe pneumonia or ARDS. More research is needed to help us understand how to better treat those with alcohol use disorders with COVID-19.

9.02 WITHDRAWAL

> "Rigor and delirium after excessive drinking are bad symptoms."
>
> —Hippocrates of Cos, "Aphorisms VII"

> "Nicknames include 'the horrors', 'the shakes', 'the bottleache', 'quart mania', 'orks orks', 'gallon distempter', 'the zoots', 'barrel fever', 'the 750 itch'. 'pint paralysis', 'seeing pink elephants'. Another nickname is 'the Brooklyn Boys' found in Eugen O'Neill's one-act play Hughie set in 1920s Times Square."
>
> —"People Who Died from Delerium Tremens," geni.com

> "For any chemical action we impose on the brain, there is eventually an equal and opposite reaction."
>
> —Cermak, "Marijuana: What's a Parent to Believe?" (2003)

Delirium is derived from a Latin word meaning "to lose track" and was also known as brain fever. Delirium tremens was first described by an army physician, Thomas Sutton, in 1813 (90201, 90207).

Alcohol withdrawal syndrome (AWS) occurs within 1 to 2 days of abrupt cessation of alcohol consumption in chronic drinkers (90202). The removal of the constant depressant effects of alcohol causes a hyperexcitability or hyperactive state (90203, 90204, 90211). Alcohol is one of the few recreational drugs where a sudden cessation can cause death. Some of the clinical features of AWS include:

- Anxiety
- Tremor
- Headache

- Disorientation
- Agitation
- Delirium tremens
- Hallucinations (tactile, visual, auditory)
- Insomnia
- Anorexia, nausea, vomiting
- Diaphoresis (heavy sweating)
- Hyper-reflexia
- Tachycardia
- Hypertension
- Seizures
- Hyperventilation

The prevalence of AWS in the general population is about 5% but it can be up to 86% in alcoholics admitted for alcohol intoxication. Different types of drugs are used to treat AWS, including benzodiazepines, antipsychotic agents, antiepileptic drugs, and barbiturates (90206).

Approximately 20% of hospitalized patients have AUD, and AWS occurs in about 30% of trauma patients (90207). Trauma patients with AWS have seven times higher rates of complications and eight times the rate of ICU admissions than non-intoxicated patients without AWS (90208, 90212). Comorbidities such as smoking (71%), diabetes mellitus (25%), and chronic liver disease (35%) are common in patients with AWS (90209). A Prediction of Alcohol Withdrawal Severity Scale (PAWSS) has been developed to predict complicated AWS in hospitalized patients (90210; see Appendix 5).

One fifty-two-year-old man who drank at least 1.5 L of wine a day for twenty years developed hypovolemic shock and acute renal failure as a result of severe sweating and fever due to AWS (90211).

Approximately 14% of the deaths that occurred in unlicensed alcohol rehabilitation facilities in Los Angeles were due to AWS (90213). A thirty-year-old male chronic, heavy drinker for 10 years who had abstained from alcohol for 3 days was found wandering semi-nude around a train station and died suddenly at hospital (90214).

Delirium tremens should also be considered in an acutely agitated patient. A thirty-one-year-old man who consumed seventeen bottles of wine a week for ten years developed auditory and visual hallucinations after 6 days of abstinence and cut open his abdomen with a glass shard (90215).

Another serious disorder that occurs in alcoholics is Wernicke-Korsakoff syndrome, typically due to malnutrition, and alcoholism is treated with thiamine (90216).

A COVID-19 lockdown involving the banning of alcohol in India increased the number of hospitalized patients with severe AWS including delirium tremens. Hospitalizations increased from four to eight per day in Bangalore (90217).

Reference Number: 90201

PORCEL, F.J. AND H.S. SCHUTTA. "From Antiquity to the N-Methyl-D-Aspartate Receptor: A History of Delirium Tremens." *Journal of the History of Neurosciences*, 24: 378–395, 2015 (62 references)

Abstract: By 3200 B.C.E., wine was already widely distributed in the Middle East. Greek alchemists had discovered distillation in the first century C.E., but there is no evidence it was used to distill alcohol. The distillation of wine to produce wine spirits was probably invented by apothecaries in Salerno, Italy, in the eleventh century C.E. Delirium (to lose track) was a word used by the Romans, but the description of delirious states associated with drinking began earlier with the Hippocratic writers. An army physician, Thomas Sutton, published a tract on delirium tremens (DT) in 1813. In 1955, H. Isabel and colleagues found withdrawal symptoms of various intensity in six volunteers if they consumed nearly an equivalent of a liter of whiskey daily for 48–87 days. The current mortality rates of DT range from 0 to 15% and is relatively high in older patients who have infections or other diseases.

Studies beginning in 1989 have shown that ethanol selectively inhibits NMDA (N-Methyl-D-Aspartate) receptors that transmit the excitatory effects of the neurotransmitter glutamate. The depressing effect of alcohol on NMDAR (N-Methyl-D-Aspartate receptors) results in a compensatory up-regulation of these receptors with consequent brain hyperexcitability that emerges upon the withdrawal of alcohol. Such neuroadaptive processes also develop in benzodiazepines users.

Reference Number: 90202

DIXIT, D., J. ENDICOTT, L. BURRY, L. RAMOS, S.Y.A. YEUNG, S. DEVABHKTUNI, S. CHAN, A. TOBIA, AND M.N. BULLOCH. "Management of Acute Alcohol Withdrawal Syndrome in Critically Ill Patients." *Psychopharmacology*, 36: 797–822, 2016 (2 tables, 46 references).

Abstract: Alcohol is the most frequently abused drug in the United States with more than 17 million Americans having alcohol use disorder (AUD). Approximately 16 to 31% of patients in ICU have AUD and are at risk of developing AWS while in care. Critically ill patients with AWS have an increased hospital and ICU stay, increased duration of mechanical ventilation, and higher mortality rates. Alcohol stimulates the inhibitory system, gamma aminobutyric acid [(GABA)A], and inhibits the excitatory N-methyl-D-aspartate (NMDA) system. Chronic alcohol consumption leads to tolerance and dependence. Neuronal hyperactivity and excitability occurs once the alcohol is ceased abruptly and the opposite occurs. The alcohol stimulation of the (GABA)A inhibitory system and the alcohol inhibition of the NMDA are removed. An additional upregulation of the dopaminergic system can lead to the hallucinations experienced during AWS. Benzodiazepines are the major drug used to control AWS, although barbiturates, propofol, baclofen, and carbamazepine have also been employed.

Table. Stages of Alcohol Withdrawal Symptoms

Stage	Time Since Last Alcohol	Signs and Symptoms
1	6–24 hours	• Tremor • Autonomic activity • Insomnia/agitation • Tachypnea/hyperventilation • Headache • Sweating • Anorexia/vomiting
2	7–48 hours	• Distractibility, tonic-clonic seizures (10% of patients) • Visual, tactile, or auditory hallucinations (30% of patients) • Autonomic instability • Diarrhea
3	49–96 hours	• Intense tremor—delirium tremens 5% of patients [25% mortality] • Severe autonomic instability • Confusion/disorientation/extreme agitation

Source: Adapted from Dixit et al (2016).

Obtaining a thorough substance use history from each patient is imperative to determine the risk of developing AWS symptoms. One of the goals of AWS treatment is to prevent the occurrence of the most severe symptoms in high-risk patients. Early identification and treatment is vital in reducing the risk of progressing to severe AWS. Unfortunately, this history can be difficult to obtain from critically ill patients who may not be able to communicate and who may not have a proxy to provide the information. Because their results are often conflicting, reports have failed to find any relationship between admission blood alcohol concentration and the likelihood of developing AWS. Patients with a history of prior withdrawal, seizures or DTs or those consuming alcohol while being treated for alcohol use disorder, are at a greater risk for withdrawal. With advancements in medical care and pharmacotherapy options, most patients survive AWS acutely. However, many patients remain at risk after acute AWS episode has subsided as a result of alcohol use after discharge. Approximately 44% of ICU patients who survive AWS are rehospitalized at least once or experience death within a year.

Reference Number: 90203

SAITZ, R. "Introduction to Alcohol Withdrawal." *Alcohol Health and Research World*, 22: 5–12, 1998 (2 figures).

Abstract: More than 1.5 million Americans are admitted to alcoholism treatment or to a general hospital as a result of alcohol dependence each year. These people and many others who do not seek professional treatment experience AWS, which may range from mild insomnia to delirium tremens and even death. AWS is due to a hyperactive or hyperexcited state caused by an abrupt removal of the constant depressive effects caused by alcohol. One of the most severe manifestations of AWS includes hallucinosis, which can occur within 2 days of decreasing or abstaining from alcohol, in which the person sees, hears, or feels things that are not there even though they are fully conscious and aware of their surroundings. AW seizures can also occur with 1 to 2 days of abstinence in which the person experiences a generalized convulsion involving a shaking of the arms, legs, and loss of consciousness. Multiple seizures may occur, resulting in status epilepticus. DTs can develop within 1 to 4 days and are more serious than the shakes. DTs cause a rapid heart rate, high blood pressure, fever, sweating, and tremors. About 5% of patients who experience DTs die from metabolic or cardiovascular complications, trauma, or infection.

Heavy drinkers who suddenly decrease their alcohol consumption or abstain completely may experience alcohol withdrawal (AW). Signs and symptoms of AW can include, among others, mild to moderate tremors, irritability, anxiety, or agitation. The most severe manifestations of withdrawal include delirium tremens, hallucinations, and seizures. These manifestations result from alcohol-induced imbalances in the brain chemistry that cause excessive neuronal severity of the patient's symptoms and of any complicating conditions as well as treatment of the withdrawal symptoms with pharmacological and nonpharmacological approaches. Treatment can occur in both inpatient and outpatient settings. Recognition and treatment of withdrawal can represent a first step in the patient's recovery process.

Reference Number: 90204

TREVIAN, L.A., N. BOUTROS, I.L. PETRAKIS, AND J.H. KRYSTAL. "Complications of Alcohol Withdrawal." *Alcohol Health and Research World*, 22: 61–66, 1998 (1 table, 1 figure, 44 references)

Abstract: GABA is an inhibitory neurotransmitter that alcohol facilitates its inhibitory function of the (GABA)A receptor, which contributes to the intoxicating and depressant effects of alcohol. Alcohol withdrawal causes reduced brain GABA and (GABA)A receptor sensitivity, which contributes to nervous system hyperactivity. The major excitatory neurotransmitter is glutamate. NMDA receptors play a role in memory, learning, and generation of seizures. Alcohol inhibits the excitatory function of NMDA receptors. AW seizures are associated with increased NMDA receptor function after alcohol cessation.

AW and its complications are among the most visible consequences of alcoholism. Those syndromes arise directly from adaptations made within nerve cell communication systems that are targets of alcohol in the brain. Among its actions, alcohol acutely facilitates the activity of (GABA)A receptor function and blocks NMDA receptor activity. The adaptations within these systems contribute to withdrawal-related symptoms, seizures, and neurotoxicity. Repeated AW episodes appear to increase the risk of future AW seizure. Acute withdrawal symptoms and complications including seizures, hallucinations, and DTs represent medical emergencies. Some complications including Wernicke-Korsakoff syndrome may be permanently disabling. In addition, the distress associated with acute and protracted withdrawal presents an ongoing motivation to relapse to alcohol use in recently detoxified patients. Thus, the early stages of sobriety represent a period of risk at many levels.

Reference Number: 90205

MCKEON, A., M.A. FRYE, AND N. DELANTY. "The Alcohol Withdrawal Syndrome." *Journal of Neurology, Neurosurgery and Psychiatry*, 79: 854–862, 2008 (2 tables, 1 figure, 122 references)

Abstract: The prevalence of AWS in the general population in the United States is generally low, about 5%, but can be up to 86% in those admitted for alcohol detoxification. Common drugs used in the treatment of AWS include lorazepam, chlordiazepoxide, diazepam, and anti-epileptic drugs such as carbamazepine. It is not recommended that patients be dispensed alcoholic beverages or alcohol IV in hospital to prevent AWS. DTs are the most serious manifestations of alcohol withdrawal. Hyponatremia (too much water in the blood, which dilutes the sodium concentration) is frequently seen in chronic alcoholics, especially for beer drinkers due to the large volume of fluid consumed, and should not be treated with saline IV. Wernicke's encephalopathy and Korsakoff psychosis may develop due to a thiamine deficiency caused by heavy alcohol consumption.

The alcohol withdrawal syndrome (AWS) is a common management problem in hospital practice for neurologists, psychiatrists, and general physicians alike. Although some patients have mild symptoms and may even be managed in the outpatient setting, others have more severe symptoms or a history of adverse outcomes that require close inpatient supervision and benzodiazepine therapy. Many patients with AWS have multiple management issues (withdrawal symptoms, delirium tremens, the Wernicke-Korsakoff's syndrome, seizures, depression, polysubstance abuse, electrolyte disturbances, and liver disease) which requires a coordinated multidisciplinary approach. Although AWS may be complex, careful evaluation and available treatment should ensure safe detoxification for most patients.

Reference Number: 90206

JESSE, S., G. BRATHEN, M. FERRARA, M. KEINDL, E. BEN-MENACHEM, R. TANASESCU, E. BRODTKORB, M. HILLBOM, M.A. LEONE, AND A.C. LUDOLPH. "Alcohol Withdrawal Syndrome: Mechanisms, Manifestations and

Management." *Acta Neurologica Scandinavica*, 135: 4–16, 2017 (4 tables, 2 figures, 104 references)

Abstract: AWS occurs in about 8% of hospitalized AUD inpatients after an abrupt cessation of heavy/consistent drinking. Severe AWS more than doubles the length of a hospital stay and frequently causes treatment in the ICU. Different types of drugs to treat AWS include benzodiazepines, antipsychotic agents, antiepileptic agents, barbiturates, clomethiazole, and baclofen.

Table. Some Common Signs and Symptoms of AWS

Autonomic Symptoms	Motor Symptoms	Awareness Symptoms	Psychiatric Symptoms
Tachycardia	Hand tremor	Insomnia	Illusions
Rapid breathing	Seizures	Agitation	Delusions
Dilated pupils	Ataxia	Irritability	Hallucinations
Elevated BP	Gait disturbances	Delirium	Paranoid ideas
Elevated body temperature	Hyperreflexia	Disorientation	Anxiety

Source: Adapted from Jesse et al (2017).

The alcohol withdrawal seizure is a symptom occurring primarily during the early phases of withdrawal and is characterized by reduction in the seizure threshold. More than 90% of acute symptomatic seizures emerge within 48 h of cessation of prolonged drinking. Seizures frequently occur in the absence of other signs of the AWS. More than half of individuals present with repeated seizures and in up to 5% they may progress to status epilepticus. More than 50% of withdrawal seizures are associated with concurrent risk factors such as prior epilepsy, structural brain lesions, or use of other drugs. It is remarkable that the development of acute symptomatic seizures during an alcohol withdrawal episode is associated with a fourfold increase in the mortality rate that is due to complications of severe AUD rather than a direct effect of seizures.

Reference Number: 90207

MAINEROVA, B., J. PRASKO, K. LATALOVA, K. AXMANN, M. CERNA, R. HORACEK, AND R. BRADACOVA. "Alcohol Withdrawal Delirium—Diagnosis, Course and Treatment." *Biomedical Papers of the Medical Faculty of the University Palacky, Olomouc, Czech Republic*, 159: 44–52, 2015 (120 references)

Abstract: The symptoms of alcohol withdrawal delirium were first described in 1813 as brain fever. In the same year, Samuel Pearson introduced the term "delirium tremens." Approximately 20% of hospitalized patients have problems with alcohol dependence. Withdrawal symptoms occur in about 30% of trauma patients and 16% of surgery patients in the postoperative period. Delirium develops in about 5–20% of patients treated for alcohol withdrawal syndrome. Delirium tremens usually develops within twenty-four to seventy-two hours of alcohol cessation as a complication of AWS and typically worsens in the evening or night. The symptoms usually subside after 1 to 7 days.

> Delirium tremens is the most severe complication of alcohol withdrawal which usually appears after longer periods of heavy drinking. This severe condition may be life-threatening and may lead to death or severe morbidity when not managed properly. The most important issue of the treatment is its prevention by early recognition of the potential risk of alcohol withdrawal and its management. When fully developed delirium tremens is better managed at the ICU or other wards capable for monitoring the vital functions and laboratory parameters of the patients. The most effective drugs used are short-acting benzodiazepines in supramaximal doses with their sequential reduction after pacification and overall calming is achieved.

Reference Number: 90208

NG, C., M. FLEURY, H. HAKMI, B. BRONSON, J.A. VOSSWINKEL, E.C. HUANG, M. SHAPIRO, R.S. JAWA. "The Impact of Alcohol Use and Withdrawal on Trauma Outcomes: A Case Control Study." *The American Journal of Surgery*, 222: 438–445, 2021 (5 tables, 39 references)

Abstract: A study was conducted of 3,896 trauma patients hospitalized in a Boston level 1 trauma center between 2015 and 2019 with a BAC measurement and/or an AWS diagnosis. Nearly 76% of the patients had a BAC $<$ 0.010 g/100 mL, 23.2% had a BAC $>$ 0.010 g/100 mL, and 1.2% had AWS. Of the forty-eight AWS patients, forty-six received psychiatric consultation. All of the AWS patients were administered benzodiazepines. Eight patients with AWS had an initial BAC $<$ 0.010 g/100 mL. The mean BAC of the patients with a positive BAC was 0.234 g/100 mL (range 0.083–0.330 g/100 mL).

Table. Odds Ratio of Adverse Hospital Outcomes in AWS Patients

Complication	Odds Ratio
Mortality	1.40×
Major complications	7.14×
ICU admissions	8.18×
Unplanned ICU	11.6×
Mechanical ventilation	3.93×

Source: Adapted from Ng et al (2021).

Trauma patients with Alcohol Withdrawal Syndrome experienced higher rates of complications and utilized greater hospital resources compared to intoxicated and non-intoxicated individuals without AWS. The complex nature of alcohol withdrawal cases, including the possibility of developing AWS despite a negative BAL on admission, emphasizes the need for early assessment. We recommend routine blood alcohol level, use of validated AWS prediction scales, and involving Psychiatrists or other substance use disorder specialists for this population, to improve the management of these complex trauma patients.

Reference Number: 90209

AL-MAQBALI, J.S., N. AL-MAQRASHI, A. AL-HURAIZI, Q.S. AL-MAMARI, K. AL ALAWA, AND A.M. AL ALAWI. "Clinical Characteristics and Health Outcomes in Patients with Alcohol Withdrawal Syndrome: An Observational Study from Oman." *Annals of Saudi Medicine*, 52–57, 2022 (2 tables, 32 references)

Abstract: An analysis was conducted of 150 male patients (median age 39.5 years) who attended a hospital in Oman for AWS between 2019 and 2020. Smoking (70.7%) and concurrent use of other drugs (29.3%) were common. Six patients (4%) were admitted to ICU and thirteen patients (9%) required care in a high dependency unit. Twenty-one patients (14%) developed seizures. The mean total dose of diazepam was 40 mg. Forty-nine patients (32.7%) were readmitted with AWS within 90 days of release.

Table. Comorbidity of Patients with AWS

Comorbidity	Percent of Patients
Smoking	70.7%
Other drugs of abuse	29.3%
Diabetes mellitus	24.7%
Chronic liver disease	35.3%
Hypertension	24.0%
Chronic kidney disease	4.7%
Epilepsy	8.7%

Source: Adapted from Al-Maqbali et al (2022).

This study demonstrated the male predominance of patients treated for AWS. Smoking and concurrent drug abuse were common. A high proportion of patients were readmitted within 90 days with AWS. Also, drug and alcohol service was poorly engaged in managing patients with AWS due to lack of service in our hospital and underutilization of the outpatient alcohol rehabilitation program. A relatively high number of patients left the hospital against medical advice before completing the treatment, indicating poor management satisfaction. High occupancy of acute medical beds and the need for treatment in high care settings (ICU, HDU) reflect the added burden of alcohol related health outcomes in our busy health care setting. AWS is an avoidable overburden on the health care system. Therefore, we strongly believe that a drug and alcohol unit is an essential service in a tertiary care setting to improve the care of patients with drug and alcohol withdrawal.

Reference Number: 90210

MALDONADO, J.R., Y. SHER, J.F. ASHOURI, K. HILLS-EVAN, H. SWENDSEN, S. LOLAK, AND A.C. MILLER. "The Prediction of Alcohol Withdrawal Severity Scale (PAWSS): Systematic Literature Review and Pilot Study of a New Scale for the Prediction of Complicated Alcohol Withdrawal Syndrome." *Alcohol*, 48: 375–390, 2014 (5 tables, 4 figures, 261 references).

Abstract: A Prediction of Alcohol Withdrawal Severity Scale (PAWSS) was developed based on a literature search of 2,802 articles resulting in 233 unique articles describing factors predictive of AWS. A total of ten items were identified as being predictive of complicated AWS (e.g., hallucinations, seizures, and DTs). A pilot study was conducted of sixty-eight patients admitted to hospital over a 2-week period and graded according to PAWSS. The sensitivity, specificity, and positive and negative predictive values of a 4 or greater score on PAWSS was 100% (see Appendix 5).

> The results of the literature search identified 10 items which may be correlated with risk for complicated AWS. These items were assembled into a tool to assist in the identification of patients at risk: PAWSS. The result of this pilot study suggests that PAWSS may be useful in identifying risk of complicated AWS in medically ill hospitalized individuals. PAWSS is the first validated tool for the prediction of severe AWS in the medically ill and its use may aid in the early identification of patients at risk for complicated AWS, allowing for prophylaxis against AWS before severe alcohol withdrawal syndromes develop.

Reference Number: 90211

FUNAYAMA, M., R. OKOCHI, S. ASADA, Y. SHIMIZU, S. KUROSE, AND T. TAKATA. "Severe Diaphoresis and Fever During Alcohol Withdrawal Cause Hypovolemic Shock: Case Report." *BMC Psychiatry*, 21: 387, 5pp, 2021 (1 table, 18 references)

Abstract: Alcohol withdrawal causes a state of CNS arousal and increased adrenergic activity due to high NMDA levels and low GABA activity. Several medical conditions have been associated with AWS, such as seizure, cardiac arrhythmia, diaphoresis (excessive abnormal sweating), and fever, but this is the first reported case of severe hypovolemic shock. A fifty-two-year-old man with a twenty-year history of AUD (consuming at least 1.5 L of wine per day) was admitted to ER with severe diaphoresis and fever, and over a period of days this led to hypovolemic shock and acute renal failure.

> This case shows that excessive diaphoresis and high fever associated with alcohol withdrawal syndrome can cause hypovolemic [shock] and its related conditions, i.e., hypotension and acute renal failure, even though a patient may consume almost all their food. Prophylactic administration of benzodiazepines immediately after admission should have been conducted and might have prevented alcohol withdrawal syndrome and these medical consequences. In our opinion, however, this clinical course might be common considering the frequent occurrence of diaphoresis and fever during alcohol withdrawal syndrome, and some patients even experience iatrogenic benzodiazepine associated delirium [during] alcohol withdrawal treatment. In fact, diaphoresis is included as one of the essential signs for

diagnosis of alcohol withdrawal syndrome in ICD-10 (international Classification of Diseases, 10th revision).

Reference Number: 90212

VIGOUROUX, A., C. GARRET, J-B. LASCARROU, M. MARTIN, A-F. MIAILHE, J. LEMARIE, J. DUPEYRAT, O. ZAMBON, A. SEGUIN, J. REIGNIER, AND E. CANET. "Alcohol Withdrawal Syndrome in ICU Patients: Clinical Features, Management, and Outcome Predictors." *PLOS One*, 16: 14pp, 2021 (4 tables, 1 figure, 48 references)

Abstract: Of the 5,641 patients admitted to the ICU at the Nantes University Hospital between 2017 and 2019, 246 (4.4%) had AWS, of which 204 were included in this study. AWS was typically diagnosed 1 day after ICU admission and lasted 5 days. Vitamin B1 and vitamin B6 and intravenous hydration were administered within the first twenty-four hours. Benzodiazepines were given to 99% of the patients. The occurrence of a complicated hospital stay in ICU patients was 48% in those with AWS and 31% in patients without AWS.

Table. Some Characteristics of Complicated and Uncomplicated Hospital Stays

	Complicated Hospital Stay	Uncomplicated Hospital Stay
Delirium tremens	58.2%	48.1%
Seizures	16.3%	21.7%
Status epilepticus	5.1%	12.3%
Pneumonia	48.0%	17.9%
Median length of stay in ICU (days)	11	4

Source: Adapted from Vigouroux et al (2021).

In conclusion, ICU patients in this sample drawn from a single hospital in France were predominately male (84%) with a median age of 53 (IQR 46–60) and were commonly admitted with additional diagnoses including sepsis, trauma, or following elective or urgent surgery. Despite having low severity scores at ICU admission, half the patients experienced an extended ICU stay or death during hospital stay. The likelihood of developing complicated hospital stay was lower in patients with seizures and higher in those with multiple organ dysfunctions at ICU admission.

Reference Number: 90213

SU, K.-C., L. NGUYEN, AND C. ROGERS. "Deaths in an Unlicensed Alcohol Rehabilitation Facilities." *Journal of Forensic Sciences*, 62: 103–106, 2017 (2 tables, 2 figures, 14 references)

Abstract: A review of forty-two deaths that occurred in unlicensed alcohol rehabilitation facilities serving Spanish-speaking men in Los Angeles County between 2003 and 2014 was undertaken. All decedents were male ranging in age between twenty-two and sixty-eight years (mean age forty-four years). The BACs ranged from 0 to 0.590 g/100 mL (mean 0.197 g/100 mL).

Table. Causes of Death and Percentage in Unlicensed Alcohol Rehabilitation Facilities

Cause of Death	Percent of Deaths (%)
Chronic alcoholism	26.2
Acute alcohol toxicity	26.2
Alcohol withdrawal	14.2
Toxicity of alcohol and other substances	7.1
Restraint	7.1
Diabetes mellitus	7.1
Atherosclerotic disease	4.8
Bronchopneumonia	2.4
Hypertensive heart disease	2.4
Blunt head trauma	2.4

Source: Adapted from Su et al (2017).

Acute complications of alcohol withdrawal include dehydration, hypoglycemia, ketoacidosis, hypokalemia, inhalation pneumonia, aggressive behavior, and hyperpyrexia. About 40% of those who misuse alcohol develop an acute withdrawal symptom when they abruptly stop drinking. This syndrome consists of anxiety, tremor, sweating, nausea, retching, tachycardia, and systemic hypertension. The onset of acute alcohol withdrawal is typically about 6–8 days after stopping alcohol, and the syndrome may last for several days.

Reference Number: 90214

BAND, R.M., M.C. MEENA, A. KANDPAL, AND S. MITTAL. "Rapid Death Due to Alcohol Withdrawal Syndrome: Case Report and Review of Literature." *Asia Pacific Journal of Medical Toxicology*, 4: 51–54, 2015 (3 figures, 25 references)

Abstract: A thirty-year-old male chronic and heavy alcohol drinker for 10 years was undergoing de-addiction treatment and abstained from alcohol for 3 days. He developed palpitations, sweating, and tremors. The next day he was taken to hospital as he was wandering around a railroad station in a semi-nude condition, talking to himself. At the ER he was stuporous (Glasgow Coma Scale, 6), feverish, with tachycardia (110 bpm), low BP ($^{90}/_{60}$ mm Hg), difficulty breathing, and developed generalized seizures. Despite treatment he died 2 hours later. At autopsy, it was found that he had a massive pulmonary hemorrhage as well as a cirrhotic, yellow discolored liver and left ventricular hypertrophy of the heart.

> Alcoholism is associated with liver dysfunction and especially in final phases with cirrhosis. Hence, and due to resultant coagulopathy, patients are vulnerable to internal bleedings. Hypertrophic cardiomyopathy also occurs in chronic alcoholics. Therefore, we can speculate that our patient developed pulmonary hemorrhage as a result of the combined effect of coagulopathy secondary to cirrhosis, alveolar damage (seizure and artificial ventilation) and congestive heart failure. For a patient with delirium, convulsions, respiratory distress and coagulopathy, diagnosis of DT should be kept in mind.

Reference Number: 90215

THOMASSON, R., V. CRAIG, AND E. GUTHRIE. "Self-Disembowelment During Delirium Tremens: Why Early Diagnosis Is Vital." *BMJ Case Reports*, 3pp, 2016 (14 references)

Abstract: A thirty-four-year-old man who drank more than seventeen bottles of wine a week for a decade was concerned about his drinking and decided to completely stop his drinking at once. Over the next few days, he developed AWS, including sweating, tremors, and escalating anxiety. Within 6 days he developed auditory and visual hallucinations and ran outside with a knife. He was detained in police custody and was diagnosed with paranoid psychosis and was transferred to a psychiatric ward. He continued to have hallucinations and within hours of his admission smashed a mirror on the wall and used a shard of glass to cut open his abdomen. He was treated at hospital for his physical injuries and his psychotic symptoms resolved quickly after the administration of chlordiazepoxide.

Delirium tremens should always be considered in the differential diagnosis of the acutely agitated patient. Psychotic symptoms may or may not be immediately apparent, and patients may be too frightened or suspicions to disclose them. Ask about command hallucinations.They may be present in addition to classically described visual hallucinations and confer grave risks to the patient and others if commands involve instructions to harm.

Reference Number: 90216

ZUBARAN, C., J.G. FERNANDES, AND R. RODNIGHT. "Wernicke-Korsakoff Syndrome." *Postgraduate Medical Journal*, 73: 27–31, 1997 (3 figures, 55 references).

Abstract: Alcohol abuse is a serious public health problem, and the Wernicke-Korsakoff syndrome (WKS) is one of the most serious consequences of alcoholism. Wernicke's disease is associated with nutritional deficiency (i.e., thiamine), especially due to alcoholism and withdrawal, which results in ataxia, nystagmus, and mental confusion. Korsakoff's psychosis is a mental disorder in which retentive memory is greatly impaired and is also associated with alcoholism and malnutrition. Patients with WKS should be treated immediately with 50–100 mg thiamine IV daily. The mortality rates with WKS are high (10%–20%).

A symptom complex comprising both a defect in learning and memory and the manifestations of Wernicke's disease is appropriately diagnosed as Wernicke-Korsakoff syndrome.

Reference Number: 90217

NARASIMHA, V.L., L. SHUKLA, D. MUKHERJEE, J. MENON, S. HUDDAR, U.K. PANDA, J. MAHADEVAN, A. KANDASAMY, P.K. CHAND, V. BENEGAL, AND P. MURTHY. "Complicated Alcohol Withdrawal—An Unintended Consequence of COVID-19 Lockdown." *Alcohol and Alcoholism*, 55: 350–353, 2020 (1 figure, 24 references)

Abstract: The first COVID-19 case in India was reported on 30 January 2020. India instituted a 21-day lockdown on 24 March 2020, and during the lockdown alcohol was banned. The incidence of severe AWS presenting at hospitals in Bangalore was determined between 1 January 2020 and 11 April 2020. During lockdown there was a four to eight per day increase in the number of severe AWS cases presenting at the hospitals. The typical severe AWS patient, especially DT patients in Bangalore, is unemployed, homeless, and suffering electrolyte abnormalities, structural brain lesions, and malnutrition.

> What are the solutions? The solutions will have to be context specific. For example, Scottish health services disseminated information to guide patients in gauging their risk of severe AWS and planning a safe domiciliary detoxification. This strategy may work in a higher income well-connected population. Most of our patients reported that they wished to stockpile and gradually reduce, but they did not have the money to buy alcohol on the last day. Nevertheless, planning, foreseeing an increase in severe AWS and ensuring that addiction treatment services are not disrupted are reasonable steps in all settings.

9.03 HEALTH RISKS

> "All the crimes on earth do not destroy so many of the human race, nor alienate so much property as drunkenness."
>
> —Attributed to Francis Bacon

> "Harmful use of alcohol is a causal factor in more than 200 diseases and injury conditions. Worldwide, 3 million deaths every year result from harmful use of alcohol. This represents 5.5% of all deaths."
>
> —World Health Organization, "Alcohol: Harmful Use of Alcohol" (2022)

In addition to the well-known effect of alcohol causing liver diseases, excessive alcohol use is also associated with:

- Cardiac arrhythmias
- Cardiovascular diseases
- Seizures
- Stroke
- Hypertension
- Respiratory disease
- Kidney diseases
- Cancers
- Dementia

Unlike tobacco, in which any use is harmful, moderate alcohol consumption has been associated with decreased risk of cardiovascular disease and a prolongation of life associated with the French paradox and a U- or J-shaped curve (90301, 90302, 90309).

But alcohol has been known to be cardiotoxic for over a century, and heavy use is associated with premature cardiovascular mortality, hypertension, cardiac arrhythmias and holiday heart syndrome, sudden cardiac deaths, seizures, and strokes (90303–90310).

Excessive alcohol consumption is also associated with alcohol-related dementia and Wernicke-Korsakoff syndrome (90311–90312).

Alcohol causes 3.6% of the cancers worldwide, especially cancers of the upper aerodigestive tract, oral cavity, pharynx, and esophagus (90313). A heavy drinker has 1.4 times the cancer risk as an abstainer (90314).

Of course, alcohol use causes all types of liver diseases, such as fatty enlarged livers, cirrhosis, fibrosis, and hepatitis (90315). Sudden unexpected deaths in alcohol misuse are common (90316).

Men and women with long-term AUD die more than *25 years or a quarter century earlier* than men and women without AUD (90317).

Reference Number: 90301

SINKIEWICZ, W., M. WEGLARZ., AND M. CHUDZIRISKA. "Wine, Alcohol and Cardiovascular Disease." *Kardiologia Polska*, 72: 771–776, 2014 (3 figures, 41 references)

Abstract: A short review of the French paradox regarding wine consumption and cardiovascular disease (CVD) is presented. The incidence of CVD in people living in the south of France is lower than those living in northern Europe (e.g., Scotland). The association between all-cause mortality and alcohol consumption is a U-shaped curve. Binge drinking (five or more drinks in one day of the week and refraining from drinking for the rest of the week) increases the risk of coronary heart disease. Regular consumption of reasonable amounts of alcoholic beverages while maintaining a healthy lifestyle can reduce morbidity and mortality.

> In conclusion, Hippocrates's statement: Wine is a matter which in a miraculous way intended for men to apply in good and bad health in the proper quantities; is surprisingly accurate and still valid in view of the hereby presented research findings.

Reference Number: 90302

LAONIGRO, I., M. CORREALE, M. DI BASE, AND E. ALTOMARE. "Alcohol Abuse and Heart Failure." *European Journal of Heart Failure*, 11: 453–462, 2009 (1 table, 136 references)

Abstract: Alcohol has been considered a cardiotoxin for more than a century, and heavy alcohol consumption can result in alcoholic cardiomyopathy (ACM). The relationship between ACM and other cardiac events and alcohol consumption is a U- or J-shaped curve. Those who consume 30 g or more of alcohol a day have increased overall mortality, higher BP, and increased liver enzymes, while smaller doses reduce the risk of coronary heart disease.

> Long term alcohol consumption is an important cause of dilated cardiomyopathy. Although the amount and duration of alcohol that results in ACM is not clearly established, men and women who consume > 90g/day of alcohol (more than eight drinks per day) for > 5 years are at risk for the development of ACM. There is a symptomatic stage of ACM which is characterized by LV dilation, increased LV mass, and diastolic function. The symptomatic stage of ACM is characterized by pronounced LV dilation, increased LV mass, wall thinning, systolic dysfunction and signs and symptoms of HF.

Reference Number: 90303

SIDORENKOV, O., O. NILSSEN, N. KLESCHINOV, AND A.M. GRIBOVSKI. "Premature Cardiovascular Mortality and Alcohol Consumption Before Death in Arkhangelsk, Russia: An Analysis of a Consecutive Series of Forensic Autopsies." *International Journal of Epidemiology*, 40: 1519–1529, 2011 (4 tables, 39 references).

Abstract: A study was conducted of 1,099 men and 519 women (ages thirty to seventy years) who died of cardiovascular disease (CVD) in Arkhangelsk, Russia, between 2008 and 2009. Postmortem BACs and UACs were determined by GC. CVDs were responsible for about 35% of all deaths in women and men less than seventy years of age. About one-third of men and women who died of CVD before the age of sixty years had consumed alcohol shortly prior to death. Alcohol was 1.55 times as likely to be found in men than women.

Consumption of large amounts of spirits in a single drinking episode is widely prevalent in Russia, primarily among middle-aged men. This drinking pattern has been shown to increase the risk of IHD by way of underlying myocardial dysfunction with increased propensity to cardiac arrhythmias and diminished myocardial contractility, increased clotting tendency and transient increase of blood pressure. Most of the current evidence for the association between high cardiovascular mortality in Russia and hazardous alcohol consumption originates from research based on combined population-level data. Research using a single sample with information on the individual level is therefore warranted.

Reference Number: 90304

MILLER, P.M., R.F. ANTON, B.M. EGON, J. BASILE, AND S.A. NGUYEN. "Excessive Alcohol Consumption and Hypertension: Clinical Implications of Current Research." *The Journal of Clinical Hypertension*, 7: 346–353, 2005 (1 table, 47 references)

Abstract: Hypertension is the leading cause of stroke and congestive heart failure and affects more than half of Americans over sixty years of age. Excessive alcohol consumption (three or more drinks per day) increases blood pressure significantly in both normotensive and hypertensive individuals. Initially alcohol causes vasodilation with secondary stimulus of the sympathetic system, which causes constriction of the blood vessels and increases the contractile force of the heart.

Of the more than 60 million hypertensive patients in the United States, approximately 9.75 million drink at levels that could negatively impact their BP. Brief physician intervention could reduce alcohol consumption considerably in these patients. Based on the studies reviewed here, reductions in drinking could lead to at least a 2 mm Hg reduction in diastolic BP. The overall result in the general population would be a 17% decrease in the prevalence of hypertension, a 15% reduction in stroke, and a 6% reduction in the risk of coronary heart disease. Routine screening and brief intervention by physicians can significantly improve BP control and overall quality of care in hypertensive patients.

Reference Number: 90305

BRUNNER, S., R. HERBEL, C. DROBESCH, A. PEERS, S. MASSEBERG, S. KAAB, AND M.F. SINNER. "Alcohol Consumption, Sinus Tachycardia, and Cardiac

Arrhythmias at the Munich Octoberfest: Results from the Munich Beer Related Electrocardiogram Workup Study (MunichBREW)." *European Heart Journal*, 38: 2100–2106, 2017 (3 tables, 3 figures, 24 references).

Abstract: Oktoberfest is a traditional public festival in Munich that has been celebrated annually since 1810. In 2015, nearly 6 million visitors attended Oktoberfest and consumed 7.5 million liters of beer. During the 16 days of the 2015 Munich Oktoberfest, 3,028 participants (mean age 34.7 years, 30% women) were administered an EEG using a smartphone-based AliveCor device. BrACs were determined with an Alcotest 7510. In addition, the chronic effects of alcohol on a 12-lead EEG were determined on 2,021 men and 2,110 women who also answered a survey regarding alcohol consumption in the KORA S4 study. The mean BrACs were 0.085 g/100 mL (range 0–0.294 g/100 mL) at Oktoberfest. Cardiac arrhythmia occurred in 30.5% of the drinkers but only 2.7% of the participants in the chronic alcohol users study.

Table. The Percentage of Men and Women with Acute and Chronic Alcohol Use and Various Related Cardiac Arrhythmias

	Acute		Chronic	
Arrhythmia	Men	Women	Men	Women
Sinus arrhythmia	1.9%	1.2%	0.2%	0.2%
Sinus tachycardia	24.2%	29.9%	0.4%	0.4%
Premature atrial complexes	1.4%	1.0%	0.7%	0.5%
Premature ventricular complexes	1.8%	1.4%	0.9%	1.3%
Atrial fibrillation	0.6%	1.4%	0.9%	0.2%

Source: Adapted from Brunner et al (2017).

Acute alcohol consumption is associated with cardiac arrhythmias and sinus tachycardia in particular. This partly reflects autonomic imbalance as assessed by significantly reduced sinus arrhythmia. Such imbalance might lead to sympathetically triggered atrial fibrillation resembling the holiday heart syndrome.

Reference Number: 90306

KAUPPILA, J.P., L. PAKANEN, K. PORVANI, J. VAHATALO, L. HOLMSROM, J.S. PERKIOMAKI, H.V. HUIKURI, AND M.J. JUNTTILA. "Blood Alcohol Levels in Finnish Victims of Non-Ischemic Sudden Cardiac Death." *Annals of Medicine*, 53: 413–419, 2021 (3 tables, 2 figures, 26 references)

Abstract: Non-ischemic heart disease (NIHD) accounts for approximately 20% of sudden cardiac deaths (SCD). Chronic heavy drinking can lead to cardiomyopathy (CM), which is a type of NIHD. The BACs of 1,301 victims of sudden cardiac disease due to NIHD in Finland were determined between 1998 and 2017. A positive postmortem BAC was found in 543 (42%) of the victims. The median BAC was 0.140 g/100 mL. Fifty-one percent of all NIHD SCD victims were known to be heavy drinkers. Sixty-one percent of the victims with a positive BAC were known to be heavy drinkers compared to 44% of those with a negative BAC. More male SCD victims had a positive BAC (45%) compared to 31% of the female victims. Recent alcohol consumption may contribute to the subsequent NIHD sudden cardiac death.

Chronic heavy drinking (more than six standard drinks per day) is associated with hypertension, myocyte hypertrophy, and increased cortisol and cholesterol levels, increasing the risk of myocardial infarction, dilated CM, heart failure and cardiac arrhythmias, such as atrial fibrillation, ventricular tachycardia, and ventricular fibrillation. NIHD consists of different conditions, such as CMs, myocarditis and valvular disease. CMs compose the majority of NIHD.

Reference Number: 90307

CRAUCIC, D.-V., C.I. STAN, L.A. RISCANU, D-C. PIRVU, AND D. BULGARU-ILIESCU. "Death-Causing Cardiac Injuries After Chronic Alcohol Intake Identified by Forensic Medicine." *Romanian Journal of Morphology and Embryology*, 62: 553–561, 2021 (2 tables, 6 figures, 74 references)

Abstract: Autopsies were conducted on 57 male and 20 female chronic alcohol consumers who died in northwest Romania in 2020. The victims ranged in age from eighteen to eighty-nine years (mean sixty-two years) and two-thirds lived in rural areas. Approximately 40% of the victims were less than sixty years of age. Postmortem blood EtG concentrations were determined. All victims had increases in heart size (especially the left ventricle), heart failure changes, myocardial fibrosis, and aortic arteriosclerosis. An elevated blood EtG concentration was observed in all victims indicating that alcohol consumption occurred within 96 hours of death.

Table. Percent of Victims with Cardiovascular Complication and Mean Postmortem Blood EtG Concentration

Cardiovascular Complication	Percent	Mean Blood EtG Concentration (ng/mL)
Dilated cardiomyopathy	80.5%	726
Myocardial fibrosis	92.2%	619
Myocardial infarction	9.0%	845

Source: Adapted from Crauciuc et al (2021).

Consumed in excessive amounts, alcohol becomes a toxic drug with pathological effects on the liver, gastrointestinal tract, cardiovascular system, kidneys, brain, etc. Practically, alcohol, due to its very small molecule penetrates almost all tissues of the body, which leads to significant changes in organ function and the appearance of diseases limited to one organ or multisystemic disorders.

Reference Number: 90308

TONELO, D., R. PROVIDENCIA, R., AND L. GONCALVES. "Holiday Heart Syndrome Revisited After 34 Years." *SciELO Brazil*, 183–189, 2013 (1 table, 2 figures, 32 references).

Abstract: The holiday heart syndrome (HHS) was first recognized by Philip Ettinger in 1978 to describe the association between his acutely alcohol-intoxicated patients and cardiac arrhythmias. The cardiac arrhythmias occurred more frequently after weekends and public holidays when alcohol intoxication was more prevalent. The most frequent symptoms reported are heart palpations, pain, dizziness, and shortness of breath. The episodes of HHS disappeared with alcohol abstinence and reappeared with continued binge alcohol use.

Alcohol has a definite role in cardiac arrhythmia, either by chronic abuse or by binge drinking. It is important for physicians to recognize HHS and be aware of the role of alcohol in its genesis, sparing patients from complex investigations when there is no clinical evidence of cardiac pathologies. During admission of a patient with palpitations or their symptoms associated with cardiac arrhythmia, a high suspicion of HHS should occur if the patient exhibits signs of alcoholic intoxication or had a recent episode or binge drinking. After confirming the cardiac arrhythmia and excluding evident heart diseases, the physician should explain the syndrome to the patient and recommend alcohol abstinence in an effort to prevent new episodes of HHS.

Reference Number: 90309

VOSKOBOINIK, A., J.M. KALMAN, A. DE SILVA, ET AL. "Alcohol Abstinence in Drinkers with Atrial Fibrillation." *The New England Journal of Medicine*, 382: 20–28, 2020 (2 tables, 3 figures, 28 references)

Abstract: Atrial fibrillation is a leading cause of stroke and affects 33 million people worldwide. A dose-dependent relationship between alcohol intake and atrial fibrillation incidence and adverse events has been reported with the consumption of seven to fourteen drinks per week. Alcohol is also linked with other risk factors for atrial fibrillation such as hypertension, obesity, obstructive sleep apnea, and left ventricular dysfunction. One hundred and forty patients in Australia with atrial fibrillation were assigned randomly to an abstinence group and a control group (no change in drinking) for 6 months. Patients in the abstinence group reduced their alcohol consumption from 16.8 to 2.1 standard drinks (12 g alcohol) per week. The control group reduced their consumption from 16.4 to 13.2 standard drinks per week. Atrial fibrillation-related hospital visits were 9% in the abstinence group and 20% in the control group. The percentage of time in atrial fibrillation was 0.5% in the abstinence group and 1.2% in the control group.

Epidemiologic studies suggest that light-to-moderate alcohol consumption is associated with a lower incidence, in a U-shaped pattern of coronary artery disease and cardiovascular events. Complete abstinence may increase the risk of these events and this study was underpowered to determine the effect on cardiovascular disease, heart failure, stroke, or mortality. Thus, potential cardiovascular benefits of moderate alcohol consumption must be reconciled with the potential for atrial proarrhythmic. Regular alcohol consumption is a potentially modifiable risk factor for atrial fibrillation. In this trial involving regular alcohol drinkers with atrial fibrillation [who] decreased their drinking from about 17 drinks per week to 2 drinks per week and had a reduction in both atrial fibrillation burden and risk of recurrence of atrial fibrillation.

Reference Number: 90310

O'KEEFE, J.H., S.K. BHATTI, A. BASJWA, J.J. DINICOLANTONIO, AND C.J. LAVIE. "Alcohol and Cardiovascular Health: The Dose Makes the Poison . . . or the Remedy." *Mayo Clinic Proceedings*, 89: 382–393, 2014 (9 figures, 99 references)

Abstract: The WHO estimates that alcohol kills 2.5 million people a year worldwide or is responsible for approximately 4% of all deaths. The harmful use of alcohol is the world's leading risk factor for deaths among males (ages fifteen to fifty-nine years) due mainly to injuries, violence, and cardiovascular deaths. Excessive alcohol consumption is also associated with seizures, strokes, poisonings, cirrhosis, and cancers of the colon, rectum, breast, larynx, and liver. It is estimated that excessive drinking in the United States costs $234 billion a year due to health costs. Responsible habitual drinking (one drink/day for women, one to two drinks/day for men) is associated with lower risks for diabetes mellitus, stroke, heart failure, coronary artery disease, and total mortality.

However, higher levels of alcohol consumption are associated with increased cardiovascular risk. Indeed, behind only smoking and obesity, excessive alcohol consumption is the third leading cause of premature death in the United States. Heavy alcohol use 1) is one of the most common causes of reversible hypertension, 2) accounts for about one-third of all cases of nonischemic dilated cardiomyopathy, 3) is a frequent cause of atrial fibrillation, and 4) markedly increased risk of stroke—both ischemic and hemorrhagic.

Reference Number: 90311

RIDLEY, N.J., B. DRAPER, AND A. WITHALL. "Alcohol-Related Dementia: An Update of the Evidence." *Alzheimer's Research and Therapy*, 5: 3, 8pp, 2013 (70 references)

Abstract: Up to 70% of individuals diagnosed with alcoholism show some degree of brain pathology at autopsy. Neuroimaging and neuropathological evidence show prominent white matter loss (mainly in the frontal lobes), which can show partial recovery upon abstention. A review was conducted on the two main cognitive-related impairments due to alcoholism, alcohol related dementia (ARD), and Wernicke-Korsakoff syndrome (WKS).

Most cases of WKS in developed countries related to the misuse of alcohol, although WKS syndrome following gastrointestinal disorders and systemic diseases can also contribute. While there is no direct correlation between the prevalence of WE and per capita consumption of alcohol, the introduction of thiamine supplementation programs in some countries as well as general dietary habits also influences overall rates. Prevalence rates of WKS identified post mortem are thought to be between 1% and 12% of the general population and around 10% of alcohol misusers in Western countries.

Reference Number: 90312

HANDING, E.P., R. ANDEL, P. KADLECOVA, M. GATZ, AND N.L. PEDERSEN. "Midlife Alcohol Consumption and Risk of Dementia Over 43 Years of Follow-Up: A Population-Based Study from the Swedish Twin Registry." *Journals of Gerontology: Medical Sciences,* 70: 1248–1254, 2015 (6 tables, 2 figures, 38 references).

Abstract: The association between alcohol consumption and various adverse health effects has been described as a J- or U-shaped curve. This could be because low alcohol doses or toxicity may boost the body's natural defense mechanism and support health and cognitive health over time, whereas high doses and toxicity overwhelm the body and cause adverse effects. This is known as hormesis theory. The midlife consumption of alcohol (beer, wine, spirits) and dementia incidence was determined over 43 years in 12,236 members of the Swedish Twin Registry, born between 1907 and 1925. The group was divided into non-drinking (0 g/d), light (1–5 g/d), moderate (5–12 g/d), heavy (12–24 g/d), and very heavy (> 12 g/d) groups. Overall, 1,958 (15%) of the participants had a recorded dementia with an average age at the first record of dementia of 83.2 years.

Table. Daily Alcohol Consumption and Hazard Ratio of Developing Dementia (Adjusted for Age, Sex, Education, Smoking Status, and Physical Activity)

Alcohol Consumption	Hazard Ratio
None	1.05
Light	ref
Moderate	0.98
Heavy	1.10
Very heavy	1.18

Source: Adapted from Handing et al (2015).

Averaging more than 12 grams of alcohol per day may increase risk of dementia. Alcohol from spirits appears particularly important for the increased dementia risk. Genetic and/or familial factors do not explain these associations. Alcohol use reduction may be a useful population-wide intervention strategy.

Reference Number: 90313

CAO, Y. AND E.L. GIOVANNUCCI. "Alcohol as a Risk Factor for Cancer." *Seminars in Oncology Nursing,* 32: 325–331, 2016 (1 table, 50 references).

Abstract: Approximately 88% of Americans have consumed alcohol at some time in their life and 72% reported drinking alcohol in the last year. It is estimated that alcohol causes 3.6% of all cancers worldwide. The cancers with the highest relative risk due to alcohol are upper aerodigestive tract, oral cavity, pharynx, larynx, and esophagus cancers. The relative risks are less for colorectal and breast cancer. The total amount of alcohol consumed over time and not the type of alcoholic beverage consumed seems to be the most important factor for the risk of cancer. Light to moderate drinking are defined as one drink (14 g) per day for women and up to two drinks per day for men. The metabolite of alcohol, acetaldehyde, is considered to be the major cancer-causing agent.

Alcohol is a complex behavior in our society. The impact of alcohol on cancer risk is just one of the concerns, albeit an important one, in regards to the overall health and social aspects of alcohol consumption. Light-to-moderate drinking, defined as up to one drink per day for women and up to two drinks per day for men is not appreciably associated with cancer risk, and may be beneficial for cardiovascular disease and overall mortality. Although it is generally not advisable for abstainers to begin alcohol drinking for health benefits, it is reasonable for those already drinking at moderate levels, including cancer survivors to continue to do so if they wish. Nonetheless, some subgroups, especially those with a family history of colorectal cancer, possibly breast cancer or experience facial flushing after alcohol consumption, may be at increased risk for some cancers if they consume alcohol.

Reference Number: 90314

XI, B., S.P. VEERANKI, M. ZHAO, C. MA, Y. YAN, AND J. MI. "Relationship of Alcohol Consumption to All-Cause, Cardiovascular, and Cancer-Related

Mortality in U.S. Adults." *Journal of the American College of Cardiology*, 70: 913–922, 2017 (3 tables, 7 figures, 34 references)

Abstract: Self-reported alcohol consumption and mortality rates were determined in 333,247 US participants (eighteen years or older) between 1997 and 2009. After a mean follow-up of 8.2 years, 34,754 died of all causes, 8,947 died of CVD, and 8,427 died of cancer.

Table. Relative Risk of Death According to Alcohol Consumption Status

Cause of Death	Lifetime Abstainer	Lifetime Infrequent Drinker	Former Drinker	Light Drinker	Moderate Drinker	Heavy Drinker
Cancer	1.0	1.05	1.12	0.89	0.95	1.40
CVD	1.0	1.06	0.93	0.73	0.72	0.96
Heart disease	1.0	1.06	0.93	0.74	0.73	0.99
Stroke	1.0	1.10	0.95	0.71	0.69	0.82
All cause	1.0	1.02	1.04	0.80	0.81	1.13

Source: Adapted from Xi et al (2017).

Using a large sample of US adults, our study re-emphasized the existence of a J-shaped curve in the alcohol-mortality association, supporting current findings that light to moderate drinking might be protective, especially for CVD, but heavy drinking or binge drinking has serious health consequences, including death. A balance between beneficial and detrimental effects of alcohol consumption on health should be considered when making individual or population-wide recommendations, but the reduction of harmful or high consumption of alcohol remains necessary and essential.

Reference Number: 90315

SAVOLAINEN, V.T., K. LIESTO, A. MANNIKKO, A. PENTTILA, AND P.J. KARHUNEN. "Alcohol Consumption and Alcoholic Liver Disease: Evidence of a Threshold Level of Effects of Ethanol." *Alcoholism: Clinical and Experimental Research*, 17: 1112–1117, 1993 (4 figures, 43 references).

Abstract: The features of alcoholic liver disease (ALD) were determined in 210 men (ages thirty-five to sixty-nine years) during autopsy at the Department of Forensic Medicine in Helsinki. The subjects were divided into rates of daily alcohol intake of controls (0–10 g), 10–40 g, 40–80 g,

80–160 g, and > 160 g. Moderate alcohol consumption was considered to be 10–80 g of alcohol daily. When compared to controls, the relative weight of the liver statistically increased in the 40–80 g and > 160 g groups. Alcohol-induced liver enlargement is the result of an accumulation of water (50%–55%), proteins (15%–25%), and fatty acids and triglycerides (20%–25%). Liver enlargement occurs in approximately 90 percent of alcoholics with fatty livers (FL). A slight fatty change of the liver (1%–10%) was a common feature of all consumption groups as well as 44% of the controls. Liver cirrhosis and bridging fibrosis increased 8.8 times for the group consuming > 80 g/day compared to controls. No positive alcoholic hepatitis (AH) cases were found at daily consumption levels less than 40 g.

In conclusion, liver enlargement and the incidence of FL and AH all increased statistically significantly with a daily intake between 40 and 80 g in this series of males, suggesting that between these margins may exist a threshold beyond which the risk of ALD increases. The highly significant increases in the incidence of bridging fibrosis and liver cirrhosis among consumers with daily intake exceeding 80 g indicated that fibrosis of the liver is not associated with moderate alcohol consumption but rather with long-term excessive alcohol consumption. Furthermore, when an individual risk level is attained increasing daily consumption may have no additional effect on the progression of ALD.

Reference Number: 90316

SANJEEWA, R.H.K., D.G. VAN PITTISU, AND M. VIDANAPATHIRANA. "Sudden Unexpected Death in Alcohol Misuse: A Case Report." *Medico-Legal Journal of Sri Lanka*, 6: 43–46, 2018 (2 figures, 10 references)

Abstract: A sixty-three-year-old man was found dead on the bathroom floor. These was no past medical history of diabetes mellitus, hypertension, or alcohol withdrawal. He stopped smoking thirty years ago. He consumed five to six bottles per day for the last 9 months but his postmortem BAC was 0.113 g/100 mL. At autopsy there was slight jaundice, pallor, mild left ventricular hypertrophy, and marked fatty changes in the liver, but no evidence of chronic diseases.

Sudden death is more common in chronic alcohol misuse. The relationship between sudden death and fatty liver has been confirmed in a number of studies which have reported a link between fatty liver and death in alcoholics. Possibilities include fat embolism, alcohol withdrawal, hypoglycemia, alcoholic ketoacidosis, and other electrolyte abnormalities. Cardiac arrhythmia is most favored as the likely mechanism. Many alcoholics have a prolonged QT interval which is associated with increased risk of sudden death. Chronic alcoholism is associated with profound electrolyte disturbances including hypomagnesaemia which can lead to fatal rythym.The term SUDAM (sudden unexpected death in alcohol misuse) has been coined recognizing the increased risk of sudden death in alcoholics. SUDAM is applied to sudden unexpected non-traumatic deaths where there is a history of chronic excess alcohol consumption and/or evidence of hepatic steatosis but no other anatomical or toxicological cause of death and no significant cardiac hypertrophy.

Reference Number: 90317

WESTMAN, J., K. WAHLBECK, T.M. LARSEN, M. GISSLER, M. NORDENTOFT, H. HALLGREN, M. ARFFMAN, AND U. OSBY. "Mortality and Life Expectancy of People with Alcohol Use Disorder in Denmark, Finland and Sweden." *Acta Psychiatrica Scandinavica*, 131: 297–306, 2015 (3 tables, 7 figures, 29 references).

Abstract: The mortality and life expectancy of people with AUD in Denmark, Finland, and Sweden between 1987 and 2006 were determined. In all three counties, people with AUD had higher mortality from all causes of death, all diseases and medical conditions, and suicides. Life expectancies were 24 to 28 years shorter in people with AUD than the general population.

Table. Life Expectancy (Years) of Men and Women with AUD and the General Population in Denmark from 1987 to 2006

	1987–1991	1992–1996	1997–2001	2002–2006
Men with AUD	46.6	46.1	46.7	47.5
General male population	72.3	72.8	74.0	75.0
Difference	–25.7	–26.7	–27.3	–27.5
Women with AUD	49.8	49.5	51.4	51.2
General female population	77.9	77.9	78.7	79.6
Difference	–28.1	–28.4	–27.3	–28.4

Source: Adapted from Westman et al (2015).

Findings from the present study show that AUD in the Nordic countries is associated with substantially increased mortality, even though alcohol control policies are restrictive compared with other countries. What might be important to add to the general restrictive alcohol policies would be selective efforts aimed at high alcohol consumers to achieve preventative effects in terms of reducing the rate of high consumers converting to AUD. In this field a wider focus is necessary including testing new preventative efforts with the aim of reducing alcohol-related harm in people with AUD. In addition, the somatic care of people with AUD should be substantially improved.

9.04 FETAL ALCOHOL SPECTRUM DISORDER

"But he said unto me, Behold, thou shalt conceive, and bear a son; and now drink no wine nor strong drink, neither eat any unclean thing: for the child shall be a Nazarite to God from the womb to the day of his death."

—Judges 13:7, *King James Bible*

"During pregnancy the placenta does not act as a protective barrier to the widespread distribution of alcohol taken by mothers; and foetal and maternal blood alcohol concentrations are virtually identical."

—Beattie, "Transplacental Alcohol Intoxication" (1986)

Fetal alcohol spectrum disorder (FASD) is a complicated condition caused by alcohol use by the mother during pregnancy, especially during the first two trimesters. Some of the possible indictors of FASD include (90403):

- Chronic homelessness
- Consistently confabulates
- Easily influenced by others
- Inability to maintain employment
- Poor coping skills
- Rage control problems
- Sexually inappropriate behaviors
- Substance abuse problems
- Impaired memory

The deleterious effect of alcohol by a pregnant woman has been known since Greek and Roman times and it was believed that alcohol intoxication at the time of procreation would result in a damaged child. The term fetal alcohol syndrome was introduced in 1973 and in 1996 the term fetal alcohol spectrum disorder was introduced (90401).

Approximately 3% of pregnant women in the United States consumed two or more drinks a day while they were pregnant. However, when the alcohol consumption is abruptly ceased both the mother and fetus developed AWS (90402).

The prevalence of FAS in Italy is eight per 100,000 births and the brain injury caused by alcohol exposure in the fetus is irreversible (90404–90405). The global prevalence of FASD is 0.77%; it is 0.19% in Europe and 2 to 5% in the United States (90406).

Youth with FASD were nineteen times more likely to be incarcerated than youth without alcohol exposure as a fetus. But only 0.1% of justice-involved adults have documented FASD (90407–90409).

Reference Number: 90401

CALHOUN, F. AND K. WARREN. "Fetal Alcohol Syndrome: Historical Perspectives." *Neuroscience and Behavioral Reviews*, 31: 168–171, 2007 (25 references)

Abstract: The deleterious effect of a pregnant woman's consumption of alcohol on the fetus has been known since ancient Greek and Roman times, who believed that alcohol intoxication at the time of procreation would result in a damaged child. Clinically, FAS was not well documented until 1968. The term FAS was introduced in 1973. In 1996 a committee of the Institute of Medicine recommended a new classification, fetal alcohol spectrum disorders (FASD), which includes FAS (with and without a history of alcohol exposure), partial FAS, ARBD (alcohol-related birth defects), and ARND (alcohol-related neurodevelopmental disorder).

Jones et al, 1973 presented a detailed case report of three Native American, three black, and two white children, including developmental delay, microcephaly, prenatal and postnatal growth deficiency, short, palpebral fissures, epicanthal folds, small jaws, flattened midface, joint anomalies, and altered palm crease patterns. The authors concluded their observations claiming the data are sufficient to establish that maternal alcoholism can cause serious aberrant fetal development.

Reference Number: 90402

THOMAS, J.D. AND E.P. RILEY. "Fetal Alcohol Syndrome: Does Alcohol Withdrawal Play a Role?" *Alcohol Health and Research World*, 22: 53, 1998 (2 figures, 26 references).

Abstract: Approximately 3.3% of pregnant women in the United States consumed two or more drinks per day during their pregnancy. When heavy alcohol consumption is abruptly ceased, both the mother and the fetus undergo AWS. In one case a newborn who had a BAC of more than 0.200 g/100 mL developed signs of alcohol withdrawal including tremors and vomiting 24 to 48 hours after birth. Newborns undergoing AWS are best treated by being placed in a calm, decreased sensory environment. The use of benzodiazepines and other drugs should be used for only the most serious AW cases (e.g., seizures).

Prenatal alcohol exposure can have devastating effects on the growth and development of the fetus. Although alcohol can disrupt development through many mechanisms, both direct and indirect, little research has addressed the issue of whether withdrawal contributes to alcohol's deleterious effects. Researchers are now beginning to understand the role of neurotransmitter receptors in excitotoxic brain damage and in the development of withdrawal symptoms. The consequences of alcohol's actions at these receptors are highly complex in the dynamic context of development because these neurotransmitters that react with these receptors also play important roles in neural development. For example, NMDA receptors activation can result in both neuronal growth promoting and excitotoxic effects and its activity must be finely balanced. Consequently, both inhibition of the NMDA receptor after alcohol exposure and activation of the receptor during withdrawal could interfere with neuronal development.

Reference Number: 90403

GUPTA, K.K., V.K. GUPTA, AND T. SHIRASAKA. "An Update on Fetal Alcohol Syndrome—Pathogenesis, Risks and Treatment." *Alcoholism: Clinical and Experimental Research*, 40: 1594–1602, 2016 (1 table, 1 figure, 129 references)

Abstract: FAS was first described in 1973. The incidence of FAS in Canada and the United States ranges between 0.5 and 3.0 per 100,000 live births.

Alcohol is a well-established teratogen. The risk of FAS is related to timing (in the first trimester) and amount of alcohol consumed (e.g., binge drinking). Other risk factors include genetic influences, lower socioeconomic status, and smoking.

Table. Psychological Deficits in Fetal Alcohol Syndrome

Psychological Deficits in FAS
• Hyperactivity • Attention deficits—sustained and focused attention • Planning difficulties • Learning memory problems • Poor consolidation of new memories • Lower IQ—arithmetic, receptive language, and verbal processing problems • Social difficulties

Source: Adapted from Gupta et al (2016).

Clearly the most effective method of FAS prevention is to stop maternal alcohol consumption during pregnancy; however, considering current incidence rates, this seems largely ineffective thus far. In 2011/2012, 40 to 52% of women were reported to drink alcohol during pregnancy in the United Kingdom, and 52.5% in the United States with 17.2% bingeing (4+ drinks/occasion). This does not however, advocate the discontinuation of programs used to educate mothers on the dangers of drinking during pregnancy. Prenatal methods to reverse or prevent alcohol's teratogenicity mechanisms are being explored, although none are currently approved for clinical use. Many trials have examined the effects of antioxidants on alcohol-exposed fetuses. For example, vitamin C, resveratrol, astaxanthin, and curcumin have been administered to cell or animal models and shown to counter ETOH-induced oxidative stress. Treating women with antioxidants as food supplements may also help reverse nutritional deficiencies commonly seen in FAS mothers.

Reference Number: 90404

LANDGRAF, M.N., M. NOTHACKER, I.B. KOPP, AND F. HEINEN. "The Diagnosis of Fetal Alcohol Syndrome." *Deutsches Ärzteblatt International*, 110: 703–710, 2013 (5 tables, 3 figures, 37 references)

Abstract: The deleterious effects of alcohol exposure of the developing fetus due to drinking by the pregnant mother is referred to as fetal alcohol spectrum disorder (FASD). This spectrum ranges from full blown FAS to partial FAS, to alcohol-related neurodevelopment disorder (ARND) to alcohol-related birth deficits (ARBD). The prevalence of FAS in Italy is approximately eight per 100,000 live births. The brain injury caused by alcohol exposure in the fetus is irreversible and causes function impairment and problems coping with daily life.

> Of the 1383 publications retrieved by searches, 178 were analyzed for the evidence they contained, it was concluded that the fully-developed clinical syndrome of FAS should be diagnosed on the basis of the following criteria: Patients must have at least one growth abnormality, e.g., short stature, as well as all three characteristic facial abnormalities—short palpebral fissure length, a thin upper lip, and a smooth philtrum. They must also have at least one diagnosed structural or functional abnormality of the central nervous system, e.g., microcephaly or impaired executive function. Confirmation of intrauterine exposure to alcohol is not obligatory for the diagnosis.

Reference Number: 90405

MEMO, L., E. GNOATO, S. CAMINITI, S. PICHINI, AND L. TARANI. "Fetal Alcohol Spectrum Disorders and Fetal Alcohol Syndrome: The State of the Art and New Diagnostic Tools." *Early Human Development*, 8951: 540–543, 2013 (22 references)

Abstract: If the fetus is exposed to alcohol during pregnancy, a spectrum of physical, cognitive, and behavioral disabilities may develop known as FASD. The most severe form of FASD is fetal alcohol syndrome. In one Italian study the prevalence of FAS was between 3.7 and 7.4 per 1,000 births and of FASD was between 20.3 and 40.5 per 1,000 births. Biomarkers of alcohol consumption such as EtG, EtS, or FAEE in the maternal blood, urine, or meconium can detect unreported gestational use of alcohol. If the pregnant patient has a urinary tract infection of *E. coli*, a false negative test may occur as the EtG can be hydrolyzed (metabolized) by the bacteria.

> Ethanol is a legal and widely available substance that is increasingly abused in our society. One of the major harmful consequences of its consumption is certainly during pregnancy for the serious and irreversible damages of fetal exposure. Indeed, a significant number of women of childbearing age who are either problem drinkers or social drinkers will not refrain from ethanol drinking during pregnancy and may give birth to an infant in utero exposed

to this toxin. In addition, many women of childbearing age may not be aware of the harm even sporadic alcohol consumption during pregnancy can cause, since the message received from health professionals is not always clear, especially in countries of moderate ethanol use. Since the evidence of maternal drinking is always a critical prerequisite for FAS, it is important to objectively assess alcohol consumption in pregnant women for a targeted intervention to stop consumption during pregnancy. More important, for an early diagnosis of prenatal exposure and proper follow up, sensitive and specific biomarkers such as meconium, FAEEs or EtG testing are needed.

Reference Number: 90406

CARITO, V., G. PARLAPIANO, D. RASIO, R. PAPARELLA, V. PAOLUCCI, G. FERRAGUTI, A. GRECO, M. RALLI, S. PICHINI, M. FIORE, G. CORIALE, M. CECCANTI, AND L. TARANI. "Fetal Alcohol Spectrum Disorders in Pediatrics: FASD and the Pediatrician." *Biomedical Reviews*, 29: 27–35, 2018 (1 table, 2 figures, 73 references)

Abstract: FASD is a complex malformative condition due to the teratogenic effect of alcohol consumed during pregnancy and ranges from minimal damage to full FASD in the newborn and child. The global prevalence of FASD is about 0.77%; the European prevalence is 0.19% and it is 2 to 5% in the United States. Subjects with FAS typically have three major facial features such as short palpebral fissures (the area between the eyelids), elongated and flattened nasolabial philtrum (deep wrinkles from the bottom of the nose to the corners of the mouth), and a thin upper lip.

The issue of lifelong disabilities caused by alcohol drinking during pregnancy is quite problematic at familial, individual, and societal levels. As far as a nontoxic consumption behavior during gestation cannot be established, for the extremely individual conditions of vulnerability to alcohol, the only suggestion for women planning pregnancies, or during gestation and lactation is to totally avoid the consumption of alcoholic beverages.

Reference Number: 90407

BOWER, C., R.E. WATKINS, R.C. MUTCH, R. MARRIOTT, J. FREEMAN, N.R. KIPPIN, B. SAFE, C. PESTELL, C.S. CHEUNG, H. SHIELD, L. TARRATT, A. SPRINGALL, J. TAYLOR, N. WALKER, E. ARGIRO, S. LEITAO, S. HAMILTON, C. CONDON, H.M. PASSMORE, AND R. GIGLIA. "Fetal Alcohol Spectrum Disorder and

Youth Justice: A Prevalence Study Among Young People Sentenced to Detention in Western Australia." *BMJ Open*, 8: e019605, 10pp, 2017 (6 tables, 50 references)

Abstract: An assessment of FASD was conducted on ninety-nine youths (ages ten to eighteen years) in the only youth detention center in Western Australia between 2015 and 2016. This group was 93% male, 74% Aboriginal, and 13% were in child protection. Eighty-eight detainees had at least one domain of severe neurodevelopmental impairment and 36% were diagnosed with FASD. Prenatal alcohol exposure was confirmed in 47% of the total group and 47% of those diagnosed with FASD were Aboriginal.

Table. Percent of Those with and Without FASD Who Have Severe Impairment of Various Neurodevelopmental Domains

Neurodevelopmental Domain Impaired	Percent of Those with FASD	Percent of Those Without FASD
Academic achievement	86%	48%
Attention	72%	44%
Executive function	78%	40%
Language	69%	32%
Memory	56%	29%
Motor skills	50%	17%
Cognition	36%	13%

Source: Adapted from Bower et al (2017).

The greater prevalence of FASD in Aboriginal populations corresponds with higher rates of high-level alcohol consumption in these populations, but this observation fails to acknowledge the complex reasons were higher alcohol use. Past colonial policies such as the removal of Aboriginal children from their families and resultant dispossession from land, community, and culture, as well as the historical role of the criminal justice system and Aboriginal incarceration was well documented. In addition, these policies have left a legacy: high levels of family violence, drug and alcohol misuse, mental health problems, poverty, disadvantage, marginalization, trauma, and incarceration have been well documented as traversing generations of Aboriginal families. High population rates of FASD in Aboriginal young people are likely to be directly responsible, in part, for the high rate of Aboriginal youth incarceration.

Reference Number: 90408

PEI, J., K. FLANNIGAN, S. KELLER, M. STEWART, AND A. JOHNSON. "Fetal Alcohol Spectrum Disorder and the Criminal Justice System: A Research Summary." *Journal of Mental Health and Clinical Psychology*, 2: 48–52, 2018 (37 references)

Abstract: FASD describes a diverse range of neurodevelopmental deficits that can occur as a result of prenatal alcohol exposure and affects 2 to 5% of the US and Canadian population. Approximately 11 to 23% of justice-involved youth were diagnosed or suspected of FASD, but only thirteen out of 14,8979 (0.1%) of justice-involved adults had documented FAS.

Individuals with FASD experience high rates of child welfare involvement, malnutrition, and increased risk for multiple placements as well as maltreatment before age 6. School disruptions, substance use, inappropriate behaviors, trouble with the law, incarceration, residential and employment instability and mental disorders are experienced much more frequently among individuals with FASD than in the general population. The FASD population is an incredibly complex group with needs that evolve and extend across the lifespan. It is believed that intervention research can provide answers for treating specific challenges and ameliorating negative outcomes for individuals with FASD, however the literature examining the effectiveness of treatment with this population is limited.

Reference Number: 90409

BROWN, J., J. LONG-MCGIE, A. WARTNIK, P. OBEROI, J. WALSH, E. WEINKAU, G. FALCONE, AND A. KERR. "Fetal Alcohol Spectrum Disorders in the Criminal Justice System: A Review." *Journal of Law Enforcement*, 3: 1–10, 2014 (64 references)

Abstract: The incidence of FASD in the US population is estimated to be between 1 and 5% and may be an invisible problem in the criminal justice system. Juveniles with FASD are nineteen times more likely to be incarcerated than those without FASD. In one study, nearly 60% of persons with FASD over the age of 12 years had a criminal record. Individuals with FASD in correctional settings can be highly susceptible and often associate with negative peer groups.

Education regarding the significance of FASD on the criminal justice system would help to promote awareness and sensitivity among criminal justice professionals (e.g., correctional officers, judges, law enforcement, lawyers, and probation officers) who may regularly come in contact with individuals diagnosed or suspected of having FASD. Once identified, a variety of skill-based interventions can be implemented with the goal of helping the individual with FASD live a more pro-social and productive life. Individuals who are incarcerated and struggle with FASD are deemed to be at high risk for recidivism after being released into the community, and typically require special consideration in order to prevent further criminal activity. Hence, current practices in working with these individuals involved in the criminal justice system appear to be relatively ineffective. Educating professionals in the early identification and subsequent referral for diagnosis is critical as well as initiating evidence-based treatments, and long-term monitoring of FASD is necessary to improve outcomes for the individual as well as for his or her community.

9.05 PUBLIC SAFETY MEASURES

"This is to certify that the post-accident convalescence of the Hon. Winston S. Churchill necessitates the use of alcoholic spirits especially at meal times. The quantity is naturally indefinite but the minimum requirements would be 250 cubic centimeters."

—A medical prescription written for Winston Churchill on 26 January 1932, which allowed him to consume alcohol during Prohibition while in the US, *The Chartwell Trust*

"Accompanying the near ubiquity of alcoholic beverages in human history has been a lively appreciation of the social and health problems caused by drinking. Whether in Greece, Palestine, or China, ancient texts speak eloquently about such problems. Every major religion has at least some strands that counsel abstinence from alcoholic beverages."

—Room et al, "Alcohol and Public Health" (2005)

Although Prohibition was a political failure, it did dramatically decrease alcohol consumption in the United States, which did not recover to its pre-Prohibition peak until the 1970s (90501).

Some of the public health measures found to mitigate alcohol harm include (90502–90509):

- Effective restrictions of alcohol sales to youth

- Increased and effective measures against drinking and driving
- Increased alcohol taxes
- Decreased availability of alcohol
- Health warnings (especially cancer) on labels of alcoholic beverages
- Restrictions in advertising especially to youth in social media
- Restrictions of alcohol sponsorship of sports

Global alcohol companies portray themselves as David fighting for freedom against government (Goliath) restrictions of alcohol (90510). Sports is the primary setting for the marketing of alcohol products, a practice that should be banned as tobacco products have been (90511). Most efforts to reduce alcohol-related harms by public health measures have faced strong resistance from the alcohol industry, which still continues to ignore the harms they created (90506–90508, 90512). As seen throughout this book, alcohol is not a harmless product.

Reference Number: 90501

BLOCKER JR, J.S. "Did Prohibition Really Work? Alcohol Prohibition as a Public Health Innovation." *American Journal of Public Health*, 96: 233–244, 2006 (4 figures, 65 references)

Abstract: Between 1900 and 1913 American beer production increased 1.2 billion gallons and the tax paid for alcohol grew from $97 million to $147 million. The Prohibitionists agreed that a powerful alcohol lobby was the greatest threat to American society and only Prohibition (making the manufacture of alcohol illegal) could stop the threat. The Anti-Saloon League (ASL) became the major Prohibitionist organization in 1905. The ALS was so focused on Prohibition that it did not require its members to pledge personal abstinence. Prohibition did dramatically decrease alcohol consumption, which did not recover to its pre-Prohibition peak until the 1970s. In 1939, 42% of Americans stated they did not consume any alcohol, which only dropped to 30% in the 1960s.

> Perhaps the most powerful legacy of National Prohibition is the widely held belief that it did not work. I agree with other historians who have argued that this belief is false: Prohibition did work in lowering per capita consumption. The lowered level of consumption during the quarter century following Repeal, together with the large minority of abstainers did socialize or maintain a significant portion of the population in temperate or abstemious habits. That it, it was partly successful as a public health

innovation. Its political failure is attributable more to a changing context than to characteristics of the innovation itself.

Reference Number: 90502

BOBAN, I.V., A. VRCA, AND M. SARAGE. "Changing Patterns of Acute Alcohol Intoxications in Children." *Medical Science Monitor*, 24: 5123–5131, 2018 (5 tables, 3 figures, 43 references)

Abstract: Of the 24,651 children (ages zero to eighteen years) hospitalized in Croatia between 2008 and 2015, 272 were treated for alcohol intoxication. The average age of the patients was 15.95 years (youngest 7.17 years) and the average BAC was 0.200 g/100 mL. Alcohol intoxication occurred mainly outside the children's home (92.4%) and on weekends or holidays (81.6%). The proportion of children hospitalized for alcohol intoxication decreased from 1.33% in 2008 to 0.75% in 2015.

> In conclusion, there was a significant decline in the number of hospitalizations for acute alcohol intoxication in children. This might be a result of better preventive and educational measures in schools and media campaigns, or the result of changing attitudes to alcohol drinking among youth. A high number of psychological treatments, more provided in girls than boys, could also be a reason for this declining trend or the small number of recurrences. Since most intoxications happen in public places to further reduce these risky behaviors, implementation of stricter laws and preventive measures are needed. In addition, prohibition of alcohol sales to youths should be better conducted and supervised. We also found an increase in non-medical drug usage indicating a need for a stricter legal procedure to ban the sale of drugs to minors and better school area supervision.

Reference Number: 90503

CHIKRITZHS, T. AND M. LIVINGSTON. "Alcohol and the Risk of Injury." *Nutrients*, 13: 277, 15pp, 2021 (1 figure, 151 references)

Abstract: Nearly 4.5 million persons died from injury globally in 2019. Alcohol intoxication plays a major role in a wide variety of injuries, such as road accidents, falls, drownings, and interpersonal violence (IV). Men (90%) and young persons ages fifteen to thirty-nine years (40%) dominate the alcohol-related injury deaths.

Table. Millions of Global Disability Adjusted Life Years (DALY) Lost Due to Alcohol Attributable Injuries

Alcohol-Related Injury	Millions of DALYs Lost
Interpersonal Violence	2.8
Suicide/Self-Harm	4.8
Road Injury	4.3
Other Transport	0.3
Falls	1.9
Drowning	0.4
Fire/Heat	0.3
Poisoning	0.2

Source: Adapted from Chikritzh et al (2021).

Nonetheless, there is reason to be optimistic. The evidence is clear; population level alcohol consumption centred policies that reduced alcohol's economic and physical availability, especially when implemented in conjunction with each other, substantially reduce alcohol-related injury in its various forms. Strategies specifically targeted at reducing alcohol-impaired driving are also highly effective and indeed essential for addressing the world's leading cause of death and disability among people in their most productive years.

Reference Number: 90504

RAZVODOVSKY, Y.E. "Alcohol, and Suicide in Belarus." *Psychiatria Danubina,* 21: 290–296, 2009 (1 table, 3 figures, 41 references)

Abstract: The autopsy reports of 64,162 suicides and 59,489 fatal alcohol poisonings were examined between 1997 and 2007 in Belarus (a former Soviet Republic). The suicide rate increased 41.2% from 17.7 in 1997 to 25 per 100,000 population in 2007. The fatal alcohol poisoning cases increased 2.1 times from 12.8 to 26.7 per 100,000 population. Alcohol was found in 62% of the suicide victims ranging from 49.3% in 1988 to 68.5% in 1981.

The results of the present study as well as findings from other settings indicated that a restrictive alcohol policy can be considered as an effective measure of suicide prevention in countries where rates of both alcohol consumption and suicide are high.

Reference Number: 90505

WIGG, S. AND L.D. STAFFORD. "Health Warnings on Alcoholic Beverages: Perceptions of the Health Risks and Intentions Towards Alcohol Consumption." *PLOS One*, 11: 12 pp, 2016 (3 tables, 2 figures, 40 references).

Abstract: Alcohol consumption is a factor in developing more than 200 diseases and is responsible for 3.3 million deaths worldwide annually. Forty-three female and seventeen male university students (ages eighteen to thirty-five years) were randomly assigned to no health warning (control), a printed health warning, or a pictorial health warning on beer and wine beverages. The effectiveness of the health warnings were measured with a survey.

> The present study produced several novel findings; participants' fear arousal, their perceptions of the health risks of consuming alcohol and their intentions to reduce and quit alcohol consumption differed significantly depending on the health warning label they were assigned. Consistent with predictions, the pictorial health warning was found to be the most effective health warning for all of the main measures. Most importantly, we observed that the pictorial health warning was found to be the most effective health warning for all of the main measures. Most importantly, we observed that the pictorial health warning led to increased intentions to reduce and quit alcohol consumption compared to the control conditions. This finding is in line with tobacco research which has found pictorial health warnings to be the most effective health warnings in increasing intentions to quit alcohol consumption. Similarly, we found that fear arousal and perceptions of health risks were highest for those participants in the pictorial health warning condition, a finding which is also in keeping with tobacco research.

Reference Number: 90506

HOBIN, E., S. SHOKAR, K. VALLANCEW, D. HAMMOND, J. MCGAVOCK, T.K. GREENFIELD, N. SCHOUERI-MYCHASIW, C. PARADIS, AND T. STOCKWELL. "Communicating Risks to Drinkers: Testing Alcohol Labels with a Cancer Warning and National Drinking Guidelines in Canada." *Canadian Journal of Public Health*, 111: 716–725, 2020 (2 tables, 2 figures, 32 references).

Abstract: Supporting safer and informed alcohol use is a critical component of public health policy to reduce alcohol-related harm. Alcohol warning labels (AWL) are an important aspect due to their low costs and high visibility to drinkers and especially to heavy drinkers. Currently forty-seven countries (but not Canada) mandate AWL. But AWL warning of drinking while pregnant and against the operation of a motor vehicle have been mandated in Yukon and the Northwest Territories since 1991. In one liquor store in Whitehorse, Yukon, AWLs with a cancer warning were placed on all liquor sold but was ceased by intense pressure from the alcohol industry in Canada. The recall of the cancer warning was thirty-two times greater in a liquor store with cancer AWL compared to stores without.

> This is the first real-world study to experimentally test the impact of alcohol labels with a cancer warning and national drinking guidelines. After a one-month intervention, significant increases were observed in recall of the cancer warning, label processing, and influence of drinking behaviours. Increases in recall of the drinking guideline label were not statistically significant, suggesting the label effects on cognitive processing and drinking behaviours were likely driven by the cancer warning. Using alcohol labels to increase consumer awareness of commonly unknown alcohol-related health risks, such as cancer, may help drinkers pay closer attention to their drinking and minimize alcohol related harms.

Reference Number: 90507

VALLANCE, K., A. VINCENT, N. SCHOUERI-MYCHASIW, T. STOCKWELL, D. HAMMOND, T.K. GREENFIELD, J. MCGAVOCK, AND E. HOBIN. "News Media and the Influence of the Alcohol Industry: An Analysis of Media Coverage of Alcohol Warning Labels with a Cancer Message in Canada and Ireland." *Journal of Studies in Alcohol and Drugs*, 81: 273–283, 2020 (2 tables, 3 figures, 66 references).

Abstract: A review was conducted of newspaper articles regarding coverage of alcohol warning labels containing a cancer message in Canada (Yukon) and Ireland between 2017 and 2019. Overall, 68.4% of the media articles in Canada and 18.9 percent in Ireland were supportive of AWLs with a cancer message. The majority of articles presented the alcohol industry arguments opposing AWL in Canada (65.8%) and Ireland (86.5%).

Table. Industry Arguments Against AWLs Reported in News Articles in Canada and Ireland

	Number of Mentions	
Industry Arguments	Canada	Ireland
Stating alcohol can cause cancer is inaccurate/misleading/unproven/incomplete/overreach	18	25
Alcohol and cancer link is too complex for a single label	5	7
AWLs are not effective/there are better less anti-trade alternative measures that the industry supports	7	23
Alcohol has health benefits and AWLs should not just mention risk	5	11
Alcohol is not the same as tobacco	4	2
Defamation and damages result from applying label stating that alcohol can cause cancer	12	0
Academic study conducting biased/flawed research	7	0

Source: Adapted from Vallance et al (2020).

Media coverage of the Yukon Study in Canada was largely supportive of AWLs with a cancer message, whereas coverage of the Ireland Bill was mainly opposed to the cancer labels and consistently foregrounded alcohol industry perspectives. Representatives of the alcohol industry in Canada and Ireland frequently made statements that distorted or unequivocally denied the validity of the labels' evidence based cancer message. Across all news coverage, industry arguments opposing the cancer label were largely consistent with the cross-industry playbook known to be used to undermine effective public health policies. Engaging with news and other media to increase awareness of the alcohol industry's playbook of messaging strategies may enable public health researchers and advocates to generate more critical coverage of industry lobbying activities and increase public support for alcohol control measures.

Reference Number: 90508

SEIDENBERG, A.B., K.P. WISEMAN, R.H. ECK, K.D. BLAKE, H.N. PLATTER, AND W.M.P. KLEIN. "Awareness of Alcohol as a Carcinogen and Support for Alcohol Control Policies." *American Journal of Preventive Medicine*, 62: 174–182, 2022 (2 tables, 35 references)

Abstract: A survey was conducted on 3,865 American adults in the 2020 Health Information National Trends Survey 5, Cycle 4 regarding adding warning labels and drinking guidelines to alcoholic beverage containers and banning outdoor advertising. Most Americans supported warning labels and drinking guidelines on alcohol containers (65.1% and 63.9% respectively), but only 34.4 percent supported banning outdoor alcohol advertising. Approximately one-half of the participants were non-drinkers (52.1%), 19.6% were post 30- to 60-day drinkers, and 28.3% were heavier drinkers. Awareness of the alcohol-cancer link was low (only 31.8% reported an increased cancer risk).

Alcohol is a leading modifiable risk factor for cancer, yet most Americans are unaware that alcohol increases cancer risk. Misperceptions about the alcohol-cancer link were associated with lower odds of support for 3 alcohol control policies. Moreover, heavier drinkers had lower odds of policy support than nondrinkers. Because public opinion is one aspect of political will, which has been described as an essential component to the implementation of public health policy, increasing awareness and subsequently policy support may help increase the adoption of preventive alcohol policies. Increasing awareness of the alcohol-cancer link, such as through multimedia campaigns and patient-provider communications, may be an important new strategy for health advocates working to implement preventive alcohol policies.

Reference Number: 90509

VENTURA-COTS, M., M.P. BALLESTER-FERRE, S. RAVI, AND R. BATALLER. "Public Health Policies and Alcohol-Related Liver Disease." *JHEP Reports*, 1: 403–413, 2019 (3 figures, 107 references)

Abstract: Alcohol-related liver disease (ALD) is a main contributor to alcohol attributable deaths and disabilities. The major factor affecting advanced ALD (i.e., cirrhosis) is the percentage of the population who drink heavily. Since the 1990s the WHO and numerous governments have developed public health policies to curb the consumption of alcohol, such as taxes and price, drinking age, restrictions to alcohol access, driving-related alcohol policies, and alcohol promotion and advertising restrictions.

Although the alcohol industry has its own self-regulation codes, a recent study detected that alcohol brands have alarmingly inadequate age-gates to social media accounts.The type and role of different advertising regulations on social media and the internet are not well defined. The first studies investigating the influence of all media advertising on alcohol consumption (including television, radio, billboards, internet, and social media) did not find robust evidence for or against implementation of alcohol advertising restrictions. Further studies focused on social media and young populations found that alcohol-related social media engagement was correlated with both greater self-reported drinking and alcohol-related problems. This is of extreme importance as young populations are more exposed to alcohol advertising content on social media than adults. The positive use of social media represents an opportunity to target young people. In fact, a recent study showed that young adults exposed to certain types of alcohol-warning advertising reduce alcohol consumption.

Reference Number: 90510

MADDEN, M. AND J. MCCAMBRIDGE. "Alcohol Marketing Versus Public Health: David and Goliath?" *Globalization and Health*, 17: 45, 6pp, 2021 (72 references).

Abstract: Alcohol harms are increasing globally, and global alcohol corporations have sought to become trusted sources of advice for policy makers and consumers. The promotion of alcohol is widespread, but the alcohol industry appears invisible, with product retail largely being undertaken by other parties such as the hospitality industry and supermarkets. Although the international alcohol manufacturers are global marketing and financial giants, they portray themselves as David, fighting for freedom and against government (Goliath) restrictions on alcohol. Reducing alcohol harms means reducing the amount of the drug (ethanol) that is consumed by increasing its price, reducing its physical availability, and marketing.

Alcohol marketing dominates people's thinking about alcohol because we currently allow this to happen. We give corporations a license to operate and we should look at the terms of the license and revise them to better protect public health. Some countries have complete bans on alcohol marketing and WHO recommend such bans should be enforced where they exist and comprehensive restrictions on advertising, sponsorship, and promotion introduced where they do not. If that idea makes you uncomfortable, you might ask yourself why.

Reference Number: 90511

O'BRIEN, K.S., P.G. MILLER, G.S. KOLT, P. MATRENS, AND A. WEBBER. "Alcohol Industry and Non-Alcohol Industry Sponsorship of Sportspeople and Drinking." *Alcohol and Alcoholism*, 46: 210–213, 2011 (1 table, 33 references)

Abstract: Sportspeople drink more alcohol, in a more hazardous manner, and with more resulting harm than non-sportspeople. A survey was conducted of 652 sportspeople (mean age 20.7 years, 51% female) at the sports grounds of two universities in New South Wales regarding sports sponsorship and their current drinking status. Nearly one-third of the sportspeople reported receiving some form of sports sponsorship, of which 95% was from the alcohol industry. About 60% of those interviewed met the AUDIT criteria of hazardous drinking and only 6% reported abstaining from alcohol. Those sportspeople who received alcohol sponsorship were predictive of higher AUDIT scores, but those who received non-alcohol sponsorship were not.

Sport is a primary setting for the marketing of alcohol products and consumption. Tobacco industry sponsorship of sport has been abolished in most western nations for over a decade with little apparent detriment to sport. The banning of alcohol industry sponsorship and advertising in sport remains contentious but is at the centre of alcohol policy debates and suggests that governmental regulation of alcohol industry sponsorship and advertising in sport may be warranted.

Reference Number: 90512

PETTIGREW, S., C. HAFEKOST, M. JONGENELIS, H. PIERCE, T. CHIKRITZHS, AND J. STRAFFORD. "Behind Closed Doors: The Priorities of the Alcohol Industry as Communicated in a Trade Magazine." *Frontiers in Public Health*, 6: Article 217, 8pp, 2018 (1 table, 52 references).

Abstract: Most efforts to reduce alcohol-related harm by public health measures have faced strong resistance from the alcohol industry. A total of 362 articles published in the Australia alcohol trade magazine—*National Liquor News*—during 2015 were evaluated. Three main themes were evident in those articles: (1) the legitimization of alcohol as an important social and economic product, (2) the portrayal of the industry as trustworthy and benign, and (3) the strategic embedding of alcohol in various facets of everyday life. There was a general failure in the articles and by the alcohol industry to acknowledge the substantial burden of disease caused by their product.

> Recommendations for future alcohol policy are consistent and clear. There is strong support for minimum unit pricing, the introduction of a volumetric tax, mandatory advertising regulations, stricter trading hours limits, limiting outlet density, and alcohol warning labels. The content of the trade magazine articles demonstrates that such interventions will be viewed by the industry as unreasonable incursions on their rights. But forewarned is forearmed, and the insights obtained from the articles provide some indication of effective approaches to address industry strategizing. First, while alcohol marketers attempt to better educate consumers to demand more of their products, the public health community needs to counter this with other forms of consumer education that draw drinkers' attention to alcohol-related harms. For example, research suggests that drinkers would be receptive to and influenced by warning labels that inform them that alcohol is a carcinogen. In addition, mass media campaigns along the lines of those used in tobacco control have the potential to ensure consumers are informed of the harms associated with alcohol consumption. This is important in the face of ubiquitous alcohol advertising that depicts alcohol as a harmless product.

CAGE Questionnaire for Alcohol Use[1]

- ○ C: Have you ever felt you needed to **Cut** down on your drinking?
- ○ A: Have people **Annoyed** you by criticizing your drinking?
- ○ G: Have you ever felt **Guilty** about drinking?
- ○ E: Have you ever felt you needed a drink first thing is the morning (**Eye-opener**) to steady your nerves or to get rid of a hangover?

If the answers to all the questions are negative then the CAGE screening is negative.

1 Developed by Dr. John A. Ewing in the 1970s.

Table of the Effects of Alcohol for the Average Drinker with Increasing BAC[1]

BAC Range	Level of Impairment
0–0.05 g/100 mL	**Mild Impairment** • Mild speech, memory, attention, coordination, balance impairments • Perceived beneficial effects such as relaxation • Sleepiness can begin
0.060–0.150 g/100 mL	**Increased Impairment** • Perceived beneficial effects of alcohol, such as relaxation, give way to increasing intoxication • Increased risk of aggression in some people • Speech, memory, attention, coordination, balance further impaired • Significant impairment in all driving skills • Increased risk of injury to self and others • Moderate memory impairments
0.160–0.300 g/100 mL	**Severe Impairment** • Speech, memory, coordination, attention, reaction time, balance significantly impaired • All driving-related skills dangerously impaired • Judgment and decision making dangerously impaired • Vomiting and other signs of alcohol poisoning common • Loss of consciousness
0.310–0.450 g/100mL	**Life Threatening** • Loss of consciousness • Danger of life-threatening alcohol poisoning • Significant risk of death in most drinkers due to suppression of vital life functions

1 National Institute of Alcohol Abuse and Alcoholism. "Alcohol Overdose, the Dangers of Drinking Too Much." 2014.

Glasgow Coma Scale (GCS)[1]

GLASGOW COMA SCALE

Eye Opening Response

- Spontaneous — open with blinking at baseline **4 points**
- To verbal stimuli, command, speech **3 points**
- To pain only (not applied to face) **2 points**
- No response **1 point**

Verbal Response

- Oriented **5 points**
- Confused conversation, but able to answer questions **4 points**
- Inappropriate words **3 points**
- Incomprehensible speech **2 points**
- No response **1 point**

Motor Response

- Obeys commands for movement **6 points**
- Purposeful movement to painful stimulus **5 points**
- Withdraws in response to pain **4 points**
- Flexion in response to pain (decorticate posturing) **3 points**
- Extension response in response to pain (decerebrate posturing) **2 points**
- No response **1 point**

1 G. Teasdale and B. Jennett. "Assessment of Coma and Impaired Consciousness." *Lancet*, 1974; 81–84.

Head Injury Classification

- Severe Head Injury — GCS score of **8 or less**
- Moderate Head Injury — GCS score of **9 to 12**
- Mild Head Injury — GCS score of **13 to 15**

DSM-5 Diagnostic Criteria of Alcohol Use Disorder[1]

- Alcohol is often taken in larger amounts over a longer period of time than was intended.
- There is a persistent desire or unsuccessful efforts to cut down or control alcohol use.
- A great deal of time is spent in activities necessary to obtain alcohol, use alcohol, or recover from its addictions.
- Craving, or a strong desire or urge to use alcohol.
- Recurrent alcohol use resulting in a failure to fulfill major role obligations at work, school, or home.
- Continued alcohol use despite having persistent or recurrent social or interpersonal problems caused or exacerbated by the effects of alcohol.
- Important social, occupational, or recreational activities are given up or reduced because of alcohol use.
- Recurrent alcohol use in situations in which it is physically hazardous.
- Alcohol use is continued despite knowledge of having a persistent or recurrent physical or psychological problem that is likely to have been caused or exacerbated by alcohol.
- Tolerance as defined by either of the following: (1) a need for markedly increased amounts of alcohol to achieve intoxication or desired effects, or (2) a markedly diminished effect with continued use of the same amount of alcohol.

1 At least two positives within the last 12-month period: W. Thompson. medscape.com (23 March 2020).

- Withdrawal, as manifested by either of the following: (1) the characteristic withdrawal syndrome of alcohol or (2) alcohol (or closely related substance such as benzodiazepine) is taken to relieve or avoid withdrawal symptoms.

Prediction of Alcohol Withdrawal Severity Score[1]

1. Have you consumed any amount of alcohol (i.e., been drinking) within the last 30 days, **or** did the patient have a positive BAC upon admission?
2. Have you ever experienced previous episodes of alcohol withdrawal?
3. Have you ever experienced alcohol withdrawal seizures?
4. Have you ever experienced delirium tremens or DTs?
5. Have you ever undergone alcohol rehabilitation treatment?
6. Have you ever experienced blackouts?
7. Have you combined alcohol with other downers like benzodiazepines or barbiturates during the last 90 days?
8. Have you combined alcohol with any other substance of abuse during the last 90 days?
9. Was the patient's BAC on presentation > 0.200 g/100 mL?
10. Is there evidence of increased autonomic activity? (e.g., HR > 120 bpm, tremor, sweating, agitation, nausea)

Scoring: One point for each affirmative answer. A score of four or more suggests a High Risk for moderate to severe AWS.

1 Maldonado et al (2014).

Abbreviations

=	equal to
>	greater than
≥	greater than or equal to
<	less than
≤	less than or equal to
%	percent
±	plus or minus
°C	degrees Celsius
4-MP	4-methylpyrazole
5-HIAA	5-hydroxyindole-3-acetic acid
5-HTOL	5-hydroxytryptophol

ABAC	arterial BAC
ABHS	alcohol-based hand sanitizer
ABV	alcohol by volume
ACA	alcohol congener analysis
ACA	Automatic Clinical Analyzer
ACM	alcoholic cardiomyopathy
ADH	alcohol dehydrogenase
ADHD	attention deficit/hyperactivity disorder
ADS	Alcohol Dependence Scale
AFM	Ambient Fail Message
AFTR-FTIR	attenuated total reflective-Fourier transformed infrared spectroscopy
AGN	alcohol gaze nystagmus

AH	alcoholic hepatitis
AHG	alcohol hand gel
AID	alcohol-impaired driving
AIS	abbreviated injury scale
ALD	alcoholic liver disease
ALDH	acetaldehyde dehydrogenase
AON	angle of onset of nystagmus
ARBD	alcohol-related birth defects
ARD	alcohol-related disease
ASAT	alanine aminotransferase
ASD	approved screening device
AST	alcohol saliva testing
AST	aspartate aminotransferase
ATC	Alcohol Test Committee
AUA	acute use of alcohol
AUC	area under the drug concentration-time curve
AUD	alcohol use disorder
AUDIT	alcohol use disorders identification test
AV	aterio-venous
AWL	alcohol warning labels
AWS	alcohol withdrawal syndrome

B	beta
BAC	blood alcohol concentration
BAL	blood alcohol level
BBR	blood:breath ratio
BEC	blood ethanol concentration
BHB	beta hydroxybutyrate
BMC	blood methanol concentration
BMI	body mass index
BP	blood pressure
BPM	beats per minute
BrAC	breath alcohol concentration
BTBPI	blunt traumatic brachial plexus injury

CA	container airspace
CAC	(red blood) cells alcohol concentration

CAGE	cut, annoyed, guilty, and eye questionnaire
CB	central blood
c.c.	cubic centimeter
CC	calcium carbimide
CDC	Centers for Disease Control
CDCC	child day care center
CDT	carbohydrate deficient transferrin
CE	common era
CEW	conducted electrical weapon
CFF	critical flicker fusion
CFFF	critical flicker fusion frequency
CFS	Centre of Forensic Sciences
CHIPS	college health intervention study
CI	confidence interval
C_{max}	maximum BAC
CNS	central nervous system
COPD	chronic obstructive pulmonary disease
COVID	coronavirus disease
CPT	continuous performance test
CRP	C reactive protein
CRT	choice reaction time
CT	computed tomography
CTI	clinical tests for impairment
CTT	compensatory tracking test
CV	coefficient of variation
CVD	cardiovascular disease
CYP	cytochrome enzyme (systems)

DALY	disability adjusted life years
DC	District of Columbia
DD	designated driver
DER	disulfiram ethanol reaction
DFSA	drug facilitated sexual assault
DM	DataMaster
DOHS	Department of Health Services
DOT	Department of Transportation
DSM-5	Diagnostic and Statistical Manual of Mental Disorders, 5th edition

DSST	digital symbol substitution test
DT	delirium tremens
DUI	driving under the influence
DVA	dynamic visual acuity
DWI	driving while impaired

E85	up to 85% ethanol gasoline
eBAC	estimated blood alcohol concentration
EBHD	ethanol-based hand disinfectant
EBS	ethanol breath standard
EBT	evidential breath (alcohol) tests
ECG	electrocardiogram
E-cigs	Electronic cigarettes
EC/IR	electrochemical/infrared
ED	emergency department
EEG	electroencephalogram
EER	ethanol elimination rate
EG	ethylene glycol
E-liquid	electronic cigarette refill liquid
EMG	electromyogram
EMS	emergency medical services
EOD	end of drinking
EOG	electro-oculogram
ERS	emergency response services
EtG	ethyl glucuronide
EtS	ethyl sulfate
EtOH	ethanol
ER	emergency room
ERP	event related potential

F	chemical symbol for fluorine
FAA	Federal Aviation Authority
FAEE	fatty acid ethyl esters
FARS	Fatality Analysis Reporting System
FAS	fetal alcohol syndrome
FASD	fetal alcohol spectrum disorder
FEV1	forced expired volume (after one second)
FID	flame ionization detector

FL	fatty liver
fMRI	functional magnetic resonance imaging
FMVA	fatal motor vehicle accident
FMVC	fatal motor vehicle collision
FPM	first pass metabolism
FT-IR	Fourier transformed infrared
FVB	femoral venous blood
FVC	forced vital capacity

g	gram
g/100 mL	grams (of alcohol) in 100 milliliters of blood
g%	grams percent or grams per 100 milliliters of blood
g/100 mL/h	the rate of elimination of alcohol from the blood measured in grams of alcohol in 100 milliliters of blood per hour
g/dL	grams of alcohol in one deciliter of blood (i.e., 100 mL)
g/kg	amount (dose) of alcohol administered to the subject in grams of alcohol for each kilogram of the subject's weight
g/L/h	rate of elimination of alcohol measured in grams of alcohol per liter of blood per hour
g/m^3	grams per cubic meter
GA	glycolic acid
GA	guardian angel
GABA	gamma aminobutyric acid
GC	gas chromatography
GC/MS	gas chromatography/mass spectroscopy
GCS	Glasgow Coma Scale
GERD	gastroesophageal reflux disease
GES	General Estimates System
GGT	gamma glutamyl transferase
GHB	gamma hydroxybutyrate
GI	gastrointestinal
GLC	gas liquid chromatography
gm/dL	grams per deciliter (100 milliliters)
GMLT	Groton Maze Learning Test
GTOL	5-HTOL glucuronide

h (hr)	hour
HAZMAT	hazardous materials

Hb	hemoglobin
HB	heart blood
HC	hydroxycotinine
HCV	hepatitis C virus
HD	heavy drinkers
HGN	horizontal gaze nystagmus—one of the tests in SFST
HHS	holiday heart syndrome
HPLC	high pressure liquid chromatography
H_2RA	H_2 receptor antagonist
HS-GC	headspace gas chromatography
HS-GC-FID	headspace gas chromatography flame ionization detector
HS-GC/MS	headspace gas chromatography mass spectroscopy
HS-SPME	headspace solid-phase microextraction

ICU	intensive care unit
ILD	interstitial lung disease
in vitro	in glass (outside a living organism)
in vivo	in a living (organism)
IPA	isopropyl alcohol
IPrOH	isopropanol
IR	infrared
IS	invalid (breath) sample
ISS	injury severity scale
IV	intravenous

J	joule

kg	kilogram
km	kilometer
KM	Michaelis-Menten constant

L	liter
LAGB	laparoscopic adjustable gastric banding
lbs	pounds
LC/MS	liquid chromatography/mass spectroscopy
LC/MS/MS	liquid chromatography/mass spectroscopy/mass spectroscopy
LD	light (social) drinker

LDH	lactate dehydrogenase
LOD	limit of detection
LOQ	limit of quantitation
LSG	laparoscopic sleeve gastrectomy
LV	left ventricle

m/s^2	meters per second per second
MADD	Mothers Against Drunk Driving
MAE	mouth alcohol effect
MAS	mandatory alcohol screening
mcg/100 mL	micrograms per 100 milliliters
MCV	mean corpuscular volume
MDI	metered dose inhaler
MEK	methyl ethyl ketone
MeOH	methanol
MIS	multiple invalid samples
mg	milligram
mg%	milligrams percent or milligrams per 100 milliliters
mg/100 mL	the BAC measured in milligrams per 100 milliliters
mg/100 mL/h	the rate of elimination of alcohol measured in milligrams per 100 milliliters of blood per hour
mg/dL	milligrams per deciliter (i.e., 100 mL)
mg/L	milligram per liter
microns	micrometer
min	minute
mL	milliliter
MLDA	minimum legal drinking age
mmol/L	millimoles per liter
mph	miles per hour
MPT	magnesium perchlorate tubes
MRS	magnetic resonance spectroscopy
ms	millisecond
MVA	motor vehicle accident
MVC	motor vehicle collision

n =	number (of subjects) is equal to
NAD(H)	nicotinamide adenine dinucleotide

NaF	sodium fluoride
NC	North Carolina
ng	nanogram
NHTSA	National Highway Traffic Safety Administration
NIC	nicotine
NIST	National Institute of Standards and Technology
NMDA	N-Methyl-D-Aspartate
NMR	nuclear magnetic resonance
NYC	New York City

OEL	occupational exposure limit
OEM	original equipment manufacturer
OFI	*Opuntia ficus indica*
OI	orthostatic intolerance
OJ	orange juice
OKRe	optokinetic response
OLS	one leg stand—one of the tests in SFST
OMSL	Ontario's mandatory seatbelt law
OR	odds ratio

p	probability of obtaining a test result at least as extreme as the one that was actually observed
PAC	plasma alcohol concentration
PAN	positional alcoholic nystagmus
PASAT	paced auditory serial addition task
PAWSS	Prediction of Alcohol Withdrawal Severity Scale
PBF	putrefactive blister fluid
PBT	preliminary (pre-arrest) breath tester
p.c.	percent
PD	physical (attributes of) drunkenness
PDOA	periodic determination of accuracy
PEFR	peak expired flow rate
PEG	polyethylene glycol
PEth	phosphatidylethanol
PG	propylene glycol
pg/mg	picograms per milligrams

pH	measure of acidity of a solution (negative of the common logarithm of hydrogen ion concentration). A pH of 7.0 is neutral. pH > 7.0 is considered basic (alkaline), pH < 7.0 is considered acidic
PM	postmortem
PO	per os (by mouth)
ppm	parts per million
propanol-2	isopropyl alcohol

QC	quality control
QT	qualified technician

r	correlation coefficient (e.g., as for the correlation of BAC and BrAC)
r	rho or Widmark factor (ratio of alcohol in the body to alcohol in the blood)
RBC	red blood cells
RBT	roadside breath tester
REA	radiative energy attenuation
RFI	radio frequency interference
RH	relative humidity
RR	relative risk
RSD	roadside screening device
RT	reaction time
RYGB	Roux-en-Y-gastric bypass

SA	steering angle
SAC	serum alcohol concentration
SBS	short bowel syndrome
SBST	standardized boating sobriety tests
SCD	sudden cardiac death
SCIT	subtle cognitive impairment test
SCR	sacculocollic reflex
SCRAM	secure continuous remote alcohol monitoring
SD	standard deviation
SDLP	standard deviation of lane position
SDRT	simulated driving reaction time
SEtGC	serum ethyl glucuronide concentration
SF	synovial fluid

SFST	standardized field sobriety tests
SG	specific gravity
SIBO	small intestine bacterial overgrowth
SIFT-MS	selective ion flow tube-mass spectrometry
SMC	serum methanol concentration
SMLL	suicide method of low lethality
SMHL	suicide method of high lethality
SMVC	single motor vehicle collision
SPME	solid-phase microextraction
SRI	self-rated impairment
SRR	steering reversal rate
SS	steering speed
StAC	stomach alcohol concentration
STP	standard temperature and pressure
SUDAM	sudden unexpected death in alcohol misuse

$t_{1/2}$	half-life
TAC	transdermal alcohol concentration
TAS	transdermal alcohol sensor
TBI	traumatic brain injury
TBW	total body water
TCA	trichloroacetic acid
THC	tetrahydrocannabinol
TIM	tracking input manipulator
TSI	total snoring incidence
TT	transthoracic
TTS	transdermal therapeutic system
TVOR	translational vestibular ocular response

UAC	urine alcohol concentration
UBV	urinary bladder volume
UDA	unsafe driving action
UFOV	useful field of view
ug	micrograms
UHPLS/MS/MS	ultra high pressure liquid chromatography/mass spectrometry/mass spectrometry
UK	United Kingdom

umol	micromoles
UMC	urine methanol concentration
UPPL	uniform policy provision law
US	United States (of America)
USP	United States Pharmacopeia

VAC	vapor alcohol concentration
VBAC	venous blood alcohol concentration
Vd	volume of distribution
VEMP	vestibular evoked myogenic potential
VFR	visual flight rules
VGN	vertical gaze nystagmus
VH	vitreous humor
VHAC	vitreous humor alcohol concentration
VOR	vestibulo-ocular reflex
VS	vehicle speed
v/v	volume/volume

WAT	walk and turn—one of the tests in SFST
WBAA	whole blood-associated acetaldehyde
WBE	waste-based epidemiology
WHO	World Health Organization
WKS	Wernicke-Korsakoff syndrome
WUI	walking under the influence
wt/v	weight/volume

y (yr)	year

ZTL	zero tolerance law

Chemical Symbols/Formulae

CH_3CHO	acetaldehyde
CH_3COOH	acetic acid
CH_3COCH_2COOH	acetoacetic acid
CH_3COCH_3	acetone
CH_3CH_2OH	alcohol (ethanol, ethyl alcohol)
Br	bromine
C_4H_{10}	butane
Ca	calcium
$CaCl_2$	calcium chloride
C	carbon
C1-C3	one to three carbon chain (i.e., methyl, ethyl, propyl)
CO_2	carbon dioxide
CO	carbon monoxide
COHb	carboxyhemoglobin
Cl	chlorine
$CHCl_3$	chloroform
$Cr_2(SO_4)_3$	chromic sulfate
D_2O	deuterium oxide or heavy water
$CH_3CH_2OCH_2CH_3$	ether
$C_8H_{14}O_7$	ethyl glucuronide
$C_2H_6O_4S$	ethyl sulfate
CH_2OHCH_2OH	ethylene glycol
$C_6H_{12}O_6$	glucose
$C_6H_{10}O_7$	glucuronic acid

CH_2OHCHO	glycolaldehyde
CH2OHCOOH	glycolic acid
$CF_3CHBrCl$	halothane
He	helium
H	hydrogen
H_2	hydrogen gas
$CH_3CHOHCH_3$	isopropanol
Mg	magnesium
$Mg(ClO_4)_2$	magnesium perchlorate
CH_3OH	methanol
$CH_3COC_2H_5$	methyl ethyl ketone
N	nitrogen
N_2	nitrogen gas
COOHCOOH	oxalic acid
O	oxygen
O_2	oxygen gas
P	phosphorus
K	potassium
$K_2Cr_2O_7$	potassium dichromate
K_2SO_2	potassium sulfate
C_3H_8	propane
Na	sodium
NaCl	sodium chloride (table salt)
NaF	sodium fluoride
$NaVO_3$	sodium metavanadate
H_2SO_4	sulfuric acid
H_2O	water

Abstracted Studies

Alphabetically by Author **(reference number in bold brackets)**

A

ABBEY, A., P.O. BUCK, T. ZAWACKI, AND C. SAENZ. "Alcohol's Effects on Perceptions of a Potential Date Rape." *Journal of Studies on Alcohol*, 64: 669–677, 2003 **(61702)**

ABBEY, A., A.M. CLINTON-SHERROD, P. MCAULSAN, ET AL. "The Relationship Between the Quantity of Alcohol Consumed and the Severity of Sexual Assaults Committed by College Men." *Journal of Interpersonal Violence*, 18: 813–833, 2003 **(61705)**

ABBEY, A., T. ZAWACKI, AND P. MCAUSLAN. "Alcohol's Effect on Sexual Perception." *Journal of Studies on Alcohol*, 61: 688–697, 2000 **(61701)**

ACEVEDO, M.B., J.C. EAGON, B.D. BARTHOLOW, ET AL. "Sleeve Gastrectomy Surgery: When 2 Alcoholic Drinks Are Converted to 4." *Surgery for Obesity and Related Diseases*, 8: 7pp, 2017 **(10132)**

ACHAPPA, B., D. MADI, T. KANCHAN, AND N.K. KISHANLAL. "Treatment of Ethylene Glycol Poisoning with Oral Ethyl Alcohol." *Case Reports in Medicine,* Article ID, 7985917, 3pp, 2019 **(80511)**

ADACHI, J., Y. MIZOI, T. FUKUNAGA, ET AL. "Degrees of Alcohol Intoxication in 117 Hospitalized Cases." *Journal of Studies on Alcohol*, 52: 448–453, 1991 **(50603)**

ADAMS, A.J. AND B. BROWN. "Alcohol Prolongs Time Course of Glare Recovery." *Nature*, 257, 481–483, 1975 **(50102)**

AFSHAR, M., G. NETZER, E. SALISBURY-AFSHAR., S. MURTHI, AND G.S. SMITH. "Injured Patients with Very High Blood Alcohol Concentrations." *Injury,* 47: 83–88, 2016 **(70413)**

AGABIO, R., C. PISANU, G.L. GESSA, AND F. FRANCONI. "Sex Differences in Alcohol Use Disorder." *Current Medicinal Chemistry*, 24: 1–10, 2017 **(90104)**

AHMED, S., M.O. KHAIUM, AND F. TAZMEEM. "COVID-19 Lockdown in India Triggers a Rapid Rise in Suicides due to the Alcohol Withdrawal Symptoms: Evidence from Media Reports." *International Journal of Social Psychiatry*, 66: 827–829, 2020 **(62021)**

AIRAKSINEN, N.K., I.S. NURMI-LUTHJE, J.M. KATAJA, ET AL. "Cycling Injuries and Alcohol." *Injury, International Journal of Care for the Injured,* 49: 945–952, 2018 **(60211)**

AL-AWADHI, A., I.A. WASFI, AND Z. ALL-HATALI. "Autobrewing Revisited: Endogenous Concentrations of Blood Ethanol in Residents of the United Arab Emirates." *Science and Justice,* 44: 149–152, 2004 **(20505)**

ALFORD, C., C. BROOM, H. CARVER, ET AL. "The Impact of Alcohol Hangover on Simulated Driving Performance During a Commute to Work—Zero and Residual Alcohol Effects Compared." *Journal of Clinical Medicine*, 9: 1435, 14 pp, 2020 **(60816)**

ALHA, A.R. AND V. TAMMINEN. "Fatal Cases with an Elevated Urine Alcohol but Without Alcohol in the Blood." *Journal of Forensic Medicine,* 11: 3–5, 1964 **(70701)**

ALI, S.S., M.P. WILSON, E.M. CASTILLO, ET AL. "Common Hand Sanitizers May Distort Readings of Breathalyzer Tests in the Absence of Acute Intoxication." *Academic Emergency Medicine*, 20: 212–215, 2013 **(30131)**

ALKANA, R.L., E.S. PARKER, H.B. COHEN, ET AL. "Interaction of Sted-eze, Nikethamide, Pipradrol, or Ammonium Chloride with Ethanol in Human Males." *Alcoholism: Clinical and Experimental Research*, 4: 84-92, 1980 **(10713)**

AL-LANQAWI, Y., A. MORELAND, F. MCEWEN, ET AL. "Ethanol Kinetics: Extent of Error in Back Extrapolation Procedures." *British Journal of Clinical Pharmacology*, 34: 316–321, 1992 **(10503)**

ALLEN, D., M. LADER, AND H.V. CURRAN. "A Comparative Study of the Interactions of Alcohol with Amitriptyline, Fluoxetine and Placebo in Normal Subjects." *Progress. Neuro-Psychopharmacology and Biological Psychiatry*, 12: 53–80, 1988 **(10712)**

ALLEN, R.W., H.R. JEX, D.T. MCRUER, AND R.J. DIMARCO. "Alcohol Effects on Driving Behavior and Performance in a Car Simulator." *IEEE Transactions on Systems, Man and Cybernetics, SMC-5*: 498–505, 1975 **(50206)**

AL-MAQBALI, J.S., N. AL-MAQRASHI, A. AL-HURAIZI, ET AL. "Clinical Characteristics and Health Outcomes in Patients with Alcohol Withdrawal Syndrome: An Observational Study from Oman." *Annals of Saudi Medicine*, 52–57, 2022 **(90209)**

ALTMAN, C.M., N.S. COMPO, D. MCQUISTON, ET AL. "Witnesses' Memory for Events and Faces Under Elevated Levels of Intoxication." *Memory*, 14pp, 2018 **(60320)**

ALTMAN, C.M., D.E. MCQUISTON, AND N.S. COMPO. "How Elevated Blood Alcohol Concentration Level and Identification Format Affect Eyewitness Memory: A Field Study." *Applied Cognitive Psychology,* 33: 426–438, 2019 **(60316)**

AMADOR, E. AND A. GAZDAR. "Sudden Death During Disulfiram-Alcohol Reaction." *Journal of Studies on Alcohol*, 28: 649–654, 1967 **(80106)**

AMMANN, D., R. BECKER, A. KOHL, ET AL. "Degradation of the Ethyl Glucuronide Content in Hair by Hydrogen Peroxide and a Non-Destructive Assay for Oxidative Hair Treatment Using Infra-Red Spectroscopy." *Forensic Science International*, 244: 30–35, 2014 **(40527)**

ANDERSON, S. AND J. DAWSON. "Neurophysiological Correlates of Alcoholic Hangover." *South African Journal of Science*, 95: 145–147, 1999 **(60809)**

ANDERSSON, A.L AND O. BUNKETORP. "Cycling and Alcohol." *Injury, International Journal of Care Injured*, 33: 467–471, 2002 **(60203)**

ANDERSSON, L. AND A.W. JONES. "Room Temperature Influences on the Performance of Some Breath Alcohol Simulators." *Proceedings ICADTS T2000, Stockholm, May 22–26, 2000, Poster 1,* 6pp (30204)

ANDRE, J.T. "Visual Functioning in Challenging Conditions: Effects of Alcohol Consumption, Luminance, Stimulus Motion and Glare on Contrast Sensitivity." *Journal of Experimental Psychology and Applications*, 2: 250–269, 1996 **(50109)**

ANDREWS, S.A. AND H.J. COLVIN. "Verification of Intoximeter 3000 Breath Alcohol Concentration by Magnesium Perchlorate Tube Method in Long-Term Field Program." *Journal of Analytical Toxicology*, 13: 113–116, 1989 **(30704)**

ANTEBI, D. "The Effects of Alcohol on Four Choice Serial Reaction Time." *Medicine Science and the Law*, 22: 181–188, 1982 **(50107)**

ANTONIDES, H. AND L MARINETTI. "Ethanol Production in a Postmortem Urine Sample." *Journal of Analytical Toxicology*, 35: 516–518, 2011 **(70706)**

APPENZELLER, B.M.R., R. AGIRMAN, P. NEUBERG, ET AL. "Segmental Determination of Ethyl Glucuronide in Hair: A Pilot Study." *Forensic Science International,* 173: 87–92, 2007 **(40508)**

APPENZELLER, B.M.R., M. SCHMAN, M. YEGLES, AND R. WENNIG. "Ethyl Glucuronide Concentration in Hair Is Not Influenced by Pigmentation." *Alcohol and Alcoholism,* 42: 326–327, 2007 **(70909)**

APPENZELLER, B.M.R., M. SCHUMAN, AND R. WENNIG. "Was a Child Poisoned by Ethanol? Discrimination Between Ante-Mortem Consumption and Post-Mortem Formation." *International Journal of Legal Medicine*, 122: 42–434, 2008 **(70220)**

ARMER, J.M., L. GUNAWARDANA, AND R.L. ALLCOCK. "The Performance of Alcohol Markers Including Ethyl Glucuronide and Ethyl Sulphate to Detect Alcohol Use in Clients in a Community Alcohol Treatment Programme." *Alcohol and Alcoholism*, 52: 29–34, 2017 **(40521)**

ARMSTRONG, E.J., D.A. ENGELHART, A.J. JENKINS, AND E.K. BALRAJ. "Homicidal Ethylene Glycol Intoxication. A Report of a Case." *American Journal of Forensic Medicine and Pathology*, 27: 151–155, 2006 **(80509)**

ARNDT, T., B. GUESSREGEN, D. HALLERMANN, ET AL. "Forensic Analysis of Carbohydrate Deficient Transferrin (CDT) by HPLC—Statistics and Extreme CDT Values." *Forensic Science International,* 175, 27–30, 2008 **(40505)**

ASADA, M. AND J.T. GALAMBOS. "Liver Disease, Hepatic Alcohol Dehydrogenase Activity, and Alcohol Metabolism in the Human." *Gastroenterology*, 45: 67–72, 1963 **(10312)**

ASBRIDGE, M., R. MANN, M.D. CUSIMANO, ET AL. "Cycling-Related Crash Risk and the Role of Cannabis and Alcohol: A Case-Crossover Study." *Preventive Medicine*, 96: 80–86, 2014 **(60212)**

ASBRIDGE, M., R.E. MANN, R. FLAM-ZALCMAN, AND G. STUDOTO. "The Criminalization of Impaired Driving in Canada: Assessing the Deterrent Impact of Canada's First Per Se Law." *Journal of Studies on Alcohol*, 65: 450–459, 2004 **(50702)**

AUCKLOO, M.B K.M. AND B.B. DAVIES. "Post-mortem Toxicology in Violent Fatalities in Cape Town, South Africa: A Preliminary Investigation." *Journal of Forensic and Legal Medicine*, 63: 18–25, 2019 **(60917)**

AUFDERHEIDE, T.P., S.M. WHITE, W.J. BRADY, AND H. STUEVEN. "Inhalation and Percutaneous Methanol Toxicity in Two Firefighters." *Annals of Emergency Medicine*, 22: 1916–1918, 1993 **(80309)**

AVELLA, J., E. BRIGLIA, G. HARLEMAN, AND M. LEHRER. "Percutaneous Absorption and Distribution of Methanol in a Homicide." *Journal of Analytical Toxicology*, 29: 734–737, 2005 **(80314)**

B

BAGGE, C.L., H-J. LEE, J.A. SCHUMACHER, K.L. GRATZ., ET AL. "Alcohol as an Acute Risk Factor for Recent Suicide Attempts: A Case-Crossover Analysis." *Journal of Studies on Alcohol and Drugs*, 74: 552–558, 2013 **(62019)**

BAILEY, D.N. "Detection of Isopropanol in Acetonemic Patients Not Exposed to Isopropanol." *Clinical Toxicology*, 28: 459–466, 1990 **(80202)**

BAILEY, K.L., D.R. SAMUELSON, AND T.A. WYATT. "Alcohol Use Disorder: A Pre-Existing Condition for COVID-19?" *Alcohol*, 90: 11–17, 2021 **(90113)**

BAND, R.M., M.C. MEENA, A. KANDPAL, AND S. MITTAL. "Rapid Death Due to Alcohol Withdrawal Syndrome: Case Report and Review of Literature." *Asia Pacific Journal of Medical Toxicology*, 4: 51–54, 2015 **(90214)**

BANKS, S., P. CATCHSIDE, L. LACK, ET AL. "Low Levels of Alcohol Impair Driving Simulator Performance and Reduce Perception of Crash Risk in Partially Sleep Deprived Subjects." *Sleep,* 27: 1063–1067, 2004 **(50202)**

BANSAL, V., D. FORTLAGE, J.G. LEE, L.L. HILL, ET AL. "Significant Injury in Cruise Ship Passengers. A Case Series." *American Journal of Preventive Medicine*, 33: 219–221, 2007 **(61111)**

BARILLO, D.J., B.F. RUSH JR., R. GOODE ET AL. "Is Ethanol the Unknown Toxin in Smoke Inhalation Injury?" *American Surgeon*, 52: 641-645, 1986 **(60601)**

BARKLEY, R.A., K.R. MURPHY, T. O'CONNELL, ET AL. "Effects of Two Doses of Alcohol on Simulator Driving Performance in Adults with Attention-Deficit/ Hyperactivity Disorder." *Neuropsychology*, 26: 77–87, 2006 **(50203)**

BARNES, E.W., N.J. COOKE, A.J. KING, AND R. PASSMORE. "Observations on the Metabolism of Alcohol in Man." *British Journal of Nutrition*, 19: 485-489, 1965 **(10309)**

BARNETT, N.P., E.B. MEADE, AND T.R. GLYNN. "Predictors of Detection of Alcohol Use Episodes Using a Transdermal Alcohol Sensor." *Experimental and Clinical Psychopharmacology*, 22: 86–96, 2014 **(40309)**

BARRY, A.E., B.H. CHANEY, AND M.L. STELLEFSON, "Breath Alcohol Concentrations of Designated Drivers." *Journal of Studies in Alcohol and Drugs*, 74: 509–513, 2013 **(50716)**

BARTL, G., C. BRANDSTATTER, A. HOSEMANN, AND C. REITER. "Saccadic Eye Movements and Reactions of Drivers with Low Alcohol Concentrations [German]." *Blutalkohol*, 35: 124–138, 1998 **(50305)**

BARTLETT, G., J. GAWRYLOWICZ, D. FRINGS, AND I.P. ALBERY. "The Intoxicated Co-Witness: Effects of Alcohol and Dyadic Discussion on Memory Conformity and Event Recall." *Psychopharmacology,* 238: 1485–1493, 2021 **(60319)**

BARZ, J., W. BONTE, C. KEULTJES, AND J. SIELAND. "Concentrations of Ethanol, Methanol, Propanol-2 and Acetone in Blood Samples of Impaired Drivers." *Acta Medicinae Legalis et Socialis*, 40: 49–60, 1990 **(30601)**

BASNAYAKE, B.M.D.B., A.W.M. WAZIL, N. NANAYAKKARA, ET AL. "Ethylene Glycol Intoxication Following Brake Fluid Ingestion Complicated with Unilateral Facial Nerve Palsy: A Case Report." *Journal of Medical Case Reports*, 13: 203, 4pp, 2019 **(80512)**

BATTEN, P.J., D.W. PENN, AND J.D. BLOOM. "A 36-Year History of Fatal Road Rage in Marion County, Oregon: 1963–1998." *Journal of Forensic Sciences*, 45: 397–399, 2004 **(60115)**

BATTERMAN, S.A. AND A. FRANTZBLAU. "Time-Resolved Cutaneous Absorption and Permeation Rates of Methanol in Human Volunteers." *International Archives Occupational Environmental Health*, 70: 341–351, 1997 **(80307)**

BAY, H.W., K.F. BLURTON, H.C. LIEB, AND H.G. OSWIN. "Electrochemical Measurements of Blood Alcohol Levels." *Nature* 240: 52–53, 1972 **(30103)**

BECK, O., M. MELLRING, C. LOWBEER, ET AL. "Measurement of the Alcohol Biomarker Phosphatidylethanol (PEth) in Dried Blood Spots and Venous

Blood—Importance of Inhibition of Post-Sampling Formation from Ethanol." *Analytical and Bioanalytical Chemistry*, 413: 5601–5606, 2021 **(70910)**

BEIRNESS, D.J. "Assessment of the Initial Impact of Mandatory Alcohol Screening on Alcohol-Involved Driver Fatalities in Canada." Final Report, Department of Justice Canada, 11pp, 5 May 2021 **(50717)**

BEIRNESS, D.J., K.W. GU, N.J. LOWE, ET AL. "Cannabis, Alcohol and Other Drug Findings in Fatally Injured Drivers in Ontario." *Traffic Injury Prevention*, 22: 6pp, 2021 **(50803)**

BELL, M.D., V.J. RAO, C.V. WETLI, AND R.N. RODRIGUEZ. "Positional Asphyxiation in Adults. A Series of 30 Cases from the Dade and Broward County Florida Medical Examiner Offices From 1982 to 1990." *American Journal of Forensic Medicine and Pathology*, 13: 101–107, 1992 **(60512)**

BELSKY, T.P. "Does It Add Up? Analyzing the Use of Extrapolation Calculations to Determine the Ability to Consent in Alcohol-Related Sexual Assault Cases." *Naval Law Review Military Justice Edition*, 62, 54–75, 2013 **(61718)**

BENDTSEN, P., J. HULTBERG, M. CARLSSON, AND A.W. JONES. "Monitoring of Ethanol Exposure in a Clinical Setting by Analysis of Blood, Breath, Saliva and Urine." *Alcoholism: Clinical and Experimental Research*, 23: 1446–1451, 1999 **(40206)**

BENDTSEN, P. AND A.W. JONES. "Impact of Water-Induced Diuresis on Excretion Profiles of Ethanol, Urinary Creatinine and Urinary Osmolality." *Journal of Analytical Toxicology*, 23: 565–569, 1999 **(40103)**

BENDTSEN, P., A.W. JONES, AND A. HELANDER. "Urinary Excretion of Methanol and 5-Hydroxytryptophol as Biochemical Markers of Recent Drinking in the Hangover State." *Alcohol and Alcoholism*, 33: 431–438, 1998 **(60804)**

BENNETT, A.T. AND K.A. COLLINS. "Suicide: A Ten-Year Retrospective Study." *Journal of Forensic Sciences*, 45: 1256–1258, 2000 **(62011)**

BENO, J.M., R. HARTMAN, C. WALLACE, ET AL. "Homicidal Methanol Poisoning in a Child." *Journal of Analytical Toxicology*, 35: 524–528, 2011 **(80323)**

BERGH, A.K. "Observations on ToxTrap Silica Gel Breath Capture Tubes for Alcohol Analysis." *Journal of Forensic Sciences*, 30: 186–193, 1985 **(30701)**

BERGGREN, S.M. AND L. GOLDBERG. "The Absorption of Ethyl Alcohol from the Gastro-Intestinal Tract as a Diffusion Process." *Acta Physiologica Scandinavia.*, 1/2: 246–270, 1940/1941 **(10101)**

BERILD, D. AND H. HASSELBALCH. "Survival After a Blood Alcohol of 1127 mg/dL [Letter]." *Lancet*, 15 August 1981, 363 **(70410)**

BERNAT, D.H., W.T.M. DUNSMUIR, AND A.C. WAGENAAR. "Effects of Lowering the Legal BAC to 0.08 on Single Vehicle Nighttime Fatal Traffic Crashes in 19 Jurisdictions." *Accident Analysis Prevention*, 36: 1089–1097, 2004 **(50704)**

BESSONNEAU, V. AND O. THOMAS. "Assessment of Exposure to Alcohol Vapor from Alcohol-Based Hand Rubs." *International Journal of Environmental Research and Public Health*, 9: 868–879, 2012 **(10127)**

BEVERIDGE, A. AND G. YORSTON. "I Drink, Therefore I Am: Alcohol and Creativity." *Journal of Royal Society of Medicine*, 92: 646–648, 1999 **(61218)**

BIASOTTI, A.A. AND T.E. VALENTINE. "Blood Alcohol Concentration Determined from Urine Samples as a Practical Equivalent or Alternative to Blood and Breath Tests." *Journal of Forensic Sciences*, 30: 194–207, 1985 **(40101)**

BILGREN, S., N. TURKMEN, B. EREN, AND R. FEDAKER. "Peripheral Vascular Injury-Related Deaths." *Turkish Journal of Trauma and Emergency Surgery*, 15: 357–361, 2009 **(60904)**

BILLINGS, C.E., T. DEMOSTHENES, T.R. WHITE, AND D. O'HARA. "Effects of Alcohol on Pilot Performance in Simulated Flight." *Aviation, Space Environmental Medicine*, 62: 233–235, 1991**(60704)**

BINZ, T. M., M.R. BAUMGARTNER, AND T.KRAEMER. "The Influence of Cleansing Shampoos on Ethyl Glucuronide Concentration in Hair Analyzed with an Optimized and Validated LC-MS/MS Method." *Forensic Science International*, 244: 20–24, 2014 **(40526)**

BISHOP, S.C., G. JOHNSON, L. SMITH, ET AL. "Manual Versus Automatic Sampling Variations of a Preliminary Alcohol Screening Device." *Journal of Analytical Toxicology*, 33: 521–524, 2009 **(30311)**

BISHOP-FREEMAN, S.C., R.L. BERTHOLF, R.H. POWERS, ET AL. "False-Positive Enzymatic Alcohol Results in Perimortem Specimens." *Laboratory Medicine*, 51: 394–401, 2020 **(70107)**

BLAIS, E., F. BELLAVANCE, A. MARCIL, AND L. CARNIS. "Effects of Introducing an Administrative .05% Blood Alcohol Concentration Limit on Alcohol-Related Collisions in Canada." *CIRRELT-2015-01*, 27pp, 2015 **(50720)**

BLOCKER JR, J.S. "Did Prohibition Really Work? Alcohol Prohibition as a Public Health Innovation." *American Journal of Public Health*, 96: 233–244, 2006 **(90501)**

BLOMBERG, R.D., R.C. PECK, H. MOSKOWITZ, ET AL. "The Long Beach/Fort Lauderdale Relative Risk Study." *Journal of Safety Research*, 40: 285–292, 2009 **(50503)**

BLUMENTHAL, R. "Suicidal Gunshot Wounds to the Head. A Retrospective Review of 406 Cases." *American Journal of Forensic Medicine and Pathology*, 28: 288–291, 2007 **(62009)**

BOATTO, G., C. TRIGNANO, L. BURRAI, ET AL. "Effects of Homeopathic Mother Tinctures on Breath Alcohol Testing." *Journal of Forensic Sciences,* 60: S1, S231–S233, 2015 **(30523)**

BOBAN, I.V., A. VRCA, AND M. SARAGE. "Changing Patterns of Acute Alcohol Intoxications in Children." *Medical Science Monitor*, 24: 5123–5131, 2018 **(90502)**

BOLLIGER, S.A., S. ROSS, L. OESTERHELWEG, ET AL. "Are Full or Empty Beer Bottles Sturdier and Does Their Fracture-Threshold Suffice to Break the Human Skull?" *Journal of Forensic and Legal Medicine*, 16: 138–142, 2009 **(60120)**

BONVENTRE, J., S. VALANJU, AND M.L. BASTOS. "Evaluation of Ethanol Analysis on Brain and Liver by Head-Space Gas Chromatography." *Forensic Science International*, 19: 75–83, 1982 **(70103)**

BOOKER, R., G.P. LEHMANN, AND S.L. KORKOSH, "Calibration Stability of the Alco-Sensor FST Over a Seven Week Period." *Canadian Society of Forensic Science Journal*, 45: 176–178, 2012 **(30216)**

BOOKER, J. L. AND K. RENFROE. "The Effects of Gastroesophageal Reflux Disease on Forensic Breath Alcohol Testing." *Journal of Forensic Sciences*, 60: 1516–1522, 2015 **(30528)**

BORGES, G., C.J. CHERPITEL, S. MACDONALD, ET AL. "A Case-Crossover Study of Acute Alcohol Use and Suicide Attempt." *Journal of Studies on Alcohol*, 65: 708–714, 2004 **(62002)**

BORGES, G. AND H. ROSOVSKY. "Suicide Attempts and Alcohol Consumption in an Emergency Room Sample." *Journal of Studies on Alcohol*, 57: 543–548, 1996 **(62001)**

BORKENSTEIN, R.F., R.F. CROWTHER, R.P. SHUMATE, ET AL. "The Role of the Drinking Driver in Traffic Accidents. The Grand Rapids Study." *Blutalkohol* 11 (Suppl. 1): 1–131, 1974 **(50501)**

BORKENSTEIN, R.F. AND H.W. SMITH, "The Breathalyzer and Its Applications." *Medicine Science and the Law*, 2: 13–23, 1961 **(30101)**

BOROWSKA-SOLONYNKO, A. SIWINSKA-ZIOLKOWSKA, M. PIOTRKOWICZ, ET AL. "Analysis of the Origin and Importance of Acetone and Isopropanol Levels in the Blood of the Deceased for Medicolegal Testimony." *Archiwum medycyny sadowej i kryminologii*, 64: 230–245, 2014 **(80411)**

BOSKER, W.M., E.L. THEUNISSEN, S. COENE, ET AL. "A Placebo-Controlled Study to Assess Standardized Field Sobriety Tests Performance During Alcohol and Cannabis Intoxication in Heavy Cannabis Users and Accuracy of Point of Collection Testing Devices for Detecting THC in Oral Fluid." *Psychopharmacology*, 223: 439–446, 2012 **(50806)**

BOSWELL, H.A. AND F.L. DORMAN. "Uncertainty of Blood Alcohol Concentration (BAC) Results as Related to Instrumental Conditions: Optimization and Robustness of BAC Analysis Headspace Parameters." *Chromatography*, 2: 691–708, 2015 **(20120)**

BOTCH, S.R. AND R.D. JOHNSON. "Alcohol-Related Aviation Accidents Involving Pilots with Previous Alcohol Offenses." *DOT/FAA/AM-08/22,* Office of Aerospace Medicine, 8pp, Final Report, October 2008 **(60710)**

BOUMBA, V.A. "Modeling Postmortem Ethanol Production/Insights into the Origin of Higher Alcohols." *Molecules*, 27: 700, 14pp, 2022 **(70219)**

BOUMBA, V.A., N. KOURKOUMELIS, P. GOUSIA., ET AL. "Modeling Microbial Ethanol Production by *E. coli* Under Aerobic/Anaerobic Conditions: Applicability to Real Postmortem Cases and to Postmortem Blood Derived Microbial Cultures." *Forensic Science International,* 232: 191–198, 2013 **(70216)**

BOUMBA, V.A., N. KOURKOUMELIS, K.S. ZIAVROU, ET AL. "Patterns of the Most Abundant Volatiles Detected in Post-Mortem Blood." *Romanian Journal of Legal Medicine* 20: 147–154, 2012 **(70218)**

BOUMBA, V.A. AND T. VOUGIOUKIAKIS. "Impact of Blood Collection Tubes on Erroneous 1-Propanol Detection and on Forensic Ethanol Analysis." *Journal of Forensic Toxicology and Pharmacology*, 4: 5pp, 2015 **(20318)**

BOWER, C., R.E. WATKINS, R.C. MUTCH, ET AL. "Fetal Alcohol Spectrum Disorder and Youth Justice: A Prevalence Study Among Young People Sentenced to Detention in Western Australia." *BMJ Open*, 8: e019605, 10pp, 2017 **(90407)**

BRAGG, B.W.E., N. DAWSON, D. KIRBY, AND G. GOODFELLOW. "Detection of Impaired Drivers Through Measurement of Speed and Alignment." *Proceedings 8th International Conference on Alcohol Drugs and Traffic Safety,* T-80 Stockholm, L. Goldberg (ed), 1341–1353, 1981 **(50403)**

BRANDSTROM, H., A. ERIKSSON, G. GIESBRECHT, ET AL. "Fatal Hypothermia: An Analysis from a Sub-Arctic Region." *International Journal of Circumpolar Health,* 71: 18502, 7pp, 2012 **(61007)**

BRATZKE, H. AND T. GILG. "Fatal Hemorrhage from a Single Scalp Wound [German]." *Archives fur Kriminologie*, 180: 101–106, 1987 **(60913)**

BREAKSPERE, R.J. AND P.M.WILLIAMS. "Breath Alcohol Instrumentation: A Proposal in Commercial Taxonomy." *Proceedings 13th International Conference on Alcohol Drugs Traffic Safety*, Vol 1. C. N. Kloeden, and A. J. McLean (eds), Australia, 1995 **(30113)**

BRECKLIN, L.R. AND S.E. ULLMAN. "The Role of Offender Alcohol Use in Rape Attacks. An Analysis of National Crime Victimization Survey Data." *Journal of Interpersonal Violence*, 16: 3–21, 2001 **(61708)**

BREITMEIER, D., I. SEELAND-SCHULZE, H. HECKER, AND U. SCHNEIDER. "The Influence of Blood Alcohol Concentrations of Around 0.03% on Neuropsychological Functions—A Double-Blind, Placebo-Controlled Investigation." *Addiction Biology*, 12: 183–189, 2007 **(50103)**

BRENNAN, D.F., S. BETZELOS, R. REED, AND J. FALK. "Ethanol Elimination Rates in an ED Population." *American Journal of Emergency Medicine*, 13: 276–280, 1995 **(10806)**

BRENNER, M. AND J.R. CASH. "Speech Analysis as an Index of Alcohol Intoxication—The EXXON Valdez Accident." *Aviation Space, Environmental Medicine,* 62: 893–898, 1991 **(61106)**

BREWER, C. AND E. STREET. "Is Alcohol in Hand Sanitizers Absorbed Through the Skin or Lungs? Implications for Disulfiram Treatment." *Alcohol and Alcoholism,* 55: 354–356, 2020 **(10128)**

BRICK, J. "Diabetes, Breath Acetone and Breathalyzer Accuracy: A Case Study." *Alcohol, Drugs and Driving*, 9: 27–28, 1993 **(30605)**

———. "Time of Death Relative to Alcohol Use: Application of Brain: Blood Ratios and Gastric Ethanol." *Journal of Addiction Medicine and Therapeutic Science*, 2: 19–22, 2016 **(70817)**

BROWN, A. ST J.M. AND P.F.W. JAMES. "Omeprazole, Ranitidine and Cimetidine Have No Effect on Peak Blood Ethanol Concentrations, First Pass Metabolism, or Area Under the Time-Ethanol Curve Under Real-Life Conditions." *Alimentary Pharmacology Therapeutics*, 12: 141–145, 1998 **(10703)**

BROWN, J., J. LONG-MCGIE, A. WARTNIK, ET AL. "Fetal Alcohol Spectrum Disorders in the Criminal Justice System: A Review." *Journal of Law Enforcement*, 3: 1–10, 2014 **(90409)**

BRUBACHER, J. R., H. CHAN, M. FANG, ET AL. "Police Documentation of Alcohol Involvement in Hospitalized Injured Drivers." *Traffic Injury and Prevention*, 14: 453–460, 2013 **(50616)**

BRUCK, D., M. BALL, AND I.R. THOMAS. "Fire Fatality and Alcohol Intake: Analysis of Key Risk Factors." *Journal of Studies on Alcohol and Drugs*, 72: 731–736, 2011 **(60611)**

BRUNNER, S., R. HERBEL, C. DROBESCH ET AL. "Alcohol Consumption, Sinus Tachycardia, and Cardiac Arrhythmias at the Munich Octoberfest: Results from the Munich Beer Related Electrocardiogram Workup Study (MunichBREW)." *European Heart Journal*, 38: 2100–2106, 2017 **(90305)**

BUCHSBAUM, R.M., ADELSON, L., AND I. SUNSHINE. "A Comparison of Post-Mortem Ethanol Levels Obtained from Blood and Subdural Specimens." *Forensic Science International*, 41: 237–243, 1989 **(70501)**

BUCKLEY, T.J., J.D. PLEIL, J.R. BOWYER, AND J.M. DAVIS, "Evaluation of Methyl tert-Butyl Ether (MTBE) as an Interference on Commercial Breath-Alcohol Analyzers." *Forensic Science International*, 123: 111–118, 2001 **(30620)**

BUCZEK, Y. AND J.G. WIGMORE. "The Significance of Breath Sampling Frequency on the Mouth Alcohol Effect." *Canadian Society of Forensic Science Journal,* 35: 185–193, 2002 **(30519)**

BUDD, R.D. "Post Mortem Brain Alcohol Levels." *Journal of Chromatography*, 259: 353–355, 1983 **(70801)**

———. "Validity of Post Mortem Chest Cavity Blood Ethanol Determinations." *Journal of Chromatography*, 449: 337–340, 1988 **(70303)**

BUIKHUISEN, W. AND R.W. JONGMAN. "Traffic Perception Under the Influence of Alcohol." *Quarterly Journal of Studies on Alcohol*, 33: 800–806, 1972 **(50207)**

BUONO, M.J. "Sweat Ethanol Concentrations Are Highly Correlated with Co-Existing Blood Values in Humans." *Experimental Physiology*, 84: 401–404, 1999 **(40304)**

BURNS, D.T. AND M.K. WALKER. "The Stability of Urine for the Forensic Analysis of Samples in Alleged Driving Under the Influence of Alcohol Cases—A Review and Case Report." *Journal of the Association of Public Analysts*, 48 001–010, 10pp, 2020 **(40111)**

BUSUITTIL, A., J.O. OBAFUNWA, AND A. AHMED. "Suicidal Inhalation of Vehicular Exhaust in the Lothian and Borders Region of Scotland." *Human, Experimental Toxicology*, 13: 545–550, 1994 **(62008)**

BUYUK, Y., M. EKE, A.S. CAGDIR, AND H.K. KARAASLAN. "Post-Mortem Alcohol Analysis in Synovial Fluid: An Alternative Method for Estimation of Blood Alcohol Level in Medico-Legal Autopsies." *Toxicology Mechanisms and Methods*, 19: 375–378, 2009 **(70815)**

BYARD, R.W. "Commercial Fishing Industry Deaths—Forensic Issues." *Journal of Forensic and Legal Medicine,* 20: 129–132, 2013 **(61108)**

———. "Lethal Injuries Occurring During Illegal Break-Ins." *American Journal of Forensic Medicine and Pathology*, 26: 121–124, 2005 **(60912)**

BYE, E.K. "Alcohol and Violence: Use of Possible Confounders in a Time-Series Analysis." *Addiction*, 102: 369–376, 2007 **(60111)**

BYE, E.K., S.T. BOGSTRAND, AND I. ROSSOW. "The Importance of Alcohol in Elderly's Hospital Admissions for Fall Injuries: A Population Case-Control Study." *Nordic Studies on Alcohol and Drugs,* 12pp, 2021 **(60518)**

C

CADDY, G.R., M.B. SOBELL, AND L.C. SOBELL. "Alcohol Breath Tests: Criterion Times for Avoiding Contamination by 'Mouth Alcohol.'" *Behaviour Research Methods and Instrumentation*, 10: 814–818, 1978 **(30501)**

CAIRNS, F.J., T.D. KOELMEYER, AND W.M.I. SMEETON. "Deaths from Drowning." *New Zealand Medical Journal*, 97: 65–67, 1984 **(60403)**

CALHOUN, F. AND K. WARREN. "Fetal Alcohol Syndrome: Historical Perspectives." *Neuroscience and Behavioral Reviews* 31: 168–171, 2007 **(90401)**

CAMERON, J.M. AND A.K. MANT. "Fatal Subarachnoid Hemorrhage Associated with Cervical Trauma." *Medicine Science and the Law*, 12: 66–70, 1972 **(60911)**

CAMPBELL, L. AND H.K. WILSON. "Blood Alcohol Concentrations Following the Inhalation of Ethanol Vapour Under Controlled Conditions." *Journal of the Forensic Science Society,* 26: 129–135, 1986 **(10122)**

CANADIAN SOCIETY OF FORENSIC SCIENCE ALCOHOL TEST COMMITTEE. "Alcohol Test Committee Position Paper, Documentation Required for Assessing the Accuracy and Reliability of Approved Instrument Breath Alcohol Results." *Canadian Society of Forensic Science Journal*, 45: 101–103, 2012 **(30135)**

CANFIELD, D., J. BRINK, R. JOHNSON, ET AL. "Clarification of Ethanol-Positive Case Using Urine Serotonin Metabolite Ratio." *Journal of Analytical Toxicology*, 31: 592–595, 2007 **(70212)**

CAO, Y. AND E.L. GIOVANNUCCI. "Alcohol as a Risk Factor for Cancer." *Seminars in Oncology Nursing,* 32: 325–331, 2016 **(90313)**

CAPLAN, Y. AND B. LEVINE. "The Analysis of Ethanol in Serum, Blood and Urine. A Comparison of the TDx REA Ethanol Assay with Gas Chromatography." *Journal of Analytical Toxicology*, 10: 49–52, 1986 **(20109)**

———. "Vitreous Humor in the Evaluation of Postmortem Blood Ethanol Concentrations." *Journal of Analytical Toxicology*, 14: 305–307, 1990 **(70604)**

CAREY, K.B. AND J.T.P. HUSTAD. "Are Retrospectively Reconstructed Blood Alcohol Concentrations Accurate? Preliminary Results from a Field Study." *Journal of Studies on Alcohol*, 63: 762–766, 2002 **(10606)**

CARITO, V., G. PARLAPIANO, D. RASIO, ET AL. "Fetal Alcohol Spectrum Disorders in Pediatrics: FASD and the Pediatrician." *Biomedical Reviews*, 29: 27–35, 2018 **(90406)**

CARPENTER, C. "How Do Zero Tolerance Drunk Driving Laws Work?" *Journal of Health Economics*, 23: 61–83, 2004 **(50708)**

CARVALHO, A.F., M. HELLIG, A. PEREZ, ET AL. "Alcohol Use Disorders." *Lancet*, 394: 781–792, 2019 **(90102)**

CARY, P.L., P.D. WHITTER, AND C.A. JOHNSON. "Abbot Radiative Energy Attenuation Method for Quantifying Ethanol Evaluated and Compared with Gas Liquid Chromatography and the Du Pont ACA." *Clinical Chemistry*, 30: 1867–1870, 1984 **(20110)**

CASAVANT, M.J., M.N. SHAH, AND R. BATTELS. "Does Fluorescent Urine Indicate Antifreeze Ingestion by Children?" *Pediatrics*, 107: 113–114, 2001 **(80504)**

CASSIN, B.J. AND W.U. SPITZ. "Concentration of Alcohol in Delayed Subdural Hematoma." *Journal of Forensic Science*, 28: 1013–1015, 1983 **(70505)**

CAUGHLIN, J.D. "An Unusual Source for Postmortem Findings of Methyl Ethyl Ketone and Methanol in Two Homicide Victims." *Forensic Science International*, 67: 27–31, 1994 **(70307)**

CECILLIASON, A.-S., M.G. ANDERSSON, E. LUNDIN, AND H. SANDLER. "Microbial Neoformation of Volatiles: Implications for the Estimation of Post-Mortem

Interval in Decomposed Human Remains in an Indoor Setting." *International Journal of Legal Medicine*, 11pp, 6 October 2020 **(70217)**

CENTOLA, C., M. TAGLIABUE, A. SPOTO, ET AL. "Enhancement of Unsafe Behaviors in Simulated Moped-Riding Performance Under the Influence of Low Dose of Alcohol." *Accident Analysis and Prevention*, 136: 105409, 8pp, 2020 **(61316)**

CHANGCHIEN, E.M., G.A. WOODARD, T. HERNANDEZ-BOUSSARD, AND J.M. MORTON, "Normal Alcohol Metabolism after Gastric Banding and Sleeve Gastrectomy: A Case-Cross-Over Trial." *American College of Surgeons*, 215: 475–479, 2012 **(10129)**

CHAPPELL, A.G. "Severe Hypothermia Due to Combination of Psychotropic Drugs and Alcohol." *British Medical Journal*, 356, 5 February 1966 **(61011)**

CHARLEBOIS, R.C., M.R. CORBETT, AND J.G. WIGMORE. "Comparison of Ethanol Concentrations in Blood, Serum, and Blood Cells for Forensic Application." *Journal of Analytical Toxicology*, 20: 171–178, 1996 **(20205)**

CHATHA, H., I. SAMMY, M. HICKNEY, ET AL. "Falling Down a Flight of Stairs: The Impact of Age and Intoxication on Injury Pattern and Severity." *Trauma,* 20: 169–174, 2018 **(60519)**

CHEN, H-M., W.W. LIN, K.H. FERGUSON, ET AL. "Studies of the Oxidation of Ethanol to Acetaldehyde by Oxyhemoglobin Using Fluorogenic High Performance Liquid Chromatography." *Alcoholism: Clinical and Experiment Research*, 18: 1202–1206, 1994 **(20307)**

CHENG, S-Y., H-Y LEE, J-C.LEE, AND S-Y.TSAI, "Comparing the Effects of Light Alcohol Consumption on Human Response to Auditory and Visual Stimuli." *Perceptual and Motor Skills*, 111: 589–607, 2010 **(50115)**

CHIANG, H-H. AND Y-H. YOUNG. "Impact of Alcohol on Vestibular Function in Relation to the Legal Limit of 0.25 mg/L Breath Alcohol Concentration." *Audiology and Neurotology*, 12: 183–188, 2007 **(61302)**

CHIAROTTI, M. AND N. DE GIOVANNI. "Acetaldehyde Accumulation During Headspace Gas Chromatographic Determination of Ethanol." *Forensic Science International*, 20: 21–25, 1982 **(20103)**

CHIAROTTI, M., N, DE GIOVANNI, AND A. CARNEVALE. "The Use of Silica Gel in Evidential Tests in Drunken Driver Problems Related to Alcohols Adsorption and Elution." *Blutalkohol*, 22: 264–271, 1985 **(30702)**

CHIHURI, S., G. LI, AND Q. CHEN. "Interaction of Marijuana and Alcohol on Fatal Motor Vehicle Crash Risk: A Case Control Study." *Injury Epistemology*, 4:8 2017 **(50808)**

CHIKRITZHS, T. AND M. LIVINGSTON. "Alcohol and the Risk of Injury." *Nutrients*, 13: 277, 15pp, 2021 **(90503)**

CHOW, B.L.C. AND J.G. WIGMORE. "Technical Note: The Stability of Aqueous Alcohol Standard Used in Breath Alcohol Testing After Twenty-Six Years Storage." *Canadian Society of Forensic Science Journal*, 38: 21–24, 2005 **(30207)**

CHRISTMAS, A.B., R.A. BRINTZENHOFF, T.M. SCHMELZER, ET AL. "MOPEDS: Motorized Objects Propelling Ethanol Drinking Subjects." *The American Surgeon*, 77: 304–306, 2011 **(61317)**

CHRISTMORE, D.S., R. KELLY, AND L.A. DOSHIER. "Improved Recovery and Stability of Ethanol in Automated Headspace Analysis." *Journal of Forensic Science*, 29: 1038–1044, 1984 **(20101)**

CHRISTOPOULOS, G., E.R. KIRCH, AND J.E. GEARIEN. "Determination of Ethanol in Fresh and Purified Postmortem Tissues." *Journal of Chromatography*, 87: 455–472, 1973 **(70101)**

CHUN, H-J., J.L. POKLIS, A. POKLIS, AND C.E. WOLF. "Development and Validation of a Method for Alcohol Analysis in Brain Tissue by Headspace Gas Chromatography with Flame Ionization Detector." *Journal of Analytical Toxicology*, 40: 653–658, 2016 **(70106)**

CHUWERS, P., J. OSTERLOH, T. KELLY ET AL. "Neurobehavioral Effects of Low-Level Methanol Vapor Exposure in Healthy Human Volunteers." *Environmental Research*, 71: 141–150, 1995 **(80308)**

CINA, S.J., J.L. KOELPIN, C.A. NICHOLS, AND S.E. CONRADI. "A Decade of Train-Pedestrian Fatalities: The Charleston Experience." *Journal of Forensic Science*, 39: 668–673, 1994 **(61501)**

CITEK, K., B. BALL AND D.A. RUTLEDGE. "Nystagmus Testing in Intoxicated Individuals." *Optometry,* 74: 695–710, 2003 **(50606)**

CITEK, K., A.D. ELMONT, C.L. JONS, ET AL. "Sleep Deprivation Does Not Mimic Alcohol Intoxication in Field Sobriety Testing." *Journal of Forensic Sciences*, 56: 1170–1179, 2011 **(50615)**

CLARKE, S.W., K.E. GLINDEMANN, AND D.M. WIEGAND. "The Epidemiology of Alcohol Consumption at College Football Tailgate Parties: Implications for Traffic Safety." *Proceedings of 17th International Conference on Alcohol, Drugs and Traffic Safety, August 8–13, 2004*, Glasgow, Scotland, Oliver, J., Williams, P., and Clayton, P. (eds), CD, 6pp **(61909)**

COHEN, J., E.J. DEARNALEY, AND C.E.M. HANSEL. "The Risk Taken in Driving Under the Influence of Alcohol." *British Medical Journal*, 1438–1442, 1958 **(50302)**

COLBURN, N., R.D. MEYER, M. WRIGLEY, AND E.L. BRADLEY. "Should Motorcycles Be Operated Within the Legal Alcohol Limits for Automobiles?" *Journal of Trauma*, 35: 183–186, 1993 **(61301)**

COLLINS, W.E., H.W. MERTENS, AND E.A. HIGGINS. "Some Effects of Alcohol and Simulated Altitude on Complex Performance Scores and Breathalyzer Readings." *Aviation, Space Environmental Medicine*, 58: 328–332, 1987 **(60708)**

CONNELL, M. "Expert Testimony in Sexual Assault Case: Alcohol Intoxication and Memory." *International Journal of Law and Psychiatry*, 8pp, 2015 **(61721)**

CONNER, C.R., H.M. RAY, R.M. MCCORMACK, ET AL. "Association of Rideshare Use with Alcohol-Associated Motor Vehicle Crash Trauma." *JAMA Surgery,* E1–E8, 2021 **(50719)**

CONNER, K.R. AND C.L. BAGGE. "Suicidal Behavior. Links Between Alcohol Use Disorder and Acute Use of Alcohol." *Alcohol Research: Current Reviews*, 40: e1–e4, 2019 **(90109)**

CONNOR, J., R. NORTON, S. AMERATUNGA, AND R. JACKSON. "The Contribution of Alcohol to Serious Car Crash Injuries." *Epidemiology*, 15: 337–344, 2004 **(50506)**

CONSTANTINO, A., E.J. DIGREGORIO, W. KORN, ET AL. "The Effect of the Use of Mouthwash on Ethylglucuronide Concentrations in Urine." *Journal of Analytical Toxicology*, 30: 659–662, 2006 **(40509)**

COOKE, A.R. "The Simultaneous Emptying and Absorption of Ethanol from the Human Stomach." *Digestive Diseases*, 15: 449–454, 1970 **(10102)**

COOKE, C.T., G.A. CADDEN, AND K.A. MARGOLIUS. "Death by Hanging in Western Australia." *Pathology,* 27: 268–272, 1995 **(62007)**

COOPER, P.J. AND J.P. ROTHE, "Drinking Establishment, Driving Risk, and Ethno-Pharmacology." *Proceedings of 35th International Congress on Alcohol and Drug Dependence, Oslo, Norway,* Vol 2, 6pp, 1988 **(10401)**

COOPER, P.N. AND C.M. MILROY. "Violent Suicide in South Yorkshire, England." *Journal of Forensic Science*, 39: 657–667, 1994 **(62010)**

COOPER, S. "Infrared Breath Alcohol Analysis Following Inhalation of Gasoline Fumes." *Journal of Analytical Toxicology*, 5: 198–199, 1981 **(30613)**

CORTOT, A., G. JOBIN, F. DUCROT, ET AL. "Gastric Emptying and Gastrointestinal Absorption of Alcohol Ingested with a Meal." *Digestive Diseases and Sciences*, 31: 343–348, 1986 **(10103)**

COWAN, J.M. "Does the Intoxilyzer 4011AS-A Conform to the Beer-Lambert Law?" *Journal of the Forensic Science Society*, 28: 179–184, 1988 **(30107)**

COWAN, J.M., J.M. BURIS, J.R. HUGHES, AND M.P. CUNNINGHAM, "The Relationship of Normal Body Temperature, End-Expired Breath Temperature, and the BAC/BrAC Ratio in 98 Physically Fit Human Test Subjects." *Journal of Analytical Toxicology*, 34: 238–242, 2010 **(30419)**

COWAN, J.M., M.E. DENNIS III, AND L.F. SMITH. "A Comparison of Equal Alcohol Doses of Beer and Whiskey on Eleven Human Test Subjects." *Canadian Society of Forensic Science Journal*, 37: 137–145, 2004 **(10405)**

COWAN, J.M., W.E. VAN TASSEL, AND M.E. DENNIS III. "Is There a Gender Factor? A Comparison of Blood: Breath Differences and Ratios Between Men and Women." *Proceedings of the 17th International Conference on Alcohol, Drugs and Traffic Safety, August 8–13, 2004, Glasgow, Scotland,* Oliver, J., Williams, P., and Clayton, P. (eds), CD, 5pp **(30418)**

COWAN, S. "The Trouble with Drink Intoxication, (In)capacity, and the Evaporation of Consent to Sex." *Akron Law Review*, 41: Article 4, 899–922, 2015 **(61720)**

CRAUCIC, D.-V., C.I. STAN, L.A. RISCANU, ET AL. "Death-Causing Cardiac Injuries After Chronic Alcohol Intake Identified by Forensic Medicine." *Romanian Journal of Morphology and Embryology*, 62: 553–561, 2021 **(90307)**

CROCKER, P., O. ZAD, T. MILLING, AND K.A. LAWSON. "Alcohol, Bicycling, and Head and Brain Injury: A Study of Impaired Cyclists' Riding Patterns R1." *American Journal of Emergency Medicine*, 28: 68–72, 2010 **(60208)**

CROCKETT, A.J., M. ROZEE, R. LASLETT, AND J.H. ALPERS. "Minimum Lung Function for Breath Alcohol Testing Using the Lion Alcolmeter SD-400." *Science and Justice*, 39: 173–177, 1999 **(30305)**

CROMBIE, I.K., D.J. POUNDER, AND P.H. DICK. "Who Takes Alcohol Prior to Suicide?" *Journal of Clinical and Forensic Medicine*, 5: 65–68, 1998 **(62003)**

CROMER, J.R., J.A. CROMER, P. MARUFF, AND P.J. SNYDER. "Perception of Alcohol Intoxication Shows Acute Tolerance While Executive Functions Remain Impaired." *Experimental and Clinical Psychopharmacology*, 18: 329–339, 2010 **(50114)**

CROWDY, K.A. AND D.E. MARPLE-HORVAT. "Alcohol Affects Eye Movements Essential for Visually Guided Stepping." *Alcoholism: Clinical and Experimental Research*, 28: 402–407, 2004 **(60507)**

CULLEN, S.A. AND R.W. MAYES. "Alcohol Discovered in the Urine After Death: Ante-mortem Ingestion or Post-Mortem Artefact?" *Medicine, Science and the Law,* 45: 196–200, 2005 **(70703)**

CURCULIC, D., A. BOSNAR, V. STEMBERGA, ET AL. "Interpretation of Blood Alcohol Concentration in Maritime Accidents—A Case Report." *Forensic Science International*, Suppl. Series 1: 35–37, 2009 **(61107)**

CURRIER, G.W., A.J. TRENTON, AND P.G. WALSH. "Relative Accuracy of Breath and Serum Alcohol Readings in the Psychiatric Emergency Service." *Psychiatric Services*, 57: 34–36, 2006 **(30409)**

D

DAHL, H., N. STEPHANSON, O. BECK, AND A. HELANDER. "Comparison of Urinary Excretion Characteristics of Ethanol and Ethyl Glucuronide." *Journal of Analytical Toxicology,* 26: 201–204, 2002 **(40506)**

DALLEY, R. "DUI and Petrol Consumption [Letter]." *Journal of the Forensic Science Society*, 25: 53–54, 1985 **(30614)**

DALLY, A.M. "Fatal Methanol Intoxication—Two Exceptional Cases." *Toxichem Krimtech,* 82(1): 27, 2015 **(80315)**

DALRYMPLE-ALFORD, J.C., P.A. KERR, AND R.D. JONES. "The Effects of Alcohol on Driving-Related Sensorimotor Performance Across Four Times of Day." *Journal of Studies on Alcohol*, 64: 93–97, 2003 **(50110)**

DANIEL, D.R., B.H. MCANALLEY, AND J.C. GARRIOTT. "Isopropyl Alcohol Metabolism After Acute Intoxication in Humans." *Journal of Analytical Toxicology*, 5: 110–112, 1981 **(80403)**

DAVIDSON, D., P. CAMARA, AND R. SWIFT. "Behavioral Effects and Pharmacokinetics of Low-Dose Intravenous Alcohol in Humans." *Alcoholism, Clinical and Experimental Research*, 21: 1294–1299, 1997 **(40303)**

DAVIS, A.R. AND A.H. LIPSON. "Central Nervous System Tolerance to High Blood Alcohol Levels." *Medical Journal of Australia*, 144: 9–12, 1986 **(62006)**

DAVIS, D.P., K.J. BRAMWELL, R.S. HAMILTON, AND S.R. WILLIAMS. "Ethylene Glycol Poisoning: A Case Report of a Record-High Level and a Review." *Journal of Emergency Medicine*, 15: 653–667, 1997 **(80507)**

DAVIS, K.C., W.H. GEORGE, J. NORRIS, ET AL. "Effects of Alcohol and Blood Alcohol Concentration Limb on Sexual Risk-Taking Intentions." *Journal of Studies on Alcohol and Drugs*, 70: 499–507, 2009 **(61711)**

DAVIS, K.C., C.S. HENDERSHOT, W.H. GEORGE, J. NORRIS, AND J.R. HEIMAN. "Alcohol Effects on Sexual Decision Making: An Integration of Alcohol Myopia and Individual Differences." *Journal of Studies on Alcohol*, 68: 843–851, 2007 **(61703)**

DAVIS, P.L., L.A. DAL CORTIVO, AND J. MATURO. "Endogenous Isopropanol: Forensic and Biochemical Implications." *Journal of Analytical Toxicology*, 8: 209–212, 1984 **(80401)**

DEAKIN, C.D., F. THOMPSON, C. GIBSON, AND M. GREEN. "Effects of International Football Matches on Ambulance Call Profiles and Volumes During the 2006 World Cup." *Emergency Medicine Journal*, 24: 405–407, 2007 **(61914)**

DECHANO, W.D. "The Effects of Dosed Tobacco in Evidentiary Breath-Testing Using Non-Drinking Subjects." *Science and Justice*, 52: 142–144, 2012 **(30521)**

DEDONNO, A., A. DEFAZIO, M.G. GRECO, ET AL. "Death in Head-Down Position in a Heavily Intoxicated Obese Man." *Legal Medicine*, 10: 204–209, 2008 **(60511)**

DE FREITAS, E.A.M., I.D. MENDES, AND L.C.M. DE OLIVEIRA. "Alcohol Consumption Among Victims of External Causes in a University General Hospital." *Rev Saude Publica*, 42: 1–8, 2008 **(60119)**

DE GIER, J.J. "A Subjective Measurement of the Influence of Ethyl Alcohol in Moderate Levels on Real Driving Performance." *Blutalkohol*, 16: 363–370, 1979 **(50402)**

DE GIONVANNI, G. DONADIO, AND M. CHIAROTTI. "The Reliability of Fatty Acid Ethyl Esters (FAEE) as Biological Markers for the Diagnosis of Alcohol Abuse." *Journal of Analytical Toxicology*, 31: 93–97, 2007 **(40510)**

DEGUTIS, L.C., R. RABINOVICI, A. SABBAJ, ET AL. "The Saliva Strip Test Is an Accurate Method to Determine Blood Alcohol Concentration in Trauma Patients." *Academy of Emergency Medicine*, 11: 885–887, 2004 **(40205)**

DE MARTINIS, B.S., C.M.C. DE PAULA, A. BRAGA, ET AL. "Alcohol Distribution in Different Postmortem Body Fluids." *Human Experimental Toxicology,* 25: 83–97, 2006 **(70803)**

DE MARTINIS B.S. AND C.C.S. MARTIN. "Automated Headspace Solid-Phase Microextraction and Capillary Gas Chromatography Analysis of Ethanol in Postmortem Specimens." *Forensic Science International*, 128: 115–119, 2002 **(70104)**

DEMING, J.E., R.E. MITTLEMAN, AND C.V. WETLI. "Forensic Science Aspects of Fatal Sexual Assaults on Women." *Journal of Forensic Science*, 28: 572–576, 1983 **(61712)**

DE MOULIN, D. "Spontaneous Combustion: An Odd Chapter in the History of Burns." *Archives Chirurgicum Neeland*, 27: 223–227, 1975 **(60609)**

DENGIZ, H., N. DAGLIOGLU, AND I.E. GOREN. "Assessment of Recent Alcohol Consumption by Detecting Ethyl Glucuronide and Ethyl Sulfate Level Among Traffic Accident Patients." *Traffic Injury Prevention*, 21: 371–374, 2020 **(40523)**

DENNEY, R.C. "Solvent Inhalation and Apparent Alcohol. Studies on the Lion Intoximeter 3000." *Journal of the Forensic Science Society*, 30: 357–361, 1990 **(30609)**

DERR, R.F. "First-Pass Metabolism of Ethanol in the Human Stomach: A Negligible Reaction." *Biochemical Archives*, 10: 197–201, 1994 **(10314)**

DE SOUZA V., J.M. RODRIGUES, R.D. BANDEIRA, ET AL. "Evaluation of the Stability of Ethanol in Water Certified Reference Material: Measurement Uncertainty Under Transport and Storage Conditions." *Accreditation Quality Assurance*, 13: 717–721, 2008 **(30212)**

DETTLING, A., F. FISCHER, S. BOHLER, ET AL. "Ethanol Elimination Rates in Men and Women in Consideration of the Calculated Liver Weight." *Alcohol,* 41: 415–420, 2007 **(10305)**

DETTLING, A., A. PREISS, G. SKOPP, AND H-T. HAFFNER. "The Influence of Luteal and Follicular Phases on Major Pharmacokinetic Parameters of Blood and Breath Alcohol Kinetics in Women." *Alcohol*, 44: 315–321, 2010 **(10316)**

DETTLING, A., S. WITTE, G. SKOPP, ET AL. "A Regression Model Applied to Gender-Specific Ethanol Elimination Rates from Blood and Breath Measurements in Non-Alcoholics." *International Journal of Legal Medicine*, 123: 381–385, 2009 **(10306)**

DEVENNEY, L.E., K.B. COYLE, AND J.C. VERSTER. "Memory and Attention During an Alcohol Hangover." *Human Psychopharmacology Clinical and Experimental*, 34: e2701, 7pp, 2019 **(60815)**

DEVIVO, M.J. AND P. SEKAR. "Prevention of Spinal Cord Injuries That Occur in Swimming Pools." *Spinal Cord*, 35: 509–515, 1997 **(60412)**

DEWAARD, D. AND K.A. BROOKHUIS. "Assessing Driver Status: A Demonstration Experiment on the Road." *Accident Analysis and Prevention*, 23: 297–307, 1991 **(50401)**

DICK, G.L. AND H.M. STONE. "Alcohol Loss Arising from Microbial Contamination of Drivers' Blood Specimens." *Forensic Science International*, 34: 17–27, 1987 **(20310)**

DIEHL, B.W. AND E. ZAILER, "Alternative Determination of BAC by Means of 1H-NMR." *Toxichem Krimtech* 80: 320–322, 2013 **(20125)**

DIENER, H.C., J. DICHGANS, M. BACHER, ET AL. "Mechanism of Postural Ataxia after Intake of Alcohol." *Zeitschrift fur Rechtsmedizin,* 90: 159–165, 1983 **(60501)**

DITT, J. AND G. SCHULZE. "The Course of the Blood Alcohol Curve in Men After Blood Loss and Infusion of a Blood Substitute [German]." *Acta Medicinae Legalis et Socialis*, 16: 71–76, 1963 **(10801)**

DITTMANN, V., O. PRIBILLA, AND T. WAGNER. "Ethanol Elimination in Man Under the Influence of Frequently Prescribed Beta Receptor Blockers [German]." *Blutalkohol*, 22: 364–370, 1985 **(10704)**

DIXIT, D., J. ENDICOTT, L. BURRY, ET AL. "Management of Acute Alcohol Withdrawal Syndrome in Critically Ill Patients." *Psychopharmacology*, 36: 797–822, 2016 **(90202)**

DOMENECH, M.S., H.M. ALCAZAR, A.A. PALLARES, ET AL. "The Murderer Is the Bed: An Unusual Case of Death by Traumatic Asphyxia in a Hotel Folding Bunk Bed." *Forensic Science International*, 220: e1–e4, 2012 **(60919)**

DOOLDENIYA, M.D., R. KHAFAGY, H. MASHALY ET AL. "Lower Abdominal Pain in Women After Binge Drinking." *British Medical Journal*, 335: 992–993, 2007 **(40110)**

DORAFSHAR, A.H., D.J. O'BOYLE, AND R.F. MCCLOY. "Effects of a Moderate Dose of Alcohol on Simulated Laparoscopic Surgical Performance." *Surgical Endoscopy,* 16: 1753–1758, 2002 **(61209)**

DOUGHTERY, D.M., J.M. BJORK, R.H. BENNETT, AND F.G. MOELLER. "The Effects of a Cumulative Alcohol Dosing Procedure on Laboratory Aggression in Women and Men." *Journal of Studies on Alcohol*, 60: 322–329, 1999 **(60102)**

DOUGHTERY, D.M., N. CHARLES, A. ACHESON, ET AL. "Comparing the Detection of Transdermal and Breath Alcohol Concentrations During Periods of Alcohol Consumption Ranging from Moderate Drinking to Binge Drinking." *Experimental and Clinical Psychopharmacology*, 20: 373–381, 2012 **(40310)**

DOUGHTERY, D.M., N. HILL-KAPTURCZAK, Y. LIANG, ET AL. "The Potential Clinical Utility of Transdermal Alcohol Monitoring Data to Estimate the Number of Alcoholic Drinks Consumed." *Addict Disorders and Their Treatment*, 14: 124–130, 2015 **(40308)**

DOWLING, G. AND B. CURRY. "Traumatic Basal Subarachnoid Hemorrhage." *American Journal of Forensic Medicine and Pathology*, 9: 23–31, 1988 **(60910)**

DOWLING, S., D. REYNOLDS, A. O'REILLY, ET AL. "A Clinical Investigation into the Ability of Subjects with a Lung Disease to Provide Breath Specimens Using the Drager 6510." *Journal of Forensic and Legal Medicine*, 72: 6pp, 2020 **(30313)**

DRESSLER, J., G. HAUCK, AND K. LEHMAN. "On the Diagnosis of Fatal Ethanol Intoxication During the Absorption Period [German]." *Blutalkohol*, 28: 302–303, 1991 **(70407)**

DRUMMOND-LAGE, A.P., R.G. DE FREITA, G. CRUZ, ET AL. "Correlation Between Blood Alcohol Concentration (BAC), Breath Alcohol Concentration (BrAC) and Psychomotor Evaluation in a Clinical Monitored Study of Alcohol Intake in Brazil." *Alcohol*, 66: 15–20, 2018 **(30425)**

DUBOIS, S., N. MULLEN, B. WEAVER, AND M. BEDARD. "The Combined Effects of Alcohol and Cannabis on Driving: Impact on Crash Risk." *Forensic Science International*, 248: 94–100, 2015 **(50807)**

DUBOWSKI, K.M. "Duplicate Breath-Alcohol Testing [Letter]." *American Journal of Forensic Medicine and Pathology*, 9: 272, 1988 **(30116)**

DUBOWSKI, K.M. AND N.A. ESSARY. "Evaluation of Commercial Breath-Alcohol Simulators: Further Studies." *Journal of Analytical Toxicology*, 15: 272–275, 1991 **(30201)**

———. "Field Performance of Current Generation Breath-Alcohol Simulators." *Journal of Analytical Toxicology*, 16: 325–327, 1992 **(30202)**

———. "Vapor-Alcohol Control Tests with Compressed Ethanol-Gas Mixtures: Scientific Basis and Actual Performance." *Journal of Analytical Toxicology*, 20: 484–491, 1996 **(30209)**

DUKE, A., P.R. GIANCOLA, D.H. MORRIS, ET AL. "Alcohol Dose and Aggression: Another Reason Why Drinking More Is a Bad Idea." *Journal of Studies on Alcohol and Drugs*, 72: 34–43, 2011 **(60116)**

DULTZ, L.A. AND S.G. FRANGOS. "The Impact of Alcohol in Pedestrian Trauma." *Trauma* 15: 64–75, 2012 **(61411)**

DUMOLLARD, C., J-F. WIART, F. HAKIM, ET AL. "Putatively Lethal Ingestion of Isopropyl Alcohol-Related Case: Interpretation of Post Mortem Isopropyl Alcohol and Acetone Concentrations Remains Challenging." *International Journal of Legal Medicine*, 135: 175–182, 2021 **(80410)**

DUNBAR, J.A., W.A. MACRAE, J.H. MURPHIE, ET AL. "Evidential Breath Testing of Drivers—Day Surgery and Halothane Anaesthesia." *Medicine Science and the Law,* 25: 162–164, 1985 **(30616)**

DUNDEE, J.W., J.G. BOVILL, AND M. ISAAC. "Failure to Demonstrate an Increased Removal of Alcohol from the Blood Stream by Fructose." *Medicine Science and the Law,* 11: 146–148, 1972 **(10715)**

DUNDEE, J.W., M. ISAAC, AND J. TAGGART. "Blood Ethanol Levels Following Rapid Intravenous Infusion." *Quarterly Journal of Studies on Alcohol* 32: 741–747, 1971 **(10115)**

DUTTA, S.K., M. ORESTES, S. VENGULEKUR, AND P. KWO. "Ethanol and Human Saliva: Effect of Chronic Alcoholism on Flow Rate, Composition and Epidermal Growth Factor." *American Journal of Gastroenterology*, 87: 350–354, 1992 **(40208)**

E

EARLL, J.M., H.H. WESTMORELAND, C.A. WENDT, ET AL. "The Influence of Temperature on Alcohol Absorption Rates in Humans." *Military Medicine*, 150: 612–613, 1985 **(10111)**

ECKENHOFF, R.G. AND C.S. OLSTAD. "Ethanol and Venous Bubbles After Decompression in Humans." *Undersea Biomedical Research*, 18: 47–51, 1991 **(60405)**

EGAN, V. AND G. CORDAN. "Barely Legal: Is Attraction and Estimated Age of Young Female Faces Disrupted by Alcohol Use, Make Up and the Sex of the Observer?" *British Journal of Psychology*, 415–427, 2009 **(60709)**

EISELE, J.W., D.T. REAY, AND H.J. BONNELL. "Ethanol in Sequestered Hematomas: Quantitative Evaluation." *American Journal of Clinical Pathology*, 81: 352–355, 1984 **(70502)**

EMADI, A. AND L. COBERLY. "Intoxication of a Hospitalized Patient with an Isopropanol-Based Hand Sanitizer [Letter]." *New England Journal of Medicine*, 356: 530–531, 2007 **(80405)**

EMESON, B. L., T. WHITFUL, C.R. BAUM, ET AL. "Effects of Alcohol-Based Hand Hygiene Solutions on Breath Alcohol Detection in the Emergency Department." *American Journal of Infection Control*, 44: 1672–1674, 2016 **(30130)**

ENDRES, H.G.E. AND O. GRUNER. "Comparison of D_2O and Ethanol Dilutions in Total Body Water Measurements in Humans." *Clinical Investigator*, 72: 830–837, 1994 **(10201)**

ENGELHART, D.A. AND A.J. JENKINS. "Evaluation of an Onsite Alcohol Testing Device for Use in Postmortem Forensic Toxicology." *Journal of Analytical Toxicology*, 25: 612–615, 2001 **(70612)**

ERICKSON, D.J., T.L. TOOMEY, K.M. LENK, ET AL. "Can We Assess Blood Alcohol Levels of Attendees Leaving Professional Sporting Events?" *Alcoholism: Clinical and Experimental Research*, 35: 689–694, 2011 **(61915)**

ERIKSSON, A. AND U. BJORNSTIG. "Fatal Snowmobile Accidents in Northern Sweden." *Journal of Trauma*, 22: 977–982, 1982 **(61805)**

ERIKSSON, C.J.P. "Problems and Pitfalls in Acetaldehyde Determination." *Alcoholism: Clinical and Experimental Research*, 4: 22–29, 1980 **(80101)**

ERNSTGARD, L., A. PEXARAS, AND G. JOHANSON. "Washout Kinetics for Ethanol from the Airways Following Inhalation of Ethanol Vapors and Use of Mouthwash." *Clinical Toxicology*, 58: 171–177, 2020 **(30530)**

F

FAIRBAIRN, C.E., W.J. VENERABLE, I.G. ROSEN, AND S.E. LUCZAK. "Estimating the Quantity and Time Course of Alcohol Consumption from Transdermal Alcohol Sensor Data: A Combined Laboratory-Ambulatory Study." *Alcohol,* 81: 111–116, 2019 **(40312)**

FEIN, G. AND D.J. MEYERHOFF. "Ethanol in Human Brain by Magnetic Resonance Spectroscopy: Correlation with Blood and Breath Levels, Relaxation, and Magnetization Transfer." *Alcoholism: Clinical and Experimental Research*, 24: 1227–1235, 2000 **(10206)**

FELL, J.C. AND R.B. VOAS. "The Effectiveness of Reducing Illegal Blood Alcohol Concentration (BAC) Limits for Driving: Evidence for Lowering the Limit to.05 BAC." *Journal of Safety Research*, 37: 233–243, 2006 **(50705)**

———. "Mothers Against Drunk Driving (MADD): The First 25 Years." *Traffic Injury Prevention*, 7: 195–212, 2006 **(50712)**

FERRARI, L.A., J.M.TRISZCZ, AND L. GIANNUZZI. "Kinetics of Ethanol Degradation in Forensic Blood Samples." *Forensic Science International*, 161: 144–150, 2006 **(70207)**

FERREIRA, S.E., M.T. DE MELLO, S. POMPEIA, AND M.L.O. DE SOUZA-FORMIGONI. "Effects of Energy Drink Ingestion on Alcohol Intoxication." *Alcoholism: Clinical and Experimental Research*, 30: 598–605, 2006 **(10719)**

FILLMORE, M.T., J.S. BLACKBURN, AND E.L.R. HARRISON. "Acute Disinhibiting Effects of Alcohol as a Factor in Risky Driving Behavior." *Drug and Alcohol Dependence,* 95: 97–106, 2008 **(50210)**

FINNIGAN, F., R. HAMMERSLEY, AND K. MILLAR. "Effects of Meal Composition on Blood Alcohol Level, Psychomotor Performance and Subjective State After Ingestion of Alcohol." *Appetite,* 31: 361–375, 1998 **(10107)**

FINNIGAN, F., D. SCHULZE, J. SMALLWOOD, AND A. HELANDER. "The Effects of Self-Administered Alcohol-Induced Hangover in a Naturalistic Setting on Psychomotor and Cognitive Performance and Subjective State." *Addiction,* 100: 1680–1689, 2005 **(60802)**

FIORENTINO, D.D. "Validation of Sobriety Tests for the Marine Environment." *Accident Analysis and Prevention*, 40: 870–877, 2011 **(60411)**

FLANAGAN, N.G., P.W. STRIKE, C.J. RIGBY, AND G. LOCHRIDGE. "The Effect of Low Doses of Alcohol on Driving Performance." *Medicine, Science, and the Law,* 22: 203–208, 1983 **(50303)**

FONTAINE, H. AND Y. GOURLET. "Fatal Pedestrian Accidents in France: A Typological Analysis." *Accident Analysis and Prevention* 29: 303–312, 1997 **(61403)**

FORNEY, R.B. AND F.W. HUGHES. "Alcohol Accumulation in Humans After Prolonged Drinking." *Clinical Pharmacology and Therapeutics,* 5: 619–621, 1963 **(10403)**

FORREST, A.R.W. "The Estimation of Widmark's Factor." *Journal of the Forensic Science Society*, 26: 249–252, 1986 **(10601)**

FOSEN, J.T., J. MORLAND, AND G. HOISETH. "The Relationship Between Ingested Dose of Ethanol and Amount of Ethyl Glucuronide Formed in Blood." *Journal of Analytical Toxicology*, 44: 861–863, 2020 **(40522)**

FRACASSO, T., B. BRINKMANN, J. BEIKE, AND H. PFEIFFER. "Clotted Blood as a Sign of Alcohol Intoxication: A Retrospective Study." *International Journal of Legal Medicine*, 122: 157–161, 2008 **(70213)**

FRANCISCO, J.T. AND T.E. BALDWIN. "Are Post Mortem Alcohols Valid?" *Medical Times*, 100 145–155, 1972 **(70205)**

FRANSSON, M., A.W. JONES, AND L. ANDERSSON. "Laboratory Evaluation of a New Evidential Breath-Alcohol Analyser Designed for Mobile Testing—The Evidenzer." *Medicine, Science and the Law*, 45: 61–70, 2005 **(30110)**

FRENI, F., M. MORETTI, S. SCARDO, ET AL. "Ethyl Glucuronide in Hair: A 5-Years Retrospective Cohort Study in Subjects Sanctioned for Driving Under the Influence of Alcohol and Psychoactive Substances." *Drug Testing Analysis*, 1–12, 2022 **(40525)**

FRIEDMAN, T.W., S.R. ROBINSON, AND G.W. YELLAND. "Impaired Perceptual Judgment at Low Blood Alcohol Concentrations." *Alcohol*, 45: 711–718, 2011 **(50116)**

FRIEL, P.N., B.K. LOGAN, AND J. BAER. "An Evaluation of the Reliability of Widmark Calculations Based on Breath Alcohol Measurements." *Journal Forensic Science*, 40: 91–94, 1995 **(10602)**

FROENTJES, W. "An Analysis of 10,000 Blood Tests in the Netherlands." *Proceedings 3rd International Conference on Alcohol and Road Traffic, BMA House, London*, 179–188, 1963 **(50614)**

FUNAYAMA, M., R. OKOCHI, S. ASADA, ET AL. "Severe Diaphoresis and Fever During Alcohol Withdrawal Cause Hypovolemic Shock: Case Report." *BMC Psychiatry*, 21: 387, 5pp, 2021 **(90211)**

G

GALLAHER, M.M., D.W. FLEMING, L.R. BERGER, AND C.M. SEWELL. "Pedestrian and Hypothermia Deaths Among Native Americans in New Mexico. Between Bar and Home." *Journal of the American Medical Association*, 267: 1345–1348, 1992 **(61004)**

GANERT, P.M. AND W.D. BOWTHORPE. "Evaluation of Breath Alcohol Profiles Following a Period of Social Drinking." *Canadian Society of Forensic Science Journal*, 33: 137–143, 2000 **(10404)**

GAO, J., J. LI, G. JIAN, ET AL. "Stability of Alcohol and Tobacco Consumption in a Real Rising Main Sewer." *Water Research*, 138: 19–26, 2018 **(40530)**

GARFINKEL, S.N., Z. DIENES, AND T. DUKA. "The Effect of Alcohol and Repetition at Encoding on Implicit and Explicit False Memories." *Psychopharmacology*, 188: 498–508, 2006 **(60311)**

GARG, U., C. FRAZEE, L. JOHNSON, AND J.W. TURNER. "A Fatal Case Involving Extremely High Levels of Ethylene Glycol Without Elevation of Its Metabolites or Crystalluria." *American Journal of Forensic Medicine and Pathology,* 30: 273–275, 2009 **(80510)**

GARRIOTT, J.C. "Skeletal Muscle as an Alternative Specimen for Alcohol and Drug Analysis." *Journal of Forensic Science,* 36: 60–69, 1991 **(70804)**

GARRISON, H., A. SCHOLEY, F. OGDEN, AND S. BENSON. "The Effects of Alcohol Intoxication on Cognitive Functions Critical for Driving: A Systematic Review." *Accident Analysis and Prevention*, 154: 11pp, 2021 **(50119)**

GATT, J.A. AND P. MATTHEWMAN. "Autobrewing: Fact or Fantasy?" *Science and Justice*, 40: 211–215, 2000 **(20506)**

GAUDET, M.P. AND G.L. FRASER. "Isopropanol Ingestion: Case Report with Pharmacokinetic Analysis." *American Journal of Emergency Medicine*, 7: 297–299, 1989 **(80404)**

GAUDIO, R.M., S. BARBIERI, P. FELTRACCO, ET AL. "Impact of Alcohol Consumption on Winter Sports-Related Injuries." *Medicine, Science and the Law*, 50: 122–125, 2010 **(61919)**

GAWRON, V.J. AND T.A. RANNEY. "The Effects of Alcohol Dosing on Driving Performance on a Closed Course and in a Driving Simulator." *Ergonomics*, 31: 1219–1244, 1988 **(50306)**

———. "The Effects of Spot Treatments on Performance in a Driving Simulator under Sober and Alcohol-Dosed Conditions." *Accident Analysis and Prevention* 22: 263–279, 1990 **(50208)**

GAWRYLOWICZ, J., A.M. RIDLEY, I.P. ALBERY, ET AL. "Alcohol-Induced Retrograde Facilitation Renders Witnesses of Crime Less Suggestible to Misinformation." *Psychopharmacology*, 9pp, 2017 **(60317)**

GEAR, A.J.L., W.D. NGUYEN, H.N. HIMEL, AND R.F. EDLICH. "Flaming Dr. Pepper—Another Cause of Recreational Burn Injury [Letter]." *American Journal of Emergency Medicine*, 15: 108–111, 1997 **(60608)**

GENGO, F.M., C. GABOS, C. STRALEY, AND C. MANNING. "The Pharmacodynamics of Ethanol: Effects on Performance and Judgment." *Journal of Clinical Pharmacology*, 30: 748–754, 1990 **(50108)**

GERBERICH, S.G., B.K. GERBERICH, D. FIFE, ET AL. "Analyses of the Relationship Between Blood Alcohol and Nasal Breath Alcohol Concentrations: Implications for Assessment of Trauma Cases." *Journal of Trauma*, 29: 338–343, 1989 **(30312)**

GERCHOW, J. "Statistical and Experimental Studies on the Differing Assessment in Subjects During Rising and Falling BAC [German]." *Heifte Unfallheik*, 66: 90–95, 1961 **(50613)**

GERSHAM, H. AND J. STEEPER. "Rate of Clearance of Ethanol from the Blood of Intoxicated Patients in the Emergency Department." *Journal of Emergency Medicine,* 9: 307–311, 1991 **(10805)**

GHADIPASHA, M. AND M. AKHGARI. "Case Report: An Unusually High Blood Alcohol Level in a Burnt Child Homicide Victim." *International Journal of Medical Toxicology and Forensic Medicine,* 9: 45–49, 2019 **(70311)**

GHOSH, A., T. MAHINTAMANI, Y.P.S. BLAHARA, ET AL. "Disulfiram Ethanol Reaction with Alcohol-Based Hand Sanitizer: An Exploratory Study." *Alcohol and Alcoholism*, 1–8, 2020 **(80111)**

GILL, R., S.E. HATCHETT, C.G. BROSTER, ET AL. "The Response of Evidential Breath Alcohol Testing Instruments with Subjects Exposed to Organic Solvents and Gases. I. Toluene, 1,1,1-Trichloroethane and Butane." *Medicine, Science, and the Law*, 31: 187–200, 1991 **(30610)**

GILL, R., H.E. WARNER, C.G. BROSTER, ET AL. "The Response of Evidential Breath Alcohol Testing Instruments with Subjects Exposed to Organic Solvents and Gases. II. White Spirit and Nonane." *Medicine, Science, and the Law,* 31: 201–213, 1991 **(30611)**

GJERDE, H., BRETTEVILLE-JENSEN, A.L., AND H. FURUHAUGEN. "Poor Correlation Between Alcohol Concentration In Oral Fluid and Breath in Subjects Consuming Beverages Immediately Before Testing." *Biochemia Medica (Zagreb)*, 32: 5pp, 2022 **(40211)**

GJERDE, H., P.T. NORMANN, AND A.S. CHRISTOPHERSEN. "The Prevalence of Alcohol and Drugs in Sampled Oral Fluid Is Related to Sample Volume." *Journal of Analytical Toxicology*, 34: 416–418, 2010 **(40209)**

GLEITER, C.H., K-H. ANTONIN, W. SCHOENLABER, AND P. BIECK. "Interaction of Alcohol and Transdermally Administered Scopolamine." *Journal of Clinical Pharmacology*, 28: 1123–1127, 1988 **(10711)**

GLOVER, E.D., S. LANE, AND M.Q. WANG. "Relationship of Alcohol Consumption and Recreational Boating in Beaufort County, North Carolina." *Journal of Drug Education*, 25: 149–157, 1995 **(60407)**

GLOVER, P.L. "The Effect of Heat on Blood Samples Containing Alcohol." *Proceedings of the 16th International Conference on Alcohol, Drugs and Traffic Safety,* T2002 CD-ROM, D. Mayhew, and C. Dussault (eds), 5pp, 2002 **(20305)**

GODING, G.S. AND R.A. DOBIE. "Gaze Nystagmus and Blood Alcohol." *Laryngoscopic* 96: 713–717, 1986 **(50608)**

GOLDBERGER, B.A. AND Y.H. CAPLAN. "Infrared Quantitative Evidential Breath Alcohol Analysers: in Vitro Accuracy and Precision Studies." *Journal of Forensic Science*, 31: 16–19, 1986 **(30108)**

GOLDBERGER, B.A., Y.H. CAPLAN, AND J.R. ZETTL. "A Long-Term Field Experience with Breath Ethanol Collection Employing Silica Gel." *Journal of Analytical Toxicology*, 10: 194–197, 1986 **(30703)**

GOLDING, J.M., AND G.S. BRADSHAW. "Alcohol in the Courtroom: The Intoxication Defense." *American Journal of Forensic Psychiatry*, 26: 37–56, 2005 **(60312)**

GOLDWAG, J.L., E.D. PORTER, A.R. WILCOX, Z ET AL. "Geriatric Snowmobile Trauma: Longer Courses After Similar Injuries." *Journal of Surgical Research*, 262: 85–92, 2021 **(61809)**

GOMM. P.J. AND C.G. BROSTER. "Study into the Ability of Healthy People of Small Stature to Satisfy the Sampling Requirements of Breath Alcohol Testing Instruments." *Medicine, Science, and the Law*, 33: 311–314, 1993 **(30301)**

GOMM, P.J., M.D. OSSELTON, Z.C.G. BROSTER, ET AL. "The Effect of Salbutamol on Breath Alcohol Testing in Asthmatics." *Medicine Science and the Law*, 31: 226–228, 1991 **(30309)**

GOODMAN, R.A., J.A. MERCY, F. LOYA, ET AL. "Alcohol Use and Interpersonal Violence: Alcohol Detected in Homicide Victims." *American Journal of Public Health*, 76: 144–149, 1986 **(60907)**

GOODWIN, D.W. "Alcohol Amnesia [Editorial]." *Addiction*, 90: 315–317, 1995 **(60302)**

GOODWIN, D.W., J.B. CRANE, AND S.B. GUZE. "Alcoholic Blackouts: A Review and Clinical Study of 100 Alcoholics." *American Journal of Psychiatry*, 126: 191–198, 1969 **(60301)**

GRAHAM, J.W. "Fatal Motorcycle Accidents." *Journal of Forensic Science*, 14: 79–86, 1969 **(61309)**

GRAHAM, T. "Alcohol Ingestion and Man's Ability to Adapt to Exercise in a Cold Environment." *Canadian Journal of Applied Sport Science*, 6: 27–31, 1981 **(61001)**

GREEN, R.S. AND R. MAIER. "The Urban Cowboy Syndrome Revisited: Case Report." *Southern Medical Journal* 96: 1262–1264, 2003 **(61213)**

GREENE, N., M.B. ESSER, R. VESSELINOV, ET AL. "Variability in Antemortem and Postmortem Blood Alcohol Concentration Levels Among Fatally Injured Adults." *American Journal of Drug and Alcohol Abuse*, 8pp, 2020 **(70224)**

GREENE, S.L., C.M. SHIEW, P. STREETE, ET AL. "What's Being Used to Spike Your Drink? Alleged Spiked Drink Cases in Inner City London." *Postgraduate Medical Journal*, 83: 754–758, 2007 **(61715)**

GRELLNER, W. AND R. IFFLAND. "Assessment of Postmortem Blood Alcohol Concentrations by Ethanol Levels Measured in Fluids from Putrefactive Blisters." *Forensic Science International*, 90: 57–63, 1997 **(70806)**

GRILLON C., R. SINHA, AND S.S. O'MALLEY. "Effects of Ethanol on the Processing of Low Probability Stimuli: An ERP Study." *Psychopharmacology,* 119: 455–465, 1995 **(50112)**

GRUHN, K.M. AND O. PRIBILLA. "Blood Alcohol Concentrations After Consumption of Brandy Chocolates [German]." *Blutalkohol,* 21: 363–365, 1984 **(10125)**

GRUSZECKI, A.C., A. ROBINSON, S. KLODA, AND R.M. BRISSIE. "High Urine Ethanol and Negative Blood and Vitreous Ethanol in a Diabetic Woman. A Case Report, Retrospective Case Survey, and Review of the Literature." *American Journal of Forensic Medicine and Pathology*, 26: 96–98, 2005 **(70702)**

GUG, S.-G., J-H. YUN, D. HARSHAPRIYA, AND J-J. HAN. "A Prefatory Study on the Effects of Alcohol on Ship Maneuvering, Navigational and Decision-Making Abilities of Navigators." *The Journal of Navigation*, 1–13, 2022 **(61112)**

GULLBERG, R.G. "A Concern Associated with Single Breath Alcohol Analysis for Forensic Purposes [Letter]." *Journal of Forensic Science*, 38: 1263–1265, 1993 **(30117)**

GULLBERG, R.G. "Breath Alcohol Analysis in One Subject With Gastroesophageal Reflux Disease." *Journal of Forensic Science*, 46: 1498–1503, 2001 **(30515)**

———. "Considering Measurement Variability When Performing Retrograde Extrapolation of Breath Alcohol Results [Letter]." *Journal of Analytical Toxicology*, 18: 126–127, 1994 **(10506)**

———. "The Elimination Rate of Mouth Alcohol: Mathematical Modeling and Implications in Breath Alcohol Analysis." *Journal of Forensic Sciences*, 37: 1363–1372, 1992 **(30504)**

———. "Employing Simulated Data to Illustrate an Important Cause of the Steepling Effect in Breath Alcohol Analysis." *Medicine, Science, and the Law,* 34: 321–323, 1994 **(10507)**

———. "Evaluation the Variability of Duplicate Breath Alcohol Analyses as a Function of Subject Age." *Medicine, Science and the Law*, 33: 110–114, 1993 **(30121)**

———. "Predicting the Second Breath Alcohol Measurement from the First: An Application of Regression Analysis [Letter]." *Journal of Forensic Sciences* 36: 10–14, 1991 **(30118)**

———. "The Relationship Between Duplicate Reproducibility and Concentration in Breath Alcohol Testing Programs [Letter]." *Journal of Analytical Toxicology,*16: 272–273, 1992 **(30123)**

———. "Repeatability of Replicate Breath Alcohol Measurements Collected in Short Time Intervals." *Science and Justice*, 35: 5–9, 1995 **(30119)**

———. "Statistical Evaluation and Reporting of Blood Alcohol/Breath Ratio Distribution Data." *Journal of Analytical Toxicology*, 15: 343–344, 1991 **(30412)**

———. "Statistical Evaluation of Truncated Breath-Alcohol Test Measurements." *Journal of Forensic Sciences*. 33: 507–510, 1988 **(30124)**

GULLBERG, R.G. AND A.W. JONES. "Guidelines for Estimating the Amount of Alcohol Consumed from a Single Measurement of Blood Alcohol Concentration: Re-Evaluation of Widmark's Equation." *Forensic Science International*, 69: 119–130, 1994 **(10603)**

GULLBERG, R.G. AND B.K. LOGAN. "Reproducibility of Within Subject Breath Alcohol Analysis." *Medicine Science and the Law*, 38: 157–162, 1998 **(30120)**

GULLBERG, R.G. AND A.J. MCELROY. "Comparing Roadside with Subsequent Breath Alcohol Analyses and Their Relevance to the Issue of Retrograde Extrapolation." *Forensic Science International*, 57: 193–201, 1992 **(10408)**

GUMBEL, D., F. SCHNEIDLER, M. FRANK, ET AL. "Urinary Bladder Volume Measured in Whole-Body CT Scans Is a Useful Marker for Alcohol Intoxication." *Alcohol*, 65: 45–50, 2017 **(40112)**

GUPTA, K.K., V.K. GUPTA, AND T. SHIRASAKA. "An Update on Fetal Alcohol Syndrome—Pathogenesis, Risks and Treatment." *Alcoholism: Clinical and Experimental Research*, 40: 1594–1602, 2016 **(90403)**

GUSTAFSON, R. "Male Alcohol-Related Aggression as a Function of Type of Drink." *Aggressive Behavior*, 25: 401–408, 1999 **(60103)**

H

HADLEY, J.A. AND G.C. SMITH. "Evidence for an Early Onset of Endogenous Alcohol Production in Bodies Recovered from the Water. Implications for Studying Alcohol and Drowning." *Accident Analysis and Prevention*, 35: 763–769, 2003 **(70204)**

HAECKEL, R. AND U. PEIFFER. "Comparison of Ethanol Concentration in Saliva and Blood from Police Controlled Persons." *Blutalkohol*, 29: 342–349, 1992 **(40203)**

HAFSTROM, A., M. PATEL, F. MODIG, ET AL. "Acute Alcohol Intoxication Impairs Segmental Body Alignment in Upright Standing." *Journal of Vestibular Research*, 24: 297–304, 2014 **(60516)**

HAGEMANN, C.T., A. HELLAND, O. SPIGSET, ET AL. "Ethanol and Drug Findings in Women Consulting a Sexual Assault Center—Associations with Clinical Characteristics and Suspicions of Drug-Facilitated Sexual Assault." *Journal of Forensic and Legal Medicine*, 20: 777–784, 2013 **(61714)**

HAHN, R.G., A. NORBERG, J. GABRIELSSON, ET AL. "Eating a Meal Increases the Clearance of Ethanol Given by Intravenous Infusion." *Alcohol and Alcoholism*, 29: 673–677, 1994 **(10304)**

HAHN, R.G., A. NORBERG, AND A.W. JONES. "Overshoot of Ethanol in the Blood After Drinking on an Empty Stomach." *Alcohol and Alcoholism*, 32: 501–505, 1997 **(10203)**

HAK, E.A., B.J. GERLITZ, P.M. DEMONT, AND W.D. BOWTHORPE. "Determination of Serum Alcohol: Blood Alcohol Ratios." *Canadian Society of Forensic Science Journal*, 28: 123–126, 1995 **(20204)**

HALSEY, L.G., J.W. HUBER, R.D.J. BUFTON, AND A.C. LITTLE. "An Explanation for Enhanced Perceptions of Attractiveness After Alcohol Consumption." *Alcohol*, 44: 307–313, 2010 **(61710)**

HALSTEAD, C.H., E.A. ROBLES, AND E. MEZEY. "Distribution of Ethanol in the Human Gastrointestinal Tract." *American Journal of Clinical Nutrition*, 26: 831–834, 1973 **(10104)**

HAMMOND, K.B., B.H. RUMACK, AND D.O. RODGERSON, "Blood Ethanol: A Report of Unusually High Levels in a Living Patient." *Journal of the American Medical Association*, 226: 63–64, 1973 **(50617)**

HANDING, E.P., R. ANDEL P. KADLECOVA, ET AL. "Midlife Alcohol Consumption and Risk of Dementia Over 43 Years of Follow-Up: A Population-Based Study from the Swedish Twin Registry." *Journals of Gerontology: Medical Sciences*, 70: 1248–1254, 2015 **(90312)**

HANNUSELA, M.L. AND S. ELAHHAM. "Benefits and Risks of Sauna Bathing." *American Journal of Medicine*, 110: 118–126, 2001 **(61603)**

HANSEN, C.S., L.H. FAERCH, AND P.L. KRISTENSEN. "Testing the Validity of the Danish Urban Myth that Alcohol Can Be Absorbed Through Feet: Open Labelled Self Experimental Study." *British Medical Journal*, 341: c6812, 3pp, 2010 **(10124)**

HANTSON, P., R. VANBINST, AND P. MAHIEU. "Determination of Ethylene Glycol Tissue Content after Fatal Oral Poisoning and Pathologic Findings." *American Journal of Forensic Medicine and Pathology*, 23: 159–161, 2002 **(80502)**

HANZLICK, R., K. POWELL, AND K. TOOMEY. "Hypothermia Related Deaths —Georgia, January 1996–December 1997 and United States, 1979–1995." *Journal of the American Medical Association*, 281: 124–125, 1999 **(61005)**

HARD, A.M., N.G. CROFTS, L.M. LEE, ET AL. "Isolated Bladder Rupture After Minor Trauma in a Patient with Alcohol Intoxication." *Journal of Emergency Medicine*, 12: 409–411, 1994 **(40109)**

HARDING, G.J. AND N.A. JARAD. "Alcohol Breath Testing: How Do Lung Diseases Interfere?" *Airways Journal*, 2: 204–207, 2004 **(30308)**

HARDING, P.M., R.H. LAESSIG, AND P.H. FIELD. "Field Performance of the Intoxilyzer 5000: A Comparison of Blood- and Breath-Alcohol Results in Wisconsin Drivers." *Journal of Forensic Sciences*, 35: 1022–1028, 1990 **(30406)**

HARDING, P.M., M.C. MCMURRAY, R.H. LAESSIG, ET AL. "The Effect of Dentures and Denture Adhesives on Mouth Alcohol Retention." *Journal of Forensic Sciences*, 37: 999–1007, 1992 **(30516)**

HARRISON, E.L.R. AND M.T. FILLMORE. "Alcohol and Distraction Interact to Impair Driving Performance." *Drug Alcohol Dependence*, 117: 31–37, 2011 **(50214)**

HARTSHORNE, N.J., R.C. HARRUFF, AND E.C. ALVORD. "Fatal Head Injuries in Ground-Level Falls." *American Journal of Forensic Medicine and Pathology*, 18: 258–264, 1997 **(60503)**

HAUM, A., W. PERBIX, H.J. HACK, ET AL. "Alcohol and Drug Abuse in Burn Injuries." *Burns*, 21: 194–199, 1995 **(60603)**

HAWKINS, E.R. AND J.H. BRICE. "Fire Jumpers: Description of Burns and Traumatic Injuries from a Spontaneous Mass Gathering and Celebratory Riot." *Journal of Emergency Medicine*, 38: 182–187, 2010 **(60612)**

HAYWARD, L., S.R. ZUBRICK, AND S. SILBURN. "Blood Alcohol Levels in Suicide Cases." *Journal of Epidemiology and Community Health*, 46: 256–260, 1992 **(62015)**

HEATLEY, M.K. AND J. CRANE. "The Blood Alcohol Concentration at Post-mortem in 175 Fatal Cases of Alcohol Intoxication." *Medicine Science and the Law,* 30: 101–105, 1990 **(70404)**

HEDLUND, J., J. AHLNER, M. KRISTIANSSON, AND J. STURUP. "Population-Based Study on Toxicological Findings in Swedish Homicide Victims and Offenders from 2007 to 2009." *Forensic Science International*, 244: 25–29, 2014 **(60918)**

HEDLUND, J., J. FORSMAN, J. STURUP, AND T. MASTERMAN. "Pre-Offense Alcohol Intake in Homicide Offenders and Victims: A Forensic Toxicological Case Control Study." *Journal of Forensic and Legal Medicine*, 56: 55–58, 2018 **(60916)**

HEGEMAN, J., V. WEERDESTEYN, B.J.F. VAN DEN BERNT, ET AL. "Even Low Alcohol Concentrations Affect Obstacle Avoidance Reactions in Healthy Senior Individuals." *BMC Research Notes*, 3: 243, 2010 **(60514)**

HEGSTAD, S., A. HELLAND, C. HAGEMANN, ET AL. "EtG/EtS in Urine from Sexual Assault Victims Determined by UPLC-MS-MS." *Journal of Analytical Toxicology*, 37: 227–232, 2013 **(61717)**

HEISE, H.A. "How Extraneous Alcohol Affects the Blood Test for Alcohol Pitfalls to Be Avoided When Withdrawing Blood for Medicolegal Purposes." *American Journal of Clinical Pathology*, 32: 169–170, 1959 **(20401)**

HELANDER, A., I. OLSSON, AND H. DAHL. "Postcollection Synthesis of Ethyl Glucuronide by Bacteria in Urine May Cause False Identification of Alcohol Consumption." *Clinical Chemistry*, 53: 1855–1857, 2007 **(40520)**

HELM, J.F. "Esophageal Acid Clearance." *Journal of Clinical Gastroenterology,* 8 (Suppl 1): 5–11, 1986 **(30518)**

HELANDER, A., O. BECK, AND A.W. JONES. "Distinguishing Ingested Ethanol from Microbial Formation by Analysis of Urinary 5-Hydroxytryptophol and 5-Hydroxyindoleacetic Acid." *Journal of Forensic Sciences*, 40: 95–98, 1995 **(70704)**

HENINGER, M. "Subdural Hematoma Occurrence. Comparison Between Ethanol and Cocaine Use at Death." *American Journal of Forensic Medicine and Pathology*, 34: 237–241, 2013 **(70506)**

HERNETKOSKI, K. AND E. KESKINEN. "Self-Destruction in Finnish Motor Traffic Accidents in 1974–1992." Accident Analysis and Prevention, 30: 697–704, 1998 **(62020)**

HETHERINGTON, H.P., F. TELANG, J.W. PAN, ET AL. "Spectroscopic Imaging of the Uptake Kinetics of Human Brain Ethanol." *Magnetic Resonance Medicine*, 2: 1019–1026, 1999 **(10207)**

HEZAVEH, A.M. AND C.R. CHERRY. "Walking Under the Influence of the Alcohol: A Case Study of Pedestrian Crashes in Tennessee." *Accident Analysis and Prevention*, 121: 64–70, 2018 **(61413)**

HICKOX, K.L., N. WILLIAMS, L.F. BECK, ET AL. "Pedestrian Traffic Death Among Residents, Visitors, and Homeless Persons—Clark County, Nevada, 2008–2011." *Morbidity and Mortality Weekly Report*, 63(28): 597–602, 2014 **(61414)**

HIEDA, Y., H. TAKESHITA, J. FUJIHARA, AND K. TAKAYAMA. "A Fatal Case of Pure Ethanol Ingestion." *Forensic Science International*, 149: 243–247, 2005 **(70406)**

HIGASHIKAWA, Y. AND S. SUZUKI. "Effect of Exercise After Drinking on Breath Alcohol Concentrations." *Japanese Journal of Forensic Toxicology*, 22: 205–208, 2004 **(30417)**

HILMI, M., P.S. LAI, L.S. KHOO, ET AL. "Relationship of Blood and Urine Alcohol Levels in Postmortem Blood Samples and Prevalence of Alcohol Level Above Legal Limit in Hospital Kuala Lumpur." *SM Journal of Forensic Research and Criminology*, 1: 1012, 4pp, 2017 **(70707)**

HINGSON, R., T. HEEREN, AND M. WINTER. "Lower Legal Blood Alcohol Limits for Young Drivers." *Public Health Reports*, 109: 738–744, 1994 **(50706)**

HIRVONEN, J. "Necropsy Findings in Fatal Hypothermia Cases." *Forensic Science*, 8: 155–164, 1976 **(61002)**

HO, E., A. COLLANTES, B.M. KAPUR, M. MORETTI, AND G. KOREN. "Alcohol and Breast Feeding: Calculation of Time to Zero Level in Milk." *Biology of Neonate*, 80: 219–222, 2001 **(40403)**

HOBIN, E., S. SHOKAR, K. VALLANCEW, ET AL. "Communicating Risks to Drinkers: Testing Alcohol Labels with a Cancer Warning and National Drinking Guidelines in Canada." *Canadian Journal of Public Health*, 111: 716–725, 2020 **(90506)**

HODGSON, B.T. AND N.K. SHAJANI. "Distribution of Ethanol: Plasma to Whole Blood Ratios." *Canadian Society Forensic Science Journal*, 18: 73–77, 1985 **(20201)**

HODGSON, B.T. AND M.D. TAYLOR. "Evaluation of the Breathalyzer 7410-CDN Evidential Breath Alcohol Analyzer." *Canadian Society of Forensic Science Journal*, 31: 263–267, 1998 **(30104)**

———. "Evaluation of the Drager Alcotest 7110 Mk III Dual C Evidential Breath Alcohol Analyser." *Canadian Society of Forensic Science Journal*, 34: 95–101, 2001 **(30112)**

HOISETH, G., J.P. BERNARD, N. STEPHANSON, ET AL. "Comparison Between the Urinary Alcohol Markers EtG, EtS, and GTOL/5-HIAA in a Controlled Drinking Experiment." *Alcohol and Alcoholism*, 43: 187–191, 2008 **(40511)**

HOISETH, G., R. KARINEN, A.S. CHRISTOPHERSON, ET AL. "A Study of Ethyl Glucuronide in Post Mortem Blood as a Marker of Ante Mortem Ingestion of Alcohol." *Forensic Science International*, 165: 41–45, 2007 **(70901)**

HOISETH, G., R. KARINEN, L. JOHNSEN, ET AL. "Disappearance of Ethyl Glucuronide During Heavy Putrefaction." *Forensic Science International*, 176: 147–151, 2008 **(70903)**

HOISETH, G., L. MORINI, A. POLETTINI, ET AL. "Serum/Whole Blood Concentration Ratio for Ethylglucuronide and Ethyl Sulfate." *Journal of Analytical Toxicology*, 33: 208–211, 2009 **(40512)**

HOISETH, G., L. MORINI, A. POLETTINI, ET AL. "Ethyl Glucuronide in Hair Compared with Traditional Alcohol Biomarkers—A Pilot Study of Heavy Drinkers Referred to an Alcohol Detoxification Unit." *Alcoholism Clinical and Experimental Research*, 33: 812–816, 2009 **(40515)**

HOISETH, G., G.H. NILSSON, R. LUNDBERG, ET AL. "Evaluating the Hip-Flask Defence Using Analytical Data from Ethanol and Ethyl Glucuronide: A Comparison of Two Models." *Forensic Science International*, 316: 8pp, 2020 **(10412)**

HOMANN, N., H. JOUSIMIES-SOMER, ET AL. "High Acetaldehyde Levels in Saliva After Ethanol Consumption Methodological Aspects and Pathogenetic Implications." *Carcinogenesis*, 18: 1739–1743, 1997 **(80108)**

HON, K.L., A.K.C. LEUNG, E. CHEUNG, ET AL. "An Overview of Exposure to Ethanol-Containing Substances and Ethanol Intoxication in Children Based on Three Illustrated Cases." *Drugs in Context*, 7: 5pp, 2018 **(40407)**

HONEYBOURNE, D., A.J. MOORE, A.K. BUTTERFIELD, AND L. AZZAN. "A Study to Investigate the Ability of Subjects with Chronic Lung Diseases to Provide Evidential Breath Samples Using the Lion Intoxilyzer 6000 UK Breath Alcohol Testing Device." *Respiratory Medicine*, 94: 684–688, 2000 **(30306)**

HONKANEN, R., L. ERTAMA, P. KUOSMANEN, ET AL. "The Role of Alcohol in Accidental Falls." *Journal of Studies on Alcohol*, 44: 231–245, 1983 **(60502)**

HOON, J.R. "Hair of the Dog." *Journal of the American Medical Association*, 229: 184–185, 1974 **(60806)**

HORAUF, J.-A., C. NAU, N. MUHLENFELD, ET AL. "Injury Patterns After Falling Down Stairs—High Ratio of Traumatic Brain Injury Under Alcohol Influence." *Journal of Clinical Medicine*, 11: 697, 10 pp, 2022 **(60520)**

HORNE, J.A., L.A. REYNER, AND P.R. BARRETT. "Driving Impairment Due to Sleepiness Is Exacerbated by Low Alcohol Intake." *Occupational Environmental Medicine*, 60: 689–692, 2003 **(50104)**

HOSTIUC, S., D. RADU, L. SERETEAN, ET AL. "Driving Under the Influence of Alcohol During the COVID-19 Pandemic." *Forensic Science International*, 329: 6pp, 2021 **(50517)**

HOURNARD, J.A., M.E. LAGENFELD, R. WILEY, AND J. SIEFERT. "Effects of Acute Ingestion of Small Amounts of Alcohol Upon 5-Mile Run Times." *Journal of Sports Medicine*, 27: 253–257, 1987 **(61902)**

HOWLAND, J., D.J. ROHSENOW, D, ALLENSWORTH-DAVIES, ET AL. "The Incidence and Severity of Hangover the Morning After Moderate Alcohol Intoxication." *Addiction*, 103: 758–765, 2008 **(60801)**

HOWLAND, J., D.J. ROHSENOW, B. GOMEZ, ET AL. "Effects of Low-Dose Alcohol Exposure on Simulated Merchant Ship Piloting by Maritime Cadets." *Accident Analysis and Prevention*, 33: 257–265, 2001 **(61102)**

HULTEN, B.A., A. HEATH, T. MELLSTRAND, AND T. HEDNER. "Does Alcohol Absorb to Activated Charcoal?" *Human Toxicology*, 5: 211–212, 1985 **(10803)**

HURST, T.S. "Ability of Subjects with Impaired Respiratory Function to Provide a Satisfactory Breath Sample for the Alcotest 7410 Breath Alcohol Device." *Canadian Society of Forensic Science Journal*, 31: 269–274, 1998 **(30303)**

HWANG, R-J., J. BELTRAN, C. ROGERS, J. BARLOW, AND G. RAZATOS. "Measurement of Uncertainty for Blood Alcohol Concentration by Headspace Gas Chromatography." *Canadian Society of Forensic Science Journal*, 50: 114–124, 2017 **(20119)**

I

INGEMANN-HANSEN, O., O. BRINK, S. SABROE, V. SORENSEN, AND A.V. CHARLES. "Legal Aspects of Sexual Violence—Does Forensic Evidence Make a Difference?" *Forensic Science International*, 180: 98–104, 2008 **(61722)**

IGNACIO-GARCIA, J.M., J.M. IGNACIO-GARCIA, J. ALMENARA-BARRIOS, ET AL. "A Comparison of Standard Inhalers for Asthma with and without Alcohol as a Propellant on the Measurement of Alcohol in Breath." *Journal of Aerosol Medicine*, 18: 193–197, 2005 **(30509)**

IMOBERSTEG, A.D., A. KING, M. CARDEMA, AND E. MULRINE. "The Effects of Occupational Exposure to Paint Solvents on the Intoxilyzer 5000: A Field Study [Letter]." *Journal of Analytical Toxicology*, 17: 254–255, 1993 **(30612)**

INNS, P., P.J. MORRISON, AND K. PAJOUMOND. "Evaluation of Fuel Cell Alcometer for Forensic and Pharmacokinetic Purposes." *British Journal of Clinical Pharmacology*, 7: 439P–440P, 1979 **(30105)**

IOAN, B.G., V. JITARU, R. DAMIAN, AND S.I. DAMIAN. "Study on the Relationship Between the Concentration of Ethanol in the Blood, Urine and Vitreous Humor." *Romanian Journal of Legal Medicine*, 23: 211–216, 2015 **(70608)**

IRWIN C., A. GOODWIN, M. LEVERITT, A.K. DAVEY, AND B. DESBROW. "Alcohol Pharmacokinetics and Risk-Taking Behavior Following Exercise-Induced Dehydration." *Pharmacology, Biochemistry and Behavior*, 101: 609–616, 2012 **(10209)**

IRWIN, J. AND S.D. COHLE. "Sudden Death Due to Diabetic Ketoacidosis." *American Journal Forensic Medicine and Pathology*, 9: 119–121, 1988 **(80205)**

IRWIN, S.T., C.C. PATTERSON, AND W.H. RUTHERFORD. "Association Between Alcohol Consumption and Adult Pedestrians Who Sustain Injuries in Road Traffic Accidents." *British Medical Journal*, 286: 522, 1983 **(61402)**

ISKIERKA, M., M. ZAWADZKI, P. SZPOR, AND T. JUREK. "Comparison of Post-Mortem Ethanol Level in Blood and Bone Marrow." *Journal of Forensic and Legal Medicine*, 61: 65–68, 2019 **(70816)**

ISOKOSKI, M., A. ALHA, AND K. LAIHO. "Bone Marrow Alcohol Content in Cadavers." *Journal of Forensic Medicine*, 15: 9–11, 1968 **(70807)**

IWASAKI, Y., M. YASHIKI, A. NAMERA, ET AL. "On the Influence of Postmortem Alcohol Diffusion from the Stomach Contents to the Heart Blood." *Forensic Science International*, 94: 111–118, 1998 **(70302)**

J

JACKSON, P.R., G.T. TUCKER, AND H.F. WOODS. "Backtracking Booze with Bayes—The Retrospective Interpretation of Blood Alcohol Data." *British Journal of Clinical Pharmacology*, 31: 55–63, 1991 **(10504)**

JACOBSEN, D., C.S. SEBASTIAN, D.F. DIES, ET AL. "Kinetic Interactions Between 4-Methylpyrazole and Ethanol in Healthy Humans." *Alcoholism: Clinical and Experimental Research*, 20: 804–809, 1996 **(10706)**

JACOBSON, M.D. "Alcohol-Related Motor Vehicle Encounter with a Cow." *The Federal Air Surgeon's Medical Bulletin*, 53: 8–9, 2015 **(60711)**

JAFFE, D.H., M. SIMAN-TOV, A. GOPHER, AND K. PERLEG. "Variability in the Blood/Breath Alcohol Ratio and Implications for Evidentiary Purposes." *Journal of Forensic Sciences*, 58: 1233–1237, 2013 **(30422)**

JANNSSON-NETTELBLADT, E., S. MEURLING, B. PETRINI, AND J. SJOLIN. "Endogenous Ethanol Fermentation in a Child with a Short Bowel Syndrome." *Acta Paediartica*, 95: 502–504, 2006 **(20508)**

JENKINS, A.J., B.S. LEVINE, AND F. SMIALEK. "Distribution of Ethanol in Postmortem Liver." *Journal of Forensic Science*, 40: 611–613, 1995 **(70809)**

JENKINS, G. AND R.A. SCHULLER. "The Impact of Negative Forensic Evidence on Mock Jurors' Perceptions of a Trial of Drug-Facilitated Sexual Assault." *Law and Human Behavior,* 31: 369–380, 2007 **(61716)**

JESSE, S., G. BRATHEN, M. FERRARA, ET AL. "Alcohol Withdrawal Syndrome: Mechanisms, Manifestations and Management." *Acta Neurologica Scandinavica,* 135: 4–16, 2017 **(90206)**

JOHNSON, M.B. AND R.B. VOAS. "Potential Risks of Providing Drinking Drivers with BAC Information." *Traffic Injury and Prevention*, 5: 42–49, 2004 **(40207)**

JOHNSON, R. D., R.J. LEWIS, M.K. ANGIER, AND N.T. VU. "The Formation of Ethanol in Postmortem Tissues." *FAA Civil Aerospace Medical Institute Report*, Oklahoma City, 14pp, 2004 **(70225)**

JOHNSTON, J.J.E. AND S.J. MCGOVERN. "Alcohol Related Falls: An Interesting Pattern of Injuries." *Emergency Medicine Journal*, 21: 185–188, 2004 **(60504)**

JONES, A.E. AND R.L. SUMMERS. "Detection of Isopropyl Alcohol in a Patient with Diabetic Ketoacidosis." *Journal of Emergency Medicine*, 19: 165–168, 2000 **(80203)**

JONES, A.W. "Are a Blood Alcohol Concentration of 256 mg/dL and Minimal Signs of Impairment Reliable Indications of Alcohol Dependence?" *Medicine Science and the Law,* 34: 265–270, 1994 **(10609)**

———. "Are Changes in Blood Ethanol Concentration During Storage Analytically Significant? Importance of Method Imprecision." *Clinical Chemistry Laboratory Medicine*, 45: 1299-1304, 2007 **(20303)**

———. "Biomarkers of Recent Drinking, Retrograde Extrapolation of Blood-Alcohol Concentration and Plasma-to-Blood Distribution Ratio in a Case of Driving Under the Influence of Alcohol." *Journal of Forensic and Legal Medicine,* 18: 213–216, 2011 **(10510)**

———. "Driving Under the Influence of Isopropanol [Letter]." *Clinical Toxicology,* 30: 153–155, 1992 **(80406)**

———. "Effects of Temperature and Humidity of Inhaled Air on the Concentration of Ethanol in a Man's Exhaled Breath." *Clinical Science,* 63: 441–445, 1982 **(30415)**

———. "Electrochemical Measurement of Breath-Alcohol Concentration: Precision and Accuracy in Relation to Blood Levels." *Clinica Chimica Acta*, 146: 175–183, 1985 **(30401)**

———. "Elimination Half-Life of Methanol During Hangover." *Pharmacology and Toxicology*, 60: 217–220, 1987 **(60805)**

———. "Enforcement of Drink-Driving Laws by Use of 'Per Se' Legal Alcohol Limits: Blood and/or Breath Concentration as Evidence of Impairment." *Alcohol, Drugs and Driving*, 4: 99–112, 1988 **(30402)**

———. "Ethanol Distribution Ratios between Urine and Capillary Blood in Controlled Experiments and in Apprehended Drinking Drivers." *Journal of Forensic Science*, 37: 21–34, 1992 **(10409)**

———. "Evidence-Based Survey of the Elimination Rates of Ethanol from Blood with Applications in Forensic Casework." *Forensic Science International*, 200: 1–20, 2010 **(10511)**

———. "Evidential Breath Alcohol Analysis and the Venous Blood-to-Breath Ratio [Letter]." *Forensic Science International* 2016 **(30424)**

———. "Excretion of Alcohol in Urine and Diuresis in Healthy Men in Relation to Their Age, the Dose Administered and the Time After Drinking." *Forensic Science International,* 45: 217–224, 1990 **(40102)**

———. "How Breathing Technique Can Influence the Results of Breath Alcohol Analysis." *Medicine Science and the Law*, 22: 275–280, 1982 **(30413)**

———."Inter- and Intra-Individual Variations in the Saliva/Blood Alcohol Ratio During Ethanol Metabolism in Man." *Clinical Chemistry*, 25: 1394–1398, 1979 **(40201)**

———. "Reference Limits for Urine/Blood Ratios of Ethanol in Two Successive Voids from Drinking Drivers." *Journal of Analytical Toxicology*, 26: 333–339, 2002 **(40104)**

———. "Relationship Between Blood and Breath Alcohol Concentration in a Subject Absorbing Alcohol at the Time of Testing [Letter]." *Journal of Analytical Toxicology*, 15: 44–45, 1991 **(30416)**

———. "Role of Rebreathing in Determination of the Blood-Breath Ratio of Expired Ethanol." *Journal of Applied Physiology*, 55: 1237–1241, 1983 **(30414)**

———. "Ultra-Rapid Rate of Ethanol Elimination from Blood in Drunken Drivers with Extremely High Blood Alcohol Concentrations." *International Journal of Legal Medicine,* 122: 129–134, 2008 **(10406)**

JONES, A.W. AND L. ANDERSSON. "Biotransformation of Acetone to Isopropanol Observed in a Motorist Involved in a Sobriety Check." *Journal of Forensic Science,* 40: 686–687, 1995 **(80204)**

———. "Variability of the Blood/Breath Alcohol Ratio in Drinking Drivers." *Journal of Forensic Sciences*, 41: 916–921, 1996 **(30408)**

JONES, A.W., R. ANDERSSON., J. SAKSHAUG, AND J. MORLAND. "Possible Formation of Ethanol in Postmortem Blood Specimens after Antemortem Treatment with Mannitol [Letter]." *Journal of Analytical Toxicology*, 15: 157–158, 1991 **(70209)**

JONES, A. W. AND J.M. COWAN. "Reflections on Variability in the Blood-Breath Ratio of Ethanol and its Importance When Evidential Breath-Alcohol Instruments are Used in Law Enforcement." *Forensic Science Research*, 9pp, 2020 **(30423)**

JONES, A.W., A. EKLUND, AND A. HELANDER. "Misleading Results of Ethanol Analysis in Urine Specimens from Rape Victims Suffering from Diabetes." *Journal of Clinical and Forensic Medicine*, 7: 144–146, 2000 **(40106)**

JONES, A.W. AND M. FRANSSON. "Blood Analysis by Headspace Gas Chromatography: Does a Deficient Sample Volume Distort Ethanol Concentration?" *Medicine Science and the Law*, 43: 241–247, 2003 **(20122)**

JONES, A.W. AND R.G. HAHN. "Pharmacokinetics of Ethanol in Patients with Renal Failure Before and After Hemodialysis." *Forensic Science International*, 90: 175–183, 1997 **(10311)**

JONES, A.W., R.G. HAHN, AND H.P STALBERG. "Distribution of Ethanol and Water Between Plasma and Whole Blood: Inter- and Intra-Individual Variations After Administration of Ethanol by Intravenous Infusion." *Scandinavian Journal of Clinical Laboratory Investigation*, 50: 775–780, 1990 **(20203)**

———. "Pharmacokinetics of Ethanol in Plasma and Whole Blood: Estimation of Total Body Water by the Dilution Principle." *European Journal of Clinical Pharmacology*, 42: 445–448, 1992 **(10202)**

JONES, A.W. AND P. HARDING. "Driving Under the Influence with Blood Alcohol Concentrations over 0.4g%." *Forensic Science International*, 231: 349–353, 2013 **(50512)**

JONES, A.W. AND P. HOLMGREN. "Comparison of Blood-Ethanol Concentration in Deaths Attributed to Acute Alcohol Poisoning and Chronic Alcoholism." *Journal of Forensic Science*, 48: 874–879, 2003 **(70405)**

———. "Uncertainty in Estimating Blood Ethanol Concentrations by Analysis of Vitreous Humor." *Journal of Clinical Pathology*, 54: 699–702, 2001 **(70605)**

———. "Urine/Blood Ratios of Ethanol in Deaths Attributed to Acute Alcohol Poisoning and Chronic Alcoholism." *Forensic Science International*, 135: 206–212, 2003 **(70408)**

JONES, A.W., R.D. JENNINGS, J. ADOLFSON, AND C.M. HESSER. "Combined Effects of Ethanol and Hyperbaric Air on Body Sway and Heart Rate in Man." *Undersea Biomedical Research*, 6: 15–25, 1979 **(60406)**

JONES, A.W. AND K.A. JONSSON. "Alcohol as a Disinfectant Resulted in Zero Per Thousand (Promille) in Blood [Swedish]." *Larkartidningen*, 95: 4052, 1998 **(20405)**

JONES, A.W., L. JORFELDT, H. HJERTBERG, AND K.A. JONSSON. "Physiological Variations in Blood Ethanol Measurements During the Post-Absorptive State." *Journal of the Forensic Science Society*, 30: 273–283, 1990 **(10508)**

JONES, A.W. AND F.C. KUGELBERG. "Relationship Between Blood and Urine Alcohol Concentrations in Apprehended Drivers Who Claimed Consumption of Alcohol After Driving with and Without Supporting Evidence." *Forensic Science International*, 194: 97–102, 2010 **(10410)**

JONES, A.W., L. LINDBERG, AND S-G. OLSSON. "Magnitude and Time-Course of Arterio-Venous Differences in Blood-Alcohol Concentration in Healthy Men." *Clinical Pharmacokinetics*, 43: 1157–1166, 2004 **(10204)**

JONES, A.W. AND H. LOWINGER. "Relationship Between the Concentration of Ethanol and Methanol in Blood Samples from Swedish Drinking Drivers." *Forensic Science International,* 37: 277–285, 1988 **(30607)**

JONES, A.W., J. NEIMAN, AND M. HILLBOM. "Elimination Kinetics of Ethanol and Acetaldehyde in Healthy Men During the Calcium Carbimide-Alcohol Flush Reaction." *Alcohol and Alcoholism, Suppl 1*: 213–217, 1987 **(80103)**

JONES, A.W. AND A. NERI. "Evaluation of Blood-Ethanol Profiles After Consumption of Alcohol Together with a Large Meal." *Canadian Society of Forensic Science Journal*, 24: 165–173, 1991 **(10108)**

JONES, A.W., A. NORBERG, AND R.G. HAHN. "Concentration-Time Profiles of Ethanol in Arterial and Venous Blood and End-Expired Breath During and After Intravenous Infusion." *Journal of Forensic Science*, 42: 1088–1094, 1997 **(10205)**

JONES, A.W. AND J. RAJS. "Appreciable Blood-Ethanol Concentration After Washing Abrased and Lacerated Skin with Surgical Spirit [Letter]." *Journal of Analytical Toxicology*, 21: 587–588, 1997 **(70308)**

JONES, A.W., A. SAGARDUY, E. ERICSSON, AND H.J. ARNQVIST. "Concentrations of Acetone in Venous Blood Samples from Drunk Drivers, Type-1 Diabetic Outpatients, and Healthy Blood Donors." *Journal of Analytical Toxicology*, 17: 182–185, 1993 **(30602)**

JONES, A.W. AND J. SCHUBERTH. "Computer-Aided Headspace Gas Chromatography Applied to Blood-Alcohol Analysis: Importance of Online Process Control." *Journal of Forensic Sciences*, 34: 1116–1127, 1989 **(20102)**

JONES, A.W., S. SKAGERBERG, S. BORG, AND E. ANGGARD. "Time Course of Breath Acetaldehyde Concentrations During Intravenous Infusions of Ethanol in Healthy Men." *Drugs and Alcohol Dependence*, 14: 113–119, 1984 **(80102)**

JONES, A.W. AND B. STERNEBRING. "Kinetics of Ethanol and Methanol in Alcoholics During Detoxification." *Alcohol and Alcoholism*, 27: 641–647, 1992 **(10302)**

JONES, A.W., J.G. WIGMORE, AND C.J. HOUSE. "The Course of the Blood-Alcohol Curve After Consumption of Large Amounts of Alcohol Under Realistic Conditions." *Canadian Society Forensic Science Journal*, 39: 125–140, 2006 **(10605)**

JONES, G.R., P.P. SINGER, AND K. RITTENBACH. "The Relationship of Methanol and Formate Concentrations in Fatalities Where Methanol Is Detected." *Journal of Forensic Science*, 52: 1376–1382, 2007 **(80313)**

JORDAN, F.B., K. SCHMECKPEPER, AND M. STROPE. "Jail Suicides by Hanging. An Epidemiological Review and Recommendations for Prevention." *American Journal of Forensic Medicine and Pathology*, 8: 27–31, 1987 **(62014)**

JORDAN, P.W. AND W. YOUNG. "The Incidence of Alcohol Amongst Injured Pedestrians." *Australian Road Research Proceedings*, 1: 87–99, 1982 **(61401)**

JORGEN, S., N.N.J.J.M. VAN DER SLUISZEN, D. BROWN, AND E.F.P.M. VUUMAN. "Single- and Dual Track Performance During On-the-Road Driving at a Low and Moderate Dose of Alcohol: A Comparison Between Young Novice and More Experienced Drivers." *Human Psychopharmacology Clinical and Experimental*, 33: e2661, 6 pp, 2018 **(50405)**

JORTANI, S.A. AND A. POKLIS. "Evaluation of the ADx REA Assay for Determination of Ethanol in Serum and Urine." *Journal of Analytical Toxicology*, 17: 307–309, 1993 **(20111)**

JOZKOWSKI, K.N. AND J.D. WIERSMA. "Does Drinking Alcohol Prior to Sexual Activity Influence College Students' Consent?" *International Journal of Sexual Health*, 27: 156–174, 2015 **(61719)**

JURIC, A., A. FIJACKO, L. BAKULIC, T. ORESIC, AND I. GMAJNICKI. "Evaluation of Breath Alcohol Analysers by Comparison of Breath and Blood Alcohol Concentrations." *Arhj Hig Rada Toksikol*, 69: 69–76, 2018 **(30426)**

K

KAHN, A. AND D. BLUM. "Methyl Alcohol Poisoning in an 8-Month Boy: An Unusual Route of Intoxication." *Journal of Pediatrics*, 94: 841–843, 1979 **(80310)**

KALANT, H. "Intoxicated Automatism: Legal Concept vs. Scientific Evidence." *Contemporary Drug Problems*, 23: 631–648, 1996 **(60306)**

KALSI, J., T. SELANDER, AND T. TERVO. "Alcohol Policy and Fatal Alcohol-Related Crashes in Finland 2000–2016." *Traffic Injury and Prevention*, 19: 476–479, 2018 **(50723)**

KANNY, D., R.D. BREWER, J.B. MESNICK, ET AL. "Vital Signs: Alcohol Poisoning Deaths—United States, 2010–2012." *Morbidity and Mortality Weekly Report*, 63: 5pp, 2015 **(70417)**

KARGER, B., K. TEIGE, M. FUCHS, AND B. BRINKMANN. "Was the Pedestrian Hit in an Erect Position Before Being Run Over?" *Forensic Science International*, 119: 217–220, 2001 **(61406)**

KARLSON-STIBER, C. AND H. PERSSON. "Ethylene Glycol Poisoning: Experiences from an Epidemic in Sweden." *Journal of Toxicology and Clinical Toxicology*, 30: 565–574, 1992 **(80506)**

KARLSSON, T. "Sharp Force Homicides in the Stockholm Area, 1983–1992." *Forensic Science International*, 94: 129–139, 1998 **(60903)**

KARNS-WRIGHT, T. E., J.D. ROACHE, N, HILL-KAPTURCZAK, ET AL. "Time Delays in Transdermal Alcohol Concentrations Relative to Breath Alcohol Concentrations." *Alcohol and Alcoholism*, 52: 35–41, 2017 **(40307)**

KASANTIKUL, V., J.V. OUELLET, T. SMITH, ET AL. "The Role of Alcohol in Thailand Motorcycle Crashes." *Accident Analysis and Prevention*, 37: 357–366, 2005 **(61307)**

KATKICI, U., M.S. OZKOK, AND M. ORSAL. "An Autopsy Evaluation of Defence Wounds in 195 Homicidal Deaths due to Stabbing." *Journal of the Forensic Science Society,* 34: 237–240, 1994 **(60902)**

KATONA, B.G., E.G. SIEGEL, J.R. ROBERTS, ET AL. "The Effect of Superactivated Charcoal and Magnesium Citrate Solution on Blood Ethanol Concentrations and Area Under the Curve in Humans." *Clinical Toxicology,* 27: 129–137, 1989 **(10804)**

KAUPPILA, J.P., L. PAKANEN, K. PORVANI, ET AL. "Blood Alcohol Levels in Finnish Victims of Non-Ischemic Sudden Cardiac Death." *Annals of Medicine*, 53: 413–419, 2021 **(90306)**

KAWAI, T., T. YASUNGI, S. HORIGUCHI, ET AL. "Biological Monitoring of Occupation Exposure to Isopropyl Alcohol Vapor by Urinalysis for Acetone." *International Archives of Occupational and Environmental Health*, 62: 409–413, 1990 **(80407)**

KAYE, S. AND H.B. HAAG. "Terminal Blood Alcohol Concentrations in Ninety-Four Fatal Cases of Acute Alcoholism." *Journal of the American Medical Association*, 165: 451–452, 1957 **(70401)**

KECHAGIAS, S., K-A. JONSSON, T. FRANZEIN, ET AL. "Reliability of Breath-Alcohol Analysis in Individuals with Gastroesophageal Reflux Disease." *Journal of Forensic Science*, 44: 814–818, 1999 **(30514)**

KECHIAGIAS, S., K.A. JONSSON, AND A.W. JONES. "Impact of Gastric Emptying on the Pharmacokinetics of Ethanol as Influenced by Cisapride." *British Journal of Clinical Pharmacology*, 48: 728–732, 1999 **(10710)**

KELLEY, D. AND J.B. LYNCH. "Burns in Alcohol and Drug Users Result in Longer Treatment Times with More Complications." *Journal of Burn Care and Rehabilitation*, 13: 218–220, 1992 **(60604)**

KEMNITZER, C., C.N. POPE, S. NWOSU, ET AL. "An Investigation of Driver, Pedestrian, and Environmental Characteristics and Resulting Pedestrian Injury." *Traffic Injury Prevention*, 20: 510–514, 2019 **(61417)**

KENDALL, M.J., F. SPANNUTH, R.P. WALT, ET AL. "Lack of Effect of H2-Receptor Antagonists on the Pharmacokinetics of Alcohol Consumed After Food at Lunchtime." *British Journal Clinical Pharmacology*, 37: 371–374, 1994 **(10701)**

KENDRICK, Z.V., M.B. AFFRIME, AND D.T. LOWENTHAL. "Effects of Caffeine or Ethanol on Treadmill Performance and Metabolic Responses of Well-Trained Men." *International Journal of Clinical Pharmacology and Therapeutics*, 32: 536–541, 1994 **(61903)**

KENTTAMES, A. AND K. KARKOLA. "Death in Sauna." *Journal of Forensic Sciences*, 53: 724–729, 2008 **(61606)**

KERNS II, W., C. TOMASZEWSKI, K. MCMARTIN, ET AL. "Formate Kinetics in Methanol Poisoning." *Clinical Toxicology*, 40: 137–143, 2002 **(80305)**

KESANIEMI, Y.A. "Ethanol and Acetaldehyde in the Milk and Peripheral Blood of Lactating Women After Ethanol Administration." *Journal of Obstetrics and Gynaecology*, 81: 84–86, 1974 **(40401)**

KETEN, A., A.R. TURNER, AND A. BALSEVEN-ODABAST. "Measuring of Ethyl Glucuronide in Vitreous Humor with Liquid Chromatography-Mass Spectrometry." *Forensic Science International*, 193: 101–105, 2009 **(70902)**

KETTNER, M., A. SCHNABEL, AND F. RAMSTHALER. "Suspected Paradoxical Undressing in a Homicide Case." *Forensic Science, Medicine, and Pathology*, 8: 426–429, 2012 **(61008)**

KHIABANI, H.Z., M.S. OPDAL, AND J. MORLAND. "Blood Alcohol Concentrations in Apprehended Drivers of Cars and Boats Suspected to Be Impaired by the Police." *Traffic Injury and Prevention*, 9: 31–36, 2008 **(60409)**

KIM, D-J., S-J. YOON, H-P. LEE, B-M. CHOI, AND H.J. GO. "The Effects of Alcohol Hangover on Cognitive Functions in Healthy Subjects." *International Journal of Neuroscience*, 113: 581–594, 2003 **(60810)**

KIM, H., C-S. YANG, B-W. LEE, ET AL. "Alcohol Effects on Navigational Ability Using Ship Handling Simulator." *International Journal of Industrial Ergonomics, 37*: 733–743, 2007 **(61104)**

KING, A.C. AND J.A. BYARS. "Alcohol-Induced Performance Impairment in Heavy Episodic and Light Social Drinkers." *Journal of Studies on Alcohol*, 65: 27–36, 2004 **(50105)**

KINNULA, S., T. TAPIANINEN, M. RENKO, AND M. UHARI. "Safety of Alcohol Hand Gel Use Among Children and Personnel at a Child Day Care Center." *American Journal of Infection Control*, 37: 318–321, 2009 **(10126)**

KINTZ, P., "Influence of Antemortem Perfusion on Autopsy Blood Ethanol Concentration." *Forensic Toxicology*, 30: 76–79, 2012 **(10810)**

KINZINGER, R., M. RISSE, AND K. PUSCHEL. "Cold-'Craziness': Paradoxical Undressing in Hypothermia [German]." *Archives fur Kriminologie*, 187: 47–56, 1991 **(61006)**

KIRCHEN, L. AND M. YEGLES. "Influence of Hair Straightening on Ethyl Glucuronide Content in Hair." *Toxichem Krimtech*, 80 (Special Issue): 357–358, 2013 **(40528)**

KIRSCH, B., C.G. BIRNGRUBER, AND R. DETTMEYER. "Senior Driving Under the Influence. A Five-Year Retrospective Study of Alcoholized Road-Users Aged 70 and Over." *Forensic Science International*, 277: 10–15, 2017 **(50516)**

KLEEMAN, W.J., M. SEIBERT, A. TEMPKA, ET AL. "Arterial and Venous Alcohol Elimination in Ten Patients with Polytrauma/Shock [German]." *Blutalkohol*, 32: 162–173, 1995 **(10807)**

KLOCKHOFF, H., I. NASLUND, AND A.W. JONES. "Faster Absorption of Ethanol and Higher Peak Concentration in Women After Gastric Bypass Surgery." *British Journal of Clinical Pharmacology,* 54: 587–591, 2002 **(10114)**

KNOTT, B. "The Facts About Workplace Evidential Breath Tester Calibration." *Data Focus*, 17–24, Spring 2013 **(30214)**

KOCAK, F.E., O.O. ISIKLAR, H. KOCAK, AND A. MERAL. "Comparison of Blood Ethanol Stabilities in Different Storage Periods." *Biochemia Medica*, 25: 57–63, 2015 **(20312)**

KOLVES, K., B.M. DRAPE, J. SNOWDON, AND D. DE LEO. "Alcohol Use Disorders and Suicides: Results from a Psychological Autopsy Study in Australia." *Alcohol* 64: 29–35, 2017 **(90107)**

KOPPEL, C. AND F. MARTENS. "Clinical Experience in the Therapy of Bites from Exotic Snakes in Berlin." *Human and Experimental Toxicology*, 11: 549–552, 1992 **(61207)**

KORKOSH, S.L., J.A. HACKETT, AND J.C. MONTPETIT. "Blood Alcohol and Breath Alcohol Comparisons Using the Intox EC/IR II." *Canadian Society of Forensic Science Journal,* 45: 195–200, 2012 **(30421)**

KORTELAINEN, M-L. "Hyperthermia Deaths in Finland in 1970–1986." *American Journal of Forensic Medicine and Pathology*, 12: 115–118, 1991 **(61604)**

KOSECKI, P.A., P. BROOKE, L. ABBOTT, AND E. CANONICO. "The Effect of Sample Hemolysis on Blood Ethanol Analysis Using Headspace Gas Chromatography." *Journal of Forensic Sciences*, 66: 1136–1142, 2021 **(20116)**

KOSECKI, P.A., L.A. ABBOTT, AND M.E. RAINES. "Large-Scale Reanalysis of Refrigerated Antemortem Blood Maples for Ethanol Content at Random Intervals." *Journal of Forensic Sciences*, 66: 1966–1972, 2021 **(20316)**

KOSECKI, P.A., P. BROOKE, AND E. CANONICO. "The Effect of Sample Temperature Variations During Sample Preparation on Measured Blood Ethanol Concentration." *Journal of Forensic Sciences*, 66: 2478–2483, 2021 **(20123)**

KOSECKI, P.A., E. CANONICO, AND P. BROOKE. "Testing Antemortem Blood for Ethanol Concentration from a Blood Kit in a Refrigerator Fire." *Journal of Forensic Sciences,* 65: 2198–2200, 2020 **(20319)**

KOSECKI, P.A. AND M.E. RAINES. "Testing Antemortem Blood Samples for Ethanol After Four to Seven Years of Refrigerated Storage." *Journal of Forensic Sciences,* 1–8, 2022 **(20317)**

KRAMER-SARRETT, M. "The Effect of Invisalign Use on Mouth Alcohol Retention." *Canadian Society of Forensic Science Journal*, 49: 52–57, 2016 **(30527)**

KRAMER-SARRETT, M., E. LIN, K.S. CHUA, ET AL. "Examination of the Effects of Breath Hydrogen and Methane Levels on the EC/IR II." *Canadian Society of Forensic Science Journal*, 50: 125–130, 2017 **(30624)**

KRISHAN, S. AND S.M.W. LUI. "A Study of Acetone Interference in Intoxilyzer 5000C." *Canadian Society of Forensic Science Journal*, 35: 159–164, 2002 **(30606)**

KRISTOFFERSON, L. AND A. SMITH-KIELLAND. "An Automated Alcohol Dehydrogenase Method for Ethanol Quantification in Urine and Whole Blood." *Journal of Analytical Toxicology*, 29: 387–389, 2005 **(20113)**

KRISTOFFERSEN L., L-E. STORMYHR, AND A. SMITH-KIELLAND. "Headspace Gas Chromatographic Determination of Ethanol: The Use of Factorial Design to Study Effects of Blood Storage and Headspace Conditions on Ethanol Stability and Acetaldehyde Formation in Whole Blood and Plasma." *Forensic Science International*, 161: 151–157, 2006 **(20117)**

KRUGER, H-P. AND M. VOLLRATH. "The Alcohol-Related Accident Risk in Germany: Procedure, Methods and Results." *Accident Analysis and Prevention* 36: 125–133, 2004 **(50502)**

KUCMANIC, J. "Long-Term Stability of Ethanol Solutions for Breath-Alcohol Tests." *Journal of Analytical Toxicology*, 33: 328–331, 2009 **(30208)**

L

LAAKSO, O., M. HAAPALA, T. PENNANEN, ET AL. "Fourier-Transformed Infrared Breath Testing After Ingestion of Technical Alcohol." *Journal of Forensic Sciences*, 52: 982–987, 2007 **(30115)**

LAAKSO, M., T. HUOPANIEMI, J. HYVARINEN, ET AL. "Inefficacy of Oxygenated Drinking Water in Accelerating Ethanol Elimination in Humans." *Life Sciences*, 25: 1369–1372, 1979 **(10716)**

LACEY, J.H., S.A. FERGUSON, T. KELLY-BAKER, AND R.P. RIDER. "Low-Manpower Checkpoints: Can They Provide Effective DUI Enforcement in Small Communities?" *Traffic Injury Prevention*, 7: 213–218, 2006 **(50713)**

LAI, C-L., Y-C. CHAO, Y-C. CHEN, ET AL. "No Sex and Age Influences on the Expression Pattern and Activities of Human Gastric Alcohol and Aldehyde Dehydrogenases." *Alcoholism: Clinical and Experimental Research*, 24: 1625–1632, 2000 **(10315)**

LANDAUER, A.A. "The Accuracy Reliability and Validity of the Breathalyzer." *Australian New Zealand Journal of Criminology*. 5: 250–254, 1972 **(30102)**

LANDAUER, A.A. AND P. HOWATT. "Low and Moderate Alcohol Doses, Psychomotor Performance and Perceived Drowsiness." *Ergonomics*, 26: 647–657, 1983 **(50201)**

LANGILLE, R.M. AND PATRICK, J. "Precision of Breath Alcohol Testing in the Field Using the Intoxilyzer 5000C and the Paradox of Truncation." *Canadian Society of Forensic Science Journal*, 39: 55–64, 2005 **(30125)**

LANGILLE, R.M. AND J.G. WIGMORE. "The Mouth Alcohol Effect After a Mouthful of Beer Under Social Conditions." *Canadian Society of Forensic Science Journal*, 33: 193–198, 2000 **(30503)**

LANDGRAF, M.N., M. NOTHACKER, I.B. KOPP, AND F. HEINEN. "The Diagnosis of Fetal Alcohol Syndrome." *Deutsches Ärzteblatt International*, 110: 703–710, 2013 **(90404)**

LAONIGRO, I., M. CORREALE, M. DI BASE, AND E. ALTOMARE. "Alcohol Abuse and Heart Failure." *European Journal of Heart Failure*, 11: 453–462. 2009 **(90302)**

LASOTA, D., A. AL-WATHINANI, P. KRAJEWSKI, ET AL. "Alcohol and the Risk of Railway Suicide." *International Journal of Environmental Research and Public Health*, 17: 70003, 10pp, 2020 **(61508)**

LATHROP, S.L., T.B. DICK, AND K.B. NOLTE, "Fatal Wrong-Way Collisions on New Mexico's Interstate Highways, 1990–2004." *Journal of Forensic Sciences*, 55: 432–437, 2010 **(50508)**

LAURENS, J.B., F.J.J. SEWELL, AND M.M. KOCK. "Pre-Analytical Factors Related to the Stability of Ethanol Concentration During Storage of Ante-Mortem Blood Alcohol Concentrations." *Journal of Forensic and Legal Medicine*, 58: 155–163, 2018 **(20315)**

LAURELL, H. "Effects of Small Doses of Alcohol on Driver Performance in Emergency Traffic Situations." *Accident, Analysis and Prevention,* 9: 191–201, 1977 **(50301)**

LAWRENCE, D.W., L.I. GIBBS, AND M.A. KOHN. "Spinal Cord Injuries in Louisiana Due to Falls from Deer Stands, 1985–1994." *Journal of Louisiana State Medical Society*, 148: 77–79, 1995 **(60510)**

LAWTON, M.E. "Alcohol in Breast Milk." *Australian and New Zealand Obstetrics and Gynaecology*, 25: 71–73, 1985 **(40402)**

LEE, S. "Navigating Under the Influence and the Threat to Maritime Safety in Korea." *Asia-Pacific Journal of Ocean Law and Policy*, 5: 228–236, 2020 **(61109)**

LEFFINGWELL, T.R., N.J. COONEY, ET AL. "Continuous Objective Monitoring of Alcohol Use: Twenty-First Century Measurement Using Transdermal Sensors." *Alcoholism: Clinical and Experimental Research*, 37:16–22, 2013 **(40311)**

LEICHLITER, J.S., P.W. MEILMAN, C. PRESLEY, AND J.R. CASHIN. "Alcohol Use and Related Consequences Among Students with Varying Levels of Involvement in College Athletics." *Journal of American College Health*, 46: 257–262, 1998 **(61907)**

LENNE, M.G., P.M. DIETZE, T.J. TRIGGS, ET AL. "The Effects of Cannabis and Alcohol on Simulated Arterial Driving: Influences of Driving Experience and Task Demand." *Accident Analysis and Prevention*, 42: 850–866. 2010 **(50805)**

LEONARD, K.E., R.L. COLLINS, AND B.M. QUIGLEY. "Alcohol Consumption and the Occurrence and Severity of Aggression: An Event-Based Analysis of Male-to-Male Barroom Violence." *Aggressive Behavior*, 29: 346–365, 2003 **(60105)**

LEONARD, R.J. "Evaluation of the Analytical Performance of a Fuel Cell Breath Alcohol Testing Instrument: A Seven-Year Comprehensive Study." *Journal of Forensic Sciences*, 57:1614–1620, 2012 **(30128)**

LEONARD, S., T. WOEHRLE, H. NIKIZAD, ET AL. "Blunt Traumatic Brachial Plexus Injuries in a Northern Rural US Setting: Increased Likelihood in Unshielded Motor-Power Crashes." *Trauma Surgery & Acute Care Open*, 5: e000558, 3pp, 2020 **(61808)**

LERER, L.B. AND R.G. MATZOPOULOS. "Fatal Railway Injuries in Cape Town, South Africa." *American Journal of Forensic Medicine and Pathology,* 18: 144–147, 1997 **(61502)**

LEVESKY, M.E. AND M.A. MILLER. "Isopropyl Alcohol Skin Prep Pads: The Extreme Case [Letter]." *Journal of Emergency Medicine*, 33: 280, 2007 **(20409)**

LEVI-FAICT, T.W. AND G. QUATREHOMME. "So-Called Spontaneous Human Combustion." *Journal of Forensic Sciences*, 56: 1334–1339, 2011 **(60610)**

LEVINE, B. AND J.E. SMIALEK. "Status of Alcohol Absorption in Drinking Drivers Killed in Traffic Accidents." *Journal of Forensic Sciences*, 45: 3–6, 2000 **(10411)**

LEVINE, B., M.L. SMITH, J.E. SMIALEK, AND Y.H. CAPLAN. "Interpretation of Low Postmortem Concentrations of Ethanol." *Journal of Forensic Sciences*, 38: 663–667, 1993 **(70203)**

LEVINE, B., J.M. TITUS, K.A. MOORE, AND D. FOWLER. "Alcohol Concentration and the Ability to Form Intent." *Science and Justice,* 45: 195–197, 2005 **(62004)**

LEWIS, M.J. "Inhalation of Ethanol Vapour: A Case Report and Experimental Test Involving the Spraying of Shellac Lacquer." *Journal of the Forensic Science Society,* 25: 5–9, 1985 **(10120)**

LEWIS, R.J., R.D. JOHNSON, M.K. ANGIER, AND N.T. VU. "Ethanol Formation in Unadulterated Postmortem Tissues." *Forensic Science International*, 146: 17–24, 2004 **(70814)**

LI, G. AND S.P. BAKER. "Alcohol in Fatally Injured Bicyclists." *Accident Analysis and Prevention*, 26: 543–548, 1994 **(60206)**

LI, G., S.P. BAKER, M.W. LAMB, ET AL. "Characteristics of Alcohol-Related Fatal General Aviation Crashes." *Accident Analysis and Prevention*, 37: 143–148, 2005 **(60707)**

LI, G., S.P. BAKER, Y. QIANG, ET AL. "Alcohol Violations and Aviation Accidents: Findings from the U.S. Mandatory Alcohol Testing Program." *Aviation, Space, Environmental Medicine*, 78(5): 510–513, 2007 **(60709)**

LI, G., S.P. BAKER, J.E. SMIALEK, AND C.A. SODERSTROM. "Use of Alcohol as a Risk Factor for Bicycling Injury." *Journal of the American Medical* Association, 285: 893–897, 2001 **(60201)**

LI, G., S.P. BAKER, S. STERLING, ET AL. "A Comparative Analysis of Alcohol in Fatal and Nonfatal Bicycling Injuries." *Alcoholism: Clinical and Experimental Research*, 20: 1553–1559, 1996 **(60205)**

LI, G., C. SHAHPAR, C.A. SODERSTROM, AND S.P. BAKER. "Alcohol Use in Relation to Driving Records among Injured Bicyclists." *Accident Analysis and Prevention,* 32: 583–587, 2000 **(60204)**

LI, J., T. MILLS, AND R. ERATO. "Intravenous Saline Has No Effect on Blood Ethanol Clearance." *Journal of Emergency Medicine*, 17: 1–5, 1999 **(10802)**

LI, R., L. HU, L. HU, ET AL. "Evaluation of Acute Alcohol Intoxication as the Primary Cause of Death: A Diagnostic Challenge for Forensic Pathologists." *Journal of Forensic Sciences*, 62: 1213–1219, 2017 **(70412)**

LI, Y.C., N.N. SZE, S.C. WONG, ET AL. "Experimental Study of the Temporal Profile of Breath Alcohol Concentration in a Chinese Population After a Light Meal." 14: 15pp, 2019 **(10319)**

LI, Y-M. "Feasibility of Identification of Alcohol Intoxication by Nurses in Emergency Departments." *Kaohsiung Journal of Medical Science*, 19: 391–396, 2003 **(50602)**

LI, Z., X. LI, X. ZHAO, AND Q. ZHANG. "Effects of Different Alcohol Dosages on Steering Behavior in Curve Driving." *Human Factors*, 61: 139–151, 2019 **(50220)**

LIEBERMAN, F.L. "The Effect of Liver Disease on the Rate of Ethanol Metabolism in Man." *Gastroenterology*, 44: 261–266, 1963 **(10313)**

LIGUORI, A., R.B. D'AGOSTINO JR., S.I. DWORKIN, ET AL. "Alcohol Effects on Mood, Equilibrium and Simulated Driving." *Alcoholism Clinical and Experimental Research*, 23: 815–821, 1999 **(50204)**

LIN, P.T. AND J.R. GILL. "Subway Train-Related Fatalities in New York City: Accident Versus Suicide." *Journal of Forensic Sciences*, 54: 1414–1418, 2009 **(61506)**

LIN, Z., H. WANG, A.W. JONES, ET AL. "Evaluation and Review of Ways to Differentiate Sources of Ethanol in Postmortem Blood." *International Journal of Legal Medicine*, 134: 2081–2093, 2020 **(70223)**

LINDBERG, L., S. BRAUER, P. WOLLMER, ET AL. "Breath Alcohol Concentration Determined with a New Analyzer Using Free Exhalation Predicts Almost Precisely the Arterial Blood Alcohol Concentration." *Forensic Science International*, 168: 200–207, 2007 **(30111)**

LINDBERG, L., D. GRUBB, D. DENCKER, ET AL. "Detection of Mouth Alcohol During Breath Alcohol Analysis." *Forensic Science International*, 240: 66–72, 2015 **(30526)**

LINDEN, C.H. AND J.R. TUCKER. "Alcoholic Beverages: Proof and Flammability [Letter]." *American Journal of Emergency Medicine*, 16: 544–555, 1998 **(60607)**

LIPPI, G., M. MERCADANTI, R. MUSA, AND R. ALOE. "The Concentration of Plasma Ethanol Measured with an Enzymatic Assay Is Decreased in Hemolyzed Specimens [Letter]." *Clinica Chimica Acta*, 413: 356–357, 2012 **(20118)**

LIPPI, G., A-M. SIMUNDIC, G. MUSILE, ET AL. "The Alcohol Used for Cleansing the Venipuncture Site Does Not Jeopardize Blood and Plasma Alcohol Measurements with Head-Space Gas Chromatography and an Enzymatic Assay." *Biochemia Medica*, 27: 398–403, 2017 **(20411)**

LIRA, M. C., T.C. HEEREN, M. BUCZEK, ET AL. "Trends in Cannabis Involvement and Risk of Alcohol Involvement in Motor Vehicle Crash Fatalities in the United States, 2000–2018." *American Journal of Public Health,* 111: 1976–1985, 2021 **(50809)**

LIU, J.J., M.R. DAYA, O. CARRASQUILLO, AND S.N. KALES. "Prognostic Factors in Patients with Methanol Poisoning." *Clinical Toxicology*, 36: 175–181, 1998 **(80304)**

LOGAN, B.K. AND S. DISTEFANO. "Ethanol Content of Various Foods and Soft Drinks and Their Potential for Interference with a Breath-Alcohol Test." *Journal of Analytical Toxicology*, 22: 181–181, 1998 **(30510)**

LOGAN, B.K., S. DISTEFANO, AND G.A. CASE. "Evaluation of the Effect of Asthma Inhalers and Nasal Decongestant Sprays on a Breath Alcohol Test." *Journal of Forensic Sciences*, 43: 197–199, 1998 **(30508)**

LOGAN, B.K. AND R.G. GULLBERG. "Lack of Effect of Tongue Piercing on an Evidential Breath Alcohol Test." *Journal of Forensic Sciences*, 43: 239–240, 1998 **(30517)**

LOGAN, B.K. AND A.W. JONES. "Endogenous Ethanol Auto-Brewery Syndrome as a Drunk-Driving Defence Challenge." *Medicine. Science and the Law*, 40: 206–215, 2000 **(20504)**

LOGAN, B.K. AND G. LINDHOLM. "Gastric Contamination of Postmortem Blood Samples During Blind-Stick Sample Collection." *American Journal of Forensic Medicine and Pathology*, 17: 109–111, 1996 **(70306)**

LOOMIS, T.A. "Blood Alcohol in Automobile Drivers: Measurement and Interpretation for Medicolegal Purposes I. Effect of Time Interval Between Incident and Sample Acquisition." *Quarterly Journal of Studies on Alcohol*, 35: 458–472, 1974 **(10501)**

LOVIBOND, S.H. AND K. BIRD. "Danger Level—The Warwick Farm Project." *Proceedings of the 29th International Conference on Alcoholism and Drug Dependence. L.G. Kiloh (ed), Butterworths (pub), Australia*, 299–305, 1971 **(50304)**

LOWE, G. AND S.B. TAYLOR. "Effects of Alcohol on Responsive Laughter and Amusement." *Psychological Reports*, 80:1149–1150, 1997 **(61203)**

LUCZAK, S.E., S.H. SHEA, A.C. HSUEH, ET AL. "ALDH2*2 Is Associated with a Decreased Likelihood of Alcohol-Induced Blackouts in Asian American College Students." *Journal of Studies on Alcohol,* 67: 349–353, 2006 **(60304)**

LUKE, L.C., C. DEWAR, M. BAILEY, ET AL. "A Little Nightclub Medicine: The Healthcare Implications of Clubbing." *Emergency Medicine*, 19: 542–545, 2002 **(60108)**

LUNA, G.K., R.V. MAIER, L. SOWDER, ET AL. "The Influence of Ethanol Intoxication on Outcome of Injured Motorcyclists." *Journal of Trauma*, 24: 695–700, 1984 **(61305)**

LUND, A. "The Rate of Disappearance of Blood Alcohol in Drunken Drivers." *Blutalkohol*, 16: 395–398, 1979 **(10502)**

———. "The Secretion of Alcohol in the Tear Fluid." *Blutalkohol*, 21: 51-54, 1984 **(40306)**

LUNETTA, P. AND K. HAIKONEN. "Land Motor Vehicle-Related Drowning in Finland: A Nation-Wide Population Based Survey." *Traffic Injury Prevention*, 21: 533–538, 2020 **(60416)**

LUTMER, B.M. "The Effect of Water-Soluble OC Pepper Spray on Select Infrared and Electrochemical Breath Alcohol Instruments." *Canadian Society of Forensic Science Journal*, 42: 266–275, 2009 **(30618)**

LUTMER, B., C. ZURFLUH, AND C. LONG. "Potential Effect of Alcohol Content in Energy Drinks on Breath Alcohol Testing." *Journal of Analytical Toxicology*, 33:167–169, 2009 **(30511)**

LYLE, C.B., J.T. MONROE JR., D.E. FLINN, AND L.E. LAMB. "Micturition Syncope: Report of 24 Cases." *New England Journal of Medicine*, 265: 982–986, 1961 **(60509)**

LYNN, M. "The Effects of Alcohol Consumption on Restaurant Tipping." *Personality and Social Psychological Bulletin*, 14: 87–91, 1988 **(61204)**

M

MACDONALD, S. "The Influence of the Age and Sex Distributions of Drivers on the Reduction of Impaired Crashes: Ontario, 1974– 1999." *Traffic Injury Prevention*, 4: 33–37, 2003 **(50709)**

MACLEOD, K.E., J.B. GRISWOLD, L.S. ARNOLD, AND D.R. RAGLAND. "Factors Associated with Hit-and-Run Pedestrian Fatalities and Driver Identification." *Accident Analysis and Prevention*, 45: 366–372, 2012 **(61409)**

MADDEN, M. AND J. MCCAMBRIDGE. "Alcohol Marketing Versus Public Health: David and Goliath?" *Globalization and Health*, 17: 45, 6pp, 2021 **(90510)**

MAEDA, H., B-L. ZHU, T. ISHIKAWA, ET AL. "Evaluation of Post-Mortem Ethanol Concentrations in Pericardial Fluid and Bone Marrow Aspirate." *Forensic Science International*, 161: 141–143, 2006 **(70808)**

MAHDI, A.S. AND A.J. MCBRIDE. "Intravenous Injection of Alcohol by Drug Injectors: Report of Three Cases." *Alcohol and Alcoholism*, 34: 918–919, 1999 **(10116)**

MAINEROVA, B., J. PRASKO, K. LATALOVA, ET AL. "Alcohol Withdrawal Delirium—Diagnosis, Course and Treatment." *Biomedical Papers of the Medical Faculty of the University Palacky, Olomouc, Czech Republic*, 159: 44–52, 2015 **(90207)**

MALATHESH, B.C., C.N. KUMAR, A. KANDASAMY, ET AL. "Legal, Social, and Occupational Problems in Persons with Alcohol Use Disorder: An Exploratory Study." *Indian Journal of Psychological Medicine*, 43: 234–240, 2021 **(90106)**

MALCOLM, R., R.F. ANTON, S.E. CONRADI, AND S. SUTHERLAND. "Carbohydrate-Deficient Transferrin and Alcohol Use in Medical Examiner Cases." *Alcohol*, 17: 7–11, 1999 **(70906)**

MALDONADO, J.R., Y. SHER, J.F. ASHOURI, ET AL. "The Prediction of Alcohol Withdrawal Severity Scale (PAWSS): Systematic Literature Review and Pilot Study of a New Scale for the Prediction of Complicated Alcohol Withdrawal Syndrome." *Alcohol*, 48: 375–390, 2014 **(90210)**

MALINGRE, M., T. VERVERS, S. BOS, ET AL. "Alcohol Swabs and Venipuncture in a Routine Hospital Setting: No Effect on Blood Ethanol Measurement [Letter]." *Therapeutic Drug Monitoring*, 27: 403–404, 2005 **(20406)**

MANN, K., D. HERMANN, AND A. HEINZ. "One Hundred Years of Alcoholism: The Twentieth Century." *Alcohol and Alcoholism*, 35: 10–15, 2000 **(90101)**

MANN, R.E., R.G. SMART, G. STODUTO, ET AL. "Alcohol Consumption and Problems among Road Rage Victims and Perpetrators." *Journal of Studies on Alcohol*, 65: 161–168, 2004 **(60114)**

MANOLAKOPOULOS, S., M. ECONOMOU, S. BETHANIS, ET AL. "A Single Alcohol Ingestion Does Not Affect Serum Hepatitis C Virus RNA in Patients with Chronic Hepatitis C." *Liver International*, 26: 1196–1200, 2006 **(10318)**

MARCZINSKI, C.A., E.L.R. HARRISON, AND M.T. FILLMORE. "Effects of Alcohol on Simulated Driving and Perceived Driving Impairment in Binge Drinkers." *Alcoholism: Clinical and Experimental Research*, 32: 1329–1337, 2008 **(50211)**

MARSDEN, G. AND J. LEACH. "Effects of Alcohol and Caffeine on Maritime Navigational Skills." *Ergonomics*, 43: 17–26, 2000 **(61101)**

MARTI, V., M. AUGSBURGER, C. WIDMER, AND C. LARDI. "Significant Postmortem Diffusion of Ethanol: A Case Report." *Forensic Science International*, 328: 5pp, 2021 **(70310)**

MARTIN, T.L., "An Evaluation of the Intoxilyzer 8000C Evidential Breath Alcohol Analyzer." *Canadian Society of Forensic Science Journal*, 44(1): 22–30, 2011 **(30619)**

MARTIN, T.L., P.A.M. SOLBECK, D. J. MAYERS, ET AL. "A Review of Alcohol-Impaired Driving: The Role of Blood Alcohol Concentration and Complexity of the Driving Task." *Journal of Forensic Sciences*, 58: 1238–1250, 2013 **(50117)**

MARTIN, T.L., J.G. WIGMORE, AND K.L. WOODALL. "A Comparison of Blood Alcohol Concentrations Estimated from Drinking Histories of Drivers Charged with Over 80 and Their Intoxilyzer 5000C Results." *Canadian Society of Forensic Science Journal*, 37: 187–195, 2004 **(10608)**

MASON, J.K. AND D.J. BLACKMORE. "Experimental Inhalation of Ethanol Vapour." *Medicine, Science, and the Law*, 12: 205–208, 1972 **(10121)**

MATTHIAS, D.J., D.C. HARVEY, AND D.E. DEFRAGE. "Concentration Verification of Ethanol/Nitrogen Compressed Gas Cylinders Prior to Use for Periodic Determinations of Accuracy in California." *Journal of Analytical Toxicology*, 25: 215–218, 2001 **(30211)**

MATTICK, A.P., R. MEHTA, H. HANRAHAN, AND J.J. O'DONNELL. "The Football World Cup 2002—Analysis of Related Attendance to an Irish Emergency Department." *Irish Medical Journal*, 96: 90–91, 2003 **(61911)**

MAYER, J.H., J.E. HERLOCHER, AND J. PARISAN. "Esophageal Rupture After Mushroom Alcohol Ingestion [Letter]." *Journal of American Medical Association*, 285: 1323, 1971 **(80105)**

MAYES, R., B. LEVINE, M.L. SMITH, ET AL. "Toxicologic Findings in the USS Iowa Disaster." *Journal of Forensic Science*, 37: 1352–1357, 1992 **(70214)**

MCCOLL, K.E.L., B. WHITING, M.R. MOORE, AND A. GOLDBERG. "Correlation of Ethanol Concentration in Blood and Saliva." *Clinical Science*, 26: 283–286, 1979 **(40202)**

MCELRAE, A., C. SU, AND L. SMITH. "Truncation of Breath Alcohol Measurements and Its Effect on Peak Concentrations." *Canadian Society of Forensic Science Journal*, 44: 13–21, 2011 **(10509)**

MCGWIN JR. G., V. CHAPMAN, M. ROUSCULP, ET AL. "The Epidemiology of Fire-Related Deaths in Alabama." *Journal of Burn Care Rehabilitation*, 21: 75–83, 2000 **(60505)**

MCHUGH, R.K. AND R.D. WEISS. "Alcohol Use Disorder and Depressive Disorders." *Alcohol Research, Current Reviews*, 40: e1–e8, 2019 **(90110)**

MCIVOR, R.A. AND S.H. COSBEY. "Effect of Using Alcoholic and Non-Alcoholic Skin Cleansing Swabs When Sampling Blood for Alcohol Estimation Using Gas Chromatography." *British Journal of Clinical Practice*, 44: 235–236, 1990 **(20403)**

MCKAY, J., M.D. RAWLINGS, I. COBDEN, AND O.F.W. JAMES. "The Acute Effects of Alcohol on Acetanilide Disposition in Normal Subjects, and in Patients with Liver Disease." *British Journal of Clinical Pharmacology*, 14: 501–504, 1982 **(10317)**

MCKEON, A., M.A. FRYE, AND N. DELANTY. "The Alcohol Withdrawal Syndrome." *Journal of Neurology, Neurosurgery and Psychiatry*, 79: 854–862, 2008 **(90205)**

MCKNIGHT, A.J., J.E. LANGE, AND A.S. MCKNIGHT. "Development of a Standardized Boating Sobriety Test." *Accident Analysis and Prevention*, 31: 147–152, 1999 **(60410)**

MCKNIGHT, A.J., E.A. LANGSTON, A.S. MCKNIGHT, AND J.E. LANGE. "Sobriety Tests for Low Blood Alcohol Concentrations." *Accident Analysis and Prevention*, 34: 305–311, 2002 **(50610)**

MCNAUGHTON, L. AND D. PREECE. "Alcohol and Its Effect on Sprint and Middle Distance Running." *British Journal of Sports Medicine*, 20: 56–59, 1986 **(61901)**

MEDA, S.A., V.D. CALHOUN, R.S. ASTUR, ET AL. "Alcohol Dose Effects on Brain Circuits During Simulated Driving: An fMRI Study." *Human Brain Mapping*, 30: 1257–1270, 2009 **(50212)**

MEKJAVOC, I.B., C.A. GAUL, M.D. WHITE, AND K.D. MITTLEMAN. "Cardiovascular Responses During 70 Degree Head-Up Tilt. The Effect of Elevated Body Temperature and High Alcohol Blood Levels." *Physiologist*, 30: S-56–S-57, 1987 **(61601)**

MELIA, A.T., J. ZHI, R. ZELASKO, D. HARTMANN, ET AL. "The Interaction of the Lipase Inhibitor Orlistat with Ethanol in Healthy Volunteers." *European Journal of Clinical Pharmacology,* 54: 773–777, 1998 **(10707)**

MENZ, V., M. PHILIPPE, E. POCECCO, ET AL. "The Use of Medication and Alcohol in Recreational Downhill Skiers: Results of a Survey Including 816 Subjects in Tyrol." *Journal of Science and Medicine in Sport*, 22: 522–526, 2019 **(61918)**

MEMO, L., E. GNOATO, S. CAMINITI, ET AL. "Fetal Alcohol Spectrum Disorders and Fetal Alcohol Syndrome: The State of the Art and New Diagnostic Tools." *Early Human Development*, 8951: 540–543, 2013 **(90405)**

MEYER, T., P.K. MONGE, AND J. SAKAHAUG. "Storage of Blood Samples Containing Alcohol." *Acta Pharmacologica et Toxicologica*, 45: 282–286, 1979 **(20301)**

MEZEY, E., A.L. IMBEBO, J.J. POTTER, ET AL. "Endogenous Ethanol Production and Hepatic Disease Following Jejunoileal Bypass for Morbid Obesity." *American Journal of Clinical Nutrition*, 28: 1277–1283, 1975 **(20502)**

MICHALODIMITRAKIS, M.N, R. LA GRANGE, AND A.M. TSATSAKIS. "Suicide by Alcohol Overdose." *Journal of Clinical and Forensic Medicine,* 4: 91–94, 1997 **(62005)**

MIDTLYNG, L., G. HOISETH, H. LUYTKIS, ET AL. "Relationship Between Betahydroxybutyrate (BHB) and Acetone Concentrations in Postmortem Blood and Cause of Death." *Forensic Science International*, 32: 6pp, 2021 **(80210)**

MIHAILOVIC, Z., S. SAVIC, I. DAMJIANJUK, ET AL. "A Case of a Fatal Himalayan Black Bear Attack in the Zoo." *Journal of Forensic Sciences*, 56: 806–809, 2011 **(61223)**

MILLER, B.A., S.M. DAY, T.E. VASQUEZ, AND F.M. EVANS. "Absence of Salting Out Effects in Forensic Blood Alcohol Determination at Various Concentrations of Sodium Fluoride Using Semi-Automated Headspace Gas Chromatography." *Science and Justice*, 44: 73–76, 2004 **(20105)**

MILLER, M.A., A. ROSON, AND C.S. CRYSTAL. "Alcohol-Based Hand Sanitizer: Can Frequent Use Cause an Elevated Blood Alcohol Level?" *American Journal of Infection Control*, 34: 150–151, 2006 **(10118)**

MILLER, P.M., R.F. ANTON, B.M. EGON, ET AL. "Excessive Alcohol Consumption and Hypertension: Clinical Implications of Current Research." *The Journal of Clinical Hypertension*, 7: 346–353, 2005 **(90304)**

MILLS, R.J., W.D.S. MCLAY, AND J.D.H. BANKIER. "Breath Sampling by the Camic Breath Alcohol Analyser in the Presence of Respiratory Impairment." *Police Surgeon*, 39: 19–22, 1991 **(30302)**

MINH, A.E. "Effects of Vaping E-Juices with and Without Alcohol on the Accuracy of the Alco-Sensor FST Approved Screening Device." *Canadian Society of Forensic Science Journal*, 54: 77–85, 2021 **(30525)**

MITCHELL JR., M.C., E.L. TEIGEN, AND V.A. RAMCHANDANI. "Absorption and Peak Blood Alcohol Concentration After Drinking Beer, Wine, or Spirits." *Alcoholism: Clinical and Experimental Research*, 38: 1200–1204, 2014 **(10131)**

MLYNCZAK, J., J. KUBICKI, AND K. KOPCZYNSKI, "Stand-Off Detection of Alcohol in Car Cabins." *Journal of Applied Remote Sensing*, 8: 7pp, 2014 **(30134)**

MODIG, F., P-A FRANSSON, M. MAGNUSSON, AND M. PATEL. "Blood Alcohol Concentration at 0.06 and 0.10% Causes a Complex Multifaceted Deterioration of Body Movement Control." *Alcohol*, 46: 75–88, 2012 **(60517)**

MOHAMMADZADEH, H., H. MOHAMMADI, M. ALI TAVAKOLI, AND S. SADEGHI. "Sudden Death Due to Acetone Toxicity." *Pharmaceutical and Biomedical Research*, 7: 217–220, 2021 **(80209)**

MOJICA, C.V., E.A. PASOL, M.L. DIZON, ET AL. "Chronic Methanol Toxicity Through Topical and Inhalational Routes Presenting as Vision Loss and Restricted Diffusion of the Optic Nerves on MRI: A Case Report and Literature Review." *eNeurologicalSci*, 20: 4pp, 2020 **(80318)**

MOORE, K.A., G.W. KUNSMAN, B.S. LEVINE, ET AL. "A Comparison of Ethanol Concentrations in the Occipital Lobe and Cerebellum." *Forensic Science International*, 86: 127–134, 1997 **(70802)**

MOORE, R.L. AND J. GULLIEN. "The Effect of Breath Freshener Strips on Two Types of Breath Alcohol Testing Instruments." *Journal of Forensic Sciences*, 49: 829–831, 2004 **(30512)**

MORIYA, F. AND Y. HASHIMOTO. "Endogenous Ethanol Production in Trauma Victims Associated with Medical Treatment." *Japanese Journal of Legal Medicine*, 50: 263–267, 1996 **(70208)**

MORRISON, P.M., N.E. NOEL, AND R.L. OGLE. "Do Angry Women Choose Alcohol?" *Addictive Behaviors*, **37**: 908–913, 2012 **(60117)**

MORROW, D., J. YESAVAGE, V. LEIRER, ET AL. "The Time-Course of Alcohol Impairment of General Aviation Pilot Performance in a Frasca 141 Simulator." *Aviation, Space, and Environmental Medicine*, 64: 697–705, 1993 **(60705)**

MOSCATI, R., J.D. HO, D.M. DAWES, AND J.R. MINER. "Physiological Effects of Prolonged Conducted Electrical Weapon Discharge in Ethanol-Intoxicated Adults." *American Journal of Emergency Medicine*, 28: 582–587, 2010 **(61219)**

MOSKAL, A., J-L MARTIN, AND B. LAUMON. "Risk Factors for Injury Accidents Among Moped and Motorcycle Riders." *Accident Analysis and Prevention*, 489: 5–11, 2012 **(61314)**

MOSKOWITZ, H., M. BURNS, AND S. FERGUSON. "Police Officers' Detection of Breath Odors from Alcohol Ingestion." *Accident Analysis and Prevention*, 31: 175–180, 1999 **(50601)**

MOUG, S.J., J.A. LYLE, AND M. BLACK. "A Review of Gunshot Deaths in Strathclyde—1989 to 1998." *Medicine, Science, and the Law*, 41: 260–265, 2001 **(60909)**

MOUNCE, N.H. AND O.J. PENDLETON. "The Relationship Between Blood Alcohol Concentration and Crash Responsibility for Fatally Injured Drivers." *Accident Analysis and Prevention*, 24: 201–210, 1992 **(50509)**

MULLINS, M.E., R.A. GRIMSBO, AND E. O'LEARY. "A Natural Sobriety Enzyme: A Party Pill or Snake Oil?" *Veterinary and Human Toxicology*, 41: 102–103, 1999 **(10718)**

MUNDT, M.P., L.I. ZAKLETSKAIA, D.D. BROWN, AND M.F. FLEMING. "Alcohol-Induced Memory Blackouts as an Indicator of Injury Risk Among College Drinkers." *Injury Prevention*, 18: 44–49, 2012 **(60314)**

MURTY, O.P. "Postmortem Production of Alcohol in Viscera." *International Journal of Medical Toxicology and Legal Medicine*, 4: 34–35, 2002 **(70221)**

MUSSHOF, F., C. BROCKMANN, B. MADEA, ET AL. "Ethyl Glucuronide Findings in Hair Samples From the Mummies of the Capuchin Catacombs of Palermo." *Forensic Science International*, 232: 213–217, 2013 **(70915)**

N

NAGATA, T., S. SETOGUCHI, D. HEMENWAY, AND M.J. PERRY. "Effectiveness of a Law to Reduce Alcohol-Impaired Driving in Japan." *Injury Prevention*, 14: 19–23, 2008 **(50701)**

NANIKAWA, R. AND S. KOTOKU. "Medico-Legal Evaluation of the Ethanol Levels in Cadaveric Blood and Urine." *Yonago Acta Medica,* 15: 61–69, 1971 **(70215)**

NARASIMHA, V.L., L. SHUKLA, D. MUKHERJEE, ET AL. "Complicated Alcohol Withdrawal—An Unintended Consequence of COVID-19 Lockdown." *Alcohol and Alcoholism*, 55: 350–353, 2020 **(90217)**

NARKIEWICZ, K., R.L. COOLEY, AND V.K. SOMERS. "Alcohol Potentiates Orthostatic Hypotension: Implications for Alcohol-Related Syncope." *Circulation*, 101: 398–402, 2000 **(60508)**

NAWROT, M., B. NORDENSTROM, AND A. OLSON. "Disruption of Eye Movements by Ethanol Intoxication Affects Perception of Depth from Motion Parallax." *Psychological Science*, 15: 858–865, 2004 **(50111)**

NELSON, T.F. AND H. WECHSLER. "School Spirits: Alcohol and Collegiate Sports Fans." *Addictive Behaviors*, 28: 1–11, 2003 **(61908)**

NESOFF, E. D., A.J. MILAM, C.C. BRANZAS, ET AL. "Alcohol Outlets, Neighborhood Retail Environments, and Pedestrian Injury Risk." *Alcoholism: Clinical and Experimental Research*, 42: 1979–1987, 2018 **(61415)**

NEUMANN, J., T. KELLER, F. MONTICELLI, ET AL. "Ethyl Glucuronide and Ethanol Concentrations in Femoral Blood, Urine, and Vitreous Humor from 117 Autopsy Cases." *Forensic Science International*, 318: 7pp, 2021 **(70911)**

NEUTEBOOM, W. AND A.W. JONES. "Disappearance Rate of Alcohol from the Blood of Drunk Drivers Calculated from Two Consecutive Samples: What Do the Results Really Mean?" *Forensic Science International*, 45: 107–115, 1990 **(10407)**

NEUTEBOOM, W. AND P.G.M. ZWEIPFENNING. "The Stability of the Alcohol Concentration in Urine Specimens." *Journal of Analytical Toxicology*, 13: 141–143, 1989 **(40107)**

NG, C., M. FLEURY, H. HAKMI, ET AL. "The Impact of Alcohol Use and Withdrawal on Trauma Outcomes: A Case Control Study." *The American Journal of Surgery*, 222: 438–445, 2021 **(90208)**

NIESCHALK, M., C. ORTMANN, A. WEST, ET AL. "Effects of Alcohol on Body-Sway Patterns in Human Subjects." *International Journal of Legal Medicine*, 112: 253–260, 1999 **(50604)**

NIXON, J., A. CORCORAN, L. FIELDING, AND J. EASTGATE. "Fatal and Nonfatal Accidents on the Railways: A Study of Injuries to Individuals, with Particular Reference to Children and to Nonfatal Trauma." *Accident Analysis and Prevention*, 17: 217–222, 1985 **(61504)**

NIXON, K. AND J.A. MCCLAIN. "Adolescence as a Critical Window for Developing an Alcohol Use Disorder: Current Findings in Neuroscience." *Current Opinions Psychiatry*, 23: 227–232, 2010 **(90103)**

NORDBY, K., R.G. WATTEN, R.T. RAANAAS, AND S. MAGNUSSEN. "Effects of Moderate Doses of Alcohol on Immediate Recall of Numbers: Some Implications for Information Technology." *Journal of Studies on Alcohol*, 60: 873–878, 1999 **(60308)**

NORHEIM, G. "Postmortem Alcohol in Vitreous Humor." *Blutalkohol*, 9: 187–191, 1972 **(70603)**

NORLANDER, T., A. NORDMAKER, AND T. ARCHER. "Effects of Alcohol and Frustration on Experimental Graffiti." *Scandinavian Journal of Psychology*, 39: 201–207, 1998 **(61216)**

NORSTROM, T. "Effects on Criminal Violence of Different Types and Private and Public Drinking." *Addiction*, 93: 689–699, 1998 **(60110)**

NYMAN, E. AND A. PALMLOV. "On the Effect of Muscular Exercise on the Metabolism of Ethyl Alcohol." *Scandinavian Archives of Physiology*, 68: 271–294, 1934 **(10308)**

———. "The Elimination of Ethyl Alcohol in Sweat." *Skandinavischae Archiv fur Physiologie*, 74: 155–159, 1936 **(40301)**

O

OAKLAND, C.D.H. "Ice Skating Injuries: Can They Be Reduced or Prevented?" *Archives of Academic Emergency Medicine*, 7: 95–99, 1990 **(61906)**

O'BRIEN, C.P. AND F. LYONS. "Alcohol and the Athlete." *Sports Medicine*, 29: 295–300, 2000 **(61917)**

O'BRIEN, K.S., P.G. MILLER, G.S. KOLT, ET AL. "Alcohol Industry and Non-Alcohol Industry Sponsorship of Sportspeople and Drinking." *Alcohol and Alcoholism*, 46: 210–213, 2011 (**90511**)

ODELL, M.S., C.F. MCDONALD, J. FARRAR, ET AL. "Breath Testing in Patients with Respiratory Disability." *Journal of Clinical and Forensic Medicine*, 5: 45–48, 1998 (**30304**)

OEHMICHEN, M., T. NORPOTH, G. STICHT, ET AL. "Interaction of H_2-Receptor Antagonists (Cimetidine and Ranitidine) and High Blood Alcohol Concentrations. Experimental Investigations." *Blutalkohol*, 33: 305–320, 1996 (**10702**)

OGDEN, E.J.D., J. GERSTNER-STEVENS, J. BURKE, AND S.J. YOUNG. "Venous Blood Alcohol Sampling and the Alcohol Swab." *Police Surgeon*, 42: 4–5, 1992 (**20404**)

OHSHIMA, T., T. KONDO, Y. SATO, AND T. TAKAYASU. "Postmortem Alcohol Analysis of the Synovial Fluid and Its Availability in Medico-Legal Practices." *Forensic Science International*, 90: 131–138, 1997 (**70810**)

O'KEEFE, J. H., S.K. BHATTI, A. BASJWA, ET AL. "Alcohol and Cardiovascular Health: The Dose Makes the Poison . . . or the Remedy." *Mayo Clinic Proceedings*, 89: 382–393, 2014 (**90310**)

OLKKONEN, S. AND R. HONKANEN. "The Role of Alcohol in Nonfatal Bicycle Injuries." *Accident Analysis and Prevention*, 22: 89–96, 1990 (**60202**)

OLSEN, H., J. SAKSHAUG, F. DUCKERT, ET AL. "Ethanol Elimination-Rates Determined by Breath Analysis as a Marker of Recent Excessive Ethanol Consumption." *Scandinavian Journal of Clinical and Laboratory Investigation*, 49: 359–365, 1989 (**10301**)

OLSEN, T. AND W.L. HEARN. "Stability of Ethanol in Postmortem Blood and Vitreous Humor in Long-Term Refrigerated Storage." *Journal of Analytical Toxicology*, 27: 517–519, 2003 (**70206**)

O'NEAL, C.L., C.E. WOLF II, B. LEVINE, ET AL. "Gas Chromatographic Procedures for Determination of Ethanol in Postmortem Blood Using T-Butanol and Methyl Ethyl Ketone as Internal Standards." *Forensic Science International*, 83: 31–38, 1996 (**70102**)

O'NEAL, E.N., S.H. DECKER, C. SPOHN, AND K. TELLIS. "Condom Use During Sexual Assault." *Journal of Forensic and Legal Medicine*, 20: 605–609, 2013 (**61723**)

OSHAUG, K., R. KRONSTRAND, F.C. KUGELBERG, ET AL. "Frequency of Postmortem Ethanol Formation in Blood, Urine and Vitreous Humor—Improving Diagnostic Accuracy with the Use of Ethyl Sulphate and Putrefactive Alcohols." *Forensic Science International*, 331: 6pp, 2022 (**70227**)

OSTROM, M. AND A. ERIKSSON. "Pedestrian Fatalities and Alcohol." *Accident Analysis and Prevention*, 33: 173–180, 2001 (**61404**)

OSUNA, E., M.D. PEREZ-CARCELES, M. MORENO, ET AL. "Vitreous Humor Carbohydrate-Deficient Transferrin Concentrations in the Postmortem Diagnosis of Alcoholism." *Forensic Science International*, 108: 205–213, 2000 **(70907)**

OUELLET, J.V., H.H. HURT JR., AND D.R. THOM. "Alcohol Involvement in Motorcycle Accidents." *SAE Technical Paper Series 870602*, 121–129, International Congress and Exposition, Detroit Michigan, 23–27 February 1987 **(61306)**

OXLEY, J., M. LENNE, AND B. CORBEN. "The Effect of Alcohol Impairment on Road-Crossing Behavior." *Transportation Research Part F*, 9: 258–268, 2006 **(61410)**

P

PACH, J., Z. MAREK, M. BOGUSZ, AND W. STASKO. "The Clinical Appearance and Blood Alcohol Level in Acute Poisoning and Blood Alcohol Level in Fatal Non-Treated Poisoning." *Acta Pharmacologica Toxicologica*, 41: 362–368, 1977 **(70402)**

PAJUNEN, T., E. VUORI, AND P. LUNETTA."Epidemiology of Alcohol-Related Unintentional Drowning: Is Post-mortem Ethanol Production a Real Challenge?" *Injury Epidemiology*, 5: 39, 5pp, 2018 **(70226)**

PALATNICK, W., L.W. REDMAN, D.S. SITAR, AND M. TENEBEIN. "Methanol Half-Life During Ethanol Administration: Implications for Management of Ethanol Poisoning." *Annals of Emergency Medicine*, 26: 202–207, 1995 **(80306)**

PALMENTIER, J.-P.F.P., R.M. LANGILLE, C.J. HOUSE, AND J. PATRICK. "Ambient Fail Exception Messages During Breath Testing of Suspected Impaired Drivers Using the Intoxilyzer 5000C: A 10-Year Retrospective Analysis." *Canadian Society of Forensic Science Journal*, 48: 46–57, 2015 **(30129)**

PALMENTIER, J-P F.P., J.G. WIGMORE, R.M. LANGILLE, AND J. PATRICK. "Incidence of Invalid Sample Screen Messages on the Intoxilyzer 5000C Obtained from Arrested Drinking Drivers in Toronto. Is a 15 to 20 Minute Wait Period Warranted?" *Canadian Society of Forensic Science Journal*, 39: 101–114, 2006 **(30507)**

PAPIERZ, P., J. BERENT, L. MARKUSZEWSKI, AND S. SZRAM. "A Comparative Study of the Ethyl Alcohol Concentration in Vitreous Humor in Relation to Ethyl Alcohol Concentration in Blood and Urine." *Problems of Forensic Science,* LVIII, 34–44, 2004 **(70609)**

PAPOZ, L., J. WEILL, Y. CHICH, ET AL. "Biological Markers of Alcohol Intake Among 4,796 Subjects Injured in Accidents." *British Medical Journal*, 292: 1234–1237, 1986 **(40501)**

PAPPAS, A.A., B.H. ACKERMAN, K.M. OLSEN, AND E.H. TAYLOR. "Isopropanol Ingestion: A Report of Six Episodes with Isopropanol and Acetone Serum Concentration Time Data." *Clinical Toxicology*, 29: 11–21, 1991 **(80402)**

PARK, C.H.K., S.H. YOO, J. LEE, ET AL. "Impact of Acute Alcohol Consumption on Lethality of Suicide Methods." *Comprehensive Psychiatry*, 75: 27–34, 2017 (**62018**)

PARKER, K.M. AND J.L. GREEN. "Delayed Ethanol Analysis of Breath Specimens: Long-Term Field Experience with Commercial Silica Gel Tubes and Breathalyzer Collection." *Journal of Forensic Science*, 35: 1353–1359, 1990 (**30705**)

PARROTT, D.J. AND P.R. GIANCOLA. "The Effect of Past-Year Heavy Drinking on Alcohol-Related Aggression." *Journal of Studies on Alcohol*, 67: 122–130, 2006 (**60104**)

PASIN, L.T. AND H. GJERDE. "Alcohol and Drug Use Among Road Users Involved in Fatal Crashes in Norway." *Traffic Injury Prevention*, 22: 267–271, 2021 (**50801**)

PATEL, M., F. MODIG, M. MASNUSSON, AND P.A. FRANSSON. "Alcohol Intoxication at 0.06 and 0.10% Blood Alcohol Concentration Changes Segmental Body Movement Coordination." *Experimental Brain Research*, 202: 431–443, 2010 (**60515**)

PEACHEY, J.E., D.H. ZILM, AND H. CAPPELL. "Burning Off the Antabuse: Fact or Fiction." *Lancet*, 943–944, 25 April 1981 (**80104**)

PEARN, J.H., A.E. PEDEN, AND R.C. FRANKLIN. "The Influence of Alcohol and Drugs on Drowning Among Victims of Senior Years." *Safety*, 5: 8, 10pp, 2019 (**60415**)

PEARSON, G.J. AND W.C. KEYS. "Local Dental Anaesthesia and Evidential Breath Testing: The Effect of Injection of Local Anaesthetic on Lip Seal." *Medicine, Science and the Law*, 29: 298–302, 1989 (**30310**)

PECK, R.C., M.A. GEBERS, R.B. VOAS, AND E. ROMANO. "The Relationship Between Blood Alcohol Concentration (BAC), Age, and Crash Risk." *Journal of Safety Research*, 39: 311–319, 2008 (**50504**)

PEEK-ASA, C. AND J.F. KRAUS. "Alcohol Use, Driver and Crash Characteristics Among Injured Motorcycle Drivers." *Journal of Trauma Injury and Infection, Critical Care*, 41: 989–993, 1996 (**61308**)

PEI, J., K. FLANNIGAN, S. KELLER, ET AL. "Fetal Alcohol Spectrum Disorder and the Criminal Justice System: A Research Summary." *Journal of Mental Health and Clinical Psychology*, 2: 48–52, 2018 (**90408**)

PELISSIER-ALICOT, A-L., N. COSTE, C. BARTOLI, ET AL. "Comparison of Ethanol Concentrations in Right Cardiac Blood, Left Cardiac Blood and Peripheral Blood in a Series of 30 Cases." *Forensic Science International*, 156: 35–39, 2006 (**70304**)

PELLA, P.A. AND B.I. DIAMONDSTORE. "Stability of Aqueous Ethanol Solutions Stored in Glass Ampules." *Journal of Forensic Science*, 20: 537–538, 1975 (**30206**)

PELLEGRINO, S., F.S. BRUNO, AND M. PETRARULO. "Liquid Chromatographic Determination of Ethyl Alcohol in Body Fluids." *Journal of Chromatography B*, 729: 103–110, 1999 (**20114**)

PELLETIER, A. "Deaths Among Railroad Trespassers.The Role of Alcohol in Fatal Injuries." *Journal of the American Medical Association*, 277: 1064–1066, 1997 **(61503)**

PENETAR, D.M., J.F. MCNEIL, E.T. RYAN, AND S.E. LUKAS. "Comparison Among Plasma, Serum, and Whole Blood Ethanol Concentrations: Impact of Storage Conditions and Collection Tubes." *Journal of Analytical Toxicology*, 32: 505–510, 2008 **(20206)**

PENNER, D.W. AND B.B. COLDWELL. "Car Driving and Alcohol Consumption: Medical Observations on an Experiment." *Canadian Medical Association Journal*, 79: 793–800, 1958 **(50611)**

PENNINGTON, J.C. "The Effect of Non-Ethanolic Substances on the Alcometer S-L2." *Canadian Society of Forensic Science Journal*, 28: 131–135, 1995 **(30617)**

PENTILLA, A., M. KATAJA, AND M. TENHU. "Examination Model for Suspected Drunken Drivers." *Blutalkohol,* 12: 24–38, 1975 **(50607)**

PEPINO, M.Y. AND J.A. MENNELLA, "Effects of Breast Pumping on the Pharmacokinetics and Pharmacodynamics of Ethanol During Lactation." *Clinical Pharmacology and Therapeutics*, 84: 710–714, 2008 **(40405)**

PEPINO, M.Y., A.L. STEINMEYER, AND J.A. MENNELLA. "Lactation State Modified Alcohol Pharmacokinetics in Women." *Alcoholism: Clinical and Experimental Research*, 31: 909–918, 2007 **(40406)**

PERESKA, Z., N. SIMONOVSKA, A. BABULOVSKA, ET AL. "Acute Severe Poisoning with Disinfectant in Senior Patient-Case Report and Overview of Literature Considering Age Influence on Treatment Decision in Alcohol-Based Intoxication." *SAGE Open Medical Case Reports*, 9: 1–6, 2021 **(70416)**

PERHAM, N., S.C. MOORE, J. SHEPHERD, AND B. CUSENS. "Identifying Drunkenness in the Night-Time Economy." *Addiction*, 102: 377–380, 2007 **(50605)**

PERNA, E.B.D.F., E.L. THEUNISSEN, K.P.C. KUYPERS, ET AL. "Subjective Aggression During Alcohol and Cannabis Intoxication Before and After Aggression Exposure." *Psychopharmacology*, 233: 331–334, 2016 **(60121)**

PERPER, J.A., A. TWERSKI, AND J.W. WIENAND. "Tolerance at High Blood Alcohol Concentrations: A Study of 110 Cases and Review of Literature." *Journal of Forensic Sciences*, 31: 212–221, 1986 **(50612)**

PERRINE, W. "Alcohol and Highway Crashes. Closing the Gap Between Epidemiology and Experimentation." *Modern Problems Pharmacopsychology*, 11: 22–41, 1976 **(50404)**

PERRINE, M.W., J.C. MUNDT, AND R.I. WEINER. "When Alcohol and Water Don't Mix: Diving Under the Influence." *Journal of Studies on Alcohol*, 55: 517–524, 1994 **(60404)**

PERRINO JR., A.C., E. RALEVSKI, G. ACAMPORA, ET AL. "Ethanol and Pain Sensitivity: Effects in Healthy Subjects Using an Acute Pain Paradigm." *Alcoholism: Clinical and Experimental Research,* 32: 952–958, 2008 **(61212)**

PERRY, P.J., T.R. ARGO, M.J. BARNETT, ET AL. "The Association of Alcohol-Induced Blackouts and Grayouts to Blood Alcohol Concentrations." *Journal of Forensic Sciences*, 51: 896–899, 2006 **(60305)**

PETKOVIC, S., S. SAVIC, D. ZGONJANIN, AND I. SAMOJLIK. "Ethanol Concentrations in Antemortem Blood Samples Under Controlled Conditions." *Alcohol and Alcoholism*, 43: 658–660, 2008 **(20304)**

PETTIGREW, S., C. HAFEKOST, M. JONGENELIS, ET AL. "Behind Closed Doors: The Priorities of the Alcohol Industry as Communicated in a Trade Magazine." *Frontiers in Public Health*, 6: Article 217, 8pp, 2018 **(90512)**

PFEIFER, P., C. BARTSCH, A. HEMMER, AND T. REISCH. "Acute and Chronic Alcohol Use Correlated with Methods of Suicide in a Swiss National Sample." *Drug and Alcohol Dependence*, 178: 75–79, 2017 **(90108)**

PHILLIPS, J.C., R.P. OGEIL, AND F. MULLER. "Alcohol Consumption and Handwriting: A Kinematic Analysis." *Human Movement Science*, 29: 619–632, 2009 **(61214)**

PHILLIPS, M., J. GREENBERG, AND J. ANDRZEJEWSKI. "Evaluation of the Alcopatch, A Transdermal Dosimeter for Monitoring Alcohol Consumption." *Alcoholism: Clinical and Experimental Research*, 19: 1547–1549, 1995 **(40302)**

PHILLIPS, S., J. MATUSKO, AND E. TOMASOVIC. "Reconsidering the Relationship Between Alcohol and Lethal Violence." *Journal of Interpersonal Violence*, 22(1): 66–84, 2007 **(60915)**

PIETTE, M., L. DECOMINCK, J. TIMPERMAN, F. THOMAS, AND W. MAJELYNE. "Correlation Between Postmortem Ethanol Levels in the Blood and Testicle." *Zeitschrift fur Rechtsmedizin*, 88: 39–48, 1982 **(70813)**

PITTLER, M.H., A.R. WHITE, C. STEVINSON, AND E. ERNST. "Effectiveness of Artichoke Extract in Preventing Alcohol-Induced Hangovers: A Randomized Controlled Trial." *Canadian Medical Association Journal*, 169: 1269–1273, 2003 **(60807)**

PLUECKHAHN, V.D. "The Significance of Alcohol and Sugar Determinations in Autopsy Blood." *Medical Journal of Australia*, 46–51, 10 January 1970 **(70201)**

———. "The Significance of Blood Alcohol Levels at Autopsy." *Medical Journal of Australia*, 118–124, 15 July 1967 **(70202)**

PLUECKHAHN, V.D. AND B. BALLARD. "Diffusion of Stomach Alcohol and Heart Blood Alcohol Concentration at Autopsy." *Journal of Forensic Science*, 12: 463–470, 1967 **(70301)**

PODSTAWSKI, R., E. WESOLOWSKA, AND D. CHOSZCZ. "Empty Alcohol Containers and Breath Alcohol Analysis Measures of Alcohol Consumption at a College

Volleyball Championship." *Journal of Studies on Alcohol and Drugs*, 76: 152–157, 2015 **(61916)**

POIKOLAINEN, K., K. LEPPANEN, AND E. VUORI. "Alcohol Sales and Fatal Alcohol Poisonings: A Time-Series Analysis." *Addiction,* 97: 1037–1040, 2002 **(70409)**

POKLIS, J.L., C.E. WOLF II, AND M.R. PEACE. "Ethanol Concentration in 56 Refillable Electronic Cigarettes Liquid Formulations Determined by Headspace Gas Chromatography with Flame Ionization Detector (HS-GC-FID)." *Drug Testing and Analysis*, 9: 1637–1640, 2017 **(30524)**

POLITI, L., L. MORINI, F. MARI, ET AL. "Ethyl Glucuronide and Ethyl Sulfate in Autopsy Samples 27 Years after Death." *International Journal of Legal Medicine*, 122: 507–509, 2008 **(70905)**

POLLACK JR, C.V., R.C. JORDEN, F.B. CARLTON, AND M.L. BAKER. "Gastric Emptying in the Acutely Inebriated Patient." *Journal of Emergency Medicine*, 10: 1–5, 1992 **(10105)**

POLLISSAR, N. L., W. SUWANVIJIT, AND R.G. GULLBERG. "The Accuracy of Handheld Pre-Arrest Breath Test Instruments as a Predictor of the Evidential Breath Alcohol Test Results." *Journal of Forensic Sciences*, 60: 482–487, 2015 **(30127)**

PORCEL, F.J. AND H.S. SCHUTTA. "From Antiquity to the N-Methyl-D-Aspartate Receptor: A History of Delirium Tremens." *Journal of the History of Neurosciences*, 24: 378–395, 2015 **(90201)**

POTOCKA-BANAS, B.K., T. JANUS, AND S. MAJDANIK. "Expert Opinions Concerning Breath Testing After Consumption of Chocolates Filled with Alcohol and Selected Preparations Containing Alcohol." *Problems of Forensic Science,* 75: 256–267, 2008 **(30529)**

POULSEN, H., R. MOAR, AND C. TRONCOSO. "The Incidence of Alcohol and Other Drugs in Drivers Killed in New Zealand Road Crashes 2004–2009." *Forensic Science International*, 223: 364–370, 2012 **(50804)**

PRESSMAN, M.R. AND D.S. CAUDILL. "Alcohol-Induced Blackout as a Criminal Defense or Mitigating Factor: An Evidence-Based Review and Admissibility as Scientific Evidence." *Journal of Forensic Sciences*, 58: 932–940, 2013 **(60313)**

PREUSSER, D.F. AND R.D. BLOMBERG. "Pedestrians and Alcohol." *Abstracts and Reviews in Alcohol and Driving*, 2: 6–10, 1981 **(61405)**

PREUSSER, D.F., A.F. WILLIAMS, AND R.G. ULMER. "Analysis of Fatal Motorcycle Crashes: Crash Typing." *Accident Analysis and Prevention*, 27:845–851, 1995 **(61310)**

PRIDEMORE, W.A. "Weekend Effects on Binge Drinking and Homicide: The Social Connection Between Alcohol and Violence in Russia." *Addiction* 99: 1034–1041, 2004 **(60914)**

PROBST, C., J. MANTHEY, A. MARTINEZ, AND J. REHM. "Alcohol Use Disorder Severity and Reported Reasons Not to Seek Treatment: A Cross-Sectional Study in European Primary Care Practices." *Substance Abuse Treatment, Prevention and Policy*, 10: 32, 10pp, 2015 **(90105)**

PZAVLIC, M., K. LIBISELLER, P. GRUBWEISER, ET AL. "Another Soberade on the Market: Does Outox Keep Its Promise?" *Wiener Klinische Wochenschrift*, 119: 104–111, 2007 **(10720)**

Q

QUIGLEY, B.M., K.E. LEONARD, AND R.L. COLLINS. "Characteristics of Violent Bars and Bar Patrons." *Journal of Studies on Alcohol*, 64: 765–772, 2003 **(60107)**

QUILLAN, W.C., D.J. COX, B.P. KOVATCHEV, AND C. PHILLIPS. "The Effects of Age and Alcohol Intoxication on Simulated Driving Performance, Awareness and Self-Restraint." *Age and Aging*, 28: 59–66, 1999 **(50209)**

QUINTAS, M.J., P. COSTA, P. MELO, ET AL. "Postmortem In Vitro Ethanol Production—It Could Be More Common Than We Think!" *Forensic Science International*, 247: 113–116, 2017 **(70229)**

R

RAINO, J., S. AHOLA, P. KANGASTUPA, ET AL. "Comparison of Ethyl Glucuronide and Carbohydrate-Deficient Transferrin in Different Body Fluids for Post-Mortem Identification of Alcohol Use." *Alcohol and Alcoholism*, 49: 55–59, 2014 **(70912)**

RAKAUSKAS, M.E., N.J. WARD, E.R. BOER, ET AL. "Combined Effects of Alcohol and Distraction on Driving Performance." *Accident Analysis and Prevention*, 40: 1742–1749, 2008 **(50205)**

RAMER, L., M. TIHY, N. GOOSSENS, ET AL. "Disulfiram-Induced Acute Liver Injury." *Case Reports in Hepatology*, Article ID 8835647, 4pp, 2020 **(80110)**

RAN, R. AND M.E. MULLINS. "Can Handling E85 Motor Fuel Cause Positive Breath Alcohol Test Results?" *Journal of Analytical Toxicology*, 37: 430–432, 2013 **(30621)**

RASH, C.J., N.M. PETRY, S.M. ALESSI, AND N.P. BARNETT. "Monitoring Alcohol Use in Heavy Drinking Soup Kitchen Attendees." *Alcohol*, 81: 139–147, 2019 **(40313)**

RAWAT, B.R. "Head Space Gas Chromatography (GC-HS) Analysis of Postmortem Unpreserved Blood Samples and Identification of Volatiles Produced." *The Indian Police Journal*, 55: 36–45, 2008 **(70105)**

RAZATOS, G., R. LUTHI, AND S. KERRIGAN. "Evaluation of a Portable Evidential Breath Alcohol Analyzer." *Forensic Science International*, 153: 17–21, 2005 **(30109)**

RAZVODOVSKY, Y.E. "Alcohol, and Suicide in Belarus." *Psychiatria Danubina*, 21: 290–296, 2009 **(90504)**

REDELMEIER, D.A. AND F. MANZOOR. "Life-Threatening Alcohol-Related Traffic Crashes in Adverse Weather: A Double-Matched Case-Control Analysis from Canada." *British Medical Journal,* 9: e024415, 7pp, 2019 **(50514)**

REDELMEIER, D.A. AND C.L.STEWART. "Driving Fatalities on Super Bowl Sunday." *New England Journal of Medicine*, 348: 368–369, 2003 **(61913)**

REFAAI, M.A., P.N. NGUYEN, T.S. STEFFENSEN, ET AL. "Liver and Adipose Tissue Fatty Acid Ethyl Esters Obtained at Autopsy Are Postmortem Markers for Premortem Ethanol Intake." *Clinical Chemistry*, 48: 77–83, 2002 **(70908)**

REILING, D.M. AND M.R. NUSBAUMER. "An Exploration of the Potential Impact of the Designated Driver Campaign on Bartenders' Willingness to Over-serve." *International Journal of Drug Policies*, 18: 458–463, 2007 **(50715)**

REILLY, T. AND F. HALLIDAY. "Influence of Alcohol Ingestion on Tasks Related to Archery." *Journal of Human Ergology*, 14: 99–104, 1985 **(61904)**

REILLY, T. AND J. SCOTT. "Effects of Elevating Blood Alcohol Levels on Tasks Relating to Dart Throwing." *Perceptual and Motor Skills*, 77: 25–26, 1993 **(61905)**

REISFIELD, G.M., B.A. GOLDBERGER, B.O. CREWS, ET AL. "Ethyl Glucuronide, Ethyl Sulfate, and Ethanol in Urine After Intensive Exposure to High Ethanol Content Mouthwash." *Journal of Analytical Toxicology,* 35: 264–268, 2011 **(40518)**

REISH, L., L.M. CARSON, AND A.F. RAY. "Associations Between Social Drinking Events and Pedestrian Behavior—An Observational Study." *Journal of Transport and Health,* 20: 8pp, 2021 **(61412)**

RETTING, R.A., R.G. ULMER, AND A.F. WILLIAMS. "Prevalence and Characteristics of Red-Light Running Crashes in the United States." *Accident Analysis and Prevention,* 31: 687–694, 1999 **(50507)**

RHEE, S.-J., J-W. CHAE, B-J SONG, ET AL. "Effect of Dissolved Oxygen in Alcoholic Beverages and Drinking Water on Alcohol Elimination in Humans." *Alcohol*, 47: 27–30, 2013 **(10721)**

RIDLEY, N.J., B. DRAPER, AND A. WITHALL. "Alcohol-Related Dementia: An Update of the Evidence." *Alzheimer's Research and Therapy*, 5: 3, 8 pp, 2013 **(90311)**

RIDOUT, F., S. GOULD, C. NUNES, AND I. HINDMARCH. "The Effects of Carbon Dioxide in Champagne on Psychometric Performance and Blood-Alcohol Concentration." *Alcohol and Alcoholism*, 38: 381–385, 2003 **(10109)**

RIEMANN, R., R. VOLK, A. MULLER, AND M. HERZOG. "The Influence of Nocturnal Alcohol Ingestion on Snoring." *European Archives Otorhinolaryngology*, 267:1147–1156, 2010 **(61217)**

RIFAAT, S.M., R. TAY, AND A. DE BARROS. "Severity of Motorcycle Crashes in Calgary." *Accident Analysis and Prevention*, 49: 44–49, 2012 **(61312)**

RIGGS, J.E., J.L. FROST, AND S.S. SCHOCHET JR. "Ethanol Level Differential Between Postmortem Blood and Subdural Hematoma." *Military Medicine*, 163: 722–724, 1998 **(70504)**

RILEY, D., J.G. WIGMORE, AND B. YEN. "Dilution of Blood Collected for Medico-legal Alcohol Analysis by Intravenous Fluids." *Journal of Analytical Toxicology,* 20: 330–331, 1996 **(10809)**

RIMM, D., D. BRIDDELL, M. ZIMMERMAN, AND G. CADDY. "The Effects of Alcohol and the Expectancy of Alcohol on Snake Fear." *Addictive Behaviours*, 6: 47–51, 1981 **(61206)**

RITZ-TIMME, S., M. THORNE, G. GRUTTERS, ET AL. "What Shall We Do with the Drunken Sailor? Effects of Alcohol on the Performance of Ship Operators." *Forensic Science International*, 156: 16–22, 2006 **(61103)**

ROBERTS, C. AND S.P. ROBINSON. "Alcohol Concentration and Carbonation of Drinks: The Effect on Blood Alcohol Levels." *Journal of Forensic and Legal Medicine,* 14: 398–405, 2007 **(10110)**

ROBERTSON, A.A., H. LIEW, AND S. GARDNER. "An Evaluation of the Narrowing Gender Gap in DUI Arrests." *Accident Analysis and Prevention*, 43: 1414–1420, 2011 **(50515)**

ROBINSON, D.W. AND D.S. REIVE. "A Gas Chromatographic Procedure of Quantitation of Ethylene Glycol in Postmortem Blood." *Journal of Analytical Toxicology*, 5: 69–72, 1981 **(80501)**

RODDA, L.N., J. BEYER, D. GEROSTAMOULOS, AND O.H. DRUMMER. "Alcohol Congener Analysis and the Source of Alcohol: A Review." *Forensic Science, Medicine, and Pathology,* 9: 194–207, 2013 **(60811)**

RODDA, L.N., S. PEARRING, C.E. HARPER, ET AL. "Inferences and Legal Considerations Following a Blood Collection Tube Recall." *Journal of Analytical Toxicology*, 4pp, 2020 **(20320)**

RODHE, A. AND A. ERIKSSON. "Sauna Deaths in Sweden, 1992–2003." *American Journal of Forensic Medicine and Pathology*, 29: 27–31, 2008 **(61605)**

ROGDE, S., H.P. HOUGEN, AND K. POULSEN. "Homicide by Blunt Force in 2 Scandinavian Capitals." *American Journal of Forensic Medicine and Pathology*, 24: 288–291, 2003 **(60905)**

ROGDE, S. AND J.H. OLVING. "Characteristics of Fire Victims in Different Sorts of Fires." *Forensic Science International*, 77: 93–99, 1996 **(60606)**

ROHNER C., S. FRANCKENBERG, N. SCHWENDENER, ET AL. "New Evidence for Old Lore—Urinary Bladder Distension on Post-Mortem Computed Tomography Is Related to Intoxication." *Forensic Science International*, 225: 48–52, 2013 **(70708)**

ROHRBAUGH, J.W., W. STAPLETON, R. PARASURAMAN, ET AL. "Alcohol Intoxication Reduces Visual Sustained Attention." *Psychopharmacology*, 96: 442–446, 1988 **(50106)**

ROHSENOW, D.J., J. HOWLAND, S. MINSKY, AND J.T. ARNEDT. "Effects of Heavy Drinking by Maritime Academy Cadets on Hangover, Perceived Sleep, and

Next-Day Ship Power Plant Operation." *Journal of Studies on Alcohol*, 67: 406–415, 2006 **(61105)**

ROINE, R.P., C.J.P. ERIKSSON, R. YLIKAHRI, ET AL. "Methanol as a Marker of Alcohol Abuse." *Alcoholism: Clinical and Experimental Research*, 13: 172–175, 1989 **(40504)**

ROINE, R.P., T.G. GENTRY, R.T. LIM JR., ET AL. "Comparison of Blood Alcohol Concentrations After Beer and Whiskey." *Alcoholism: Clinical and Experimental Research*, 17: 709–711, 1993 **(10113)**

ROINE, R.P., U.M. KORRI, R. YLIKAHRI, ET AL. "Increased Serum Acetate as Marker of Problem Drinking Among Drunken Drivers." *Alcohol and Alcoholism*, 23: 123–126, 1988 **(40503)**

ROINE, R., O.J. LUURILAS, A. SUOKAS, ET AL. "Alcohol and Sauna Bathing: Effects on Cardiac Rhythm, Blood Pressure, and Serum Electrolyte and Cortisol Concentrations." *Journal of Internal Medicine*, 231: 333–338, 1992 **(61602)**

ROMAIN-GLASSEY, N., M. GUTT, A-S. FEINER, ET AL. "When Nightclub Security Agents Assault Clients." *Journal of Forensic and Legal Medicine,* 19: 341–344, 2012 **(60118)**

ROSANO, T.G., T.A. SWIFT, C.J. KRANICK, AND M. SIKIRICA. "Ethylene Glycol and Glycolic Acid in Postmortem Blood From Fatal Poisonings."*Journal of Analytical Toxicology*, 33: 508–513, 2009 **(80503)**

ROSLAND, M., J. MONTPETIT, AND V. MENDES. "Practical Use of Commercially Available Compressed (Dry Gas) Alcohol Standards." *Canadian Society of Forensic Science Journal*, 50: 197–207, 2017 **(30213)**

ROSLAND, M. AND R. PON. "A Statistical Evaluation of Calibration Check Intervals." *Canadian Society of Forensic Science Journal*, 43: 41–46, 2010 **(30215)**

ROSS, L.E. AND J.C. MUNDT. "Multiattribute Modeling Analysis of the Effects of a Low Blood Alcohol Level on Pilot Performance." *Human Factors*, 30: 293–304, 1988 **(60702)**

ROSS, L.E., L.M. YEAZEL, AND A.W. CHAU. "Pilot Performance with Blood Alcohol Concentrations Below 0.04%." *Aviation, Space and Environmental Medicine*, 63: 951–956, 1992 **(60703)**

ROTHSCHILD, M.A. AND V. SCHNEIDER. "Terminal Burrowing Behaviour—A Phenomenon of Lethal Hypothermia." *International Journal of Legal Medicine*, 107: 250–256, 1995 **(61009)**

ROWE, B. AND G. BOTA. "Serious Snowmobile Trauma in a Northern Ontario Community: A Case Series." *Annals of the Royal College of Physicians and Surgeons of Canada*, 24: 501–505, 1991 **(61802)**

ROWE, B., R. MILMNER, C. JOHNSON, AND G. BOTA. "The Association of Alcohol and Night Driving with Fatal Snowmobile Trauma: A Case-Control Study." *Annals of Emergency Medicine*, 24: 842–848, 1994 **(61804)**

ROWE, B.H., S.A. THERRIEN, J.A. BRETZLAFF, ET AL. "The Effect of a Community-Based Police Surveillance Program on Snowmobile Injuries and Deaths." *Canadian Journal of Public Health,* 89: 57–61, 1998 **(61807)**

ROY, M., B. BAILEY, D. CHALUT, ET AL. "What Are the Adverse Effects of Ethanol Used as an Antidote in the Treatment of Suspected Methanol Poisoning in Children?" *Journal of Toxicology and Clinical Toxicology*, 41: 155–161, 2003 **(80311)**

RUDRAM, D.A. "The Incidence of Clotted Blood Samples in Road Safety Act Cases." *Journal of Forensic Science Society*, 14: 19–22, 1974 **(20115)**

RUITER, J.E., F. WEINBERG, AND A. MORRISON. "The Stability of Glucose in Serum." *Clinical Chemistry*, 9: 356–359, 1963 **(20311)**

RYAU, Y., D. BARCELO, L.P. BARRON, ET AL. "Comparative Measurement and Quantitative Assessment of Alcohol Consumption Through Wastewater-Based Epidemiology: An International Study in 20 Cities." *Science of the Total Environment*, 565: 977–983, 2016 **(40531)**

RYDER, K.W. AND M.R. GLICK. "The Effect of Skin Cleansing Agents on Ethanol Results Measured with the Du Pont Automatic Clinical Analyzer." *Journal of Forensic Science*, 31: 574–579, 1986 **(20407)**

RYU, J., K.H. LIM, D-R. RYU, ET AL. "Two Cases of Methyl Alcohol Intoxication by Sub-Chronic Inhalation and Dermal Exposure During Aluminum, CNC Cutting in a Small-Sized Subcontracted Factory." *Annals of Occupational and Environmental Medicine,* 28: 65–72, 2016 **(80319)**

S

SAITZ, R. "Introduction to Alcohol Withdrawal." *Alcohol Health and Research World*, 22: 5–12, 1998 **(90203)**

SAKAI, J.T., S.K. MIKULICH-GILBERTSON, R.J. LONG, AND T.J. CROWLEY. "Validity of Transdermal Alcohol Monitoring: Fixed and Self-Regulated Dosing." *Alcoholism: Clinical and Experimental Research*, 30: 26–33, 2006 **(40305)**

SALASPURO, M.K., K.O. LINDROS, AND P.H. PIKKARAINEN. "Effect of 4-Methylpyrazole on Ethanol Elimination Rate and Hepatic Redox Changes in Alcoholics with Adequate or Inadequate Nutrition and in Nonalcoholic Controls." *Metabolism, Clinical and Experimental,* 27: 631–639, 1978 **(10705)**

SANJEEWA, R.H.K., D.G. VAN PITTISU, AND M. VIDANAPATHIRANA. "Sudden Unexpected Death in Alcohol Misuse: A Case Report." *Medico-Legal Journal of Sri Lanka*, 6: 43–46, 2018 **(90316)**

SANTTILA, P., M. EKHOLM, AND P. NIEMI. "The Effects of Alcohol on Interrogative Suggestibility: The Role of State-Anxiety and Mood States as Mediating Factors." *Legal Criminological Psychology*, 4: 1–13, 1999 **(60310)**

SANTUNIONE, A.L., P. VERRI, F. MARCHESI, ET AL. "The Role of Ethyl Glucuronide in Supporting Medico-Legal Investigations: Analysis of This Biomarker in Different Postmortem Specimens from 21 Selected Autopsy Cases." *Journal of Forensic and Legal Medicine*, 53: 25–30, 2018 **(70913)**

SASTRE, C., V. BAILLIF-COUNION, F. MUSCARELLA, ET AL. "Can Subclavian Blood Be Equated with a Peripheral Blood Sample? A Series of 50 Cases." *International Journal of Legal Medicine*, 127: 379–384, 2013 **(70312)**

SAVINI, F., A. TARTAGLIA, L. COCCIA, ET AL. "Ethanol Determination in Post-Mortem Samples: Correlation Between Blood and Vitreous Humor Concentration." *Molecules*, 25: 2724, 9pp, 2020 **(70611)**

SAVOLA, O., O. NIEMELA, AND M. HILLBOM. "Blood Alcohol Is the Best Indicator of Hazardous Alcohol Drinking in Young Adults and Working-Age Patients with Trauma." *Alcohol and Alcoholism*, 39: 340–345, 2004 **(40502)**

SAVOLAINEN, P. AND F. MANNERING. "Probabilistic Models of Motorcyclists' Injury Severities in Single- and Multi-Vehicle Crashes." *Accident Analysis and Prevention*, 39: 955–963, 2007 **(61311)**

SAVOLAINEN, V.T., K. LIESTO, A. MANNIKKO, ET AL. "Alcohol Consumption and Alcoholic Liver Disease: Evidence of a Threshold Level of Effects of Ethanol." *Alcoholism: Clinical and Experimental Research*, 17: 1112–1117, 1993 **(90315)**

SAYETTE, M.A., E.D. REICHLE, AND J.W. SCHOOLER. "Lost in the Sauce. The Effects of Alcohol on Mind Wandering." *Psychological Science*, 20: 747–752, 2009 **(61215)**

SAYETTE, M.A., G.T. WILSON, AND M.J. ELIAS. "Alcohol and Aggression: A Social Information Processing Analysis." *Journal of Studies on Alcohol*, 54: 399–407, 1993 **(60101)**

SCHAFFER, K.B., G. SCHWENDIG, F. NASRALLAH, ET AL. "Falls from a Balcony While Intoxicated: A New Injury Among Young Adults?" *Injury Epidemiology*, 6: 4, 6pp, 2019 **(60522)**

SCHLOEGL, H., S. DRESEN, K. SPACZYNSKI, ET AL. "Stability of Ethyl Glucuronide in Urine, Post-Mortem Tissue and Blood Samples." *International Journal of Legal Medicine*, 120: 83–88, 2006 **(70904)**

SCHMAL, F., R. KUNZ, C. ORTMANN, ET AL. "Effect of Ethanol on Dynamic and Visual Acuity During Vertical Body Oscillation in Healthy Volunteers." *European Archives Otorhinolaryngology*, 257: 485–489, 2000 **(50101)**

SCHMINKE, L.H., V. JEGER, D.S. EVANELOPOULOS, ET AL. "Riding the Escalator: How Dangerous Really?" *Western Journal of Medicine*, 14: 141–145, 2013 **(60521)**

SCHOLZ, C., M.R. BAUMGARTNER, AND M.M. MADRY. "Use of Ethanol-Based Hand Disinfectants: Source of Increased Ethyl Glucuronide Levels in Hair?" *Alcohol and Alcoholism*, 1–4, 2020 **(40529)**

SCHMITT, G., P. DROENNER, G. SKOPP, AND R. ADERJAN. "Ethyl Glucuronide Concentration in Serum of Human Volunteers Teetotalers, and Suspected Drinking Drivers." *Journal of Forensic Science*, 42: 1099–1102, 1997 **(40507)**

SCHNEIR, A.B. AND R.F. CLARK. "Death Caused by Ingestion of an Ethanol-Based Hand Sanitizer." *Journal of Emergency Medicine*, 1–3, 2013 **(70415)**

SCHROT, M., K. PUSCHEL, AND C. EDLER. "Drunken by a Bath in Champagne?—Error: No Relevant Ethanol Absorption Through Intact Skin [German]." *Blutalkohol*, 47: 275–281, 2010 **(10123)**

SCHUETZE, P., R.D. EIDEN, AND A.W.K. CHAN. "The Effects of Alcohol in Breast Milk on Infant Behavioral State and Mother-Infant Feeding Interactions." *Infancy*, 3: 349–363, 2002 **(40404)**

SCHUSTER, R., G. SCHEWE, O. LUDWIG, ET AL. "Driving Tests on Alcohol-Caused Unsafe Driving at Night [German]." *Blutalkohol,* 28: 287–301, 1991 **(50307)**

SCHWARTZ, R.H., R. MILTEER, M.J. SHERIDAN, AND C.P. HORNER. "Beach Week: A High School Graduation Rite of Passage for Sun Sand, Suds and Sex." *Archives of Pediatric and Adolescent Medicine*, 153: 180–183, 1999 **(61704)**

SCOTT, C.L. "Evaluating Amnesia for Criminal Behavior: A Guide to Remember." *Psychiatric Clinics of North America,* 35: 797–819, 2012 **(60315)**

SCOTT, W., I. ROOT, AND B. SANBORN. "The Use of Vitreous Humor for Determination of Ethyl Alcohol in Previously Embalmed Bodies." *Journal of Forensic Science*, 9: 913–916, 1974 **(70607)**

SCOTT-HAM, M. AND F.C. BURTON. "A Study of Blood and Urine Alcohol Concentration in Cases of Alleged Drug-Facilitated Sexual Assault in the United Kingdom Over a 3-Year Period." *Journal of Clinical Forensic Medicine*, 13: 107–111, 2006 **(61706)**

SCRADER, J., M. ROTHE, AND F. PRAGST. "Ethyl Glucuronide Concentrations in Beard Hair After a Single Alcohol Dose: Evidence for Incorporation in Hair Root." *International Journal of Legal Medicine*, 126: 791–799, 2012 **(40524)**

SECCOMBE, L.M., P.G. ROGERS, L. BUBBLE, ET AL. "The Impact of Severe Lung Disease on Evidential Breath Analysis Collection." *Science and Justice*, 56: 256–259, 2016 **(30314)**

SEIDENBERG, A.B., K.P. WISEMAN, R.H. ECK, ET AL. "Awareness of Alcohol as a Carcinogen and Support for Alcohol Control Policies." *American Journal of Preventive Medicine*, 62: 174–182, 2022 **(90508)**

SENDLER, D.J. "Physicians Working Under the Influence of Alcohol: An Analysis of Past Disciplinary Proceedings and Their Outcomes." *Forensic Science International* 285: 29–37, 2018 **(61222)**

SENKOWSKI, C.M. AND K.A. THOMPSON. "The Accuracy of Blood Alcohol Analysis Using Automated Headspace Gas Chromatography When Performed on Clotted Samples." *Journal of Forensic Science*, 35: 176–180, 1990 **(20104)**

SETHI, M., J. HEYER, S. WALL, ET AL. "Alcohol Use by Urban Bicyclists Is Associated with More Severe Injury, Greater Hospital Resource Use, and Higher Mortality." *Alcohol,* 53: 1–7, 2016 **(60209)**

SHAJANI, N.K., B.A. IMAGE, AND E.B. CHU. "The Stability of Ethanol in Stored Forensic Blood Samples." *Canadian Society of Forensic Science Journal*, 22: 335–339, 1989 **(20302)**

SHAN, X., N.B. TISCIONE, I. ALFORD, AND D.T. YEATMAN. "A Study of Blood Alcohol Stability in Forensic Antemortem Blood Samples." *Forensic Science International*, 211: 47–50, 2011 **(20313)**

SHAPOVALOV, K. A. "Injuries of the Floating Crew of the Northern Water Pool in a State of Alcohol Intoxication." *International Maritime Health*, 64: 41–50, 2013 **(61110)**

SHARMA, A. AND J.D. MORROW. "Isopropyl Alcohol Swabs as a Preferred Substance of Abuse." *Journal of Psychoactive Drugs*, 49: 258–261, 2017 **(80409)**

SHARP, D. "Safe Bubbly [Comment]." *Lancet*, 364: 2165, 2004 **(61220)**

SHEPHERD, J., M. IRISH, C. SCULLY, AND I. LESLIE. "Alcohol Intoxication and Severity of Injury in Victims of Assault." *British Medical Journal*, 296: 1299, 1988 **(60106)**

SHIELDS, L.B.E., D.M. HUNSAKER, J.C. HUNSAKER III, AND M.K. WARD. "Toxicologic Findings in Suicide. A 10-Year Retrospective Review of Kentucky Medical Examiner Cases." *American Journal of Forensic Medicine and Pathology*, 27: 106–112, 2006 **(62012)**

SHIELDS, L.B.E., J.C. HUNSAKER III, AND D.M. STEWART. "Russian Roulette and Risk-Taking Behavior. A Medical Examiner Study." *American Journal of Forensic Medicine and Pathology*, 29: 32–39, 2008 **(62013)**

SHITAI, Y., T. TSUDA, S. KITAGAWA, ET AL. "Alcohol Ingestion Stimulated Mosquito Attraction." *Journal of American Mosquito Control Association*, 18: 91–96, 2002 **(61201)**

SIDORENKOV, O., O. NILSSEN, N. KLESCHINOV, AND A.M. GRIBOVSKI. "Premature Cardiovascular Mortality and Alcohol Consumption Before Death in Arkhangelsk, Russia: An Analysis of a Consecutive Series of Forensic Autopsies." *International Journal of Epidemiology*, 40: 1519–1529, 2011 **(90303)**

SILVERMAN, L.D., K. WONG, AND S. MILLER. "Confirmation of Ethanol Compressed Gas Standard Concentrations by an NIST-Traceable, Absolute Chemical Method and Comparison with Wet Breath Alcohol Simulators." *Journal of Analytical Toxicology*, 21: 369–372, 1997 **(30210)**

SIMIC, M., N. AJDUKOVIC, I. VESELINOVIC, ET AL. "Endogenous Ethanol Production in Patients with Diabetes Mellitus as a Medicolegal Problem." *Forensic Science International*, 216: 97–100, 2012 **(20507)**

SINGER, P.P., G.R. JONES, R. LEWIS, AND R. JOHNSON. "Loss of Ethanol from Vitreous Humor in Drowning Deaths." *Journal of Analytical Toxicology*, 31: 522–525, 2007 **(70606)**

SINKIEWICZ, W., M. WEGLARZ, AND M. CHUDZIRISKA. "Wine, Alcohol and Cardiovascular Disease." *Kardiologia Polska*, 72: 771–776, 2014 **(90301)**

SIVILOTTI, M.L.A., M.J. BURNS, K.E. MCMARTIN, AND J. BRENT. "Toxicokinetics of Ethylene Glycol During Fomepizole Therapy: Implications for Management." *Annals of Emergency Medicine*, 36: 114–125, 2000 **(80508)**

SJOBERG, L. "Alcohol and Gambling." *Psychopharmacology*, 14: 284–298, 1969 **(61205)**

SLADE, M., L.J. DANIEL, AND C.J. HEISLER. "Application of Forensic Toxicology to the Problem of Domestic Violence." *Journal of Forensic Science,* 36: 708–713, 1991 **(60908)**

SLAMA, G., F. BRUZZO, J.P. DUPEYRON, ET AL. "Ketone Bodies Do Not Give Falsely Positive Alcohol Tests." *Diabetic Medicine*, 6: 142–143, 1989 **(30603)**

SMART, R.G. AND R.E. MANN. "Causes and Consequences of Air Rage in Canada." *Canadian Journal of Public Health*, 94: 251–253, 2003 **(60113)**

SMIALEK, J.E., W.U. SPITZ, AND J.A. WOLFE. "Ethanol in Intracerebral Clot: Report of Two Homicidal Cases Involving Prolonged Survival After Injury." *American Journal of Forensic Medicine and Pathology*, 1: 149–150, 1980 **(70503)**

SMITH, F.J. AND D. HARRIS. "Effects of Low Blood Alcohol Levels on Pilots' Prioritization of Tasks During a Radio Navigation Task." *International Journal of Aviation Psychology*, 4: 349–358, 1994 **(60701)**

SMITH, G.S., P.M. KEYL, J.A. HADLEY, ET AL. "Drinking and Recreational Boating Fatalities. A Population-Based Case-Control Study." *Journal of the American Medical Association*, 286: 2974–2980, 2001 **(60408)**

SMOPLLE, K.H., G. HOFMANN, P. KAUFMANN, ET AL. "Q.E.D. Alcohol Tests: A Simple and Quick Method to Detect Ethanol in Saliva of Patients in Emergency Departments." *Intensive Care Medicine,* 25: 492–495, 1999 **(40204)**

SMREKAR, M., S. CUKLIEK, A.M. HOSNIAK, ET AL. "Alcoholism: Success of Long-Term Treatment—a Systematic Review." *Croatian Nursing Journal*, 2: 63–71, 2018 **(90111)**

SOLNICK, S.J. AND D. HEMENWAY. "The Hit and Run in Fatal Pedestrian Accidents: Victims, Circumstances and Drivers. Accident." *Analysis and Prevention,* 27: 643–649, 1995 **(61407)**

SOMMERS, M.S., J.M. DYEHOUSE, S.R. HOWE, ET AL. "Nurse, I Only Had a Couple of Beers: Validity of Self-Reported Drinking Before Serious Vehicular Injury." *American Journal of Critical Care*, 11: 106–114, 2002 **(10607)**

SOUSA, A.P., D.N. VIEIRA, M.M.F. OLIVEIRA, ET AL. "Comparison Between Ethanol Levels of Vitreous Humor of Both Eyes in the Same Individual." *Proceedings of the 35th The International Association of Forensic Toxicology, Padova, Italy*, 574–578, 1997 **(70601)**

SOUSA, S., L. SANTOS, R.J. DINIS-OLIVEIRA, ET AL. "Pedestrian Fatalities Resulting from Train-Persons Collisions." *Traffic Injury Prevention*, 16: 208–212, 2015 **(61507)**

SPECK, P.R., A.J. MCELROY, AND R.G. GULLBERG. "The Effect of Breath Alcohol Simulator Solution Volume on Measurement Results." *Journal of Analytical Toxicology*, 15: 332–335, 1991 **(30203)**

SPRUNG, R., W. BONTE, E. RUDELL, ET AL. "On the Problem of Endogenous Alcohols [German]." *Blutalkohol*, 18: 65–70, 1981 **(20503)**

SQUIRES, T. AND A. BUSUTTIL. "Alcohol and House Fire Fatalities in Scotland, 1980–1990." *Medicine, Science and the Law*, 37: 321–325, 1997 **(60602)**

SREERAMA, L. AND G.G. HARDIN. "Improper Sealing Caused by the Styrofoam Integrity Seals in Leakproof Plastic Bottles Lead to Significant Loss of Ethanol in Frozen Evidentiary Urine Samples." *Journal of Forensic Sciences*, 48: 672–676, 2003 **(40108)**

STEELE, C.M. AND R.A. JOSEPHS. "Alcohol Myopia. Its Prized and Dangerous Effects." *American Psychologist*, 45: 921–933, 1990 **(60112)**

STEENSBERG, J. "Epidemiology of Accidental Drowning in Denmark 1989–1993." *Accident Analysis and Prevention*, 30: 755–762, 1998 **(60401)**

STEFFEN, K.J., S.G. ENGEL, G.A. POLLERT, ET AL. "Blood Alcohol Concentrations Rise Rapidly and Dramatically Following Roux-en-Y Gastric Bypass." *Surgery for Obesity and Related Diseases*, 9: 470–473, 2013 **(10130)**

STEIN, I., A.M. BACHANI, AND C. HOE. "The Alcohol Industry's Involvement with Road Safety NGOs." *Globalization and Health*, 18: 18, 9pp, 2022 **(50722)**

STEPHENS, A. "A Survey of Hand-Poured Measures of Spirit." *Science and Justice*, 26: 191–194, 1996 **(10610)**

STEPHENS, A. AND S.D.A. FRANKLIN. "Level of Lung Function Required to Use the Camic Datamaster Breath Alcohol Testing Device." *Science and Justice*, 41: 49–52, 2001 **(30307)**

STEPHENS, A. AND S. PHEASEY. "Petrol Effects on the New Camic Machine [Letter]." *Journal of the Forensic Science Society*, 34: 106, 1994 **(30615)**

STEPHENSON, L., P. STOCKHAM, C. VAN DEN HEUVEL, AND R.W. BYARD. "Characteristics of Drowning Deaths in an Inner City River." *Legal Medicine*, 47: 3pp, 2020 **(60414)**

STERLING, K. "The Rate of Dissipation of Mouth Alcohol in Alcohol Positive Subjects." *Journal of Forensic Sciences*, 57: 802–805, 2012 **(30520)**

STERN, E.L., R. MOONEY, E. UKESTAD, AND S. JEJURIKAR. "Field Study Comparison of Intoxilyzer 5000 Breath Alcohol Tests with GLC and Urine Alcohol Tests."

Proceedings 11th International Conference on Alcohol Drugs Traffic Safety, National Safety Council, Chicago, 250–259, 1990 **(30407)**

STEWART, R.L. AND G.B. BLACK. "Snowmobile Trauma: 10 Years' Experience at Manitoba's Tertiary Trauma Centre." *Canadian Journal of Surgery*, 47: 90–94, 2004 **(61803)**

STILLMAN, M.A. AND J. SUTCLIFF. "Predictors of Relapse in Alcohol Use Disorder: Identifying Individuals Most Vulnerable to Relapse." *Addiction and Substance Abuse*, 1: 3–8, 2020 **(90112)**

STOWELL, A.R., A.R. GAINSFORD, AND R.G. GULLBERG. "New Zealand's Breath and Blood Alcohol Testing Programs: Further Data Analysis and Forensic Implications." *Forensic Science International*, 178:83–92, 2008 **(30410)**

STOWELL, A.R. AND L.I. STOWELL. "Estimation of Blood Alcohol Concentrations After Social Drinking" *Journal of Forensic Sciences*, 43: 14–21, 1998 **(10505)**

STRAKA, L., F. NOVOMESKY, M. MARCINKOVA, AND J. KRAJCOVIC. "An Unusual Case of Highly False-Positive Breath-Alcohol Test in a Motor Vehicle Driver." *Romanian Journal of Legal Medicine*. 25: 293–296, 2017 **(30133)**

STRANGER, J., M. GRAW, K. BESSERER, AND H.T. HAFFNER. "Nutritive Influences on Endogenous Methanol Concentrations and Endogenous Methanol Formation." *Blutalkohol*, 36: 269–275, 1999 **(80301)**

STRASSGUTL, L. AND C. EVERS. "Long-Term Effects of the German Zero Tolerance Law for Novice Drivers." *Journal of Safety Research*, 80: 46–53, 2022 **(50721)**

STRAUCH, H., I. WIRTH, AND G. GESERICK. "Fatal Accidents Due to Train Surfing in Berlin." *Forensic Science International*, 94: 119–127, 1998 **(61505)**

STRAUCH, H., I. WIRTH, U. TAYMOORIAN, AND G. GESERICK. "Kicking to Death—Forensic and Criminological Aspects." *Forensic Science International*, 123: 165–171, 2001 **(60906)**

STRAWSINE, E. AND B. LUTMER. "The Effect of Alcohol-Based Hand Sanitizer Vapors on Evidential Breath Alcohol Test Results." *Journal of Forensic Sciences*, 63: 1284–1290, 2018 **(30132)**

STREUFERT, S., R. POGASH, J. ROACHE, ET AL. "Alcohol and Managerial Performance." *Journal of Studies on Alcohol*, 55: 230–238, 1994 **(61208)**

STROMBERG, C., T. SEPPALA, AND M.J. MATTILA. "Acute Effects of Maprotiline, Doxepin and Zimeldine with Alcohol in Healthy Volunteers." *Archives International Pharmacodynamics*, 291: 217–228, 1988 **(10708)**

STUBIG, T., M. PETRI, C. ZECKEY, ET AL. "Alcohol Intoxication in Road Traffic Accidents Leads to Higher Impact Speed Difference, Higher ISS and MAIS and Higher Preclinical Mortality." *Alcohol*, 46: 681–686, 2012 **(50510)**

STUSTER, J. "Validation of the Standardized Field Sobriety Test Battery at 0.08% Blood Alcohol Concentration." *Human Factors*, 48: 608–614, 2006 **(50609)**

SU, K.-C., L. NGUYEN, AND C. ROGERS. "Deaths in an Unlicensed Alcohol Rehabilitation Facilities." *Journal of Forensic Sciences*, 62: 103–106, 2017 **(90213)**

SULKOWSKI, H.A., A.H.B. WU, AND Y.S. MCCARTER. "In-Vitro Production of Ethanol in Urine by Fermentation." *Journal of Forensic Science*, 40: 990–993, 1995 **(40105)**

SULWAY, M.J. AND J.M. MALINS. "Acetone in Diabetic Ketoacidosis." *Lancet,* ii: 736–740, 1970 **(80201)**

SUN, S.W., D.M. KAHN, AND K.G. SWAN. "Lowering the Legal Blood Alcohol Limit for Motorcyclists." *Accident Analysis and Prevention,* 30: 133–136, 1998 **(61304)**

SUTLOVIC, D., M. MESTIC, Z. KOVACIC, ET AL. "Microbial Ethanol Production in Postmortem Urine Sample." *Medicine, Science, and the Law*, 53: 243–246, 2013 **(70228)**

SUTLOVIC, D., M. VERSIC-BRATINCEVIC, AND M. DEFINIS-GOJANOVIC. "Blood Alcohol Stability in Postmortem Blood Samples." *American Journal of Forensic Medicine and Pathology*, 35: 55–58, 2014 **(70222)**

SWIHART, G., J. YUILLE, AND S. PORTER. "The Role of State-Dependent Memory in Red-Outs." *International Journal of Law and Psychiatry*, 22: 199–212, 1999 **(60307)**

SZEREMETA, M., E. MIRONIUK, M. JANICA, ET AL. "Vitreous Humor as an Alternative Material for the Determination of Alcohol Concentration in Human Corpses." *Archiwum Medycyny Sadowej i Kryminologii,* 68: 108–118, 2018 **(70610)**

T

TALBOT, R. AND L. LA GRANGE. "The Effects of Salty and Nonsalty Food on Peak Breath Alcohol Concentration and Divided Attention Task Performance in Women." *Substance Abuse*, 20: 77–84, 1999 **(10112)**

TANGERMAN, A. "Highly Sensitive Gas Chromatographic Analysis of Ethanol in Whole Blood, Serum, Urine, and Fecal Supernatants by the Direct Injection Method." *Clinical Chemistry*, 43: 1003–1009, 1997 **(20107)**

TAYLOR, A.J., G. MCGWIN JR, G.G. DAVIS, ET AL. "Hypothermia Deaths in Jefferson County, Alabama." *Injury Prevention*, 7: 141–145, 2007 **(61010)**

TAYLOR, G.F., G.H. TURRILL, AND N.G. CARTER. "Blood Alcohol Analysis: A Comparison of the Gas-Chromatographic Assay with an Enzymatic Assay." *Pathology*, 16: 157–159, 1984 **(20408)**

TAYLOR, H.L. AND R.P. HUDSON. "Acute Ethanol Poisoning: A Two Year Study of Deaths in North Carolina." *Journal of Forensic Sciences,* 22: 639–653, 1977 **(70403)**

TAYLOR, L., V. REMESKEVICIUS, L. SASKOY, ET AL. "Determination of Ethanol in Micro-Volumes of Blood by Headspace Gas Chromatography: Statistical Comparison Between Capillary and Venous Sampling Sites." *Medicine, Science, and the Law*, 11pp, 2020 **(20121)**

TAYLOR, M.D. AND B.T. HODGSON. "Blood/Breath Correlations: Intoxilyzer 5000C, Alcotest 7110 and the Breathalyzer 900A Breath Alcohol Analyzers." *Canadian Society Forensic Science Journal*, 28: 153–164, 1995 **(30404)**

TERESINSKI, G., G. BUSZEWICZ, AND R. MADRO. "Acetonaemia as an Initial Criterion of Evaluation of a Probable Cause of Sudden Death." *Legal Medicine*, 11: 18–24, 2009 **(80206)**

———. "Biochemical Background of Ethanol-Induced Cold Susceptibility." *Legal Medicine*, 7: 15–23, 2005 **(80207)**

THELANDER, G., F.C. KUGELBERG, AND A.W. JONES. "High Correlation Between Ethanol Concentrations in Postmortem Femoral Blood and in Alternative Biological Specimens but Large Uncertainty When the Linear Regression Model Was Used for Prediction in Individual Cases." *Journal of Analytical Toxicology*, 44: 415–421, 2020 **(70818)**

THIERAUF, A., H. GNANN, A. WOHLFARTH, ET AL. "Urine Tested Positive for Ethyl Glucuronide and Ethyl Sulphate After the Consumption of Non-Alcoholic Beer." *Forensic Science International*, 202: 82–85, 2010 **(40516)**

THIERAUF, A., A. SERR, C.C. HALTER, ET AL. "Influence of Preservatives on the Stability of Ethyl Glucuronide and Ethyl Sulphate in Urine." *Forensic Science International*, 182: 41–45, 2008 **(40513)**

THIERAUF, A., A. WOHLFARTH, V. AUWATER, ET AL. "Urine Tested Positive for Ethyl Glucuronide and Ethyl Sulfate After the Consumption of Yeast and Sugar." *Forensic Science International*, 202: e45–e47, 2010 **(40517)**

THIERAUF-EMBERGER, A., J. ECHLE, M. DACKO, AND T. LANGE. "Comparison of Ethanol Concentrations in the Human Brain Determined by Magnetic Resonance Spectroscopy and Serum Ethanol Concentrations." *International Journal of Legal Medicine*, 134: 1713–1718, 2020 **(10208)**

THOKALA, M.R., S.P.R. DORANKULA, K. MUDDANA, AND S.R. VELDANDLA. "Alcohol Saliva Strip Test." *Journal of Clinical and Diagnostic Research*, 8: 307–308, 2014 **(40210)**

THOMAS, J.D. AND E.P. RILEY. "Fetal Alcohol Syndrome: Does Alcohol Withdrawal Play a Role?" *Alcohol Health and Research World*, 22: 53, 1998 **(90402)**

THOMASSON, R., V. CRAIG, AND E. GUTHRIE. "Self-Disembowelment During Delirium Tremens: Why Early Diagnosis Is Vital." *BMJ Case Reports*, 3pp, 2016 **(90215)**

THORNTON, D., M.B. HILL, D. VITEK, ET AL. "Botulism from Drinking Prison-Made Illicit Alcohol—Utah 2011." *Morbidity and Mortality Weekly Report*, 61, 782–784, 2012 **(61221)**

THYSSEN, H.H., J. BRYNSKOV, AND E.C. JANSEN. "Alcohol and Postural Imbalance. A Forced Plate Study." *Zeitschrift fur Rechtsmedizin*, 87: 257–260, 1981 **(60506)**

TIAN, M., H. HE, Y. LIU, ET AL. "Fatal Methanol Poisoning with Different Clinical and Autopsy Findings: Case Report and Literature Review." *Legal Medicine*, 54: 6pp, 2022 **(80321)**

TILLONEN, J., N. HOMANN, M. RAUTIO, ET AL. "Ciprofloxacin Decreases the Rate of Ethanol Elimination in Humans." *Gut*, 43: 347–352, 1999 **(10709)**

TINTINALLI, J.E. "Serum Methanol in the Absence of Methanol Ingestion [Letter]." *Annals of Emergency Medicine*, 26: 393, 1995 **(80302)**

TIPPETTS, A.S., R.B. VOAS, J.C. FELL, AND J.L. NICHOLS. "A Meta-Analysis of .08 BAC Laws in 19 Jurisdictions in the United States." *Accident Analysis Prevention*, 37: 149–161, 2005 **(50703)**

TISCIONE, N.B., R.E. VACHA, B. ALFORD, ET AL. "Long-Term Blood Alcohol Stability in Forensic Antemortem Whole Blood Samples." *Journal of Analytical Toxicology*, 39: 419–425, 2015 **(20314)**

TONELLATO, D.J., J.R. RANSOHOFF, C. NASH, ET AL. "Traumatic Pedestrian and Bicyclist Injuries Associated with Intoxication." *American Journal of Emergency Medicine*, 4pp, 2020 **(60210)**

TONELO, D., R. PROVIDENCIA, AND L. GONCALVES. "Holiday Heart Syndrome Revisited After 34 Years." *SciELO Brazil*, 183–189, 2013 **(90308)**

TORMEY, W.P. AND T.M. MOORE. "Ethanol as a Single Toxin in Non-Traumatic Deaths—A Toxicology Perspective." *Legal Medicine*, 15: 122–125, 2013 **(70411)**

TRELA, F. AND M. BOGUSZ. "Usefulness of Ethanol Determination in Perilymph and Skeletal Muscle in the Case of Advanced Putrefaction of the Body." *Blutalkohol*, 17: 198–206, 1980 **(70805)**

TREMBLAY, J. "A Comparison of Paired Calibration Check Results of Alco-Sensor IV RBT IV and Intoxilyzer 5000C in Real Cases." *Canadian Society of Forensic Science Journal*, 46: 112–119, 2013 **(30217)**

TREMBLAY, J. AND G. NOLIN. "Lack of Response of Breath Alcohol Screening Devices to Sugar Alcohols Contained in Chewing Gum." *Canadian Society of Forensic Science Journal*, 47: 46–54, 2014 **(30522)**

TREMBLAY, M., F. GALLANT, M. LAVALLIERE, ET AL. "Driving Performance on the Descending Limb of Blood Alcohol Concentration (BAC) in Undergraduate Students: A Pilot Study." *Public Library of Science ONE*, 10(2): 15pp, 27 February 2015 **(50118)**

TREVIAN, L.A., N. BOUTROS, I.L. PETRAKIS, AND J.H. KRYSTAL. "Complications of Alcohol Withdrawal." *Alcohol Health and Research World*, 22: 61–66, 1998 **(90204)**

TSE, T.J., S.K. PURDY, J. SHEN, ET AL. "Toxicology of Alcohol-Based Hand Rubs Formulated with Technical-Grade Ethanol." *Toxicology Reports*, 8: 785–792, 2021 **(80316)**

TU, G.C. AND Y. ISRAEL. "Alcohol Consumption by Orientals in North America is Predicted Largely by a Single Gene." *Behavioral Genetics*, 25: 59–65, 1995 **(80107)**

TUCKER, A. AND C. TRETHEWY. "Lack of Effect on Blood Alcohol Level of Swabbing Venipuncture Sites with 70% Isopropyl Alcohol." *Emergency Medicine Australasia*, 22: 9–12, 2010 **(20410)**

TUERO, G., J. GONZALEZ, L. SAHUQUILLO, ET AL. "Value of Glycolic Acid Analysis in Ethylene Glycol Poisoning: A Clinical Case Report and Systematic Review of the Literature." *Forensic Science International*, 290: e9–e14, 2018 **(80513)**

TUMER, A. R., A. LALE, M. GURLER, ET AL. "The Effects of Traditional Fermented Beverages on Ethanol, Ethyl Glucuronide and Ethyl Sulphate Levels." *Egyptian Journal of Forensic Sciences*, 8: 33, 5pp, 2018 **(40519)**

TUMRAM, N.K., V.N. AMBRADE, AND P.G. DIXIT. "Compression Asphyxia in Upright Suspended Position." *American Journal of Forensic Medicine and Pathology*, 35: 80–82, 2014 **(60513)**

TURNER, P., B. SAEED, AND M.C. KELSEY. "Dermal Absorption of Isopropyl Alcohol from a Commercial Hand Rub: Implications for Its Use in Hand Decontamination." *Journal of Hospital Infection*, 56: 287–290, 2004 **(80408)**

TWISK, D.A.M. AND M. REURINGS. "An Epidemiological Study of the Risk of Cycling in the Dark: The Role of Visual Perception, Conspicuity and Alcohol Use." *Accident Analysis and Prevention*, 60: 134–140, 2013 **(60207)**

U

UMEH, C., R.C. GUPTA, R. GUPTA, ET AL. "Acetone Ingestion Resulting in Cardiac Arrest and Death." *Cureus, Open Access Case Report*, 5pp, 2021 **(80208)**

V

VALDERRAMA-ZURIAN, J.C., D. MELERO-FUENTES, F.J. ALVAREZ, AND F. HERRERA-GOMEZ. "Worldwide Research Output Trends on Drinking and Driving from 1956 to 2015." *Accident Analysis and Prevention*, 135: 5pp, 2020 **(50406)**

VALLANCE, K., A. VINCENT, N. SCHOUERI-MYCHASIW, ET AL. "News Media and the Influence of the Alcohol Industry: An Analysis of Media Coverage of Alcohol Warning Labels with a Cancer Message in Canada and Ireland." *Journal of Studies in Alcohol and Drugs*, 81: 273–283, 2020 **(90507)**

VAN DE LOO, M.M., G. KORTE-BOUWS, K. BROOKHUIS, ET AL. "Urine Ethanol Concentration and Alcohol Hangover Severity." *Psychopharmacology*, 234: 73–77, 2017 **(60814)**

VAN DIJKEN, J.H., J.L. VELDSTRA, A.J.A.E.VAN DE LOO, ET AL. "The Influence of Alcohol (0.5%) on the Control and Maneuvering Level of Driving Behaviour, Finding Measures to Assess Driving Impairment: A Simulator Study." *Transportation Research Part F*, 73: 119–127, 2020 **(50216)**

VAN DYKE, N.A., AND M.T. FILLMORE. "Distraction Produces Over-Additive Increases in the Degree to Which Alcohol Impairs Driving Performance." *Psychopharmacology,* 232: 4277–4284, 2015 **(50215)**

VARGA, M., L. BURIS, AND M. FODOR. "Ethanol Elimination in Man under the Influence of Hepatoprotective Silibinin." *Blutalkohol*, 28: 405–408, 1991 **(10717)**

VARGA, M., G. SOMOYGI, J. POSTA, AND L. BURIS. "Effect of Different Columns and Internal Standards on the Quality Assurance of the Gas Chromatographic Determination of Blood Ethanol." *European Journal of Clinical Chemistry and Clinical Biochemistry*, 31: 773–776, 1993 **(20108)**

VENTURA-COTS, M., M.P. BALLESTER-FERRE, S. RAVI, AND R. BATALLER. "Public Health Policies and Alcohol-Related Liver Disease." *JHEP Reports*, 1: 403–413, 2019 **(90509)**

VERSTER, J.C., L.D. KRUISSELBRINK, K.A. SLOT, ET AL. "Sensitivity to Experiencing Alcohol Hangovers: Reconsideration of the 0.11% Blood Alcohol Concentration (BAC) Threshold for Having a Hangover." *Journal of Clinical Medicine,* 9: 179, 7pp, 2020 **(60813)**

VEZZOLI, S., M. BERNINI, AND F. DE FERRARI. "Ethyl Glucuronide in Vitreous Humor and Blood Postmortem Specimens: Analysis by Liquid Chromatography-Electrospray Tandem Mass Spectrometry and Interpreting Results of Neo-Formation of Ethanol." *Annali dell'Istituto Superiore di Sanità*, 51: 19–27, 2015 **(70613)**

VIGOUROUX, A., C. GARRET, J-B. LASCARROU, ET AL. "Alcohol Withdrawal Syndrome in ICU Patients: Clinical Features, Management, and Outcome Predictors." 16: 14pp, 2021 **(90212)**

VOAS, R.B., J.H. LACEY, K. JONES, ET AL. "Drinking Drivers and Drug Use on Weekend Nights in the United States." *Drug and Alcohol Dependence*, 130: 215–221, 2013 **(50513)**

VOAS, R.B., E. ROMANO, AND R. PECK. "Validity of the Passive Alcohol Sensor for Estimating BACs in DWI-Enforcement Operations." *Journal of Studies on Alcohol,* 67: 714–721, 2006 **(30106)**

VOAS, R.B., A.S. TIPPETTS, AND J.C. FELL. "Assessing the Effectiveness of Minimum Legal Drinking Age and Zero Tolerance Laws in the United States." *Accident Analysis Prevention*, 35: 579–587, 2003 **(50707)**

VOLOSHYNA, D.M., E.E. BONAR, R.M. CUNNINGHAM, ET AL. "Blackouts Among Male and Female Youth Seeking Emergency Department Care." *American Journal of Drug and Alcohol Abuse,* 44: 129–139, 2018 **(60318)**

VONLANTHEN, R., J.H. BEER, AND B.H. LAUTERBURG. "Effect of Methylene Blue on the Disposition of Ethanol." *Alcohol and Alcoholism*, 35: 424–426, 2000 **(10714)**

VOSKOBOINIK, A., J.M. KALMAN, A. DE SILVA, ET AL. "Alcohol Abstinence in Drinkers with Atrial Fibrillation." *The New England Journal of Medicine*, 382: 20–28, 2020 **(90309)**

W

WAGENAAR, A.C. AND M.M. MALDONADO-MOLINA. "Effects of Drivers' License Suspension Policies on Alcohol-Related Crash Involvement: Long-Term Follow-Up in Forty-Six States." *Alcoholism: Clinical and Experimental Research*, 31: 1399–1406, 2007 **(50711)**

WAGENAAR, A.C., M.M. MALDONADO-MOLINA, D.J. ERICKSON, ET AL. "General Deterrence Effects of U.S. Statutory DUI Fine and Jail Penalties: Longer-Term Follow-Up in 32 States." *Accident Analysis and Prevention*, 39: 982–994, 2007 **(50714)**

WALDER, A.D. AND C.K.G.TYLER. "Ethylene Glycol Antifreeze Poisoning." *Anaesthesia*, 49: 964–967, 1994 **(80505)**

WALKER, B., M. BUTLER, AND M. PLATE. "Assessment of the Calibration of the Intoxilyzer 5000C Following Extensive Use of an Alcohol Standard." *Canadian Society of Forensic Science Journal*, 37: 155–162, 2004 **(30205)**

WALKER, D., L. SMARANDESCU, AND B. WANSINK. "Half Full or Empty: Cues That Lead Wine Drinkers to Unintentionally Overpour." *Substance Use and Misuse*, Early Online: 1–8, 2013 **(10611)**

WALKER, G.W. AND A.S. CURRY. "Endogenous' Alcohol in Body Fluids." *Nature*, 210: 1368, 25 June 1966 **(20501)**

WALL, T.L., S.M. HORN, M.L. JOHNSON, ET AL. "Hangover Symptoms in Asian Americans with Variations in the Aldehyde Dehydrogenase (ALDH2) Gene." *Journal of Studies on Alcohol*, 61: 13–17, 2000 **(60803)**

WALLAGE, H.R. AND I.M. BUGYRA. "Interferent Detect on the Intoxilyzer 8000C in an Individual with an Elevated Blood Acetone Concentration due to Ketoacidosis." *Canadian Society of Forensic Science Journal*, 50: 157–163, 2017 **(30622)**

WALLE, A.J., O. GRUNER, AND W. NIEDERMAYER. "Measurement of Total Body Water in Patients on Maintenance Hemodialysis Using an Ethanol Dilution Technique." *Nephron*, 26: 286–290, 1980 **(10310)**

WALLER, J.A. AND K.R. LAMBORN. "Snowmobiling: Characteristics of Owners, Patterns of Use and Injuries." *Accident Analysis and Prevention*, 7: 213–223, 1975 **(61801)**

WANG, J. AND J.B. CICCHINO. "Fatal Pedestrian Crashes on Interstates and Other Freeways in the United States." *Journal of Safety Research*, 74: 1–7, 2020 **(61416)**

WARGOTZ, E.S. AND M. WERNER. "Asymptomatic Blood Methanol in Emergency Room Patients." *American Journal of Clinical Pathology*, 87: 773–775, 1987 **(80303)**

WATERS, B., K. HARA, N. IKEMATSU, ET AL. "An Unusual Case of Suicide by Methanol Ingestion." *Forensic Science International*, 289: e9–e14, 2018 **(80322)**

WATHAN, M.M., D.S. SEWELL, R.A. MARLOW, ET AL. "The Economic Impact of Acute Sunburn." *Archives of Dermatology*, 139: 1003–1006, 2003 **(61202)**

WATKINS, R.L. AND E.V. ADLER. "The Effect of Food on Alcohol Absorption and Elimination Patterns." *Journal of Forensic Science*, 38: 285–291, 1993 **(10106)**

WATSON, P.E., I.D. WATSON, AND R.D. BATT. "Predictions of Blood Alcohol Concentrations in Human Subjects. Updating the Widmark Equation." *Journal of Studies on Alcohol*, 42: 547–556, 1981 **(10604)**

WATSON, W.A., AND J.C. GARRIOTT. "Alcohol and Motorcycle Riders: A Comparison of Motorcycle and Car/Truck DWIs." *Veterinary and Human Toxicology*, 34: 213–215, 1992 **(61303)**

WATTEN, R.G. AND I. LIE. "The Effects of Alcohol on Eye Movements During Reading." *Alcohol and Alcoholism*, 32: 275–290, 1997 **(61210)**

WATTERSON, J.H. AND K.N. ELLEFSEN. "Examination of Some Performance Characteristics of Breath Alcohol Measurements Obtained with the Intoxilyzer 8000C Following Social Drinking Conditions." *Journal of Analytical Toxicology*, 33: 514–520, 2009 **(30405)**

WEAFER, J. AND M.T. FILLMORE. "Acute Tolerance to Alcohol Impairment of Behavioral and Cognitive Mechanisms Related to Driving: Drinking and Driving on the Descending Limb." *Psychopharmacology,* 220: 697–706, 2012 **(50213)**

WEATHERMON, A.R., J.R. MCCUTCHEON, AND J.M. COWAN. "Results of Analyses for Alcohol of Near Simultaneously Collected Venous Blood and Alveolar Breath Specimens." *Alcohol, Drugs and Driving*, 9: 19–25, 1993 **(30403)**

WEBB, E., J.P. WYATT, J. HENRY, AND A.A. BUSUTTIL. "A Comparison of Fatal with Non-Fatal Knife Injuries in Edinburgh." *Forensic Science International*, 99: 179–187, 1999 **(60901)**

WEDIN, B., L. VANGGAARD, AND J. HIRVONEN. "Paradoxical Undressing in Fatal Hypothermia." *Journal of Forensic Science*, 24: 543–553, 1979 **(61003)**

WEGNER, A.J. AND M. FAHLE. "Alcohol and Visually Guided Saccades: Gap Effect and Predictability of Target Location." *Psychopharmacology,* 146: 24–32, 1999 **(50113)**

WEILER, G. "Are Postmortem Alcohol Determinations Useful in Cases of Severe Hemorrhagic Shock Treated with Numerous Blood Transfusions? [German]." *Blutalkohol*, 16: 306–309, 1979 **(70309)**

WELLS, D. "Drug Administration and Sexual Assault: Sex in a Glass." *Science and Justice*, 41: 197–199, 2001 **(61707)**

WENTWORTH, P., A.E. CROAL, L.A. JENTZ, ET AL. "Water-Related Deaths in Brant County 1969–1992: A Review of Fifty-Seven Cases." *Canadian Society of Forensic Science Journal*, 26: 1–17, 1993 **(60402)**

WENZEL, F.J. AND R.A. PETERS. "A Ten-Year Survey of Snowmobile Accidents, Injuries and Fatalities in Wisconsin." *Physician and Sports Medicine*, 14: 140–149, 1986 **(61806)**

WERFEL, P. "Beware of Patients Under the Influence." *Journal of Emergency Medical Services*, 22: May 2000 **(61408)**

WESTMAN, J., K. WAHLBECK, T.M. LARSEN, ET AL. "Mortality and Life Expectancy of People with Alcohol Use Disorder in Denmark, Finland and Sweden." *Acta Psychiatrica Scandinavica*, 131: 297–306, 2015 **(90317)**

WHITE, A.M., M.L. SIGNER, C.L. KRAUS, AND H.S. SWARTZWELDER. "Experiential Aspects of Alcohol-Induced Blackouts Among College Students." *American Journal of Drug Alcohol Abuse*, 30: 205–224, 2004 **(60303)**

WHITE, M.D., C.E. JOHNSTON, M.P. WU, ET AL. "Ethanol Ingestion Prolongs Orthostatic Intolerance in Hyperthermic Humans." *Aviation, Space Environmental Medicine*, 69: 577–582, 1998 **(61607)**

WICK, R.L. "Alcohol and Pilot Performance Decrements." *Alcohol, Drugs and Driving*, 8: 207–215, 1992 **(60706)**

WIEDERMANN, K., F. NAUJOKS, J. WORLE, ET AL. "Effect of Different Alcohol Levels on Take-Over Performance in Conditionally Automated Driving." *Accident, Analysis and Prevention*, 115: 89–97, 2018 **(50217)**

WIESE, J., S. MCPHERSON, M.C. ODDEN, AND M.G. SHLIPAK. "Effect of Opuntia ficus indica on Symptoms of the Alcohol Hangover." *Archives of Internal Medicine*, 164: 1334–1340, 2004 **(60808)**

WIESE, J.G., M.G. SHILPAK, AND W.S. BROWNER. "The Alcohol Hangover." *Annals of Internal Medicine*, 132: 897–902, 2000 **(60812)**

WIGG, S. AND L.D. STAFFORD. "Health Warnings on Alcoholic Beverages: Perceptions of the Health Risks and Intentions towards Alcohol Consumption." *PLOS One*, 11: 12 pp, 2016 **(90505)**

WIGMORE, J.G. "Blood Ethanol Concentrations are Less Stable than Serum or Plasma Upon Storage Because of Oxyhemoglobin-Mediated Oxidation of Ethanol to Acetaldehyde [Letter]." *Journal of Analytical Toxicology*, 33: 182–183, 2009 **(20308)**

———. "The Effect of an Elevated Serum Methanol Concentration on the Intoxilyzer 5000C Results of a Drinking Driver." *Canadian Society of Forensic Science Journal*, 41: 171–174, 2008 **(30608)**

———. "The Purell Defence: Can the Use of Alcohol-Containing Hand Sanitizers Cause an Elevated Breath or Blood Alcohol Concentration?" *Canadian Society of Forensic Science Journal*, 42: 147–151, 2009 **(10119)**

———. "An Unusual Postmortem Urine–Blood Alcohol Ratio: Beware of Urine Dilution from Catheter Use." *Canadian Society of Forensic Science Journal,* 39: 25–27, 2006 **(70705)**

———."Up to Their Necks in Hot Water: Body Temperature and the BAC/BrAC Ratio [Letter]." *Journal of Analytical Toxicology*, 34: 605–606, 2010 **(30420)**

WIGMORE, J.G. AND I.M. BUGYRA. "Decreasing the Mouth Alcohol Effect by Increasing the Salivary Flow Rate." *Canadian Society of Forensic Science Journal*, 36: 211–216, 2003 **(30505)**

WIGMORE, J.G. AND B.L.C. CHOW. "Case Report: Detection of Neo-Formation of Ethanol in a Postmortem Blood Sample Using N-Propanol and a Urine Sample." *Canadian Society of Forensic Science Journal*, 33: 145–149, 2000 **(70211)**

WIGMORE, J.G., C.J. HOUSE, AND R.M. LANGILLE. "Duplicate Breath Alcohol Testing: Should the Statutory Wait in Canada of at Least 15 Minutes Between Tests Be Changed?" *Canadian Society of Forensic Science Journal*, 38: 1-8, 2005 **(30122)**

WIGMORE, J.G., C.J. HOUSE, AND J.W. PATRICK. "Characteristics of Arrested Drinking Drivers with the Highest Intoxilyzer 5000C Results in Toronto: Drinking and Driving Not Only at Night or on Weekends." *Canadian Society of Forensic Science Journal,* 37: 1–8, 2004 **(50511)**

WIGMORE, J.G. AND G.M. LESLIE. "The Effect of Swallowing or Rinsing Alcohol Solution on the Mouth Alcohol Effect and Slope Detection of the Intoxilyzer 5000." *Journal of Analytical Toxicology*, 25: 112–114, 2001 **(30502)**

WIGMORE, J.G. AND M.J. WARD. "The Incidence of Ethanol and Acetone in the Blood and Urine of Victims of Sexual Assault." *Canadian Society of Forensic Science Journal,* 19: 49–58, 1986 **(61713)**

WIGMORE, J.G., M.J. WARD, AND J. WELLS. "Assessing Breath Test Estimation of Blood Alcohol Concentration [Letter]." *Journal of Analytical Toxicology*, 13: 244–245, 1989 **(30411)**

WIGMORE, J.G. AND M.P. WILKIE. "A Simulation of the Effect of Blood in the Mouth on Breath Alcohol Concentrations of Drinking Subjects." *Canadian Society of Forensic Science Journal,* 35: 9–16, 2002 **(30513)**

WILKIE, M.P., J.G. WIGMORE, AND J.W. PATRICK. "The Performance of the Approved Screening Device, the Alcotest 7410 GLC in the Field: Low Incidence of False Positive Results in the Identification of Drinking Drivers." *Canadian Society of Forensic Science Journal,* 36: 165–171, 2003 **(30506)**

WILLIAMS, A.F. "Alcohol-Impaired Driving and its Consequences in the United States: The Past 25 Years." *Journal of Safety Research*, 37: 123–138, 2006 **(50710)**

WILSON, C.I., S.S. IGNACIO, AND G.A. WILSON. "An Unusual Form of Fatal Ethanol Intoxication." *Journal of Forensic Science*, 50: 676–678, 2005 **(10117)**

WILSON, P.F., C.G. FREEMAN, M.J. MCEWAN, ET AL. "Alcohol in Breath and Blood: A Selected Ion Flow Tube Mass Spectrometric Study." *Rapid Communications Mass Spectrometry*, 15: 413–417, 2001 **(30114)**

WINEK, C.L., J. BAUER, W.W. WAHBA, AND W.D. COLLOM. "Blood Versus Synovial Fluid Ethanol Concentrations in Humans." *Journal of Analytical Toxicology*, 17: 233–235, 1993 **(70811)**

WINEK, C.L. AND M. CARFAGNA. "Comparison of Plasma, Serum, and Whole Blood Ethanol Concentrations." *Journal of Analytical Toxicology*, 11: 267–268, 1987 **(20202)**

WINEK, C.L. AND T. EASTLY. "Factors Affecting Contamination of Blood Samples for Ethanol Determinations." *Legal Medicine Annual*, 147–162, 1976 **(20402)**

WINEK, C.L., D. HENRY, AND L. KIRKPATRICK. "The Influence of Physical Properties and Lipid Content of Bile on the Human Blood/Bile Ethanol Ratio." *Forensic Science International*, 22: 171–178, 1983 **(70812)**

WINEK, C.L., W.W. WAHBA, R.M. WINDISCH, AND C.L. WINEK JR. "Serum Alcohol Concentrations in Trauma Patients Determined by Immunoassays Versus Gas Chromatography." *Forensic Science International*, 139: 1–3, 2004 **(20112)**

WINEK JR., C.L., C.L. WINEK, AND W.W. WAHBA. "The Role of Trauma in Post-mortem Blood Alcohol Determination." *Forensic Science International*, 71: 1–8, 1995 **(70305)**

WINEK, T., C.L. WINEK, AND W.W. WAHBA. "The Effect of Storage at Various Temperatures on Blood Alcohol Concentration." *Forensic Science International*, 78: 179–185, 1996 **(20306)**

WINGREN, C.J. AND A. OTTOSSON. "The Association Between Obesity and Lethal Blood Alcohol Concentrations: A Nationwide Register-Based Study of Medicolegal Autopsy Cases in Sweden." *Forensic Science International*, 244: 285–288, 2014 **(70414)**

WISSEL, P.S. "Dietary Influences on Ethanol Metabolism." *Drug-Nutrient Interactions*, 5: 161–168, 1987 **(10307)**

WOLFE, J., R. MARTINEZ, AND W.A. SCOTT. "Baseball and Beer: An Analysis of Alcohol Consumption Patterns Among Male Spectators at Major-League Sporting Events." *Annals of Emergency Medicine*, 31: 629–632, 1998 **(61912)**

WOODALL, K.L., B.L.C. CHOW, A. LAUWERS, AND D. CASS. "Toxicological Findings in Fatal Motor Vehicle Collisions in Ontario, Canada." *Journal of Forensic Sciences*, 60(3): 669–674, 2015 **(50802)**

WOODALL, K.L., AND J-P.F.P. PALMENTIER. "Intoxilyzer 8000C Breath Results Obtained from a Suspected Impaired Driver Following Reported Occupational

Solvent Exposure." *Canadian Society of Forensic Science Journal*, 50: 84–89, 2017 **(30623)**

WOODROW, K.M. AND L.G. ELTHERINGTON. "Feeling No Pain: Alcohol as an Analgesic." *Pain,* 32: 159–163, 1988 **(61211)**

WRIGHT, N.R. "A Day at the Cricket: The Breath Alcohol Consequences of a Type of Very English Binge Drinking." *Addiction Research and Theory*, 14: 133–137, 2006 **(61910)**

WU CHEN, N.B., E.R. DONOGHUE, AND M.I. SCHAFFER. "Methanol Intoxication: Distribution in Postmortem Tissues and Fluids Including Vitreous Humor." *Journal of Forensic Sciences*, 30: 213–216, 1985 **(80312)**

WUNDER, C., S. HAIN, S.C. KOELZER, ET AL. "Lack of Effects of a Sobering Product Eezup on the Blood Ethanol and Congener Alcohol Concentration." *Forensic Science International*, 278: 101–105, 2017 **(10722)**

WUNDER, C., W. POGODA, A. PAULKE, AND S.W. TOENNES. "Assay of Ethanol and Congener Alcohols in Serum and Beverages by Headspace Gas Chromatography/Mass Spectrometry." *MethodsX*, 8, 7 pp, 2021 **(20124)**

WURST, F.M., R. VOGEL, K. JACHAU, ET AL. "Ethyl Glucuronide Discloses Recent Covert Alcohol Use Not Detected by Standard Testing in Forensic Psychiatric Inpatients." *Alcoholism Clinical Experimental Research*, 27: 471–476, 2003 **(40514)**

WYATT, J.P., D. BEARD, AND A. BUSUTTIL. "Fatal Falls Down Stairs." *Injury, International Journal of Care Injured,* 30: 31–34, 1999 **(60505)**

X

XI, B., S.P. VEERANKI, M. ZHAO, ET AL. "Relationship of Alcohol Consumption to All-Cause, Cardiovascular, and Cancer-Related Mortality in U.S. Adults." *Journal of the American College of Cardiology*, 70: 913–922, 2017 **(90314)**

Y

YADAV, A.K. AND N.R. VELAGA. "Effect of Alcohol Use on Accelerating and Braking Behaviors of Drivers." *Traffic Injury Prevention*, 20: 353–358, 2019 **(50218)**

———. "Laboratory Analysis of Driving Behavior and Self-Perceived Physiological Impairment at 0.03%, 0.05% and 0.08% Blood Alcohol Concentrations." *Drug and Alcohol Dependence*, 205: 7pp, 2019 **(50219)**

YAJIMA, D., H. MOTANI, K. KAMEI, ET AL. "Ethanol Production by *Candida Albicans* in Postmortem Human Blood Samples: Effects of Blood Glucose Levels and Dilution." *Forensic Science International,* 164: 116–121, 2006 **(70210)**

YANG, J., X. GUO, M. XU, ET AL. "Alcohol-Impaired Motorcyclists Versus Car Drivers: A Comparison of Crash Involvement and Legal Consequences from Adjudication Data." *Journal of Safety Research*, 79: 292–303, 2021 **(61313)**

YANG, K., B.H. CHOI, B. LEE, AND S.H. YOO. "Bath-Related Deaths in Korea Between 2008–2015." *Journal of Korean Medicine and Science*, 33: e108, 9 pp, 2018 **(60413)**

YANG, K.-M., B-W. LEE, J. OH, AND S.H. YOO. "Characteristics of Sauna Deaths in Korea in Relation to Different Blood Alcohol Concentrations." *Forensic Science, Medicine and Pathology*, 14: 307–313, 2018 **(61608)**

YAO, J., M.B. JOHNSON, AND K.H. BECK. "Predicting DUI Decisions in Different Legal Environments: Investigating Deterrence with a Conjoint Experiment." *Traffic Injury Prevention*, 15: 213–221, 2014 **(50718)**

YELLAND, L.N., J.P. BURNS, D.N. SIMS, ET AL. "Inter- and Intra-Subject Variability in Ethanol Pharmacokinetic Parameters: Effects of Testing Interval and Dose." *Forensic Science International*, 175: 65–72, 2008 **(10303)**

YIP, D.C.P. AND S.F. SHUM. "A Study on the Correlation of Blood and Vitreous Humor Alcohol Levels in the Late Absorption and Elimination Phases." *Medicine Science and the Law,* 30: 29–33, 1990 **(70602)**

YIP, L., D. BIXLER, D.E. BROOKS, ET AL. "Serious Adverse Health Events, Including Death, Associated with Ingesting Alcohol-Based Hand Sanitizers Containing Methanol—Arizona and New Mexico, May–June 2020." *MMWR*, 69: 1070–1073, 2020 **(80317)**

YORK, J.L., J. WELTE, AND J. HIRSCH. "Gender Comparison of Alcohol Exposure on Drinking Occasions." *Journal of Studies on Alcohol*, 64: 790–801, 2003 **(10402)**

YOSHIZAWA, T., Y. KAMIJO, Y. FUJITA, ET AL. "Mild Manifestations of Methanol Poisoning Half a Day After Massive Ingestion of a Fuel Alcohol Product Contain 30% Ethanol and 70% Methanol: A Case Report." *Acute Medicine and Surgery*, 5: 28–291, 2018 **(80320)**

YUILLE, J.G. AND P.A.TOLLESTRUP. "Some Effects of Alcohol on Eyewitness Memory." *Journal of Applied Physiology*, 75: 268–273, 1990 **(60309)**

Z

ZADOR, P.L., S.A. KRAWCHUK, AND R.B. VOAS. "Alcohol-Related Relative Risk of Driver Fatalities and Driver Involvement in Fatal Crashes in Relation to Driver Age and Gender: An Update Using 1996 Data." *Journal of Studies on Alcohol,* 61: 387–395, 2000 **(50505)**

ZAILER, E. AND B.W.K. DIEHL. "Alternative Determination of Blood Alcohol Concentration by 1H NMR Spectroscopy." *Journal of Pharmaceutical and Biomedical Analysis*, 119: 59–64, 2016 **(20126)**

ZAPATA, E. AND A. ORWIN. "Severe Hypertension and Bronchospasm During Disulfiram-Ethanol Test Reaction [Letter]." *British Medical Journal*, 305: 870, 1992 **(80109)**

ZDOLSEK, H.J., F. SJOBERG, B. LISANDER, AND A.W. JONES. "The Effect of Hypermetabolism Induced by Burn Trauma on the Ethanol-Oxidizing Capacity of the Liver." *Critical Care Medicine*, 27: 2622–2625, 1999 **(10808)**

ZERBINI, T., J. DE CARVALHO PONCE, D.M. SINGAWA, ET AL. "Blood Alcohol Levels in Suicide by Hanging Cases in the State of Sao Paulo, Brazil." *Journal of Forensic and Legal Medicine*, 19: 294–296, 2012 **(62016)**

ZEREN, C., A. KETEN, S. CELIK, ET AL. "Demonstration of Ethyl Glucuronide in Dental Tissue Samples by Liquid Chromatography/Electro-Spray Tandem Mass Spectrometry." *Journal of Forensic and Legal Medicine*, 20: 706–710, 2013 **(70914)**

ZHANG, L., W.F. WIECZOEK, AND J.W. WELTE. "The Nexus Between Alcohol and Violent Crime." *Alcoholism: Clinical and Experimental Research*, 21: 1264–1271, 1997 **(60109)**

ZITTEL, D.B. AND G.G. HARDIN. "Comparison of Blood Ethanol Concentrations in Samples Simultaneously Collected into Expired and Unexpired Venipuncture Tubes." *Journal of Analytical Toxicology*, 30: 317–318, 2006 **(20309)**

ZUBA, D. "Accuracy and Reliability of Breath Alcohol Testing by Handheld Electrochemical Analysers." *Forensic Science International*, 178: e29–e33, 2008 **(30126)**

———. "Measurement Uncertainty in Determination of Blood Alcohol Concentration." *Problems of Forensic Sciences*, 54: 113–136, 2003 **(20106)**

ZUBARAN, C., J.G. FERNANDES, AND R. RODNIGHT. "Wernicke-Korsakoff Syndrome." *Postgraduate Medical Journal*, 73: 27–31, 1997 **(90216)**

ZUBE, K., T. DALRUP, M. LAU, R. MAATZ, ET AL. "E-Scooter Driving Under the Acute Influence of Alcohol—A Real Fitness Study." *International Journal of Legal Medicine*, 10pp, 26 February 2022 **(61315)**

ZUPANC, A.M., A.V. PASKA, AND P. PREGELJI. "Blood Alcohol Concentration of Suicide Victims by Partial Hanging." *Journal of Forensic and Legal Medicine*, 20: 976–979, 2013 **(62017)**

Subject Index

About the Author

James Wigmore has worked as a forensic toxicologist for over 29 years at one of the foremost forensic laboratories in North America—the Centre of Forensic Sciences in Toronto, Ontario. He has testified in over 700 criminal cases throughout Canada and in numerous personal injury civil cases and coroner's inquests. He has published over seventy scientific articles in forensic toxicology that have been cited by the Supreme Court of Canada and the High Court of South Africa. James has been interviewed numerous times on the CBC and other media on the issues arising out of the legalization of cannabis in Canada and on vaping. He was on Health Canada's expert panel on public information regarding cannabis. He received the prestigious Derome Award from the Canadian Society of Forensic Sciences for his outstanding contributions to the field of forensic science. His book series on the medicolegal aspects of alcohol, cannabis, and nicotine has received international acclaim.

www.ingramcontent.com/pod-product-compliance
Lightning Source LLC
LaVergne TN
LVHW020429080826
844660LV00034B/1374

* 9 7 8 1 5 5 2 2 1 6 8 3 5 *